MW01204076

SAP® Administration—Practical Guide

SAP PRESS is a joint initiative of SAP and Rheinwerk Publishing. The know-how offered by SAP specialists combined with the expertise of Rheinwerk Publishing offers the reader expert books in the field. SAP PRESS features first-hand information and expert advice, and provides useful skills for professional decision-making.

SAP PRESS offers a variety of books on technical and business-related topics for the SAP user. For further information, please visit our website: *www.sap-press.com*.

Sebastian Schreckenbach

SAP® Administration—Practical Guide

Bonn • Boston

Editor Sarah Frazier
Acquisitions Editor Kelly Grace Weaver
German Edition Editor Janina Schweitzer
Translation Lemoine International, Inc., Salt Lake City, UT
Copyeditor Julie McNamee
Cover Design Janina Conrady, Graham Geary
Photo Credit Shutterstock.com: 95662684/© senticus, 95538487/© Antonov Roman, 116485294/© Rashevskyi Viacheslav
Layout Design Vera Brauner
Production Graham Geary
Typesetting III-satz, Husby (Germany)
Printed and bound in the United States of America, on paper from sustainable sources

ISBN 978-1-4932-1024-4

2nd edition 2015
3rd German edition published 2015 by Rheinwerk Verlag, Bonn, Germany

Library of Congress Cataloging-in-Publication Data
Schreckenbach, Sebastian.
[Praxishandbuch SPA Administration. English]
SAP administration : practical guide / Sebastian Schreckenbach. -- 2nd edition.
pages cm
Includes index.
ISBN 978-1-4932-1024-4 (print : alk. paper) -- ISBN 1-4932-1024-6 (print : alk. paper) --
ISBN 978-1-4932-1025-1 (ebook) -- ISBN 978-1-4932-1026-8 (print and ebook) 1. SAP NetWeaver.
2. Computer networks--Management. 3. Database management. 4. Industrial management--
Data processing. I. Title.
TK5105.8885.S24S3713 2015
004.6--dc23
2015001119

Contents at a Glance

Dear Reader,

The term *SAP administration* casts broad strokes. The depth of coverage on such a topic seems beyond the bonds of this book's binding. And yet, author Sebastian Schreckenbach and we at SAP PRESS were once again up for the challenge. Updated for SAP NetWeaver 7.4 and SAP ERP 6.0, it is our pleasure to present to you the second edition of *SAP Administration—Practical Guide*.

Providing expertise and guidance for both commonly-performed and specialized system administrator tasks, this book scales the big picture topic of SAP administration down to size. With step-by-step instructions and hundreds of screenshots, explore everything from SAP admin fundamentals to what actions should be taken when disaster strikes. Whether you're a beginner SAP Basis administrator, or just looking to brush up on your skills, I'm certain this book will be a vital resource in your continued administration education.

What did you think about the second edition of *SAP Administration—Practical Guide*? Your comments and suggestions are the most useful tools to help us make our books the best they can be. Please feel free to contact me with any praise or criticism you may have.

Thank you for purchasing a book from SAP PRESS!

Sarah Frazier
Editor, SAP PRESS

Rheinwerk Publishing
Boston, MA

sarahf@rheinwerk-publishing.com
www.sap-press.com

Contents

Preface

This book introduces you to the tasks associated with the role of an SAP system administrator. An SAP system administrator ensures that the SAP Basis components of every SAP system and their functions are working correctly during live operation. If this isn't the case, specialized SAP components, such as Financials (FI), Materials Management (MM), and Sales and Distribution (SD), won't be able to run smoothly.

The software components within SAP Basis include the SAP NetWeaver Application Server (formerly known as the SAP Web Application Server, component `SAP_BASIS`) and the cross-application component `SAP_ABA`. These software components supply the basic functions, transactions, and programs that every SAP system needs.

This book includes many real-world examples, step-by-step guides, and checklists to provide an overview of the wide range of tasks involved in SAP administration and to familiarize you with the most important tools available to administrators.

Who Is This Book For?

This book is aimed, in particular, at the following groups of readers:

- Newcomers to SAP administration
- System administrators in SMEs and large enterprises
- Administrators who are in a position to focus on an SAP system and are only involved to a limited extent in the administration of the operating system and database
- Junior consultants

Large sections of this book may offer information that is too basic for senior consultants, experienced system administrators, and database administrators who would need to consult more specialized literature to answer specific questions. However, this book may prove useful as a reference.

Content and Structure

An SAP administrator is responsible for a wide range of tasks, and so this book is also designed to cover a broad range of topics. Each chapter provides essential information about the most commonly used and most significant elements that are fundamental to the day-to-day operation of SAP systems.

The book's broad focus means that it's not possible to enter into the finer details of each individual topic; thus, wherever the discussion is cut short in this book, you'll find references to additional sources of information, such as specialist literature, help pages, and SAP Notes.

The key tasks of administrators and the tools and transactions they can use are explained in detail using many screenshots and step-by-step guides based on real-world examples. The content of the book is structured as follows.

Chapter 1, Fundamentals of SAP System Administration, provides basic information about system administration. This is followed in **Chapter 2**, SAP System Administration, by a detailed discussion of the key tasks and transactions associated with SAP administration, such as starting and stopping the server and controlling the most important functions. Monitoring of SAP systems is examined in **Chapter 3**, System Monitoring. **Chapter 4**, System Administration with SAP Solution Manager, explains how the SAP Solution Manager can be used as part of system administration.

Chapter 5, Scheduled Tasks, consists mainly of checklists that can be used for tasks that must be carried out on a regular basis and can be scheduled in advance. You'll find general information about how to perform data backups in SAP systems in **Chapter 6**, Backup and Restore, while **Chapter 7**, Disaster Recovery, explains how to restore a system in the event of a disaster.

Chapter 8, Database Administration, and **Chapter 9**, Operating System Administration, briefly discuss the essential transactions used for the administration of databases and operating systems. **Chapter 10**, Security Administration, describes how to increase and monitor the security level in SAP systems. **Chapter 11**, Performance, then provides an introduction to the analysis and handling of performance issues.

Next, **Chapter 12**, SAP GUI, is devoted to the SAP Graphical User Interface, which enables you to use an SAP system from a PC—apart from the browser. **Chapter 13**, User Administration, and **Chapter 14**, Authorization Management, cover such topics as the creation of user master data records and the assignment of authorizations.

Chapter 15, Background Processing, describes how to schedule and manage batch jobs in SAP systems. This is followed in **Chapter 16**, Output Management, by a discussion of how data can be output (primarily via printing).

Chapter 17, Change and Transport Management, includes a description of the SAP transport system and how you can use it to distribute changes to the SAP systems in your system landscape. The following chapter, **Chapter 18**, System Maintenance, provides instructions on importing support packages. Finally, **Chapter 19**, Diagnostics and Troubleshooting, provides information about how to use the SAP Support Portal and how to import SAP Notes.

The appendices list useful, security-related transactions (**Appendix A** and **Appendix B**) as well as important tables (**Appendix C**) and provide recommendations on the design of specific forms (**Appendix D**). All sources and publications referred to in this book are listed in the bibliography in **Appendix E**.

The Basis Layer of SAP Components

The various SAP components that belong to the application layer, such as SAP Customer Relationship Management (SAP CRM), SAP Advanced Planning & Optimization (SAP APO), and SAP Business Warehouse (SAP BW), are all based on a shared Basis layer. The tasks and tools associated with system administration are always the same for this Basis layer. In other words, capabilities and expertise in the area of system administration can be transferred between SAP applications because administration of the Basis layer always remains the same. However, some administration tasks may also be component-specific and therefore fall outside the scope of this book.

The administration of the Java stack in SAP systems is also omitted. The Java stack is used for web applications such as the SAP Enterprise Portal. However, this book is limited to the administration of the ABAP layer of SAP systems.

Version and Visual Differences

The screenshots in this book originate in systems with SAP NetWeaver version 7.40. The transaction screens in earlier or later releases may differ from those shown here. For this reason, the screen in your system may not look the same as the screen shown in the screenshot. In addition to possible release-specific differences, your system's support package level is also relevant. However, the differences, if any, will be minute.

Other factors influencing the appearance of the transaction screens include the version used and the activated design of the SAP GUI. The screenshots included in this book were created with the Blue Crystal theme of SAP GUI 7.40.

Prerequisites

This book assumes that you already have a certain level of knowledge and that specific system prerequisites are in place. Details of the required knowledge and system configuration are set out next.

Requirements for Users

We assume that you possess a basic level of knowledge of the SAP components, the operating system, and the database.

You should also be able to perform the following tasks:

- **SAP component level**
  - Log on to the SAP system.
  - Use menus and transaction codes for navigation in the SAP system.
- **Operating system level**
  - Be familiar with the file and directory structure.
  - Use the command line for navigation and to run programs.
  - Set up a printer.
  - Perform a backup using the standard tools of the operating system or third-party tools.
  - Use the operating system's basic security functions.
  - Copy and move data.
  - Start up and shut down the operating system and server correctly.
- **Database level**
  - Stop and start the database correctly.
  - Use the tools provided in the database system.
  - Create a database backup copy.

You should have access to the SAP system, the database, and the operating system, and be familiar with basic navigation in each. In addition, you should have sufficient authorization to execute the tasks described.

Requirements for the System

The SAP system must be fully and correctly installed, and its infrastructure must be set up and in full working order. Installation and related one-off tasks are not described in this book.

You can use the following checklist to determine whether your system has been set up in accordance with the prerequisites for this book. If you can log on to your SAP system, you know that most of these tasks have already been completed:

- **SAP level**
  - Has the SAP system been installed in accordance with SAP recommendations?
  - Are the profile files available?
  - Is the Transport Management System (TMS) configured?
  - Is the SAProuter configured?
  - Is the ABAP Workbench configured?
  - Were any security functions configured for logon (e.g., default passwords changed)?
  - Is the online documentation installed?
- **Database level**
  - Is the database configured?
  - Does the database have a working connection to the SAP system?
- **Operating system level**
  - Are all drives configured (e.g., *sapmnt*)?
- **Software**
  - Is a backup program installed?
  - Is a hardware monitor installed?
  - Is a system monitor installed?
  - Is an uninterrupted power supply (UPS) control installed?

- **Hardware**
  - Is the hardware of the application and database server working?
  - Have the backup devices been installed and tested?
- **Infrastructure**
  - Is the network configured?
  - Is aUPS installed?
  - Is a server monitor or system monitor available?
- **Desktop**
  - Is the SAP GUI installed on the desktop PC?
  - Can users log on to the SAP system from their desktops?

Check whether these prerequisites are in place. If in doubt, ask for assistance from a colleague from the operating system, database, or network administration, or from an external consultant.

How to Use This Book

Important points to note and additional information are provided throughout this book in info boxes. These boxes can be divided into various categories depending on their focus, and these categories are indicated using various icons:

[!] **Note**: Please take particular care when performing this task or executing this step. An explanation of why particular care is needed in these cases is also provided.

[+] **Tip**: This icon identifies useful hints and shortcuts, which are intended to make your job easier.

[Ex] **Example**: Useful real-world examples are indicated by this symbol.

[⚙] **Tech talk**: Information indicated by this icon will help you understand the topic at a deeper level. This information is not essential to performing the task.

I hope that this book will help you fulfill your tasks in relation to SAP administration, and I wish you every success and happy reading! Any feedback would be gratefully appreciated.

Sebastian Schreckenbach

This chapter deals with the general description of the tasks of a system administrator. It also explains the terms that occur most frequently in connection with SAP system administration.

1 Fundamentals of SAP System Administration

Depending on the size of the enterprise and the available resources, either a single individual is responsible or several specialists in one or more departments are responsible for the administration of an SAP system. The allocation of tasks, positions, and roles for system administration depends on the following factors:

- Size of the enterprise
- Available resources (size of the SAP Basis team)
- Available infrastructure support for the following:
  - Desktop support
  - Databases
  - Networks
  - Implementations

Depending on the circumstances, the system administrator may be responsible for performing only a few or, alternatively, a large number of the tasks described next, all of which are related directly or indirectly to the SAP system.

1.1 System Administrator Tasks

The tasks of an SAP system administrator can be divided into a number of different areas. Each area is represented by a specific role, which is, in turn, assigned to one or more individuals. System administrators may be assigned the following roles that relate directly to the SAP system:

- **System administrator**
  Keeps the system in good working order and monitors and manages system performance and system logons.
- **User administrator**
  Creates and manages user accounts.
- **Authorization administrator**
  Creates and manages SAP roles.
- **Security administrator**
  Guarantees the security of the SAP system and monitors breaches of security.
- **Transport administrator**
  Transports changes between systems and manages change requests.
- **Background job administrator**
  Creates, monitors, and manages background jobs.
- **Data backup administrator**
  Schedules, performs, and monitors backup jobs in the SAP database and in all required files at the system level.
- **Disaster recovery manager**
  Creates, tests, and executes the plan for an SAP system restore following a disaster.
- **Programmer**
  Imports SAP Notes and, if necessary, makes changes to the ABAP Dictionary.

Additional tasks arise in relation to an SAP system that play a key role in influencing system operation. These tasks are related more or less indirectly to the SAP system and mainly have to do with the underlying infrastructure:

- **Database administrator**
  Performs database-specific tasks and keeps the database in good working order.
- **Operating system administrator**
  Manages access to the operating system and performs operating system-specific tasks.
- **Network administrator**
  Manages network access and guarantees network support and maintenance.
- **Server administrator**
  Manages servers and virtual machines.

- **Desktop support specialist**
  Provides support for users' desktop PCs.
- **Print operator**
  Manages network and desktop printers.
- **Facility manager**
  Manages the technical/physical infrastructure (e.g., power supply, air conditioning, etc.).

From an organizational perspective, these roles must be assigned to one or more individuals to distribute the tasks that need to be performed and guarantee system operation.

Another important aspect are substitute rules to ensure that tasks will be taken care of by another person if the administrator is on vacation or ill. Checklists, sets of instructions, and documentation relating to key tasks must be created because not all employees will possess all of the information required. This approach improves availability and the transfer of knowledge within the enterprise.

1.2 Guiding Principles for System Administrators

In your role as SAP system administrator, you should follow some basic guiding principles.

Protect the System

Everything you do as system administrator should serve a single purpose: to secure and protect system integrity. If the integrity of the system—and, in particular, the data it contains—cannot be guaranteed, the wrong decisions may be made on the basis of incorrect information. Your enterprise may suffer serious losses if the system can't be restored following a system failure.

It's your responsibility to guarantee system operation and system availability for employees, customers, suppliers, and so on. You need to minimize both the risk of downtime and the length of downtime because every minute that the system can't be used may have a negative economic impact on your own enterprise and any enterprises associated with it.

Given these considerations, it's essential that the system administrator takes positive, responsible action. After all, the system administrator is responsible for the enterprise's data backbone and, as such, must proceed with particular caution because any mistake may cost the enterprise dearly.

Another important task of a system administrator is to protect the system from attack. Such attacks may be external (hackers) or internal (e.g., unauthorized access by "curious" employees).

Don't Be Afraid to Ask for Help

Some SAP components are so large and complex that it's impossible for a single person to know all there is to know about them. Without the requisite knowledge, tasks are difficult to perform, and errors are almost inevitable. In some cases, these errors can't be undone. Often, asking for help is the only way to avoid errors and bridge knowledge gaps. There are no stupid questions!

Help can come from many different sources: SAP Notes and documentations, various websites and forums (e.g., SAP Service Marketplace and SAP Community Network) or consultants. For more information, also read the following principles.

Make Contact with Other Customers and with Consultants

To broaden your knowledge base, you can contact the Basis team and system administrators in other enterprises. Other SAP customers may have solutions to the problems you encounter based on their own experience in the same area. If a colleague can answer your question, you can save yourself a consultant's fee.

Good networking opportunities are provided by training courses, professional organizations, SAP events (such as the TechEd and SAPPHIRE conferences organized by SAP), and user groups (such as the Americas' SAP Users' Group [ASUG] and the SAP Community Network ,formerly the SAP Developer Network).

Use the KISS Principle (Keep It Short and Simple)

If you follow this important principle, you won't make tasks more complicated than they already are. Large or complex tasks become easier to handle if you can break them down into smaller, manageable units.

Sometimes a technically simple solution is best. Depending on the situation, a solution that appears to be rather primitive may actually work more reliably than a highly sophisticated solution and also reduce your costs.

Document Every Step

Make sure to document all processes, procedures, hardware changes, configuration changes, checks, problems, errors, and so on. If you're ever in doubt as to how much detail you should include in your documentation, it's best to write everything down.

Over time, you may forget important details of a process or a problem. If this occurs, you can rest assured that you can access your detailed documentation of the procedures to refresh your memory. Detailed documentation can also help others perform your tasks when you're not there. Because high staff turnover is the norm in the working world, detailed documentation also facilitates the training of new employees.

The documentation must grow and develop in tandem with the system. Make sure that older documents are updated on an ongoing basis. Any change to the system must also be reflected in the documentation. Inaccuracies in the documentation may result in costly errors. Your documentation should be comprehensive, clearly structured, and easily understood. Where relevant, use graphics, flow charts, and screenshots to illustrate content and provide additional information.

Make sure that the documentation is stored in an easily accessible location. Keep a log book for each server, where you can note any changes made.

Document Your Work Promptly and Thoroughly [!]

It's easy to forget about documentation in the "hot" phase of a project or in the event of an emergency. You should record everything done in the system—ideally while it's being done. Never put the task of documentation on the back burner, or you may never get around to it.

Use Checklists

Checklists allow you to standardize processes and minimize the risk of overlooking important steps. By using a checklist, you're also forced to document events (such as runtimes) that may prove to be significant at a later stage. Checklists are particularly useful in the case of complex or important tasks. Serious errors may occur if one step is omitted or not executed correctly (e.g., you may be unable to restore the database).

You'll find a checklist helpful the first time you perform a task or for any tasks that you only need to perform occasionally. Some pre-prepared checklists are provided in various parts of this book. You can use these as a starting point for creating lists that meet your own requirements. These checklists serve as documentation of your work and ensure that your steps can be retraced later.

Perform Planned Maintenance

By scheduling regular, preventive maintenance measures, you can prevent minor nuisances from spiraling into major issues. In this way, potential problems are eliminated before they can impact negatively on the system and on business processes.

[Ex]

Losses Are Often Due to Neglected Maintenance Tasks

The database stops when the available memory for the log files drops to zero. This can shut down the entire SAP system. The system can then only be restarted when a sufficient amount of memory has been freed up. The resulting delays may hinder business processes, such as shipping. By permanently monitoring the memory and timely extending or regularly cleaning up the file system, you can avoid such issues.

Proactive troubleshooting should therefore form part of your routine tasks and should be done at a time when the disruption to users can be kept to a minimum. You should keep an eye on the various logs and event monitors and be on the lookout for potential sources of problems. In addition, you should check the integrity and consistency of the database on a regular basis.

Remember, however, that physical maintenance is also required. Check whether the hardware is located in a clean and cool environment. If necessary, perform hardware updates, for example, to provide additional disk storage space. And, finally, check that you have a fully functional, uninterrupted power supply (UPS).

Only Change What Needs to Be Changed

In today's high-tech world, we may feel compelled to constantly equip ourselves with the latest and best hardware and software. However, it's not always advisable to give in to this temptation. If your system is running without any problems, then you should leave it alone. Don't perform upgrades simply because you can. Upgrading with new software or hardware may introduce new elements and therefore new risks to a previously stable system. In addition, upgrades are frequently costly, in terms of time, resources, money, or potential system downtime.

You should only make changes to the system environment if this is necessitated by the business structures or by legal requirements. Of course, if hardware or software is no longer supported by the manufacturer, this is also a good reason to perform an upgrade.

If you're planning to change your system environment, you should first make sure that the system can be reset to its original status before the change. Conduct regression tests with the operational functions team and users to ensure that the changes do not impact other parts of the system. We recommend planning and testing a change using the following sequence of system steps:

1. Test system (sandbox)
2. Development system
3. Quality assurance system
4. Production system

Even if your enterprise doesn't have all of these systems in place—for instance, a sandbox system—you should still follow this general sequence of development, quality assurance, and production systems.

Don't Change the System During Critical Phases

We strongly recommend that you never make any changes to the system during critical phases. A critical phase refers to a time during which a system failure could result in serious operational problems and business losses.

You should always inform users about any system events that may potentially disrupt their use of the system. Your scheduling must take account of the fact that various user groups, such as accounting users and order entry users, have certain periods of relatively low activity during the year. Schedule potentially disruptive system events during quiet phases, when the effects of any problems on users are minimized. Organize the times at which urgent and less important maintenance tasks are to be performed and decide how users are to be informed. Define contact persons for system administration and SAP users, and coordinate the maintenance plan with all involved.

[Ex]

Critical Phases

Examples of critical phases include the following:

- The start of the month, when the accounting department prepares the month-end closing for the previous month
- The final month of the year (calendar year or fiscal year), when the posting and shipping activities of the sales and distribution department and the shipping department are intensified to maximize revenue for the current year
- The start of the year, when the accounting department is performing the year-end closing for the previous year and preparing for the financial audit
- Key project phases, such as training, testing, or go-live of a new SAP component

Minimize Single Points of Failure

With a single point of failure, the failure of a single component, task, or activity causes the failure of the entire system or leads to a critical event. Any risk of a single point of failure therefore simultaneously increases the risk of a system failure or critical event.

To avoid single points of failure, proceed as follows:

- Configure your system with an integrated system backup.
- Ensure redundancy, for example, with a redundant power supply system.
- Keep replacement parts on hand.
- Ensure that you have enough human resources, and distribute knowledge.
- Have consultants on call.
- Consider cross-training.
- Consider outsourcing.

[Ex]

Single Point of Failure

Some examples of single-point-of-failure scenarios are provided here:

- You only have a single tape drive. The tape drive fails. You can no longer save your database on tape.
- You depend on the main power supply because you have no UPS. In the event of a power outage, the server crashes and may damage the database.
- You are the only person capable of performing a specific task. If you go on a vacation or are ill, this task can't be performed until you return to work.

Prevent Direct Database Access

Direct database access means that a user can query or change the database directly without authorization in the SAP system. If a user has direct access to the database, there's a risk that the database may suffer damage. Direct access also interferes with the synchronization of the database with the SAP-internal buffers.

SAP applications usually write their data to several tables in the database when a specific transaction or document is saved, for example. If a user writes data to the database tables directly, the database may be damaged if a single table is omitted because a mismatch then exists between the tables. With direct database access, a user may also accidentally change or delete the database instead of reading data from it.

Outlaw All Non-SAP Activities on the SAP Server

The servers on which your SAP instances are running should only ever be used for this purpose. If other services also run on these servers, they may make the server run more slowly and also increase the risk of unintentional data changes or deletions.

Preventing Access to the Server [!]

Don't allow users to access the SAP server directly by Telnet or external access. This is necessary to protect confidential or sensitive information. Don't use the SAP application server as a file server. In this way, you can ensure that no data can be deleted or changed by mistake. Don't run any programs on the servers of the SAP components that aren't directly related to the application. As a result, system resources remain open for SAP tasks.

1.3 Definitions

This book uses some terms with a very specific meaning. These terms are defined next for the purpose of clarification.

Database Server

The *database server* comprises the database of the SAP system, for example, MS SQL Server, DB2, or Oracle. The system clock of the database server sets the time for the SAP application.

Application Server

The *application server* runs the SAP application, that is, the kernel program. An SAP system can consist of one or more application servers. The application server can also run on the database server (physical or virtual). Application servers can be set up for online users, for background processing, or for both.

Instance

An *instance* refers to an installation of the SAP application on an application server. We can distinguish between a central instance and dialog instances. The central application is the *central instance* on which the SAP enqueue server (or *lock server*) runs. It exists only once in the system environment. *Dialog instances* are all other (noncentral) instances. Any system environment may have several dialog instances. More than one instance may be installed on a physical or virtual server. During installation, separate directories and profile files are created for each instance.

System

A *system* comprises the complete SAP installation for a system ID (SID), for example, V14. A system logically consists of the SAP central instances and the dialog instances for the SID. Physically, it comprises the database server and the application servers for this SID.

SAP Configuration with Three Layers

Table 1.1 shows an SAP configuration with three layers.

Layer	Physical Device	What Runs on This Layer?
Display	Several desktop PCs	SAP GUI, browser
Application	One or more application servers	SAP central or dialog instance
Databases	A single database server	Database: MS SQL Server, DB2, Oracle

Table 1.1 Configuration with Three Layers

In a two layer configuration, the SAP application and the database are run on one single server.

Client

A *client* is an area containing independent application data within an SAP system. You log on to the SAP system in a specific client. Several clients may exist in parallel in a single SAP system, with each client representing a self-contained unit in terms of master data and application data. This delineation is often used to map organizational or project-related structures, for example, scenarios where separate clients for system maintenance tests from running operation and a project go-live are set up in a quality assurance system. The clients in a system share various cross-client system resources, such as the SAP instances, the database, and the ABAP Dictionary.

1.4 Summary

This chapter has familiarized you with the essential areas of responsibility of an SAP system administrator. Based on this knowledge, you can decide how to distribute the tasks in your administration group from an organizational perspective. In addition, we set out some basic principles to guide administrators in their tasks. These should be followed as part of routine system operation to maximize system availability and minimize the risk of downtime. The terms and definitions provided here should also assist you in your understanding of the rest of the book.

Your main role as an SAP system administrator is to manage the day-to-day operation of the SAP system. This chapter describes the tasks, tools, and transactions that you need to know for system administration.

2 SAP System Administration

On a day-to-day basis, most of your time as an SAP administrator will be taken up with general system administration. The system must be configured in a way that ensures stable operation with the available resources and avoids *system downtimes*. As administrator, you're also required to eliminate errors that inevitably occur during operation. You must investigate the problem, determine its cause, and find an appropriate solution.

In addition, critical situations will regularly occur that don't originate in the SAP system directly but are, instead, caused by a problem at database or operating system level. In cases like these, you're expected to quickly and accurately assess system status and to use the information obtained to make the right decision concerning how to proceed.

This chapter introduces you to the essential tasks and SAP tools in the system administration environment that you need to use for routine system operation. If you require further information on the administration of SAP systems, refer to *SAP NetWeaver AS ABAP—System Administration* by Föse, Hagemann, and Will (4th edition, SAP PRESS, 2012).

2.1 Starting and Stopping the SAP System

Today's SAP systems comprise three layers: the operating system layer, database layer, and application layer. The individual layers build on one another in this sequence. As a result, the individual components must be started in exactly the same sequence because each layer can only run if the underlying layer is active.

The *operating system layer* provides a basis for the database and application layers, and it runs on a server—this can involve a physical or virtual server. The database and SAP system are installed on this server, or, if necessary, the database and application can also be operated on two separate servers. The server and operating system must be running for you to start the database and application. The operating system manages the hardware resources of the server, and makes it available to the running applications. This book doesn't cover the individual steps involved in the startup and shutdown of a server or of the installed operating system. If necessary, refer to the documentation provided by your operating system or hardware manufacturer.

All SAP system data is stored in the database. This includes the application data (e.g., POs, invoices, etc.) generated by daily transactions, as well as the system settings (*Customizing*) and the source code of programs, functions modules, and so on. The database must be active if you want to start an SAP application because this is the only way to ensure that the application can access the data. Chapter 8 describes how to start and stop the database.

[!]

Steps to Follow When Stopping the System

If you stop the database without stopping the SAP system first, the application can't save buffered data that hasn't yet been stored. In this case, data loss is inevitable. The same also applies if you shut down the operating system or server without closing the SAP system and database properly. The application and database buffers can't be emptied, and the buffered data can't be saved.

You can only start the SAP application itself if the operating system and database are already running. While it's running, the application accesses the information stored in the database. To stop an SAP system, it's necessary to repeat the same steps in exactly the reverse order. You stop the SAP system before stopping the database. The operating system and the physical or virtual server can then be shut down.

2.1.1 Starting the SAP System

Follow these steps to start the SAP system:

1. Start the server and the operating system. Check the operating system log to determine whether the start has been successful.
2. Start the database (see Chapter 8). Check the database log to determine whether the start has been successful.

Starting the Database [+]

This step is optional because the database is started first automatically by the start script when you start the SAP system. However, if you start the database manually, you can check the database log *before* starting the SAP system.

SAP Microsoft Management Console [+]

The following section describes how to start and stop an SAP system using SAP Microsoft Management Console (SAP MMC). SAP MMC can only be installed on Microsoft operating systems. However, you can use it to manage SAP systems from your Windows frontend. These SAP systems can run on any other operating systems (e.g., UNIX).

In addition, you always have the option to directly start the SAP system on the server via the console or by using terminal client software, such as PuTTY, on your frontend computer. For this purpose, log in using the `<sid>adm` user, and start the SAP system by entering the `startsap` command in your console.

3. Open *SAP Microsoft Management Console* by choosing START • (ALL) PROGRAMS • SAP MANAGEMENT CONSOLE from the taskbar.
4. Right-click on the system ID of the system you want to start (e.g., V14), and choose the START entry from the context menu (see Figure 2.1).

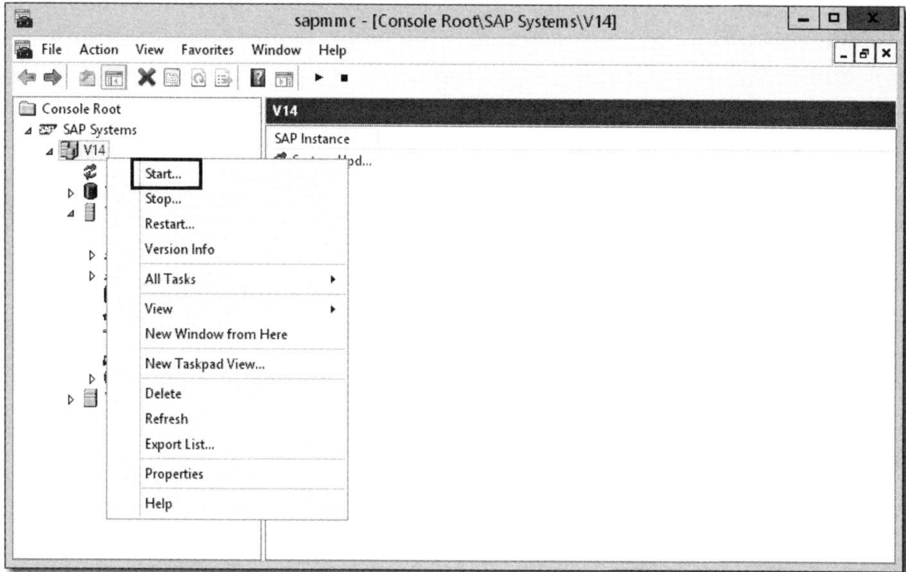

Figure 2.1 Starting the System

5. Enter a START TIMEOUT PERIOD in seconds in the dialog box that opens. If you're only running a single instance, simply click on OK to confirm (see Figure 2.2).

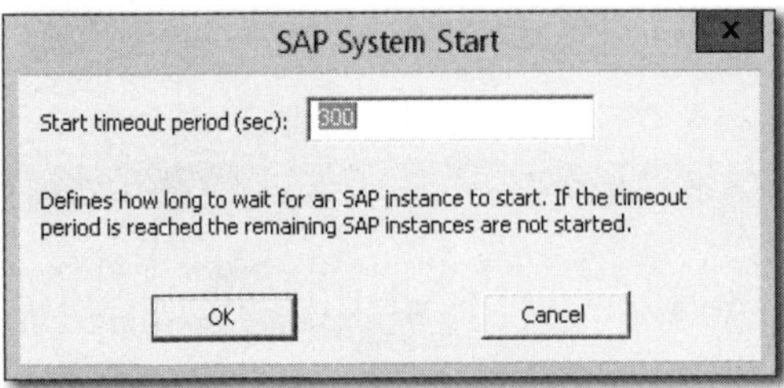

Figure 2.2 Defining the Start Timeout

[+]

Start Timeout

A start timeout is only relevant if you're running other system instances alongside the central instance. The central instance must be running before you can start the other instances.

Entering a start timeout value indicates how many seconds the system should wait before starting the other instances. The value is based on the length of time it takes to start your central instance, based on past experience.

6. Another dialog box opens in which you must authenticate yourself as the administrator of the SAP system (see Figure 2.3). Only administrators are authorized to start and stop an SAP system.

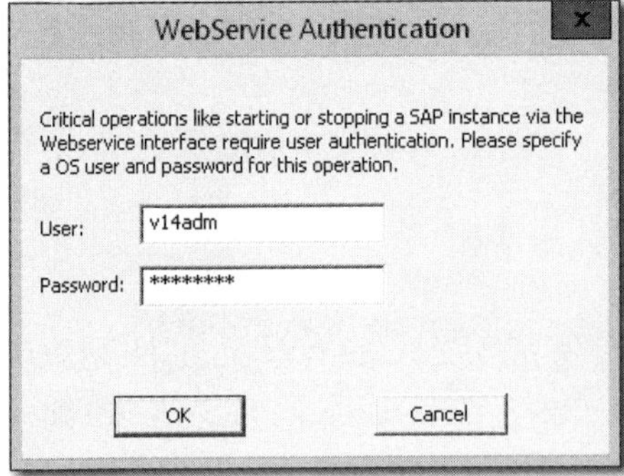

Figure 2.3 System Administrator Authentication

7. This automatically starts the database (if it hasn't already been started) and then the SAP system. In the SAP Microsoft Management Console, the status is

initially yellow, which changes to green after a successful start. In the PROCESS LIST, all processes have the RUNNING status (see Figure 2.4).

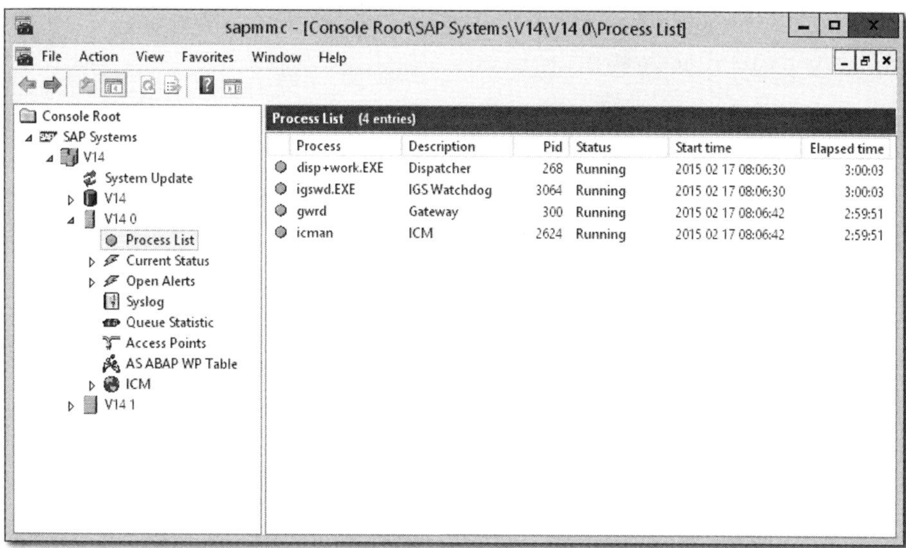

Figure 2.4 Process List of the System Started

Patience Is a Virtue [+]

It may take several minutes to start an SAP instance. Patience really is an essential characteristic of good system administrators. You need to wait and remain calm if it takes longer than expected. A red traffic light icon will alert you to the occurrence of errors. As long as you don't see any red traffic lights, simply give the system the time it needs.

8. The system has started. To check whether the SAP system is running, log on to the system with the SAP GUI. You know that the system has been started correctly if the logon screen appears (see Figure 2.5).

Checking the Start Logs [⚙]

If problems occur when starting the system, you need to check the start logs. You'll find these logs at the operating system level in the */usr/sap/<SID>/<instance>/work* directory. Check for error messages in the following files:

- *sapstart.log*
- *sapstartsrv.log*

- *dev_disp*
- *dev_ms*
- *dev_w0*

Eliminate the error, and restart the system.

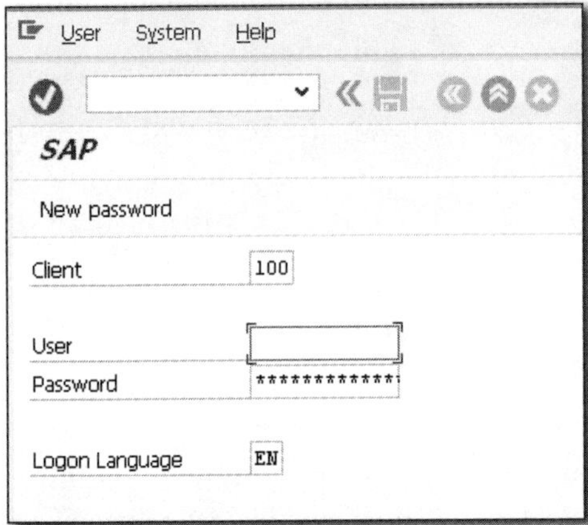

Figure 2.5 Logon Screen of the System Started

9. Log on, and check the *system log* (Transaction SM21—see Section 2.4.1) to determine whether any errors occurred at startup.

[⚙]

Checking the System Log after Startup

You should wait for a minute or so after starting the SAP system. This makes it easier to read the system log. Several entries may still be in the process of being written to the log during the start phase. If you wait, you won't need to refresh the system log view several times to display all of these.

2.1.2 Stopping the SAP System

There are several reasons you may need to stop or restart the SAP system:

- An unplanned hardware or software failure
- Planned hardware or software maintenance
- Changes to profile parameters that can't be switched dynamically
- Planned complete backup of the server

If you need to stop the SAP system, it's essential that you do so in consultation with your end users. Stopping the system at your own discretion and without any prior warning is very likely to infuriate users because all unsaved data are lost.

Preparing for a System Stop

Before you stop the system, you must perform checks and take precautions to ensure that system activities have ceased at the time of the system stop.

Checking System Activities before Stopping the System [!]

For certain activities, such as large posting jobs, you may find that some transactions have already been posted, while others have not. A subsequent restore may be problematic in such cases.

Follow these steps before a system shutdown:

- Coordinate the system shutdown with all departments affected. If a group of users has already scheduled an activity for the period during which you want to shut the system down, and the activity is dependent on a live SAP system, you may have to postpone your system stop and give a higher priority to the needs of these users.
- Create a system message (Transaction SM02) to inform all users of the planned system stop.
- Before you stop the system, make sure that no users are still logged on or active in the system (Transaction SM04 or AL08—see Chapter 13).
- In Transaction SM37 (see Chapter 15), check whether any jobs are active or have been scheduled for the time during which the system stop is to take place. Reschedule all jobs, or cancel the jobs that are due to either run or be started during the planned system stop.
- Check whether any active processes are still running (Transaction SM50 or SM51—see Section 2.4.3).
- Use Transaction SMGW to search for any active RFC connections, which may indicate interfaces that are currently running.

Use the checklist in Table 2.1 as preparation for stopping the system.

Task	Date	Initials
The following tasks must be completed in sufficient time before the SAP system is stopped:		
Coordinate the system stop with all departments affected (e.g., accounting, shipping, distribution, etc.).		
Create a system message to inform all users of the planned system stop (Transaction SM02).		
Send an additional email notification to all users affected.		
Reschedule jobs or cancel the jobs that are either due to run or be started during the planned system stop (Transaction SM37).		
The following additional tasks must also be completed shortly before the SAP system is stopped:		
Make sure that no active users are still logged on to the system (Transactions SM04 and AL08).		
Make sure that no active background jobs are running (Transaction SM37).		
Make sure that no active processes are running (Transactions SM50 and SM51).		
Check for active external interfaces (Transaction SMGW).		
How to stop the SAP system:		
Stop the application server instances.		
Stop the central instance.		
Stop the database (optional).		

Table 2.1 Checklist for Preparing for a System Stop

In the event of an emergency, or if the system stop has priority over all other requirements (e.g., if you have a file system overflow, log storage overflow, device failure, etc.), the system must be stopped immediately. In such cases, end users are forced by circumstances to adapt. However, you should still try to work through the checklist.

Stopping the SAP System

You shouldn't stop the SAP system until you've completed all necessary checks and are certain that all system activities have ceased. To stop the SAP system, follow these steps:

1. Open the SAP Microsoft Management Console by selecting START • (ALL) PROGRAMS • SAP MANAGEMENT CONSOLE.
2. You can choose to stop the SAP system only or to stop both the SAP system and the database. To stop the SAP system only, right-click on the name of the instance you want to stop (e.g., V14 0), and choose the STOP entry from the context menu (see Figure 2.6).
3. If you also want to stop all other instances of the SAP system (e.g., another ABAP or Java instance belonging to the system) as well as the database, right-click on the system ID (e.g., V14), and choose STOP from the context menu (see Figure 2.7).

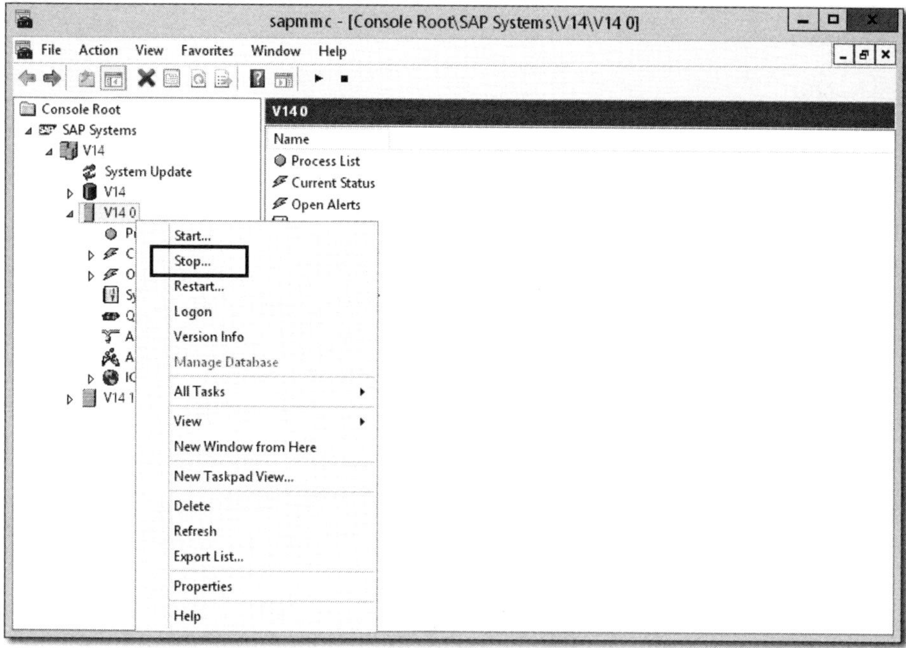

Figure 2.6 Stopping the SAP System

[+]

Stopping without the SAP Microsoft Management Console

You can also stop the SAP system using the console. To do so, open a shell or the command prompt, and use the `stopsap r3` console command. To stop the SAP system and the database, execute the `stopsap` or `stopsap all` command.

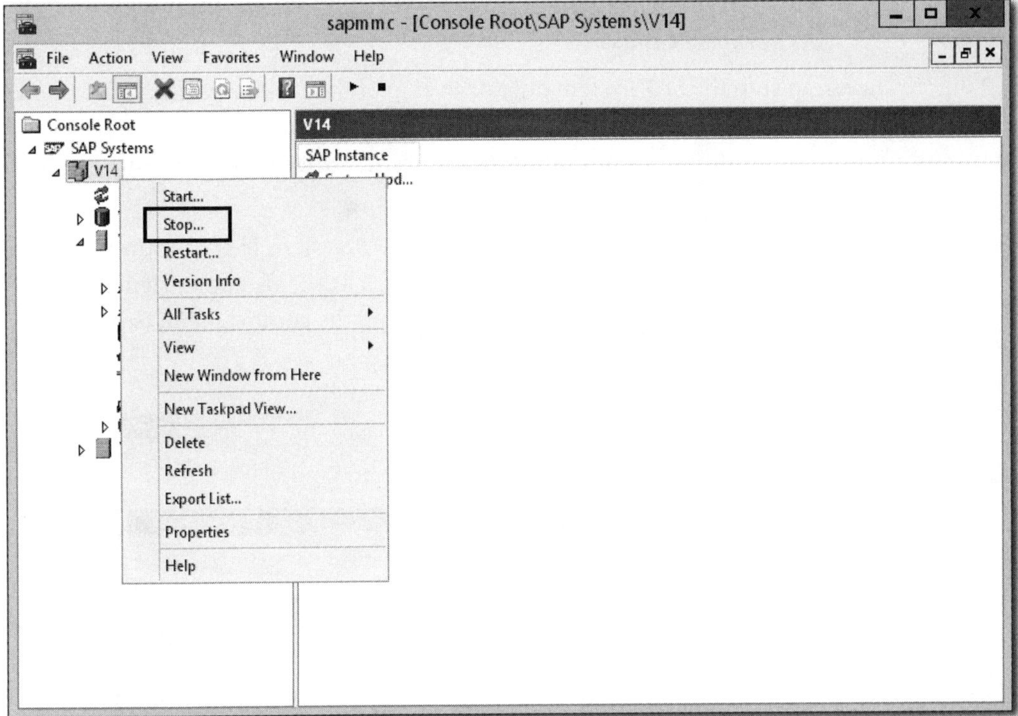

Figure 2.7 Stopping All Instances and the SAP System Database

4. Select the shutdown type in the dialog box that opens (see Figure 2.8):
   - HARD (SIGINT): The SAP system is shut down immediately.
   - SOFT (SIGQUIT/SIGINT): The SAP system first attempts a *soft shutdown*. If the specified period elapses without a successful shutdown of the SAP system, a *hard shutdown* is executed instead.
5. Choose OK to continue.
6. A dialog box opens, in which you're required to authenticate as an administrator. The SAP system may only be shut down by administrators.
7. Next, the database is stopped, followed by the SAP system, or, alternatively, only the SAP system is stopped, depending on which selection you've made. The status changes from green to gray in the SAP Microsoft Management Console. The processes in the PROCESS LIST change their status to STOPPED (see Figure 2.9).

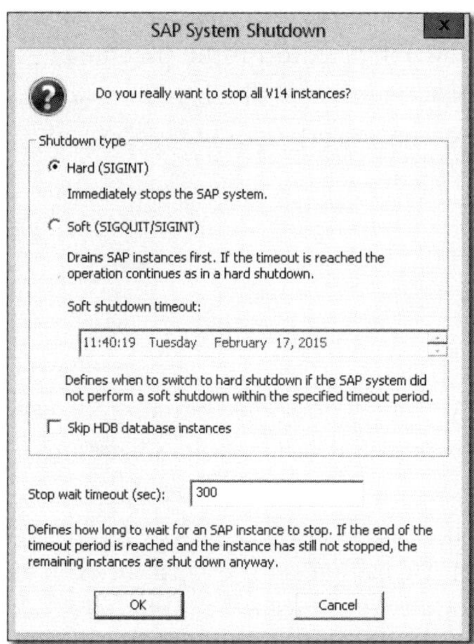

Figure 2.8 Selecting the Shutdown Type

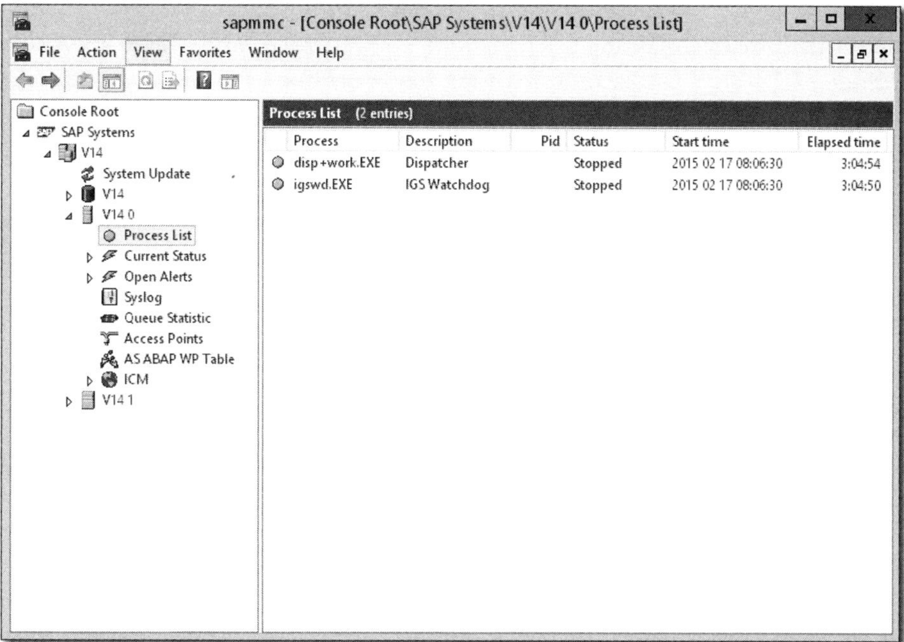

Figure 2.9 Process List with Stopped Processes

You've now stopped the SAP system or both the database and SAP system. If you've stopped the SAP system only to allow changes to profile parameters to become effective, you can now restart the system immediately. If you've stopped both the SAP system and the database, you can now stop the operating system if necessary and shut down the physical server.

2.2 Instances and Operation Modes

Servers at the SAP application level are referred to as *instance servers* or *application servers* in the SAP system architecture. The SAP application (application server) and the database usually share a server. More powerful system landscapes have an SAP system and a database running on two separate servers. The next step up from this configuration is to create instance clusters, in other words, to set up various SAP instances, which can run on different servers. This enhances the capabilities of the system at the application level. However, the individual instances all still access the same database, which can only be clustered if this is supported by the database system (e.g., DB2 PureScale and Oracle Real Application Clusters).

Each instance provides a configurable number of *work processes* that are responsible for the processing of the tasks that are transferred to the system. These may include executing a transaction in a user dialog or processing a background job, for example. Work processes are divided into various types based on the tasks for which they are reserved:

- **Dialog work processes**
  Execute ABAP dialog programs.
- **Batch work processes**
  Execute background jobs.
- **Update work processes**
  Control asynchronous database changes.
- **En queue work processes**
  Execute lock operations.
- **Spool work processes**
  Process print data.

As an SAP administrator, you must consider, on the one hand, whether your SAP system should comprise one or more instances. On the other, you can also determine the number and distribution of the work process types of the instances. For example, you could have one instance for dialog logons and a second instance for background processing only.

The total number of work processes in an instance is relatively static because it can only be changed by restarting the application server. However, you can use *operation modes* to influence the type distribution of the work processes dynamically (i.e., during live operation). As a rule, work processes are switched in synchronization with different times of the day. For example, more dialog processes can be made available during daytime hours to handle the higher number of users logging on. At night, when only a small number of users at most are using the system, and the focus is on the processing of scheduled background jobs, the dialog processes can be switched to batch processes. This ensures that more processes are available for background processing.

Operation modes therefore allow you to adjust the SAP system configuration in accordance with your enterprise's requirements. However, the total number of work processes remains unchanged. In small installations where at most a handful of batch jobs are processed at night, you may be able to dispense with the additional process of configuring and managing operation modes. Fewer operation modes mean less administrative work to maintain the system. However, after the system has been configured correctly, the subsequent administrative effort required is low.

Dynamic Work Processes

Since SAP NetWeaver 7.02 with kernel 7.20, you can define two further *dynamic work processes* in addition to the statically defined number of work processes. The dynamic work processes are created if the kernel determines system deadlocks (*not* database deadlocks!).

The barriers for creating further dynamic work processes are defined by the kernel and are very high. For this reason, dynamic work processes aren't a magic bullet and can only be used to a limited extent to avoid resource bottlenecks and performance issues. You can find an overview of the profile parameters for defining dynamic work processes in SAP Note 1636252.

Creating Instance Definitions

To use operation modes, you must create the instances of your system as instance definitions by following these steps:

1. Enter Transaction RZ04 in the command field and press the [Enter] key (or select the menu option TOOLS • CCMS • CONFIGURATION • RZ04—OPERATION MODES/INSTANCES).
2. Click on INSTANCES/OPERATION MODES (see Figure 2.10).

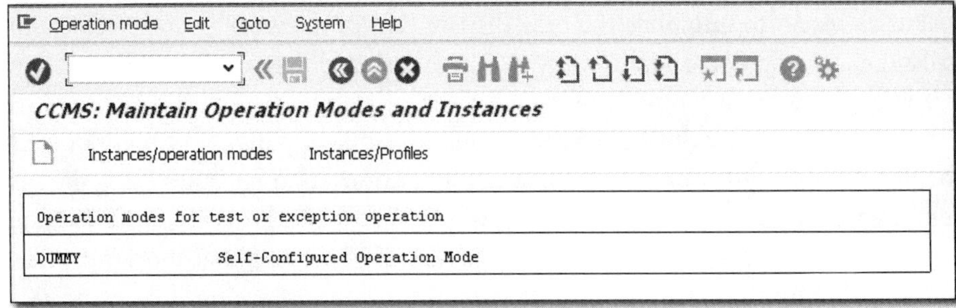

Figure 2.10 Maintaining Instances and Operation Modes

3. Click on the CREATE NEW INSTANCE icon (see Figure 2.11).

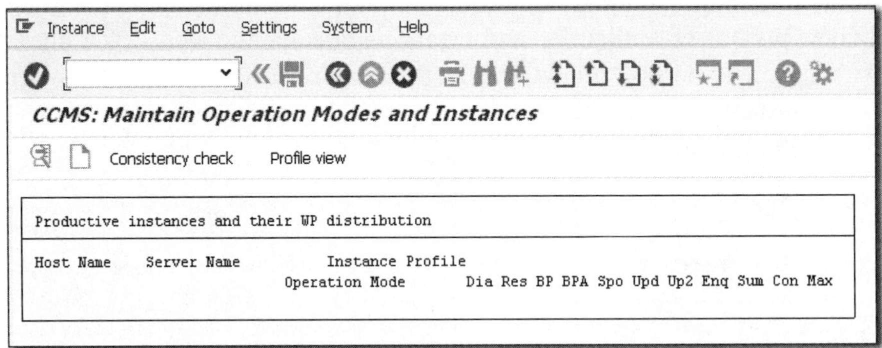

Figure 2.11 Creating a New Instance

4. The instance data must be maintained on the next screen (see Figure 2.12):
   - Enter the name of the server under HOST NAME.
   - Enter the system number in the SAP SYSTEM NO. field.
   - Enter the name of the instance profile under INSTANCE PROFILE.
   - When you've finished, click on SAVE.

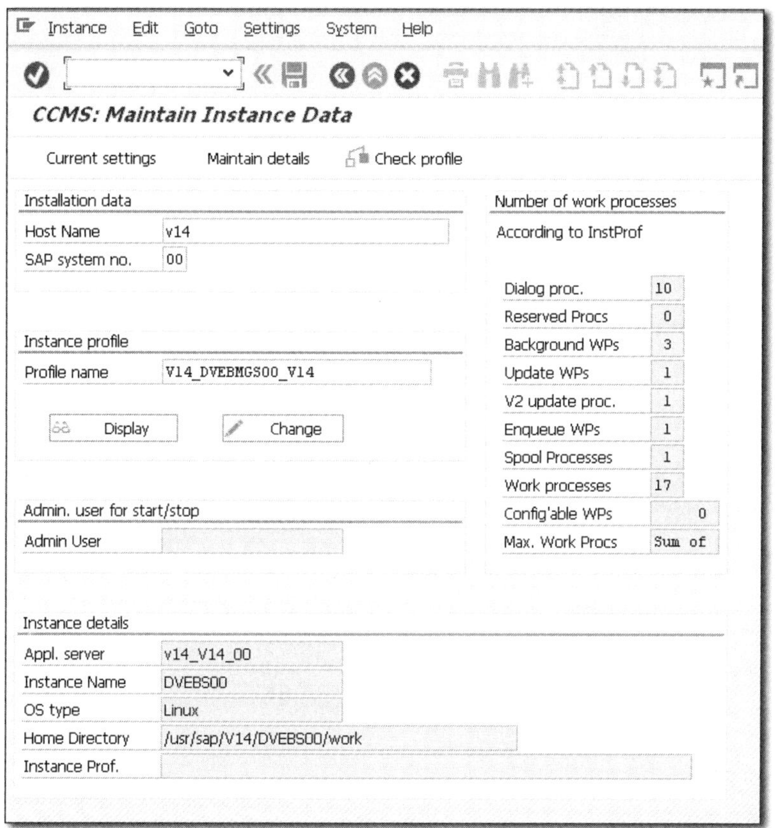

Figure 2.12 Maintaining Instance Data

Creating an Instance for the First Time [+]

If no instances have been created, and you want to create the current instance as an instance definition, fill in the Host Name and SAP system no., and click on the Current settings button. The system automatically determines the data required from the current instance configuration.

5. A dialog box appears, in which you must specify how the work process types are to be distributed (see Figure 2.13). Because these settings are to be defined later by operation modes, enter the placeholder "*" in the Operation Mode field, and leave the other settings unchanged. Click on Save.

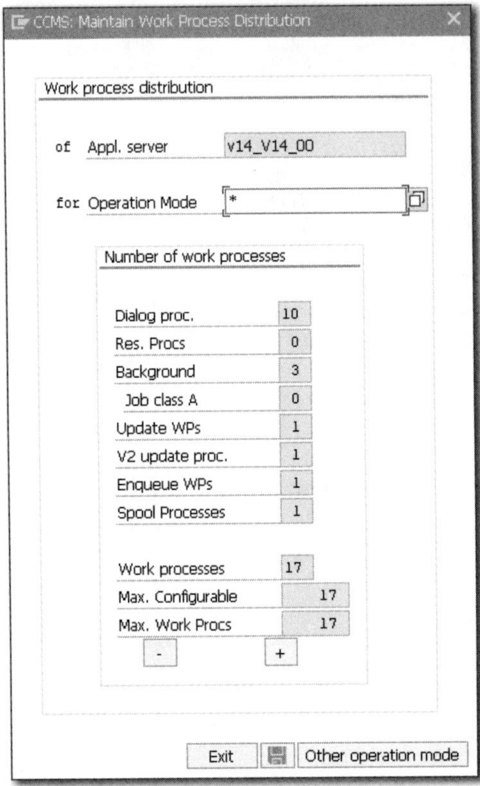

Figure 2.13 Defining the Distribution of Work Processes

6. Click on No in the dialog box that opens (see Figure 2.14).

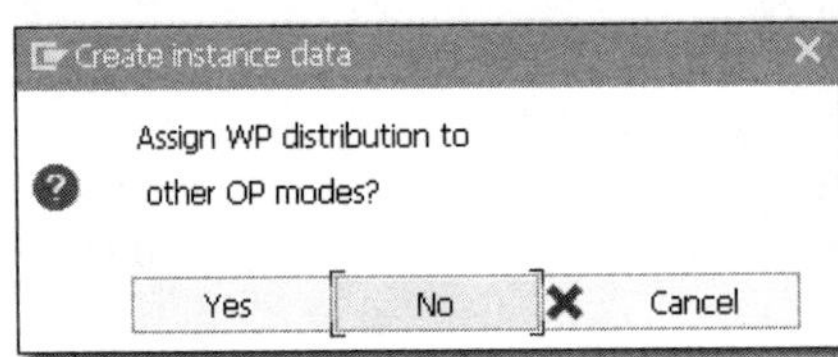

Figure 2.14 Assigning Further Work Process Distributions

7. The instance definition is created, and you return automatically to the initial screen. The table displays the production instances, their detailed data, and the distribution of work processes (see Figure 2.15). Click on Save.

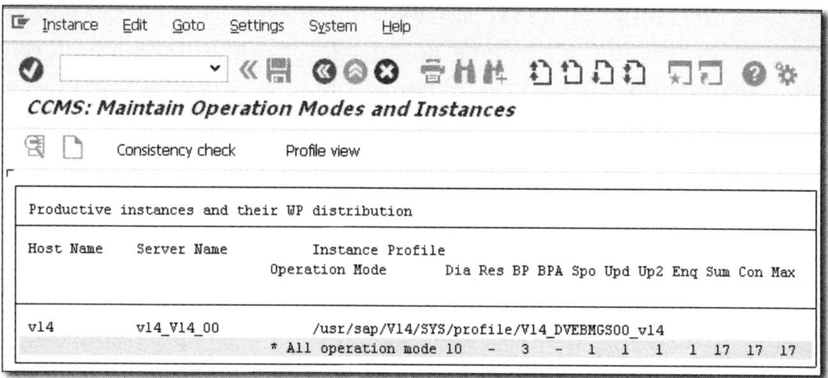

Figure 2.15 Overview of Instances and Operation Modes

Creating Additional Instance Definitions [!]

At this point, you can add more application servers as instance definitions. However, the corresponding instances must already be installed and running on a separate server.

Defining Operation Modes

Next, create the operation modes you want your system to have:

1. Call Transaction RZ04.
2. Click on the Create Operation Mode icon (see Figure 2.16).

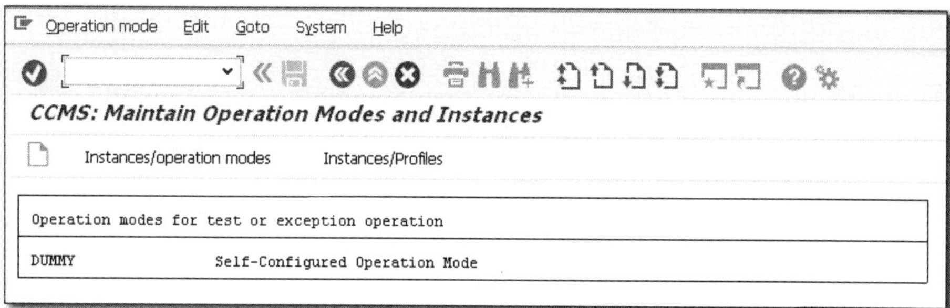

Figure 2.16 Creating a New Operation Mode

3. On the next screen, enter a name (e.g., "Daytime") in the Operation Mode field, then enter a description that is as meaningful as possible in the Short Description field (see Figure 2.17). Click on Save.

4. You return automatically to the initial screen of the existing operation modes. The operation mode you just created is now displayed in the list of PRODUCTIVE OPERATION MODES (NORMAL OPERATION) (see Figure 2.18). Choose CREATE OPERATION MODE to create another operation mode.

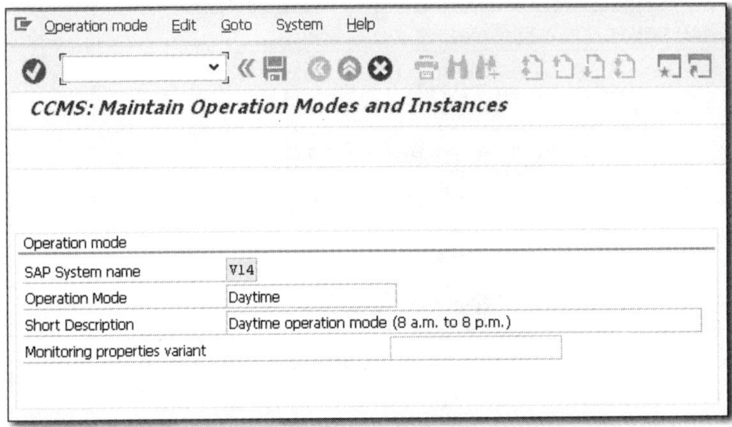

Figure 2.17 Entering the Name and Description for an Operation Mode

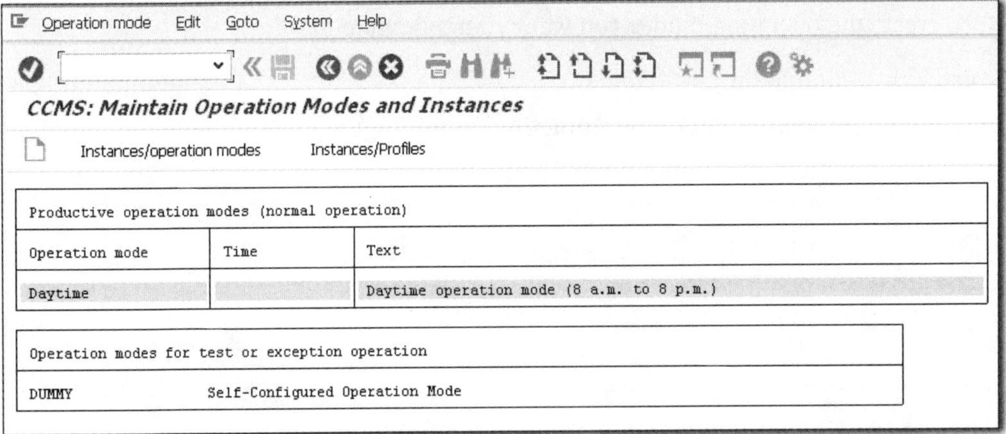

Figure 2.18 Overview of Operation Modes

[+]

Distinguishing Between Different Operation Modes

Production operation modes refer to normal SAP operation, while *test* or *special operation modes* are used, for example, for development systems, test systems, or for specific tasks (such as system maintenance or year-end closing activities).

5. Enter a name (e.g., "Nighttime") and a SHORT DESCRIPTION for the operation mode (see Figure 2.19), and click on SAVE .

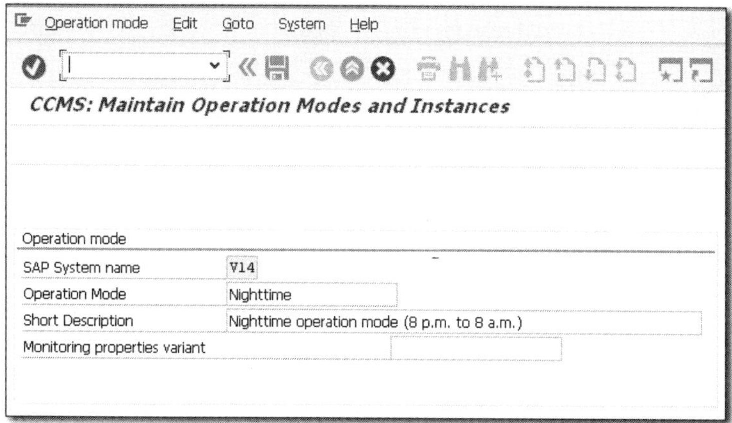

Figure 2.19 Creating Another Operation Mode

Both definitions you created are then shown in the list of PRODUCTIVE OPERATION MODES (see Figure 2.20).

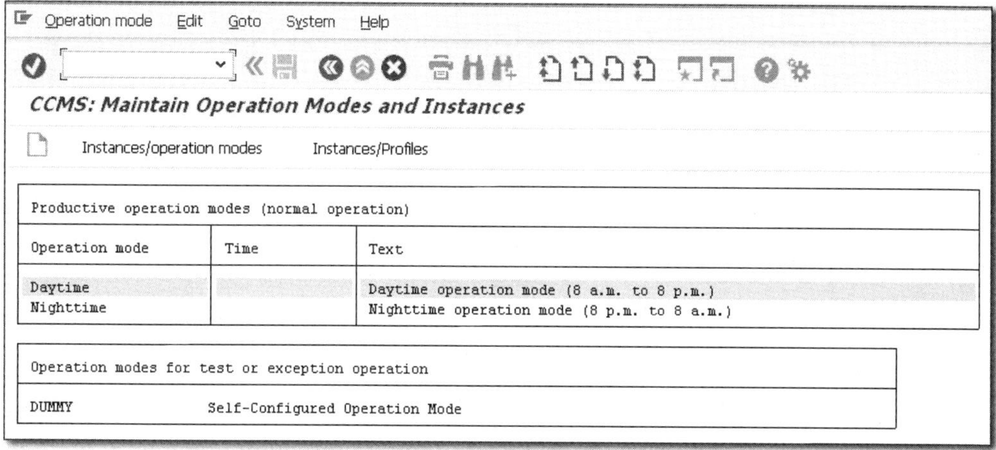

Figure 2.20 Overview of Operation Modes

Useful Operation Modes [+]

The operation modes that will prove useful for your enterprise will be determined by the question of whether or not your system is used differently at different times. In an enterprise with a single location, for example, it may make sense to define one operation mode for daytime operation and one for nighttime operation, with these two modes differing largely in terms of the distribution of dialog and background processes. However, if you need to ensure smooth operation in dialog mode 24/7 (e.g., because various locations in time zones that are very far apart need access to the system), the distribution described here would not make much sense. In a case like this, you would need to base your operation modes on the working hours and needs of all locations, for example.

Assigning Operation Modes and Defining Work Process Distribution

After you've created the operation modes, you can assign these to the instance definitions:

1. Again, call Transaction RZ04.
2. Click on the INSTANCES/OPERATION MODES button (refer to Figure 2.20).
3. On the following screen, position the cursor on the first operation mode row (entry *; see Figure 2.21), and click on CHOOSE.

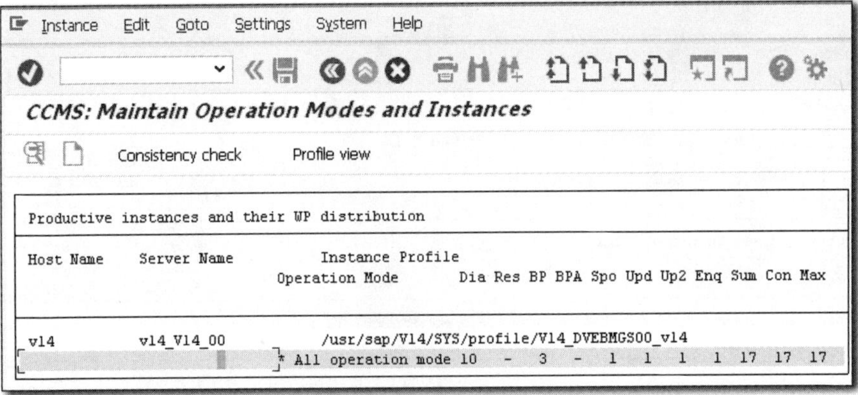

Figure 2.21 Selecting the Operation Mode Row

4. In the dialog box that opens, click on the OTHER OPERATION MODE button.
5. Enter one of the operation modes you created (e.g., "Daytime") in the OPERATION MODE field, or use the input help to select an operation mode. You can use the [-] and [+] buttons to change the number of work processes (see Figure 2.22). When you've finished, click on SAVE.

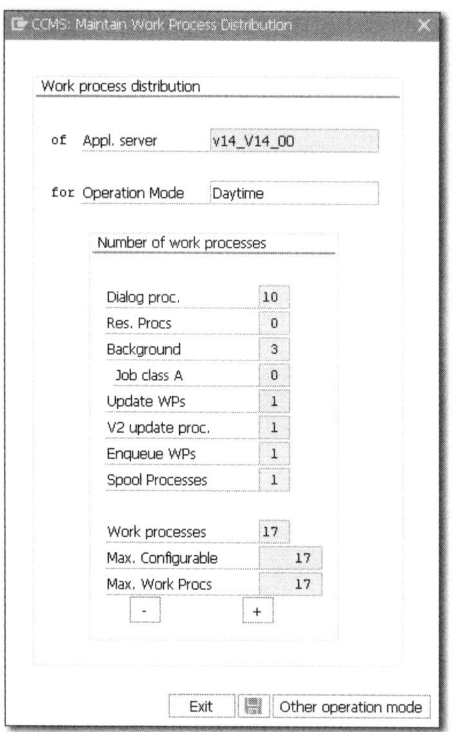

Figure 2.22 Maintaining the Distribution of Work Processes

Changing the Number of Work Processes [+]

In previous releases (SAP NetWeaver 7.3 or lower), the number of dialog work processes is always determined by the other work process types. In other words, you can't configure the dialog processes using the plus and minus buttons. You can, for example, reduce the number of batch processes so that the number of dialog processes increases.

In newer releases, the configuration is more convenient. When you're done with the configuration, always confirm that the number in the MAX. WORK PROCS field is identical to the number displayed in MAX. CONFIGURABLE.

6. Repeat steps 3 and 4, and select the next OPERATION MODE (e.g., NIGHTTIME). Configure the work process distribution, and click on SAVE.

Minimum Number of Dialog Work Processes [!]

Note that an instance must have at least two dialog work processes. The system won't allow you to configure fewer dialog processes for any operation mode.

7. In the table view, position your cursor on the * entry, which isn't needed, and select the INSTANCE • DELETE ENTRY menu option to delete it (see Figure 2.23).

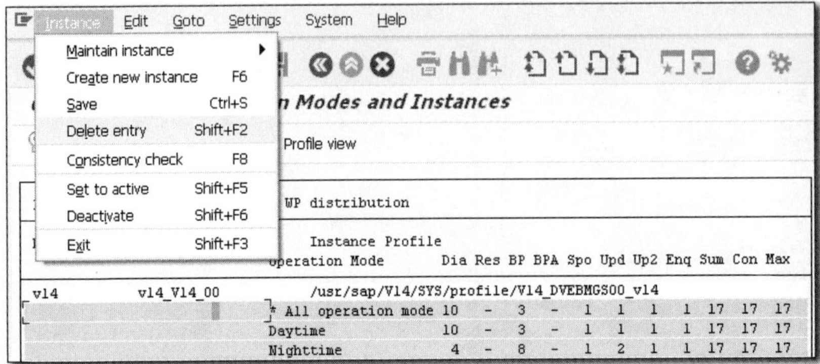

Figure 2.23 Deleting an Operation Mode

8. Choose YES to confirm the dialog box in Figure 2.24, and then choose SAVE.

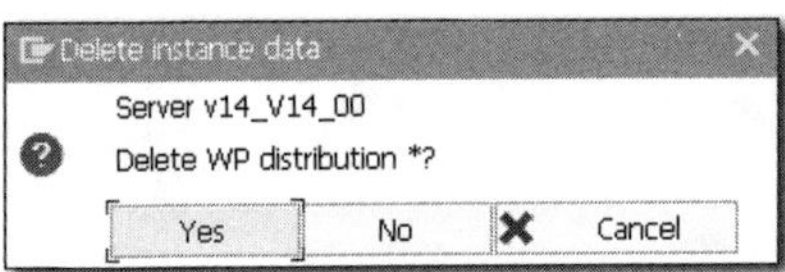

Figure 2.24 Confirming a Deletion

By following these steps, you've assigned the relevant operation modes to the instance and defined how the work processes are to be distributed for each operation mode. Next, you need to configure time-dependent operation mode switching.

Configuring a Time Allocation for Operation Modes

The operation modes and associated work process distribution are subject to time-dependent switching. To define how this switching is to be executed, follow these steps:

1. Enter Transaction SM63 in the command field and press the Enter key (or select the menu option TOOLS • CCMS • CONFIGURATION • SM63—OPERATION MODE CALENDAR).
2. Select NORMAL OPERATION (24 HR), and click on the CHANGE button (see Figure 2.25).

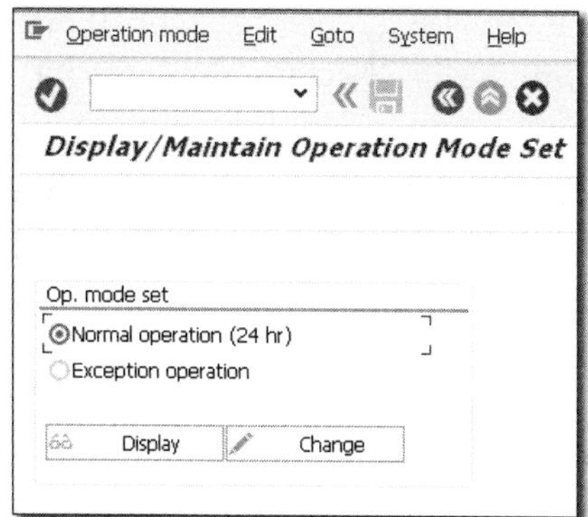

Figure 2.25 Changing the Work Process Distribution for Normal Operation

3. On the next screen, you define the time interval for which the operation mode is to be valid. Position your cursor at the start of the period (e.g., 08.00 – 09.00, if daytime operations are to start at 8:00 am; see Figure 2.26). Select the OPERATION MODE • SELECT INTERVAL menu option, or press the [F2] key.

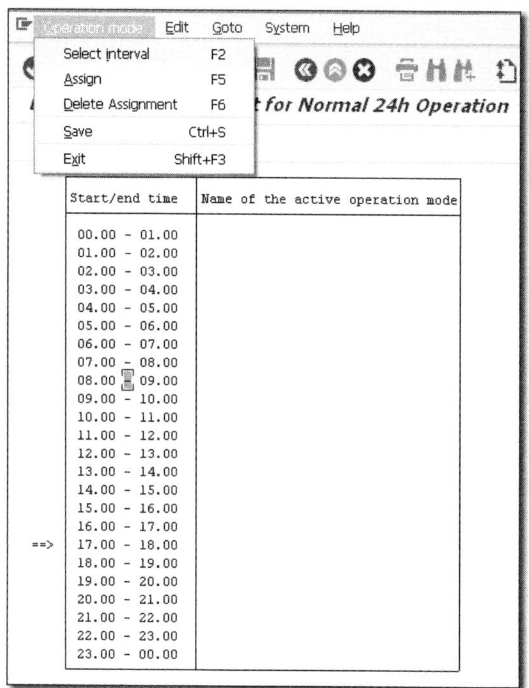

Figure 2.26 Defining the Start of the Time Interval for an Operation Mode

4. Then position your cursor at the end of the interval (e.g., 19.00 – 20.00, if daytime operations are to end at 20.00, or 8:00pm). Again, select OPERATION MODE • SELECT INTERVAL, or press the F2 key.
5. The interval has been selected. Click on the ASSIGN button. In the dialog box that opens, use the input help to select the relevant operation mode, and click on CONTINUE ✓ (see Figure 2.27).

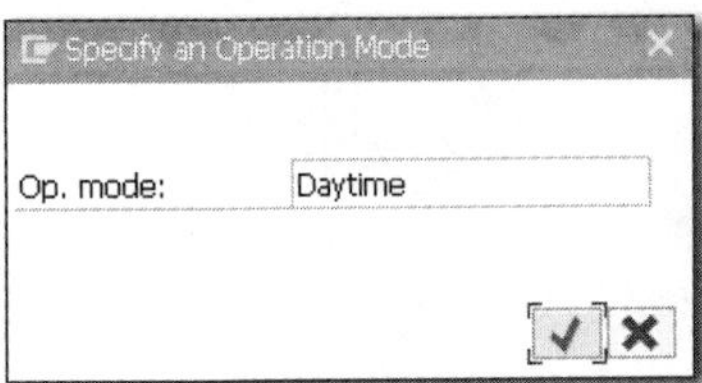

Figure 2.27 Selecting the Operation Mode for the Define Interval

6. The assignment is shown in the table (see Figure 2.28).
7. Repeat steps 3 to 5 to assign an operation mode to the other times.

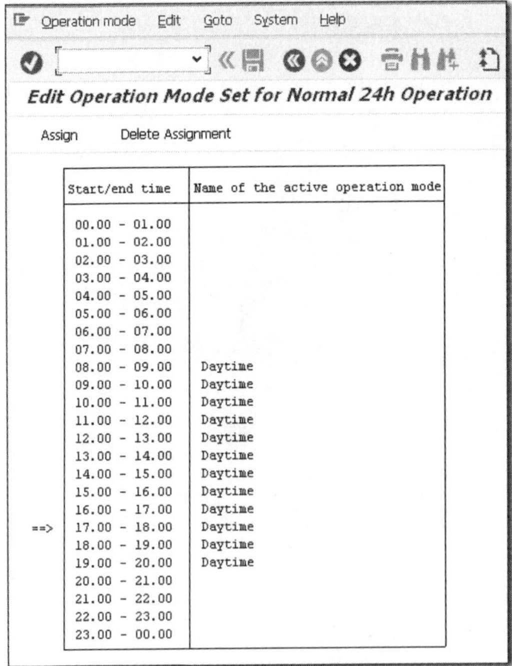

Start/end time	Name of the active operation mode
00.00 - 01.00	
01.00 - 02.00	
02.00 - 03.00	
03.00 - 04.00	
04.00 - 05.00	
05.00 - 06.00	
06.00 - 07.00	
07.00 - 08.00	
08.00 - 09.00	Daytime
09.00 - 10.00	Daytime
10.00 - 11.00	Daytime
11.00 - 12.00	Daytime
12.00 - 13.00	Daytime
13.00 - 14.00	Daytime
14.00 - 15.00	Daytime
15.00 - 16.00	Daytime
16.00 - 17.00	Daytime
17.00 - 18.00	Daytime
18.00 - 19.00	Daytime
19.00 - 20.00	Daytime
20.00 - 21.00	
21.00 - 22.00	
22.00 - 23.00	
23.00 - 00.00	

Figure 2.28 Table with Interval Assignment

8. When you've finished (see Figure 2.29), click on SAVE.

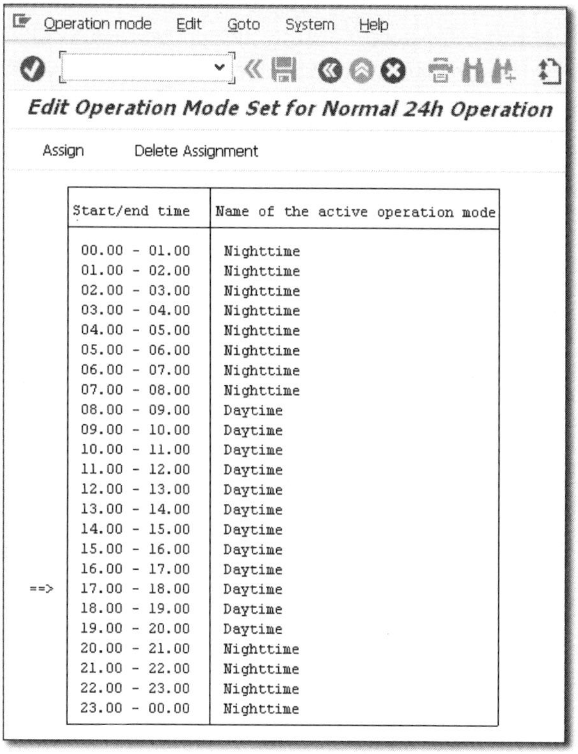

Operation mode Edit Goto System Help

Edit Operation Mode Set for Normal 24h Operation

Assign Delete Assignment

	Start/end time	Name of the active operation mode
	00.00 - 01.00	Nighttime
	01.00 - 02.00	Nighttime
	02.00 - 03.00	Nighttime
	03.00 - 04.00	Nighttime
	04.00 - 05.00	Nighttime
	05.00 - 06.00	Nighttime
	06.00 - 07.00	Nighttime
	07.00 - 08.00	Nighttime
	08.00 - 09.00	Daytime
	09.00 - 10.00	Daytime
	10.00 - 11.00	Daytime
	11.00 - 12.00	Daytime
	12.00 - 13.00	Daytime
	13.00 - 14.00	Daytime
	14.00 - 15.00	Daytime
	15.00 - 16.00	Daytime
	16.00 - 17.00	Daytime
==>	17.00 - 18.00	Daytime
	18.00 - 19.00	Daytime
	19.00 - 20.00	Daytime
	20.00 - 21.00	Nighttime
	21.00 - 22.00	Nighttime
	22.00 - 23.00	Nighttime
	23.00 - 00.00	Nighttime

Figure 2.29 Table with Complete Interval Assignment

9. The status bar displays the message OPERATION MODE SET SAVED, which indicates that the operation mode set has been saved for normal operation.

From this point on, the operation modes will be switched using this timetable. A log entry is generated in the system log (Transaction SM21) when a switch is made. Both the old and new process types are recorded for each work process that is switched.

However, the type of a work process can't be switched until the process becomes available. In other words, a delay may be experienced while the work process is still occupied. For example, if all background processes to be switched are still executing jobs, the processes are switched one by one, as soon as the corresponding jobs have been completed. Processing isn't interrupted, and normal system operation proceeds without disruption during switching.

Manual Switching of Operation Modes

You can switch operation modes manually if necessary. This function is required if, for example, you want to switch to a special operation mode, use a new operation mode immediately, or nighttime operations need to be brought forward for an important reason. To switch operation modes manually, follow these steps:

1. Enter Transaction RZ03 in the command field and press the Enter key (or select the menu option TOOLS • CCMS • CONTROL/MONITORING • RZ03—CONTROL PANEL).
2. Position the cursor on the application server whose operation mode you want to select (see Figure 2.30). Click on CHOOSE OPERATION MODE.

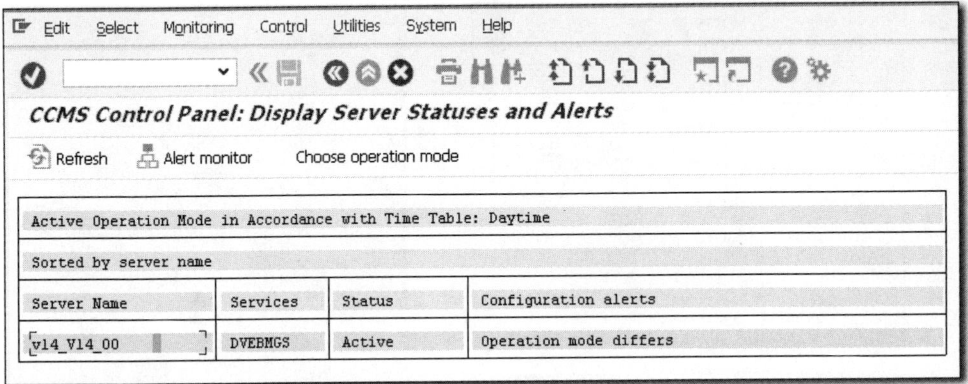

Figure 2.30 Selecting the Application Server

3. Place the cursor on the operation mode to which you want to switch (see Figure 2.31), and click on CHOOSE.

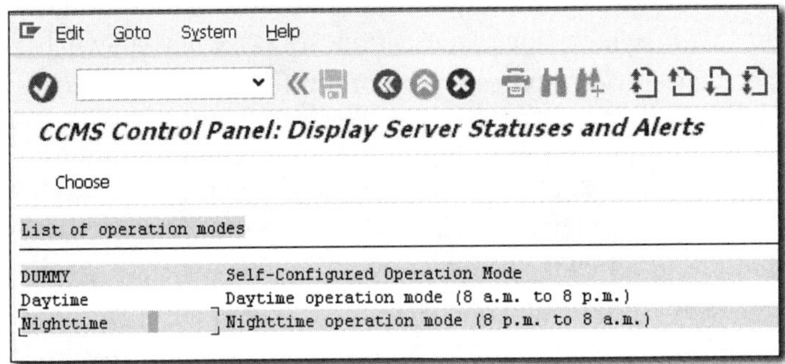

Figure 2.31 Selecting the Operation Mode

4. The view switches back to the DISPLAY SERVER STATUSES AND ALERTS screen. Your selected operation mode is now displayed as the ACTIVE OPERATION MODE. Position the cursor on the relevant server, and select the CONTROL • SWITCH OPERATION MODE • SELECTED SERVERS (see Figure 2.32).

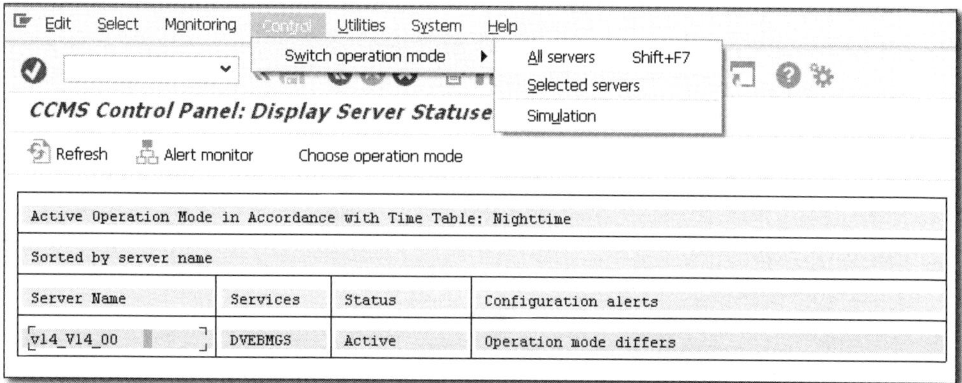

Figure 2.32 Switching the Operation Mode for Selected Servers

5. Click on YES in the dialog box that opens (see Figure 2.33).

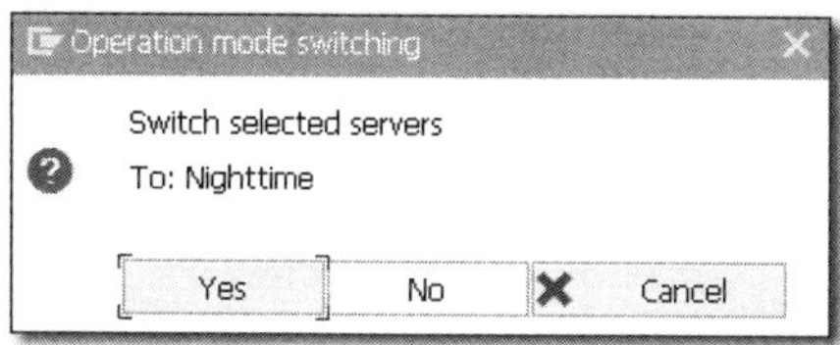

Figure 2.33 Confirming the Operation Mode Switch

The operation mode has now been switched. You can verify the work process distribution in Transaction SM50 (see Section 2.4.3). The manually selected operation mode remains active until the next scheduled switch point.

2.3 Maintaining Profile Parameters

Profile parameters are used in the SAP system to control basic technical settings that are required to start the system. For example, you can use parameters to specify the number of work processes a system should have or the required minimum number of characters in a user password.

Profile parameters are stored in three different profiles:

- **Start profile**
  This profile defines the name of the system and which SAP services are started. This profile type is only available in releases before SAP NetWeaver 7.10 unless you have a system for which an appropriate upgrade was implemented. As of release 7.10, the instance profile assumes the start profile function.
- **Default profile**
  This profile contains all parameters that must be identical for all instances of the system.
- **Instance profile**
  This profile determines the detailed configuration of a specific instance. This makes it possible to have different configurations for individual application servers (or instances) that are intended for different tasks.

The profiles are loaded in the sequence given in the preceding list at startup.

[⚙]

File Directory at the Operating System Level

The profiles are saved as files at the operating system level. They are located in the */usr/sap/<System-ID>/SYS/profiles* directory. These profiles may only be changed in Transaction RZ10 (System Profiles) and must *not* be changed at the operating system level. You should only edit the files directly as an emergency measure if the system can't be started after a change.

Changes to profile parameters are critical for system operation and must only be carried out by administrators. If a parameter is set incorrectly, it may no longer be possible to start the SAP system. Only change a value for a specific purpose, and be very sure of *what* you want to change and *why*.

[!]

Saving the Profile Files

Before you change system profiles, make sure that you have a current backup copy of the system profile files. This backup copy may be your only hope if a profile change means you can no longer start the SAP system.

Follow these steps to maintain profile parameters:

1. Enter Transaction RZ10 in the command field and press the Enter key (or select the menu option TOOLS • CCMS • CONFIGURATION • RZ10—SYSTEM PROFILES).

2. Enter the relevant system profile in the PROFILE field, or use the input help to select it (see Figure 2.34).

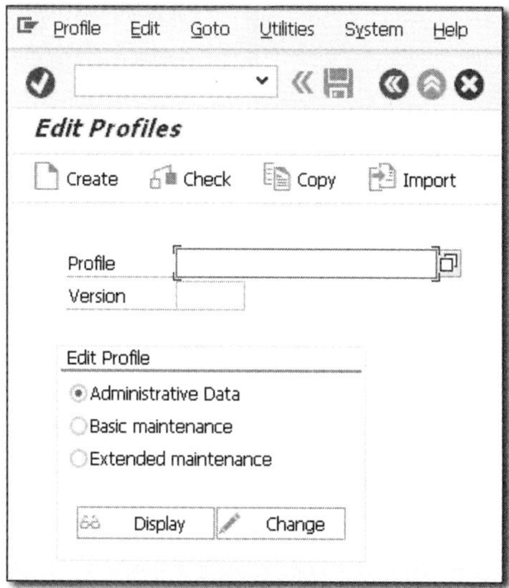

Figure 2.34 Initial Screen of the Profile Maintenance

3. Three options are already available in the EDIT PROFILE area:
   - ADMINISTRATIVE DATA: This option isn't a maintenance option. Instead, it's used to change the file name if you need to change the profile.
   - BASIC MAINTENANCE: In this mode, you can define buffers, work processes, and directories in the system profiles. You can also specify which SAP components are to be started in start profiles (e.g., message server, application server, SNA gateway). This type of maintenance protects most profile parameters from being changed by potentially incorrect settings.
   - EXTENDED MAINTENANCE: This This mode enables full access to all profile parameters.

   Select the EXTENDED MAINTENANCE option, and click on CHANGE (see Figure 2.35).
4. Position the cursor on the row below the new row you want to be inserted with the profile parameter. Click on the CREATE PARAMETER button to create the parameter (see Figure 2.36).

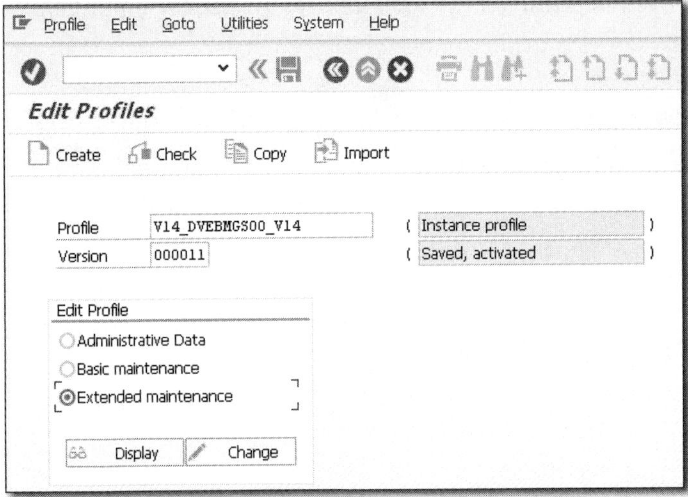

Figure 2.35 Starting the Extended Maintenance of a Profile

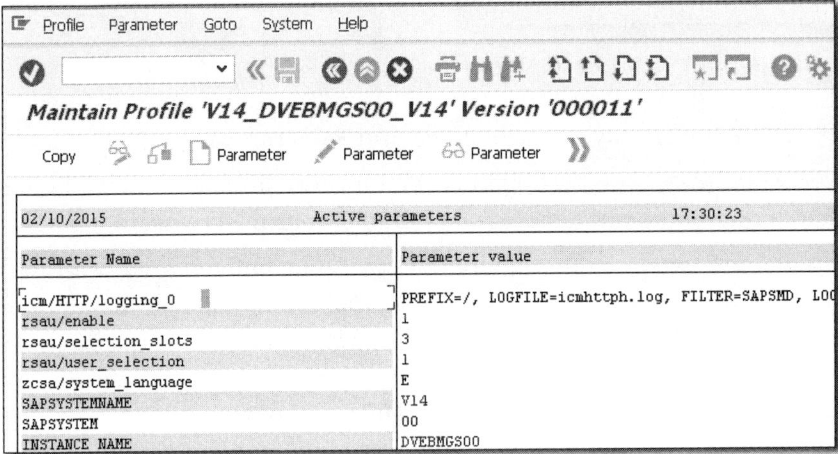

Figure 2.36 Creating Parameters

[+]

Adding New Parameters

The location in which you insert the new profile parameter has no effect on the process. However, for the sake of clarity, we recommend grouping or sorting the parameters (e.g., by keeping all logon parameters together). It's difficult to move profile parameters after they've been entered. You should therefore give careful consideration to where you insert the parameters.

5. Enter the name of the new parameter in the PARAMETER NAME field (see Figure 2.37). The SAP default value of the parameters is displayed under UNSUBSTITUTED STANDARD VALUE. Enter the desired value in the PARAMETER VAL. field. Under COMMENT, enter the reason for the change for documentation purposes. When you've finished, click on COPY.

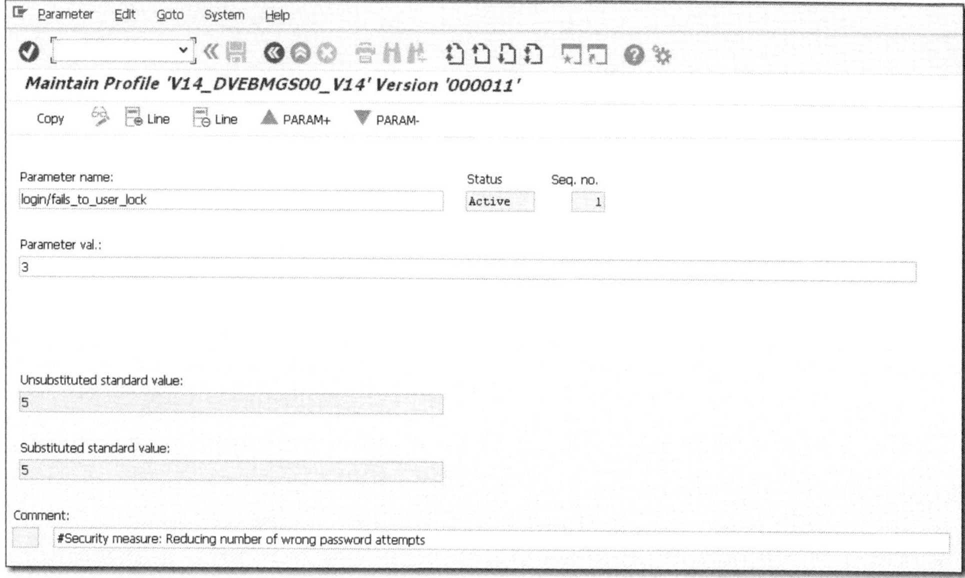

Figure 2.37 Maintaining Parameter Values and Comments

6. The system enters your user ID and the current date in the COMMENT field (see Figure 2.38). This feature allows you to keep track of which persons have made profile changes at which times. A message is also displayed to confirm that the changes have been applied. Click on BACK .

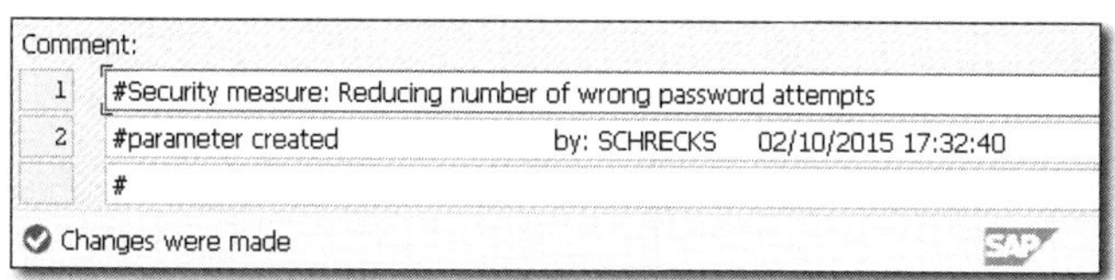

Figure 2.38 Logging the Processor and Confirming Changes

7. You're then returned automatically to the list of profile parameters. The new parameter has been added to the list (see Figure 2.39). Click on COPY.

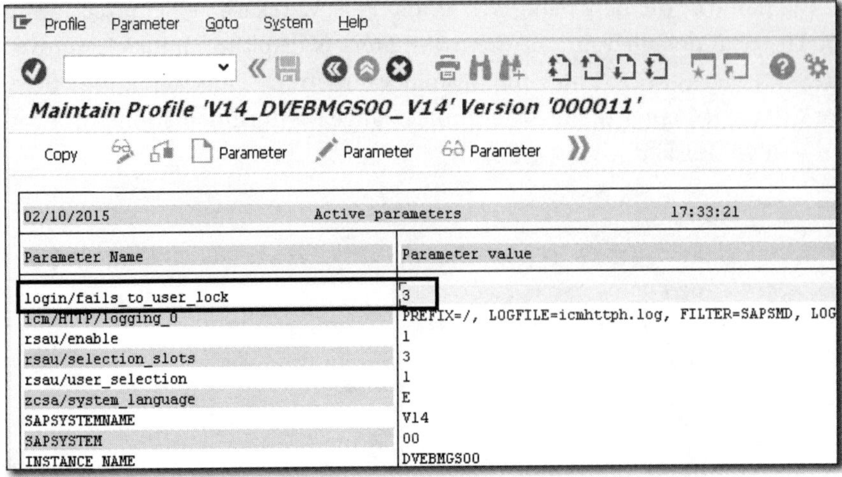

Figure 2.39 List with New Profile Parameter

8. The message THE CHANGED PROFILE WAS TRANSFERRED is displayed at the bottom of the screen to confirm that the profile has been changed. Click on BACK.
9. The system takes you back to the EDIT PROFILES screen (refer to Figure 2.35). Click on SAVE.
10. Choose YES to confirm activation of the profile (see Figure 2.40).

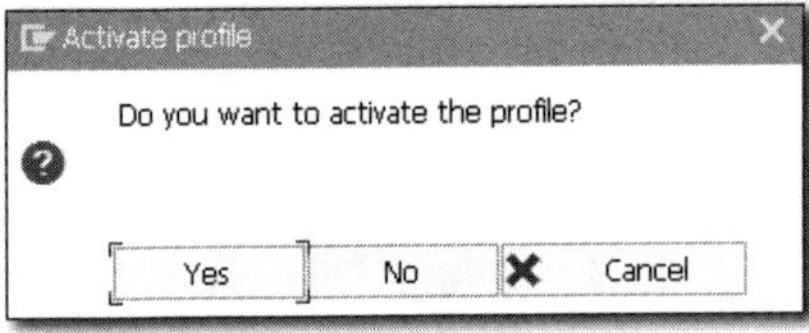

Figure 2.40 Activating the Profile

11. In the dialog box that opens, click on CONTINUE (see Figure 2.41).

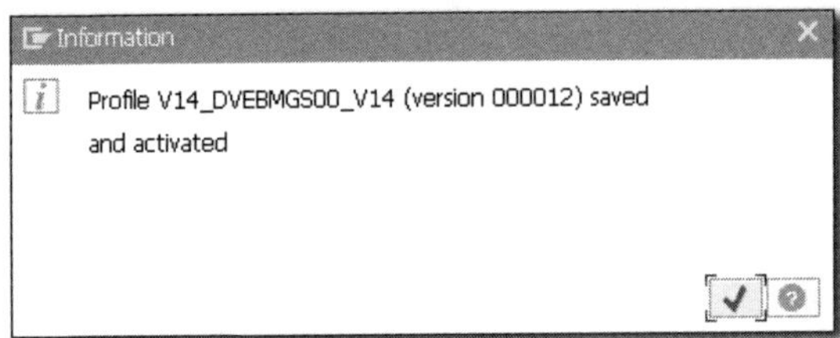

Figure 2.41 Activation Confirmation

12. The system informs you that changes to the profile parameters usually become active after the application server has been restarted. Confirm this system message by clicking on CONTINUE (see Figure 2.42).

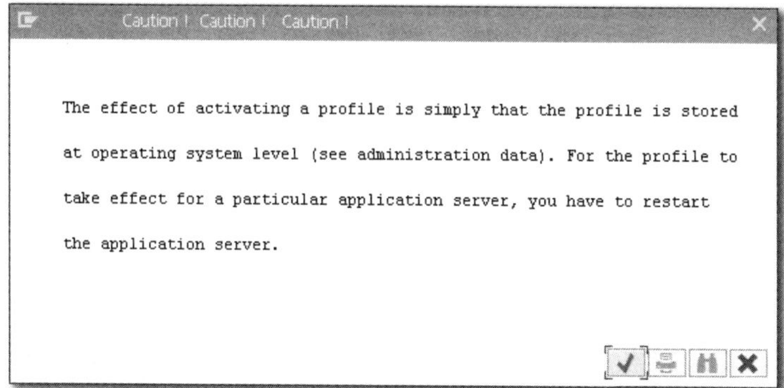

Figure 2.42 Message Confirmation

13. The EDIT PROFILES screen is displayed (see Figure 2.43). Note that the version number of the profile has now changed.

Figure 2.43 Changed Version Number

Your change to the parameter file has been saved at the operating system level. When maintaining profiles, you normally need to restart the SAP application server for your changes to become effective because only changes to dynamic profile parameters take immediate effect. Use Transaction RZ11 to find out whether a profile parameter is dynamic. The metadata of the parameters contains the entry DYNAMIC PARAMETER • YES/NO (see Figure 2.44).

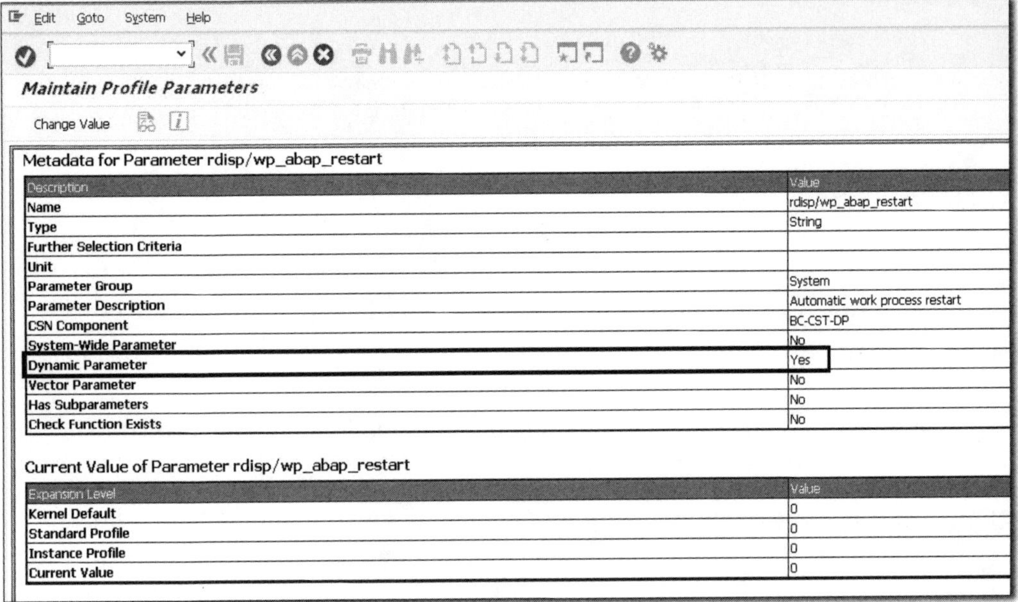

Figure 2.44 Parameter Details in Transaction RZ11

[+]

Displaying Profile Parameters in Transaction RZ11

Use Transaction RZ11 (Maintain Profile Parameters) to display the profile parameters that are available in the system. You can display a detailed parameter documentation in this transaction.

2.4 Specific Monitoring Transactions

The SAP system provides a range of transactions that you can use to monitor general or very specific system statuses or problems. This section explains how to use the most widely used tools. Additional transactions may be relevant, depending on the type and scope of your SAP system. However, those described here are very important in all systems.

2.4.1 System Log

The system log records all events, errors, problems, and other system messages. This is an important log because unexpected or unfamiliar warning and error messages may indicate serious problems. You should therefore check your system log several times a day.

As your experience grows, you'll find it increasingly easy to monitor the system log. Over time, you'll learn which log entries normally appear in your system log and which are unusual and need to be investigated. To check the system log, follow these steps:

1. Enter Transaction SM21 in the command field and press the Enter key (or select the menu option Tools • Administration • Monitor • SM21—System Log).
2. In the From Date/Time field, enter the start of the period you want to examine (see Figure 2.45).

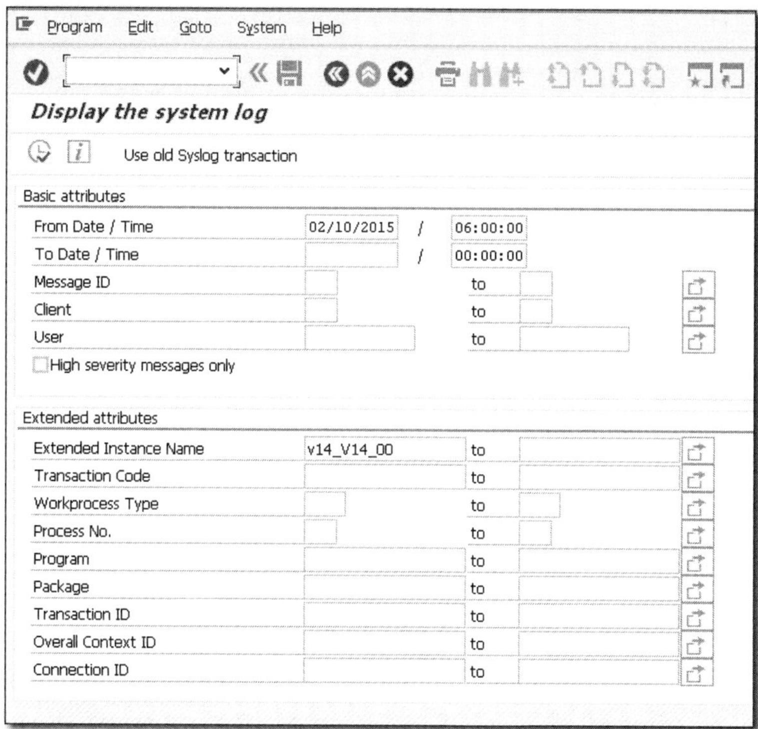

Figure 2.45 Evaluating the System Log

3. You can restrict your selection further if required, for example, to a specific client, user, or transaction.
4. Click on the EXECUTE button.
5. A chronological list of logged system events appears (see Figure 2.46). Check the entries for errors or warnings, using the colored icons in the PRIORITY column as a guide.

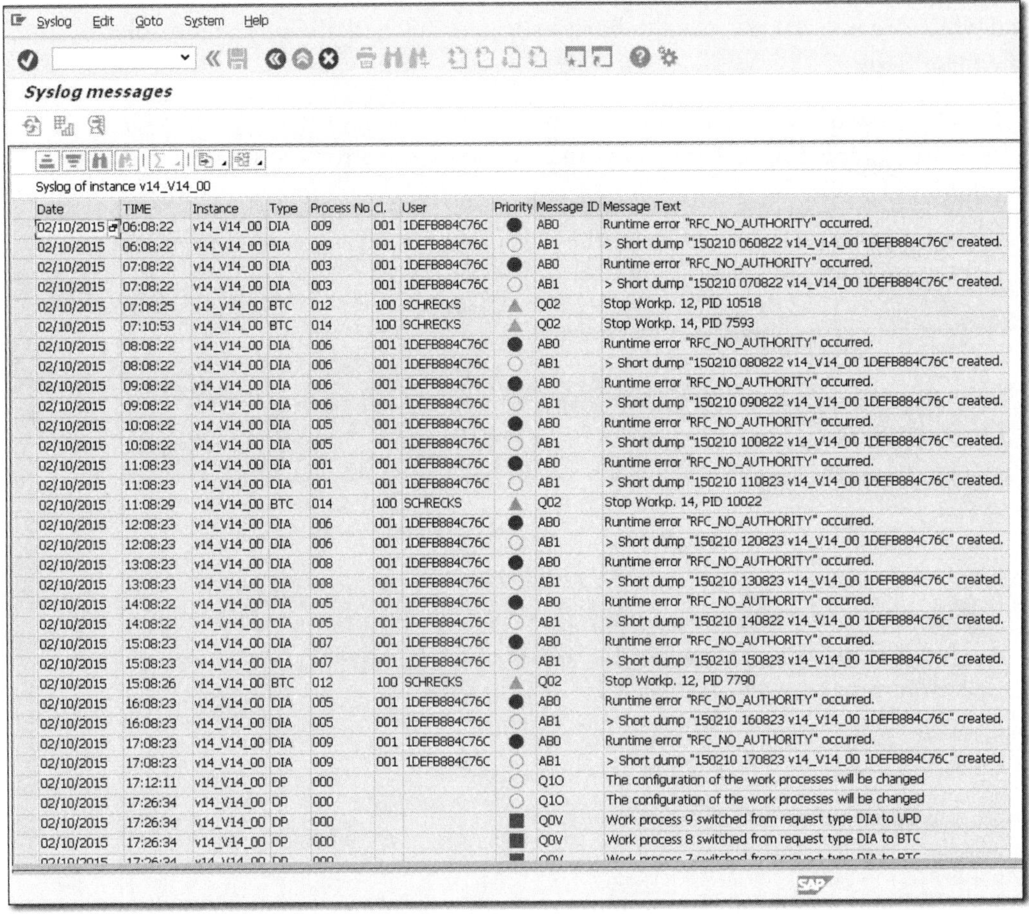

Date	TIME	Instance	Type	Process No	Cl.	User	Priority	Message ID	Message Text
02/10/2015	06:08:22	v14_V14_00	DIA	009	001	1DEFB884C76C		AB0	Runtime error "RFC_NO_AUTHORITY" occurred.
02/10/2015	06:08:22	v14_V14_00	DIA	009	001	1DEFB884C76C		AB1	> Short dump "150210 060822 v14_V14_00 1DEFB884C76C" created.
02/10/2015	07:08:22	v14_V14_00	DIA	003	001	1DEFB884C76C		AB0	Runtime error "RFC_NO_AUTHORITY" occurred.
02/10/2015	07:08:22	v14_V14_00	DIA	003	001	1DEFB884C76C		AB1	> Short dump "150210 070822 v14_V14_00 1DEFB884C76C" created.
02/10/2015	07:08:25	v14_V14_00	BTC	012	100	SCHRECKS		Q02	Stop Workp. 12, PID 10518
02/10/2015	07:10:53	v14_V14_00	BTC	014	100	SCHRECKS		Q02	Stop Workp. 14, PID 7593
02/10/2015	08:08:22	v14_V14_00	DIA	006	001	1DEFB884C76C		AB0	Runtime error "RFC_NO_AUTHORITY" occurred.
02/10/2015	08:08:22	v14_V14_00	DIA	006	001	1DEFB884C76C		AB1	> Short dump "150210 080822 v14_V14_00 1DEFB884C76C" created.
02/10/2015	09:08:22	v14_V14_00	DIA	006	001	1DEFB884C76C		AB0	Runtime error "RFC_NO_AUTHORITY" occurred.
02/10/2015	09:08:22	v14_V14_00	DIA	006	001	1DEFB884C76C		AB1	> Short dump "150210 090822 v14_V14_00 1DEFB884C76C" created.
02/10/2015	10:08:22	v14_V14_00	DIA	005	001	1DEFB884C76C		AB0	Runtime error "RFC_NO_AUTHORITY" occurred.
02/10/2015	10:08:22	v14_V14_00	DIA	005	001	1DEFB884C76C		AB1	> Short dump "150210 100822 v14_V14_00 1DEFB884C76C" created.
02/10/2015	11:08:23	v14_V14_00	DIA	001	001	1DEFB884C76C		AB0	Runtime error "RFC_NO_AUTHORITY" occurred.
02/10/2015	11:08:23	v14_V14_00	DIA	001	001	1DEFB884C76C		AB1	> Short dump "150210 110823 v14_V14_00 1DEFB884C76C" created.
02/10/2015	11:08:29	v14_V14_00	BTC	014	100	SCHRECKS		Q02	Stop Workp. 14, PID 10022
02/10/2015	12:08:23	v14_V14_00	DIA	006	001	1DEFB884C76C		AB0	Runtime error "RFC_NO_AUTHORITY" occurred.
02/10/2015	12:08:23	v14_V14_00	DIA	006	001	1DEFB884C76C		AB1	> Short dump "150210 120823 v14_V14_00 1DEFB884C76C" created.
02/10/2015	13:08:23	v14_V14_00	DIA	008	001	1DEFB884C76C		AB0	Runtime error "RFC_NO_AUTHORITY" occurred.
02/10/2015	13:08:23	v14_V14_00	DIA	008	001	1DEFB884C76C		AB1	> Short dump "150210 130823 v14_V14_00 1DEFB884C76C" created.
02/10/2015	14:08:22	v14_V14_00	DIA	005	001	1DEFB884C76C		AB0	Runtime error "RFC_NO_AUTHORITY" occurred.
02/10/2015	14:08:22	v14_V14_00	DIA	005	001	1DEFB884C76C		AB1	> Short dump "150210 140822 v14_V14_00 1DEFB884C76C" created.
02/10/2015	15:08:23	v14_V14_00	DIA	007	001	1DEFB884C76C		AB0	Runtime error "RFC_NO_AUTHORITY" occurred.
02/10/2015	15:08:23	v14_V14_00	DIA	007	001	1DEFB884C76C		AB1	> Short dump "150210 150823 v14_V14_00 1DEFB884C76C" created.
02/10/2015	15:08:26	v14_V14_00	BTC	012	100	SCHRECKS		Q02	Stop Workp. 12, PID 7790
02/10/2015	16:08:23	v14_V14_00	DIA	005	001	1DEFB884C76C		AB0	Runtime error "RFC_NO_AUTHORITY" occurred.
02/10/2015	16:08:23	v14_V14_00	DIA	005	001	1DEFB884C76C		AB1	> Short dump "150210 160823 v14_V14_00 1DEFB884C76C" created.
02/10/2015	17:08:23	v14_V14_00	DIA	009	001	1DEFB884C76C		AB0	Runtime error "RFC_NO_AUTHORITY" occurred.
02/10/2015	17:08:23	v14_V14_00	DIA	009	001	1DEFB884C76C		AB1	> Short dump "150210 170823 v14_V14_00 1DEFB884C76C" created.
02/10/2015	17:12:11	v14_V14_00	DP	000				Q1O	The configuration of the work processes will be changed
02/10/2015	17:26:34	v14_V14_00	DP	000				Q1O	The configuration of the work processes will be changed
02/10/2015	17:26:34	v14_V14_00	DP	000				Q0V	Work process 9 switched from request type DIA to UPD
02/10/2015	17:26:34	v14_V14_00	DP	000				Q0V	Work process 8 switched from request type DIA to BTC

Figure 2.46 Log of System Events

6. To display the details of a log entry, double-click on the relevant row. You can also position the cursor on the row and choose DISPLAY DETAILS.

7. Check for indications of the cause of the error or the solution to the problem in the detailed information for the log entry (see Figure 2.47). Click on BACK to return to the system log.

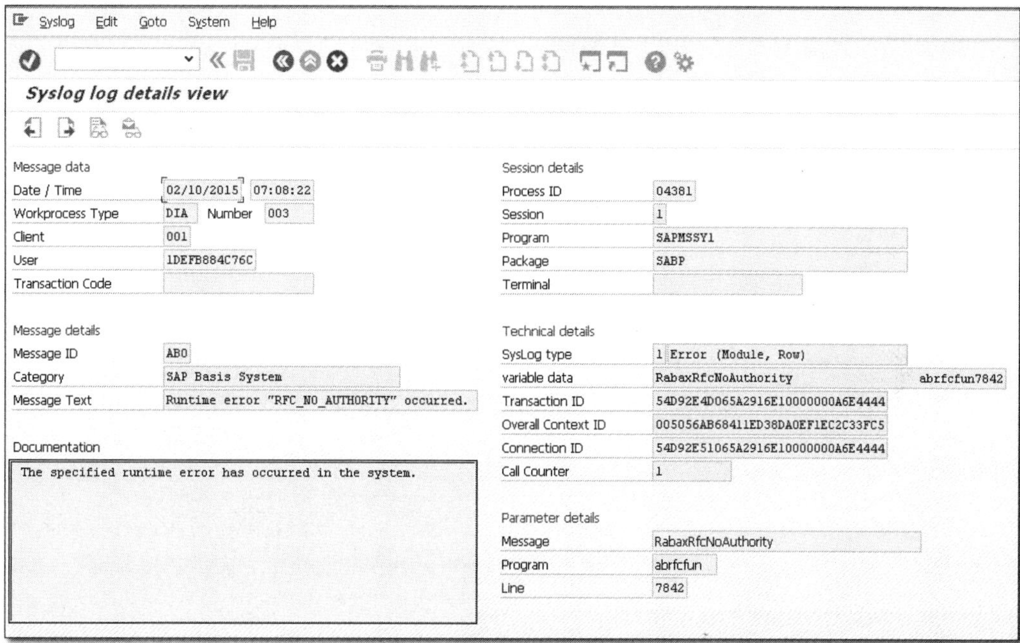

Figure 2.47 Detail View of a System Log Entry

You can use the system log to gain an initial overview of recent events at a superficial level and to track error messages. When checking the log, focus on errors (red) and warnings (yellow), as well as any unusual entries. Learning to filter the relevant entries is largely a matter of experience.

2.4.2 ABAP Dump Analysis

An *ABAP dump* (also known as a *short dump*) is a runtime error that is always generated whenever a report or transaction is terminated due to a serious error. If a short dump occurs in dialog mode, an error message is displayed for the user (see Figure 2.48).

The system records the error in the system log (Transaction SM21), where it also generates a brief explanation (the dump) of the program termination. You can use

Transaction ST22 (Dump Analysis) to analyze ABAP dumps in detail and draw conclusions regarding the cause of the error and a possible solution.

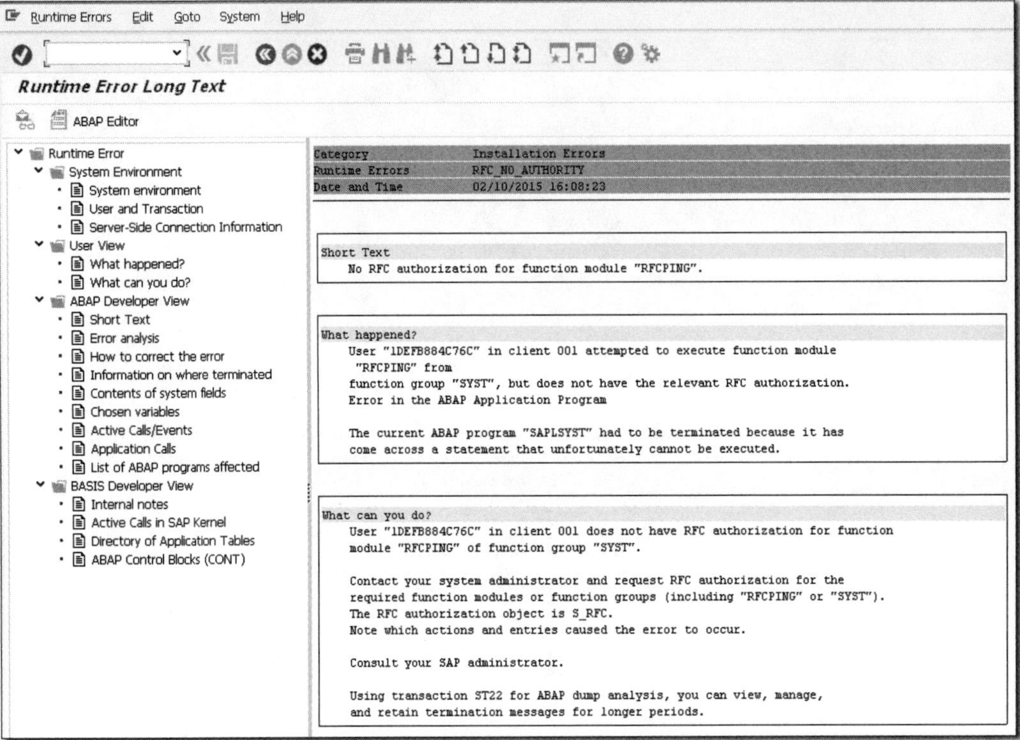

Figure 2.48 ABAP Short Dump in a Transaction

To analyze an ABAP dump, follow these steps:

1. Enter Transaction ST22 in the command field and press the Enter key (or select the menu option TOOLS • ADMINISTRATION • MONITOR • ST22—DUMP ANALYSIS).
2. You can select the dumps to be displayed in one of the following ways (see Figure 2.49):
   - For a simple selection of the current dumps, select one of the buttons TODAY or YESTERDAY in the STANDARD screen area.
   - To restrict the selection using precise criteria, you can also enter the relevant parameters in the OWN SELECTION area, and click on START.

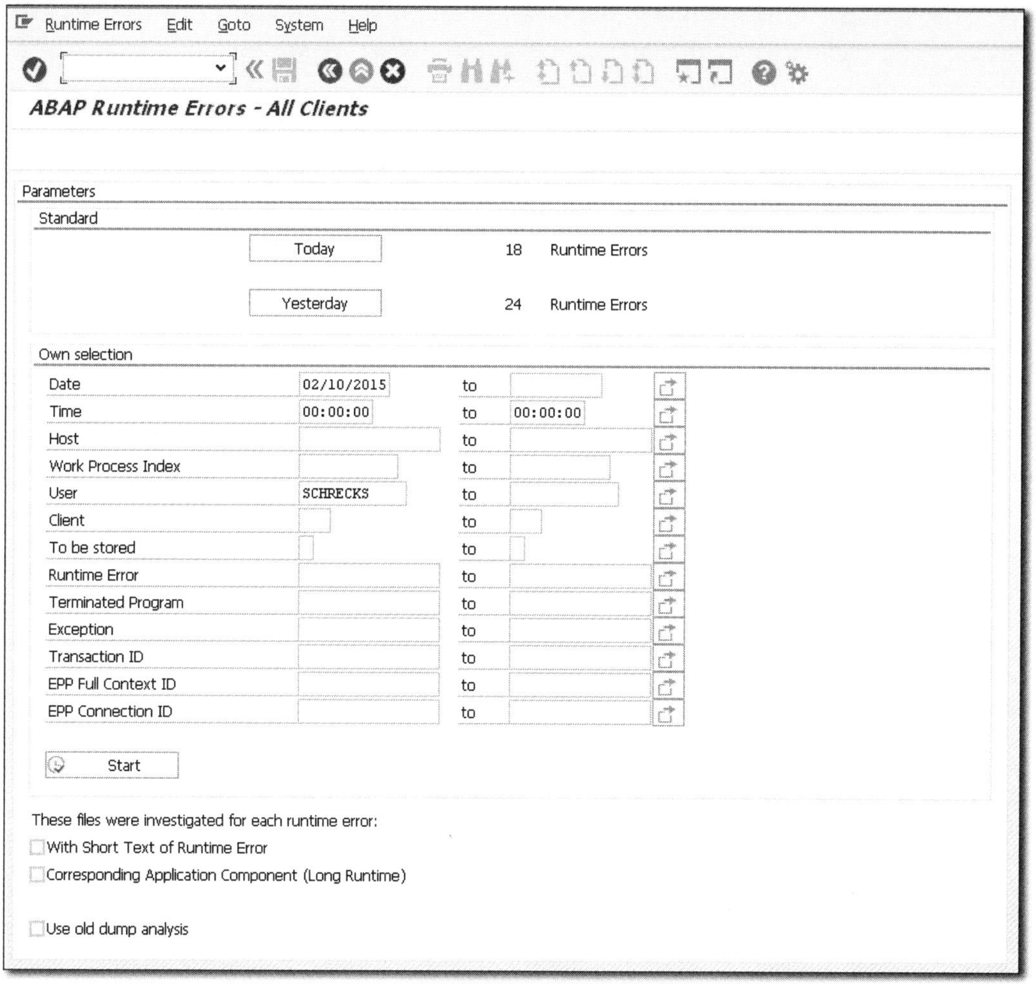

Runtime Errors Edit Goto System Help

ABAP Runtime Errors - All Clients

Parameters

Standard

Today 18 Runtime Errors

Yesterday 24 Runtime Errors

Own selection

Date	02/10/2015	to	
Time	00:00:00	to	00:00:00
Host		to	
Work Process Index		to	
User	SCHRECKS	to	
Client		to	
To be stored		to	
Runtime Error		to	
Terminated Program		to	
Exception		to	
Transaction ID		to	
EPP Full Context ID		to	
EPP Connection ID		to	

Start

These files were investigated for each runtime error:

With Short Text of Runtime Error

Corresponding Application Component (Long Runtime)

Use old dump analysis

Figure 2.49 Selecting the ABAP Short Dumps to Be Displayed

Initial Screen for Runtime Error Analysis [!]

The number of runtime errors displayed on the initial screen of Transaction ST22 when you click on the TODAY or YESTERDAY buttons provides a rough indication of the system status. If a large number of short dumps have been recorded, there may be a general problem with the system that is affecting a large number of users. In this case, a quick response is essential. If the number of short dumps is small, the system obviously has a more or less stable status. Check the recorded ABAP runtime errors at regular intervals several times a day.

3. A list of the runtime errors that have occurred is displayed (see Figure 2.50). Double-click on the dump you want to analyze, or position the cursor accordingly. Click on the DISPLAY LONG TEXT button.

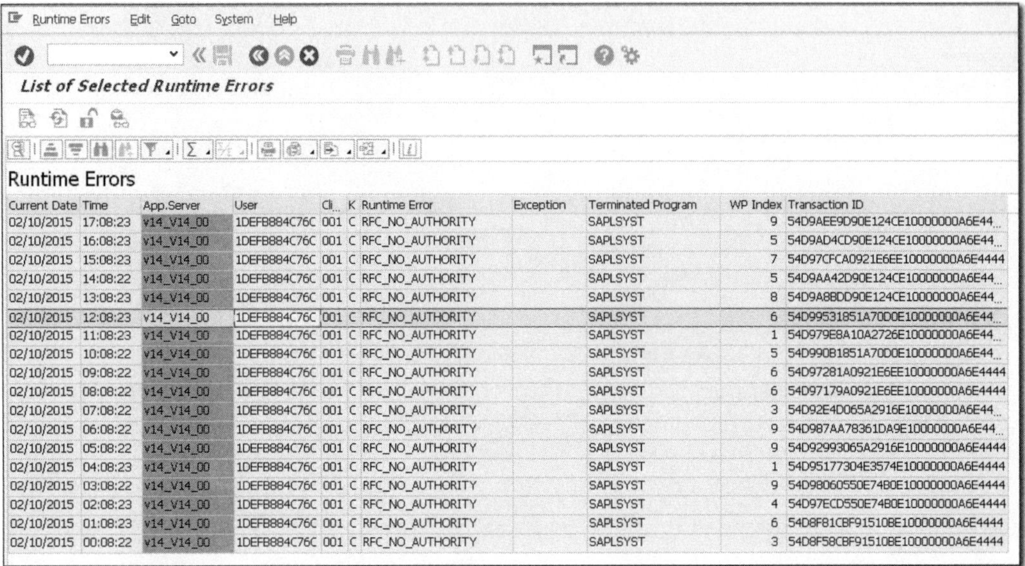

Current Date	Time	App.Server	User	Cli...	K	Runtime Error	Exception	Terminated Program	WP Index	Transaction ID
02/10/2015	17:08:23	v14_V14_00	1DEFB884C76C	001	C	RFC_NO_AUTHORITY		SAPLSYST	9	54D9AEE9D90E124CE10000000A6E44...
02/10/2015	16:08:23	v14_V14_00	1DEFB884C76C	001	C	RFC_NO_AUTHORITY		SAPLSYST	5	54D9AD4CD90E124CE10000000A6E44...
02/10/2015	15:08:23	v14_V14_00	1DEFB884C76C	001	C	RFC_NO_AUTHORITY		SAPLSYST	7	54D97CFCA0921E6EE10000000A6E4444
02/10/2015	14:08:22	v14_V14_00	1DEFB884C76C	001	C	RFC_NO_AUTHORITY		SAPLSYST	5	54D9AA42D90E124CE10000000A6E44...
02/10/2015	13:08:23	v14_V14_00	1DEFB884C76C	001	C	RFC_NO_AUTHORITY		SAPLSYST	8	54D9A8BDD90E124CE10000000A6E44...
02/10/2015	12:08:23	v14_V14_00	1DEFB884C76C	001	C	RFC_NO_AUTHORITY		SAPLSYST	6	54D99531851A70D0E10000000A6E44...
02/10/2015	11:08:23	v14_V14_00	1DEFB884C76C	001	C	RFC_NO_AUTHORITY		SAPLSYST	1	54D979E8A10A2726E10000000A6E44...
02/10/2015	10:08:22	v14_V14_00	1DEFB884C76C	001	C	RFC_NO_AUTHORITY		SAPLSYST	5	54D990B1851A70D0E10000000A6E44...
02/10/2015	09:08:22	v14_V14_00	1DEFB884C76C	001	C	RFC_NO_AUTHORITY		SAPLSYST	6	54D97281A0921E6EE10000000A6E4444
02/10/2015	08:08:22	v14_V14_00	1DEFB884C76C	001	C	RFC_NO_AUTHORITY		SAPLSYST	6	54D97179A0921E6EE10000000A6E4444
02/10/2015	07:08:22	v14_V14_00	1DEFB884C76C	001	C	RFC_NO_AUTHORITY		SAPLSYST	3	54D92E4D065A2916E10000000A6E44...
02/10/2015	06:08:22	v14_V14_00	1DEFB884C76C	001	C	RFC_NO_AUTHORITY		SAPLSYST	9	54D987AA78361DA9E10000000A6E44...
02/10/2015	05:08:22	v14_V14_00	1DEFB884C76C	001	C	RFC_NO_AUTHORITY		SAPLSYST	9	54D92993065A2916E10000000A6E4444
02/10/2015	04:08:23	v14_V14_00	1DEFB884C76C	001	C	RFC_NO_AUTHORITY		SAPLSYST	1	54D95177304E3574E10000000A6E4444
02/10/2015	03:08:22	v14_V14_00	1DEFB884C76C	001	C	RFC_NO_AUTHORITY		SAPLSYST	9	54D98060550E74B0E10000000A6E4444
02/10/2015	02:08:23	v14_V14_00	1DEFB884C76C	001	C	RFC_NO_AUTHORITY		SAPLSYST	4	54D97ECD550E74B0E10000000A6E4444
02/10/2015	01:08:23	v14_V14_00	1DEFB884C76C	001	C	RFC_NO_AUTHORITY		SAPLSYST	6	54D8F81CBF91510BE10000000A6E4444
02/10/2015	00:08:22	v14_V14_00	1DEFB884C76C	001	C	RFC_NO_AUTHORITY		SAPLSYST	3	54D8F58CBF91510BE10000000A6E4444

Figure 2.50 List of Runtime Errors Occurred

4. The short dump is then displayed (see Figure 2.51). Scroll through the display to analyze the error and obtain information about the cause of the problem.
5. If you come to a dead end in your analysis and need to ask SAP Support for assistance, it's useful to save the short dump as a file and attach it to a problem notification, for example. To do this, select SYSTEM • LIST • SAVE • LOCAL FILE in the RUNTIME ERROR LONG TEXT screen, and save the short dump to your PC (see Figure 2.52).

[+]

Scope of Runtime Errors

The term *short dump* doesn't reflect the length of the explanation of the runtime error that is provided. ABAP short dumps may, in fact, run to several dozen pages because when a runtime error occurs, the log records very detailed information about the system status and the cause of the error. It's recommended that you save important dumps locally, and only print out the section of the long text that you actually need.

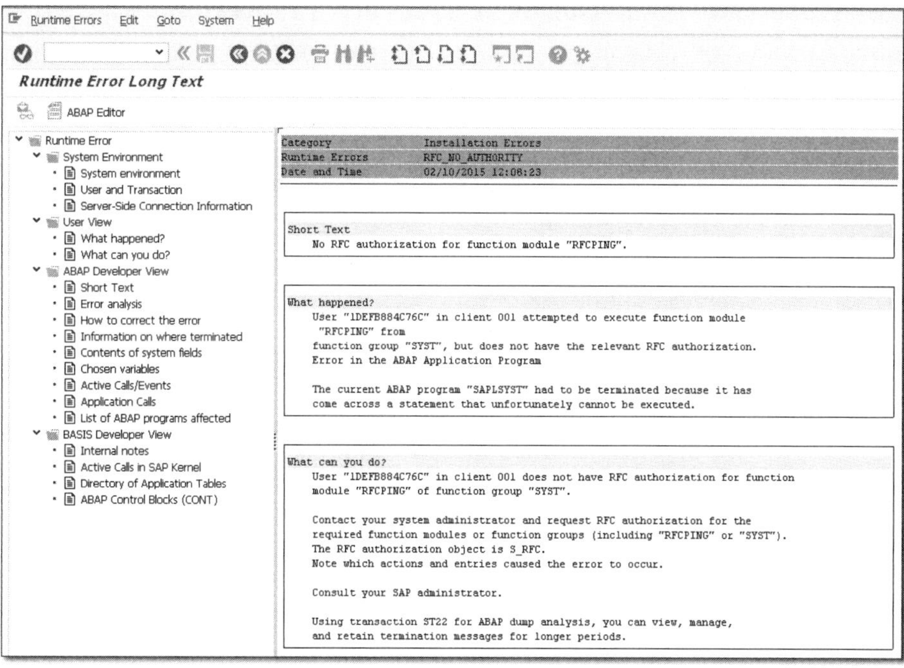

Figure 2.51 Detail View of a Short Dump

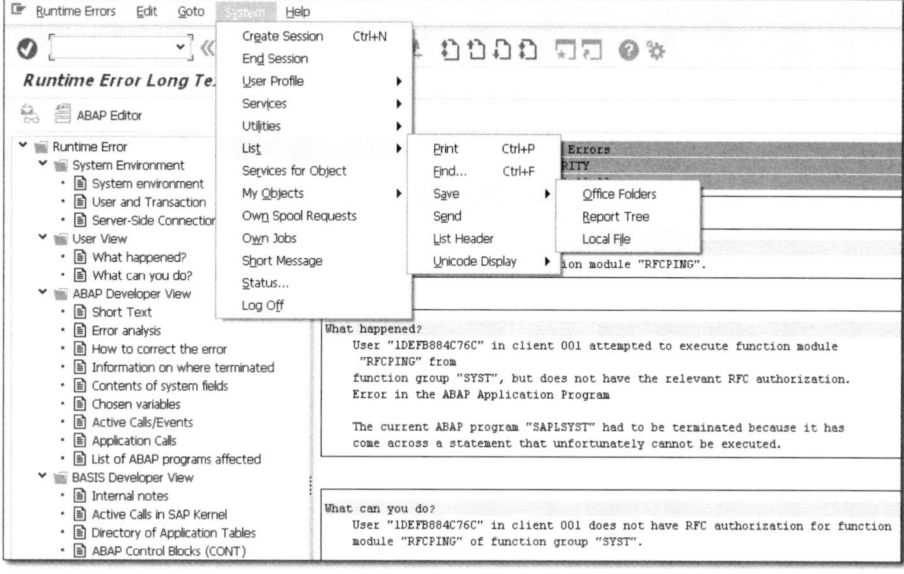

Figure 2.52 Saving the Short Dump as a File

2.4.3 Checking Application Servers and Work Processes

During system operation, you can use Transactions SM50 and SM51 to monitor the application servers and work processes in your SAP system. This monitoring function is important for the following reasons:

- When a dialog application server is inactive, users who normally log on to this server are unable to log on.
- When the batch application server is inactive, batch jobs that have been scheduled for this server can't be executed.
- When all work processes are occupied, no further tasks can be processed. This situation may arise if too many users are logged on, too many background jobs are running in parallel, or if a posting problem occurs.

In the event of problems like these, you can use Transactions SM50 and SM51 to determine whether an application server is inactive or whether all work processes are occupied.

First, check whether the application servers are active:

1. Enter Transaction SM51 in the command field and press the Enter key (or select the menu option Tools • Administration • Monitor • System Monitoring • SM51—Servers).
2. Take a look at the servers listed (see Figure 2.53). Check whether the list contains all servers that should be active. Check whether the Server State column contains the entry Active.

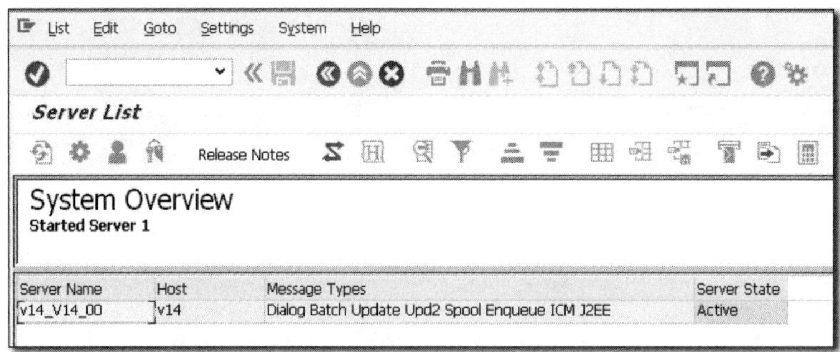

Figure 2.53 Overview of Started Servers

If all applications are displayed as active, you can begin checking the work processes:

1. Enter Transaction SM50 in the command field and press the [Enter] key (or select the menu option TOOLS • ADMINISTRATION • MONITOR • SYSTEM MONITORING • SM50—PROCESS OVERVIEW).

Global Process Overview [+]

Instead of Transaction SM50, you can also use Transaction SM66 (Global Process Overview). Using this transaction, you can display work processes also across instances if your system comprises several instances.

2. Check the STATUS of the individual work processes. Processes that have the status WAITING are available, while processes with the status RUNNING are currently occupied by the system (see Figure 2.54). The WORK PROCESS ACTION column provides details about the processes that are currently running.

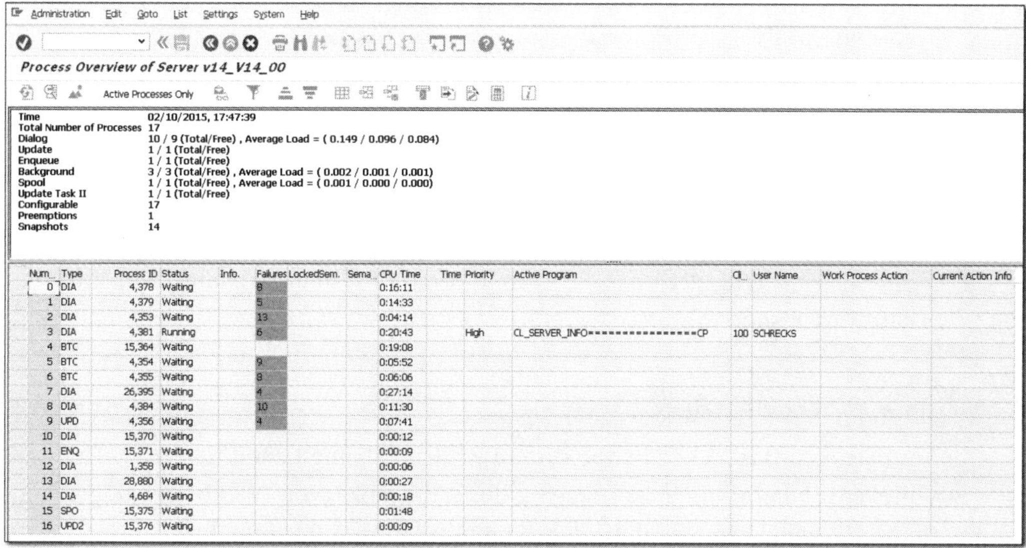

Figure 2.54 Checking the Status of Work Processes

Checking Processes [+]

When checking the process overview, focus on the following information provided:

- **Dialog work processes (DIA) with high time values**
  This may point to a problem or to a step in a background process that is taking a long time to execute and that starts a dialog process.

- **Stopped processes**
  If STOPPED is shown in the STATUS column for a work process, this may also indicate a problem because this process may have failed or been interrupted.

In certain cases, you may need to cancel processes manually to eliminate a blockage in the system.

[+]

Canceling Processes Manually

If necessary, you can select the PROCESS • CANCEL WITH/WITHOUT CORE menu option to make system resources available. This procedure is described in connection with performance problems in Chapter 11.

[⚙]

dpmon

In particularly critical situations, you may no longer be able to log on to the system because all dialog work processes are occupied. In this case, the `dpmon` program is available at the operating system level. Using this program, you can display the table of work processes (as in Transaction SM50) as well as cancel processes manually (see SAP Note 42074).

The application server overview and process overview provide you with a quick initial impression of the system status. Using this approach, you may be able to detect, even at this early stage, any indications of system instability or insufficient hardware resources.

2.4.4 Lock Entries

A data record is locked by the system while it's being edited by a user. This lock prevents other users from changing this same data record while it's being edited. The following example illustrates the importance of this function.

[Ex]

The Advantage of Using Locks

You're in the process of changing a customer's postal address, while, at the same time, another user is changing the telephone number for this same customer. You save your change first, followed by the other user. The other user's change overwrites your change, and, as a result, your entry is lost.

Sometimes, an old lock still exists in the system, for example, after a system failure or after a user abruptly loses a connection due to a network problem. These locks must be removed so that the relevant data record can be accessed and changed.

Check the log entries regularly, paying particular attention to older lock entries (entries that are more than a day old). However, a user may inform you of a lock, and you may discover that the user responsible for triggering the lock is no longer logged on to the system.

1. Enter Transaction SM12 in the command field and press the [Enter] key (or select the menu option TOOLS • ADMINISTRATION • MONITOR • SM12—LOCK ENTRIES).
2. If you only want to analyze lock entries in general, clear all fields. To restrict the selection, enter the relevant parameters in the fields provided (see Figure 2.55). Click on the LIST button.

Figure 2.55 Selecting Lock Entries

3. Check the lock entries (see Figure 2.56). Pay particular attention to any locks from the previous day that appear in the DATE/TIME column. A lock dating from the previous day suggests that the user may have lost his connection to the network and the SAP system.

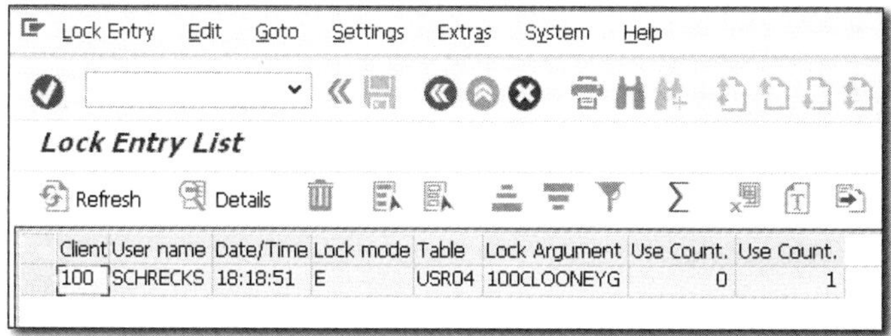

Client	User name	Date/Time	Lock mode	Table	Lock Argument	Use Count.	Use Count.
100	SCHRECKS	18:18:51	E	USR04	100CLOONEYG	0	1

Figure 2.56 Checking Lock Entries

4. Double-click on a lock entry, or click on the DETAILS button. Details of the selected lock are displayed (see Figure 2.57). Click on CONTINUE ✓ to return to the list view.

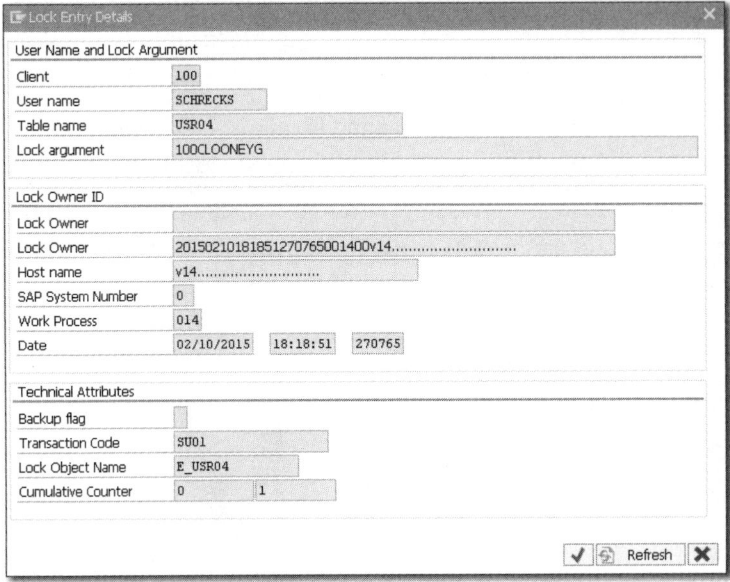

Figure 2.57 Lock Details

5. To release a lock, select it in the list display, and click on DELETE 🗑.

[!]

Deleting Locks

Deleting a lock may involve some risks. Before deleting a lock, it's imperative that you check whether the lock is currently in use. If you delete a lock that is currently in use, you risk database inconsistencies. No further steps should be executed until you're certain that the user ID specified in the lock entry is no longer active in the system.

6. Choose YES to confirm the dialog box of Figure 2.58.

Figure 2.58 Confirming a Deletion

Deleting a lock is critical, so it shouldn't be done lightly or without due consideration. Before you delete a lock, you should clarify and answer the questions in Table 2.2.

Task	Transaction Code for This Task
Is the relevant user logged on to a server?	Transaction SM04 (User List) or Transaction AL08 (User List—All Instances) If the user isn't logged on to the system but is displayed in Transaction SM04 or Transaction AL08, delete the user session (see Chapter 13). In some cases, this step is sufficient to remove the lock.
Are any processes running under the user ID?	Transaction SM50 (Process Overview) or Transaction SM66 (Process Overview of All Instances) Even if the user isn't logged on to the system, processes may still be active under the user ID. Wait until there are no longer any active processes under the user ID, or, in case of an emergency, cancel the process.
Are any background jobs running under the user ID?	Transaction SM37 (Job Overview) Check whether any background job is active for the relevant user ID. Wait until the job is finished, or, in case of an emergency, cancel it.
Are update records currently being processed for this user ID?	Transaction SM13 (Update Requests) The data records will remain locked until the update has been completed in the database. Wait until all update requests have been processed. In some cases, there may be a problem, which you must eliminate first.

Table 2.2 Things to Check Before Deleting a Lock

Take Care When Deleting Locks [!]

Check the user ID again before deleting the lock. You may damage the database by deleting the wrong lock. Delete locks in sequence. Never use the Delete All option because this option deletes all locks, not just those you've selected.

2.4.5 Canceled Update Requests

The SAP system sends update requests to cancelation in the database so that data changes are saved there permanently. In certain cases, an update request may fail, and the update may be canceled.

[Ex]

The Update Concept

The following example explains the update concept:

- An accountant hands a file to a clerical assistant. This is the equivalent of saving a transaction in the system.
- The clerical assistant issues the accountant with an acknowledgement of receipt. This equates to the creation of an SAP document number.
- On the way to the filing cabinet, the clerical assistant stumbles and is injured. As a result, the file isn't filed in the filing cabinet. We can compare this incident with an update error.
- The result is that the file is *not* in the filing cabinet, even though the accountant has received an acknowledgement. The same thing happens in an SAP update environment. The document isn't in the SAP system, even though the user has been given a document number for it.

When users receive a document number, they assume that the corresponding entry has been successfully entered in the system. However, if the update record is canceled, the entry doesn't exist in the system, even though the user has a document number for it.

You should therefore check the system for canceled update records several times a day. In global systems, you should adjust the times at which you search for canceled update records in accordance with the various time zones. Employees located within the relevant time zone should also be involved in this check.

Asynchronous Updates

To enhance performance, changes to the database are made in asynchronous mode. In this mode, the user continues working while the system takes charge of the update process and then waits until the database change has been completed. In synchronous mode, users must wait until the database has been successfully changed before continuing with their work.

The more time that elapses between the cancelation of the update and your detection of it, the more difficult it is for users to remember exactly what they were doing when the updated record was canceled. If you act quickly, you can also reduce the frequency with which update records are canceled.

1. Enter Transaction SM13 in the command field and press the Enter key (or select the menu option Tools • Administration • Monitor • SM13—Update).

2. Complete the selection fields and make sure that you don't restrict the selection for an initial analysis (see Figure 2.59). In particular, leave the FROM DATE field blank, or enter a date in the distant past. When you've finished, choose EXECUTE.

Figure 2.59 Update Requests Selection Screen

3. Search the STATUS column for entries with the status ERROR (see Figure 2.60). This status indicates a terminated update record. You can double-click on an entry to display its details.

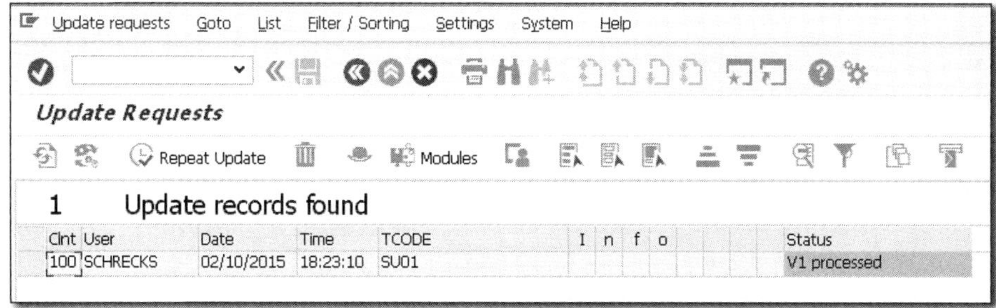

Figure 2.60 Overview of Update Records

4. The Status of Update Module screen provides details of the user, transaction, and function that is to be updated (see Figure 2.61). Click on the Error Information button.

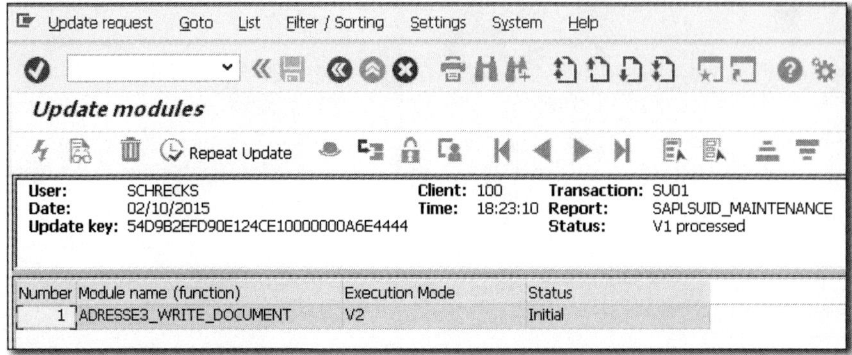

Figure 2.61 Update Modules

5. Details of the update status are then displayed, which may indicate an error (see Figure 2.62).

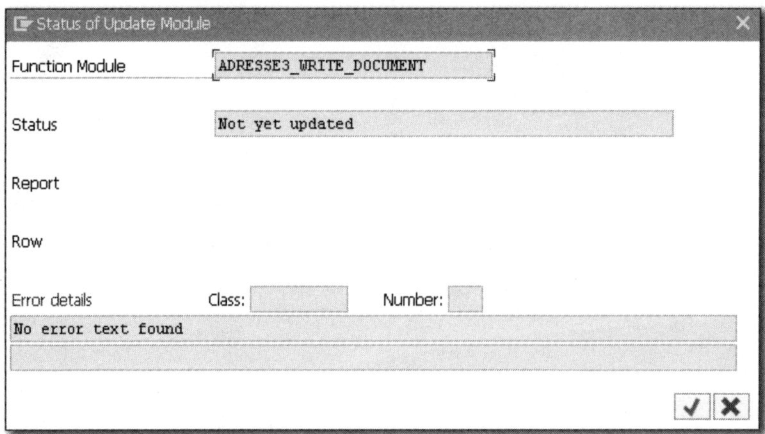

Figure 2.62 Status Details of an Update

If you detect the occurrence of update errors, you must then notify the affected users. These users should search for missing entries and reenter the data records that haven't been updated.

Reposting Canceled Update Records [!]

Don't try to update a canceled update record again! In certain cases, this may damage the database. Instead, you should *always* ask the users to execute the failed transaction again.

When an update request ends in an error, the user receives the following notification: EXPRESS DOCUMENT RECEIVED. SAP uses express messages to notify users immediately of canceled update records. It's therefore easiest for the user to repair the damage as soon as the problem occurs. The user should stop working immediately and ask for help with pinpointing the problem. Users should be made aware of this procedure during training.

Administration of the Update System 

In certain exceptional cases, it's recommended that you deactivate the update system. For example, it may not be possible to save data following a serious database error. As a result, the update requests that can't be executed begin to accumulate.

In *Update Program Administration* (Transaction SM14), you can deactivate updates in the SAP system as a whole. If you do this, update requests are no longer sent to the database, and the error can be eliminated without any further interruptions.

While the update system is deactivated, the following information is displayed to users in the status bar: UPDATE DELAYED. PLEASE WAIT. The work process stops and remains blocked until the update function is reactivated. Data can be sent to the database after the update system has been reactivated.

2.5 System Messages

A system message is a dialog box that is displayed for all users. System messages are useful for making information available to all users (e.g., if you need to carry out unplanned system maintenance). After a new message is created, this dialog box is displayed once per day and each time a user executes an action (e.g., clicking on a button). To create a system message, follow these steps:

Display System Messages at Each Logon 

As of SAP NetWeaver release 6.00, system messages are displayed only once per day to the user; previously, they were displayed at each logon (see SAP Note 302696). Customers can make modifications to restore the old system behavior. For more details, refer to SAP Note 604495.

1. Enter Transaction SM02 in the command field and press the [Enter] key (or select Tools • Administration • Administration • SM02—System Messages in the SAP standard menu).
2. On the System Messages screen (see Figure 2.63), click on the Create button.

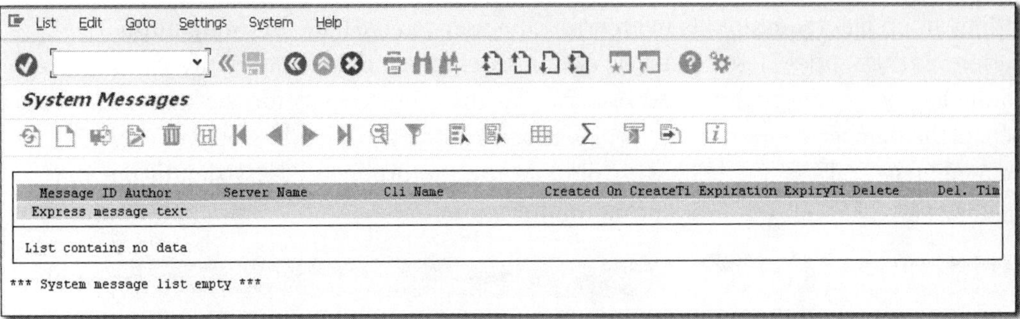

Figure 2.63 Overview of System Messages

3. The Create System Messages dialog box opens (see Figure 2.64). The following can be done here:
   - Enter the text of your message under System Message Text.
   - If you only want the message to apply to a specific application server (e.g., because you only need to shut down one specific instance), you can specify this server in the ServerName field.

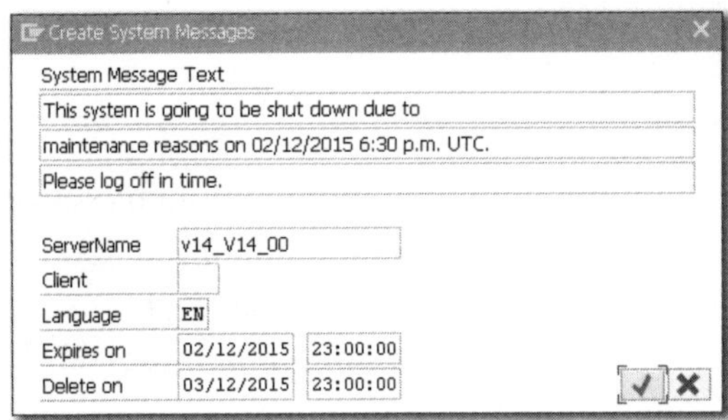

Figure 2.64 Creating a System Message

   - If the message is only relevant for users of a specific client (e.g., because postings are locked in that client due to the year-end closing), you can specify this client in the Client field.

- The LANGUAGE field allows you to restrict your message to a single logon language. In international enterprises, you can define a translated system message for each logon language.
- In the EXPIRES ON field, enter the date and time as of which you no longer want the message to be displayed.
- In the DELETE ON field, enter the date and time at which you want the message to be permanently deleted.

4. Click on CONTINUE ✓.

Specifying Exact Times in System Messages [+]

Always enter the exact time of the system stop, including the time zone and date (e.g., Tuesday, May 13th, 2014, 06:30:00 PM CST). If you provide vague information such as "in 15 minutes," it isn't clear when the system is to be stopped because users have no way of knowing when the message was created.

5. A message in the status bar indicates that the system message has been saved (see Figure 2.65).

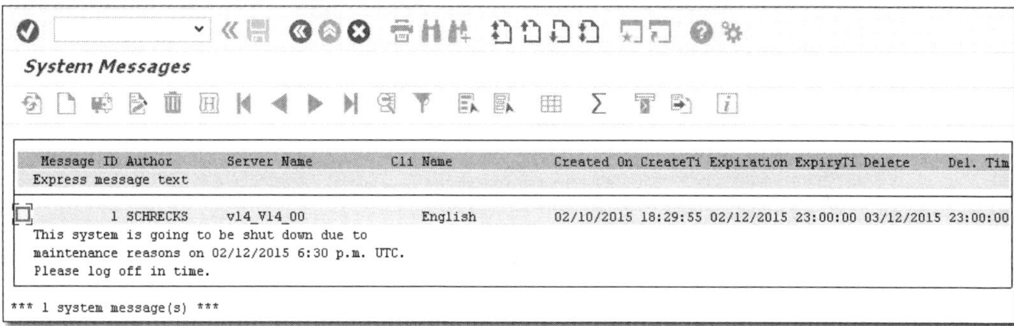

Figure 2.65 New System Message in the Overview

6. The message will then be displayed in a dialog box whenever a user logs on to the SAP system or whenever a user who is already logged on executes an action (see Figure 2.66).

Using System Messages [+]

Use system messages with caution. Users may feel that automatically displayed dialog boxes interfere with their work. Note also that whenever you make a change to a system message, it will be displayed again for all users.

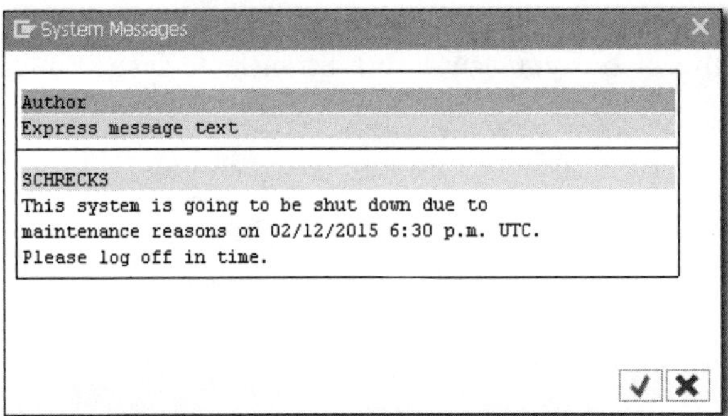

Figure 2.66 System Message as Displayed to the User

2.6 Connections

The SAP system offers a range of interfaces with other systems. Various standard logs can be used for communication purposes. You, as the SAP administrator, are responsible for configuring and monitoring these connections, and for correcting any errors that occur. This section describes the various forms that communication with external systems may take and presents the tools that can be used for monitoring and administering these connections.

2.6.1 RFC Destinations

Remote Function Calls (RFCs) can be used, for example, to call ABAP function modules in remote SAP systems, which then trigger a transaction in those systems. Communication is based on the RFC interface. The destinations of the function call (e.g., a server, system, client, etc.) are defined in *RFC destinations* (or *RFC connections*).

It's essential for you to know how to create and maintain these destinations because RFC connections need to be used relatively frequently in the ABAP environment.

1. Enter Transaction SM59 in the command field and press the Enter key (or select the menu option Tools • Administration • Administration • Network • SM59—RFC Destinations).
2. On the Configuration of RFC Connections screen (see Figure 2.67), select the ABAP Connections folder under RFC Connections.

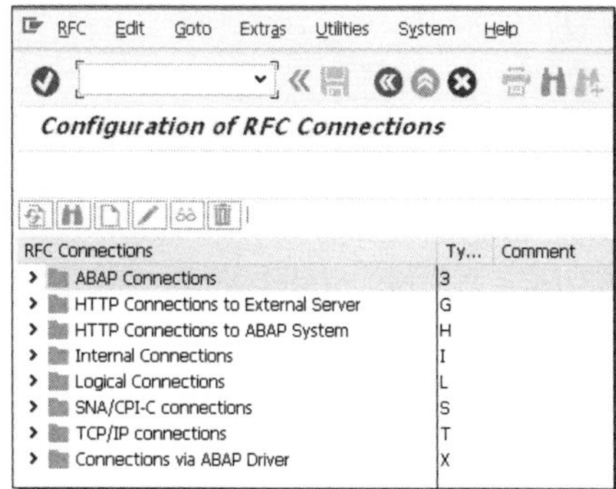

Figure 2.67 Configuring the RFC Connections

3. The existing RFC connections are displayed (see Figure 2.68). Double-click on any destination you want to display. To set up a new connection, click on CREATE.

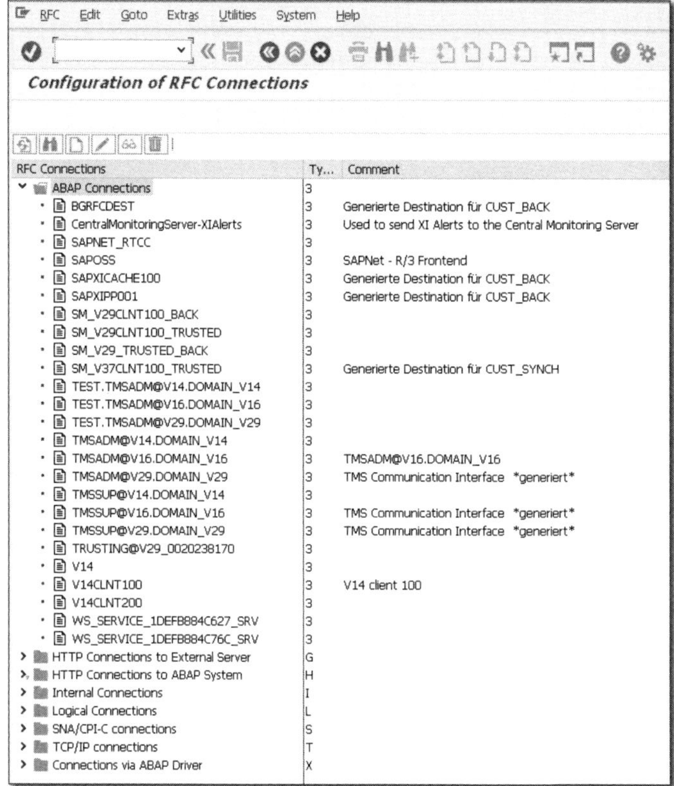

Figure 2.68 Overview of RFC Connections

4. Enter the following details (see Figure 2.69):
   - Enter a name in RFC DESTINATION.
   - Select a CONNECTION TYPE; for example, type "3" for a new ABAP connection.
   - Enter explanatory texts in the DESCRIPTION fields.
   - Press the Enter key to confirm.

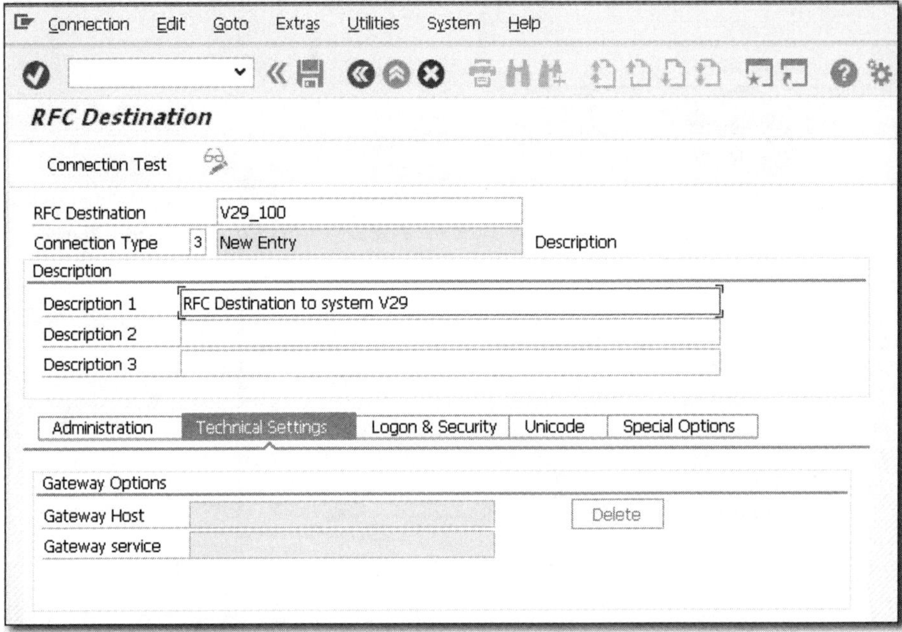

Figure 2.69 Creating an RFC Connection

5. New input fields are provided on the TECHNICAL SETTINGS tab (see Figure 2.70) based on the connection type you selected. Enter the following data here:
   - Enter the name or IP address of the SAP server that is to be called in the TARGET HOST field.
   - Enter the SYSTEM NUMBER.
6. Switch to the LOGON & SECURITY tab (see Figure 2.71). Make the following settings:

- Enter a logon language in the LANGUAGE field.
- In the CLIENT field, enter the client in which you want to use the RFC logon function.
- In the USER field, enter the user ID with which the function is to be executed in the target system.
- Enter the PASSWORD of the user in the target system.

Press the Enter key.

Figure 2.70 Maintaining the Technical Settings of the Connection

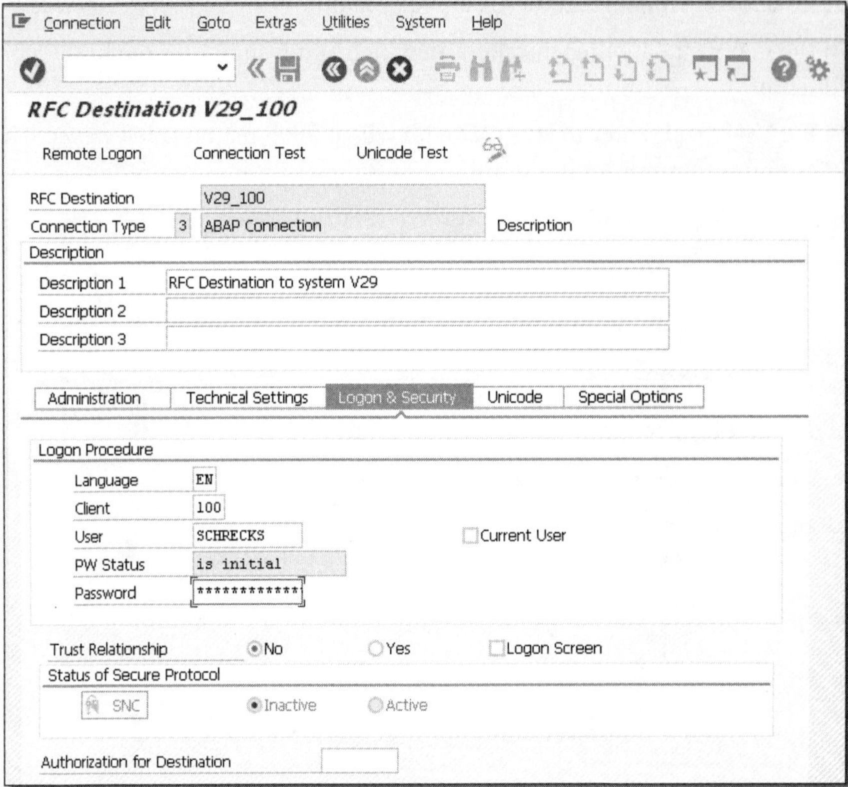

Figure 2.71 Saving Logon and Security Settings

7. Choose CONTINUE ✓ to confirm the dialog box (see Figure 2.72).

Figure 2.72 Confirming the Dialog Box

8. The RFC DESTINATION <NAME OF DESTINATION> view is displayed again (see Figure 2.73). Here you can see that your entries have been copied into the LOGON

PROCEDURE field group. Click on SAVE [icon]. A message in the status bar confirms that your RFC connection has been saved.

Figure 2.73 Saving an RFC Connection

9. To check the proper functioning of the RFC connection, click on the CONNECTION TEST button. The system now attempts to reach the remote server in the network using the `ping` command (see Figure 2.74). If this test is successful, a connection can be set up at the TCP/IP level. Click on BACK [icon].

10. On the RFC DESTINATION screen, click on REMOTE LOGON to verify that the logon data you entered is correct. The screen shown in Figure 2.75 is dis-

played if the connection is working. You're now in the target system, as you can see on the bottom-right of the screen.

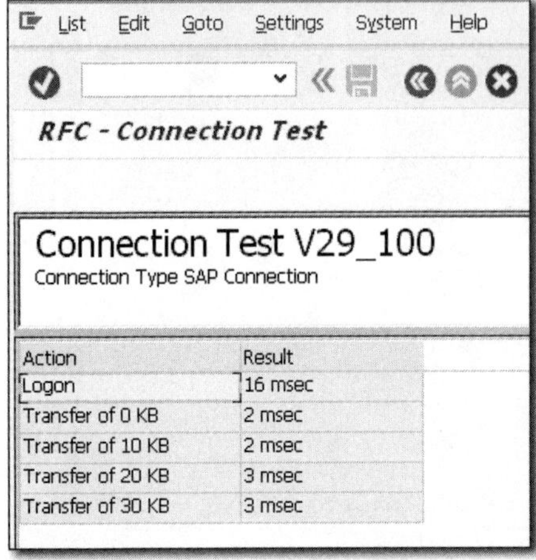

Figure 2.74 Results of the Connection Test

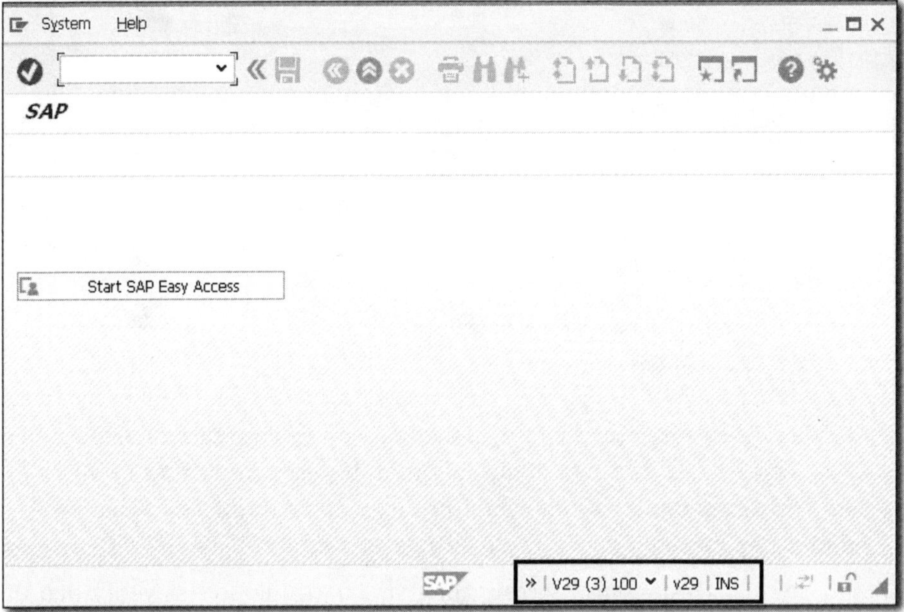

Figure 2.75 Successful Logon to the Target System via RFC Connection

11. If the connection can't be set up, for example, because the password entered is incorrect, a logon screen is displayed instead (see Figure 2.76). Check the data you entered on the LOGON & SECURITY tab, and test the connection again.

[!]

Testing RFC Connections

If nothing happens when a remote logon is attempted, this usually means that the connection is working and the logon was successful. This may happen, for example, if you entered a user of the "Communication" type for the RFC logon. To make sure that the destination is working and the user is authorized to set up RFC connections in the target system, you should implement an authorization test via UTILITIES • TEST • AUTHORIZATION TEST. To verify the settings in the UNICODE tab, choose UTILITIES • TEST • UNICODE TEST.

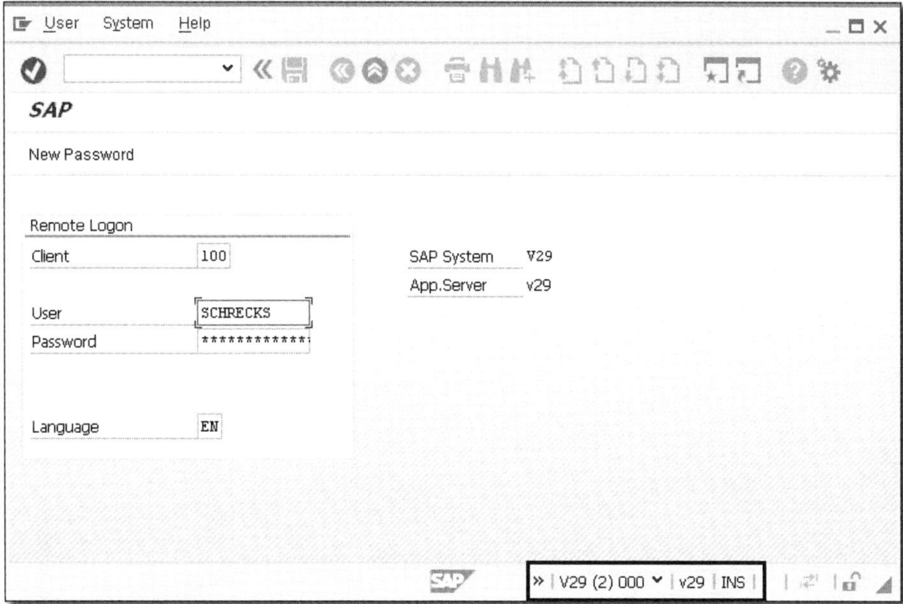

Figure 2.76 Logon Screen for a Failed RFC Connection

12. The RFC connection has now been set up. Choose BACK to exit the view. The new connection is displayed in the list of destinations (see Figure 2.77).

RFC connections not only allow you to call ABAP function modules in other SAP systems but also to start programs in non-SAP systems. These connections have many and varied applications.

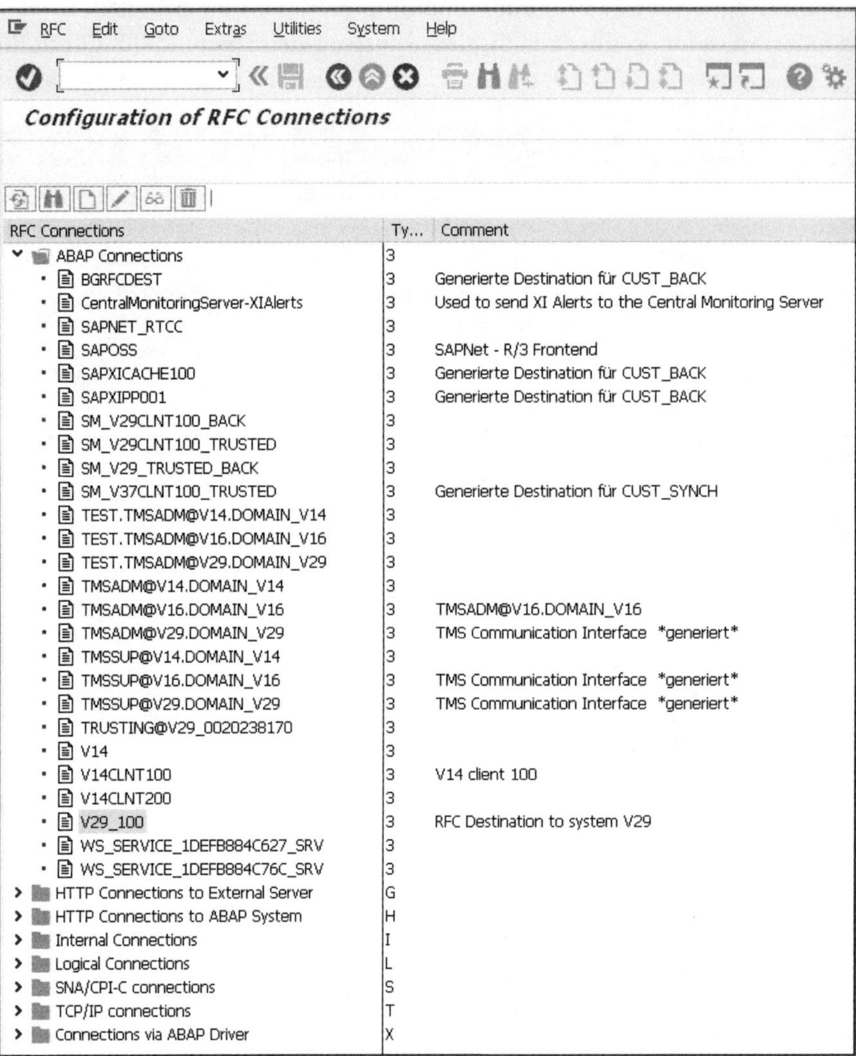

Figure 2.77 Display of New RFC Connection in the Connection Overview

[+]

Testing RFC Connections

If errors occur with RFC connections, perform a connection test as described before attempting a remote logon. In most cases, the server you're calling can't be reached due to problems with the network or because incorrect logon data was entered for the connection. For example, an RFC connection can't be set up if the user entered is locked in the target system, has been deleted, or has changed his password.

2.6.2 SAP Gateway Monitor

The SAP Gateway is used to create connections between external systems and programs that use TCP/IP. In the SAP environment, this category includes all RFC connections of type 3 (ABAP), for example. The Gateway Monitor (Transaction SMGW) is used for monitoring, analysis, and administration of the SAP Gateway. To use the monitor, follow these steps:

1. Enter Transaction SMGW in the command field and press the Enter key (or select the menu option Tools • Administration • Monitor • System Monitoring • SMGW—Gateway Monitor).
2. All existing inbound and outbound RFC connections are initially displayed (see Figure 2.78). Click on Refresh to refresh the display.

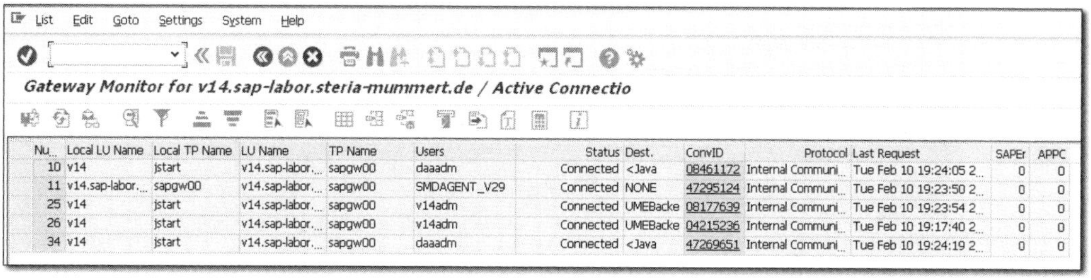

List Edit Goto Settings System Help

Gateway Monitor for v14.sap-labor.steria-mummert.de / Active Connectio

Nu...	Local LU Name	Local TP Name	LU Name	TP Name	Users	Status	Dest.	ConvID	Protocol	Last Request	SAPEr	APPC
10	v14	jstart	v14.sap-labor....	sapgw00	daaadm	Connected	<Java	08461172	Internal Communi...	Tue Feb 10 19:24:05 2...	0	0
11	v14.sap-labor....	sapgw00	v14.sap-labor....	sapgw00	SMDAGENT_V29	Connected	NONE	47295124	Internal Communi...	Tue Feb 10 19:23:50 2...	0	0
25	v14	jstart	v14.sap-labor....	sapgw00	v14adm	Connected	UMEBacke	08177639	Internal Communi...	Tue Feb 10 19:23:54 2...	0	0
26	v14	jstart	v14.sap-labor....	sapgw00	v14adm	Connected	UMEBacke	04215236	Internal Communi...	Tue Feb 10 19:17:40 2...	0	0
34	v14	jstart	v14.sap-labor....	sapgw00	daaadm	Connected	<Java	47269651	Internal Communi...	Tue Feb 10 19:24:19 2...	0	0

Figure 2.78 Gateway Monitor

3. Double-click on a list entry to display detailed information about it, or click on Choose Detail. The system switches to the Detailed Connection Information view (see Figure 2.79).

On this screen, you can see, for example, the IP addresses that are connected by the new connection (HOSTADDR list entry). You can also identify the connection partner for any suspicious-looking RFC connections.

Gateway Security [⚙]

Because the gateway manages connections from the outside, it represents a vulnerable point and it's security-relevant for possible system attacks. You can control the security settings of the gateway using the files *sec_info* (starting external server programs) and *reg_info* (as of kernel release 6.40, registration of external server programs). Further information on this topic is available in SAP Notes 614971, 1069911, and 1408081 or in the linked detail notes.

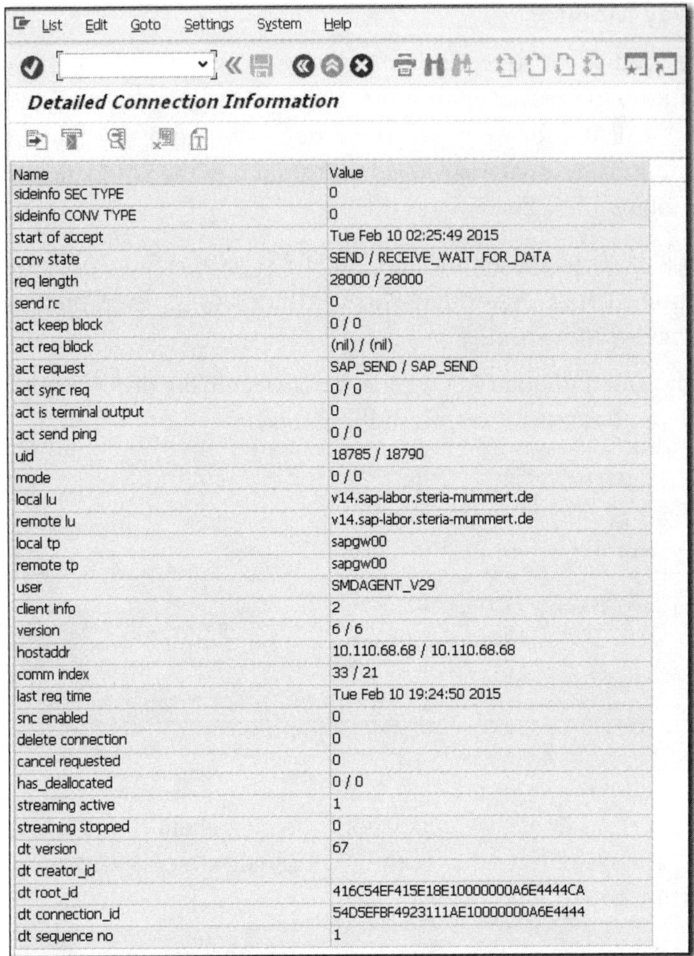

Name	Value
sideinfo SEC TYPE	0
sideinfo CONV TYPE	0
start of accept	Tue Feb 10 02:25:49 2015
conv state	SEND / RECEIVE_WAIT_FOR_DATA
req length	28000 / 28000
send rc	0
act keep block	0 / 0
act req block	(nil) / (nil)
act request	SAP_SEND / SAP_SEND
act sync req	0 / 0
act is terminal output	0
act send ping	0 / 0
uid	18785 / 18790
mode	0 / 0
local lu	v14.sap-labor.steria-mummert.de
remote lu	v14.sap-labor.steria-mummert.de
local tp	sapgw00
remote tp	sapgw00
user	SMDAGENT_V29
client info	2
version	6 / 6
hostaddr	10.110.68.68 / 10.110.68.68
comm index	33 / 21
last req time	Tue Feb 10 19:24:50 2015
snc enabled	0
delete connection	0
cancel requested	0
has_deallocated	0 / 0
streaming active	1
streaming stopped	0
dt version	67
dt creator_id	
dt root_id	416C54EF415E18E10000000A6E4444CA
dt connection_id	54D5EFBF4923111AE10000000A6E4444
dt sequence no	1

Figure 2.79 Detailed Connection Information

2.6.3 SAPconnect

SAPconnect is an RFC interface used for external communication (or *information broadcasting*). For example, you can use SAPconnect to send and receive emails via SMTP. The following communication types are provided by SAPconnect:

- Fax
- Internet (SMTP)
- X.400

- SAP to SAP
- Paging (SMS)
- Printer

You use Transaction SCOT (SAPconnect) for SAPconnect administration. Here you can configure and monitor the communication services.

Classic Node Maintenance [+]

Transaction SCOT was completely redesigned for release 7.31. Although all functions are still available in the new transaction, it may take a while to get used to it. To change to the old design, select the UTILITIES • CLASSIC NODE MAINTENANCE menu option.

1. Enter Transaction SCOT in the command field and press the Enter key (or select the menu option TOOLS • BUSINESS COMMUNICATION • COMMUNICATION • SCOT—SAPCONNECT).
2. To configure the SMTP service, for example, select BUSINESS COMMUNICATION ADMINISTRATION • SETTINGS • OUTBOUND MESSAGES in the tree structure and position the cursor on the SMTP NODE entry. In the menu bar on the right-hand side of the screen, click on the CREATE NODE button (see Figure 2.80).

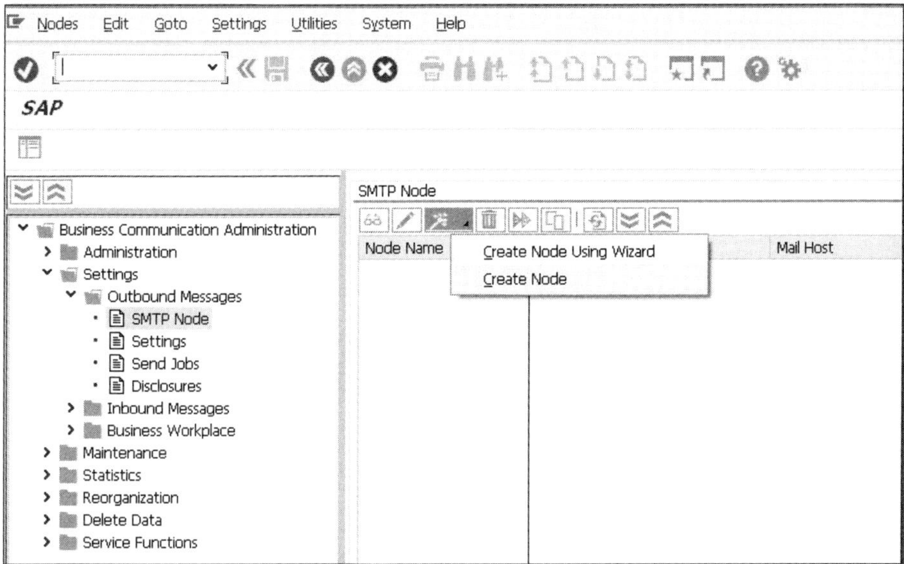

Figure 2.80 Creating SMTP Nodes

3. Maintain the settings for the SMTP service (see Figure 2.81). Under SMTP CONNECTION, enter the SMTP server and the corresponding port. Choose CONTINUE ✓ to save your entries.

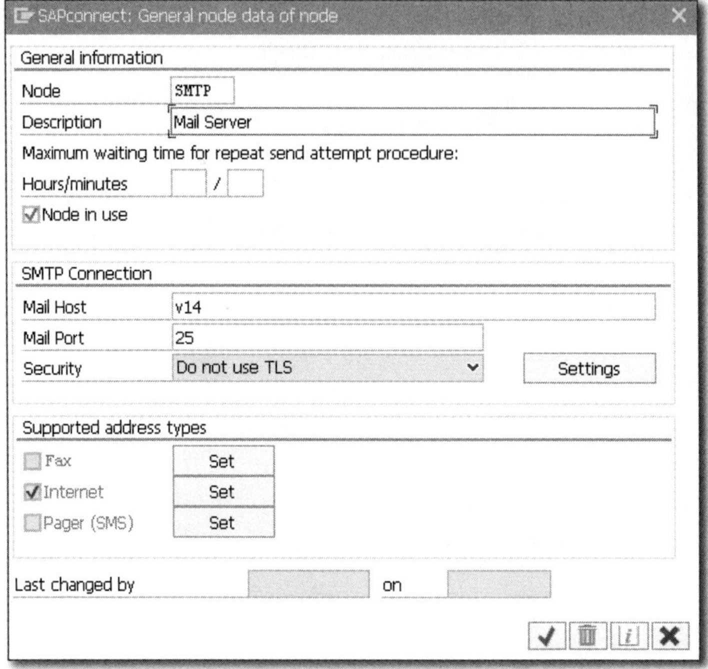

Figure 2.81 Maintaining the Settings for the SMTP Service

4. If you want emails to be sent via the SMTP server, you need to run a corresponding *send job*, which transfers the communication items. In the tree structure under OUTBOUND MESSAGES, double-click on the SEND JOBS entry (see Figure 2.82).
5. All planned or active send jobs are listed in the right screen frame. To define a new send job, click on SCHEDULE JOB, and select the relevant communication type (e.g., SCHEDULE JOB FOR INT; see Figure 2.83).

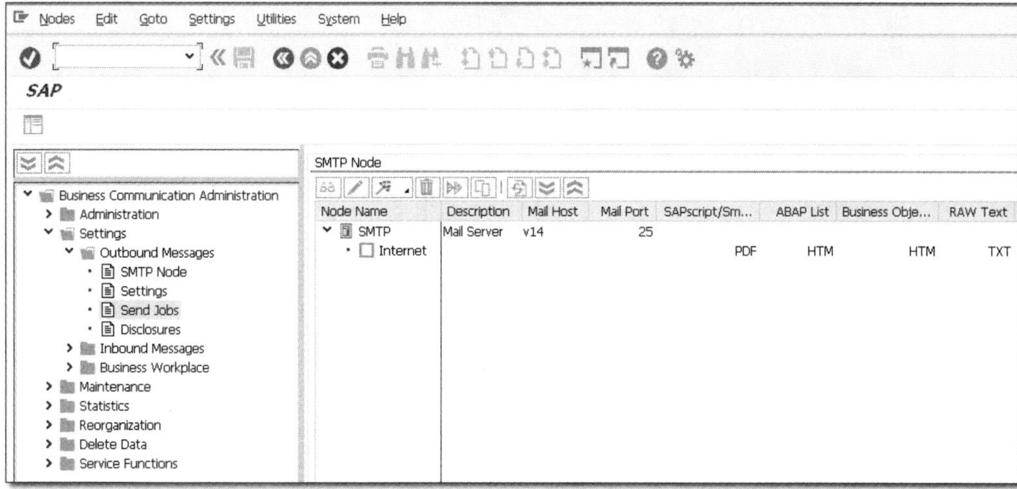

Figure 2.82 Switching to Send Job Configuration

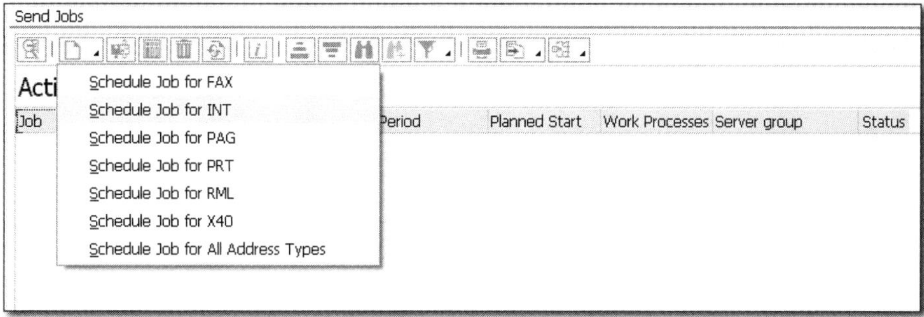

Figure 2.83 Creating a New Send Job

6. Make the following settings on the next screen (see Figure 2.84):
   - Enter a name for the job (try to make it as meaningful as possible) in the JOB field.
   - Enter an execution interval for the job in the PERIOD field.
   - Enter a time for the first job run in the PLANNED START field.
   - In the BACKGROUND USER field, enter the SAP user ID with which the job is to be scheduled.

   Choose CONTINUE to accept the settings.

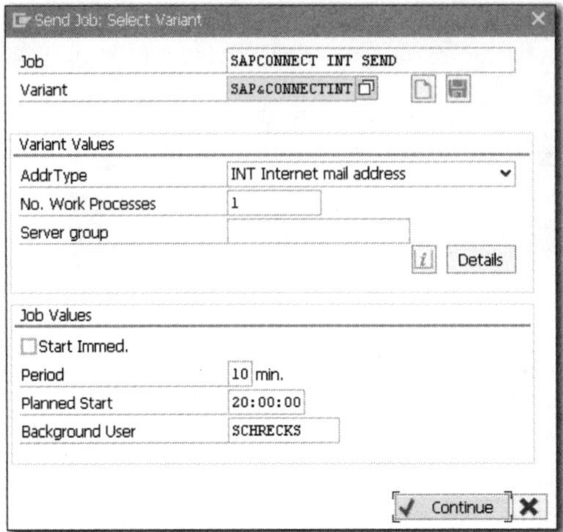

Figure 2.84 Settings for the New Send Job

7. The data you enter here is copied to the Define Background Job view (see Figure 2.85 and Chapter 15 for more information). To schedule the job, click on Save.

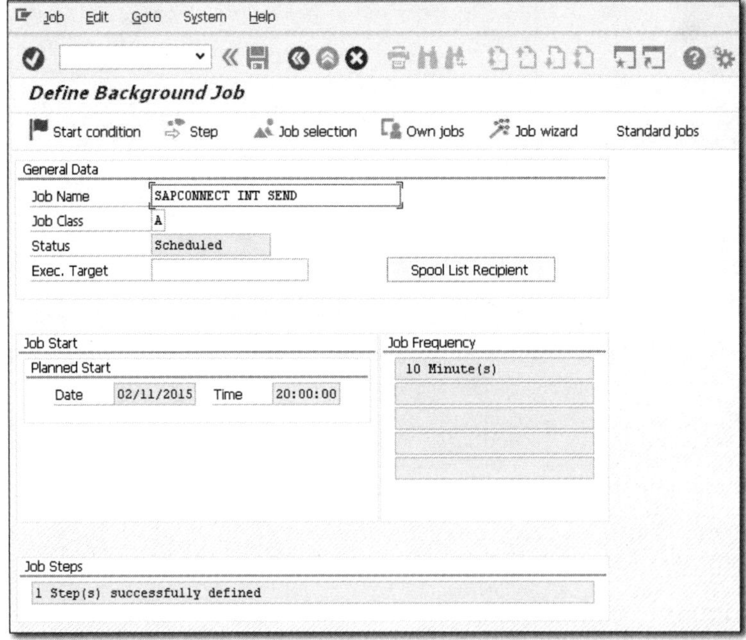

Figure 2.85 Job Scheduling Details

8. The display switches back to the ACTIVE AND SCHEDULED SEND JOBS window (see Figure 2.86). The new job you've just defined is now included in the list. The SCHEDULED icon in the STATUS column indicates that the send job has been scheduled. Choose BACK to exit the view.

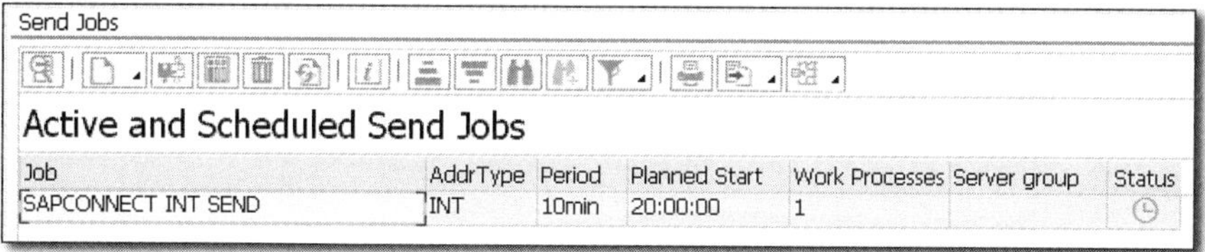

Figure 2.86 Active and Scheduled Send Jobs Window

After you set up the communication type and schedule the send job, the emails created in the system (e.g., SAP Business Workplace (Transaction SBWP)) are sent at the correct time. You can also follow the same steps for sending faxes and SMS messages, for example.

[!]

Activating the SMTP Service

Note that the SAPconnect service must be activated in Transaction SICF (see Section 2.6.5) for your configuration to work.

2.6.4 Message Server Monitor

The message server is a system process of the central instance, which manages the communication between the individual instances of an SAP system (see Figure 2.87). If load distribution is configured in your system, the message server also selects the application server to which the user logs on, for example.

If problems occur, use the Message Server Monitor (Transaction SMMS) to monitor the message server. The Message Server Monitor also provides access to the administration functions of the message server. To check the status of the message server, follow these steps:

1. Enter Transaction SMMS in the command field and press the Enter key (or select the menu option TOOLS • ADMINISTRATION • MONITOR • SYSTEM MONITORING • SMMS—MESSAGE SERVER MONITOR).

2. The message server data are displayed. The SERVER STATUS column indicates whether the server is active. The SAP SERVICE column, meanwhile, specifies the services that are available on the individual application servers.

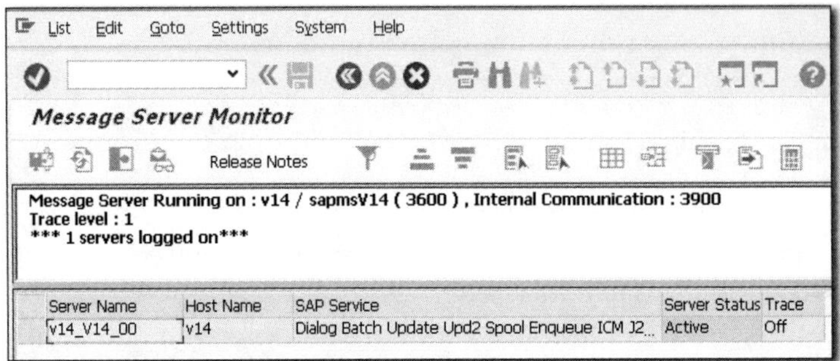

Figure 2.87 Message Server Monitor

3. To restart the message server following an error, select the menu option GOTO • EXPERT FUNCTIONS • SERVERS • SHUT DOWN SERVER (HARD)/(SOFT) (see Figure 2.88).

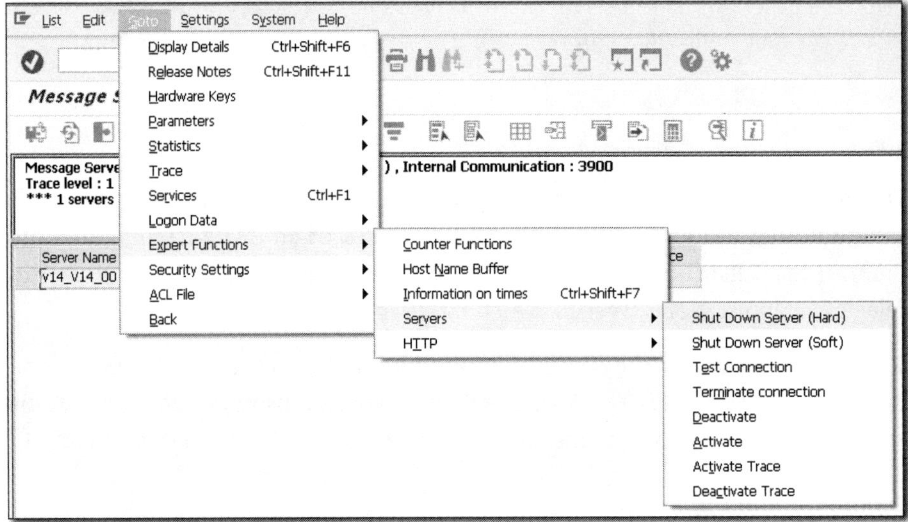

Figure 2.88 Message Server Restart

If there's an error on the message server, communication between the instances may be threatened in certain cases. In other words, it may no longer be possible to reach certain application servers. The other advanced functions of the Message Server Monitor (see Figure 2.88) allow you to bring about this status deliberately (DEACTIVATE TRACE), and to analyze and eliminate errors (e.g., ACTIVATE TRACE).

2.6.5 Internet Communication Framework

The *Internet Communication Framework* (ICF) enables communication with the SAP system via the HTTP, HTTPS, and SMTP Internet protocols. For example, the ICF receives HTTP calls sent from a web browser to the SAP system and forwards these to the relevant application.

You can use Transaction SICF for administration and monitoring ICF. You can also activate the services required for specific applications on this screen.

1. Enter Transaction SICF in the command field and press the Enter key (or select the menu option TOOLS • ADMINISTRATION • ADMINISTRATION • NETWORK • SICF—HTTP SERVICE HIERARCHY MAINTENANCE).
2. SERVICE is always preconfigured as the HIERARCHY TYPE to be maintained (see Figure 2.89). Click on the EXECUTE button ✓.

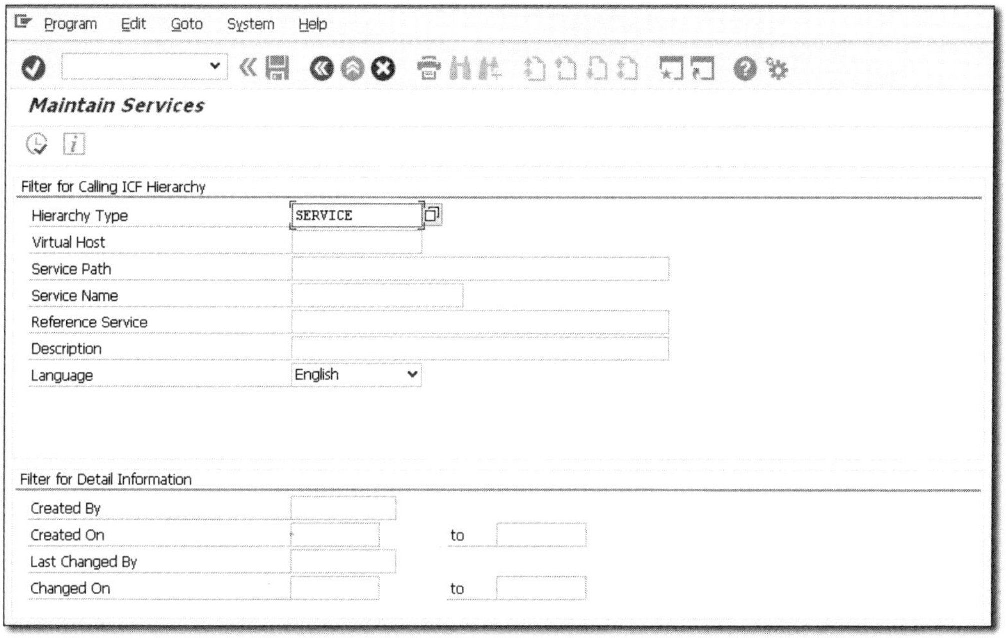

Figure 2.89 Maintenance of the ICF Hierarchy

3. You can activate or deactivate services on the next screen (see Figure 2.90). You can use the fields in the FILTER DETAILS area to restrict your search for a service based on specific criteria. Alternatively, expand the tree structure below VIRTUAL HOSTS/SERVICES.

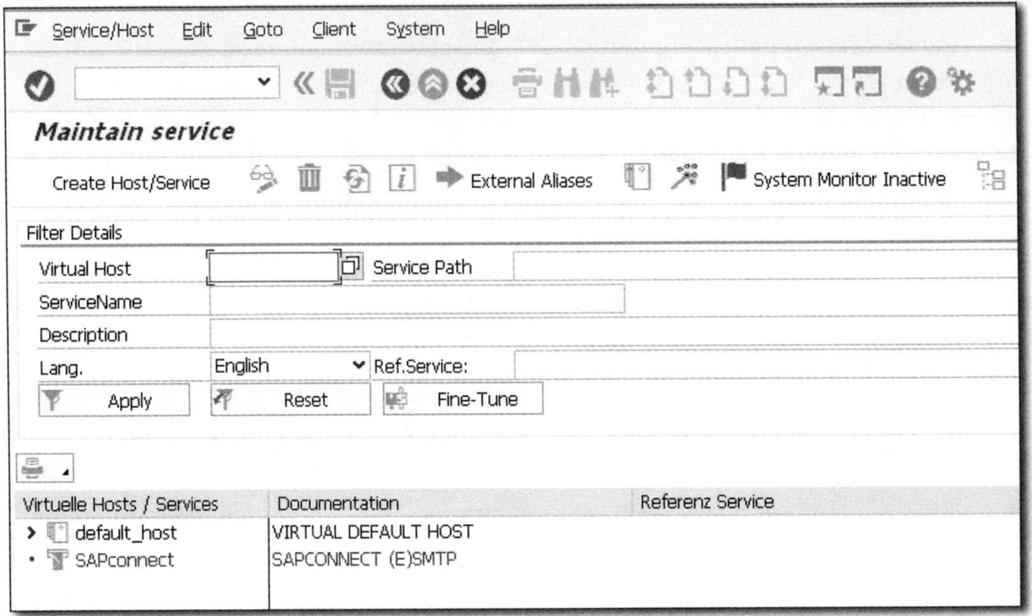

Figure 2.90 Detail Maintenance of an ICF Service

4. For example, expand the path DEFAULT_HOST • SAP • PUBLIC • BC • CCMS • MONITORING. Inactive services are displayed in gray font, while active services are indicated by black font (see Figure 2.91).
5. Right-click on the service you want to activate (e.g., MONITORING), and select the ACTIVATE SERVICE entry from the context menu.
6. Choose YES to confirm activation (see Figure 2.92). If you also want to activate all lower-level services within a node, click on the YES button with the icon .

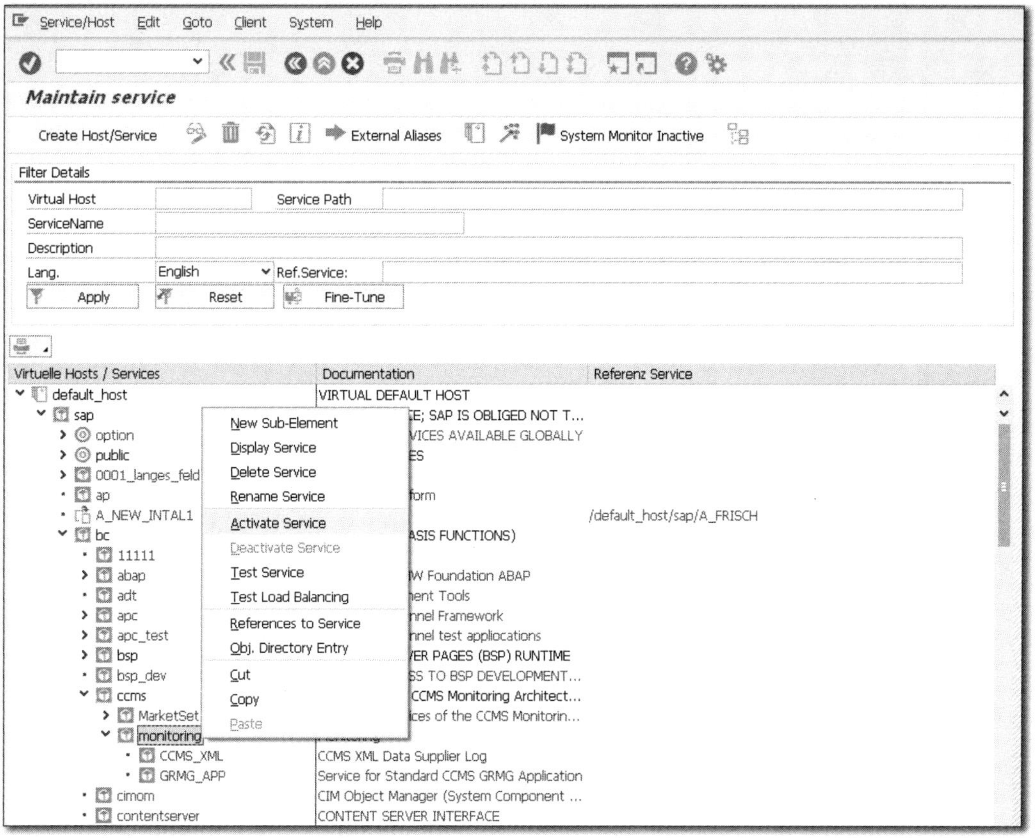

Figure 2.91 Activating the ICF Service

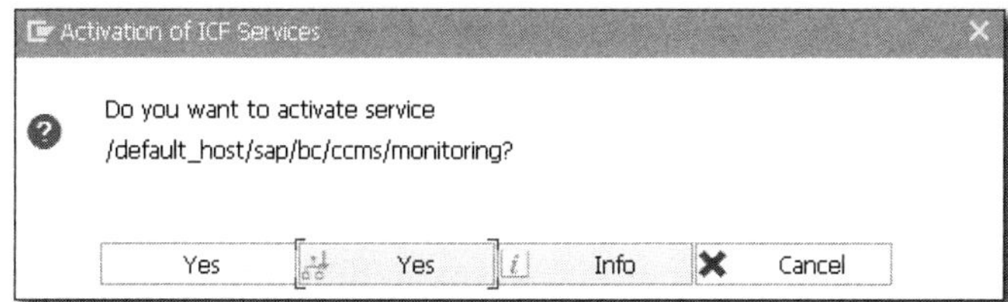

Figure 2.92 Confirmation of Activation

The services have been activated and are now shown in black font (see Figure 2.93).

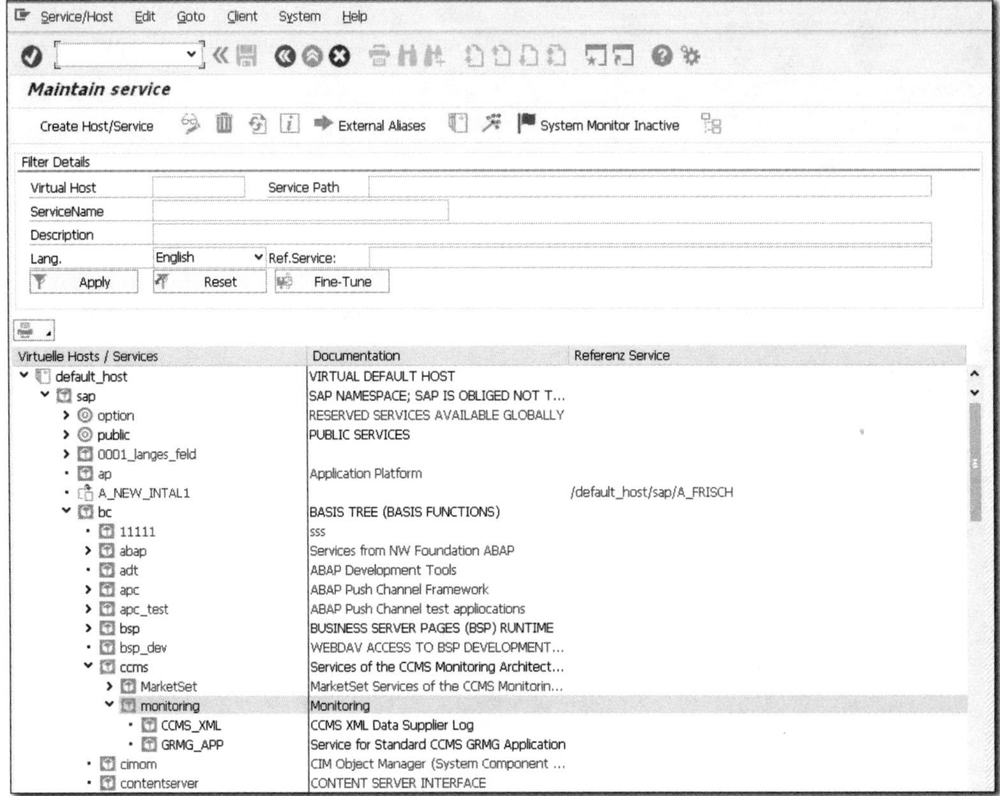

Figure 2.93 Newly Activated Services in the Tree View

[+]

Which Services to Activate

If you aren't sure which services to activate, seek the assistance of a programmer or consultant. In most cases, the services that need to be activated are specified in an error message when a user calls the relevant function.

In addition to the administration of services, Transaction SICF also offers other monitoring and administration functions for the ICF. These functions are available in the EDIT menu.

2.6.6 ICM Monitor

The *Internet Communication Manager* (ICM) is responsible for any communication between the SAP system and external applications made via the ICF using HTTP,

HTTPS, and SMTP. This applies to both inbound and outbound data communication. The ICM is particularly useful if you run web applications on your SAP system. It decides whether a browser call is intended for the ABAP or Java part of the SAP system and forwards it accordingly.

If problems arise with web applications, you'll need to check whether the ICM is running and if any errors have occurred. You can use the ICM Monitor (Transaction SMICM) for this purpose:

1. Enter Transaction SMICM in the command field and press the Enter key (or select the menu option TOOLS • ADMINISTRATION • MONITOR • SYSTEM MONITORING • SMICM—ICM MONITOR).
2. The initial screen of the ICM Monitor shows the status of the ICM (see Figure 2.94). Check whether the ICM is currently RUNNING (this is indicated by a green traffic-light icon). You should also check the list of threads, in particular, the entry in the STATUS column. Click on REFRESH to refresh the display.

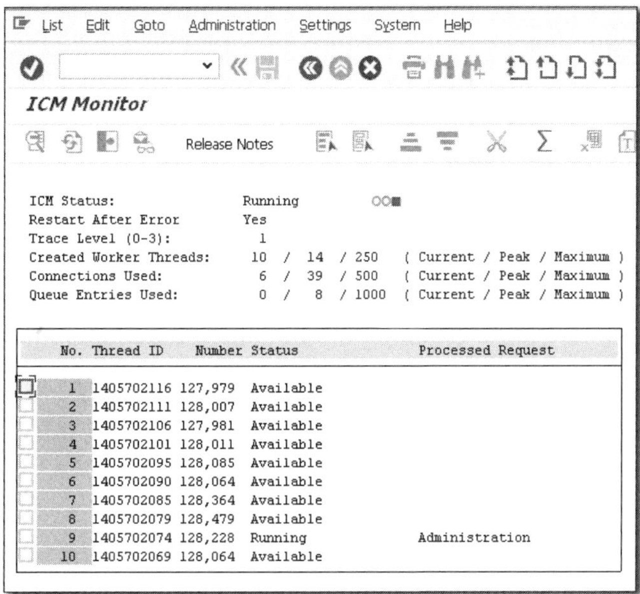

Figure 2.94 ICM Monitor

ICM-Threads

The work processes of the ICM, called *threads* or *worker threads*, are responsible for accepting external requests and sending responses.

3. If you want to know which services are provided by the ICM and via which ports you can reach them, click on the SERVICES button. You're provided with a list of all configured protocols including the most important parameter (see Figure 2.95).

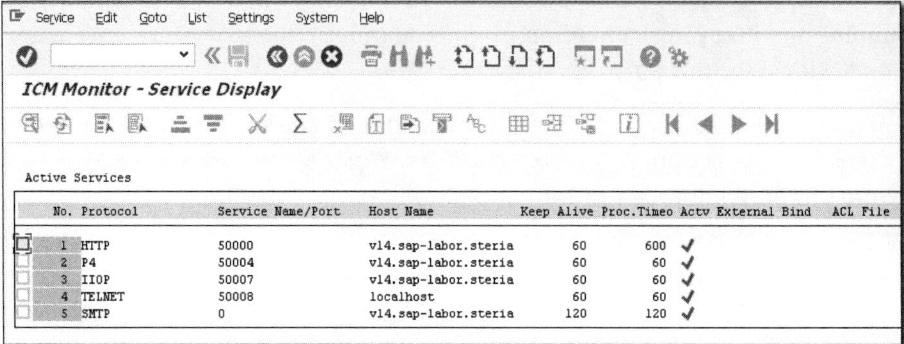

Figure 2.95 Service Overview of the ICM Monitor

4. You may need to restart the ICM if an error occurs. To do this, in the initial screen of the ICM Monitor, select the menu option ADMINISTRATION • ICM • EXIT HARD • LOCAL/GLOBAL (see Figure 2.96).

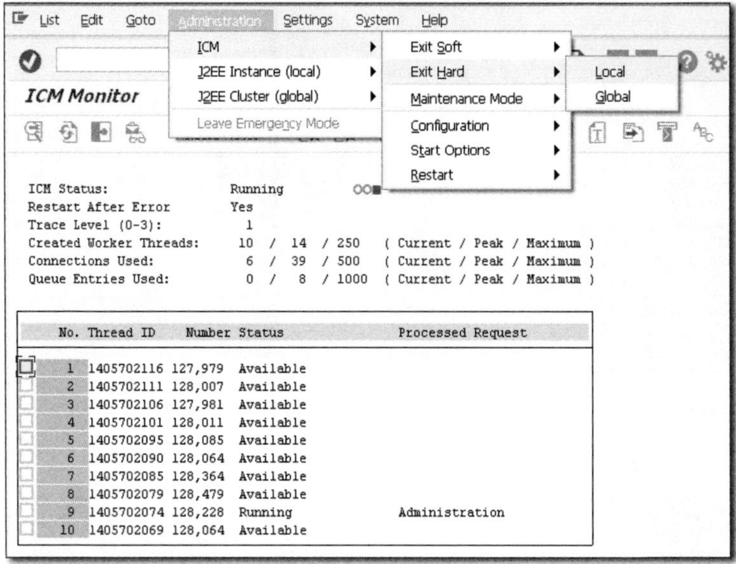

Figure 2.96 ICM Restart

"Exit Soft" or "Exit Hard" [+]

Sometimes, you need to restart the ICM to eliminate an error. You can perform a *soft* or *hard* restart in this case. With a soft shutdown, the ICM stops accepting requests but tries to complete any tasks that are still open. With a hard shutdown, the ICM shuts down immediately, without taking account of any open connections.

2.7 Client Administration

A *client* is, by definition, an organizationally and technically self-contained unit within an SAP system. While all clients in the system access the same repository objects (programs, tables, etc.; in other words, cross-client data), the Customizing settings and system master data are largely client-specific.

As a result, clients are often used to keep data separate to comply with commercial or corporate law requirements. In theory, for example, several enterprises may each operate their own client in a shared SAP system. In this case, the use of clients ensures a very clear separation between the data belonging to individual enterprises (which isn't the case if you use company codes, for example).

Multiple Enterprises in one SAP System [!]

With regard to the client concept, you must note that the SAP software can involve multiple clients; however, this doesn't apply to the database. In other words, if the database fails or if a recovery must be performed, this affects the entire system (and thus all clients).

Client administration, which involves the following tasks, is one of your responsibilities as system administrator:

- Creating, changing, and deleting clients
- Copying clients within a system
- Copying clients across systems

This section describes the main functions of client administration.

2.7.1 Creating Clients

A client is identified within a system by a unique three-digit code. Avoid using letters or special characters when you create new clients because this limits the functionality of the client to a considerable degree (e.g., in relation to transport management and certain application modules).

Three clients are reserved in every SAP standard system delivered: 000, 001, and 066. These clients aren't intended for live operation. Before you fill a system with Customizing settings or data, you create a new client (e.g., client 100); however, you can also create more clients.

A new client is normally created using the following two steps:

1. Create a new entry in the client table.
2. Execute a client copy.

You therefore begin by maintaining the client table:

1. Enter Transaction SCC4 in the command field and press the [Enter] key (or select the menu option Tools • Administration • Administration • Client Administration • SCC4—Client Maintenance).
2. The client table is then displayed (see Figure 2.97). Click on Display <-> Change.

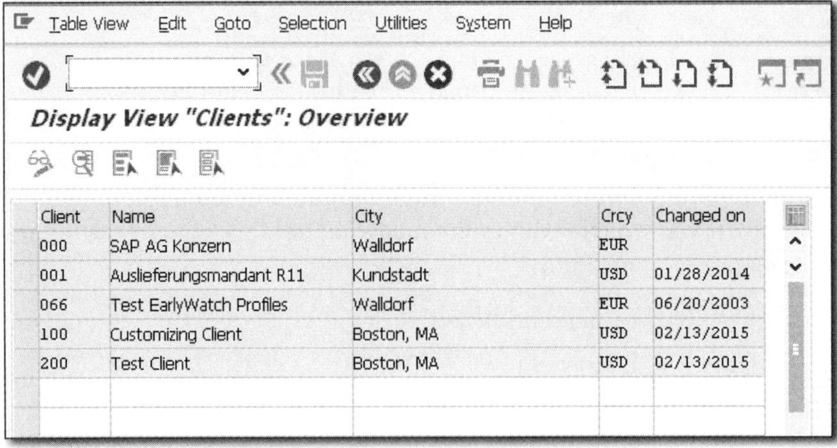

Figure 2.97 Client Table

3. In the dialog box that opens (see Figure 2.98), click on Continue.

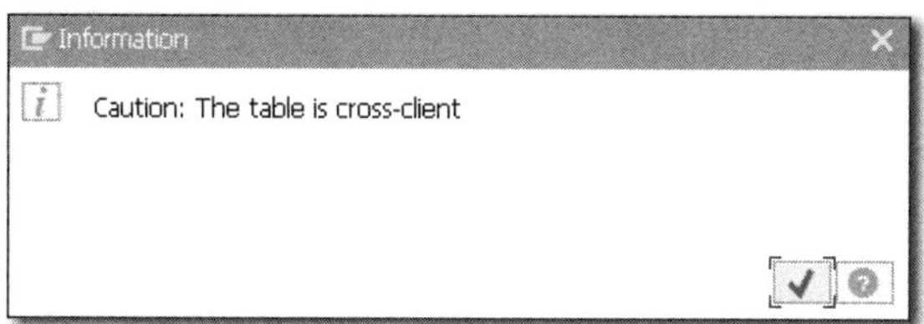

Figure 2.98 Confirming a Message about the Maintenance of a Cross-Client Table

4. Click on the New Entries button (see Figure 2.99).

Table View Edit Goto Selection Utilities System Help

Change View "Clients": Overview

New Entries

Client	Name	City	Crcy	Changed on
000	SAP AG Konzern	Walldorf	EUR	
001	Auslieferungsmandant R11	Kundstadt	USD	01/28/2014
066	Test EarlyWatch Profiles	Walldorf	EUR	06/20/2003
100	Customizing Client	Boston, MA	USD	02/13/2015
200	Test Client	Boston, MA	USD	02/13/2015

Figure 2.99 Client Table in Change Mode

5. Complete the fields in the detailed view for new clients as follows (see Figure 2.100):
   - In the Client text boxes, enter a client number (e.g., "300") and a name (e.g., "Test Client").
   - Enter the location name in the City field (e.g., "Boston, MA").
   - In Std currency, enter a default currency for the client (e.g., "USD").
   - Select an entry from the Client role dropdown list (e.g., "Test").
   - Enter the relevant option under Changes and Transports for Client-Specific Objects (see Chapter 10).
   - Select the relevant option from the Cross-Client Object Changes dropdown list.

- Under Client Copy and Comparison Tool Protection, select Protection level 0: No restriction from the dropdown list. The protection level can't be increased until the client copy is complete because copying would not be possible otherwise.
- If you want to enable the execution of CATT and eCATT runs, select the eCATT and CATT option under CATT and eCATT Restrictions.

Finally, click on Save.

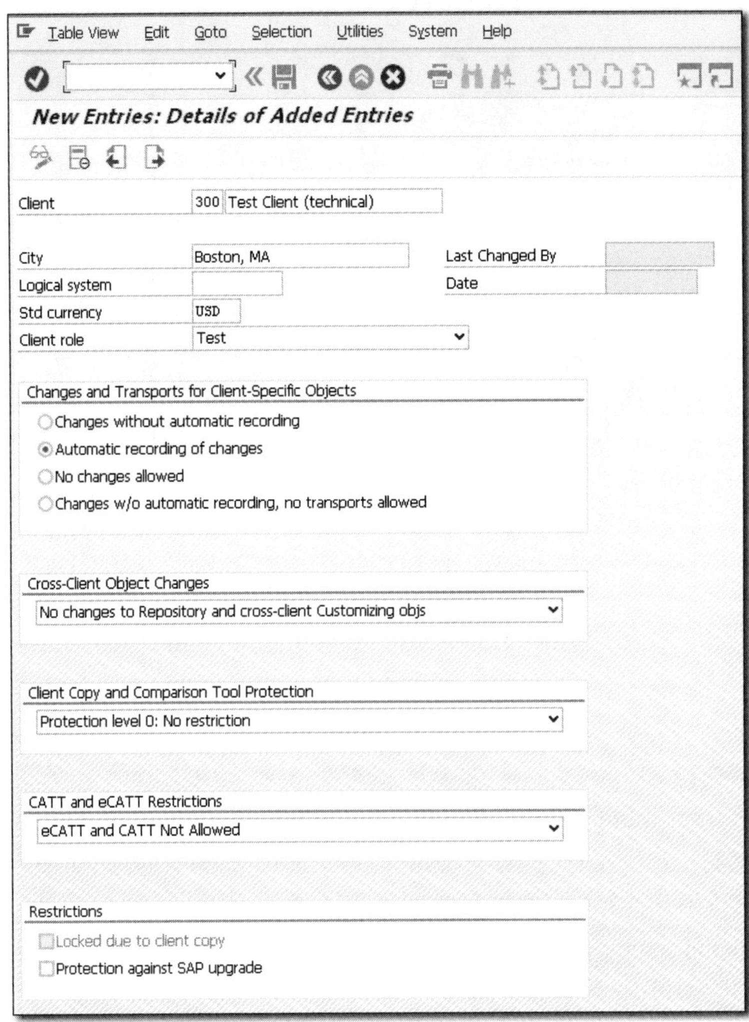

Figure 2.100 Adding a New Client Entry

6. The message DATA WAS SAVED appears in the status bar to confirm that the client has been created. Click on BACK.

   The client you just created is now also listed in the table (see Figure 2.101).

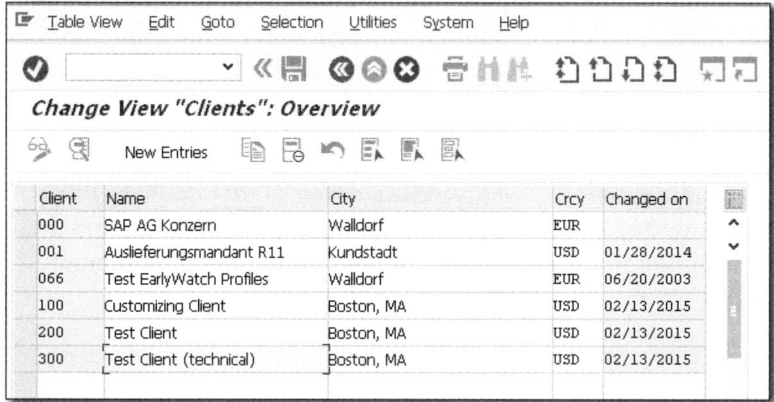

Figure 2.101 Table with New Client

The client is now ready to be used as the target client in a client copy. The new client contains no Customizing, master, or application data. You therefore need to fill the client with data using a client copy. In addition, the new client doesn't contain any user master records. The first time you log on to the client, you therefore use the user `SAP*` and the default password `pass`.

The SAP* User in New Clients [!]

The user `SAP*` and default password `pass` represent generally recognized logon data, and this user account also has unrestricted authorizations. You should therefore create an actual `SAP*` user and change the password as soon as possible.

Access by this user is only possible if the `login/no_automatic_user_sapstar` profile parameter has the value `0`. As soon as you've finished the client copy, check whether the passwords for all system IDs are secure in the new client.

2.7.2 Copying Clients

You use the client copy function to copy or transport client-specific Customizing settings or data from a source client into a target client. This function doesn't copy any cross-client objects such as ABAP programs or table structures. You can use copy profiles to determine the scope of the data copy, which means that you don't need to copy all of the data in a client.

The target client may be in the same or another system. A copy within the same system is known as a *local client copy*. Cross-system copies can be executed either as a *remote copy* (using an RFC connection) or as a *client transport* using the Transport Management System (TMS).

It may take several hours or longer to copy a client because the datasets may be very large in some cases. For the duration of the copy, all users should be locked and the scheduling of all background jobs canceled; otherwise, data inconsistencies may occur in the target client. Note also that the new client requires additional memory in the database. Make sure that you have sufficient memory in reserve because the client copy is otherwise very likely to terminate.

[+]

SAP Notes Relating to Client Copies

For more information about tools you can use for client copies, refer to SAP Notes 24853 and 552711. SAP Note 118823 provides information about the database memory required for the additional client. If you have problems involving long runtimes when copying large clients, refer to SAP Note 489690 for some solution approaches.

Local Client Copy

You perform a client copy to copy a client within the same system. This is the fastest way to copy a client.

1. To log on to your newly created client, use the `SAP*` user ID and the password `pass`.

[!]

Log On to the Correct Client

It's essential to ensure that you're logged on to the *correct* target client. Otherwise, you may unintentionally destroy another client.

2. Enter Transaction SCCL in the command field and press the [Enter] key (or select the menu option TOOLS • ADMINISTRATION • ADMINISTRATION • CLIENT ADMINISTRATION • CLIENT COPY • SCCL—LOCAL COPY).
3. On the CLIENT COPY - COPY A CLIENT screen, open the input help for the SELECTED PROFILE field (see Figure 2.102).

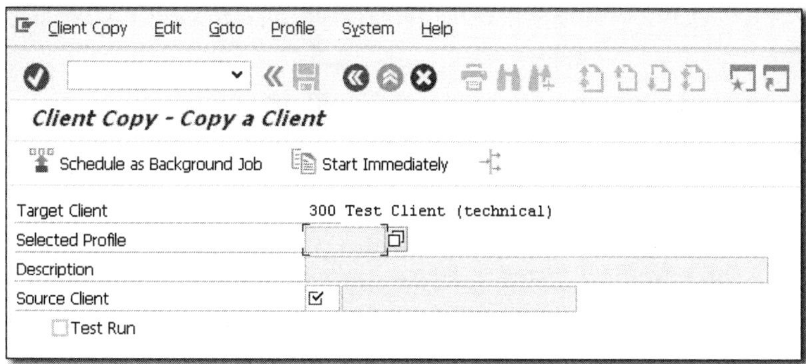

Figure 2.102 Initial Screen of the Local Client Copy

4. Select a copy profile (e.g., SAP_ALL; see Figure 2.103). The profile determines the type and scope of the data to be copied (see the MEANING column). Click on CHOOSE.

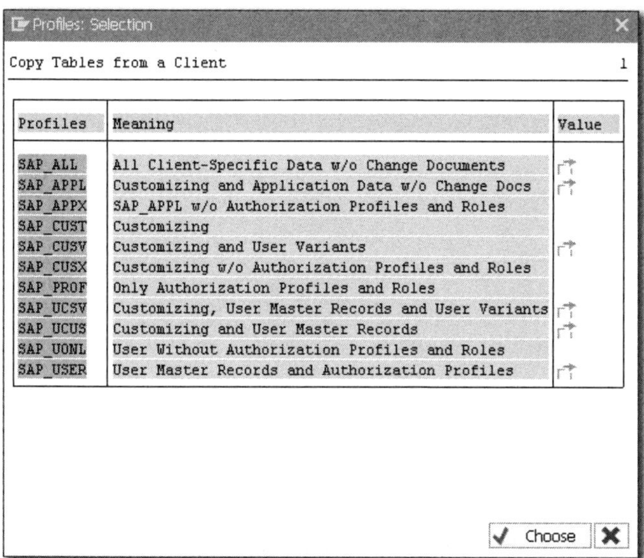

Figure 2.103 Selecting the Copy Profile

5. Enter the number of the source client (e.g., "100") in the SOURCE CLIENT field. You may also need to enter a value in the SOURCE CLIENT USER MASTERS field, depending on the copy profile selected. You can specify two different source

clients for the data. Click on the SCHEDULE AS BACKGROUND JOB button (see Figure 2.104).

6. Click on the SCHEDULE JOB button (see Figure 2.105).
7. Enter a start time for the job (see Figure 2.106). The job is scheduled the same way as any other background process (see Chapter 15). Click on SAVE.
8. The copy options are then displayed (see Figure 2.107). The selected contents result from the copy profile selected in step 4. Check the settings, and click on CONTINUE.

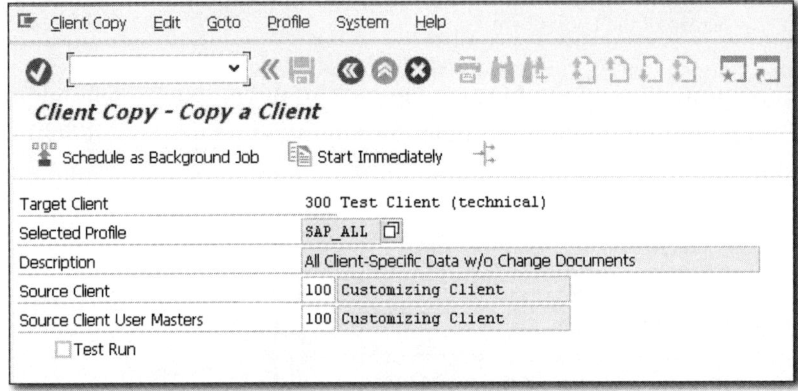

Figure 2.104 Starting the Client Copy with the Profile Selected

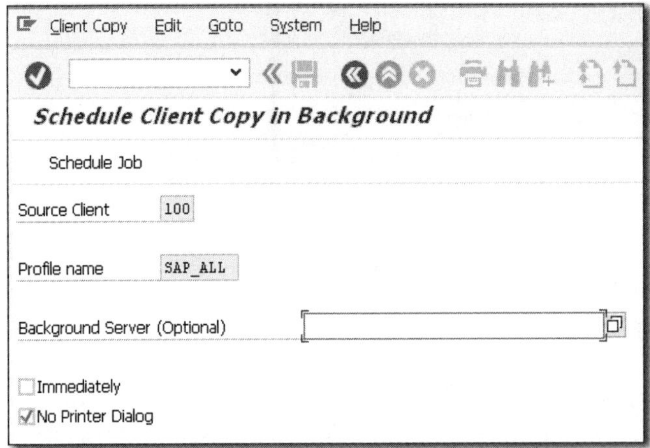

Figure 2.105 Scheduling the Client Copy as a Background Job

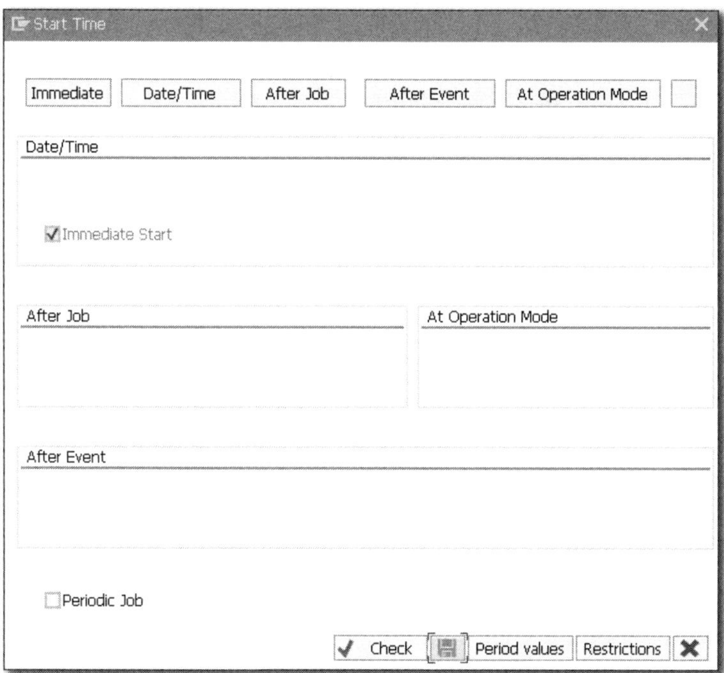

Figure 2.106 Defining the Start Time for the Background Job

Figure 2.107 Checking the Copy Options

9. Scheduling of the copy job is confirmed in a dialog box (see Figure 2.108), which you can close by choosing CONTINUE ✓.

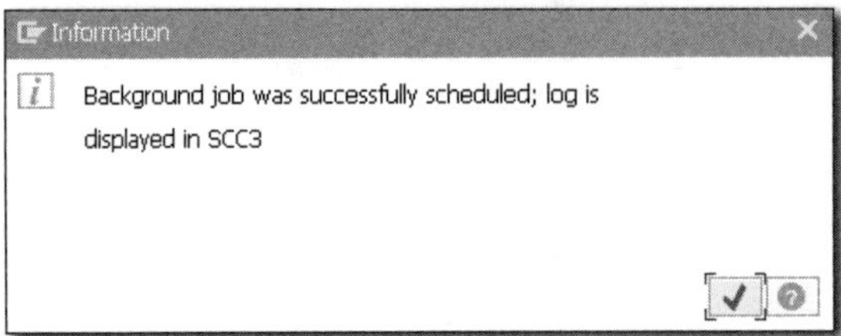

Figure 2.108 Message for Successful Job Scheduling

The client copy is executed in the background. You can monitor the job using Transaction SM37 (Job Monitor) (see Chapter 15) or analyze the log in Transaction SCC3 (Client Copy Log) (see Section 2.7.3).

[+]

Local Client Copy Using Transport Requests

A special variant of the local client copy is available with Transaction SCC1 (Client Copy by Transport Request). With this variant, only the objects included in a specific transport request are copied from a client into the local target client (in the same system).

This function is useful, for example, in development systems that have a client reserved exclusively for development, and a separate client for developer testing. Often, the creation of test cases isn't possible in the development client, which means that Customizing settings must be tested with data in another environment. With Transaction SCC1, it isn't necessary to transfer every transport request to the test system; an initial test can be performed in the development system.

Remote Copy

If you want to copy a client into another system (with a different system ID), perform a remote client copy. The RFC interface of the systems involved is used for the remote copy. To prepare for the copy, you must therefore create a new client and use Transaction SM59 to set up an RFC connection to the source system (see Section 2.6.1) by following these steps:

1. Log on to the target system and client.

[!]

Log On to the Correct Client

It's essential to ensure that you're logged on to the *correct* target client in order to not destroy another client.

2. Enter Transaction SCC9 in the command field and press the [Enter] key (or select the menu option Tools • Administration • Administration • Client Administration • Client Copy • SCC9—Remote Copy).
3. On the Client Copy – Copy a Client screen, open the input help for the Selected Profile field (see Figure 2.109).
4. Select a copy profile (e.g., SAP_ALL; refer to Figure 2.103). The profile determines the type and scope of the data to be copied. Click on Choose.

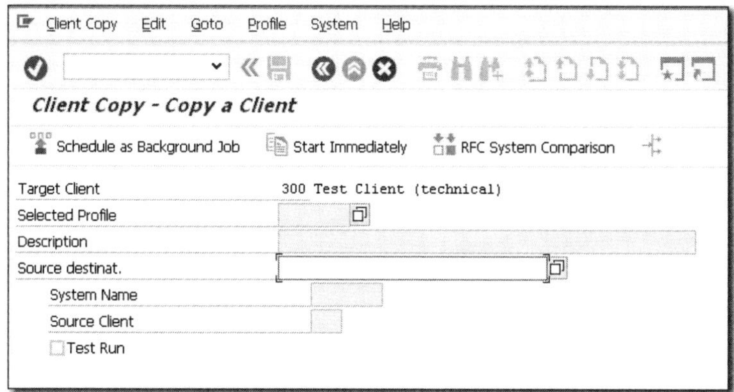

Figure 2.109 Remote Copy of a Client

5. Enter the RFC connection to the source system in the Source Destinat. field (see Figure 2.110). The System Name and Source Client fields are filled automatically using the settings of the RFC connection. Click on the Schedule as Background Job button.

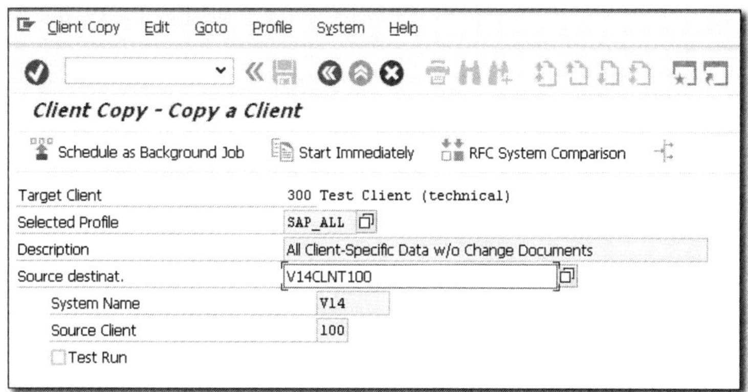

Figure 2.110 Specifying the Source Destination

6. On the next screen, click on the SCHEDULE JOB button (see Figure 2.111).

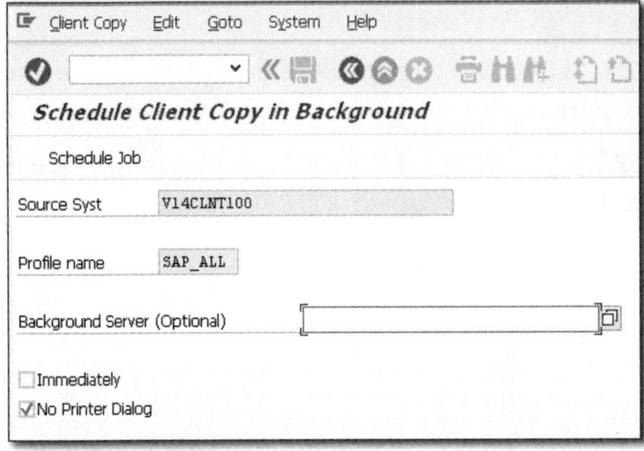

Figure 2.111 Scheduling a Background Job

7. Enter a start time for the job (refer to Figure 2.106; see Chapter 15). Click on SAVE.

8. The copy options are then displayed (see Figure 2.112). Check the settings, and click on CONTINUE.

Figure 2.112 Checking the Copy Options

9. Scheduling of the copy job is confirmed in a dialog box, which you can close by choosing CONTINUE ✓.

When you perform a remote copy, the data are transferred by RFC connection. This places a corresponding load on the network. The performance of the copy depends on the dimensions of your network infrastructure.

[+]

Client Copies within a System

Although a remote copy will also work within a system, it's recommended that you use a local client copy for this purpose instead.

Client Transport

The second option for copying a client across systems is a client transport. This comprises three steps:

1. Client export
2. Client import
3. Import postprocessing

The client export generates transport files, which are then imported into another system using the TMS (see Chapter 17). After the import, a postprocessing job must also be run to adapt the copied data to the new system.

The client export also allows you to save a client, for example, by burning the generated files to a CD or using another external storage medium.

To perform the client export, follow these steps:

1. Log on to the source client.
2. Enter Transaction SCC8 in the command field and press the Enter key (or select the menu option TOOLS • ADMINISTRATION • ADMINISTRATION • CLIENT ADMINISTRATION • CLIENT TRANSPORT • SCC8—CLIENT EXPORT).
3. On the CLIENT EXPORT screen, open input help for the SELECTED PROFILE field (see Figure 2.113).
4. Select a copy profile (e.g., SAP_ALL; refer to Figure 2.103). The profile determines the type and scope of the data to be copied. Click on CHOOSE.

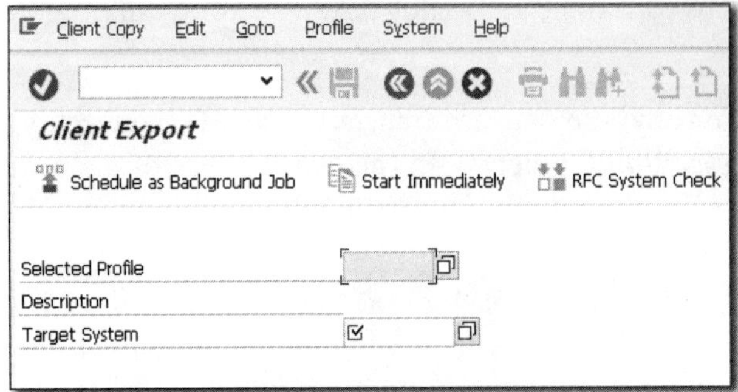

Figure 2.113 Initial Screen of the Client Export

5. Enter the system into which you want the export file to be imported later in the TARGET SYSTEM field (see Figure 2.114). You may only select systems that are part of the transport landscape. Click on the SCHEDULE AS BACKGROUND JOB button.

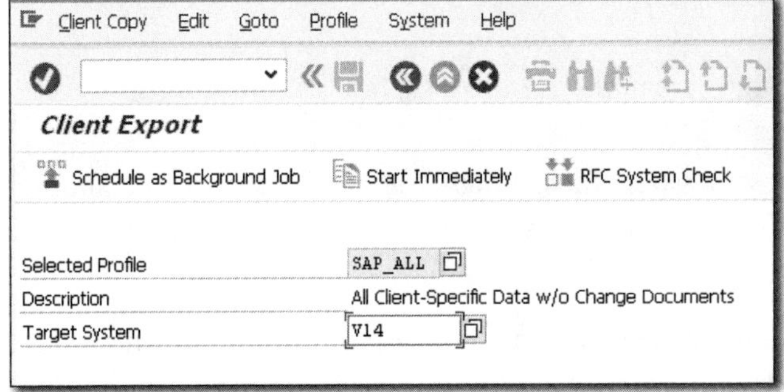

Figure 2.114 Specifying the Target System for the Client Export

[+]

Selecting the Target System

You can also enter the name of the system in which you're currently logged on as the target system. The generated transports are initially placed in the import queue of the system without importing them immediately. You can subsequently import the relevant transport requests into a system other than the system specified in the client export.

6. On the next screen, click on the SCHEDULE JOB button (refer to Figure 2.105).
7. Enter a start time for the job, and click on SAVE (refer to Figure 2.106).
8. The copy options are then displayed. Check the settings (see Figure 2.115), and click on CONTINUE.

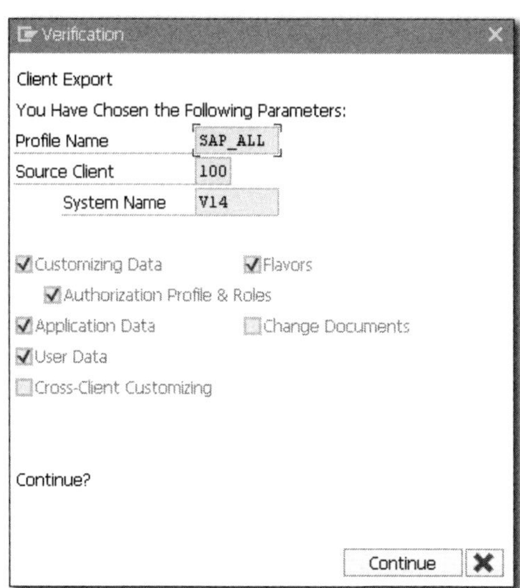

Figure 2.115 Checking the Export Options

9. The transport request files created by the export are displayed in a dialog box (see Figure 2.116). Take note of the file names, and choose the CONTINUE button ✓.

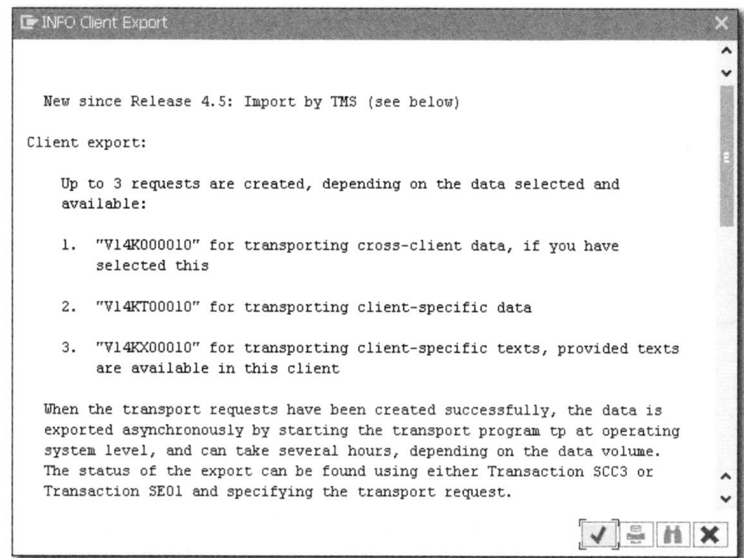

Figure 2.116 Transport Files Created During the Client Export

10. Scheduling of the copy job is confirmed in a dialog box, which you can close by choosing CONTINUE ✓.

Depending on the copy options, up to three transport requests are generated by the client export:

- *<SID>KO<number>*: Cross-client data
- *<SID>KT<number>*: Client-specific data
- *<SID>KX<number>*: Texts and forms

These files are saved to your system's transport directory (*<drive>:\usr\sap\trans* or */usr/sap/trans*). To save the client or transfer it to a system outside of your transport landscape, you can copy these files and archive them or insert them into the transport directory of the remote system.

If you specify a system within your transport landscape as the target system for the client export, the transport requests are displayed in the system's transport queue after the export is completed (see Figure 2.117). You can then *import* the transport requests as described in Chapter 17. To do this, select the requests, and click on IMPORT REQUEST.

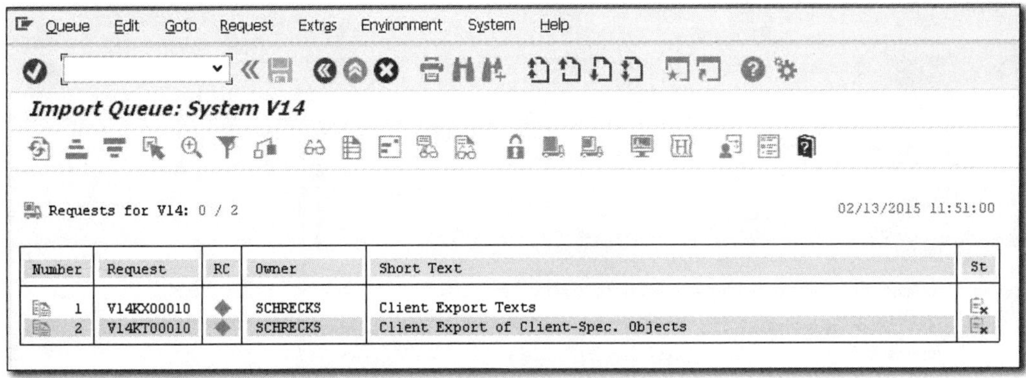

Figure 2.117 Transport Requests in the Transport Queue

Now you only need to specify the TARGET CLIENT (see Figure 2.118), before starting the transport with the START IMPORT button.

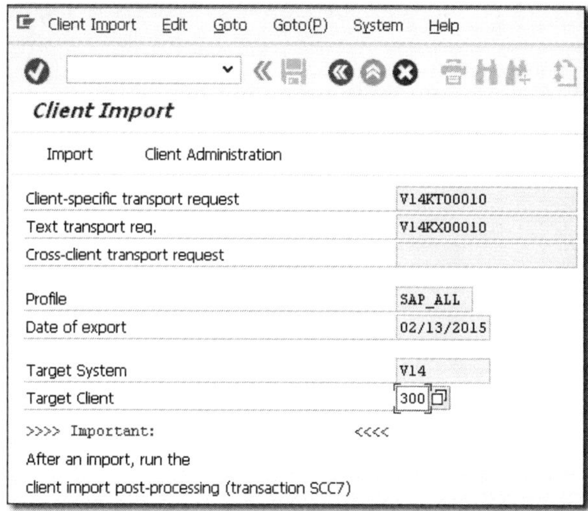

Figure 2.118 Specifying the Target Client for the Import

The client data are then imported into the new client via the transport system. Wait until the import is completed, and then execute *import postprocessing*.

1. Log on to the target system and client.
2. Enter Transaction SCC7 in the command field and press the Enter key (or select the menu option TOOLS • ADMINISTRATION • ADMINISTRATION • CLIENT ADMINISTRATION • CLIENT TRANSPORT • SCC7—IMPORT EDITING).
3. Click on the SCHEDULE AS BACKGROUND JOB button (see Figure 2.119).

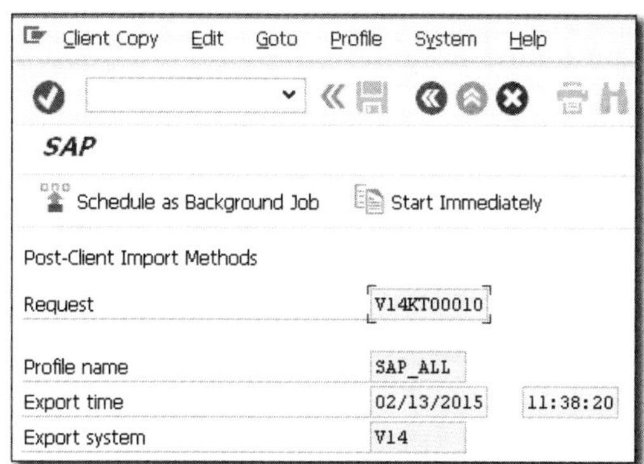

Figure 2.119 Scheduling the Import Postprocessing as a Background Job

4. In the dialog box that opens, click on the SCHEDULE JOB button (refer to Figure 2.105).
5. Enter a start time for the job. Click on SAVE (refer to Figure 2.106).
6. The copy options are then displayed. Check the settings (see Figure 2.120), and click on CONTINUE.

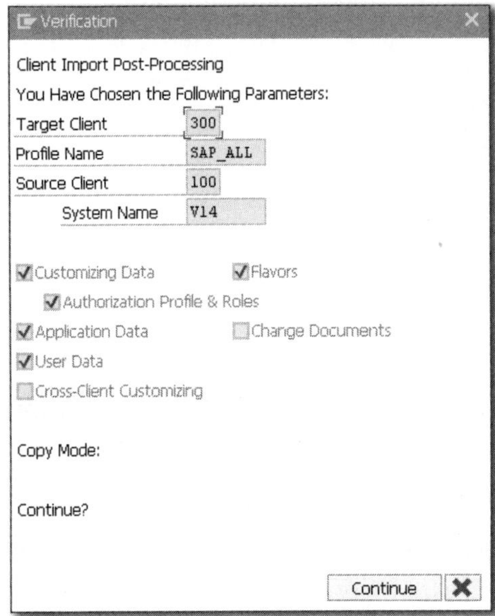

Figure 2.120 Checking and Confirming Options for the Import Postprocessing

7. Scheduling of the postprocessing job is confirmed in a dialog box, which you can close by choosing CONTINUE.

The client transport essentially produces the same result as a remote client copy. However, whereas the remote copy is significantly faster because it allows for a "live" data copy, the client export option offers the advantage of being network-independent. In addition, the transport requests generated during the export can be used more than once, for example, for several remote systems or as backup files.

2.7.3 Deleting Clients

You can delete clients in Transaction SCC5 (Delete Client). If you choose to do so, all client-specific data are deleted from the database. To delete a client, it's not enough to merely remove the corresponding entry from the client table (Transaction SCC4). To delete a client, you should follow these steps:

1. Log on to the client you want to delete.
2. Enter Transaction SCC5 in the command field and press the Enter key (or select the menu option TOOLS • ADMINISTRATION • ADMINISTRATION • CLIENT ADMINISTRATION • SPECIAL FUNCTIONS • SCC5—DELETE CLIENT).
3. On the DELETE CLIENT screen, activate the DELETE ENTRY FROM T000 checkbox if you want to delete the table entry from Transaction SCC4 at the same time as your deletion of the client.
4. Click on the DELETE IN BACKGROUND button (Figure 2.121).

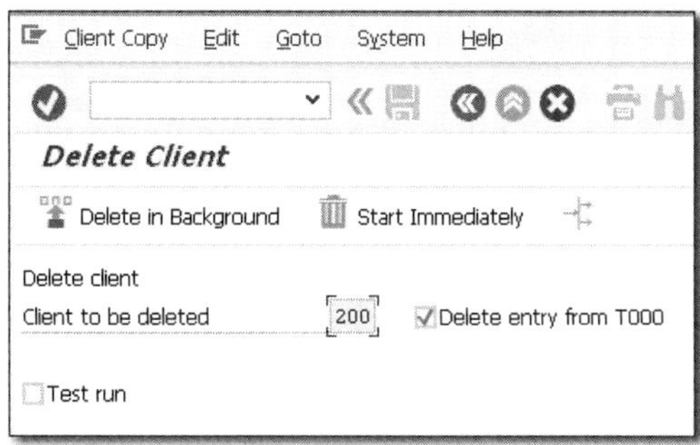

Figure 2.121 Deleting a Client

5. In the dialog box that opens, click on the SCHEDULE JOB button (see Figure 2.122).

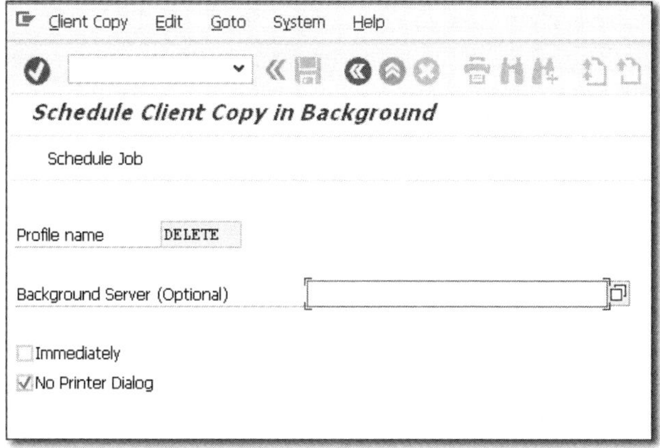

Figure 2.122 Scheduling a Background Job for Deleting a Client

6. Enter a start time for the job, and click on SAVE (refer to Figure 2.106).
7. The copy options are then displayed. Check the settings, and click on CONTINUE (see Figure 2.123).

Figure 2.123 Confirming Deletion Options

8. Scheduling of the deletion job is confirmed in a dialog box, which you can close by choosing CONTINUE.

Following deletion, all client data are permanently lost. You should therefore only execute this action if you're certain that you no longer need the client. If necessary, create a backup copy of the client beforehand using a client export, or create a full backup of the entire database.

2.7.4 Checking the Client Copy Log

You can check the client log to determine the progress and results of the operations just described:

1. Enter Transaction SCC3 in the command field and press the Enter key (or select the menu option TOOLS • ADMINISTRATION • ADMINISTRATION • CLIENT ADMINISTRATION • SCC3—COPY LOGS).

2. Use the buttons in the title bar, for example, to display a cross-client view (ALL CLIENTS button) or to switch to the client exports (EXPORTS button; see Figure 2.124).

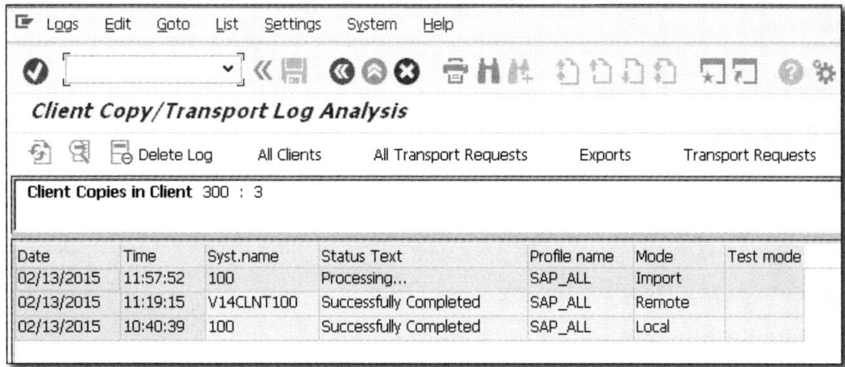

Date	Time	Syst.name	Status Text	Profile name	Mode	Test mode
02/13/2015	11:57:52	100	Processing...	SAP_ALL	Import	
02/13/2015	11:19:15	V14CLNT100	Successfully Completed	SAP_ALL	Remote	
02/13/2015	10:40:39	100	Successfully Completed	SAP_ALL	Local	

Figure 2.124 Log Overview for Client Administration

3. The detailed view provides additional information (see Figure 2.125), such as the time at which an error occurred. You can double-click on a log entry or click on CHOOSE to display its details.

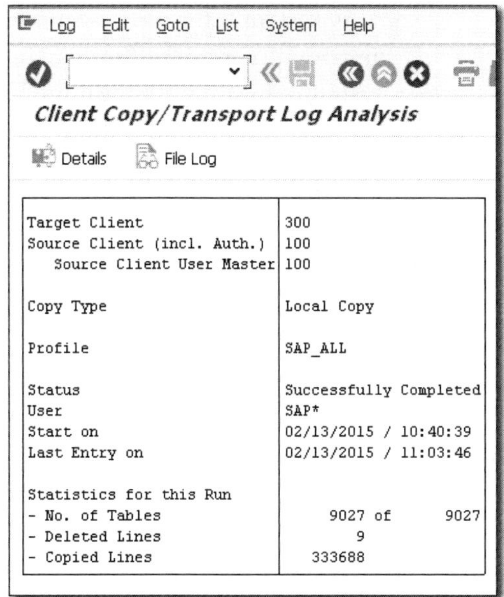

Target Client	300
Source Client (incl. Auth.)	100
Source Client User Master	100
Copy Type	Local Copy
Profile	SAP_ALL
Status	Successfully Completed
User	SAP*
Start on	02/13/2015 / 10:40:39
Last Entry on	02/13/2015 / 11:03:46
Statistics for this Run	
- No. of Tables	9027 of 9027
- Deleted Lines	9
- Copied Lines	333688

Figure 2.125 Detailed View of the Local Client Copy

The display works in all clients, which means you don't need to be logged on to the correct client. If an operation hasn't yet been completed, it's displayed with the status EXECUTING. Choose the REFRESH button to refresh the display of the list view.

2.8 System Copy

There are several reasons for executing a system copy:

- Transferring data from the production system into a test or QA system to make a large dataset available for testing.
- Preparing for an upgrade. The upgrade test system should be an exact replica of the production system so that the upgrade can be tested in as realistic a manner as possible.
- Synchronizing the configuration in the test and development system with the production system. The configuration in various systems may diverge over time so that they no longer correspond to the production system. This makes Customizing, programming, and testing more difficult.

Synchronizing the production system and the quality system is the most common reason for creating a system copy. Following the copy process, the test system contains the current data from the production system. This enables meaningful testing and should reduce the time and effort required to create test cases.

Note that large volumes of data are involved in the creation of a system copy. A production system may be several hundred gigabytes or terabytes in size, and a system copy requires just as much storage space as the original system. However, this argument against their use has faded in recent years given the current costs of hard disk space.

Another point to consider is that data from the production system is actual data. This involves a risk from the point of view of data security because this data may be of a confidential and sensitive nature. The development and test systems should therefore meet security standards that are at least as high as those that apply to the production system. Anonymization programs are an alternative as they manipulate real data and thus allow for better usage. However, these tools aren't included in the standard SAP solution; in other words, you must develop or purchase them yourself. Test data, in contrast, is usually invented data, so the issue of data security is of much less concern in this case.

There are two ways to perform a system copy:

- A database copy of the production system
- A client copy of the production client

A database copy is usually performed with the tools available in the database management system. If in doubt, consult your database administrator. The steps involved in a client copy are described in Section 2.7.2. The benefits and drawbacks of the two variants are briefly outlined next.

2.8.1 A Database Copy of the Production System

You can reproduce the complete production database using a database copy.

- **Benefits**
  The benefits of using a database copy are as follows:
  - The updated system is an exact copy of the production system.
  - Client-specific changes are also recorded and copied to the target system.
  - The copy can then be made using standard backup media to avoid impacting the production system. The creation of the copy simultaneously tests the backup-and-restore process.
- **Drawbacks**
  The drawbacks of using a database copy are as follows:
  - The version history of the current system is lost. This loss is usually acceptable for the test system, but, in most cases, it's unacceptable for the development system.
  - The target database must be the same size as the source database.
  - The target system has to be reconfigured after the copy.
  - The client structure in the target system is lost because it's overwritten with the client structure from the source system. If the source system has a single client, and the target system has three, only a single client will remain in the target system after the database copy is created. The other two clients are lost if they haven't been backed up using a client export prior to the copy.

Copying the database alone isn't particularly time-consuming, provided that the relevant infrastructure is available in the data center. Most of the work involves reconfiguring the target system in this case. This complex process comprises many steps and can't be described here. If necessary, consult with an internal or external expert in relation to this option.

2.8.2 Client Copy with Data

In a client copy, the active client is copied from the source system (instead of the complete database, as in a database copy, for example).

- **Benefits**
  The benefits of using a client copy with data are as follows:
  - In contrast to a database copy, you don't need to reconfigure the target system.
  - The client structure of the target system isn't overwritten.
- **Drawbacks**
  The drawbacks of using a client copy with data are as follows:
  - Users can't work in the source or target system during the execution of a client copy. This constitutes a disadvantage for many enterprises because the time required to complete the client copy may cause the limits of acceptable downtime to be exceeded. If the source client is very large, it may take days to create the client copy.
  - Client-specific objects (e.g., programs, table structures, etc.) that were changed and aren't identical in both systems aren't copied.

[+]

RFC System Comparison

You should perform an RFC system comparison to verify whether a copy of the production client could fail due to different statuses of the cross-client repository objects. For this purpose, call Transaction SCC9 in the target system, enter an RFC connection to the source system, and click on the RFC SYSTEM COMPARISON button.

While a client copy is an alternative to a database copy, you must ensure that it's appropriate for your enterprise.

2.8.3 Client Copy without Data

With this option, you can create a basic client copy, including Customizing settings, for example. No master data, transaction data, or, in most cases, user data are copied. The required (test) data are then loaded into the new client. The following tools are used for this purpose:

- CATT or eCATT
- Data Transfer Workbench (Transaction LSMW, Legacy System Migration Workbench)
- Application Link Enabling (ALE)

This option offers the following benefits, in addition to those listed earlier for the client copy option:

- You can control which data are loaded into the new clients.
- Data can be created to test specific objects.
- You don't need to access production data to test specific objects.
- Production data may not include data that are suitable for the testing of specific objects. Test data must then be created in any case.

The disadvantages of this option are the same as those specified for the creation of a client copy of the production system with data.

2.9 Summary

This chapter described the main tasks involved in system maintenance. You now know how to start and stop the SAP system. You also understand the significance of instances, operation modes, and work processes. You know how to maintain profile parameters to adapt the system configuration to the needs of your enterprise.

This chapter also introduced you to transactions that you can use to monitor the main areas of an SAP system. You can use these transactions to find out very quickly if any problems have occurred in your system. In addition, this chapter discussed the administration of connections from, to, and between SAP systems, as well as client administration.

The transactions described are standard tools for an SAP system administrator. You should therefore familiarize yourself with those transactions extensively.

As a system administrator, you must be able to get a quick overview of the system status and be notified immediately of critical situations. This chapter presents the CCMS Alert Monitor, which is the most essential tool for live system monitoring besides SAP Solution Manager.

3 System Monitoring

Chapter 2 described how to manually monitor your system and check its status. In some systems, however, it may require a lot of time and effort to call the relevant transactions individually and to investigate warning and error messages.

For this reason, SAP offers tools to help you set up automatic *system monitoring* to continuously collect data about your system. You can use these tools to gain a quick overview of the system status. They also notify you automatically if the system status becomes critical. One of these tools is the CCMS Alert Monitor, which is described in this chapter. Another tool for monitoring SAP systems is the SAP EarlyWatch Alert, which is described in Chapter 4, Section 4.3.4.

The following section provides essential information about the system monitoring techniques that are possible with the CCMS Alert Monitor. For more information about setting up a monitoring concept and implementing this concept with SAP Solution Manager, see Chapter 4, Section 4.3.1.

3.1 CCMS Alert Monitor

The *CCMS Alert Monitor* (Computing Center Management System Alert Monitor) enables real-time, live monitoring of SAP systems. You can use Transaction RZ20 to monitor the servers in your system environment. You can use the tool to monitor individual systems or several systems from a central system.

The CCMS Alert Monitor has a hierarchical tree structure:

- At the highest level, the monitor consists of several *monitor sets*.
- These, in turn, comprise several *monitors*.
- Monitors represent a grouping of *monitoring tree elements* (MTEs).
- In the hierarchy, the level below MTEs comprises *monitor objects*, which are the components of the system that are to be monitored.
- Each monitor has one or more *monitor attributes*, such as a value or a status.
- Threshold values are defined for each monitor attribute. As soon as a value exceeds or falls short of a threshold value, an *alert* is triggered. These alert messages usually indicate a serious problem that should be eliminated quickly. If a problem of this kind isn't eliminated, an emergency situation may arise.

The CCMS Alert Monitor comes with a range of standard monitor sets for general system monitoring tasks. However, you can also define your own monitor sets, consisting exclusively of the monitor objects that you actually need. The advantage of doing so is that you can then obtain an even faster overview of the system components that are important to you, as well as their statuses.

[!]

Replaced by Monitoring and Alerting Infrastructure

Note that the CCMS technology is outdated and has been replaced by the *Monitoring and Alerting Infrastructure* (MAI) of SAP Solution Manager. If you don't use any monitoring system yet and are considering implementing such a system, you shouldn't reconfigure CCMS-based monitoring, but should use MAI instead.

Nevertheless, many SAP customers still use carefully configured CCMS monitoring that will probably serve its purpose for many years. To take this into account, the following first describes the basic functions of the CCMS Alert Monitor, using the SAP standard monitor sets as examples. We'll then explain how to create your own monitor sets.

Customizing the CCMS Alert Monitor

This book doesn't include a discussion of the technical settings of the CCMS Alert Monitor, which are defined in Transaction RZ21. Very detailed information about the configuration of this tool is provided in the SAP Help Portal (*http://help.sap.com*) under ALERT MONITOR. This chapter assumes that your monitoring system landscape has already been preconfigured and is fully functional.

3.2 System Monitoring with the Standard CCMS Alert Monitor

Follow these steps to display alerts with the CCMS Alert Monitor:

1. Enter Transaction RZ20 in the command field and press the [Enter] key (or select Tools • CCMS • Control/Monitoring • RZ20—CCMS Monitor Sets).

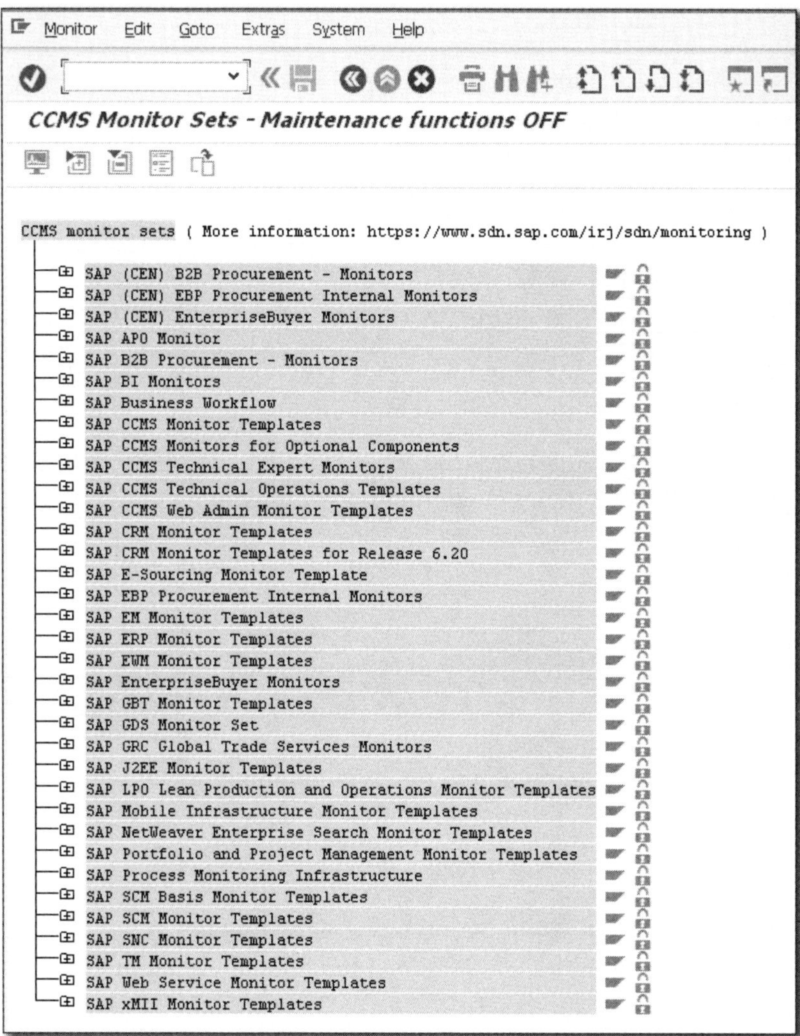

Figure 3.1 Initial Screen of CCMS Monitoring

2. The screen displays all monitor sets provided in the SAP standard system (see Figure 3.1). You can expand a monitor set (e.g.,CCMS MONITOR TEMPLATES) to view the monitors it contains.

[+]

CCMS Monitor Sets in the SAP Standard System

The SAP standard sets are indicated by the MONITOR SET DELIVERED BY SAP icon. These monitor templates can't be changed (as indicated by the NOT MODIFIABLE icon. Only user-defined monitor sets can be adjusted.

3. To start a monitor (e.g., ENTIRE SYSTEM; see Figure 3.2), double-click on it, or position the cursor on the relevant row, and choose LOAD MONITOR at the top left of the screen.

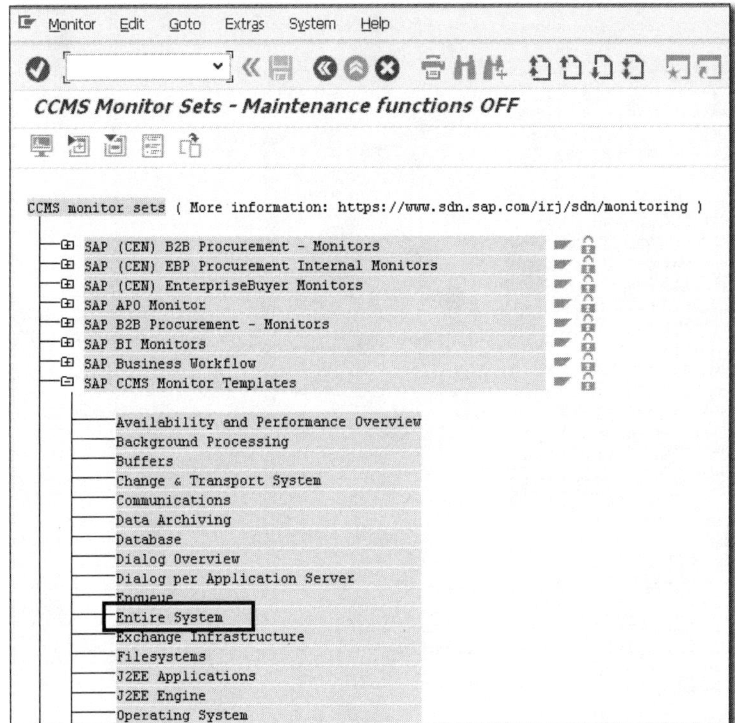

Figure 3.2 Displaying the Monitor

4. The selected monitor is displayed in the CURRENT SYSTEM STATUS view (see Figure 3.3). The monitor objects belonging to the monitor are arranged in a tree

structure. The color coding used in the monitor indicates immediately whether any alerts exist:

- Green: No alerts exist.
- Yellow: Less serious alerts exist (warnings).
- Red: Serious alerts exist (errors).

Expand the tree structure to display the individual monitor objects.

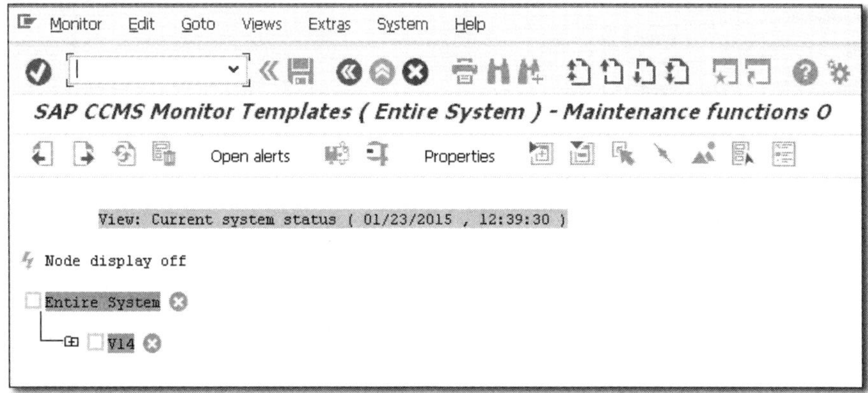

Figure 3.3 Checking the Monitor Status

[+]

CCMS Alert Monitor Views

The CCMS Alert Monitor offers two different views: one view of the *current system status* (in which the current alert situation is displayed), and one view of alerts that are *currently open* (displaying alerts that have been generated but haven't yet been confirmed). You should eliminate the problems shown in the view showing the current system status before turning your attention to the open alerts.

5. The lowest level in the tree structure shows the monitor objects (see Figure 3.4), that is, the components or aspects of the system that are being monitored (e.g., available memory on the *C:* drive). Each monitor object has a monitor attribute (such as available memory in megabytes). To display detailed information, position the cursor on a monitor object, and click on DISPLAY DETAILS.
6. The detailed view (see Figure 3.5) shows additional data about the current status and about the progression of the measurements over time. Choose BACK to return to the monitor view.

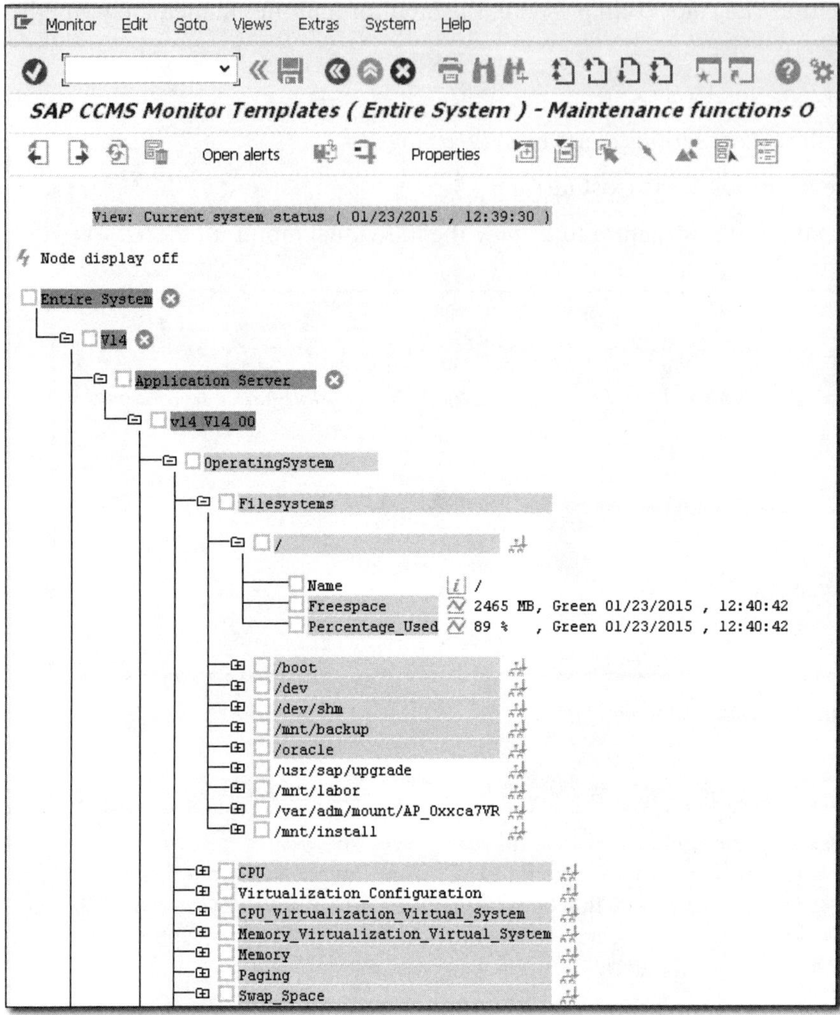

Figure 3.4 Tree Structure of the Monitored Individual Components

7. To display the threshold values of a monitoring object, position your cursor on the object in the monitor view (refer to Figure 3.4), and click on PROPERTIES.
8. On the PERFORMANCEATTRIBUTE tab, the THRESHOLD VALUES area indicates the values at which an alert changes from green to yellow, and from yellow to red, as well as the values at which these alert levels are reset (see Figure 3.6).
9. Click on BACK to return to the monitor.

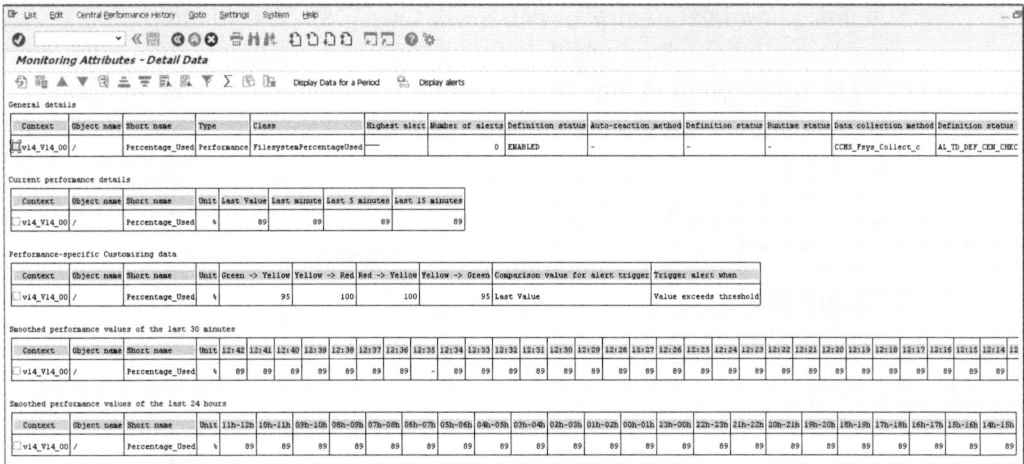

Figure 3.5 Detail View of the Monitor Attributes

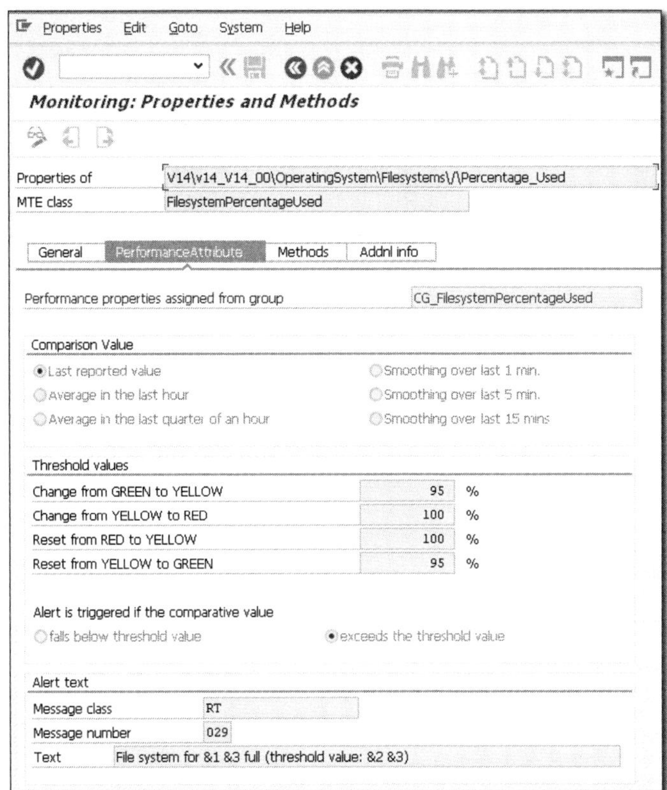

Figure 3.6 Displaying Threshold Values of the Performance Attributes

You now know how to display alerts with the CCMS Alert Monitor. You should always start by checking whether the current view contains any alerts. These must be investigated as high-priority issues to prevent or resolve serious problems in the system. Next, check whether any older open alerts also exist using the following steps:

1. Click on OPEN ALERTS in the monitor to switch to the view of open alerts (refer to Figure 3.4).
2. Expand the tree structure to display any yellow or red alerts it contains. If you click on DISPLAY ALERTS, a list of all alerts is displayed (Figure 3.7).

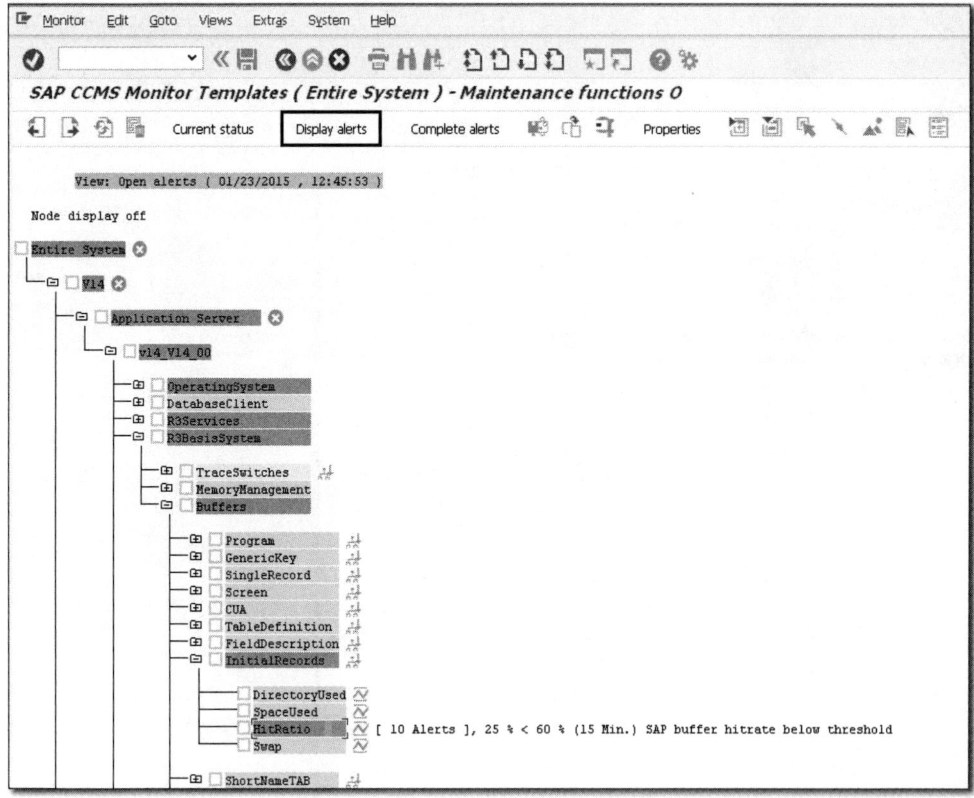

Figure 3.7 Displaying Alerts

3. All alerts that have occurred are shown here (see Figure 3.8). From here, you can also navigate to the details or properties of a monitor, for example, to show the history of the alert's occurrence and the threshold values.

4. Click on Display Details.

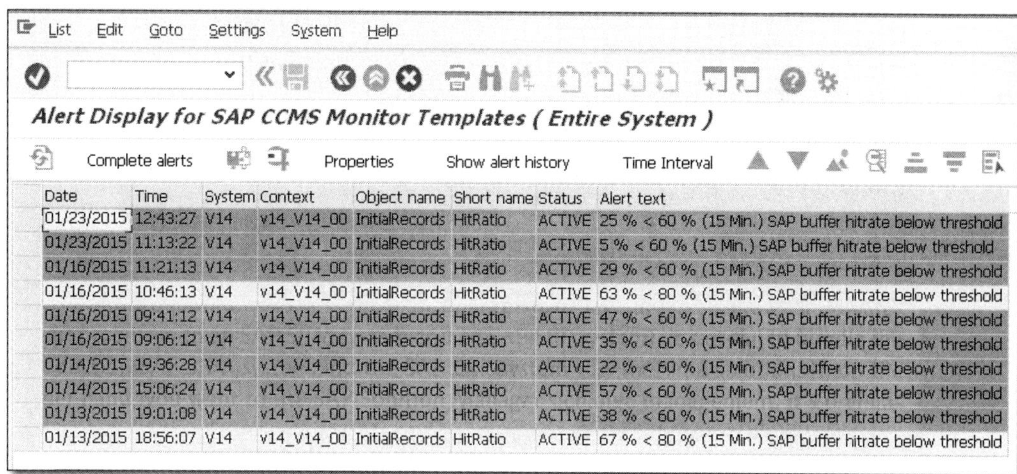

Date	Time	System	Context	Object name	Short name	Status	Alert text
01/23/2015	12:43:27	V14	v14_V14_00	InitialRecords	HitRatio	ACTIVE	25 % < 60 % (15 Min.) SAP buffer hitrate below threshold
01/23/2015	11:13:22	V14	v14_V14_00	InitialRecords	HitRatio	ACTIVE	5 % < 60 % (15 Min.) SAP buffer hitrate below threshold
01/16/2015	11:21:13	V14	v14_V14_00	InitialRecords	HitRatio	ACTIVE	29 % < 60 % (15 Min.) SAP buffer hitrate below threshold
01/16/2015	10:46:13	V14	v14_V14_00	InitialRecords	HitRatio	ACTIVE	63 % < 80 % (15 Min.) SAP buffer hitrate below threshold
01/16/2015	09:41:12	V14	v14_V14_00	InitialRecords	HitRatio	ACTIVE	47 % < 60 % (15 Min.) SAP buffer hitrate below threshold
01/16/2015	09:06:12	V14	v14_V14_00	InitialRecords	HitRatio	ACTIVE	35 % < 60 % (15 Min.) SAP buffer hitrate below threshold
01/14/2015	19:36:28	V14	v14_V14_00	InitialRecords	HitRatio	ACTIVE	22 % < 60 % (15 Min.) SAP buffer hitrate below threshold
01/14/2015	15:06:24	V14	v14_V14_00	InitialRecords	HitRatio	ACTIVE	57 % < 60 % (15 Min.) SAP buffer hitrate below threshold
01/13/2015	19:01:08	V14	v14_V14_00	InitialRecords	HitRatio	ACTIVE	38 % < 60 % (15 Min.) SAP buffer hitrate below threshold
01/13/2015	18:56:07	V14	v14_V14_00	InitialRecords	HitRatio	ACTIVE	67 % < 80 % (15 Min.) SAP buffer hitrate below threshold

Figure 3.8 List View of Errors

5. To view a graphical representation of the alert history, select the values from the past 30 minutes, and click on Display Performance Values Graphically (see Figure 3.9).

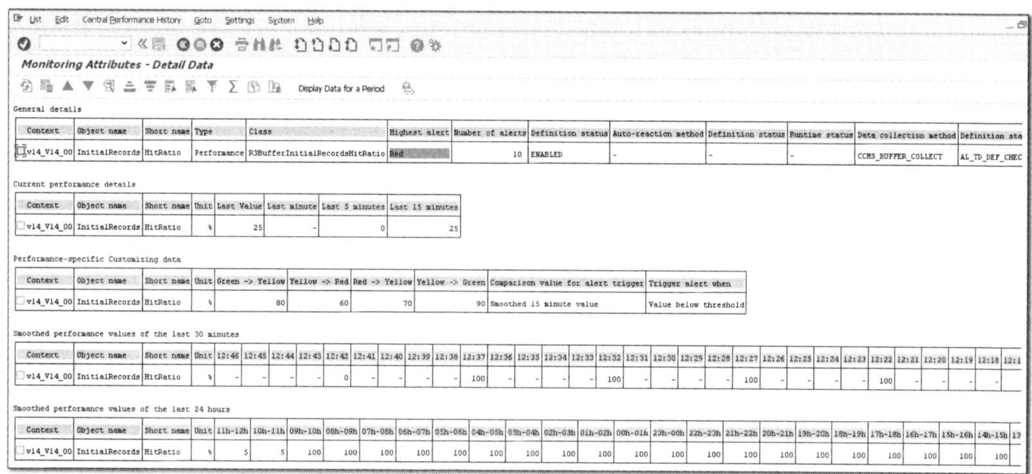

General details

Context	Object name	Short name	Type	Class	Highest alert	Number of alerts	Definition status	Auto-reaction method	Definition status	Runtime status	Data collection method	Definition sta
v14_V14_00	InitialRecords	HitRatio	Performance	R3BufferInitialRecordsHitRatio	Red	10	ENABLED	-	-	-	CCMS_BUFFER_COLLECT	AL_TD_DEF_CHEC

Current performance details

Context	Object name	Short name	Unit	Last Value	Last minute	Last 5 minutes	Last 15 minutes
v14_V14_00	InitialRecords	HitRatio	%	25	-	0	25

Performance-specific Customizing data

Context	Object name	Short name	Unit	Green -> Yellow	Yellow -> Red	Red -> Yellow	Yellow -> Green	Comparison value for alert trigger	Trigger alert when
v14_V14_00	InitialRecords	HitRatio	%	80	60	70	90	Smoothed 15 minute value	Value below threshold

Smoothed performance values of the last 30 minutes

Context	Object name	Short name	Unit	12:46	12:45	12:44	12:43	12:42	12:41	12:40	12:39	12:38	12:37	12:36	12:35	12:34	12:33	12:32	12:31	12:30	12:29	12:28	12:27	12:26	12:25	12:24	12:23	12:22	12:21	12:20	12:19	12:18	12:1
v14_V14_00	InitialRecords	HitRatio	%	-	-	-	-	0	-	-	-	-	100	-	-	-	-	100	-	-	-	-	100	-	-	-	-	100	-	-	-	-	

Smoothed performance values of the last 24 hours

Context	Object name	Short name	Unit	11h-12h	10h-11h	09h-10h	08h-09h	07h-08h	06h-07h	05h-06h	04h-05h	03h-04h	02h-03h	01h-02h	00h-01h	23h-00h	22h-23h	21h-22h	20h-21h	19h-20h	18h-19h	17h-18h	16h-17h	15h-16h	14h-15h	13
v14_V14_00	InitialRecords	HitRatio	%	5	5	100	100	100	100	100	100	100	100	100	100	100	100	100	100	100	100	100	100	100	100	

Figure 3.9 Detail View of the Monitor

6. The graphical display in Figure 3.10 indicates how the values have changed over the past half hour. Click on BACK to return to the previous screen.

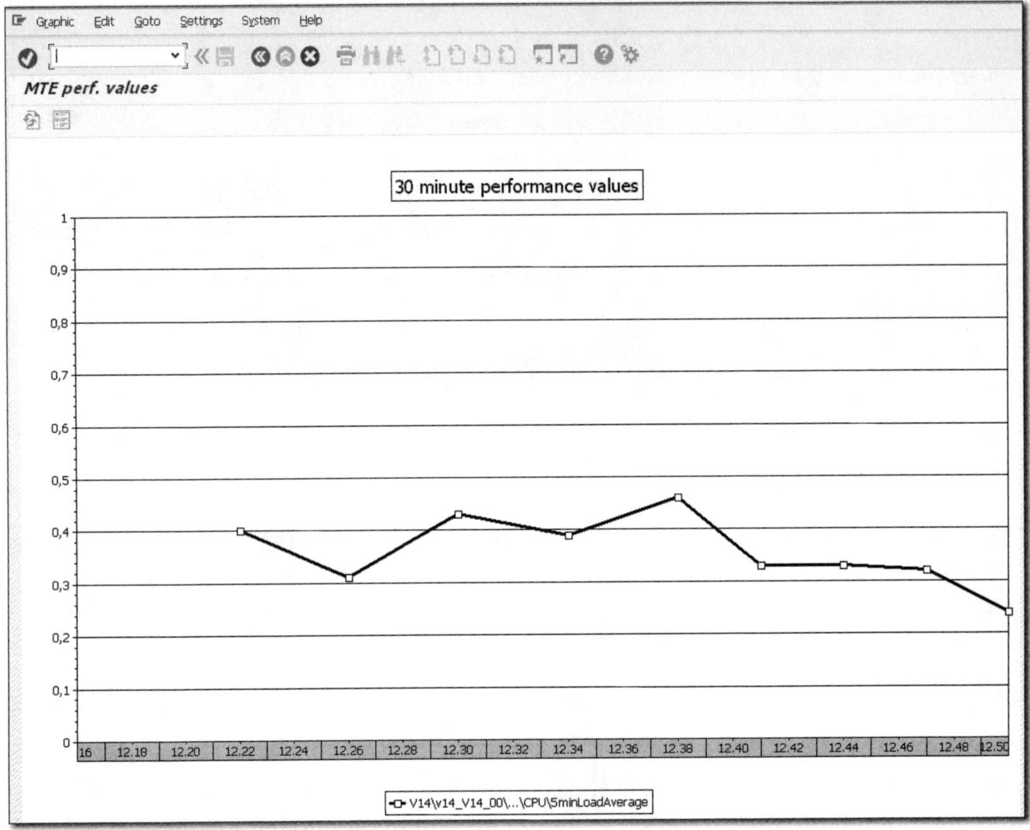

Figure 3.10 Graphical Representation of the Alert Behavior

7. Alerts remain open until they are confirmed. After analyzing and resolving the problem, select one or more alerts in the ALERT DISPLAY, and click on COMPLETE ALERTS (see Figure 3.11).
8. A message in the status bar confirms that the alerts have been processed (see Figure 3.12). Click on BACK to return to the monitor view.
9. If you've set all alerts to COMPLETED, the background color in the tree structure of the monitor display changes to green (see Figure 3.13). It now contains no more open alerts.

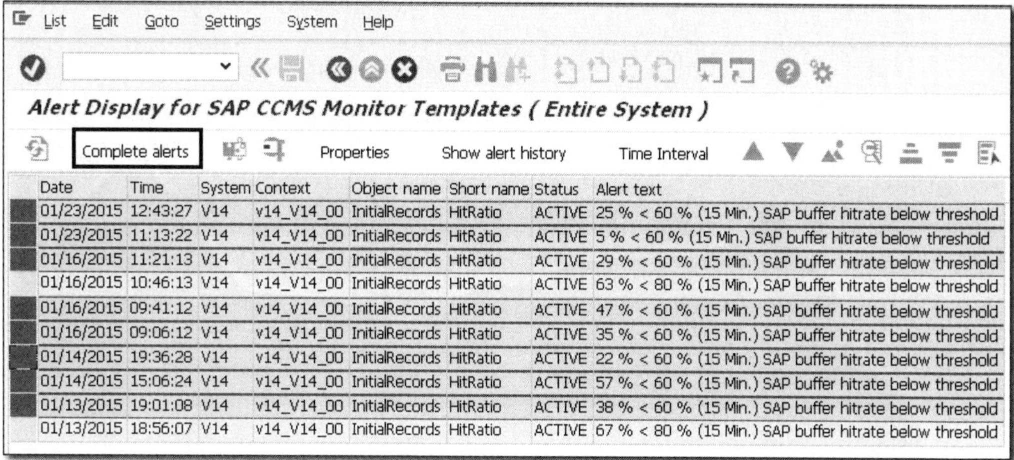

Figure 3.11 Completing Alerts

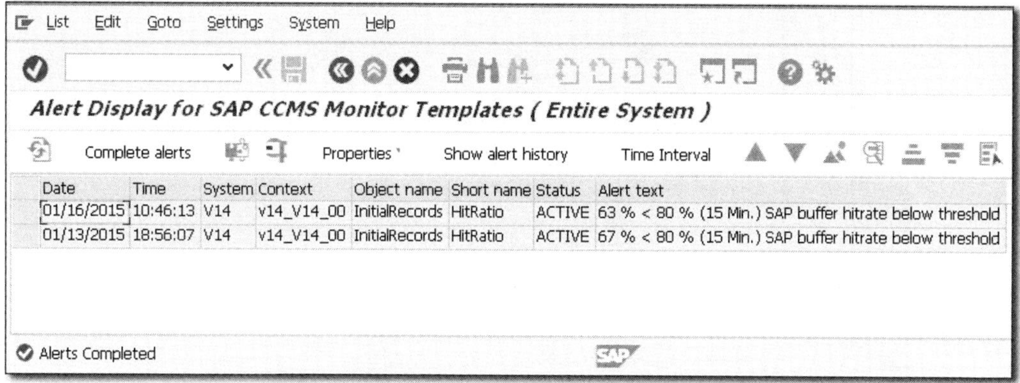

Figure 3.12 Confirmation for Completed Alerts

By completing alerts, you also delete them from the Open Alerts view. The list of open alerts will fill up again as soon as the system detects any new threshold violations.

Completing Alerts [!]

You still need to resolve the issue highlighted by the alert. Confirming an alert merely indicates that you've taken note of it.

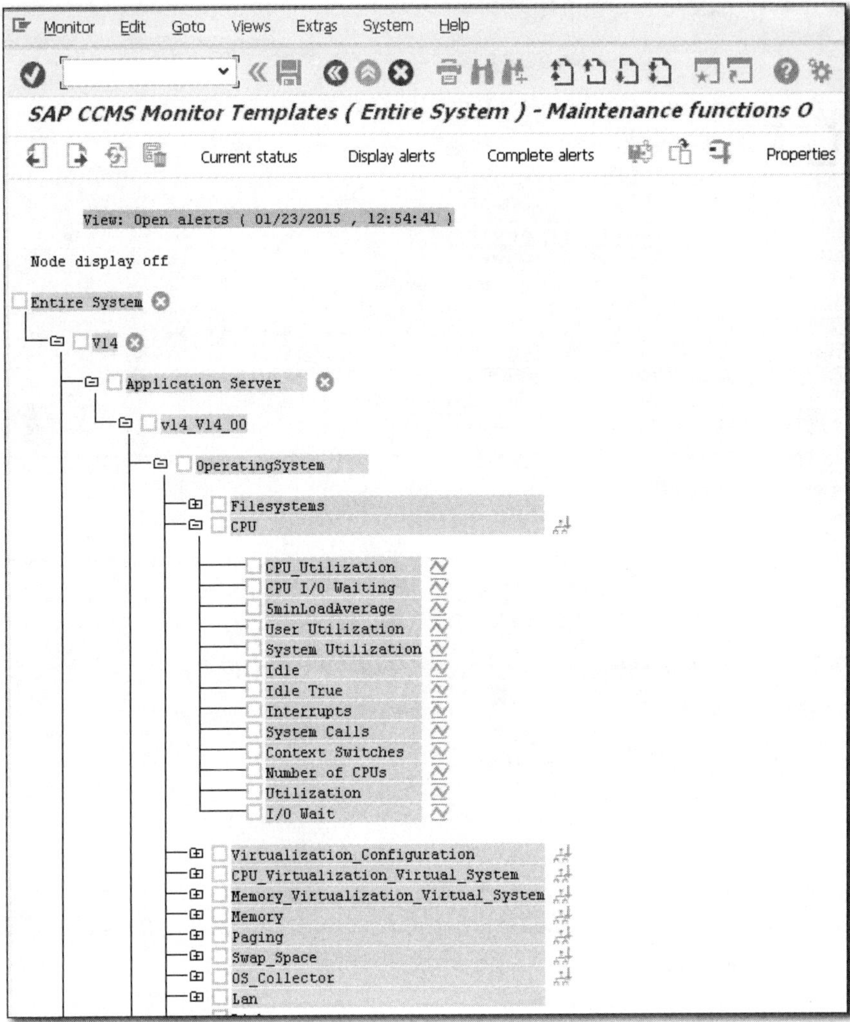

Figure 3.13 Monitor View for Completed Alerts

3.3 Adapting the CCMS Monitor Sets

The standard CCMS monitors offer very extensive monitoring options. Not all of these options will be relevant for your system landscape. Moreover, the extensive nature of the monitors hampers fast access to the really important information.

You can therefore use one of the following two options to adjust the CCMS Alert Monitor sets to meet your needs:

- Hide CCMS monitor sets that aren't needed.
- Create your own monitor sets.

In this way, you can reduce the number of CCMS monitors to those that are essential and make system monitoring more efficient.

3.3.1 Hiding Monitor Sets

You can hide the monitor sets you don't need as follows:

1. Call Transaction RZ20.
2. On the CCMS Monitor Sets – Maintenance Functions OFF screen, select the menu option Extras • Activate maintenance function (see Figure 3.14).

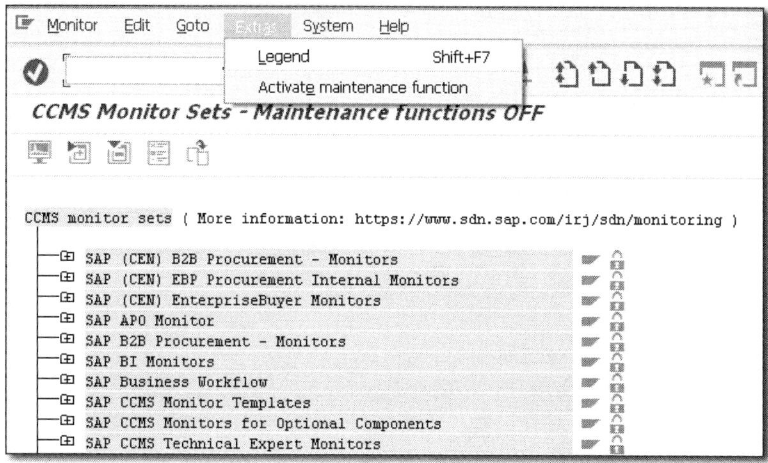

Figure 3.14 Activating Maintenance Functions

3. The screen title then changes to CCMS Monitor Sets – Maintenance Functions ON. The tree structure of the monitor sets is divided into the two root nodes My Favorites and All (see Figure 3.15).
4. To hide a CCMS monitor set, position your cursor on the relevant set (e.g., SAP J2EE Monitor Templates if you only want to monitor ABAP systems), and click on Change.

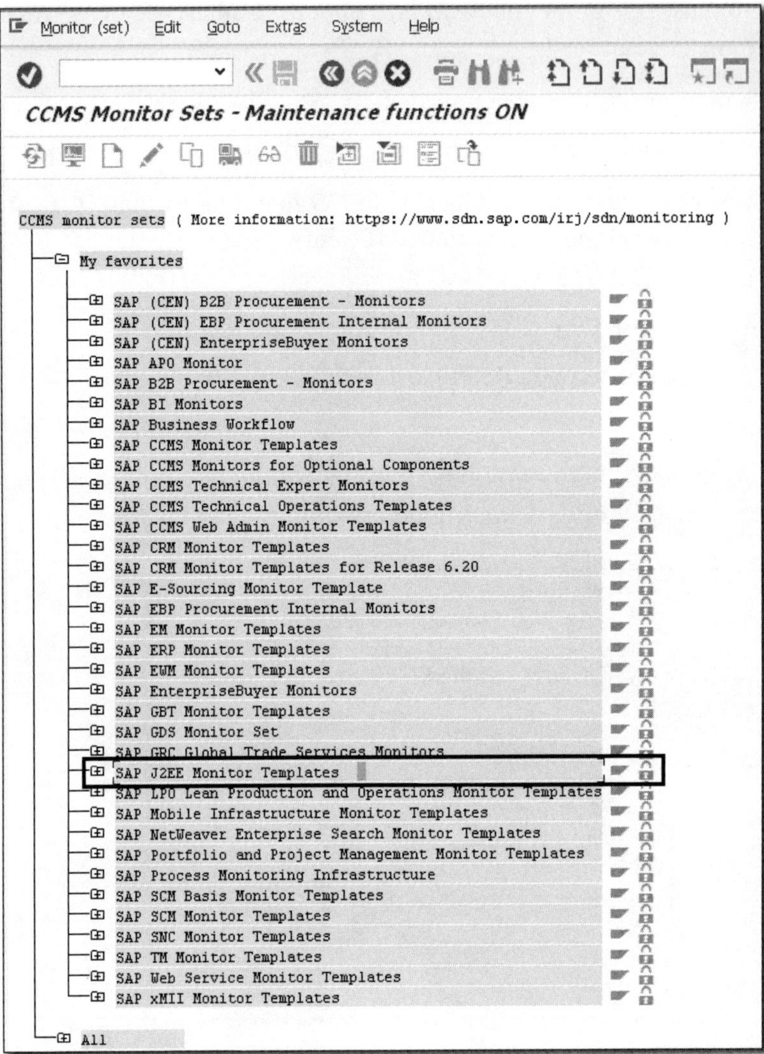

Figure 3.15 Selecting a Monitor Set

5. In the dialog box that opens, remove the checkmark from the PUBLIC (VISIBLE FOR ALL USERS) field (see Figure 3.16). Then click on COPY .

6. A message in the status bar confirms that your changes have been saved (see Figure 3.17). The monitor set has been deleted from the MY FAVORITES node. Repeat these steps for all monitors that aren't required.

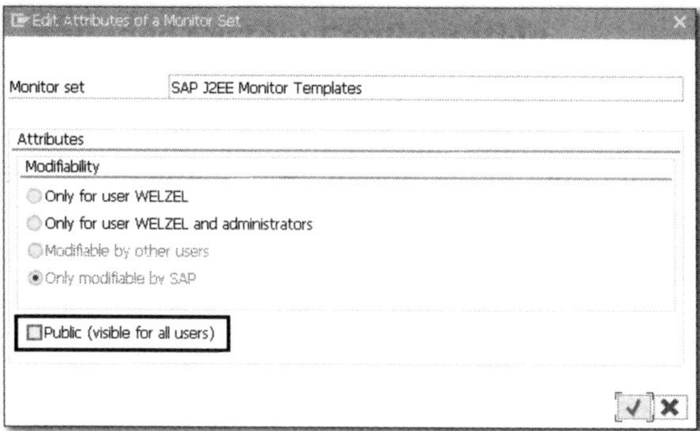

Figure 3.16 Setting the Visibility of a Monitor Set

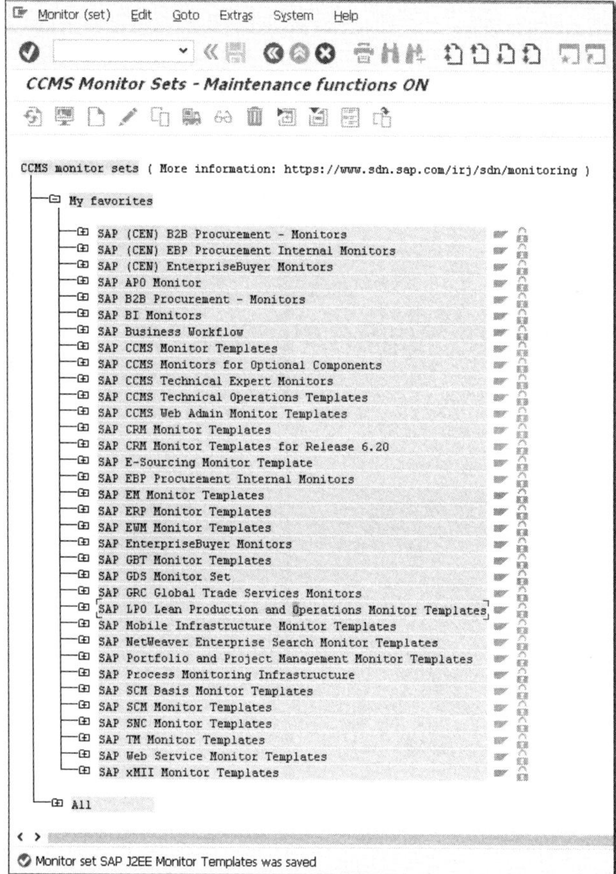

Figure 3.17 Changed Favorites in the Monitor View

7. To check your change, select the EXTRAS • DEACTIVATE MAINTENANCE FUNCTION menu option. When you do so, the monitor set is no longer shown on the initial screen of Transaction RZ20 (see Figure 3.18).

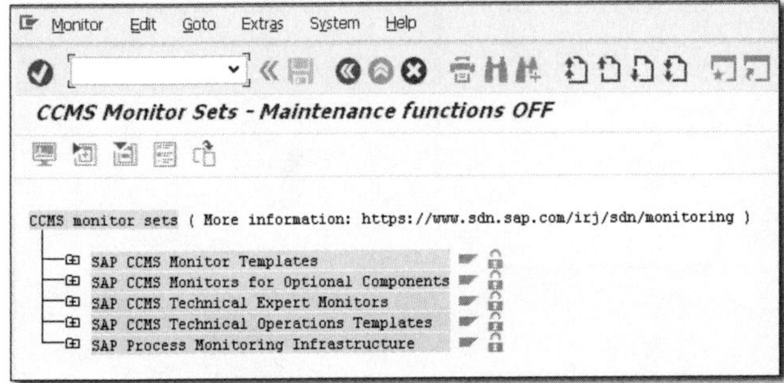

Figure 3.18 Checking the Adaptation in the Initial Screen of Transaction RZ20

8. If you want to show the hidden CCMS monitor set again, activate the maintenance functions, and find the monitor set under ALL • SAP in the tree structure (see Figure 3.19). Position your cursor on the monitor set you want to show, and click on CHANGE.

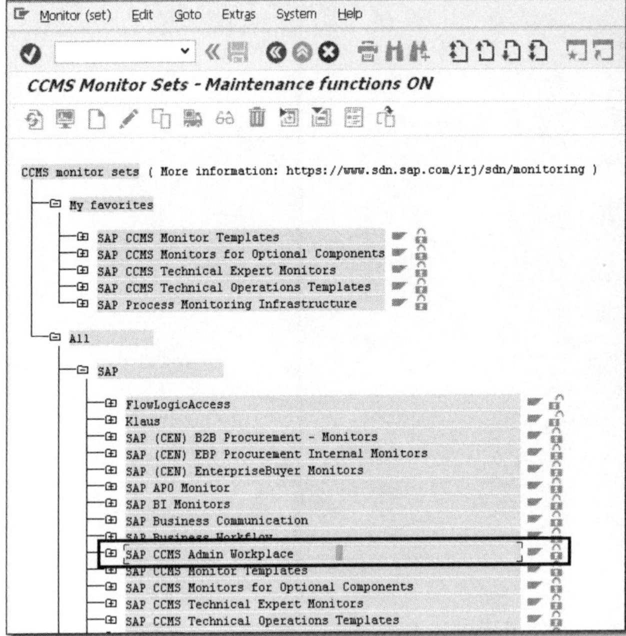

Figure 3.19 Selecting a Monitor Set for Display

9. Activate the PUBLIC (VISIBLE FOR ALL USERS) field in the dialog box from Figure 3.20, and click on COPY.

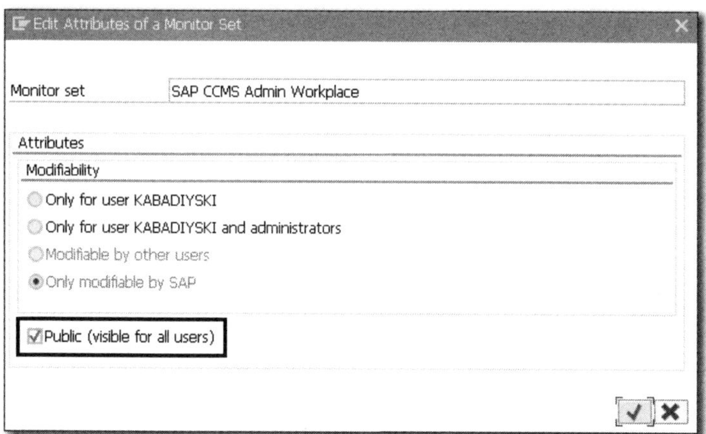

Figure 3.20 Activating Public Visibility of the Monitor Set

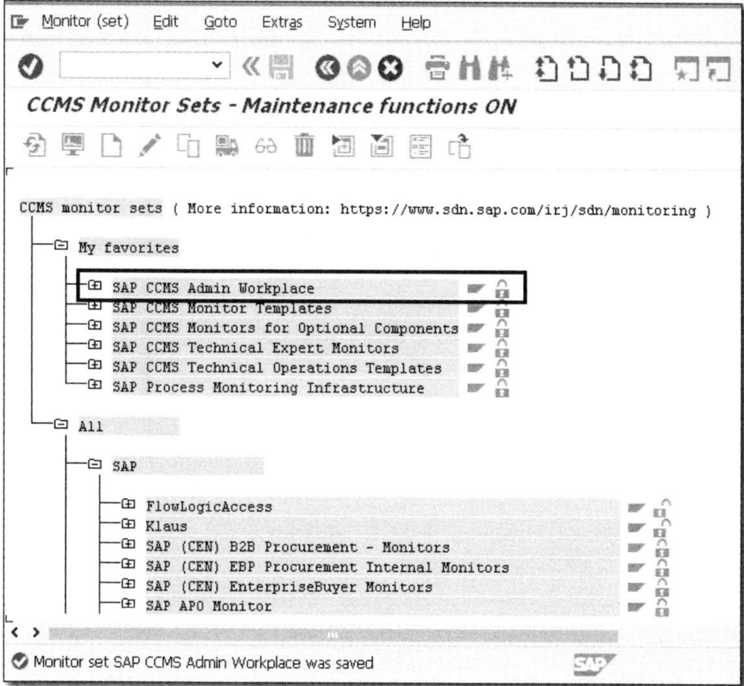

Figure 3.21 Displayed Monitor in the Overview

10. Save to confirm, and the monitor is displayed under the My Favorites node (see Figure 3.21).

By hiding unnecessary CCMS monitor sets, you've taken a first step toward making monitoring more manageable. This may be sufficient for your routine monitoring tasks. If not, you can make further adjustments.

3.3.2 Defining a New Monitor Set

If the standard monitor sets don't meet your requirements, you can create or build your own monitor sets:

1. Call Transaction RZ20.
2. Select the Extras • Activate maintenance function menu option to activate the maintenance functions (refer to Figure 3.14).
3. Click on Create (see Figure 3.22).

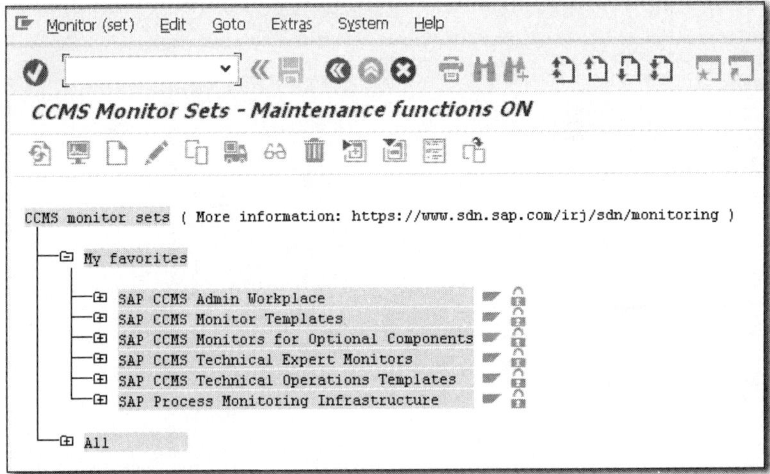

Figure 3.22 Creating a New Monitor Set

[+]

Copying Monitor Sets

An alternative option to creating a new monitor set is to copy an existing one. This is useful if, for example, you want to copy most of one of the standard monitor sets but eliminate a small number of monitors that aren't required. In this case, click the Copy button.

4. In the dialog box that opens, select the NEW MONITOR SET option, and click on CONTINUE (see Figure 3.23).

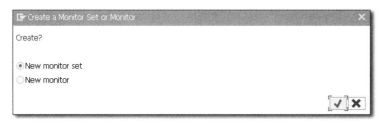

Figure 3.23 Selecting New Monitor Set

5. Enter the following details on the next screen (see Figure 3.24):
   - Enter a name for the set in the MONITOR SET field.
   - Under MODIFIABILITY, specify which users are permitted to modify the set.
   - If you want the monitor set to be displayed on the initial screen of Transaction RZ20, activate the PUBLIC field.
6. Click on COPY.

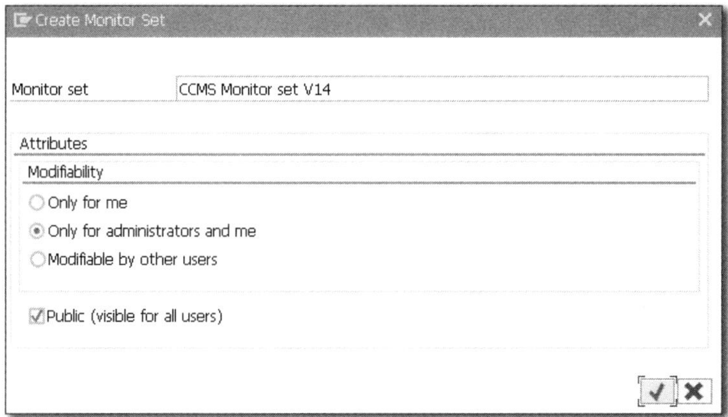

Figure 3.24 Defining a Name and Attributes for the New Monitor Set

7. The new monitor set is now shown under MY FAVORITES (see Figure 3.25). The PUBLIC MONITOR SET icon indicates entries that you've created yourself. The MODIFIABLE icon signals that the set can be edited.

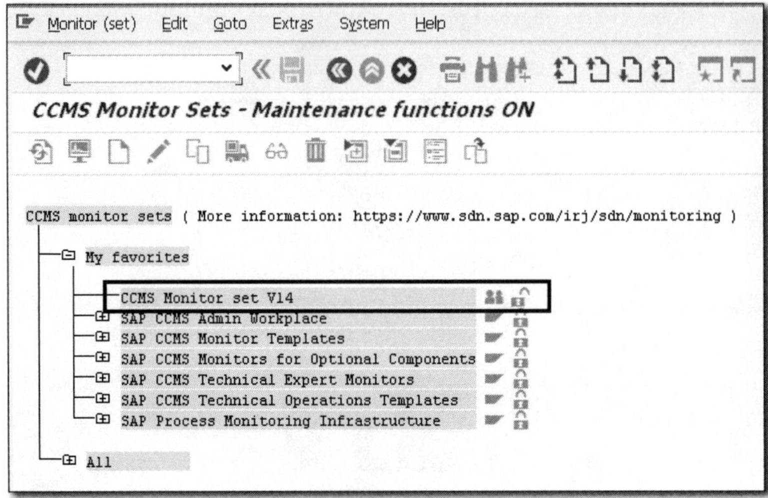

Figure 3.25 New Monitor Set in My Favorites

Your CCMS monitor set has now been created. The next step involves making changes to the monitors contained in the set. You can add new monitors and remove any that you don't need.

3.3.3 Adding a Monitor to a Monitor Set

You can add monitors to CCMS monitor sets you created yourself. This option allows you to adapt the scope and content of your monitor set to meet your needs.

1. Call Transaction RZ20.
2. Activate the maintenance functions, position your cursor on your monitor set (see Figure 3.26), and choose CREATE.
3. The monitor objects you added are displayed in a tree structure (see Figure 3.27). Expand the monitor tree, and select the node you want to add to your monitor set (e.g., BACKGROUND). When you've selected all of the monitor objects you want to add, click on GENERATE MONITOR.

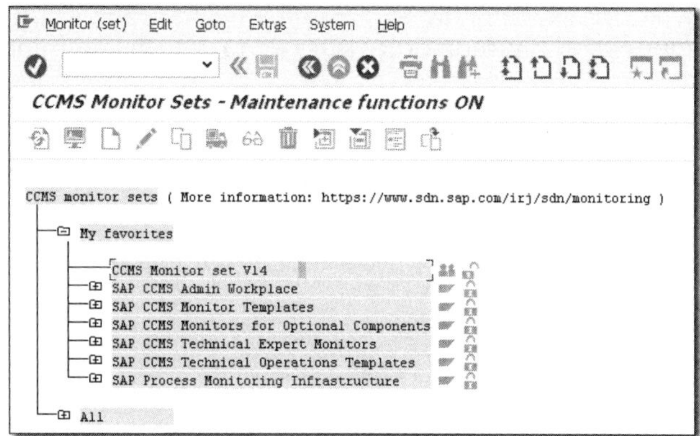

Figure 3.26 Selecting a Monitor Set for Adding a Monitor

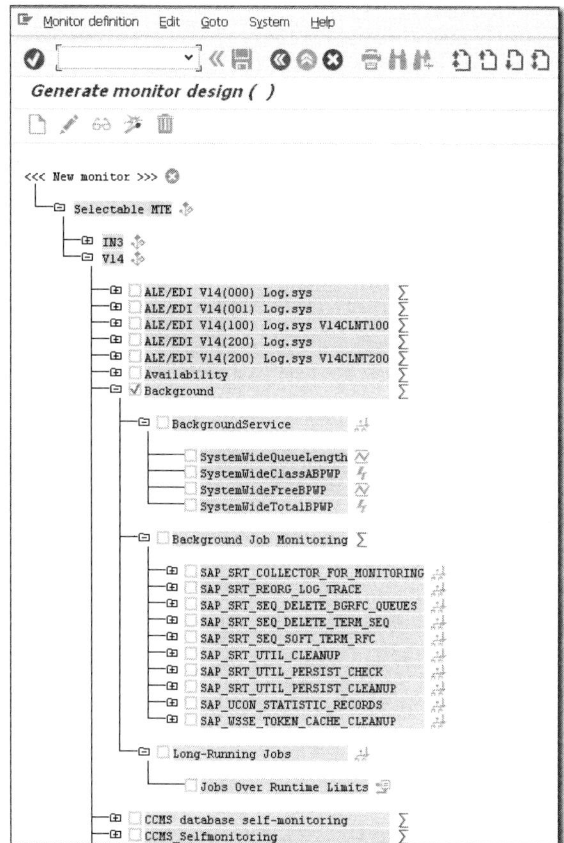

Figure 3.27 Displaying Available Monitor Objects

4. In the dialog box that opens, enter a meaningful name for your new monitor in the MONITOR field (see Figure 3.28). Click on CONTINUE ✔ to save the monitor definition.

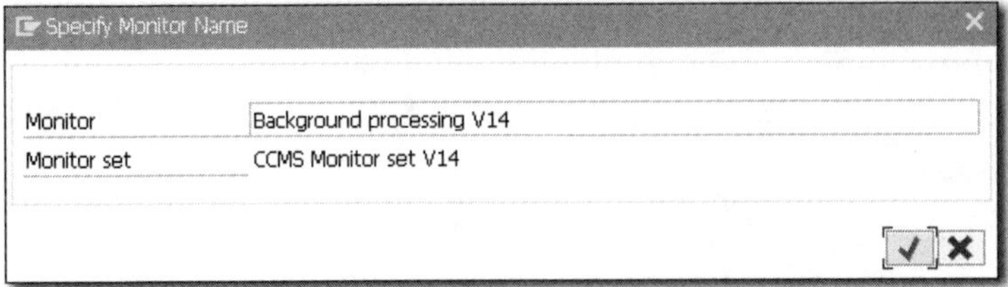

Figure 3.28 Defining New Monitors

5. You can now deactivate the maintenance functions again. Expand your monitor set in the initial screen of Transaction RZ20, and position the cursor on the new monitor. Click on LOAD MONITOR (see Figure 3.29).

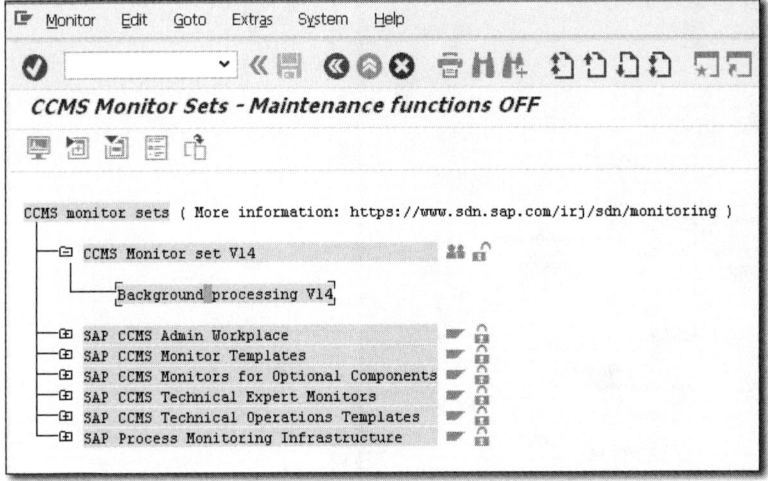

Figure 3.29 New Monitor in the Initial Screen of Transaction RZ20

6. Expand the monitor tree. This new monitor only displays the nodes you selected (see Figure 3.30). In the example provided here, the monitor is used for monitoring background processing by the system.

It may be useful to build your own user-defined monitors if you use CCMS Alert Monitoring on a frequent basis and want to be able to view the most important alerts at a glance. This allows you to monitor critical areas of SAP systems with greater efficiency. Even if you monitor several systems, having your own monitor sets is still useful. You can, for example, check certain aspects of all monitored systems (e.g., background processing) and create a new monitor for this purpose.

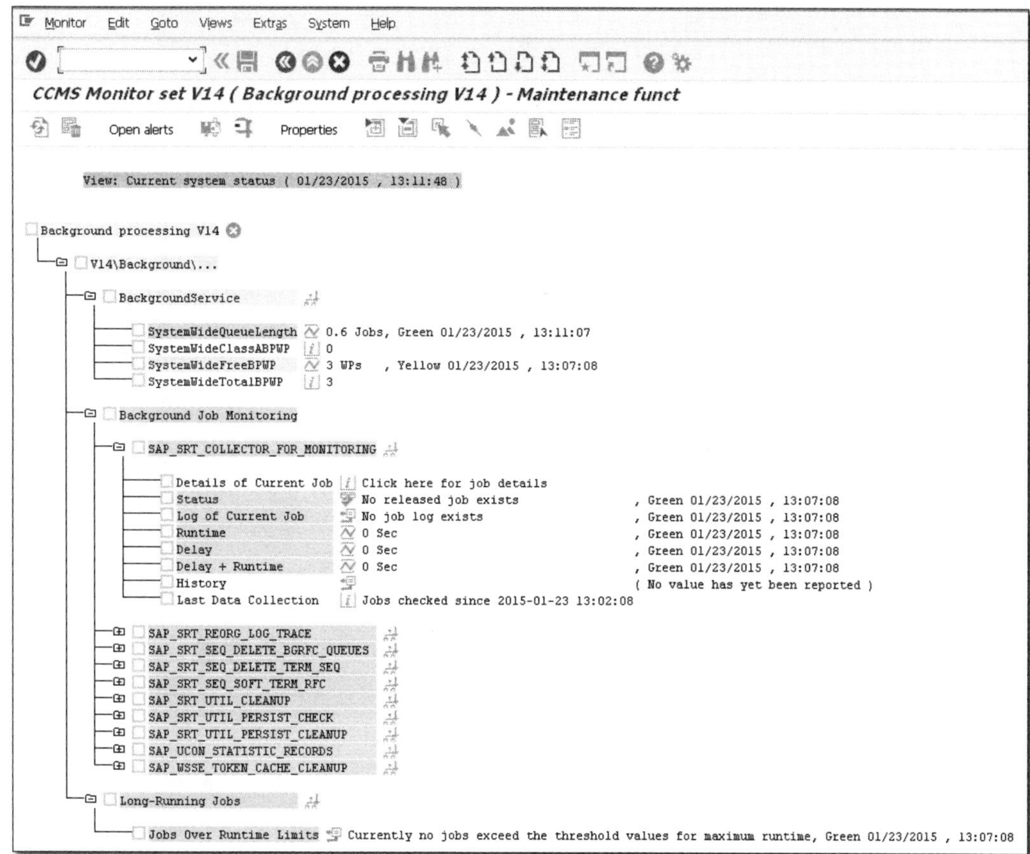

Figure 3.30 View of the New Monitor with the Monitor Objects Selected

3.3.4 Deleting a Monitor from a Monitor Set

SAP standard monitors provide a sound starting point for creating customer-specific monitor sets. After copying these standard monitor sets, you can eliminate any monitors you don't need from your copy. This allows you to create your own custom monitoring solution.

1. Call Transaction RZ20.
2. Activate the maintenance functions, and expand the monitor structure in your copy of the monitor set (see Figure 3.31).

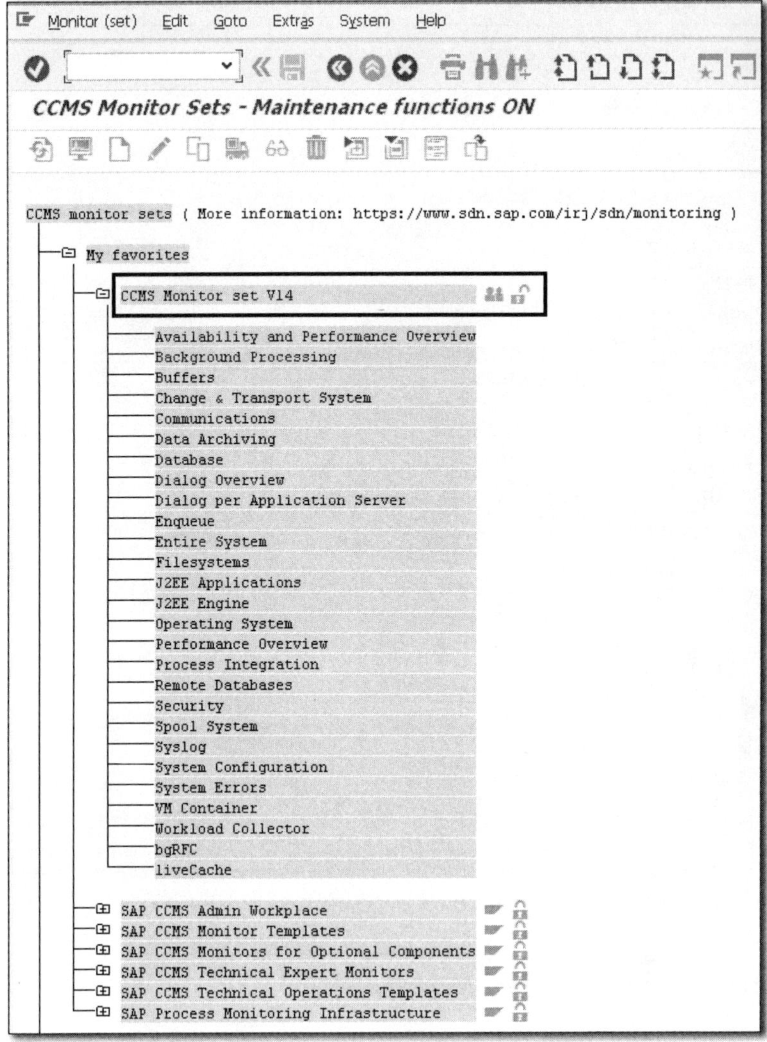

Figure 3.31 Expanding the Structure of the Monitor Set Copy

3. Position the cursor on the monitor you want to delete (e.g., J2EE ENGINE in Figure 3.32), and click on DELETE .

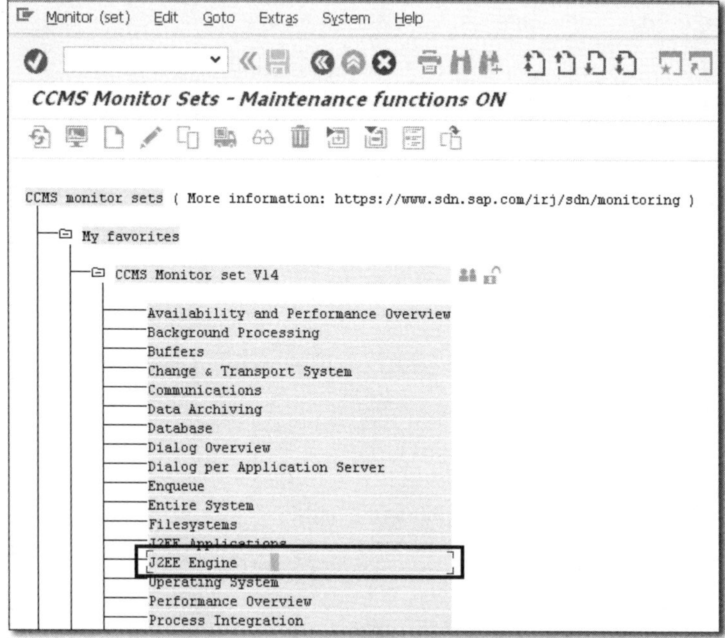

Figure 3.32 Selecting a Monitor for Deletion

4. Confirm the deletion in the dialog box with YES (see Figure 3.33).

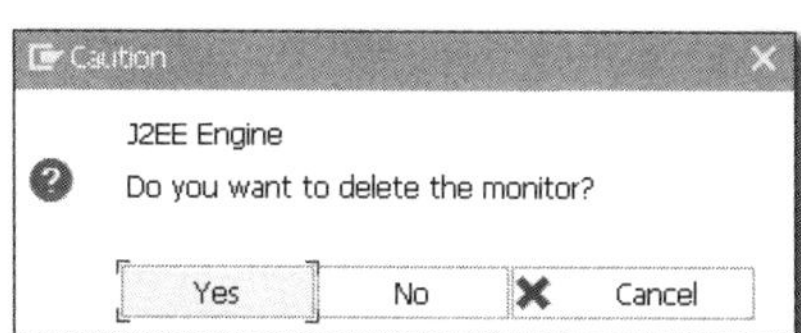

Figure 3.33 Confirming the Monitor Deletion

5. The message MONITOR <YX> HAS BEEN DELETED appears in the status bar to confirm deletion.
6. Repeat these steps until you're only left with the monitors you require (see Figure 3.34).

Transporting Monitor Sets [+]

If you've created your own CCMS monitor set, which you also want to use in other systems, you can use the transport function: Select the monitor set, and click on TRANSPORT MONITOR SET. You can then use a transport request to import the monitor set into other systems.

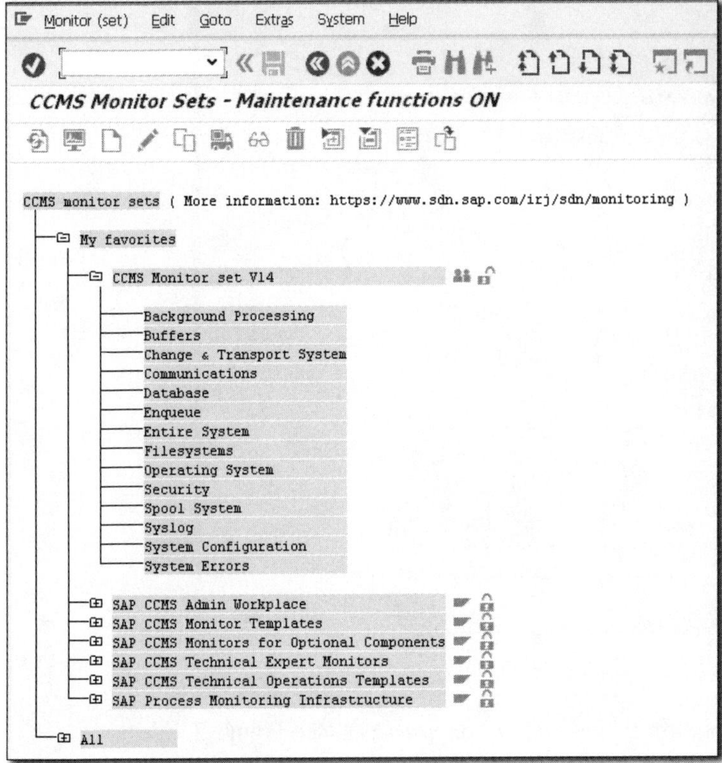

Figure 3.34 Modified Monitor Set

3.3.5 Changing Alert Thresholds

An alert threshold value is a value at which an alert indicator changes color. The color changes from green to yellow and from yellow to red, depending on the severity of the problem to which you're being alerted. The indicator then switches back from red to yellow and yellow to green, when the system returns to an uncritical status.

Because every SAP installation is unique, various threshold values may be useful. You may want to change the threshold values in the example scenarios described here:

- A large amount of paging (or, more accurately, swapping, that is, the removal of data from the main memory [RAM] to the virtual memory on the hard disk) is problematic in the production system but isn't critical in the development system.

- The database file is the only file on a drive, and it takes up all of that drive. A *file system full alert* is therefore superfluous because the configuration of the database allows it to occupy the entire drive.
- You need to be informed at an early stage of a high level of CPU utilization because, based on experience, you know that you need large system reserves during live operation.

You can adjust the threshold values of the monitor objects to meet your requirements by following these steps:

1. In Transaction RZ20, select the monitor object for which you want to change the alert threshold value (e.g., CPU_UTILIZATION in Figure 3.35), and click on PROPERTIES.

Figure 3.35 Selecting a Monitor Object for Changing the Threshold Value

2. Click on Display <-> Change to switch to change mode (see Figure 3.36).

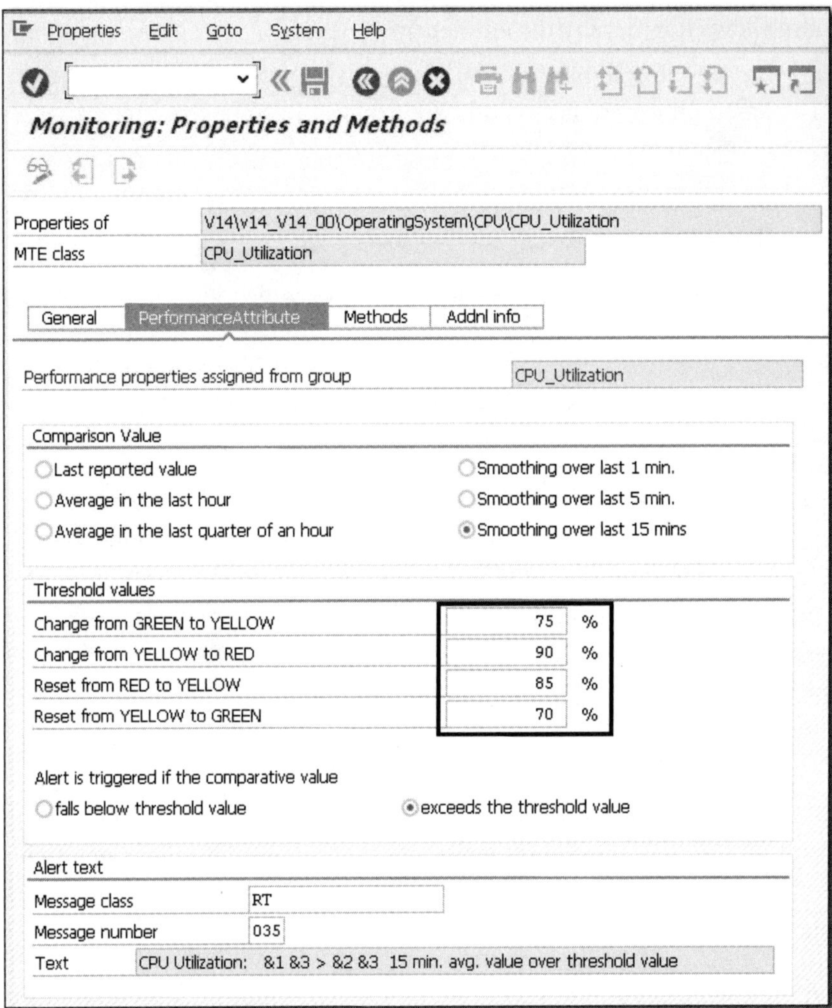

Figure 3.36 Changing Threshold Values

3. Under THRESHOLD VALUES, enter the values that meet your requirements. Click on SAVE .
4. The message PROPERTIES HAVE BEEN SAVED in the status bar confirms that the values have been saved. Click on BACK to return to the monitor.

From now on, the alerts of the monitor object will be switched as soon as the relevant values exceed or fall short of the threshold values you defined.

3.4 Auto-Reaction Methods

Auto-reaction methods are key components of the CCMS Alert Monitor. You can use these methods to determine how the system responds in the event of an alert. Possible auto-reaction methods include the following:

- **Automatic alert notification**
  You can ensure that the system automatically sends you a notification, for example, by email or text message, whenever an alert occurs (`CCMS_OnAlert_Email` method).
- **Execute operating system commands**
  The system can execute commands or scripts when certain threshold values are reached (`CCMS_AUTO_REACT_OP_COMMAND` method).

As an example of these methods, the next section explains how you can set up automatic email notification as an auto-reaction to an alert.

3.4.1 Changing an Auto-Reaction Method

The auto-reaction method for sending notifications is provided standard in the SAP system. All you need to do, therefore, is adapt this method to your requirements as follows:

1. Enter Transaction RZ21 in the command field and press the Enter key (or select TOOLS • CCMS • CONFIGURATION • RZ21—ATTRIBUTES AND METHODS).

2. Make sure that the METHOD DEFINITIONS entry is selected in the METHODS area (see Figure 3.37), and click on DISPLAY OVERVIEW.
3. Scroll in the list until you find the `CCMS_OnAlert_Email` method, and then select it (see Figure 3.38). Click on COPY.

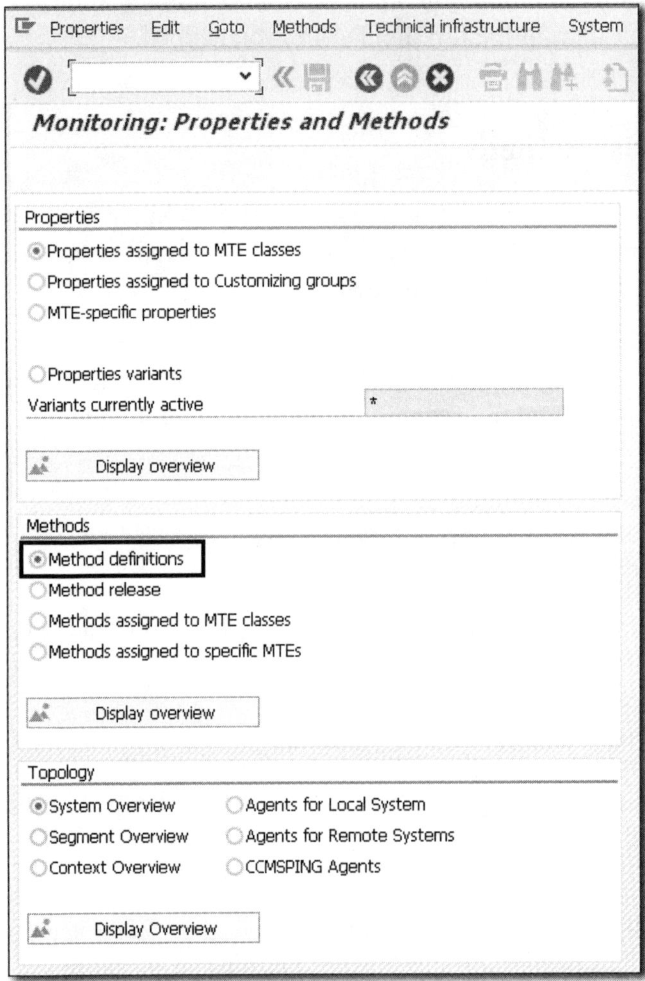

Figure 3.37 Displaying Method Definitions

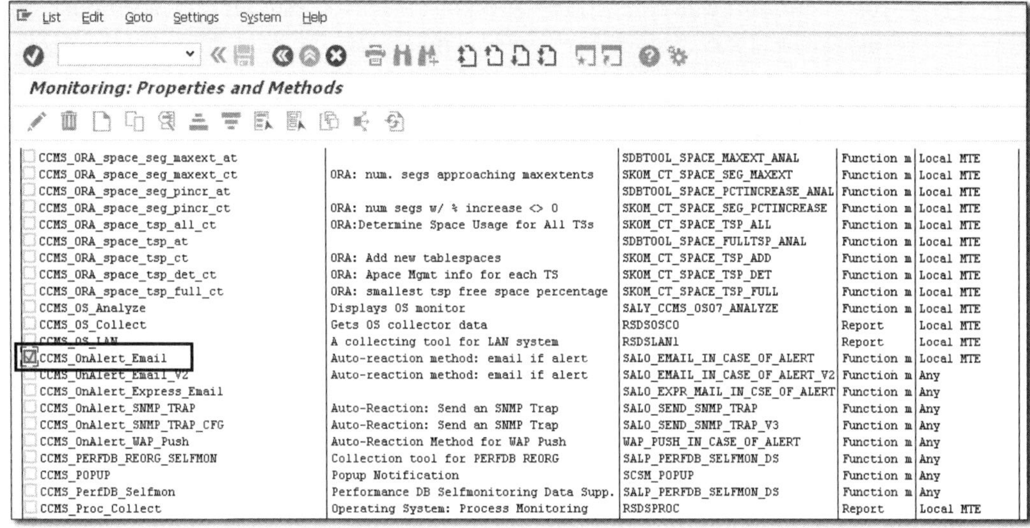

Figure 3.38 Copying the "CCMS_OnAlert_Email" Method

Copying Auto-Reaction Methods

[+]

Avoid changing the SAP standard auto-reaction methods. Instead, make a copy of these methods, and then modify your copies. This approach means that you'll always have access to the unaltered original method definitions should you need them again.

You may need to make several copies of an auto-reaction method in certain cases, for example, to send notification to a different set of recipients, depending on the alert.

4. In the dialog box displayed, give the auto-reaction method a new name (e.g., "Z_CCMS_OnAlert_Email_01" in Figure 3.39), and click Continue ✓ to confirm.

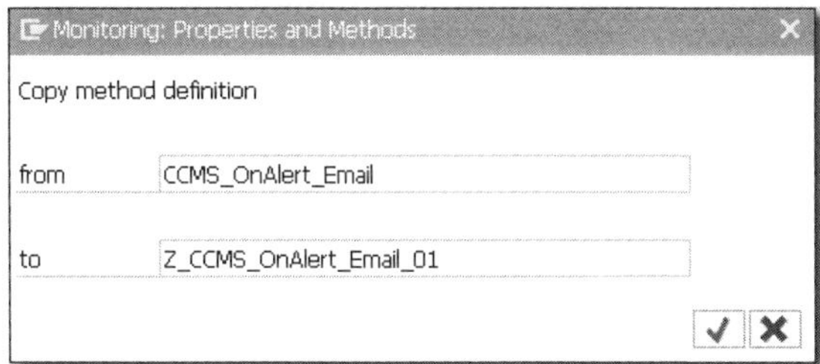

Figure 3.39 Entering a Name for the New Auto-Reaction Method

5. Your copy of the auto-reaction method is displayed (see Figure 3.40). Click on DISPLAY <-> CHANGE to switch to change mode.

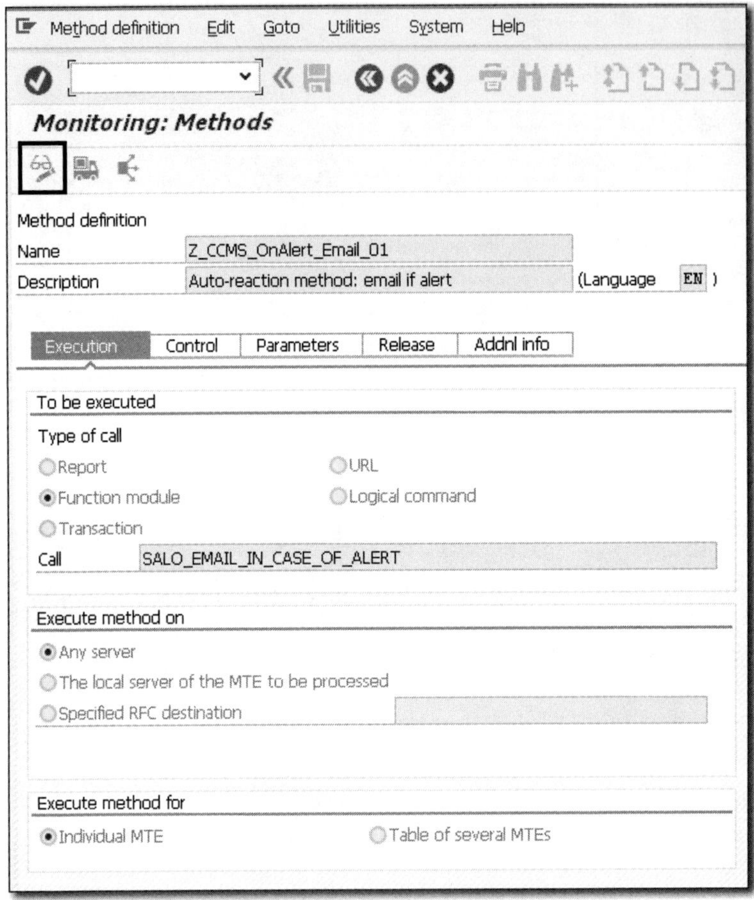

Figure 3.40 Changing the Newly Created Auto-Reaction Method

6. Go to the PARAMETERS tab, and make the following settings (see Figure 3.41):
   - As a parameter value for the `SENDER` parameter, enter the SAP user you want to be used as the sender of the notification.
   - For the `RECIPIENT` parameter, enter the user you want to receive the notification (e.g., an email address).

- Use the `RECIPIENT-TYPEID` parameter to define the address type of the address you entered as a `RECIPIENT` (e.g., U for an Internet address).

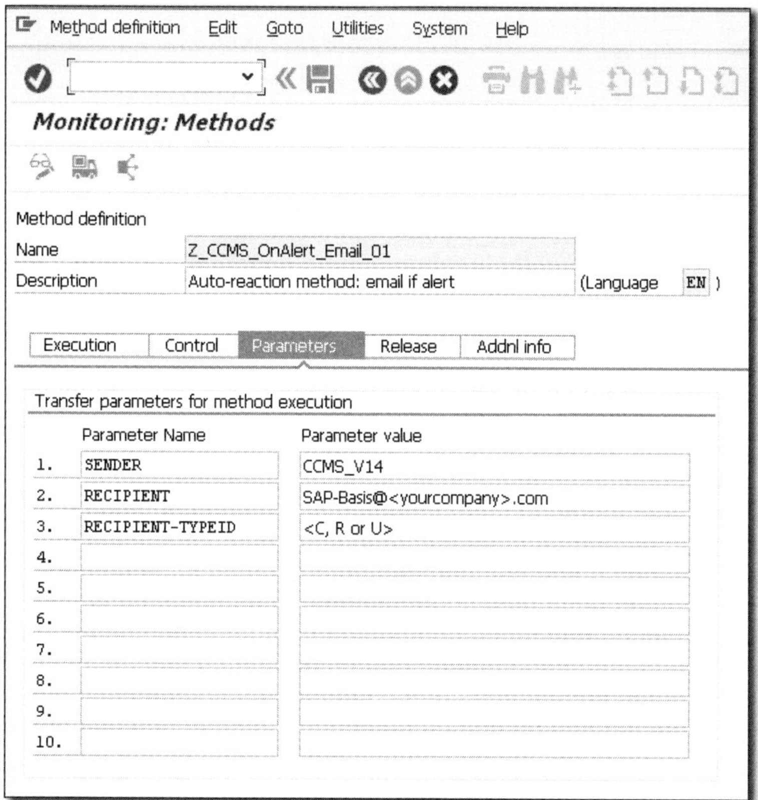

Figure 3.41 Adapting the Parameters of the Auto-Reaction Method

Email Distribution Lists [!]

You can also use distribution lists when defining the recipients of a notification. Distribution lists are created in the SAP Business Workplace (Transaction SBWP). Note that distribution lists must be created and maintained in client 000 because the CCMS agent communicates exclusively with this client.

7. Switch to the RELEASE tab, and select the AUTO-REACTION METHOD checkbox (see Figure 3.42). Choose SAVE to save your settings.

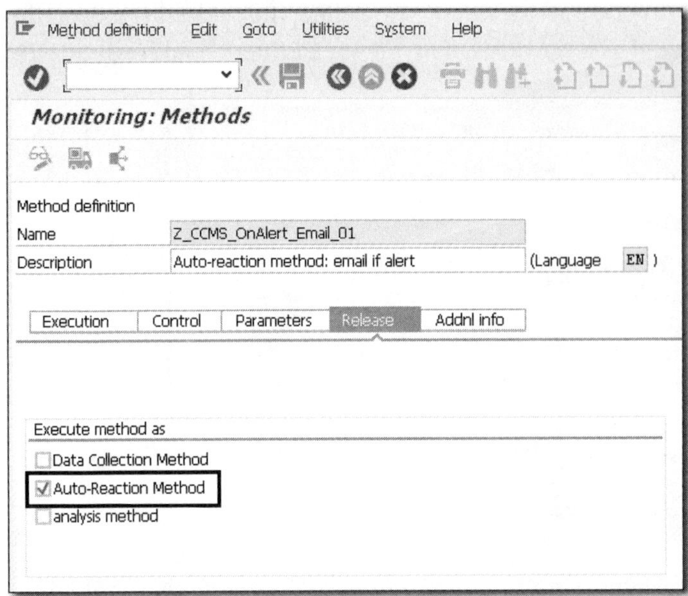

Figure 3.42 Releasing the Auto-Reaction Method

8. A message in the status bar confirms that the method definition has been saved and released. Choose BACK to exit Transaction RZ21.

You've now defined an auto-reaction method, which sends a notification in the desired format to the desired recipients. You've also released the method for use in the CCMS Alert Monitor. In the next step, you'll assign the new method to a monitor object.

3.4.2 Assigning an Auto-Reaction Method to a Monitor Object

After an auto-reaction method has been created, configured, and released, it can be used in the CCMS Alert Monitor.

1. Call Transaction RZ20.
2. Expand the monitor set, and position the cursor on the relevant monitor (e.g., FILESYSTEMS in Figure 3.43). Click on LOAD MONITOR.
3. Expand the monitor's tree structure, and select the relevant monitor (e.g., FREESPACE in Figure 3.44). Click on PROPERTIES.

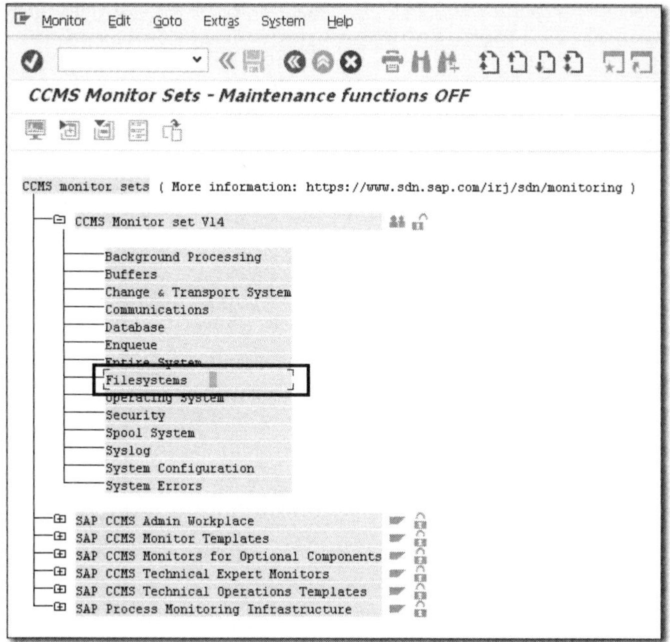

Figure 3.43 Selecting a Monitor for the Auto-Reaction Method

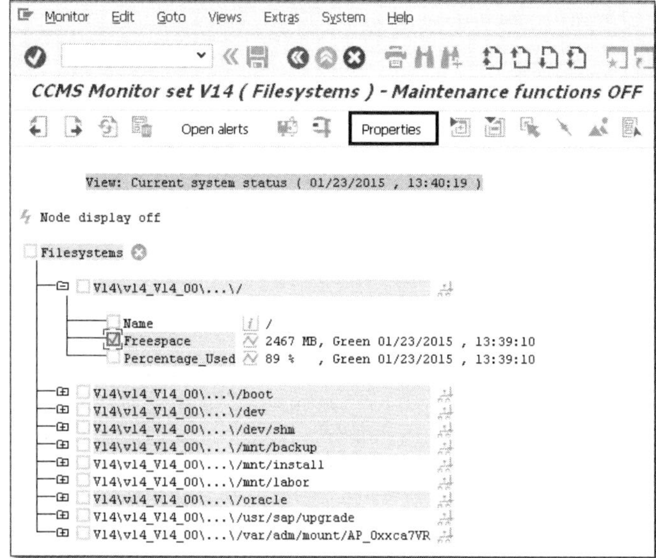

Figure 3.44 Calling the Properties of the Monitor Object

4. Go to the METHODS tab, and click on the METHOD ASSIGNMENT button (see Figure 3.45).

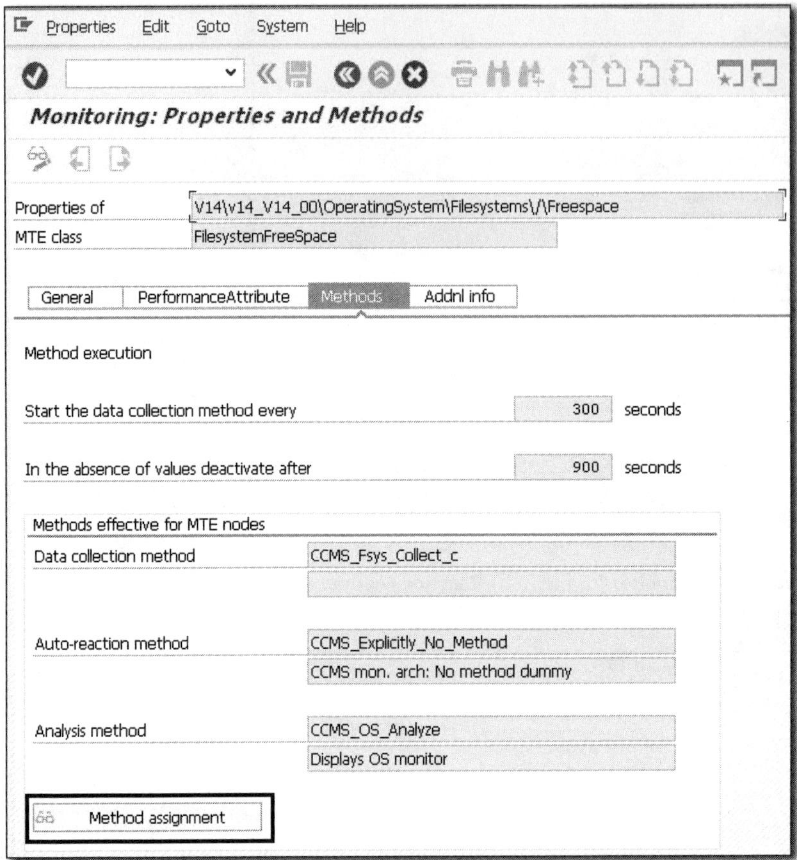

Figure 3.45 Calling the Method Assignment

[✪]

Assigning Methods

You can assign methods to an individual monitor object directly or to the MTE class to which the object belongs. If you assign the auto-reaction method to the MTE class of the monitor object, it will be inherited by all objects in this class.

To assign the method to the MTE class, double-click on the MTE CLASS field in the MONITORING: PROPERTIES AND METHODS view. On the next screen, you can assign the method to the selected class.

5. Click on DISPLAY <-> CHANGE to activate the change mode, and select the AUTO-REACTION tab (see Figure 3.46). In the METHOD ALLOCATION area, select the METHOD NAME entry. Enter your auto-reaction method (e.g., "Z_CCMS_OnAlert_Email_01") in the relevant field. Click SAVE to save your entries.

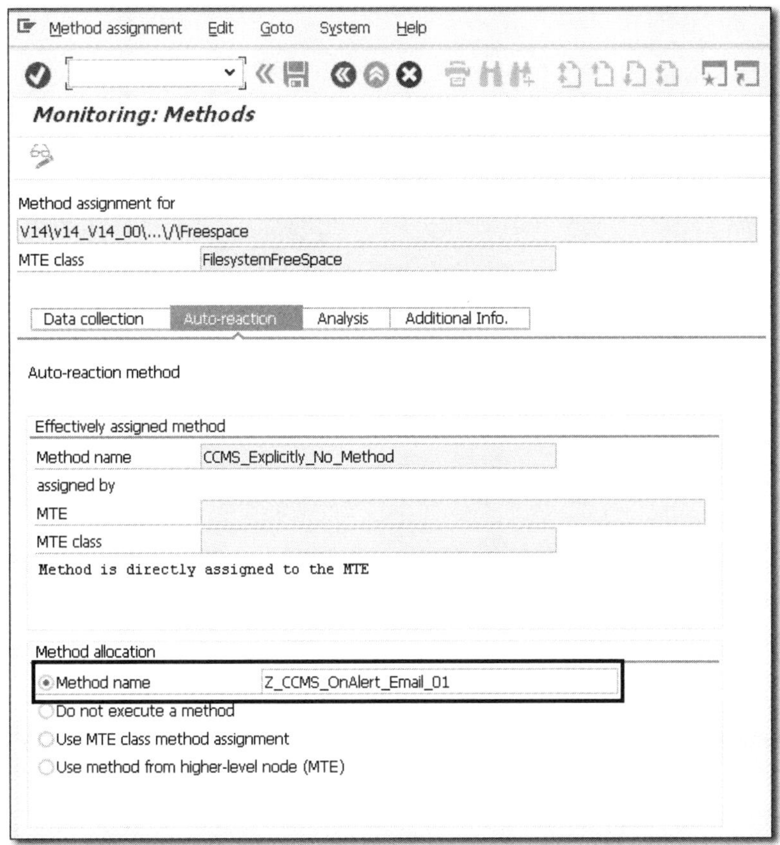

Figure 3.46 Entering an Auto-Reaction Method for the Monitor Object

Case Sensitivity [!]

Note that the field in which you enter the method name is case-sensitive. Make sure that you enter uppercase/lowercase characters correctly. Otherwise, your method won't be found.

6. The assigned auto-reaction method is now displayed in the METHOD NAME field under METHOD ALLOCATION (see Figure 3.47). Choose BACK to exit the view.

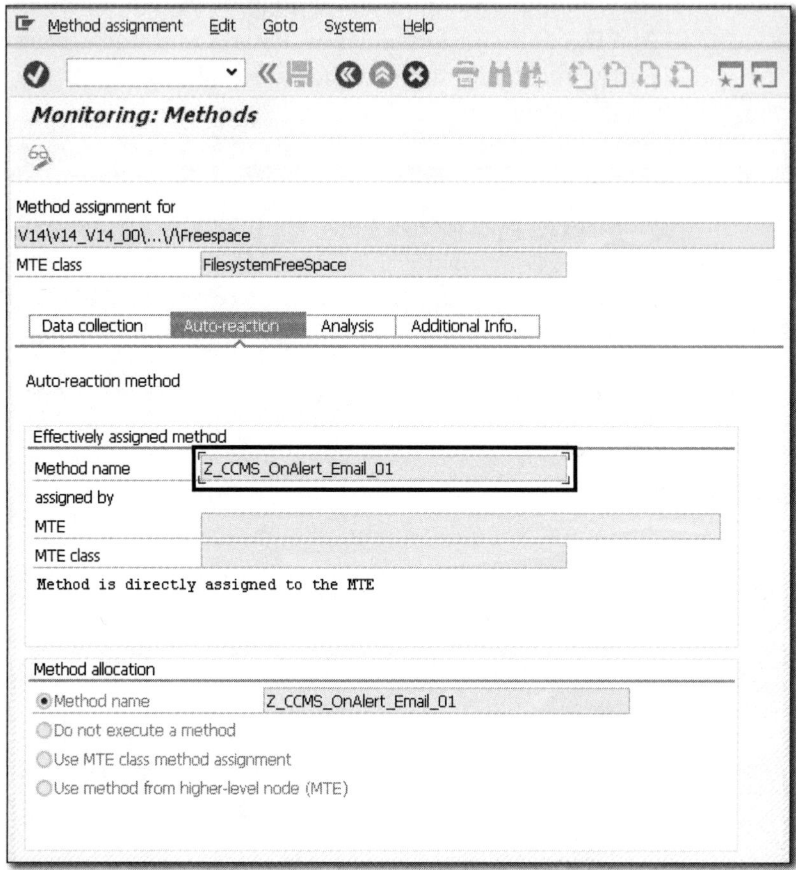

Figure 3.47 Checking the Assignment of the Auto-Reaction Method

7. The assigned auto-reaction method is now also displayed on the MONITORING: PROPERTIES AND METHODS screen (see Figure 3.48). Choose BACK to return to the monitor's tree structure.

[!]

Configuring SAPconnect

SAPconnect must be set up in client 000 if you want to send notifications to external email addresses, for example. You configure SAPconnect in Transaction SCOT (SAPconnect Administration) (see also Chapter 2, Section 2.6.3).

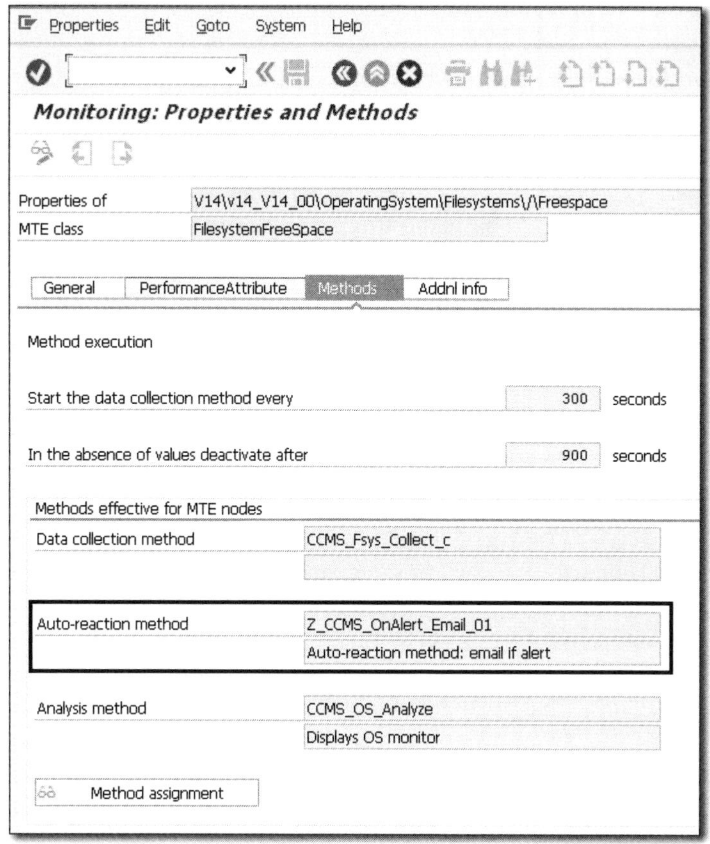

Figure 3.48 Auto-Reaction Method in the Properties of the Monitoring Object

Your auto-reaction method has now been assigned to a specific monitor object. From now on, a notification will be sent as soon as an alert is triggered.

Follow the same steps just described if you want the system to execute an operating system command when a certain alert occurs. In this case, use the CCMS_AUTO_REACT_OP_COMMAND method as your starting point.

Registering Operating System Commands [+]

Before an operating system command can be executed as a method, it must be registered in Transaction SM69 (Maintain External OS Commands).

3.5 Summary

The CCMS Alert Monitor is still a very powerful tool for monitoring SAP systems, even though it was replaced by the Monitoring and Alerting Infrastructure (MAI) of SAP Solution Manager in the long run. It allows you to keep track of virtually all conceivable aspects of a system. Several monitors are included in the standard system, which you can easily use for basic monitoring. You can use auto-reaction methods to ensure that the system informs you by email whenever any critical situations arise, without you having to constantly keep an eye on CCMS alerts.

The options offered by this tool don't stop there. User-defined monitors, modified methods, and central system monitoring are all possible, so that you can set up an extensive, effective monitoring concept. However, it's necessary to immerse yourself deeply in this subject—don't underestimate the complexity of the Customizing settings for the CCMS Alert Monitor. You also shouldn't rely exclusively on a single tool. You should use parallel monitors at the operating, database, and possibly also hardware level to safeguard system monitoring in the event of an emergency.

SAP Solution Manager has become an indispensable tool for enterprises that run SAP software. However, the value added by its integration into the system landscape varies significantly between one enterprise and the next. This chapter shows you how to use SAP Solution Manager for administration of your SAP systems.

4 System Administration Using SAP Solution Manager

All SAP customers need to use *SAP Solution Manager*: It's no longer possible to download support packages without this tool. For this reason, any enterprise or business that runs SAP software also uses SAP Solution Manager.

In practice, however, opinions are still divided. While some regard it as a necessary evil, others try to use the functions of SAP Solution Manager as extensively as possible and to incorporate them profitably into the value chain. The resources available within the enterprise or SAP administrator group often determine the fate of an SAP Solution Manager installation. It takes time, money, and patience to become familiar with its functions, set up a stable two-system or even three-system landscape, and map projects and business processes in the "SolMan."

However, a great deal has happened. With SAP Solution Manager 7.1, both functionality and the look and feel have been improved considerably. New functions are delivered with almost every support package stack for SAP Solution Manager. Also with regard to error-proneness and administration effort, SAP Solution Manager 7.0 and the well-maintained SAP Solution Manager 7.1 are worlds apart.

This chapter explains how to use SAP Solution Manager for SAP system administration. It explains the basic settings required to use the essential functions. However, it also introduces other instruments that may be of interest to administrators and may help make your life a lot easier.

4.1 Functional Spectrum of SAP Solution Manager

SAP Solution Manager seeks to manage and document the entire lifecycle of SAP systems, from the initial project phase, through the implementation of a new software solution, and, ultimately, to live system operation. SAP Solution Manager provides a central or higher-level starting point from which you can navigate to all connected systems.

Details of some of the main applications are provided as follows:

- **System landscape administration**
  SAP Solution Manager collects data of the systems in your landscape via the *System Landscape Directory* (SLD). It then stores the data in the *Landscape Management Database* (LMDB). This data forms the basis for the system landscape's lifecycle management, particularly for system maintenance and upgrades (see Chapter 18).

  In addition, the SAP EarlyWatch Alert function enables proactive system monitoring and supports service level reporting for management. If a problem occurs, SAP Solution Manager allows you to contact the SAP support and track its resolution (Issue Management). In addition, SAP Solution Manager can manage licenses and maintenance certificates.

- **System and technical monitoring**
  SAP Solution Manager provides functions for monitoring the performance of the system landscape both via the old CCMS architecture (*system monitoring*, see also Chapter 3) and the new *Monitoring and Alerting Infrastructure* (MAI), which replaces the CCMS Alert Monitor technically and extends the functional scope considerably.

- **Root cause analysis**
  New functions such as *root cause analysis* (RCA) significantly expand the usage scope in the area of error analysis. Moreover, you can synchronize the system settings in your landscape regularly and automatically by using the *configuration validation*. By means of *system recommendations*, you identify the SAP Notes that are available for your system.

- **Data volume management**
  Data volume management (DVM) supports you in monitoring the data volumes within your system landscape. You can use this tool to forecast the data growth and simulate procedures to reduce the amount of data. In the best case, it

allows you to save memory space and thus reduce the costs for your system landscape.

- **Implementation and upgrade of SAP solutions**
  You can use SAP Solution Manager to map an implementation or upgrade project. It contains best-practice guidelines known as *roadmaps* for a range of commonly occurring scenarios. You can use a *business blueprint* to model business processes. This process structure provides a basis for configuration, Customizing, and documentation of the solution. SAP Solution Manager can also be used for administration of customer developments. It also offers basic functions for project administration and controlling.
- **Test management**
  SAP Solution Manager provides a central platform for software testing, both within projects and during live operation. Test cases (e.g., manual test cases or eCATT tests) can be structured using test plans and packages, and they can be assigned to testers in the form of a worklist. Testers execute the test cases in SAP Solution Manager, which provides automatic navigation to the system that is to be tested. The test process is documented and evaluated in SAP Solution Manager.
- **IT service management**
  SAP Solution Manager can be used as a service desk, for example, for your enterprise's IT hotline support. Since release 7.1, the *Web User Interface* (Web UI) is available as a new browser-based technology that makes the service desk even more appealing.
- **Change management**
  Change management offers a workflow for requesting, implementing, rolling out, documenting, and tracking changes in the system. You can implement and control all transport management functions (see Chapter 17) using a change request process to create a consistent workflow comprising change request, approval, programming/Customizing, testing, acceptance, and transport into the production system.

The preceding list illustrates what a powerful tool SAP Solution Manager has become. It's impossible to cover all aspects of SAP Solution Manager in this book, much less discuss them in detail. This chapter therefore focuses on the topic of system administration with SAP Solution Manager. For further information on many of the topics mentioned, refer to Appendix E.

[!] **Release Status**

This chapter describes the functions of SAP Solution Manager 7.1 with Support Package Stack (SPS) 12. If you use another SPS status, there may be differences in terms of content and display.

4.2 Maintaining the System Landscape

You must make your system landscape known in SAP Solution Manager before you can use it for administration of your systems. This process has been automated, and the systems send their data to the System Landscape Directory (SLD). The SLD is a Java application that can run either on the Java stack of SAP Solution Manager or another Java stack or system. The SLD information is then forwarded to the Landscape Management Database (LMDB) of SAP Solution Manager. As a result, the information is then available for further usage. Manual maintenance of systems (e.g., via Transaction SMSY) is usually no longer required. Communication between SAP Solution Manager and the systems is based on RFC connections, which are created or generated automatically when managed systems are linked.

[+] **Work Centers**

In SAP Solution Manager help documentation available in the SAP Help Portal (*http://help.sap.com*), *work centers* are frequently mentioned in connection with various SAP Solution Manager functions. The background is that almost all SAP Solution Manager functions can now be reached via central Transaction SOLMAN_WORKCENTER. There, the various functions are organized on tabs, which are referred to as work centers. You can call the work centers via the mentioned transaction from within the SAP GUI. Alternatively, you can also use Transaction SM_WORKCENTER, which starts the work centers in a browser.

4.2.1 Transferring System Data to SAP Solution Manager

Before SAP Solution Manager can manage a system, it requires the system data. The system data isn't read by SAP Solution Manager itself nor directly sent to SAP Solution Manager. Instead, the SLD functions as a collection point that collects the data of all SAP systems and forwards it to SAP Solution Manager. The advantage of this procedure is that each system provides all necessary data independently without you having to maintain extensive information (e.g., product versions, etc.) in SAP Solution Manager. This results in an automatism that works perfectly.

To ensure that an ABAP system sends its data to the SLD, follow these steps:

1. Start Transaction RZ70 in the system to be managed.
2. Under RFC CONNECTION TO SLD, enter the GATEWAY HOST name and the GATEWAY SERVICE ("sapgw<instance number>") of your SLD server (see Figure 4.1).

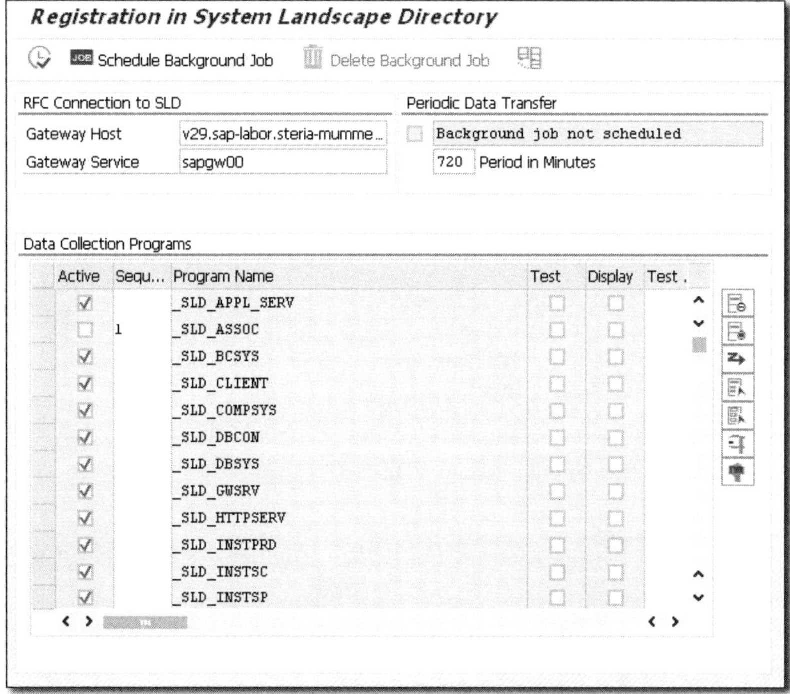

Figure 4.1 Registering an ABAP System in the System Landscape Directory

3. To transfer the system data to the SLD once, click the IMMEDIATE DATA TRANSFER TO SLD icon. However, it makes more sense to schedule a job that provides the data on a regular basis. Then, you don't need to make any manual modifications after a system maintenance takes place that changes the system data (e.g., kernel and component versions). To do so, click the SCHEDULE AS BACKGROUND JOB button.

[+]

Sending Java System Data to the SLD

The data of ABAP and Java stacks or systems is transferred separately to the SLD. It isn't sufficient to execute Transaction RZ70 in a dual stack system (e.g., SAP Solution Manager or old ABAP/Java installations). In Java systems up to SAP NetWeaver 7.02 (which also includes SAP Solution Manager 7.1), you must configure the data transfer in the *Visual Administrator*. As of SAP NetWeaver 7.30, you can use the *SAP NetWeaver Administrator* of the Java stack.

4. Your work in the system to be connected is done. Log off, and check the result of the data transfer to the SLD. To do so, log on to your SLD server by calling the URL *http://<host name>:<Port>/sld* in the browser (see Figure 4.2). Then click the TECHNICAL SYSTEMS link.

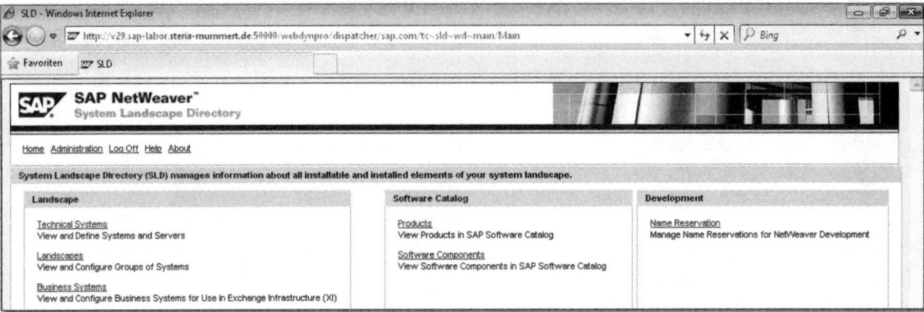

Figure 4.2 Checking the Result of the Data Transfer in the SLD

[+]

Protocol and Port

Make sure that you select a port that matches the log. The server won't be available via HTTP on the HTTPS port and vice versa. Also note—particularly if you use the SLD of your SAP Solution Manager (dual stack system)—that the SLD is an application of the Java application server, and you thus must log on to the Java stack and not the ABAP stack. By default, the HTTP port of the Java stack is 5<instance number>00, for example, 50000 for the instance number 00. The default HTTP port of the ABAP stack, in turn, is 80<instance number>, for example, 8000. However, you can't call the SLD on this port.

5. Choose WEB AS ABAP in the TYPE OF TECHNICAL SYSTEM dropdown list. Under TECHNICAL SYSTEMS, you're provided with a list of ABAP system that sent their data to the SLD (see Figure 4.3). Select the desired system, and go through the tabs to view the detail information on this system.

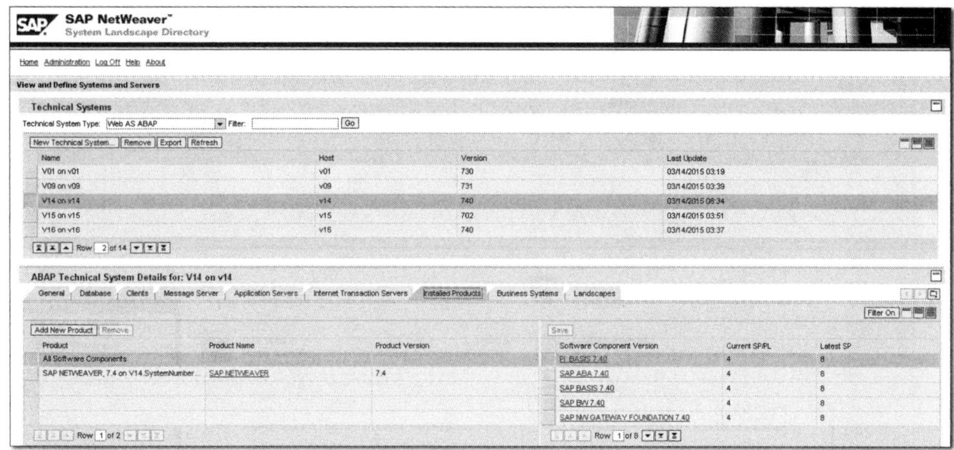

Figure 4.3 List of Systems in the System Landscape Directory

6. After you've made sure that the data reached the SLD, you can log off again. Now check whether SAP Solution Manager also received the information. For this purpose, log on to SAP Solution Manager, and start Transaction LMDB to call the LMDB (see Figure 4.4).

SAP Solution Manager Configuration [!]

In this chapter, we assume that your SAP Solution Manager has already been configured; that is, the steps for system preparation and basic configuration have already been performed in Transaction SOLMAN_SETUP. For managing the system landscape, the steps SELECT SLD and SETUP LMDB under SYSTEM PREPARATION • PREPARE LANDSCAPE DESCRIPTION are of particular importance.

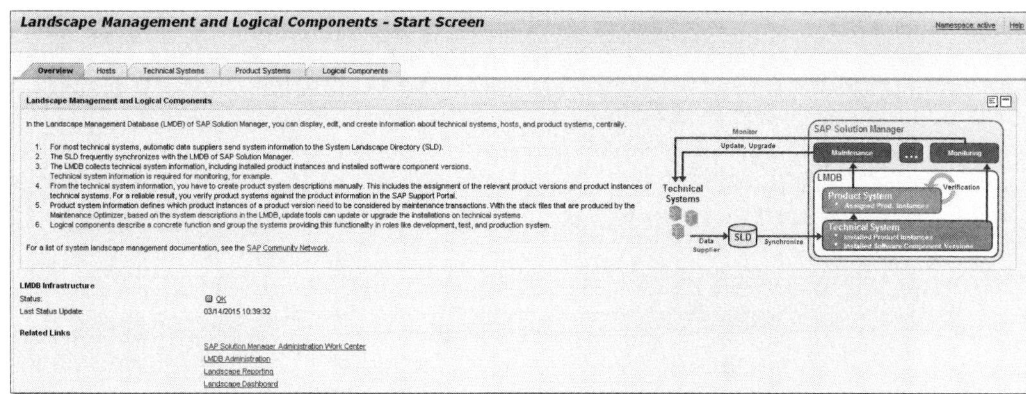

Figure 4.4 Initial Screen of the Landscape Management Database

7. Choose the TECHNICAL SYSTEMS tab. Under EXTENDED SYSTEM ID, enter the system ID of your system, and click on DISPLAY (see Figure 4.5).

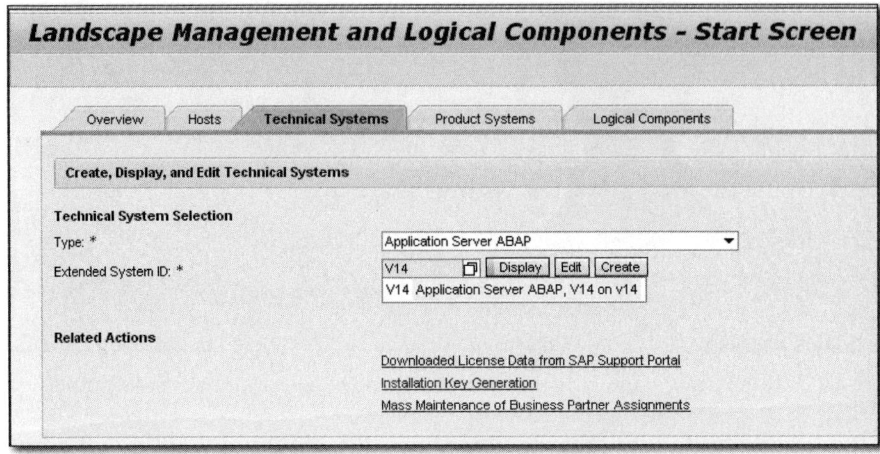

Figure 4.5 Calling the Technical System in the Landscape Management Database

8. The LMDB receives all technical information from the SLD and saves it. Choose an area in the navigation tree to display the information (see Figure 4.6). By clicking on the LMDB START SCREEN button, you return to the previous view.

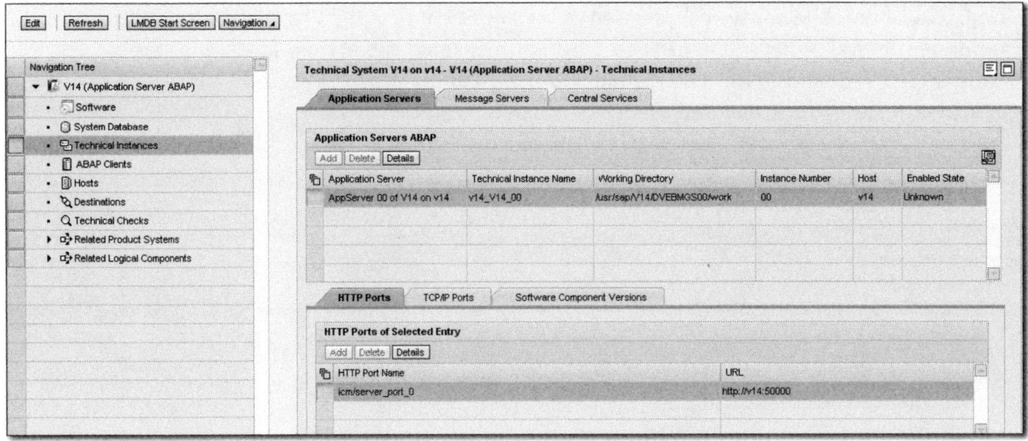

Figure 4.6 Viewing Detailed Information about a Technical System

You configured the system to be managed in such a way that it transfers its system data to the SLD. You then made sure that the technical information has reached both the SLD and the LMDB of SAP Solution Manager. A technical system was created automatically in SAP Solution Manager. In the following sections, we described how to use this technical system. To be able to run maintenance transactions, you must make the following preparations, which are also discussed later on:

1. Create a *product system* for the technical system.
2. Assign the product system to a *logical component*.
3. Define a *solution* in which you insert the logical component.

[+]

Steps for Assigning a Product

You implement these three steps conveniently in the ASSIGN PRODUCT step of the wizards for configuring managed systems (see Section 4.2.5). For better understanding and to reproduce the "magic" in the system, the following sections describe the steps individually.

4.2.2 Creating a Product System

After the technical system has been generated automatically, you can continue with creating the product system. A product system describes how the individual components of your enterprise's SAP product (e.g., SAP CRM, SAP ERP, or SAP Solution Manager) are distributed to technical systems (e.g., to an ABAP and a Java system in SAP Solution Manager). The assignment of products to technical systems is necessary so that SAP Solution Manager can calculate correct maintenance transactions.

1. In SAP Solution Manager, start Transaction LMDB, and switch to the PRODUCT SYSTEMS tab.
2. Assign a name to the product system, and click on CREATE (see Figure 4.7).

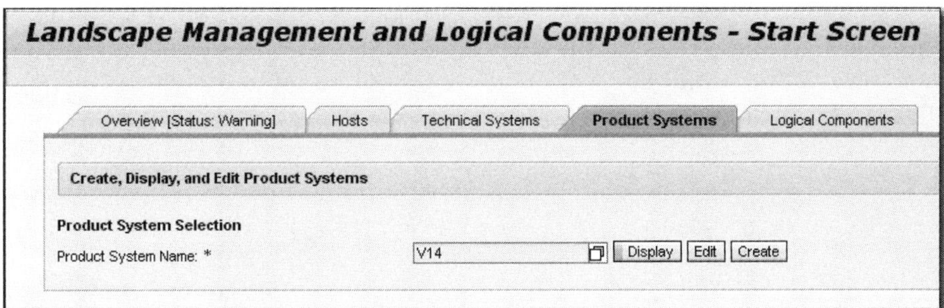

Figure 4.7 Creating a New Product System

3. Assign one or more technical systems to the product system by clicking on the ASSIGNED TECHNICAL SYSTEMS tab, and then clicking on the ADD button (see Figure 4.8).

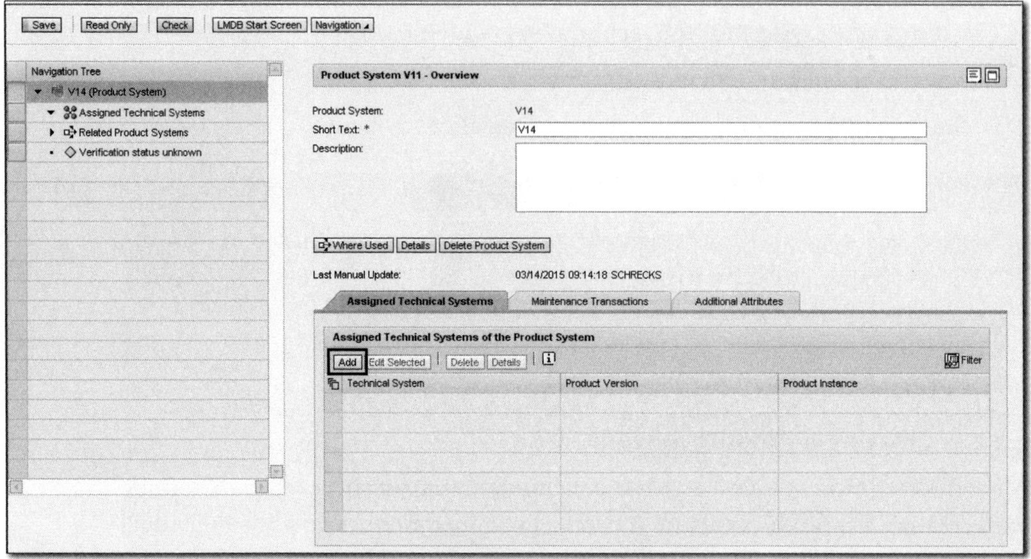

Figure 4.8 Assigning Technical Systems to the Product System

4. Under TECHNICAL SYSTEM SELECTION, search for the system that you want to assign using the extended system ID, and click on SELECT (see Figure 4.9).

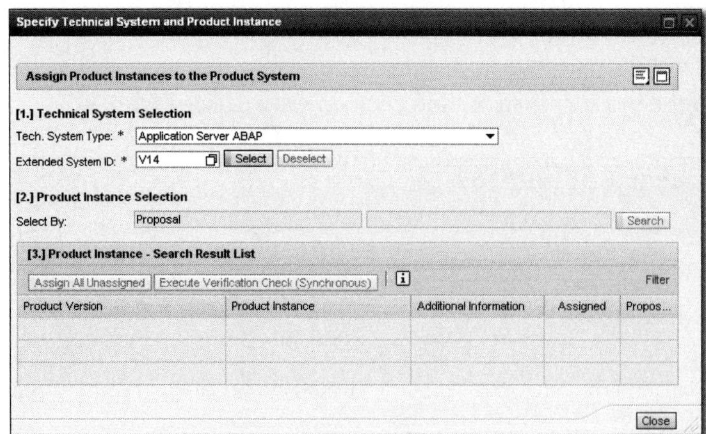

Figure 4.9 Selecting the Technical System

5. In the next step, click on the SEARCH button under PRODUCT INSTANCE SELECTION. By means of the installed products that are known from the system data, SAP Solution Manager searches for a proposal for the product version (see Figure 4.10).

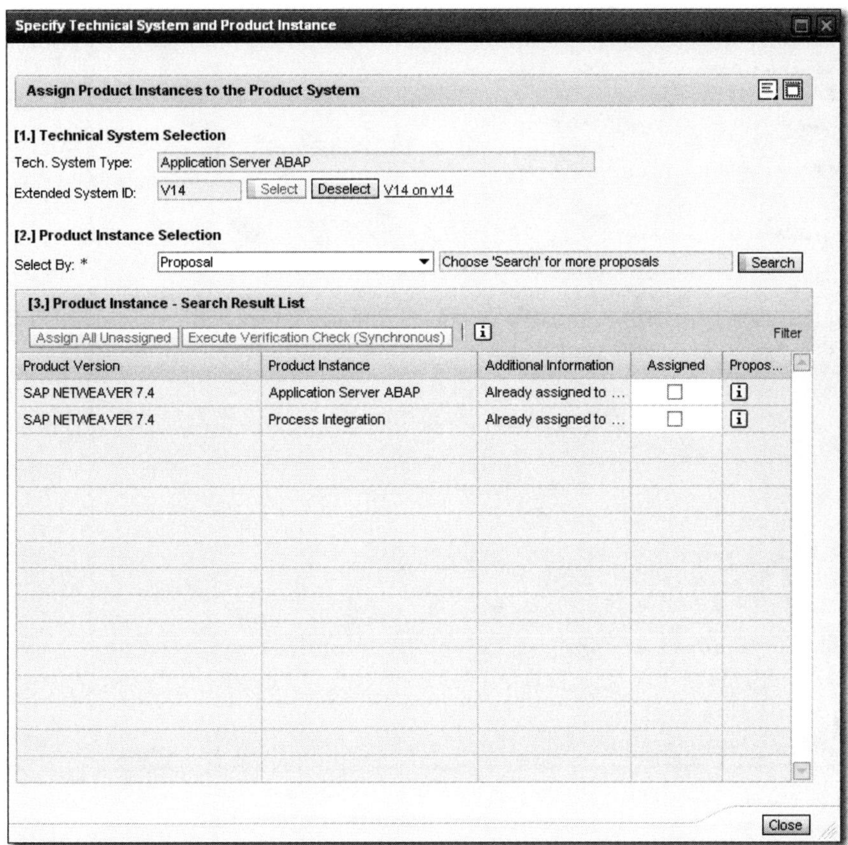

Figure 4.10 Proposal List for the Product Instance

6. In the PRODUCT INSTANCE – SEARCH RESULT LIST area, activate the checkmark in the ASSIGNED column for the appropriate product instance(s). Then click on the EXECUTE VERIFICATION CHECK (SYNCHRONOUS) button to check the assignment.

7. Check the verification log, that is, the message in the upper area of the dialog box, and remedy any errors (see Figure 4.11). If no problems were found, you can close the dialog box.

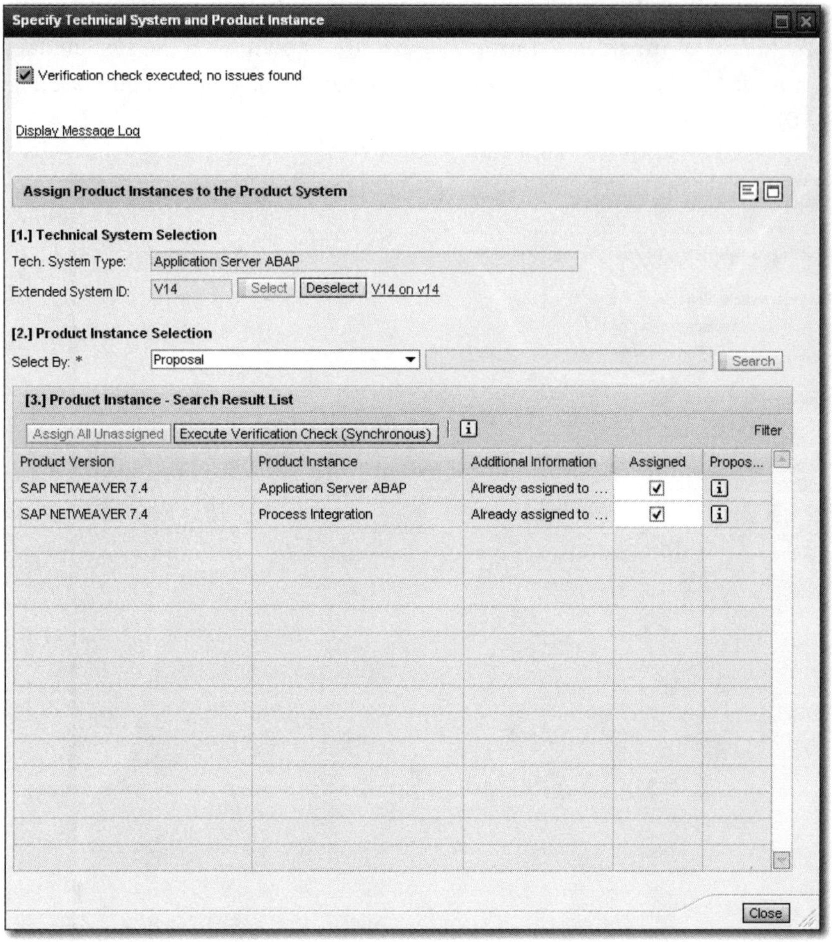

Figure 4.11 Executing a Verification Check

8. In our example, a Java stack was assigned to the ABAP system, and this Java system was added as another technical system (see Figure 4.12). If required, you can repeat the verification check. The system will then submit proposals for a solution in case of an error. It's important that you complete verification successfully.

You've assigned a product system to the technical system, which is essential for the maintenance transactions in the Maintenance Optimizer for example. Next, you create a *logical component* and assign the system. The logical component is then assigned to a *solution*.

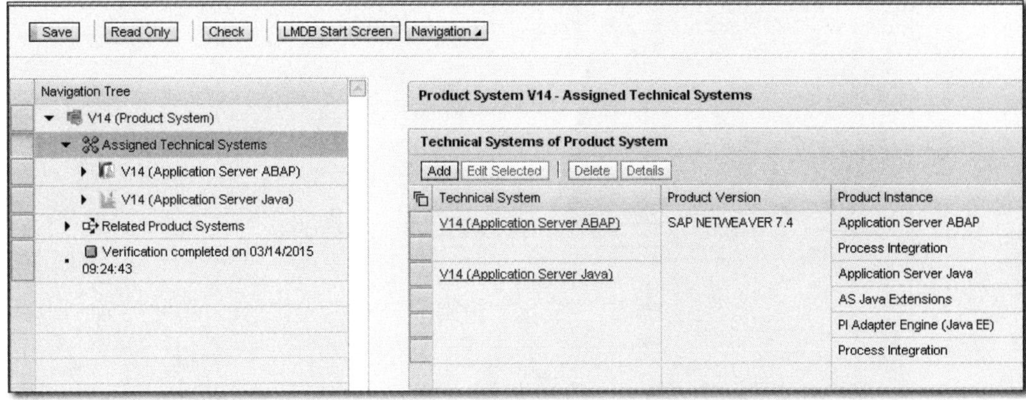

Figure 4.12 Product System Overview with Additional Technical System (Java Stack)

4.2.3 Creating a Logical Component

By means of logical components, you can combine the systems of a multi-system landscape into one administration unit. In this process, roles are assigned to the individual technical systems. These roles uniquely identify them within the logical component, for example, the development, quality assurance, or production system. To assign a logical component to your product system, follow these steps:

1. In SAP Solution Manager, start Transaction LMDB, and switch to the LOGICAL COMPONENTS tab.
2. Assign a name to the logical component, and click on CREATE (see Figure 4.13). Use a name from the customer namespace starting with "Z".

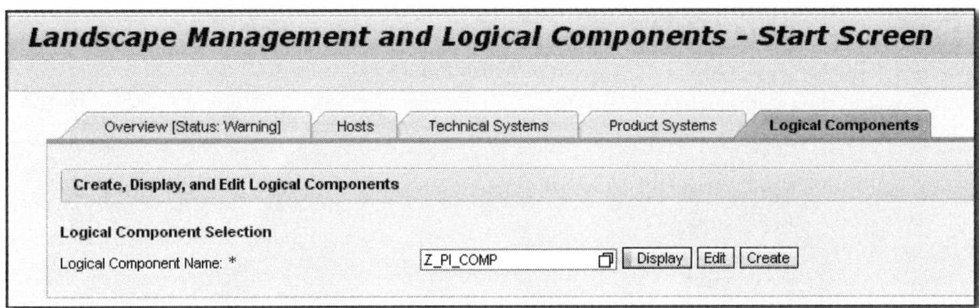

Figure 4.13 Creating a Logical Component

3. Assign a product instance to the logical component that corresponds to your product system by clicking on the MAINTAIN button (see Figure 4.14).

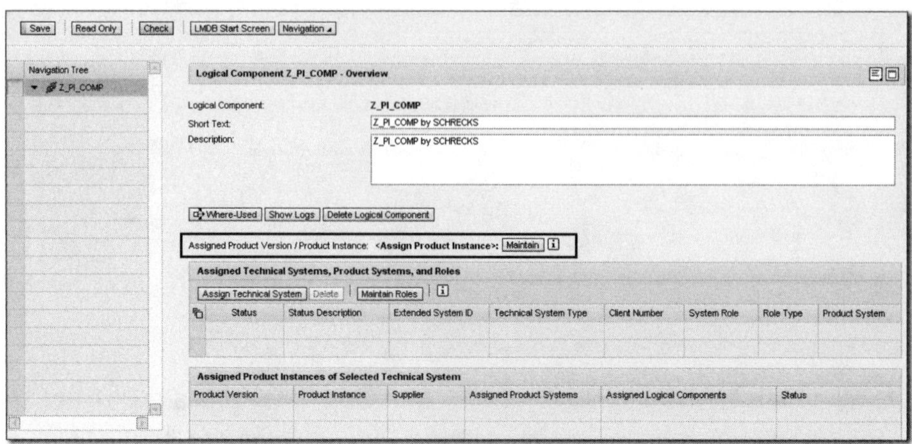

Figure 4.14 Assigning a Product Instance

4. In the PRODUCT INSTANCE list shown in Figure 4.15, search for the product instance that matches your system, and activate the checkmark in the SELECT column. Close the dialog window.

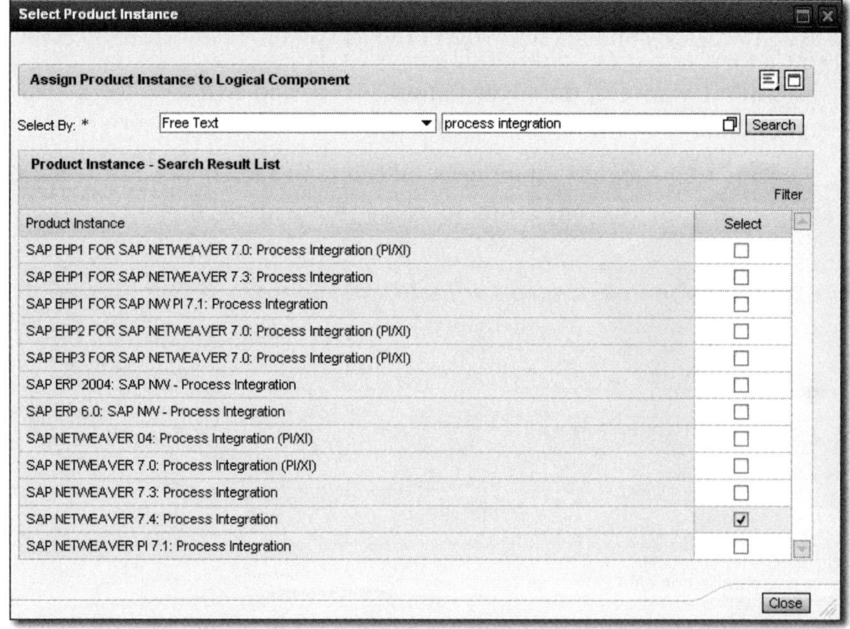

Figure 4.15 Selecting the Product Instance

5. Add your technical systems to the logical component by clicking the ASSIGN TECHNICAL SYSTEM button (see Figure 4.16).

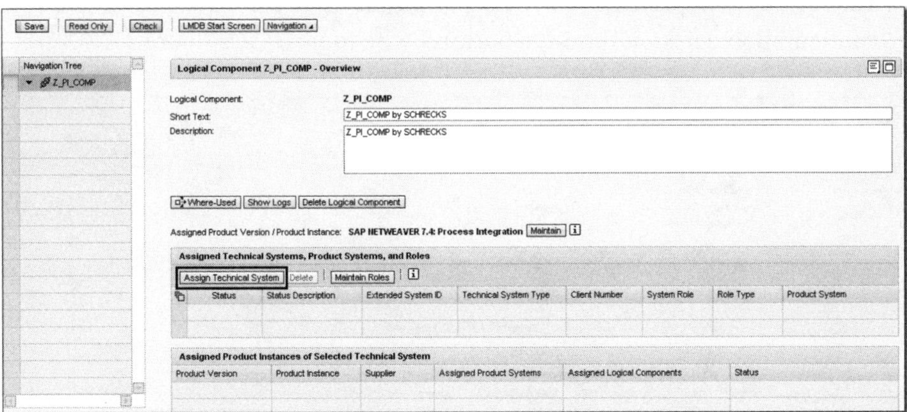

Figure 4.16 Adding a Technical System

6. In the dialog window, choose the technical system, client, and the corresponding system role (see Figure 4.17).

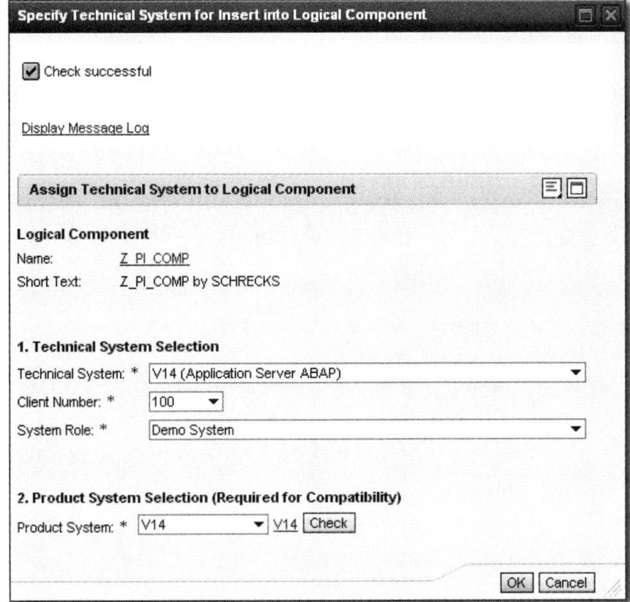

Figure 4.17 Adding a Technical System and a Product System

The product system is proposed based on your selection. Run a check by clicking on the CHECK button. If no errors are found, click on OK.

7. The system is displayed in the overview of the assigned systems. To save your configuration, click on the SAVE button in the toolbar (see Figure 4.18).

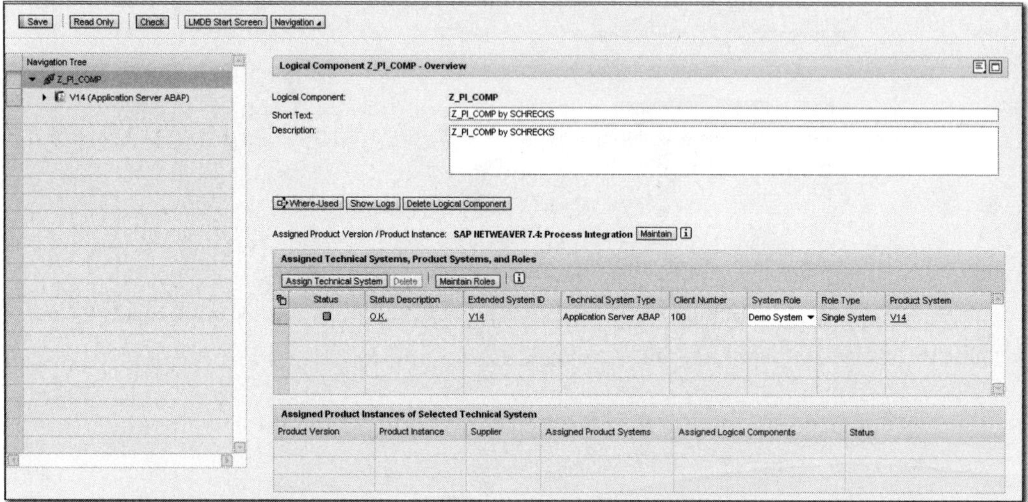

Figure 4.18 Saving the Configuration of the Logical Component

Use this procedure to assign a logical component to your systems, and sort the technical systems based on their role (SYSTEM ROLE column). For example, you can group the systems of a three-system landscape comprising a development system, test system, and production system in a logical component and then assign the relevant system role. The next step is to create a *solution* and assign the logical component that you previously created to this solution.

[+]

Using Logical Components

Logical components are particularly useful for implementation or upgrade projects because these projects distinguish among the development, test, and production systems. This also applies to test and change management. However, logical components are also required for system monitoring.

4.2.4 Solutions

Solutions give you the option of bundling individual systems together and managing them as a unit. The way in which you group systems together as solutions ultimately depends on the system landscape you're managing and on which SAP Solution Manager functions you use. You can also add the same system to several different solutions to enable system administration in accordance with your requirements and based on a range of criteria.

> **Defining Solutions** [Ex]
>
> If you want to monitor business processes that involve several systems (e.g., a procurement process with an SAP SRM system and an SAP ERP system), it's useful to bundle the production SAP SRM system and the SAP ERP system together in a solution. If, on the other hand, you want to use SAP Solution Manager's change management, it's preferable to bundle the development, QA, and production systems of the SAP ERP landscape together.
>
> Another option is to structure the solutions in accordance with your enterprise structure (e.g., by subsidiary) or based on the geographical locations of the sites involved.

To create a new solution, follow these steps:

1. In SAP Solution Manager, start Transaction SOLMAN_WORKCENTER (or Transaction SM_WORKCENTER for execution in the browser). Select the SAP Solution Manager Administration tab (e.g., the work center), and then click on the Solutions link (see Figure 4.19).

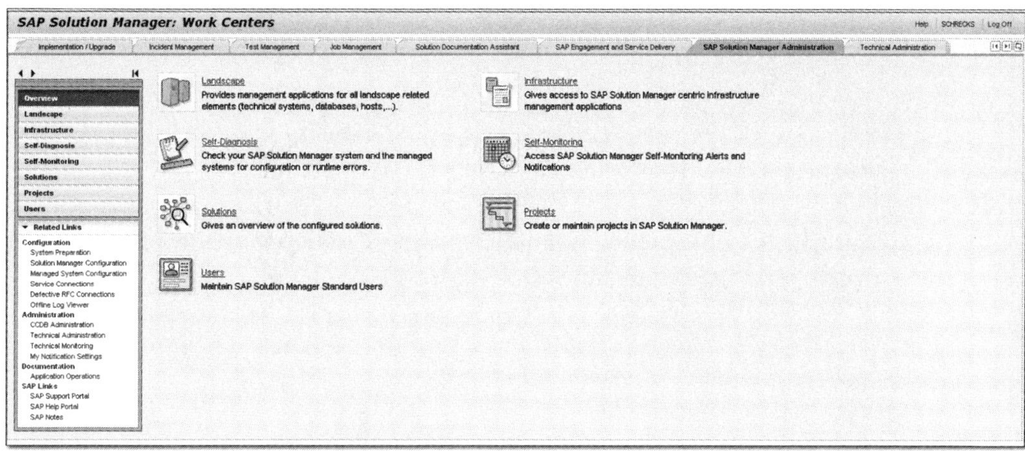

Figure 4.19 SAP Solution Manager Work Center

2. To create a solution in the solution overview, click on the NEW button (see Figure 4.20).

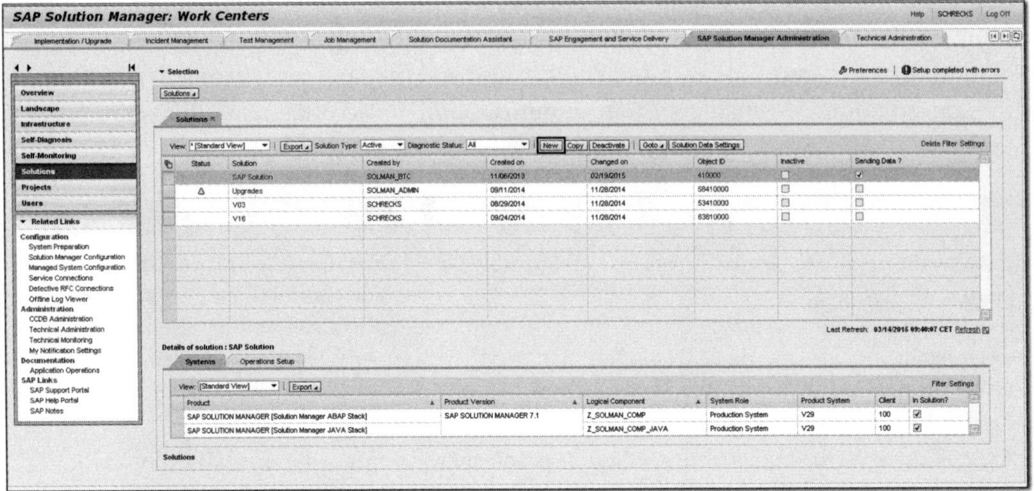

Figure 4.20 Creating a New Solution

3. In the dialog window that opens, enter a name for the solution, for instance, "Process Integration", and click on OK (see Figure 4.21).

Figure 4.21 Entering a Name for the New Solution

4. This takes you back to the solution overview. Click on the name of the solution that you just created to edit it (see Figure 4.22).

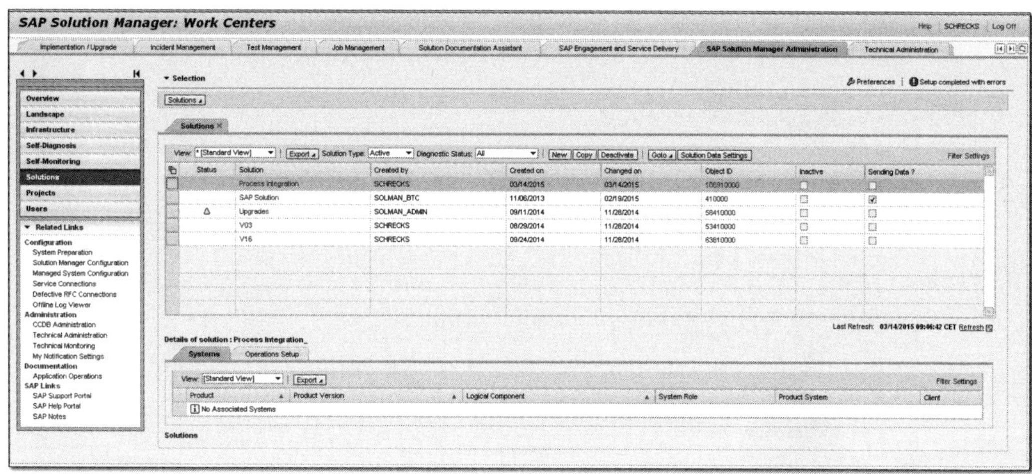

Figure 4.22 Selecting a Created Solution for Editing

5. The SOLUTION DIRECTORY opens (see Figure 4.23). Assign a logical name to the solution by calling the input help in the relevant column.

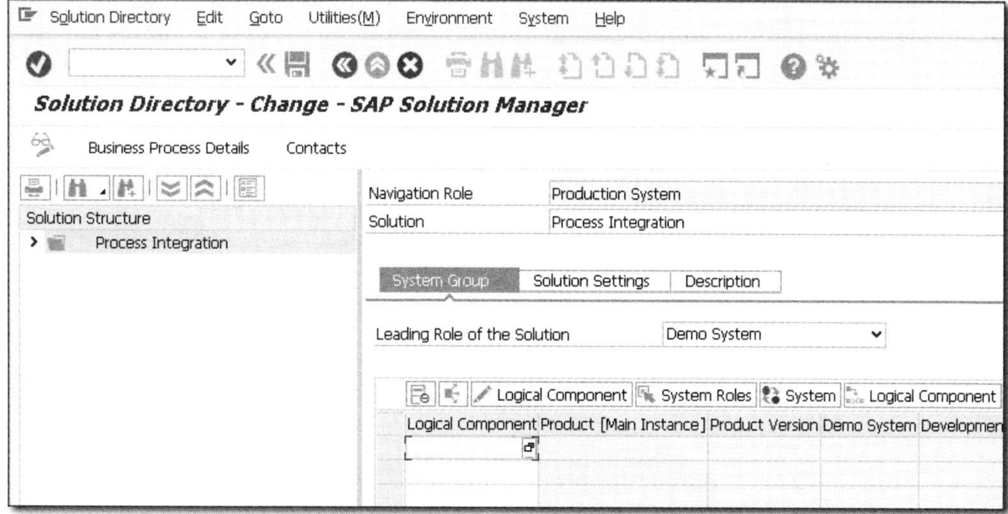

Figure 4.23 Solution Directory

6. In the dialog window, search for your logical component (in our example, Z_PI_COMP), and select it (see Figure 4.24). Click on CONTINUE.

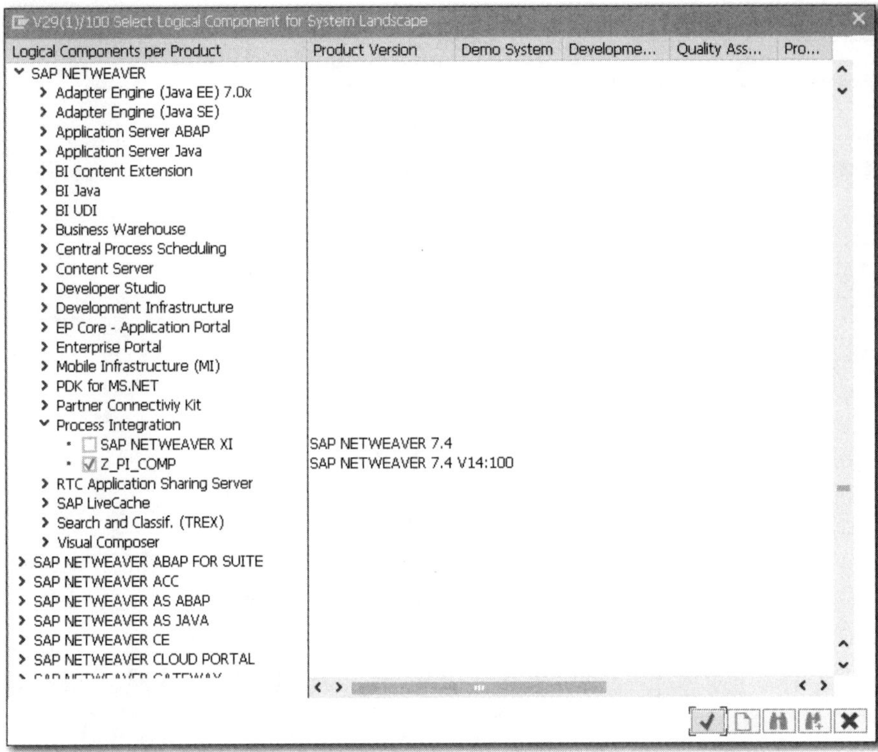

Figure 4.24 Selecting the Logical Component

7. The logical component has been assigned to your solution (see Figure 4.25). Click on SAVE. Then choose BACK to exit Solution Directory maintenance.

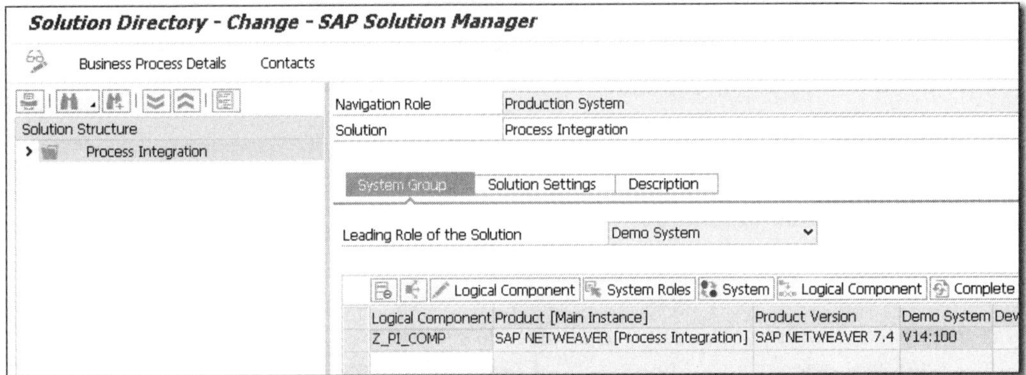

Figure 4.25 Solution with Assigned Logical Component

8. The work center's solution overview now displays the assignment to the logical component and the systems contained therein under DETAILS OF SOLUTION: PROCESS INTEGRATION (see Figure 4.26).

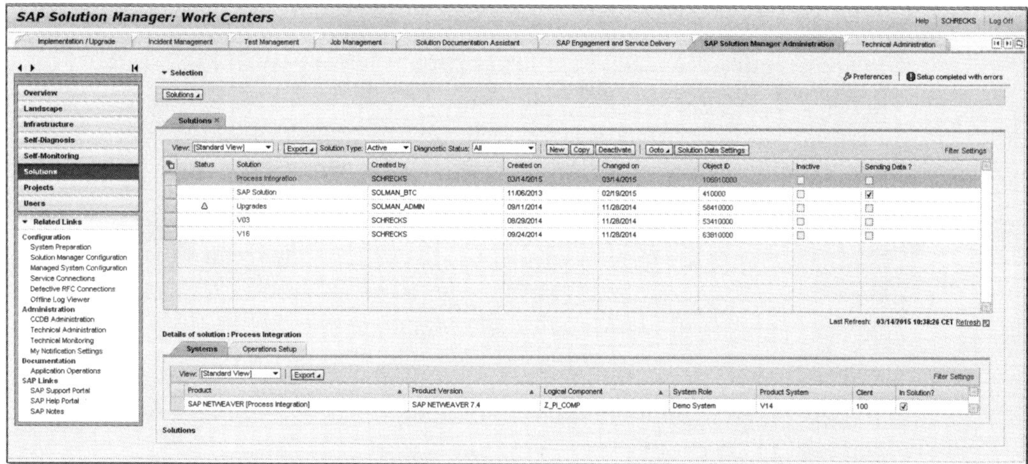

Figure 4.26 Solution Details in the Work Center

Your solution is now created, and its basic configuration has been completed. You can now use it for maintenance transactions in the Maintenance Optimizer (see Section 4.4).

Deactivating and Deleting Solutions [+]

You can deactivate solutions in the solution overview if you don't want to use them any longer or want to delete them. You can delete inactive solutions only.

4.2.5 Configuring Managed Systems

To be able to use all functions of SAP Solution Manager, you must configure the managed systems. Configuration is incremental and supported by a wizard—similar to the system preparation and the basic configuration of SAP Solution Manager.

Within the scope of configuring managed systems, you establish RFC connections between SAP Solution Manager and the managed system, connect the diagnostics or host agents that are installed on the target system, and run additional manual or automatic configuration steps. The tasks can be rather comprehensive and go beyond the scope of this book. Nevertheless, we want to give you a rough impression of the necessary activities.

To configure a managed system, follow these steps:

1. In SAP Solution Manager, start Transaction SOLMAN_WORKCENTER or Transaction SM_WORKCENTER. Choose the SAP SOLUTION MANAGER: CONFIGURATION work center. Then, click on MANAGED SYSTEMS CONFIGURATION.
2. A list of known technical systems is displayed (see Figure 4.27). Unconfigured systems are labeled with the NOT PERFORMED status ◇; in this case, the SYSTEM STATUS is ERROR. Initially, make sure that the SUCCESS icon ■ is displayed in the PLUG-IN STATUS table column for your technical system. If this isn't the case, you must update the ABAP software component ST-PI in the system to be managed.
3. To start the configuration wizard for a system, select the system in the list, and click on the CONFIGURE SYSTEM button.

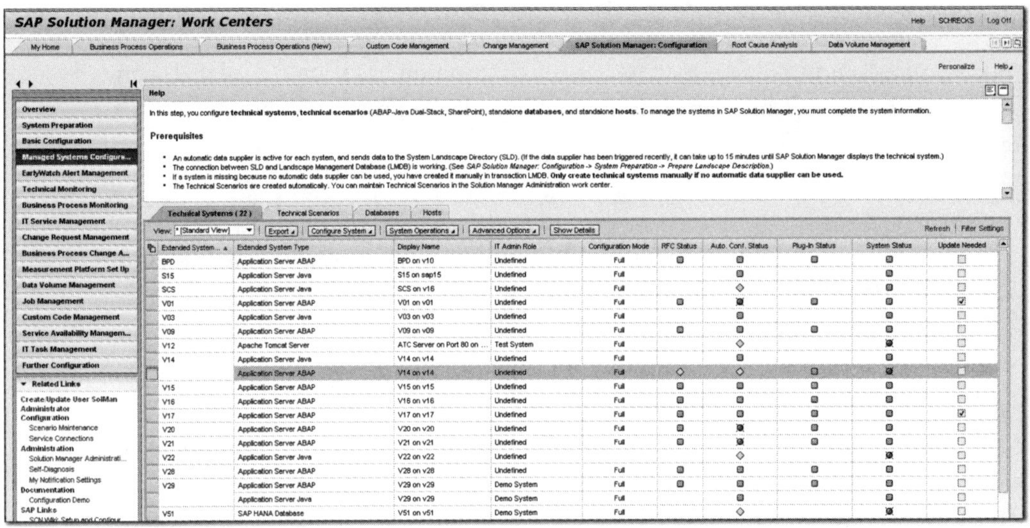

Figure 4.27 Initial Screen for Configuring the Managed System

4. Click on the EDIT button to switch to change mode (see Figure 4.28).

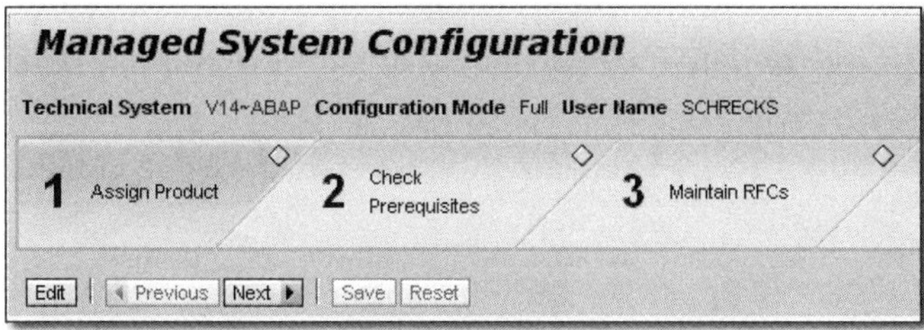

Figure 4.28 Initial Screen of the Configuration Wizard

Help [+]

If you get stuck in the configuration of individual steps, read the text in the HELP area first. Often, a DOCUMENTATION column is available containing links to additional information. In case of errors, a link is available right next to the message (LONG TEXT or DETAILS) in the LOG area. This link provides you with further information and solution approaches.

5. Now go through the individual steps of the wizard. The HELP area informs you about the meaning and the background of the respective step (see Figure 4.29). In case of an error, the LOG area displays messages including long text and usually a solution approach. After you've edited a configuration screen, click on NEXT to go to the next step.

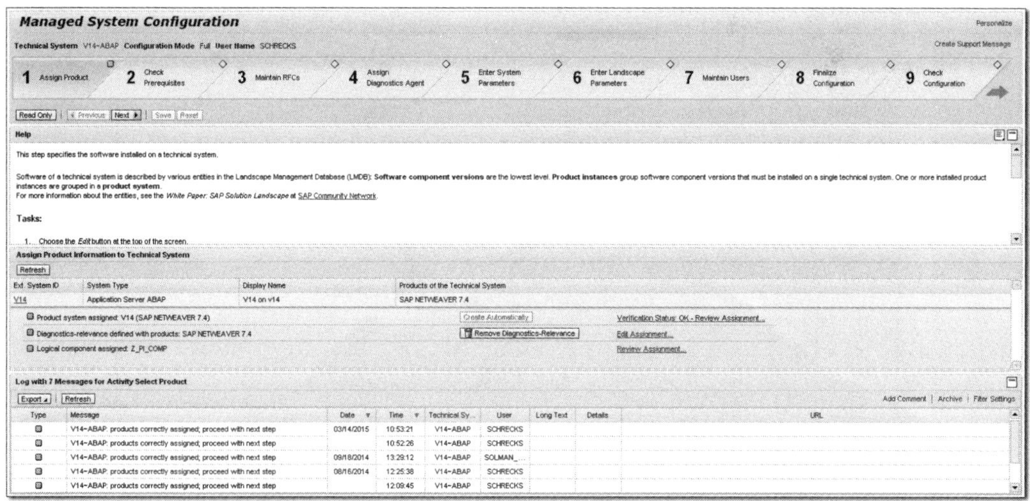

Figure 4.29 "Assign Product" Step Completed

6. If a step comprises AUTOMATIC ACTIVITIES, as in step 2 in Figure 4.30, either click on EXECUTE ALL or select the required activities, and then click on the EXECUTE SELECTED button. SAP Solution Manager starts a background job that executes the activity automatically.

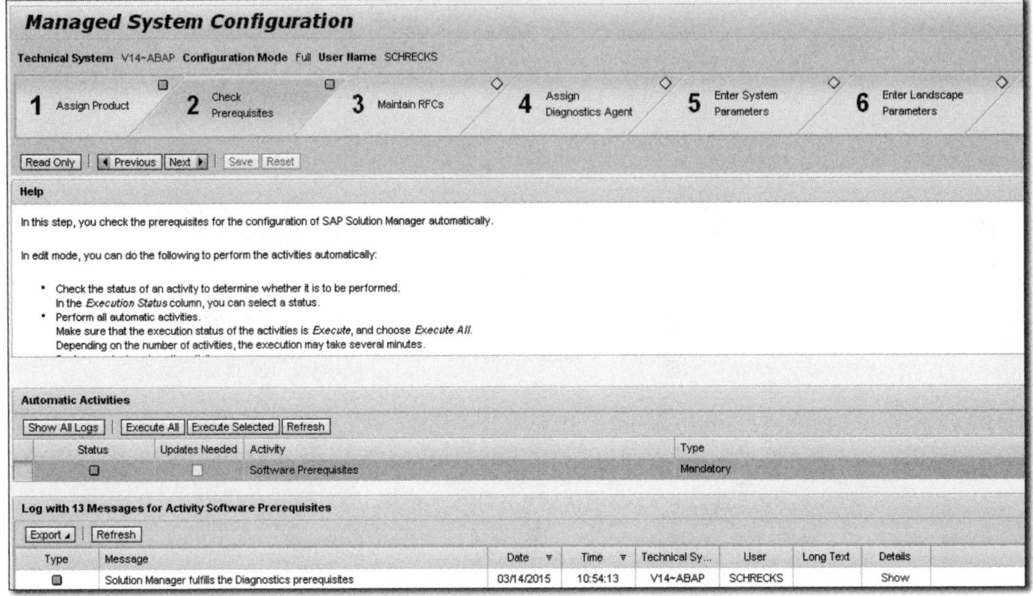

Figure 4.30 Executing Automatic Activities in Step 2

7. In the MAINTAIN RFCs step, create at least the RFC connections to the leading client of the system to be managed (e.g., CLIENT 100; see Figure 4.31). No separate RFC connections are usually required for Clients 000, 001, and 066.

[+]

Trusted System Connections

Trusted system connections eliminate the need for password logons and therefore also the transfer of passwords within the network. Trusted system connections can be identified in RFC destination maintenance (Transaction SM59; see Chapter 2, Section 2.6.1) by the setting TRUSTED SYSTEM • YES on the LOGON & SECURITY tab.

If you want to use a trusted system connection, you must create a relationship of trust between the two systems involved. You use Transaction SMT1 to define which systems are trusted systems. The counterpart of a *trusted* system is its *trusting* system, which you can view in Transaction SMT2. These entries are generated automatically in the partner system when it's created as a trusted system.

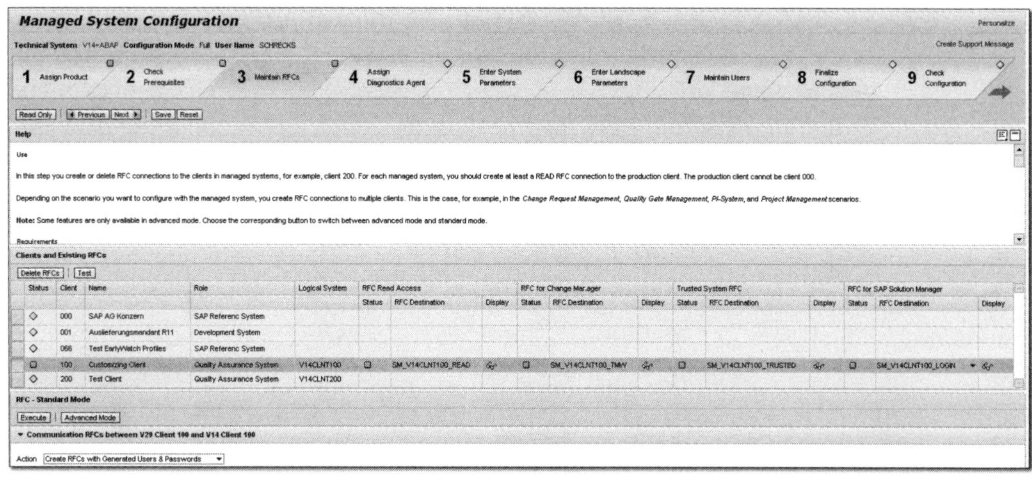

Figure 4.31 Generating RFC Connections

8. If you want to use the MAI or end-to-end/root cause analysis functions of SAP Solution Manager, you must link the diagnostics agent and the host agent of the managed system with SAP Solution Manager in the Assign Diagnostics Agent step (see Figure 4.32).

Diagnostics Agents

You can find essential additional information on the installation, configuration, and updates of diagnostics agents in SAP Notes 1365123, 1833501, and 1858920.

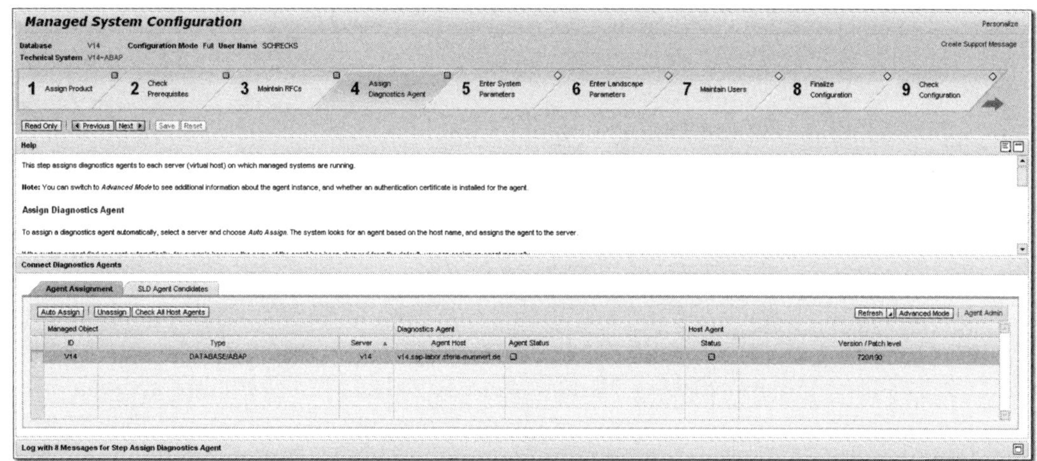

Figure 4.32 Assign Diagnostics Agent

9. The ENTER SYSTEM PARAMETERS step is particularly important for the root cause analysis (see Figure 4.33). Under COMMON PARAMETERS, you can right-click to open the context menu where you can access the quick help to obtain further information. Note that the database extractor for collecting database-specific monitoring data must be licensed before you may use it.

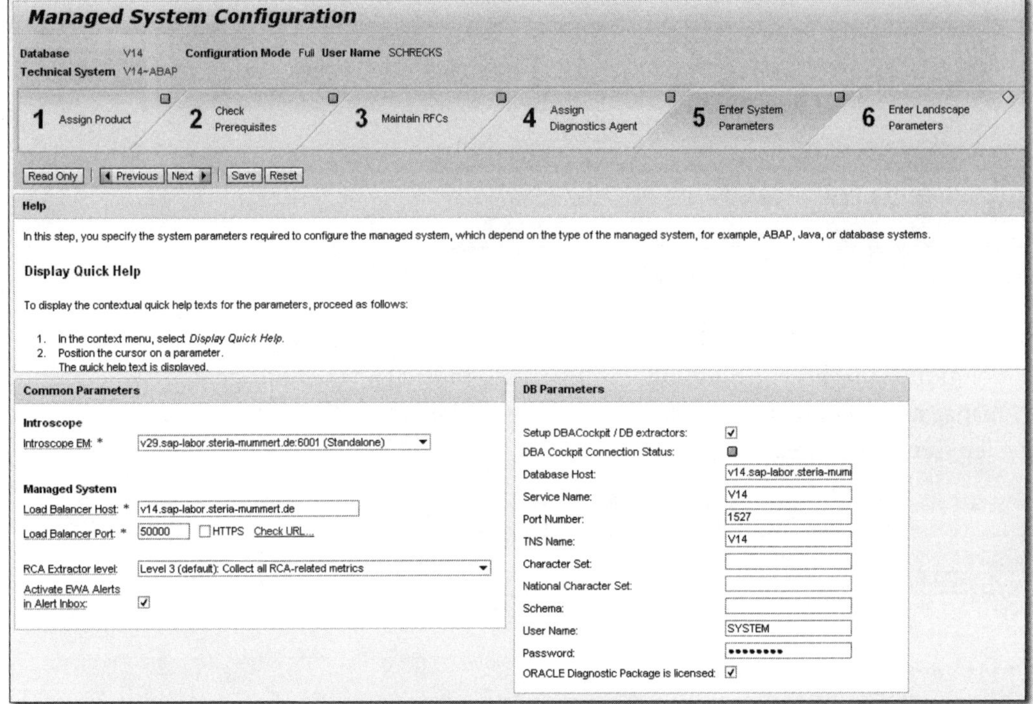

Figure 4.33 Entering the Wiley Introscope System Parameter

10. In the ENTER LANDSCAPE PARAMETERS step, you just need to edit a few details for which you can usually keep the default values (see Figure 4.34). By selecting the CHECK EXISTENCE OF PATHS WHEN SAVING checkbox, the system ensures the correctness of your entries.

11. In the MAINTAIN USERS step, you create users in the managed system (see Figure 4.35). Ensure that the proposed role names comply with your security conventions—making changes retroactively is usually more tedious than adhering to the security concept upon creation.

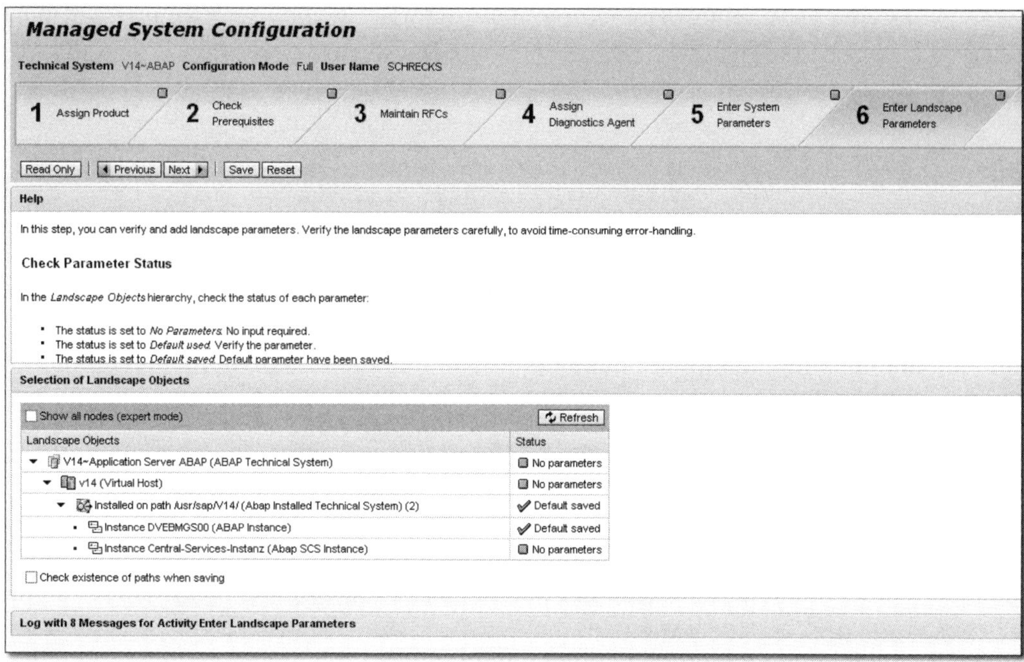

Figure 4.34 Entering Landscape Parameters

Figure 4.35 Maintaining Users in the Managed System

12. The Finalize Configuration step comprises several automatic and manual steps (see Figure 4.36). As a minimum requirement, execute the steps that are marked as Mandatory.

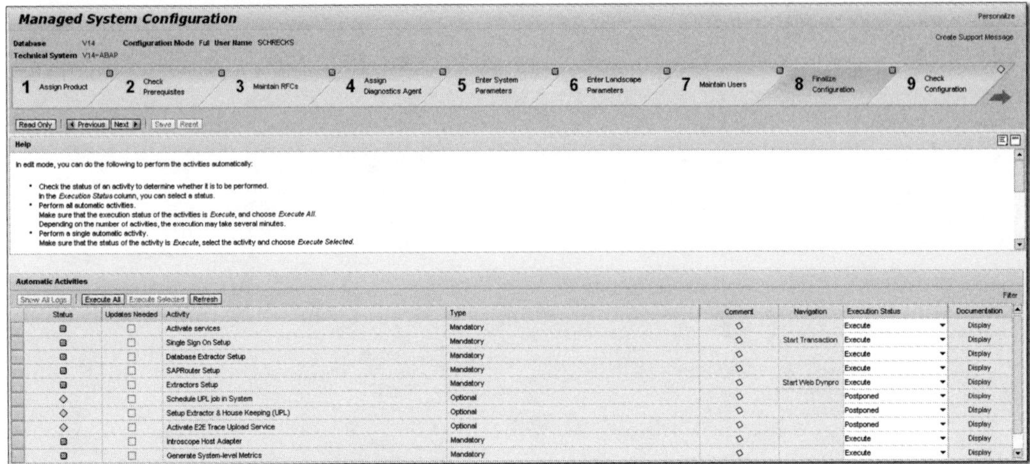

Figure 4.36 Finalize Configuration

13. Finally, in the Check Configuration step, you start a job that verifies all settings of the managed system (see Figure 4.37). If no error occurs, you complete the configuration wizard in the next step.

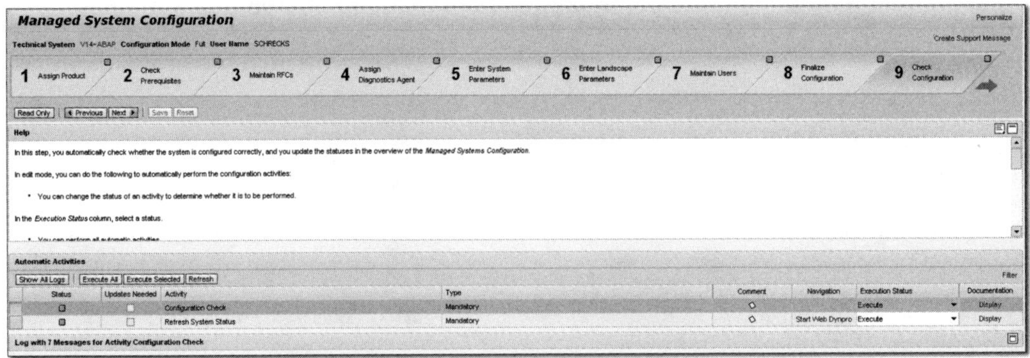

Figure 4.37 Check Configuration

14. The configurations made are summarized for you. Click on FINISH to close the window (see Figure 4.38).

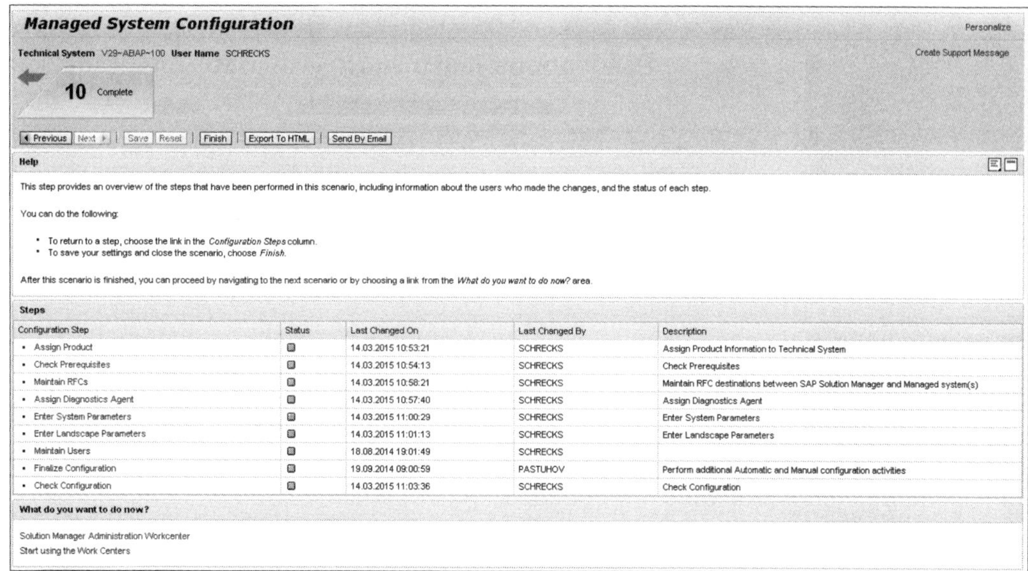

Figure 4.38 Finishing the Configuration

15. The initial screen of the configuration for managed systems displays the updated status of the system configuration (see Figure 4.39).

Technical Systems (22) | Technical Scenarios | Databases | Hosts

View: * [Standard View] | Export | Configure System | System Operations | Advanced Options | Show Details | Refresh | Filter Settings

Extended System...	Extended System Type	Display Name	IT Admin Role	Configuration Mode	RFC Status	Auto. Conf. Status	Plug-In Status	System Status	Update Needed
SCS	Application Server Java	SCS on v16	Undefined	Full					
V01	Application Server ABAP	V01 on v01	Undefined	Full					
V03	Application Server Java	V03 on v03	Undefined	Full					
V09	Application Server ABAP	V09 on v09	Undefined	Full					
V12	Apache Tomcat Server	ATC Server on Port 80 on ...	Test System	Full					
V14	Application Server Java	V14 on v14	Undefined	Full					
	Application Server ABAP	V14 on v14	Undefined	Full					
V15	Application Server ABAP	V15 on v15	Undefined	Full					

Figure 4.39 Updated Overview of Managed Systems

Configuring managed systems is a prerequisite for most of the application cases of SAP Solution Manager that go beyond the scope of Maintenance Optimizer. If you also want to use functions such as end-to-end analysis or root cause analysis as well as the MAI, you can't skip complete configuration. This ultimately means that you must install *CA Wily Introscope*, which considerably increases the complexity of your system landscape and thus the administration effort.

[+]

CA Wily Introscope Enterprise Manager

CA Wily Introscope Enterprise Manager processes the performance data of your managed systems that is collected by the agents. It then provides the data to SAP Solution Manager for evaluation. SAP Note 797147 CA provides information on how to install Wily Introscope Enterprise Manager. A requirement for connecting managed systems with CA Wily Introscope Enterprise Manager is that you've successfully completed the CONFIGURE CA INTROSCOPE step of the basic configuration within Transaction SOLMAN_SETUP.

4.3 System Administration

System administrators are likely to be most interested in finding out about the functions provided by SAP Solution Manager for administration and technical administration of the SAP systems. SAP Solution Manager covers the following areas:

- System and application monitoring
- Technical analyses
- Root cause analysis and exception management
- Central system administration

This section describes how you can use these functions for the administration of your system landscape.

4.3.1 Technical Monitoring and Alerting

The *Monitoring and Alerting Infrastructure* (MAI) is an essential improvement that was introduced with SAP Solution Manager 7.1. It succeeds the CCMS Alert Monitor (see Chapter 3) and comprises a much more complex architecture based on diagnostics agents and CA Wily Introscope Enterprise Manager, among other things. The *solution tool plug-ins* in the ABAP system (components ST-PI and ST-A/PI) play a significant role by providing functions in the target system that SAP Solution Manager requires for extracting data. SAP BW technology is used within SAP Solution Manager to store and format the data collected.

You must successfully complete the system preparation and the basic configuration of SAP Solution Manager in Transaction SOLMAN_SETUP to use MAI. In particular, you must install CA Wily Introscope Enterprise Manager and connect the diagnostics agents. Furthermore, you must link the systems to be monitored as managed systems in SAP Solution Manager as described in Section 4.2.

Configuring the Technical Monitoring

After you've made all necessary preparations, you can set up the technical monitoring using one of the tried and tested wizards. The following section describes the essential steps:

1. In SAP Solution Manager, start Transaction SOLMAN_SETUP, and then click on TECHNICAL MONITORING.
2. Make sure that the SYSTEM MONITORING option under TECHNICAL MONITORING is activated (see Figure 4.40). Switch to change mode, and click on NEXT.

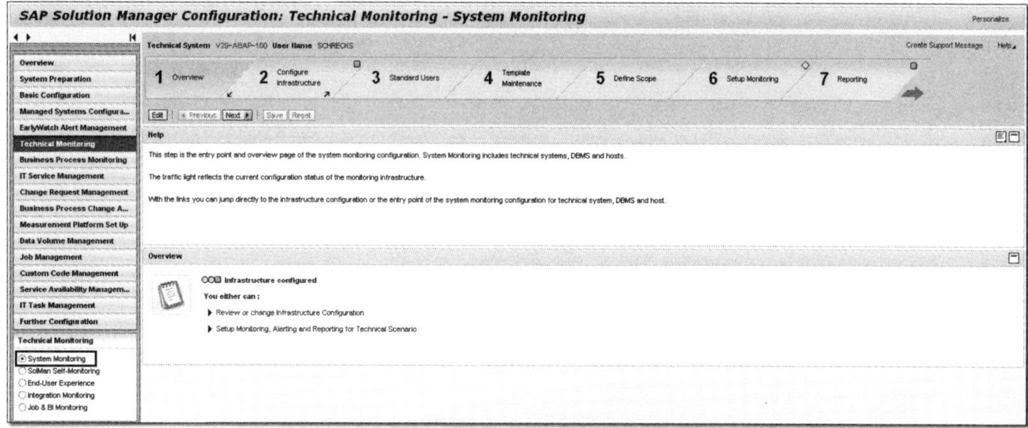

Figure 4.40 Initial Screen for Configuring the System Monitoring

3. In the DEFAULT SETTINGS step, for example, you define on the NOTIFICATIONS tab which users are informed with which notification method (email/text message) if alerts occur during monitoring (see Figure 4.41).
4. Because a large amount of data can be collected, and your SAP Solution Manager database could grow massively depending on how many systems you include in monitoring, you have the option to specify the retention period of measurement data (*metrics*) (see Figure 4.42).

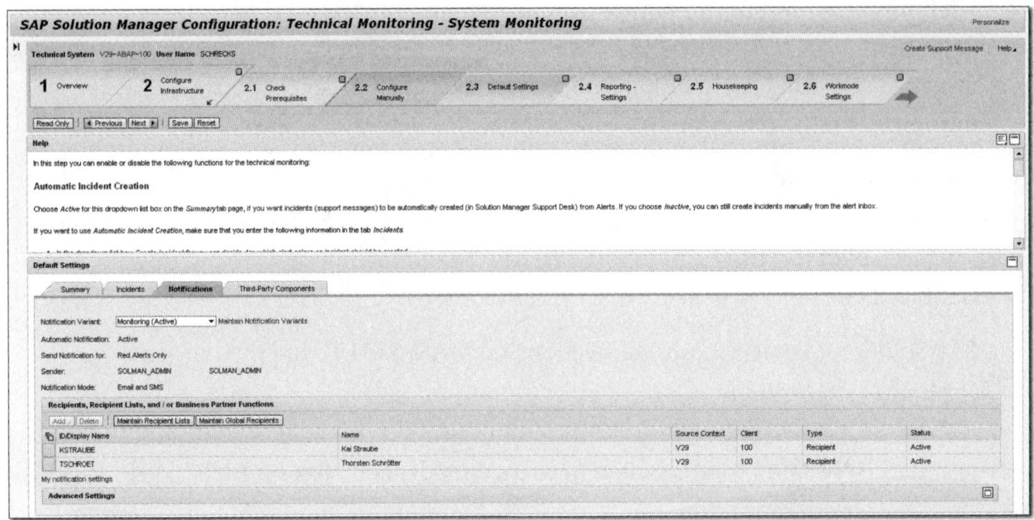

Figure 4.41 Making Settings for Notifications

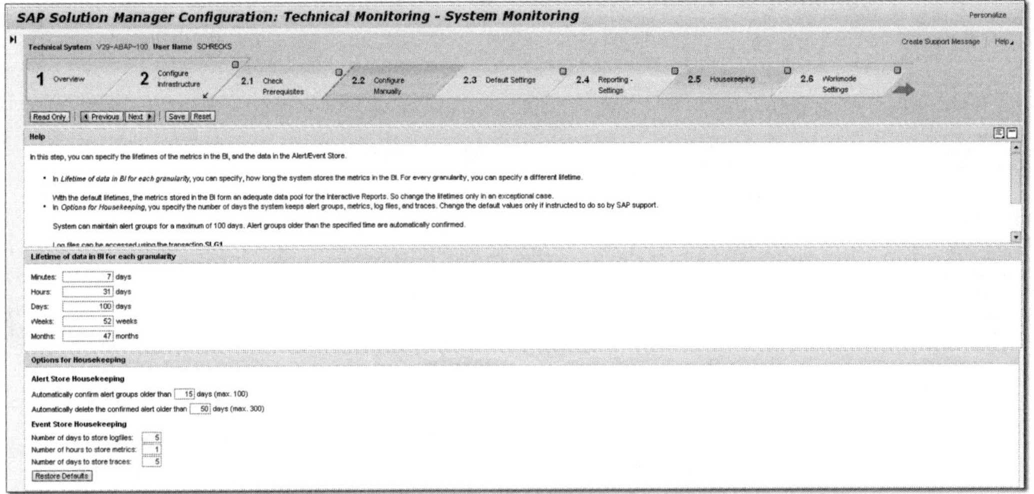

Figure 4.42 Defining the Retention Period for Metrics

5. You can also determine the work modes for which you want to activate monitoring (see Figure 4.43). For example, it's useful to deactivate monitoring during system maintenance or scheduled unavailability of the system. Otherwise, this would cause unnecessary alerts that might prevent you from noticing important messages.

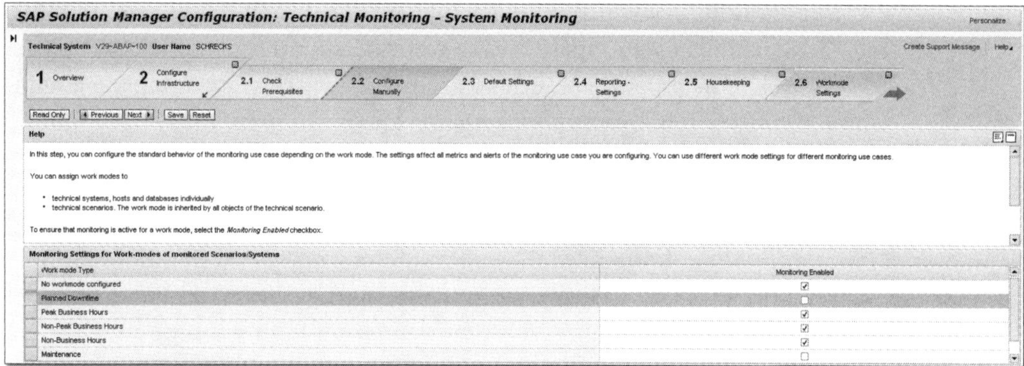

Figure 4.43 Defining Work Modes for Monitoring

[+]

Work Mode Management

Work modes are maintained centrally in *Work Mode Management*, which you can find in the TECHNICAL ADMINISTRATION work center. Here, you make the settings for the work modes and can switch individual systems to a specific mode.

6. SAP regularly provides updates for the monitoring content, which you can download and import in the setup area. Simple updates of content are usually unproblematic. After you've downloaded new content, you must activate or apply it (see Figure 4.44). However, you should first analyze it using the COMPARE button because the template that you've used for monitoring so far (see the TEMPLATE MAINTENANCE step) could be subjected to major changes otherwise.

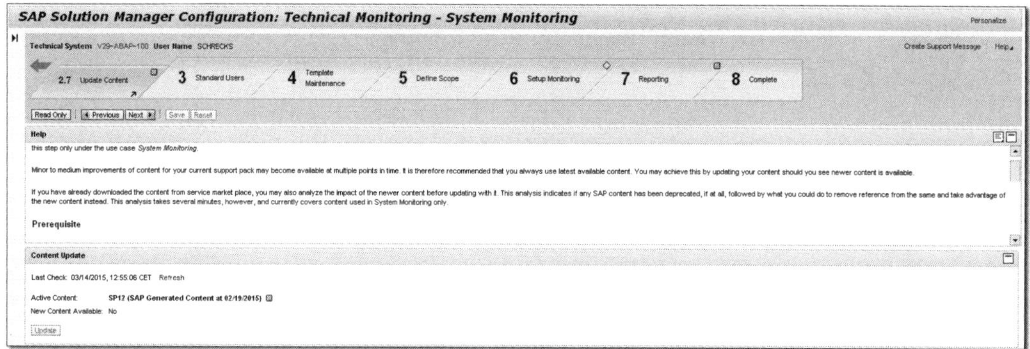

Figure 4.44 Activating the Monitoring Content

7. SAP's monitoring content provides templates for setting the system monitoring. These templates are based on the respective system types and are preset accordingly. If necessary, you can adapt the templates in the template administration to your requirements (see Figure 4.45).

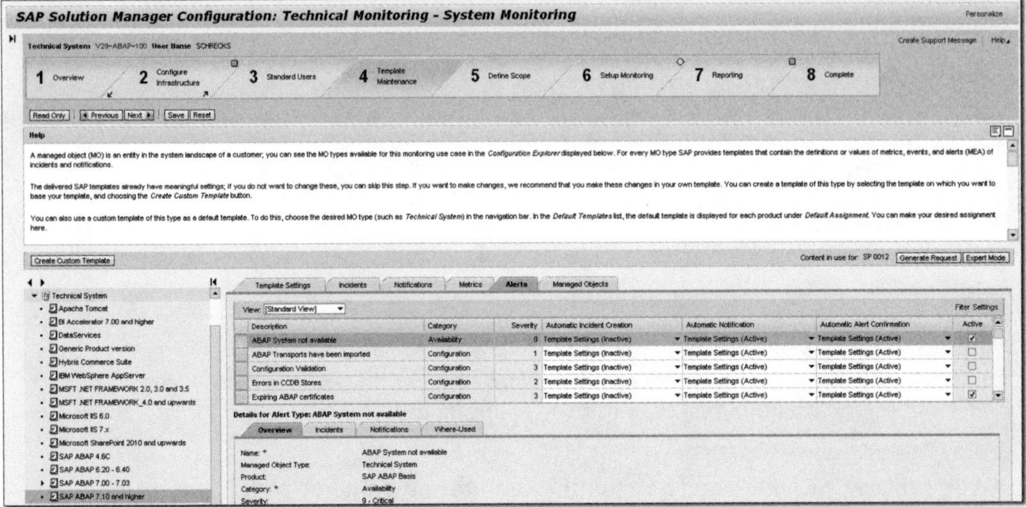

Figure 4.45 Adapting the Monitoring Templates

8. Specify which systems you want to add to your monitoring. Select these systems in the DEFINE SCOPE step, and click on NEXT (see Figure 4.46).

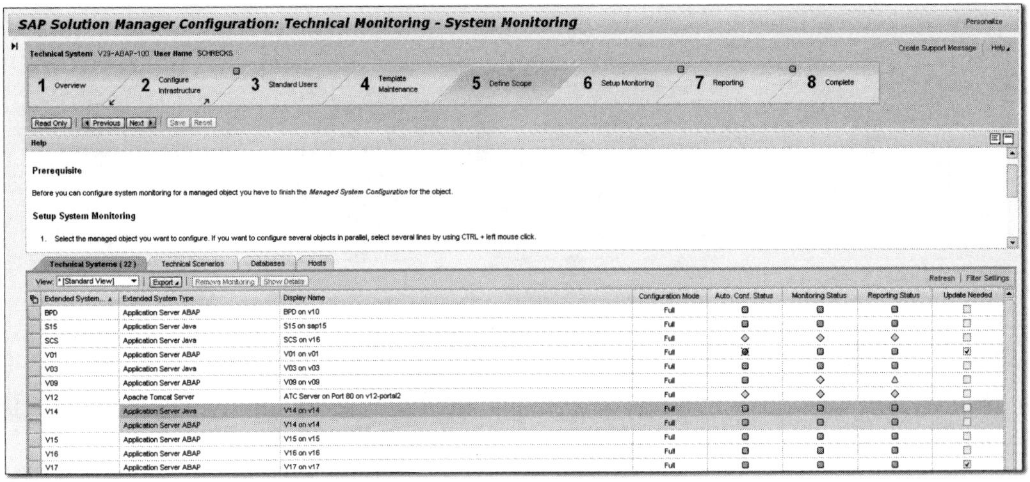

Figure 4.46 Defining the Systems to Be Monitored

9. In the next step, assign an appropriate template to the systems you've selected (see Figure 4.47). If you click on RESTORE DEFAULTS during initial configuration, SAP Solution Manager proposes templates. Then click on APPLY AND ACTIVATE.

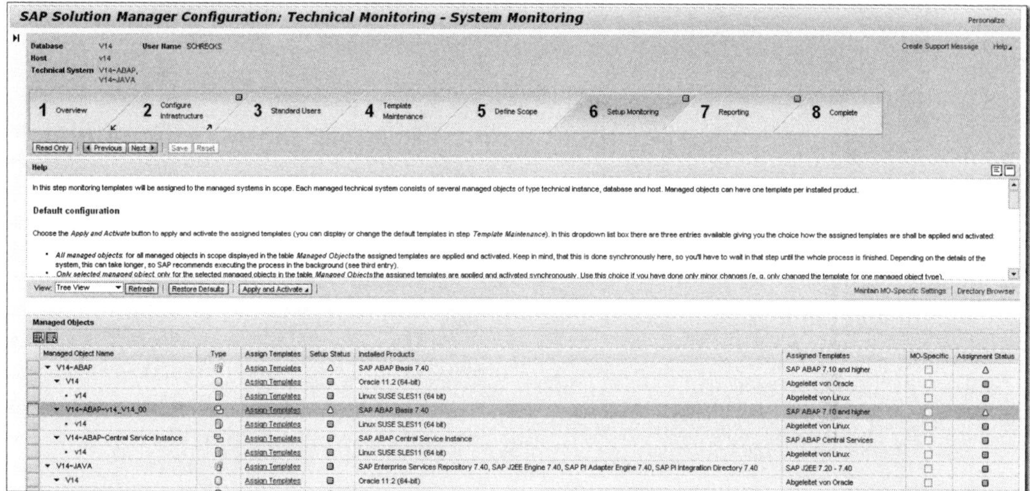

Figure 4.47 Assigning Monitoring Templates

10. Next, check the extraction settings, and, if required, activate the collection of metrics for individual systems using the ACTIVATE button. All systems should have the status REPORTING ACTIVE ■ (see Figure 4.48).

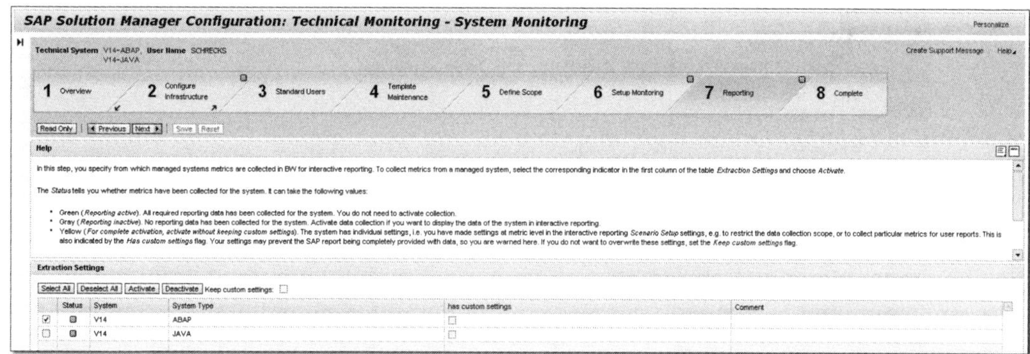

Figure 4.48 Checking the Extraction Settings

11. After you've successfully completed all steps, you can finish the technical monitoring setup (see Figure 4.49).

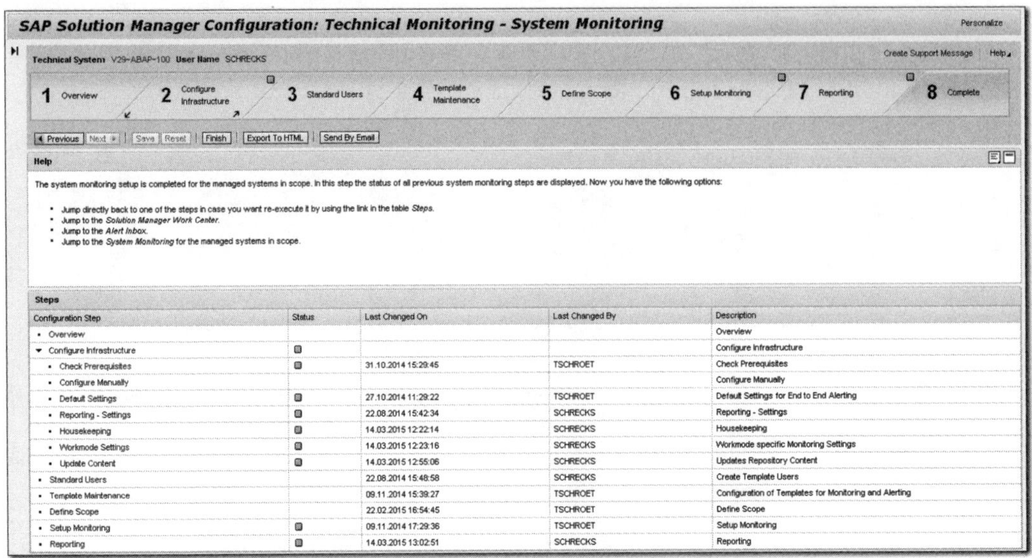

Figure 4.49 Finishing the Configuration of System Monitoring

Monitoring Systems with Technical Monitoring

As soon as you've completed the setup of the technical monitoring, you can evaluate the collected alerts and performance data centrally in SAP Solution Manager. The TECHNICAL MONITORING work center is the entry point. Technical monitoring comprises various functions:

- **Alerting**
  Central inbox for warning messages.
- **System monitoring**
  Overview of the current status of systems.
- **Job and BI monitoring**
  Monitoring of jobs and BI processes.
- **Monitoring integration**
  Interface monitoring.
- **End user monitoring**
  Performance evaluations from the end user's perspective (*End User Experience Monitoring*, EEM).

- **Automated evaluations**
  EarlyWatch alerts and Service Level Agreement (SLA) reports.
- **Interactive evaluations**
  Various reports on performance topics.

To not go beyond the scope of this book, we only provide a short description of the classic monitoring functions of alerting and system monitoring in the following:

1. In SAP Solution Manager, start Transaction SOLMAN_WORKCENTER (or Transaction SM_WORKCENTER), and then go to the TECHNICAL MONITORING tab.
2. Select one of the options from the overview, for example, ALERT INBOX (see Figure 4.50).

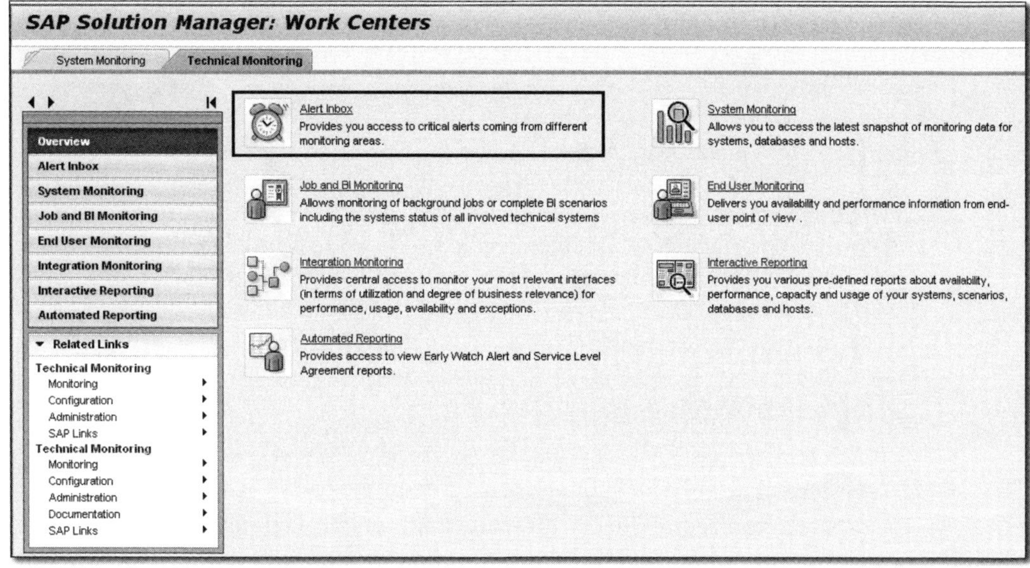

Figure 4.50 Technical Monitoring Work Center

3. The system displays a table which includes alerts that were received since a specific point in time and which are sorted by message priority in descending order (see Figure 4.51).
4. Choose an alert from the inbox list. In the alert view (the table at the bottom), for example, click on the first row and the entry in the STATUS column.

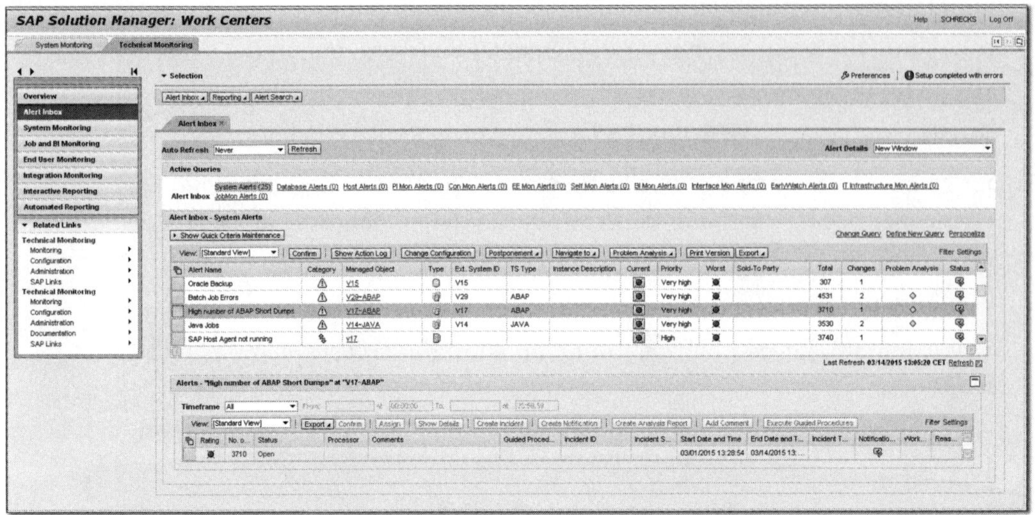

Figure 4.51 Alert Inbox List

[⚙]

Alert Groups

Compared to the old CCMS technology, a major benefit of alerting in MAI is that you can *group* alerts. So, if an alert was triggered and the corresponding threshold value is no longer exceeded afterwards, all measurements are combined in an alert group (e.g., "CPU utilization > 90%" as a group of alerts for value exceedances for a period of 30 minutes). MAI recognizes that the individual events belong together and notifies you only once.

In the CCMS architecture, every measurement is handled as a separate alert. As a result, you receive a notification on threshold value exceedances for each measurement (e.g., every five minutes).

5. The alert details provide more information on the error cause (see Figure 4.52). Moreover, you're provided with many additional functions:
   - You can assign the alert to a processing user using the Assign button.
   - You can use the Create Incident button to integrate alerts with Incident Management in SAP Solution Manager and to generate a message in the service desk.
   - You can use the Create Notification button to send the alert (e.g., by email) to your expert contact person on the user side.

- After the alert has been processed and the problem has been eliminated, you can close it with the CONFIRM button. It's then removed from the alert inbox.
- If you establish that the alerting settings you've made during setup don't meet your requirements, you can modify them in the list view using the CHANGE CONFIGURATION button—either for the entire template (and thus for all systems assigned to it) or for the selected system only (see Figure 4.53).

6. Return to the initial technical monitoring screen. Now choose the SYSTEM MONITORING option (see Figure 4.54).

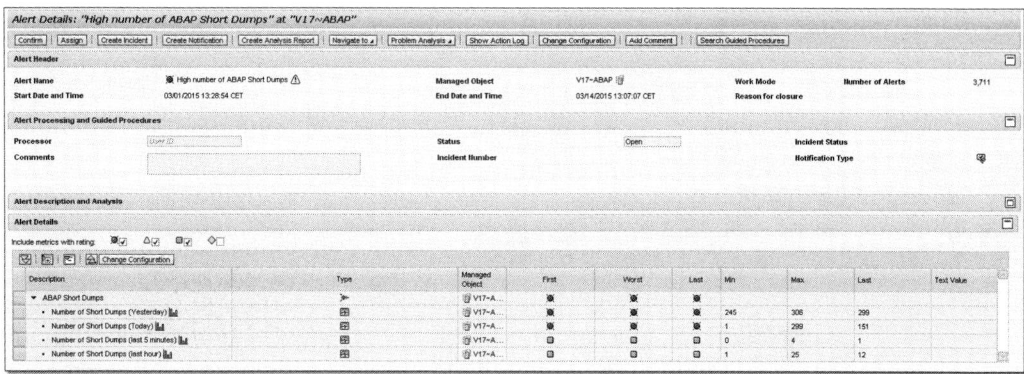

Figure 4.52 Alert Details

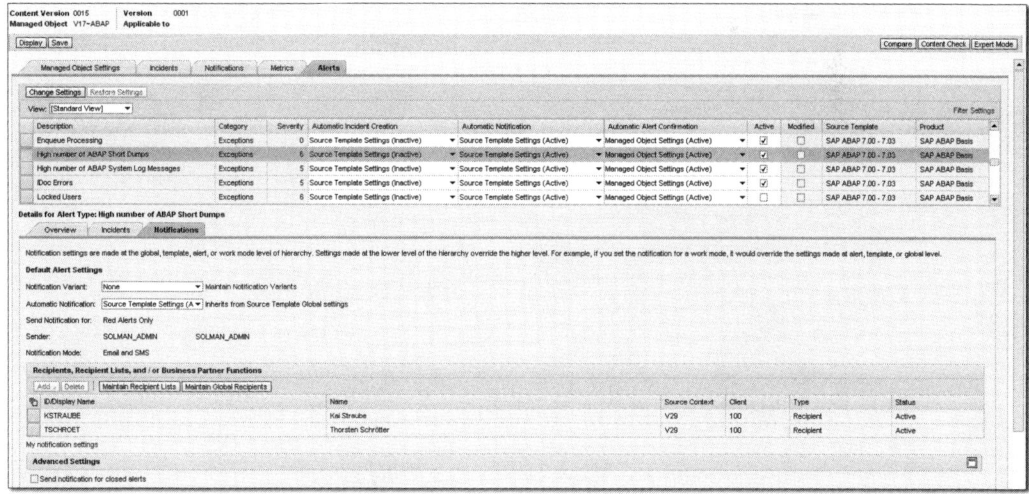

Figure 4.53 Modifying the Alert Settings

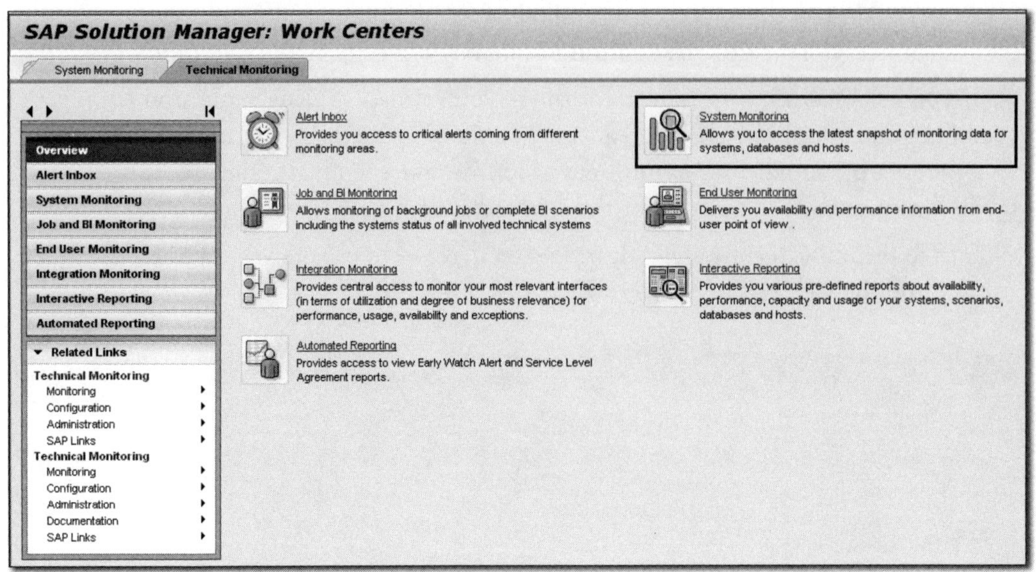

Figure 4.54 Initial Screen of System Monitoring

7. On the SYSTEMS tab, choose a system for which you want to start system monitoring, and click on SYSTEM MONITORING (see Figure 4.55). You can also choose multiple systems.

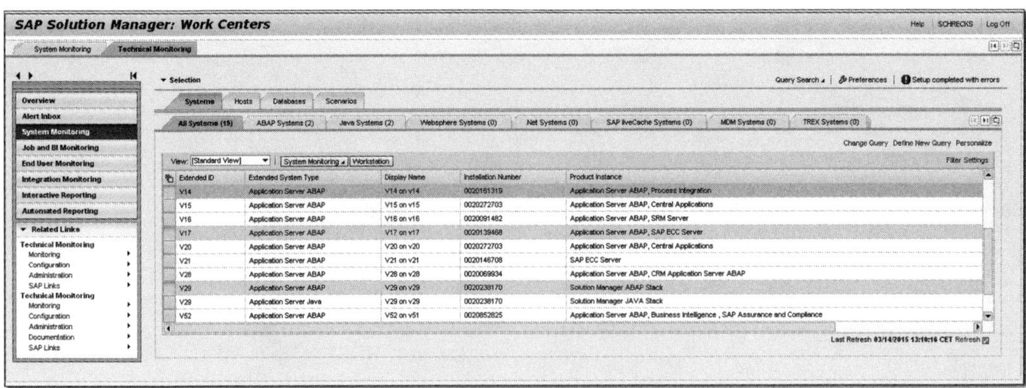

Figure 4.55 Selecting a System for Monitoring

8. The systems selected are displayed in a list. The system statuses are represented with traffic light colors respectively. This considers the availability, perfor-

mance, system configuration, handling of exceptions, alerting, and configuration status of technical monitoring. Click on a row to go to the detail view (see Figure 4.56).

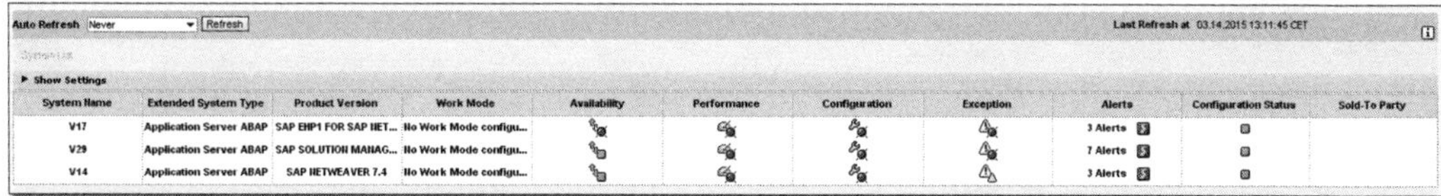

Figure 4.56 Status Overview of Monitored Systems

9. The system view provides a graphical display of the statuses of the individual system components, such as host, database, instance, and technical system (see Figure 4.57). Click on one of the traffic light icons to navigate to the detail view of this system component.

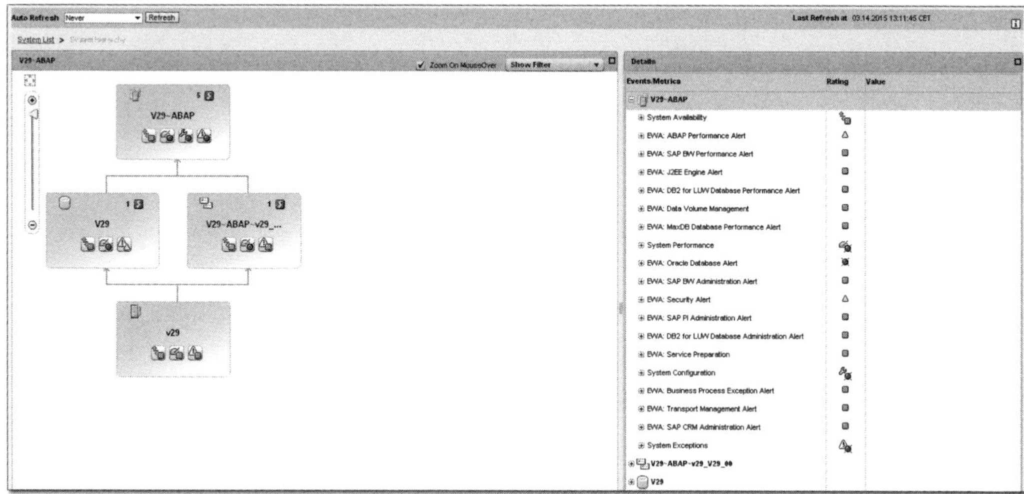

Figure 4.57 Detail View for a Monitored System

10. In the graphic on the left-hand side of the system component view, you can choose individual monitoring categories (e.g., CPU, memory; see Figure 4.58). The tree structure on the right-hand side then displays a node for this area with its key figures and current measurement values.
11. The details for the measurement and the threshold values are displayed if you position the cursor on a value (see Figure 4.59).

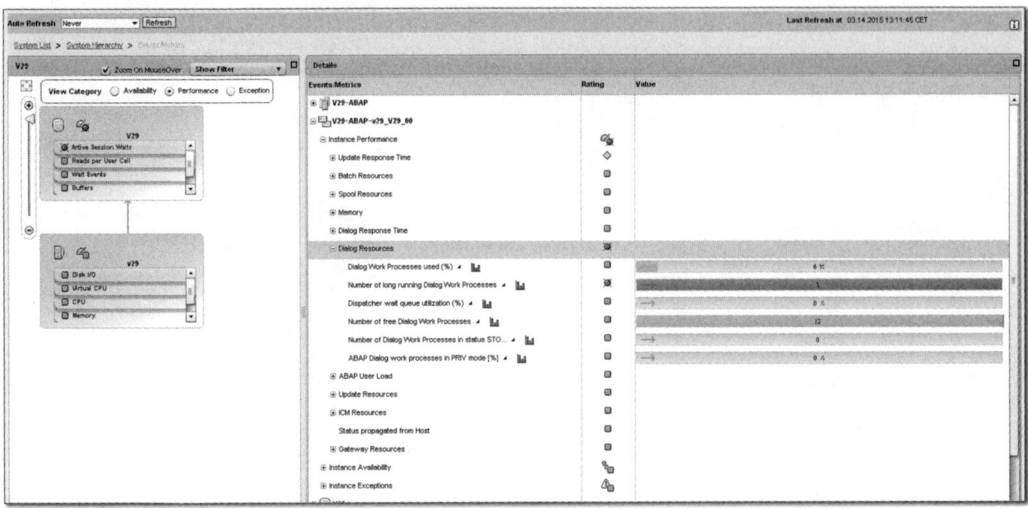

Figure 4.58 Display of Measurement Values for the Dialog Resources Area

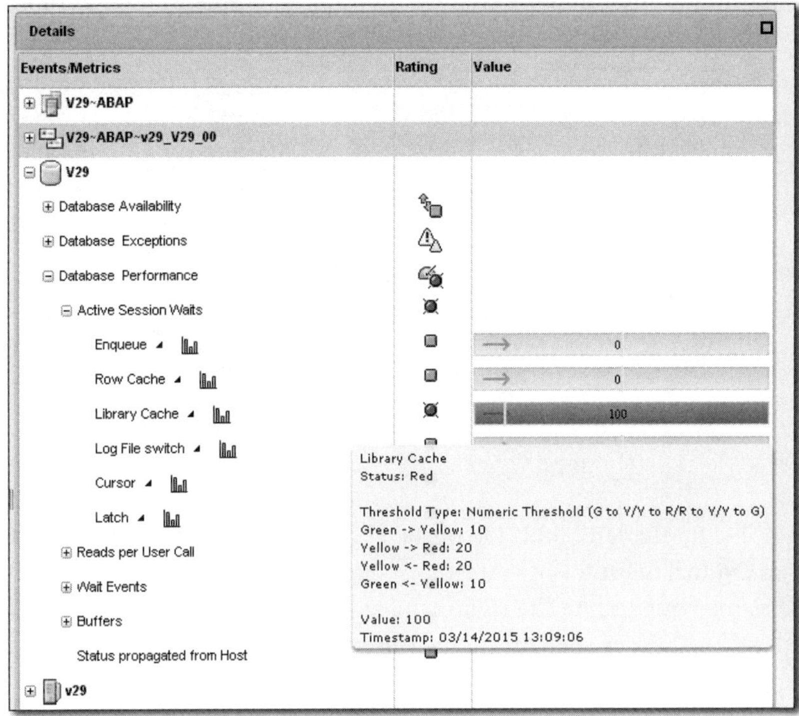

Figure 4.59 Measurement Details and Threshold Values

12. You can open the context menu of metrics by clicking on the small triangle next to a node. It contains some options; for example, you can call the documentation of the key figure, modify the configuration (e.g., threshold values), and view details for data collection (see Figure 4.60).

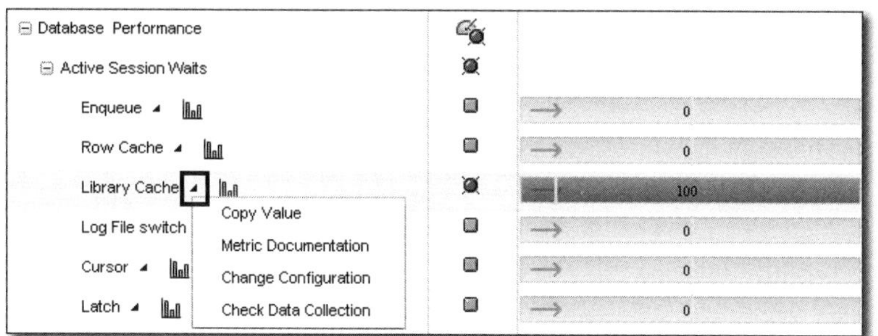

Figure 4.60 Context Menu with Additional Functions

13. The data collection details, for example, inform you whether the measurement is up to date and when the next measurement takes place (see Figure 4.61).

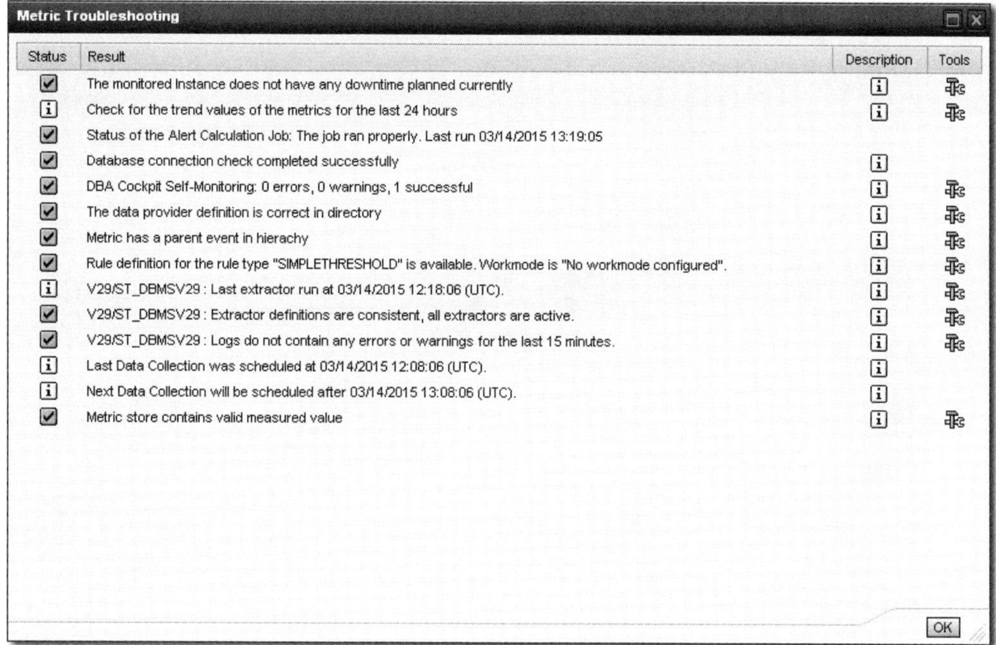

Figure 4.61 Details for Collecting Measurement Data

14. The *metric monitor* provides information on the measurement progress. For this purpose, click on the Launch Metric Monitoring icon in the measurement value list (see Figure 4.62).

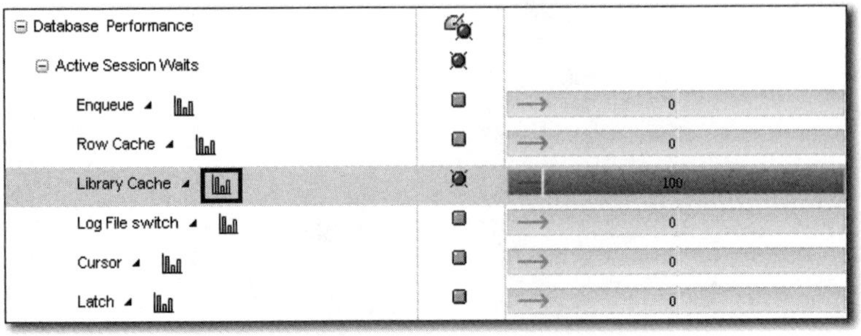

Database Performance
Active Session Waits
Enqueue 0
Row Cache 0
Library Cache 100
Log File switch 0
Cursor 0
Latch 0

Figure 4.62 Calling the Metric Monitor

15. The metric monitor presents the measurement values on a time bar (see Figure 4.63). If you position the cursor on a specific point of the curve, the corresponding measurement value is displayed. The period of time to be considered can be set via the Calendar icon at the beginning and the end of the time bar. You can also define the desired curve section by drawing a marker box while keeping the left mouse button pressed.

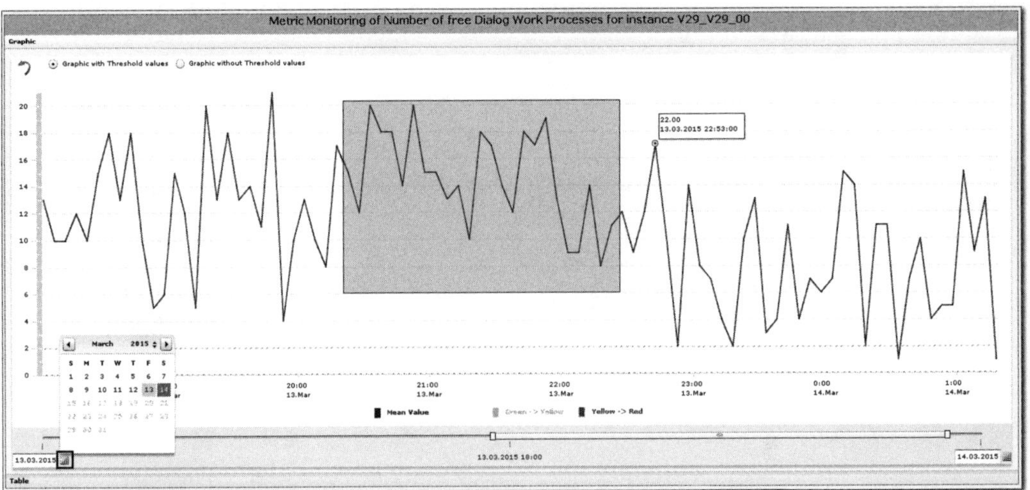

Figure 4.63 Metric Monitor

16. Both the system hierarchy view and the system components view include the icon, which allows you to directly navigate to the alert inbox list of the

respective system (see Figure 4.64). Here you can edit the alerts as described in step 3 (refer to Figure 4.51).

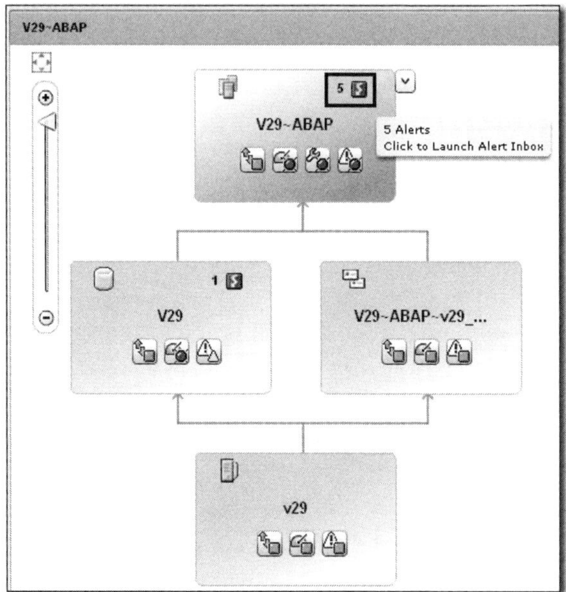

Figure 4.64 Navigating to the Alert Inbox

17. The Workstation button in the system selection view of the Technical Monitoring tab is another interesting detail (see Figure 4.65). If you click on this button, the system takes you to the CA Wily Introscope Workstation.

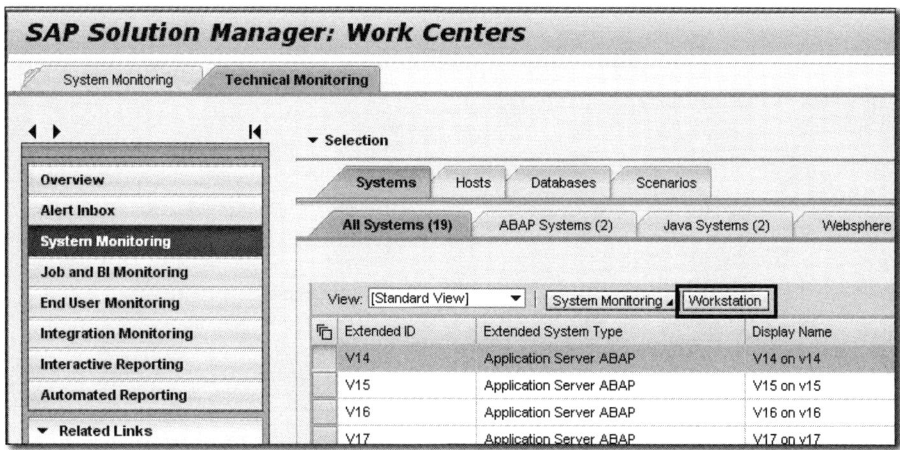

Figure 4.65 Navigating to the CA Wily Introscope Workstation

18. Select a CA Wily installation, and click on START INTROSCOPE (see Figure 4.66). You must authenticate yourself for CA Wily Introscope Enterprise Manager before you're granted access to the workstation.

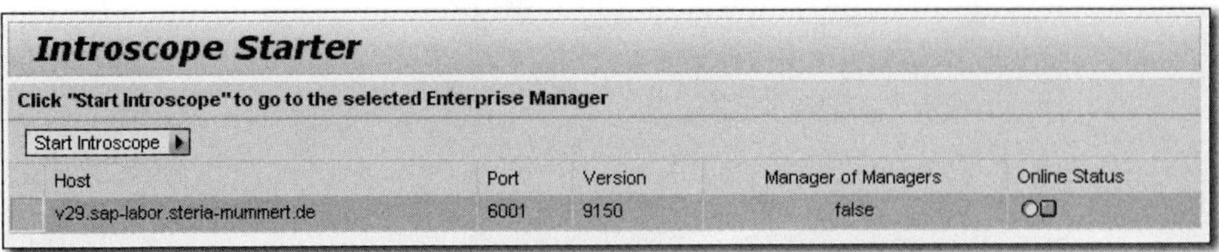

Figure 4.66 Starting CA Wily Introscope Workstation

19. Select one of the displayed dashboards in the workstation, for example, ABAP, and start it by double-clicking (see Figure 4.67).
20. Here, you have direct access to the measurement data collected by CA Wily Introscope Enterprise Manager (see Figure 4.68).

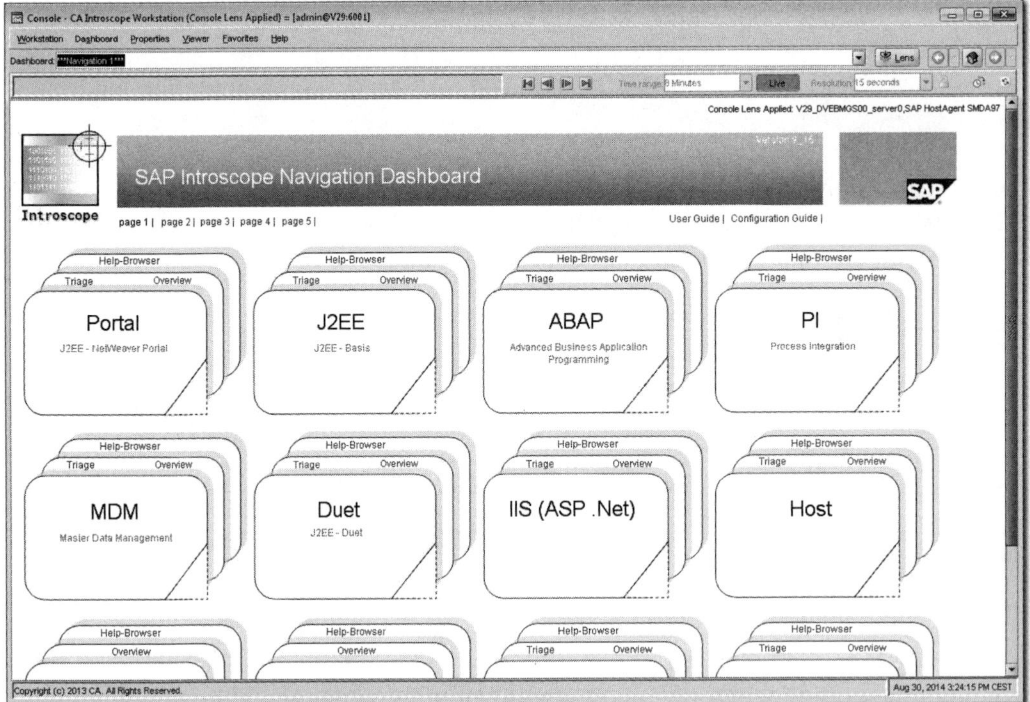

Figure 4.67 Dashboard Overview in the CA Wily Introscope Workstation

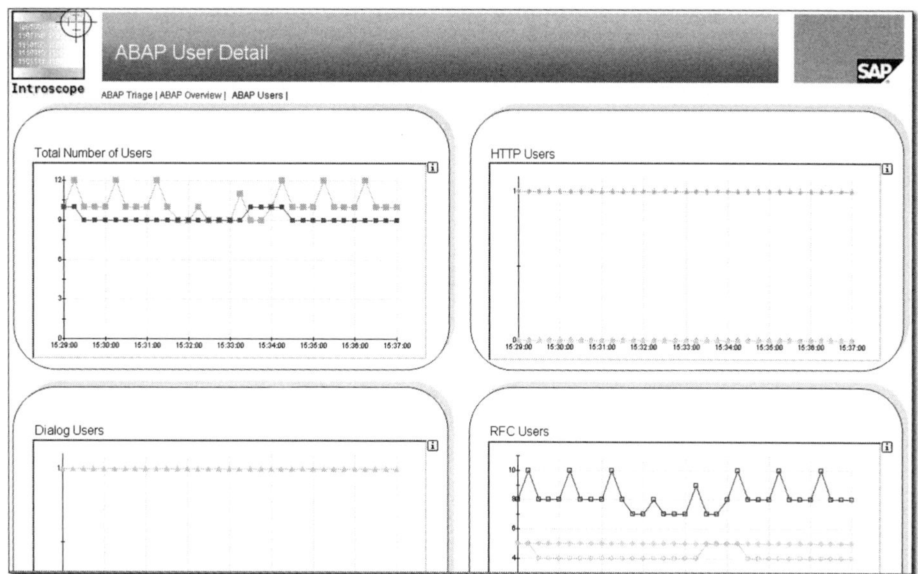

Figure 4.68 Measurement Data Charts of CA Wily Introscope Enterprise Manager

The new MAI is a powerful tool for monitoring system statuses and system performance. In addition to the functions presented here, there are numerous other usage options, for example, monitoring of interfaces, BI or SAP PI systems, and end-user experience monitoring.

4.3.2 End-to-End Analysis

End-to-end analysis (not to be confused with end-user experience monitoring) is part of *root cause analysis* (RCA) of SAP Solution Manager 7.1. Its basic idea is to solve a problem within the system landscape as quickly as possible and with a cause-oriented approach. For this purpose, the end-to-end analysis provides some interesting tools that support your analysis:

- Trace analysis
- Workload analysis
- Change analysis
- Exception analysis

Beyond that, the root cause analysis provides functions for host, system, and database analysis, which we won't discuss here.

Like technical monitoring, end-to-end analysis uses data that is collected by diagnostics agents and via the solution tool plug-ins and then provided to SAP Solution Manager. For this reason, a large amount of data is available for evaluation. We'll outline the end-to-end analysis options based on some usage examples.

[+]

Further Information on Root Cause Analysis

SAP Note 1483508 describes the requirements for using root cause analysis. Additionally, you should also refer to the corresponding wiki page in the SAP Community Network (SCN): *http://wiki.scn.sap.com/wiki/display/TechOps/RCA_Home*.

1. In SAP Solution Manager, start Transaction SOLMAN_WORKCENTER (or Transaction SM_WORKCENTER). Open the Root Cause Analysis work center, and then click on the End-to-End Analysis link (see Figure 4.69).

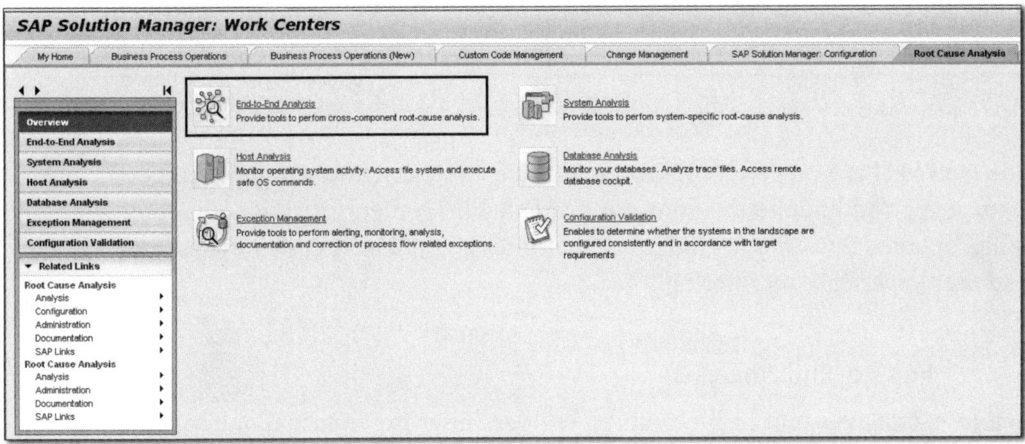

Figure 4.69 Calling the End-to-End Analysis

2. Select a system from the system list, and click on the Workload Analysis button (see Figure 4.70).

Trace Analysis

In addition to the workload analysis, you can also navigate to the trace analysis from the End-to-End Analysis work center. The trace analysis is primarily used in case of performance problems in browser-based applications. Here, a plug-in, which must be installed and started on the user's PC, logs the user's activities so that you can run an analysis that considers trace information both from the frontend and from the SAP NetWeaver Java and ABAP system.

We won't discuss trace analysis here. For more information, refer to the SCN wiki under *http://wiki.scn.sap.com/wiki/display/TechOps/RCA_Trace_Home*.

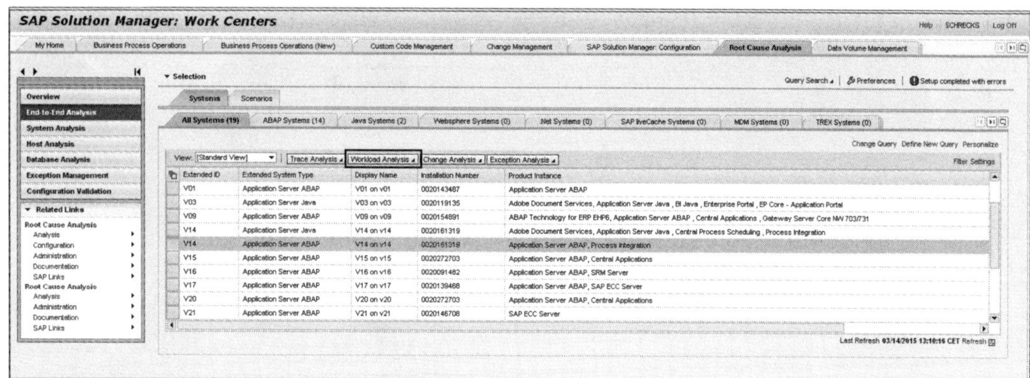

Figure 4.70 Starting the Workload Analysis

3. The workload analysis allows you to evaluate performance data of the selected system, for instance, the transactions with the longest dialog response times (see Figure 4.71).

Timeframe Last month From 02/01/2015 at 00:00 To 02/28/2015 at 24:00 CET Granularity hour Apply Filter

Overview | V14 - Application Server ABAP | V14 - Process Integration

ABAP Basis | RFC | Host

Workload Summary | Top Dialog | Top Update | Top Batch | Top HTTP | User Load | Top HTTP Server | ICM Load | Work Process Load | GW RegisteredTP | WS Provider | WS Consumer

▷ Conditions

▷ Navigation

▽ Metric Data Display

Transaction	Tot. Resp. Time (s)	Avg. Resp. Time (ms)	Avg. CPU Time (ms)	Avg. DB Time (ms)	# Dialog Steps
Overall Result	1,299	1,190	43	496	1,092
SU01	208	3,056	47	536	68
SESSION_MANAGER	188	1,938	66	912	97
DB12	155	15,465	261	11,860	10
SM21	92	4,584	139	2,176	20
SE38	87	3,006	28	156	29
#	79	1,458	26	912	54
SXMB_ADM	77	931	24	445	83
I18N	36	2,025	65	767	18
SM59	32	539	33	168	60
SCOT	32	508	33	169	63
RZ10	31	369	28	206	83
SE16	28	1,996	94	1,086	14
SXMB_MONI	24	718	39	193	34
RZ11	22	2,010	81	1,027	11
S_BCE_68001409	21	1,780	128	691	12
SICF	19	519	29	141	36
SM37	13	663	22	343	19
SCC3	12	1,008	172	219	12
SPAM	11	2,762	200	1,337	4
SCC9	11	597	14	187	18

Figure 4.71 Evaluating the Dialog Response Times

4. Here, you can also evaluate the key figures of the operating system, for example, utilization of CPU and memory (see Figure 4.72).

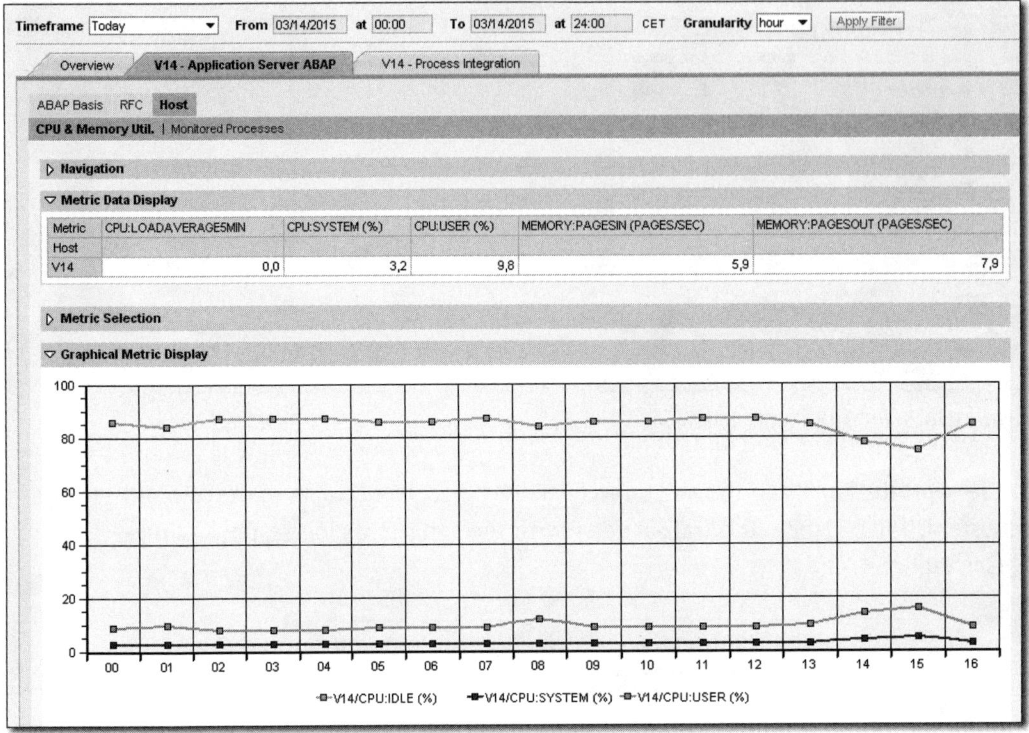

Metric	CPU:LOADAVERAGE5MIN	CPU:SYSTEM (%)	CPU:USER (%)	MEMORY:PAGESIN (PAGES/SEC)	MEMORY:PAGESOUT (PAGES/SEC)
Host					
V14	0,0	3,2	9,8	5,9	7,9

Figure 4.72 Evaluating the CPU and Memory Utilization

5. Now, return to the initial screen of the end-to-end analysis (refer to Figure 4.70), and click on the CHANGE ANALYSIS function. By means of the change analysis, you can obtain detailed information about the changes that were made in the system in a freely selectable period of time (see Figure 4.73).

6. These changes include, among others, imported support packages and notes, imported transports, and adjusted profile parameters (see Figure 4.74), which you can trace for the respective systems on the tabs on the right-hand side of the OVERVIEW tab.

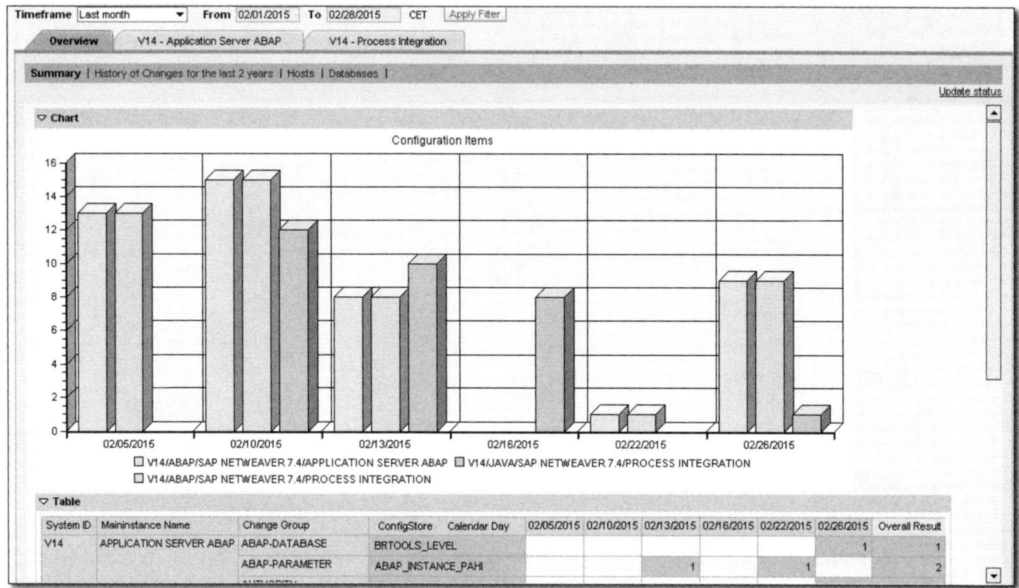

Figure 4.73 Overview Tab in the Change Analysis

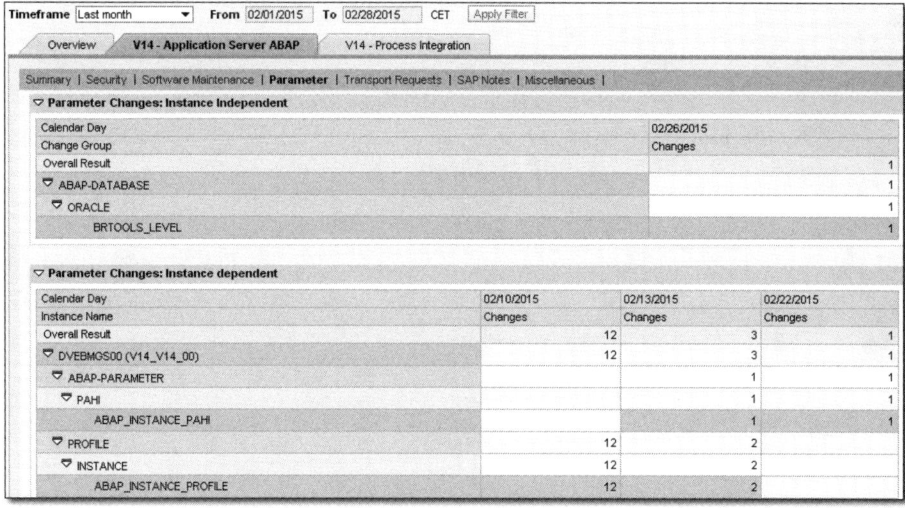

Figure 4.74 Change Overview for Parameters of a System

7. Most objects that can be analyzed allow you to navigate to the detail evaluation; you can, for example, examine all SAP Notes implemented within a specific period of time (see Figure 4.75).

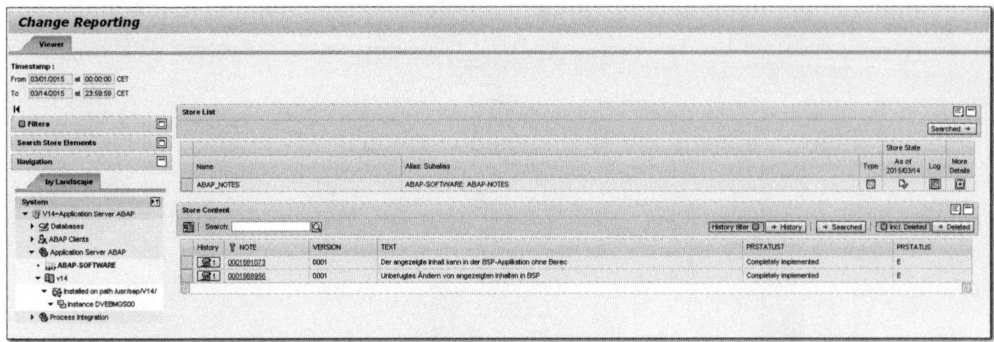

Figure 4.75 Detail Analysis of Imported SAP Notes

8. Click on the Exception Analysis button in the initial screen of the end-to-end analysis (refer to Figure 4.70).
9. Exceptions involve, for example, errors that are logged in the system log (Transaction SM21). Short dumps, update terminations, and IDoc errors are also exceptions. The number of events is displayed in a graphical overview (see Figure 4.76).

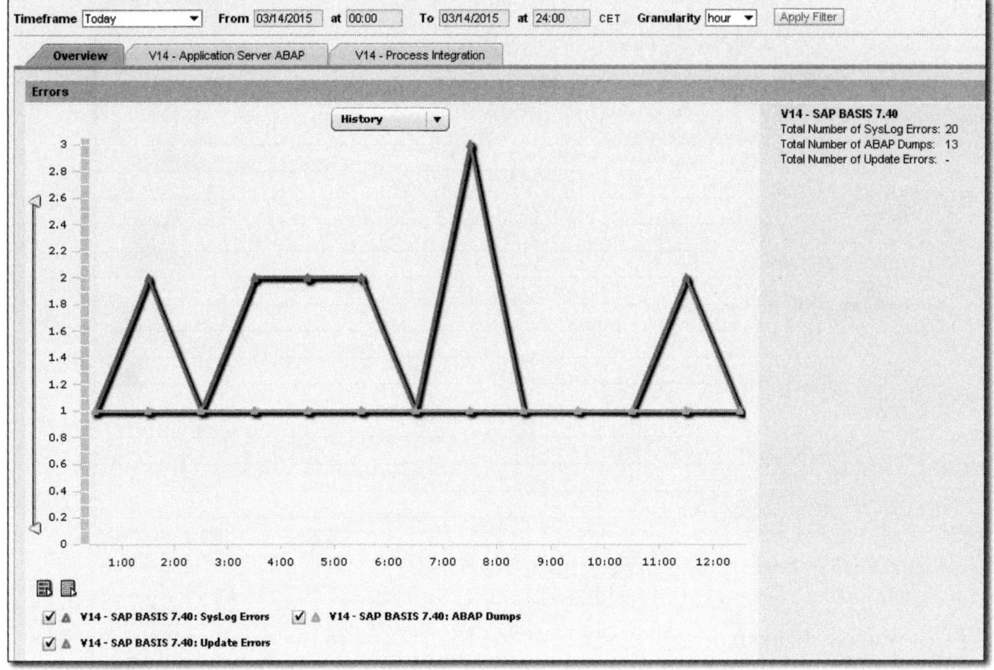

Figure 4.76 Exception Analysis Overview Page

10. The individual exception types are analyzed in the detail view. This view corresponds to a tree structure whose entries you can expand (see Figure 4.77).

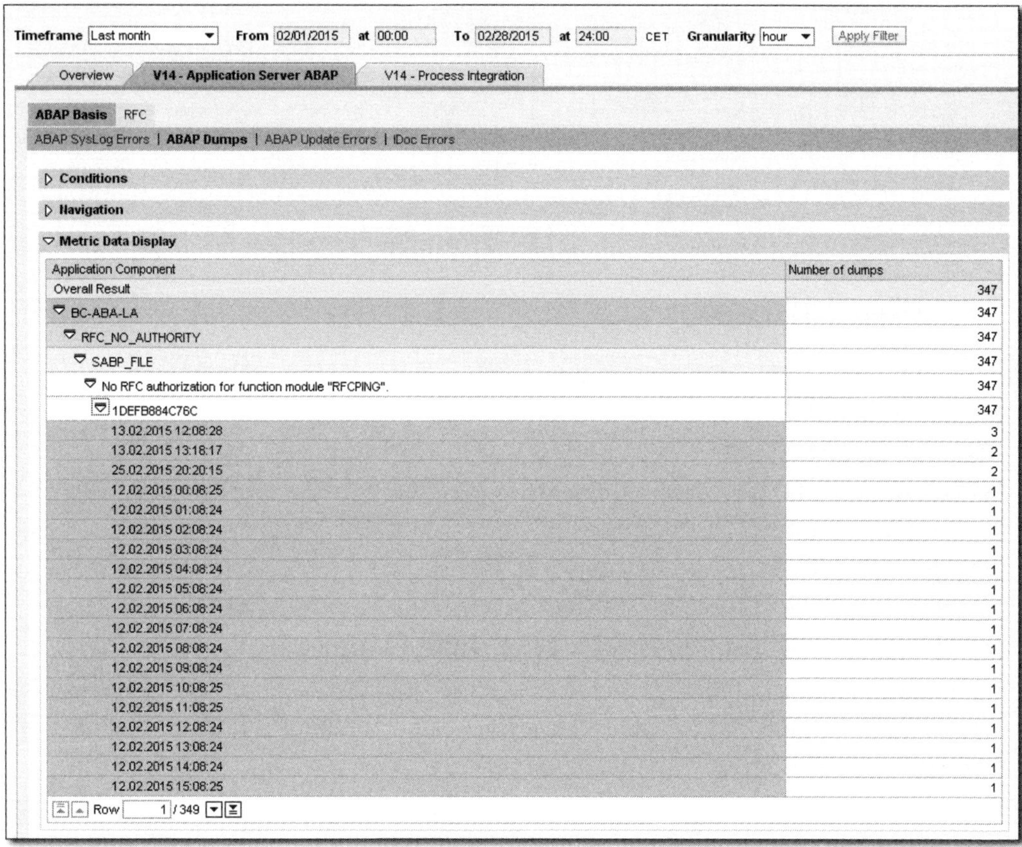

Figure 4.77 Detail View of the ABAP Dump

11. Click on an individual event, for example, a specific short dump, and navigate to the corresponding target system. There you can use the functions of the default transactions (e.g., Transaction ST22) to examine the problem in detail (see Figure 4.78).

The end-to-end analysis provides comprehensive options to monitor your systems during running operation. The central entry point facilitates the evaluation of data, in particular for larger system landscapes.

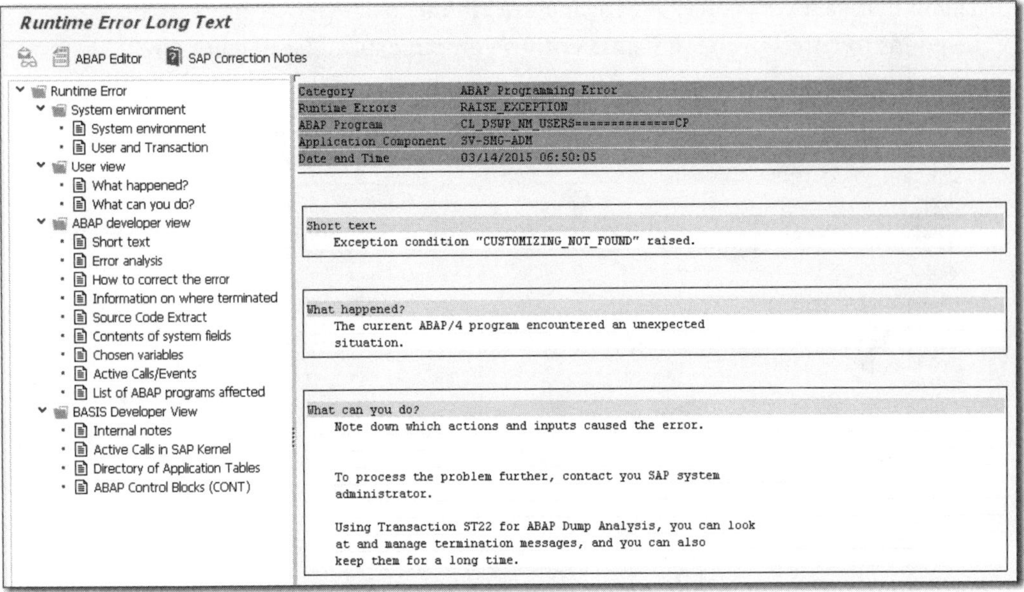

Figure 4.78 Detail Analysis in the Target System

4.3.3 Configuration Validation

The *configuration validation* is a powerful tool for monitoring your system settings. Instead of logging on to each system individually and checking the parameters or settings, you can evaluate the system landscape via SAP Solution Manager.

For example, you can use the configuration validation to map the security guidelines of your enterprise in electronic form. The guidelines can define, for example, that the system and client change option must be set to NOT MODIFIABLE in all production systems. It involves a lot of work and time if you have to check this manually on an ongoing basis. But you can reduce this effort considerably using the configuration validation.

[+]

Wiki for Configuration Validation

In the following, we describe the configuration validation based on a short example. Discussing all options of this tool would go far beyond the scope of this book. Instead, refer to the wiki page of the SCN, where you can find additional information on this topic: *http://wiki.scn.sap.com/wiki/display/TechOps/ConfVal_Home*.

Follow these steps to set up the configuration validation:

1. In SAP Solution Manager, start Transaction SOLMAN_WORKCENTER (or Transaction SM_WORKCENTER). Open the ROOT CAUSE ANALYSIS work center, and then click on the CONFIGURATION VALIDATION link (see Figure 4.79).

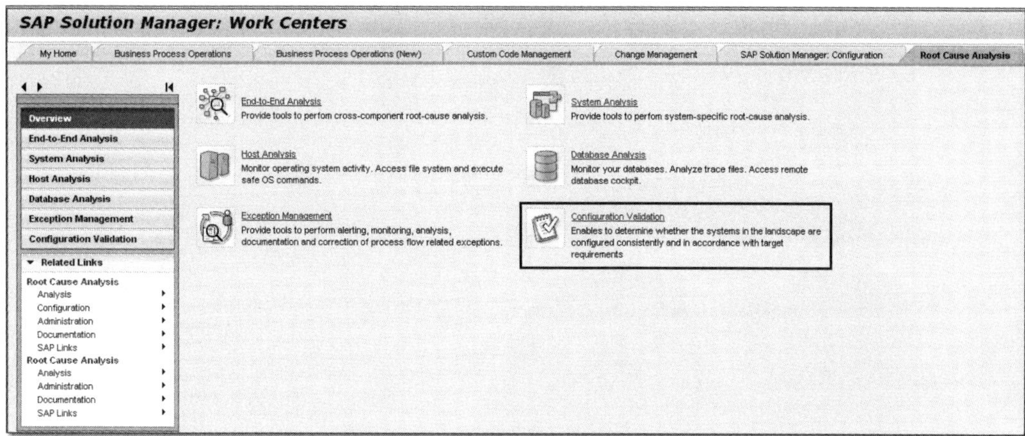

Figure 4.79 Calling the Configuration Validation

2. Now create a target system. The target system is a virtual reference system with which you compare your real systems. Open the TARGET SYSTEM MAINTENANCE tab, and click on the DISPLAY ALL button in the SOURCE SYSTEM area (see Figure 4.80).

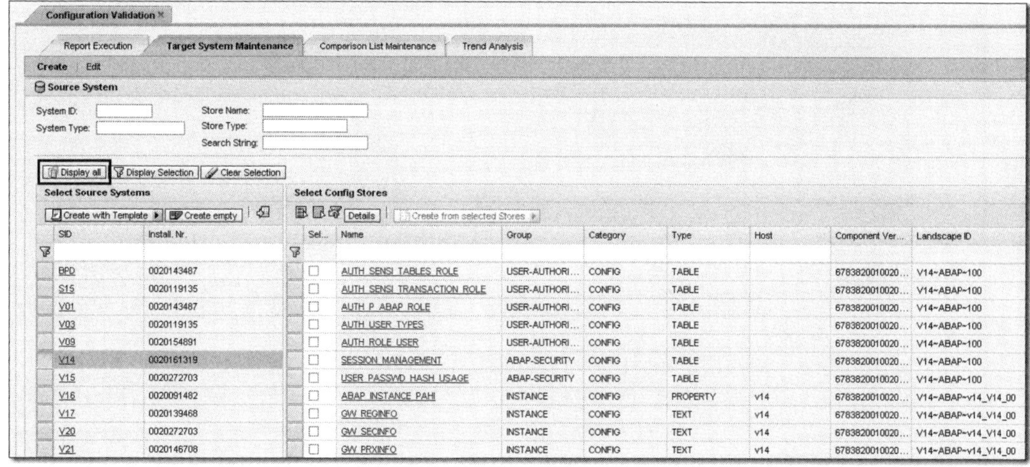

Figure 4.80 Displaying the Source Systems

3. Then select a configuration store. A configuration store contains various preconfigured characteristics based on which you can compare systems. This example deals with the client settings mentioned previously, so we select the CLIENTS configuration store here. Click on CREATE FROM SELECTED STORES (see Figure 4.81).

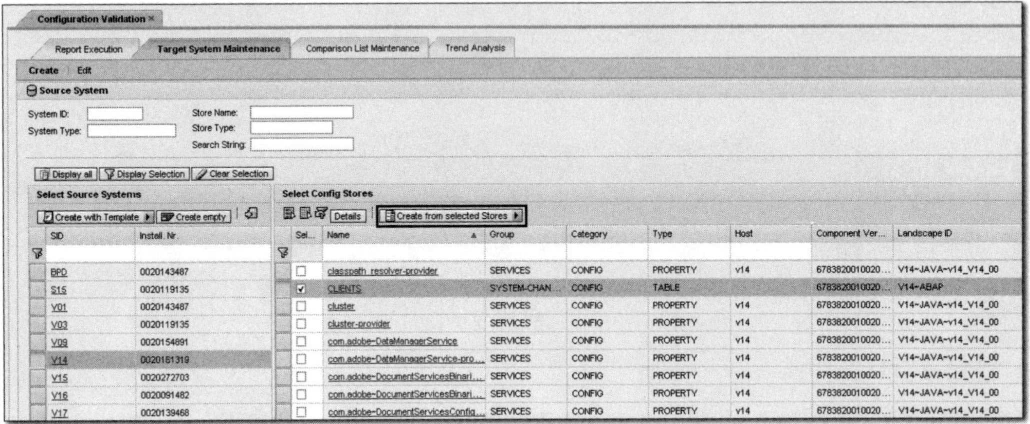

Figure 4.81 Selecting a Configuration Store

4. The target system is created. In the header of the TARGET SYSTEM MAINTENANCE tab, click on EDIT, and select the configuration store you just copied. The lower area of the screen displays the detail information of the configuration store (see Figure 4.82).

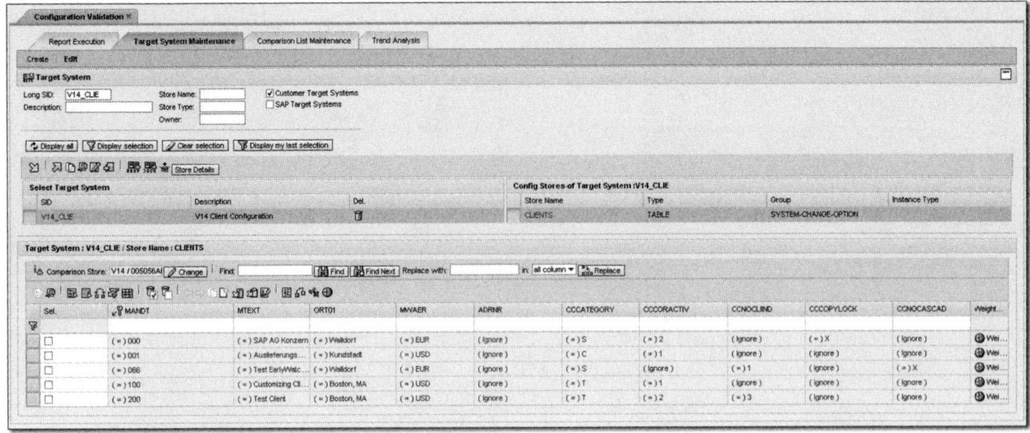

Figure 4.82 Editing the Target System

Content of the Configuration Store

The configuration store contains highly technical information. In this example, the CLIENTS configuration store represents table T000 of the SAP system to be compared, that is, a table that stores the technical data of the client administration. The columns of the configuration store thus correspond to the columns of table T000.

5. Select CLIENT 100, for example. Another detail table opens that contains the comparison field values and operators (see Figure 4.83). In our example, we adapt the four fields for the client role (CCCATEGORY), changeability of client-dependent (CCCORACTIV) and client-independent (CCNOCLIND) objects, as well as for the protection level for client copier (CCCOPYLOCK) by entering the desired target values and clicking on APPLY CHANGES. Then click SAVE to save your settings.

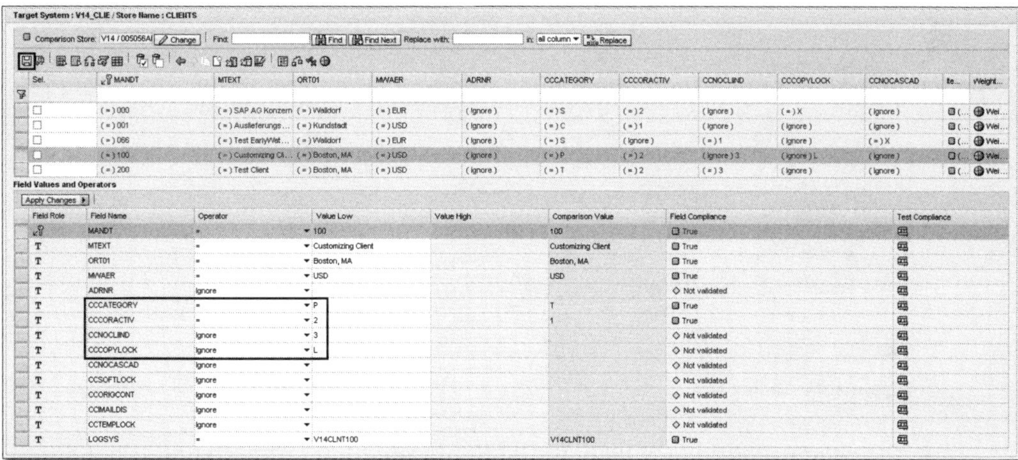

Figure 4.83 Entering Target Values in the Configuration Store

6. If you click the CHECK COMPLIANCE WITH REFERENCE STORE icon, you can compare your current settings of the system. Compliant or noncompliant field values are indicated with corresponding traffic light icons in the FIELD COMPLIANCE column (see Figure 4.84).
7. For all clients or more systems, you should display the results of the check as a report to obtain a better overview. To do so, go to the REPORT EXECUTION tab, and select the REPORTING TEMPLATES option. Choose your reference system (see Figure 4.85).

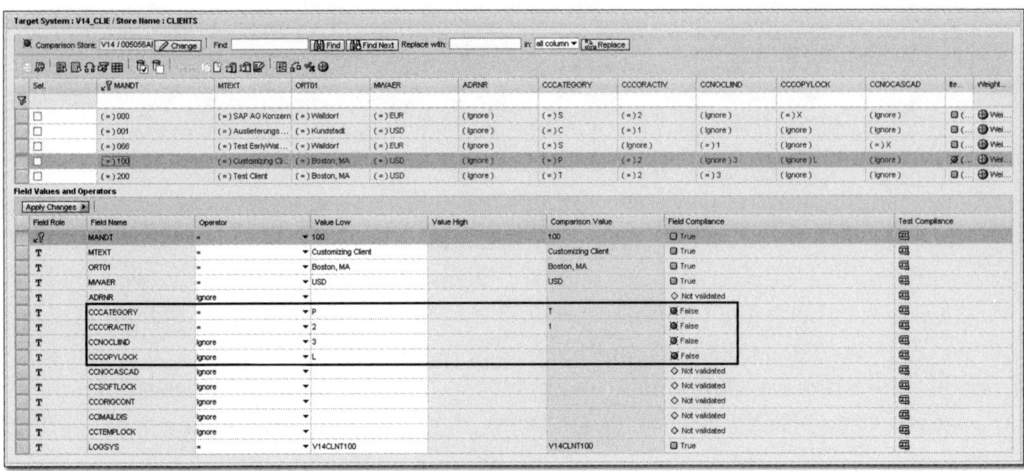

Figure 4.84 Checking the Compliance with Target Values

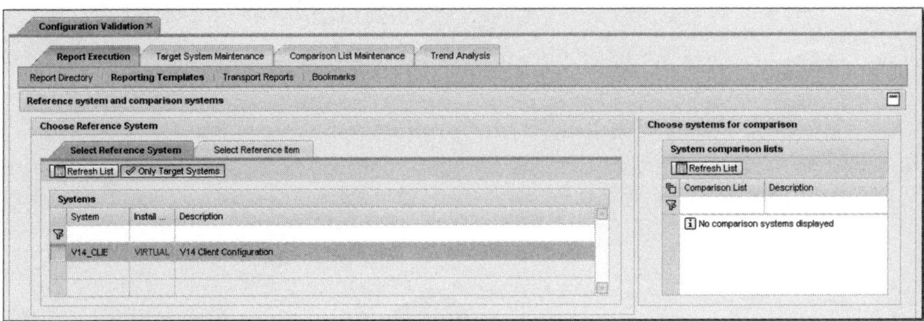

Figure 4.85 Calling the Comparison Result via a Report

8. Choose a report to compare the reference system with the technical system (see Figure 4.86). Then click on START OPERATOR VALIDATION REPORTING.

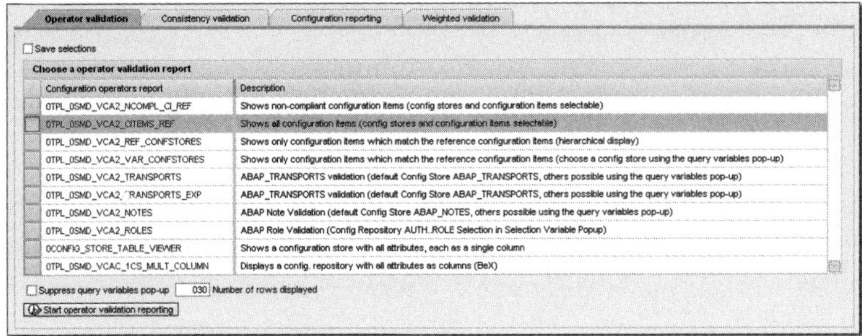

Figure 4.86 Starting the Validation Report

9. The report may query selection variables. In our example, select the appropriate comparison system (see Figure 4.87). Click on Execute.

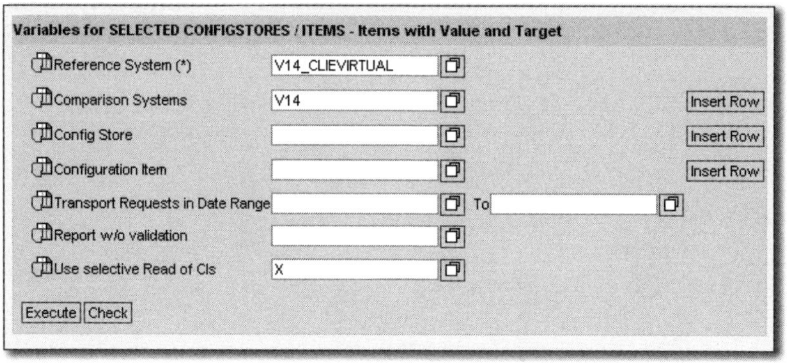

Figure 4.87 Selecting the Appropriate Comparison System

10. The report is executed and displayed in a new window (see Figure 4.88). Clients that meet the target values are displayed in green or with the numeric value 1. Objects that don't meet the target values are highlighted in orange and displayed with the value –1. This value is inherited from the single characteristics upward; in other words, *one* failed check makes the entire client noncompliant.

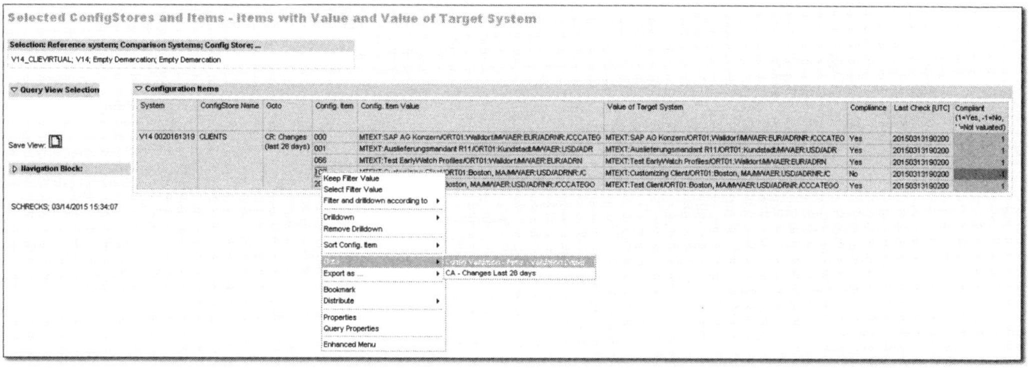

Figure 4.88 Validation Report

11. To display the individual values, right-click on the corresponding cell to open the context menu, and choose Goto • Config. Validation – Elements – Validation Details.

12. In the detail view, you can see which settings don't correspond with the preset target values (see Figure 4.89). In our example, the client settings (see step 5) are set incorrectly.

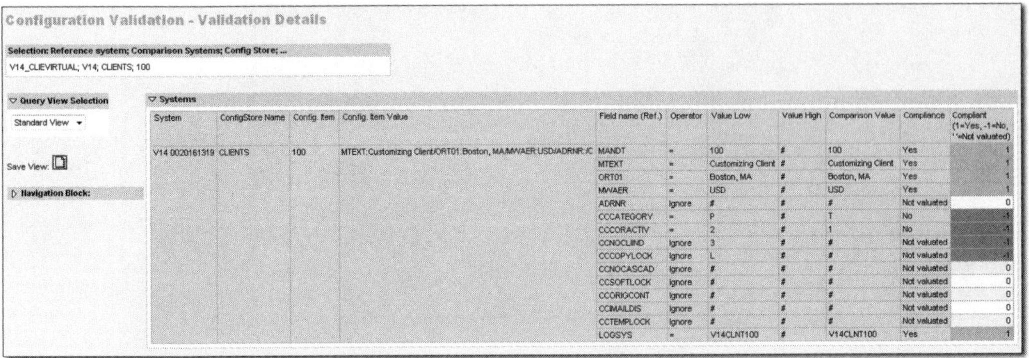

Figure 4.89 Detail View of the Validation Report

The configuration validation provides many more options to validate your system landscape; for example, you can compare the system parameters or check further security-relevant settings. All comparisons that are relevant for you can be bundled in custom reports and be executed periodically, for example, on a weekly basis. SAP Solution Manager can send you the results by email. At this point, we can only give a small insight into the comprehensive options because the actual configuration is very extensive and has a strong technical orientation.

4.3.4 SAP EarlyWatch Alert

SAP EarlyWatch Alert (hereafter, EarlyWatch Alert) is part of system reporting. However, unlike system monitoring, it analyzes the status of an SAP system on a regular basis (usually weekly) rather than in real time. For analysis purposes, this report accesses data that has been gathered over a longer period to provide both a snapshot and a long-term evaluation of the following system-critical aspects:

- System configuration (hardware, software, service availability)
- System performance (performance development, transaction profiles)
- Workload distribution (per module, database load)

- System operation (update terminations, transports, short dumps)
- Hardware capacity (CPU, main memory, paging)
- Database performance (locks, read and write times, indexes)
- Database administration (growth, objects with a critical size)
- Security (users with critical authorizations, security gaps)
- Trend analysis (system availability, response times, hardware)

Information about EarlyWatch Alert [+]

For more information about the EarlyWatch Alert, see the SAP Support Portal at *www.service.sap.com/ewa*.

The EarlyWatch report is based on the *Service Data Control Centers* (SDCC; Transaction SDCCN) data gathered in the target system. You must therefore ensure that the SDCC is fully configured before you can use the EarlyWatch Alert. With release 7.0 of SAP Solution Manager, SDCC still had to be activated manually for the respective system. In SAP Solution Manager 7.1, the configuration was integrated with the connection of managed systems (see Section 4.2.5). Further manual activities aren't necessary.

Configuring the EarlyWatch Alert

The following basic configuration settings are required before you can execute the EarlyWatch Alert and retrieve the report. To do this, follow these steps:

1. In SAP Solution Manager, start Transaction SOLMAN_SETUP, and then click on EARLYWATCH ALERT MANAGEMENT.

Transaction SOLMAN_SETUP [+]

You can also reach the functions of Transaction SOLMAN_SETUP via Transaction SOLMAN_WORKCENTER (or Transaction SM_WORKCENTER). The corresponding work center is called SAP SOLUTION MANAGER: CONFIGURATION.

2. As usual, configuration is supported by a wizard. The first screen displays the available technical systems (see Figure 4.90). Click on NEXT.

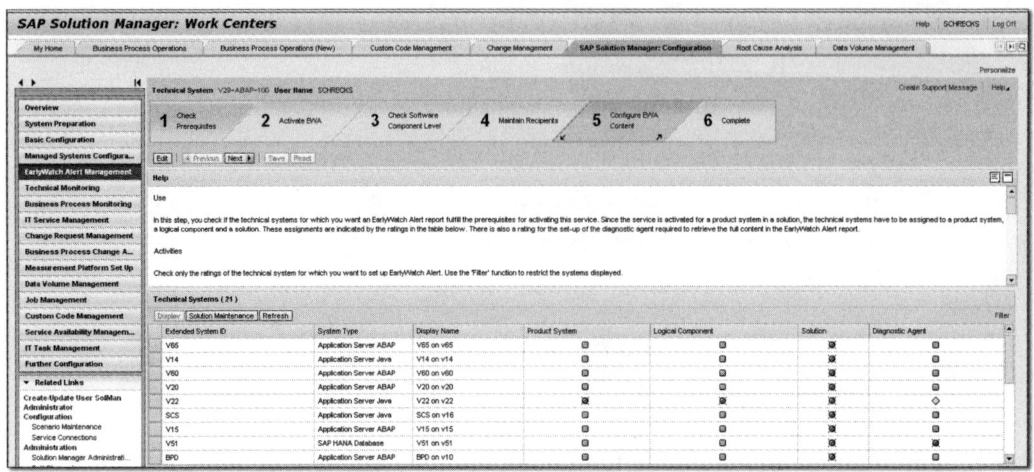

Figure 4.90 Wizard for Configuring the EarlyWatch Alert

3. In the second step, you must check whether the status of the EarlyWatch activation is marked as ACTIVE. If required, set the checkmark (see Figure 4.91). In this step, you can also choose the day on which the EarlyWatch report is supposed to be generated. Then click on NEXT.

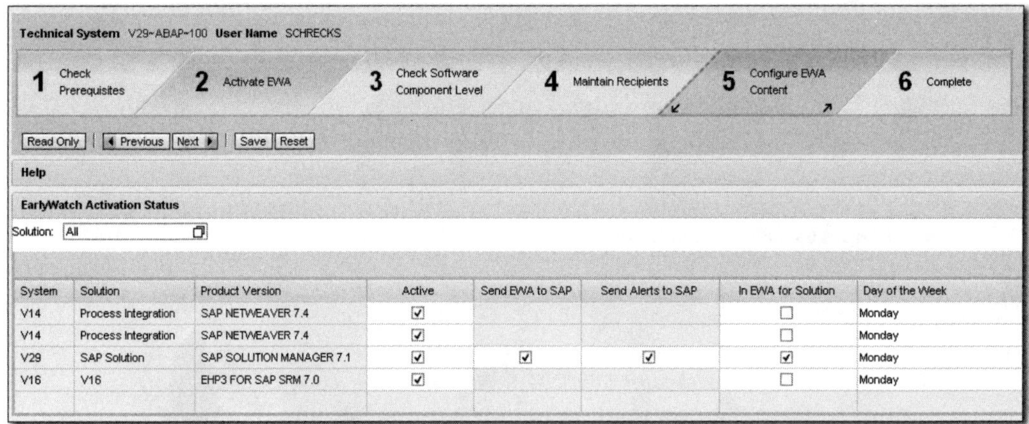

Figure 4.91 Activating the EarlyWatch Alert

4. In the third step, you ensure that the system components ST-PI and ST-A/PI of your systems are up to date (see Figure 4.92).

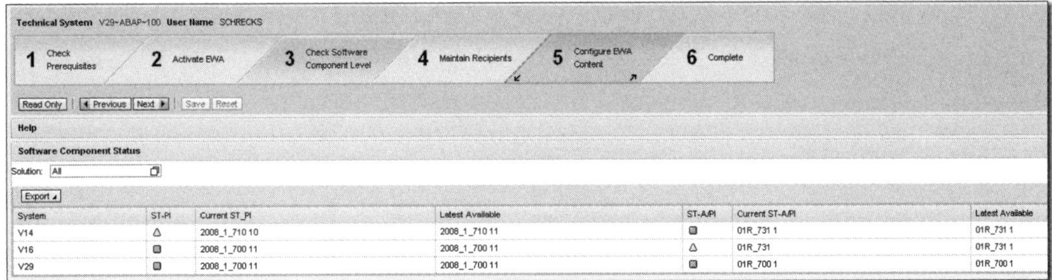

Figure 4.92 Checking the Status of the Software Components

Service Preparation Check

[⚙]

The EarlyWatch Alert uses the *Application Service tools* (component ST-A/PI), which needs to be updated from time to time. In addition, SAP makes new *service definitions* available on a regular basis. These serve as a basis for the recommendations of the EarlyWatch Alert. You can use program `RTCCTOOL` to check whether your systems have the current version of the ST-A/PI add-on and the latest service definitions. The `RTCCTOOL` report provides specific actions for ensuring that your system is up to date.

5. Next, you can define the recipient of the EarlyWatch report (see Figure 4.93).

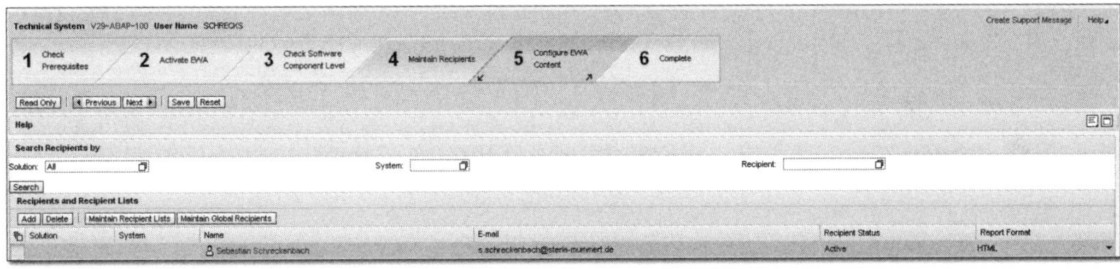

Figure 4.93 Defining Recipients

You may define individual recipients or work with RECIPIENT LISTS. Furthermore, you can specify the REPORT FORMAT in which the report is to be sent. The dispatch can be differentiated based on solutions and systems.

Notification Management

[+]

The central entry point for maintaining and managing recipient lists and so on is the *notification management*, which you can find in the TECHNICAL ADMINISTRATION work center.

6. Next, the system displays the initial screen of the EarlyWatch content configuration (see Figure 4.94). Click on NEXT to go to the first substep of configuration.

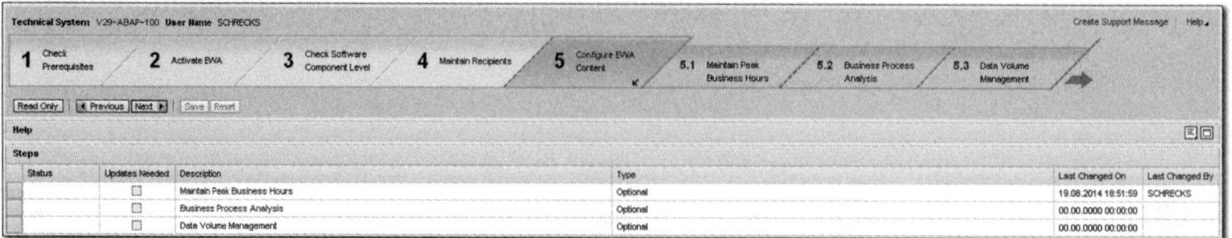

Figure 4.94 EarlyWatch Content Configuration

7. First, you can MAINTAIN PEAK BUSINESS HOURS (see Figure 4.95); in other words, you define when your system is fully utilized. It's also possible to ignore certain days in the EarlyWatch report, for example, Saturday and Sunday.

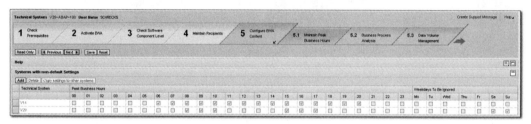

Figure 4.95 Maintaining Peak Business Hours

8. In the BUSINESS PROCESS ANALYSIS substep, you can activate the *Business Process Analysis* (BPA), that is, the MAI-based business process and interface monitoring (see Figure 4.96). For more detailed information, refer to SAP Note 1430754.

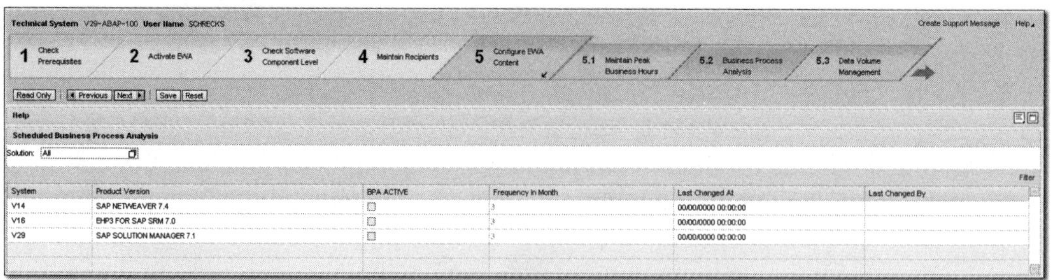

Figure 4.96 Activating Business Process Analysis

9. Finally, you specify whether analyses from *data volume management* (DVM) are to be included in the EarlyWatch report. A separate work center exists for DVM in Transaction SOLMAN_WORKCENTER (or Transaction SM_WORKCENTER),

in which you must define an appropriate configuration (see Figure 4.97). If you deploy DVM, it makes sense to add the evaluation to the EWA report.

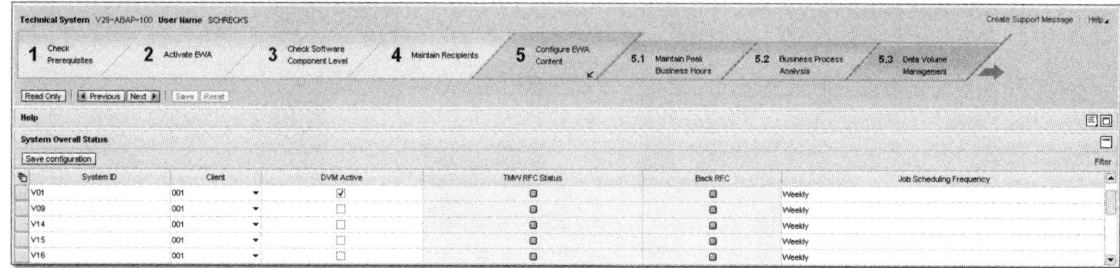

Figure 4.97 Adding Data Volume Management to the EarlyWatch Report

10. Close the configuration of the EarlyWatch Alert administration by clicking on the FINISH button (see Figure 4.98).

Technical System V29~ABAP~100 User Name SCHRECKS

1 Check Prerequisites | 2 Activate EWA | 3 Check Software Component Level | 4 Maintain Recipients | 5 Configure EWA Content | 6 Complete

Previous | Next | Save | Reset | Finish | Export To HTML | Send By Email

Help

Steps

Configuration Step	Status	Last Changed On	Last Changed By	Description
• Check Prerequisites				Check Prerequisites
• Activate EWA				Activate EWA
• Check Software Component Level				Check Software Component Level
• Maintain Recipients		19.08.2014 18:37:46	SCHRECKS	Maintain Recipients
▾ Configure EWA Content				Configure EWA Content
• Maintain Peak Business Hours		19.08.2014 18:51:58	SCHRECKS	Maintain Peak Business Hours
• Business Process Analysis				Business Process Analysis
• Data Volume Management				Data Volume Management

Figure 4.98 Closing the EarlyWatch Configuration

The EarlyWatch Alert has been configured. A report is generated for each system in the interval set and is then sent to the recipients defined. The reports provide key information about the general status of your system. They give specific instructions as to how problems can be eliminated. You should run the EarlyWatch Alert on a weekly basis and always check the report thoroughly after each execution to ensure that your SAP systems remain in good working order.

Displaying the EarlyWatch Alert in SAP Solution Manager

In addition to sending the EarlyWatch reports by email, they can also be displayed directly in SAP Solution Manager.

1. In SAP Solution Manager, start Transaction SOLMAN_WORKCENTER or Transaction SM_WORKCENTER. Choose the SYSTEM MONITORING work center, and then click on REPORTS.

2. Choose a product system and a report in the SAP EARLYWATCH ALERT report view. Click on DISPLAY HTML REPORT to call the alert (see Figure 4.99).

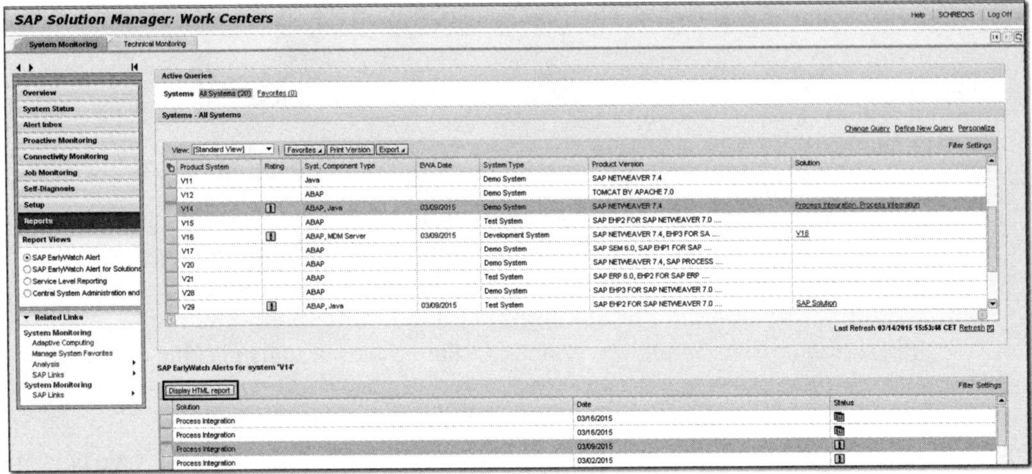

Figure 4.99 Calling the EarlyWatch Report

3. The report is displayed in a new browser window (see Figure 4.100). Scroll through the individual sections to get an overview of the examined system and its status.

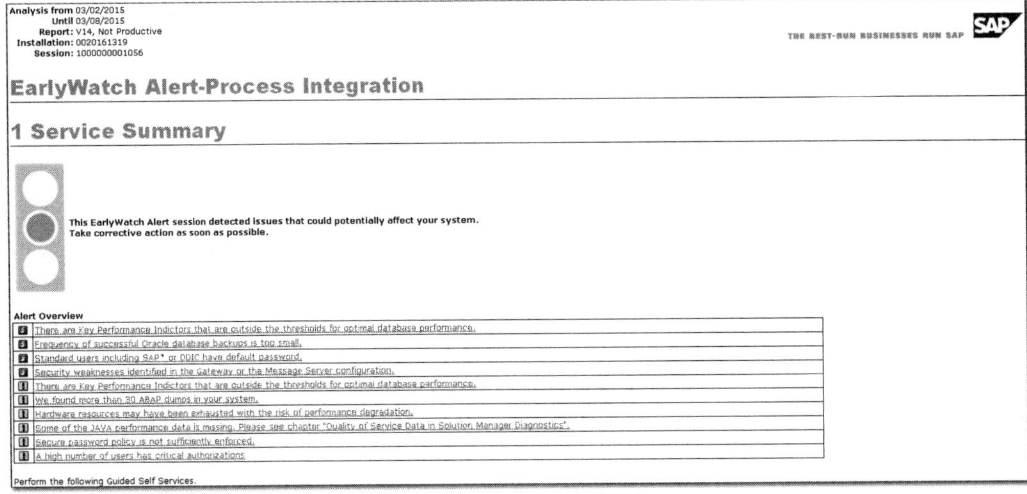

Figure 4.100 EarlyWatch Report

4.3.5 System Recommendations

System recommendations is another function of SAP Solution Manager that is rather useful and can be configured with little effort. This function periodically compares the current status of the respective system with the SAP Notes published by SAP and prepares a list of SAP Notes that can be imported. This way, you obtain a quick overview of the *HotNews* (notes with highest priority) as well as upcoming repairs, for example, regarding topics such as security, performance, and legal changes.

Follow these steps to configure system configurations:

1. In SAP Solution Manager, start Transaction SOLMAN_WORKCENTER (or Transaction SM_WORKCENTER). Open the CHANGE MANAGEMENT work center, and then click on SYSTEM RECOMMENDATIONS.
2. Follow the SETTINGS link in the top-right corner of the view (see Figure 4.101).

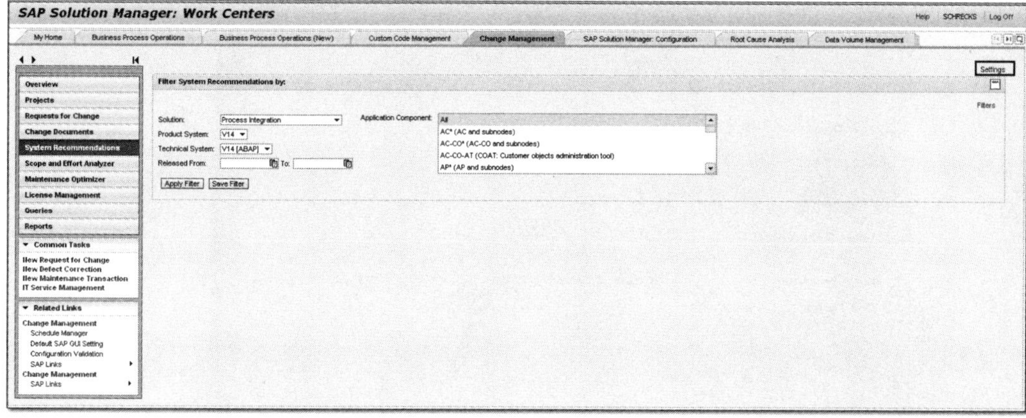

Figure 4.101 Configuration of System Settings

3. Set the switch to TURN ON AUTOMATICAL CHECK – RECOMMENDED, and choose an appropriate interval as well as a start time for the periodic job `SM:SYSTEM RECOMMENDATIONS`. Then click on NEXT (see Figure 4.102).
4. Add the technical systems for which you want to retrieve system recommendations to the list of selected systems using the relevant solution. To finish configuration, click on SAVE (see Figure 4.103).

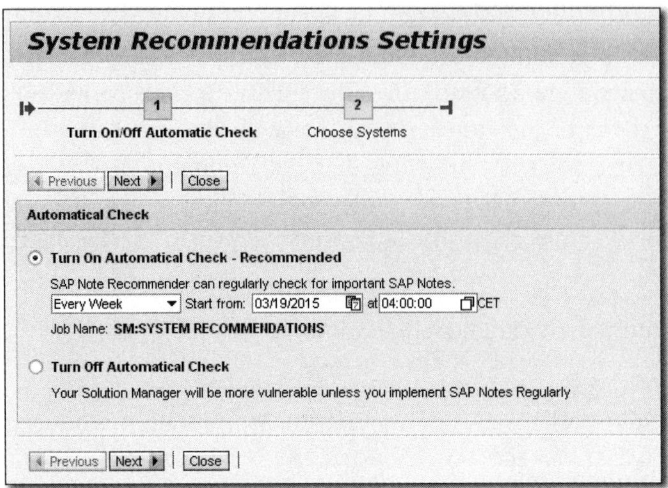

Figure 4.102 Activating Automatic Check

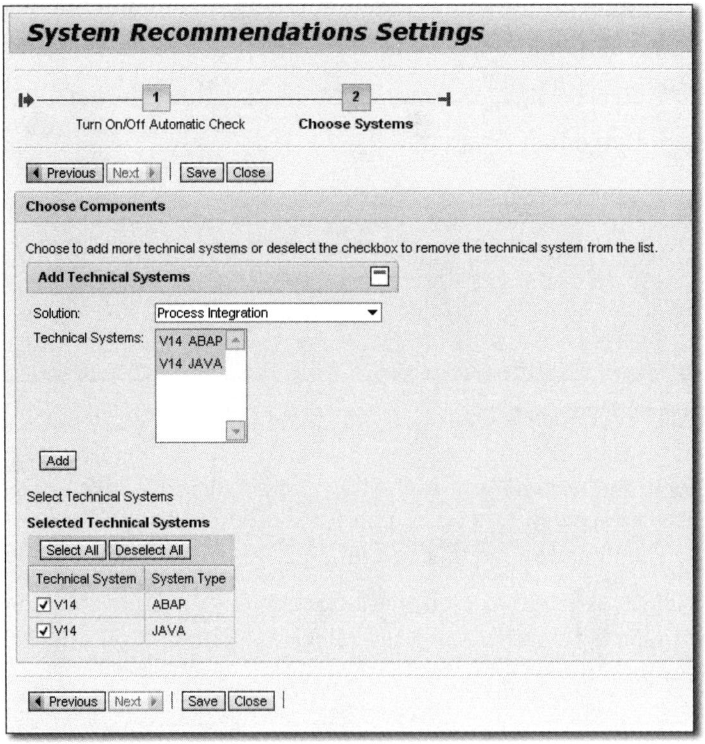

System Recommendations Settings

1 Turn On/Off Automatic Check — 2 Choose Systems

Previous | Next | Save | Close

Choose Components

Choose to add more technical systems or deselect the checkbox to remove the technical system from the list.

Add Technical Systems

Solution: Process Integration

Technical Systems: V14 ABAP, V14 JAVA

Add

Select Technical Systems

Selected Technical Systems

Select All | Deselect All

Technical System	System Type
☑ V14	ABAP
☑ V14	JAVA

Previous | Next | Save | Close

Figure 4.103 Selecting Systems

5. Now choose a system in the initial screen of the system recommendations, and restrict the desired period of time. Then, click on REFRESH. The list of notes is updated. Based on the various tabs, check which notes are relevant for your system (see Figure 4.104).

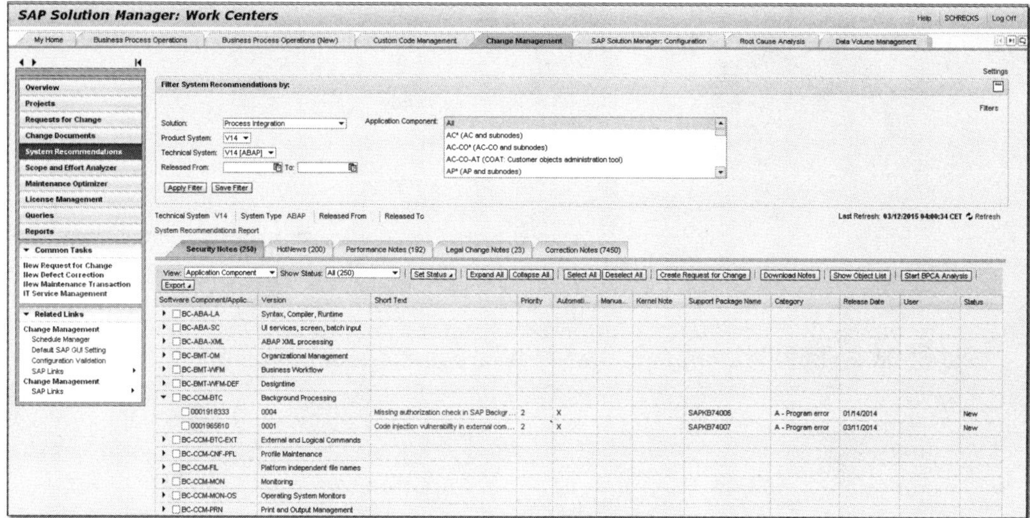

Figure 4.104 List of Available Security Notes

The SAP Notes are already filtered by their relevance for the selected system; that is, if a note has already been implemented in the target system via a support package, it's no longer displayed in the system recommendations.

4.3.6 Managing Service Connections

Chapter 19, Section 19.3, describes how to open a service connection manually for the SAP support team using the SAP Support Portal. You can also complete this task using SAP Solution Manager.

1. In SAP Solution Manager, start Transaction SOLMAN_CONNECT. Alternatively, you can also call the SAP SOLUTION MANAGER ADMINISTRATION work center, and click on the SERVICE CONNECTIONS link.
2. You must first configure the administration of service connections. Select a system, and choose SETUP • CREATE SETUP... (see Figure 4.105).
3. Choose a SERVICE CONNECTION TYPE under SYSTEM DETAILS (e.g., R/3 SUPPORT). Then, click on NEXT (see Figure 4.106).

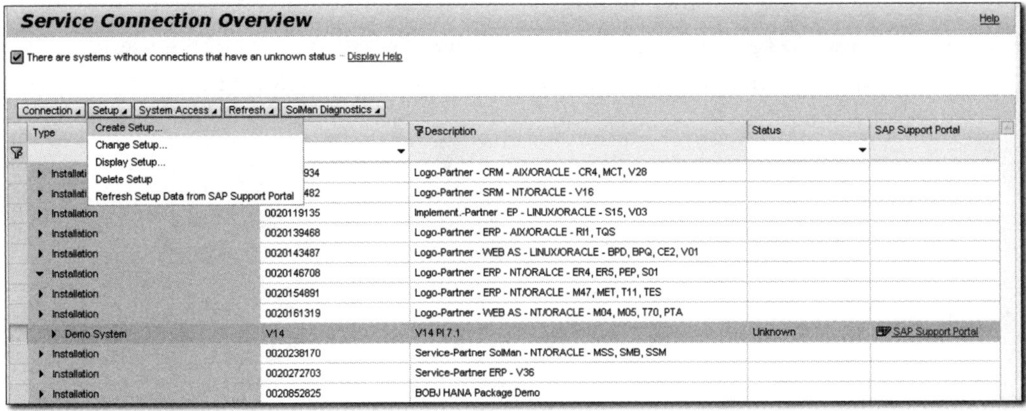

Figure 4.105 Creating the Configuration for Service Connections

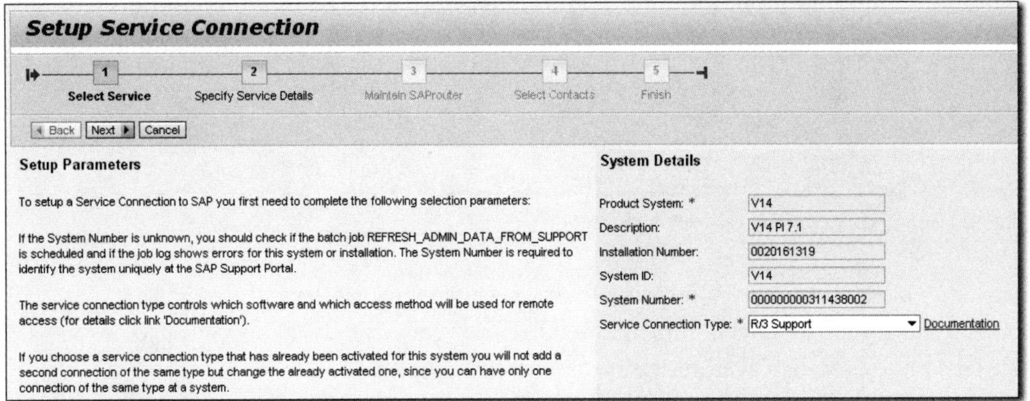

Figure 4.106 Selecting a Service Connection Type

4. Check the information for the server, and then click on the Next button (see Figure 4.107).

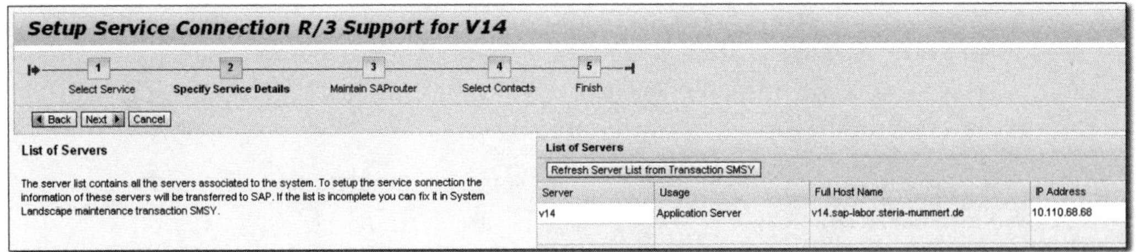

Figure 4.107 Checking the Server Information

5. Choose the correct SAProuter, and go to the next step by clicking on NEXT (see Figure 4.108).

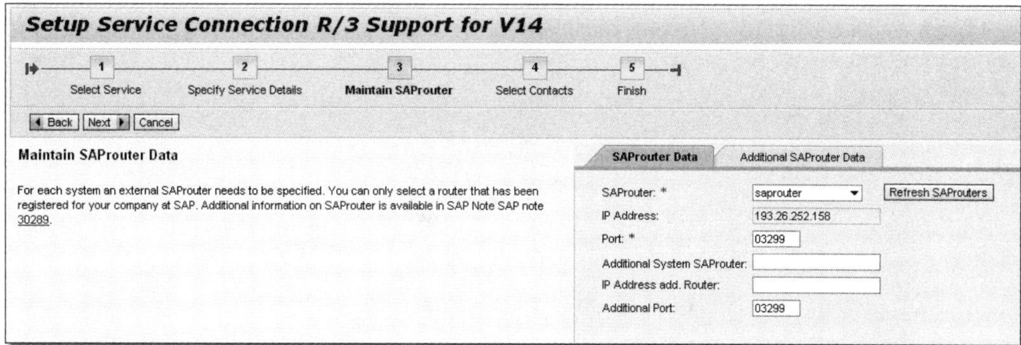

Figure 4.108 Selecting the SAProuter

6. Specify a contact person for the support team and a substitute if required (see Figure 4.109). Click NEXT.

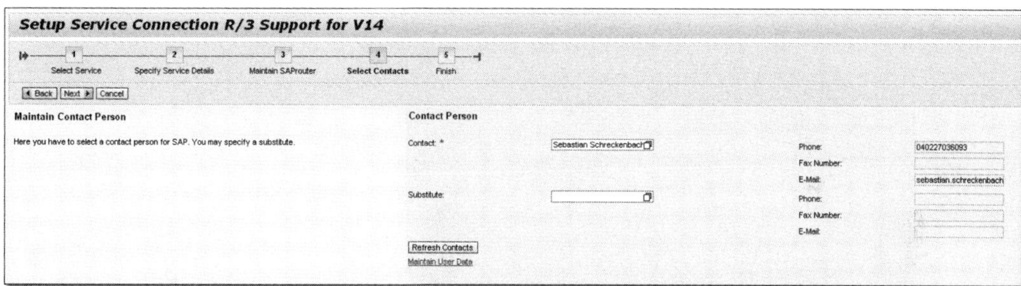

Figure 4.109 Specifying a Contact Person

7. Complete the configuration by clicking the FINISH button (see Figure 4.110).

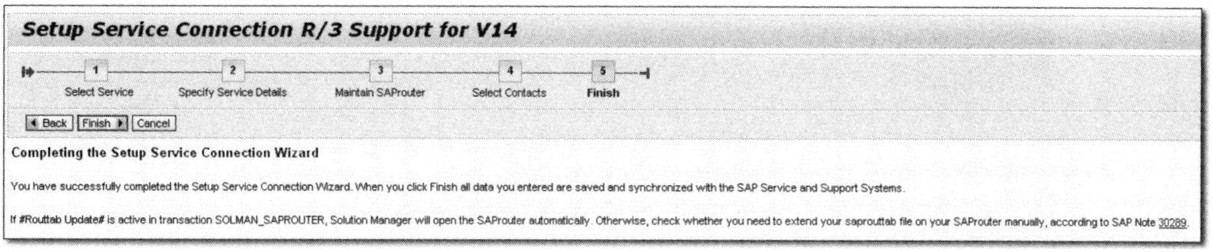

Setup Service Connection R/3 Support for V14

1 Select Service — 2 Specify Service Details — 3 Maintain SAProuter — 4 Select Contacts — 5 Finish

Back | Finish | Cancel

Completing the Setup Service Connection Wizard

You have successfully completed the Setup Service Connection Wizard. When you click Finish all data you entered are saved and synchronized with the SAP Service and Support Systems.

If #Routtab Update# is active in transaction SOLMAN_SAPROUTER, Solution Manager will open the SAProuter automatically. Otherwise, check whether you need to extend your saprouttab file on your SAProuter manually, according to SAP Note 30289.

Figure 4.110 Finishing the Configuration

8. You can now select the previously created service connection in the overview of service connections. To open it, choose Change • Open/Change Connection... (see Figure 4.111).

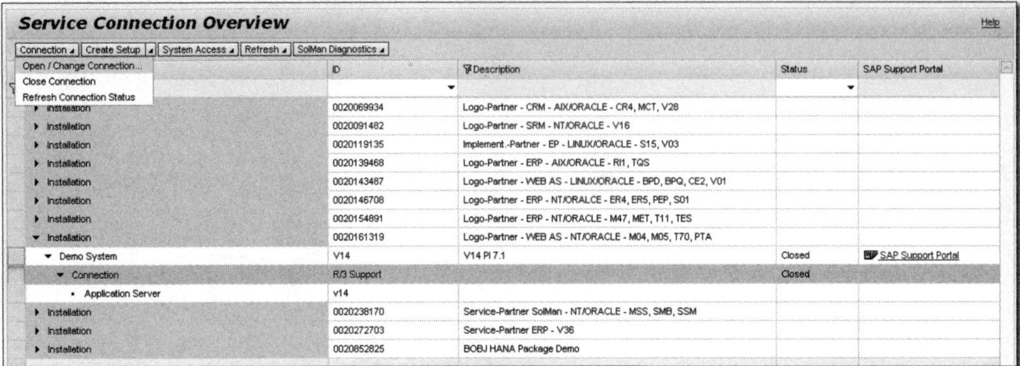

Figure 4.111 Opening the Service Connection

9. Define for how long the connection is supposed to remain open, and then click on Submit (see Figure 4.112).

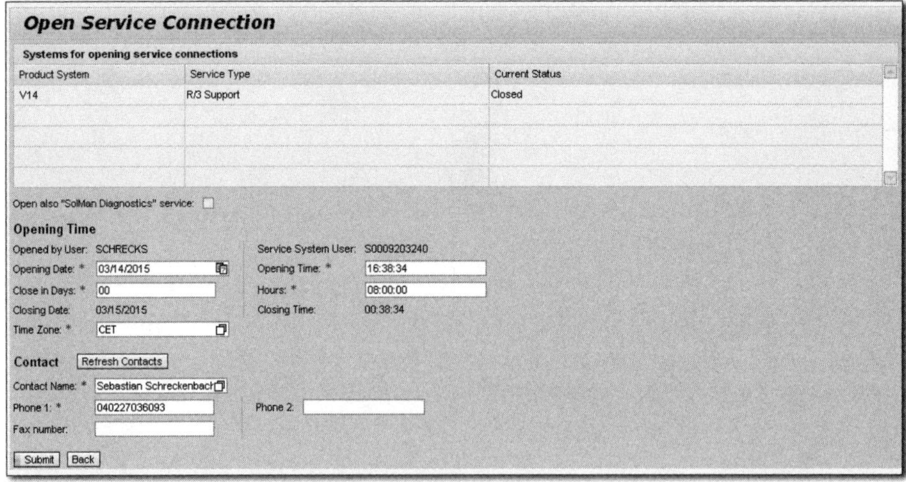

Figure 4.112 Setting the Connection Time

10. The service connection is opened. The connection overview displays the status (e.g., Open) and the remaining connection time (see Figure 4.113).

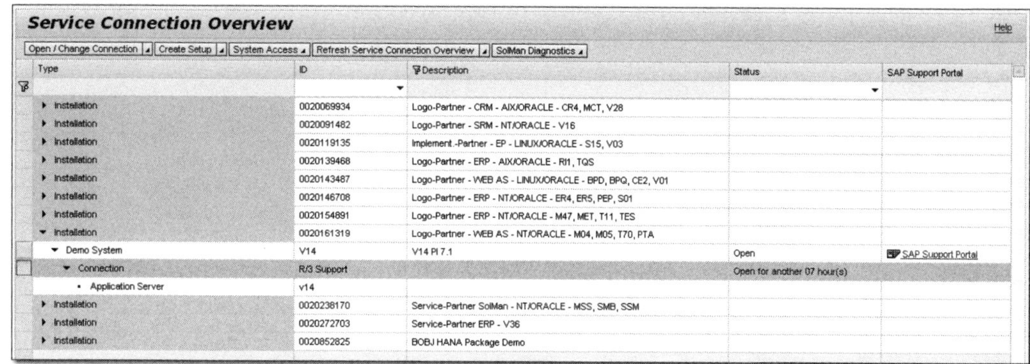

Figure 4.113 Connection Overview

Opening the service connections via SAP Solution Manager facilitates your work because a separate logon to the SAP Support Portal isn't required. The cross-system overview of all open connections provides benefits compared with the status control in the SAP Support Portal.

4.3.7 License Administration

SAP Solution Manager 7.1 provides the option to automate your SAP license administration centrally. This function particularly facilitates the renewal of maintenance certificates, which are required for importing support packages. By default, however, they are only valid for three months, respectively. Particularly for large system landscapes, this facilitates your work considerably: SAP Solution Manager transfers the data of the managed system to SAP's global support system. If it's established that the maintenance certificate has expired, a new one is requested automatically and then retrieved by SAP Solution Manager. SAP Solution Manager in turn distributes the new certificates to the connected systems so that this process no longer requires any manual intervention.

License administration is set up when connecting the managed systems. To check and change the configuration, follow these steps:

1. In SAP Solution Manager, start Transaction SOLMAN_WORKCENTER (or Transaction SM_WORKCENTER). Open the CHANGE MANAGEMENT work center, and then click on LICENSE MANAGEMENT.
2. The license status of the managed product systems is displayed in a table. Expired licenses and certificates are represented with a red traffic light, and valid data are displayed in green (see Figure 4.114).

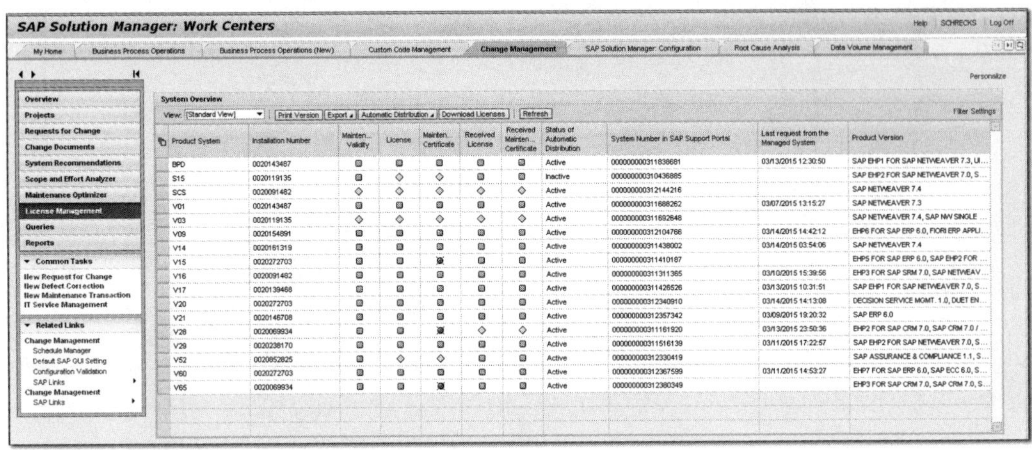

Figure 4.114 Initial Screen of the License Administration

3. When you select a system, the detail view provides you with detailed expiry dates of the individual licenses and certificates (see Figure 4.115).

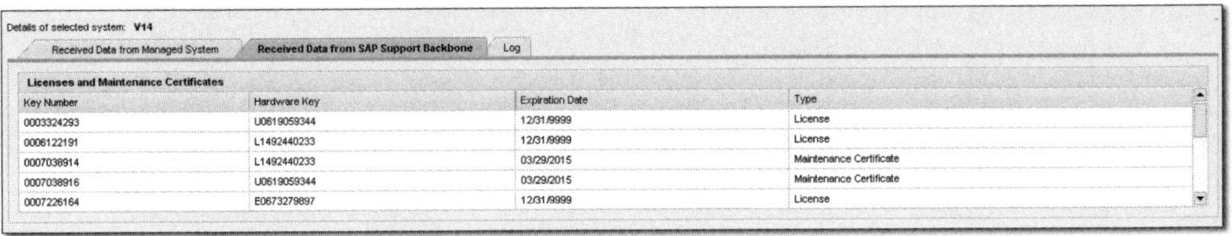

Details of selected system: **V14**

Received Data from Managed System | **Received Data from SAP Support Backbone** | Log

Licenses and Maintenance Certificates

Key Number	Hardware Key	Expiration Date	Type
0003324293	U0619059344	12/31/9999	License
0006122191	L1492440233	12/31/9999	License
0007038914	L1492440233	03/29/2015	Maintenance Certificate
0007038916	U0619059344	03/29/2015	Maintenance Certificate
0007226164	E0673279897	12/31/9999	License

Figure 4.115 Detail View of the Licenses and Certificates

4. With the Automatic Distribution button, you can activate or deactivate the forwarding of certificates to the managed system, for example, if you want to log off the system (see Figure 4.116).

System Overview

View: [Standard View] | Print Version | Export | Automatic Distribution | Download Licenses | Refresh

Activate Automatic Distribution
Deactivate Automatic Distribution

Product System	Installation Number	Mainten... Validity	License	Mainten... Certificate	Received License	Received Mainten... Certificate	Status of Automatic Distribution
BPD	0020143487	□	□	□	□	□	Active
S15	0020119135	□	◇	◇	□	□	Inactive
SCS	0020091482	◇	◇	◇	◇	◇	Active
V01	0020143487	□	□	□	□	□	Active
V03	0020119135	◇	◇	◇	◇	◇	Active
V09	0020154891	□	□	□	□	□	Active
V14	0020161319	□	□	□	□	□	Active
V15	0020272703	□	□	⊠	□	□	Active

Figure 4.116 Activating/Deactivating Automatic Distribution

The license administration allows you to reduce the administration work in the system administration by automating recurring tasks.

4.4 Maintenance Optimizer

SAP Solution Manager supports the process of maintaining your SAP systems (see Chapter 18) with the *Maintenance Optimizer*. The Maintenance Optimizer guides you step-by-step through the maintenance process. Use of the Maintenance Optimizer is mandatory for all systems based on SAP NetWeaver 7.0 or higher. As of this platform release, support packages and support package stacks can only be downloaded from the SAP Support Portal using SAP Solution Manager. (More precisely, SAP Solution Manager is required for approving downloads.)

Old-school administrators were highly skeptical about this procedure because it initially involves more work compared to the conventional download of software components because a maintenance process must be created each time. However, in addition to offering better documentation and an assisted process, another benefit of this method is that it reduces the likelihood of errors. Because the Maintenance Optimizer is based on your predefined system landscape, it can retrieve the release and component information directly from the systems that are to be maintained.

A complete list of required support packages is then provided, which means that you don't need to gather this information yourself manually. In addition, the correct support package levels are determined, and the relevant updates selected automatically. The Maintenance Optimizer thus prevents you from downloading incorrect or incomplete maintenance packages. With SAP Solution Manager 7.1, the Maintenance Optimizer has become an even more user-friendly and fully fledged tool.

Prerequisites for Using the Maintenance Optimizer [+]

For the Maintenance Optimizer to function, the basic configuration of SAP Solution Manager must be completed, and it must be possible to connect to the SAP Support Portal using the RFC destination SAP-OSS (connection test and remote login are successful). In addition, the SAP system for which you want to download support packages must have been created as a product system in the system landscape and assigned to a logical component and a solution.

Finally, you must have assigned your user ID in the SAP Support Portal to your SAP user in Transaction AISUSER. This user is used to connect to the SAP Support Portal in the background.

To download support packages with the Maintenance Optimizer, create a maintenance transaction, and allow the Maintenance Optimizer to guide you through the process:

1. In SAP Solution Manager, start Transaction SOLMAN_WORKCENTER or SM_WORKCENTER. Choose the CHANGE MANAGEMENT work center, and then click on MAINTENANCE OPTIMIZER.
2. Create a new maintenance transaction by clicking the NEW button (see Figure 4.117).

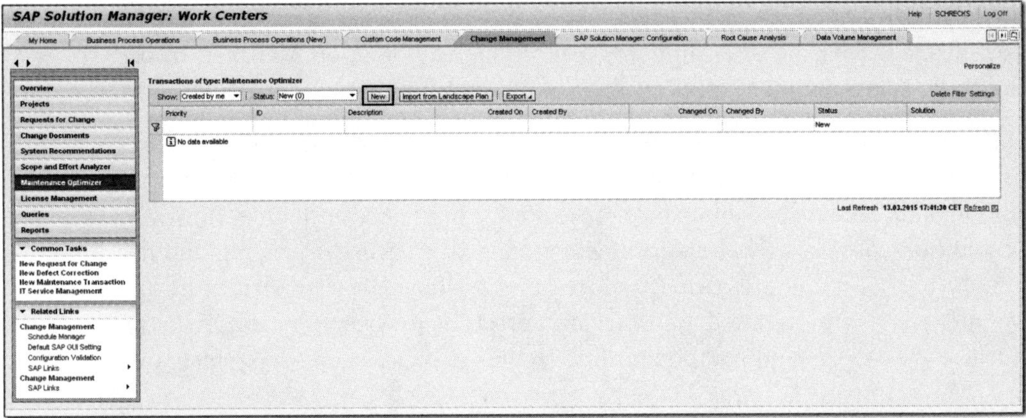

Figure 4.117 Creating a Maintenance Transaction

3. Enter a meaningful text for your maintenance process in the DESCRIPTION field. Restrict your selection using the PRODUCT SYSTEM, SOLUTION, and PRODUCT VERSION fields, and select the desired system (see Figure 4.118). Click the CONTINUE button.

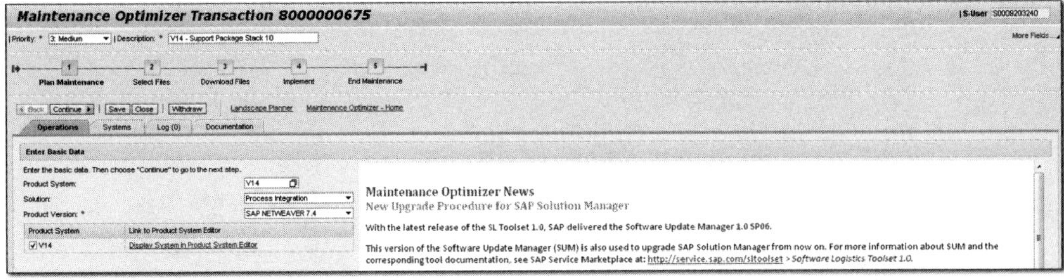

Figure 4.118 Selecting a System for Maintenance

4. In the CHOOSE FILE SELECTION MODE area, leave the setting as CALCULATE FILES AUTOMATICALLY – RECOMMENDED (see Figure 4.119). Choose CONTINUE to proceed to the next step.

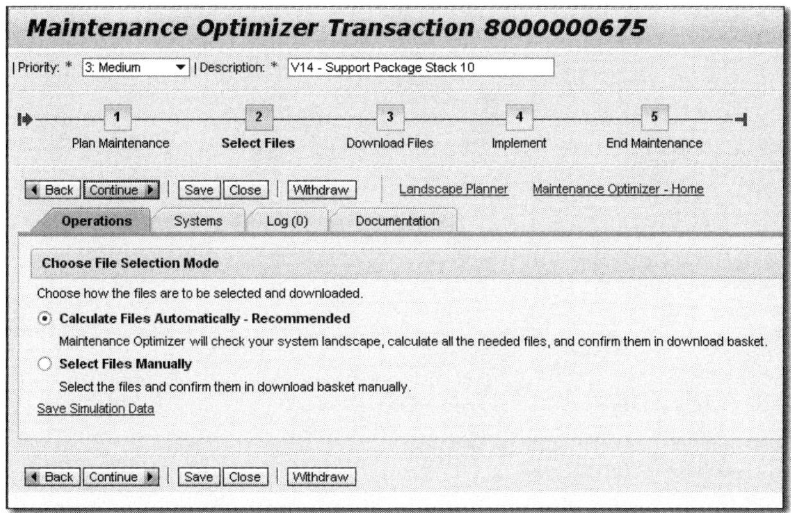

Figure 4.119 Automatic File Calculation

5. Choose the desired maintenance option, for example, SUPPORT PACKAGE STACKS (see Figure 4.120). Click on CONTINUE.

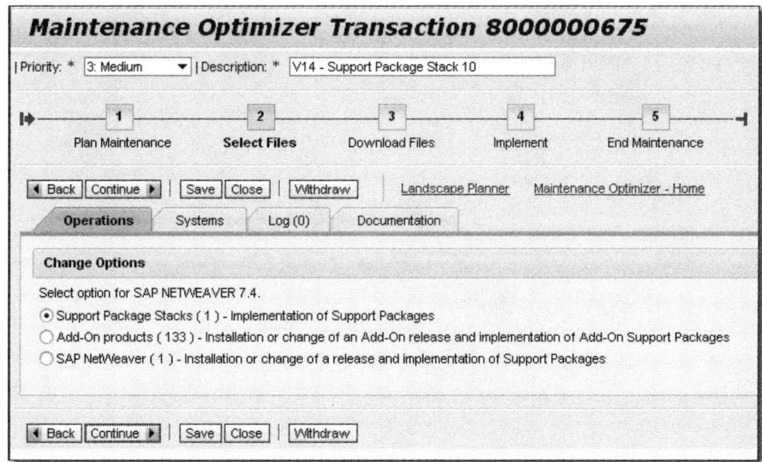

Figure 4.120 Selecting a Maintenance Option

6. Use the dropdown lists in the SELECT TARGET area to select the system's TARGET STACK (see Figure 4.121). Click on CONTINUE.

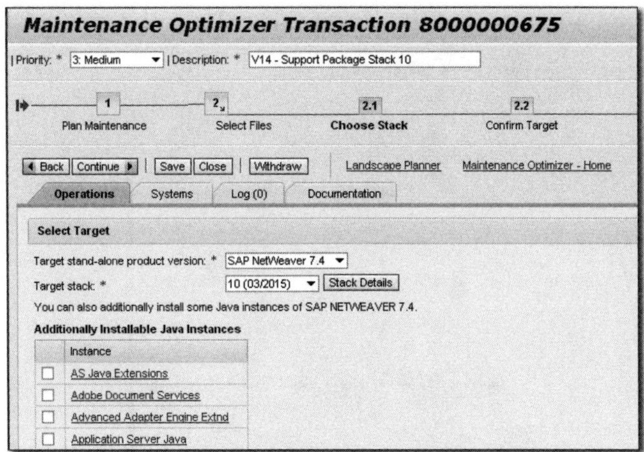

Figure 4.121 Selecting the Target Support Package Stack

7. In the next step, the maintenance target is confirmed once again (see Figure 4.122). Make sure that the Maintenance Optimizer has selected the correct target version, and click on CONTINUE.

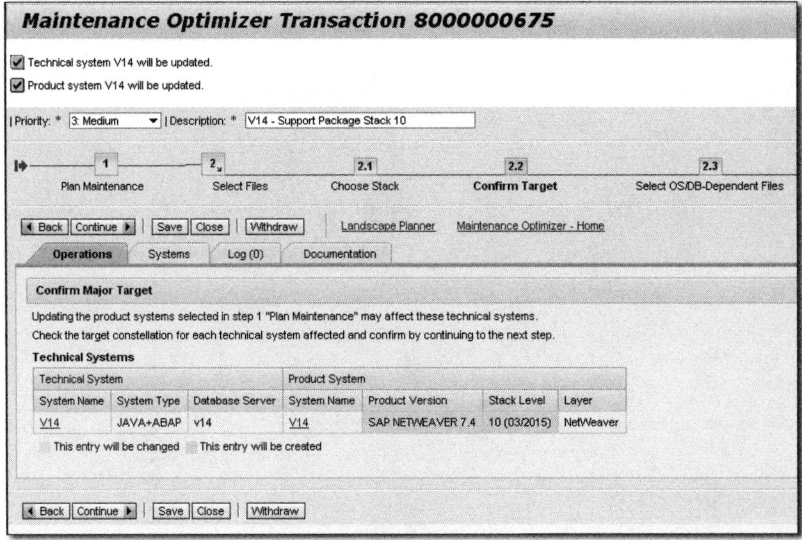

Figure 4.122 Confirming the Maintenance Target

8. You can also choose add-on products that you want to install (see Figure 4.123). This selection is optional. For this sample configuration, don't make any selection, and click on CONTINUE.

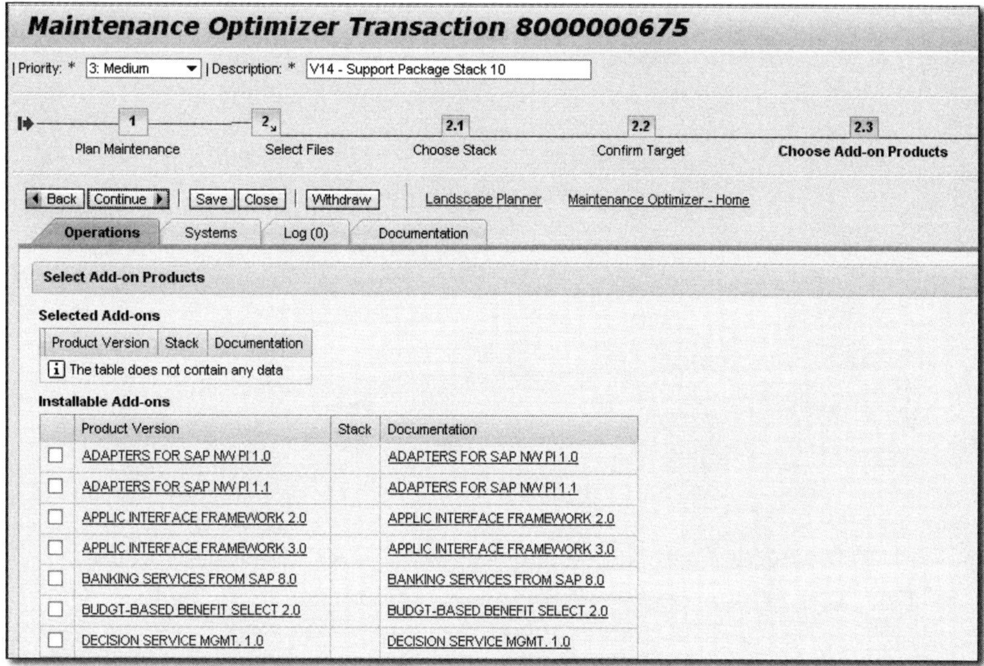

Figure 4.123 Selecting Add-On Products

9. In the next step, you choose download files that depend on the operating system and the database (see Figure 4.124). This includes the kernel components (part I + II, IGS), SAP host agent, the patch for the SAP Java Virtual Machine (for Java systems), and the current version of the Software Update Manager, which ultimately runs the maintenance. Click on CONTINUE.

10. Now add the files to your selection that are independent of the support package stack to be imported (see Figure 4.125). These include, for example, the latest SPAM/SAINT patch (see Chapter 18, Section 18.4). Click on CONTINUE.

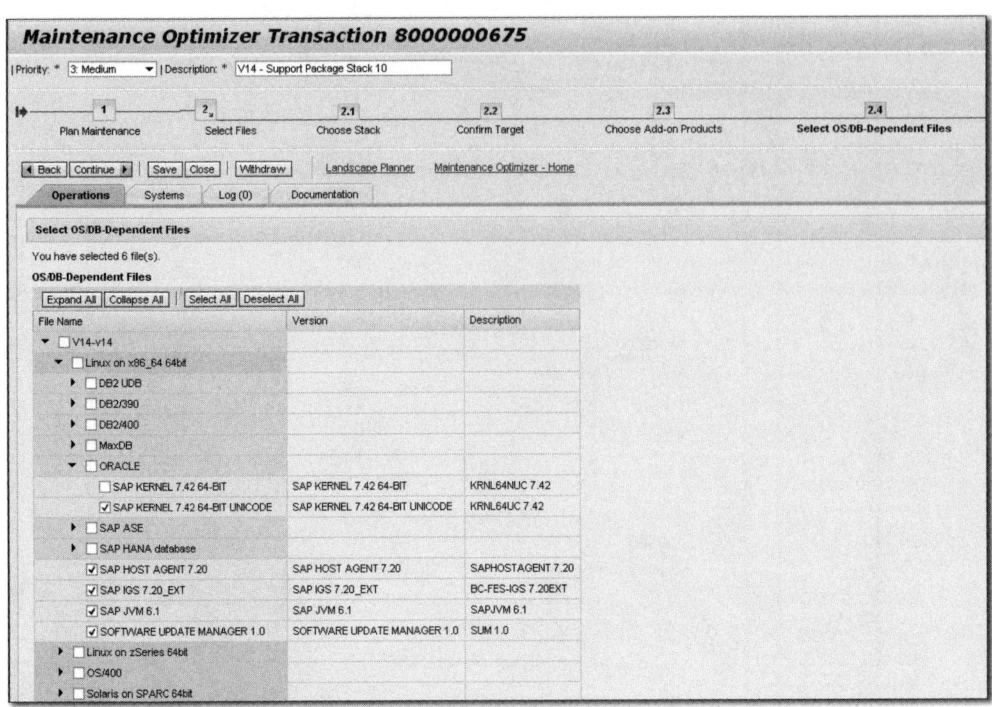

Figure 4.124 Selecting the Download Files

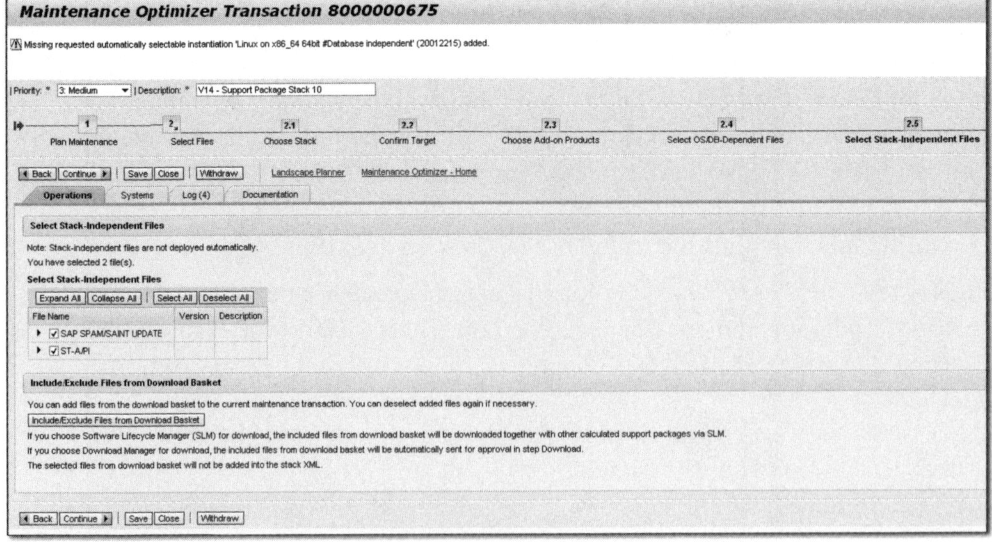

Figure 4.125 Selecting Stack-Independent Data

11. In the next screen, check the selection of the ABAP and non-ABAP support packages. If you maintain a system with Java components, don't miss the ADD JAVA PATCHES button (see Figure 4.126)!

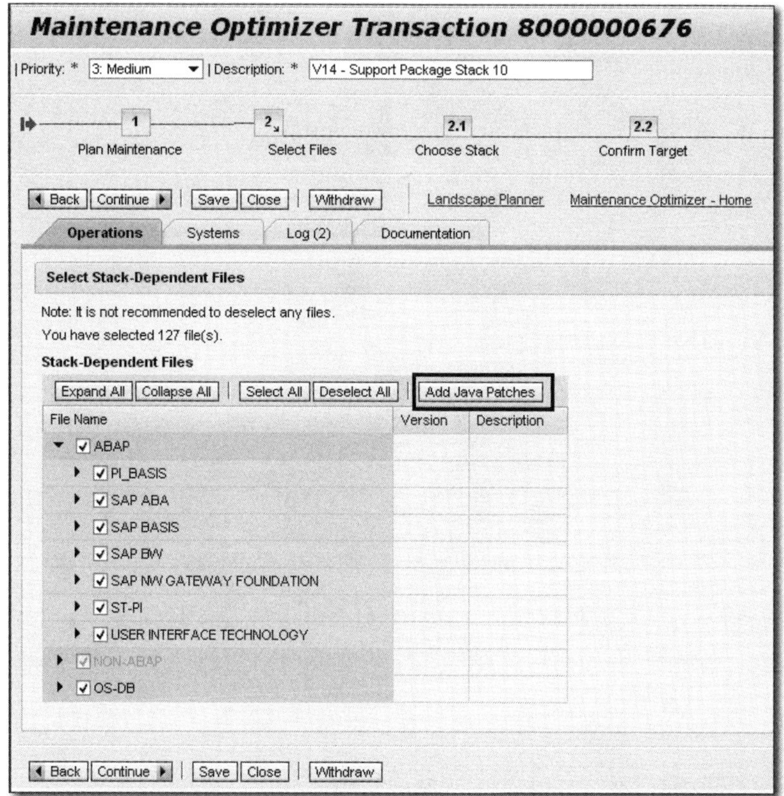

Figure 4.126 Add Java Patches Button

12. If you clicked the ADD JAVA PATCHES button, select the Java packages with SELECT ALL in the dialog box with the same name (see Figure 4.127). Select the INCLUDE SELECTED JAVA PATCHES INTO STACK XML option so that the Java files are automatically included when SUM runs the maintenance transaction. Click on OK.
13. In the next step of the Maintenance Optimizer, choose the DOWNLOAD BASKET as the download tool, and click on CONTINUE (see Figure 4.128).

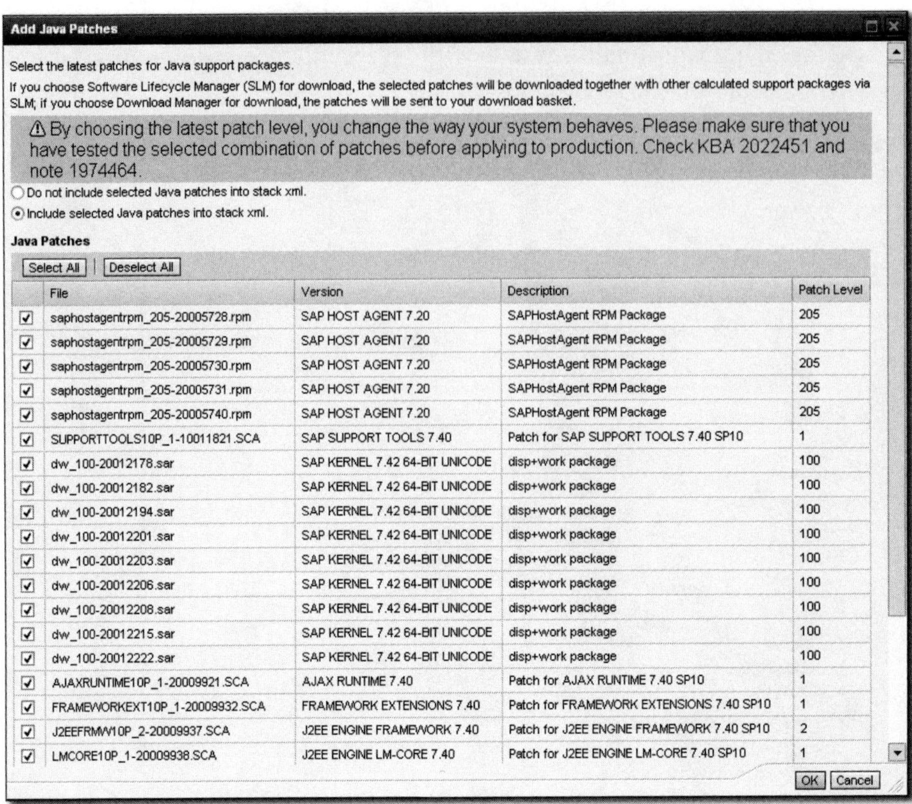

Figure 4.127 Selecting Java Patches

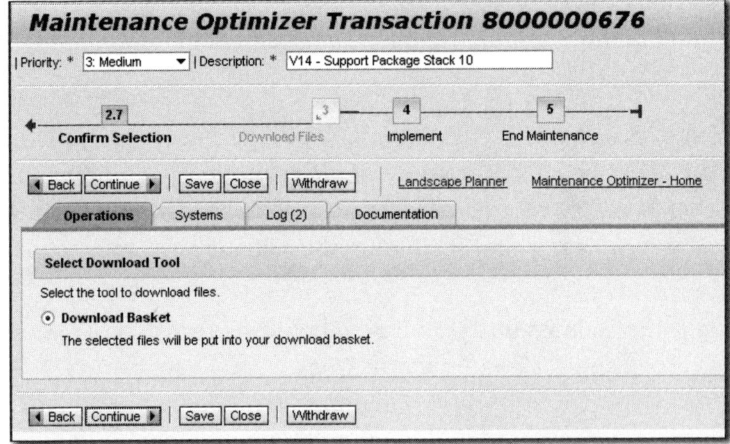

Figure 4.128 Selecting the Download Basket as the Download Tool

14. The files are automatically stored in your Download Basket (see Figure 4.129) and can be downloaded using SAP Download Manager (see Chapter 18, Section 18.1.3). Moreover, a stack delta file (*SMSDXML_<...>.xml*) is generated and added to the *trans* directory of SAP Solution Manager. You require this file later on for SUM. You can also download this file directly on the STACK FILES tab. When you're finished, click on CONTINUE.

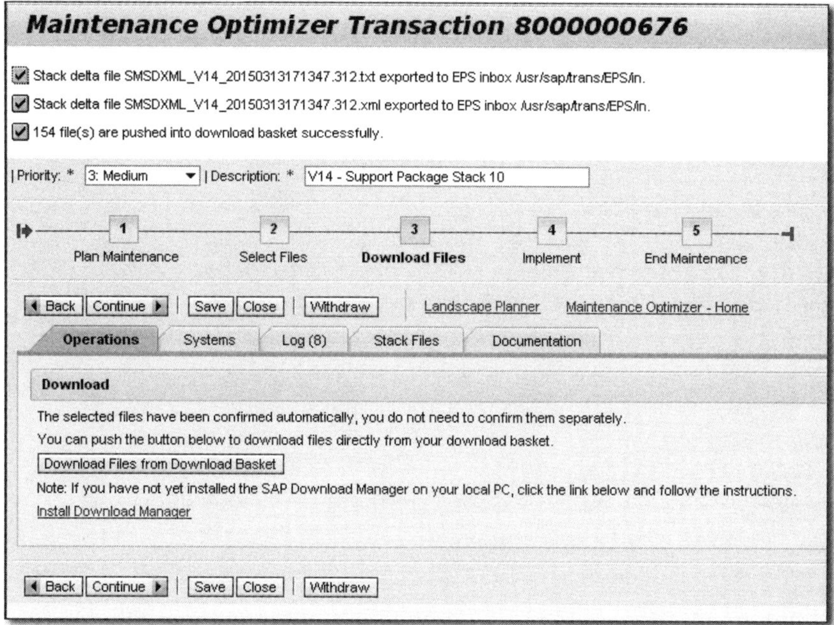

Figure 4.129 Maintenance Files Ready for Download

The "Download Files from Download Basket" Button [!]

A direct download using the DOWNLOAD FILES FROM DOWNLOAD BASKET button is *not* recommended because this method is particularly laborious if you have a very large number of files to download.

Downloading the SAP Download Manager [+]

If the SAP Download Manager isn't yet installed on your PC, you can download it from the SAP Support Portal in this step by clicking on the INSTALL DOWNLOAD MANAGER link.

15. The next step manages the status of the maintenance transaction and doesn't directly influence the subsequent process. For example, set the STATUS OF IMPLEMENTATION to IN PROCESS, and save the Maintenance Optimizer process using the SAVE button (see Figure 4.130).

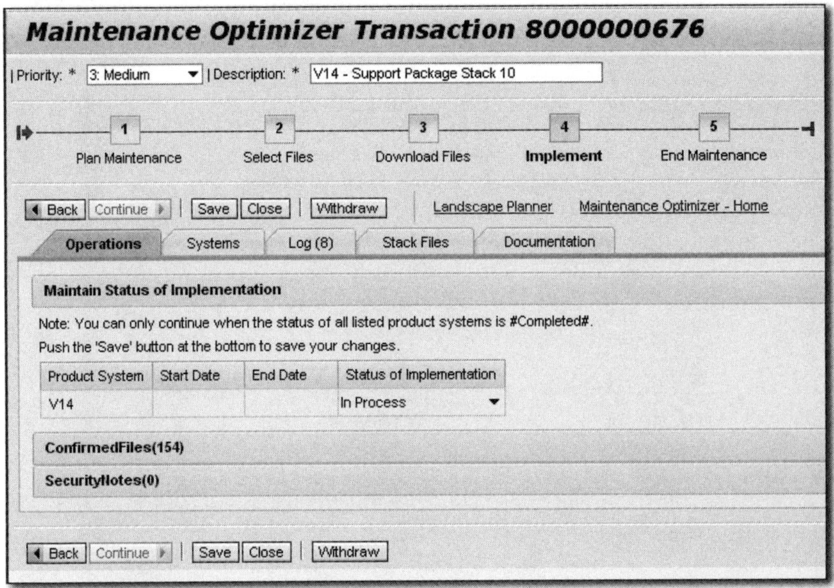

Figure 4.130 Setting the Implementation Status

16. You can now proceed to import the support packages (see Chapter 18). SAP Solution Manager is no longer required here, so you can close the Maintenance Optimizer. After you've completed the maintenance, reopen the Maintenance Optimizer transaction, and set the implementation status to COMPLETED. Click on CONTINUE.

17. To finish the maintenance transaction, finally click on COMPLETE TRANSACTION (see Figure 4.131).

[!]

Completing the Transaction

To go from step 4 (IMPLEMENTATION) to step 5 (END MAINTENANCE), you must set the status of the implementation to COMPLETED. SAP Solution Manager won't allow you to move on to step 5 until you do so.

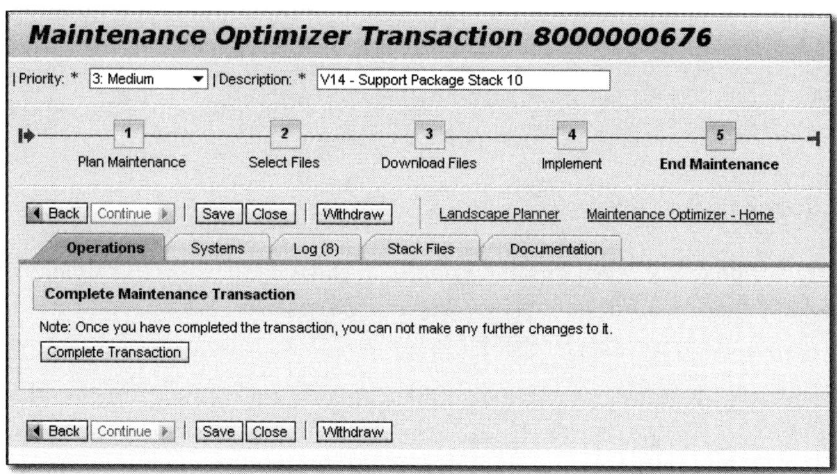

Figure 4.131 Complete Maintenance Transaction

18. The maintenance transaction has been completed, and no further changes can be made to it. Your transaction is now displayed as COMPLETED in the overview of maintenance transactions (see Figure 4.132).

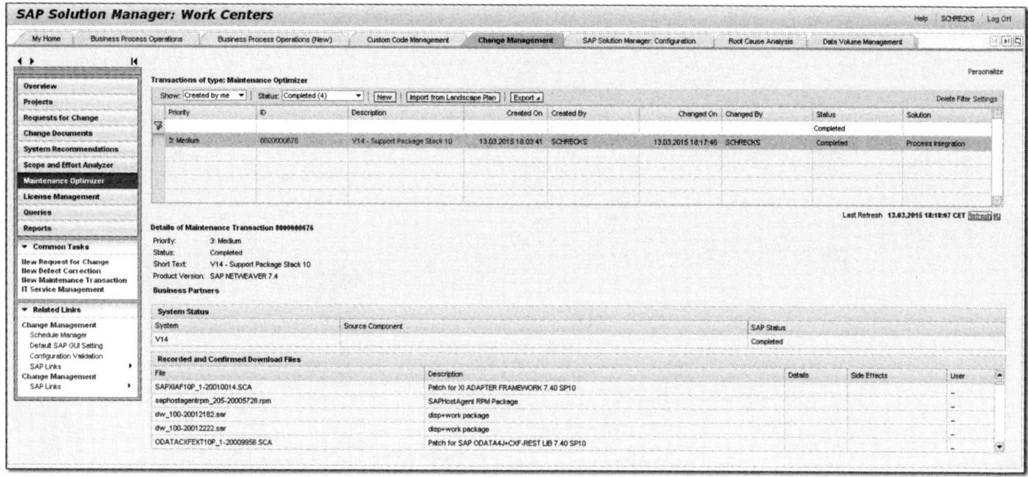

Figure 4.132 Overview of Maintenance Transactions

You now know how to download support package files from the SAP Support Portal using SAP Solution Manager and the Maintenance Optimizer tool. Chapter

18 describes how to import these files into your SAP system manually. We recommend using SUM for importing support packages because in this case the maintenance transaction runs automatically to a large extent.

4.5 Summary

SAP Solution Manager is indispensable for utilizing SAP services, for example, the download of support packages. It also offers a range of tools that make the job of SAP system administrator more efficient.

The system administration and system monitoring functions described in this chapter help you manage a system landscape of a medium to very large size enterprise. This makes it easy for you to leverage synergy effects. SAP Solution Manager also offers some functions that are of interest in the context of SAP projects. Incident Management and Change Request Management enhance the functions of this central system to provide you with an even broader range of options.

This chapter provides you with specific points of reference and checklists to help you plan and execute tasks that you need to perform on a regular basis.

5 Scheduled Tasks

Certain areas of your SAP system need to be monitored on a regular basis to ensure reliable operation. To handle these tasks, it's useful to have a schedule to work through at specific intervals. This chapter presents sample checklists that you can use and modify to suit your own specific requirements. The chapter is structured so that the tasks are divided into groups based on the frequency with which they occur. Here you'll find lists that need to be performed once a day, once a week, and once a year.

Benchmark – Frequency of Execution [!]

Note, however, that the classification used here is merely intended as a rough guideline. The type of your SAP system and the scope of its use will determine whether a task that is listed here as having to be performed on a weekly basis may actually need to be executed once a day.

The individual checklists are, in turn, based on the following aspects:

- Critical tasks
- SAP system
- Databases
- Operating system
- Other
- Notes

Checklists Available for Download [+]

To make things simpler, you can also download the individual checklists as PDF files from the publisher's web site at *www.sap-press.com/3639*.

Use the tables from this chapter as checklists. They provide basic information about the relevant transactions. For more information about these transactions, refer to the chapters specified in each checklist.

5.1 Critical Tasks

Some critical tasks have to be performed every morning. You can use these tasks to determine whether the SAP system is running as normal and whether your backups have been successful. If you detect that your system isn't running smoothly or that the backups weren't successfully completed, you need to resolve these issues promptly to prevent system outages or data loss.

5.1.1 Check Whether the SAP System Is Running

Your first task of the day is to perform a high-level check to ascertain whether the SAP system is running as normal. If there are any problems, users will ask you for information about the cause of the problem and when the issue will be resolved.

You can use the following as a general principle: If you can set up a connection to the SAP system, you can assume that the system is running and that the network between you and the system is functioning. If you work from a workstation, log in using the SAP GUI. If you can log in, your test has been successful.

5.1.2 Checks to Determine Whether Your Backups Have Been Successful

You need to verify whether the backups that were scheduled to be performed overnight have been successfully completed. Backups of the SAP database and the corresponding nondatabase files at the operating system level are required to restore the SAP system should the need arise. The following are examples of non-database files:

- Database log dumps
- Files for third-party applications that don't save their data in the system, for example, external control files
- Transport files
- Files for inbound and outbound interfaces
- Externally stored print files

Problems with backups need to be resolved as quickly as possible. If the database fails, necessitating a restore, and the most recent backup wasn't completed successfully, you have to use the most recent successful backup for the restore. The further back in time you need to go to find a successful backup, the more time you will have to spend restoring and updating the database.

As soon as the problem is resolved, you should perform an online backup as a precaution, provided that this doesn't have a significant impact on performance. Indeed, this precautionary backup in enshrined in some corporate policies.

Some files need to be synchronized with the SAP database at the operating system level. If you restore the SAP system without these files, you will be unable to use the restore (e.g., in the case of external control files that must be synchronized with the system files for the control reports to match the SAP reports).

Conducting Backup Tests and Troubleshooting [!]

You must execute these critical tasks first thing each Monday morning. If a shift is worked between the hours of 10:00pm and 7:00am, you should conduct backup testing as soon as the backups are completed. Each defective backup identified must be investigated immediately, and the underlying problem resolved. You should never simply have blind faith in the backup working properly during the coming night. If this backup also fails, you'll already be missing a backup for another whole day.

An overview of all critical tasks is provided in Table 5.1.

Transaction	Code	Action	Explanation
Users	AL08/ SM04	Display all users currently logged on to the system, together with their user ID and terminal.	Allows administrators to detect faulty or multiple logons.
OS Monitor	ST06	Display operating system logs.	Allows administrators to detect possible OS and hardware problems (e.g., a failed drive).
Select background jobs/Job Scheduling Monitor	SM37/ RZ01	Select and monitor batch jobs scheduled in the background.	Allows the administrator to detect any critical jobs that have been executed incorrectly. Other tasks may depend on the successful execution of these jobs.

Table 5.1 Critical Tasks – Checking the SAP System and Backups

Transaction	Code	Action	Explanation
CCMS Alert Monitor	RZ20	Monitor servers (DEV, QAS, Test, PRD, etc.) in your environment using a central program.	Alerts indicate potentially serious problems that require an immediate solution.
Select lock entries	SM12	Display a list of all lock entries. Locks prevent other users from changing data records that you're in the process of editing.	Allows the administrator to remove old locks or locks that need to be removed.
Update records	SM13	Display, process, test, reset, delete, and access statistics for update records.	Administrators can process any update records that haven't yet been processed.
System log	SM21	Analyze system logs.	Supports the administrator in the early detection of system problems in the SAP system.
Batch input	SM35	Manage batch input sessions.	Alerts the administrator to the existence of new or faulty batch input sessions.
Work processes	SM50/ SM51	Display the status of work processes; Transaction SM50 is used for systems without an application server. ▸ Transaction SM51 is the central transaction. ▸ Transaction SM50 is started for each application server.	Allows users to monitor work processes and check whether any have been processed incorrectly or have been running for too long.
Spool requests	SP01	SAP System Output Manager.	Helps you resolve time-critical print job issues.
Tune summary	ST02	Display statistics relating to SAP buffer performance, fine-tuning of buffer parameters, SAP database parameters, and operating system parameters.	Enables the solving of problems with extensive buffer swaps. Search for entries shown in red in the SWAPS column, and monitor the time details to identify trends.

Table 5.1 Critical Tasks – Checking the SAP System and Backups (Cont.)

Transaction	Code	Action	Explanation
Load analysis in the SAP system	ST03N	Determine system performance.	If you know the normal load distribution when the system is running, you can make minor adjustments that may help when problems occur.
Database performance analysis	ST04	High-level database performance monitor.	Allows you to monitor the growth of the database, capacity, input/output statistics, and alerts. You can drill down to display additional information.
ABAP dump analysis	ST22	Display the logs of ABAP short dumps.	Allows you to determine why a report or transaction terminated.
Transport Management System	STMS	Check transport queues and logs.	Allows you to detect errors in the import of transport requests.

Table 5.1 Critical Tasks – Checking the SAP System and Backups (Cont.)

Profile Parameter for Automatic User Logoff [⚙]

We assume that the `rdisp/gui_auto_logout` profile parameter has been set. This parameter defines an automatic user logoff if no user activity is detected for a predefined number of minutes.

5.2 Daily Tasks

This section lists the tasks that we recommend you perform once a day.

Using the Checklists [+]

When using checklists, you should ensure that you always record the system in which the checks are performed, when they are performed, and the person responsible. We therefore recommend that you enter the following details at the top of each checklist:

System: __________

Date: ____/____/____

Administrator: ____________________

Possible changes should be recorded immediately at the bottom of the checklist. We recommend that you use a table similar to that shown in Table 5.2 for this purpose:

Problems	Action	Solution

Table 5.2 Sample for Notes

General information and documentation of changes should be included in every checklist you use. However, we've omitted these elements from the checklists in this chapter to save space.

5.2.1 Critical Tasks

An overview of all daily tasks is provided in Table 5.3.

Task	Transaction	Chapter	Procedure	Done/ Initials
Check whether the SAP system is running.			Log on to the SAP system.	
Check whether the daily backup was executed without errors.	DB12/DB13	8	Test the database backup. Duration of backup:	
			Check the backup at the operating system level. Duration of backup:	

Table 5.3 Critical Tasks – Summary

For more information about critical tasks, see Section 5.1.

5.2.2 SAP System

The checklist in Table 5.4 provides an overview of tasks relating to the SAP system.

Task	Transaction	Chapter	Procedure	Done/ Initials
Check whether all application servers are running.	SM51	2	Check whether all servers are running.	
Check the work processes.	SM50	2	Check for all work processes with the status RUNNING or WAITING.	
Check the CCMS Alert Monitor.	RZ20	3	Look for alerts.	
Look for any update records that have terminated. An unusually high number of unprocessed update records indicates a processing problem, for example, a bottleneck for update work processes in a background job.	SM13	2	▸ Set the date to one year ago today. ▸ Enter the placeholder "*" under USER. ▸ Select the status ALL. ▸ Check for any rows with ERR.	
Check the system log.	SM21	2	Set the time and date to the time and date before the most recent log check. Look for: ▸ Errors ▸ Warnings ▸ Security notifications ▸ Terminations ▸ Database problems ▸ Other unusual events	
Look for any terminated jobs.	SM37	16	Enter the placeholder "*" under USER NAME. Check whether all critical jobs have been executed successfully. Check the log of terminated jobs.	

Table 5.4 Daily Tasks – SAP System

Task	Transaction	Chapter	Procedure	Done/ Initials
Look for errors in the import of transport requests.	STMS	17	Check the import queues and import histories of the individual systems for any transports with the return code of 8 or higher.	
Look for "old" locks. An unusually high number of lock entries indicates a processing problem, for example, a background job that wasn't completed correctly.	SM12	2	Enter "*" as the user name. Look for entries for previous days.	
Look for users logged on to the system.	SM04/AL08	13	Look for unknown or unusual users and terminals. This task should be executed several times a day.	
Look for spool problems.	SP01	15	Look for spool requests that have been "in process" for more than an hour.	
Check the batch input log.	SM35		Look for: ▸ New jobs ▸ Jobs with errors	
Check dumps.	ST22	2	Check whether a large number of dumps occurred. Look for any unusual dumps.	
Check the statistics for system load.	ST03N	11	Check whether the response or processing times of the system are unusually high.	
Check the buffer statistics.	ST02	11	Look for swaps.	
If necessary, check the user administration log.	SCUL	13	Look for warning and error messages.	

Table 5.4 Daily Tasks – SAP System (Cont.)

5.2.3 Databases

The checklist in Table 5.5 provides an overview of tasks relating to the database.

Task	Transaction	Chapter	Procedure	Done/ Initials
Check the error log.	ST04	8	Look for error messages or problems.	
Check tables and memory usage.	DB02	8	Check how much memory is occupied in the database. Check whether inconsistencies in the database are reported.	

Table 5.5 Daily Tasks – Database

5.2.4 Operating System

The checklist in Table 5.6 provides an overview of tasks relating to the operating system.

Task	Transaction	Chapter	Procedure	Done/ Initials
Check for problems in the system log.	ST06	9	Check the operating system log.	

Table 5.6 Daily Tasks – Operating System

5.2.5 Other

The checklist in Table 5.7 provides an overview of all other tasks.

Task	Transaction	Chapter	Procedure	Done/ Initials
Check the uninterrupted power supply (UPS).	UPS program log	9	Check the following: ▸ Events ▸ UPS self-test ▸ Errors	

Table 5.7 Daily Tasks – Other

5.3 Weekly Tasks

The following tasks should be performed on a weekly basis.

5.3.1 SAP System

The checklist in Table 5.8 provides an overview of tasks relating to the SAP system.

Task	Transaction	Chapter	Procedure	Done/ Initials
Check the spool for problems and error-free processing.	SP01	16	Check and remove old spool requests.	
Perform TemSe consistency check.	SP12	16	Check and remove any inconsistencies.	
Check the Security Audit Log.	SM20	10	Analyze the Security Audit Log.	
Check the EarlyWatch Alert.	SOLUTION_MANAGER	4	Check the EarlyWatch report for instructions on system optimization.	

Table 5.8 Weekly Tasks – SAP System

5.3.2 Databases

The checklist in Table 5.9 provides an overview of tasks relating to the database.

Task	Transaction	Chapter	Procedure	Done/ Initials
Check the database for available memory.	DB02	8	Record the available memory.	
Monitor the growth of the database and estimate its future growth.	DB02	8	Record the database's memory history.	
Check database consistency (DBCC).		8	Check the output of the DBCC job for errors (Microsoft SQL Server).	

Table 5.9 Weekly Tasks – Database

Task	Transaction	Chapter	Procedure	Done/ Initials
Refresh the Microsoft SQL Server statistics.		8	Check whether the statistics were refreshed successfully.	

Table 5.9 Weekly Tasks – Database (Cont.)

5.3.3 Operating System

The checklist in Table 5.10 provides an overview of tasks relating to the operating system.

Task	Transaction	Chapter	Procedure	Done/ Initials
Check that the file system has sufficient memory.	RZ20	9	Check memory usage and whether a sufficient amount of memory is available in the file system.	

Table 5.10 Weekly Tasks – Operating System

5.3.4 Other

The checklist in Table 5.11 provides an overview of all other tasks.

Task	Transaction	Chapter	Procedure	Done/ Initials
Check the system monitor for updates.	System monitor	3	Search for events that need to be added or deleted.	
Check the alert mechanism of the system monitor.	System monitor	3	Send test email and test paging.	
Clean the tape drive.	Tape drive	6	Clean the tape drive with a cleaning cartridge.	

Table 5.11 Weekly Tasks – Other

5.3.5 Overview of Transactions

Table 5.12 provides basic information about the transactions specified in the checklists. For more information about these transactions, refer to the chapters specified in each checklist.

Task	Transaction	Action	Explanation
Database performance	DB02	Analyze the database assignment.	Allows the administrator to monitor the history of the database memory and to monitor execution of the database analysis.
CCMS Alert Monitor	RZ20	Monitor servers (DEV, QAS, Test, PRD, etc.) in your environment using a central program.	Alerts indicate potentially serious problems that require an immediate solution.
Spool requests	SP01	SAP System Output Manager.	Helps you resolve time-critical print job issues.
Consistency check of the temporary sequential (TemSe) database	SP12	Compare the data of the TemSe objects (TST01) with the TemSe data tables (TST03).	Relationships between objects and data in TemSe may be destroyed as the result of a restore, database copy, faulty client copy, or client deletion without previous deletion of corresponding objects.

Table 5.12 Weekly Tasks – Transactions

5.4 Monthly Tasks

We recommend that you execute the tasks listed in this section on a monthly basis.

5.4.1 SAP System, Database, Operating System, Other

The checklist in Table 5.13 provides an overview of all tasks relating to the data archiving system (DAP) system, database, and operating system, as well as other tasks.

Task	Trans-action	Chap-ter	Procedure	Done/ Initials
SAP System				
Defragment the memory.		2	Restart the system.	
Databases				
Monitor the growth of the database.	DB02	8	Record and monitor database usage.	
Operating System				
Back up your file server.		9	Perform a full backup of the server.	
Check file system usage.		9	Record file system usage; monitor usage. ▸ Do you need the additional memory? ▸ Do you need to run cleanup programs?	
Other				
Check consumable items.		6	Do you have a replacement cleaning cartridge for all tape drives/drive cards? ▸ DAT (digital audio tape) ▸ DLT (digital linear tape) Do you have replacement media for swappable data carriers? ▸ ZIP ▸ MO (magneto-optical) ▸ DVD/CD blanks Do you have preprinted forms? ▸ Shipping documents ▸ Invoices ▸ Checks Do you have supplies of special materials, such as toner cartridges? Do you have office supplies in stock? ▸ Toner for laser printers ▸ Paper (for printers) ▸ Batteries ▸ Pens, etc.	

Table 5.13 Monthly Tasks – SAP System, Database, Operating System, Other

5.4.2 Checking Consumable Items

You should check your supplies of consumable items at regular intervals. Consumable items are items that you need on a regular basis, including the following:

- Cleaning cartridges
- Data cartridges (tapes and disks)
- Toner for laser printers
- Ink cartridges
- Batteries
- Forms
- Envelopes
- CD and DVD blanks

Some consumable items must be classified as critical. When you run out of these supplies, it has an immediate impact on business processes, which may even need to be interrupted as a result. Your stock of available consumable items should be sufficient to cover a scale of different levels of demand and to last until new items can be added to your supplies.

[Ex]

Critical Consumables

If you run out of toner cartridge for the check printer, you're unable to continue printing checks from the system. Your only option then is to complete the checks manually (provided that you've already printed out sufficient copies). Particular attention must be paid to special or customer-specific consumable items, such as the following:

- **Special cartridges for inkjet printers used to print MICR characters on checks**
  These cartridges aren't available from all suppliers.
- **Preprinted forms (with the corporate letterhead, instructions, or other customer-specific details)**
  These consumable items are often so specific that the lead time for their replenishment is usually far longer than for nonspecific items.

Make sure that you have sufficient supplies of consumable items. To check your consumable items, follow these steps:

1. Check the expiration date of items that expire. This applies both to materials that are currently in use and those currently in stock.

2. Check items that expire at designated intervals, for example, after a certain number of hours or number of operating cycles.

Materials with an Expiration Date [Ex]

Certain DATs may be used for a maximum of 100 full backups, after which they must be replaced.

3. Keep in touch with your buyers and suppliers. Market conditions may make it more difficult to procure certain items. In this case, the replenishment lead times for these items will be longer, and you'll need to order larger quantities.
4. Keep track of consumption, and adjust your stocks and purchasing plans accordingly.

Taking Account of Replenishment Lead Times [+]

Some items have longer replenishment lead times for procurement, production, or shipping.

5.5 Quarterly Tasks

The following tasks should ideally be performed once each quarter.

5.5.1 SAP System

The checklist in Table 5.14 provides an overview of tasks relating to the SAP system.

Task	Transaction	Chapter	Procedure	Done/ Initials
Archive quarterly backup.			Send the tapes with your quarterly backup to external long-term storage locations.	
Perform security check.	SU01/SUIM	13	Check the user IDs and search for users that are no longer current and which need to be locked or deleted.	

Table 5.14 Quarterly Tasks – SAP System

Task	Transaction	Chapter	Procedure	Done/ Initials
	SM30	13	Check the list of "prohibited" passwords (table USR40).	
	RZ10	13	Check the profile parameters for password standards.	
Check scheduled jobs.	SM37	15	Check all scheduled jobs and determine whether they are still relevant.	

Table 5.14 Quarterly Tasks – SAP System (Cont.)

5.5.2 Databases

The checklist in Table 5.15 provides an overview of tasks relating to the database.

Task	Transaction	Chapter	Procedure	Done/ Initials
Archive quarterly backup.		7	Send the tapes with your quarterly backup to external long-term storage locations.	
Check scheduled jobs.	DB13	8	Check all jobs scheduled with the DBA Planning Calendar, and determine whether they are still relevant.	
Test the database restore process.		7	Restore the database on a test server. Test the restored database.	
Clean up the BR*TOOLS logs (Oracle)	Clean up BR*TOOLS.		Check/maintain *init<SID>.dba*.	

Table 5.15 Quarterly Tasks – Database

5.5.3 Operating System

The checklist in Table 5.16 provides an overview of tasks relating to the operating system.

Task	Transaction	Chapter	Procedure	Done/ Initials
Archive quarterly backup.		7	Send the tapes with your quarterly backup to external long-term storage locations.	
Archive old transport files.		6	Archive old transport files and logs.	

Table 5.16 Quarterly Tasks – Operating System

5.5.4 Other

The checklist in Table 5.17 provides an overview of all other tasks.

Task	Transaction	Procedure	Done/ Initials
Check service contracts.		▸ Check whether any contracts have expired. ▸ Check whether any changes in use have occurred.	

Table 5.17 Quarterly Tasks – Other

5.6 Yearly Tasks

Certain tasks are best performed on an annual basis.

5.6.1 SAP System

The checklist in Table 5.18 provides an overview of tasks relating to the SAP system.

Task	Transaction	Chapter	Procedure	Done/ Initials
Archive end-of-year backup.		7	Send the tapes with your end-of-year backup to external long-term storage locations.	

Table 5.18 Yearly Tasks – SAP System

Task	Transaction	Chapter	Procedure	Done/ Initials
Check user security.		13	Check the user security authorization forms using the assigned profiles. You can also use report RSUSR100 for this purpose.	
Check profiles and authorizations.	SU02	14	Execute with report RSUSR101.	
	SU03	14	Executed with report RSUSR102.	
	PFCG	14	Check authorization roles.	
Check the separation of duties (SOD).	PFCG	14	Check the authorization concept for critical overlapping.	
Check user IDs SAP* and DDIC.	SU01/SUIM	13, 14	Check whether the users are locks, or change the password if necessary.	
Start SAP programs to track user activity.	SUIM, SA38 (or SE38)	14	Start SAP programs to track user activities: RSUSR003, RSUSR006, RSUSR007, RSUSR008_009_NEW, RSUSR100, RSUSR101, and RSUSR102.	
Check whether the system status has been set to NOT MODIFIABLE.	SE03	10	Check whether the system status has been set to NOT MODIFIABLE.	
	SCC4	10	Check whether the relevant clients have a modifiable status.	
Check locked transactions.	SM01	10	Check transactions against the list of locked transactions.	

Table 5.18 Yearly Tasks – SAP System (Cont.)

5.6.2 Databases

The checklist in Table 5.19 provides an overview of tasks relating to the database.

Task	Transaction	Chapter	Procedure	Done/ Initials
Archive end-of-year backup.		7	Send the tapes with your end-of-year backup to external long-term storage locations.	

Table 5.19 Yearly Tasks – Database

5.6.3 Operating System

The checklist in Table 5.20 provides an overview of tasks relating to the operating system.

Task	Transaction	Chapter	Procedure	Done/ Initials
Archive end-of-year backup.		7	Send the tapes with your end-of-year backup to external long-term storage locations.	

Table 5.20 Yearly Tasks – Operating System

5.6.4 Other

The checklist in Table 5.21 provides an overview of all other tasks.

Task	Transaction	Chapter	Procedure	Done/ Initials
Perform a disaster recovery.		7	▸ Restore the entire system on a disaster recovery test system. ▸ Test whether normal business can be resumed.	

Table 5.21 Yearly Tasks – Other

5.6.5 Overview of Transactions

The checklist in Table 5.22 provides an overview of important transactions.

Transaction	Transaction code	Action	Explanation
User administration.	SU01	All users who leave your enterprise should be refused access to the SAP system as soon as they leave. By locking or deleting these user IDs, you ensure that the SAP system can only be accessed by users with the required authorization. Check that this task has been completed on a regular basis.	User maintenance also involves blocking user access to the SAP system for users who are no longer employees of your enterprise. This also prevents other users from logging on with this ID.
Change the object catalog entry of objects.	SE03/SCC4	Test and apply changes correctly.	Users should be unable to make changes to objects in the QA or production system. This prevents changes to objects and the configuration in the production system before testing is performed. You can protect the integrity of the pipeline by setting the status of the production system to NOT MODIFIABLE.
Lock transaction codes.	SM01	Lock transactions.	This prevents users from causing damage to the system by running transactions.

Table 5.22 Yearly Tasks – Transactions

You can use switches to prevent changes from being made to the system. In the production system, these should be set to NOT MODIFIABLE (see Chapter 10, Section 10.3.5). This prevents any changes being made through the development pipeline.

Changes go through the following stages in the development pipeline:

1. Creation in the development system
2. Testing in the development system
3. Transport from the development system to the test system
4. Testing in the test system
5. Transport from the test system to the production system

This method ensures that changes are properly tested in the pipeline and applied to systems.

Critical Transactions [+]

Critical transactions are transactions that may result in the following outcomes:

- Damage to the system
- Creation of a security risk
- Negative impact on performance

An overview of critical transactions is provided in Appendix B.

If a user accesses a transaction by mistake, resulting in one of the outcomes listed in the preceding box, the entire SAP system may be damaged or even destroyed. Access to these transactions is more critical in the production system than in the development or test system. This has to do both with live data and the fact that the business processes depend on the SAP system.

Therefore, some transactions should be locked in the production system but not in the development, test, or training system. Standard security measures normally prevent access to these transactions. However, some administrators, programmers, consultants, and key technical users may have access to these transactions, depending on the specific system in question. In this case, the transaction lock acts, in a way, as a second line of defense. For more information about security in the SAP system, see Chapter 10.

5.7 Summary

Certain tasks need to be executed regularly in an SAP system to ensure that operation remains as smooth as possible. The transactions specified in this chapter will remind you which tasks need to be performed and when, and they can be used as a basis for formulating your own schedule for system administration. The SAP Solution Manager enables technical mapping of this schedule (see Chapter 4, Section 4.3), so that you can be reminded on a regular basis about open tasks.

This chapter explains how to develop a backup and restore strategy. After covering the main backup methods, we'll explore the benefits and drawbacks of each. You can then use this information to develop an appropriate backup concept for your own SAP system.

6 Backup and Restore

An effective backup and restore strategy forms the backbone of SAP system operation. The goal of this strategy is to enable a full or partial recovery of the database in as short a time as possible following system failure, an emergency situation (see Chapter 7), or a hardware/software error.

The information provided in this chapter is intended to help you develop a concept to optimize the continuous backup of your data and allow you to restore your database quickly and efficiently in the event of an emergency. We begin by discussing the two aspects of backup and restore, before turning to the issue of performance. Details relating to individual databases are provided in Chapter 8.

The goal of a backup strategy is to minimize data loss in the event of an emergency, in other words, to make sure that no data are lost or to minimize the period during which data are lost. To achieve this objective, your backup strategy should be as clearly defined as possible because an unnecessarily complicated strategy may also make your backup and restore processes unnecessarily complicated. You should also ensure that your procedures and handling of problems are well documented and that your backup strategy doesn't impact negatively on your enterprise's routine business operations.

6.1 Backup

The purpose of a system backup is to allow you to access the data currently stored in the system and to import that data back into the system following an emergency. This is a safeguarding measure because you'll only need to use the backup if your system needs to be restored, unless you plan, for example, to build a quality assurance system from a system backup. Nevertheless, backups aren't a trivial matter and shouldn't be treated as such. On the contrary, you should take a moment to consider how much data can be lost in the event of a system failure and what ramifications this may have for the enterprise. Even if you lose order data for only an hour or a day, the economic impact on your business may be huge.

6.1.1 What Has to Be Saved?

Three categories of data require backup:

- Databases
- Transaction logs
- Operating system files

You may need to use different tools to back up different data. For example, SAP tools only allow you to back up one or two of the data categories; for example, the DBA Planning Calendar (Transaction DB13; see also Chapter 8) is capable of backing up your database and transaction logs but not your system files.

Databases

The database represents the very heart of your SAP system. Without a backup of your database, you won't be able to restore the system. The frequency with which you perform a full database backup determines how far back in time you must go when restoring the system:

- If a full backup is performed every day, you require the full backup from the previous day, as well as the transaction log files from the last day or last half-day to restore the system.
- If a full backup is performed every week, you require the full backup from the previous week. However, you must also recover the log files from the last number of days to update the system.

A daily backup reduces the risk of your being unable to restore the current database status if you're unable to use the relevant log files.

If you don't perform a daily backup, you require a large number of log files to update the system. This step increases the duration of the restore process due to the volume of files involved and also increases the risk of your being unable to restore the database to the current status due to individual defective transaction logs.

Weekly Backups [Ex]

A restore is performed using the full backup from the previous week, which dates from four days ago. Keep the following in mind:

- Ten log files are created every day.
- As a result, the system must be updated with 40 files (10 log files × 4 days).
- You require 120 minutes to load the log files from the tape to the hard drive (40 files × 3 minutes per file).
- You require 200 minutes to update the database with the log files (40 files × 5 minutes per file).

The total time required for the restore—not taking account of the actual database files—is 320 minutes (or 5.3 hours).

Daily Backup [Ex]

A restore is performed using the full backup from the night before. Keep the following in mind:

- A maximum of 10 log files are created every day.
- You require 30 minutes to load the log files from the tape to the hard drive (10 files × 3 minutes per file).
- You require 50 minutes to update the database with the log files (10 files × 5 minutes per file).

The total time required for the restore—not taking account of the actual database files—is 80 minutes (or 1.3 hours).

As illustrated in these examples, a restore takes much longer to perform if backups are made on a weekly rather than a daily basis. These examples also demonstrate that the time required to restore the log files depends on the size of the files and on the number of days that have elapsed since the last full backup was performed. The process can quickly become unmanageable in the case of large log files (e.g., 100MB or more per hour). By performing full database backups on a more frequent basis (i.e., by leaving fewer days between backups), you can automatically reduce the time required for a restore.

You therefore need to weigh the question of whether performing a full database backup on a daily basis with fewer files is a more viable option for your system, based on the volume of transactions involved, than, for example, performing a full backup on a weekly basis with an accordingly higher number of transaction logs to be reloaded. Of course, this decision also depends on the importance of the SAP system in the context of your enterprise's business processes.

[+]

Daily Full Database Backups

You should have a very good reason not to perform a daily backup of your production database (e.g., your database is too big to be backed up overnight). In recent years, the cost of storage space has fallen to such a degree that a backup strategy based on a full daily backup is no longer impractical. SAP recommends that you perform a fully daily backup of the production database and that you store the 28 most recent backups.

Transaction Logs

Transaction logs form part of a database backup and are essential to performing a database restore. These logs contain all changes made to the database. They allow you to undo these changes and to restore the database to its most recent status after a system failure. It's essential to have a complete backup copy of all transaction logs. If even a single log can't be used when you need to perform a restore, the database can't be restored beyond the point at which this gap occurs.

[Ex]

Damaged Log Files

A log file from Tuesday is damaged. The system fails two days later, on Thursday. You can only restore the database up to the last error-free log from Tuesday. From the point at which the damaged log occurs, all subsequent transactions are lost.

The frequency of log backups is also a business decision, based on the following factors:

- Transaction volume
- Critical periods for the system
- Volume of data that management can tolerate losing
- Resources required for the backup

[+]

Intervals Between Log Backups

The following principle applies here: The greater the volume of transactions, the shorter the intervals that you should leave between the individual log backups. In this way, the volume of data that can be lost in the event of a potential disaster in the data center is automatically reduced.

To back up the transaction logs, follow these steps:

1. Save the transaction log to the hard disk.
2. Copy this backup to a backup file server located at another site. You should always use verifications when you save your logs across a network.

   The backup file server should ideally be located in another building or another city. A remote location increases the chances of your backup remaining intact if the primary data center (containing the SAP servers) is destroyed.
3. Save the transaction log backups from both servers (the SAP server and backup file server), together with the other files from the operating system level to tape on a daily basis.

Database Stops When the Backup Directory Is Full [!]

Transaction logs are stored in a directory, which must have sufficient storage space. The database stops when the available memory in the directory is completely occupied by the transaction logs. If no further processing can take place in the database, the entire SAP system stops also. It's therefore important to think ahead and to back up transaction logs on a regular basis.

If a backup file server in a separate location isn't available to you, you must save the transaction log backups to tape after each log backup operation and send the tapes to another location on a regular basis.

No Backups in Append Mode [!]

Don't back up the logs to tape in *append mode*. In this mode, several backups are written to the same tape. In the event of an emergency, all backups on this tape may be lost.

Files at the Operating System Level

You also need to back up files at the operating system level:

- Configuration of the operating environment (e.g., system and network configuration)
- SAP files (e.g., kernels)
- System profiles

- Spool files
- Transport files
- Other SAP-related applications
- Interfaces or add-on products that save their data or configurations outside of the SAP database

The data volume of these files is relatively small compared to the SAP database. Depending on how your system works, the backup of the files in the list may only comprise a few hundred megabytes to a few gigabytes. In addition, some of the files may contain static data, which remains unchanged for months at a time.

The frequency of backups at the operating system level depends on the applications involved. If you need to ensure synchronicity between these application files and the SAP system, they must be backed up with the same frequency as the logs.

[Ex]

Synchronizing Application Files and the SAP System

One example of this scenario is a tax calculation program, which stores VAT data outside of the SAP system. These files must correspond exactly to the sales orders in the system.

A quick and easy method of backing up operating system files is to copy all files to the hard drive of a second server. A range of products for backing up data at the operating system level is available on the market at the present time. You can then back up all required files to tape from the second server. This approach minimizes the periods during which files are unavailable.

6.1.2 Backup Types

We can distinguish between different types of database backups based on the following three questions:

- What is backed up? Is the backup a full or incremental backup?
- How is it backed up? Online or offline?
- When is it backed up? Is the backup scheduled or ad hoc?

You can, in principle, combine the various answers to these questions to produce a range of options. Each variant has its benefits and drawbacks, which are discussed next.

What Is Backed Up?

In terms of the scope of the database backup, you can choose between a full or partial backup, as described here:

- **Full database backup**
  Note the following considerations:
  - *Advantages*: The database as a whole is backed up, which makes a database restore faster and easier to perform. Fewer transaction logs are required to update the database.
  - *Disadvantages*: A full backup takes longer to complete than an incremental backup. As a result, users are disrupted for a longer period. You should therefore only perform full backups outside of normal business hours.
- **Incremental backup with transaction logs**
  Note the following considerations:
  - *Advantages*: An incremental backup is much quicker than a full database backup. Because the backup takes less time to complete, users are impacted for shorter periods and, in most cases, to a barely noticeable degree.
  - *Disadvantages*: A full backup is required to restore the database. Restoring the database with incremental transaction logs takes much longer and is more complicated than a restore based on a full backup. The most recent full backup must be used for the restore, and the system then has to be updated with all logs dating from the time when the full backup was made. If several days have elapsed since the last full backup, a very large number of logs have to be restored if the system fails. If you're unable to restore one of these logs, you'll also be unable to restore any subsequent log.

A third option may also be available to you, depending on your database and operating system (see Table 6.1):

- **Differential backup**
  In this case, you only back up the changes that have been made since the most recent full backup. One commonly used approach is to perform a full backup every weekend and differential backups during the week.
  - *Advantages*: The risk of your being unable to perform a full restore because of damaged log backups is reduced. A differential backup saves all changes made to the database since the last full backup.

- *Disadvantages*: As with an incremental backup, you still require a full backup as a basis for restoring the database. A differential backup may take longer to complete than a backup of the transaction logs. Initially (after the full backup), it will take less time, but the process will gradually become longer over time as more data are changed.

[!]

Full Backup as a Basis for an Incremental Backup

Note that an incremental backup always comprises a full backup *and* a backup of the subsequent transaction logs. A restore based on incremental backups becomes problematic as soon as the underlying full backup or one of the transaction logs is damaged or lost.

How Is It Backed Up?

In terms of backup mode, we can distinguish between *offline* and *online*, based on the system status of the SAP system and the database. To perform an offline backup, you must disconnect the SAP system from the database and stop work in the SAP system. An online backup, on the other hand, is performed during normal operation of the database and SAP system.

- **Offline**

  Benefits

  - An offline backup is faster than an online backup.
  - There are no complications caused by changes to data in the database during the backup.
  - All files are backed up at the same time and give a consistent picture of the system; the corresponding operating system files are synchronized with the SAP database.
  - You can execute a binary verification during an offline backup. However, this doubles the time required to perform the backup.
  - An offline backup doesn't require the SAP system to be stopped. The SAP buffer is therefore preserved.

  Drawbacks

  - The SAP system isn't available during an offline backup.
  - When the database is stopped, the database buffer is also cleared of all data. This operation has a negative impact on performance, with this effect lasting until the buffer is filled with data once again.

- **Online**

  Benefits

  - The SAP system is available to users during the backup. This is essential if the system is in constant demand 24/7.
  - The buffers aren't cleared. As a result, there is no negative impact on performance following the backup.

  Drawbacks

  - An online backup is slower than an offline backup. The time taken to complete the backup increases over time because the backup runs during normal operation and uses system resources.
  - Online performance deteriorates during the backup.
  - The data in the database may change while the backup is still in progress. Transaction logs are therefore particularly important to ensure a successful restore.
  - The corresponding files at the operating system level may possibly no longer be synchronized with the SAP database.

Transaction Logs in an Online Backup [!]

If you use online backups, transaction logs are particularly important to ensure a successful restore.

When Is It Backed Up?

You can select the time at which a database backup is performed based on a backup schedule or spontaneously as the need arises in a specific situation. For more information about the tools and transactions mentioned in the following, refer to Chapter 8:

- **Planned**

  Planned backups are performed on a regular basis, for example, daily or weekly. For normal operation, you can use the DBA Planning Calendar (Transaction DB13) to configure an automated backup schedule for the database and transaction logs. You can use this calendar to set up and check backup cycles. You also have the option of performing important database checks and updating the statistics. You can display the status of your backups in the DB Backup Monitor (Transaction DB12).

- **Ad hoc**
  Ad hoc backups are spontaneous backups performed on an as-needed basis, for example, prior to large-scale system changes, in preparation for an SAP upgrade, or after a structural change to the database (such as the addition of a data file). Backups that are monitored directly by the user or are performed on an as-needed basis can either be initiated using the DBA Planning Calendar or at the database or operating system level.

The DBA Scheduling Calendar can be used for both regular, planned backups and spontaneous backups. However, tools at the database level, such as SQL Server Management Studio for Microsoft SQL Server or BR* Tools under Oracle, are more commonly used for these ad hoc backups. Regardless of the backup method you select, you should always set the following goals:

- Create a reliable backup that can be used to restore the database.
- Use a simple backup strategy.
- Reduce the number of interdependencies required for operation.
- Try to eliminate or minimize the impact on the work being done in the system by business department users.

Weigh up the needs of system security and performance to use the available options to develop the best possible backup strategy for your system.

Database System-Specific Terminology

Table 6.1 compares the terminology that is used in relation to the various methods outlined in the previous sections and for backing up various database systems. The backup methods and jobs have different names, depending on which database your system uses. However, the underlying principle is always the same. If in doubt, consult your database administrator or the documentation provided for your database system.

	Full Database Backup	Content	Partial Database Backup	Log Backup
DB2 UDB	Full database backup in TSM (Tivoli Storage Manager)	Offline/online tablespace backup in TSM	Incremental database backup with DB2 UDB in TSM	Archiving of inactive log files in TSM

Table 6.1 Terminology of Backups

	Full Database Backup	Content	Partial Database Backup	Log Backup
	Full database backup to storage device	Offline/online tablespace backup to storage device	Incremental database backup with DB2 UDB to storage device	Archiving of inactive log files on storage device
	Full database backup with vendor library	Offline tablespace backup with vendor library	Incremental database backup with DB2 UDB and vendor library	One-step archiving in storage software
SQL Server	Full database backup		Differential database backup	Transaction log backup
Oracle	Full database backup offline and new log backup	Full offline database backup	Partial offline database backup	New log backup
	Full database backup online and new log backup	Full online database backup	Partial online database backup	

Table 6.1 Terminology of Backups (Cont.)

6.1.3 Backup Strategy

Your backup strategy unites and defines all measures used to back up your system and specifies when exactly backups are to be performed, the intervals at which they are to be performed, and the backup method that is to be employed. You should document this strategy in the form of a *backup frequency table* in a backup concept and ensure that it meets the needs of management and the business departments.

You then implement your *backup strategy* with the appropriate backup tools. Ultimately, however, your choice of tool to implement the strategy is of little relevance, be it one of the SAP-internal tools mentioned previously or the standard tools provided in your database or operating system. The most important criteria when selecting tools are manageability, reliability, and the monitoring options.

To develop a backup strategy, follow these steps:

1. **Determine your requirements for performing a restore and your tolerance range in the event of a system failure.**
   A generally acceptable system downtime can't be defined because this will differ significantly between one enterprise and the next. The costs incurred by system downtime include the cost of production downtime, plus the costs of performing a restore, such as time, money, and so on. These costs should have a sliding scale, similar to that used for insurance premiums. With insurance, the more coverage you require, the greater the premium you have to pay. If we apply this model to a system restore, we get the following rule: The faster a restore is completed, the more expensive the solution you'll have to use.
2. **Determine which combination of hardware, software, and processes is used in the desired solution.**
   Better hardware makes a backup and restore faster, better software makes these operations easier, and well-defined processes make them more efficient. Of course, this all comes at a price, and the benefits will have to be weighed against the costs. However, it's even more important that your method be reliable.
3. **To test your backup method, implement the hardware, and check the actual runtimes and test results.**
   Ensure that you obtain results for all backup types used in your environment and not only those you intend to use. This information will facilitate future evaluation and capacity planning decisions and, if necessary, provide a sound basis for comparison.
4. **Test your restore method by simulating various system failure scenarios.**
   Document all aspects of the restore; include questions such as who will take care of specific tasks, which users are to be notified, and so on (see Chapter 7). You should also consider the likelihood that a restore may occur exactly when you least expect it. You should therefore conduct testing on an ongoing basis and perform additional tests whenever changes are made to hardware or software components.

Schedule additional backups on specific dates (e.g., end of the month, end of the year) alongside your daily and weekly backup cycles. These aren't strictly necessary but can, for example, be archived separately as a safeguard against a disaster (see Chapter 7).

6.1.4 Strategy Recommendations

This section provides some further tips and recommendations for developing a backup strategy.

Databases

As discussed previously, we recommend that you perform a full database backup every day, provided that the cost of doing so isn't prohibitively high. If your database is too large for a daily backup, you should perform a full backup once a week instead.

Testing Your Backups

Your backups need to be tested on a regular basis. To do this, you need to restore the system and then conduct a test to determine whether the restore has been completed to your satisfaction. Without testing your backups, you can't tell whether all of the required data has actually been backed up on the tape or hard disk.

Why Testing Your Backups Is Essential [Ex]

Various files were backed up, but the APPEND switch was set incorrectly for the second file and all subsequent files. As a result, the files weren't saved to tape in sequence. Instead, the tape was rewound after each file was backed up and prior to the backup of the next file. The outcome is that all files except for the last file to be backed up were overwritten.

Test Finished Backups Only [!]

You can only test a backup after *all* files have been backed up. If you test your backup after each individual file, the system will be unable to detect whether the previous file has been overwritten.

Database Integrity

You need to check the integrity of the database regularly to ensure that it contains no damaged blocks. Otherwise, defective blocks may remain undetected during a backup. If possible, conduct an integrity test once a week outside of business hours. This can be scheduled with the DBA Planning Calendar.

Transaction Logs

It's extremely important that you back up your transaction logs. The database and, therefore, also the SAP system, stops when the memory that is available for storing the transaction logs is full.

For this reason, monitor the number of transaction logs in your system, and define your own backup interval, for example, hourly, based on your monitoring findings. The intervals between the backups correspond to the maximum data volume that you can tolerate losing. The risk is naturally higher for an enterprise with a large transaction volume. In this case, it would be advisable to perform a backup every 30 minutes, for example. If your enterprise has a shipping department that starts work at 3:00am, or a production line that works until 10:00pm, you should begin making backups earlier or stop later as required. Transaction logs can be backed up during normal operation without any impact on users.

Files at the Operating System Level

The frequency of backups at the operating system level depends on the applications involved. If you need to ensure synchronicity between the application files and the SAP system, they must be backed up with the same frequency as the database and logs. If perfect synchronicity is less important, you can also back up the application files less frequently.

Backup Strategy Checklist

You need to develop an appropriate system for backing up valuable system data. You should define a suitable strategy as soon as possible to avoid a possible loss of data. You should have worked through a checklist covering all backup-relevant topics before your system goes live (see Table 6.2).

Question, Task, or Decision	Done
Decide how frequently you want to perform a full database backup.	
Decide whether partial or differential backups are required.	
Decide whether to use automatic backups. If you want to use automatic backups, decide where to do this (in the DBA Planning Calendar or elsewhere).	

Table 6.2 Backup Strategy Checklist

Question, Task, or Decision	Done
Decide how frequently the transaction logs are to be backed up.	
Define which backup media (hard disks, tapes, etc.) you want to use.	
Ensure that you can store a day's volume of logs on the server.	
Ensure that you have sufficient memory in the directory for transaction logs.	
Set up the authorizations required for the SAP system, the operating system, and the database.	
Consider whether you want to use the DBA Planning Calendar to schedule the backup of transaction logs.	
Work out guidelines for labeling data carriers to ensure a smooth workflow.	
Decide on the period for which your backups are to be stored.	
Acquire the required hardware (hard disks) or define the size of the tape pool required (tapes required per day × retention period + 20%).	
Take account of future growth and special requirements.	
Initialize the tapes.	
Define a storage strategy for the tapes.	
Document the backup procedures in an instruction manual.	
Train users in the backup procedures.	
Implement a backup strategy.	
Perform a backup and restore for testing purposes.	
Define a contingency plan for emergencies, and decide which users are to be contacted in the event of an emergency.	

Table 6.2 Backup Strategy Checklist (Cont.)

6.2 Restore

You usually perform a restore for one of the following reasons:

- Disaster recovery following an emergency situation (see Chapter 7)
- Testing of your disaster recovery plan (see Chapter 7)
- Copying your database into another system (see Chapter 2)

You access the backups that are made on a regular basis to perform a system restore. In the context of disaster recovery, you usually restart the database and, if necessary, the operating system, using the most recent full backup. You then import the transaction logs that have been created since the full backup. When this procedure is successfully completed, the system once again has the status it had at the time the last error-free log backup was made. The duration of this restore is of critical importance. You want it to be completed as quickly as possible so that the system can be used again after an outage, and the disruption to business processes can be kept to a minimum.

For a *database copy* (e.g., in the context of regular updating of the QA system using a copy of the production system), you normally either import the most recent full backup or generate a live copy using data streaming. Transaction logs are usually ignored.

As in your system backup strategy, you should also have a *restore strategy* in your arsenal, which can be deployed in the event of an emergency. The following factors may influence your restore strategy:

- Business costs incurred by system downtimes
- Operational schedules
- Global or local users
- Number of transactions per hour
- Budget

The development of a restore strategy is discussed in detail in Chapter 7. The actual process of restoring the SAP system and database isn't discussed in this book because this task varies widely between different systems and databases. If in doubt, consult an expert (e.g., your database administrator or an external Basis consultant) who can provide you with operational support for this critical process. You should also collaborate with your database administrator or consultant to test and document the restore process. This transfer of knowledge will soon enable you to perform a restore on your own.

[!]

An Incomplete or Incorrect Restore

If the restore is performed incorrectly or incompletely, it may fail and have to be restarted to avoid the possibility of some files being excluded. Certain data must be entered via your database so that it can be restored subsequently. Work with an expert to identify and document this data.

Because the restore process is one of the most important tasks in the SAP system, you need to test database restores at regular intervals. Chapter 7 provides additional information on this.

6.3 Performance

The key objectives of a database restore are to restore the data as completely as possible and to minimize the time required to do so. The length of time that the SAP system is unavailable to users and, as a result, certain business processes are halted, is of critical importance to an enterprise. System performance is therefore a key factor when performing a restore.

The performance of your backup process is also important, in particular if your system is used globally 24/7. Disruption to users should be kept to a minimum during a backup. As a result, you need to strive to reduce the duration of the backup (in particular, in the case of offline backups) and to ensure adequate system reserves to guarantee acceptable system operation during an online backup.

The performance of your backup and restore processes are largely determined by data throughput on your devices. To improve throughput, you need to identify bottlenecks or devices that are limiting the throughput and eliminate or replace these. This process is subject to economic considerations because performance enhancement with additional or more modern devices is naturally also a cost factor.

This section provides tips for improving the performance of your data backups and restores by implementing some specific measures.

6.3.1 Performance Factors

The main variables, which are provided in the following list, affect the performance of both the backup and the restore:

- **Size of the database**
  The larger the database, the longer it takes to back it up.
- **Hardware throughput**
  This variable determines how quickly the backup can be performed. Throughput is always determined by the weakest link in the backup chain, for example:

  - Database driver array
  - Input/output channel (I/O) channel used
  - Hard disk or tape drive
- **Time of backup**
  This is the time or period available to you for regular system backups. Your objective here should be to minimize disruption to users. Consider both online and offline backups:
  - *Online backup*: The appropriate times for performing online backups are periods during which there is a low level of system activities, which is usually early in the morning.
  - *Offline backup*: The appropriate times for performing offline backups are periods during which you can shut down the SAP system, which is usually at the weekend.

  The times at which you perform system restores are less critical because the system can't run in any case unless you do so.

[+]

Take into Account the Time Differences Between Different Sites

Remember to take into account the time differences between the various sites in which your enterprise is located. For example, when it's 12:00 midday in Central Europe, it's only 6:00am in New York.

6.3.2 Backup Performance

The following approaches to improving backup performance assume that you save your backup locally on the database server. Although a backup via the network is technically possible, performance in this case depends to a large degree on network topology, overhead, and data traffic, while the throughput values of the disk systems take a backseat. In any case, the full capacity of the network is rarely available. If you perform a backup via the network, network performance also deteriorates for other users. As a result, other applications in your enterprise may be slowed down.

Backup to Faster Devices

All approaches to optimizing performance aim to prevent bottlenecks occurring on the backup device. The backup device, usually a hard disk or tape drive, is the device that limits throughput. You should consider the following aspects in this context:

- **Advantages**
  Faster hard disks or tape drives allow you to save an entire database within a reasonable amount of time.
- **Disadvantages**
  Fast memory is more expensive. Hard disks or tape devices with high data throughput require willingness to invest.

Parallel Backup

A parallel backup to more than one tape drive uses a RAID-0 array (Redundant Array of Independent Disks), whereby data can be written to several media (hard disks/tapes) simultaneously. In some environments, for example, Oracle, individual tablespaces or files are backed up on separate drives at the same time. Overall performance is better than when you use a single drive.

If you have a sufficient number of tape drives that can be used in parallel, the bottleneck can be shifted from the tape drives to another component. For this reason, you also need to take account of the performance of other subsystems if you want to use the parallel backup option. These subsystems include the controller, CPU, and I/O bus. In many configurations, the controller or bus represents the limiting factor.

Restoring a Parallel Backup [!]

When you restore a parallel backup, you need to be able to read all media in the set. If a single tape is damaged, the backup can't be used. The more tapes you have in a set, the higher the risk of one of them being damaged.

Backup to Hard Disk before Backup to Magnetic Tape

The backup on hard disks and then on tape is the fastest method to back up a database. The backup to hard disk is usually faster than the backup to tape. With this method, you can quickly save several identical copies to hard disks and, for example, store some in external enterprise locations and others at your own site.

As soon as the backup to the hard disk is complete, the impact on system performance is minimal. Because the backup to tape is made from the copy already made on the hard disk rather than from the production database, there are no competing drains on resources from the backup and database activities. During a disaster recovery process, the data can ideally be restored from the backup on the hard disk. However, this method also has a number of disadvantages:

- You require additional hard disk space equivalent to the size of the database. If your database is large, this may give rise to immense additional costs.
- Until the backup to tape is completed, you have no protection against the risk of potential disasters occurring in the data center. In a disaster recovery scenario, you must recover the files on the hard disk first and then restore the database from the hard disk.

Other options for faster backups are also available, for example, *high availability (HA)* or modern *snapshot procedures*. However, a discussion of these options falls outside the scope of this book.

6.3.3 Restore Performance

The performance requirements for a restore are more important than those for a backup. The restore performance determines when the system will be available again and how quickly business can be resumed. Your objective in this regard is to restore the database and corresponding files quickly and make the system generally available as soon as possible.

The measures to enhance backup performance that we outlined previously also essentially result in shorter restore times. You can therefore examine these proposals from the point of view of both backup and restore performance, for example:

- **Dedicated drives**
  Together with a parallel backup, restoring files and tablespaces to individual, dedicated drives accelerates the process considerably. Only one tablespace or file is written to the drive. As a result, competition for drive resources is avoided.
- **RAID systems**
  RAID 0+1 is faster than RAID5, although these speeds depend on the hardware used. In more cases, the calculation of parity data for the parity drive (RAID5) is more time-consuming than writing the data twice (RAID 0+1). This option is

costly because the usable capacity only amounts to 50% of total capacity, which is significantly less with RAID5:

- *RAID 0+1 = [single_drive_capacity × (number_of_drives/2)]*
- *RAID5 = [single_drive_capacity × (number of drives – 1)]*

- **Drives with better write performance**
  You can generally read data more quickly from modern drives that offer a higher write performance. Enhanced reading capacity reduces the time required to perform the restore.
- **Drive array systems with better write performance**
  The benefit of a faster single drive also applies to drive arrays: As a rule, read speeds generally improve in tandem with write performance, which reduces the time required for a restore.

Measures to improve backup performance are often viewed by management as not being particularly urgent. The reason for this is that backups are usually performed out of core business hours and that enhanced performance isn't usually obvious to users. As a result, it can be difficult to obtain the additional means required for modern technology.

However, if you make the argument that clear time savings can be made in terms of the restore process, you may find that your pleas no longer fall on deaf ears. After all, you'll be able to ensure that the system is available after a disaster or emergency much sooner thanks to this technology.

6.4 Summary

The information provided in this chapter was intended to help you develop a backup strategy for your SAP systems, based on your enterprise's business framework. You can protect your systems from the worst-case scenario by combining full and incremental database backups, as well as by backing up your transaction logs and operating system files. You should aim to be able to restore the system completely within a short space of time should such a scenario arise.

The next chapter, Chapter 7, provides additional specific instructions for managing a disaster situation. Chapter 8 introduces you to the SAP-internal database tools, which you can use for automatic backups.

Even the most conscientious system administrator can become overwhelmed when faced with a system failure, a loss of data, or destruction caused by a natural disaster. For such situations, it's always good to have a plan of action and not to be caught completely off guard. This chapter suggests ways in which you can brace yourself for a disaster and prepare for a subsequent system recovery.

7 Disaster Recovery

Thousands of business processes occur on a daily basis and usually without any problems whatsoever. However, even a very brief system outage can seriously disrupt business processes and result in a loss of time, money, and resources. It's therefore advisable to plan for emergency situations so that you aren't entirely helpless when faced with such problems, irrespective of their size and complexity.

This chapter discusses a system administrator's most important task, namely *disaster recovery*, which is a form of system recovery (see Chapter 6).

7.1 Preliminary Considerations

The goal of disaster recovery is to restore the system after an *emergency* in such a way that the enterprise can continue its business processes. Because business processes come to a standstill not only during the system failure itself but also during system recovery, disaster recovery must be performed as quickly as possible. For this reason, it's even more important to have a tried-and-tested recovery plan. Furthermore, the earlier you start to plan, the better prepared you'll be in an actual emergency.

Note on the Following Explanations [!]

This chapter isn't a guide to disaster recovery. Instead, its sole purpose is to increase your awareness of disaster recovery and to stress how important it is to develop a plan.

An emergency is anything that will damage an SAP system or cause a system failure. This includes damage to a database (e.g., accidental loading of test data into a production system), a serious hardware failure, or a complete loss of the SAP system and the infrastructure (e.g., as a result of a natural disaster or fire). In the event of such an emergency, the most important task of the system administrator is to successfully restore the SAP system. Above all else, however, the administrator should ensure that such an emergency doesn't occur in the first place.

A system administrator should be prepared for the worst and have suitable "emergency plans" in place. Disaster recovery isn't the time to try out something new because unwelcome surprises could ruin the entire recovery process.

When developing a plan, ask yourself the following questions:

- If the SAP system fails, will the entire business process fail?
- How high is the loss of earnings, and how high are the resulting costs during a system failure?
- Which important business functions can no longer be performed?
- How are customers supported?
- How long can a system failure last before an enterprise is incapable of conducting business?
- Who will coordinate and manage a disaster recovery?
- What will users do while the SAP system is down?
- How long will the system failure last?
- How long will it take to restore the SAP system?
- Which SAP system components need to be restored so that a remote recovery is possible?

Careful planning will ensure that you're less stressed in the event of an emergency because you'll already know that the system can be restored and the length of time it will potentially take to perform this system recovery.

If you discover that the time required for a system recovery is too long, and the associated losses are too high, management should consider making an additional investment in equipment, facilities, and personnel. Even though a *high availability* (HA) solution is often costly, these costs may not be as high as those associated with possible losses incurred during a disaster.

7.2 Planning for an Emergency

Creating a disaster recovery plan is considered a large project because development, testing, and documentation require a great deal of time, possibly more than a year. The documentation alone may be very extensive, possibly comprising several hundred pages.

Seek advice from experts if you don't know how to plan for an emergency. A plan that doesn't work is worse than having no plan at all because poor planning lulls an enterprise into a false sense of security. Third-party disaster recovery consultants and suppliers can support you during disaster recovery planning.

7.2.1 Which Measures Apply to Disaster Recovery?

The requirements for disaster recovery can be derived directly from the requirements for system availability, which are laid down by management. The guidelines for the requisite system availability are based, for example, on the losses that an enterprise is expected to incur in the event of a system disaster. The monetary loss is usually calculated by management and specified in USD per time unit, while the failure costs depend not only on the enterprise or sector (e.g., industry/public administration) but also on the division in which the software is used (e.g., production/purchasing).

The desired system availability is usually agreed upon in *Service Level Agreements* (SLAs) that you, as an administrator, must fulfill. Therefore, from your perspective, it's also important to know which investments (e.g., for technical equipment or service personnel) are needed to ensure a certain level of availability for the relevant system. Note that the higher the recovery costs, the less time it will take to perform a recovery. However, you can influence these costs through preventive measures (see Chapter 10) and a good recovery plan.

When it comes to technical business units, you must bear in mind that HA comes at a price. If savings are made in the wrong areas, you could be in for a rude awakening. Such costs must be included in the administrative or IT budget.

Financial Effects of a Disaster [Ex]

The following discusses three examples of how to calculate financial and entrepreneurial impacts for a disaster:

- **Example 1**
  When forecasting the monetary loss associated with a system failure, your enterprise discovered that transaction data can only be lost for a period of one hour. The resulting costs assume that 1,000 transactions (entered in the SAP system and not restored) will be lost each hour. Such a loss in transactions can lead to a loss in sales as well as extremely annoyed customers. If orders urgently required by customers disappear, the situation can become critical. In this case, you must ensure that the frequency with which data is backed up is sufficiently high (e.g., an hourly backup of the transaction logs).
- **Example 2**
  In your enterprise, you discovered that a system can't be offline for more than three hours. The resulting costs (e.g., at an hourly rate of USD $20,000) are based on the fact that no sales can be posted. In this case, you require a sufficiently efficient emergency strategy or infrastructure to ensure that the system is operational again within three hours.
- **Example 3**
  In the event of an emergency (e.g., the loss of a building that houses the SAP data center), the enterprise can only survive a downtime of two days. After two days, customers start to conduct their business elsewhere. Consequently, an alternative method must be found to continue business (e.g., an alternative data center is built, or an emergency contract is agreed upon with an external provider).

7.2.2 When Should the Disaster Recovery Procedure Begin?

For each disaster recovery plan, you must use a unique set of criteria to determine when such a plan will come into effect and when the procedure will begin. Ask yourself the following questions:

- Which characteristics define an emergency?
- Have these characteristics been fulfilled in the current situation?
- Who must be consulted to assess the situation? The relevant person should know not only how a failure can impact the business process but also be aware of the problems associated with a recovery.

These considerations should help you decide whether or not to initiate your disaster recovery procedure. Alternatively, form a committee that will contribute and assess all of the information required to make a decision within the shortest possible time as well as make a decision in relation to implementing the recovery procedure.

7.2.3 Expected Downtime

Downtime is the period during which a system is unavailable. Even though you can only estimate downtime, it's usually longer than the restore time because, after a system recovery, some tests must be performed, user master records must be unlocked, and notifications must be sent, among other things. It's even more important to have an accurate idea of the restore time.

During downtime, it isn't possible, for example, to process orders or dispatch products. The resulting losses are just one part of the costs associated with a disaster recovery. To minimize disruption, you need to examine alternative processes that can be used while the SAP system is being restored.

During downtime, the following factors generate costs:

- The time during which the SAP system can't be used. The longer the system doesn't work, the longer it will take, after a successful recovery, to make up for the losses incurred during downtime. The transactions from the alternative processes deployed during downtime must be fed into the system to update it. This situation may be problematic in an environment that has extensive transactions.
- A failed system generates more costs than an operational system because additional technology or personnel must be used.
- Customers who can't be served or supported by the enterprise may conduct their business elsewhere.
- If follow-up processes also come to a standstill, your customers may have a claim for recourse.

What is deemed to be an acceptable downtime depends, to a large extent, on the enterprise and the nature of its business.

7.2.4 Restore Time

Restore time is the time required to restore lost data and system operability. Different emergency scenarios have different restore times, depending on the operational needs (e.g., the volume of data to be restored).

The restore time must be adapted to the requirements of the enterprise. If the current restore time exceeds the time limit for these measures, the relevant managers must be informed of this disparity. Such a disparity can be resolved as follows:

- By investing in equipment, processes, and facilities that will shorten the restore time
- By changing the requirements of the enterprise so that longer restore times are possible

[Ex]

Minimizing Restore Times via Additional Resources

In an enterprise, it would take a week to restore the system if just one employee was entrusted with this task. The enterprise can't afford the resulting costs or losses in revenue because, during this time, customers would conduct their business elsewhere, vendor invoices would fall due, and invoices would not be paid. In such situations, the management would have to provide additional resources to reduce the restore time to an acceptable level.

If you don't test your recovery procedure (see Section 7.8), the required restore time simply remains an estimate. Use basic testing to ensure that, in the event of an emergency, you can accurately state how much time a system recovery will require (assuming that you have a broad range of experience in this area). You can then also make more accurate statements (to the users) in relation to the expected downtime.

7.2.5 Communication in the Event of a Disaster

A communication concept should form part of your emergency plan. Even if a system failure is usually very noticeable, users can find it annoying if they are left in the dark about their situation.

In certain enterprise areas, a system failure may cause the entire operation to come to a standstill. However, those responsible can't respond appropriately if they aren't informed about when the system is expected to be available again.

If necessary, discuss the following factors with end users:

- Who is affected in the event of a system failure?
- What are the implications of a system failure for the user departments, or which particular dependencies arise?
- What is the timeframe during which information about the system failure must be imparted?

- Which information should be provided (e.g., type, cause, and extent of the disruption, and anticipated downtime)?
- Which contact persons should be informed?
- How should the information be conveyed, or what are the chains of communication?
- Which paths of communication are still available in the event of a disaster? How does communication occur if, for example, the email system is also down?
- After a system has been restored, how do we convey that the system is available again?
- To what extent is information about incident analysis and processing conveyed?

Actively incorporate communication into your recovery plan and coordinate this with the user departments. Good communication can have a calming effect in the event of an emergency because you don't have to deal with complaints and can instead concentrate on restoring the system.

7.3 Recovery Team and Role Distribution

Several people, known collectively as the *recovery team*, are usually involved in a system recovery. A highly coordinated team is the secret to implementing disaster recovery as quickly and as efficiently as possible. There are four key roles within a recovery team:

- **Recovery manager**
  The recovery manager, who coordinates all activities, is responsible for the complete technical recovery.
- **Communications officer**
  The communications officer looks after the users (by telephone, email, etc.) and informs upper management about the current recovery status. If one person assumes responsibility for all communication, the rest of the group can devote themselves to the actual recovery procedure without any interruptions.
- **Technical recovery team**
  This team works to restore the system. If the original plans need to change during the recovery, the technical recovery team must manage such changes and coordinate the technical system recovery.

- **Test and acceptance manager**
  After a recovery has taken place, the test and acceptance manager coordinates and plans the test and acceptance procedures.

The number of employees who assume these roles varies depending on the size of the enterprise. In a small enterprise, for example, one person can assume the role of recovery manager and communications officer. In addition, the descriptions and range of tasks will most likely vary depending on the needs of your enterprise.

Structure your disaster recovery concept in such a way that each team member and each role knows exactly which tasks are to be performed and when. Describe the dependencies and coordination processes between the roles, and create checklists for each team member.

[+]

Status Notice

To prevent incidents involving employees working on the recovery, we recommend that you create a status notice. Key points in the recovery plan are listed here as well as estimates in relation to when the system will be restored and operational again.

Also bear in mind that key employees may not be available in the event of an emergency (e.g., due to vacations or sick leave). Therefore, the team must also be able to perform a successful recovery without these people. In an actual emergency, this issue can be very urgent.

[!]

Planning with Employees from Other Locations

If the emergency is a major natural disaster, your on-site employees will be extremely concerned about their own families as well as the enterprise itself. In some cases, key employees may be badly or even fatally injured. You should also prepare for such situations and formulate plans accordingly. Allow for the fact that employees would have to be flown in from other locations and integrated into the recovery team.

7.4 Types of Disaster Recovery

Disaster recovery scenarios can be divided into two types:

- **In-house recovery**
  In-house recovery is disaster recovery that you perform yourself at your enterprise location. The in-house infrastructure must remain intact as far as possible

(this is usually the case). Ideally, the recovery is made using the original hardware. In the worst-case scenario, the original hardware must be replaced with a backup system.

- **Remote recovery**
  Remote recovery is disaster recovery performed at a special disaster recovery location. In this scenario, the entire hardware and infrastructure has been destroyed as a result of a fire, flood, earthquake, or similar. Consequently, the new servers have to be configured from scratch.

In the case of a remote recovery, you must bear in mind that a second system recovery must take place at the original location as soon as the original facility has been rebuilt. Plan and schedule the second recovery in such a way that as few users as possible are inconvenienced by the fact that the system won't be operational during this recovery.

7.5 Emergency Scenarios

Although numerous emergency scenarios are conceivable, it's impossible to develop plans for all possible scenarios. Therefore, to keep this task manageable, you should limit yourself to approximately three to five probable scenarios. If an emergency occurs, you can adhere to the scenario that best corresponds to the actual emergency. An emergency scenario comprises the following points:

- Description of the emergency
- Planning the main tasks at a high level
- Estimated downtime

The best way to prepare for an emergency is to use emergency scenarios:

1. Use Section 7.5.1 through Section 7.5.3 as a starting point, and prepare three to five scenarios that cover the largest possible range of emergencies.
2. For each scenario, create a plan for the main tasks at a high level.
3. Test the planned scenarios by simulating different emergencies and checking whether your scenarios could be applied to the actual emergency.
4. If this isn't the case, change the scenarios or develop new ones.
5. Repeat the process.

The following three examples are arranged in order of increasing severity. Note that the downtimes cited are merely examples to illustrate the situations you may encounter. Your own downtime will differ from those specified here. You must therefore replace the sample downtime with a downtime that applies to your environment. It will become clear that, depending on the specific emergency, various extensive measures must be taken and that extremely long downtimes may occur even if the damage appears to be minor.

7.5.1 Damaged Database

A database may be damaged if test data are inadvertently loaded into the production system or if data incorrectly transported into the production system causes a crash. If such an incident occurs, the SAP database and associated operating system files must be restored. The downtime is, for example, four hours.

7.5.2 Hardware Failure

The following hardware can fail:

- Processors
- Hard disks or their control unit
- RAID controller (known as an array failure)

If such a failure occurs, the following steps are necessary:

1. Replace the failed hardware.
2. If required, rebuild the server (operating system and programs).
3. Restore the SAP database and associated files.

The downtime is, for example, three days, broken down as follows:

- Two days to procure replacement hardware
- One day to rebuild the server (by one person), that is, eight working hours in total

[+]

Planning a Production Server Replacement

Plan and test the use of your test system (QAS) as a backup server if the production server (PRD) fails.

7.5.3 Complete Loss or Destruction of the Server Facility

The following components may be destroyed if a catastrophe occurs:

- The servers
- The entire supporting infrastructure
- All of the documentation and materials in the building
- The building itself

Such a complete loss of facilities may be the result of a natural disaster such as a fire, flood, hurricane, or a manmade catastrophe. If such a catastrophe occurs, the following steps are necessary:

1. Replace the destroyed facilities.
2. Replace the destroyed infrastructure.
3. Replaced the destroyed hardware.
4. Rebuild the server and the SAP environment (hardware, operating system, database, etc.).
5. Restore the SAP database and associated files.

The downtime is, for example, eight days, broken down as follows:

- At least five days to procure the hardware. If it's a regional catastrophe, it may take longer to procure the hardware because vendors may also be affected by the catastrophe.

National Vendors [+]

Turn to national vendors that have several regional distribution centers. As an additional backup measure, you should look for alternative vendors in distant regions.

- Two days to rebuild the server (by one person), that is, 16 working hours in total.
- While the hardware is being procured and the server is being rebuilt, an alternative facility in which a minimal emergency network can be constructed must work. The integration into the emergency network may take one day, for example.

A complete loss makes it necessary to perform a recovery in a new facility or in a different building. Depending on the size of the enterprise, how important the

SAP system is for the enterprise's business processes, and the regional risk of a natural disaster, it may make sense to build a redundant data center. If one of your data centers is destroyed, operation of the system landscape can then switch to the other data center. However, both of these data centers must be built at least a few kilometers apart from each other. If housed in the same building, it's highly likely that both data centers would fail in the event of a disaster.

If your enterprise doesn't have or want to use the resources necessary for a redundant data center, you can agree on a contract for a disaster recovery location with an external provider. Then, if a disaster occurs, the provider's hardware will be available for your emergency use.

[!]

Recovery Location in an Emergency

Having a contract for a disaster recovery location doesn't guarantee that this location will be available in the event of an emergency. If a catastrophe that affects an entire region occurs, many other enterprises will want to access the same disaster recovery locations as you. In such a situation, you may have to cope without a recovery location because other enterprises will have booked the location before you.

Sometimes, the equipment in a disaster recovery location or emergency data center isn't as efficient as your production system. Therefore, when making plans, bear in mind that you'll be faced with lower performance and limited transactions. For example, reduce background jobs to only the most urgent jobs. Alternatively, only grant recovery system access to those users who need to perform essential business tasks.

7.6 Recovery Script

A recovery script is a document that contains step-by-step instructions for the following aspects:

- The procedure for restoring the SAP system
- The individuals responsible for each step
- The estimated time required for lengthy steps
- The interdependencies between steps

A script helps you implement suitable steps for restoring the SAP system and avoids the risk of any steps being omitted. If you inadvertently omit an important step, you may have to start the entire procedure from scratch, thus delaying the system recovery.

To create a recovery script, you need the following:

- A checklist for each step
- A document that contains screenshots that explain the instructions (if required)
- Flow charts if the sequence in which the steps or activities are performed is complex or confusing

If the main person responsible for the recovery is unavailable, a recovery script will help his representative fulfill this task. The script must therefore fully describe all tasks in an easy-to-understand manner.

Important Steps in the Recovery Procedure

If you want to shorten the recovery process, you can define a procedure whereby as many tasks as possible are handled concurrently. Provide a schedule for each step. The most important steps are as follows:

1. During an emergency, you can support the recovery by doing the following:
   - Gather facts.
   - Retrieve the backup tapes from the remote storage location.
   - Have the crash kit ready (see Section 7.7).
   - Notify all relevant employees (e.g., the in-house SAP team, key users affected by the emergency, infrastructure support, IT, facilities, on-call consultants, etc.).
   - Prepare functional organizations (sales, accounting, and shipping) for alternative procedures for important business transactions and procedures.
   - Notify non-SAP systems that have interfaces from and to the SAP system about the system failure.
2. Minimize the effects of the failure by implementing the following measures:
   - Stop all additional transactions into the system (e.g., interfaces from other systems).
   - Collect transaction documents that will have to be entered again manually.

3. Start the planning process by implementing the following measures:
   - Analyze the problem.
   - Select the scenario plans that best correspond to the emergency that has actually occurred.
   - Change the plans, if necessary.
4. Decide when the disaster recovery procedure will begin:
   - Which criteria formed the basis for determining that an emergency had occurred? Were these criteria satisfied?
   - Who makes the final decision in relation to confirming that an emergency has occurred?
5. Ascertain whether an emergency has occurred.
6. Implement the recovery procedure.
7. Test and approve the restored system. Key users should conduct the relevant tests. Such users use a checklist to clarify whether the system has been restored to a satisfactory level.
8. Update the system with transactions that alternative processes handled during the system failure. As soon as this step is complete, the outcome should be approved again.
9. Notify users that the system is operational again.
10. Arrange a postmortem meeting to ascertain why the disaster occurred.
11. Assess the recovery team's experience of the system recovery, and optimize your disaster recovery plans accordingly.

The recovery script must be easily accessible in the event of a disaster. It must not be stored on a server that may no longer be accessible in the event of a network failure. Also bear in mind that a paper copy could be destroyed in a fire. Prepare yourself for such emergency scenarios and store the recovery script redundantly. Make sure that the storage location is widely known and accessible to those individuals responsible for a recovery in the event of an emergency.

Dependency on Other Applications

Your SAP system is usually connected, via interfaces, to other upstream or downstream systems. If the SAP system fails, feeder systems may also come to a standstill because RFCs accumulate en masse and can't be processed. In addition, downstream systems may not work because your SAP system doesn't make the necessary data available. You can therefore see how easy it is to experience a chain reaction that will have far-reaching consequences for the system landscape and business processes.

In your recovery script, give some thought to communication with those individuals responsible for the applications connected to the SAP system. Make sure that the interfaces are stopped or stop them yourself. Decide how the data will be resynchronized after a system recovery.

7.7 Crash Kit

A *crash kit* contains everything you need to rebuild the SAP server, reinstall the SAP system, and restore the SAP database, including all related files. You must therefore store everything you need to restore your SAP environment in one or more containers physically—in the form of backup tapes, hardware, and documents—and/or digitally. If your location needs to be evacuated, you won't have any time to gather everything you need at the last minute.

You should therefore check your crash kit regularly and check whether all of the elements are still up to date and operational. A service agreement is a good example of a crash kit component that requires such a regular check. If the agreement is no longer valid because its validity period wasn't extended in time, you may not be able to access the services provided by external providers in an emergency, or you may have to enter into negotiations first.

Updating the Crash Kit [!]

If a (hardware or software) component on the server is changed, replace the obsolete component in your crash kit with the latest, tested element.

The crash kit should be stored in a room separate from the servers. If the crash kit is stored in the server room, the crash kit will also be affected if servers are lost. Examples of suitable storage options include the following:

- A commercial data storage location outside the enterprise's location
- Other enterprise locations
- Another secure part of the building

Next, we'll name the most important items that should form part of any crash kit. You can add or omit items, depending on your particular environment. The inventory is sorted according to documentation and software.

Documentation

A crash kit must contain the following documentation:

- A disaster recovery script.
- A test and verification script for functional user groups, which is used to ascertain the functionality of the restored system.
- Installation instructions:
  - Operating system
  - Databases
  - SAP system
- Special installation instructions for the following:
  - Drivers that must be installed manually
  - Programs that must be installed in a certain way
- Copies of the following:
  - SAP licenses for all instances
  - Service agreements (with telephone numbers) for all servers

[!]

Checking the Validity of the Service Agreements

Make sure that the service agreements are still valid. You should perform this check regularly.

- Instructions for retrieving backup tapes from external data stores outside the enterprise's location.
- A list of individuals authorized to retrieve backup tapes from data stores outside the enterprise's location. This list must correspond to the list available at the external data store.
- A parts list that contains enough information to ensure that new hardware can be purchased or leased if the server is destroyed. After a certain length of time, original parts may no longer be available. You should then draft an alternative parts list. At this time, you should also give some thought to updating your equipment.

- Layout of the file system.
- Layout of hardware.
- Telephone numbers of the following:
  - Key users
  - Information service employees
  - Facilities personnel
  - Other infrastructure personnel
  - Consultants (SAP, network, etc.)
  - SAP hotline
  - Data stores outside the enterprise's location
  - Security department or security employees
  - Contact partners within the framework of service agreements
  - Hardware vendors

Software

The crash kit should contain all of the software components required to completely rebuild a server.

- Operating system:
  - Installation kit
  - Hardware drivers not contained in the installation kit (e.g., network cards or SCSI controllers)
  - Service packs, updates, and patches
- Database:
  - Installation kit
  - Service packs, updates, and patches
  - Recovery script for automating a database recovery
- SAP system:
  - New installation files of the SAP release used and the database
  - Currently installed kernel
  - System profile files

- *tpparam* file
- *saprouttab* file
- *saplogon.ini* files (for SAP GUI)

- Other programs integrated into the SAP system (e.g., a control package)
- Other software for the SAP installation:
  - Auxiliary programs
  - Backup
  - UPS control program
  - Hardware monitor
  - FTP client
  - Remote control program
  - System monitors

[+]

Crash Kit Inventory

The person who seals the crash kit should also compile a signed and dated inventory. If the seal is broken, you must assume that some items have been removed or changed, and, as a result, the kit could be completely useless in an emergency.

7.8 Testing the Disaster Recovery Procedure

By simulating a disaster recovery, you can ensure that your system can actually be restored and that all of the tasks listed in the disaster recovery plan can be executed. By performing a simulation, you can ascertain whether the following are true:

- Your disaster recovery procedure works
- Changes have occurred, steps haven't been documented, or the necessary updates haven't been performed
- Some steps require additional explanation
- Steps that are quite clear to the person writing the documentation are also clear to other individuals
- Older hardware is no longer available

If one of these scenarios arises, you must revise your recovery plan. You may also have to upgrade your hardware so that it's compatible with the equipment currently available. Furthermore, you should draft an alternative procedure in response to inconsistencies that previously went unnoticed in an emergency.

Because many factors influence the actual recovery time, it can only be determined through testing. As soon as you have actual time values instead of estimates, your emergency plan will become credible. If the procedure is practiced on a regular basis, everyone will know what to do in an emergency, thus making it possible to avoid the worst-case scenario.

To test your disaster recovery procedure, follow these steps:

1. Implement your disaster recovery plan in a backup system or at a remote location.
2. Envisage a random emergency scenario.
3. Implement your emergency plan to see if it's effective in such a situation.
4. Perform disaster recovery at the same location where it will occur in the event of an emergency. If you have more than one recovery location, run the tests in each of these locations. The equipment, facilities, and configurations may differ from location to location. Document all of the steps that need to be executed at each location. You're now immune to not being able to restore the system at a certain location in the event of an emergency. Other options for locations where you can test your disaster recovery scenario include the following:
    - A backup server at your location
    - Another enterprise location
    - Another enterprise with which you have a mutual support agreement
    - An enterprise that provides disaster recovery locations and services

During a real disaster recovery, your permanent employees will carry out the relevant tasks. However, you should take precautions in case some of your key employees are unavailable during the disaster recovery. A test procedure can therefore include the random selection of an individual who won't be available and won't participate in the test procedure. This procedure reflects a real situation in which a key employee is absent or has been seriously injured, for example.

Furthermore, employees from other locations should also participate in testing. Integrate these individuals into the tests because you may also require them during a real disaster recovery. These employees can fill the gap arising from unavailable personnel.

At least once a year, you should run through your disaster recovery from start to finish. However, the frequency with which you do this is a commercial decision that should be made while considering the costs involved.

[!]

Maintaining the Production System

Note that during disaster recovery testing, employees are still needed to maintain the real production system.

7.9 Minimizing the Risk of Failure

There are many ways to minimize the risk of failure. Some of the suggestions listed here may seem obvious. In reality, however, they are frequently ignored.

7.9.1 Minimizing the Risk of Human Error

Many emergencies are triggered by human error (caused, for example, by an exhausted operator). For potentially dangerous tasks (such as deleting the test database, moving a file, or formatting a new drive), a script should be created with a checklist that can be used to verify the individual steps.

[+]

Critically Assessing Your Own Capabilities

Don't perform any dangerous tasks if you feel tired. If you nevertheless have to do it, seek a second opinion before you start.

7.9.2 Minimizing Single Points of Failure

A *single point of failure* occurs when the failure of a single component causes the entire system to fail. You can minimize the risk as follows:

- Ascertain the situations in which a single point of failure can occur.
- Devise a forecast of what happens when this component or process fails.
- Eliminate as many single points of failure as possible.

Single points of failure may include the following:

- The backup SAP server is in the same data center as the production SAP server. If the data center is destroyed, the backup server will also be destroyed.
- All SAP servers are connected to the same power supply. If the power supply is interrupted, this affects all of the equipment connected to this power supply. In other words, all servers crash.

Cascading Failures

A *cascading failure* occurs if one failure triggers a whole series of failures, thus making the problem even more complex. In this case, the recovery comprises a coordinated solution for numerous problems.

[Ex]

Cascading Failure

The following is an example of a cascading failure:

- A power outage that affects the air conditioning unit can cause the air-conditioning controls in a server room to fail.
- If the server room can't be cooled, the temperature in the room rises above the permissible operating temperature for the equipment.
- Overheating causes a hardware failure on the server.
- The hardware failure causes damage to the database.
- Overheating can also affect numerous other pieces of equipment and systems (e.g., network devices, the telephone system, and other servers).

A system recovery after a cascading failure can be complex because, when solving one problem, you may discover other problems or other damaged pieces of equipment. Alternatively, some equipment can't be tested or repaired until other pieces of equipment become operational again. In the air-conditioning example, a system could monitor the air-conditioning unit or the temperature of the server room and notify the relevant employees when a certain threshold value is exceeded.

7.10 Continuing Business During a System Recovery

During disaster recovery, any affected business processes must continue as soon as possible to avoid or minimize an enterprise's financial losses. Give some thought to which alternative procedures can support key business processes when an SAP system fails, for example:

- Collection of cash
- Order processing
- Product shipping
- Invoice payments
- Payroll
- Alternative locations for continuing business

If there's no alternative process, your business operations will decline or come to a complete standstill, which may result in the following problems:

- Orders can't be entered
- Products can't be shipped
- Cash can't be collected

The following alternative processes are conceivable:

- Manual data entry in paper form (e.g., handwritten purchase orders)
- Working on standalone PC systems

Together with your end users, plan how certain business processes can continue to run during a system recovery. Define when or during which expected downtime an alternative process will enter into force. Furthermore, give some thought to how data generated during the emergency process can be transferred to the SAP system after the system recovery.

7.11 Summary

Disaster recovery is a special type of system recovery that requires proper advance preparation. An in-depth concept, the necessary tools, and planned testing on a regular basis will all contribute to helping you prepare for an emergency. This chapter helps you think of everything you need.

Calculate the costs that your enterprise and systems would incur as a result of a system failure or the losses that would arise if a system were unavailable for a period of one hour. Concrete figures are the easiest way to convince everyone of the need to invest in disaster recovery.

Every SAP system requires a database, which, like the SAP system itself, needs to be managed. In this chapter, we'll discuss typical database administration tasks as well as the tools that you can use to perform these tasks on various types of databases.

8 Database Administration

The database is another important component within the SAP system architecture. In addition to the files at the operating system level, the database contains the ABAP programs, system settings, and data required to operate the SAP system.

Depending on the size of your enterprise and the way in which it's organized, database administration is also one of the tasks of the SAP administrator. In this case, you require extensive knowledge of database systems, in general, and knowledge of the database system used for your SAP system, in particular. In some cases, however, database system administration is organizationally separate from SAP Basis maintenance. Then, you only need to have general knowledge of database management, which will form part of this chapter. Additional literature is available (e.g., from SAP PRESS or in publications provided in close cooperation with the respective database management system manufacturer; see Appendix E).

Next, we'll introduce you to tasks and SAP tools that are relevant to you irrespective of the database used. We'll use the database management systems DB2 (IBM), Oracle, Microsoft SQL Server, MaxDB, and SAP HANA to highlight differences between database systems. We'll explain specific tools and procedures for each database.

Transaction DBACOCKPIT [+]

The functions described in the following sections can also be accessed centrally via the *DBA Cockpit* (Transaction DBACOCKPIT). We'll nevertheless describe the transactions individually so that you can decide whether to use the central screen (available via Transaction DBACOCKPIT) or to call each special transaction directly. If individual transactions aren't intended specifically for your database system, the system either informs you of this when calling the transaction or directs you to Transaction DBACOCKPIT. Because the DBA Cockpit view may vary depending on the database system, we won't make any general statements in this chapter.

8.1 Planning Database Administration Tasks

In the SAP system, the Database Administration Planning Calendar (DBA Planning Calendar; Transaction DB13) is available for planning database administration tasks. The DBA Planning Calendar is a planning tool for database administration. You can use this calendar to plan periodic recurring database tasks such as the following:

- Archiving log files
- Reorganizing
- Updating statistics
- Backing up the database
- Backing up the database log and transaction log
- Backing up the difference database
- Checking database inconsistencies
- Initializing tapes

Managing and planning tasks from within the SAP system is easier than using the command-line interface because you can manage and plan the tasks comfortably without having to call the tools of the respective database manufacturer. The tasks are automatically executed in the intervals that you define. All you have to do is perform certain preparatory tasks (e.g., providing tapes for backup purposes) and check the results.

8.1.1 Planning Database Tasks

In this section, you'll learn how to plan new database administration tasks that are to be performed regularly.

1. Enter Transaction DB13 in the command field and press the Enter key (or select the menu option Tools • CCMS • DB Administration • Planning Calendar • DB13—Local).

2. The DBA Planning Calendar screen is displayed (see Figure 8.1). To plan a database administration task, select a date and time in the calendar, and choose Add.

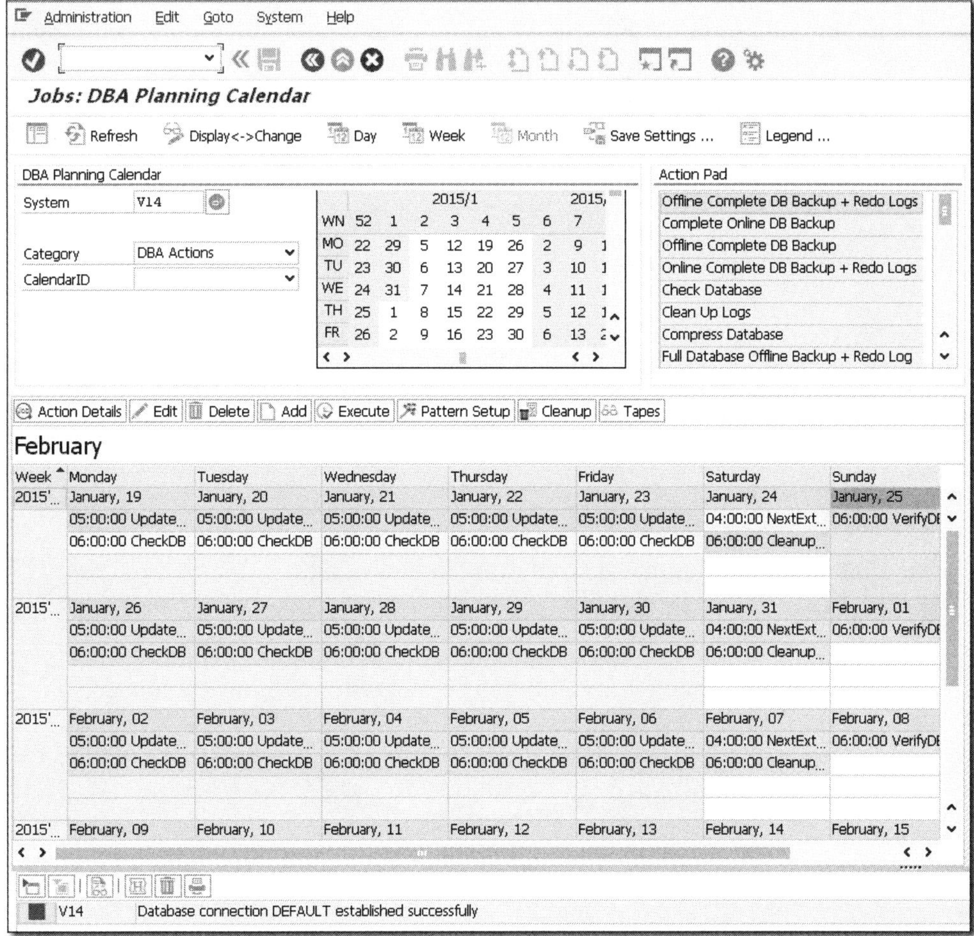

Figure 8.1 DBA Planning Calendar

Available Database Activities [+]

The actions available in the DBA Planning Calendar depend on the type of database you have. The jobs offered for a certain database (e.g., SAP MaxDB) differ from those offered for others, such as an Oracle database.

3. In the Schedule a New Action dialog box, choose the task you require (e.g., Check Database) in the Action field. In the Planned Start fields, enter the start date and start time (see Figure 8.2).

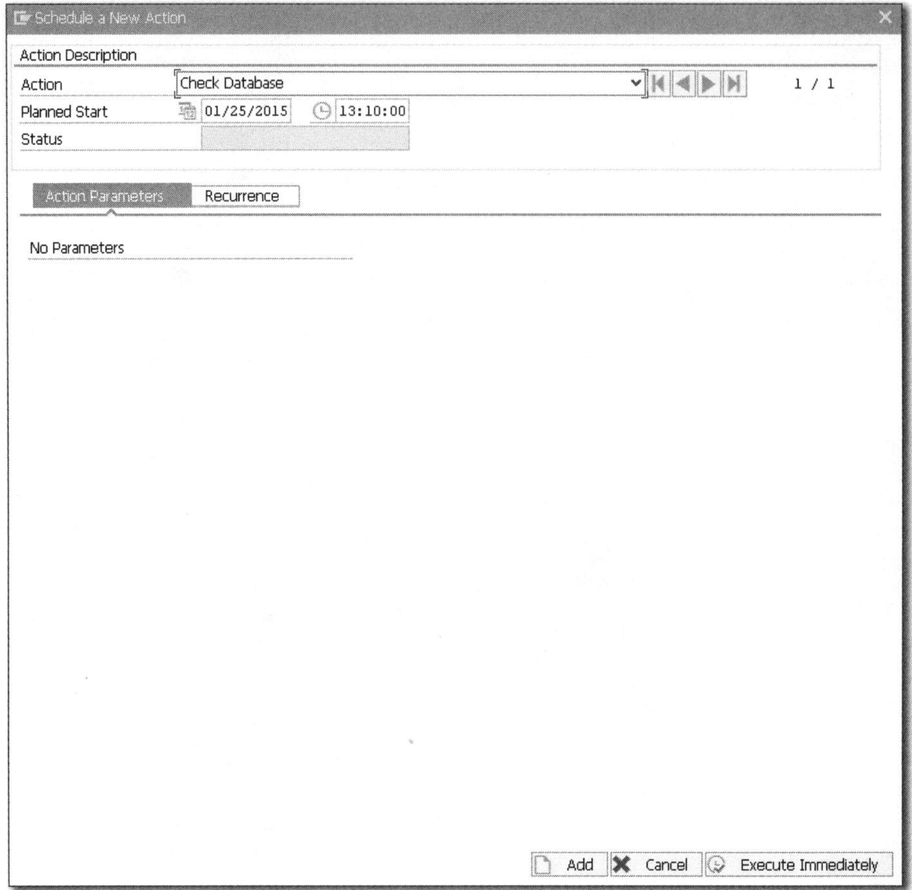

Figure 8.2 Planning a New Database Job

[+]

Action Parameter

Depending on which action you want to schedule, different parameters are queried on the Action Parameters tab (e.g., the type, name, and properties of your backup tool or the name of the tape). These parameters also depend on the database used and your backup system.

4. Switch to the RECURRENCE tab. In the RECURRENCE PATTERN area, specify the intervals in which the action is to be executed (e.g., every three days at 02:00; see Figure 8.3). Click on ADD.

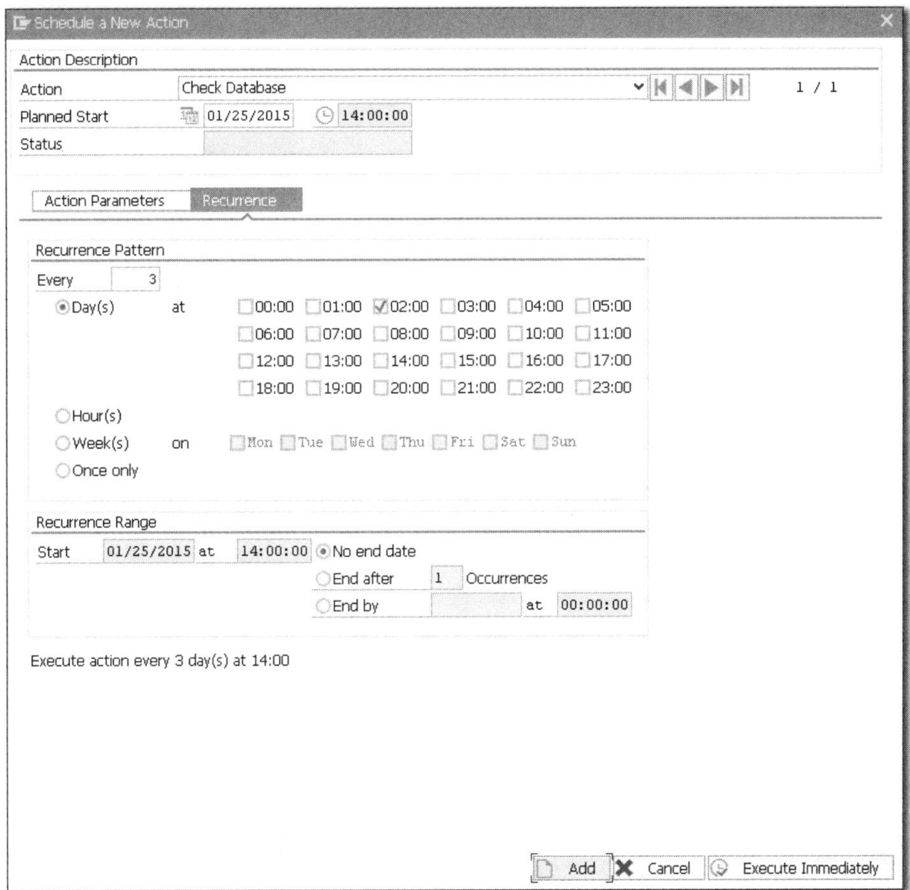

Figure 8.3 Defining the Start Time and Recurrence

Checking Storage Capacities for Backups [!]

With the DBA Planning Calendar, you must plan a backup so that it can be fully automated without any additional manual actions. In other words, you don't have to manually change the storage medium (e.g., tapes). First, check whether a single tape with sufficient capacity is available or whether several tapes with a combined sufficient capacity are available.

5. In the lower screen area, the system issues a message indicating that the action has been added to the calendar. The scheduled actions are displayed in the weekly view (see Figure 8.4).

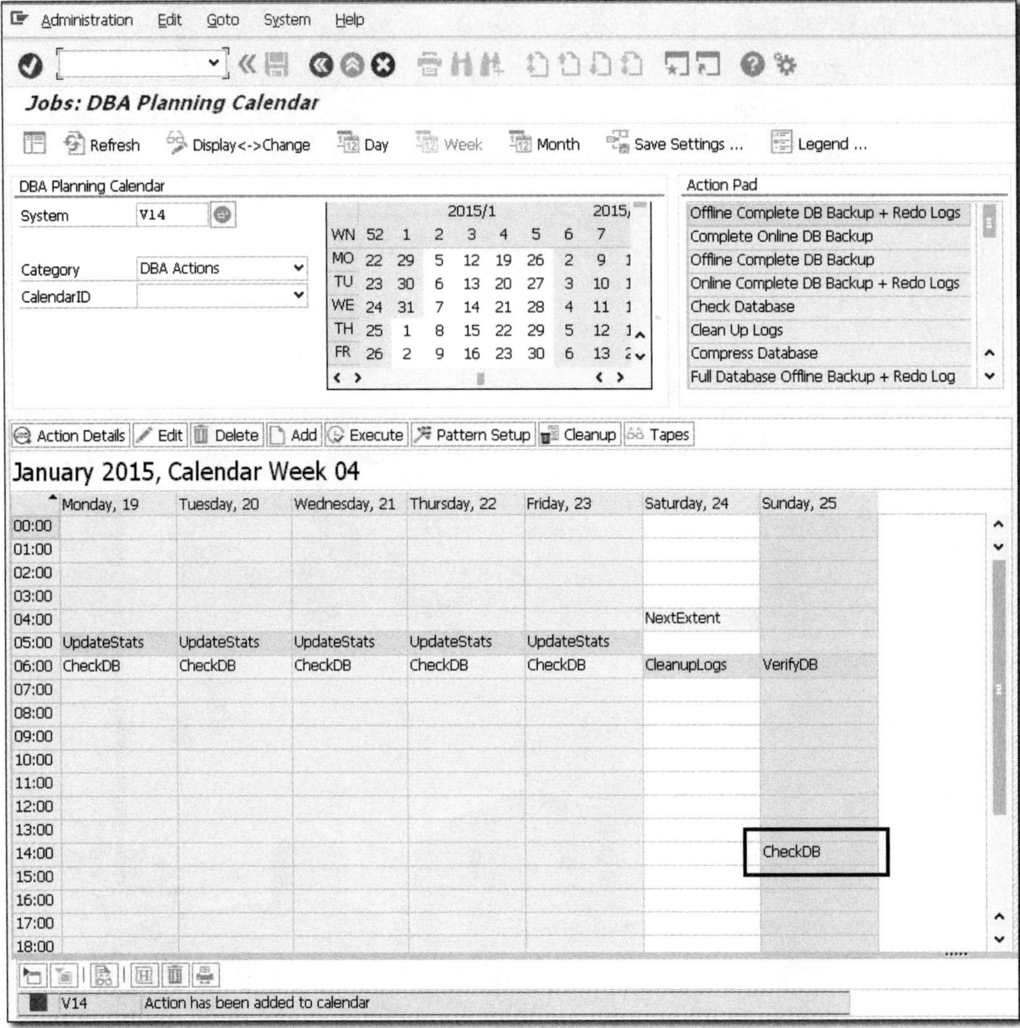

Figure 8.4 Weekly View of Planned Actions

You've now scheduled the database action you require, which will be automatically executed at the defined start time.

[+]

Action Pattern

Action patterns predefined by SAP can make it easier for you to schedule database tasks. Action patterns are summaries of recommended actions and useful intervals. In the DBA PLANNING CALENDAR screen, choose PATTERN SETUP to choose an action pattern for planning regular database actions. You're then guided step by step through the planning process.

8.1.2 Changing and Deleting Database Tasks

You can retroactively edit tasks that haven't been executed yet. You can change the action parameters, or you can delete the tasks from the DBA Planning Calendar.

1. Call Transaction DB13.
2. In the DBA PLANNING CALENDAR screen, navigate to the required date. Position your cursor on the planned task that you want to change. Click on EDIT (see Figure 8.5).

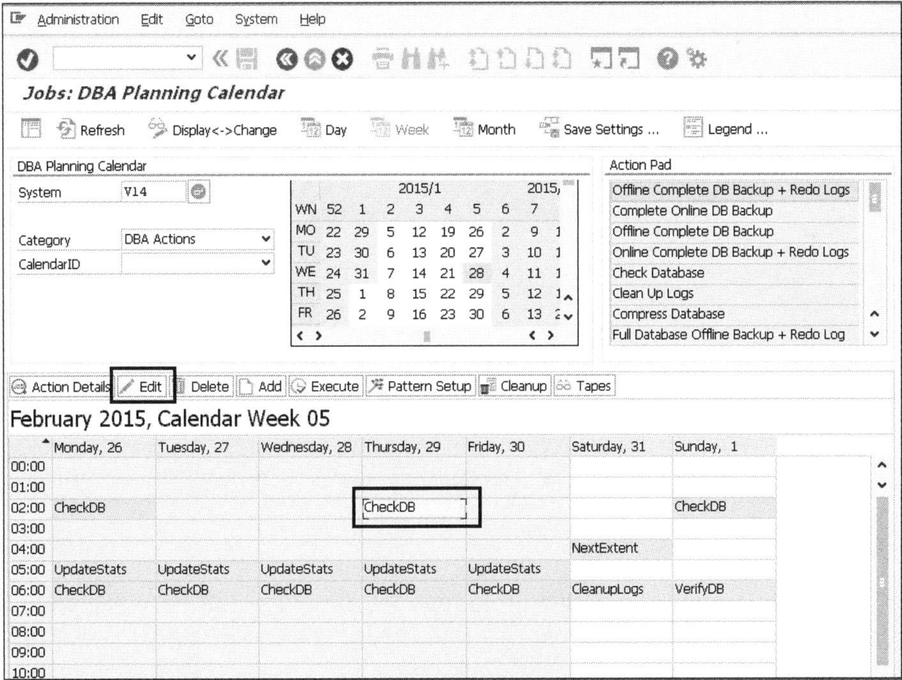

Figure 8.5 Editing an Action in the DBA Planning Calendar

3. You can adjust the action parameters for the task in the EDIT DETAILS OF ACTION dialog box (see Figure 8.6). You can also change recurrence data such as the start date/time and recurrence interval here. If your adjustment applies only to the action on the day selected, choose CHANGE CURRENT OCCURRENCE. If you want the change to apply to all other periodic recurrence dates, click on CHANGE ALL OCCURRENCES.

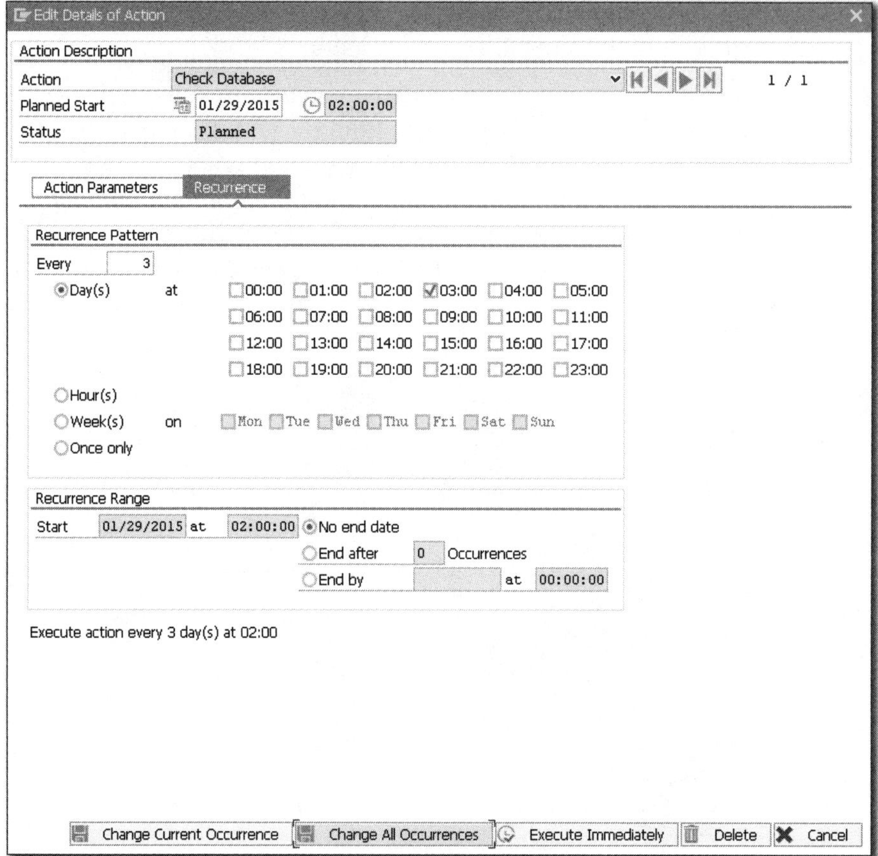

Figure 8.6 Adapting the Action Parameters

The system issues a message indicating that the action has been successfully changed.

4. If you want to delete an action, position your cursor on the task, and click on DELETE (see Figure 8.7).

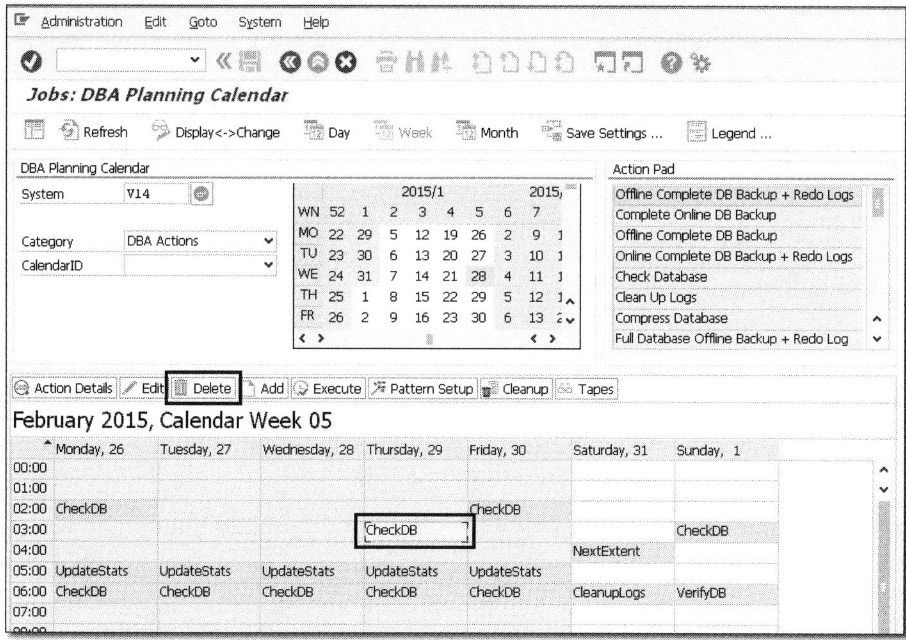

Figure 8.7 Deleting an Action from the Calendar

5. For periodically scheduled tasks, the system displays a dialog box in which you must select the execution times to be deleted (see Figure 8.8). Set the checkmark, and click on DELETE.

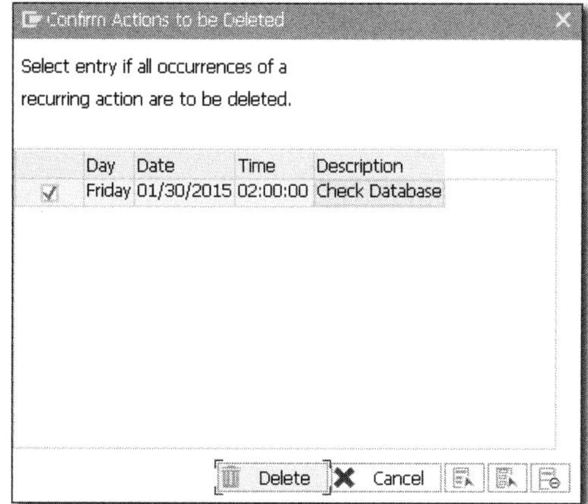

Figure 8.8 Deleting Periodically Scheduled Actions

6. A dialog box for one-time planned actions is also displayed (see Figure 8.9). Confirm this by choosing DELETE again.

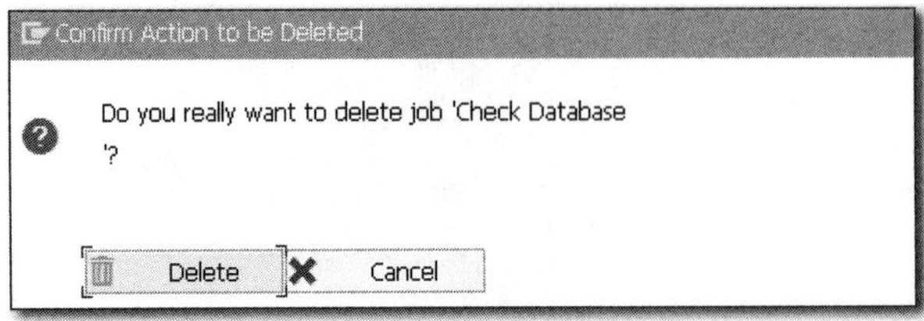

Figure 8.9 Deleting One-Time Planned Actions

By deleting the action, you remove it from the DBA Planning Calendar and undo the occurrence.

8.1.3 Checking the DBA Planning Calendar

You can also use the DBA Planning Calendar to check the status of a database administration task. For example, you can use the DBA Planning Calendar to check whether or not a task has been successfully performed by following these steps:

1. Call Transaction DB13.
2. Check the colors assigned to the tasks in the calendar view. The color indicates the status:
   - Red: Error.
   - Yellow: Warning.
   - Green: Success.
   - Blue: Currently running.
3. Position your cursor on the action you require, and click on ACTION DETAILS to check the log (see Figure 8.10).
4. In the DISPLAY DETAILS OF ACTION window, switch to the JOB LOG tab (see Figure 8.11).
5. Check the job log, for example, for warnings or error messages. You can double-click on a log entry to display the long text of the message. To exit the detail view, choose CONTINUE.

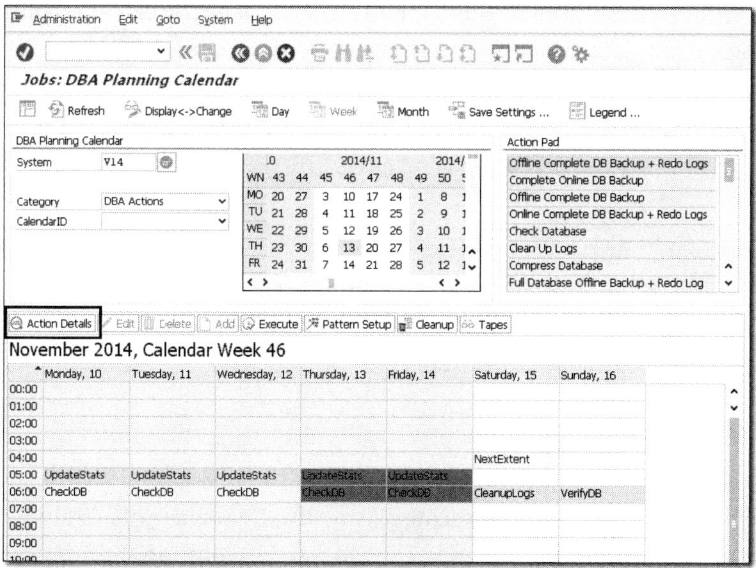

Figure 8.10 Calling Details of a Database Action

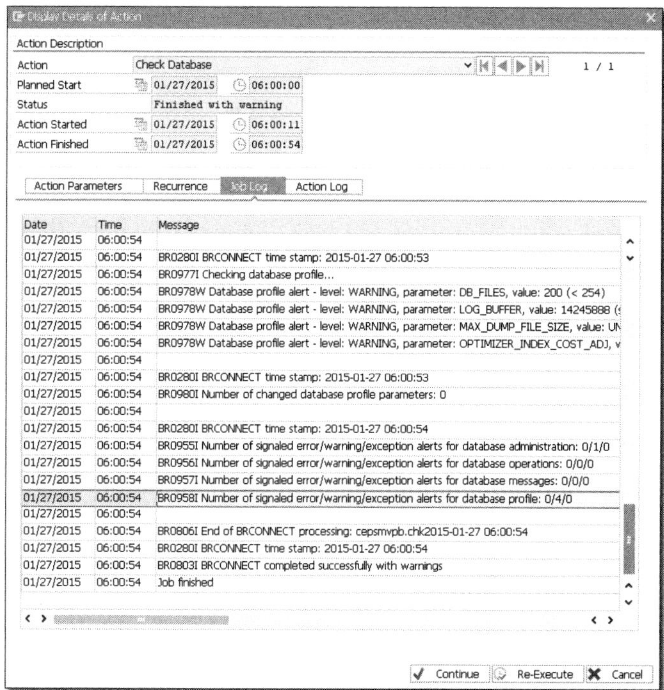

Figure 8.11 Checking the Job Log

6. In the detail view, you can directly go to the ACTION LOG tab. You can also check the action logs of the database job separately using Transaction DB14 (see Section 8.2).

At least once a day (preferably every morning), check whether the database actions, which are usually scheduled for nighttime, have been successfully executed.

[+] **Re-execute Actions**

After eliminating an error, you can choose RE-EXECUTE to restart canceled actions.

8.2 Checking Database Actions

You can use Transactions DB12 (Backup Logs) and DB14 (Operations Monitor—for Oracle only) to check the actions executed using the DBA Planning Calendar. This transaction gives you central access to the DBA action logs for tasks such as database backups. Let's first take a look at the backup logs.

1. Enter Transaction DB12 in the command field and press the Enter key (or select the menu option TOOLS • CCMS • DB ADMINISTRATION • DB12—BACKUP LOGS).
2. On the BACKUP LOGS: OVERVIEW FOR DATABASE V14 screen, choose the DISPLAY LOG button in the DATABASE BACKUPS area to check the time and content of the last database backup (see Figure 8.12).
3. The files that have been backed up are listed in the action log (see Figure 8.13). Click BACK to exit the view.
4. On the BACKUP LOGS: OVERVIEW FOR DATABASE V14 screen (see Figure 8.12), choose LIST OF LOGS to navigate to the list of all database actions that have been performed.

Figure 8.12 Initial Screen of the Backup Logs

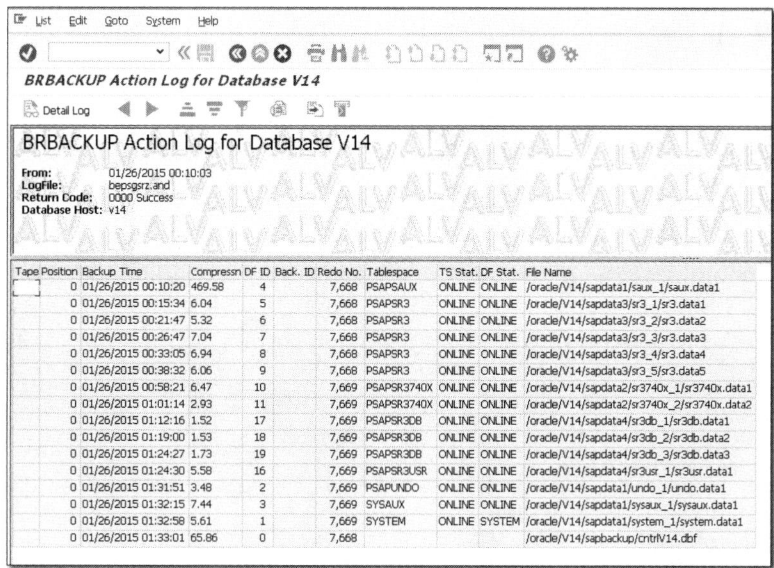

Tape Position	Backup Time	Compressn	DF ID	Back. ID	Redo No.	Tablespace	TS Stat.	DF Stat.	File Name
0	01/26/2015 00:10:20	469.58	4		7,668	PSAPSAUX	ONLINE	ONLINE	/oracle/V14/sapdata1/saux_1/saux.data1
0	01/26/2015 00:15:34	6.04	5		7,668	PSAPSR3	ONLINE	ONLINE	/oracle/V14/sapdata3/sr3_1/sr3.data1
0	01/26/2015 00:21:47	5.32	6		7,668	PSAPSR3	ONLINE	ONLINE	/oracle/V14/sapdata3/sr3_2/sr3.data2
0	01/26/2015 00:26:47	7.04	7		7,668	PSAPSR3	ONLINE	ONLINE	/oracle/V14/sapdata3/sr3_3/sr3.data3
0	01/26/2015 00:33:05	6.94	8		7,668	PSAPSR3	ONLINE	ONLINE	/oracle/V14/sapdata3/sr3_4/sr3.data4
0	01/26/2015 00:38:32	6.06	9		7,668	PSAPSR3	ONLINE	ONLINE	/oracle/V14/sapdata3/sr3_5/sr3.data5
0	01/26/2015 00:58:21	6.47	10		7,669	PSAPSR3740X	ONLINE	ONLINE	/oracle/V14/sapdata2/sr3740x_1/sr3740x.data1
0	01/26/2015 01:01:14	2.93	11		7,669	PSAPSR3740X	ONLINE	ONLINE	/oracle/V14/sapdata2/sr3740x_2/sr3740x.data2
0	01/26/2015 01:12:16	1.52	17		7,669	PSAPSR3DB	ONLINE	ONLINE	/oracle/V14/sapdata4/sr3db_1/sr3db.data1
0	01/26/2015 01:19:00	1.53	18		7,669	PSAPSR3DB	ONLINE	ONLINE	/oracle/V14/sapdata4/sr3db_2/sr3db.data2
0	01/26/2015 01:24:27	1.73	19		7,669	PSAPSR3DB	ONLINE	ONLINE	/oracle/V14/sapdata4/sr3db_3/sr3db.data3
0	01/26/2015 01:24:30	5.58	16		7,669	PSAPSR3USR	ONLINE	ONLINE	/oracle/V14/sapdata4/sr3usr_1/sr3usr.data1
0	01/26/2015 01:31:51	3.48	2		7,669	PSAPUNDO	ONLINE	ONLINE	/oracle/V14/sapdata1/undo_1/undo.data1
0	01/26/2015 01:32:15	7.44	3		7,669	SYSAUX	ONLINE	ONLINE	/oracle/V14/sapdata1/sysaux_1/sysaux.data1
0	01/26/2015 01:32:58	5.61	1		7,669	SYSTEM	ONLINE	SYSTEM	/oracle/V14/sapdata1/system_1/system.data1
0	01/26/2015 01:33:01	65.86	0		7,668				/oracle/V14/sapbackup/cntrlV14.dbf

Figure 8.13 Displaying the Backup Log

5. The individual database backups are listed in descending order by date (see Figure 8.14). The FUNCTION column specifies what has been backed up (e.g., ALL), how the backup was done (e.g., ONLINE/OFFLINE), and to which medium it was saved (e.g., DISK). Double-click on a backup to go to the corresponding action log. Click on BACK to return to the initial screen.

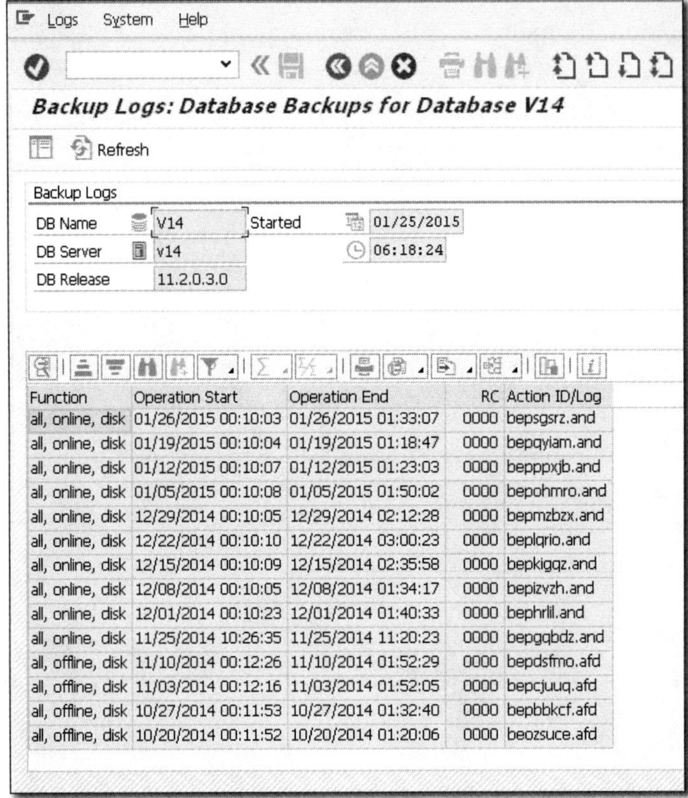

Function	Operation Start	Operation End	RC	Action ID/Log
all, online, disk	01/26/2015 00:10:03	01/26/2015 01:33:07	0000	bepsgsrz.and
all, online, disk	01/19/2015 00:10:04	01/19/2015 01:18:47	0000	bepqyiam.and
all, online, disk	01/12/2015 00:10:07	01/12/2015 01:23:03	0000	bepppxjb.and
all, online, disk	01/05/2015 00:10:08	01/05/2015 01:50:02	0000	bepohmro.and
all, online, disk	12/29/2014 00:10:05	12/29/2014 02:12:28	0000	bepmzbzx.and
all, online, disk	12/22/2014 00:10:10	12/22/2014 03:00:23	0000	beplqrio.and
all, online, disk	12/15/2014 00:10:09	12/15/2014 02:35:58	0000	bepkiggz.and
all, online, disk	12/08/2014 00:10:05	12/08/2014 01:34:17	0000	bepizvzh.and
all, online, disk	12/01/2014 00:10:23	12/01/2014 01:40:33	0000	bephrlil.and
all, online, disk	11/25/2014 10:26:35	11/25/2014 11:20:23	0000	bepgqbdz.and
all, offline, disk	11/10/2014 00:12:26	11/10/2014 01:52:29	0000	bepdsfmo.afd
all, offline, disk	11/03/2014 00:12:16	11/03/2014 01:52:05	0000	bepcjuuq.afd
all, offline, disk	10/27/2014 00:11:53	10/27/2014 01:32:40	0000	bepbbkcf.afd
all, offline, disk	10/20/2014 00:11:52	10/20/2014 01:20:06	0000	beozsuce.afd

Figure 8.14 List of Database Backups Implemented

[!]

Log File View

This list of logs that can be displayed in Transaction DB12 depends on the type of database used. Consequently, the view in your system may differ from the view shown in these screenshots.

You can view the backup logs of the database using Transaction DB12. To check the logs of all other database actions (e.g., the job created in Section 8.1), use Transaction DB14 in an Oracle database. To do this, follow these steps:

1. Enter Transaction DB14 in the command field, and press the Enter key (or select the menu option Tools • CCMS • DB Administration • DB14—Operations Monitor; see Figure 8.15).

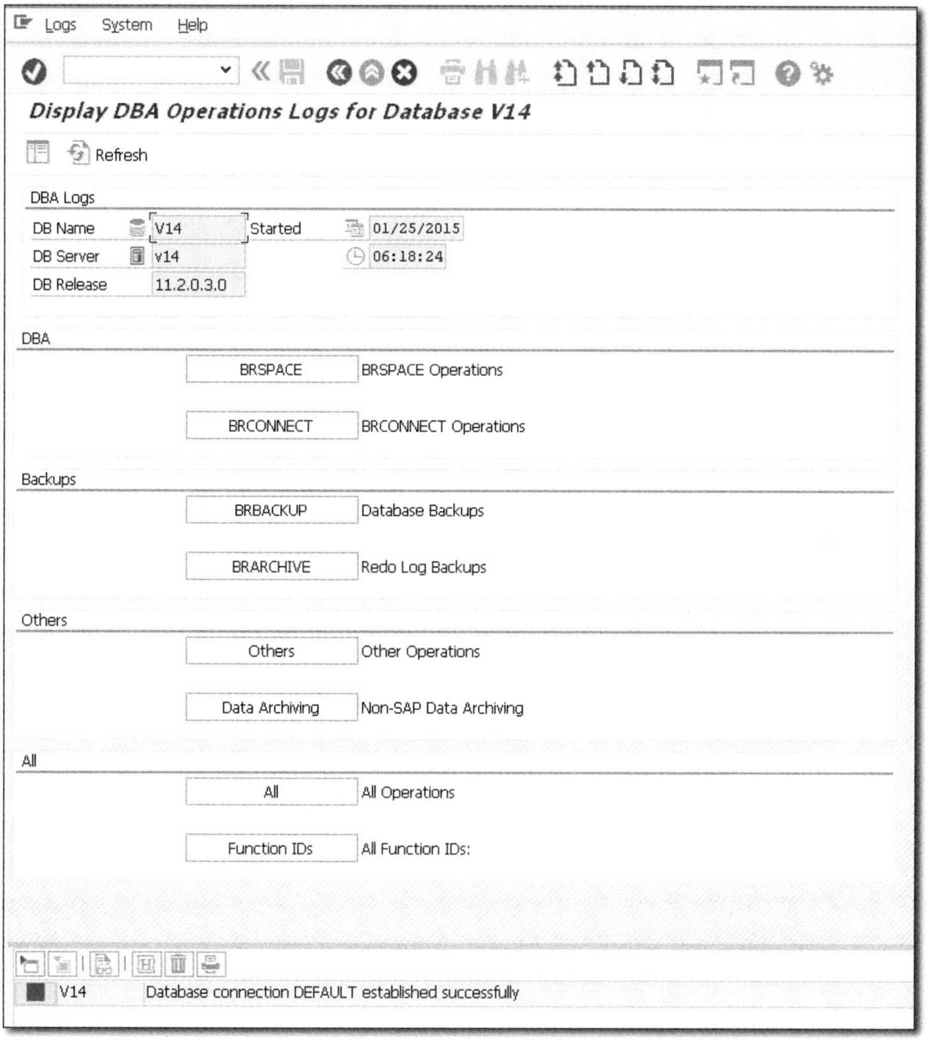

Figure 8.15 DBA Operation Monitor for Oracle Databases

2. Click on BRCONNECT, for example. The system displays a list of actions performed with this tool (see Figure 8.16). Double-click on an entry to open the overview of messages for the action selected.

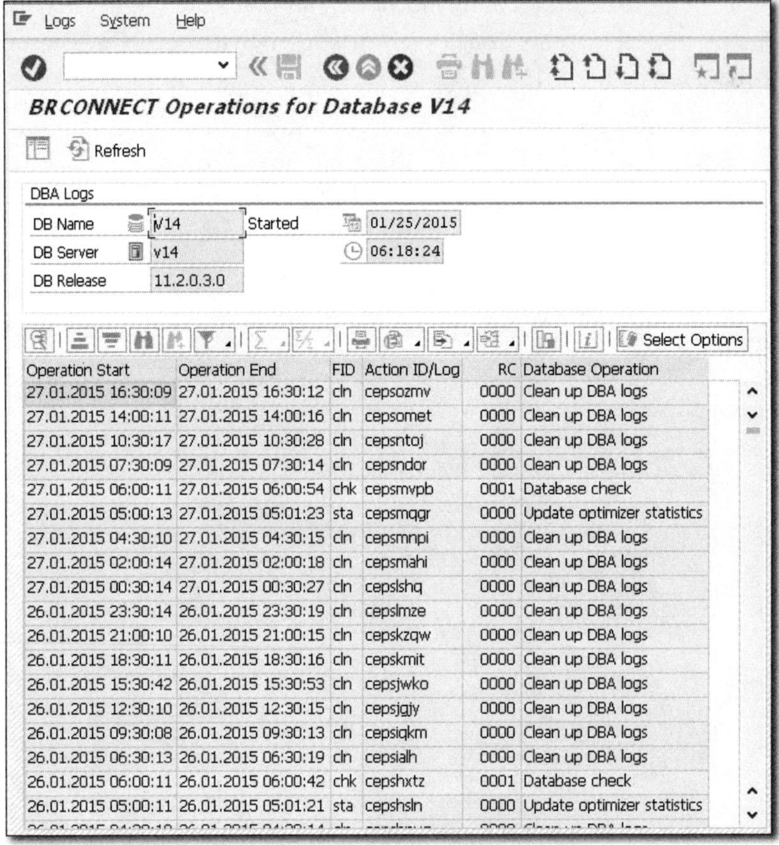

Figure 8.16 Log for the Actions Executed with BRCONNECT

3. Click on the DETAIL LOG button to display the warnings or errors (see Figure 8.17).
4. In the detail view, you can check the log messages individually. Errors and warnings are highlighted in color so that you can find them more easily among the vast number of log entries (see Figure 8.18).

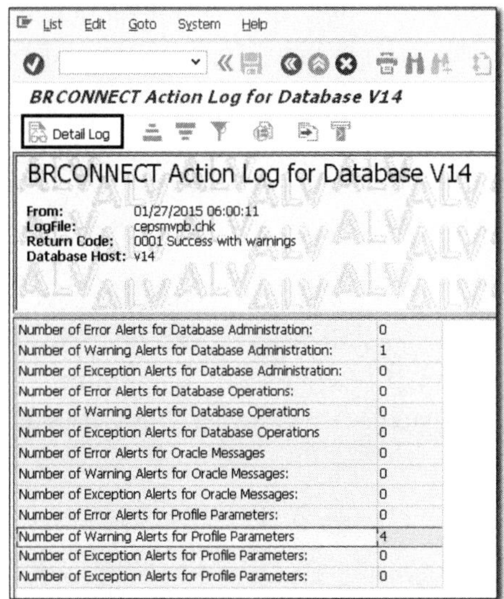

Figure 8.17 Calling the Detailed Action Log

Log Edit Goto System Help

BRCONNECT Detail Log for Database V14

```
Detail log:                  cepsmvpb.chk

 33   Y    W   TIMED_STATISTICS
 34   Y    W   TRACE_ENABLED
 35   Y    E   UNDO_MANAGEMENT                  <>                 AUTO
 36   Y    W   UNDO_TABLESPACE                  <>             PSAPUNDO
 37   Y    W   USER_DUMP_DEST
BR0280I BRCONNECT time stamp: 2015-01-27 06:00:51
BR0807I Name of database instance: V14
BR0808I BRCONNECT action ID: cepsmvpb
BR0809I BRCONNECT function ID: chk
BR0810I BRCONNECT function: check
BR0951I Number of active/inactive check conditions for database administration: 23/0
BR0952I Number of active/inactive check conditions for database operations: 8/2
BR0953I Number of active/inactive check conditions for database messages: 58/0
BR0954I Number of active/inactive check conditions for database profile: 37/0
BR0960I Last successful BRCONNECT check run: cepshxtz.chk 2015-01-26 06:00:11
BR0126I Unattended mode active - no operator confirmation required
BR0280I BRCONNECT time stamp: 2015-01-27 06:00:51
BR0969I Checking database administration...
BR0970W Database administration alert - level: WARNING, type: CRITICAL_TABLESPACE, object: PSAPSR3, value: (max_extn of 5 files on disk 2065) 24043520 KB (> 14940960 KB)
BR0280I BRCONNECT time stamp: 2015-01-27 06:00:52
BR0972I Checking database operations...
BR0280I BRCONNECT time stamp: 2015-01-27 06:00:52
BR0974I Checking database messages in /oracle/V14/saptrace/diag/rdbms/v14/V14/trace/alert_V14.log ...
BR0280I BRCONNECT time stamp: 2015-01-27 06:00:53
BR0977I Checking database profile...
BR0978W Database profile alert - level: WARNING, parameter: DB_FILES, value: 200 (< 254)
BR0978W Database profile alert - level: WARNING, parameter: LOG_BUFFER, value: 14245888 (set in parameter file)
BR0978W Database profile alert - level: WARNING, parameter: MAX_DUMP_FILE_SIZE, value: UNLIMITED (>< 40000,10000)
BR0978W Database profile alert - level: WARNING, parameter: OPTIMIZER_INDEX_COST_ADJ, value: 100 (>< 40,10)
BR0280I BRCONNECT time stamp: 2015-01-27 06:00:53
BR0980I Number of changed database profile parameters: 0
BR0280I BRCONNECT time stamp: 2015-01-27 06:00:54
BR0955I Number of signaled error/warning/exception alerts for database administration: 0/1/0
BR0956I Number of signaled error/warning/exception alerts for database operations: 0/0/0
BR0957I Number of signaled error/warning/exception alerts for database messages: 0/0/0
BR0958I Number of signaled error/warning/exception alerts for database profile: 0/4/0
BR0806I End of BRCONNECT processing: cepsmvpb.chk 2015-01-27 06:00:54
BR0280I BRCONNECT time stamp: 2015-01-27 06:00:54
BR0803I BRCONNECT completed successfully with warnings
```

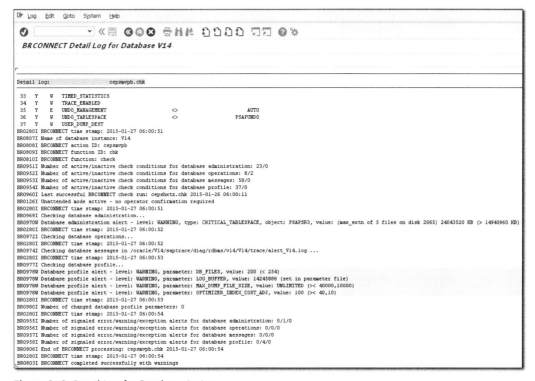

Figure 8.18 Detail Log for Database Actions

Use Transactions DB12 and DB14 (under Oracle) to check the logs for these database actions. For the database system SAP MaxDB, the logs of Transaction DB14 can also be called via Transaction DB12.

8.3 Performing a Database Analysis

Here, you can use Transaction DB02 (Tables/Indexes) to perform extensive checks on your database system. The results are stored as statistics that can be used for analysis purposes. As an SAP administrator, you can use this data to monitor and analyze the system and to identify potential database problems. The following aspects can be examined:

- Database size and database fill level
- Growth rates
- Tables and indexes
- Objects that occupy a critical amount of storage space
- Consistency of the database, objects, and so on

[+]

Monitoring the Size of the Database

Monitoring the size of the database is an important issue. You can use the growth rate to forecast the rate at which the database will grow and therefore determine when additional storage space will be required on the hard disk.

To perform an analysis, follow these steps:

1. Enter Transaction DB02 in the command field and press the Enter key (or select the menu option Tools • Administration • Monitor • Performance • Database • DB02—Tables/Indexes).
2. On the Space Overview initial screen, the system displays an overview of the most important information for about the database (in Figure 8.19 and the subsequent screenshots, we'll use an Oracle database as an example):
   - Database name and database server
   - Size and occupancy statistics
   - Number of tables and indexes

Check the date and time of the last update before you call detailed information about individual areas. If the time is too far in the past, click on REFRESH ALL DATASETS. The system may issue a message indicating that the update may take some time. Choose YES to confirm the dialog box of Figure 8.20.

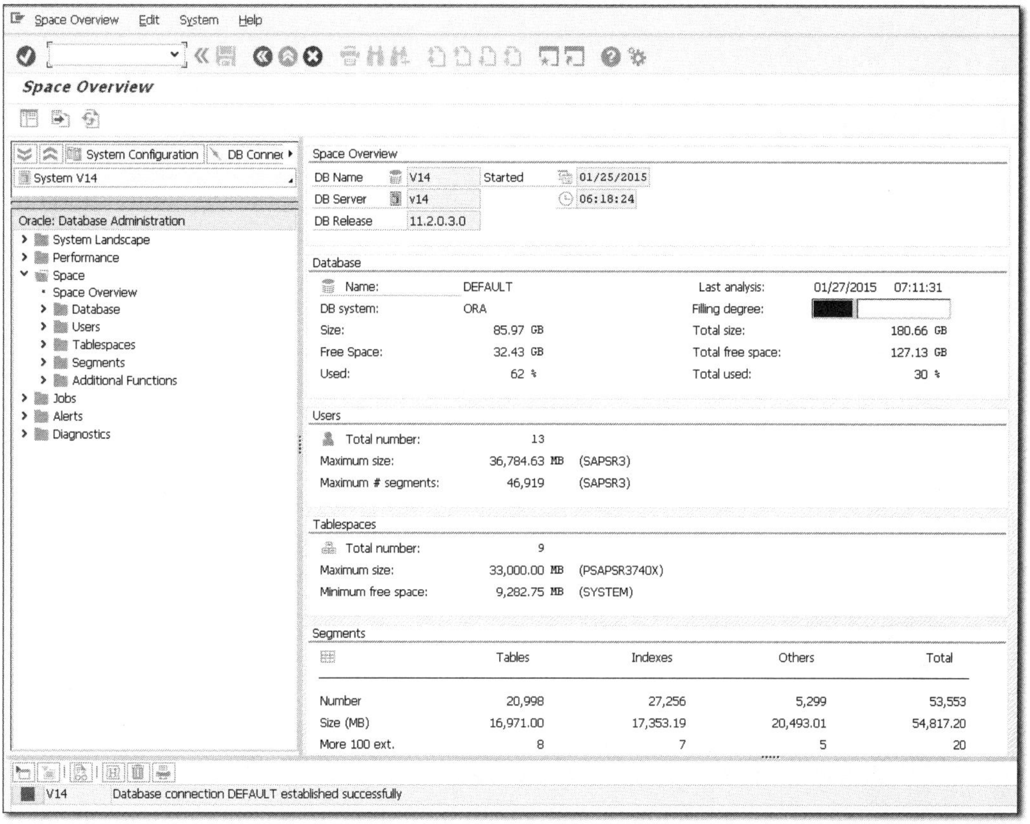

Figure 8.19 Space Overview of an Oracle Database

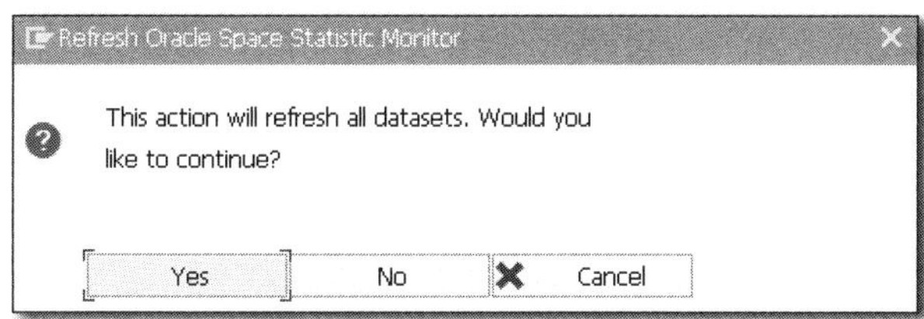

Figure 8.20 Confirming an Update

3. In the navigation structure, expand the folders on the left-hand side to navigate to the detail view of the individual analysis areas. For example, choose SPACE • TABLESPACES, and double-click on DETAILED ANALYSIS (see Figure 8.21). The data is displayed on the right-hand side of the screen.

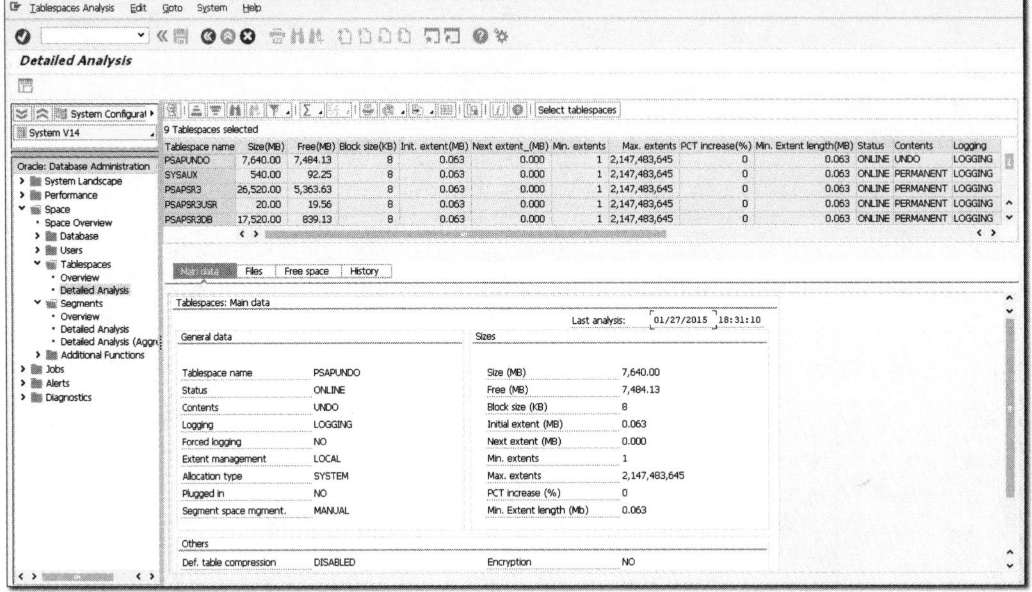

Figure 8.21 Selecting the Detailed Analysis

4. If you select SPACE • SEGMENTS • DETAILED ANALYSIS, the system takes you to the initial screen of the individual analysis for specific database objects. In the SELECT DATA dialog box, enter the name of a table in the SEGMENT/OBJECT field, for example (see Figure 8.22), and press Enter.

5. In the detail view, you can use the corresponding tabs to retrieve data about the general properties, columns, indexes, statistics, and growth rate of the table (see Figure 8.23).

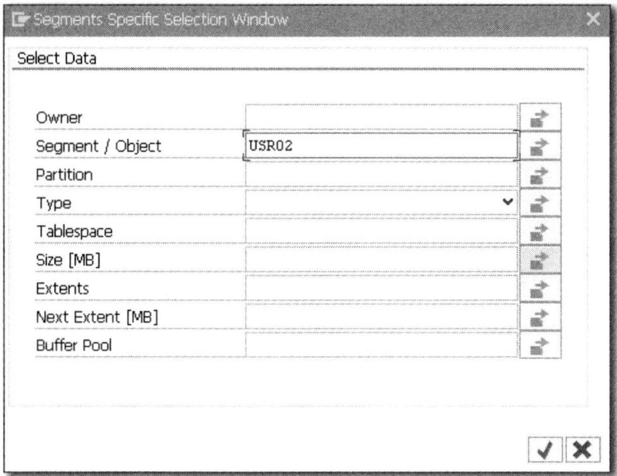

Figure 8.22 Specifying the Database Object to Be Analyzed

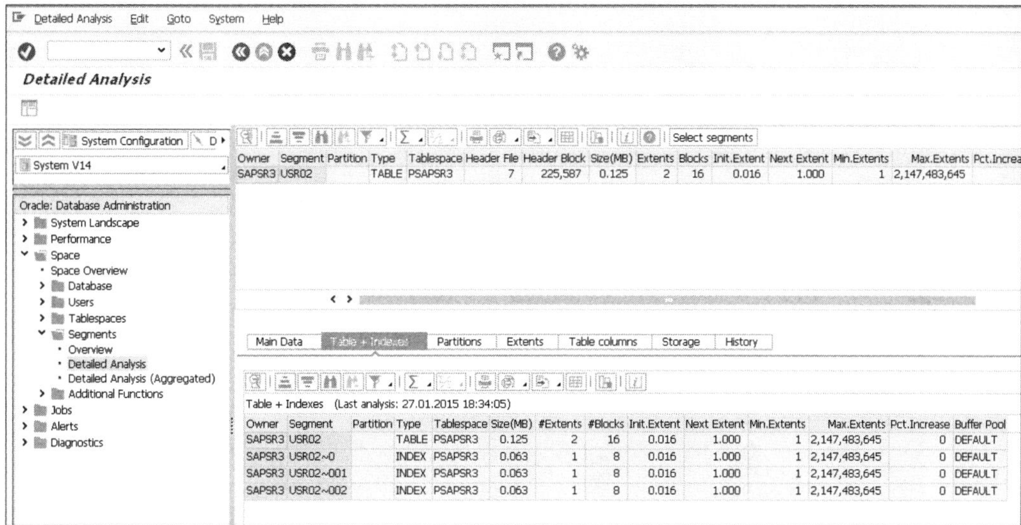

Figure 8.23 Detail Analysis of a Database Object

6. Use the Alerts • Database Check function to examine the results of the database check (see Figure 8.24).
7. Under Alerts • Alert Monitor you can find further information on the database's state of health (see Figure 8.25).

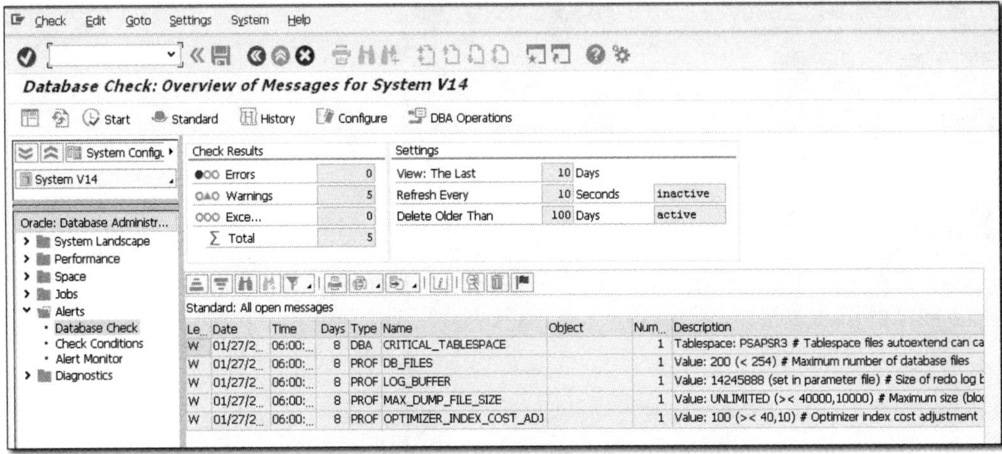

Figure 8.24 Viewing the Results of the Database Check

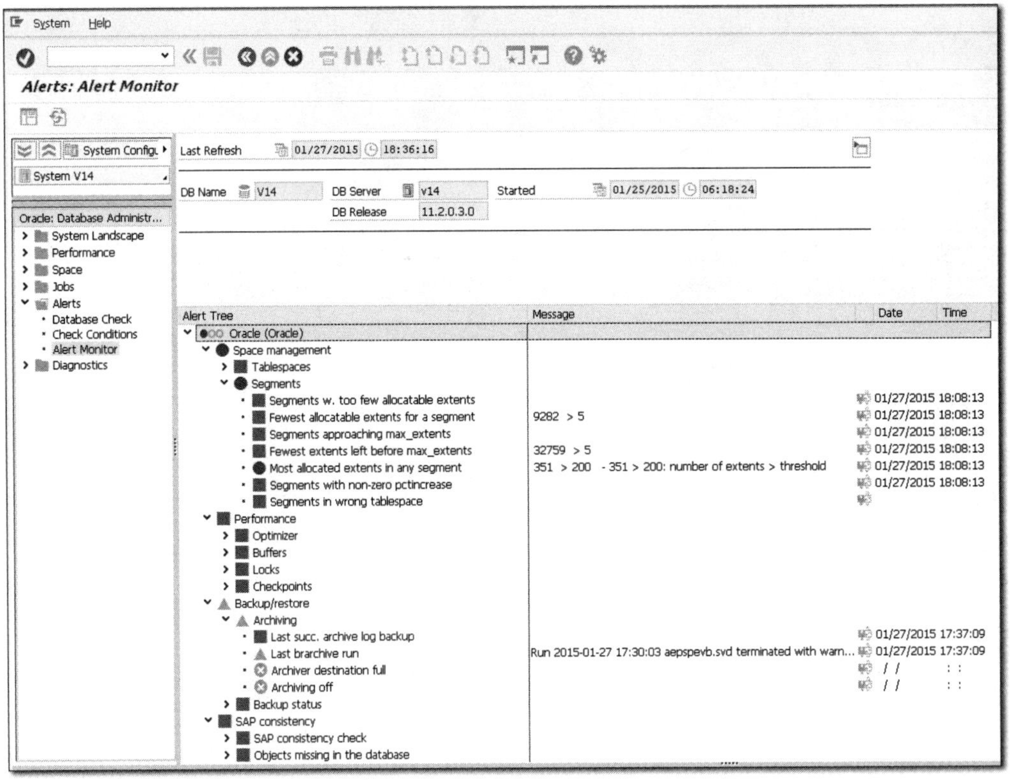

Figure 8.25 Alert Monitor

8. Under the DIAGNOSTICS folder, double-click on MISSING TABLES AND INDEXES (see Figure 8.26). On the next detail screen, check the entries relating to incorrect database objects.

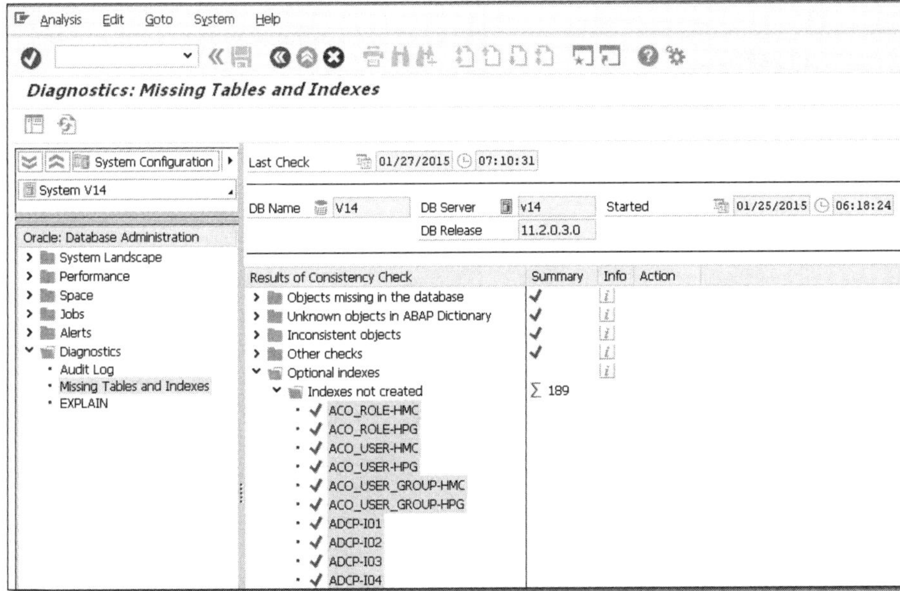

Figure 8.26 Missing Tables and Indexes

Use the database analysis if you want to examine the database with regard to space occupied and consistency.

Database Objects

Note that Transaction DB02 analyzes database objects from the perspective of the database administrator. This perspective focuses on the consistency of an object within the database. This perspective may differ significantly from the perspective of a programmer who primarily understands a table or view as part of the ABAP Dictionary. This may lead to misunderstandings.

8.4 Monitoring Database Performance

The *database performance monitor* (Transaction ST04) is a database-independent tool for analyzing and monitoring the performance-relevant parameters of a database management system such as the following:

- Storage use and buffer use
- Storage space occupancy
- CPU usage
- Input/output
- SQL requests
- SQL cache
- Detailed SQL components
- Locks and deadlocks
- Connected applications

The performance monitor is the main entry point for monitoring the database within the SAP system. The performance statistics available can be used to optimize the database. For example, you can also retrieve the database error log without having to explicitly log on to the database.

[!]

View of the Performance Monitor Transaction

The screen layout and the information available in the performance monitor depend on the type of database you have. In this section, we'll discuss the transaction using an Oracle database as an example.

To use the performance monitor, follow these steps:

1. Enter Transaction ST04 in the command field and press the Enter key (or select the menu option Tools • Administration • Monitor • Performance • Database • ST04—Activity).
2. The initial screen provides an overview of various database performance key figures (see Figure 8.27).
3. Use the navigation frame on the left side to perform a detailed analysis. Choose the path Performance • Wait Event Analysis • Session Monitor to display all queries that are currently active in the database (see Figure 8.28). With this function, you can determine whether a process of the SAP system is still active in the database and which actions it currently performs.

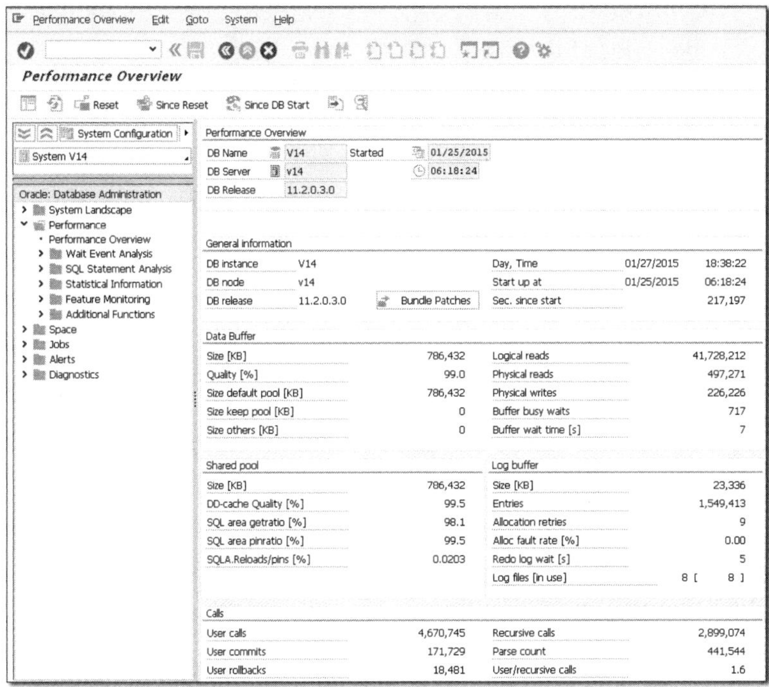

Figure 8.27 Initial Screen of the Database Performance Monitor

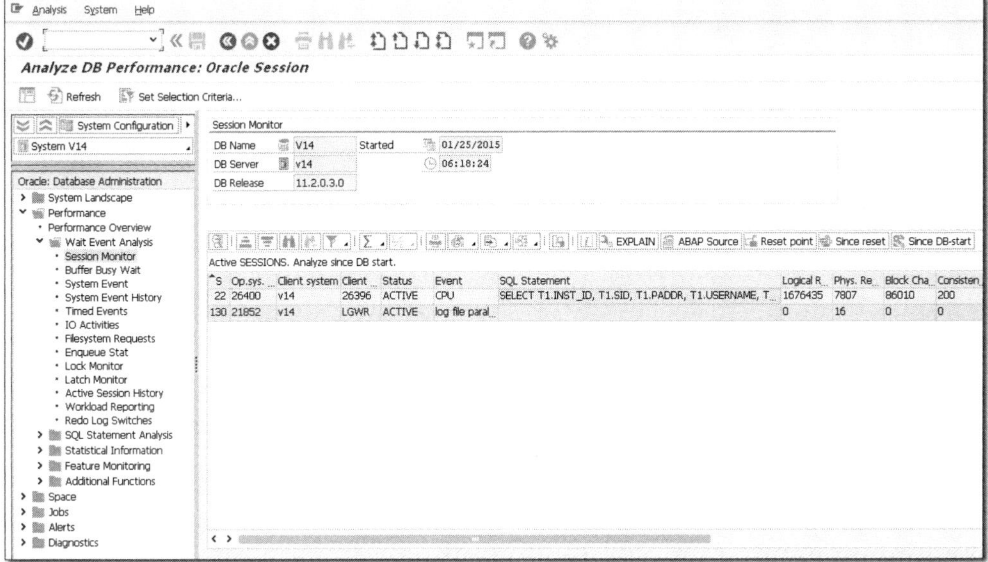

Figure 8.28 Displaying Active Database Sessions

4. Under PERFORMANCE • SQL STATEMENT ANALYSIS • SHARED CURSOR CACHE, you can evaluate the behavior of the database cache (see Figure 8.29).

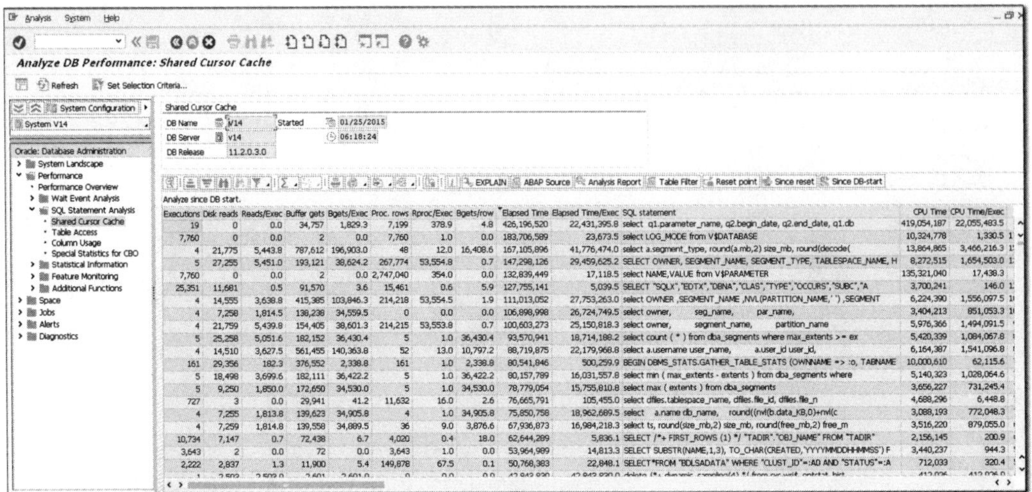

Figure 8.29 Evaluating the Shared Cursor Cache

5. You can access various bits of time-dependent information via the STATISTICAL INFORMATION entry. For example, double-click on SYSTEM STATISTICS, and go to the KEY FIGURES tab to identify the times with particularly high database usage (see Figure 8.30).
6. If you expand the FEATURE MONITORING node, you can, for example, check the ASSM settings of the various tablespaces and tables under AUTOMATIC SEGMENT SPACE MANAGEMENT (ASSM) (see Figure 8.31).
7. Under ADDITIONAL FUNCTIONS, you can display the database parameters (see Figure 8.32) or read the alert log, among other things.

Use the performance monitor to analyze and resolve performance problems in the database. If in doubt, consult with an expert before you make a change.

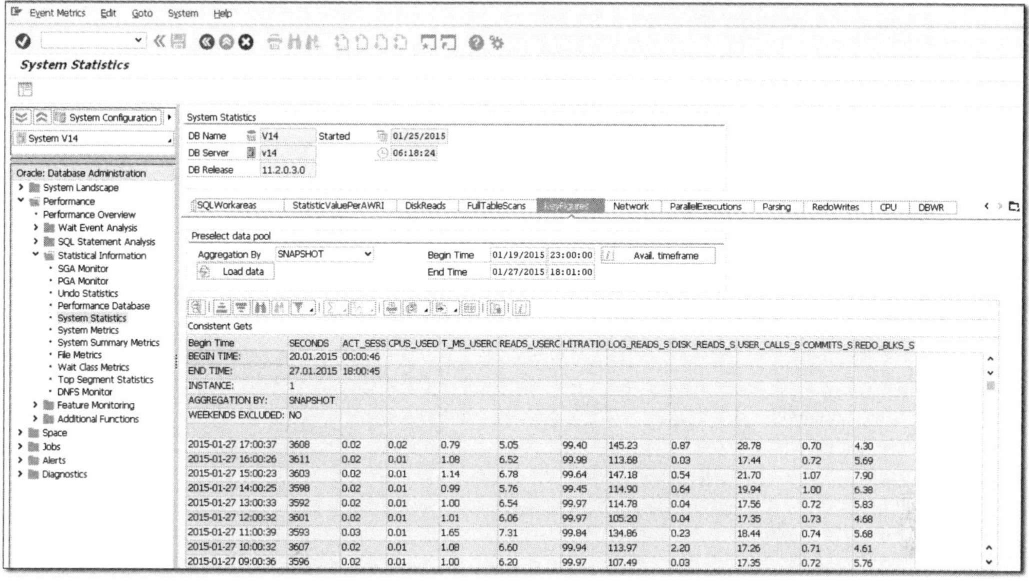

Figure 8.30 Displaying System Statistics and Key Figures

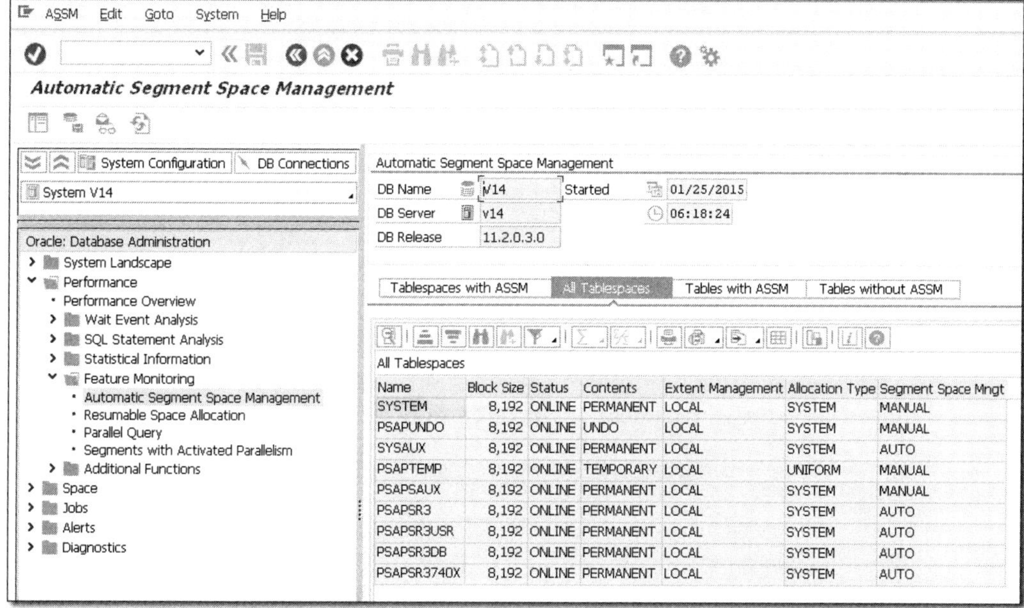

Figure 8.31 Checking the ASSM Settings

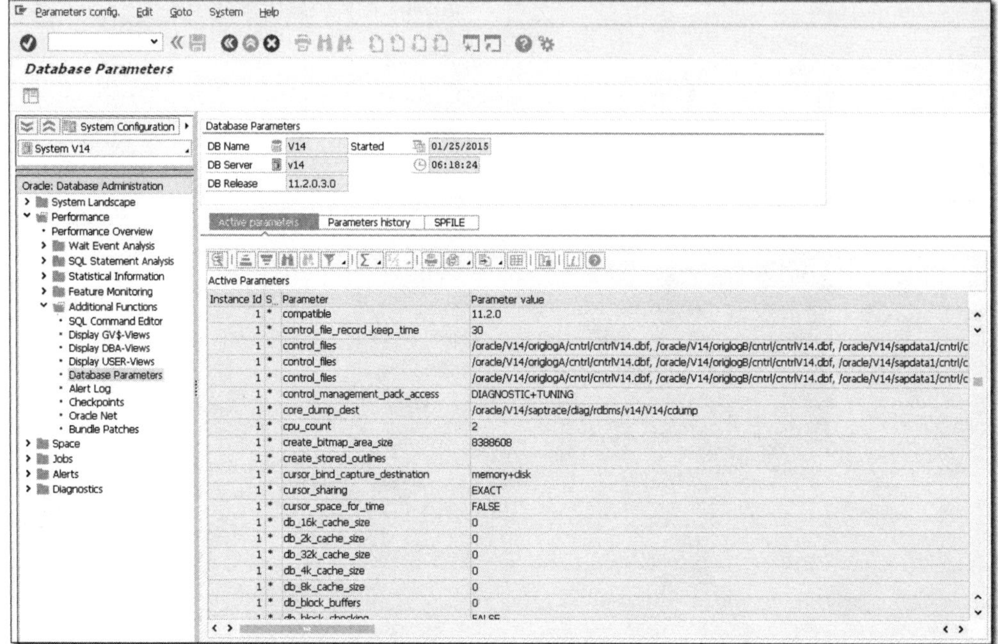

Figure 8.32 Displaying the Database Parameters

8.5 Database Administration—DB2

When managing a DB2 database in the SAP environment, two options are available to you: the DB2 Command Line Processor (CLP) at the operating system level and Transaction DBACOCKPIT in the SAP system, which you can now also operate via a web interface. We'll describe both options in this section. The DBA Cockpit is definitely the recommended and more user-friendly variant for many administration and monitoring tasks. However, there are also some commands, such as starting and stopping the database, which can only be run via the DB2 CLP.

[+]

DB2 Control Center

IBM also provides a graphical user interface (GUI) known as the *DB2 Control Center* (DB2CC), which can be used to manage a DB2 database. You can execute this via the command `db2cc`. It's available up to and including release DB2 for Linux, UNIX, and Microsoft Windows LUW (DB2 for LUW) 9.7. As of DB2 for LUW 10.1, this tool is no longer included in the delivery.

Additional Information [+]

In the SAP environment, the terms *DB2 Common Server* (DB2 CS), DB2 Universal Database (DB2 UDB), and DB6 are often used for an *IBM DB2 for LUW* database. In the SAP environment, the term DB2 describes an IBM DB2 for the operating system z/OS.

Documentation on the DB2 database and the DB2 CLP is available online at *http://www.ibm.com/software/data/db2/library/*, while documentation on managing DB2 databases in the SAP environment is available at *http://help.sap.com/* under TECHNOLOGY • SAP NETWEAVER PLATFORM • SAP NETWEAVER 7.4 • SYSTEM ADMINISTRATION AND MAINTENANCE INFORMATION • ENGLISH • ADMINISTRATION OF DATABASES • DATABASE ADMINISTRATION FOR IBM DB2 FOR LINUX, UNIX, AND WINDOWS.

8.5.1 DB2 Command Line Processor

You can use the DB2 CLP to manage your DB2 database via a command line and to execute SQL statements. The DB2 CLP is available for all platforms supported by the DB2 for LUW.

SQL Statements and DB2 Commands [+]

The DB2 database distinguishes between DB2 commands and SQL statements:

- An *SQL statement* is a logged database operation that can be restored. For example, you can use the SQL statement `db2 alter tablespace` to change the structure of the database. These changes are applied again when you restore the database.
- A *DB2 command*, on the other hand, is analyzed by the DB2 instance, for example.

You can use the DB2 CLP to perform the following tasks, among other things:

- Starting, stopping, activating, and deactivating the database
- Executing SQL statements
- Backing up the database
- Restoring the database
- Checking and updating the Database Manager configuration
- Checking and updating the database configuration
- Managing tablespaces and the associated containers

Checking the Database [+]

You could also check the database, for example. However, SAP recommends that you perform this check within the SAP system (see Section 8.3).

You can't execute the tasks of the first bullet point in the DBA Cockpit because this transaction requires a running SAP system. We recommend using the DBA Cockpit for the last three administration functions because handling is easier, and you can display and use default values provided by the application.

For most of these tasks, you need to set up a connection to the DB2 database. The DB2 CLP uses the command `connect to <db-sid>` to establish this connection.

[+]

Additional Information about a Command

If you require additional information about a command, you can use the question mark (?). For example, you can use the command `db2 "?" connect` to display all options relating to the command for setting up a connection.

8.5.2 Establishing a Connection to the DB2 Database

The DB2 CLP can be used in two variants. You can start the DB2 CLP directly (by entering the command `db2` and then working in its environment), or you can control the DB2 CLP in the command line environment in your operating system.

To work in the DB2 CLP environment, follow these steps:

1. Log on as database user `db2<db-sid>` (e.g., "su – db2t01").
2. Enter the command "db2" (see Figure 8.33).

```
vm44:db2t01 53> db2
(c) Copyright IBM Corporation 1993,2007
Command Line Processor for DB2 Client 10.5.3

You can issue database manager commands and SQL statements from the command
prompt. For example:
    db2 => connect to sample
    db2 => bind sample.bnd

For general help, type: ?.
For command help, type: ? command, where command can be
the first few keywords of a database manager command. For example:
 ? CATALOG DATABASE for help on the CATALOG DATABASE command
 ? CATALOG          for help on all of the CATALOG commands.

To exit db2 interactive mode, type QUIT at the command prompt. Outside
interactive mode, all commands must be prefixed with 'db2'.
To list the current command option settings, type LIST COMMAND OPTIONS.

For more detailed help, refer to the Online Reference Manual.

db2 =>
```

Figure 8.33 Calling the DB2 Command Line Processor

3. Use the command `connect to <db-sid>` (e.g., `connect to T01`) to establish a connection to the database (see Figure 8.34).

```
db2 => connect to T01

   Database Connection Information

 Database server        = DB2/LINUXX8664 10.5.3
 SQL authorization ID   = DB2T01
 Local database alias   = T01

db2 =>
```

Figure 8.34 Establishing a Connection to the DB2 Database

You've now established a connection to the database and can use the DB2 CLP for administration purposes. However, if you want to work with the command line in your operating system, proceed as follows:

1. Log on as `db2<db-sid>` (e.g., `su - db2t01`).
2. Enter the command "db2 connect to <db-sid>" (e.g., "db2 connect to T01").

[+]

Command "db2"

Note that if you use the command line of the operating system, the command `db2` must precede all other DB2 commands and SQL statements.

Usually, using the command line is more convenient because you can revert to the history of triggered commands and adapt or repeat them if you made a typing error, for example. This isn't possible in the DB2 CLP environment.

3. You can use the `disconnect <db-sid>` command (e.g., `disconnect T01`) if you want to log off from your DB2 database (see Figure 8.35).

```
db2 => disconnect T01
DB20000I  The SQL DISCONNECT command completed successfully.
db2 =>
```

Figure 8.35 Logging Off from the DB2 Database

4. To explicitly terminate the connection of the DB2 CLP to the active database, for example, to deactivate the database and shut down the instance, use command `terminate` (see Figure 8.36).

```
db2 => terminate
DB20000I  The TERMINATE command completed successfully.
vm44:db2t01 56> ▌
```

Figure 8.36 Terminating the Connection to the DB2 Database

After you've established a connection to the database, you can trigger additional commands or statements to work with the database.

8.5.3 Starting and Stopping the Database

There are two ways to start a DB2 database in the SAP environment:

- Using the commands delivered with the DB2 installation
- Using the `startdb` command provided by SAP

Starting the Database

To start the DB2 database using DB2 commands, follow these steps (Figure 8.37):

1. Log on to the server with the database user `<db2<db-sid>` (e.g., using the command `su - db2t01`).
2. Enter the command "db2start" to start the DB2 instance.
3. Activate the DB2 database `<DB-SID>` (e.g., using the command `db2 activate db T01`).

```
vm44:db2t01 59> db2start
06/22/2014 18:13:28     0   0   SQL1063N  DB2START processing was successful.
SQL1063N  DB2START processing was successful.
vm44:db2t01 60> db2 activate db T01
DB20000I  The ACTIVATE DATABASE command completed successfully.
```

Figure 8.37 Starting the Database Using DB2 Commands

If you want to use the command `startdb` to start the database, follow these steps (see Figure 8.38):

1. Log on to the server as `<sap-sid>adm` (e.g., using the command `su - t01adm`).
2. Enter the command "startdb", and press the [Enter] key.

```
vm44:t01adm 54> startdb
06/22/2014 18:22:09     0   0   SQL1063N  DB2START processing was successful.
SQL1063N  DB2START processing was successful.
Database activated
vm44:t01adm 55> ▌
```

Figure 8.38 Starting the Database Using the "startdb" Command

The database is now started. Next we'll cover how to stop the database.

Stopping the Database

Similar to starting the DB2 database, there are also two ways to stop the database. To stop the DB2 database using DB2 commands, follow these steps (see Figure 8.39):

1. Log on to the server as `db2<db-sid>` (e.g., `su - db2t01`).
2. Deactivate the DB2 database using `<DB-SID>` (e.g., using `db2 deactivate db T01`).
3. Enter the command "db2stop" to stop the DB2 instance.

```
vm44:db2t01 61> db2 deactivate db T01
DB20000I  The DEACTIVATE DATABASE command completed successfully.
vm44:db2t01 62> db2stop
06/22/2014 18:14:24     0   0   SQL1064N  DB2STOP processing was successful.
SQL1064N  DB2STOP processing was successful.
vm44:db2t01 63>
```

Figure 8.39 Stopping the Database Using DB2 Commands

When stopping, you don't necessarily need to deactivate the database separately because the command `db2stop` automatically deactivates the database in newer releases.

If you want to use the command `stopdb` to stop the database, follow these steps (see Figure 8.40):

1. Log on to the server as `<sap-sid>adm` (e.g., using the command `su - t01adm`).
2. Enter the command "stopdb", and press the [Enter] key.

```
vm44:t01adm 56> stopdb
Database is running
Continue with stop procedure
DB20000I  The DEACTIVATE DATABASE command completed successfully.
06/22/2014 18:22:48     0   0   SQL1064N  DB2STOP processing was successful.
SQL1064N  DB2STOP processing was successful.
Database sucessfully stopped
vm44:t01adm 57>
```

Figure 8.40 Stopping the Database Using the "stopdb" Command

To start and stop the DB2 for LUW, we recommend using the SAP `startdb` and `stopdb` programs or the `startsap` and `stopsap` scripts, which in turn call the two programs previously mentioned. This way, you ensure that the database is activated or deactivated correctly, and the instance is started or stopped.

8.5.4 Executing SQL Statements

You can use the DB2 CLP and the DBA Cockpit to execute SQL statements in your DB2 database. If, for example, you want to display all clients in your SAP system via DB2 CLP, follow these steps (see Figure 8.41):

1. Log on as `db2<dbsid>` (e.g., `su - db2t01`).
2. Enter the command "db2".
3. Establish a connection to the DB2 database (e.g., `connect to T01`).
4. Enter the command "select mandt from sap<sap-sid>.t000" (e.g., "select mandt from sapt01.t000").

```
db2 => select mandt from sapt01.t000

MANDT
---------
000
001
066
200
201
997
998
999

  8 record(s) selected.

db2 =>
```

Figure 8.41 Displaying Clients in the System

[!]

Executing SQL Statements via the DB2 CLP

We explicitly advise against executing SQL statements. You have full access to the data in the SAP system and can manipulate this data beyond the SAP transaction logic. However, this may lead to inconsistencies in the SAP system. If you can't avoid the execution of SQL statements in some circumstances, check whether a current backup of the database is available, and take due care and consideration.

8.5.5 Updating and Checking the Database Manager Configuration

The settings for the DB2 instance are managed in the Database Manager configuration. Any changes to these settings affect the DB2 instance in question as well as the DB2 databases running in the DB2 instance.

To display the current Database Manager configuration in the DB2 CLP, follow these steps (see Figure 8.42):

1. Log on with the user name `<db2<db-sid>` (e.g., using the command `su - db2t01`).
2. Enter the command "db2".
3. Enter the command "get database manager configuration".

Short Forms for Keywords [+]

The DB2 CLP environment facilitates the use of short forms for some keywords. Therefore, you can also use the command `get dbm cfg` to determine the configuration.

```
db2 => get database manager configuration

         Database Manager Configuration

    Node type = Enterprise Server Edition with local and remote clients

 Database manager configuration release level            = 0x1000

 CPU speed (millisec/instruction)             (CPUSPEED) = 3.660668e-07
 Communications bandwidth (MB/sec)      (COMM_BANDWIDTH) = 1.000000e+02

 Max number of concurrently active databases     (NUMDB) = 32
 Federated Database System Support           (FEDERATED) = NO
 Transaction processor monitor name        (TP_MON_NAME) =

 Default charge-back account           (DFT_ACCOUNT_STR) =

 Java Development Kit installation path       (JDK_PATH) = /db2/db2t01/sqllib/java/jdk64

 Diagnostic error capture level              (DIAGLEVEL) = 3
 Notify Level                              (NOTIFYLEVEL) = 3
 Diagnostic data directory path               (DIAGPATH) = /db2/T01/db2dump/
 Current member resolved DIAGPATH                        = /db2/T01/db2dump/
 Alternate diagnostic data directory path (ALT_DIAGPATH) =
```

Figure 8.42 Displaying the Database Manager Configuration

To get a detailed display for the configuration, follow these steps (see Figure 8.43):

1. Log on as `db2<db-sid>` (e.g., `su - db2t01`).
2. Enter the command "db2".
3. Enter the command "attach to db2<db-sid>" (e.g., "attach to db2t01").
4. Enter the command "get dbm cfg show detail".

In order to not establish an `ATTACH` connection separately, you need to enter the command "db2 get dbm cfg show detail" as a complete command. If you want to change one or more values of the Database Manager configuration, you can use the command update dbm cfg using <parameter> <value>. Note that you must be logged on as the database user db2<db-sid> in this case.

```
db2 => get dbm cfg show detail

          Database Manager Configuration

     Node type = Enterprise Server Edition with local and remote clients

 Description                                       Parameter   Current Value                  Delay
ed Value
 ---------------------------------------------------------------------------------------------------
---------------------
 Database manager configuration release level              = 0x1000

 CPU speed (millisec/instruction)              (CPUSPEED) = 3.660668e-07                  3.660
668e-07
 Communications bandwidth (MB/sec)       (COMM_BANDWIDTH) = 1.000000e+02                  1.000
000e+02

 Max number of concurrently active databases      (NUMDB) = 32                            32

 Federated Database System Support            (FEDERATED) = NO                            NO

 Transaction processor monitor name         (TP_MON_NAME) =
```

Figure 8.43 Calling the Detail View of the Database Manager Configuration

If, for example, you want to change the maximum number of databases that can be active in parallel from 32 (default value) to 64, follow these steps (see Figure 8.44):

1. Log on as db2<db-sid> (e.g., su - db2t01).
2. Enter the command "db2".
3. Enter the command "update dbm cfg using numdb 64".

The error SQL1362W indicates that the system can't change at least one of the parameters that was transferred for immediate modification. For these configuration parameters, you must disconnect all applications from the database so that the changes take effect.

```
db2 => update dbm cfg using numdb 64
DB20000I  The UPDATE DATABASE MANAGER CONFIGURATION command completed
successfully.
SQL1362W  One or more of the parameters submitted for immediate modification
were not changed dynamically. Client changes will not be effective until the
next time the application is started or the TERMINATE command has been issued.
Server changes will not be effective until the next DB2START command.
db2 =>
```

Figure 8.44 Changing the Maximum Number of Databases That Run in Parallel

8.5.6 Updating and Checking the Database Configuration

The settings for a DB2 database are managed in the database configuration. Changes only affect the specified DB2 database. If you want to display the current configuration via the DB2 CLP, follow these steps (see Figure 8.45):

1. Log on as db2<db-sid> (e.g., su - db2t01).
2. Enter the command "db2".
3. Establish a connection to the DB2 database (e.g., connect to T01).
4. Enter the command "get db cfg".

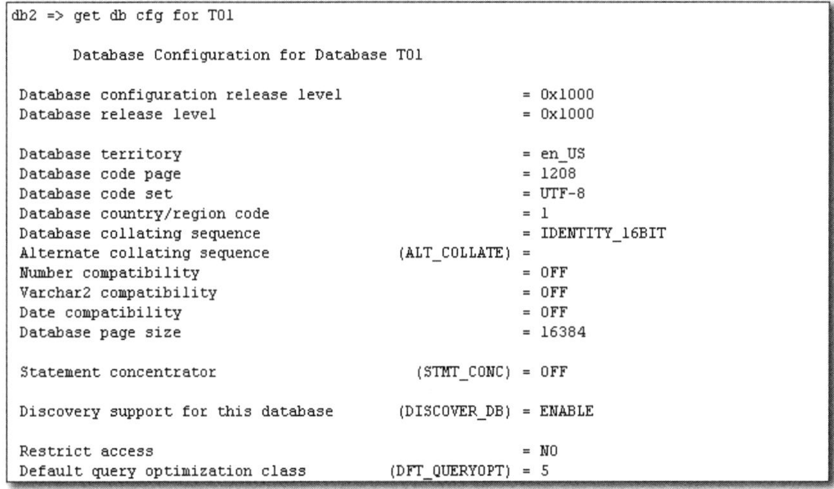

```
db2 => get db cfg for T01

       Database Configuration for Database T01

 Database configuration release level                    = 0x1000
 Database release level                                  = 0x1000

 Database territory                                      = en_US
 Database code page                                      = 1208
 Database code set                                       = UTF-8
 Database country/region code                            = 1
 Database collating sequence                             = IDENTITY_16BIT
 Alternate collating sequence              (ALT_COLLATE) =
 Number compatibility                                    = OFF
 Varchar2 compatibility                                  = OFF
 Date compatibility                                      = OFF
 Database page size                                      = 16384

 Statement concentrator                      (STMT_CONC) = OFF

 Discovery support for this database       (DISCOVER_DB) = ENABLE

 Restrict access                                         = NO
 Default query optimization class         (DFT_QUERYOPT) = 5
```

Figure 8.45 Displaying the Database Configuration

"for <DB-SID>" Addition [+]

You don't need to set up a separate connection to the database if you use the for <DB-SID> addition (e.g., get db cfg for T01).

If you want to change one or more values of the database configuration, execute the command update db cfg using <parameter> <value>. Make sure you're connected to the database. The number of primary log files can be changed as follows (see Figure 8.46):

1. Log on as db2<db-sid> (e.g., su - db2t01).

2. Enter the command "db2".
3. Establish a connection to the DB2 database (e.g., `connect to T01`).
4. Enter the command "update dbm cfg using logprimary 5".

```
db2 => update db cfg using logprimary 5
DB20000I  The UPDATE DATABASE CONFIGURATION command completed successfully.
SQL1363W  One or more of the parameters submitted for immediate modification
were not changed dynamically. For these configuration parameters, the database
must be shutdown and reactivated before the configuration parameter changes
become effective.
db2 =>
```

Figure 8.46 Changing the Number of Primary Log Files

[+] **Implementing Changes**

If possible, changes to the Database Manager configuration and database configuration are implemented immediately. If you want to avoid this, simply add the keyword `deferred` to the `UPDATE` commands. You must then restart the DB2 instance or DB2 database for the changes to take effect. This is necessary for parameters such as `logprimary`.

In the DB2 Profile Registry, you can use the `db2set` to make additional settings for your DB2 instance or DB2 database. You can use the command `db2set -all` to get a list of all possible parameters. To change a setting, execute the command `db2set <parameter>=<value>` (e.g., `db2set DB2TRC_DEF_BUFFSIZE=16M`). Note that you have to restart the DB2 instance after making changes to the settings.

[+] **Configuration of the Database and Database Manager in the DBA Cockpit**

You can configure the database and the Database Manager via a web interface using the DBA Cockpit. The SAP system must run in this case. Additionally, a parameter check is available in the DBA Cockpit. For this purpose, you need to download an SAP Note, including parameter recommendations from SAP and IBM, which are then compared with the currently set parameters for evaluation. The system then displays proposals.

8.5.7 Automatic Storage Management

Automatic Storage Management (ASM) was introduced with release DB2 for LUW 9. It's activated by default during installation and manages your tablespaces and associated containers. As a result, manual or semi-automatic storage management, which you might still know from previous releases, is no longer required.

For ASM, you only provide storage paths in which the DB2 database can work. The DB2 database then fully automates the creation and extension of the necessary containers.

Automatic Storage Management Can No Longer Be Deactivated [!]

ASM is activated during database installation when you create a tablespace and can no longer be deactivated.

If the existing storage paths are reserved for ASM, you can provide the DB2 database with another path. To do so, you must use the DB2 CLP command `alter database add storage on <path>`. Follow these steps (see Figure 8.47):

1. Log on as `db2<db-sid>` (e.g., `su - db2t01`).
2. Enter the command "db2".
3. Establish a connection to the DB2 database (e.g., `connect to T01`).
4. Enter the command "alter database add storage on '/db2/T01/sapdata5'".

```
db2 => alter database add storage on '/db2/T01/sapdata5'
DB20000I  The SQL command completed successfully.
db2 =>
```

Figure 8.47 Adding a Storage Path for Automatic Storage Management

We recommend using Transaction DBACOCKPIT for routine monitoring and administration of your database with ASM. Here, you can also easily add a storage path via the web interface. We discussed this example in Section 8.5.10.

8.5.8 Backing Up the Database

The security of data is essential for enterprises—in the worst case, an enterprise can go bankrupt if data is lost. Hardware problems, such as a defective storage system, not only lead to data loss but also to system downtime and nonavailability of the system for production, sales, and internal/external services. To avoid loss of data due to software, hardware, and user errors or external influencing factors, it's important to back up your tablespaces in the DB2 database and the log files on a regular basis. The DB2 database supports two types of backup:

- Offline backup
- Online backup

[!]

Infrastructure Planning for Data Security

You should provide any technical and structural means to reduce the probability of failure or disaster to almost zero. Plan the infrastructure and hardware of the data center with due care. Particularly for data backup, you should consider the isolation or physical separation of the data backup system from the actual hardware. Because this book can only provide you with basic information, please seek professional help if necessary.

For an *offline backup*, you must stop both the SAP system and the database. This is the major disadvantage of this type of backup. Users and customers can't access the SAP system during the backup. For systems that must be up and running 24/7, offline backup is hardly an option. For this reason, offline backups of live SAP systems are made in rare cases only. Furthermore, the buffers of the database and the SAP system are lost in this variant. This causes performance problems. The system must be used for a while until the buffers are restored. Because no activities take place on the database, an offline backup is, by its very nature, consistent. This is a major benefit.

If you want to perform an offline backup, you can use the command `backup db <dbname> to <device>, <device no.> parallelism <no. of tablespaces to be backed up in parallel>`. Follow these steps (see Figure 8.48):

1. Log on as SAP administration user `<sid>adm` (e.g., `su - t01adm`).
2. Stop the SAP system using the command `stopsap`.
3. Now log on as database user `db2<db-sid>` (e.g., `su - db2t01`).
4. Make sure that the database instance is running. If this isn't the case, start it using the command `db2start`.
5. Enter the command "db2".
6. Execute the command `backup db T01 to /db2_backup parallelism 2`.

```
db2 => backup db T01 to /db2_backup parallelism 2

Backup successful. The timestamp for this backup image is : 20140706010235

db2 =>
```

Figure 8.48 Offline Backup

[+]

Backup Information

The exact definition of individual values, devices, or paths for the backup and the number of tablespaces to be backed up in parallel depend on numerous factors and must be adjusted to the relevant environment.

For an *online backup*, you can continue to run the database and SAP system. The key advantage of this is that the users and customers can work with the SAP system. Also, the buffers of the database and the SAP system are kept and don't need to be rebuilt as in the offline backup. As a result, the performance doesn't decrease after the actual backup. The disadvantage is that you also activate the log archiving of the database and back up the database log files to keep the online backup consistent. It's also important that you run the online backup at a time when the SAP system's load is low. In most cases, you should do this at night. The backup influences the performance of the hardware components used, for example, the server, Storage Area Network (SAN), and network. This may result in longer response times in the SAP system.

If you want to perform a consistent online backup, you can use the command `backup db <dbname> online to <device>, <device no.> parallelism <no. of tablespaces to be backed up in parallel> include logs`. Follow these steps (see Figure 8.49):

1. Log on as `db2<db-sid>` (e.g., `su - db2t01`).
2. Enter the command "db2".
3. Enter the command "backup db T01 online to /db2_backup parallelism 2 include logs".

```
db2 => backup db T01 online to /db2_backup parallelism 2 include logs

Backup successful. The timestamp for this backup image is : 20140706014424

db2 =>
```

Figure 8.49 Online Backup with Two Tablespaces to Be Backed Up in Parallel

Incremental and Differential Backup [!]

In addition to a complete backup whereby the entire database is always backed up, the DB2 database also supports incremental and differential backups. However, you must set the `TRACKMOD` parameter in the database configuration for this purpose.

In the period between two database backups, you must make sure to archive the log files on a regular basis. You do this using the *DB2 Log Managers*, which you configure by making the relevant settings in the database configuration (see Figure 8.50). For example, you can use the parameter `LOGARCHMETH1` to determine how and to where the logs are to be backed up.

```
First log archive method                    (LOGARCHMETH1) = USEREXIT
Archive compression for logarchmeth1      (LOGARCHCOMPR1) = OFF
Options for logarchmeth1                    (LOGARCHOPT1) =
Second log archive method                  (LOGARCHMETH2) = OFF
Archive compression for logarchmeth2      (LOGARCHCOMPR2) = OFF
Options for logarchmeth2                    (LOGARCHOPT2) =
```

Figure 8.50 Database Configurations for Archiving Log Files

You can make snapshot backups using the `use snapshot` option of the `backup db` command. Here, the internal behavior of the database is temporarily changed as follows:

1. Changes are no longer written.
2. The database is backed up at the file level.
3. All changes are supplemented.

The backup at file level includes all containers, the database directory, and the directory with activated log files. The key advantage is that this approach has minimum effect on the system users. DB2 provides DB2 Advanced Copy Services (ACS) API drivers that allow for fluent integration of storage systems that can handle snapshots.

8.5.9 Restoring the Database

Commands are available for restore if an error occurs or if the database is defective. The restore process essentially comprises two steps. First, you must use an existing backup to restore the database. You must then use the archived log files to "roll back" the database to a time before the error occurred. The second step is necessary only if the database that was restored from the backup isn't consistent, or if the time of consistency is too far away from the time of error and thus causes considerable data loss. As the system administrator, you should have theoretical restore knowledge and make practical arrangements in the form of periodic restore tests for different error scenarios.

[+] **Backing Up a Damaged Database**

If an error occurs, remain calm and don't do anything rash. Before you undertake a restore attempt, always create a backup of the damaged database.

To fully restore the database, follow these steps (see Figure 8.51):

1. Log on as database administration user db2<db-sid> (e.g., su - db2t01).
2. Make sure that the database instance is running. If this isn't the case, start it using the command db2start.
3. Enter the command "db2".
4. Restore the database. The corresponding command is as follows: restore db <dbname> from <device>, <device no.> taken at <time stamp> (e.g., restore db T01 from /db2_backup taken at 20140607014424).
5. Enter the value "y" to confirm the security prompt.

```
db2 => restore db T01 from /db2_backup taken at 20140706014424
SQL2539W  The specified name of the backup image to restore is the same as the
name of the target database.  Restoring to an existing database that is the
same as the backup image database will cause the current database to be
overwritten by the backup version.
Do you want to continue ? (y/n) y
DB20000I  The RESTORE DATABASE command completed successfully.
db2 =>
```

Figure 8.51 Restoring the DB2 Database

6. Roll the database forward (see Figure 8.52). The corresponding command is rollforward db <dbname> to <time stamp> and stop (e.g., rollforward db t01 to end of logs and stop).

```
db2 => rollforward db T01 to end of logs and stop

                                 Rollforward Status

 Input database alias                   = T01
 Number of members have returned status = 1

 Member ID                              = 0
 Rollforward status                     = not pending
 Next log file to be read               =
 Log files processed                    = S0000068.LOG - S0000072.LOG
 Last committed transaction             = 2014-07-06-09.10.28.000000 UTC

DB20000I  The ROLLFORWARD command completed successfully.
db2 =>
```

Figure 8.52 Subsequent Rollforward of the DB2 Database

Since DB2 for LUW 8.2, you can use the recover command, which performs both steps together. The corresponding command is recover db <dbname> to <time stamp>. Follow these steps (see Figure 8.53):

1. Log on as user db2<db-sid> (e.g., su - db2t01).

2. Make sure the database instance is running. If this isn't the case, start it using the command `db2start`.
3. Enter the command "db2".
4. Execute the command `recover db T01 to end of logs`.

```
db2 => recover db T01 to end of logs

                                Rollforward Status

 Input database alias                   = T01
 Number of members have returned status = 1

 Member ID                              = 0
 Rollforward status                     = not pending
 Next log file to be read               =
 Log files processed                    = S0000068.LOG - S0000075.LOG
 Last committed transaction             = 2014-07-06-13.05.22.000000 Local

DB20000I  The RECOVER DATABASE command completed successfully.
db2 =>
```

Figure 8.53 Using the Recover Command

If you want to get information about the progress of the backup or restore, you can use the command `list utilities [show detail]` (see Figure 8.54):

1. Log on as `db2<db-sid>` (e.g., `su - db2t01`).
2. Enter the command "db2".
3. Enter the command "list utilities" or "list utilities show detail" to get detailed information.

```
db2 => list utilities show detail

ID                               = 1
Type                             = RESTORE
Database Name                    = T01
Member Number                    = 0
Description                      = db
Start Time                       = 07/06/2014 11:23:42.668529
State                            = Executing
Invocation Type                  = User
Progress Monitoring:
      Completed Work             = 4161769472 bytes
      Start Time                 = 07/06/2014 11:23:42.668547


db2 =>
```

Figure 8.54 Obtaining Information on the Database Restore

8.5.10 DBA Cockpit for DB2 for LUW

The previous two sections on DB2 CLP occasionally mentioned the DBA Cockpit. The DBA Cockpit combines the administration and monitoring tasks in a graphical web interface (or also in the SAP GUI) and provides many ad hoc query options as well as information gathered on the state of your DB2 database.

To use the DBA Cockpit without any errors, you must make the following configuration settings:

- In the system, the Internet Communication Manager (ICM) must be configured via the instance parameter `icm/server_port_0`.
- Logon must be set via single sign-on (parameter `login/accept_sso2_ticket = 1` as well as `login/create_sso2_ticket = 2`).
- The Internet Communication Framework (ICF) service activation for the Web Dynpro DBA Cockpit must be made using Transaction SICF_INST with the technical names `WEB DYNPRO ABAP` and `WEB DYNPRO DBA COCKPIT`.

After you've started Transaction DBACOCKPIT, the system opens the web interface with the initial screen of the system landscape, which, by default, includes the DB2 database of the system you're logged on to. You can add further DB2 databases of other SAP systems to create a central administration and monitoring point for all of your DB2 databases. By clicking on the ID of your database, you open a dashboard that provides a clear overview of all information (see Figure 8.55).

The menu bar of the DBA Cockpit offers the following entries which provide you with further actions, tasks, and activities on a specific topic:

- OVERVIEW
  Here you can find the dashboard we've already mentioned.
- PERFORMANCE
  This area provides a pool of all activities that are relevant with regard to the DB2 system performance, such as workload statistics or the analysis of SQL statements.
- SPACE
  This area includes all information and administration tasks for storage management, for example, for ASM, tablespaces, tables, and indexes.

- **Backup and Restore**
  This area provides an overview of the backup history and log archiving.
- **Configuration**
  In this area, you can modify the database and Database Manager configuration, configure automatic database maintenance, and set the data collection framework.
- **Jobs**
  In this area, you can find the planning calendar and the scheduled DB2 tasks.
- **Alerts**
  This area comprises all activities for alerts on the DB2 database's state, such as the Alert Monitor, alert message log, and alert configuration.
- **Diagnosis**
  This area includes all activities and tasks that support the analysis of problems and detailed troubleshooting, such as missing tables and indexes, access to the DB2 dump directory, diagnostic logs, or querying of predefined DB2 CLP commands.
- **BW Administration**
  This area provides you with all SAP BW-specific activities, such as SAP BW data distribution and the MDC Advisor.

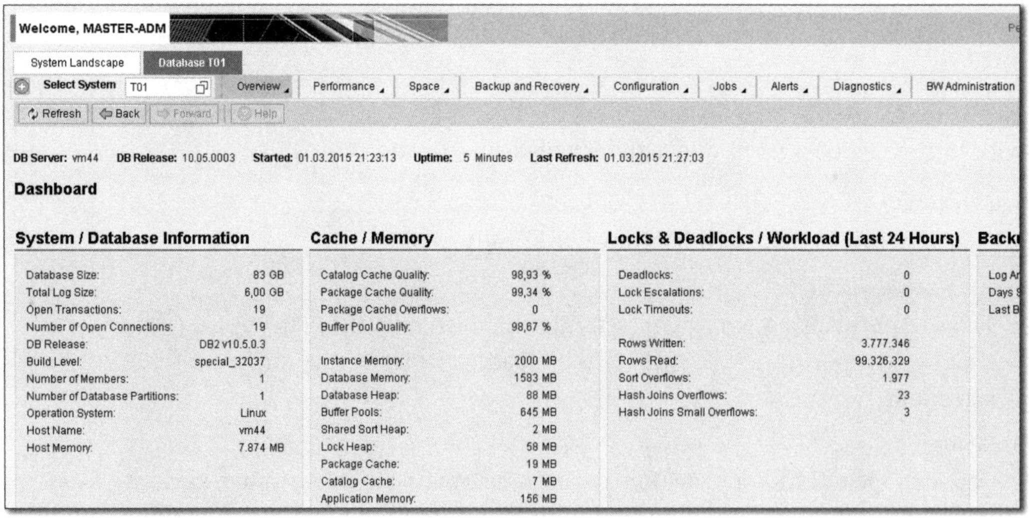

Figure 8.55 DBA Cockpit Dashboard for DB2 Database T01

In Section 8.5.7, we discussed the creation of another storage path for ASM using the DB2 CLP. As an example for using the DBA Cockpit, we now perform these steps in the DBA Cockpit:

1. Call Transaction DBACOCKPIT, and go to the database you want to manage.
2. Choose SPACE • AUTOMATIC STORAGE MANAGEMENT.
3. Select the default storage group name IBMSTOGROUP, and click on the CHANGE button.
4. A dialog box opens in which you can change the automatic storage. Enter the new storage path (e.g., "/db2/T01/sapdata5") in addition to the already existing paths (see Figure 8.56).
5. Choose CHECK to make sure that all entries are correct. You can also see which SQL statement will be generated.
6. Click on the SAVE button to add the new storage path.

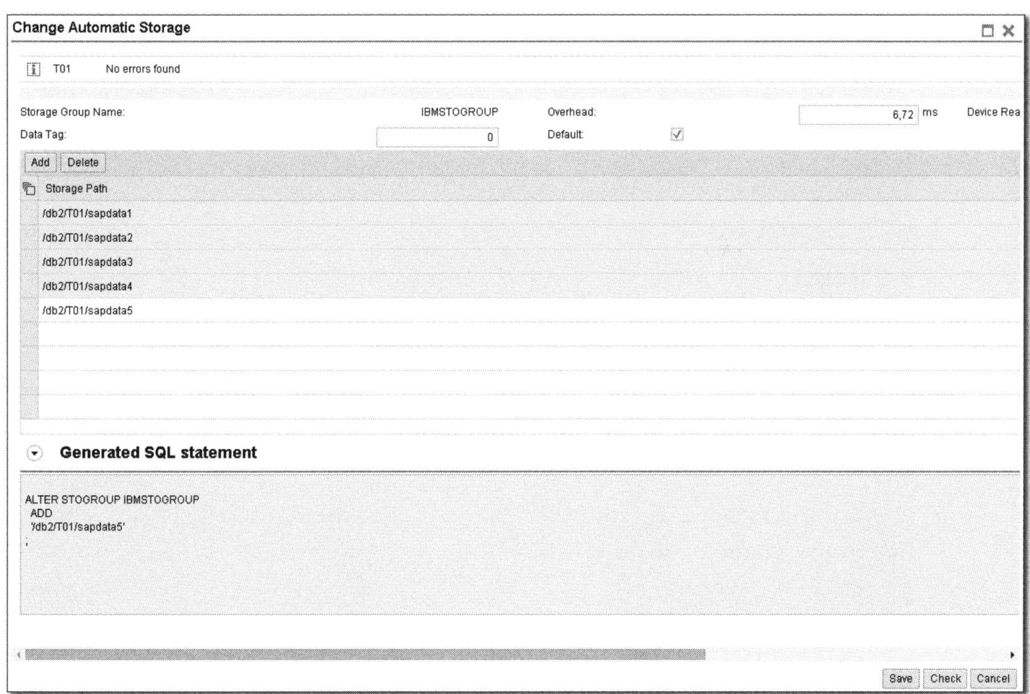

Figure 8.56 Adding a Storage Path via the DBA Cockpit

8.6 Database Administration—Oracle

When managing an Oracle database in the SAP environment, three options are available to you. The Oracle Client tool SQL*Plus and the BR*Tools provided by SAP are available at the operating system level, and the collective Transaction DBACOCKPIT is available in the SAP system.

[+]

Additional Information on SQL*Plus and BR*Tools

Documentation for the Oracle database and the Oracle Client tool SQL*Plus is available online at *http://www.oracle.com/technology/documentation*, whereas documentation on managing Oracle databases in the SAP environment and the BR*Tools is available in the operations area at *http://help.sap.com/* under TECHNOLOGY • SAP NETWEAVER PLATFORM • SAP NETWEAVER 7.4 • APPLICATION HELP • FUNCTION ORIENTED VIEW • ENGLISH • DATABASE ADMINISTRATION • DATABASE ADMINISTRATION FOR ORACLE.

8.6.1 SQL*Plus

The Oracle Client tool SQL*Plus is automatically installed when you install the Oracle database. You can use this tool to perform the following tasks, among other things:

- Starting and stopping the database
- Configuring the SQL*Plus environment
- Executing SQL statements and SQL scripts
- Managing the database

Next, we'll describe how to use SQL*Plus to manage Oracle databases.

Connecting to the Database

Before you can work with the SQL*Plus tool, it's important to establish a connection to the database. To do this, follow these steps:

1. Use user `ora<dbname>` to log on at the operating system level (e.g., using the command `su - orav14`).
2. Enter the command "sqlplus". The system now prompts you to log on to the database (see Figure 8.57).

```
v14:orav14 52> sqlplus

SQL*Plus: Release 11.2.0.3.0 Production on Tue Jul 22 18:23:44 2014

Copyright (c) 1982, 2011, Oracle.  All rights reserved.

Enter user-name:
```

Figure 8.57 Calling SQL*Plus

3. Log on as the SAP schema user, for example, sapsr3 (see Figure 8.58).

Schema User

The schema is a separation mechanism in the database. SAPSR3 is the default schema for SAP NetWeaver AS ABAP. This schema includes the SAP table (e.g., separated from the Oracle system tables).

```
v14:orav14 76> sqlplus

SQL*Plus: Release 11.2.0.3.0 Production on Tue Jul 22 19:16:31 2014

Copyright (c) 1982, 2011, Oracle.  All rights reserved.

Enter user-name: sapsr3
Enter password:

Connected to:
Oracle Database 11g Enterprise Edition Release 11.2.0.3.0 - 64bit Production
With the Partitioning, OLAP, Data Mining and Real Application Testing options

SQL>
```

Figure 8.58 Log On as SAP Schema User

4. If you want to perform database administration tasks, you must also specify the role SYSDBA. To do this, enter the command "connect / as sysdba" (see Figure 8.59).

```
SQL> connect / as sysdba
Connected.
SQL>
```

Figure 8.59 Assigning Roles for Database Administration Tasks

You've now established a connection to the database. If you want to log on directly using the role SYSDBA, you can also follow these steps (see Figure 8.60):

1. Log on as ora<dbname> (e.g., su - orav14).

2. Enter the command "sqlplus / as sysdba".

```
v14:orav14 54> sqlplus / as sysdba

SQL*Plus: Release 11.2.0.3.0 Production on Tue Jul 22 18:31:11 2014

Copyright (c) 1982, 2011, Oracle.  All rights reserved.


Connected to:
Oracle Database 11g Enterprise Edition Release 11.2.0.3.0 - 64bit Production
With the Partitioning, OLAP, Data Mining and Real Application Testing options

SQL> 
```

Figure 8.60 Direct Logon to the Oracle Database with the SYSDBA Role

Configuring the SQL*Plus Environment

You can influence the behavior of the SQL*Plus environment to a certain extent by setting variables. If, for example, you want to facilitate better logging of your work, you can copy the SQL*Plus output to a file.

If you want to view the current settings, follow these steps (see Figure 8.61):

1. Log on as ora<dbname> (e.g., su - orasl1).
2. Start SQL*Plus (e.g., sqlplus / as sysdba).
3. Enter the command "show all".

```
SQL> show all
appinfo is OFF and set to "SQL*Plus"
arraysize 15
autocommit OFF
autoprint OFF
autorecovery OFF
autotrace OFF
blockterminator "." (hex 2e)
btitle OFF and is the first few characters of the next SELECT statement
cmdsep OFF
colsep " "
compatibility version NATIVE
concat "." (hex 2e)
copycommit 0
COPYTYPECHECK is ON
define "&" (hex 26)
describe DEPTH 1 LINENUM OFF INDENT ON
echo OFF
```

Figure 8.61 Viewing the Settings of the SQL*Plus Environment

If you want to change the configuration in the SQL*Plus environment, you can do this using the command set <variable> <value>. If, for example, you want to deactivate the line break in SQL*Plus, enter the command "set wrap off" (see Figure 8.62).

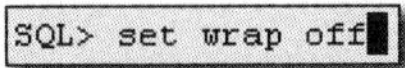

Figure 8.62 Deactivating the Line Break in SQL*Plus

If you also want to copy the SQL*Plus output to a text file, you must use the command spool <file> (e.g., spool output.txt, see Figure 8.63).

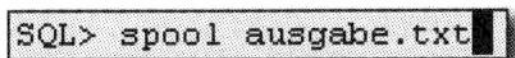

Figure 8.63 Copying SQL*Plus to a Text File

8.6.2 Starting and Stopping the Database

There are three ways to start an Oracle database in the SAP environment:

- Using the Oracle client tool SQL*Plus
- Using the SAP command startdb
- Using the BR*Tools provided by SAP

If you want to use startdb, you must first start a program that facilitates communication between the Oracle database and the clients. This program is called *Oracle Listener*. You start this listener as follows:

1. Log on as the user ora<dbname> at the operating system level (e.g., su - orav14).
2. To start the listener of the Oracle instance, enter the command "lsnrctl start", and press the Enter key (see Figure 8.64).

Oracle Listener [!]

If you want to use the command startdb to start the database, the listener must already be running. For the other two options, you can also start the listener retroactively. The listener must run at the latest when you want to start the SAP system.

```
v14:orav14 61> lsnrctl start

LSNRCTL for Linux: Version 11.2.0.3.0 - Production on 22-JUL-2014 18:45:02

Copyright (c) 1991, 2011, Oracle.  All rights reserved.

Starting /oracle/V14/112_64/bin/tnslsnr: please wait...

TNSLSNR for Linux: Version 11.2.0.3.0 - Production
System parameter file is /oracle/V14/112_64/network/admin/listener.ora
Log messages written to /oracle/V14/saptrace/diag/tnslsnr/v14/listener/alert/log.xml
Listening on: (DESCRIPTION=(ADDRESS=(PROTOCOL=ipc)(KEY=V14.WORLD)))
Listening on: (DESCRIPTION=(ADDRESS=(PROTOCOL=ipc)(KEY=V14)))
Listening on: (DESCRIPTION=(ADDRESS=(PROTOCOL=tcp)(HOST=v14.sap-labor.steria-mummert.de)(PORT=1527)))

Connecting to (ADDRESS=(PROTOCOL=IPC)(KEY=V14.WORLD))
STATUS of the LISTENER
------------------------
Alias                     LISTENER
Version                   TNSLSNR for Linux: Version 11.2.0.3.0 - Production
Start Date                22-JUL-2014 18:45:02
Uptime                    0 days 0 hr. 0 min. 0 sec
Trace Level               off
Security                  ON: Local OS Authentication
SNMP                      OFF
Listener Parameter File   /oracle/V14/112_64/network/admin/listener.ora
Listener Log File         /oracle/V14/saptrace/diag/tnslsnr/v14/listener/alert/log.xml
Listening Endpoints Summary...
  (DESCRIPTION=(ADDRESS=(PROTOCOL=ipc)(KEY=V14.WORLD)))
  (DESCRIPTION=(ADDRESS=(PROTOCOL=ipc)(KEY=V14)))
  (DESCRIPTION=(ADDRESS=(PROTOCOL=tcp)(HOST=v14.sap-labor.steria-mummert.de)(PORT=1527)))
Services Summary...
Service "V14" has 1 instance(s).
  Instance "V14", status UNKNOWN, has 1 handler(s) for this service...
The command completed successfully
v14:orav14 62>
```

Figure 8.64 Starting the Oracle Listener

Starting the Database

If you want to use the client tool SQL*Plus to start the Oracle database, follow these steps (see Figure 8.65):

1. Log on to the server as the operating system user `ora<dbname>` (e.g., `su - orav14`).
2. Start SQL*Plus, and log on as the user `SYSDBA` (e.g., `sqlplus / as sysdba`). The output `Connected to an idle instance` indicates that the database isn't running.
3. Enter the command "startup", and press the [Enter] key.

```
v14:orav14 63> sqlplus / as sysdba

SQL*Plus: Release 11.2.0.3.0 Production on Tue Jul 22 18:48:54 2014

Copyright (c) 1982, 2011, Oracle.  All rights reserved.

Connected to an idle instance.

SQL> startup
ORA-32004: obsolete or deprecated parameter(s) specified for RDBMS instance
ORACLE instance started.

Total System Global Area 1670295552 bytes
Fixed Size                  2228904 bytes
Variable Size             838864216 bytes
Database Buffers          805306368 bytes
Redo Buffers               23896064 bytes
Database mounted.
Database opened.
SQL>
```

Figure 8.65 Starting the Oracle Database Using SQL*Plus

If you want to use the command `startdb` to start the database, follow these steps (see Figure 8.66):

1. Log on to the server as the operating system user `ora<dbname>` (e.g., `su - orav14`).
2. Enter the command "startdb", and press the [Enter] key.

```
v14:orav14 65> startdb
Trying to start V14 database ...
Log file: /oracle/V14/startdb.log
V14 database started
v14:orav14 66>
```

Figure 8.66 Starting the Database Using the "startdb" Command

If you want to use the BR*Tools to start the Oracle database, follow these steps:

1. Log on to the server as `ora<dbname>` (e.g., `su - orav14`).
2. Enter the command "brtools", and press the [Enter] key. The system displays the BR*Tools menu (see Figure 8.67). Select the INSTANCE MANAGEMENT entry by entering the value "1" and pressing the [Enter] key.

```
v14:orav14 69> brtools
BR0651I BRTOOLS 7.40 (6)

BR0280I BRTOOLS time stamp: 2014-07-22 18:58:35
BR0656I Choice menu 1 - please make a selection
-------------------------------------------------------------------------------
BR*Tools main menu

 1 = Instance management
 2 - Space management
 3 - Segment management
 4 - Backup and database copy
 5 - Restore and recovery
 6 - Check and verification
 7 - Database statistics
 8 - Additional functions
 9 - Exit program

Standard keys: c - cont, b - back, s - stop, r - refr, h - help
-------------------------------------------------------------------------------
BR0662I Enter your choice:
1
```

Figure 8.67 BR*Tools Menu

3. In the next menu, select the START UP DATABASE option (see Figure 8.68) by entering the value "1" and pressing the [Enter] key.

```
Database instance management

 1 = Start up database
 2 - Shut down database
 3 - Alter database instance
 4 - Alter database parameters
 5 - Recreate database
 6 - Manage online redolog
 7 - Manage data encryption
 8 - Additional instance functions
 9 - Reset program status

Standard keys: c - cont, b - back, s - stop, r - refr, h - help
-------------------------------------------------------------------------------
BR0662I Enter your choice:
1
```

Figure 8.68 Database Instance Management Menu

4. Check the parameters displayed. Then, enter the value "c", and press the [Enter] key. To confirm the security prompt, enter the value "c" again. The BRSPACE tool is started (see also Section 8.6.5 and Figure 8.69).

```
BR0280I BRSPACE time stamp: 2014-07-22 19:00:37
BR0656I Choice menu 201 - please make a selection
-------------------------------------------------------------------------------
Database instance startup main menu

 1 = Start up database
 2 - Show instance status
 3 * Exit program
 4 - Reset program status

Standard keys: c - cont, b - back, s - stop, r - refr, h - help
-------------------------------------------------------------------------------
BR0662I Enter your choice:
1
```

Figure 8.69 Starting the Database Using the BR*Tools

5. To start the database, select the START UP DATABASE option by entering the value "1" and pressing the [Enter] key.
6. Check the parameters displayed. Then, enter the value "c", and press the [Enter] key. To confirm the security prompt, enter the value "c" again (see Figure 8.70).

```
BR0280I BRSPACE time stamp: 2014-07-22 19:02:55
BR0657I Input menu 203 - please enter/check input values
-------------------------------------------------------------------------------
Options for starting up database instance V14

 1 - Database startup to-state (state) . [open]
 2 - Database open mode (mode) ......... [normal]
 3 - Force instance restart (force) .... [no]
 4 - SQLPLUS command (command) ......... [startup open]

Standard keys: c - cont, b - back, s - stop, r - refr, h - help
-------------------------------------------------------------------------------
BR0662I Enter your choice:
c
```

Figure 8.70 Checking the Parameters

The database is now started (see Figure 8.71).

```
BR0280I BRSPACE time stamp: 2014-07-22 19:03:28
BR0304I Starting and opening database instance V14 ...

BR0280I BRSPACE time stamp: 2014-07-22 19:03:45
BR0305I Start and open of database instance V14 successful
```

Figure 8.71 Log for Starting the Oracle Database

Stopping the Database

Similar to starting the Oracle database, there are also three ways to stop the database. If you want to use the client tool SQL*Plus to stop the Oracle database, follow these steps (see Figure 8.72):

1. Log on to the server as the operating system user `ora<dbname>` (e.g., `su - orav14`).
2. Start SQL*Plus, and log on as `SYSDBA` (e.g., `sqlplus / as sysdba`).
3. Enter the command "shutdown", and press the [Enter] key.

```
v14:orav14 70> sqlplus / as sysdba

SQL*Plus: Release 11.2.0.3.0 Production on Tue Jul 22 19:05:52 2014

Copyright (c) 1982, 2011, Oracle.  All rights reserved.


Connected to:
Oracle Database 11g Enterprise Edition Release 11.2.0.3.0 - 64bit Production
With the Partitioning, OLAP, Data Mining and Real Application Testing options

SQL> shutdown
Database closed.
Database dismounted.
ORACLE instance shut down.
SQL> 
```

Figure 8.72 Stopping the Oracle Database Using SQL*Plus

[!] **Shutdown Command**

When you enter the shutdown command, make sure that you're actually in the SQL*Plus program. Otherwise, you may accidentally shut down the entire database server instead of the database instance.

If you want to use the command `stopdb` to stop the database, follow these steps (see Figure 8.73):

1. Log on to the server as the operating system user `ora<dbname>` (e.g., `su - orav14`).
2. Enter the command "stopdb", and press the [Enter] key.

```
v14:orav14 71> stopdb
Trying to stop V14 database ...
Log file: /oracle/V14/stopdb.log
V14 database stopped
v14:orav14 72> 
```

Figure 8.73 Stopping the Database Using the "stopdb" Command

If you want to use the BR*Tools to stop the Oracle database, follow these steps:

1. Log on to the server as `ora<dbname>` (e.g., using the command `su - orav14`).
2. Enter the command "brtools", and press [Enter]. The system displays the BR* Tools menu.
3. Select the INSTANCE MANAGEMENT entry by entering the value "1" and pressing the [Enter] key.
4. In the next menu, select the SHUT DOWN DATABASE entry by entering the value "2" and pressing the [Enter] key.
5. Check the parameters displayed. Then, enter the value "c", and press the [Enter] key.
6. To confirm the security prompt, enter the value "c" again. The BRSPACE tool starts.
7. To stop the database, select the SHUT DOWN DATABASE option again by entering the value "1" and pressing the [Enter] key (see Figure 8.74).

```
BR0280I BRSPACE time stamp: 2014-07-22 19:10:47
BR0656I Choice menu 204 - please make a selection
-------------------------------------------------------------------------------
Database instance shutdown main menu

 1 = Shut down database
 2 - Show instance status
 3 * Exit program
 4 - Reset program status

Standard keys: c - cont, b - back, s - stop, r - refr, h - help
-------------------------------------------------------------------------------
BR0662I Enter your choice:
1
```

Figure 8.74 Stopping the Database Using the BR*Tools

8. Check the parameters displayed. Then, enter the value "c", and press the [Enter] key.
9. To confirm the security prompt, enter the value "c" again. The database is now stopped (see Figure 8.75).

```
BR0280I BRSPACE time stamp: 2014-07-22 19:11:22
BR0307I Shutting down database instance V14 ...

BR0280I BRSPACE time stamp: 2014-07-22 19:11:29
BR0308I Shutdown of database instance V14 successful
```

Figure 8.75 Shutdown Log of the Database

You can then also stop the listener, for example, if you then want to shut down the entire database server. To do this, follow these steps (see Figure 8.76):

1. Log on to the server as `ora<dbname>` (e.g., `su - orav14`).
2. To stop the listener of the Oracle instance, enter the command "lsnrctl stop", and press the [Enter] key.

```
v14:orav14 73> lsnrctl stop

LSNRCTL for Linux: Version 11.2.0.3.0 - Production on 22-JUL-2014 19:13:32

Copyright (c) 1991, 2011, Oracle.  All rights reserved.

Connecting to (ADDRESS=(PROTOCOL=IPC)(KEY=V14.WORLD))
The command completed successfully
v14:orav14 74>
```

Figure 8.76 Stopping the Oracle Listener

8.6.3 Executing SQL Statements and SQL Scripts

SQL*Plus enables you to execute SQL statements and SQL scripts in the database. If, for example, you want to display all of the clients in your SAP system, follow these steps:

1. Log on as `ora<dbname>` (e.g., `su - orav14`).
2. Start SQL*Plus (e.g., `sqlplus / as sysdba`).
3. Enter the command "select mandt from sap<schemaid>.t000";(e.g., "select mandt from sapsr3.t000"; see Figure 8.77).

```
SQL> select mandt from sapsr3.t000;

MANDT
---------
000
001
066
100
200

SQL>
```

Figure 8.77 Executing the SQL Command Using SQL*Plus

If you want to execute an SQL script, place `@` in front of the script to be executed. If, for example, you want to execute the script `test.sql`, follow these steps (see Figure 8.78):

1. Log on as ora<dbname> (e.g., su - orav14). Make sure that you're in the directory which also includes the SQL script.
2. Start SQL*Plus (e.g., sqlplus / as sysdba).
3. Enter the command "@test.sql".

```
v14:orav14 79> pwd
/oracle/V14
v14:orav14 80> ls *.sql
test.sql
v14:orav14 81> sqlplus / as sysdba

SQL*Plus: Release 11.2.0.3.0 Production on Tue Jul 22 19:28:09 2014

Copyright (c) 1982, 2011, Oracle.  All rights reserved.


Connected to:
Oracle Database 11g Enterprise Edition Release 11.2.0.3.0 - 64bit Production
With the Partitioning, OLAP, Data Mining and Real Application Testing options

SQL> @test.sql

MANDT
---------
000
001
066
100
200

SQL> █
```

Figure 8.78 Executing the SQL Script Using SQL*Plus

Take Care When Executing SQL Statements [!]

Take due care and consideration when executing SQL statements. You have full access to the data in the SAP system and can manipulate this data beyond the SAP transaction logic. However, this may lead to inconsistencies in the SAP system.

8.6.4 Managing the Database Using SQL*Plus

You can also use SQL*Plus to perform database administration tasks. For example, you can use the command alter table-space to make changes to the tablespaces in your database (see Figure 8.79).

```
 9 - SQL command (command) ................. [alter tablespace PSAPSR3DB add datafile '/oracle/V14/
sapdata4/sr3db_4/sr3db.data4' size 4540M autoextend on next 20M maxsize 10000M]
```

Figure 8.79 Changing the Tablespaces of the Database

[+]

Displaying Available Commands

In general, the BR*Tools show you which command to execute against the database. If, for example, you're interested in learning how to use SQL*Plus to create a new data file, you can view the command in `BRSPACE`.

However, you can use the BR*Tools to perform these tasks from the menu. The BR*Tools, which are discussed in more detail in the following section, make your work easier and protect you against forgetting information. For this reason, we'll detail the database administration using SQL*Plus.

8.6.5 Managing the Database Using the BR*Tools

The BR*Tools provided by SAP enable you to perform database administration tasks from the menu. You can use the BR*Tools to perform the following tasks, among other things:

- Starting and stopping the database
- Checking and changing the status of the database instance
- Checking and updating the database configuration
- Managing tablespaces and the associated data files
- Backing up the database
- Restoring the database
- Checking the database and database statistics

[+]

Options When Using the BR*Tools

The BR*Tools enable you to perform a range of additional tasks. Therefore, take some time to familiarize yourself with these tools.

The BR*Tools comprise the `BRARCHIVE`, `BRBACKUP`, `BRCONNECT`, `BRRECOVER`, `BRRESTORE`, `BRSPACE`, and `BRTOOLS` programs, each of which is used to perform particular tasks. To make it easier for you to use the BR*Tools as a central entry point, the `BRTOOLS` program displays an interactive menu that can be used to control the other programs.

[+]

SAPDBA and the BR*Tools

The BR*Tools replace the SAP administration tool `SAPDBA` for all SAP systems running on an Oracle 9i database or newer. Even if `SAPDBA` is still available, SAP recommends that you only use the BR*Tools.

Starting and Using the BR*Tools

You can start BRTOOLS as follows (see Figure 8.80):

1. Log on as ora<dbname> (e.g., su - orav14).
2. Enter the command "brtools".

```
v14:orav14 83> brtools
```

Figure 8.80 Starting the BRTOOLS Program

You can also use the option -c to start BRTOOLS. In this case, some additional prompts are displayed in the BR*Tools. The corresponding command is then brtools -c. After you've started BRTOOLS, the system displays the main menu in which you can select individual entries by entering the corresponding number (see Figure 8.81). If, for example, you want to select the SEGMENT MANAGEMENT option, enter the value "3", and press the [Enter] key.

```
v14:orav14 83> brtools
BR0651I BRTOOLS 7.40 (6)

BR0280I BRTOOLS time stamp: 2014-07-22 19:35:58
BR0656I Choice menu 1 - please make a selection
------------------------------------------------
BR*Tools main menu

 1 = Instance management
 2 - Space management
 3 - Segment management
 4 - Backup and database copy
 5 - Restore and recovery
 6 - Check and verification
 7 - Database statistics
 8 - Additional functions
 9 - Exit program
```

Figure 8.81 Main Menu of the BRTOOLS Program

In addition to selecting the menu options, you can also use standard keys to control the BR*Tools (see Figure 8.82). Among other things, you can stop the BR*Tools or display the Help documentation. If, for example, you want to stop the BR*Tools, select the STOP standard key by entering the value "s" and pressing the [Enter] key.

```
Standard keys: c - cont, b - back, s - stop, r - refr, h - help
```

Figure 8.82 Standard Keys for the BR*Tools

Checking and Changing the Status of the Database Instance

You can use the `BRSPACE` program to display information about the current status of your database instance. To do this, follow these steps:

1. Log on as `ora<dbname>` (e.g., `su - orav14`).
2. Start `BRTOOLS` (e.g., `brtools -c`).
3. Select the INSTANCE MANAGEMENT option.
4. Select the ADDITIONAL INSTANCE FUNCTIONS option, and then select the SHOW INSTANCE STATUS entry. To do this, enter the value "8" and then the value "1", and press the [Enter] key for each value (see Figure 8.83).

```
BR0280I BRTOOLS time stamp: 2014-07-22 19:39:29
BR0656I Choice menu 3 - please make a selection
-------------------------------------------------------------------------------
Database instance management

 1 = Start up database
 2 - Shut down database
 3 - Alter database instance
 4 - Alter database parameters
 5 - Recreate database
 6 - Manage online redolog
 7 - Manage data encryption
 8 - Additional instance functions
 9 - Reset program status

Standard keys: c - cont, b - back, s - stop, r - refr, h - help
-------------------------------------------------------------------------------
BR0662I Enter your choice:
8
BR0280I BRTOOLS time stamp: 2014-07-22 19:40:09
BR0663I Your choice: '8'

BR0280I BRTOOLS time stamp: 2014-07-22 19:40:09
BR0656I Choice menu 4 - please make a selection
-------------------------------------------------------------------------------
Additional database instance functions

 1 = Show instance status
 2 - Show database parameters
 3 - Show database owners
 4 - Show flashback status
 5 - Show encryption status

Standard keys: c - cont, b - back, s - stop, r - refr, h - help
-------------------------------------------------------------------------------
BR0662I Enter your choice:
1
BR0280I BRTOOLS time stamp: 2014-07-22 19:40:11
BR0663I Your choice: '1'
```

Figure 8.83 Displaying the Status of the Database Instances

5. You get an overview of the status and the most critical settings of the database instance (see Figure 8.84). Check the parameters displayed, and select the CONT

option by entering the value "c", and pressing the [Enter] key. You then get information about the status of your Oracle database instance.

```
BR0280I BRSPACE time stamp: 2014-07-22 19:40:20
BR0692I Display menu 256 # no input possible
-------------------------------------------------------------------------------
Information about the status of database instance V14

 1 - Instance number (number) ........... 1
 2 - Instance thread (thread) ........... 1
 3 - Instance status (status) ........... OPEN
 4 - Instance start time (start) ........ 2014-07-22 19:15:34
 5 - Oracle version (version) ........... 11.2.0.3.0
 6 - Database creation time (create) .... 2010-08-13 02:04:35
 7 - Last resetlogs time (resetlogs) .... 2013-10-22 15:40:24
 8 - Archivelog mode (archmode) ......... ARCHIVELOG
 9 - Archiver status (archiver) ......... STARTED
10 - Current redolog sequence (redoseq) . 4942
11 - Current redolog SCN (redoscn) ...... 280898373
12 - Flashback status (flashback) ....... OFF
13 - Block change tracking (tracking) ... OFF
14 - Data encryption (encryption) ....... OFF
15 - Database vault (dbvault) ........... OFF
16 - Number of SAP connections (sapcon) . 0

Standard keys: c - cont, b - back, s - stop, r - refr, h - help
-------------------------------------------------------------------------------
BR0662I Enter your choice:
```

Figure 8.84 Displaying Information on the Database Instance

You can also use the BRSPACE program to change the status of your database instance. If, for example, you want to set your database instance to NOARCHIVELOG mode to disable archiving of the redo log files, follow these steps:

1. Stop the SAP system.
2. Log on as ora<dbname> (e.g., su - orav14).
3. Start the program BRTOOLS (e.g., brtools -c).
4. Select the INSTANCE MANAGEMENT option.
5. Select the ALTER DATABASE INSTANCE option by entering the value "3" and pressing the [Enter] key. You get an overview of the parameters used to start BRSPACE.
6. Check the parameters displayed, and select the CONT option by entering the value "c" and pressing the [Enter] key.
7. Select the SET NOARCHIVELOG MODE option by entering the value "4" and pressing the [Enter] key (see Figure 8.85). You get information about the current and target statuses of the database instance. The command to be executed is also displayed (see Figure 8.86).

```
BR0280I BRSPACE time stamp: 2014-07-22 19:52:02
BR0656I Choice menu 207 - please make a selection
-------------------------------------------------------------------------------
Alter database instance main menu

 1 - Switch redolog file
 2 - Force database checkpoint
 3 - Set archivelog mode
 4 - Set noarchivelog mode
 5 - Show instance status
 6 * Exit program
 7 - Reset program status

Standard keys: c - cont, b - back, s - stop, r - refr, h - help
-------------------------------------------------------------------------------
BR0662I Enter your choice:
4
```

Figure 8.85 Set Database Instance to "NOARCHIVELOG" Mode

```
BR0280I BRSPACE time stamp: 2014-07-22 19:55:13
BR0657I Input menu 209 - please enter/check input values
-------------------------------------------------------------------------------
Options for alter of database instance V14

 1 * Current archivelog mode (mode) .. [archivelog]
 2 * Alter database action (action) .. [noarchlog]
 3 - Force instance shutdown (force) . [no]
 4 - SQL command (command) .......... [alter database noarchivelog]

Standard keys: c - cont, b - back, s - stop, r - refr, h - help
-------------------------------------------------------------------------------
BR0662I Enter your choice:
c
```

Figure 8.86 Confirming the Operation Execution

8. Check the parameters displayed, and select the CONT option again.

The BRSPACE program now sets the database instance to NOARCHIVELOG mode.

Checking and Updating the Database Configuration

Originally, the Oracle database configuration was stored alone in the initialization parameter text file, which is usually called *init<DBNAME>.ora* (e.g., *initU14.ora*). However, because the Oracle database is unable to update this file dynamically, a binary server parameter file, which is usually called *spfile<DBNAME>.ora* (e.g., *spfileU14.ora*) or *spfile.ora*, is available since release 9i. Because some transactions in the SAP system (e.g., Transaction ST04) access initialization parameter text files, you must ensure that the content of both files remains the same.

Using the BR*Tools to Make Changes [+]

The BR*Tools support you in making changes to the two parameter files by automatically updating both files in parallel, thus keeping them consistent. You should therefore use the BR*Tools to make changes to your Oracle database configuration.

You can use the `BRSPACE` program to display information about your current database configuration by following these steps:

1. Log on as `ora<dbname>` (e.g., `su - orav14`).
2. Start `BRTOOLS` (e.g., `brtools -c`).
3. Select the INSTANCE MANAGEMENT option.
4. Select the ADDITIONAL INSTANCE FUNCTIONS option.
5. Select the SHOW DATABASE PARAMETERS option. You get an overview of the parameters used to start `BRSPACE` (see Figure 8.87).

```
BR0280I BRSPACE time stamp: 2014-07-22 20:00:06
BR0659I List menu 257 + you can select one or more entries
--------------------------------------------------------------------------------
List of database parameters

Pos.  Parameter                            Modif.  Spfile  Inst.    Deft. Value

  1 - _fix_control                         both     yes      *       no    '5099019:ON','5705630:ON','6055658:OFF','612048
84:OFF','8937971:ON','9196440:ON','9495669:ON','13077335:ON','13627489:ON','14255600:ON','14595273:ON'
  2 - _mutex_wait_scheme                   both     yes      *       no    1
  3 - _mutex_wait_time                     both     yes      *       no    10
  4 - _optim_peek_user_binds               both     yes      *       no    FALSE
  5 - _optimizer_adaptive_cursor_sharing   both     yes      *       no    FALSE
  6 - _optimizer_extended_cursor_sharing_rel both     yes      *       no    NONE
  7 - _optimizer_use_feedback              both     yes      *       no    FALSE
  8 - active_instance_count                spfile   no       *       yes   <null>
  9 - aq_tm_processes                      both     no       *       yes   1
 10 - archive_lag_target                   both     no       *       yes   0
 11 - asm_diskgroups                       both     no       *       yes   <null>
 12 - asm_diskstring                       both     no       *       yes   <null>
 13 - asm_power_limit                      both     no       *       yes   1
 14 - asm_preferred_read_failure_groups    both     no       *       yes   <null>
 15 - audit_file_dest                      defer    yes      *       no    /oracle/V14/saptrace/audit
 16 - audit_sys_operations                 spfile   no       *       yes   FALSE
 17 - audit_syslog_level                   spfile   no       *       yes   <null>
 18 - audit_trail                          spfile   no       *       yes   NONE
 19 - awr_snapshot_time_offset             both     no       *       yes   0
 20 - background_core_dump                 spfile   no       *       yes   partial
 21 - background_dump_dest                 both     no       *       yes   /oracle/V14/saptrace/diag/rdbms/v14/V14/trace
 22 - backup_tape_io_slaves                defer    no       *       yes   FALSE
 23 - bitmap_merge_area_size               spfile   no       *       yes   1048576
 24 - blank_trimming                       spfile   no       *       yes   FALSE
 25 - buffer_pool_keep                     spfile   no       *       yes   <null>
 26 - buffer_pool_recycle                  spfile   no       *       yes   <null>
 27 - cell_offload_compaction              both     no       *       yes   ADAPTIVE
 28 - cell_offload_decryption              both     no       *       yes   TRUE
 29 - cell_offload_parameters              both     no       *       yes   <null>
 30 - cell_offload_plan_display            both     no       *       yes   AUTO
 31 - cell_offload_processing              both     no       *       yes   TRUE
 32 - circuits                             both     no       *       yes   <null>
 33 - client_result_cache_lag              spfile   no       *       yes   3000
 34 - client_result_cache_size             spfile   no       *       yes   0
 35 - clonedb                              spfile   no       *       yes   FALSE
```

Figure 8.87 Overview of Database Parameters

6. Check the parameters displayed, and select the CONT option to get an overview of your Oracle database configuration.

You can also use BRSPACE to change your Oracle database configuration. If, for example, you want to change the size of the shared pool, follow these steps:

1. Log on as `ora<dbname>` (e.g., `su - orav14`).
2. Start the program BRTOOLS (e.g., `brtools -c`).
3. Select the INSTANCE MANAGEMENT option.
4. Select the ALTER DATABASE PARAMETERS option by entering the value "4" and pressing the Enter key. You get an overview of the parameters used to start BRSPACE.
5. Check the parameters displayed, and select the CONT option.
6. Select the CHANGE PARAMETER VALUE option by entering the value "1" and pressing the Enter key (see Figure 8.88). You get an overview of all parameters.

```
BR0280I BRSPACE time stamp: 2014-07-22 20:02:02
BR0656I Choice menu 210 - please make a selection
-------------------------------------------------------------------------------
Alter database parameter main menu

 1 = Change parameter value
 2 - Reset parameter value
 3 - Create init.ora from spfile
 4 - Create init.mem from memory
 5 - Show database parameters
 6 - Show init.ora profile
 7 * Exit program
 8 - Reset program status

Standard keys: c - cont, b - back, s - stop, r - refr, h - help
-------------------------------------------------------------------------------
BR0662I Enter your choice:
1
```

Figure 8.88 Changing the Database Parameters

7. Select the `shared_pool_size` parameter by entering the value "322" and pressing the Enter key (see Figure 8.89). Among other things, you get information about the parameter to be changed, the current value, and the value in the *SPFILE* configuration file. The command to be executed is also displayed.

```
320 - shared_memory_address              spfile  no    *   yes  0
321 - shared_pool_reserved_size          spfile  yes   *   no   79017541
322 - shared_pool_size                   both    yes   *   no   805306368
323 - shared_server_sessions             both    no    *   yes  <null>
324 - shared_servers                     both    no    *   yes  0
325 - skip_unusable_indexes              both    no    *   yes  TRUE
326 - smtp_out_server                    both    no    *   yes  <null>
327 - sort_area_retained_size            defer   no    *   yes  0
328 - sort_area_size                     defer   no    *   yes  65536
329 - spfile                             both    no    *   yes  /oracle/V14/112_64/dbs/spfileV14.ora
330 - sql92_security                     spfile  no    *   yes  FALSE
331 - sql_trace                          both    no    *   yes  FALSE
332 - sqltune_category                   both    no    *   yes  DEFAULT
333 - standby_archive_dest               both    no    *   yes  ?/dbs/arch
334 - standby_file_management            both    no    *   yes  MANUAL
335 - star_transformation_enabled        both    yes   *   no   true
336 - statistics_level                   both    no    *   yes  TYPICAL
337 - streams_pool_size                  both    no    *   yes  0
338 - tape_asynch_io                     spfile  no    *   yes  TRUE
339 - thread                             both    no    *   yes  0
340 - timed_os_statistics                both    no    *   yes  0
341 - timed_statistics                   both    no    *   yes  TRUE
342 - trace_enabled                      both    no    *   yes  TRUE
343 - tracefile_identifier               spfile  no    *   yes  <null>
344 - transactions                       spfile  no    *   yes  272
345 - transactions_per_rollback_segment  spfile  no    *   yes  5
346 - undo_management                    spfile  no    *   yes  AUTO
347 - undo_retention                     both    yes   *   no   43200
348 - undo_tablespace                    both    yes   *   no   PSAPUNDO
349 - use_indirect_data_buffers          spfile  no    *   yes  FALSE
350 - use_large_pages                    spfile  no    *   yes  TRUE
351 - user_dump_dest                     both    no    *   yes  /oracle/V14/saptrace/diag/rdbms/v14/V14/trace
352 - utl_file_dir                       spfile  no    *   yes  <null>
353 - workarea_size_policy               both    no    *   yes  AUTO
354 - xml_db_events                      both    no    *   yes  enable

Standard keys: c - cont, b - back, s - stop, r - refr, h - help
-------------------------------------------------------------------------------
BR0662I Enter your selection:
322
```

Figure 8.89 Selecting Parameters for the Size of the Shared Pool

8. Select the New parameter value option by entering the value "5" and pressing the [Enter] key (see Figure 8.90).

```
BR0280I BRSPACE time stamp: 2014-07-22 20:06:16
BR0657I Input menu 212 - please enter/check input values
-------------------------------------------------------------------------------
Options for alter of database parameter 'shared_pool_size'

 1 * Parameter description (desc) ..... [size in bytes of shared pool]
 2 * Parameter type (type) ............ [big integer]
 3 * Current parameter value (parval) . [805306368]
 4 * Value in spfile (spfval) ......... [<same>]
 5 ? New parameter value (value) ...... []
 6 - Scope for new value (scope) ...... [both]
 7 # Database instance (instance) ..... []
 8 ~ Comment on update (comment) ...... []
 9 - SQL command (command) ............ [alter system set shared_pool_size =  scope = both]

Standard keys: c - cont, b - back, s - stop, r - refr, h - help
-------------------------------------------------------------------------------
BR0662I Enter your choice:
5
```

Figure 8.90 Changing the Parameter Value

9. Enter the new value for the parameter (in bytes), and press the `Enter` key.
10. Check the parameters displayed, and select the CONT option by entering the value "c" and pressing the `Enter` key (see Figure 8.91). The size of the shared pool is changed. The files *init<DBNAME>.ora* and *spfile<DBNAME>.ora* are also updated.

```
BR0280I BRSPACE time stamp: 2014-07-22 20:09:31
BR0657I Input menu 212 - please enter/check input values
-------------------------------------------------------------------------------
Options for alter of database parameter 'shared_pool_size'

 1 * Parameter description (desc) ..... [size in bytes of shared pool]
 2 * Parameter type (type) ............ [big integer]
 3 * Current parameter value (parval) . [805306368]
 4 * Value in spfile (spfval) ......... [<same>]
 5 - New parameter value (value) ...... [1073741824]
 6 - Scope for new value (scope) ...... [both]
 7 # Database instance (instance) ..... []
 8 ~ Comment on update (comment) ...... []
 9 - SQL command (command) ............ [alter system set shared_pool_size = 1073741824 scope = both]

Standard keys: c - cont, b - back, s - stop, r - refr, h - help
-------------------------------------------------------------------------------
BR0662I Enter your choice:
c
```

Figure 8.91 Entering a New Parameter Value and Continuing the Operation

[+] **Dynamic and Static Parameters**

For Oracle databases, a distinction is made between *dynamic* and *static* parameters. Any changes made to dynamic parameters are implemented immediately, whereas changes to static parameters only take effect after you restart the Oracle database.

The documentation on the Oracle database will help you determine which parameters are dynamic and which are static.

Managing Tablespaces and Associated Data Files

You can also use the `BRSPACE` program to manage the storage space on your Oracle database. For example, you can display the current size and space occupied by the tablespaces, extend the tablespaces by creating new data files, and change the properties of the individual data files.

If you want to view the current size and space occupied by the tablespaces in your Oracle database, follow these steps:

1. Log on as `ora<dbname>` (e.g., `su - orav14`).

2. Start BRTOOLS (e.g., `brtools -c`).
3. Select the SPACE MANAGEMENT option by entering the value "2" and pressing the [Enter] key.
4. Select the EXTEND TABLESPACE option by entering the value "1" and pressing the [Enter] key (see Figure 8.92). You get an overview of the parameters used to start BRSPACE.

```
BR0280I BRTOOLS time stamp: 2014-07-23 17:30:00
BR0656I Choice menu 5 - please make a selection
-------------------------------------------------------------------------------
Database space management

 1 = Extend tablespace
 2 - Create tablespace
 3 - Drop tablespace
 4 - Alter tablespace
 5 - Alter data file
 6 - Move data file
 7 - Additional space functions
 8 - Reset program status

Standard keys: c - cont, b - back, s - stop, r - refr, h - help
-------------------------------------------------------------------------------
BR0662I Enter your choice:
1
```

Figure 8.92 Tablespace Management Using the BR*Tools

5. Check the parameters displayed, and select the CONT option by entering the value "c" and pressing the [Enter] key.
6. Select the SHOW TABLESPACES option by entering the value "2" and pressing the [Enter] key (see Figure 8.93).

```
BR0280I BRSPACE time stamp: 2014-07-23 17:30:33
BR0656I Choice menu 301 - please make a selection
-------------------------------------------------------------------------------
Tablespace extension main menu

 1 = Extend tablespace
 2 - Show tablespaces
 3 - Show data files
 4 - Show disk volumes
 5 * Exit program
 6 - Reset program status

Standard keys: c - cont, b - back, s - stop, r - refr, h - help
-------------------------------------------------------------------------------
BR0662I Enter your choice:
2
```

Figure 8.93 Displaying the Tablespaces

You get an overview of all tablespaces in your Oracle database (see Figure 8.94).

```
BR0280I BRSPACE time stamp: 2014-07-23 17:39:05
BR0658I List menu 302 - please select one entry
-------------------------------------------------------------------------------
List of tablespaces for extension

Pos.  Tablespace        Files/AuExt.    Total[KB]    Used[%]     Free[KB]  MaxSize[KB]

  1 - PSAPSAUX              1/1            204800       0.06       204672     10240000
  2 - PSAPSR3               5/5          27156480      75.99      6519616     51200000
  3 - PSAPSR3740X           2/1          33792000      47.31     17804672     46080000
  4 - PSAPSR3DB             3/3          17838080      95.18       859200     30720000
  5 - PSAPSR3USR            1/1             20480       2.19        20032     10240000
  6 - PSAPTEMP              1/1           1904640       0.00      1904640     10240000
  7 - PSAPUNDO              1/1           7823360       0.00      7823296     10240000
  8 - SYSAUX                1/1            552960      82.45        97024     10240000
  9 - SYSTEM                1/1            747520      98.24        13120     10240000
```

Figure 8.94 Overview of Tablespaces

If you are certain that there is no longer sufficient space in a tablespace, you can use BRSPACE to extend this tablespace by creating new data files. To do this, follow these steps:

1. Log on as ora<dbname> (e.g., su - oravl4).
2. Start BRTOOLS (e.g., brtools -c).
3. Select the SPACE MANAGEMENT option.
4. Select the EXTEND TABLESPACE option to get an overview of the parameters used to start BRSPACE.
5. Check the parameters displayed, and select the CONT option.
6. Select the EXTEND TABLESPACE option again by entering the value "1" and pressing the [Enter] key. You get an overview of all tablespaces in your Oracle database.
7. Select the tablespace to be extended by entering the relevant number and pressing the [Enter] key. Among other things, you get information about the last data file created as well as information about the values for the new data file. The command to be executed is also displayed (see Figure 8.95).
8. If you want to change the size of the new data file, select the SIZE OF THE NEW FILE IN MB (SIZE) option by entering the value "5" and pressing the [Enter] key. You're prompted to specify the new size.

```
BR0280I BRSPACE time stamp: 2014-07-23 17:41:28
BR0657I Input menu 303 - please enter/check input values
-------------------------------------------------------------------------------
Options for extension of tablespace PSAPSR3DB (1. file)

 1 * Last added file name (lastfile) ....... [/oracle/V14/sapdata4/sr3db_3/sr3db.data3]
 2 * Last added file size in MB (lastsize) . [4540]
 3 - New file to be added (file) ........... [/oracle/V14/sapdata4/sr3db_4/sr3db.data4]
 4 ~ Raw disk / link target (rawlink) ...... []
 5 - Size of the new file in MB (size) ..... [4540]
 6 - File autoextend mode (autoextend) ..... [yes]
 7 - Maximum file size in MB (maxsize) ..... [10000]
 8 - File increment size in MB (incrsize) .. [20]
 9 - SQL command (command) ................. [alter tablespace PSAPSR3DB add datafile '/oracle/V14/
sapdata4/sr3db_4/sr3db.data4' size 4540M autoextend on next 20M maxsize 10000M]

Standard keys: c - cont, b - back, s - stop, r - refr, h - help
-------------------------------------------------------------------------------
BR0662I Enter your choice:
```

Figure 8.95 Options for Extending a Tablespace

9. If you're satisfied with the values displayed, select the CONT standard key. The BRSPACE program asks you whether you want to create additional data files (see Figure 8.96).

```
BR1091I Next data file can be specified now

BR0280I BRSPACE time stamp: 2014-07-23 17:44:20
BR0675I This is a optional action - do you want to execute it now?
BR0676I Enter 'y[es]' to execute the action, 'n[o]/c[ont]' to skip it, 's[top]' to abort:
```

Figure 8.96 Prompt for Creating Additional Data Files

10. If you want to do this, select the YES standard key by entering the value "y" and pressing the Enter key.
11. If you've defined enough data files, select the NO or CONT option by entering the value "n" or "c" and pressing the Enter key. The data files are now created for the tablespace that you've selected.

In addition to the option of creating data files of a fixed size, Oracle also offers you the option of automatic extension. This type of storage administration is known as *autoextend*. If you want to use autoextend, set the FILE AUTOEXTEND MODE (AUTOEXTEND) option to the value YES in the menu for creating new data files. You can also use the MAXIMUM FILE SIZE IN MB (MAXSIZE) and FILE INCREMENT SIZE IN MB (INCRSIZE) values to determine the maximum permissible size for the data file or the number of megabytes by which the data file is to be extended, if required.

[+] **Autoextend**

If you use autoextend, it makes sense to restrict the maximum size of the data files. Otherwise, the data files can be extended without restriction, and the file system can be filled completely. This may lead to some nasty surprises.

You can also use BRSPACE to manage and edit individual data files. If, for example, you want to deactivate autoextend for a data file, follow these steps:

1. Log on as ora<dbname> (e.g., `su - orav14`).
2. Start BRTOOLS (e.g., `brtools -c`).
3. Select the SPACE MANAGEMENT option.
4. Select the ALTER DATA FILE option (refer to Figure 8.92) by entering the value "5" and pressing the Enter key. You get an overview of the parameters used to start BRSPACE.
5. Check the parameters displayed, and select the CONT option. A list of available options is displayed (see Figure 8.97).

```
BR0280I BRSPACE time stamp: 2014-07-23 17:52:07
BR0656I Choice menu 314 - please make a selection
-------------------------------------------------------------------------------
Alter data file main menu

 1 - Set data file online
 2 - Set data file offline
 3 - Turn on and maintain autoextend
 4 - Turn off autoextend
 5 - Resize data file
 6 - Rename data file
 7 - Drop empty data file
 8 - Show data files
 9 - Show tablespaces
10 - Show disk volumes
11 * Exit program
12 - Reset program status

Standard keys: c - cont, b - back, s - stop, r - refr, h - help
-------------------------------------------------------------------------------
BR0662I Enter your choice:
```

Figure 8.97 Option Menu for Changing a Data File

6. Select the TURN OFF AUTOEXTEND option by entering the value "4" and pressing the Enter key. You get an overview of all data files currently in autoextend (see Figure 8.98).

```
List of data files for alter

 Pos.  Tablespace      Status  Type      Size[KB] AuExt. File

   1 - PSAPSAUX        ONLINE  FILE        204800   YES   /oracle/V14/sapdata1/saux_1/saux.data1
   2 - PSAPSR3         ONLINE  FILE       5447680   YES   /oracle/V14/sapdata3/sr3_1/sr3.data1
   3 - PSAPSR3         ONLINE  FILE       5386240   YES   /oracle/V14/sapdata3/sr3_2/sr3.data2
   4 - PSAPSR3         ONLINE  FILE       5488640   YES   /oracle/V14/sapdata3/sr3_3/sr3.data3
   5 - PSAPSR3         ONLINE  FILE       5406720   YES   /oracle/V14/sapdata3/sr3_4/sr3.data4
   6 - PSAPSR3         ONLINE  FILE       5427200   YES   /oracle/V14/sapdata3/sr3_5/sr3.data5
   7 - PSAPSR3740X     ONLINE  FILE       3072000   YES   /oracle/V14/sapdata2/sr3740x_2/sr3740x.data2
   8 - PSAPSR3DB       ONLINE  FILE       6594560   YES   /oracle/V14/sapdata4/sr3db_1/sr3db.data1
   9 - PSAPSR3DB       ONLINE  FILE       6594560   YES   /oracle/V14/sapdata4/sr3db_2/sr3db.data2
  10 - PSAPSR3DB       ONLINE  FILE       4648960   YES   /oracle/V14/sapdata4/sr3db_3/sr3db.data3
  11 - PSAPSR3USR      ONLINE  FILE         20480   YES   /oracle/V14/sapdata4/sr3usr_1/sr3usr.data1
  12 - PSAPTEMP        ONLINE  FILE       1904640   YES   /oracle/V14/sapdata1/temp_1/temp.data1
  13 - PSAPUNDO        ONLINE  FILE        782336 0   YES   /oracle/V14/sapdata1/undo_1/undo.data1
  14 - SYSAUX          ONLINE  FILE        552960   YES   /oracle/V14/sapdata1/sysaux_1/sysaux.data1
  15 - SYSTEM          SYSTEM  FILE        747520   YES   /oracle/V14/sapdata1/system_1/system.data1

Standard keys: c - cont, b - back, s - stop, r - refr, h - help
--------------------------------------------------------------------------------
BR0662I Enter your selection:
```

Figure 8.98 Overview of All Data Files in Autoextend Mode

7. Select a data file by entering the number displayed and pressing the Enter key. Among other things, you get information about the data file and the target status. The command to be executed is also displayed (see Figure 8.99).

```
BR0280I BRSPACE time stamp: 2014-07-23 17:54:54
BR0657I Input menu 316 - please enter/check input values
--------------------------------------------------------------------------------
Options for alter of data file /oracle/V14/sapdata2/sr3740x_2/sr3740x.data2

 1 * Current data file status (status) ....... [AUTOEXTEND]
 2 * Current data file size in MB (currsize) . [3000]
 3 * Alter data file action (action) ......... [fixsize]
 4 # Maximum file size in MB (maxsize) ....... [15000]
 5 # File increment size in MB (incrsize) .... [200]
 6 # New data file size in MB (size) ......... []
 7 # New data file name (name) ............... []
 8 # Force data file alter (force) ........... [no]
 9 - SQL command (command) ................... [alter database datafile '/oracle/V14/sapdata2/sr374
0x_2/sr3740x.data2' autoextend off]

Standard keys: c - cont, b - back, s - stop, r - refr, h - help
--------------------------------------------------------------------------------
BR0662I Enter your choice:
```

Figure 8.99 Options for Changing the Data File

8. Check the parameters displayed, and select the CONT option.

The autoextend function is deactivated for the data file you've selected.

8.6.6 Backing Up the Database

To avoid a loss of data in the event of damage, it's important to back up your Oracle database and redo log files on a regular basis. The Oracle database supports two types of backup:

- Offline backup
- Online backup

[+]

Take Care When Backing Up the Database

Because this book can only provide you with basic information, please seek professional help when backing up your database, if necessary.

For an *offline backup*, you must stop both the SAP system and the database. Because no activities take place on the database, an offline backup is, by its very nature, consistent. However, the performance of the SAP system may deteriorate temporarily after an offline backup because the database and SAP system buffers have to be reconfigured. To perform an offline backup using the BRBACKUP program, follow these steps:

1. Stop the SAP system.
2. Log on as ora<dbname> (e.g., su - orav14).
3. Start BRTOOLS (e.g., brtools -c).
4. Select the BACKUP AND DATABASE COPY option by entering the value "4" and pressing the [Enter] key (see Figure 8.100).

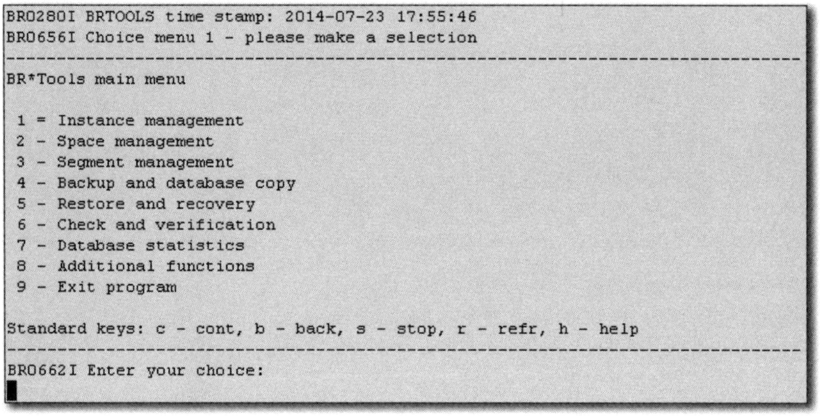

```
BR0280I BRTOOLS time stamp: 2014-07-23 17:55:46
BR0656I Choice menu 1 - please make a selection
-------------------------------------------------------------------------------
BR*Tools main menu

 1 = Instance management
 2 - Space management
 3 - Segment management
 4 - Backup and database copy
 5 - Restore and recovery
 6 - Check and verification
 7 - Database statistics
 8 - Additional functions
 9 - Exit program

Standard keys: c - cont, b - back, s - stop, r - refr, h - help
-------------------------------------------------------------------------------
BR0662I Enter your choice:
```

Figure 8.100 Selecting the Backup Option

5. Select the DATABASE BACKUP option by entering the value "1" and pressing the [Enter] key. You get an overview of the parameters for performing the backup (see Figure 8.101).

```
BR0280I BRTOOLS time stamp: 2014-07-23 18:00:47
BR0657I Input menu 15 - please enter/check input values
-------------------------------------------------------------------------------
BRBACKUP main options for backup and database copy

 1 - BRBACKUP profile (profile) ....... [initV14.sap]
 2 - Backup device type (device) ...... [disk]
 3 # Tape volumes for backup (volume) . []
 4 # BACKINT/Mount profile (parfile) .. []
 5 - Database user/password (user) .... [/]
 6 - Backup type (type) ............... [offline_force]
 7 # Disk backup for backup (backup) .. [no]
 8 # Delete disk backup (delete) ...... [no]
 9 ~ Files for backup (mode) .......... [all]

Standard keys: c - cont, b - back, s - stop, r - refr, h - help
-------------------------------------------------------------------------------
BR0662I Enter your choice:
```

Figure 8.101 Parameters for Performing the Offline Backup

6. For example, select the OFFLINE_FORCE value for the BACKUP TYPE (TYPE) option. Also check whether the BACKUP DEVICE TYPE (DEVICE) option meets your requirements, for example, whether the correct backup target is specified. Then select the CONT standard key. You get an overview of additional parameters. The command to be executed is also displayed.

7. Check the parameters displayed, and select the CONT option (see Figure 8.102). An offline backup of the database is created.

```
BR0280I BRTOOLS time stamp: 2014-07-23 18:04:17
BR0657I Input menu 16 - please enter/check input values
-------------------------------------------------------------------------------
Additional BRBACKUP options for backup and database copy

 1 - Confirmation mode (confirm) ....... [yes]
 2 - Query mode (query) ................ [no]
 3 - Compression mode (compress) ....... [yes]
 4 - Verification mode (verify) ........ [no]
 5 - Fill-up previous backups (fillup) . [no]
 6 - Parallel execution (execute) ...... [0]
 7 - Additional output (output) ........ [no]
 8 - Message language (language) ....... [E]
 9 - BRBACKUP command line (command) ... [-p initV14.sap -d disk -t offline_force -m all -k yes -e 0 -l E]

Standard keys: c - cont, b - back, s - stop, r - refr, h - help
-------------------------------------------------------------------------------
BR0662I Enter your choice:
```

Figure 8.102 Confirming the Backup Parameters

[+]

Backup Information

The exact definition of the individual parameters for the backup depends on numerous factors and must be adjusted to the relevant environment. You can also make additional settings in the *init<DBNAME>.sap* file (e.g., *initV14.sap*). Among other things, you can use the parameter `backup_root_dir` to determine where the backup is to be written for backups to the hard disk.

For an *online backup*, you can continue to run the database and SAP system. The advantage of this is that, among other things, the database and SAP system buffers are retained. However, you must also back up the database redo logs so that this backup is consistent. To perform a consistent online backup using `BRBACKUP`, follow these steps:

1. Log on as `ora<dbname>` (e.g., `su - orav14`).
2. Start `BRTOOLS` (e.g., `brtools -c`).
3. Select the BACKUP AND DATABASE COPY option.
4. Select the DATABASE BACKUP option by entering the value "1" and pressing the [Enter] key. You get an overview of the parameters for performing the backup.
5. Select the value ONLINE_CONS for the BACKUP TYPE (TYPE) option. Check whether the BACKUP DEVICE TYPE (DEVICE) option meets your requirements. Then select the CONT standard key. You get an overview of additional parameters. The command to be executed is also displayed.
6. Check the parameters displayed, and select the CONT option.

An online backup of the database is created.

[+]

Incremental and Differential Backup

In addition to a complete backup whereby the entire database is always backed up, the Oracle database also supports incremental and differential backups (see Chapter 6).

In the period between two database backups, you must make sure to back up the archived redo log files on a regular basis. You can do this using the `BRARCHIVE` program:

1. Log on as `ora<dbname>` (e.g., `su - orav14`).
2. Start `BRTOOLS` (e.g., `brtools -c`).

3. Select the BACKUP AND DATABASE COPY option.
4. Select the ARCHIVELOG BACKUP option by entering the value "2" and pressing the Enter key. You get an overview of the parameters for performing the backup (see Figure 8.103).

```
BR0280I BRTOOLS time stamp: 2014-07-23 18:08:14
BR0657I Input menu 17 - please enter/check input values
-------------------------------------------------------------------------------
BRARCHIVE main options for archivelog backup and verification

 1 - BRARCHIVE profile (profile) ...... [initV14.sap]
 2 - BRARCHIVE function (function) .... [save]
 3 - Backup device type (device) ...... [disk]
 4 # Tape volumes for backup (volume) . []
 5 # BACKINT/Mount profile (parfile) .. []
 6 - Database user/password (user) .... [/]
 7 ~ Maximum number of files (number) . []
 8 # Back up disk backup (archive) .... [no]

Standard keys: c - cont, b - back, s - stop, r - refr, h - help
-------------------------------------------------------------------------------
BR0662I Enter your choice:
```

Figure 8.103 Overview of Parameters for Performing the Backup

5. Check whether the BACKUP DEVICE TYPE (DEVICE) option meets your requirements (DISK or TAPE). Then select the CONT standard key. You get an overview of additional parameters (see Figure 8.104). The command to be executed is also displayed. Check the parameters displayed, and select the CONT option again.

```
BR0280I BRTOOLS time stamp: 2014-07-23 18:09:29
BR0657I Input menu 18 - please enter/check input values
-------------------------------------------------------------------------------
Additional BRARCHIVE options for archivelog backup

 1 - Confirmation mode (confirm) ....... [yes]
 2 - Query mode (query) ................ [no]
 3 - Compression mode (compress) ....... [yes]
 4 - Verification mode (verify) ........ [no]
 5 - Fill mode, group size (fill) ...... [no]
 6 - Modify mode, delay apply (modify) . [no]
 7 - Additional output (output) ........ [no]
 8 - Message language (language) ....... [E]
 9 - BRARCHIVE command line (command) .. [-p initV14.sap -save -d disk -k yes -l E]

Standard keys: c - cont, b - back, s - stop, r - refr, h - help
-------------------------------------------------------------------------------
BR0662I Enter your choice:
```

Figure 8.104 Confirming the Backup Parameters

A backup of the archived redo log files is now created.

[+]

Double Backup

To ensure that your backup of the archived redo log files is as secure as possible, you should back up these files twice. To do this, select the SAVE value for the BRARCHIVE FUNCTION (FUNCTION) option during the first backup, and select the SECOND_COPY_DELETE value during the second backup.

8.6.7 Restoring the Database

In the event of damage, you can use the `BRRECOVER` and `BRRESTORE` programs to restore your Oracle database by means of database backups and redo log files. The BR*Tools provide several restore options:

- Full database recovery
- Point-in-time recovery
- Database reset

Before you try to restore the database, you should err on the side of caution and create a backup of the damaged database. During a *full database recovery*, damaged or missing data files are replaced with the data files from the backup (*restore*). The redo log files are then used to set each data file to the status it had just before the damage occurred. To perform a full database recovery, follow these steps:

1. Log on as `ora<dbname>` (e.g., `su - orav14`).
2. Start `BRTOOLS` (e.g., `brtools -c`).
3. Select the RESTORE AND RECOVERY option by entering the value "5" and pressing the Enter key.
4. Select the COMPLETE DATABASE RECOVERY option by entering the value "1" and pressing the Enter key (see Figure 8.105). You get an overview of the parameters used to start `BRRECOVER` (see Figure 8.106).
5. Check the parameters displayed, and select the CONT option.
6. Now follow the step-by-step instructions provided for the `BR-RECOVER` program. Starting at the top, go through each of the options displayed (see Figure 8.107). After you've successfully processed the OPEN DATABASE AND POST-PROCESSING option, your database is operational again.

```
BR0280I BRTOOLS time stamp: 2014-07-23 18:15:37
BR0656I Choice menu 11 - please make a selection
-------------------------------------------------------------------------------
Restore and recovery

 1 = Complete database recovery
 2 - Database point-in-time recovery
 3 - Tablespace point-in-time recovery
 4 - Whole database reset
 5 - Restore of individual backup files
 6 - Restore and application of archivelog files
 7 - Disaster recovery
 8 - Manage flashback database
 9 - Reset program status

Standard keys: c - cont, b - back, s - stop, r - refr, h - help
-------------------------------------------------------------------------------
BR0662I Enter your choice:
```

Figure 8.105 Starting the Database Recovery

```
BR0280I BRTOOLS time stamp: 2014-07-23 18:16:17
BR0657I Input menu 34 - please enter/check input values
-------------------------------------------------------------------------------
BRRECOVER options for restore and recovery

 1 * Recovery type (type) ............ [complete]
 2 - BRRECOVER profile (profile) ...... [initV14.sap]
 3 ~ BACKINT/Mount profile (parfile) .. []
 4 - Database user/password (user) .... [/]
 5 - Recovery interval (interval) ..... [30]
 6 - Confirmation mode (confirm) ...... [yes]
 7 - Scrolling line count (scroll) .... [20]
 8 - Message language (language) ...... [E]
 9 - BRRECOVER command line (command) . [-p initV14.sap -t complete -i 30 -s 20 -l E]

Standard keys: c - cont, b - back, s - stop, r - refr, h - help
-------------------------------------------------------------------------------
BR0662I Enter your choice:
```

Figure 8.106 Checking the Recovery Parameters

```
BR0280I BRRECOVER time stamp: 2014-07-23 18:17:09
BR0655I Control menu 101 - please decide how to proceed
-------------------------------------------------------------------------------
Complete database recovery main menu

 1 = Check the status of database files
 2 * Select database backup
 3 * Restore split/standby control files
 4 * Restore data files
 5 * Restore split incremental control files
 6 * Restore and apply incremental backup
 7 * Restore and apply archivelog files
 8 * Open database and post-processing
 9 * Exit program
10 - Reset program status

Standard keys: c - cont, b - back, s - stop, r - refr, h - help
-------------------------------------------------------------------------------
BR0662I Enter your choice:
```

Figure 8.107 List of Steps to Be Performed for the Recovery

For a *point-in-time recovery*, you can determine the point in time that is to be used as the restore time. For this purpose, all of the data files are replaced with the data files from a backup. The redo log files are then used to set each data file to the status it had at the defined point in time. To perform a point-in-time recovery, follow these steps:

1. Log on as ora<dbname> (e.g., su - orav14).
2. Start BRTOOLS (e.g., brtools -c).
3. Select the RESTORE AND RECOVERY option by entering the value "5" and pressing the [Enter] key.
4. Select the DATABASE POINT-IN-TIME RECOVERY option by entering the value "2" and pressing the [Enter] key. You get an overview of the parameters used to start BRRECOVER.
5. Check the parameters displayed, and select the CONT option.
6. Now follow the step-by-step instructions provided for BR-RECOVER. Starting at the top, go through each of the options displayed (see Figure 8.108). After you've successfully processed the OPEN DATABASE AND POST-PROCESSING option, your database is operational again.

```
BR0280I BRRECOVER time stamp: 2014-07-23 18:19:03
BR0655I Control menu 103 - please decide how to proceed
--------------------------------------------------------------------------------
Database point-in-time recovery main menu

 1 = Set point-in-time for recovery
 2 * Select database backup or flashback
 3 * Check the status of database files
 4 * Restore control files
 5 * Restore data files
 6 * Restore split incremental control files
 7 * Restore and apply incremental backup
 8 * Restore and apply archivelog files
 9 * Restore archivelog files and flashback
10 * Open database and post-processing
11 * Exit program
12 - Reset program status

Standard keys: c - cont, b - back, s - stop, r - refr, h - help
--------------------------------------------------------------------------------
BR0662I Enter your choice:
```

Figure 8.108 List of Steps for a Point-in-Time Recovery

When resetting the database (*restore*), the database is set to the status associated with the selected backup. Here, all of the data files are replaced with the data files from a backup, and, for an online backup, the backed-up redo log files are used to reset the database to a consistent status. To reset the database, follow these steps:

1. Log on as `ora<dbname>` (e.g., `su - orav14`).
2. Start `BRTOOLS` (e.g., `brtools -c`).
3. Select the RESTORE AND RECOVERY option.
4. Select the WHOLE DATABASE RESET option by entering the value "4" and pressing the [Enter] key. You get an overview of the parameters used to start `BRRECOVER`.
5. Check the parameters displayed, and select the CONT option.
6. Now follow the step-by-step instructions provided for the `BR-RECOVER` program. Starting at the top, go through each of the options displayed (see Figure 8.109).

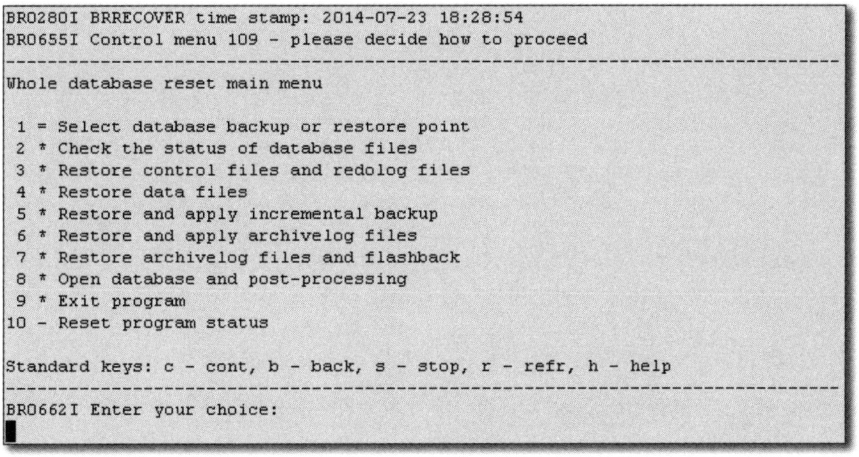

```
BR0280I BRRECOVER time stamp: 2014-07-23 18:28:54
BR0655I Control menu 109 - please decide how to proceed
-------------------------------------------------------------------------------
Whole database reset main menu

 1 = Select database backup or restore point
 2 * Check the status of database files
 3 * Restore control files and redolog files
 4 * Restore data files
 5 * Restore and apply incremental backup
 6 * Restore and apply archivelog files
 7 * Restore archivelog files and flashback
 8 * Open database and post-processing
 9 * Exit program
10 - Reset program status

Standard keys: c - cont, b - back, s - stop, r - refr, h - help
-------------------------------------------------------------------------------
BR0662I Enter your choice:
```

Figure 8.109 List of Steps to Be Performed for the Database Restore

After you've successfully processed the OPEN DATABASE AND POST-PROCESSING option, your database is operational again.

8.6.8 Checking the Database

You can use the `BRCONNECT` program to check your database. If you perform this check on a regular basis, you can identify problems in advance and respond accordingly.

To check the Oracle database, follow these steps:

1. Log on as `ora<dbname>` (e.g., `su - orav14`).
2. Start `BRTOOLS` (e.g., `brtools -c`).
3. Select the CHECK AND VERIFICATION option by entering the value "6" and pressing the Enter key.
4. Select the DATABASE SYSTEM CHECK option by entering the value "1" and pressing the Enter key (see Figure 8.110).

```
BR0280I BRTOOLS time stamp: 2014-07-23 18:30:20
BR0656I Choice menu 12 - please make a selection
-------------------------------------------------------------------------------
Database check and verification

 1 = Database system check
 2 - Validation of database structure
 3 - Verification of database blocks
 4 - Reset program status

Standard keys: c - cont, b - back, s - stop, r - refr, h - help
-------------------------------------------------------------------------------
BR0662I Enter your choice:
```

Figure 8.110 Starting the Database System Check

5. You get an overview of the parameters for performing a database check. Check the parameters displayed, and select the CONT option (see Figure 8.111).

```
BR0280I BRTOOLS time stamp: 2014-07-23 18:32:50
BR0657I Input menu 36 - please enter/check input values
-------------------------------------------------------------------------------
BRCONNECT main options for database system check

 1 - BRCONNECT profile (profile) .......... [initV14.sap]
 2 - Database user/password (user) ........ [/]
 3 - Use default check settings (default) . [no]
 4 ~ Database owner for check (owner) ..... []
 5 ~ Ignore DBCHECKORA table (ignore) ..... []
 6 ~ Ignore DBSTATC table (igndbs) ........ []
 7 ~ Exclude from check (exclude) ......... []

Standard keys: c - cont, b - back, s - stop, r - refr, h - help
-------------------------------------------------------------------------------
BR0662I Enter your choice:
c
```

Figure 8.111 Parameters for the Database Check

6. You get an overview of additional parameters. The command to be executed is also displayed. Check these parameters, and select the CONT option (see Figure 8.112).

```
BR0280I BRTOOLS time stamp: 2014-07-23 18:33:11
BR0657I Input menu 37 - please enter/check input values
-------------------------------------------------------------------------------
Additional BRCONNECT options for database system check

 1 - Confirmation mode (confirm) ...... [yes]
 2 - Query mode (query) ............... [no]
 3 - Extended output (output) ......... [no]
 4 - Message language (language) ...... [E]
 5 - BRCONNECT command line (command) . [-p initV14.sap -l E -f check]

Standard keys: c - cont, b - back, s - stop, r - refr, h - help
-------------------------------------------------------------------------------
BR0662I Enter your choice:
c
```

Figure 8.112 Checking and Confirming the Parameters

The database is checked. If you want to view the result of the check, follow these steps:

1. Log on as `ora<dbname>` (e.g., `su - orav14`).
2. Start `BRTOOLS` (e.g., `brtools -c`).
3. Select the ADDITIONAL FUNCTIONS option by entering the value "8" and pressing the Enter key.
4. Select the SHOW PROFILES AND LOGS option by entering the value "1" and pressing the Enter key (see Figure 8.113).

```
BR0280I BRTOOLS time stamp: 2014-07-23 18:35:39
BR0656I Choice menu 2 - please make a selection
-------------------------------------------------------------------------------
Additional BR*Tools functions

 1 = Show profiles and logs
 2 - Clean up DBA logs and tables
 3 - Adapt NEXT extents
 4 - Change password of database user
 5 - Create/change synonyms for DBA tables
 6 - Reset program status

Standard keys: c - cont, b - back, s - stop, r - refr, h - help
-------------------------------------------------------------------------------
BR0662I Enter your choice:
1
```

Figure 8.113 Displaying the Result of the Database Check

5. Select the BRCONNECT LOGS option to display the check logs by entering the value "7" and pressing the Enter key (see Figure 8.114).

```
BR0280I BRTOOLS time stamp: 2014-07-23 18:38:09
BR0656I Choice menu 14 - please make a selection
-------------------------------------------------------------------------------
Show profiles and logs

 1 = Oracle profile
 2 - BR*Tools profile
 3 - BRBACKUP logs
 4 - BRARCHIVE logs
 5 - BRRESTORE logs
 6 - BRRECOVER logs
 7 - BRCONNECT logs
 8 - BRSPACE logs

Standard keys: c - cont, b - back, s - stop, r - refr, h - help
-------------------------------------------------------------------------------
BR0662I Enter your choice:
7
```

Figure 8.114 Calling BRCONNECT Logs

6. Select the relevant log by entering the relevant number and pressing the Enter key (see Figure 8.115). You then identify the log you require by the timestamp and the check addition.

```
BR0280I BRTOOLS time stamp: 2014-07-23 18:39:04
BR0658I List menu 52 - please select one entry
-------------------------------------------------------------------------------
Display of BRCONNECT logs

Pos.  Log              Start                  Function   Rc   Object

  1 = ceojbakw.cln   2014-07-23 18:30:10   cleanup     0
  2 - ceojaslf.cln   2014-07-23 17:00:11   cleanup     0
  3 - ceojaklo.cln   2014-07-23 15:30:12   cleanup     0
  4 - ceojaclv.cln   2014-07-23 14:00:11   cleanup     0
  5 - ceoizume.cln   2014-07-23 12:30:12   cleanup     0
  6 - ceoizmmk.cln   2014-07-23 11:00:10   cleanup     0
  7 - ceoizemx.cln   2014-07-23 09:30:15   cleanup     0
  8 - ceoiytvz.cln   2014-07-23 07:30:15   cleanup     0
  9 - ceoiyonn.cln   2014-07-23 06:30:15   cleanup     0
 10 - ceoiylww.chk   2014-07-23 06:00:30   check       1
 11 - ceoiyjfa.cln   2014-07-23 05:30:14   cleanup     0
 12 - ceoiygom.sta   2014-07-23 05:00:32   stats       0   ALL
 13 - ceoiybfg.cln   2014-07-23 04:00:12   cleanup     0
 14 - ceoixtfp.cln   2014-07-23 02:30:13   cleanup     0
 15 - ceoixqoq.cln   2014-07-23 02:00:20   cleanup     0
 16 - ceoixnxm.cln   2014-07-23 01:30:22   cleanup     0
```

Figure 8.115 Selecting a Log

The check log is now displayed (see Figure 8.116).

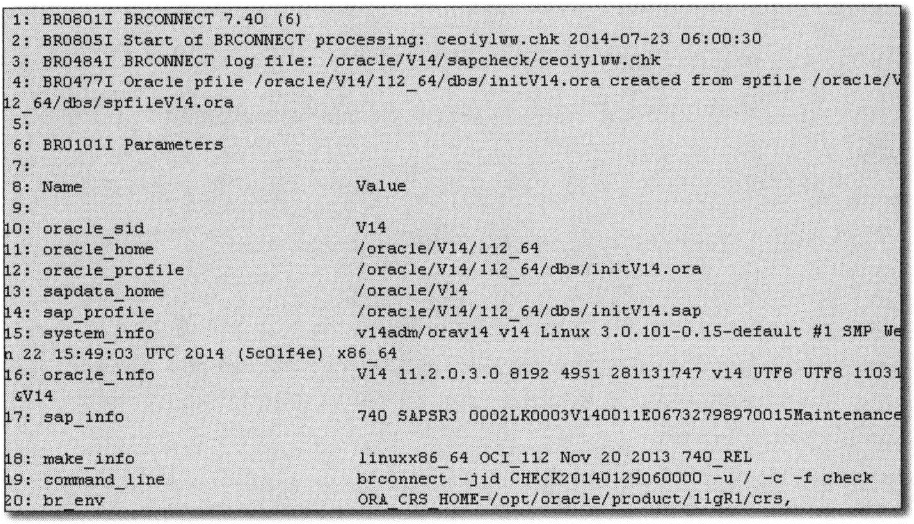

```
BR0801I BRCONNECT 7.40 (6)
BR0805I Start of BRCONNECT processing: ceoiylww.chk 2014-07-23 06:00:30
BR0484I BRCONNECT log file: /oracle/V14/sapcheck/ceoiylww.chk
BR0477I Oracle pfile /oracle/V14/112_64/dbs/initV14.ora created from spfile /oracle/V
12_64/dbs/spfileV14.ora

BR0101I Parameters

Name                              Value

oracle_sid                        V14
oracle_home                       /oracle/V14/112_64
oracle_profile                    /oracle/V14/112_64/dbs/initV14.ora
sapdata_home                      /oracle/V14
sap_profile                       /oracle/V14/112_64/dbs/initV14.sap
system_info                       v14adm/orav14 v14 Linux 3.0.101-0.15-default #1 SMP We
h 22 15:49:03 UTC 2014 (5c01f4e) x86_64
oracle_info                       V14 11.2.0.3.0 8192 4951 281131747 v14 UTF8 UTF8 11031
&V14
sap_info                          740 SAPSR3 0002LK0003V140011E06732798970015Maintenance

make_info                         linuxx86_64 OCI_112 Nov 20 2013 740_REL
command_line                      brconnect -jid CHECK20140129060000 -u / -c -f check
br_env                            ORA_CRS_HOME=/opt/oracle/product/11gR1/crs,
```

Figure 8.116 Log of the Database Check

[+]

Database Check in Transaction DB12

Evaluating logs using the BR*Tools is relatively inconvenient. You should use Transaction DB12 instead, which was described in Section 8.2, to analyze logs in prepared form.

8.7 Database Administration—Microsoft SQL Server

Of all the databases introduced here, Microsoft SQL Server is the easiest system to manage. The SQL Server is nevertheless a complex "enterprise-grade" database system that, first, demands full attention and, second, demands that the administrator acquire the requisite expertise to manage it. If the SQL Server contains enterprise-critical data, administration can't be of a "casual" nature. The SQL Server is no longer in its infancy. This product is now suitable for large environments with high performance requirements.

In particular, this section will discuss how to create a data backup. Even though data backup is by no means the only feature of the SQL Server, it's undoubtedly one of its most important features. The requirements for a database backup can be defined very quickly and are already known from Chapter 6:

- Back up all of the SAP databases together with the log files.
- Back up the `master` and `msdb` system databases.

Performing a backup is easy if you use the resources available to you in SQL Server Management Studio.

8.7.1 SQL Server Management Studio

You use SQL Server Management Studio to manage the Microsoft SQL Server on a daily basis. This is the successor to Enterprise Manager. Even though SQL Server Management Studio is comparably easy to use, you must, thanks to the large number of possible options available, pay particular attention to its many possibilities and procedures.

To use SQL Server Management Studio, follow these steps:

1. Generally, you don't have to start SQL Server Management Studio directly on the server. Instead, it can be installed on the administrator's workstation PC, which means that an interactive logon to the database server isn't required (see Figure 8.117).

Figure 8.117 Starting SQL Server Management Studio

2. After you've started SQL Server Management Studio, you're prompted to specify the server to which you want to establish a connection. There are three configuration options (see Figure 8.118):

   - SERVER TYPE
     In our example, you connect to the database module. In addition to the database module, there are other possible server types such as Analysis Services or Reporting Services.
   - SERVER NAME
     Here, you enter the name of the server to which you want to establish a connection. Most administration tasks also work via the network, which means that, for the usual administration tasks, there's no need to log on directly to the server.

     Microsoft SQL Server knows several database instances on a database server. If you want to address a particular instance (not the standard instance), insert the instance name as the server name (e.g., *servername\sapdb1*).
   - AUTHENTICATION
     If you select WINDOWS AUTHENTICATION, you'll be connected using your current logon information (the identity you used to log on to the Windows PC or server). Alternatively, you can log on using SQL Server authentication. SQL Server-specific accounts are used here (i.e., no active directory logon information). The authentication type used in your environment depends on the individual system configuration. Microsoft recommends using Windows authentication.

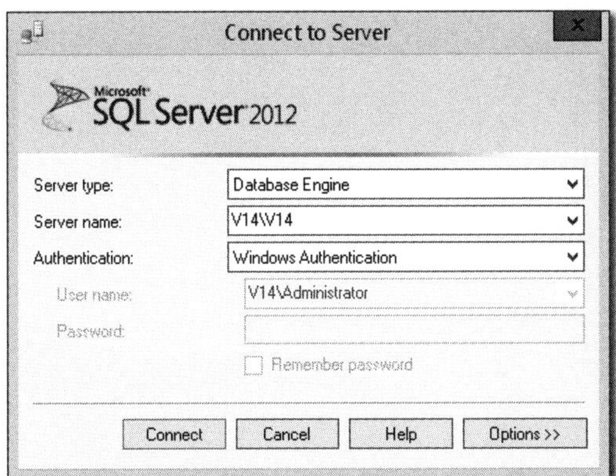

Figure 8.118 Establishing a Connection to the Database

3. Choose CONNECT to start SQL Server Management Studio.

[+]

Connecting to Several SQL Servers

With SQL Server Management Studio, you can connect to multiple SQL servers simultaneously.

After you've started SQL Server Management Studio, you also get the tree view from the "old" SQL Enterprise Manager (see Figure 8.119).

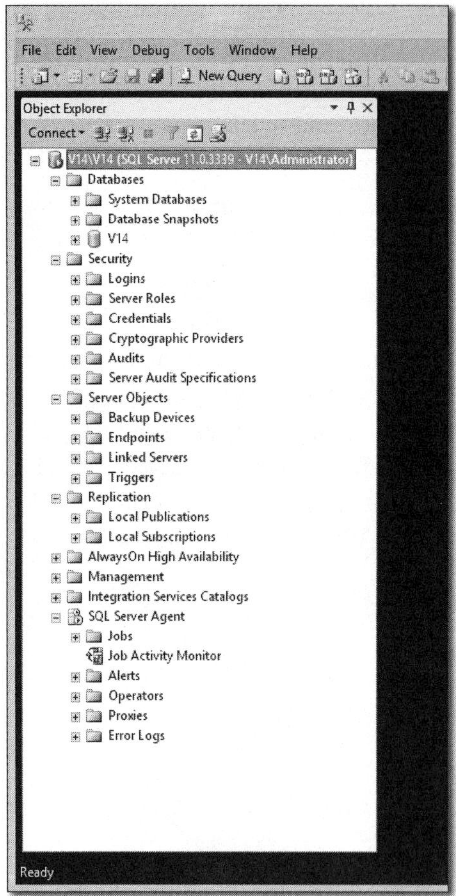

Figure 8.119 Tree Structure of the Database

For example, you see that, under SECURITY, the databases on the server can manage the logons (and much more). Here, you also see advanced configuration options such as replication, backup, or performance analysis.

8.7.2 Starting and Stopping the Database

To start the Microsoft SQL Server, follow these steps (see Figure 8.120):

1. Right-click on to call the context menu for the database instance displayed.
2. Select the START menu option.
3. Confirm the mandatory question in the dialog box (ARE YOU SURE ...). The database instance should run a short time later.

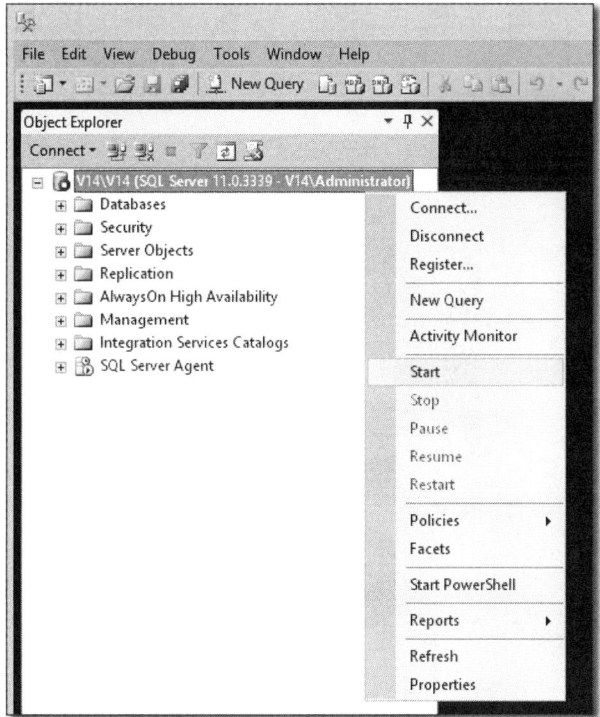

Figure 8.120 Starting the Database

You stop a database instance in a similar way. Here, you must only select the STOP menu option.

In our example, you see that the standard database instance of the server V14 (you recognize the standard instance by the fact that no other instance name is appended to it) is stopped, which is indicated by the red stop icon that precedes the database name. If the database/database instance is stopped, it can't provide any data for clients, nor can it perform any administration tasks.

[+]

Starting and Stopping the Database

Essentially, the SQL Server service (i.e., the Windows service) is started or stopped when you start or stop a database instance. However, you shouldn't simply start or stop the service. Instead, you should always follow the SQL Server-specific procedure.

SQL Server Agent

After you've started the database instance, you should take a quick look at the status of the SQL Server Agent. The fact that the actual database is running doesn't necessarily mean that the agent is running. Because the agent is required for all automation tasks, you should check that it's also running (see Figure 8.121).

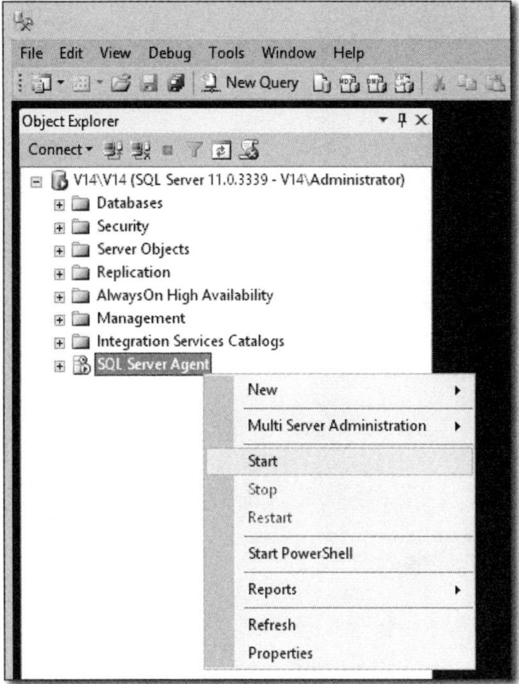

Figure 8.121 Starting the SQL Server Agent

Each database instance has its own SQL Server Agent, so greater care is required here. If the SQL Server Agent isn't running, the maintenance plans, data backup processes, or similar, which are to be called in a time-controlled manner, aren't executed.

The SQL Server Agent is implemented as a separate Windows service. If it isn't started automatically, you can configure this in the services administration area of the operating system. This service is called SQL SERVER AGENT, followed by the name of the database instance in parentheses (see Figure 8.122).

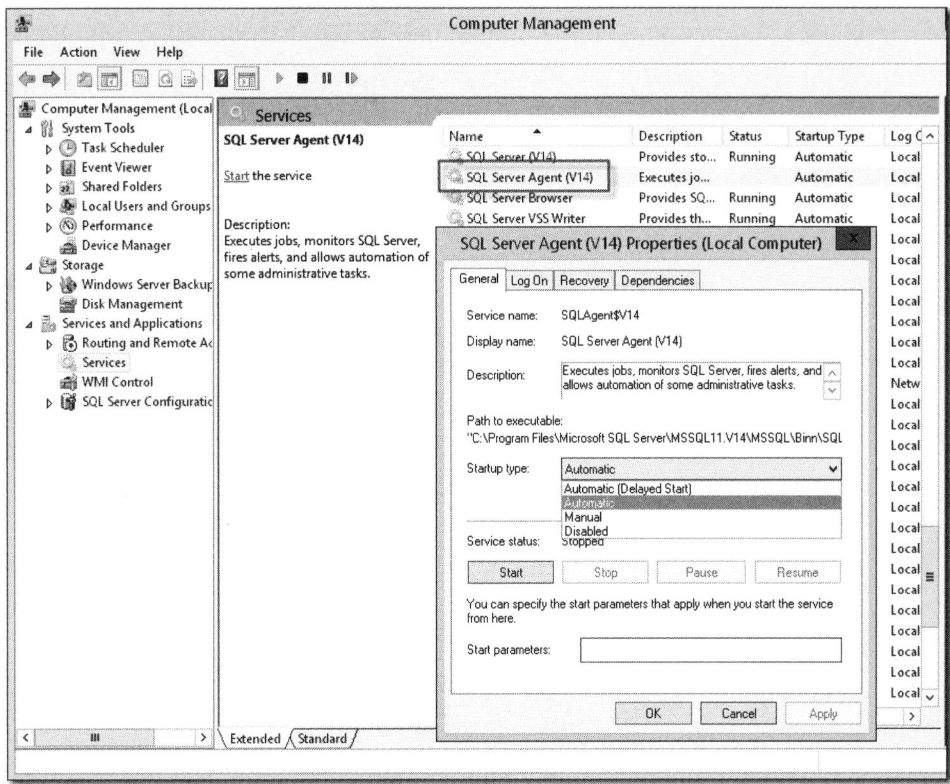

Figure 8.122 Windows Service of the SQL Server Agent

If a server has several instances, several SQL Server Agent services are created, which you can then configure to start automatically.

8.7.3 Files and Logs

This section provides some detailed information about how the SQL Server stores data on the hard disk. This information isn't only important for preparing to plan and implement a data backup but also to create disk space areas to achieve maximum performance.

Pages and Blocks

The largest SQL Server database file is also organized into pages and blocks. The following principles apply:

- A page is approximately 8KB in size, that is, 8,192 bytes.
- A block comprises 8 pages and is therefore 64KB in size, that is, 65,536 bytes.

The following example has a size of 5,976,883,200 bytes (see Figure 8.123). With this knowledge of pages and blocks, you can calculate how many blocks and pages are contained in this database file:

5,976,883,200 ÷ 8,192 = 729,600 pages = 91,200 blocks

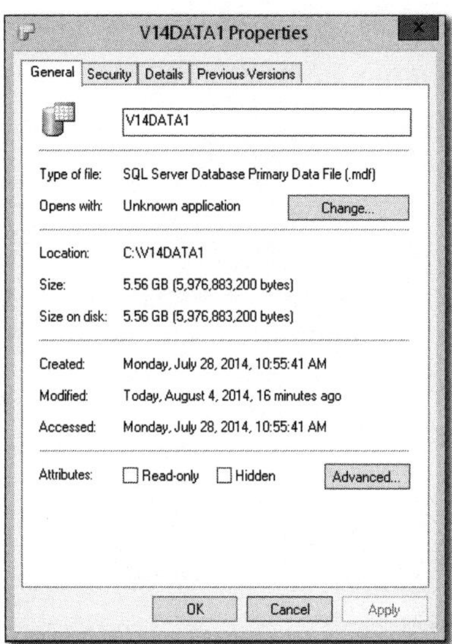

Figure 8.123 Size of the Database File

When the SQL Server accesses disk storage, it works in blocks (i.e., in 64KB units). For this reason, it makes sense to also set the physical block sizes for the RAID sets used by the SQL Server to this value.

[!]

Block Sizes

Here, we're talking about the block sizes that the RAID controller uses to format the disk areas and not the NTFS blocks. If the disk areas used by the SQL Server aren't formatted with this block size, this won't impair the function initially. However, you won't get the best performance out of your hardware later.

Let's take a look at the structure of a page (see Figure 8.124), which begins with a 96 byte page header. This is followed by one or more data rows. The row offset, which contains information about the distance between the first byte in the data row and the start of the page, is stored at the end of the file.

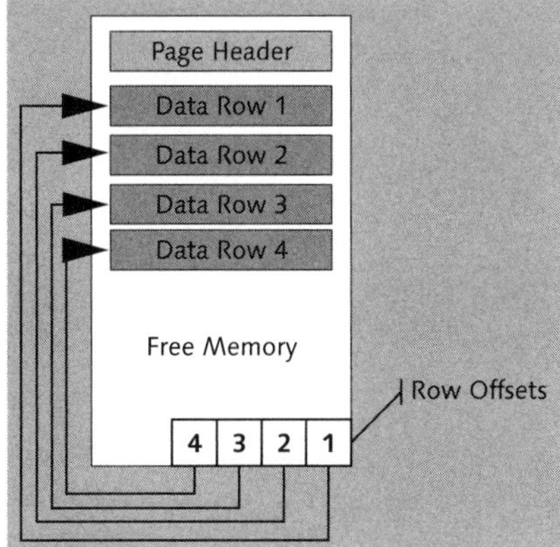

Figure 8.124 Page Structure

You see that a page may contain several data rows. If data rows are larger than one page, they are distributed across several pages.

File Groups and Files

An SQL Server database requires at least two files. One file stores the actual database, and one stores the transaction log. In Figure 8.125, you see a corresponding dialog box that contains the properties of a database. Here, you define, for example, a file type, path, or behavior for autoextend for each file.

You can create several files for both the actual database and the logs. For larger databases, this makes sense for the following reasons:

- The size of the individual file can be kept to a reasonable level, thus making it easier to manage and reducing the storage space needed. For performance reasons, it may make sense to distribute the files across several physical RAID sets.
- However, this is only possible if the database is distributed across several files.
- If only one of the files in a database is damaged (e.g., as a result of disk problems on a special RAID set), you only need to restore this one database.

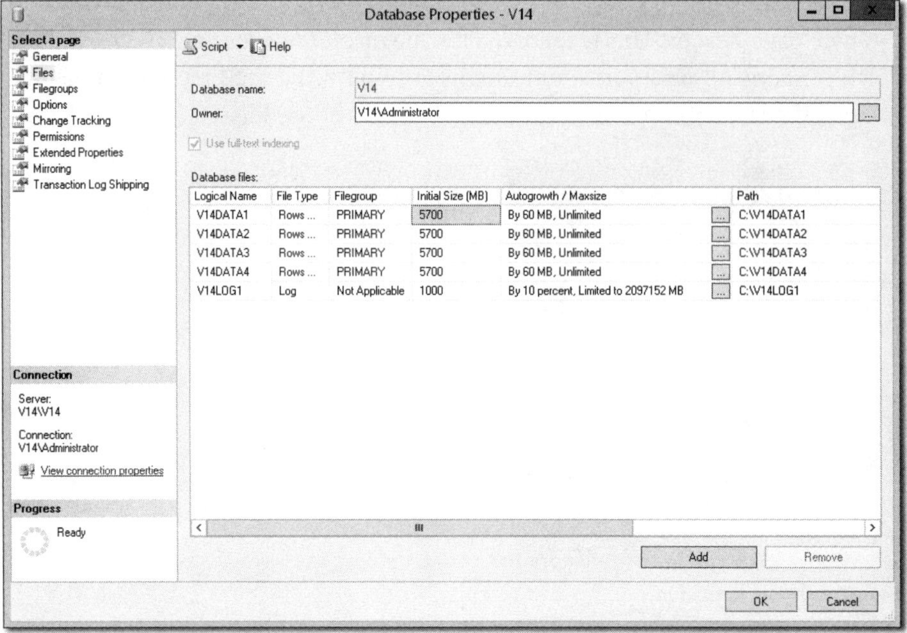

Figure 8.125 Overview of Database Files

If you want to improve administration and management, you can create file groups. Note that a database has one primary file and any number of secondary files (0 to n files). The following file name extensions are used by default:

- **.mdf* for primary database files
- **.ndf* for secondary database files
- **.ldf* for log files

Transaction Logs (Logs)

Transaction logs, also known as *logs* or *log files*, play an extremely important role in all database servers. Transaction logs are particularly important when backing up and restoring databases (see Chapter 6). In the SQL Server, a transaction log is written for each database (as is the case for every other server-based database system). Initially, a transaction log is simply one file. The database module then divides this file into multiple virtual log files. The system determines the number and size of the virtual log files that it creates and extends. You as the administrator can't influence this process.

Let's take a closer look at the log file (see Figure 8.126):

- At the start, you have two virtual log files with free storage space, which were created by truncating older entries in the transaction log.
- The logical log starts in the third virtual log file. Here, you find, among other things, a position known as the *Minimum Recovery Log Sequence Number* (Mini LSN). This identifies the log entry required for a cross-database rollback. When you truncate the log, all of the virtual log files that precede the Mini LSN position are deleted.
- The fifth virtual log file isn't used at present.

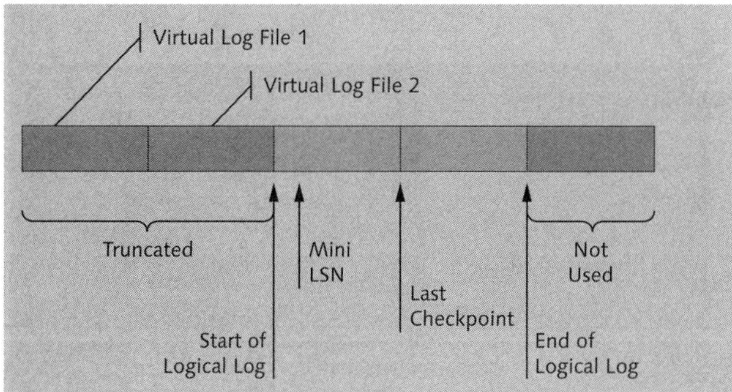

Figure 8.126 Transport Logs (I)

The following situation arises some time later (after a few transactions):

- The log is initially expanded to the fifth virtual log file. The end of the physical file may then be reached.
- If the end of the physical file is reached, the system returns to the start of the file (see Figure 8.127).

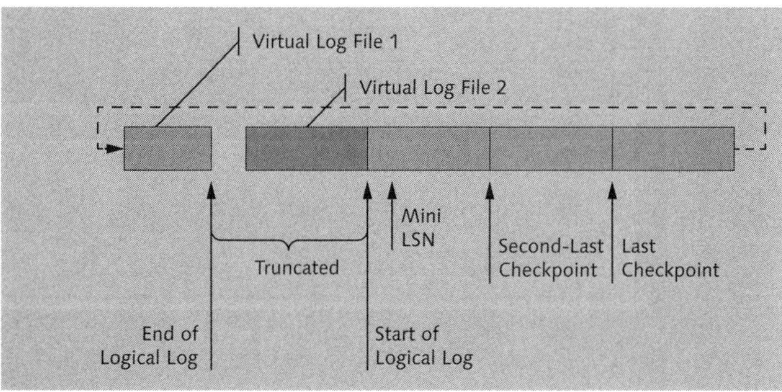

Figure 8.127 Transport Logs (II)

Ideally, the transactions are continuously written to this one physical transaction log file. A prerequisite here is that the logical log is truncated often enough to ensure that there is always enough free storage space (i.e., empty virtual log files). If there isn't enough free storage space in the physical file (as a result of a high transaction volume, a log file that is too small, or a transaction log that isn't truncated often enough), the following situation may arise:

- If autoextend is configured for the file, the database module extends the file.
- If it isn't possible to extend the file because there isn't enough space on the data carrier, the write processes are terminated (error 9002).
- If additional log files have been created, the data are written to these files.
- If autoextend isn't configured, and no additional log files are available, the write processes are terminated (error 9002).

[+]

Size of the Transaction Log Files

Sometimes, the transaction log file is several gigabytes in size and partly larger than the actual database. This happens if the log isn't truncated.

If the transaction log file continues to grow and grow, you should immediately read the rest of this chapter to find out how you can deal with transaction logs correctly.

When you truncate transaction logs, the physical file doesn't automatically become smaller. Free space is only created within the file.

If a transaction log file becomes very large (e.g., because it was not possible to truncate the transaction log for a while as a result of an error in the data backup environment), it must be reduced in size by executing an SQL command or by using SQL Server Management Studio.

8.7.4 Initiating a Backup Process

Next, we'll use SQL Server Management Studio to demonstrate how to perform a backup so that it's possible to work with the command line (i.e., with SQL commands). Because many administrators prefer to work with the graphical interface, we've chosen this display here.

[!]

SQL Commands

However, note that much of the work to be executed can only be performed using SQL commands—either because they can't be initiated in the GUI or because not all parameters can be transferred via the SQL Server Management Studio.

Fortunately, you can display the SQL commands for most of the tasks initiated via the SQL Server Management Studio. Most of the dialog boxes have the SCRIPT button for this purpose.

To start a database backup, follow these steps:

1. In the context menu for the database, choose the menu path TASKS • BACK UP (see Figure 8.128). The system displays a two-screen dialog box in which you can configure the backup.

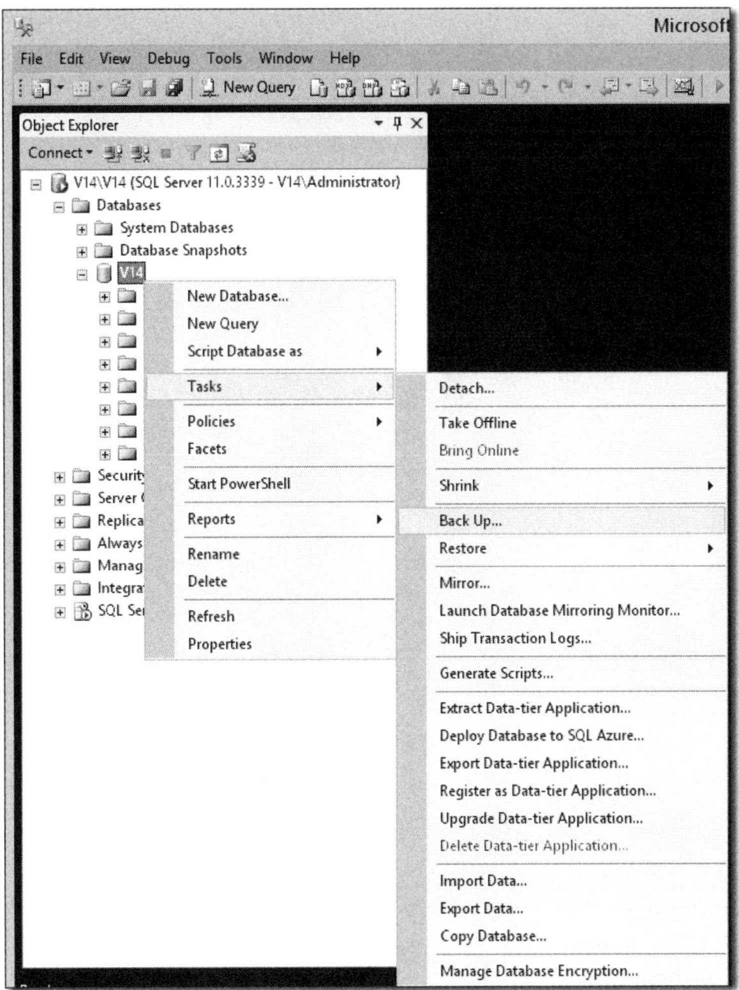

Figure 8.128 Calling the Backup Dialog

2. On the first screen (GENERAL), you make the basic configuration for the backup (e.g., whether it concerns a database backup or file backup, or which backup type is to be used, see Figure 8.129). You either specify the file to which you want to back up the data directly (as in this example), or you save the backup to a previously defined backup medium, which you select and assign by using the ADD button. If the server has a local tape drive, the backup can be written directly to this drive. In real life, however, this is unusual because, on the one hand, media management on the Microsoft SQL Server is very rudimentary, and, on the other hand, a more central solution for writing data to the tape drive is favored.

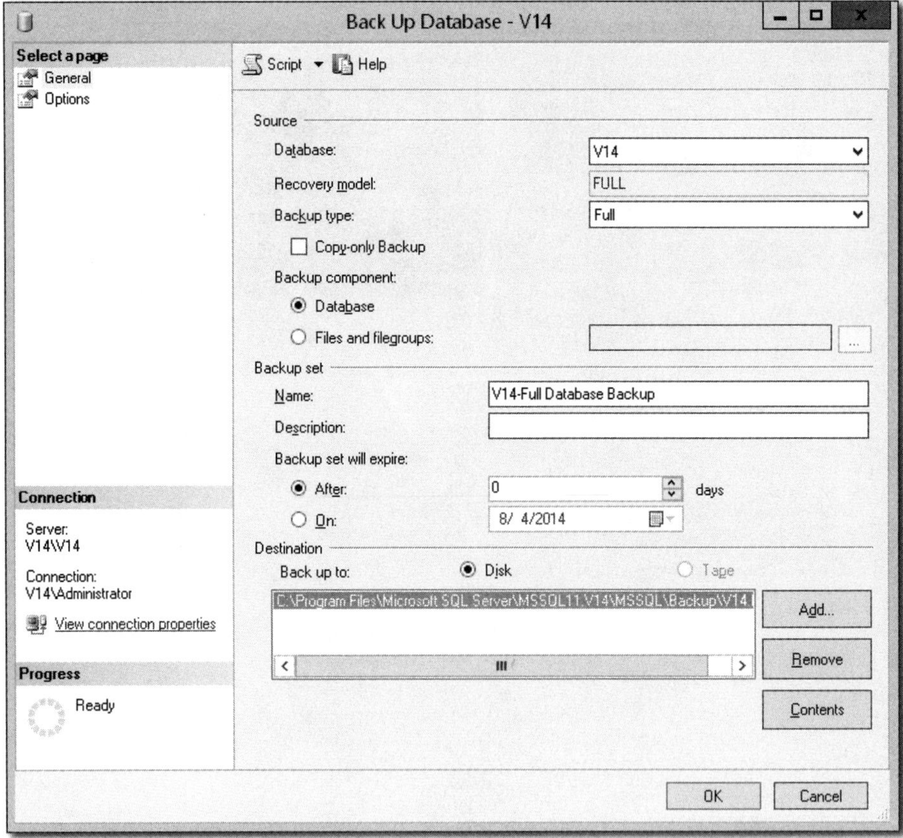

Figure 8.129 General Backup Settings

3. The second screen in the dialog box (OPTIONS) provides various different options that are largely self-explanatory (see Figure 8.130).

   The option fields that affect the transaction log are only available if you've selected TRANSACTION LOG as the BACKUP TYPE on the first screen.

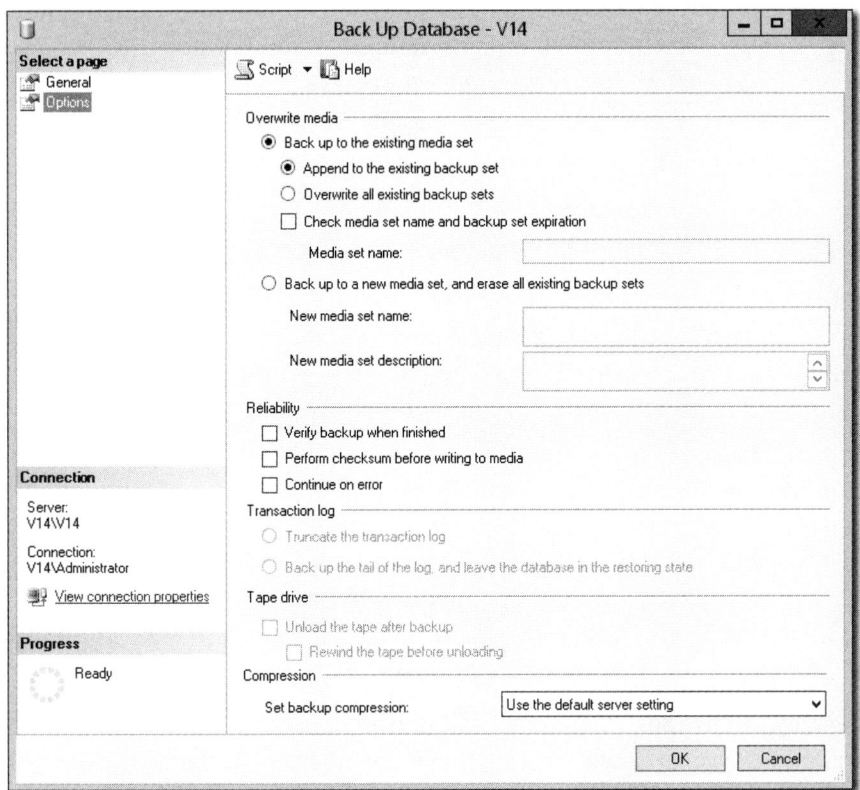

Figure 8.130 Advanced Configuration Options

4. Confirm your settings with OK. If you want to use SQL commands to start this backup process, you have to use the following code. If you aren't (yet) proficient enough to use these command lines to write this code, you can simply generate the code using the SCRIPT button.

```
BACKUP DATABASE [V14] TO DISK = N'C:\...\V14.bak'
 WITH NOFORMAT, NOINIT, NAME = N'V14-Full Database Backup', SKIP,
NOREWIND, NOUNLOAD, STATS = 10
GO
```

This is an online backup. In other words, there's no need to interrupt system operation. From a user perspective, however, an extensive backup can impair performance.

8.7.5 Setting Up Maintenance Plans for a Backup

Because starting each backup manually is tedious, you can handle this within a maintenance plan. For an SQL Server, you can set up any number of maintenance plans that start at a certain time and then execute various actions on one or more databases. You can also perform backups.

If you're running several servers, you can configure and perform backups on every single server. You must bear the following two key aspects in mind:

- **Monitoring**
  If you execute the data backup mechanisms locally on each server, you also have to monitor each machine separately to determine whether the data backup is actually performed.
- **Backup devices**
  In a production environment, backups are mostly saved to tape. Of course, you could give each SQL Server its own tape drive, but this would require a lot of administration and monitoring effort. A central solution is much more elegant here. As mentioned previously, the media management on the SQL Server is very rudimentary (i.e., you as the administrator have to store tapes, overwrite the data, and do many other things manually).

Despite these limitations, the use of a maintenance plan isn't entirely unsuitable. It works perfectly, is easy to handle, and you don't have to deal with the idiosyncrasies of other backup software. Maintenance plans are also used for other tasks. As an SQL Server administrator, you must always deal with this issue.

To create a maintenance plan, follow these steps:

1. The easiest way to create a new maintenance plan is to use the Maintenance Plan Wizard, which you can call via the menu path MANAGEMENT • MAINTENANCE PLANS • MAINTENANCE PLAN WIZARD (see Figure 8.131).
2. The Maintenance Plan Wizard (see Figure 8.132) initially guides you through the process of creating a schedule during which the maintenance plan is to be executed. You can more or less store any individual plan, which may also include recurrence intervals. Click on NEXT.

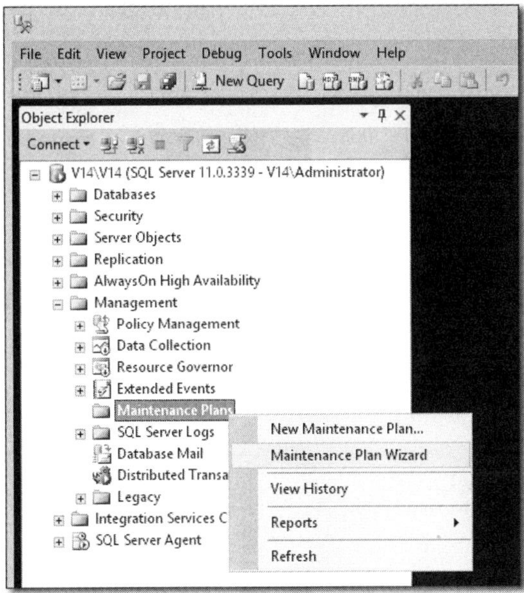

Figure 8.131 Calling the Maintenance Plan Wizard

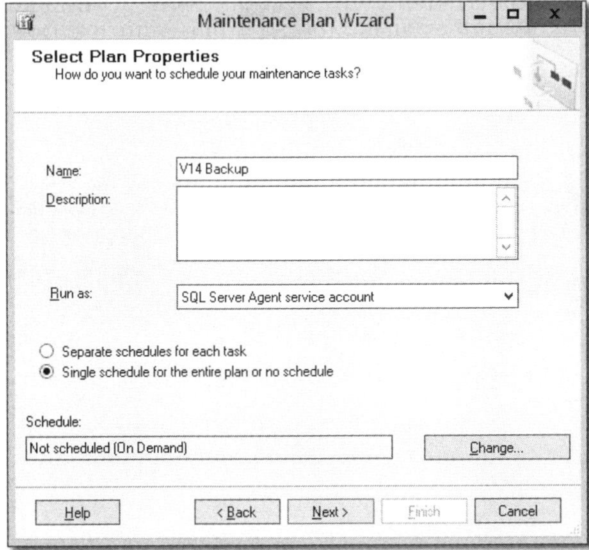

Figure 8.132 Initial Screen of the Maintenance Plan Wizard

3. The next dialog box contains the most important point, namely selecting the maintenance task (i.e., the task to be executed, see Figure 8.133). Here, you can

choose from almost a dozen options, including the complete, differential, and transaction log backup. Click on NEXT.

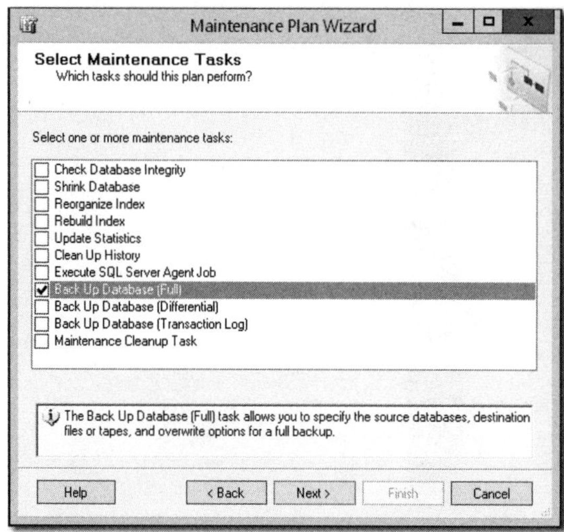

Figure 8.133 Selecting the Maintenance Task

4. If you've selected several maintenance tasks to be executed, the execution sequence will be essential. This can also be configured but not until you access the next dialog box (see Figure 8.134).

Figure 8.134 Defining the Sequence for the Tasks Selected

Using the options displayed, you determine the sequence in which the maintenance tasks in this maintenance plan are processed. Click on NEXT.

5. Most maintenance tasks require additional information about the configuration (see Figure 8.135). The wizard will display the required dialog boxes. In this example, only a complete backup is performed. The configuration options in the dialog box are similar to those for a backup that is triggered manually. One difference here is the option to create each new backup in a new file that is automatically created (see the CREATE A SUB-DIRECTORY FOR EACH DATABASE checkbox). Click on NEXT.

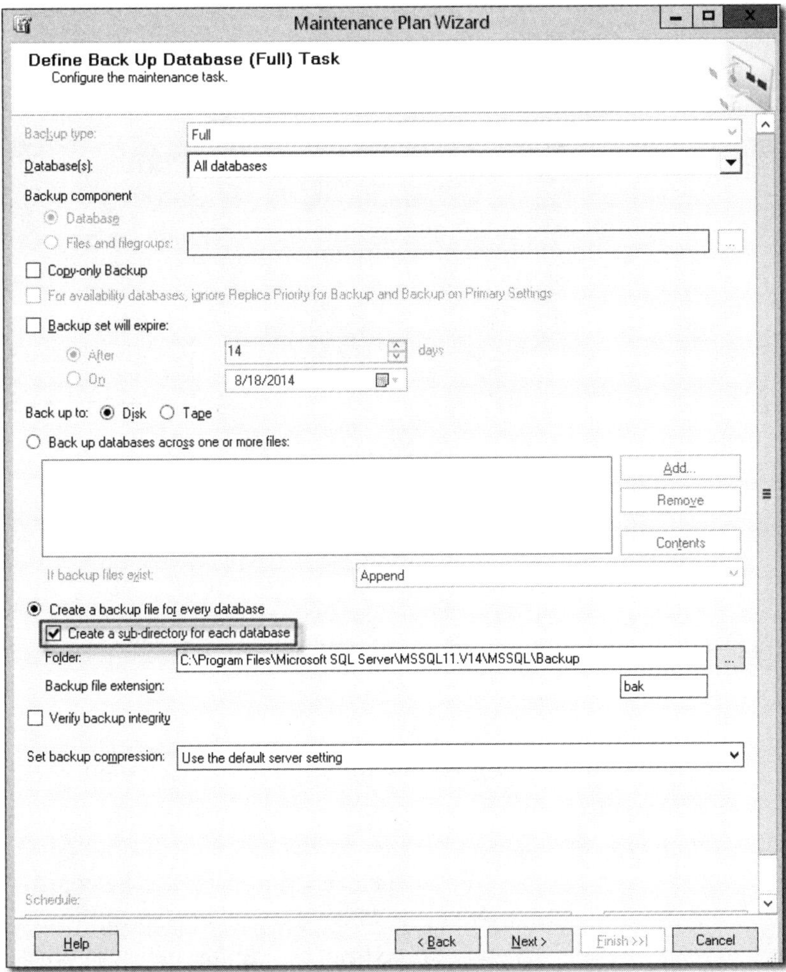

Figure 8.135 Detail Configuration of the Task Selected

After you've closed the wizard, the maintenance plan is active and works.

[!] **Executing a Maintenance Plan**

To ensure that the maintenance plan is actually executed, the SQL Server Agent must be running. Because this isn't necessarily the case by default, you should check whether it's actually active in the SQL Server Management Studio. Specify that the SQL Server Agent is automatically started after a server restart.

You can modify any maintenance plan that is created by following these steps:

1. In the context menu for the maintenance plan, choose MODIFY to display the view shown in Figure 8.136.

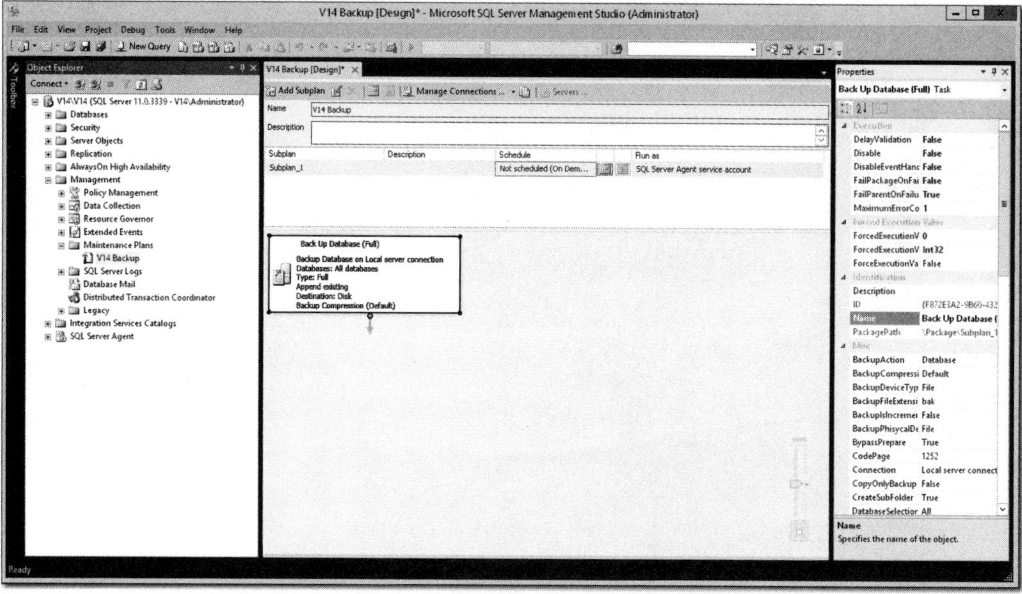

Figure 8.136 Editor for Maintenance Plans

2. If you've already worked with *SQL Server Integration Services* (SSIS), you'll immediately recognize this view and feel at home here. For all other cases, it's worth mentioning that maintenance plan task elements can be positioned and configured from the TOOLBOX. You define the execution sequence by connecting the elements in the required sequence. This editor gives you full control over your maintenance plans. As you can see from the comprehensive PROPERTIES window, you can configure the maintenance plan tasks in great detail.

3. If you want to execute the maintenance plan immediately, you can start it directly. You can do this in two places because the maintenance plan is displayed below the MANAGEMENT • MAINTENANCE PLANS and below the SQL SERVER AGENT • JOBS node (see Figure 8.137).

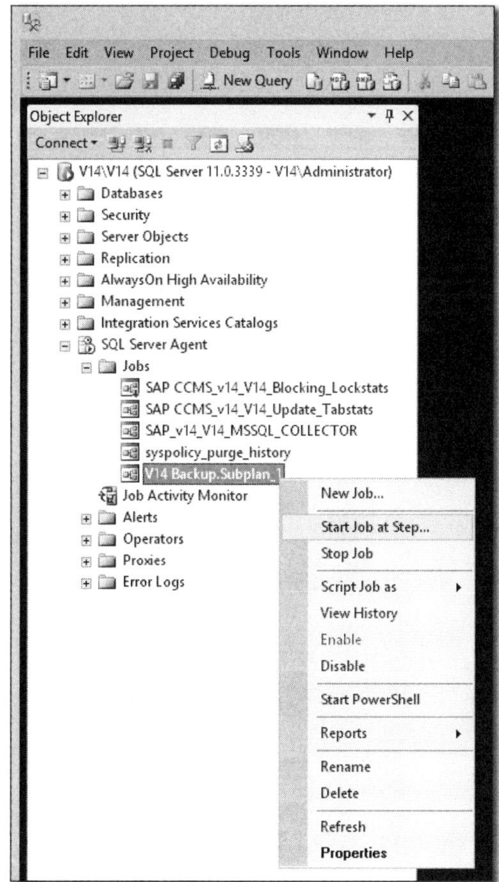

Figure 8.137 Starting the Maintenance Job Directly

An SQL Server Agent job is created for the maintenance plan. This is the reason why the SQL Server Agent must be started to execute the maintenance plans.

8.7.6 Backing Up System Databases

In addition to the databases that you create and fill with user data, there are some system databases the SQL Server uses for internal purposes (e.g., to save the configuration). The `master` database, in particular, is extremely important and must be backed up. Table 8.1 shows the system databases from a backup perspective.

Databases	Description	Backup Required?	Description
`master`	All of the system settings for the SQL Server are saved in the `master` database.	Yes	This database is extremely important. It should/must be backed up on a regular basis. The only way to back up the `master` database is by means of a complete backup. The SQL Server can't work without the `master` database. If it's damaged or lost, you can create a new `master` database. However, you then lose all of the logon information, for example.
`msdb`	The SQL Server Agent uses this database. Jobs, progression logs, and so on are stored here.	Yes	Even though losing this database would not be as dramatic as losing the `master` database, a regular backup is necessary because it also contains important information for system operation.
`model`	This is the template used for new databases.	Yes	Even though losing this database would not be as dramatic as losing the `master` database, we nevertheless recommend that you back up this database after every change.
`tempdb`	This database is used to cache temporary result sets. When you shut down the instance, any data stored there is deleted.	No	You can't back up this database because it only contains temporary data.

Table 8.1 System Databases – Backup

master Database

As already mentioned in Table 8.1, you must back up the `master` database on a regular basis. The following processes bring about a change in the database and therefore make a backup necessary:

- Creating or deleting a user database. If a user database is extended to include new data, this doesn't affect the `master` database.
- Adding or removing files or file groups.
- Adding logon names or other processes that relate to logon security. Database backup processes such as adding a user to a database don't affect the `master` database.
- Changing server-wide configuration options or database configuration options.
- Creating or removing logical backup media.
- Configuring the server for distributed queries and *Remote Procedure Calls* (RPCs) such as adding connection servers or remote logon names.

However, it has proven beneficial to include the database in a backup job to be executed on a daily basis, for example. The only way to back up the `master` database is by means of a complete database backup. Other procedures aren't supported. Because the `master` database isn't too large, this isn't a problem.

msdb and model Databases

As already mentioned in Table 8.1, the `msdb` database contains information for and about the execution of SQL Server Agent jobs. The database changes in the following cases:

- Planning tasks
- Saving integration services packages that were created using the import/export wizard in an instance of the SQL Server
- Managing an online backup and restore run
- Replication
- *setup.exe* resetting the restore model to SIMPLE
- Additions or changes to guidelines or conditions for guideline-based administration

Even though you would only need to back up the `msdb` database in the event of changes, the easiest option is to back up this database on a regular basis (e.g., daily), in the same way as you back up the `master` database.

The `model` database only changes if an administrator makes adjustments (this rarely happens). We recommend that you back up the `model` database as part of the regular backup of the `master` and `msdb` databases. Even though this is too often in principle, it's much more complicated to manage a separate backup record for this extremely small database than to simply back it up as part of the regular backup.

8.7.7 SQL Server Logs

When a server is running, you must view its logs. The SQL server logs are available below the MANAGEMENT node for this purpose (see Figure 8.138).

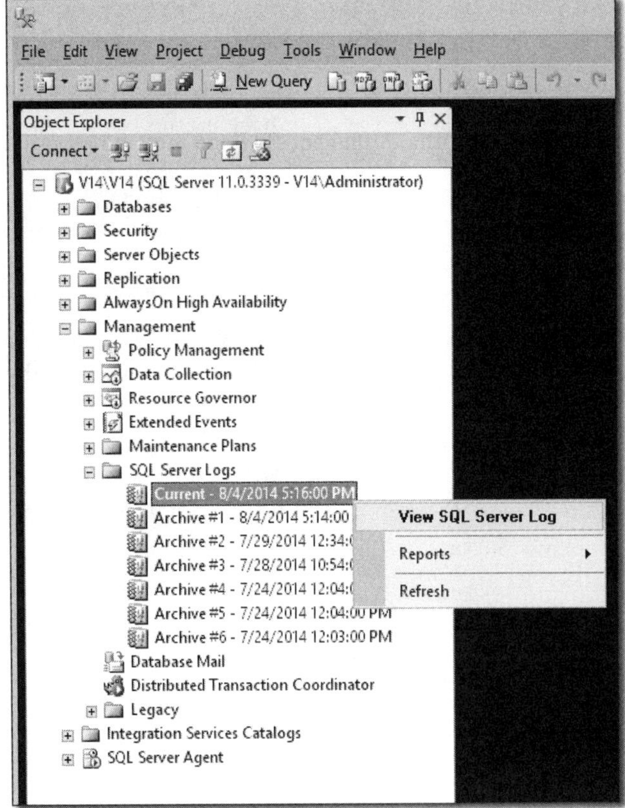

Figure 8.138 Displaying the SQL Server Logs

You can open current or archived logs. You call the LOG FILE VIEWER to "read" the logs (see Figure 8.139).

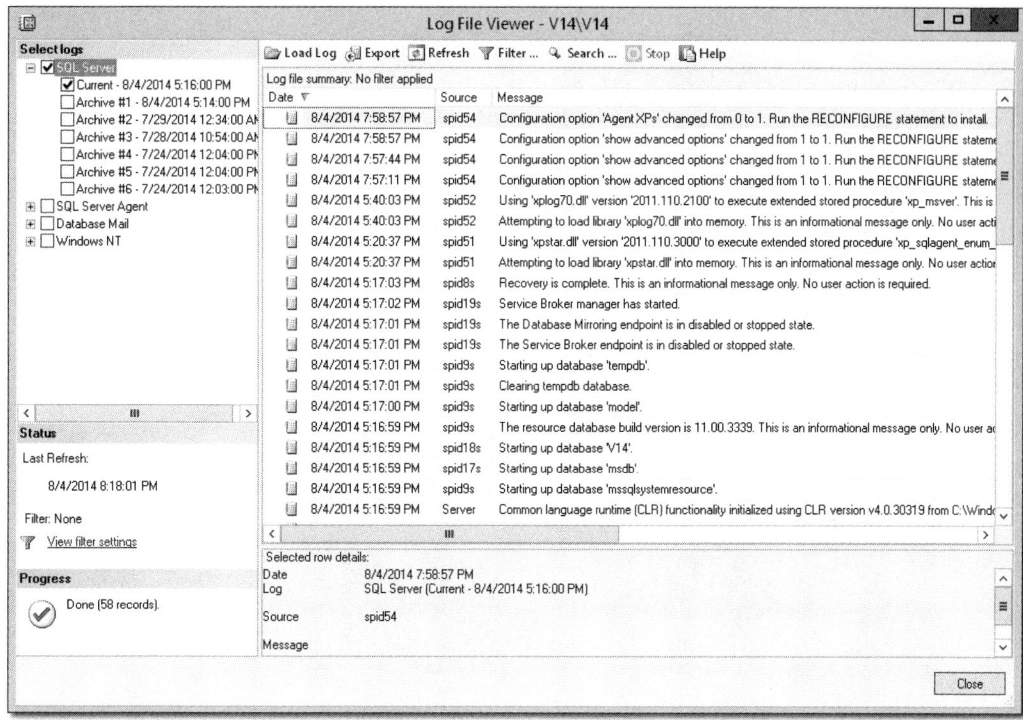

Figure 8.139 Log File Viewer

The log file entries are displayed in the LOG FILE VIEWER.

8.8 Database Administration—SAP MaxDB

SAP MaxDB is SAP's database management system, which was known as *SAP DB* before version 7.5. From a functional scope, the database is comparable with other database systems. However, it isn't as powerful as an Oracle database, for example. SAP MaxDB is primarily intended for small- and medium-sized enterprises where the focus is on low administration efforts and low costs.

8.8.1 Database Studio

MaxDB databases are managed in *Database Studio*, which replaces the two tools *Database Manager GUI* and *SQL Studio* as of MaxDB version 7.7. You can use the

Database Studio for all MaxDB databases as of version 7.5. The Database Studio provides a GUI you can use to perform all important database tasks, including the following:

- Starting and stopping the database
- Monitoring the database
- Analyzing performance
- Backing up and restoring the database

We'll describe some of these features here.

[+] **Additional Information about SAP MaxDB and Database Studio**

Additional information about SAP MaxDB and the Database Studio as well as extensive documentation is available at *http://help.sap.com/* under DATABASE • SAP MAXDB • SAP MAXDB <RELEASE>, on the MaxDB home page at *http://maxdb.sap.com*, and in the SAP Community Network at *http://scn.sap.com/community/maxdb*.

You can download the Database Studio in the SAP Support Portal under *https://support.sap.com*. For this purpose, select the path SOFTWARE DOWNLOADS • DATABASES • SAP MAXDB • DATABASE PATCHES • MAXDB GUI COMPONENTS/TOOLS • MAXDB DATABASE STUDIO <RELEASE>.

8.8.2 Starting and Stopping the Database

If necessary, you can use the Database Studio to start or stop the MaxDB database by following these steps (see Figure 8.140):

1. Under MICROSOFT WINDOWS, select the DATABASE STUDIO application.
2. Log on to the database as the database user (`SAP<DBID>`, `CONTROL`, or `SUPERDBA`).
3. Select your database in the EXPLORER window under MY LANDSCAPE • SERVERS (e.g., V14). A traffic light icon indicates the current status:
   - Green: The database is active (online).
   - Yellow: The database is in administration mode (admin).
   - Red: The database is stopped (offline).
4. To start the database, right-click on the context menu, and choose ADMINISTRATION TASKS • SET OPERATIONAL STATE • ONLINE (see Figure 8.141).

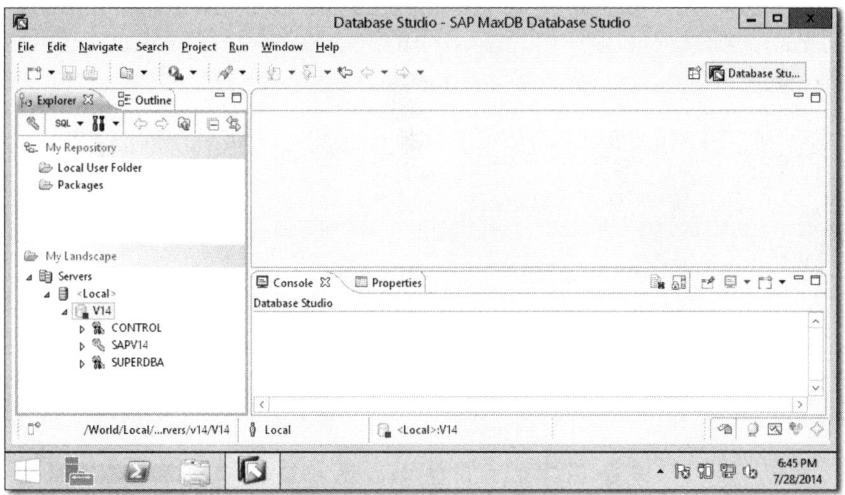

Figure 8.140 Status of the MaxDB Database in the Database Studio

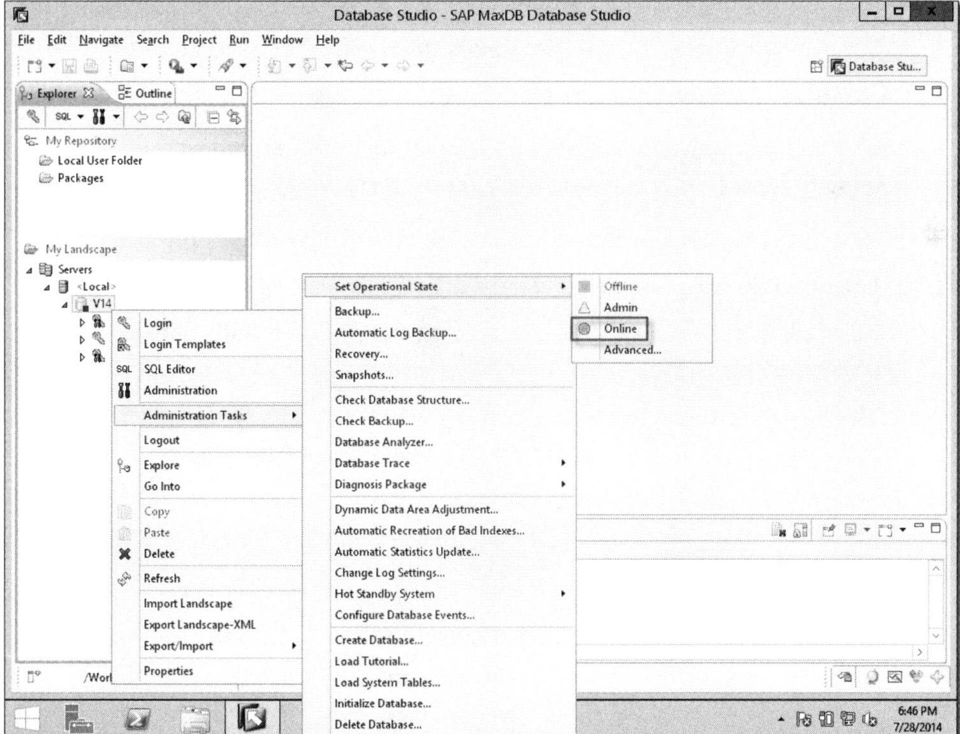

Figure 8.141 Starting the MaxDB Database

5. The database is started. After you've successfully completed the process, a green traffic light is displayed. To stop the database, select ADMINISTRATION TASKS • SET OPERATIONAL STATE • OFFLINE.

[+]

Admin Status

The ADMIN mode is intended for administrative tasks. Certain actions can only be performed in this mode (e.g., a database restore). The database is stopped for this purpose. In other words, the SAP system can't access the database.

8.8.3 Database Monitoring

You can use the Database Studio to monitor various aspects of the database, for example:

- Occupied storage space and available storage space
- Status of the log files
- Access rate on the database cache
- Database backups that have been performed
- Database activities (read/write, lock, etc.)

You should monitor the database so that you can detect errors early on and therefore avoid problems. To do so, follow these steps:

1. Under MICROSOFT WINDOWS, select the DATABASE STUDIO application.
2. Log on to the database as the database user (`CONTROL` or `SUPERDBA`).
3. Right-click to open the context menu for your database, and choose the ADMINISTRATION entry.
4. The ADMINISTRATION window opens in the screen area on the right side. General information is summarized on the OVERVIEW tab (see Figure 8.142).
5. Switch to the DATA AREA tab. The number, size, storage location, and fill level of the database files are displayed here (see Figure 8.143). Under USAGE, you can see, at a glance, how much space is still available in the database.

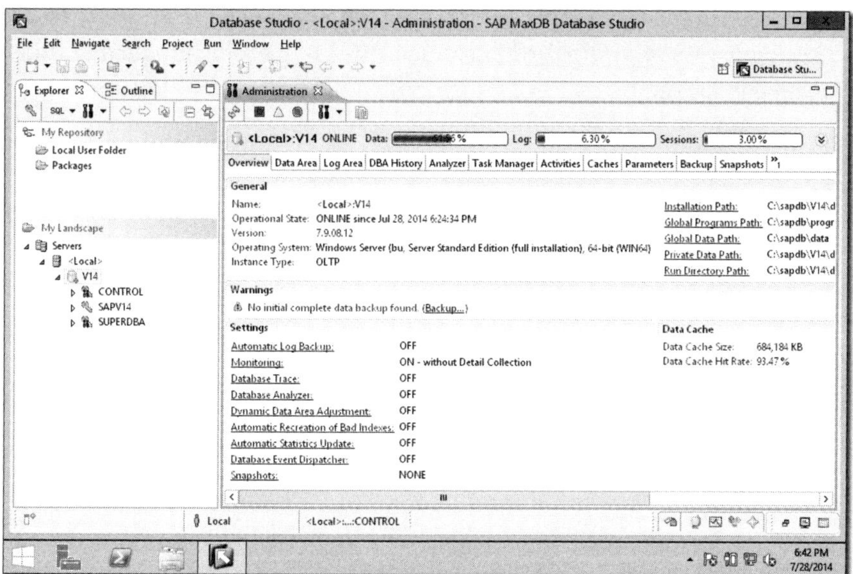

Figure 8.142 Administration Window – Overview

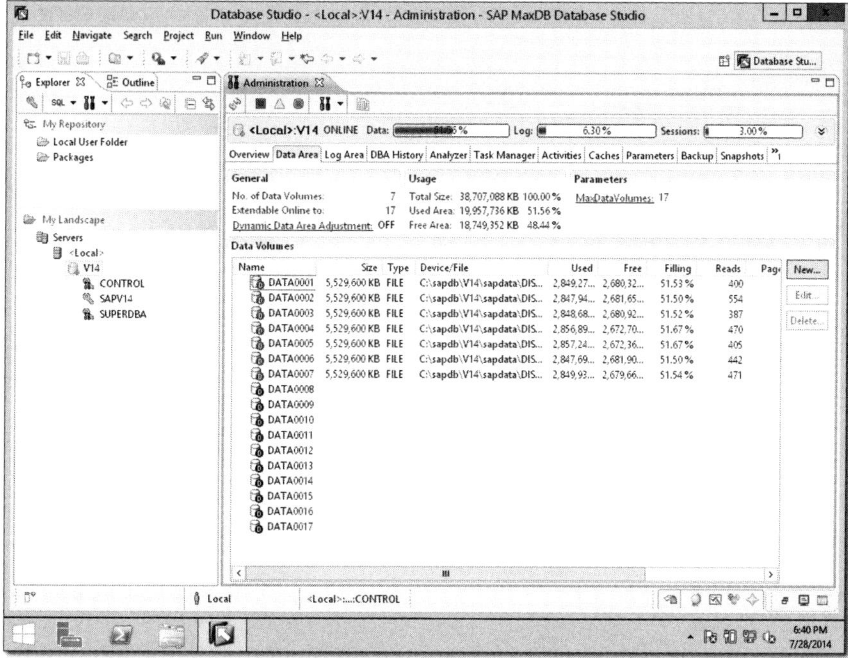

Figure 8.143 Data Area

6. Select the Log Area tab, which informs you about the status of the database logs (see Figure 8.144). If no further storage space is available, no further transaction log entries can be created, which causes the SAP system to stop.

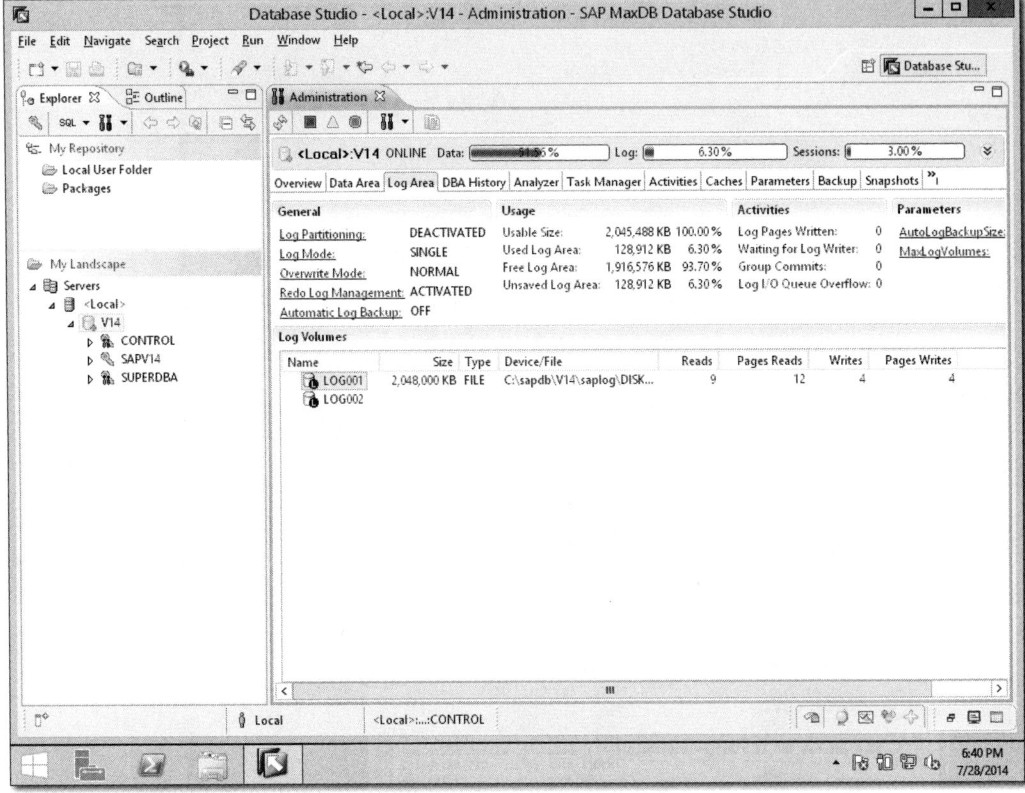

Figure 8.144 Log Areas

7. The Activities tab contains the statistical data for database activities (e.g., read and write accesses or locks, see Figure 8.145).

8. The Caches tab also contains statistical values (see Figure 8.146). Here you can see how many database accesses from cache storage can be handled by the system. A high Hit Rate indicates that the accesses are executed in a particularly efficient manner.

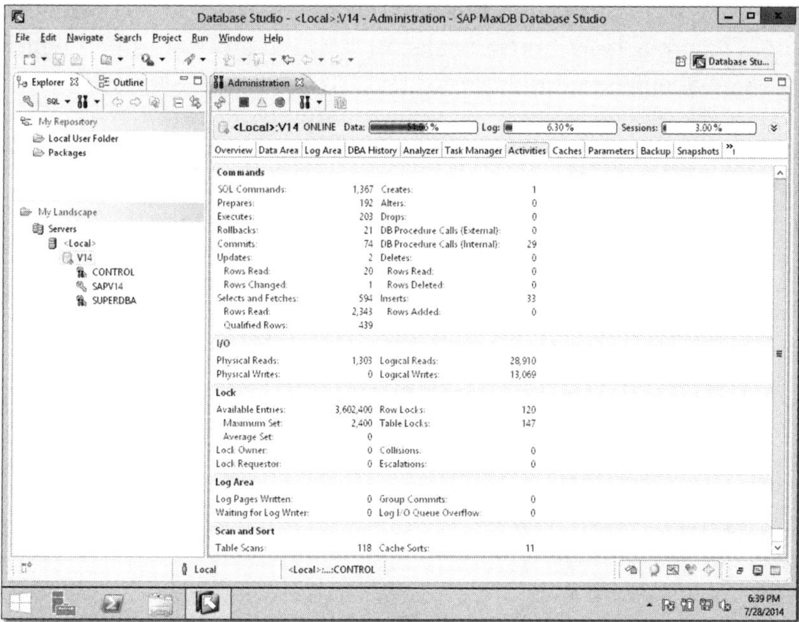

Figure 8.145 Evaluating the Database Activities

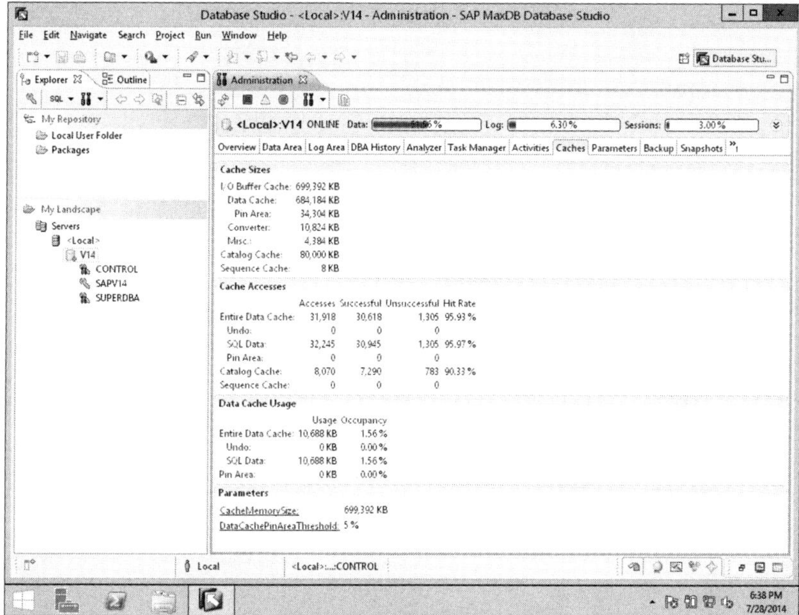

Figure 8.146 Analyzing the Database Cache

9. Switch to the BACKUP tab. You can use this overview to monitor your database backups (see Figure 8.147). Pay particular attention to error messages, which indicate that a backup wasn't fully performed.

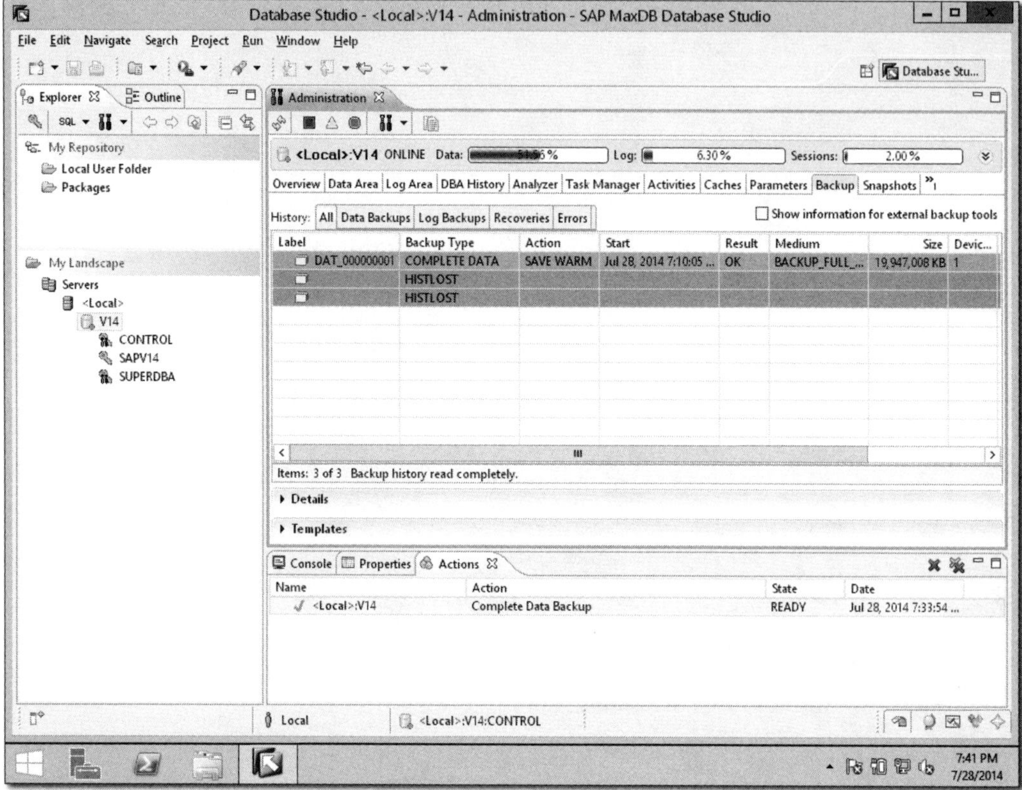

Figure 8.147 Database Backups

[+]

Automatic Notification If Problems Occur

If you want to automate database monitoring, you can use *database events* to send email notifications if certain threshold values are exceeded. For example, you can be informed if the database fill level exceeds a value of 90% or if an error occurs during a database backup.

8.8.4 Backing Up the Database

You can use the Database Studio to create database backups (for more information, see Chapter 6), including the following:

- Complete database backups
- Incremental database backups
- Database log backup

Automating the Backup [+]

Database backups are extremely important when restoring the system after a serious problem. You should therefore automate the process as far as possible (preferably using the DBA Planning Calendar, see Section 8.1) and only using the manual procedures described here on special occasions (e.g., before you import support packages).

To perform a database backup, follow these steps:

1. Under Microsoft Windows, select the Database Studio application.
2. Log on to the database as the database user (`SAP<DBSID>`, `CONTROL`, or `SUPERDBA`).
3. Right-click to open the context menu for your database, and choose Administration Tasks • Backup.

Incremental Database Backup [!]

A complete backup must exist before you can create an incremental backup.

4. Choose the option you require (e.g., Complete Data Backup), and click on Next (see Figure 8.148).

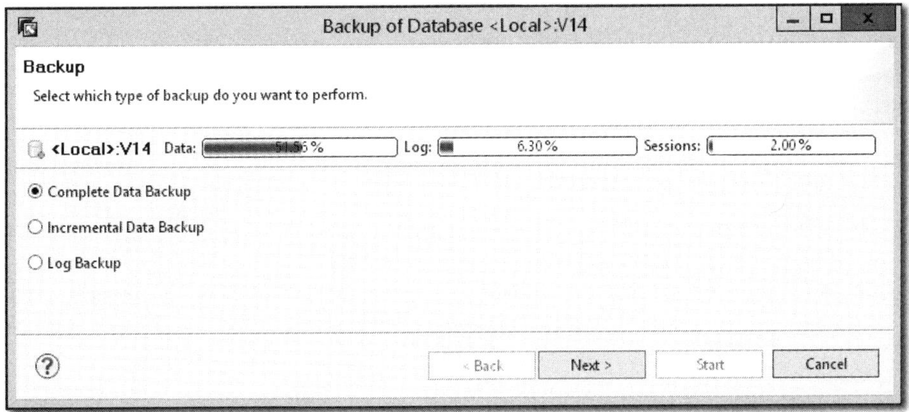

Figure 8.148 Selecting the Backup Option

5. You need a *backup template* so that you can execute a database backup. Select an existing template or choose NEW to create a new template (see Figure 8.149).

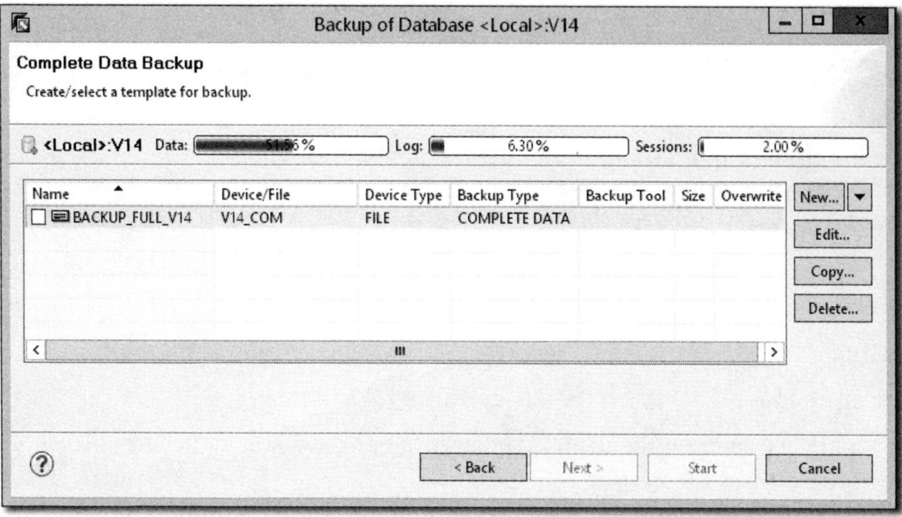

Figure 8.149 Selecting the Backup Template

6. Make the following settings (see Figure 8.150):
   - NAME: Assign a name to the template.
   - BACKUP TYPE: Select the backup type.
   - DEVICE TYPE: Find a storage medium.
   - BACKUP TOOL: This is optional if you're using a third-party tool.
   - DEVICE/FILE: Specify the name or path of the storage medium.

   Then choose OK.
7. The template has been created. Click on NEXT.
8. To start the backup, click on START (see Figure 8.151).

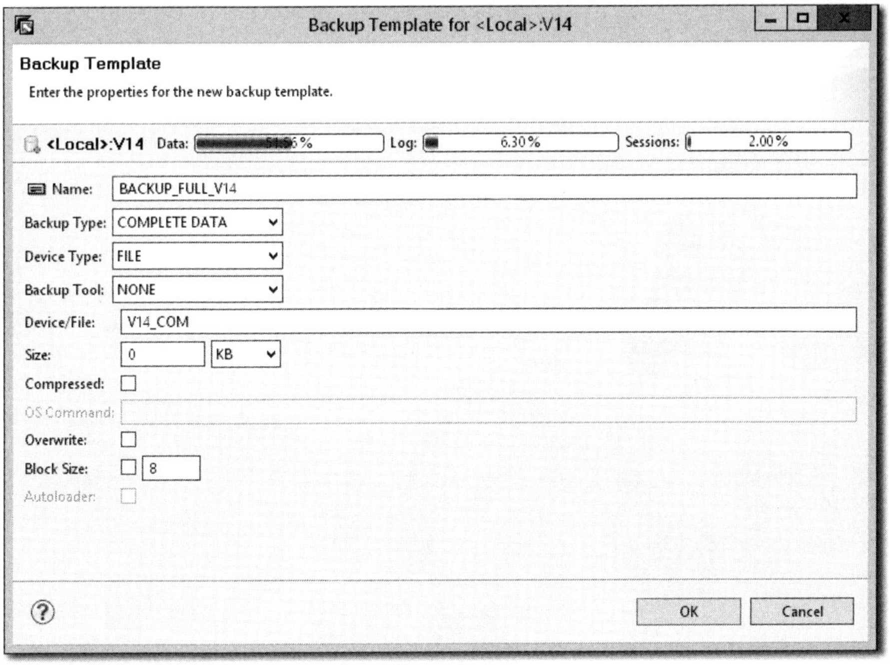

Figure 8.150 Creating a New Template

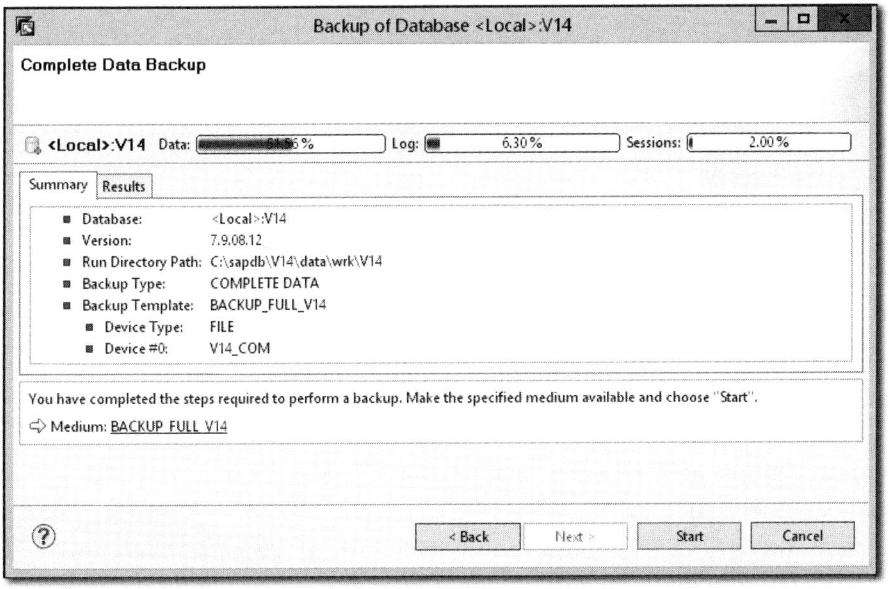

Figure 8.151 Starting the Backup

9. After you've completed the backup, the system displays the result of the process (see Figure 8.152).

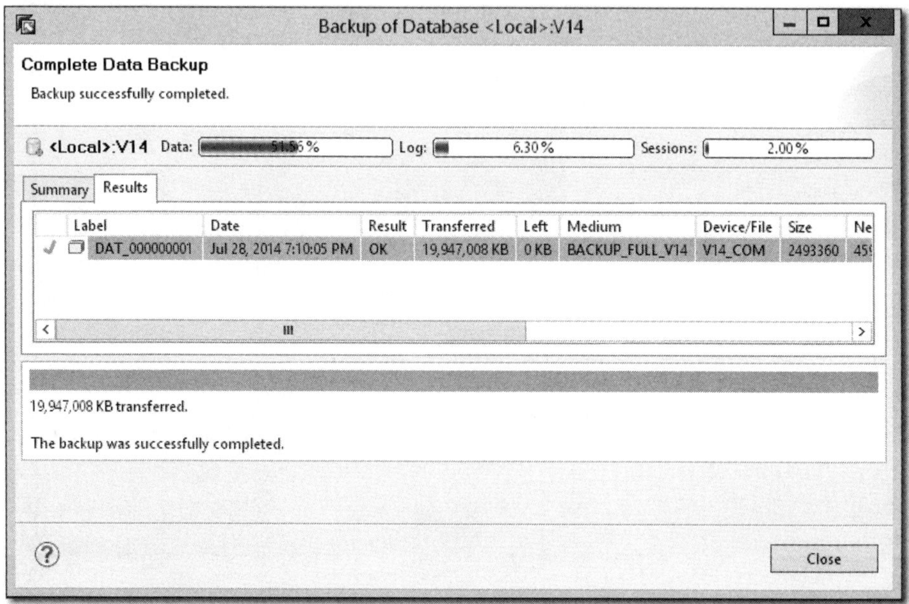

Figure 8.152 Result of the Backup

[+]

Restoring the Database

You can use existing backups to restore the database after an error occurs. To restore the database, choose RECOVERY in the context menu for the database. The database must have the admin status for this purpose.

8.9 Database Administration—SAP HANA

In 2011, SAP launched SAP HANA, which triggered an evolution among all major database manufacturers. The uncompromising implementation of technologies, which previously had only been used in special databases, has accelerated the further development of all databases. Because the underlying technology differs considerably from other databases, this section first discusses it briefly. Subsequently, we describe the standard tasks of SAP system operation using SAP HANA.

8.9.1 Technical Background

SAP HANA is a database that is designed for fast processing of large amounts of data. It's also intended to accelerate existing applications such as SAP Business Suite and allow for new processes, for which no technological background has been available so far. SAP HANA primarily yields its speed advantage from three core technologies:

- Keeping all data in the memory
- Column-based storage of tables
- Transferring functionality from the application to the database

In-Memory Technology

Keeping all data in the memory (in-memory) accelerates the processing of data by several orders of magnitude. Nevertheless, all data must also be written to non-volatile memory to prevent loss of data in case of database restarts or power interruptions. For SAP HANA, just like for other databases, this is done using data and log files, whereas the log files are written to *solid state disks* for performance reasons. Furthermore, SAP HANA databases require a lot of memory to keep all that data. When this book was written, the RAM sizes for SAP HANA servers ranged between 128 GB (for the smallest variant) and 2 TB (for the largest single-node systems). For larger systems, you can combine several server nodes (also referred to as *scale-out solutions*).

Column Store

Besides outsourcing data from the hard disk to the memory, the column-based storage of tables (*column store*) is also supposed to increase the processing speed (in contrast to row-based data storage). For column-based storage, all entries of a column are written one after another and not in the individual rows (see Figure 8.153).

This principle leads to considerably faster access speed for selective queries because fewer data blocks need to be skipped. At the same time, this principle of data storage lays the foundation for a very efficient, lightweight compression because repetitive values of a column can be indexed more easily. However, a disadvantage of this technology is the high effort for `INSERT` and `UPDATE` statements, which are considerably slower than in row-based storage methods.

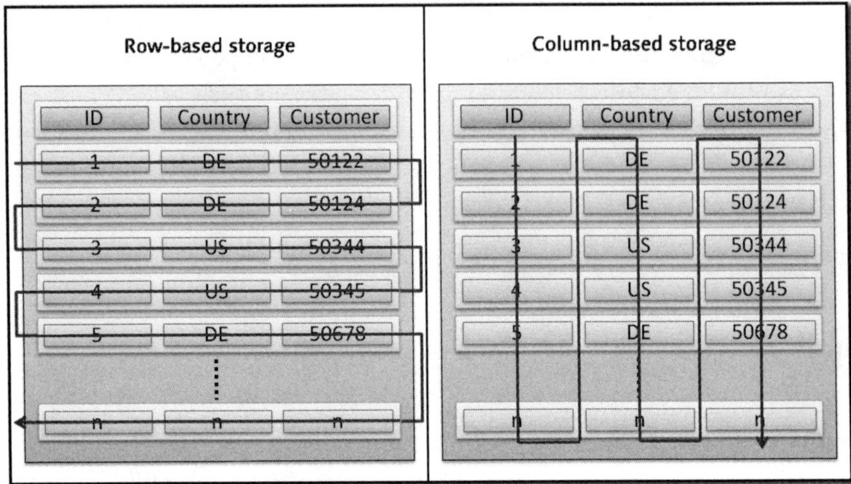

Figure 8.153 Difference Between Row-Based and Column-Based Storage

Stored Procedures

The third technology used by SAP HANA to gain higher processing speed is to transfer the functionality from the application server (e.g., SAP NetWeaver) to the database. Frequently used and data-intensive functions are transferred to the database as *stored procedures*. The effort for transporting data between the database and the application server is thus omitted, and the functions can utilize the computing power of the high-performance database server. However, you must note here that this optimization only applies if the application and the function are optimized, as is the case, for example, for parts of the SAP ERP system since Enhancement Package (EHP) 6.

[+]

SAP HANA-Optimized Applications

Not all transactions have been optimized for SAP HANA in the release mentioned. Refer to SAP Note 1761546 to get a complete list of all SAP HANA-optimized transactions in SAP ERP.

8.9.2 SAP HANA Studio

Different tools are available for the administration of the SAP HANA database. SAP HANA Studio is the tool with the more comprehensive functional scope and is recommended for daily use.

[!]

Tools for Database Configuration

You can perform almost all tasks, which you can fulfill in SAP HANA Studio, via command line programs on the database server (e.g., using SQL). But you should only use these tools if you have extensive SAP HANA knowledge.

Setting Up an Administration Environment

SAP HANA Studio is an Eclipse-based administration and working tool for SAP HANA. To open SAP HANA Studio, choose Start • Programs • SAP HANA • SAP HANA Studio.

You first need to set up the administration environment for your SAP HANA system by following these steps:

1. Add a new SAP HANA system by right-clicking on the Systems window on the initial screen and selecting the Add System entry from the context menu (see Figure 8.154).

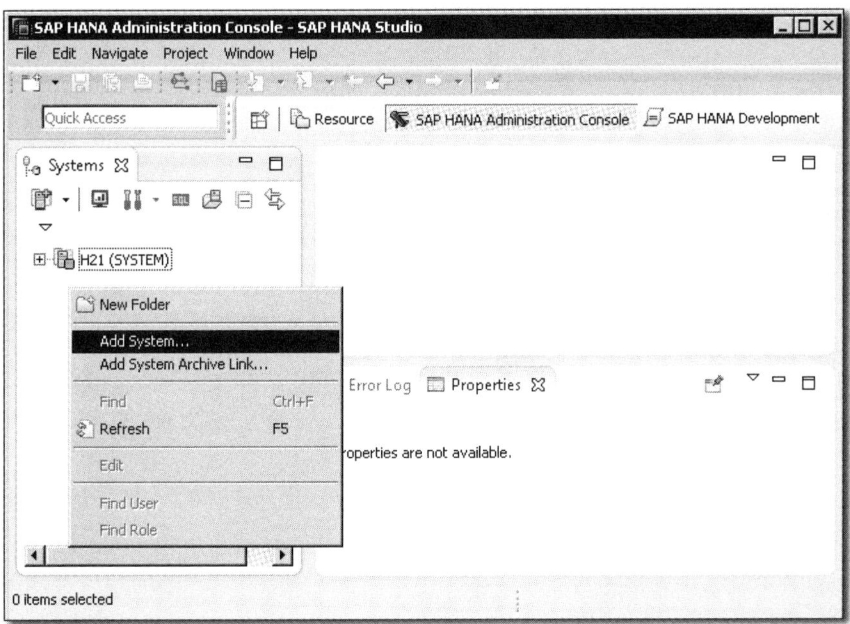

Figure 8.154 Adding a New System in SAP HANA Studio

2. Add the system using the user SYSTEM. This user has extensive authorizations to perform administration tasks.
3. Now switch to the SAP HANA ADMINISTRATION CONSOLE perspective by choosing the OPEN PERSPECTIVE button (see Figure 8.155).

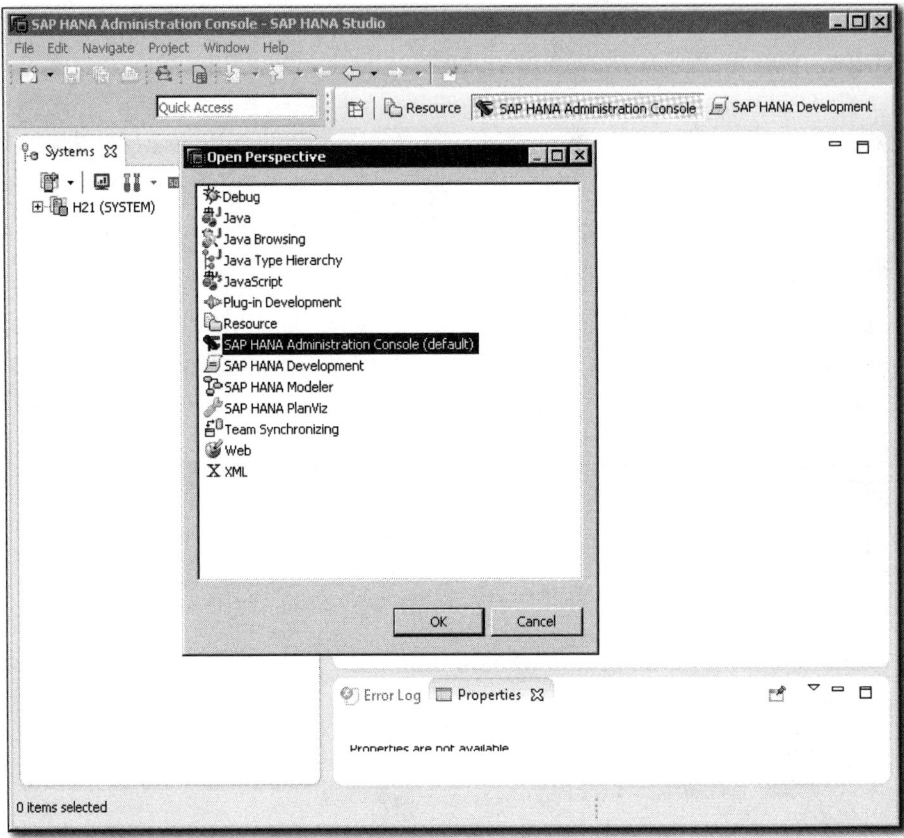

Figure 8.155 Changing the Perspective in SAP HANA Studio

4. Select the system, and click on the ADMINISTRATION button to open the administration window for the system.
5. The window which opens in the center of the SAP HANA Studio interface contains all the tools you need for basic administration tasks (see Figure 8.156).

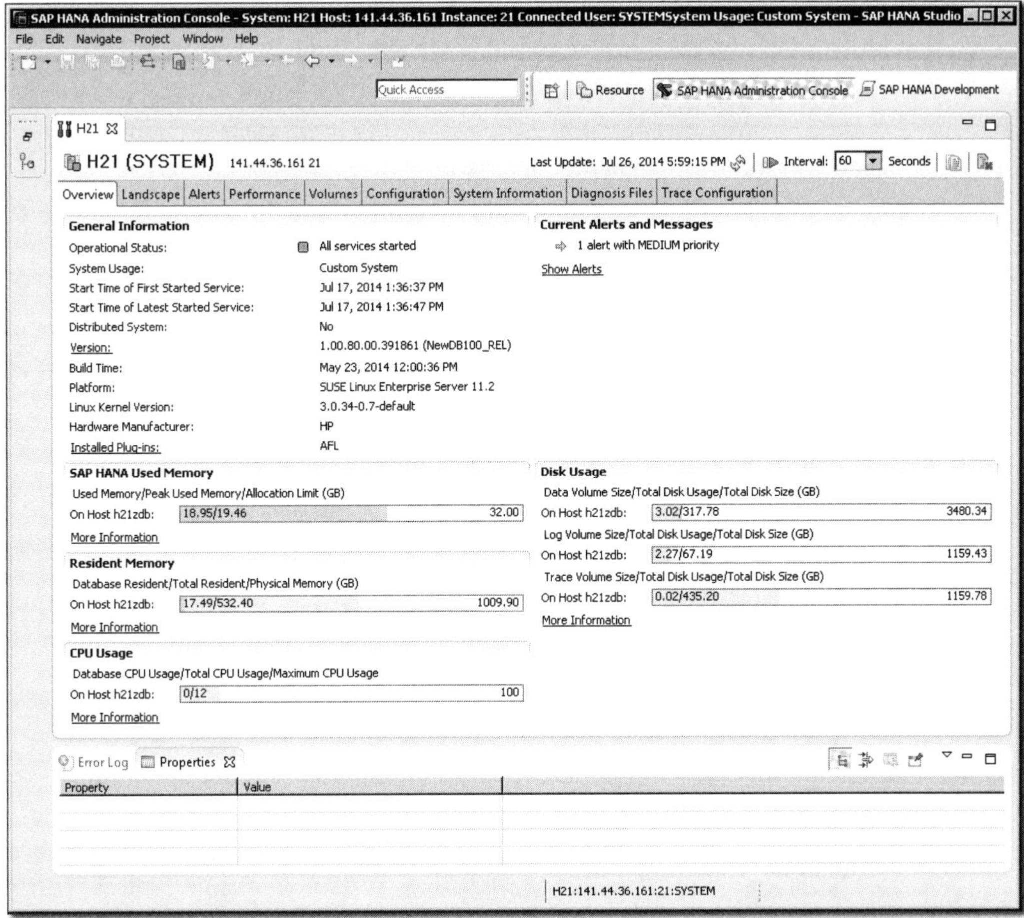

Figure 8.156 Administration Overview in SAP HANA Studio – Overview Tab

Functions of the User Interface

The upper part of the administration window comprises new tabs that you require for different tasks:

- OVERVIEW
  Provides a quick overview of the database status, including the utilization of the memory, processor, and hard disk memory. In the top-right corner, you can view an overview of current alerts and warnings.

- LANDSCAPE
  Provides information on the system landscape's state (see Figure 8.157).

  The tab is subdivided into four additional tabs. For single-node systems without replication, only the first tab (SERVICES) is interesting for administrators because it informs them about the state and utilization of the various database processes. The two tabs HOSTS and REDISTRIBUTION in the middle identify and monitor the running services and optimize data distribution in case of distributed SAP HANA databases. The last tab SYSTEM REPLICATION is used for monitoring replications.

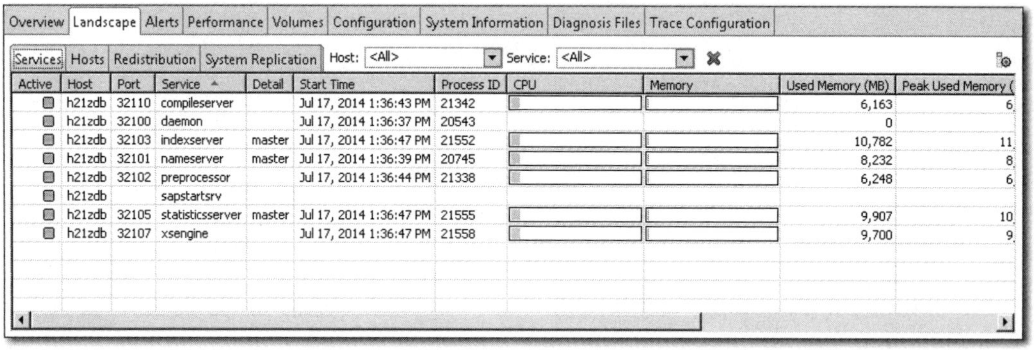

Active	Host	Port	Service	Detail	Start Time	Process ID	CPU	Memory	Used Memory (MB)	Peak Used Memory (
	h21zdb	32110	compileserver		Jul 17, 2014 1:36:43 PM	21342			6,163	6
	h21zdb	32100	daemon		Jul 17, 2014 1:36:37 PM	20543			0	
	h21zdb	32103	indexserver	master	Jul 17, 2014 1:36:47 PM	21552			10,782	11
	h21zdb	32101	nameserver	master	Jul 17, 2014 1:36:39 PM	20745			8,232	8
	h21zdb	32102	preprocessor		Jul 17, 2014 1:36:44 PM	21338			6,248	6
	h21zdb		sapstartsrv							
	h21zdb	32105	statisticsserver	master	Jul 17, 2014 1:36:47 PM	21555			9,907	10
	h21zdb	32107	xsengine		Jul 17, 2014 1:36:47 PM	21558			9,700	9

Figure 8.157 Landscape Tab

- ALERTS
  Displays all current and historic database errors and warnings (see Figure 8.158). By means of the CONFIGURE button, you can configure both the alerts themselves and email notifications for alerts.

- PERFORMANCE
  Displays performance-related properties of the database (see Figure 8.159).

  The subordinate tabs of this tab provide you with comprehensive information on the database: from detailed information of currently running threads (THREADS tab), to active sessions (SESSIONS tab), to creation of load profiles (LOAD tab).

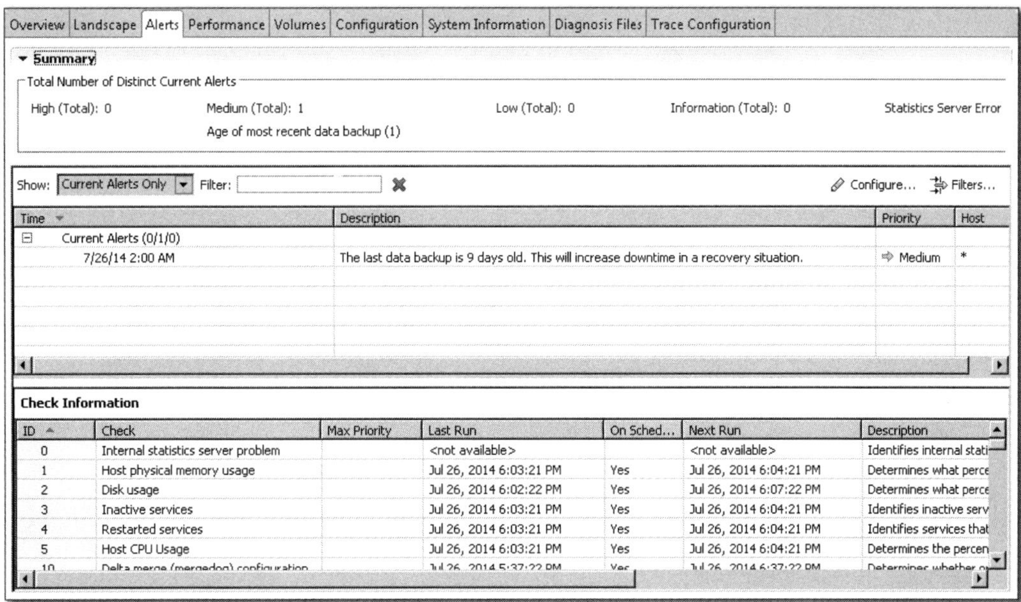

Figure 8.158 Alerts Tab

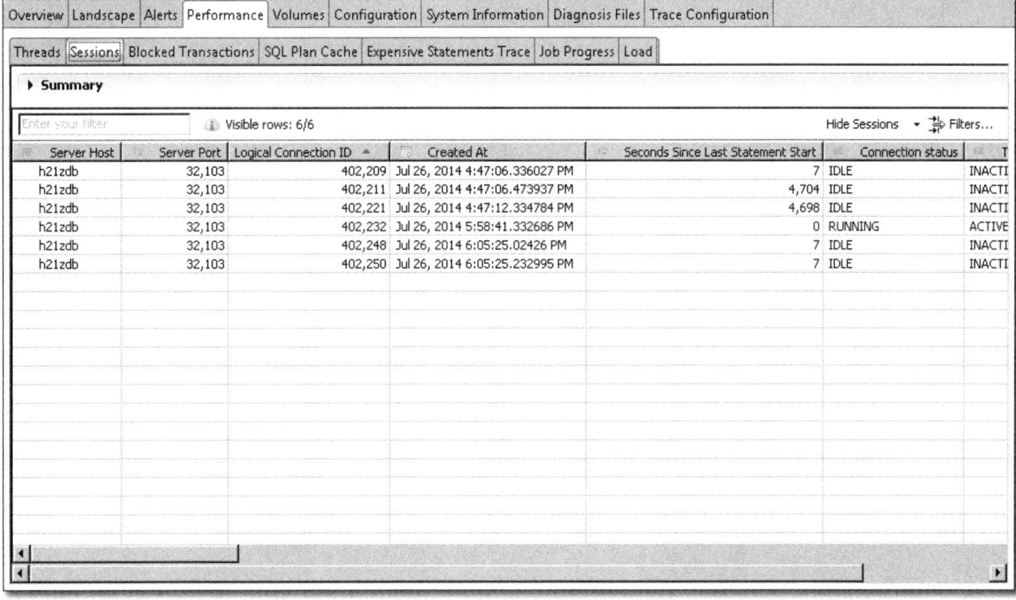

Figure 8.159 Performance Tab

- **VOLUMES**
  Displays the various active files of the database, both data and log files (see Figure 8.160). If you switch from SERVICE mode to STORAGE mode via the dropdown menu SHOW, the details provide more information on the individual written data files.

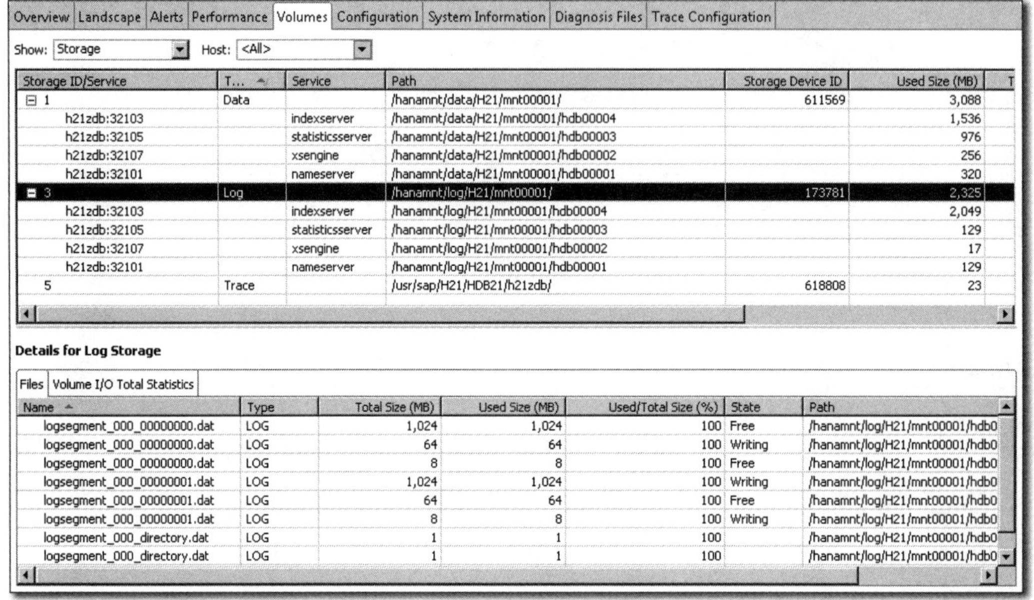

Figure 8.160 Volumes Tab

- **CONFIGURATION**
  Allows you to specify the configuration for the individual components of the various server processes (see Figure 8.161). This tab is one of the most important tabs after the system installation. Note that an incorrect configuration can lead to errors in the database or even a system stop.

- **SYSTEM INFORMATION**
  Displays different information on the SAP HANA system. The options displayed are predefined SQL statements, which you can supplement with your own options (see Figure 8.162).

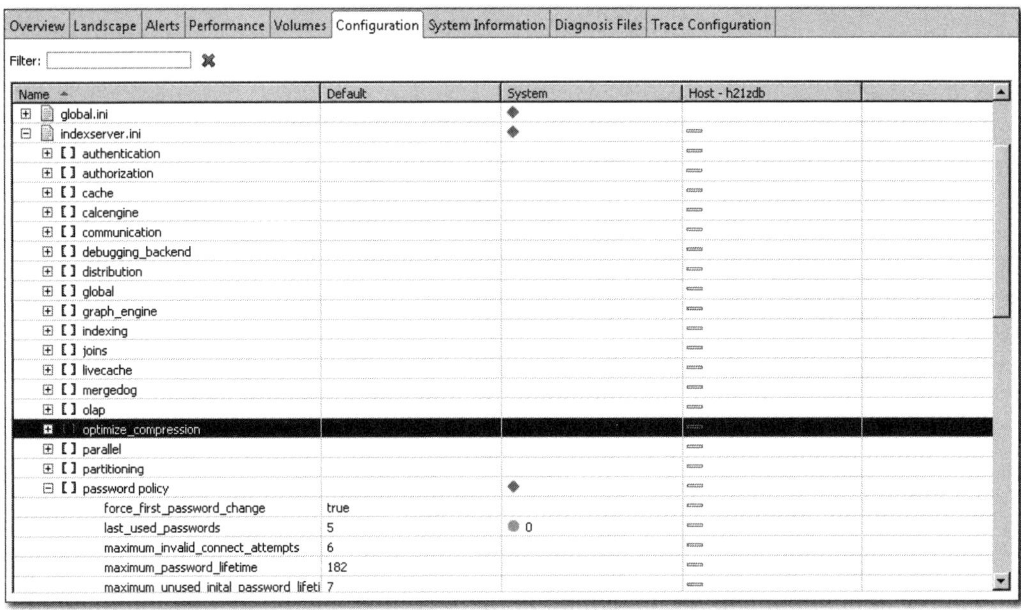

Figure 8.161 Configuration Tab

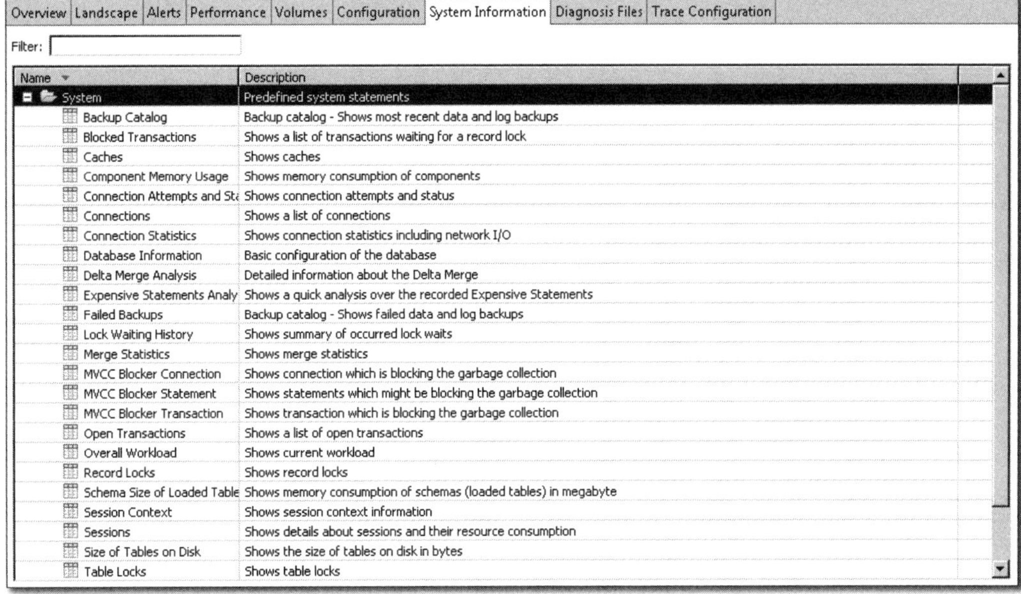

Figure 8.162 System Information Tab

- Diagnosis Files
  Enables you to directly access all log and trace files, which are written by the database, from SAP HANA Studio (see Figure 8.163). The files displayed are located on the server under */hana/shared/<SID>/HDB<number/<host>/trace/*. You should delete the files on a regular basis using the Delete Trace Files button to prevent the directory from overflowing.

Overview | Landscape | Alerts | Performance | Volumes | Configuration | System Information | Diagnosis Files | Trace Configuration

Filter: Host: <All> Merge Diagnosis Files... Delete Trace Files... Diagnosis Information

Host	Name	Type	Size (Byte)	Modified
h21zdb	available.log	Log	648	7/26/14 6:15 PM
h21zdb	nameserver_history.trc	Trace	6,921,368	7/26/14 6:15 PM
h21zdb	scriptserver_h21zdb.32104.000.trc	Trace	10,224	7/26/14 6:11 PM
h21zdb	nameserver_h21zdb.32101.000.trc	Trace	1,018,637	7/26/14 6:11 PM
h21zdb	daemon_h21zdb.32100.000.trc	Trace	580,986	7/26/14 6:11 PM
h21zdb	backup.log	Log	123,838	7/26/14 6:11 PM
h21zdb	hdbdaemon.status		1,136	7/26/14 6:11 PM
h21zdb	indexserver_alert_h21zdb.trc	Trace	20,881	7/25/14 11:11 AM
h21zdb	indexserver_h21zdb.32103.000.trc	Trace	1,002,217	7/25/14 11:11 AM
h21zdb	nameserver_alert_h21zdb.trc	Trace	3,578	7/23/14 12:41 PM
h21zdb	xsengine_h21zdb.32107.000.trc	Trace	1,039,337	7/17/14 3:19 PM
h21zdb	xsengine_alert_h21zdb.trc	Trace	62,517	7/17/14 3:19 PM
h21zdb	statisticsserver_h21zdb.32105.unloads.000.trc	Trace	527,628	7/17/14 1:37 PM
h21zdb	statisticsserver_h21zdb.32105.000.trc	Trace	1,006,467	7/17/14 1:37 PM
h21zdb	icm_port_list		38	7/17/14 1:37 PM
h21zdb	dev_webdisp		5,707	7/17/14 1:37 PM
h21zdb	dev_icm_sec		3,080	7/17/14 1:37 PM
h21zdb	indexserver_h21zdb.32103.unloads.000.trc	Trace	107,934	7/17/14 1:37 PM
h21zdb	preprocessor_h21zdb.32102.000.trc	Trace	18,619	7/17/14 1:36 PM
h21zdb	compileserver_h21zdb.32110.000.trc	Trace	17,373	7/17/14 1:36 PM
h21zdb	sapstart2.trc	Trace	274	7/17/14 1:36 PM
h21zdb	shutdown.sap		14	7/17/14 1:36 PM
h21zdb	dev_sapstart		756	7/17/14 1:36 PM
h21zdb	sapstart.log	Log	2,339	7/17/14 1:36 PM
h21zdb	stderr2		580	7/17/14 1:36 PM
h21zdb	stdout2		0	7/17/14 1:36 PM

Figure 8.163 Diagnosis Files Tab

- Trace Configuration
  Enables you to activate traces for various database components for diagnosis purposes (see Figure 8.164). The Database Trace, User-Specific Trace, and SQL Trace are particularly interesting for administrators. The other trace options are primarily used by the SAP support team.

[+] **Using the Database Trace**

Depending on the configuration, the database trace can write a very high amount of data (multiple megabytes per second). For this reason, make sure to only execute commands in the database or database component that you want to examine and for which you activate the trace. Also make sure to deactivate the trace again after you've completed the commands.

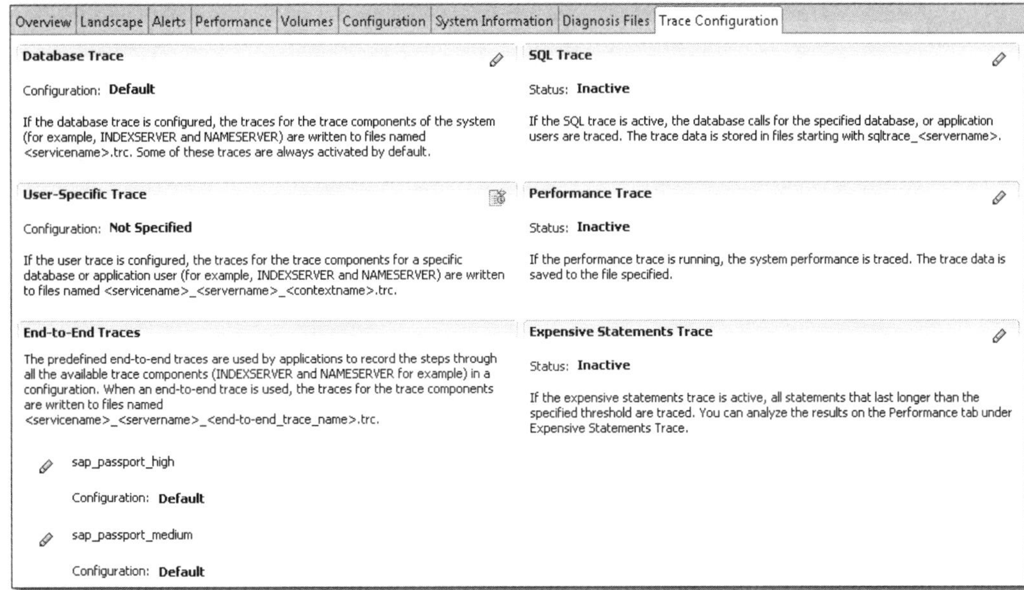

Figure 8.164 Trace Configuration Tab

8.9.3 Starting and Stopping the Database

If necessary, you have various options to start and stop the database via SAP HANA Studio or the command line.

Starting and Stopping via SAP HANA Studio

If you've already installed SAP HANA Studio, you can use it for these tasks.

1. Start SAP HANA Studio, and switch to the ADMINISTRATION CONSOLE perspective (refer to Figure 8.154). Add the SAP HANA system that you want to manage as described in Section 8.9.2.
2. On the SYSTEMS tab, right-click on the system, and choose CONFIGURATION AND MONITORING • STOP SYSTEM in the context menu (see Figure 8.165).

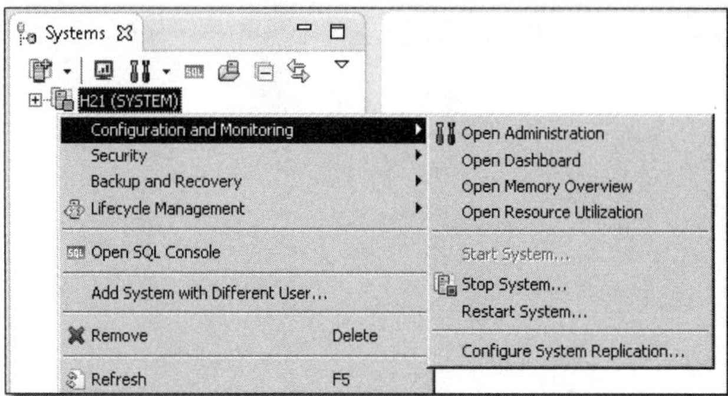

Figure 8.165 Context Menu for Configuring the System

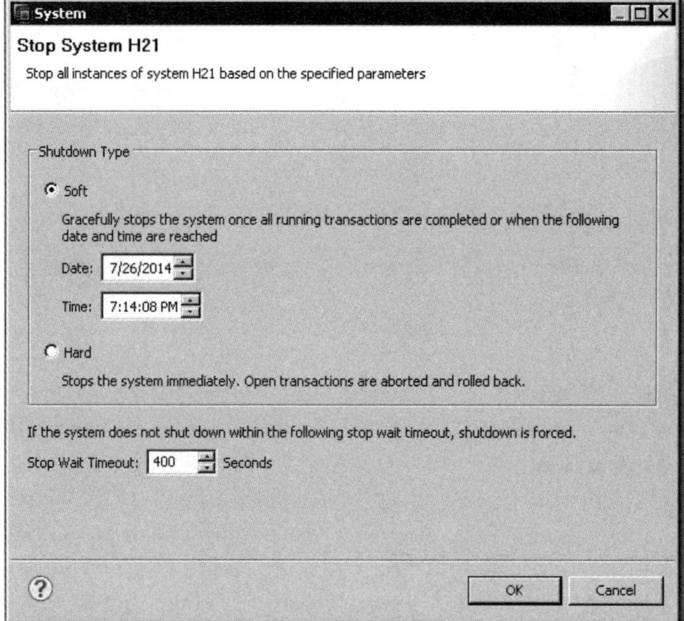

Figure 8.166 System Stop Options

3. A window opens in which you can select from various stop options (SHUTDOWN TYPE; see Figure 8.166):
   - When you choose the SOFT type, the database waits until all open transactions are completed and then shuts down the database. This ensures that the work of users in the database isn't impacted. In the DATE and TIME boxes,

you specify a time at which the last open transactions are canceled at the latest so that the database can be shut down.

- When you choose the HARD type, the database is terminated immediately, and any open transactions are rolled back. This can impact users of the database.

The STOP WAIT TIMEOUT field indicates the time until the database is shut down. If database processes are still running after this time, they are terminated immediately. It isn't recommended to reduce the preset time of 400 seconds because this can result in inconsistencies in the dataset.

4. The database is shut down after you select an option and confirmed it with OK.
5. If you haven't stored the password of the user `<sid>adm` in the password manager of SAP HANA Studio yet, the system prompts you to enter the password (see Figure 8.167).

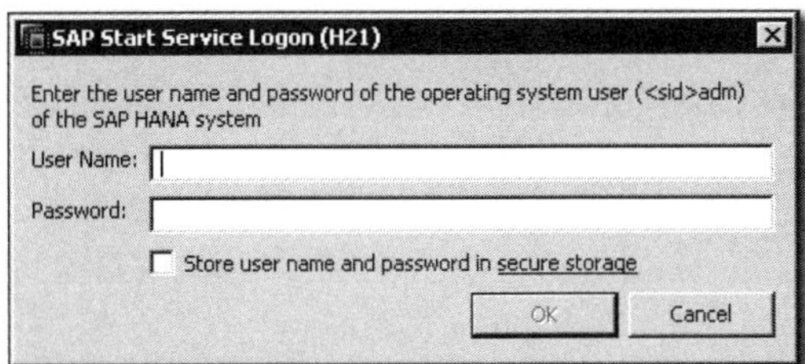

Figure 8.167 Prompt for Entering the Password of <sid>adm

After you've shut down the database, SAP HANA Studio switches to the diagnosis view for the SAP HANA system (see Figure 8.168). Here you can view the current status of the various server processes.

H21 (SYSTEM) 141....1 21 Last Update: Jul 26, 2014 7:09:46 PM Interval: 5 Seconds

Version: 1.00.80.00.391861 (NewDB100_REL)

Processes | Diagnosis Files | Emergency Information

Host: <All>

Active	Host	Process	Description	Process ID	Status	Start Time	Elapsed Time
	h21zdb	hdbcompileserver	HDB Compileserver	21342	Running	Jul 17, 2014 1:36:43 PM	221:32:25
	h21zdb	hdbdaemon	HDB Daemon	20543	Stopping	Jul 17, 2014 1:36:37 PM	221:32:31
	h21zdb	hdbindexserver	HDB Indexserver	21552	Stopping	Jul 17, 2014 1:36:46 PM	221:32:22
	h21zdb	hdbnameserver	HDB Nameserver	20745	Running	Jul 17, 2014 1:36:38 PM	221:32:30
	h21zdb	hdbpreprocessor	HDB Preprocessor	21338	Running	Jul 17, 2014 1:36:43 PM	221:32:25
	h21zdb	hdbscriptserver	HDB Scriptserver		Scheduled		
	h21zdb	hdbstatisticsserver	HDB Statisticsserver	21555	Stopping	Jul 17, 2014 1:36:46 PM	221:32:22
	h21zdb	hdbxsengine	HDB XSEngine		Scheduled		
	h21zdb	sapwebdisp_hdb	SAP WebDispatcher		Scheduled		

Figure 8.168 Diagnosis View of the SAP HANA System During Shutdown

To start a stopped database, again right-click on the database on the SYSTEMS tab in SAP HANA Studio, and choose CONFIGURATION AND MONITORING • START SYSTEM in the context menu.

A window opens in which you can specify the wait time until all processes are started (see Figure 8.169). If all processes haven't been started after the time specified, the start process is canceled.

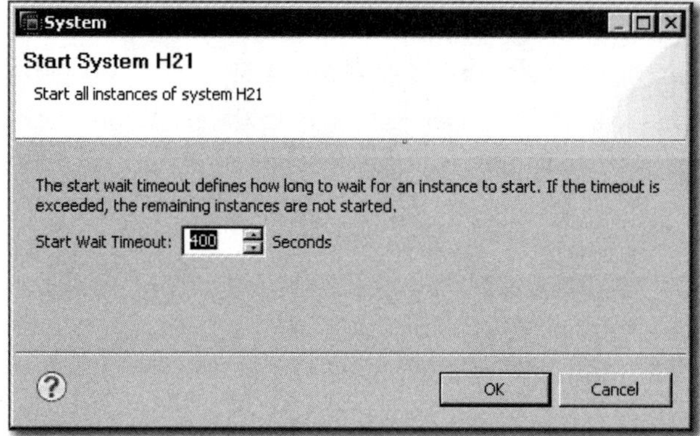

Figure 8.169 Timer Dialog before System Start

Starting and Stopping via the Command Line

You can also start and stop the database via the command line. To do this, use the user `<sid>adm` in the command line to log on to the server on which the SAP HANA database is running. For standard installations, the console switches to the */usr/sap/<SID>/HDB<number>/* directory after you've logged on with `<sid>adm`. This system directory of the SAP HANA system includes the `HDB` script with which you can start, stop, and restart the database.

Execute the command `./HDB start` to start the database. With the command `./HDB stop`, you can stop the database. Using the `./HDB -?` command, you can view all options of the script.

In case of an emergency, you can perform a hard stop with the `./HDB kill` command. As a result, the script executes the command `kill -9 <PID>` for each database process. However, we explicitly advise against using this command because it can result in loss of data and inconsistencies.

8.9.4 Database Monitoring

You have various options to monitor an SAP HANA database with standard SAP tools. The fastest way to get an overview of the SAP HANA system status is to use the diagnosis views of SAP HANA Studio. As described in Section 8.9.2, the LANDSCAPE, ALERTS, PERFORMANCE, VOLUMES, and SYSTEM INFORMATION tabs provide a good general overview of the database. This section now details how you can configure automatic email dispatch for alerts and display an overview of resource consumption of the SAP HANA database.

To configure the dispatch of emails for alerts, follow these steps:

1. Open the ADMINISTRATION view, and go to the ALERTS tab.
2. Click on the CONFIGURE button in the top-right corner (refer to Figure 8.158).
3. Three tabs are available in the window that opens. On the first tab—CONFIGURE E-MAIL FUNCTIONS—you can configure the email dispatch (see Figure 8.170).

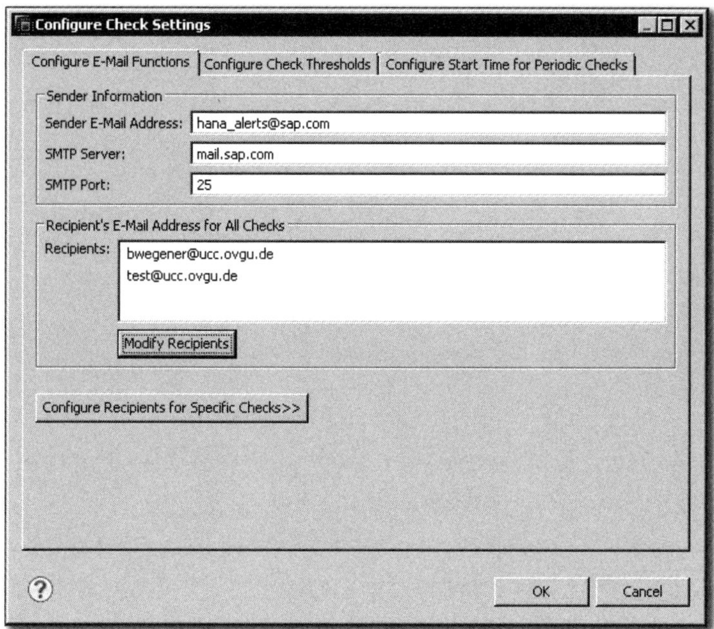

Figure 8.170 Email Configuration for SAP HANA Alerts

Enter an existing sender address in the SENDER E-MAIL ADDRESS field as well as the SMTP outgoing mail server in the SMTP SERVER field. If the email server doesn't use the default port, change it. Use the MODIFY RECIPIENTS or CONFIGURE RECIPIENTS FOR SPECIFIC CHECKS buttons to add email recipients for all or specific alerts. The emails are sent for any alert change.

4. You can adapt the threshold values for the various system alerts on the CONFIGURE CHECK THRESHOLDS tab (see Figure 8.171). Click on a threshold value to change it. In our example, the existing threshold values are very good and don't need to be changed necessarily.

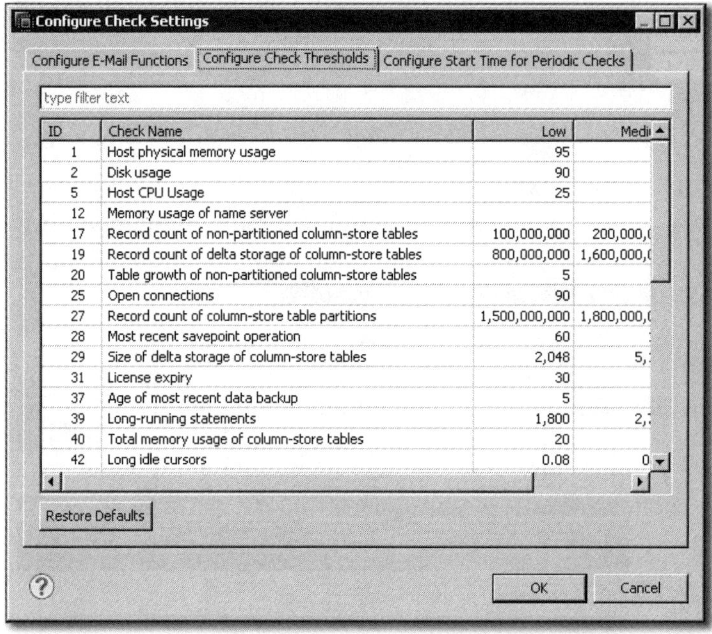

Figure 8.171 Threshold Value Configuration for SAP HANA Alerts

5. On the CONFIGURE START TIME FOR PERIODIC CHECKS tab, you can change the start time for checks with a 6-hour or 24-hour interval.

6. To get a complete overview of the current resource allocation of the system, you can use two views: MEMORY OVERVIEW and RESOURCE UTILIZATION. To be able to use them, you require the additional role `sap.hana.admin.roles::Monitoring` (also as user `SYSTEM`). You can assign the role to a user in an SQL editor. Open the SQL editor by selecting your SAP HANA database in the SYSTEMS window and clicking on the SQL EDITOR button. Enter the following command, and click on EXECUTE (see Figure 8.172):

```
CALL _SYS_REPO.GRANT_ACTIVATED_ROLE ('sap.hana.admin.roles::
Monitoring','SYSTEM')
```

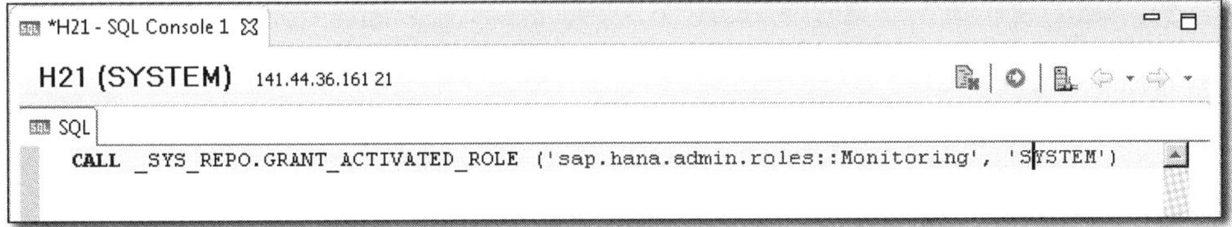

Figure 8.172 Role Assignment in the SQL Editor

You can now access the two additional views. To open them, right-click on your SAP HANA system in the SYSTEMS tab, and choose CONFIGURATION AND MONITORING • OPEN MEMORY OVERVIEW or OPEN RESOURCE UTILIZATION in the context menu.

The MEMORY OVERVIEW provides an overview of the database's and host's memory consumption as well as the distribution of the memory consumption (see Figure 8.173).

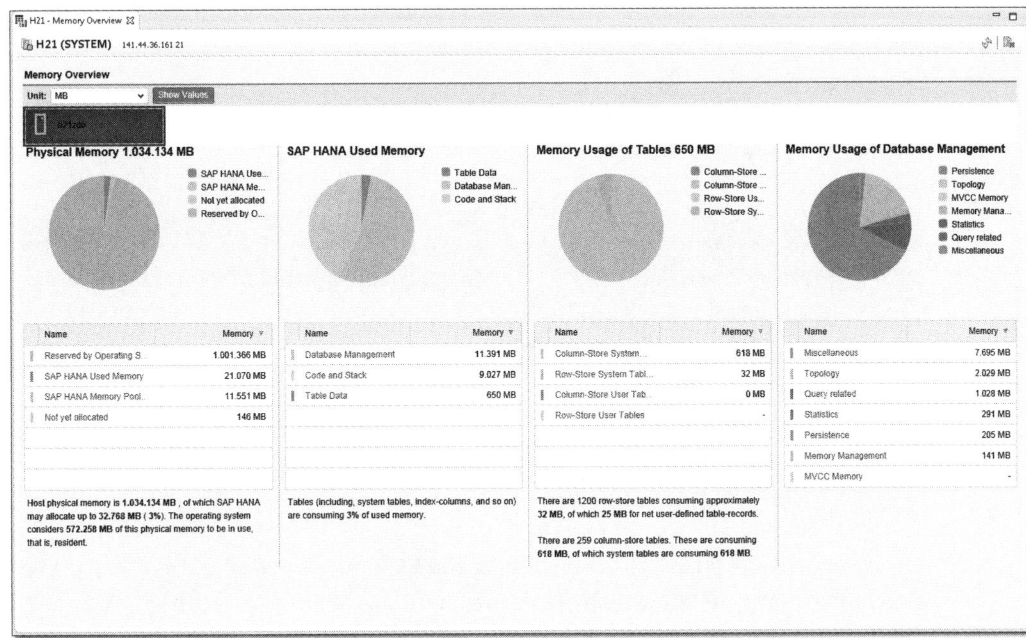

Figure 8.173 Memory Overview View

The RESOURCE UTILIZATION view, in contrast, provides an overview of many additional resources that are available on the host, for instance, CPU utilization and fill level of the log area (see Figure 8.174).

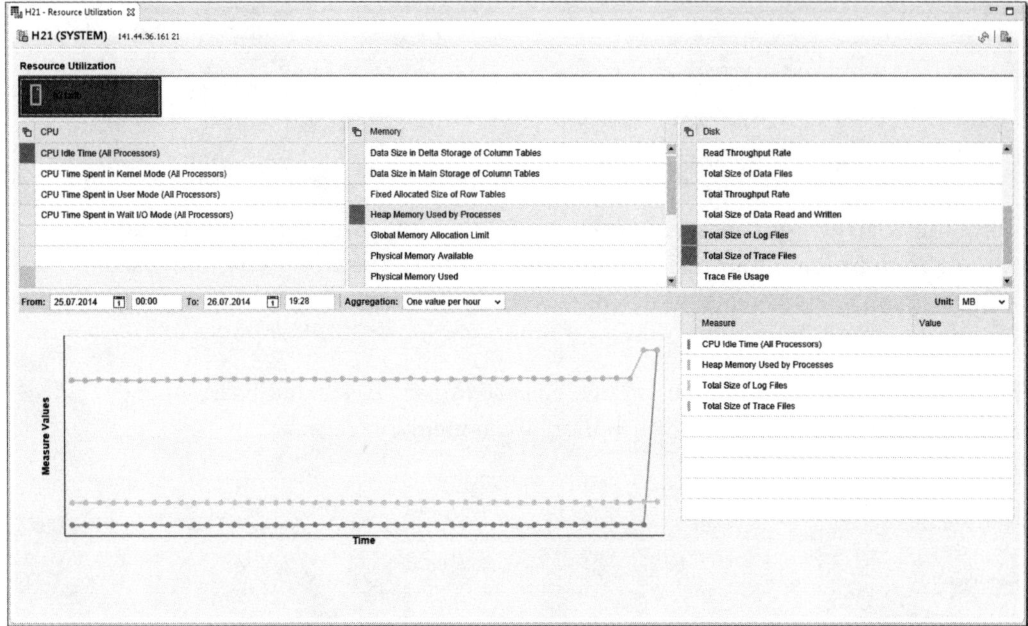

Figure 8.174 Resource Utilization View

[+]

Monitoring of Databases in Live Operation

For live operation of databases, we recommend adapting the monitoring configuration to the operation requirements and integrating them with a comprehensive monitoring system such as SAP Solution Manager.

If you want to set up very detailed monitoring of the SAP HANA system, you can also use SAP Solution Manager, which supports SAP HANA as of release 7.1 SPS 5. A prerequisite for monitoring the database using SAP Solution Manager is to install and configure the SAP host agent, configure the SAP diagnostic agent, and to register the system in the System Landscape Directory (SLD). A complete and detailed list of requirements as well as a setup guide is available at *http://wiki.scn.sap.com/wiki/display/SMSETUP/Managed+System+Setup+of+HANA+in+Solution+Manager+7.1*.

8.9.5 Configuring the Database Backup

SAP HANA provides two options for data backup. The first option is to back up data and logs on a hard disk. This type of backup can be set up quickly. However, you must also run a downstream backup of these files (e.g., by backing up the files in a backup library). The second option is the *backint interface*. The advantage of this option is that many backup programs such as HP Data Protector or IBM Tivoli Storage Manager can communicate directly with this interface, and a backup can thus be planed, performed, and restored using backup software. A list of certified backup programs is available in SAP Note 1730932. This section only describes the backup in files.

Backup Configuration [+]

The correct configuration of the backup tool is just as important as the configuration of the backup in the database. Moreover, you should pay attention to the backup scheduling and the integration with monitoring.

Like the other topics discussed in this section, you can configure the database backup via SAP HANA Studio:

1. Open SAP HANA Studio, switch to the ADMINISTRATION CONSOLE perspective, and add the SAP HANA system that you want to manage (see Section 8.9.2).
2. Expand the system, and double-click on the BACKUP node. The backup configuration and administration opens in the main window (see Figure 8.175).

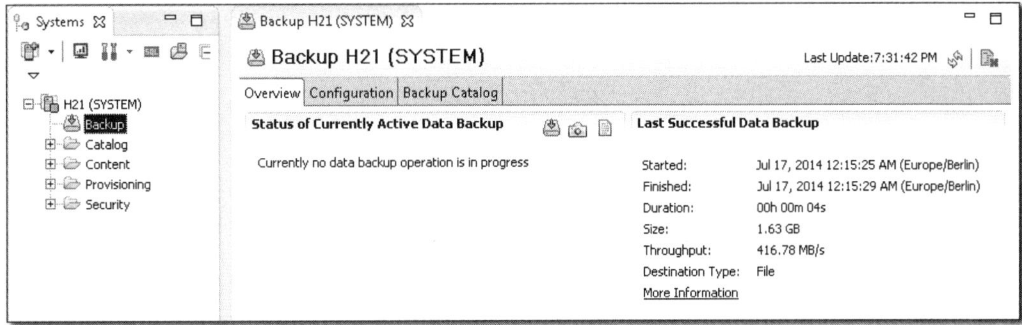

Figure 8.175 Backup Overview

3. On the OVERVIEW tab, you can view the status of running backups and the return code of the last backup.

4. For file-based backups, the CONFIGURATION tab is split into two parts: FILE-BASED DATA BACKUP SETTING and LOG BACKUP SETTINGS (see Figure 8.176).

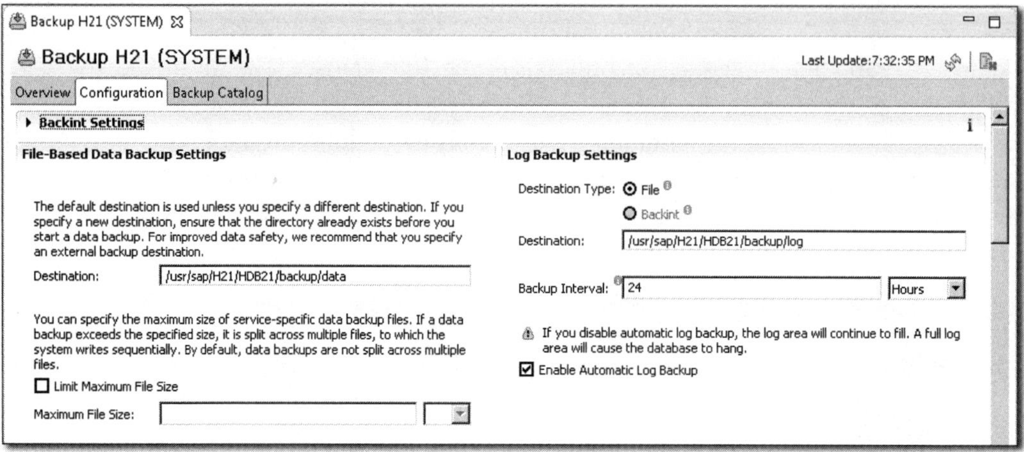

Figure 8.176 Tab for Backup Configuration

The *data backups* describe full database backups; in other words, via data backups, you can restore the status of the database at the time of the backup. When you configure the data backups, you can specify the location of the backup files. We recommend selecting a directory whose physical memory is outside the actual SAP HANA server, for example, a network file system (NFS) share, or subsequently backing up the files that you backed up on the physical SAP HANA server on an external medium.

In addition, you can restrict the maximum size of the backup files. SAP HANA writes exactly one file for each of the main server processes if no limit is set.

You can also define a target path for the backup of the *log files*, that is, the changes to the database. You can also specify after which period of time a log backup is to be written definitely, even if the active log file isn't full yet. You thus ensure that a database status with less activity can be restored. If no full database backup has been done yet, no archive logs are written.

[!]

Automatic Log Backups

Only in exceptional cases does it make sense to deactivate the ENABLE AUTOMATIC LOG BACKUP flag. If the log files aren't backed up, the normal log area of the SAP HANA database is filled until the database stops.

On the BACKUP CATALOG tab, you can view a list of all backups that were implemented on the database and their return values (see Figure 8.177).

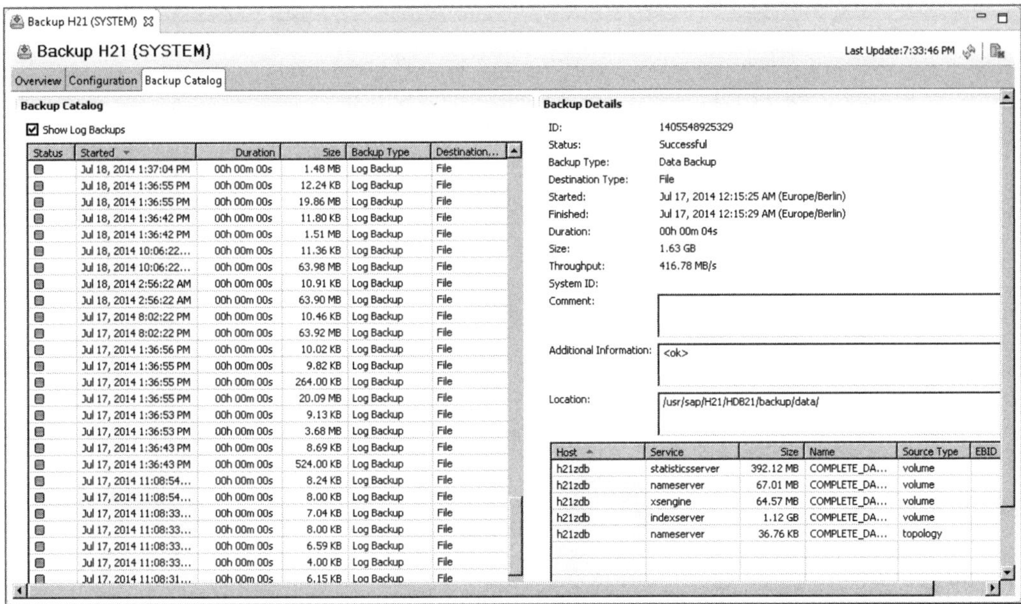

Figure 8.177 Backup Catalog

8.9.6 Backing Up the Database

To run a full backup of the database, follow these steps:

1. Open SAP HANA Studio. Switch to the ADMINISTRATION CONSOLE perspective, and add the SAP HANA system of which you want to create a backup.
2. In the SYSTEMS window, right-click on the SAP HANA system, and choose BACKUP AND RECOVERY • BACK UP SYSTEM.
3. A window is displayed in which you select the destination of the backup (the default destination is entered here) and the backup prefix (see Figure 8.178). The prefix is part of the file name of the backup files, and you should select a prefix that allows for easy identification of the backups later on.

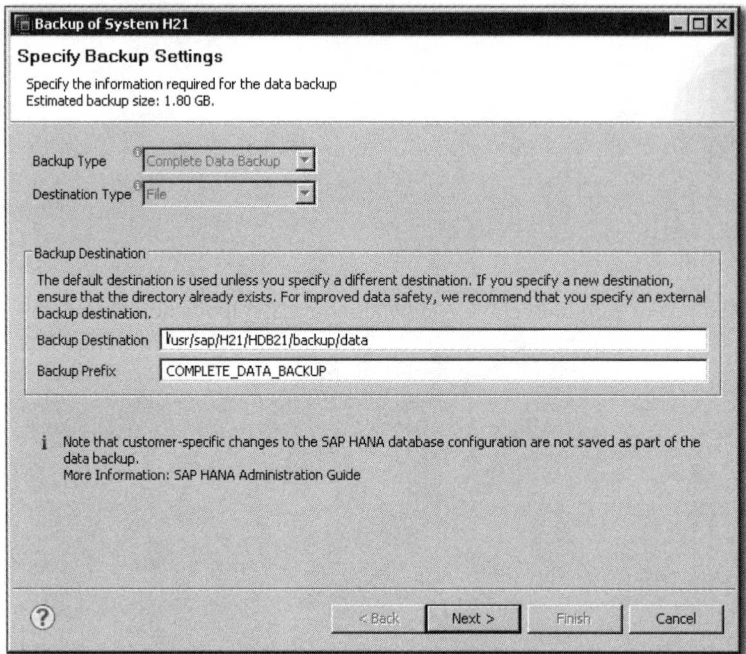

Figure 8.178 Backup Settings

[!]

Backing Up the Database Configuration

The backup mechanism described here doesn't back up the configuration of the database. The **.ini* files of the following directories must be backed up separately:

- */usr/sap/<sid>/SYS/global/hdb/custom/config*
- */usr/sap/<sid>/HDB<instance number>/<hostname>*

4. After you click on NEXT, you can check your settings once again. The backup is started as soon as you click on START.
5. After the backup is complete, the system displays an overview of the actions performed (see Figure 8.179).

[!]

Strategy for Backing Up Databases

The backup of databases and the strategies required for this go far beyond the processes described in this section. If you want to back up live SAP systems, we recommend additional training geared toward your database.

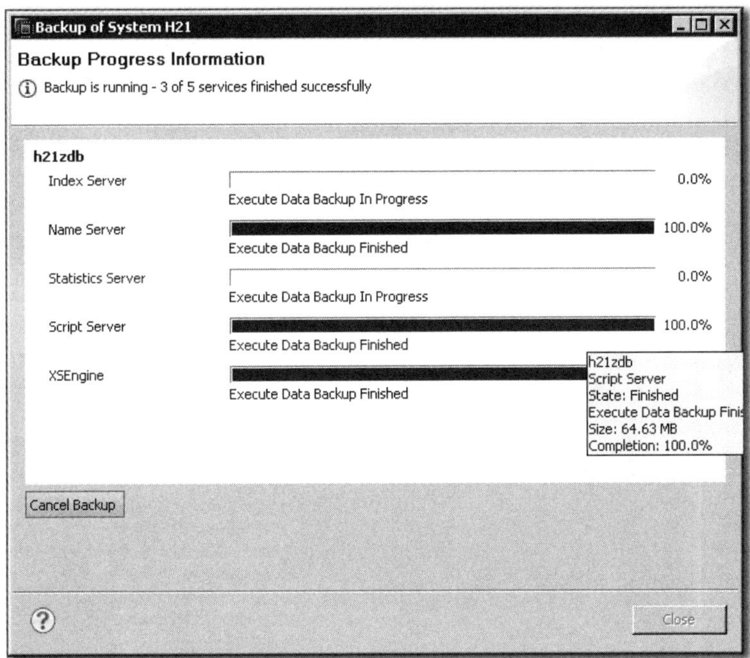

Figure 8.179 Backup Overview

8.9.7 Restoring the Database

If you performed a full backup of the database, you can restore the database using this full backup and (optionally) the archive logs. You start a restore as follows:

1. Open SAP HANA Studio. Switch to the ADMINISTRATION CONSOLE perspective, and right-click on the system that you want to restore. Choose BACKUP AND RECOVERY • RECOVER SYSTEM in the context menu.
2. If the database is still running, the system informs you that the database must be shut down (see Figure 8.180).

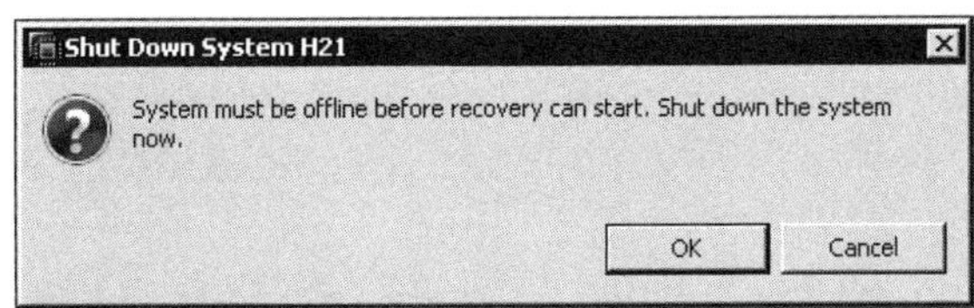

Figure 8.180 Shutdown Dialog before Restore

3. You're provided with various options as soon as the database is stopped (see Figure 8.181). With the RECOVER THE DATABASE TO ITS MOST RECENT STATE and RECOVER THE DATABASE TO THE FOLLOWING POINT IN TIME options, a full backup, and the backup of the subsequently written log files, you can restore the most recent state of the database or the state at a specific point in time.

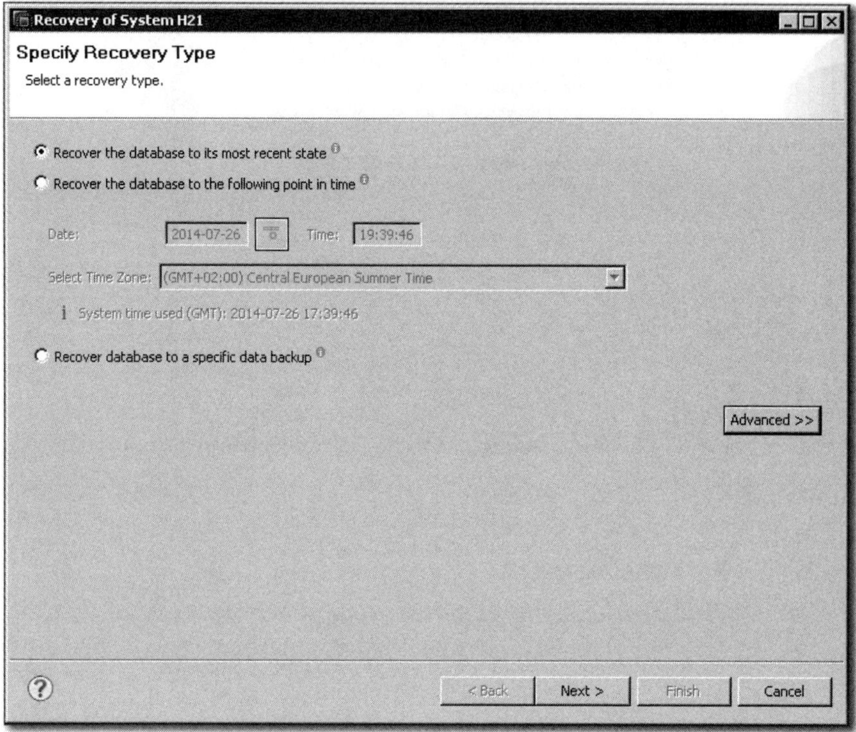

Figure 8.181 Different Restore Options

4. If you choose the third option—RECOVER DATABASE TO A SPECIFIC DATA BACKUP—and click on NEXT, you can restore the state of the database that you backed up with your full backup.

5. Via the DESTINATION TYPE dropdown menu, you can choose the source from which you want to start the recovery (backup from file or backup from the backint interface, see Figure 8.182). Under the path that you specify for LOCATION, the system searches for the backup with the name defined under BACKUP PREFIX.

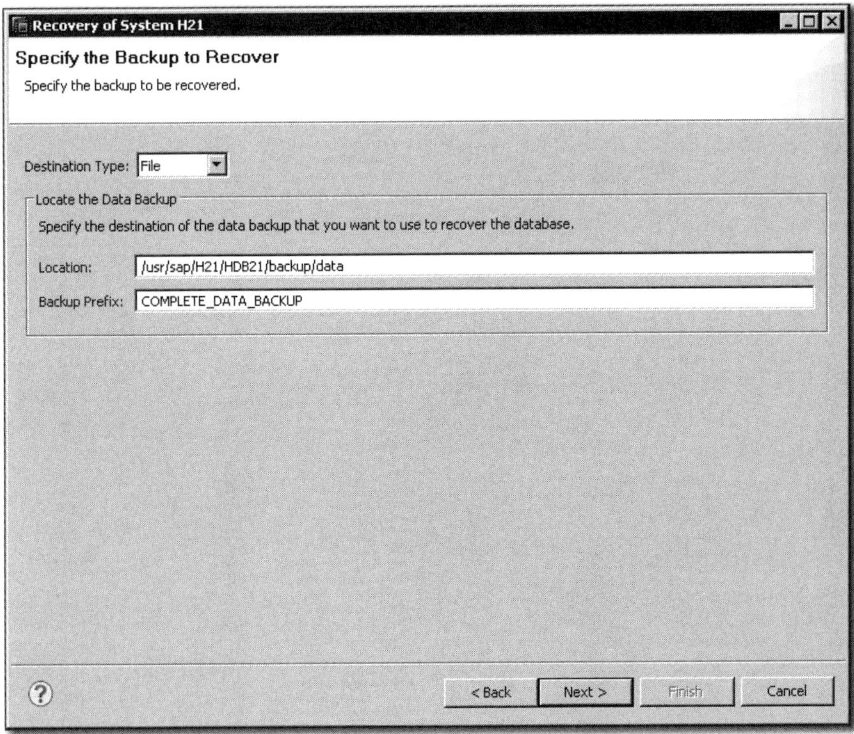

Figure 8.182 Selecting the Location and Prefix of the Backup to Be Restored

[+]

Backup/Restore as a System Copy

You can also use the backup and restore mechanisms of SAP HANA to make system copies. Note, however, that you must adapt the configuration of the target database to the source database before the restore.

6. In the next step, you can enter a new license key if the backup to be recovered originates from a different database (see Figure 8.183). If you don't import a new license, and the backup originates from a different database, the system is locked until licensing is correct.
7. In the last step before the recovery, you're provided with a summary of steps to be performed.

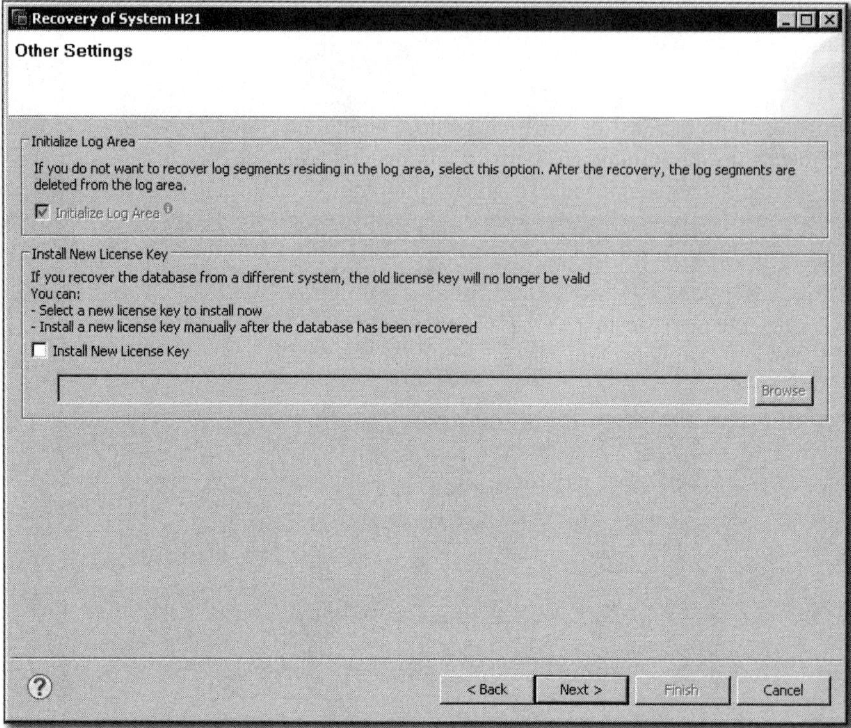

Figure 8.183 Importing a New License Key after a Recovery

The database is started after you've recovered it.

[!]

Database Recovery

Note that the recovery of databases isn't trivial and should only be made by trained experts. The processes described in this section only form the basis of measures that must be taken for a system recovery.

[+]

Additional Information

The tasks described in this chapter only described a small part of SAP HANA system administration. If you want to perform tasks on this database on a regular basis or deepen your knowledge in this area, you should consult specialist literature, for example, *SAP HANA Administration* by Richard Bremer and Lars Breddemann (SAP PRESS, 2014). Additional information on SAP HANA is also available in the *SAP HANA Administration Guide* (*http://help.sap.com/hana/SAP_HANA_Administration_Guide_en.pdf*) and at *www.saphana.com*.

8.10 Summary

Database administration isn't solely the task of an SAP system administrator. Consequently, this chapter describes only general concepts and SAP tools that can be used irrespective of the database system. The database-specific sections in this chapter provide a brief introduction to the special idiosyncrasies of various database systems. If you're entrusted with the task of managing a database, you should read additional specialist literature to prepare yourself sufficiently for this complex task.

This chapter describes the use of SAP transactions for calling operating system information—irrespective of the platform. It also explains the most important aspects of operating system monitoring.

9 Operating System Administration

The tasks that this chapter describes are usually carried out by data center employees. Depending on the size and structure of an enterprise, SAP administrators may be responsible for server administration at the operating system level. Consequently, they need to know the scope of the monitoring process for the operating system and which SAP transaction can be used.

Like any other program, an SAP system runs on an operating system (e.g., Microsoft Windows Server 2012 R2 or UNIX). The operating system manages the hardware of the physical or virtualized server and provides resources (i.e., memory, processor time, and hard disk memory) for the SAP software. If these resources become scarce, this usually affects the performance and functioning of the SAP system; in a worst-case scenario, this can result in system downtime.

9.1 Checking the Memory Usage of the File System

The operating system's file system must have sufficient memory for the operation of the SAP system. When tasks are carried out, the system sometimes creates files that occupy memory. If no hard disk memory is available, the database can't write to a file.

This may lead to downtime and thus to a breakdown of the SAP system. Consequently, monitoring the memory is one of the most important tasks at the operating system level. Files that are stored in the file system need to be checked from time to time and then may have to be moved, archived, or deleted.

The following objects occupy a large amount of memory, so you need to observe them carefully when monitoring the memory:

- Transport requests
- Support packages
- Extract files from the SAP system
- Program logs
- Backup logs
- Error logs
- Inbound interface files
- Third-party programs that store data outside the SAP database
- Trace files
- Spool files

To prevent the file system from overflowing, you should observe the following:

- Plan future memory on the disk.
- Determine whether the memory needs to be extended. If this is the case, you must plan the procurement and installation of additional memory elements. Interruptions of the normal business operation should be kept to a minimum.
- Determine whether the file system needs to be cleaned. If files have to be archived, use high-quality storage media only, for example, backup tapes or other long-term storage media. Avoid optical media such as CD-ROMs or DVDs.
- You must also check whether the standard cleanup jobs run properly (see SAP Note 16083).

You can check the memory usage using the standard tools of the operating system (e.g., Explorer in Windows) or with a monitoring tool. This can be third-party software, the SAP system's CCMS Alert Monitor, or the technical monitoring of SAP Solution Manager.

9.1.1 Monitoring the File System Using the CCMS Alert Monitor

Chapter 3 already introduced the CCMS Alert Monitor, which you can use to monitor the memory during the operating system administration. The following example briefly describes the procedure again:

1. Enter Transaction RZ20 in the command box and press the Enter key (or select TOOLS • CCMS • CONTROL/MONITORING • RZ20—CCMS MONITOR SETS).
2. Expand the SAP CCMS MONITOR TEMPLATES monitor set, and position the cursor on the FILESYSTEMS monitor (see Figure 9.1). Start the monitor by clicking the LOAD MONITOR icon.

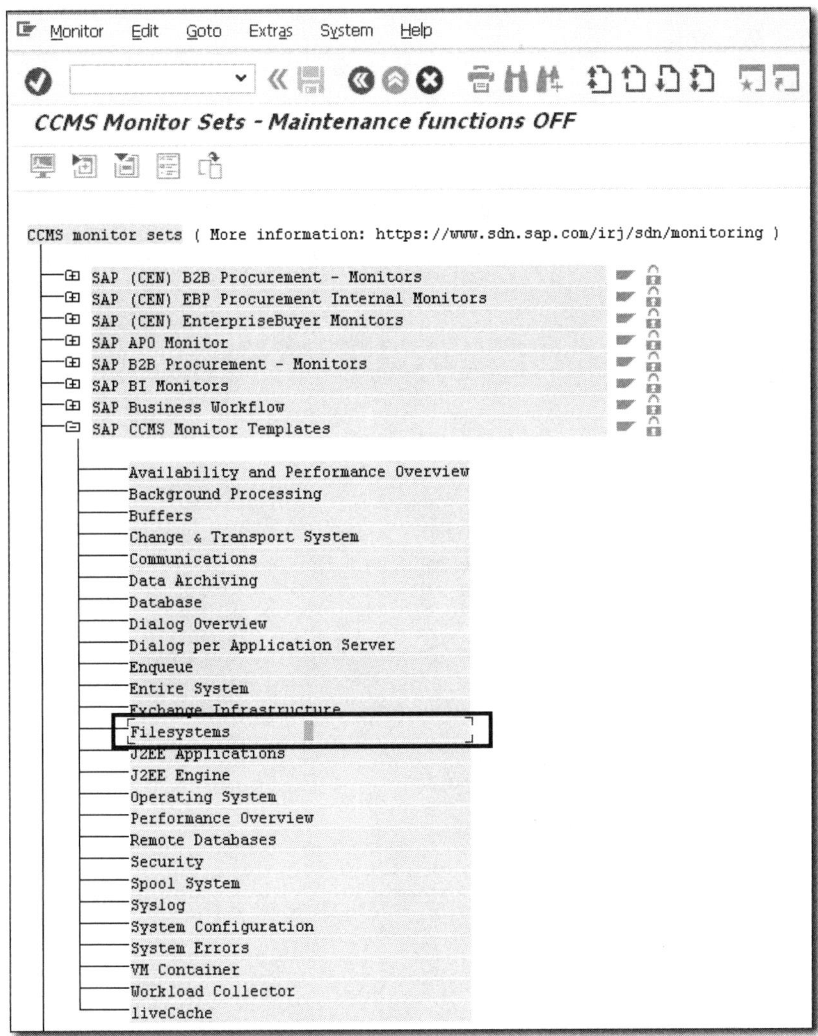

Figure 9.1 Starting the CCMS Alert Monitor

3. The system displays the data that is determined by the CCMS Alert Monitor in a tree structure, which depends on the structure of your file systems (see Figure 9.2). Expand a node to view the alert values (e.g., FREESPACE and PERCENTAGE_USED). The alert values are highlighted, and the color specifies the respective alert status:
   - Green: Okay
   - Yellow: Warning
   - Red: Critical

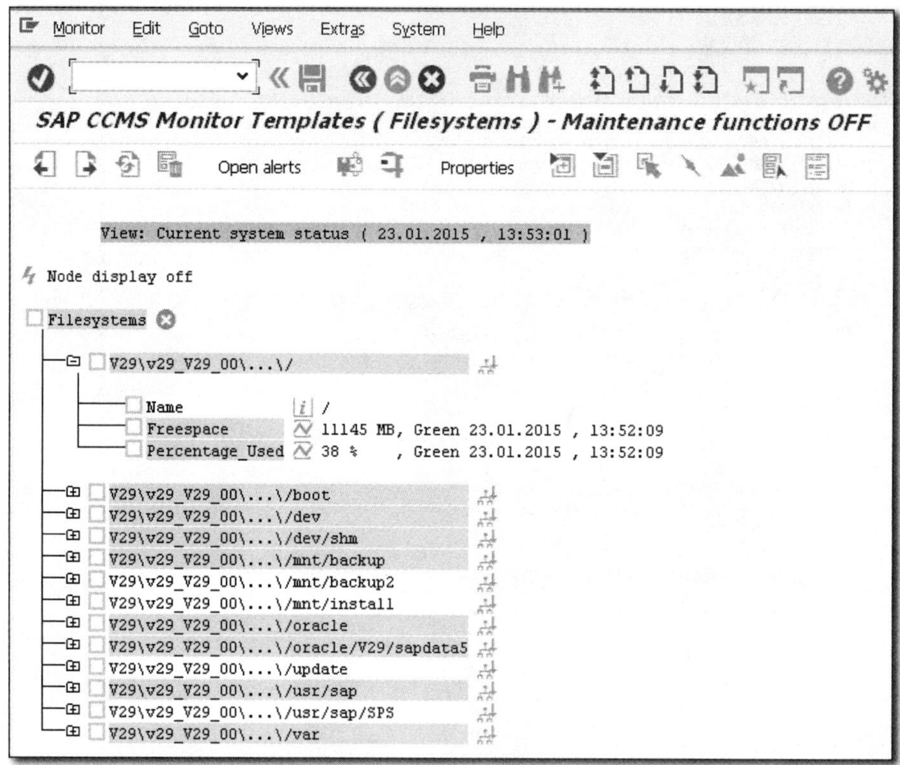

Figure 9.2 Evaluating the CCMS Alert Monitor

This enables you to determine the file system's current memory situation and assess the need for action regarding the available memory.

9.1.2 Changing Alert Thresholds

You can configure the CCMS monitor according to your individual requirements to be informed adequately in case of potential memory problems. For this purpose, customize the thresholds for the CCMS alert status display:

1. Expand the node of the drive for which you want to change the threshold, and select an alert (e.g., Freespace in Figure 9.3). Click on Properties.

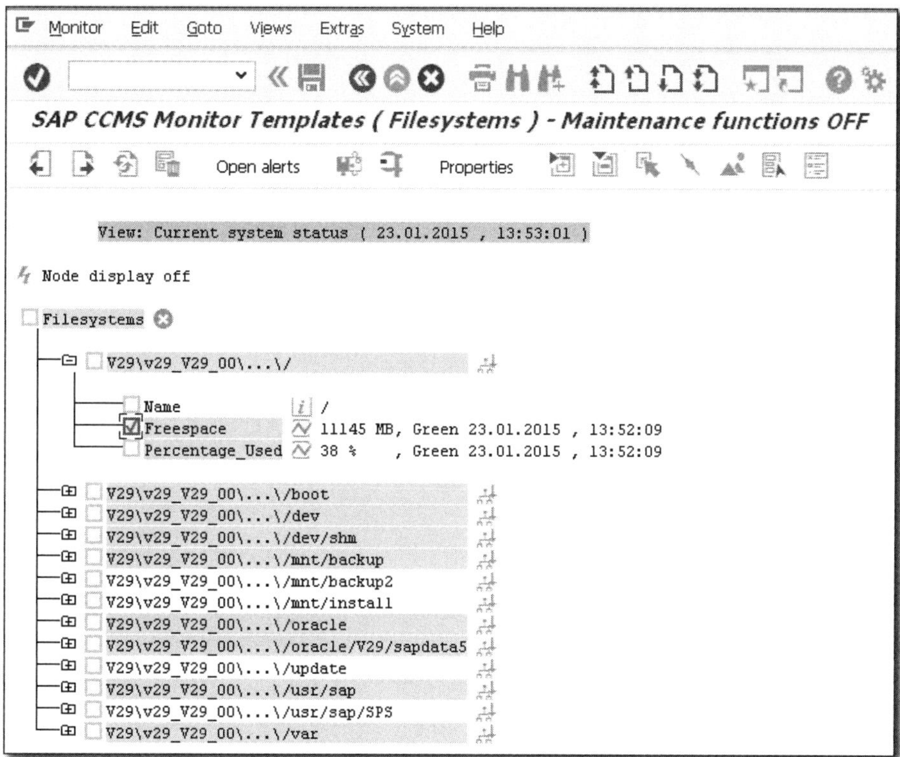

Figure 9.3 Selecting the Monitor Value

2. To change the thresholds, use Display <-> Change to switch to change mode. Enter the desired thresholds for which the status is supposed to change (see Figure 9.4).

For more information on alert thresholds, refer to Chapter 3, which also describes how you can have the system inform you when thresholds are exceeded.

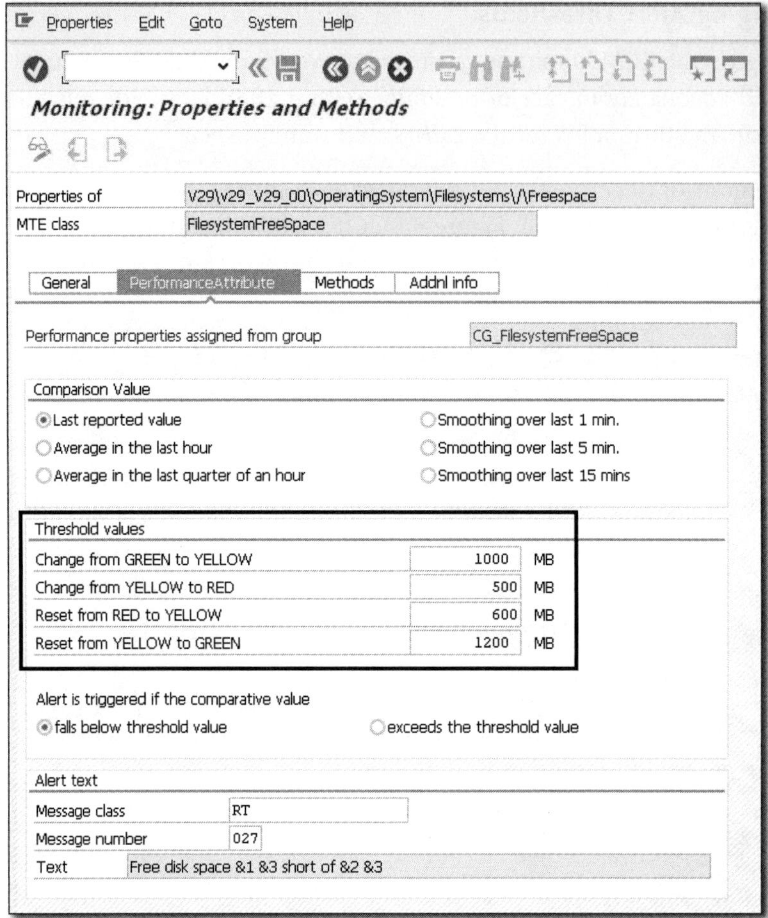

Figure 9.4 Changing the Threshold Value

9.1.3 Releasing Memory at the Operating System Level

When you encounter memory problems at the operating system level, and you can't add additional memory space, you have to check where files can be deleted. This section names directories and file categories to be considered in such a situation.

Deleting Trace Files

Trace files log the processes and actions of the SAP system's work processes. Every work process has its own file. These trace files are stored at the operating system level and can increase enormously during operation. That's reason enough to check them when memory problems occur:

1. Check the */usr/sap/<SID>/<instance>/work* directory:
   - *dev_rfc<number>[.old]* (RFC trace)
   - *dev_w<number>[.old]* (work process trace)
2. Sort the directory by size to determine the distribution of the memory usage. If the trace files have become very large (i.e., greater than 100MB), you should first save and then delete them. This way, you release free memory at the operating system level.
3. Call Transaction SM50 (Process Overview).
4. To save the trace files before deleting them, select the corresponding work process, and then choose ADMINISTRATION • TRACE • SAVE AS LOCAL FILE (see Figure 9.5). The system asks for a file path under which you want to store the copy of the trace file.
5. Delete the trace file via ADMINISTRATION • TRACE • RESET • WORK PROCESS FILES.
6. Confirm the deletion in the dialog box with YES (see Figure 9.6).

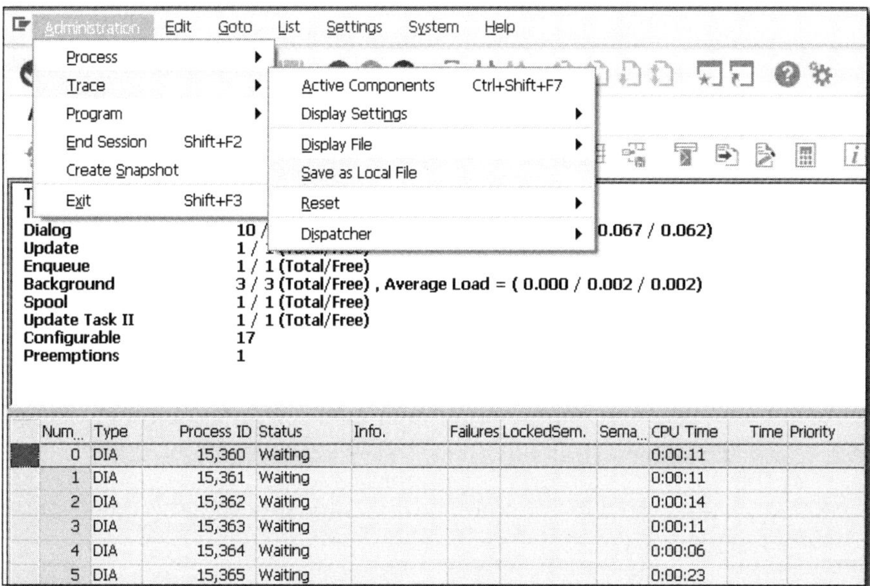

Figure 9.5 Saving the Trace Files Locally

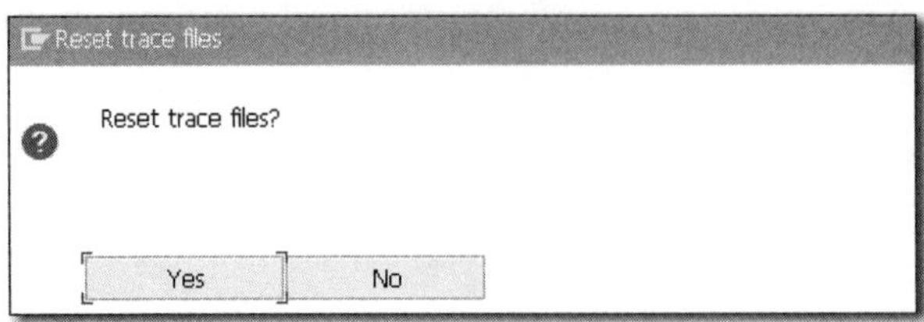

Figure 9.6 Reset Confirmation

7. Return to the */usr/sap/<SID>/<instance>/work* directory at the operating system level, and manually delete the files with the *.old* extension after having saved them if required.

> **Old Trace Files (.old Extension)**
>
> The system does not write log entries into trace files with the *.old* extension; however, they contain older entries that you may need for troubleshooting.

Deleting Spool Files, Job Logs, and Batch Input Logs

Print or output requests (see Chapter 16), background jobs, and running batch input sessions (see Chapter 15) generate files at the operating system level. The size of these files depends on the scope of the respective request or log. If necessary, check the following directories:

- */usr/sap/<SID>/SYS/global/<client>JOBLG* (job logs)
- */usr/sap/<SID>/SYS/global/<client>SPOOL* (spool requests)
- */usr/sap/<SID>/SYS/global/<client>BDCLG* (batch input sessions)

First, sort the files of the directories by size to identify the objects that occupy a large amount of memory. The creation date or last change date of the files enables you to determine when the output request, job log, or batch input log was created. Furthermore, the file names always refer to the original object in the SAP system, which allows for a clear allocation.

- The job log that is stored in the *<client>JOBLG* directory contains the ID of the job from Transaction SM37 (Job Overview).
- The file name in the *<client>SPOOL* directory ends with the spool number of the spool request in Transaction SP01 (Output Controller).

- The TEMSE ID field of the batch input session logs in Transaction SM35 (Batch Input) contains the file name in the *<client>BDCLG* directory.

If you've detected exceptionally large files at the operating system level, search for the corresponding object in the SAP system. Before deleting files, ask the owner of the print request, job, or session whether they are still required, and archive the files if necessary.

Spool requests, job logs, and batch input logs have an expiry date after which they can be deleted from the SAP system so that the memory at the operating system level is released. The following standard jobs check whether an object has reached its deletion date and, if this is the case, remove it from the database:

- `SAP_REORG_JOBS` (job logs)
- `sap_reorg_spool` (spool requests)
- `SAP_REORG_BATCHINPUT` (batch input logs)

If you determine that older files haven't been reorganized, use Transaction SM37 to check if these *reorganization jobs* are regularly scheduled in your system and completed without errors. If this isn't the case, correct the scheduling of the standard jobs using Transaction SM36.

Deleting Support Package Files

You use support packages or support package stacks to import corrections or enhancements into your SAP system (for more information, see Chapter 18). You download support packages from the SAP Support Portal and usually store them locally on a PC. To update the system, you need to copy the files to the SAP server where they accordingly occupy space in the file system; depending on the type of the SAP system and scope of the update, this can involve several hundred megabytes.

Therefore, check the size of the */usr/sap/trans/EPS/in* directory at the operating system level. When the support packages have been successfully imported to the SAP system, you can remove them from the directory. Usually, you don't need them again at a later stage. If required, create a backup copy.

Deleting Transport Files

Transport files are used to transport SAP objects and Customizing changes or transfer them between clients and systems. If transport files aren't monitored, they can occupy a disproportionally large amount of memory. You should check the transport directory in the following cases:

- After a large implementation for which numerous transports have been generated that occupy a large amount of memory.
- Directly before (or after) a database is copied; if you don't use a central transport directory, most of (or even all) the files with a date that lies before the copy process become useless.

Follow these steps to check the transport directory:

1. Check the following directories under */usr/sap/trans*:
   - *data*
   - *cofiles* (command files)
   - *log*

   Sort the directory by date to view the creation date of the files.
2. Archive all files that are no longer required, for example, files that were created before an update of a database or that have been used successfully for all target systems.
3. Optionally, archive obsolete transports on storage media, such as tapes or CDs.

Note that transport requests whose transport files have been deleted are no longer available for the Transport Management System; that is, they can no longer be imported.

9.2 Retrieving Operating System Information

The SAP system provides its own operating system monitor. The data for this monitor is determined by program `saposcol`, which is part of the SAP kernel and runs at the operating system level. You can use the operating system monitor to analyze performance problems (see Chapter 11). It also provides an operating system log that collects messages on critical events at the operating system level. Depending on the operating system, one or more logs are created.

The logs can contain information on potential problems (e.g., errors that occur at the hard disk level may indicate that the hard disk is defective and needs to be replaced). Follow these steps to use the monitor to determine the state of the operating system and have the system display the operating system log:

1. To call the operating system monitor, enter Transaction ST06 in the command box and press the [Enter] key (or select Tools • CCMS • Control/Monitoring • Performance • Operating System • Local • ST06—Operating System Monitor).
2. The initial screen provides an overview of the current status of the operating system resources (see Figure 9.7).

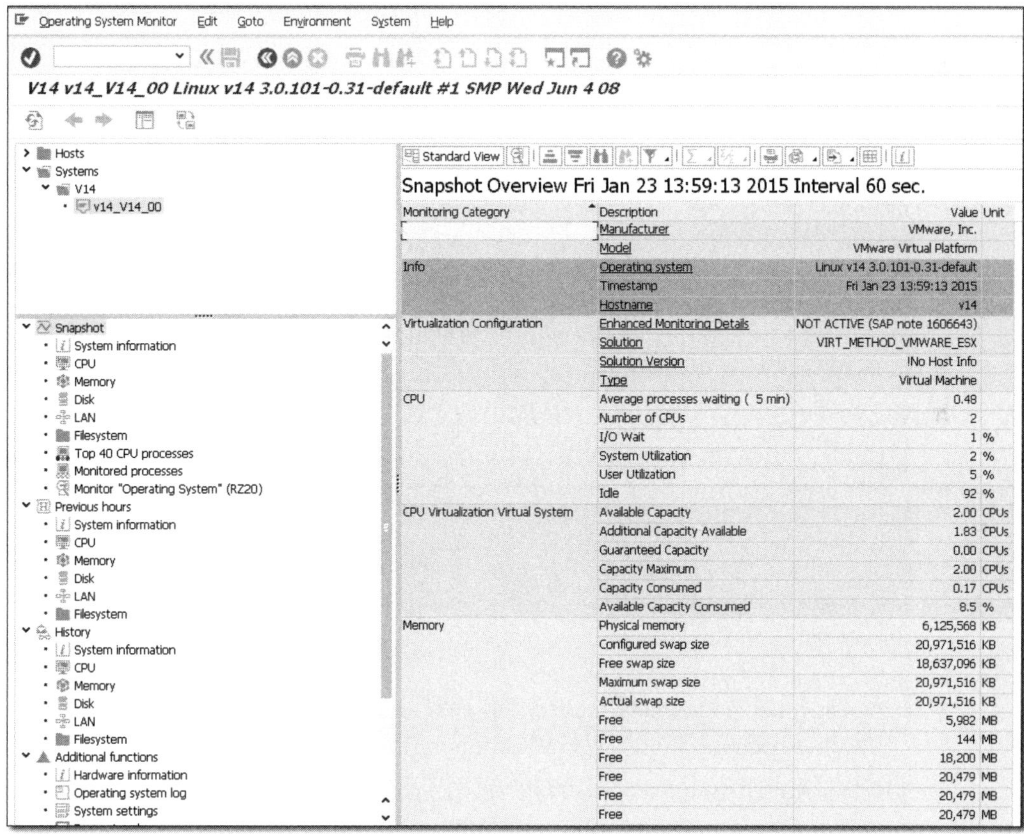

Figure 9.7 Operating System Monitor

[✿]

Transaction for the Operating System Monitor

The operating system monitor has been revised for the various SAP releases. Depending on the release, the latest version is available via Transaction ST06 (as of release 7.10) or OS07N (from release 6.20 through 7.02). An overview of release-dependent usage of these transaction codes is available in SAP Note 1483047.

3. In the navigation area on the left, you can call further functions. For example, call SNAPSHOT • TOP 40 CPU PROCESSES to view the distribution of CPU resources among the operating system processes (see Figure 9.8).

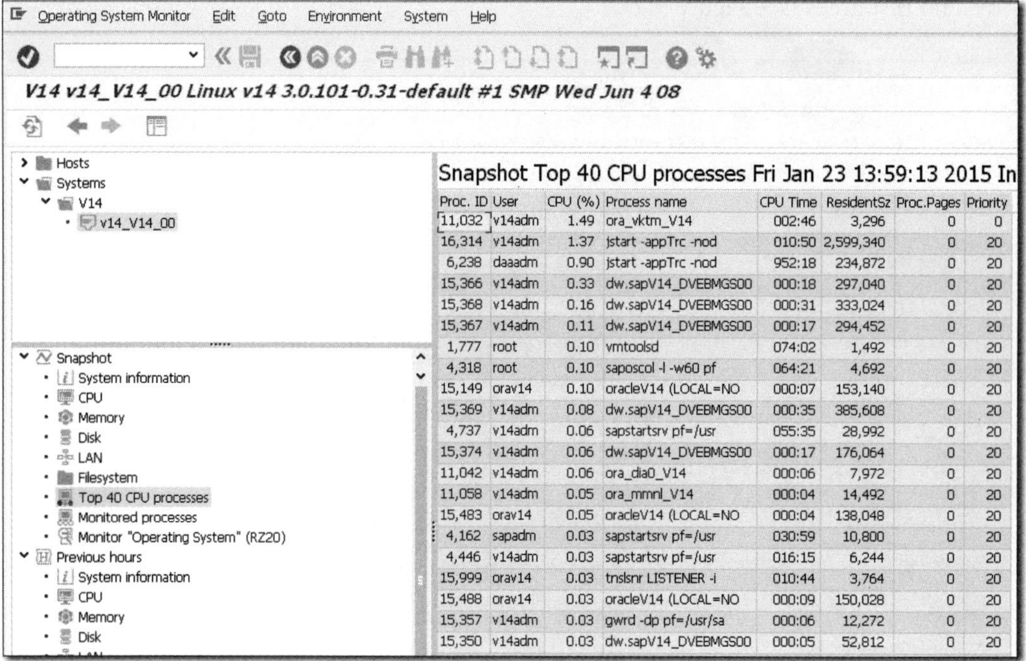

Proc. ID	User	CPU (%)	Process name	CPU Time	ResidentSz	Proc.Pages	Priority
11,032	v14adm	1.49	ora_vktm_V14	002:46	3,296	0	0
16,314	v14adm	1.37	jstart -appTrc -nod	010:50	2,599,340	0	20
6,238	daaadm	0.90	jstart -appTrc -nod	952:18	234,872	0	20
15,366	v14adm	0.33	dw.sapV14_DVEBMGS00	000:18	297,040	0	20
15,368	v14adm	0.16	dw.sapV14_DVEBMGS00	000:31	333,024	0	20
15,367	v14adm	0.11	dw.sapV14_DVEBMGS00	000:17	294,452	0	20
1,777	root	0.10	vmtoolsd	074:02	1,492	0	20
4,318	root	0.10	saposcol -l -w60 pf	064:21	4,692	0	20
15,149	orav14	0.10	oracleV14 (LOCAL=NO	000:07	153,140	0	20
15,369	v14adm	0.08	dw.sapV14_DVEBMGS00	000:35	385,608	0	20
4,737	v14adm	0.06	sapstartsrv pf=/usr	055:35	28,992	0	20
15,374	v14adm	0.06	dw.sapV14_DVEBMGS00	000:17	176,064	0	20
11,042	v14adm	0.06	ora_dia0_V14	000:06	7,972	0	20
11,058	v14adm	0.05	ora_mmnl_V14	000:04	14,492	0	20
15,483	orav14	0.05	oracleV14 (LOCAL=NO	000:04	138,048	0	20
4,162	sapadm	0.03	sapstartsrv pf=/usr	030:59	10,800	0	20
4,446	v14adm	0.03	sapstartsrv pf=/usr	016:15	6,244	0	20
15,999	orav14	0.03	tnslsnr LISTENER -i	010:44	3,764	0	20
15,488	orav14	0.03	oracleV14 (LOCAL=NO	000:09	150,028	0	20
15,357	v14adm	0.03	gwrd -dp pf=/usr/sa	000:06	12,272	0	20
15,350	v14adm	0.03	dw.sapV14_DVEBMGS00	000:05	52,812	0	20

Figure 9.8 Top 40 CPU Processes

4. You can then go to PREVIOUS HOURS • CPU and double-click this entry to evaluate the development of the CPU utilization in the past 24 hours (see Figure 9.9).

5. Select ADDITIONAL FUNCTIONS • OPERATING SYSTEM LOG to view the log files of the operating system (see Figure 9.10).

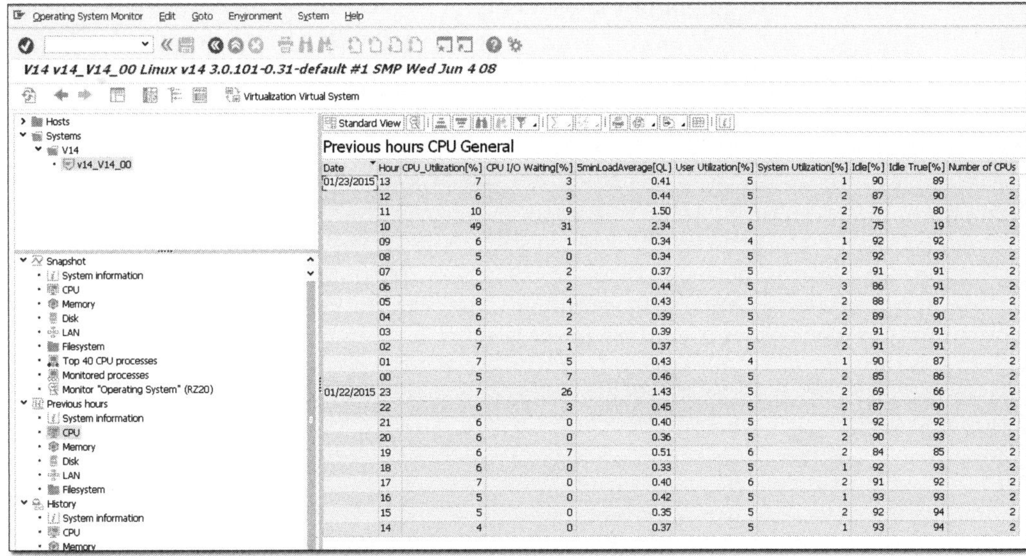

Figure 9.9 CPU Utilization in the Past 24 Hours

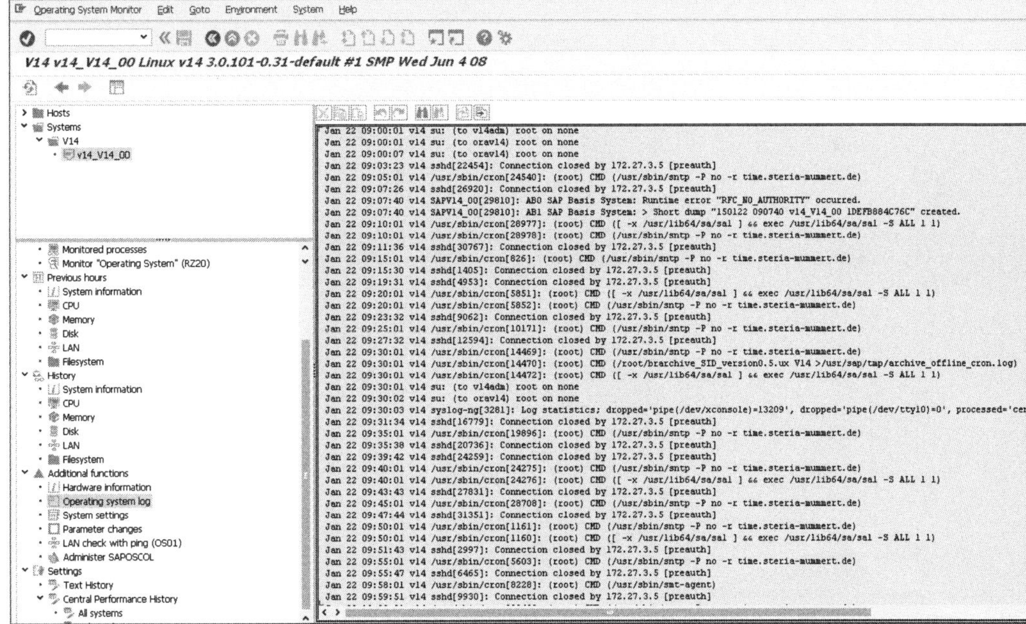

Figure 9.10 Operating System Log

6. All data available in this transaction is collected by kernel Program `saposcol`. Choose Additional Functions • Manage SAPOSCOL, and double-click this entry to view the data for Program `saposcol` (see Figure 9.11).

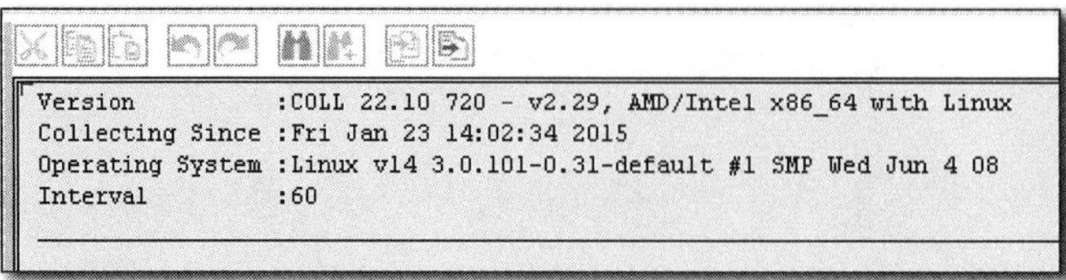

Figure 9.11 Administration of Program saposcol

7. Click on the Status button to retrieve the state of Program `SAPOSCOL` (see Figure 9.12).

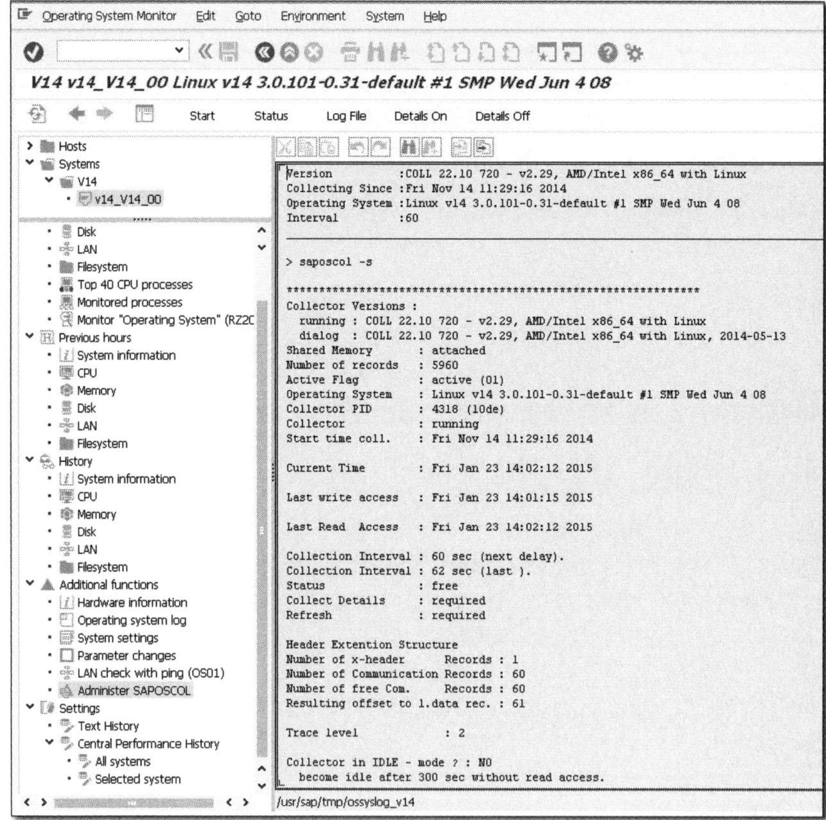

Figure 9.12 Displaying the Status of Program saposcol

[+]

Status of the OS Collector

Here, the COLLECTOR entry indicates whether Program `saposcol` is running (RUNNING status) and collects information about the operating system or whether it's inactive at the moment (NOT RUNNING status). The old versions of Transaction ST06 or OS07N (see menu path ENVIRONMENT • ST06 OLD ENVIRONMENT • OS07 OLD) allow you to manually enable or disable Program `saposcol` using the START and STOP buttons.

[⚙]

Program Directory for saposcol

Program `saposcol` is stored in the */usr/sap/<SID>/<instance>/exe* directory at the operating system level and can be controlled from there using the `saposcol` command.

Instead of using Program `saposcol`, you can also use third-party software or tools that the operating system provides (e.g., *Windows Task Manager* under Microsoft Windows or *nmon* under AIX) to monitor your servers and operating systems. If you do so, you should still run Program `saposcol` in parallel. Otherwise, you can't use the functions of the SAP operating system monitor for analyses or other statistical purposes.

9.3 Summary

A stable operating system is a prerequisite for the reliable operation of an SAP system. Irrespective of the products you use—Windows, Linux, or UNIX—you should know the respective characteristics in detail. Similar to databases, servers and operating systems on which SAP systems run are usually supervised by specialist administrators and not by SAP system administrators. This chapter is therefore limited to basic aspects, such as memory and process administration. For more detailed information, refer to the relevant specialist literature on the respective operating system.

As an SAP administrator, you bear a large responsibility for security issues such as protecting the SAP system and preparing for a security audit.

10 Security Administration

The security of an IT system is always a highly sensitive topic. The primary goals of security are to protect data against loss and theft, and to safeguard system operations on a daily basis. This chapter not only differentiates between various aspects of security administration but also names some key individual aspects and introduces tools that can be used to analyze and monitor the SAP system.

If an internal or external auditor examines the SAP system with a fine-toothed comb, the system administrator is responsible for analyzing the results of such an audit. Because each auditing company has its own procedures and may therefore check completely different aspects of security administration, this chapter prepares you for core aspects that auditing companies normally check.

The topic of computer security is so comprehensive that this chapter can only provide a brief introduction. We strongly recommend that you collaborate with everyone associated with system security (external auditors, internal auditors, the financial department, the legal department, etc.). More information is available in additional literature (see Appendix E) or at *www.service.sap.com/security*.

We'll first explain the concept of (information) security and the levels into which it can be divided. We'll then explain the various measures that can influence the security of your SAP systems. Finally, we'll discuss system audits and introduce you to some internal SAP auditing tools.

10.1 What Is Security?

Security is far more than simply assigning SAP access rights or keeping unauthorized users at bay. In the context of data, security also comprises the following aspects:

- Protecting data against hardware problems
- Ensuring data integrity
- Restoring data after a failure

In this chapter, we'll discuss those security aspects that will help you not only protect the data in your SAP system but also adhere to legal provisions. In Chapter 13, you'll learn how you can use user administration to keep unauthorized individuals at bay, while Chapter 14 will show you how to grant access authorizations and protect certain data against unwanted access.

10.1.1 Protecting Data against Damage or Loss

Security means protecting data against damage or loss. The causes of damage or loss can be divided into two categories:

- Unintentional damage or loss, for example:
  - Loading test data into the production system
  - Hardware failure
  - Destruction of the data center through fire
  - Flooding, hurricanes, earthquakes, or other natural disasters
- Malicious damage or loss, for example:
  - Deletion or damage of files by an employee
  - Deletion or damage of files by hackers

10.1.2 Adhering to Legal or Quasi-Legal Provisions

Security is a sensitive subject that also encompasses some legal aspects. Insider trading is a good example for highlighting the importance of security aspects. Insider knowledge or insider information is information that isn't in the public domain. If such knowledge were to enter the public domain, it could potentially affect the share price.

Insider trading occurs when insider information is used in the purchase or sale of shares to make a profit or minimize a loss. Even if you personally don't profit from the purchase of shares, you can still be held liable. If insider trading occurs, consult with your legal department.

[Ex]

Trading with Insider Information

The wife of an employee passed on some insider information to a relative who purchased shares and then sold them for a profit. When the relative sold the shares, he made a profit before declaring it (insider trading). The Securities and Exchange Commission imposed a fine on both the wife and the relative. The wife was found guilty of passing on insider information to the relative who, in turn, was able to profit from the sale of the shares. Consequently, both were found guilty of insider training.

10.2 Security Levels

To keep security administration simple, we recommend that you use levels to differentiate between different aspects of security. A model could, for example, comprise the following three main levels:

- Access security
  - Physical security
  - Network security
  - Application security
- Operational security
- Data security

Next, we'll describe each level in this security model in greater detail.

10.2.1 Access Security

Access security comprises all aspects of security associated with accessing a system whereby the term *access* can be considered from several perspectives.

Physical Security

Physical security controls physical access to the SAP system and network environment. To access data, an intruder must first gain access to the facility, then the building, and then the part of the building in which the users or pieces of equipment are located (e.g., the server room, cable terminal cabinet, or network room). Moreover, this level is probably the most important level. If an intruder gains access to your equipment, he can, in theory, breach the other security levels.

If the physical security level is breached, the following may happen:

- Equipment may be physically damaged or destroyed.
- The intruder may gain access to the system via the user console, which may result in a breach of network security.
- Equipment may be stolen.
- Data may be misused by hackers.

If the intruder doesn't gain physical access to the building, he must use electronic means to gain access to the system on the network. The server on which the SAP system is running should be housed in a secure room, and access to this room should be secured by a lockable door. Furthermore, it's imperative that access to the server room is controlled or monitored by video.

[!]

Access Log for the Server Room

If you use an access system with an electronic keycard, you should check the access log for the server room at regular intervals. Auditors may examine this security aspect (checking the access log on a regular basis).

Network Security

The goal of network security is to control external access and logons to the network. Logon access controls both on-site and remote access. It also determines the access rights of individual users within the network.

If intruders access your network, they may have an electronic connection to your computers. Network security specialists should configure the various access points to your network. User activities should also be tracked. The following access points, for example, should be checked:

- Outside access
  - Dial-up access
  - Internet access
  - Other remote access methods (e.g., via a Virtual Private Network [VPN])
- Network logon (e.g., Windows domain)
- Access to parts of the network (e.g., via router tables)

[+]

Recommendations for Windows

For Windows domains, we recommend the following:

- Have a separate SAP domain to which only system administrators can log on.
- Have other domains to which users can log on. These domains should "trust" the SAP domain but not vice versa.

Application Security

Application security concerns the security mechanisms of the application itself (e.g., the SAP system). These include the following:

- Access to the application (e.g., the logon to the SAP system)
- User access point to the application
- User authorizations within the application
- User authorization to certain system data in the application (e.g., in the SAP system by limiting the user to company code 1000 or cost center 47110815)
- Type of user access rights (e.g., read—don't change!—posting data).
- Use of SAP tools, for example:
  - Profile Generator (Transaction PFCG—see Chapter 14)
  - Audit Information System (see Section 10.5.1)
  - Security Audit Log (see Section 10.5.2)

For the system as a whole, it's important that all levels are protected using suitable measures to ensure optimum security.

10.2.2 Operational Security

The operational security level concerns definitions, procedures, and control functions for daily operation rather than computers and systems. Such procedures and control functions concern both the organization and its employees, and may cause problems. Employees should adhere to various rules and regulations, but they don't always do so.

Examples of operational control methods include the following:

- Segregation of Duties
- Avoiding shared usage of user IDs

- Defining password standards
- Logoff and backup mechanisms for work breaks or for the end of a shift (e.g., locking the PC when leaving a work center)

Often, employees aren't sufficiently sensitized to the issue of security, which may lead to them adopting a lax approach to daily, security-related activities. This may mean, among other things, that the physical security isn't taken too seriously, and, as a result, PCs and similar pieces of technical equipment are left unattended or unsecured (e.g., office door not locked, PC not locked). You must strive to increase awareness of security within the enterprise. Having said that, access systems (e.g., keycards) or PC settings (e.g., time until the PC locks) may enforce certain behavioral patterns.

10.2.3 Data Security

This level is closely related to disaster recovery (see Chapter 7), which represents an important part of data security. Data security involves protecting the following:

- **Server data**
  The data on the server is protected against damage or loss. Even though this protection is achieved using different resources, the goal is always to keep any data loss caused by an incident as low as possible or to avoid it altogether.
- **Backup data**
  At this level, the application data is saved to magnetic tape, which can be used to restore the system. Backup tapes must be stored securely for the following reasons:
  - To use them in the event of a disaster
  - To protect them against theft

At this point, we must highlight the following security-relevant points in relation to disaster recovery:

- Lower the likelihood of data loss.
- Treat the server as the most important location for storing data securely.
- Protect the backup data against damage or loss.
- Make sure that the system can be fully restored after a failure.

When it comes to backing up data to the server, note the following:

- In the event of an emergency, you must do everything possible to prevent data loss. The following options ensure high availability (HA):
  - RAID arrays for drives
  - Redundant equipment
  - Reliable equipment and vendors
  - Support contracts for the hardware used in the production system
- The following options refer to the facilities:
  - Uninterrupted power supply (UPS)
  - Fire alarms and fire protection devices
  - Alarm system
  - Surround alarm
- Backup
  - Backup tapes should be dispatched to a secure location outside the enterprise.
  - This measure will protect backup data against damage or complete destruction in the event of an incident.
  - The storage locations for the backup tapes—both on-site and outside the enterprise—must be secure to protect the tapes against theft.
  - If the tapes are stolen, the data may be restored and misused. If database tools are used, it's possible to bypass most SAP security functions because the tables can be read directly.

Chapter 7 and Chapter 8 provide additional information on how to ensure that your system data is secure.

10.3 Safeguarding the SAP System

In this section, you'll learn how you can use specific measures to safeguard an SAP system. It's best to use a *security concept* to document any security precautions that you take. By documenting the individual measures and the reason and purpose associated with each, you avoid any unintentional easing up of security measures.

10.3.1 Preventing Multiple User Logons

Preventing multiple user logons means that any user ID can only be logged on to the SAP system once. Multiple user logons occur if users share a user ID or if someone uses someone else's user ID without that user knowing. If several individuals use the same user ID, this is deemed to be a security threat for the following reasons:

- You can't trace a data change or posting back uniquely.
- You can't determine who is performing an activity that is considered to be a security threat.
- If training is required, you can't determine who requires training.
- You potentially violate the terms of your license agreement with SAP if multiple users share an SAP license to save money.

The fact that multiple logons are possible in a live SAP system is generally frowned upon in the event of a security audit. In test systems and QA systems, the use of multiple logons may be less restrictive.

To ensure that a user ID isn't shared by multiple users, you must use Transaction RZ10 to configure the system profile parameter `login/disable_multi_gui_login`. The following values are possible here:

- `1`: Forbid multiple user logons.
- `0`: Permit multiple user logons.

We recommend that you set the parameter value to `1` to prevent multiple user logons under the same user ID. Another advantage associated with this measure is that it's easier to identify any possible misuse of passwords. If the owner of a user ID wants to log on to an SAP system but receives a message indicating that the user ID is already logged on, he can assume that someone else knows the password.

Despite the aforementioned security concerns, there are times when it isn't practical (from a technical or organizational perspective) to use individual user IDs. Such situations are usually caused by certain organizational or technical conditions within the enterprise and must therefore be handled and assessed on an individual basis. In each case, management must approve, monitor, and document any exceptions of this type as well as any internal or external audits that are performed.

To enable certain users to log on multiple times, you must enter the relevant user IDs in the parameter `login/multi_login_users` without any blank characters and separated by commas.

10.3.2 Passwords

The password is the "key" that a user requires to access the SAP system. Just like a door key, a password must also be protected so that "uninvited guests" can't intrude. Your enterprise should have a unique yet practical password rule that is known to all users. In particular, you shouldn't use passwords that are easy to guess.

Don't Use Highly Complex Password Rules [!]

A password rule that is too restrictive or very difficult to adhere to could be counterproductive because users would then jot down their passwords and possibly store them somewhere that is easy to access, thus endangering security.

Defining Password Standards

The SAP system provides system parameters that you can use to technically implement a password guideline (e.g., defining the minimum password length or validity period for passwords). The most important password parameters are listed here:

- **Minimum password length** (`login/min_password_lng`)
  A long password is more difficult to guess. The standard length is usually at least eight characters.
- **Password validity period** (`login/password_expiration_time`)
  This parameter specifies the validity period of a password. When this period expires, the user must change his password. Auditors normally recommend a period of 30 days. However, most customers opt for a period of 90 days.
- **User lock** (`login/fails_to_user_lock`)
  This parameter is used to lock users who repeatedly enter an incorrect password at logon. Users are usually locked after three failed logon attempts. Here, you can specify the number of failed attempts that must occur before a user is locked.

Other parameters relating to password restrictions are listed in Chapter 13, Section 13.10.3. If you want to specify password parameters, use Transaction RZ10. By using appropriate parameters, you can make it considerably more difficult for anyone to gain unauthorized access to your system.

[+]

Auditing Security Parameters

Your external auditors may check whether you've configured security parameters.

Preventing the Use of Trivial Passwords

Certain passwords (e.g., 123, QWERTY, abc, sap, <your company name>) are already known and easy to guess. If users use such passwords, this endangers security and therefore the system. Various lists of frequently used user passwords are freely available on the Internet. Using one of these passwords increases the likelihood that an unauthorized person will gain access to a user account.

You can prevent the use of easy-to-guess passwords by defining forbidden character strings in table `USR40`. When a user wants to save a new password, the system checks this table. Maintenance of table `USR40` can't substitute for a sensible password guideline that users adhere to. However, it can complement it effectively.

[!]

Audit—Easy-to-Guess Passwords

External auditors may check whether you've configured a mechanism that prevents the use of easy-to-guess passwords.

The following passwords are examples of possible table entries:

- *SAP*
- *GOD*
- *QWERTY*
- *PASSWORD*
- Simple letter sequences (*abc*, *xyz*, etc.) and simple number sequences (*123*, *321*, etc.)
- Weekdays (*Monday*, *Tuesday*, etc.), months (*January*, *February*, etc.), and seasons (*Summer*, *Winter*, etc.)
- The name of your company, one of your company's product names, the name of your competitor, or one of your competitor's product names

We recommend that you use the placeholder * at the start and end of each entry in table `USR40`. By doing so, you can help prevent the entry from being used in any part of the password.

Other Password Security Options [+]

Table USR40 is only one basic measure for password security. This table must be managed manually. Third parties provide password security programs that you can integrate into the SAP system.

You can use Transaction SM30, which is the general transaction for table maintenance, to change table USR40 (for more information about this transaction, see Chapter 13). This change triggers a transport that can be passed through the entire system landscape.

Documenting Changes to Table USR40 [+]

Maintain a log of changes that are made in table USR40.

Storing System Passwords

In principle, passwords should never be written down. In real-life system administration, however, there are occasionally situations in which you have to log on to the system using an administrative user ID (e.g., when maintaining RFC connections or in the event of an emergency) and therefore need the administrative password. Because you can't select a trivial password for these powerful users but you don't require it often enough to learn it by heart, you must reluctantly jot it down.

In general, the following administrative user IDs are required for the SAP system:

- SAP*
- DDIC
- SAPCPIC (see SAP Note 29276)
- EarlyWatch (client 066)
- TMSADM
- All user-defined, technical administrative user IDs (e.g., for interfaces, RFC connections, etc.)
- All non-SAP user IDs required for system operation (e.g., for the operating system, the database, and other connected applications)

Depending on your operating system and the database used, the following user IDs are important at the operating system level and the database level:

- `<SID>ADM` (or `<sid>adm`)
- `sa`
- `SAPR3` or `sapr3`
- `SAPService<SID>`
- `SYS` (or `sys`)
- `SYSTEM` (or `system`)
- `root`
- `Ora<sid>`
- `op$<sid>adm`
- `ops$sapservice<sid>`

At the very least, the system administrator and his representative must know the password for the aforementioned user IDs. Depending on the size of your enterprise, even more individuals will need to be entrusted with this information.

Add a procedure for retaining and managing these critical passwords to your security concept. Also check the use of third-party software for password administration (password vaults are offered for this purpose). We recommend that you write down all of the passwords for all relevant system IDs, place them in a sealed envelope, and store them in a safe to which only authorized individuals have access (selected employees).

[!]

Creating a Password List

Two employees should compose the list, change passwords, and confirm new passwords separately and successively for each user ID. If an incorrect password is recorded in the list, you may no longer be able to log on to the system.

The password list must be updated to include any password changes.

10.3.3 Limiting Access for SAP* or DDIC Users

SAP* and DDIC are system user IDs that should not be used for regular system operation. In principle, you should lock the SAP* user and change the password. Don't delete the user because this would disable one of the SAP system's important protection mechanisms. You can use the profile parameter login/no_automatic_user_sapstar to control whether a logon using the SAP* ID and the password "pass" is possible if the SAP* user has been deleted. We recommend setting the parameter value to 1 so that a logon using the SAP* user isn't possible by default.

The DDIC user is required for certain system administration functions. Therefore, don't delete or lock it. Instead, change the password and store it securely. For more information about the administrative user IDs SAP* and DDIC, see Chapter 13, Section 13.10.1.

10.3.4 Locking Critical Transactions

Critical transactions are transaction codes that can damage the system, represent a general security risk, or significantly impair system performance. Access to these transactions is more critical in the production system than in the development or test system. Therefore, some transactions should be locked in the production system but not in the development, test, or training systems. Standard security normally prohibits access to these transactions. Depending on the respective system, however, some administrators, programmers, consultants, and important technical users may require access. In such cases, the transaction lock provides a second line of defense in addition to authorization management.

Depending on the scope of the component in the relevant installation, an SAP system may contain tens of thousands of transaction codes. From a transparency perspective, only highly critical transaction codes should be locked. Appendix B contains a table of transactions that should be locked. This table was created in collaboration with SAP Basis consultants and end users. The transactions are categorized as follows:

- Critical
- Impairing security
- Impairing performance

Contact your technical consultants and the persons responsible for the specific components. They can provide you with more information on further critical transactions in your components.

Table TSTCT [*]

Table TSTCT contains the transaction codes and the names of the transactions.

Appendix B also contains a table of transactions that potentially can't be locked because they are used regularly. These transactions are used in production systems for specific reasons. Because they are critical, access to these transactions should be granted via authorization roles to a limited extent only.

Add the list of locked transactions to your security concept. At the very least, this list should contain the following information:

- Which transactions are locked?
- Why are they locked?
- Who locked them?
- When were they locked?

It's important to maintain this information because someone may want to know who locked the transaction and why.

To lock a transaction, follow these steps:

1. Enter Transaction SM01 in the command field and press the [Enter] key (or select the menu option TOOLS • ADMINISTRATION • ADMINISTRATION • SM01—TRANSACTION CODE ADMINISTRATION).
2. In the TRANSACTION CODE search field (see Figure 10.1), enter the transaction code that you want to lock (e.g., "SM14"), and click on SEARCH TRANSACTION.

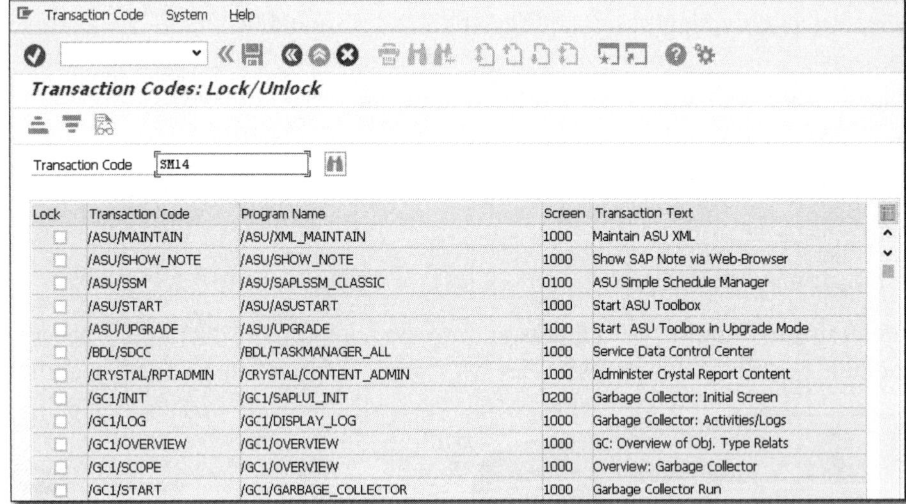

Figure 10.1 Entering the Transaction to Be Locked

3. The required transaction is now displayed in the first row in the table. To lock a transaction, select the relevant checkbox in the LOCK column. To unlock the transaction, remove the checkmark (see Figure 10.2). Then click on SAVE.

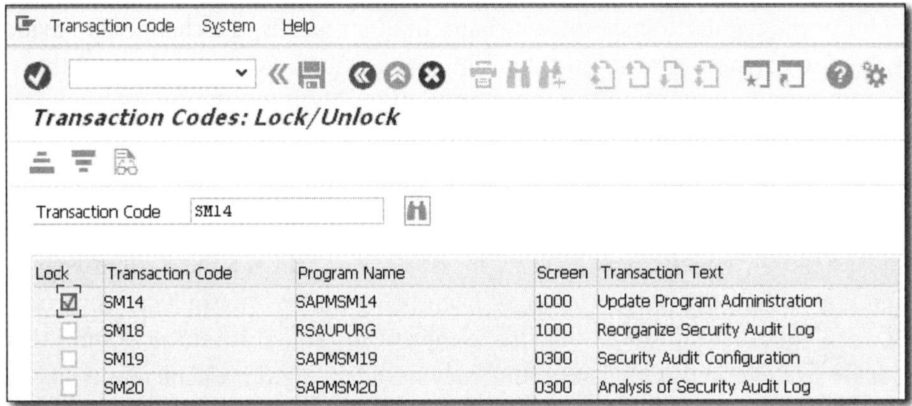

Figure 10.2 Locking a Transaction

4. Click on BACK in the toolbar. If you now try to call the locked transaction, the system displays a message in the status bar indicating that the transaction is locked (see Figure 10.3).

Transaction SM14 is locked (in transaction SM01)

Figure 10.3 System Message for Locked Transactions

Carefully Locking Transactions [!]

Take care when locking transactions because there is a risk that you'll inadvertently lock an important transaction. If this happens, you may no longer be able to unlock this or other transactions. Therefore, determine whether the best option is to lock a transaction or to use roles to restrict the access authorization.

List of Locked Transactions [+]

You can use the standard report RSAUDITC_BCE from the *Audit Information System* (see Section 10.5.1) to display a list of locked transactions.

10.3.5 Preventing Changes in the Production System

Controlling and monitoring any changes made in the SAP system is an important security aspect. In principle, any changes to Customizing or repository objects (e.g., programs or data elements) should enter the production system by means of the regular transportation chain. In other words, the changes are made in the development system and then imported into the QA system via a transport request. Such changes are therefore thoroughly tested before being transported into the production system. This procedure ensures that changes are tested properly and then consistently applied to the entire system landscape (see Chapter 17).

For systems in which changes can't be made, you can set the system change option to technically prevent changes from being made. This applies, in particular, to the production system but also to the QA system. This setting ensures that changes are checked. Otherwise, this may result in significant incidents in the production system because changes haven't been tested or because they don't correspond to changes in the development system or test system.

Often, changes are made directly in the production system because it would take too long to transport such changes. However, this doesn't produce a synchronous system landscape in which the settings in the production system correspond to those in the development system and test system. In such a situation, you can't ensure that tests performed in the QA system will be reliable. Having said that, this may give rise to a high number of emergency transports.

Setting the Production System to "Not modifiable"

You can use several switches to prevent changes to a system. In the production system, such switches should be set to NOT MODIFIABLE. You can use Transactions SE03 and SCC4 to make this setting.

1. Enter Transaction SE03 in the command field, and press the [Enter] key.
2. Choose TRANSPORT ORGANIZER TOOLS • ADMINISTRATION • SET SYSTEM CHANGE OPTION (see Figure 10.4).
3. If you want to lock the system, use the dropdown list to set the GLOBAL SETTING field to the value NOT MODIFIABLE (see Figure 10.5). If you want to unlock the system, select the value MODIFIABLE. When you've finished, click on SAVE.

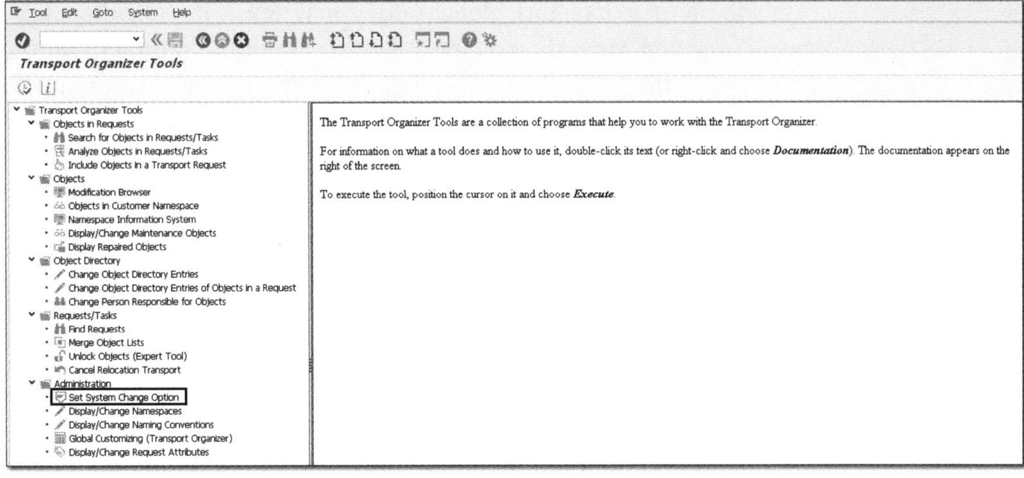

Figure 10.4 Calling the System Change Settings

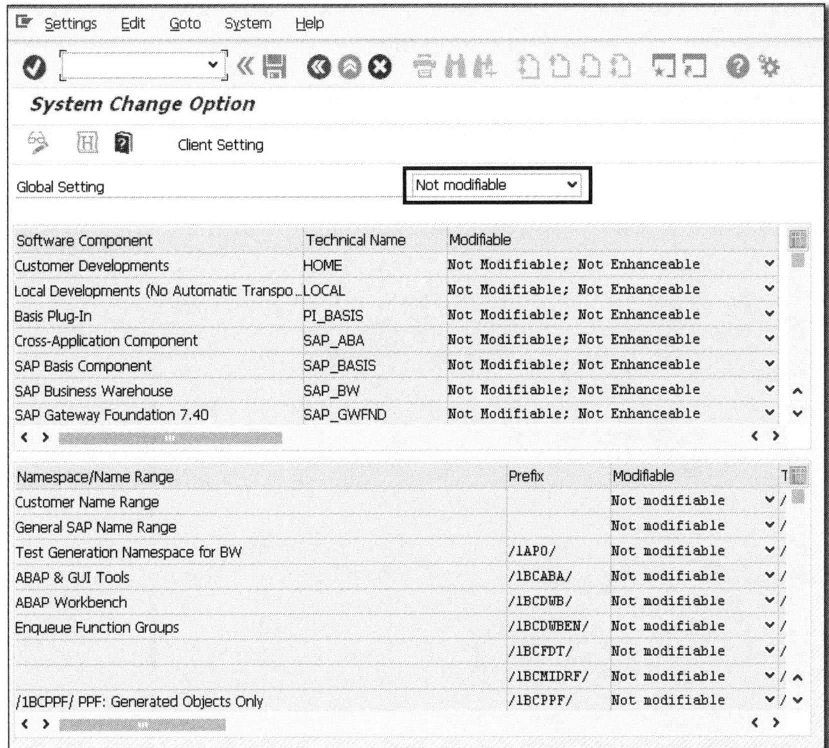

Figure 10.5 Setting the System Change Option

In some cases, the NOT MODIFIABLE global setting may result in certain applications not being executed correctly. You must then set the global setting to MODIFIABLE. You can nevertheless protect the system by restricting the change option for SOFTWARE COMPONENT and NAMESPACE/NAME RANGE and only leave the components that you actually require with the status MODIFIABLE. You can use the menu functions EDIT • SOFTWARE COMPONENTS/NAMESPACE MODIFIABLE/NOT MODIFIABLE to set all entries accordingly.

[+]

Transaction SE06

You can also set the system changeability via Transaction SE06. For this purpose, in the initial screen of the transaction, click on the SYSTEM CHANGEABILITY button.

In Transaction SE03 (Transport Organizer Tools), you control, on a cross-client basis, whether changes to repository objects and cross-client Customizing are permitted throughout the system. In Transaction SCC4 (Client Administration), you can configure this setting for a specific client, for example, if you want programming to take place in only one client within the development system.

However, Transaction SCC4 is also used to prevent changes to client-specific objects and to prohibit the creation of transport requests. To lock clients against changes, follow these steps:

1. Enter Transaction SCC4 in the command field and press the Enter key (or select the menu option TOOLS • ADMINISTRATION • ADMINISTRATION • CLIENT ADMINISTRATION • SCC4—CLIENT MAINTENANCE, see Figure 10.6).

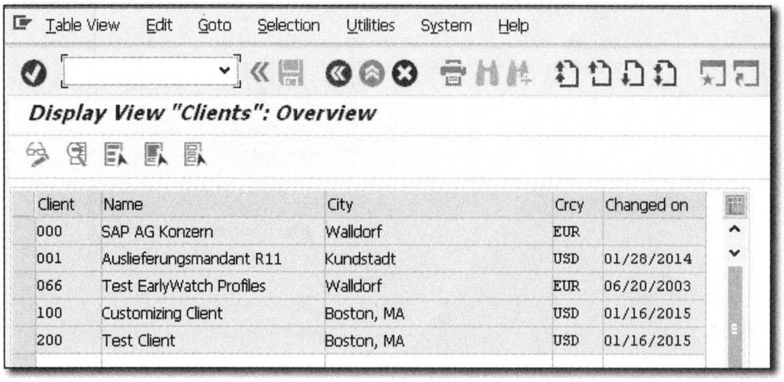

Table View   Edit   Goto   Selection   Utilities   System   Help

Display View "Clients": Overview

Client	Name	City	Crcy	Changed on
000	SAP AG Konzern	Walldorf	EUR	
001	Auslieferungsmandant R11	Kundstadt	USD	01/28/2014
066	Test EarlyWatch Profiles	Walldorf	EUR	06/20/2003
100	Customizing Client	Boston, MA	USD	01/16/2015
200	Test Client	Boston, MA	USD	01/16/2015

Figure 10.6 Initial Screen of Client Maintenance

2. Click on DISPLAY <-> CHANGE to switch to change mode.
3. In the dialog box that opens (see Figure 10.7), click on CONTINUE.

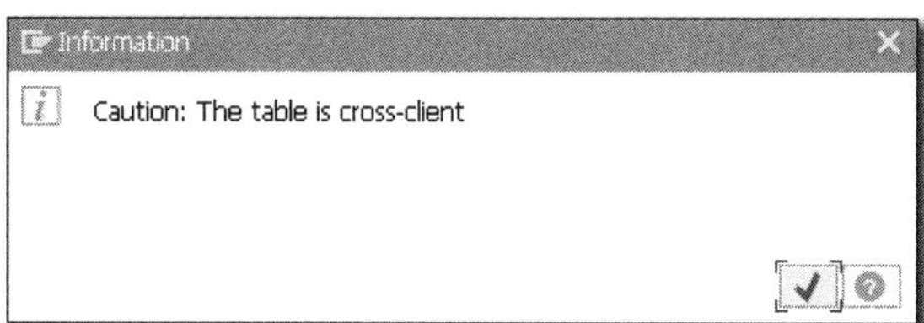

Figure 10.7 Message for the Maintenance of a Cross-Client Table

4. Select the clients to be changed, and click the DETAILS button, or double-click the relevant row (see Figure 10.8).

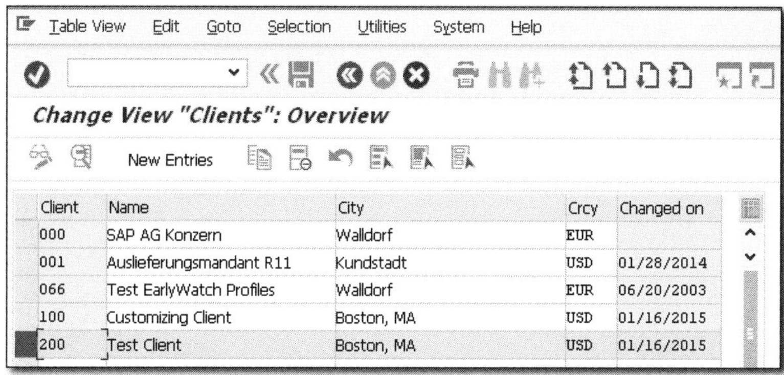

Figure 10.8 Selecting Clients

5. To lock the client, follow these steps (see Figure 10.9):
   - In the CHANGES AND TRANSPORTS FOR CLIENT-SPECIFIC OBJECTS area, choose the NO CHANGES ALLOWED option.
   - Under CROSS-CLIENT OBJECT CHANGES, use the dropdown box to select the NO CHANGES TO REPOSITORY AND CROSS-CLIENT CUSTOMIZING OBJS option.
   - In the CLIENT COPY AND COMPARISON TOOL PROTECTION area, use the dropdown box to choose PROTECTION LEVEL 2: NO OVERWRITING, NO EXTERNAL AVAILABILITY.
   - Under CATT AND ECATT RESTRICTIONS, use the dropdown box to choose the ECATT AND CATT NOT ALLOWED option.

6. When you've finished, click on SAVE .

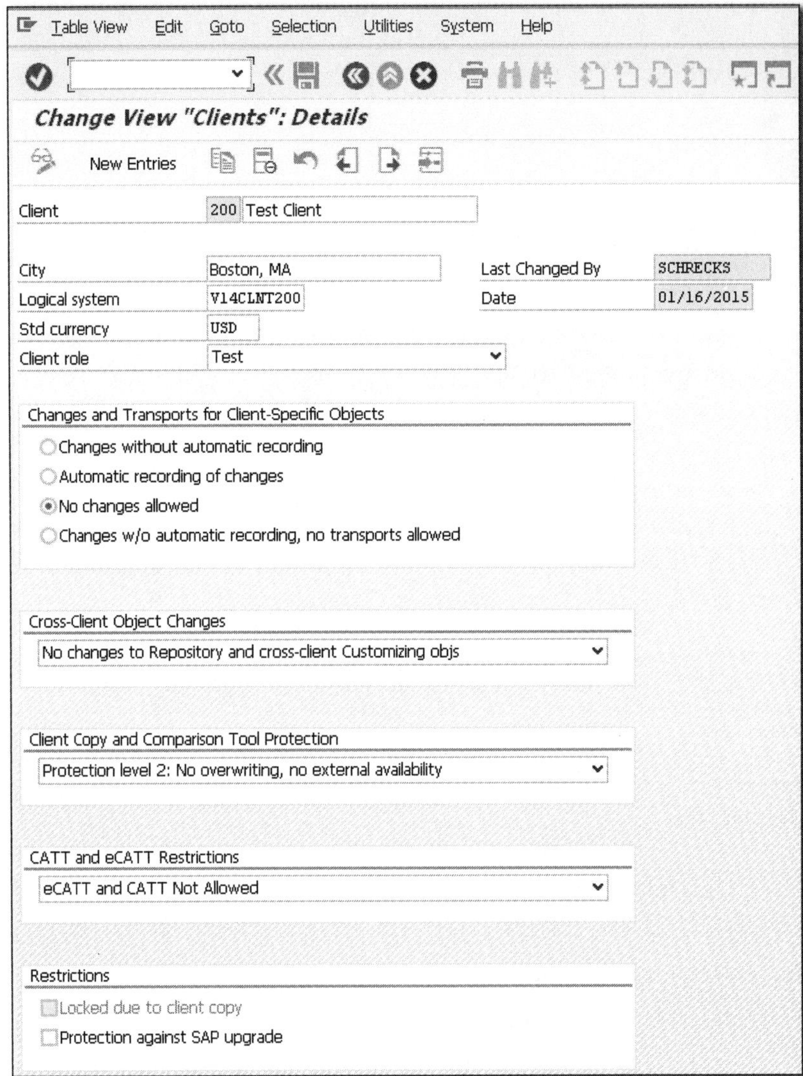

Figure 10.9 Settings for Locking a Client against Changes

The client is now protected against changes. Execute the procedure for all relevant clients in the systems to be secured.

Exceptions

There are some exceptions to this process if a change can't be transported or if a direct change is required as a result of an SAP Note. If a change can't be transported, you must implement the following procedure:

1. Confirm that the change can't be transported. Some objects may require an ABAP program for the transport.
2. Initially, make this change in the development system and QA system, and test whether you get the desired effect without any negative side effects. Then make the change in the production system. Proceed in exactly the same way for nonproduction systems.
3. Unlock the system so that changes can be made.
4. Make the change.
5. Immediately lock the system again.

Limiting Manual Changes to Essential Changes Only [!]

Implement this procedure *only* if a change can't be transported. Manual changes increase the likelihood of errors.

10.3.6 Operational Security

Operational security includes organizational regulations and definitions that aim to reduce risks in daily operation. Measures for increasing operational security aren't necessarily application-specific. Mostly, they are heavily dependent on the enterprise structure.

In the case of the SAP system, you can use the authorization concept to influence operational security (see Chapter 14). A well-defined authorization concept ensures that critical combinations of tasks and authorizations are technically separated from each other (known as *functional separation* or *segregation of duties*, SOD). Standard auditing guidelines now exist for high-risk combinations of tasks. Examples of critical combinations of authorizations include the following:

- Vendor maintenance and check creation
- Customer maintenance and cash receipt
- ABAP development and transport control

Your external auditors can support you in defining such high-risk combinations. A task sharing audit is a standard auditing procedure.

[Ex]

Task Sharing

If an employee is responsible for outgoing payments, he should not be responsible for entering vendor master data. The danger here is that the employee will enter his account details in a vendor record and transfer money to this account.

Often, smaller enterprises have to assign several functions to one person as a result of their organizational structure. In this case, you should be aware of and consider the potential risks. If you have to combine functions, choose combinations that carry the lowest possible risk. In return, accurately audit the activities performed by the employees in question.

10.4 Audits

As a system administrator, you encounter the following two audit types:

- Security audit
- Account audit

Performing a Security Check

The primary goal of a security audit is to test the security of the SAP environment. This audit is normally performed as an account audit to ensure that it complies with the relevant legal requirements. An enterprise's internal audit managers can also perform a security audit. The security of the following confidential data is audited:

- Financial data
- Customer data
- Product data
- Employee data (from SAP ERP Human Capital Management, SAP ERP HCM)

In general, the security audit is performed by a technically minded or experienced external auditor.

[+]

Preparing for an Audit

This section doesn't address all SAP security audit issues. Instead, we'll only discuss some aspects that may be important for a security audit. We recommend that you collaborate with the auditors before an account audit, so that you can test the system in advance and prepare it for the audit.

Account Audit

During an account audit, an auditor audits the financial statements of your enterprise. The purpose of this audit is to paint a picture of the enterprise's financial statements. Essentially, the financial statements reflect the enterprise's financial situation. An account audit is usually mandatory (e.g., if the enterprise's shares are traded on the stock market). If your enterprise is a private enterprise, the creditors can initiate an account audit.

As part of the account audit, the auditor usually performs a security audit of the SAP system and any connected systems. The purpose of the security audit is to ascertain the extent to which the data in the SAP system is confidential. External auditors evaluate your system and determine which tests need to be performed and how extensive these tests will be.

If the evaluation results aren't satisfactory, it may be necessary to perform more extensive audits. Consequently, the audit costs rise, and, as a result of this additional expense, it may not be possible to perform the audit until a later time. In the worst-case scenario, the security precautions may be so poor that it isn't possible to make a statement in relation to the enterprise's financial situation.

10.4.1 Auditing Aspects

During the account or security audit, the auditors consider certain auditing aspects such as the following:

- Physical security
- Network security
- User administration procedures
  - Appropriate task sharing
  - Suitable training
  - Passwords

- Data security
  - Protection against hardware errors, mirrored drives, RAID, failover, HA, and so on
  - Backup and restore procedures
  - Protecting the production system against unauthorized changes
  - Locking dangerous transactions

As the administrator, you should familiarize yourself with these aspects of account or security audits. If you don't know what the auditors will test, you can't be sufficiently prepared, nor can you protect the system accordingly.

10.4.2 Auditing Tasks for SAP Administrators

As an SAP system administrator, you support the security and account audits performed by internal and external auditors. However, such audits only occur at regular intervals (usually annually) because they are too extensive to occur at shorter intervals. Therefore, during the time between official audits, you should perform other audits on a regular basis (e.g., monthly or quarterly) to ensure that the system remains secure throughout the year. Examples of such audits include the following:

- **Checking user accounts**
  Access to the SAP system should be revoked immediately for any user who leaves your enterprise. By locking or deleting the user ID, you ensure that only users who have to work with the system actually have access to the SAP system. Regularly check whether users have been fully locked or deleted. This will also prevent other users from logging on under the respective IDs. For more information about locking users, see Chapter 13.

[+]

Auditing User IDs

Among other things, the external auditors will check whether individuals who don't have to access the SAP system nevertheless have valid user IDs.

- **Checking authorizations**
  Over time, a user can obtain an increasing number of authorization roles in the SAP system. If this isn't checked on a regular basis, these roles may result in a user obtaining more authorizations than necessary. Over time, a user may

obtain authorizations or combinations of authorizations that violate the definitions for functional separation or the SOD. Therefore, regularly audit the authorizations assigned to users and compare them with the relevant requests. Investigate whether there are any functional separation conflicts.

Auditing Authorizations [+]

External auditors may check not only the rise in the number of authorizations but also the request procedure.

Depending on the number of users, these audits may be quite extensive. In the meantime, tools that support such audits are available (e.g., the SAP products from the area of Governance, Risk & Compliance, GRC). If you don't have any technical support, it's best to perform at least one random check. Your auditor should define the minimum scope of the sample.

SAP Security Notes [+]

SAP provides security-relevant SAP Notes on the SAP Support Portal (see Chapter 19) under the path HELP & SUPPORT • SAP NOTE SEARCH • SAP SECURITY NOTES. You can use SAP Solution Manager to check whether all relevant security notes have been imported into your system. To do so, configure the SYSTEM RECOMMENDATIONS function in the CHANGE MANAGEMENT work center of SAP Solution Manager.

10.5 Auditing Tools

By default, the SAP system has several tools that support you when you perform security-relevant system administration tasks. These tools include the Audit Information System (AIS) and the Security Audit Log, which will be described in this section.

10.5.1 Audit Information System

The Audit Information System (AIS) was developed for system and business audits, and it comprises reports that automatically analyze certain aspects of system security. Thanks to these reports, it's no longer necessary to manually process individual audit points, analyze tables, or write audit programs. Consequently, auditors like to use the AIS during a system audit.

Up to Release 4.6B, the AIS was called via Transaction SECR (Audit Information System). As of Release 4.6C, SAP made the transition to a role-based auditing tool. In other words, the audit reports are now delivered in standard SAP roles. Before using the AIS, you must copy the roles into your customer namespace, complete any open authorization objects, generate authorization profiles, and transport the roles into the system to be audited.

[+]

AIS Roles

For information about release-dependent AIS roles and how to combine them to assign appropriate authorizations, see SAP Notes 451960 and 754273. To learn how to create and define authorization roles, see Chapter 14.

After you've generated and assigned the AIS roles, you can call the individual reports directly from the user menu (see Figure 10.10). You can also call the reports via Transaction SA38.

The following are some key reports in the AIS:

- **RSUSR003**
  Checks the standard passwords of standard SAP users (`SAP*`, `DDIC`, etc.).
- **RSUSR006**
  Lists users who have been locked as a result of failed logons.
- **RSUSR007**
  Lists users who have incomplete address data.
- **RSUSR008_009_NEW**
  Lists users who have critical combinations of authorizations or transactions.
- **RSUSR100**
  Lists change documents for users and displays changes made to user security.

[+]

Audit for Critical Authorizations

You must define the critical authorizations or authorization combinations checked in report RSUSR008_009_NEW (Transaction S_BCE_68002111) yourself (using the same report). The SAP standard version doesn't provide any set of rules for this purpose. Because the maintenance can be very extensive, you should check in advance whether it would be better to purchase a tool for supporting your audits. A list of critical authorizations is available in the book *100 Things You Should Know About Authorizations in SAP* by Andrea Cavalleri and Massimo Manara (SAP PRESS, 2012).

- **RSUSR101**
  Lists change documents for profiles and displays changes made to the security profiles.
- **RSUSR102**
  Lists change documents for authorizations and displays changes made to security authorizations.

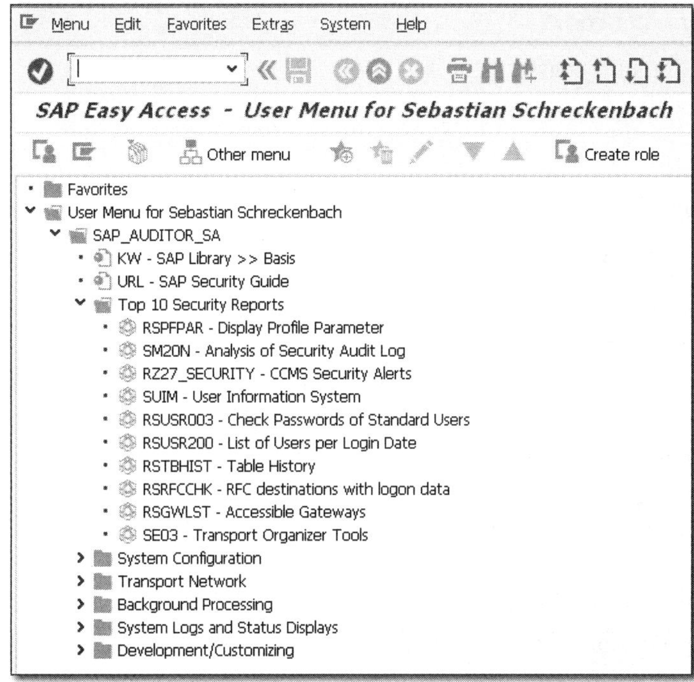

Figure 10.10 User Menu of the Audit Information System

Use the AIS to analyze and assess the security of your SAP system on a regular basis. In your security concept, define the intervals at which AIS reports are to be executed routinely. In collaboration with your user departments, check whether certain commercial audit reports are of interest to your management level.

10.5.2 Security Audit Log

The Security Audit Log plays an important role for SAP system administrators when they monitor security-relevant actions in the system. The Security Audit

Log can be used to log and subsequently analyze various types of user activities, for example:

- Dialog, RFC, and Gateway (Common Programming Interface Communication, CPIC) logon attempts to the system
- RFCs for function modules
- Transaction and program starts
- Locking/unlocking transactions
- Changing and locking user master data
- Changing and generating authorizations
- Virus detection
- Starting and stopping the application server
- Changes to the Security Audit Log configuration

The Security Audit Log is deactivated by default. After you've configured and activated the Security Audit Log, the actions to be logged are recorded in log files. These files are read when analyzing the Security Audit Log. The log files are stored at the operating system level. Because they are neither deleted nor overwritten, the number and size of the log files grows continuously. We therefore recommend that you regularly check the size of the log directory, archive the logs, and manually delete them if necessary.

[⚙]

Log Files—Names and Directories

The names and storage directories of log files are defined by the profile parameters `DIR_AUDIT` and `FN_AUDIT`.

The Security Audit Log supports the system administrator in the following tasks:

- Reconstructing and analyzing incidents
- Optimizing security through the detection of critical actions
- Tracking unusual user activities
- Understanding the effects of changes to transactions or users

[!]

Data Protection

Note that, depending on the configuration, the Security Audit Log records person-related data that may be subject to data protection laws. Therefore, before you activate logging, check whether you would be violating any data protection laws or internal agreements. If necessary, consult with auditors or the works council, and weigh the pros and cons.

Configuring the Security Audit Log

The Security Audit Log is configured in two steps:

- Maintaining profile parameters for the Security Audit Log
- Configuring audit profiles and filters

Before you activate the Security Audit Log, use a range of profile parameters to define the general conditions for logging (see Table 10.1).

Parameter	Explanation	Sample Parameter Values
`DIR_AUDIT`	Storage directory for log files on the application server	`/usr/sap/<SID>/DVEBMGS00/log`
`FN_AUDIT`	Naming convention for log files	`audit_++++++++_########.AUD`
`rsau/enable`	Security Audit Log activated/deactivated	0: Audit not activated 1: Audit activated
`rsau/max_diskspace/local`	Maximum size of the log directory	200M (200 megabytes)
`rsau/max_diskspace/per_day`	Maximum size of the log files written in one day	30M (30 megabytes)
`rsau/max_diskspace/per_file`	Maximum size of a single log file	5M (5 megabytes)
`rsau/selection_slots`	Number of configurable filters	1 to 5
`rsau/user_selection`	Use of placeholders during user selection	0: User selection with placeholders not activated 1: User selection with placeholders activated

Table 10.1 Profile Parameters – General Logging Conditions

[+]

Profile Parameter

You can display the profile parameters and settings relevant for the Security Audit Log in Transaction SM19 (Security Audit Configuration) under the menu path ENVIRONMENT • PROFILE PARAMETER. You maintain the profile parameters in Transaction RZ10. Note that you can't toggle dynamically between any of these parameters. In other words, you must restart the application server for any changes to become effective.

[!]

Parameter rsau/user_selection

When configuring the parameter `rsau/user_selection`, please read SAP Note 574914 if you want to use the generic selection (i.e., the selection using placeholders) for user names.

After you've implemented the basic configuration and restarted the application server, use Transaction SM19 to define the log filters. In the filter settings, you can define which data are to be logged. You can define up to five filters (see the profile parameter `rsau/selection_slots`).

It's necessary to distinguish between a *static* and *dynamic* configuration of the Security Audit Log:

- **Static**
  The static audit configuration is permanently saved to the database and used by all application servers that have this database. The settings only become active after you restart the application server. However, they are retained the next time the server is shut down.
- **Dynamic**
  Dynamically configured filters can be activated individually for individual application servers, or they can be distributed to several servers. The filter settings take effect immediately, but they aren't saved to the database and therefore are lost the next time you restart the server.

To define log filters, follow these steps:

1. Enter Transaction SM19 in the command field and press the [Enter] key (or select the menu option TOOLS • ADMINISTRATION • MONITOR • SECURITY AUDIT LOG • SM19—CONFIGURATION).
2. If you want to configure static filters, choose CREATE on the STATIC CONFIGURATION tab (see Figure 10.11).

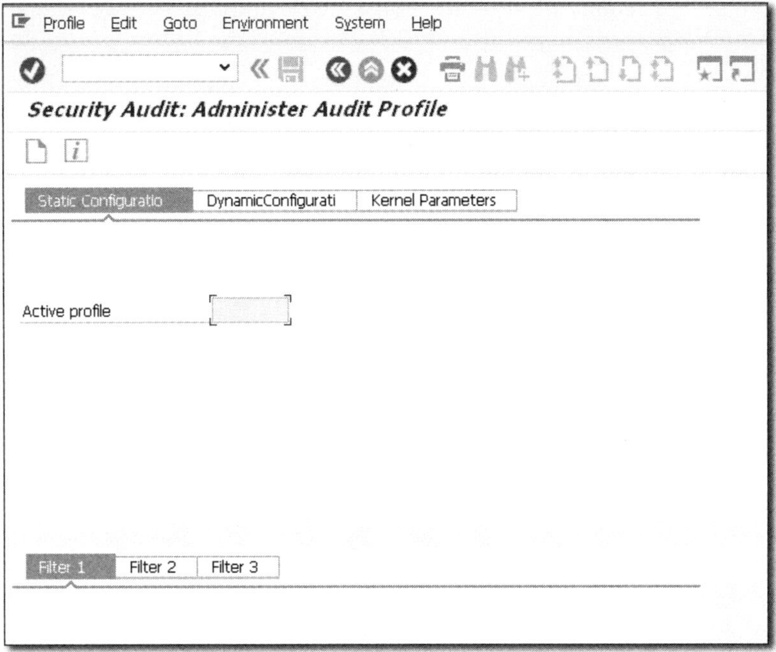

Figure 10.11 Creating Static Filters in the Security Audit Log

3. Enter a PROFILE NAME (e.g., "AUDIT"), and choose CONTINUE (see Figure 10.12).

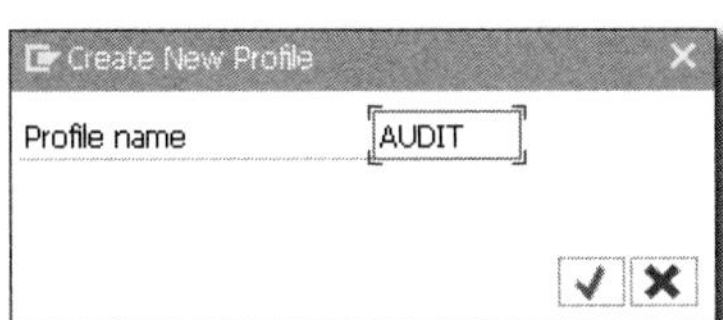

Figure 10.12 Creating a Security Audit Log Profile

4. In this example, you can specify a maximum of three different filters and define the scope of the actions to be logged in each case. Configure the following settings on the FILTER 1 tab (see Figure 10.13):
   - Activate the FILTER ACTIVE checkbox.
   - In the CLIENT field, enter the client to be monitored (e.g., "100" for an individual client or "*" for all clients).

- In the USER field, enter the user ID whose actions are to be logged (e.g., "DDIC" for the user DDIC or "*" for all users).
- In the AUDIT CLASSES column, select the logging scope you require.
- Under EVENTS, restrict logging to certain actions (e.g., ONLY CRITICAL), if necessary.
- Choose DETAIL CONFIGURAT to define additional settings.

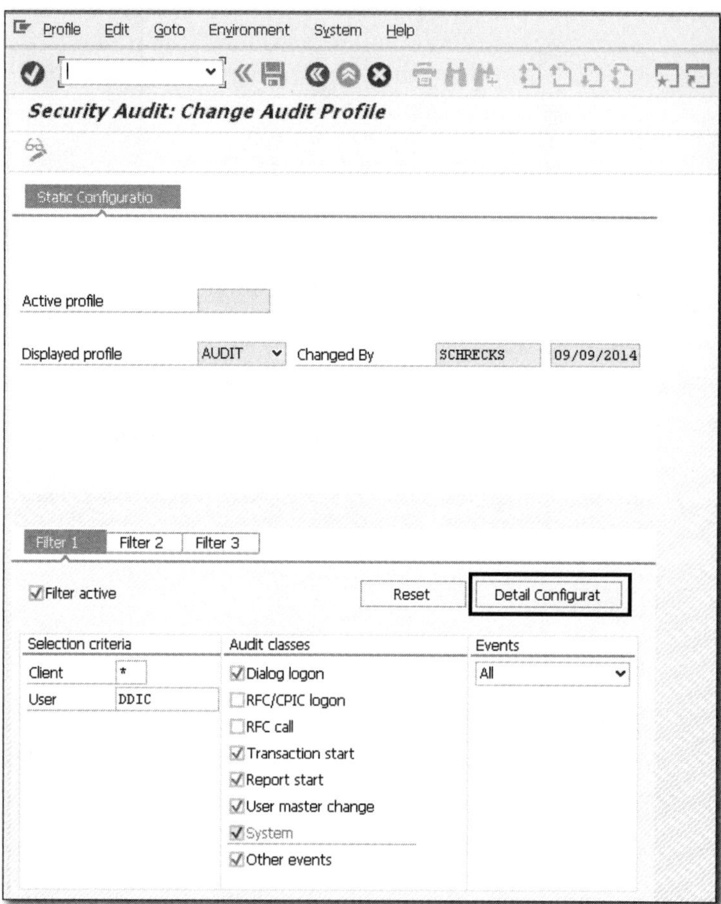

Figure 10.13 Making Filter Settings

5. Scroll through the list of loggable audit events, and make your selection by activating or deactivating event logging in the RECORDING column (see Figure 10.14). When you're finished, click on CONTINUE ✔.

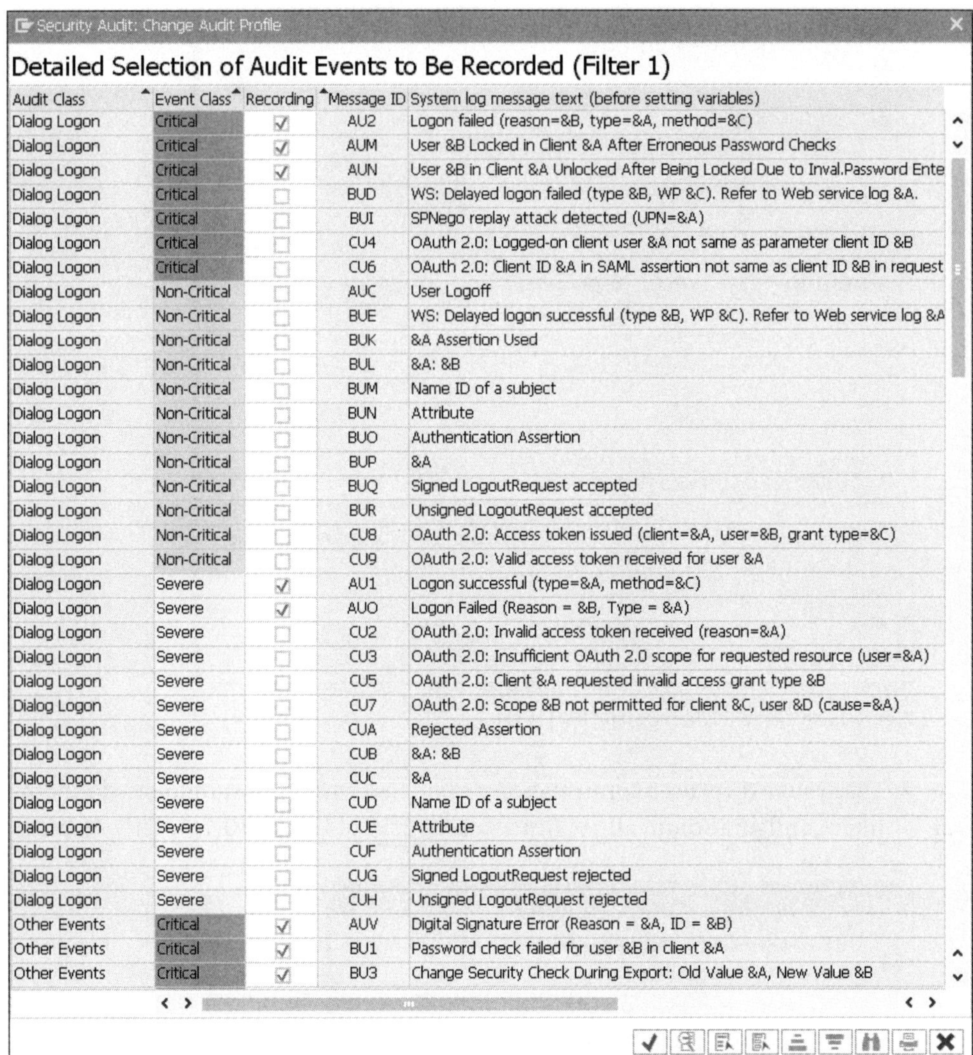

Security Audit: Change Audit Profile

Detailed Selection of Audit Events to Be Recorded (Filter 1)

Audit Class	Event Class	Recording	Message ID	System log message text (before setting variables)
Dialog Logon	Critical	☑	AU2	Logon failed (reason=&B, type=&A, method=&C)
Dialog Logon	Critical	☑	AUM	User &B Locked in Client &A After Erroneous Password Checks
Dialog Logon	Critical	☑	AUN	User &B in Client &A Unlocked After Being Locked Due to Inval.Password Ente
Dialog Logon	Critical	☐	BUD	WS: Delayed logon failed (type &B, WP &C). Refer to Web service log &A.
Dialog Logon	Critical	☐	BUI	SPNego replay attack detected (UPN=&A)
Dialog Logon	Critical	☐	CU4	OAuth 2.0: Logged-on client user &A not same as parameter client ID &B
Dialog Logon	Critical	☐	CU6	OAuth 2.0: Client ID &A in SAML assertion not same as client ID &B in request
Dialog Logon	Non-Critical	☐	AUC	User Logoff
Dialog Logon	Non-Critical	☐	BUE	WS: Delayed logon successful (type &B, WP &C). Refer to Web service log &A
Dialog Logon	Non-Critical	☐	BUK	&A Assertion Used
Dialog Logon	Non-Critical	☐	BUL	&A: &B
Dialog Logon	Non-Critical	☐	BUM	Name ID of a subject
Dialog Logon	Non-Critical	☐	BUN	Attribute
Dialog Logon	Non-Critical	☐	BUO	Authentication Assertion
Dialog Logon	Non-Critical	☐	BUP	&A
Dialog Logon	Non-Critical	☐	BUQ	Signed LogoutRequest accepted
Dialog Logon	Non-Critical	☐	BUR	Unsigned LogoutRequest accepted
Dialog Logon	Non-Critical	☐	CU8	OAuth 2.0: Access token issued (client=&A, user=&B, grant type=&C)
Dialog Logon	Non-Critical	☐	CU9	OAuth 2.0: Valid access token received for user &A
Dialog Logon	Severe	☑	AU1	Logon successful (type=&A, method=&C)
Dialog Logon	Severe	☑	AUO	Logon Failed (Reason = &B, Type = &A)
Dialog Logon	Severe	☐	CU2	OAuth 2.0: Invalid access token received (reason=&A)
Dialog Logon	Severe	☐	CU3	OAuth 2.0: Insufficient OAuth 2.0 scope for requested resource (user=&A)
Dialog Logon	Severe	☐	CU5	OAuth 2.0: Client &A requested invalid access grant type &B
Dialog Logon	Severe	☐	CU7	OAuth 2.0: Scope &B not permitted for client &C, user &D (cause=&A)
Dialog Logon	Severe	☐	CUA	Rejected Assertion
Dialog Logon	Severe	☐	CUB	&A: &B
Dialog Logon	Severe	☐	CUC	&A
Dialog Logon	Severe	☐	CUD	Name ID of a subject
Dialog Logon	Severe	☐	CUE	Attribute
Dialog Logon	Severe	☐	CUF	Authentication Assertion
Dialog Logon	Severe	☐	CUG	Signed LogoutRequest rejected
Dialog Logon	Severe	☐	CUH	Unsigned LogoutRequest rejected
Other Events	Critical	☑	AUV	Digital Signature Error (Reason = &A, ID = &B)
Other Events	Critical	☑	BU1	Password check failed for user &B in client &A
Other Events	Critical	☑	BU3	Change Security Check During Export: Old Value &A, New Value &B

Figure 10.14 Adapting Filter Details

6. You now return to the initial screen for the static configuration. The Audit classes and Events columns are no longer displayed because the settings are displayed or edited at the detail level (see Figure 10.15). Click on Save.

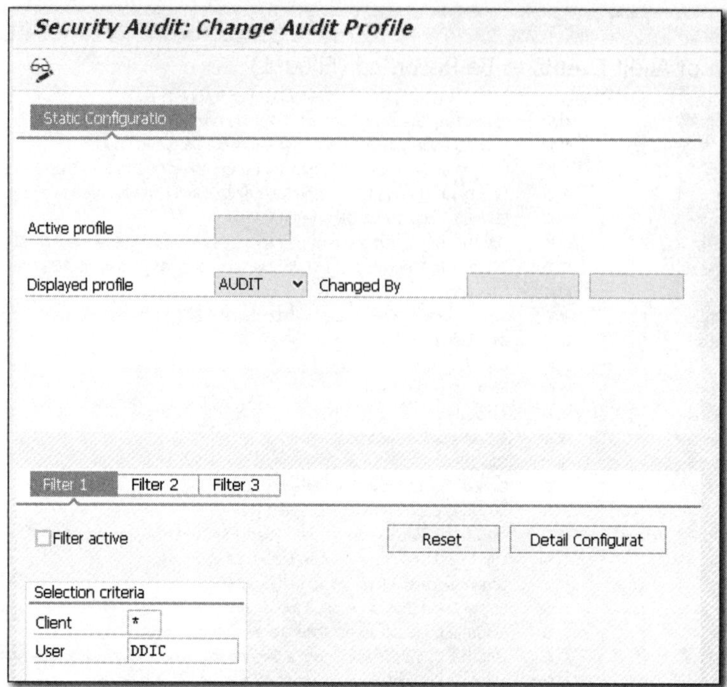

Figure 10.15 Screen When Detail Filter Is Set

7. The system displays a confirmation prompt asking if you want to distribute this filter configuration to all application servers (see Figure 10.16). Choose Yes.

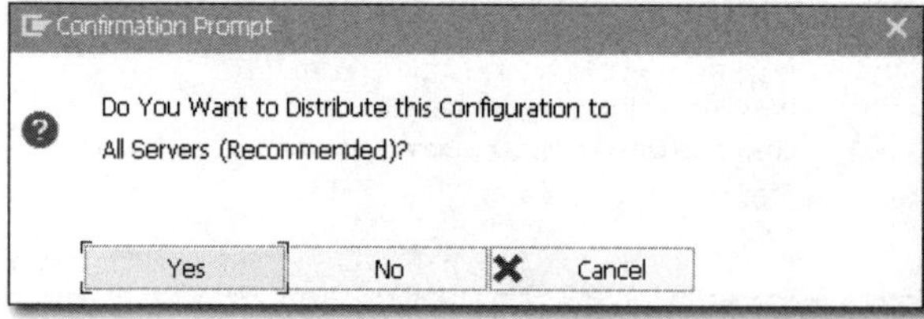

Figure 10.16 Distributing the Filter Configuration to All Application Servers

8. A message in the status bar confirms that the filter has been saved and distributed to all active instances (see Figure 10.17). For the settings to take effect, click on Activate.

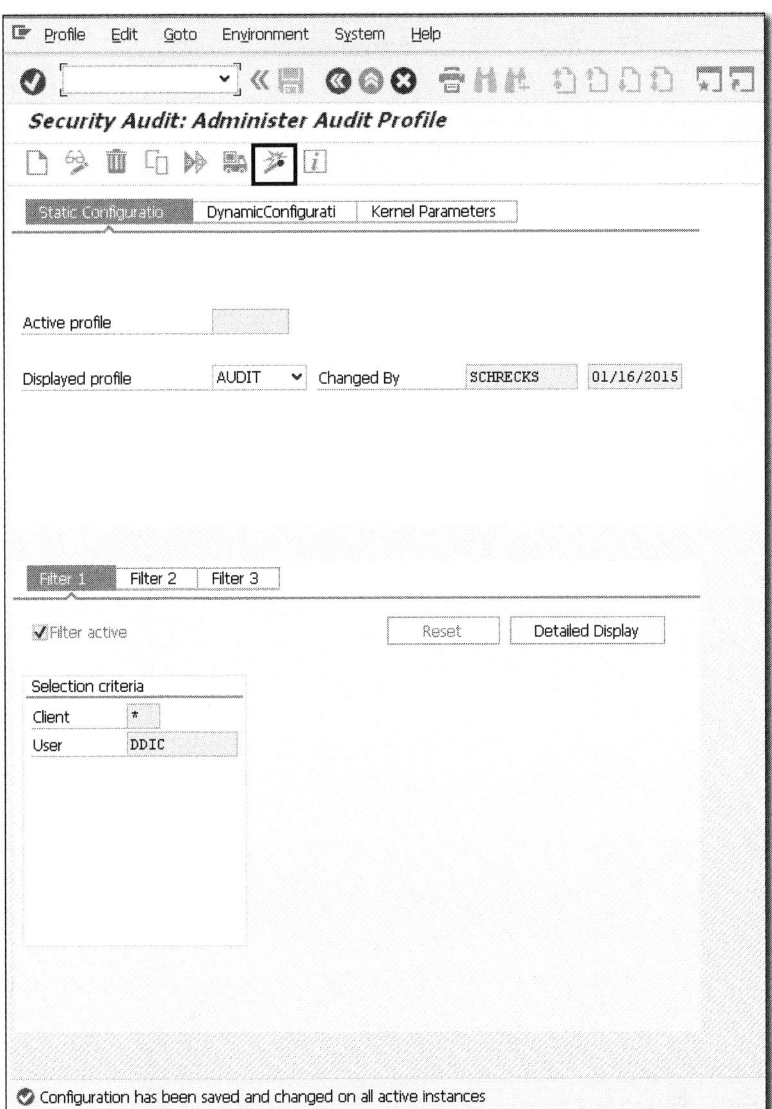

Figure 10.17 Activating the Settings

9. The name of your profile is now displayed in the Active profile field, and the message in the status bar confirms that the profile has been activated for the next system start (see Figure 10.18). Define additional filters, if necessary.

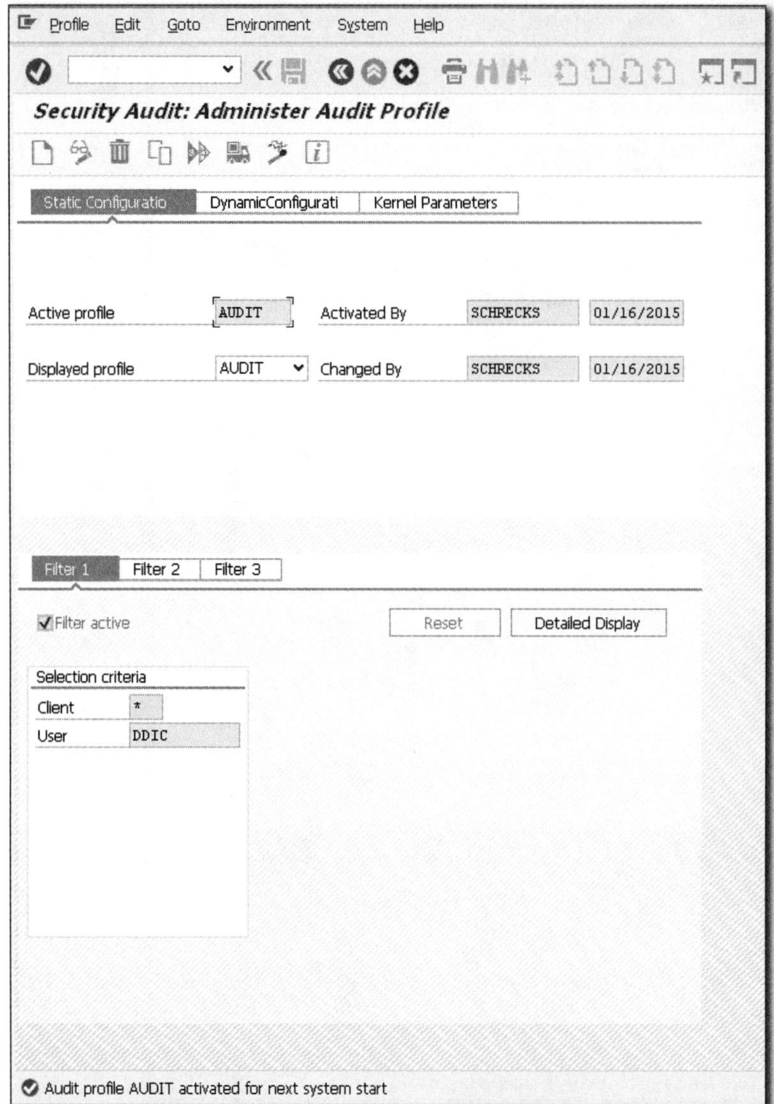

Figure 10.18 Status Bar Confirming the Activation of the Profile

[!] **When Does the Configuration Take Effect?**

Note that the static configuration doesn't take effect until you restart the application server. However, when you activate a static filter in newer releases, the system automatically creates an identical filter in the dynamic configuration so that logging is activated immediately.

If you want to change the logging criteria for one or more application servers while the system is running, follow these steps:

1. Switch to the Dynamic Configuration tab, and check whether the logging status is Activate Audit (see Figure 10.19). To create a dynamic filter, click on Display <-> Change to switch to change mode.

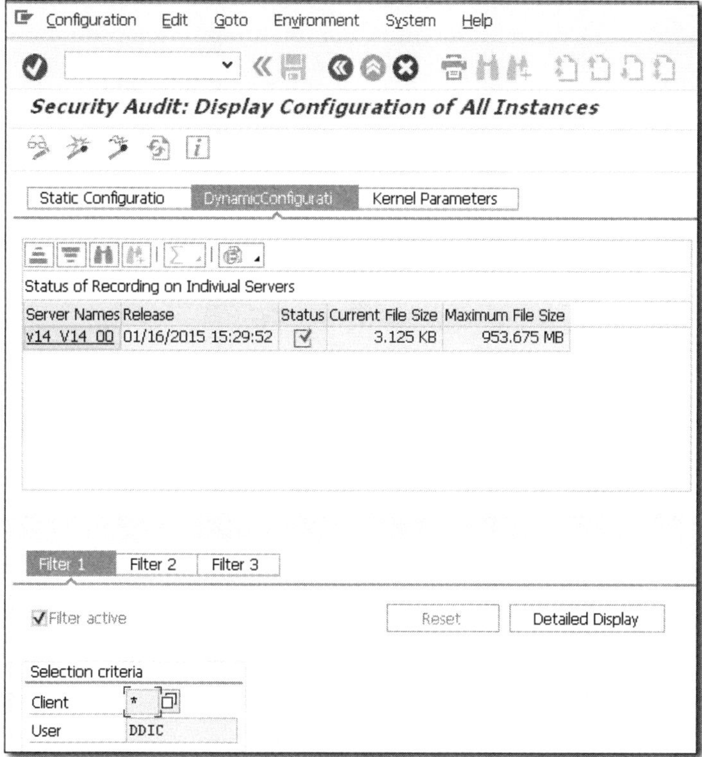

Figure 10.19 Checking the Logging Status

2. Switch to an available configuration slot (e.g., to the Filter 2 tab; see Figure 10.20).
3. Configure the required settings (see step 4 of the static configuration). When you're finished, click on Activate Audit .

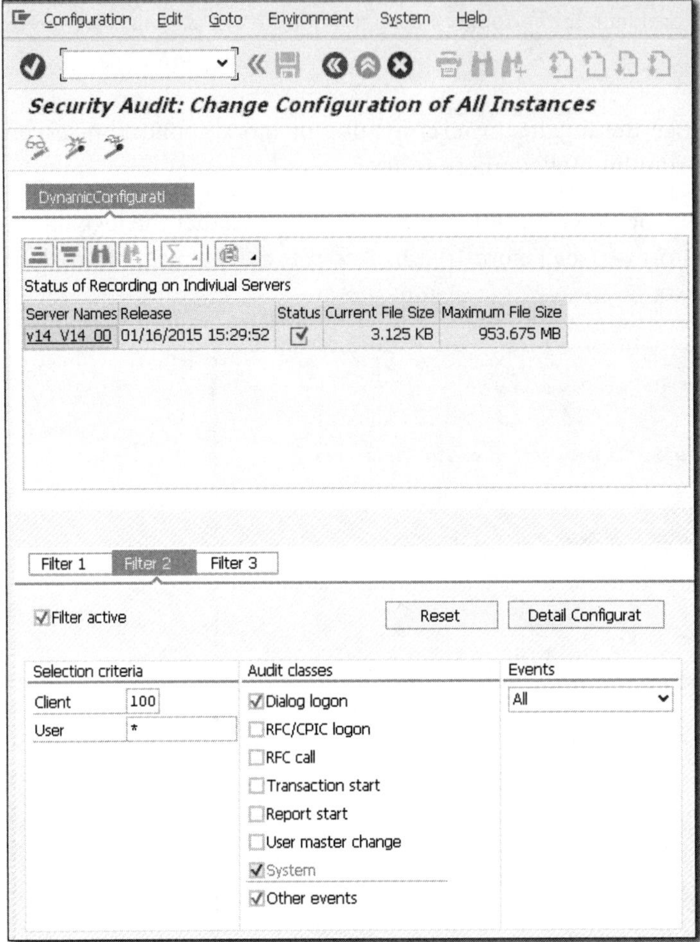

Figure 10.20 Creating Dynamic Filters

4. Click YES to confirm the security prompt (see Figure 10.21).

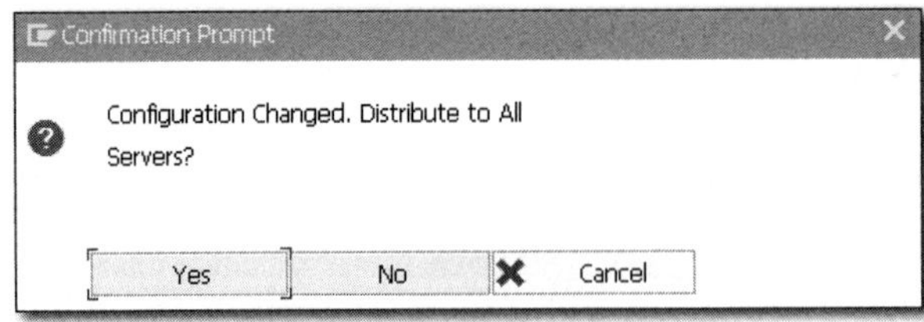

Figure 10.21 Distributing the Configuration to All Application Servers

5. A message in the status bar confirms that the filter has been activated on all instances (see Figure 10.22).

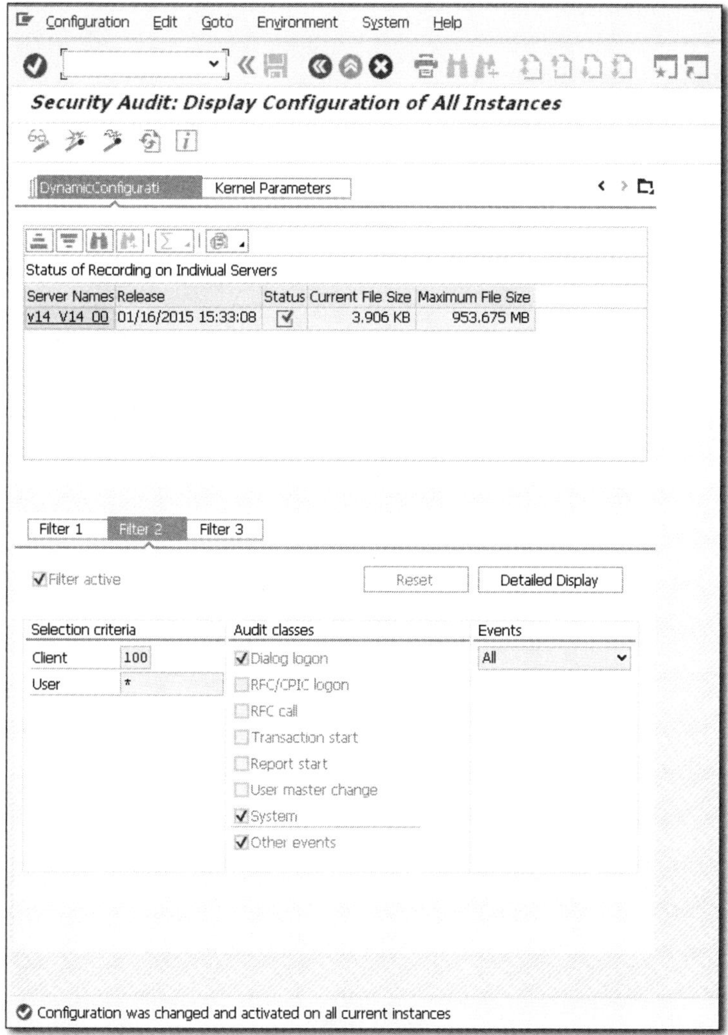

Figure 10.22 Updated Filter for All Instances

As soon as the log filters have been defined and activated, the selected events are recorded. Depending on the filter setting for a large number of users or a large number of logged system actions, the volume of data accumulates very quickly, and therefore the log files grow accordingly.

In the worst-case scenario, your file system may overflow, which will cause the SAP system to shut down. Therefore, monitor the size of your audit files or the fill level of your log directory.

Analyzing the Security Audit Log

Transaction SM20 is used to analyze the files created by the Security Audit Log. Follow these steps:

1. Enter Transaction SM20 in the command field and press the [Enter] key (or select the menu option Tools • Administration • Monitor • Security Audit Log • SM20—Analysis).
2. If necessary, you can use the following selection parameters to restrict the analysis (see Figure 10.23):
   - In the From Date/Time field, enter the start date and start time of the period to be considered.

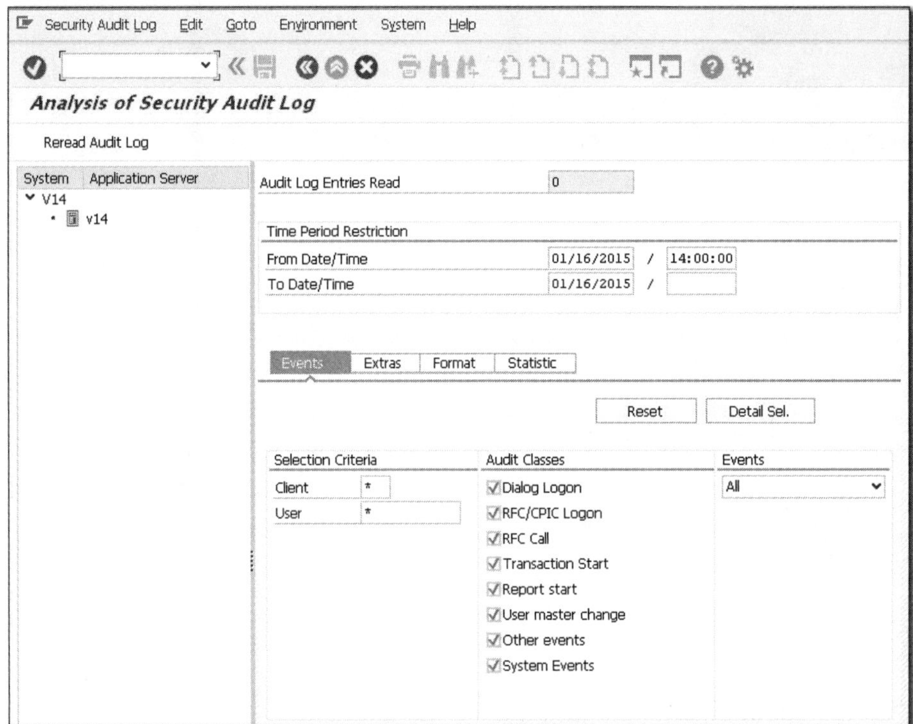

Figure 10.23 Selecting the Data to Be Analyzed

- In the To Date/Time field, enter the end date and end time of the period to be considered.
- On the Events tab, use the Client, User, and Audit Classes fields to adjust your analysis.
- Click on the Reread Audit Log button to display the log.

3. The logged system events are displayed (see Figure 10.24).

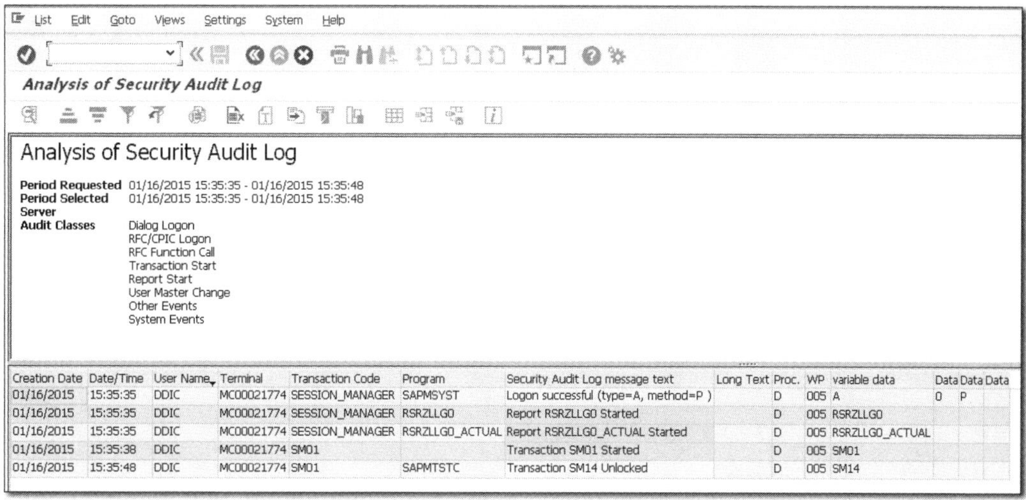

Figure 10.24 Analyzing the Security Audit Log

In this example, an anonymous user account (user DDIC) was used to remove a transaction lock (for Transaction SM14) that may have developed into a system risk. At first glance, however, you can't identify which person made the change. The entry in the Terminal column can help you determine which PC the user used to log on to the SAP system. The change documents for the relevant user master record (here: DDIC) provide another clue. In Transactions SU01 (User Maintenance) or SUIM (User Information System), you can determine who was the last person to change the user account, in other words, who was the last person to reset the password.

Transaction STAD [+]

In certain circumstances, the data protection regulations may not allow you to run the Security Audit Log continuously. In the worst-case scenario, no logs are available for analysis after a system incident. With Transaction STAD (Business Transaction Analysis), however, you don't need an active Security Audit Log to analyze which user has executed which transaction or program in the system and which PC was used to log on to the system. The standard configuration only contains data from the past 48 hours. However, you can use the profile parameters `stat/max_files` and `stat/as_max_files` to extend this period to a maximum of 99 hours.

Deleting Security Audit Log Files

Files created by the Security Audit Log aren't automatically deleted. In other words, the volume of data constantly increases if logging is active. You must therefore delete old audit files from time to time. You can do this directly at the operating system level, or you can use Transaction SM18 (Reorganize Security Audit Log).

1. Enter Transaction SM18 in the command field and press the [Enter] key (or select the menu option TOOLS • ADMINISTRATION • MONITOR • SECURITY AUDIT LOG • SM18—REORGANIZATION).
2. In the MINIMUM AGE field, enter the number of past days for which you want to retain files (e.g., data from the past 30 days). Click on EXECUTE (see Figure 10.25).

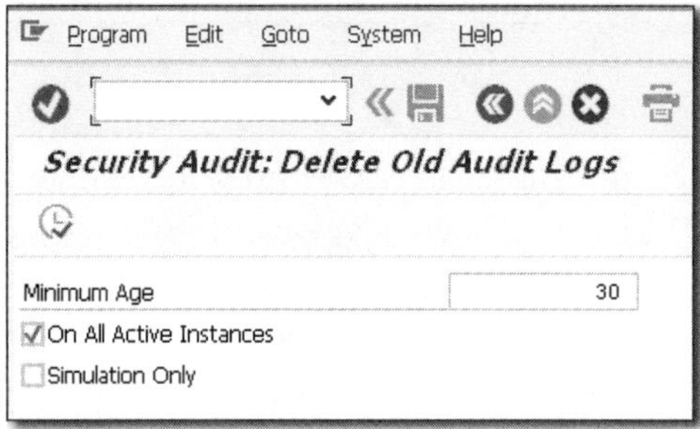

Figure 10.25 Deleting Old Security Audit Log Files

[+] **Minimum Age**

The MINIMUM AGE must be 3 or more. In other words, you can't use Transaction SM18 to delete log files from the past three days.

3. The audit files are deleted. The log shows the number of files that have been deleted and the number of files that have been retained (see Figure 10.26).

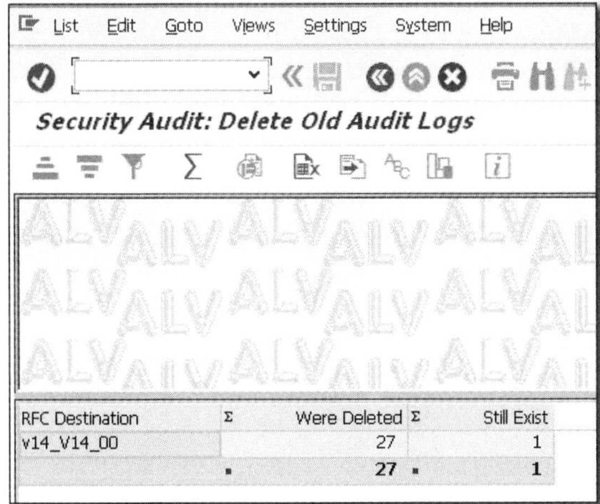

Figure 10.26 Deletion Log

Deleting Log Entries [!]

When you delete files, the log entries are permanently lost if they weren't first saved at the operating system level. Resourceful users could try to cover their tracks. For this reason, only a few users should be granted access to Transaction SM18.

10.6 Summary

All kinds of sensitive business data are stored in your SAP system. Because legislation demands that companies take appropriate measures to protect their data, you must give some thought to the security of your SAP systems.

This topic is complex because it comprises all systems levels—application, database, operating system, and infrastructure. A gap in security may result in all other measures becoming ineffective. For this reason, a usable security concept can only be created in conjunction with the relevant experts. Regular checks then ensure that no new weak spots arise.

This chapter deals with performance issues in SAP systems. In addition to providing general recommendations on the handling of short-term performance bottlenecks, this chapter introduces tools for analyzing and optimizing the system's performance.

11 Performance

Performance problems usually affect all users and most of the business processes in an SAP system. As an administrator, your highest priority is to eliminate bottlenecks as soon as possible and ensure that the users can work again. When the worst is over, you can analyze the problem in detail and try to avoid similar incidents by introducing the appropriate countermeasures. The complex area of performance analysis and optimization in an SAP system is further described in *SAP Performance Optimization Guide: Analyzing and Tuning SAP Systems* by Thomas Schneider (7th edition, SAP PRESS, 2013). This chapter introduces you to the most important tools for managing performance problems quickly and effectively.

A prerequisite is that the hardware, operating system, database, and SAP system have all been installed correctly, that they are dimensioned appropriately according to the SAP Sizing Guides (see *www.service.sap.com/sizing*), and that performance bottlenecks don't occur on a daily basis. If this is the case, there's either a general problem in the system landscape, or your system doesn't have enough resources for stable operation. You then have to analyze the infrastructure in detail or assess the resource requirements anew.

11.1 Short-Term Remedy of Performance Problems

You usually recognize temporary performance bottlenecks due to unusually long response times during the execution of dialog transactions. As an administrator, you get informed either by users or because you work in the system and are affected directly.

It may just be a short-term *peak load*; that is, a lot of users perform resource-intensive activities in the system simultaneously. In such a case, as soon as one or several users have completed their work, the system may no longer be overloaded within a short space of time without you having done anything. On the other hand, you mustn't waste time by hoping that the problem will resolve itself because it's also possible that a serious error has occurred in the system infrastructure that you have to eliminate actively (e.g., network problems or hardware defects). So, you should immediately gain an overview of the system's state by carrying out the following steps:

1. Enter Transaction SM50 in the command field and press the [Enter] key (or select the TOOLS • ADMINISTRATION • MONITOR • SYSTEM MONITORING • SM50—PROCESS OVERVIEW).
2. In the process overview, search for abnormalities, for example, whether all dialog processes are occupied or whether there are processes with exceptionally long runtimes (see Figure 11.1). Update the display several times using REFRESH to identify permanently running processes.

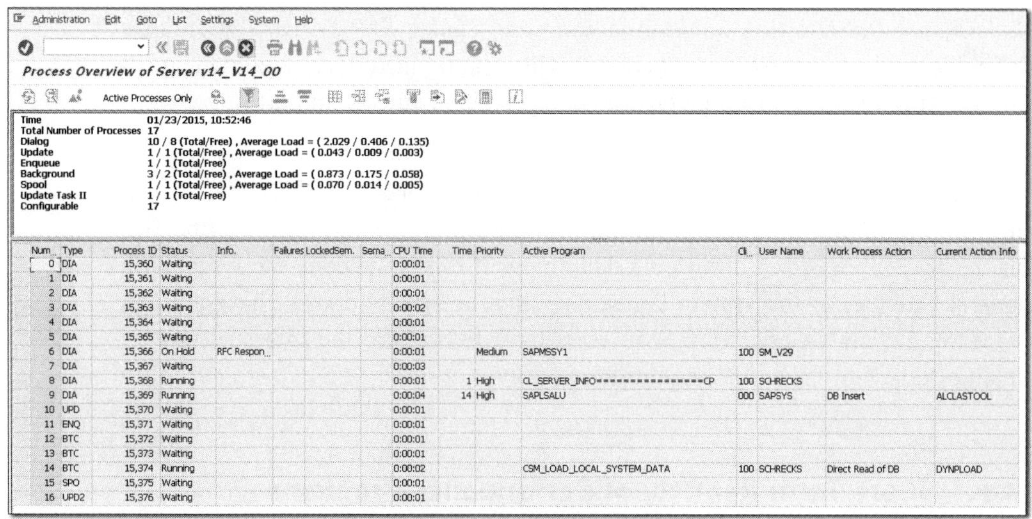

Num...	Type	Process ID	Status	Info.	Failures	LockedSem.	Sema...	CPU Time	Time	Priority	Active Program	Cli...	User Name	Work Process Action	Current Action Info
0	DIA	15,360	Waiting					0:00:01							
1	DIA	15,361	Waiting					0:00:01							
2	DIA	15,362	Waiting					0:00:01							
3	DIA	15,363	Waiting					0:00:02							
4	DIA	15,364	Waiting					0:00:01							
5	DIA	15,365	Waiting					0:00:01							
6	DIA	15,366	On Hold	RFC Respon...				0:00:01		Medium	SAPMSSY1	100	SM_V29		
7	DIA	15,367	Waiting					0:00:03							
8	DIA	15,368	Running					0:00:01	1	High	CL_SERVER_INFO=================CP	100	SCHRECKS		
9	DIA	15,369	Running					0:00:04	14	High	SAPLSALU	000	SAPSYS	DB Insert	ALCLASTOOL
10	UPD	15,370	Waiting					0:00:01							
11	ENQ	15,371	Waiting					0:00:01							
12	BTC	15,372	Waiting					0:00:01							
13	BTC	15,373	Waiting					0:00:01							
14	BTC	15,374	Running					0:00:02			CSM_LOAD_LOCAL_SYSTEM_DATA	100	SCHRECKS	Direct Read of DB	DYNPLOAD
15	SPO	15,375	Waiting					0:00:01							
16	UPD2	15,376	Waiting					0:00:01							

Figure 11.1 Searching the Process Overview for Abnormalities

[+]

Program dpmon

If all dialog work processes of the SAP system are occupied, you may no longer be able to log on to the system or start a new transaction. In such cases, you can also manage the work processes at operating system level using program `dpmon`, which you can find in the kernel directory. The menu options, `p` and `l`, show you the work processes tables analogous to Transaction SM50 and provide an option to terminate processes in a targeted manner.

3. In addition, you can use Transaction SM04 (User List) to obtain an overview of the users that are currently logged on to the system (see Figure 11.2, and see Chapter 13). One of the reasons for performance problems can be a particularly large number of users logged on to the system.

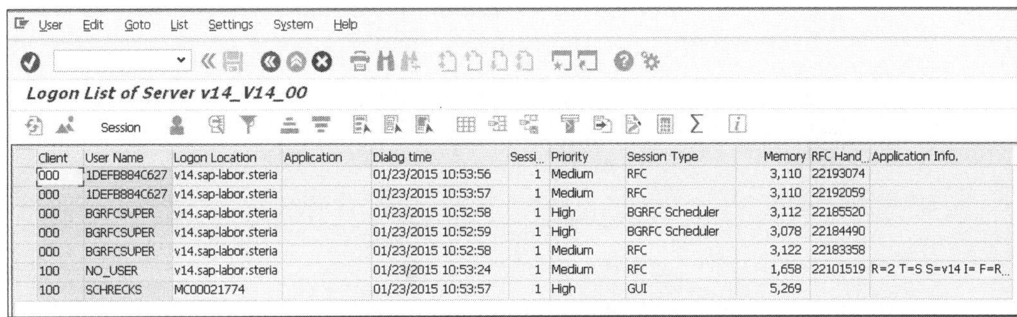

Figure 11.2 Checking the Number of Logged-On Users

4. Start a system monitor at the operating system level (e.g., *Task Manager* in Microsoft Windows, `nmon` in UNIX, or `top` in Linux). Analyze the current system load with regard to CPU, memory, virtual memory, and hard disk activity (input/output; see Figure 11.3).

Checking Processes [+]

Check whether certain processes have a particularly large share in the CPU usage, occupy a large amount of memory, or have exceptional I/O rates. Especially when objects are swapped to the virtual memory, this has a negative effect on system performance. In this case, you should increase the system's memory, if possible.

Real-Time Files at the Operating System Level [+]

Operating system tools are usually more suitable than the SAP system's operating system monitor (Transaction ST06; see Chapter 9) to solve serious performance bottlenecks because you're provided with real-time data that is updated much more often.

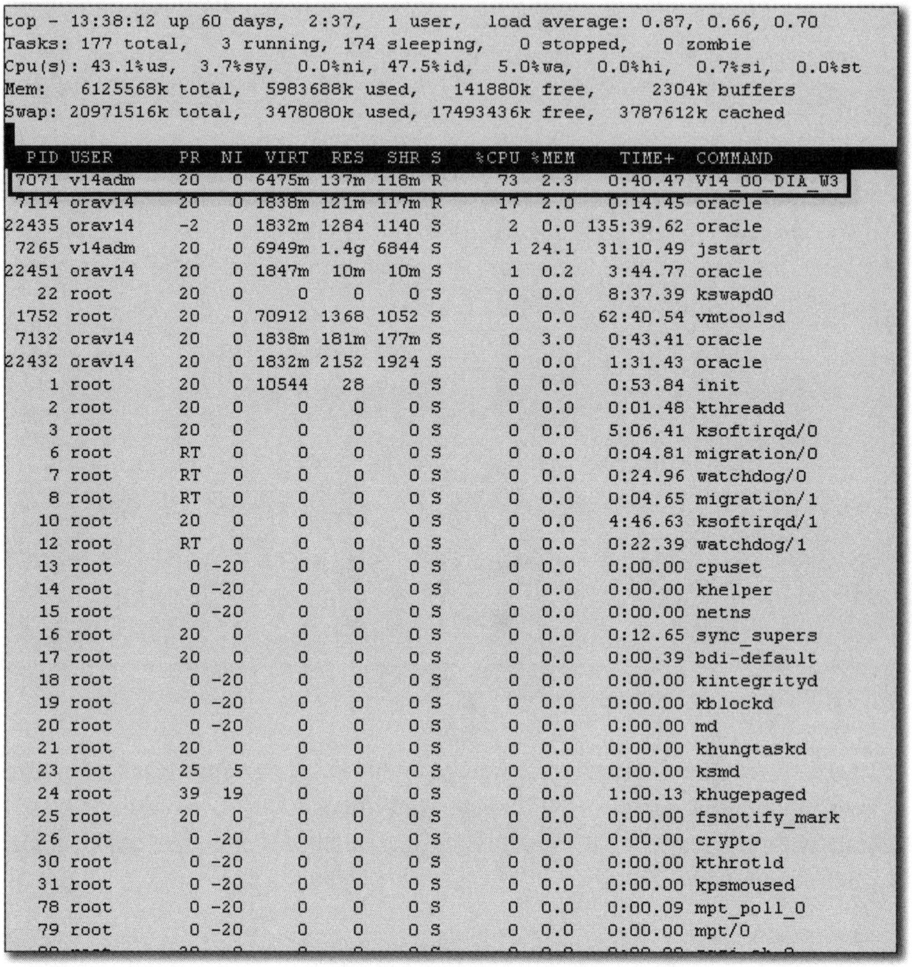

```
top - 13:38:12 up 60 days,  2:37,  1 user,  load average: 0.87, 0.66, 0.70
Tasks: 177 total,   3 running, 174 sleeping,   0 stopped,   0 zombie
Cpu(s): 43.1%us,  3.7%sy,  0.0%ni, 47.5%id,  5.0%wa,  0.0%hi,  0.7%si,  0.0%st
Mem:   6125568k total,  5983688k used,   141880k free,     2304k buffers
Swap: 20971516k total,  3478080k used, 17493436k free,  3787612k cached

  PID USER      PR  NI  VIRT  RES  SHR S %CPU %MEM    TIME+  COMMAND
 7071 v14adm    20   0 6475m 137m 118m R   73  2.3   0:40.47 V14_00_DIA_W3
 7114 orav14    20   0 1838m 121m 117m R   17  2.0   0:14.45 oracle
22435 orav14    -2   0 1832m 1284 1140 S    2  0.0 135:39.62 oracle
 7265 v14adm    20   0 6949m 1.4g 6844 S    1 24.1  31:10.49 jstart
22451 orav14    20   0 1847m  10m  10m S    1  0.2   3:44.77 oracle
   22 root      20   0     0    0    0 S    0  0.0   8:37.39 kswapd0
 1752 root      20   0 70912 1368 1052 S    0  0.0  62:40.54 vmtoolsd
 7132 orav14    20   0 1838m 181m 177m S    0  3.0   0:43.41 oracle
22432 orav14    20   0 1832m 2152 1924 S    0  0.0   1:31.43 oracle
    1 root      20   0 10544   28    0 S    0  0.0   0:53.84 init
    2 root      20   0     0    0    0 S    0  0.0   0:01.48 kthreadd
    3 root      20   0     0    0    0 S    0  0.0   5:06.41 ksoftirqd/0
    6 root      RT   0     0    0    0 S    0  0.0   0:04.81 migration/0
    7 root      RT   0     0    0    0 S    0  0.0   0:24.96 watchdog/0
    8 root      RT   0     0    0    0 S    0  0.0   0:04.65 migration/1
   10 root      20   0     0    0    0 S    0  0.0   4:46.63 ksoftirqd/1
   12 root      RT   0     0    0    0 S    0  0.0   0:22.39 watchdog/1
   13 root       0 -20     0    0    0 S    0  0.0   0:00.00 cpuset
   14 root       0 -20     0    0    0 S    0  0.0   0:00.00 khelper
   15 root       0 -20     0    0    0 S    0  0.0   0:00.00 netns
   16 root      20   0     0    0    0 S    0  0.0   0:12.65 sync_supers
   17 root      20   0     0    0    0 S    0  0.0   0:00.39 bdi-default
   18 root       0 -20     0    0    0 S    0  0.0   0:00.00 kintegrityd
   19 root       0 -20     0    0    0 S    0  0.0   0:00.00 kblockd
   20 root       0 -20     0    0    0 S    0  0.0   0:00.00 md
   21 root      20   0     0    0    0 S    0  0.0   0:00.00 khungtaskd
   23 root      25   5     0    0    0 S    0  0.0   0:00.00 ksmd
   24 root      39  19     0    0    0 S    0  0.0   1:00.13 khugepaged
   25 root      20   0     0    0    0 S    0  0.0   0:00.00 fsnotify_mark
   26 root       0 -20     0    0    0 S    0  0.0   0:00.00 crypto
   30 root       0 -20     0    0    0 S    0  0.0   0:00.00 kthrotld
   31 root       0 -20     0    0    0 S    0  0.0   0:00.00 kpsmoused
   78 root       0 -20     0    0    0 S    0  0.0   0:00.09 mpt_poll_0
   79 root       0 -20     0    0    0 S    0  0.0   0:00.00 mpt/0
```

Figure 11.3 Analyzing the System Load at the Operating System Level

5. If you notice suspicious SAP processes (process name: DISP+WORK) at the operating system level, the process number allows you to draw conclusions about abnormalities in the SAP process overview (Transaction SM50). This enables you to identify the process type (dialog process: DIA type; background job: BTC type) and the user that executes the process. If it's a background process, check the active jobs (see Figure 11.4) using Transaction SM37 (Job Overview; see Chapter 15).

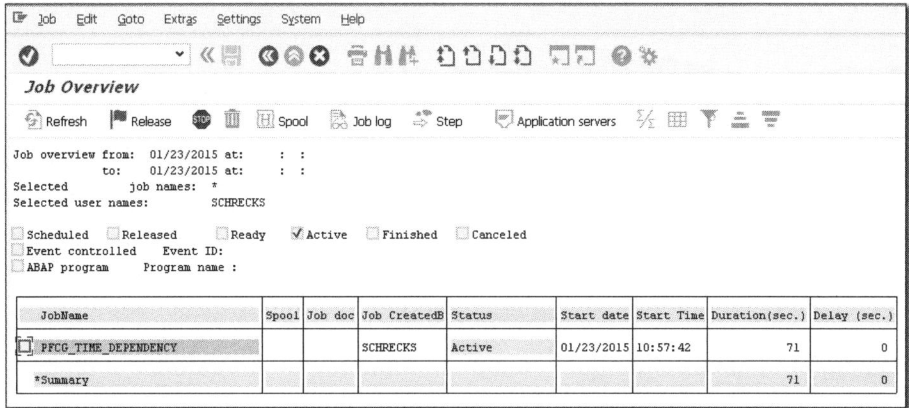

Figure 11.4 Checking Jobs

For a dialog process, contact the user.

Identifying SAP Processes

If the suspicious processes aren't SAP processes (DISP+WORK), the problem usually isn't located in the SAP system. Continue to check the programs or database processes (e.g., Oracle) that run at the operating system level.

6. When you're sure that an SAP process has caused the performance bottleneck, terminate the process if absolutely necessary, that is, if the performance problems are too severe. To do so, select the process in the process overview, and choose PROCESS • CANCEL • WITHOUT CORE (see Figure 11.5).

Generating Core Dumps [+]

If you use the CANCEL WITH CORE option, the system creates an error log file for the process and writes very detailed information to the trace file of the respective work process. You can analyze this file using Transaction ST11 (Error Log Files). Usually it's sufficient to use the CANCEL WITHOUT CORE menu option. In this case, the system doesn't generate a core dump.

7. The termination attempts in the process overview may not be successful; that is, the process isn't canceled. In this case, terminate the process at the operating system level (e.g., via END PROCESS in the Windows Task Manager or using the `kill [-KILL] <process ID>` console command under UNIX/Linux; see Figure 11.6).

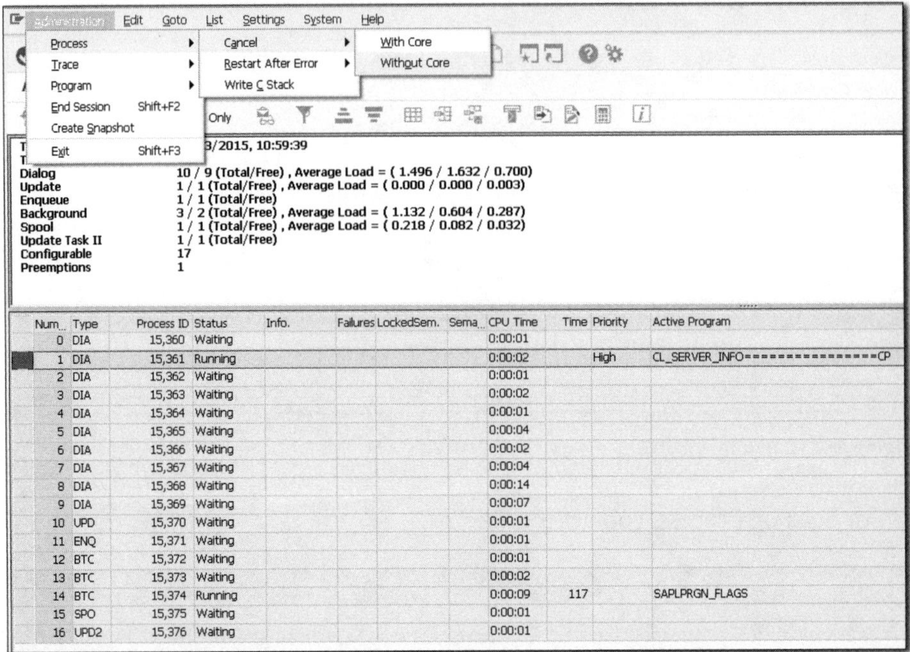

Figure 11.5 Canceling a Process

```
v14:v14adm 59> kill -KILL 7071
```

Figure 11.6 Terminating the Process via the Console (UNIX/Linux)

[!]

Caution When Terminating Processes

Be careful when terminating processes because you cancel running SAP programs ruthlessly. This can have severe consequences, particularly for critical background jobs.g

11.2 Detailed Analysis of Performance Problems

In addition to fast troubleshooting, the SAP system provides numerous analysis tools that you should use if your SAP system frequently suffers from performance bottlenecks. A prerequisite for using them is that SAP OS Collector (SAPOSCOL) is active, and the periodical job, SAP_COLLECTOR_FOR_PERFMONITOR, runs regularly (see Chapter 9). This ensures that the data required for analyses is collected. You should collect data for at least one week to obtain meaningful statistics.

11.2.1 System Load Analysis

Load analyses enable you to determine detailed data on the system's performance (see Figure 11.7). You should check these statistics and record trends to get a feel for the system performance. It also enables you to identify transactions with a high system load or bottlenecks in individual system components.

1. Enter Transaction ST03N in the command field and press the Enter key (or select TOOLS • ADMINISTRATION • MONITOR • PERFORMANCE • WORKLOAD • ST03N—AGGREGATED STATISTIC RECORDS LOCAL).

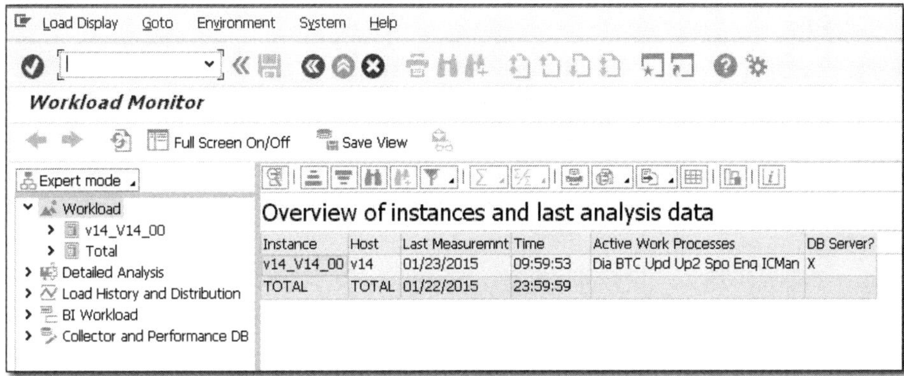

Figure 11.7 Workload Monitor

2. Ensure that the EXPERT MODE is selected in the left screen area. Expand the hierarchy entry DETAILED ANALYSIS • LAST MINUTE'S LOAD (see Figure 11.8).

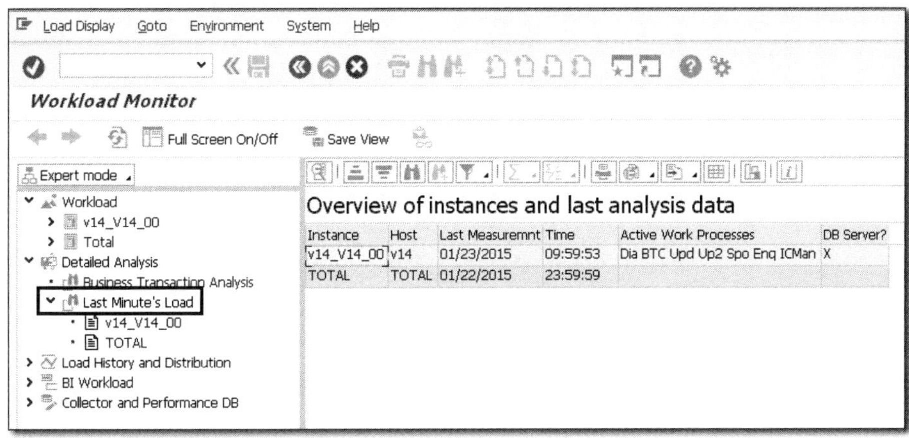

Figure 11.8 Checking the Workload of the Last Minutes

3. Double-click on the instance name (e.g., v14_V14_00). In the next screen (see Figure 11.9), you can restrict the analysis period.
   - In Analysis Interval, enter the Date and Time Period that are supposed to be analyzed.
   - If necessary, enter the Client, User, or Work process number if the data needs to be restricted.
   - Depending on the time period to be analyzed, you can also modify the value for the Time profile granularity under Analysis Parameters. For a short analysis interval (e.g., 30 minutes), it's perfectly fine to set the resolution to 1 min.
   - Click the Continue button ✓.

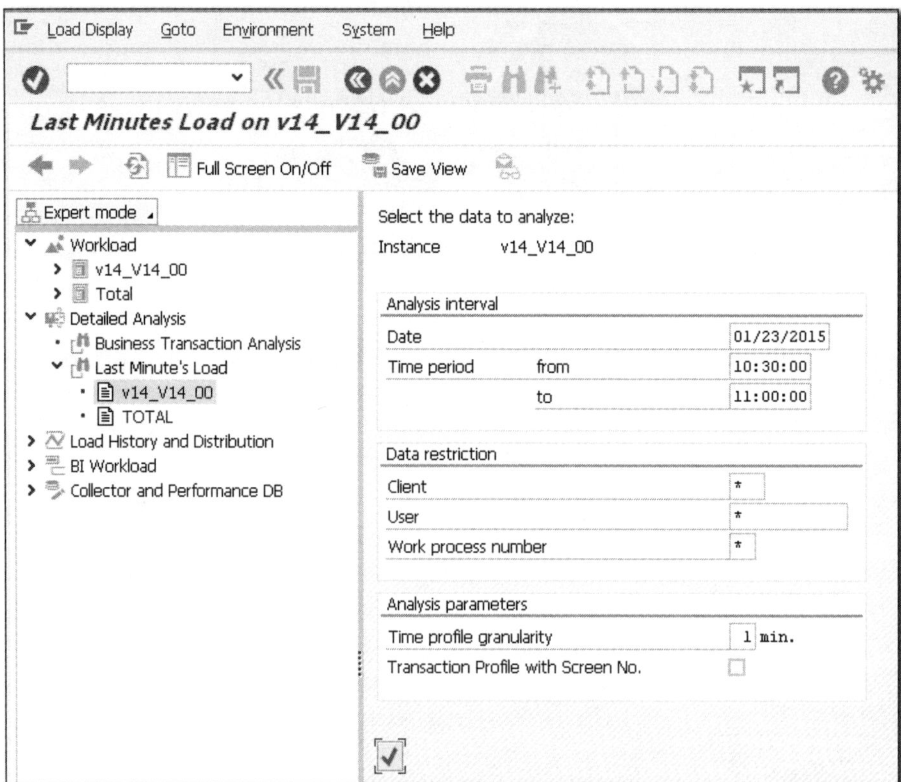

Figure 11.9 Restricting the Analysis Period

[+]

Using Notes

For subsequent analysis, you should make the corresponding notes on suspicious processes and users when using the fast troubleshooting process as described earlier in Section 11.1.

4. The WORKLOAD OVERVIEW analysis view (see Figure 11.10) displays data on various task types. The information is distributed across several tabs. The first tab, TIMES, includes a table that enables you to determine which task type occupies the most resources in your system. Under TASK TYPE, select the required type. Click on DETAILS to view the performance values for the selected task type. The most important task types are the following:
   - DIALOG: User transactions that are executed in the foreground.
   - BACKGROUND: Transactions in background processing.
   - HTTP: Internet transactions on an HTTP basis.
   - RFC: Remote function calls.
   - SPOOL: Spool work processes.
   - UPDATE: Update processes.

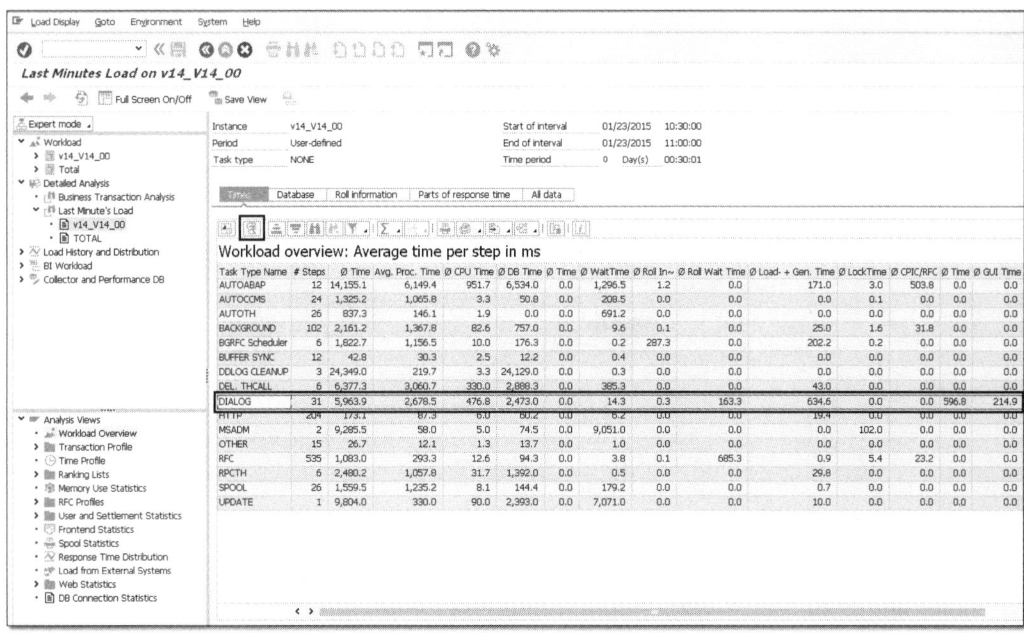

Load Display Goto Environment System Help
Last Minutes Load on v14_V14_00
Full Screen On/Off
Save View
Expert mode
Workload
v14_V14_00
Total
Detailed Analysis
Business Transaction Analysis
Last Minute's Load
v14_V14_00
TOTAL
Load History and Distribution
BI Workload
Collector and Performance DB
Analysis Views
Workload Overview
Transaction Profile
Time Profile
Ranking Lists
Memory Use Statistics
RFC Profiles
User and Settlement Statistics
Frontend Statistics
Spool Statistics
Response Time Distribution
Load from External Systems
Web Statistics
DB Connection Statistics
Instance v14_V14_00
Period User-defined
Task type NONE
Start of interval 01/23/2015 10:30:00
End of interval 01/23/2015 11:00:00
Time period 0 Day(s) 00:30:01
Times
Database
Roll information
Parts of response time
All data
Workload overview: Average time per step in ms
Task Type Name | # Steps | Ø Time | Avg. Proc. Time | Ø CPU Time | Ø DB Time | Ø Time | Ø WaitTime | Ø Roll In~ | Ø Roll Wait Time | Ø Load- + Gen. Time | Ø LockTime | Ø CPIC/RFC | Ø Time | Ø GUI Time
AUTOABAP | 12 | 14,155.1 | 6,149.4 | 951.7 | 6,534.0 | 0.0 | 1,296.5 | 1.2 | 0.0 | 171.0 | 3.0 | 503.8 | 0.0 | 0.0
AUTOCCMS | 24 | 1,325.2 | 1,065.8 | 3.3 | 50.8 | 0.0 | 208.5 | 0.0 | 0.0 | 0.0 | 0.1 | 0.0 | 0.0 | 0.0
AUTOTH | 26 | 837.3 | 146.1 | 1.9 | 0.0 | 0.0 | 691.2 | 0.0 | 0.0 | 0.0 | 0.0 | 0.0 | 0.0 | 0.0
BACKGROUND | 102 | 2,161.2 | 1,367.8 | 82.6 | 757.0 | 0.0 | 9.6 | 0.1 | 0.0 | 25.0 | 1.6 | 31.8 | 0.0 | 0.0
BGRFC Scheduler | 6 | 1,822.7 | 1,156.5 | 10.0 | 176.3 | 0.0 | 0.2 | 287.3 | 0.0 | 202.2 | 0.2 | 0.0 | 0.0 | 0.0
BUFFER SYNC | 12 | 42.8 | 30.3 | 2.5 | 12.2 | 0.0 | 0.4 | 0.0 | 0.0 | 0.0 | 0.0 | 0.0 | 0.0 | 0.0
DDLOG CLEANUP | 3 | 24,349.0 | 219.7 | 3.3 | 24,129.0 | 0.0 | 0.3 | 0.0 | 0.0 | 0.0 | 0.0 | 0.0 | 0.0 | 0.0
DEL. THCALL | 6 | 6,377.3 | 3,060.7 | 330.0 | 2,888.3 | 0.0 | 385.3 | 0.0 | 0.0 | 43.0 | 0.0 | 0.0 | 0.0 | 0.0
DIALOG | 31 | 5,963.9 | 2,678.5 | 476.8 | 2,473.0 | 0.0 | 14.3 | 0.3 | 163.3 | 634.6 | 0.0 | 0.0 | 596.8 | 214.9
HTTP | 204 | 173.1 | 87.3 | 6.0 | 60.2 | 0.0 | 6.2 | 0.0 | 0.0 | 19.4 | 0.0 | 0.0 | 0.0 | 0.0
MSADM | 2 | 9,285.5 | 58.0 | 5.0 | 74.5 | 0.0 | 9,051.0 | 0.0 | 0.0 | 0.0 | 102.0 | 0.0 | 0.0 | 0.0
OTHER | 15 | 26.7 | 12.1 | 1.3 | 13.7 | 0.0 | 1.0 | 0.0 | 0.0 | 0.0 | 0.0 | 0.0 | 0.0 | 0.0
RFC | 535 | 1,083.0 | 293.3 | 12.6 | 94.3 | 0.0 | 3.8 | 0.1 | 685.3 | 0.9 | 5.4 | 23.2 | 0.0 | 0.0
RPCTH | 6 | 2,480.2 | 1,057.8 | 31.7 | 1,392.0 | 0.0 | 0.5 | 0.0 | 0.0 | 29.8 | 0.0 | 0.0 | 0.0 | 0.0
SPOOL | 26 | 1,559.5 | 1,235.2 | 8.1 | 144.4 | 0.0 | 179.2 | 0.0 | 0.0 | 0.7 | 0.0 | 0.0 | 0.0 | 0.0
UPDATE | 1 | 9,804.0 | 330.0 | 90.0 | 2,393.0 | 0.0 | 7,071.0 | 0.0 | 0.0 | 10.0 | 0.0 | 0.0 | 0.0 | 0.0

Figure 11.10 Workload Overview

5. In the DETAILS dialog box (see Figure 11.11), check the displayed data, for example, the AVERAGE CPU TIME (MS). For the DIALOG task type, the expected standard response time is less than 1,000 ms (1 second), for instance. When you're finished, click on CLOSE WINDOW.

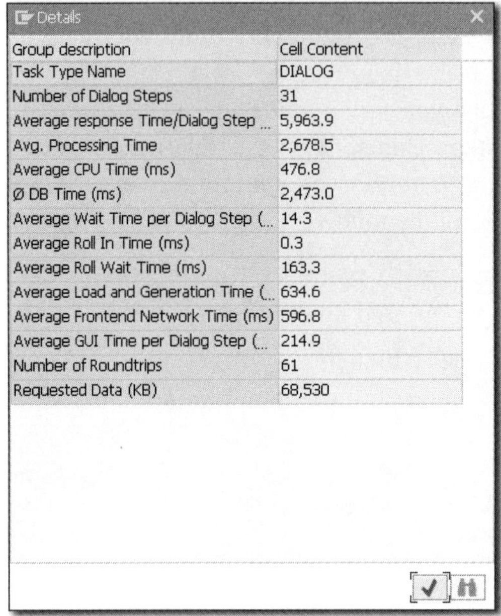

Details
Group description | Cell Content
Task Type Name | DIALOG
Number of Dialog Steps | 31
Average response Time/Dialog Step ... | 5,963.9
Avg. Processing Time | 2,678.5
Average CPU Time (ms) | 476.8
Ø DB Time (ms) | 2,473.0
Average Wait Time per Dialog Step (... | 14.3
Average Roll In Time (ms) | 0.3
Average Roll Wait Time (ms) | 163.3
Average Load and Generation Time (... | 634.6
Average Frontend Network Time (ms) | 596.8
Average GUI Time per Dialog Step (... | 214.9
Number of Roundtrips | 61
Requested Data (KB) | 68,530

Figure 11.11 Detailed Analysis for a Task Type

[+]

Evaluating Performance Statistics

These values differ depending on the task type and system component; their evaluation is mainly a matter of experience. You may have to leave it to experts. Thomas Schneider's book, which we mentioned at the beginning of this chapter, provides information on this. But you can also refer to the SAP Service Marketplace under *www.service.sap.com/performance*.

6. In the lower-left area of the screen, under ANALYSIS VIEWS, select the TRANSACTION PROFILE folder. Double-click on STANDARD (see Figure 11.12).
7. Select the AVERAGE RESPONSE TIME (Ø TIME) column heading, and click on the DESCENDING ORDER icon. The system sorts the programs and transactions by the average response time, which enables you to analyze which transactions place a particularly high load on your system (see Figure 11.13).

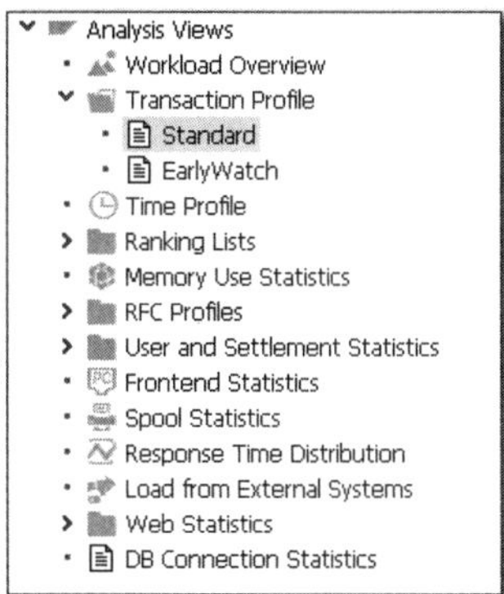

Figure 11.12 Selecting a Standard Transaction Profile

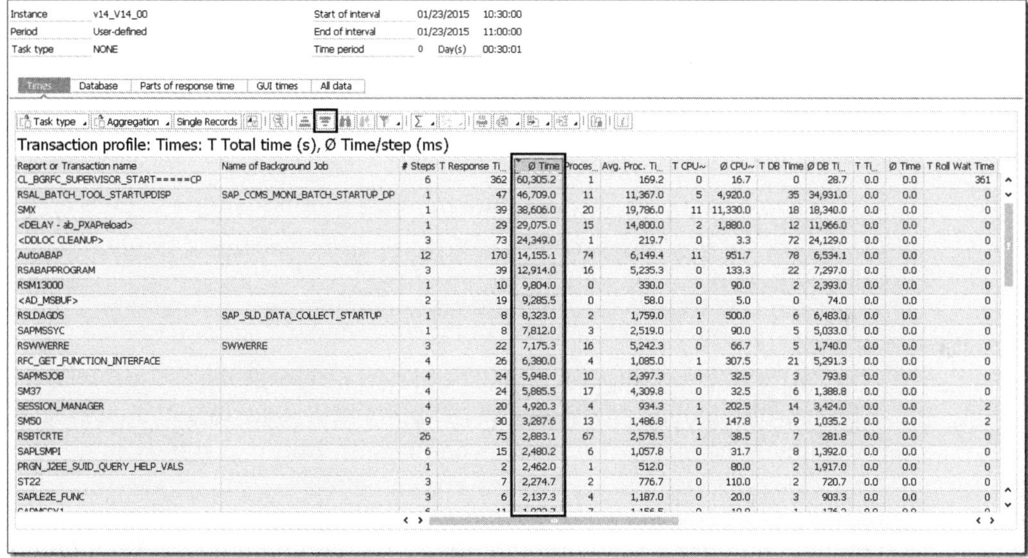

Transaction profile: Times: T Total time (s), Ø Time/step (ms)

Report or Transaction name	Name of Background Job	# Steps	T Response Ti...	Ø Time	Proces...	Avg. Proc. Ti...	T CPU~	Ø CPU~	T DB Time	Ø DB Ti...	T Ti...	Ø Time	T Roll Wait Time
CL_BGRFC_SUPERVISOR_START=====CP		6	362	60,305.2	1	169.2	0	16.7	0	28.7	0.0	0.0	361
RSAL_BATCH_TOOL_STARTUPDISP	SAP_CCMS_MONI_BATCH_STARTUP_DP	1	47	46,709.0	11	11,367.0	5	4,920.0	35	34,931.0	0.0	0.0	0
SMX		1	39	38,606.0	20	19,786.0	11	11,330.0	18	18,340.0	0.0	0.0	0
<DELAY - ab_PXAPreload>		1	29	29,075.0	15	14,800.0	2	1,880.0	12	11,966.0	0.0	0.0	0
<DDLOC CLEANUP>		3	73	24,349.0	1	219.7	0	3.3	72	24,129.0	0.0	0.0	0
AutoABAP		12	170	14,155.1	74	6,149.4	11	951.7	78	6,534.1	0.0	0.0	0
RSABAPPROGRAM		3	39	12,914.0	16	5,235.3	0	133.3	22	7,297.0	0.0	0.0	0
RSM13000		1	10	9,804.0	0	330.0	0	90.0	2	2,393.0	0.0	0.0	0
<AD_MSBUF>		2	19	9,285.5	0	58.0	0	5.0	0	74.0	0.0	0.0	0
RSLDAGDS	SAP_SLD_DATA_COLLECT_STARTUP	1	8	8,323.0	2	1,759.0	1	500.0	6	6,483.0	0.0	0.0	0
SAPMSSYC		1	8	7,812.0	3	2,519.0	0	90.0	5	5,033.0	0.0	0.0	0
RSWWERRE	SWWERRE	3	22	7,175.3	16	5,242.3	0	66.7	5	1,740.0	0.0	0.0	0
RFC_GET_FUNCTION_INTERFACE		4	26	6,380.0	4	1,085.0	1	307.5	21	5,291.3	0.0	0.0	0
SAPMSJOB		4	24	5,948.0	10	2,397.3	0	32.5	3	793.8	0.0	0.0	0
SM37		4	24	5,885.5	17	4,309.8	0	32.5	6	1,388.8	0.0	0.0	0
SESSION_MANAGER		4	20	4,920.3	4	934.3	1	202.5	14	3,424.0	0.0	0.0	2
SM50		9	30	3,287.6	13	1,486.8	1	147.8	9	1,035.2	0.0	0.0	2
RSBTCRTE		26	75	2,883.1	67	2,578.5	1	38.5	7	281.8	0.0	0.0	0
SAPLSMPI		6	15	2,480.2	6	1,057.8	0	31.7	8	1,392.0	0.0	0.0	0
PRGN_J2EE_SUID_QUERY_HELP_VALS		1	2	2,462.0	1	512.0	0	80.0	2	1,917.0	0.0	0.0	0
ST22		3	7	2,274.7	2	776.7	0	110.0	2	720.7	0.0	0.0	0
SAPLE2E_FUNC		3	6	2,137.3	4	1,187.0	0	20.0	3	903.3	0.0	0.0	0

Figure 11.13 Sorting Processes by Average Response Time

8. The other tabs (Database, Parts of response time, GUI times, All data) provide additional information.

Checking Customer-Specific Programs [+]

Customer-specific transactions where little attention was paid to efficient programming are frequently responsible for performance bottlenecks in the system. Initiate performance checks for this kind of transaction in your programming department. Queries with standard SAP programs that address large tables, however, can also lead to performance problems. For regular, performance-intensive activities, it can be useful to create specific transactions or programs whose performance is optimized for these special requirements.

Transaction ST03N (Workload Monitor) enables you to process urgent, short-term performance problems; analyze the performance of your system over a long period of time; and use the results for optimization purposes.

11.2.2 Buffer Analysis

The buffer analysis enables you to view data with regard to the buffer or main memory performance of the SAP system and use this data to reconcile buffer parameters. This is important because *swapping* (transferring data from the main memory to the virtual memory on the hard disk) can considerably impact performance. You can avoid frequent swapping by extending the system's main memory. Check the buffer behavior regularly to determine trends and get a feel for the behavior.

1. Enter Transaction ST02 in the command field and press the [Enter] key (or select TOOLS • ADMINISTRATION • MONITOR • PERFORMANCE • SETUP/BUFFER • ST02—BUFFERS).
2. In the next screen (see Figure 11.14), the following two areas are of interest:
   - HIT RATIO %: This value specifies with which percentage the user requests for the corresponding program can be processed; that is, no swapping is required. The target value is 95% and higher. After the system starts, this value is usually lower because the system buffers are still empty. The more users log on and the more data is written to the buffers, the higher the hit ratio. Normally, it takes two hours to one day until the used buffers are filled with data.
   - SWAPS: The swapping target value for the program buffer (PROGRAM) is smaller than 1,000. All other buffers have a target value of 0. If a buffer doesn't contain the required data, the system retrieves the data from the database. This data, however, can't be buffered additionally due to the fill level or fragmentation of the buffer.

     Consequently, the system must first remove other objects from the buffer to create memory for the new data (swapping). If the system is restarted, the swap value is reset to zero (0). If a strikingly large number of swaps take place in your system, optimize the system buffers.

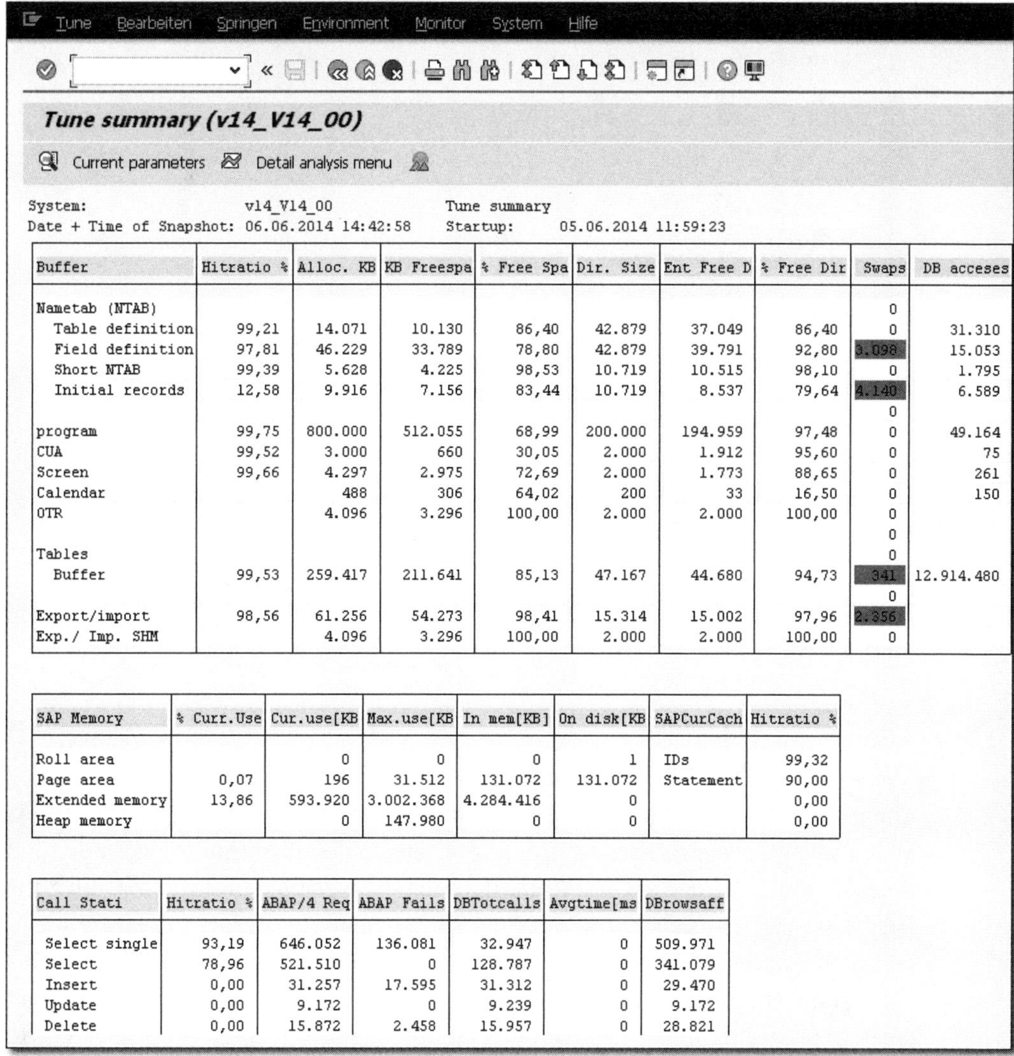

Buffer	Hitratio %	Alloc. KB	KB Freespa	% Free Spa	Dir. Size	Ent Free D	% Free Dir	Swaps	DB acceses
Nametab (NTAB)								0	
Table definition	99,21	14.071	10.130	86,40	42.879	37.049	86,40	0	31.310
Field definition	97,81	46.229	33.789	78,80	42.879	39.791	92,80	3.098	15.053
Short NTAB	99,39	5.628	4.225	98,53	10.719	10.515	98,10	0	1.795
Initial records	12,58	9.916	7.156	83,44	10.719	8.537	79,64	4.140	6.589
								0	
program	99,75	800.000	512.055	68,99	200.000	194.959	97,48	0	49.164
CUA	99,52	3.000	660	30,05	2.000	1.912	95,60	0	75
Screen	99,66	4.297	2.975	72,69	2.000	1.773	88,65	0	261
Calendar		488	306	64,02	200	33	16,50	0	150
OTR		4.096	3.296	100,00	2.000	2.000	100,00	0	
								0	
Tables								0	
Buffer	99,53	259.417	211.641	85,13	47.167	44.680	94,73	341	12.914.480
								0	
Export/import	98,56	61.256	54.273	98,41	15.314	15.002	97,96	2.356	
Exp./ Imp. SHM		4.096	3.296	100,00	2.000	2.000	100,00	0	

SAP Memory	% Curr.Use	Cur.use[KB	Max.use[KB	In mem[KB]	On disk[KB	SAPCurCach	Hitratio %
Roll area		0	0	0	1	IDs	99,32
Page area	0,07	196	31.512	131.072	131.072	Statement	90,00
Extended memory	13,86	593.920	3.002.368	4.284.416	0		0,00
Heap memory		0	147.980	0	0		0,00

Call Stati	Hitratio %	ABAP/4 Req	ABAP Fails	DBTotcalls	Avgtime[ms	DBrowsaff
Select single	93,19	646.052	136.081	32.947	0	509.971
Select	78,96	521.510	0	128.787	0	341.079
Insert	0,00	31.257	17.595	31.312	0	29.470
Update	0,00	9.172	0	9.239	0	9.172
Delete	0,00	15.872	2.458	15.957	0	28.821

Figure 11.14 Analyzing the Hit Ratio and Swaps

3. Check whether the SWAPS column contains entries that are highlighted in red. If this is the case, double-click on a value that is highlighted in red. The details view contains further information (see Figure 11.15).

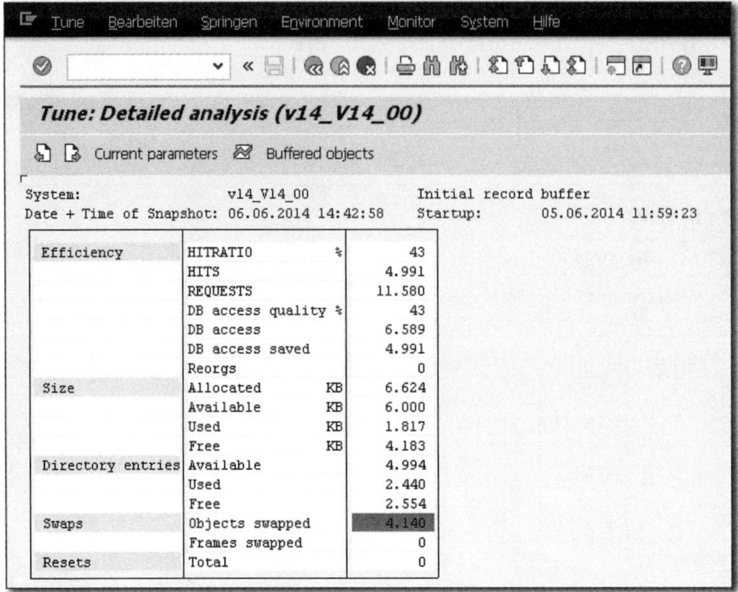

Figure 11.15 Detail View for Swapping

Analyzing and optimizing buffer parameters requires some knowledge and experience with the operating system. If in doubt, consult your operating system administrator or another expert.

11.2.3 Memory Defragmentation

The memory for the execution of the program basically functions like a hard disk. When several programs are executed, they are first loaded into the memory and deleted from it later on. Over time, the memory becomes fragmented—like the hard disk. Segments that aren't occupied are distributed across the entire memory. So it's possible that you have sufficient memory space (total of all segments that aren't occupied) but no contiguous segment that is large enough to load specific programs into the memory and run them. Restart the SAP system to defragment the system memory. To do so, stop the SAP system as described in Chapter 2, Section 2.1.2. Then, restart the SAP system.

[⚙]

Defragmenting the Program Buffer

To defragment the PXA buffer (Program Execution Area), it's sufficient to stop the SAP system. You don't have to restart the database and can keep the database cache.

It can also be useful to restart the server at the operating system level to cleanse the main memory. For this purpose, you must first stop the SAP system, including the database, and then shut down the server. Restart the server, database, and SAP system.

Buffers Are Filled Anew after a Restart

When the SAP system is restarted, the buffers (see Section 11.2.2) are updated, which means you can expect a long response time when the buffer object is accessed for the first time because the system first has to load data from the database into the buffer. When the data are accessed the second time, the response time is short again. This process repeats itself until all commonly used objects are loaded into the buffer. This usually takes one day. Without fragmentation, the program buffer is filled with the programs that the buffer contained during the shutdown process.

11.3 Analysis at Other Levels

The reasons for performance problems can also be outside of the SAP system. In persistent or implausible cases, you should therefore also analyze the other levels that affect your SAP system:

- Databases
- Operating system
- Hardware/network

If in doubt, consult your internal experts in your enterprise for the analysis—they can provide advice and help.

11.3.1 Analysis at the Database Level

For more information on the monitoring and performance balancing of the database, refer to Chapter 8 regarding the following transactions:

- Transaction ST04 (Database Assistant/DB Monitoring)
- Transaction DB02 (Database Analysis)

11.3.2 Analysis at the Operating System Level

The operating system monitor (Transaction OS06) described in Chapter 9 enables you to monitor the relevant performance data at the operating system level. This includes the following in particular:

- Memory paging (swapping at the operating system level)
- Operating system log entries

Some operating system problems affect the SAP system performance. You should therefore also analyze the operating system when the system performance is poor.

11.3.3 Analysis at the Hardware Level

You can also use Transaction OS06 (Operating System Monitor), which is further detailed in Chapter 9, to display the performance values of the hardware, for example:

- CPU usage
- Main memory utilization
- Hard disk performance and available memory
- Network statistics

Even if you implement optimizations at the SAP level, database level, and operating system level, if the hardware of your system is defective or can no longer meet the requirements, you won't obtain satisfying results. You should therefore also check the usage of your hardware components, and extend them, if necessary, or replace them.

11.4 Summary

Performance problems can be due to numerous reasons: defective hardware, problems with the operating system, an unoptimized database, or simply bad programming. Correspondingly, you have to analyze the reasons systematically.

Because an entire book could be written about this complex topic alone, this chapter only introduces the basic principles for superficial research with SAP-internal tools, such as load and buffer analysis. If you experience regular problems, you should consult your database, operating system, or network administrators, or ask a programmer if custom-developed programs are involved.

Without SAP GUI, you can't access most of the functions of the SAP system; SAP GUI needs to be installed locally on the PCs of the SAP users. Depending on the size of your enterprise, this can be quite time-consuming. This chapter describes how you can install the SAP GUI locally or via an installation server.

12 SAP GUI

To log on to an SAP system (or more precisely, to log on to an ABAP application server), the frontend software, SAP GUI, must be installed on the user's PC. The SAP GUI (Graphical User Interface) is responsible for the communication between the PC and the SAP server; that is, it forwards the user's commands to the server and outputs the information provided by the server on the PC of the user in a readable format.

The installation of the SAP GUI is—apart from access at the network level—the first obstacle on the way to the SAP system. You can positively influence the security of the system by installing the SAP GUI rather restrictively. Users shouldn't be able to install software on the enterprise's PCs. Ensure that only a restricted group of administrators has the necessary authorizations at the operating system level. Don't make the required installation files freely accessible in the network.

This chapter describes how you install SAP GUI locally or via an installation server and what you need to do to use SAP GUI to log on to an SAP system.

12.1 Installation Requirements

You can download the installation files for the SAP GUI via the SAP Software Distribution Center in the SAP Support Portal (*www.support.sap.com*).

12.1.1 Minimum Requirements for the User's PC

Before you install the SAP GUI, check whether the user's PC meets the following criteria:

- Does the system configuration meet the minimum requirements?
- Is the resolution set to at least 800 × 600?
- Is sufficient memory available on the hard disk to install the SAP GUI and execute the application?

Depending on the scope of the installation, between 100 and 500MB of memory are required on the PC's hard disk. These figures and requirements, however, depend on the current version and patch level; you should therefore first read SAP Note 26417 and refer to the installation manual of the SAP GUI compilation that is supposed to be installed.

12.1.2 Network Functions

Ensure that the user can log on to the network. Check if the following activities can be performed from the user's computer:

- Can you ping the SAP application servers to which the user will log on?
- If the SAP GUI is procured from a network resource (e.g., network drive, SAP GUI installation server), can you access the server from the user's computer on which the SAP GUI will be installed?

[+]

SAP GUI Version

Currently, SAP GUI is available in versions 7.30 (since June 2012) and 7.40 (since October 2014). Support for older SAP GUI versions has already ended, so you should no longer use version 7.20 or lower. Maintenance for SAP GUI version 7.30 ends in July or October 2015. Additional information on the maintenance strategy for the individual versions is available in SAP Note 147519.

12.2 Installation Scenarios

You have several options for installing the SAP GUI:

- Installation from an installation medium, for example, CD or network drive
- Installation from an SAP GUI installation server

Which procedure is best suited for your enterprise mainly depends on the number of employees who use the SAP system.

12.2.1 Installing SAP GUI from an Installation Medium

If you want to install the SAP GUI on a few PCs only, it doesn't pay to set up an SAP GUI installation server. You can store the installation files on a network drive or—if the network connection isn't fast enough—use the presentation CD and run the installation manually from the respective PC. You can find the instructions for the installation of the SAP GUI in the *SAP Frontend Installation Guide* in the *BD_NW_7.0_Presentation_7.40_Comp._1_\PRES1\GUI\WINDOWS\WIN32\ReadMe* directory of the presentation CD.

Follow these steps to install SAP GUI locally from an installation medium:

1. In Windows Explorer, navigate to the corresponding network or CD-ROM drive, select the setup directory of the SAP GUI (e.g., *C:\BD_NW_7.0_Presentation_7.40_Comp._1_\PRES1\GUI\WINDOWS\WIN32*), and double-click on SETUPALL.EXE (see Figure 12.1). The installation program starts.

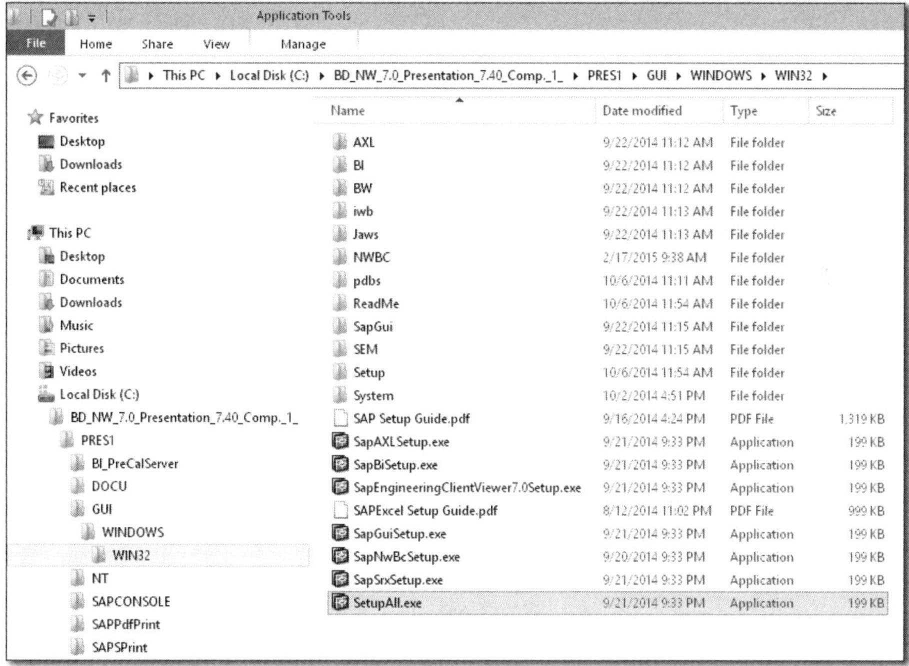

Figure 12.1 Starting the Installation Program

2. Click on NEXT (see Figure 12.2).

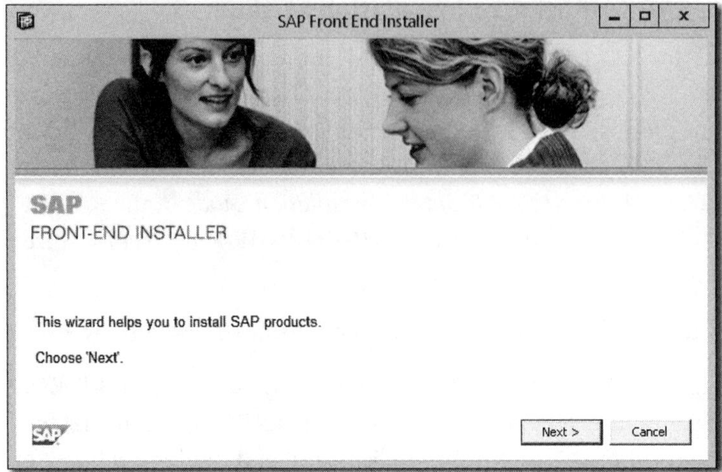

Figure 12.2 Initial Screen of the SAP GUI Installation

3. Choose the components that you require (e.g., SAP GUI, SAP LOGON, and SAP LOGON PAD). Alternatively, you can run a full installation using SELECT ALL. Click on NEXT (see Figure 12.3).

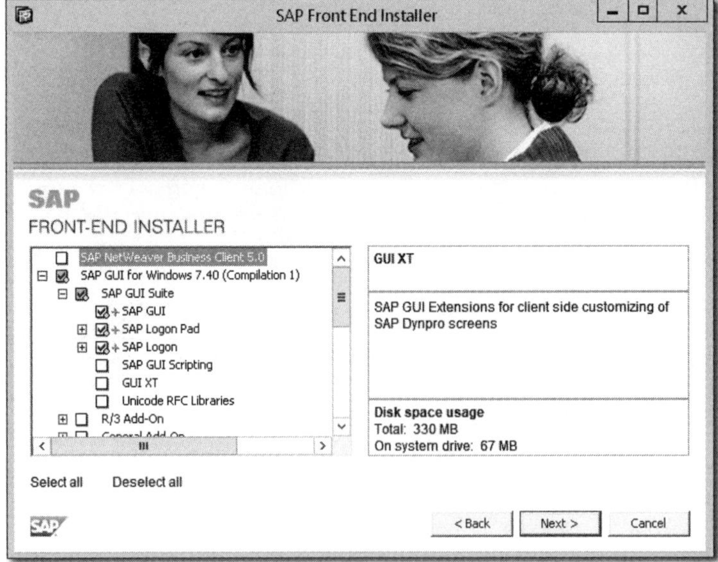

Figure 12.3 Selecting the Components to Be Installed

4. If necessary, change the target directory for the installation, and click on NEXT (see Figure 12.4).

Figure 12.4 Selecting the Target Directory for Installation

5. The SAP FRONT-END INSTALLER window displays the installation progress. When the installation is completed, click on CLOSE (see Figure 12.5).

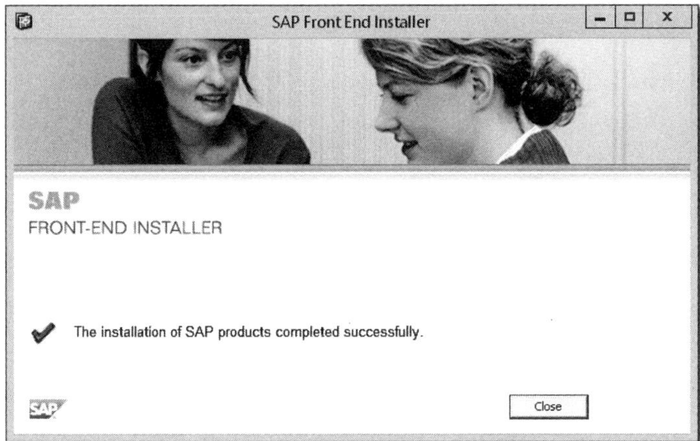

Figure 12.5 Confirmation for the Completed Installation

SAP GUI is now locally installed on your PC. Click the desktop icon or the entry in the START menu to start SAP GUI.

12.2.2 Installing SAP GUI from an Installation Server

If there are numerous SAP users, it's usually too time-consuming to install the SAP GUI manually via an installation medium on every PC. SAP GUI alternatively enables you to set up a central installation server from which you can perform the installation. The SAP GUI installation server provides extensive functions to facilitate the installation for you as the administrator:

- You can define standardized installation packages that only contain the respectively required components, which you can provide offline as single installation files.
- You can carry out the installation either with an interaction option for the user or automatically in the background.
- You can use *Local Security Handling* (LSH) to have a user without administrator authorizations run the installation.
- You can use Visual Basic scripts to distribute standardized *saplogon.ini* files, for example (see the tip box in the "Creating an SAP GUI Installation Package" section later in this chapter).
- You can keep frontend installations easily up to date by importing SAP GUI patches to the installation server and then distributing them to the users' PCs.

Setting Up an SAP GUI Installation Server

To set up an SAP GUI installation server, you need a server with a Windows operating system that is permanently available and can be accessed via a fast network connection from all PCs on which the SAP GUI is supposed to be installed.

In a medium-sized enterprise, a PC that is provided for this purpose only may be sufficient, for example. If you have to support a large number of users, you should select an appropriately fail-safe and powerful platform, of course.

1. Ensure that you have administration rights for the server.
2. In Windows Explorer, navigate to the setup directory on the presentation CD (e.g., *C:\BD_NW_7.0_Presentation_7.40_Comp._1_\PRES1\GUI\WINDOWS\WIN32\Setup*), and double-click on the NwCreateInstServer.exe file to start the installation program (see Figure 12.6).
3. Click on Next (see Figure 12.7).

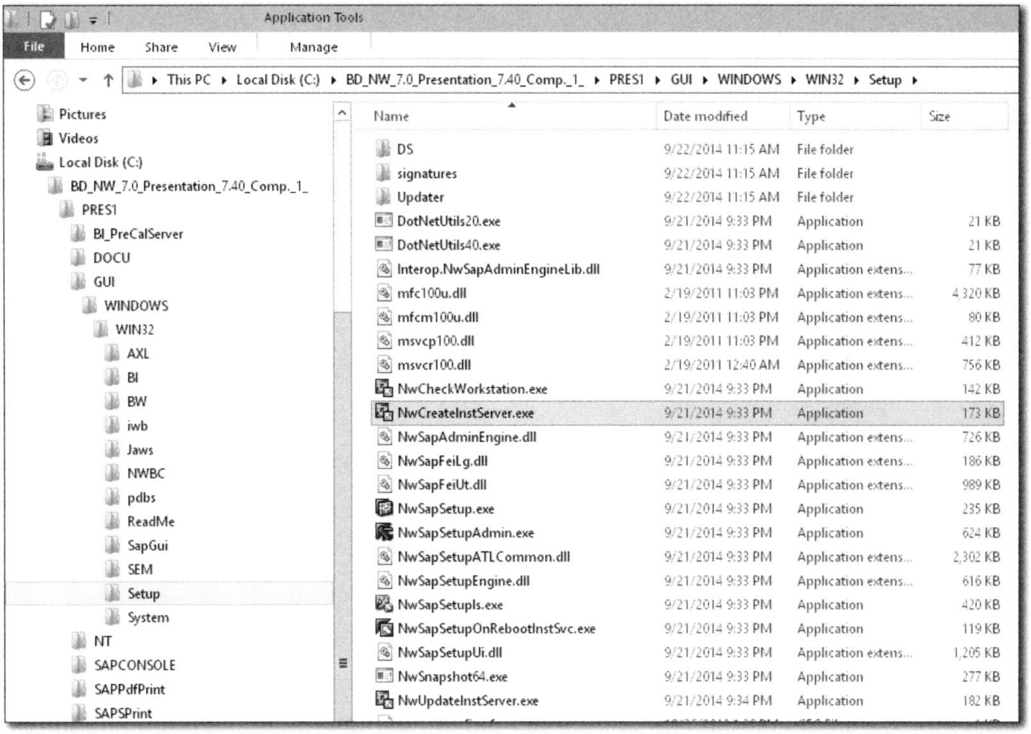

Figure 12.6 Starting the Server Installation

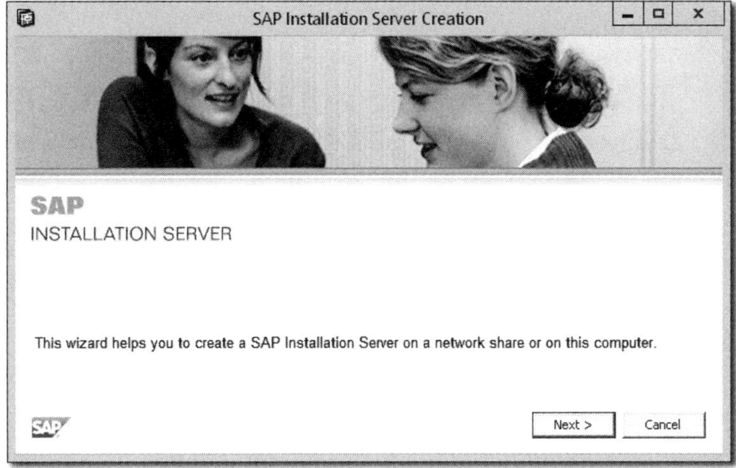

Figure 12.7 Initial Screen for Installing the Installation Server

4. Enter the directory in which the installation server is supposed to be set up. Click VERIFY to have the system verify your entry (see Figure 12.8). If the verification was successful, a corresponding message is displayed and the button text changes to CONTINUE.

Figure 12.8 Selecting the Target Directory for Installation

5. The installation directory needs to be shared in the network to allow access from the users' PCs. Choose the SHARE button to configure sharing. The process may look different depending on the version and configuration of your operating system (see Figure 12.9).
6. Assign read permissions for the directory (see Figure 12.10). You have to adhere to the security conventions in your enterprise. Apply the changes and return to the SAP GUI setup.

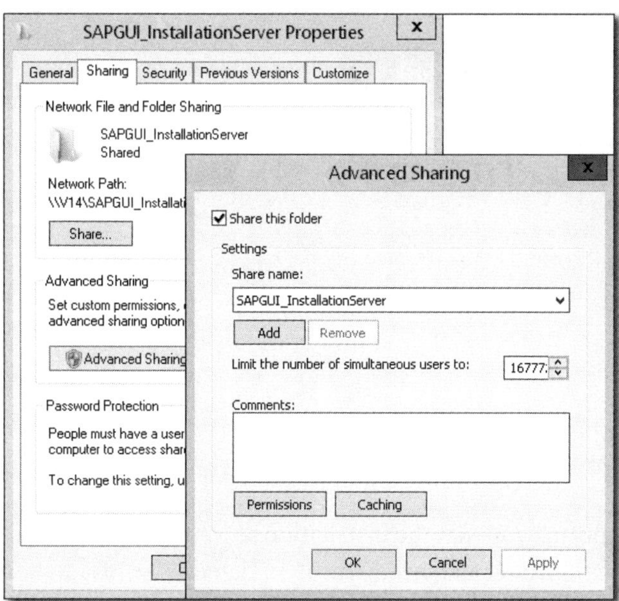

Figure 12.9 Sharing the Installation Directory

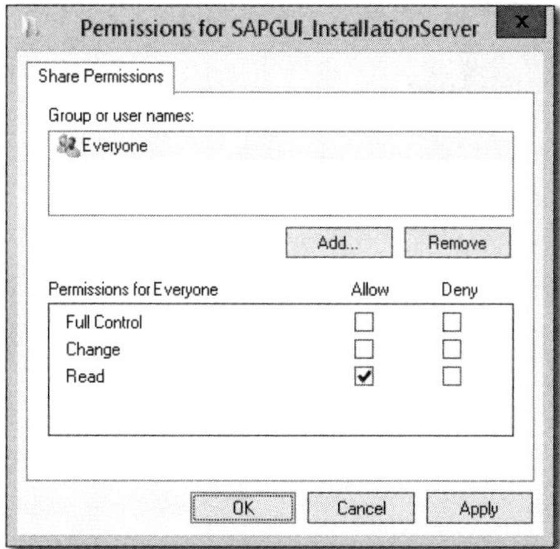

Figure 12.10 Configuring Authorizations for the Installation Directory

7. In the installation window, click on NEXT again.
8. The files that are required for the installation server are copied to the specified directory. Confirm the process with NEXT (see Figure 12.11).

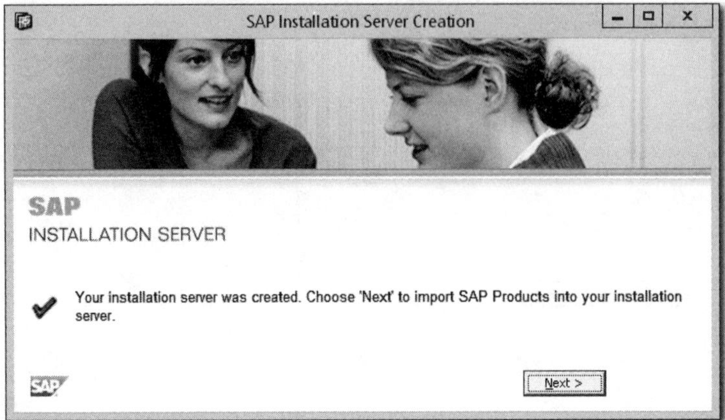

Figure 12.11 Confirming the Installation Server Setup

9. The installation wizard informs you that the installation server still doesn't contain any SAP GUI installation files and needs to be updated. The installation wizard automatically updates and informs you when the process is complete. Complete the setup process with CLOSE (see Figure 12.12).

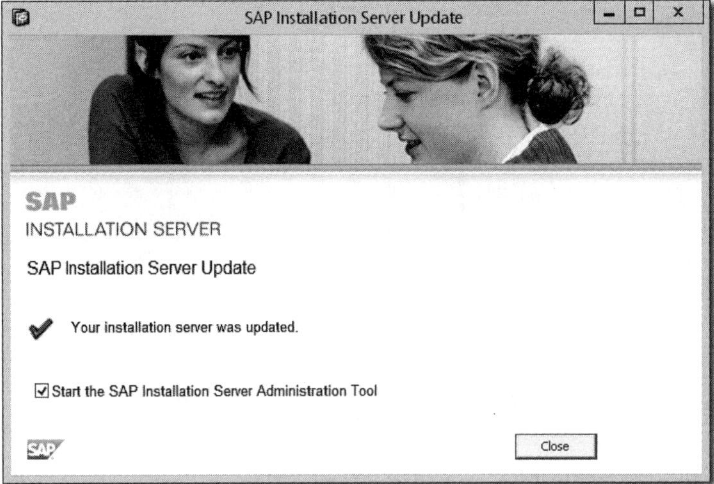

Figure 12.12 Completing the Installation

The *SAP Installation Server Administration Tool* starts automatically if you haven't deactivated the corresponding checkbox.

Creating an SAP GUI Installation Package

The basic configuration of the SAP GUI installation server is now set up, and the server is ready for operation. Further customizing is done via the SAP Installation Server Administration Tool. This administration tool provides numerous functions that can't be described in detail, for example, patching the installation server or user PCs. The *SAP Frontend Installation Guide* on the presentation CD examines the individual options in detail.

To implement the SAP GUI installation that is described in Section 12.1 via the installation server and not via an installation medium, you have to create the respective installation package first. To do so, follow these steps:

1. Start the administration tool by double-clicking on the NWSAPSETUPADMIN.EXE file in the installation server directory (e.g., *C:\SAPGUI_InstallationServer\Setup*; see Figure 12.13).

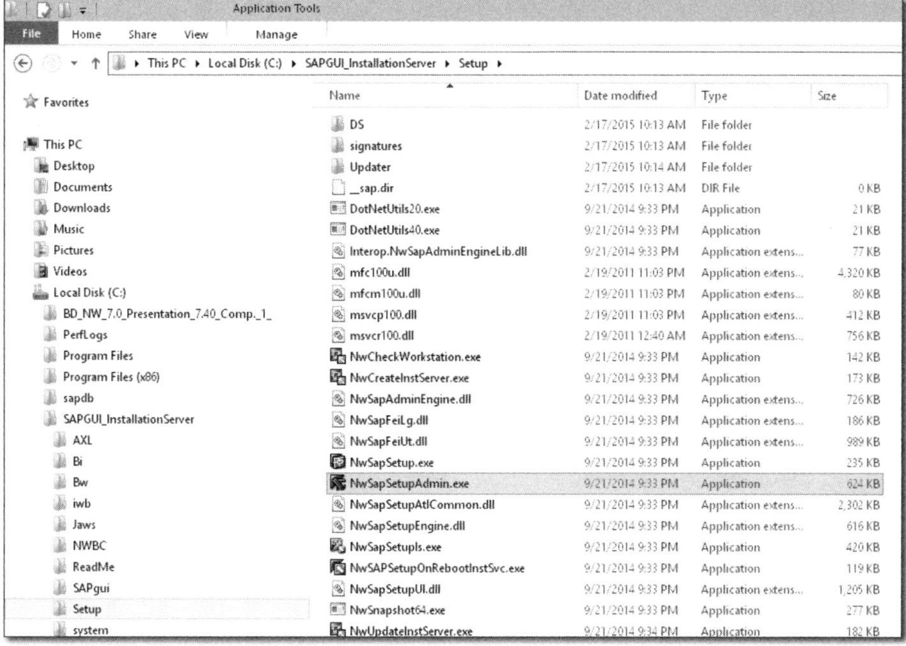

Figure 12.13 Starting the Administration Tool

2. To create a standard installation package for the users' PCs, select NEW PACKAGE in the menu bar (see Figure 12.14).

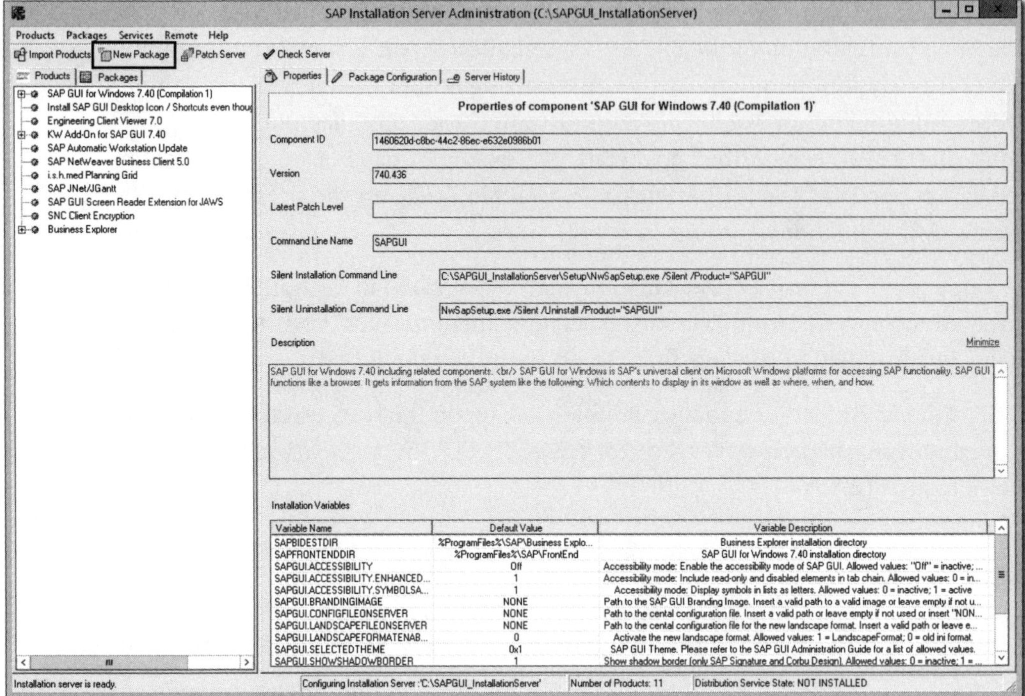

Figure 12.14 Creating a Standard Installation Package

3. Click on NEXT (see Figure 12.15).

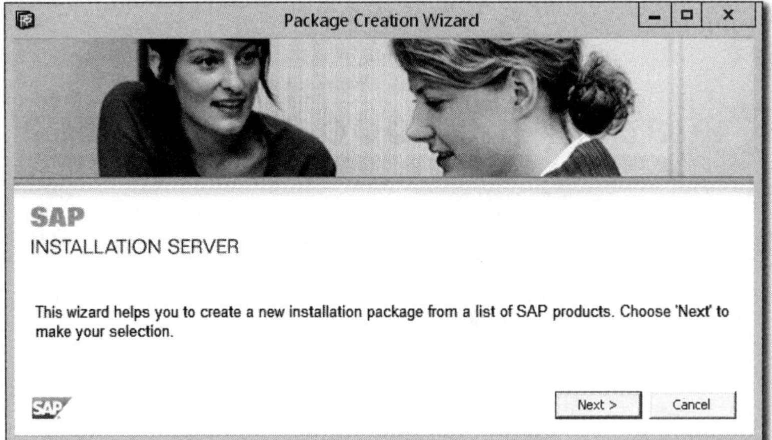

Figure 12.15 Starting the Package Creation Wizard

4. Choose the components that the installation package is supposed to contain. Confirm your choice with NEXT (see Figure 12.16).

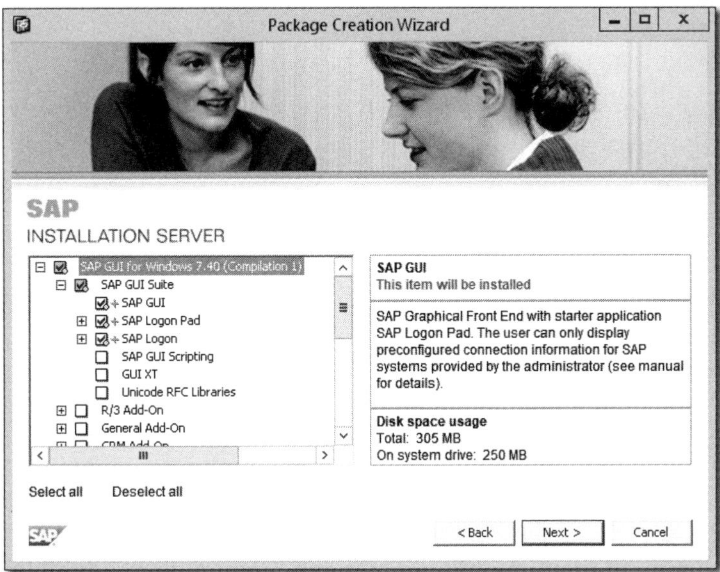

Figure 12.16 Selecting Components for a New Package

5. Assign a name to the new package, and click on NEXT (see Figure 12.17).

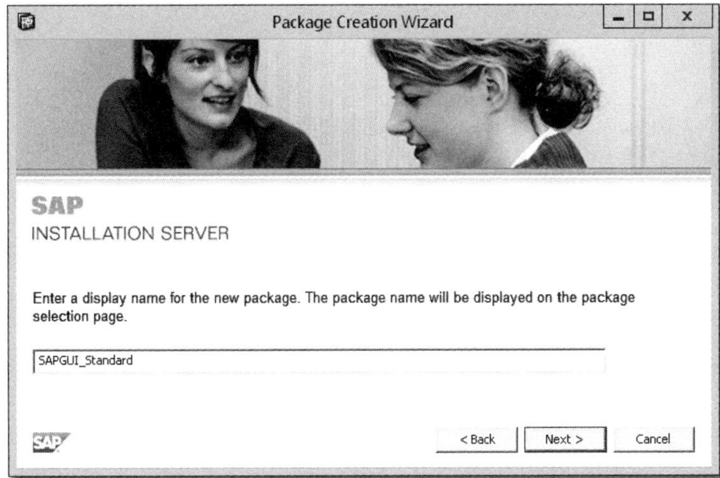

Figure 12.17 Entering a Name for the New Package

6. In the next step, you have to specify the command-line name for the package. If you want to install the SAP GUI with a command-line command later, you have to use this name in conjunction with the `/package` parameter. Ensure that the command-line name doesn't contain blanks or special characters that aren't supported. Click on CONTINUE.
7. The configuration of the installation package is now completed. Finish the process with CLOSE (see Figure 12.18).

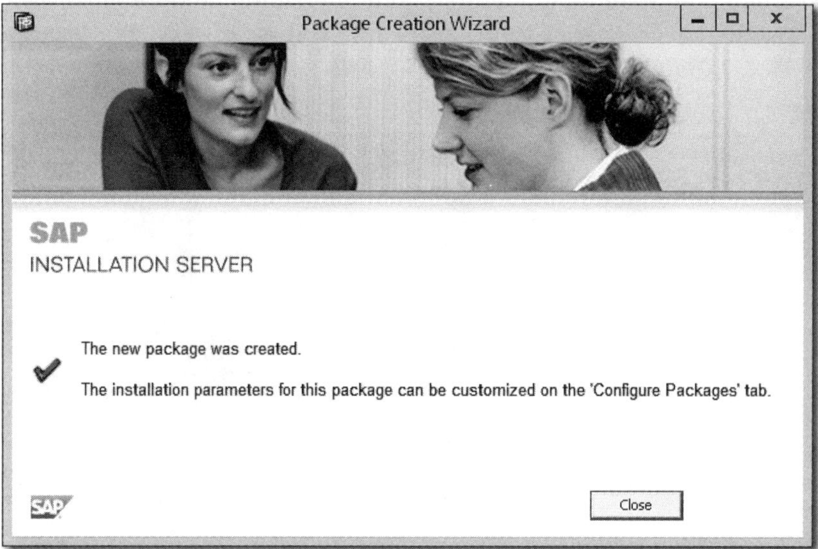

Figure 12.18 Completing the Package Creation

8. The administration tool now displays the package and the components contained therein in the PACKAGE CONFIGURATION tab (see Figure 12.19). Here you can further adapt the configuration of the package as required.

[+]

Event Scripting

When it's being installed, updated, or removed, your package triggers *script events*, which you can populate with Visual Basic commands. This is a powerful means, for example, to distribute standardized *saplogon.ini* files that you store on your installation server across the users' PCs after the installation (see SAP Note 1426178). You can find some examples of event scripting in the SAP Installation Server Help, which you can call via the HELP menu item in the administration tool.

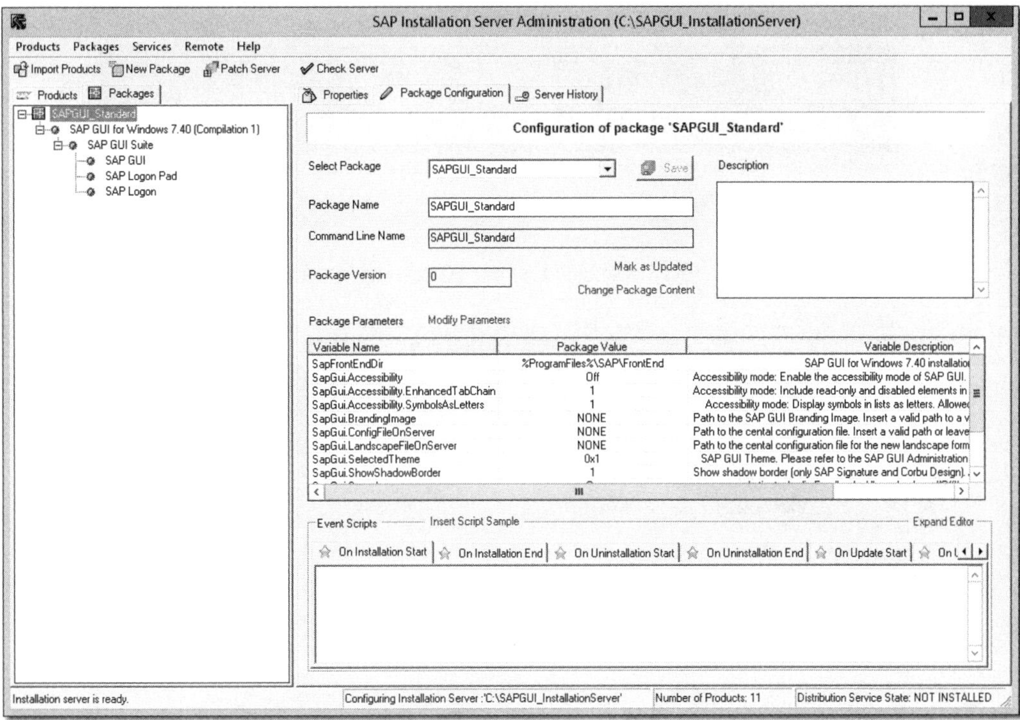

Figure 12.19 Viewing the Configuration of the New Package

Installing an SAP GUI Installation Package from the Installation Server

You can install a preconfigured installation package on a PC in dialog mode or in the background by following these steps:

1. Log on to the PC on which the SAP GUI is supposed to be installed. Ensure that you're authorized to install software.
2. On the installation server, call the *NwSapSetup.exe* file using Windows Explorer or the command line (see Figure 12.20; *\\<server name or IP address of the server>\<share name>\Setup\NwSapSetup.exe*, such as *\\V14\SAPGUI_InstallationServer\Setup\NwSapSetup.exe*).

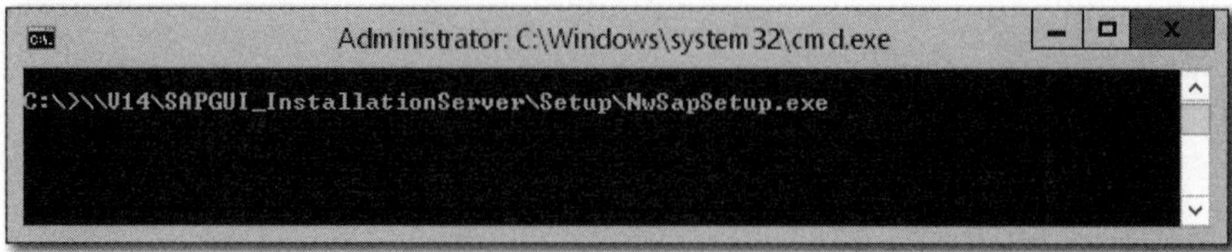

Figure 12.20 Calling NwSapSetup.exe

3. The SAP FRONT-END INSTALLER starts. Click on NEXT (see Figure 12.21).

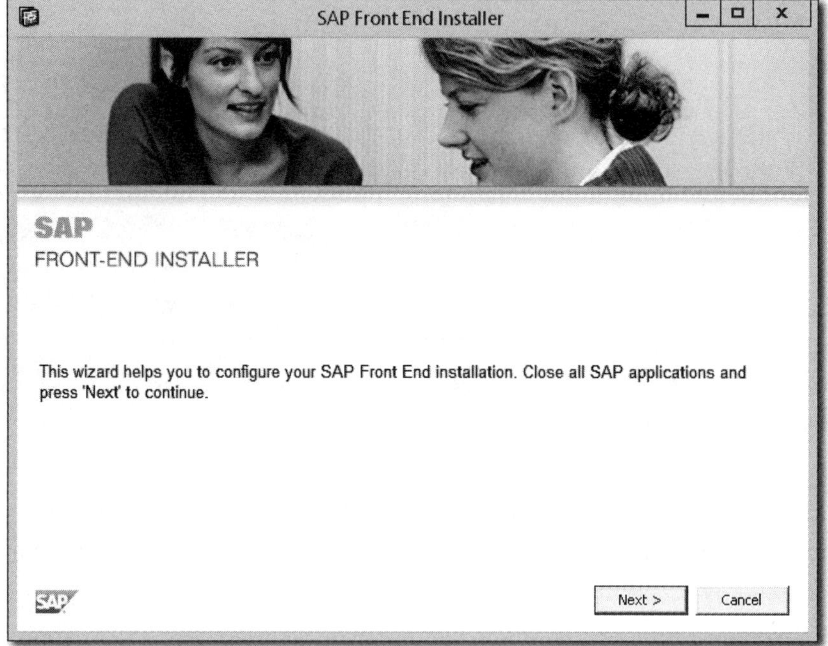

Figure 12.21 Starting the SAP Front-End Installer

4. On the left, the window first displays the list of the available components. Change this view using the PREDEFINED PACKAGES link at the lower left (see Figure 12.22).
5. The installer now displays the package that was created on the installation server. Select it, and click on NEXT (see Figure 12.23).

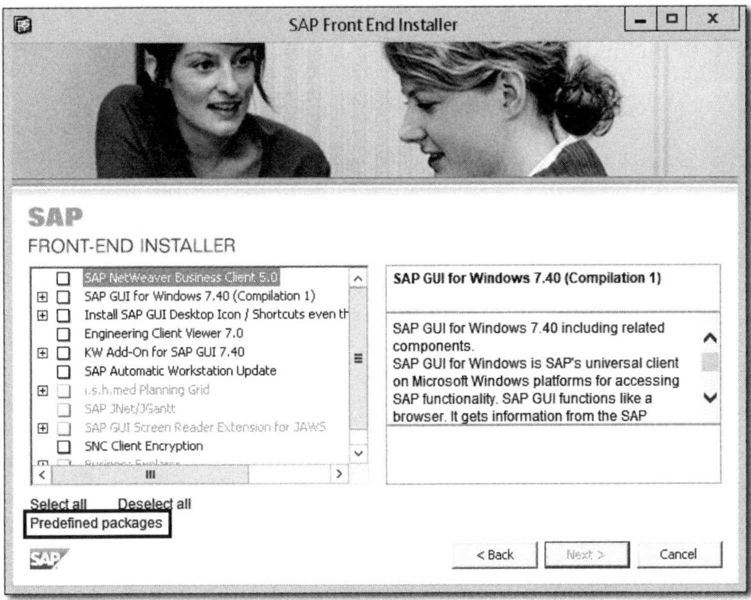

Figure 12.22 Selecting the Predefined Packages View

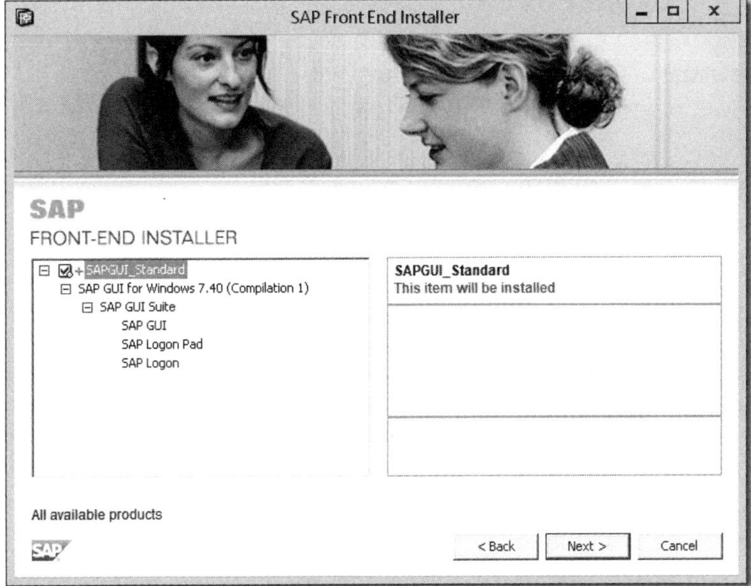

Figure 12.23 Selecting an Installation Package

6. The installer installs the components and displays the installation progress. When the process is completed, click on CLOSE (see Figure 12.24).

Figure 12.24 Closing the SAP Front-End Installer

If you know the name of the installation package, you can also carry out step 2—that is, calling *NwSapSetup.exe*—by entering the command line name. Add the `/package=<command line name of the installation package>` (e.g., *\\V14\SAPGUI_InstallationServer\Setup\NwSapSetup.exe/package=SAPGUI_Standard*; see Figure 12.25).

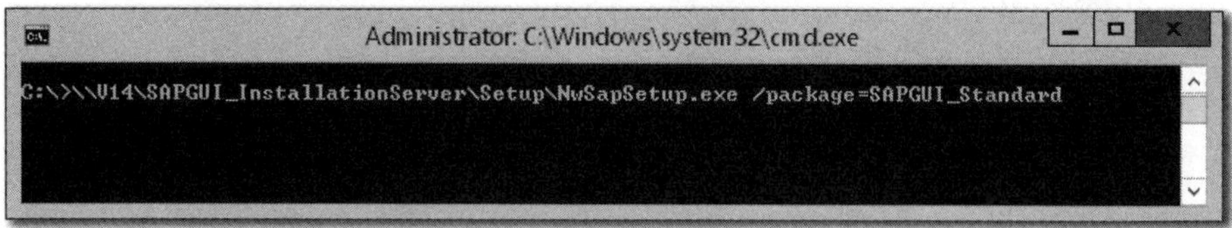

Figure 12.25 Starting the Installer via the Command Line

After the package that is supposed to be installed has been specified, the SAP FRONT-END INSTALLER starts, and the user can't modify the content of the installation. Steps 5 and 6 are carried out automatically (see Figure 12.26).

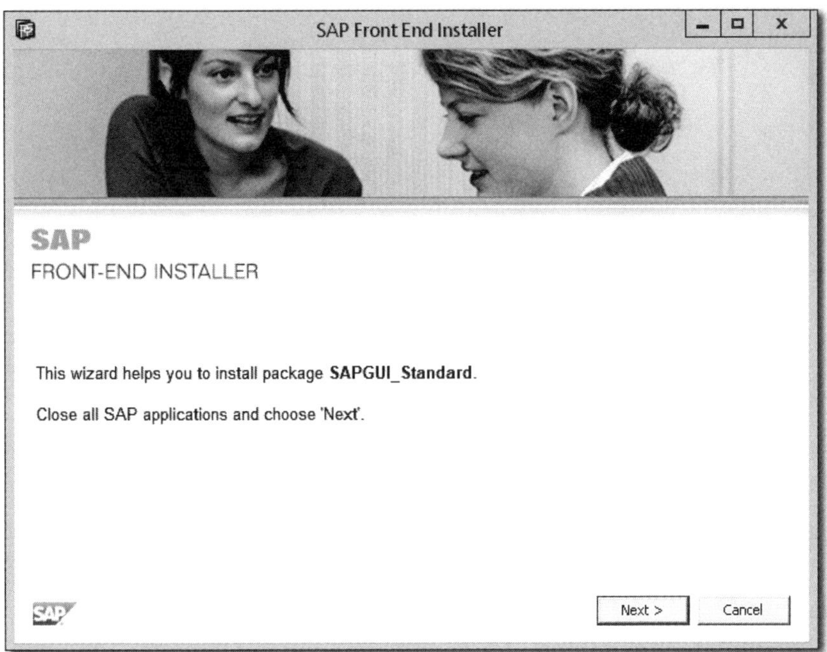

Figure 12.26 Automatic Installation of a Package

If you have the system implement the installation, you can suppress the user dialog with the /nodlg command line parameter (e.g., *\\V14\SAPGUI_InstallationServer\Setup\NwSapSetup.exe/package=SAPGUI_Standard/nodlg*; see Figure 12.27).

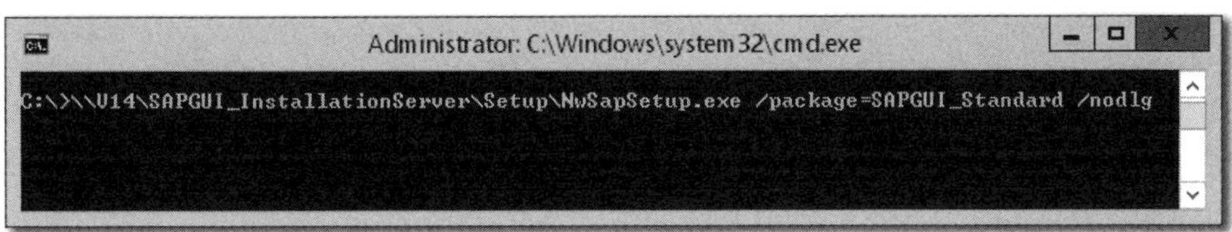

Figure 12.27 Suppressing the User Dialog for Installation

The installation starts and finishes without the user having to initiate or complete it with a mouse click. The user is only informed about the progress of the installation (see Figure 12.28).

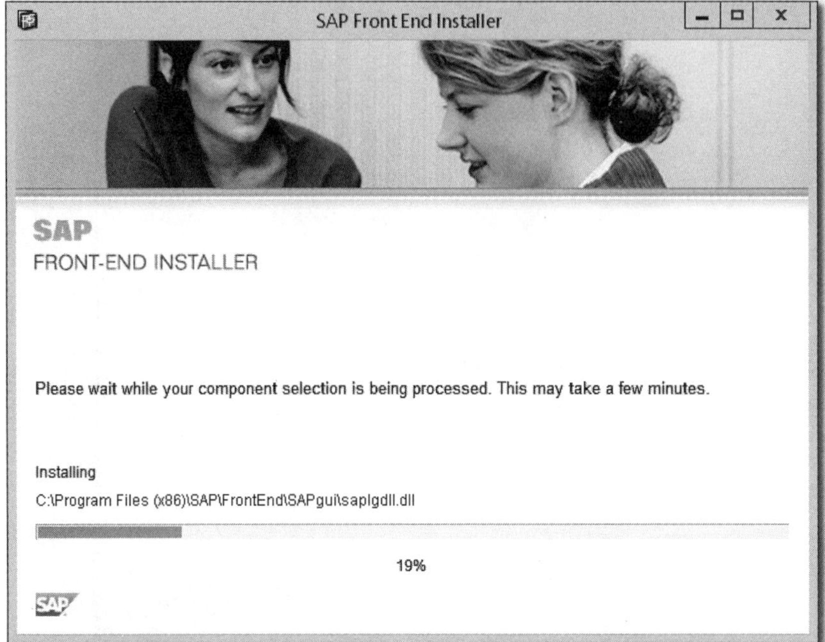

Figure 12.28 Installation Progress

If you also want to hide the progress during the installation, use the `/silent` parameter instead of `/nodlg` in the command line (see Figure 12.29).

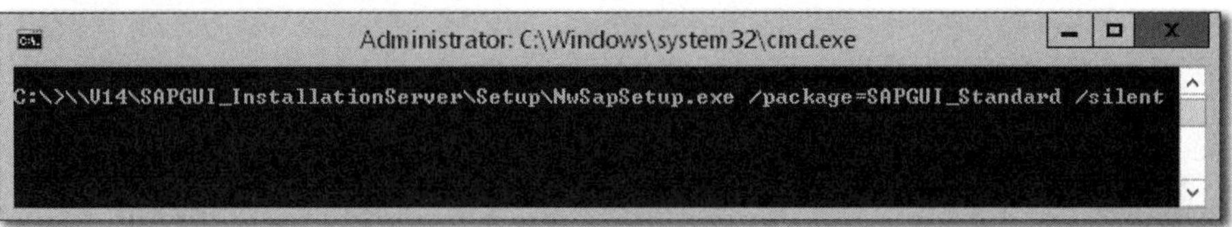

Figure 12.29 Suppressing the Progress Display

The `/noDlg` or `/silent` parameters enable you to control the SAP GUI installation also via a third-party software distribution product, for example. Table 12.1 provides an overview of possible command-line parameters when calling the *NWSapSetup.exe* file. You can find a complete list in the *SAP Setup Guide* on the installation DVD.

Parameter	Description
/package=<commando-line name of the installation package>	Installs a predefined installation package.
/product=<command-line name of the product or SAP GUI component>	Installs a specific component (product) of the SAP GUI, for example, SAP Business Explorer.
/force	Overwrites all registry entries and SAP GUI components already installed.
/ForceWindowsRestart	Restarts the PC after the installation has been completed.
/noDlg	Displays the progress of the installation. The user doesn't have to make any specifications.
/repair	Repairs the frontend installation.
/silent	Implements the installation completely in the background. The progress isn't displayed.
/uninstall	Uninstalls a package or component (in conjunction with /package or /product); can be supplemented by /all but can also be used to remove the SAP GUI completely from the PC.
/update	Updates the SAP GUI installation of the PC if a higher patch level is available on the installation server.

Table 12.1 Command Line Parameters for NWSapSetup.exe

[+]

Log Files

The installation log files are stored on your PC in the SAP GUI installation directory, for example, under *C:\Programs (x86)\SAP\SapSetup\LOGs*. If the SAP GUI installation outputs an error, you should check these files first.

Depending on whether the user under which the installation on the PC is supposed to be implemented has administrative rights or not, you may have to install LSH on the installation server first. For this purpose, you need a user account with administration authorization that is also available on the respective PC (e.g., a corresponding domain user).

12.3 Adding Systems to SAP Logon

After successfully completing the SAP GUI installation, you can add the SAP systems to SAP Logon. To do so, follow these steps:

1. Start SAP Logon by double-clicking on the respective desktop icon.
2. In the SAP LOGON 740 window (see Figure 12.30), click on the NEW button.

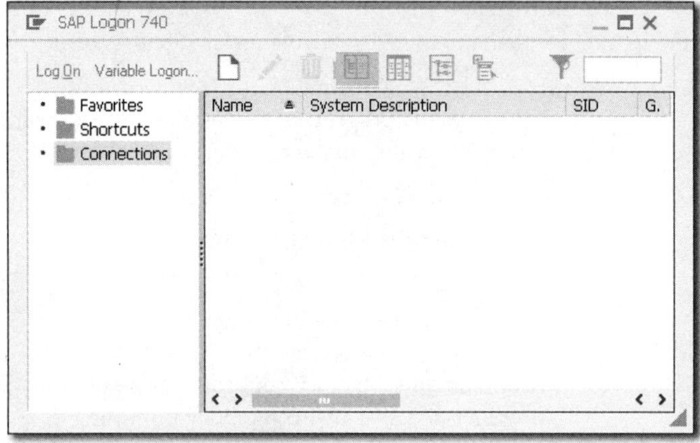

Figure 12.30 SAP Logon 740

3. The CREATE NEW SYSTEM ENTRY user dialog opens (see Figure 12.31). In the first screen, you usually don't have to make any specifications, so click on NEXT.
4. In the next entry screen (see Figure 12.32), enter the data for the new system:
   - DESCRIPTION: Text displayed in the SAP Logon system list later on (e.g., "V14").
   - APPLICATION SERVER: Name or IP address of the server on which the SAP system runs (e.g., "v14").
   - INSTANCE NUMBER: System or instance number for which you configure the logon (e.g., "00").
   - SYSTEM ID: Three-digit system ID of the SAP system (e.g., "V14")
   - SAPROUTER STRING: Remains empty if the SAP server is available directly via a network.

   When you're finished, click on NEXT.

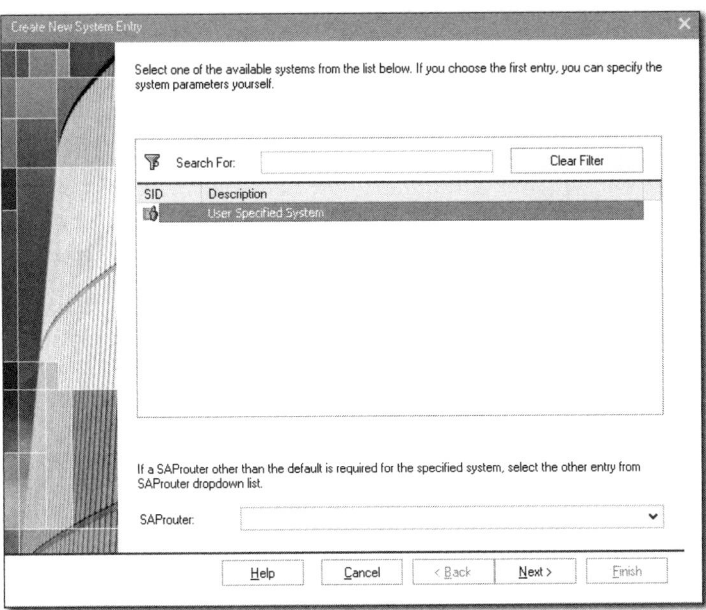

Figure 12.31 Create New System Entry – Initial Screen

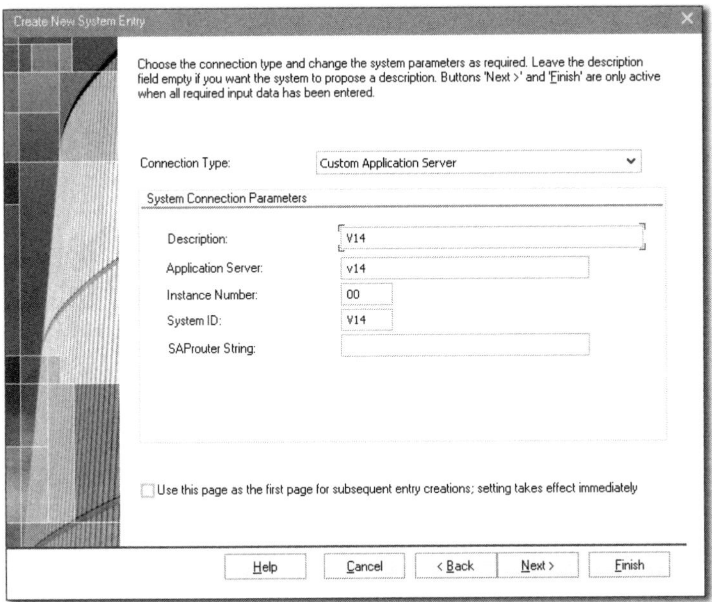

Figure 12.32 Entering Data for the New System

[+]

Information about SAProuter

You can find more information on the SAProuter in the SAP Support Portal (*www.service.sap.com/saprouter*).

5. For example, if you encrypt the communication between the frontend and server in your enterprise via Secure Network Communication (SNC), change the network settings in the next step (see Figure 12.33), and click on NEXT.

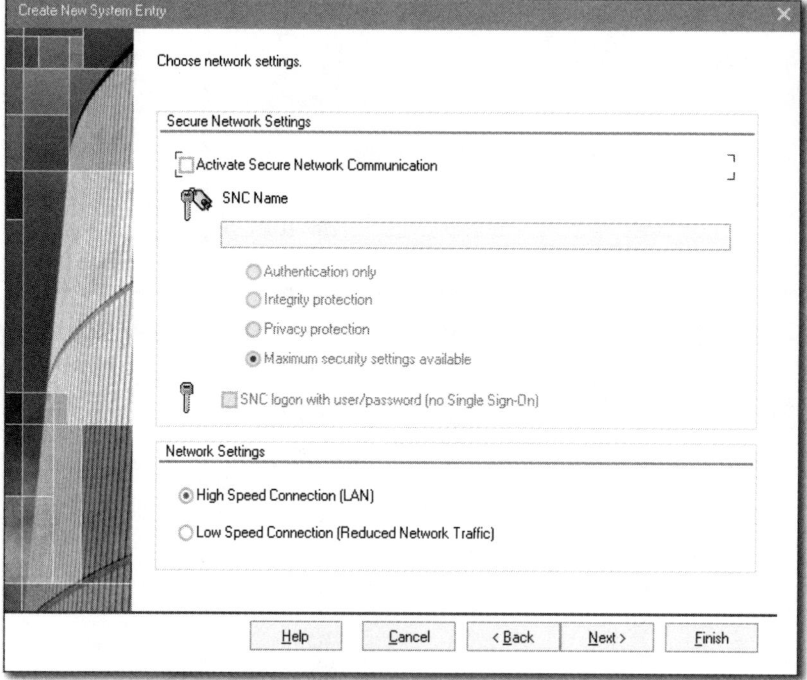

Figure 12.33 Adapting the Network Settings

6. If necessary, customize the language and coding settings (see Figure 12.34), and click on FINISH.
7. The new system is added to SAP Logon (see Figure 12.35). You can now log on to the added system using the button that has the same name as the system.

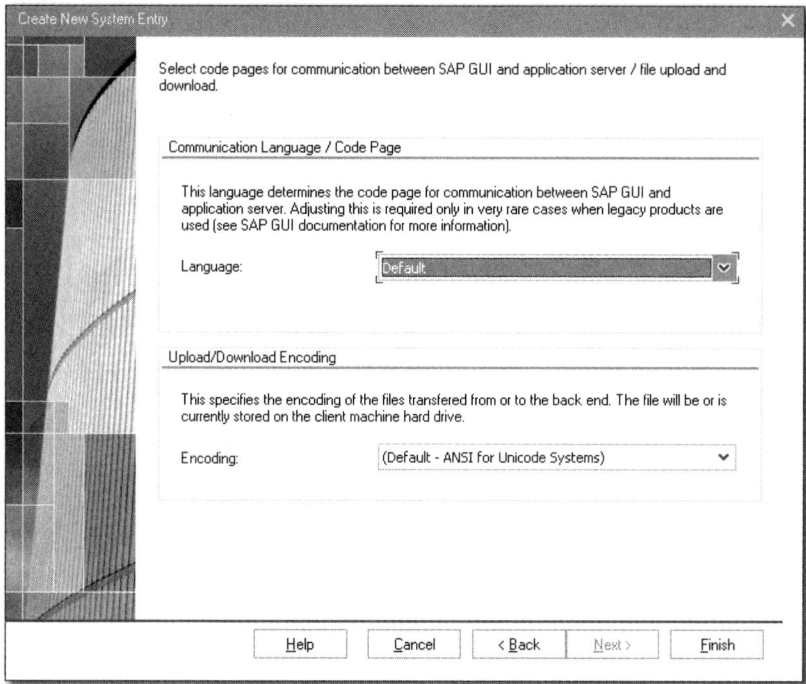

Figure 12.34 Adapting the Language and Coding Settings

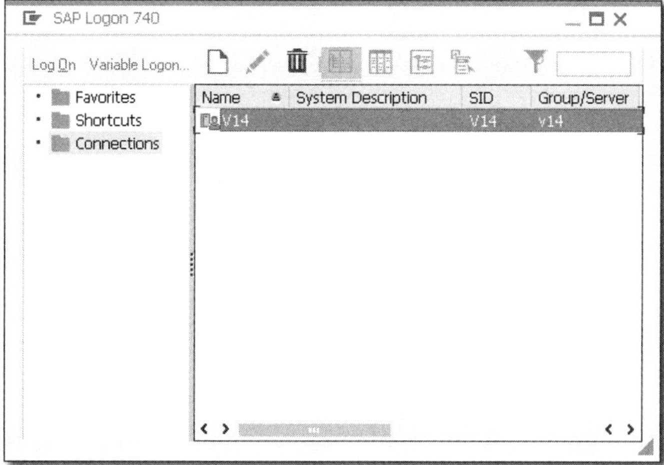

Figure 12.35 SAP Logon with the New System

[+]

File saplogon.ini

The information that you add in the steps described is entered in the *saplogon.ini* file. You can determine the location of the file via the SAP GUI options under OPTIONS FOR SAP LOGON • LOCAL CONFIGURATION FILES.

After the *saplogon.ini* file has been created, you can reuse it on other PCs by replacing the "empty" file with the predefined file after the installation of the SAP GUI. Afterwards, restart SAP Logon.

[+]

Tree View and File

Since SAP GUI version 7.30, you can switch the traditional list view of system entries to a tree view. In this view, you can sort the systems according to your requirements using folders, for example, based on the system type (SAP ERP, SAP SRM, etc.) or by status within the system line (development system, quality assurance system, or production system). For this purpose, drag and drop the system entries to the folders that you've created.

Information about your defined structure is stored in the *SapLogonTree.xml* configuration file. If you maintain the system list centrally in your enterprise and create a tree structure, you should therefore share the *saplogon.ini* and *SapLogonTree.xml* files with all employees.

12.4 Summary

Apart from access via a browser, SAP GUI is indispensable for logging on to SAP systems. It must be installed on every PC to use SAP systems. There are numerous options for the installation of the SAP GUI, from a local installation from CD to an installation via the automated installation server. The variant that is best suited for your enterprise mainly depends on the number of PCs on which the SAP GUI needs to be installed.

User accounts are an essential component of the SAP access concept. Your task as administrator is primarily to make user administration secure. Also, the increase in efficiency via a Central User Administration can be an interesting case if a high number of users or several SAP systems have to be managed.

13 User Administration

Via the user administration, you can check who has access to the SAP system. User administration is a security-relevant aspect of SAP system administration because each access to the system potentially jeopardizes the security of the system and the data stored in it. User administration is closely associated with authorization management. Both terms are now often used in connection with identity management, which provides technical support for user administration and authorization management with regard to the entire enterprise. This chapter only focuses on the pure user administration in the SAP system. It describes the fundamentals of user administration such as the administration of user master data and user groups, the assignment of passwords, and so on. Among other things, the chapter also explains how to configure a Central User Administration.

13.1 General

Be aware that you may be asked on whose request a user has been created in the system and issued with certain authorizations. Therefore, in the context of user administration, you must always ensure a comprehensive, continuous documentation and a suitable approval procedure. Some of the tasks described in this book are created to correspond to general check procedures. Consult your internal and external auditors with regard to legal and other requirements (enterprise-internal) that are made on proper and secure user administration.

The following are among the tasks of user administration:

- **Specifying naming conventions for user IDs**
  There are several naming convention alternatives for choosing a naming convention, for example:
  - Employee ID number of the enterprise (e.g., e0123456)
  - Surname, first letter of the first name or first name, first letter of the last name (e.g., SmithJS)
  - Clearly identifiable user IDs for temporary employees and consultants (e.g., T123456 or C123456)
  - Special conventions for system or interface users (e.g., `RFC_TIVOLI`, `BATCH_HCM`)
- **Creating or changing a user**
  Take into consideration the following aspects when you define your process for user requests:
  - Create or change users only if you have a completely filled-out request form (see Appendix D). The form should contain information on the person, position, and communication, as well as on the authorizations required for the task area. The form should have been authorized with a signature from the employee's supervisor.
  - If the requested authorizations concern several departments or organizations or are particularly comprehensive, the respective managers should issue their approval.
  - If it concerns a nonpermanent employee or when SAP access is limited in terms of time (e.g., in the case of external employees and consultants), the period of employment and the end of validity should be specified.
  - The responsible SAP administrator should sign the form after he has created or changed the user master data.
  - The forms should be archived based on an appropriate principle, for example, according to employee name or organizational unit.
  - The approved authorizations should be compared regularly with the authorizations assigned to the user.
  - If possible, don't allow a reference user to be specified in a user request that is supposed to be used as a template (e.g., the account of a specific colleague).

There is the danger that more authorizations are copied than actually required. Have the necessary roles or profiles listed explicitly.

- Particular attention should be paid to changing users because often only additional authorizations are requested in the case of transfers or similar organizational events. Authorizations often accumulate with time, and the removing of current roles and profiles is neglected. Always check each change request, and if in doubt, ask the employee or his responsible supervisor.

- **Deactivating or deleting a user**
  You should specify special rules when you delete users:
  - Design a procedure in collaboration with the HR department on how you're notified about an employee leaving the enterprise. Experience has shown that deleting employees no longer required is often dealt with as carelessly as removing authorizations that are no longer appropriate.
  - If the leaving of an employee is announced in advance, define a respective validity date in the user master record.
  - Lock the user ID, deactivate the password, and add it to a special user group (e.g., TERM) if the employment contract has been terminated.
  - Specify an appropriate period in which the user master record of an employee who has left the enterprise can remain in the system (e.g., three months) and after which the user is deleted from the system.
  - Search your system for users with an expired validity date and/or user group TERM on a regular basis.
  - Regularly analyze which users didn't log on to the system in a specific period of time.
  - Before you lock and delete users and define the validity date, check whether released or planned background jobs exist under this user ID (Transaction SM37, Job Overview). The jobs can't be executed if the user ID has been locked, deleted, or is no longer valid.

It would be best to maintain the conventions specified for the user administration and the procedures in a user administration concept or in a separate section of the authorization concept (see Chapter 14). In this context, also consider how the segregation of duties (SOD) for user administration and authorization management can be implemented in your enterprise.

13.2 Setting Up New Users

Before you set up a new user, you must have the respective form with the required information and approvals. You can create new users by copying an existing user or by setting up a new user profile.

13.2.1 Copying Existing Users

If an appropriate user exists, you can copy this user. During the operation, you can select which sections of the master record are supposed to be copied.

[+]

Creating User Templates

Create user templates for typical functions of your enterprise. When you set up a new user, you can then copy these templates.

1. Call Transaction SU01.
2. Enter the user ID that you want to copy in the User box (e.g., "BCUSER"), and click on Copy (see Figure 13.1).

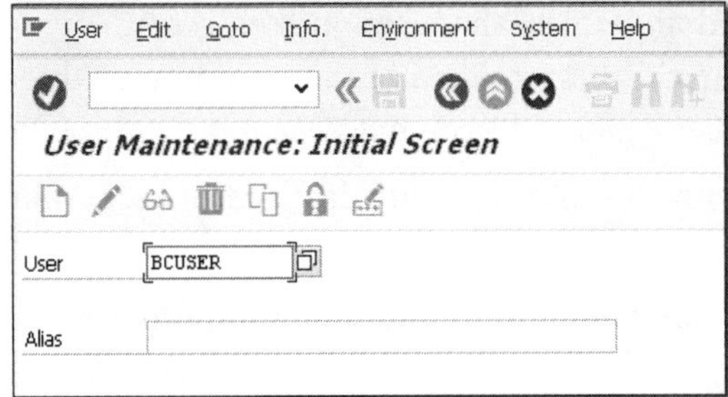

Figure 13.1 Initial Screen of User Maintenance – Enter a User

3. In the Copy Users dialog box, implement the following settings (see Figure 13.2):
   - Enter a new user ID in the To field (e.g., "BCUSER2").
   - Activate the tabs that you want to transfer from the original user.
   - Click on Copy.

[+]

Stick to Your Naming Conventions

When setting up new user IDs, remember to comply with the naming conventions of your enterprise.

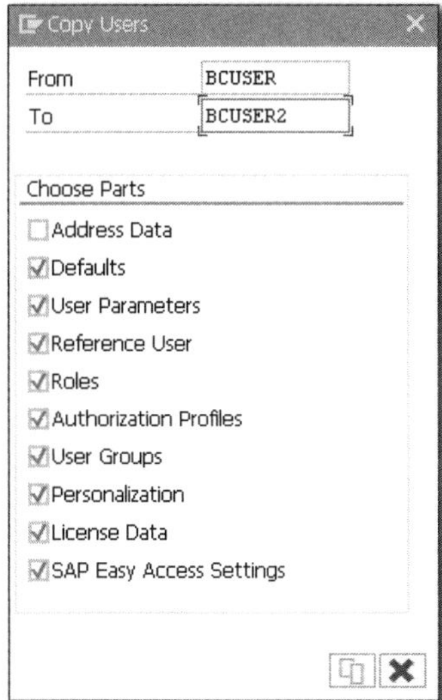

Figure 13.2 Specifying the Targer User Name and Selecting the Master Data to Be Copied

Copy Authorization Data Carefully [!]

Only copy roles and authorization profiles when there is a reference user with manageable authorizations. You should not allow user requests such as "the same authorizations as colleague Miller."

4. Select Generate Password to generate an *initial password* via a random number generator (see Figure 13.3). You can also enter a password manually in the New Password field (e.g., "Initial1"). In this case, you need to reenter it in the Repeat Password field.

Using Generated Random Passwords [+]

For security reasons, where possible, use initial passwords generated via the random password generator instead of manually assigned passwords.

Random Number Generator for Passwords

The random generator for passwords can be customized via several parameters, which can be maintained via Transaction SM30 (Table View Maintenance) in table PRGN_CUST:

- GEN_PSW_MAX_LENGTH: Maximum total length of password
- GEN_PSW_MAX_DIGITS: Maximum number of digits in password

- GEN_PSW_MAX_LETTERS: Maximum number of letters in password
- GEN_PSW_MAX_SPECIALS: Maximum number of special characters in password

Read SAP Notes 662466 and 915488 before you use these parameters.

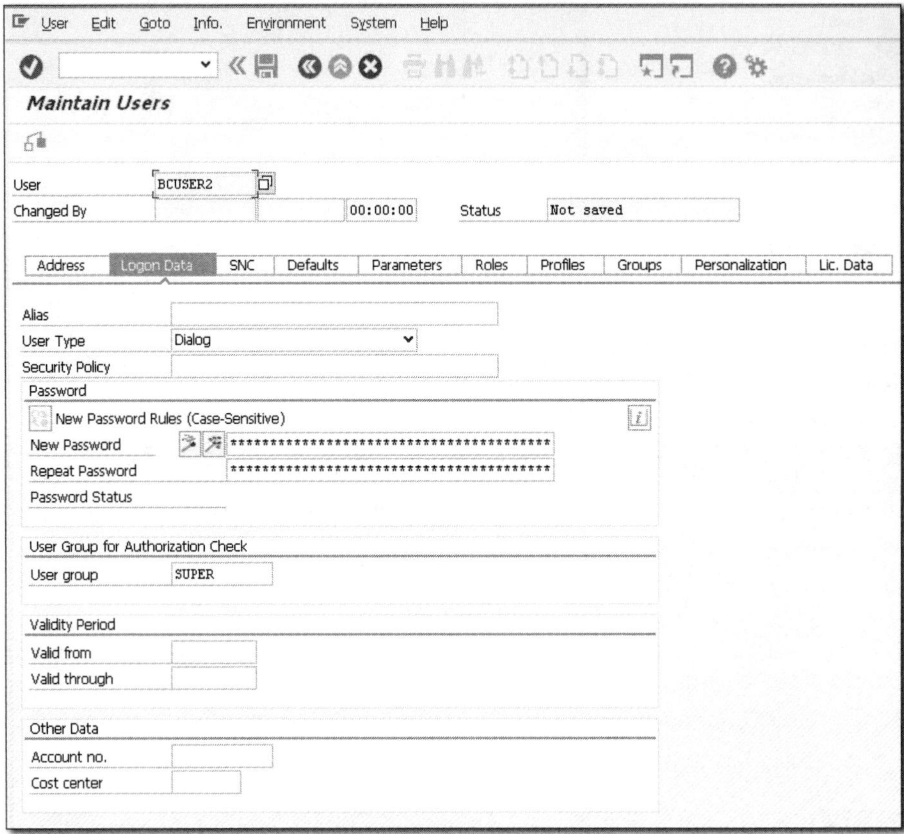

Figure 13.3 Entering an Initial Password for a User

5. Enter the USER GROUP (e.g., "SUPER") to which the user is supposed to belong in the USER GROUP FOR AUTHORIZATION CHECK area, or use the input help to select the user group from a list.

[+]

Creating User Group First, Then Assigning User

The user group must exist before the user can be assigned. If required, create it first using Transaction SUGR.

6. Enter the period in the VALID FROM and VALID THROUGH fields within which the user is authorized to access the system.
7. Choose the ADDRESS tab if you want to change the user's address data (see Figure 13.4).

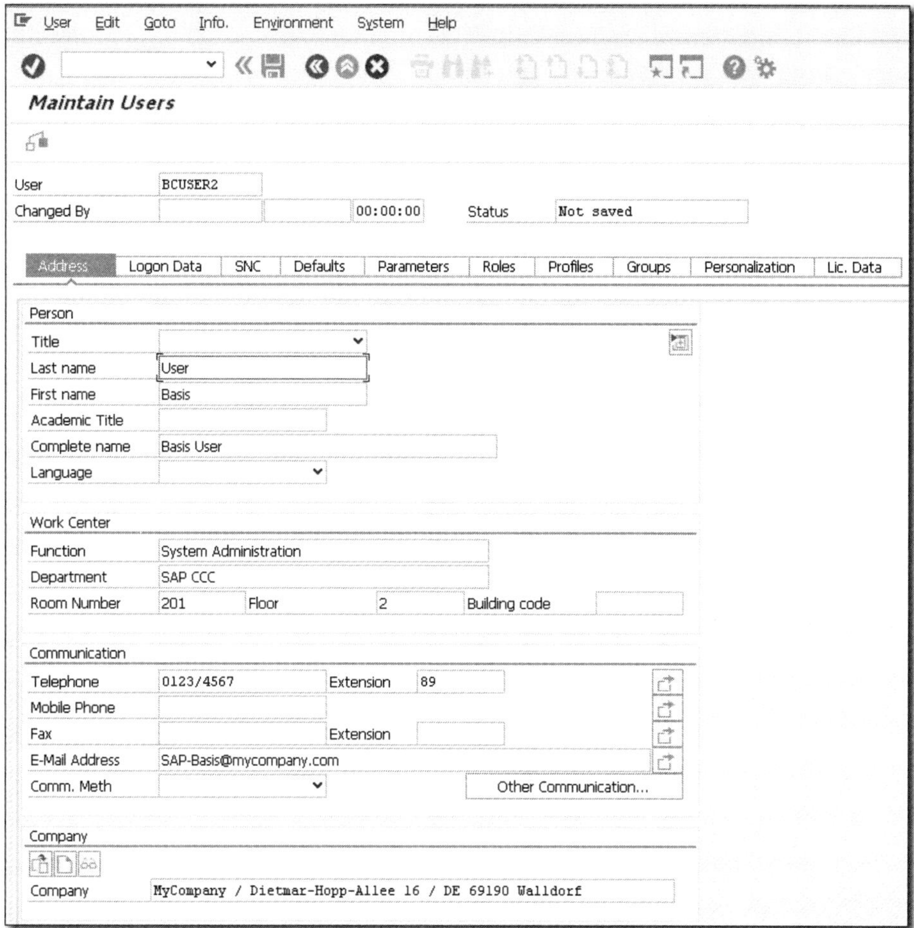

Figure 13.4 Maintaining Address Data of the User

- In the PERSON area, enter the user's LAST NAME and FIRST NAME.
- In the WORK CENTER area, enter the user's FUNCTION, DEPARTMENT, and location (e.g., ROOM NUMBER, FLOOR, BUILDING CODE).
- In the COMMUNICATION area, enter the user's TELEPHONE and E-MAIL ADDRESS.

[+]

Maintaining Contact Details and Company Addresses

Either the Telephone field or the E-Mail Address field should be a required entry field. Should a system problem in connection with the user occur, you need to be able to contact the user.

Use Transaction SUCOMP to create company addresses.

8. Select the Defaults tab (see Figure 13.5).
   - Make sure that the Logon Language is set correctly. If a default language has been defined in the system parameters, this field is only required to define a different logon language (e.g., "EN" for English) for the individual user.
   - Under Decimal Notation, select the desired option.

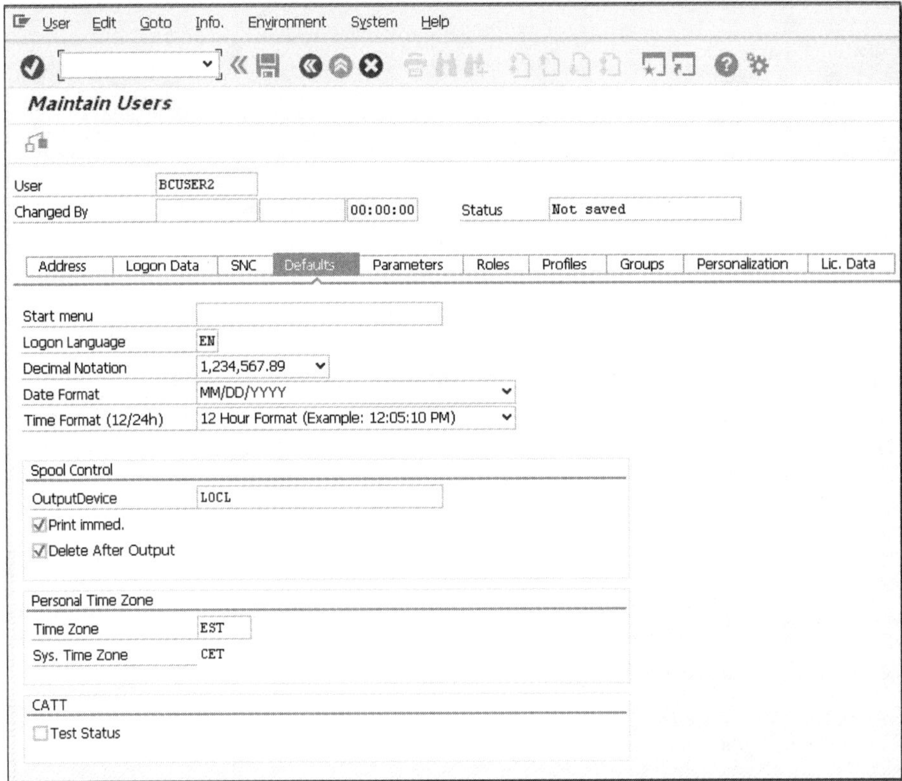

Figure 13.5 Specifying Defaults for a User

Decimal Notation [!]

The DECIMAL NOTATION displays decimal numbers. The correct setting prevents errors and misunderstandings.

- Under DATE FORMAT, select the desired date format (e.g., "MM/DD/YYYY").
- Implement the following settings in the SPOOL CONTROL area:
  - Enter a standard printer in the OUTPUT DEVICE field, or use the input help function to select one from a list.
  - Activate the two PRINT IMMED. and DELETE AFTER OUTPUT checkboxes.
- Check the PERSONAL TIME ZONE, and use the input help function if required to change a specified time zone.

9. Select the PARAMETERS tab, and enter parameters and parameter values in the table (see Figure 13.6).

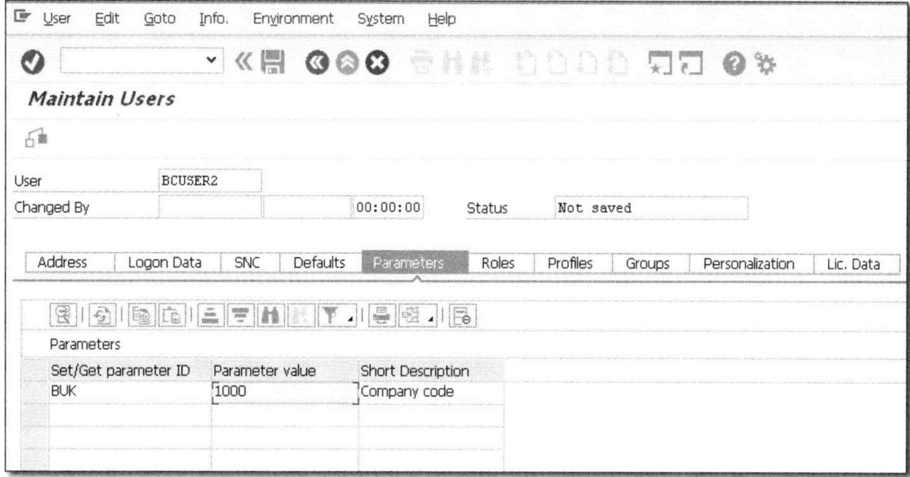

Figure 13.6 Maintaining User Parameters

Parameter [+]

There is a wide range of user parameters that can work in a completely diverse way. You can usually store default values via parameters for specific fields in SAP transactions.

10. Select the ROLES tab, and assign the requested authorization roles to the user (see Figure 13.7). You may assign a restrictive validity date.

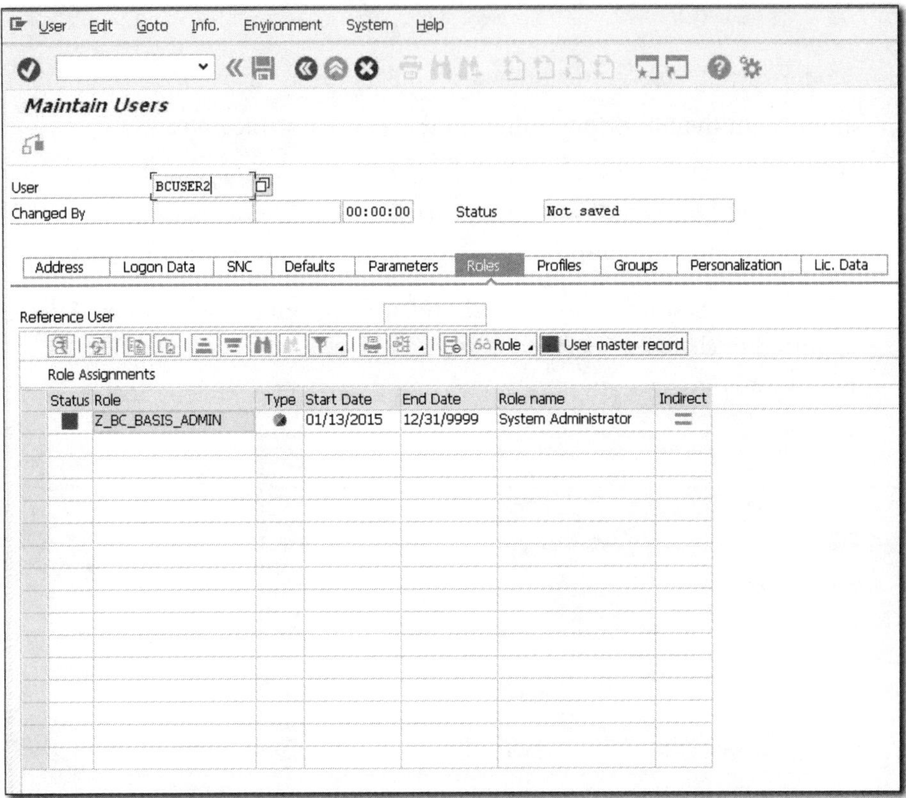

Figure 13.7 Assigning Authorization Roles

11. Go to the PROFILES tab, and assign the requested authorization profiles (see Figure 13.8).

[+]

Generated Profiles

The profiles generated and assigned via authorization roles are indicated via the icon and can't be changed.

12. Select the GROUPS tab, and enter the user groups to which you want to assign the user (see Figure 13.9).

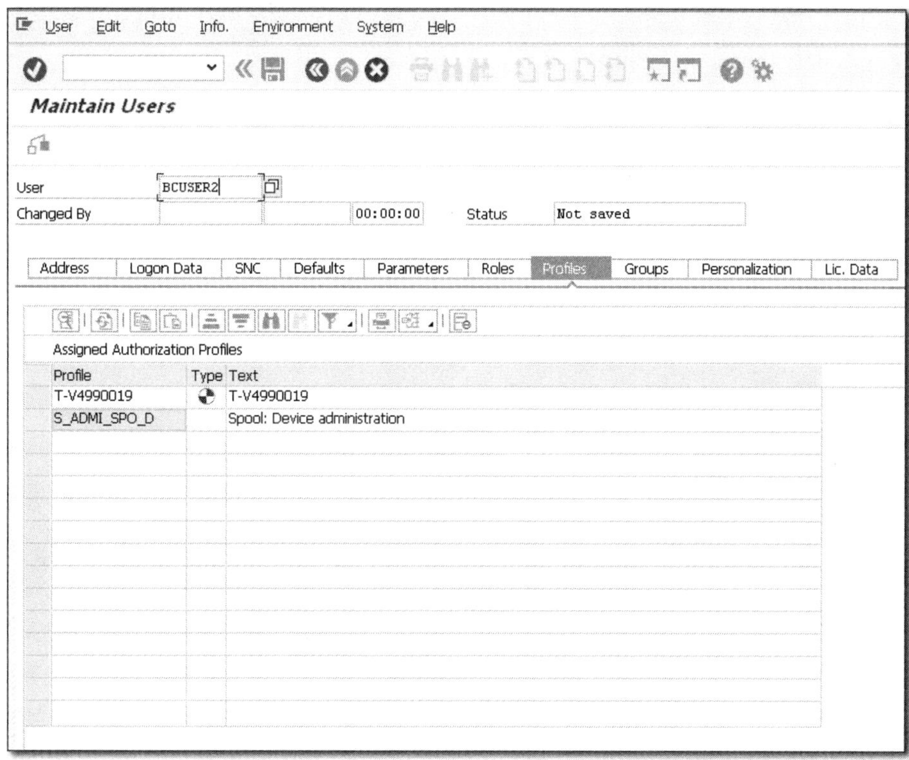

Figure 13.8 Assigning Authorization Profiles

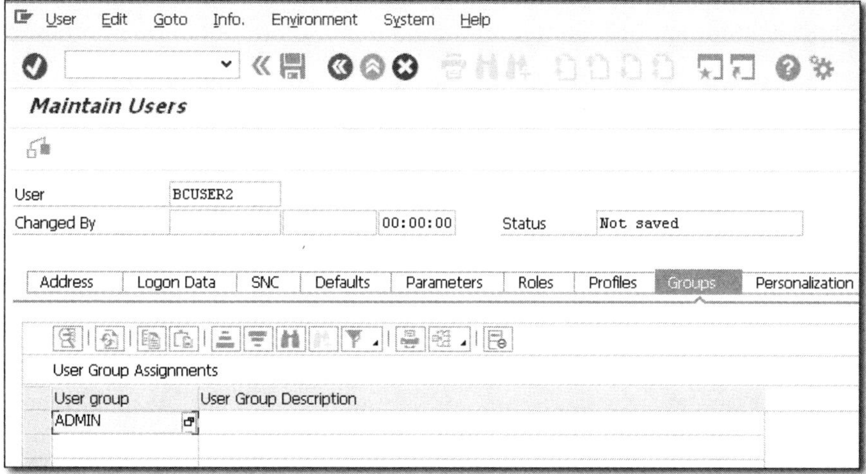

Figure 13.9 Assigning Users to User Groups

[+]

User Groups

Unlike the user group assigned in step 6, these groups aren't included in the authorization check but instead serve as an additional grouping characteristic, for example, for selections or similar.

13. Choose the PERSONALIZATION tab, and change the personalization options if required (see Figure 13.10).

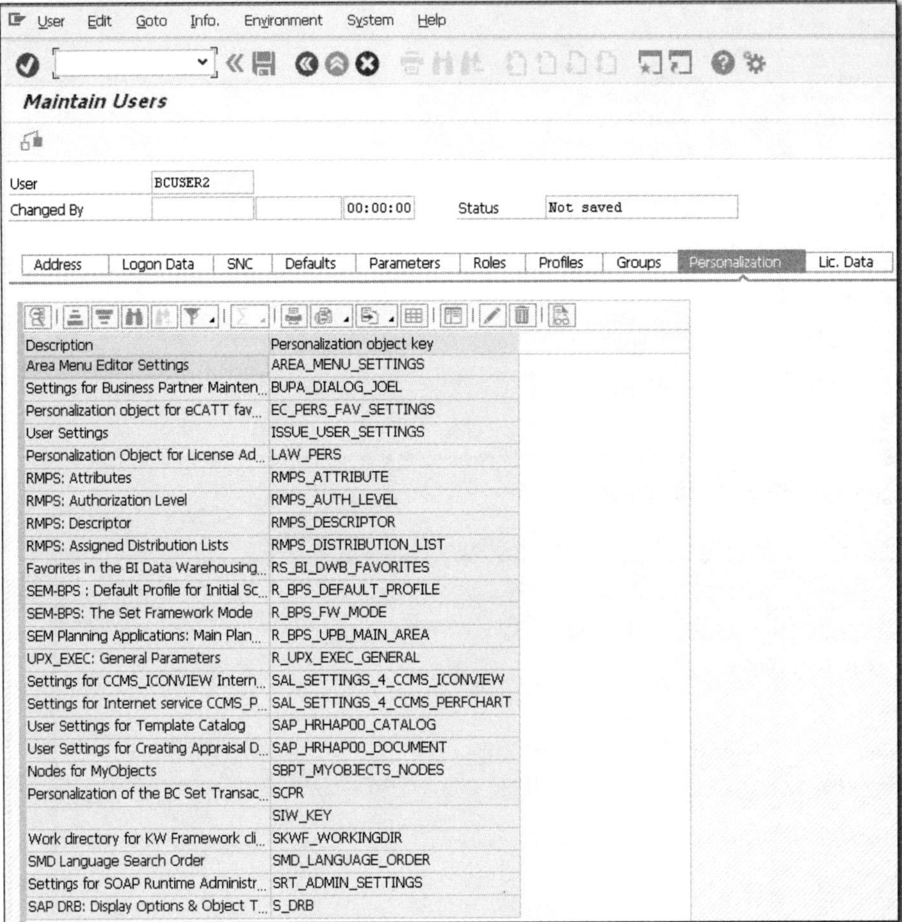

Figure 13.10 Changing the Personalization Options

14. Go to the LIC. DATA tab, and store the CONTRACTUAL USER TYPE ID corresponding to your license agreement (see Figure 13.11).

15. Click on SAVE.

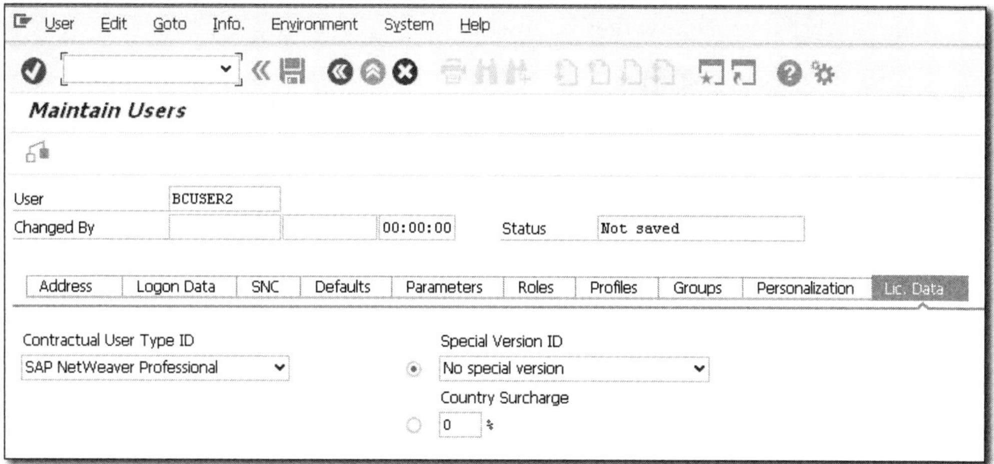

Figure 13.11 Storing the Contractual User Type

A message is displayed in the status bar, which confirms that the user has been saved.

13.2.2 Creating a New User

If there isn't a user you can copy, you must create a new user.

1. Call Transaction SU01.
2. Enter the user ID (e.g., "BCUSER3") to be created, and click on CREATE (refer to Figure 13.1).

Proceed in the remaining steps, as described in Section 13.2.1.

13.3 Maintaining Users

Before you start with the user maintenance, you should have a filled-out and approved form for changing users.

Document User Changes! [+]

The documentation of user changes is checked during a security check.

You must maintain the users in case the job or position of the employee changes, new authorizations are added, or user data (e.g., name, address, telephone number, etc.) change. Follow these steps:

1. Call Transaction SU01.
2. Enter the user ID (e.g., "BCUSER") to be maintained, and click on CHANGE (refer to Figure 13.1).

In the MAINTAIN USER screen, you can change the master data of an already existing user, as described in Section 13.2.1.

13.4 Mass Changes

In certain situations, it's helpful to not have to individually maintain the master data of a large number of users via Transaction SU01 (User Maintenance) but instead to use the mass maintenance function of Transaction SU10 (User Mass Maintenance). The following are application cases that frequently arise:

- Assigning a new company address due to organizational changes
- Changing the validity period for a consulting team's SAP accesses due to project delays
- Locking users of a specific enterprise area for system maintenance

[+]

Restrictions Regarding Mass Maintenance

Mass maintenance is subject to certain restrictions that arise from the nature of user master data or security aspects. For example, you can't change the name of users via Transaction SU10 or reset their passwords.

In appropriate cases, mass maintenance results in a considerable administration effort reduction.

1. Call Transaction SU10.
2. Enter the user IDs (e.g., "BCUSER" and "BCUSER2") to be changed, and click on CHANGE (see Figure 13.12).
3. Select the tab in which you want to implement changes (e.g., LOGON DATA, see Figure 13.13).

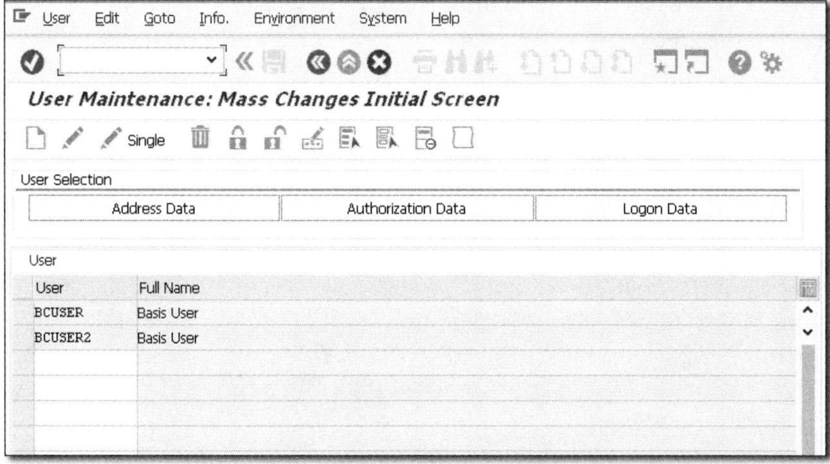

Figure 13.12 Initial Screen of the User Mass Change

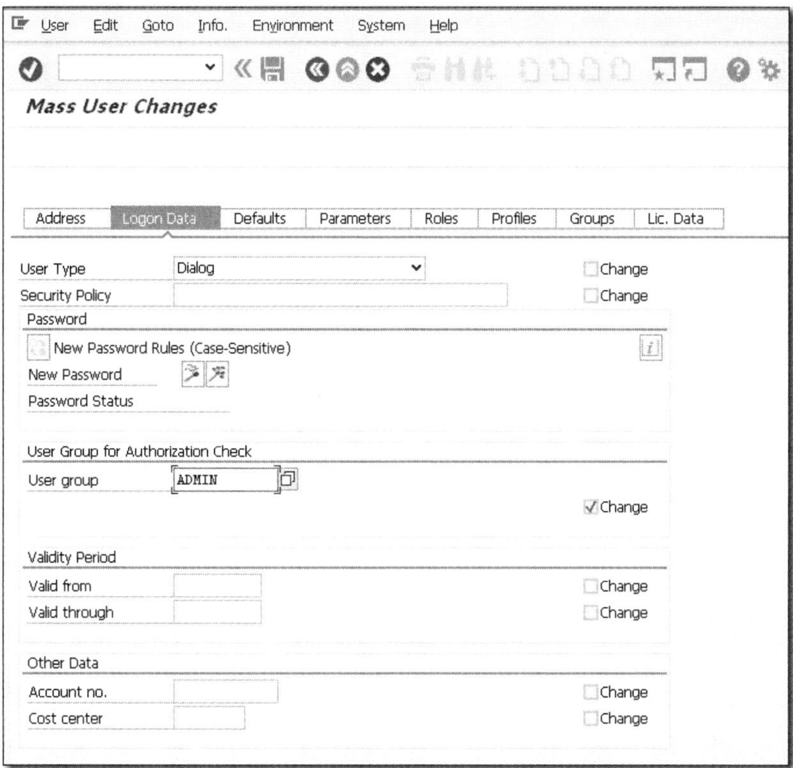

Figure 13.13 Changing User Groups of Several Users

4. Enter the data that you want to maintain (e.g., a new user group), and activate the CHANGE checkbox.
5. When you've made the desired changes, click on SAVE.
6. Check the log of implemented changes (see Figure 13.14). Click BACK to exit the log display.

[+]

Using Mass Maintenance

You can use the mass maintenance function to create, change, delete, lock, and unlock users as well as to set a new initial password. In the initial screen of Transaction SU10, you can select the users to be processed based on their address data (e.g., name, enterprise, etc.) or their authorization data (e.g., user groups, assigned roles or profiles, etc.).

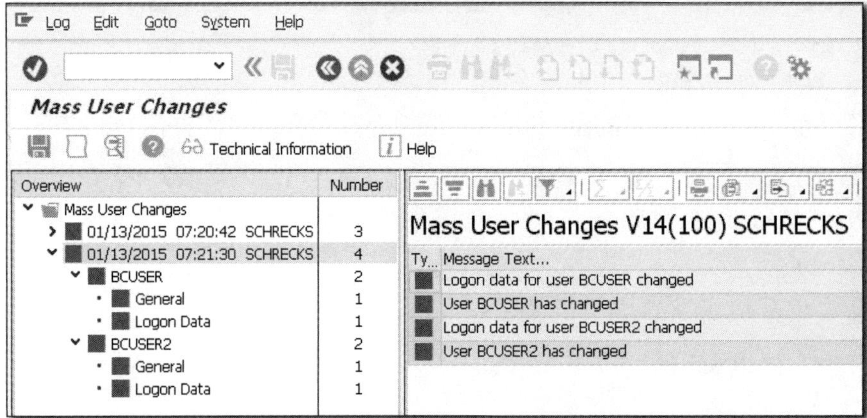

Figure 13.14 Change Log of the User Mass Change

13.5 Resetting the Password

The most frequent reason for resetting a password is that a user has forgotten his password. A user may have also exceeded the permissible number of logon attempts; that is, his user ID is locked and must also be unlocked.

[!]

Identifying the Correct User

Confirm the identity of the person who wants to reset his password. A simple method to identify the user is to compare telephone numbers on a telephone with a display. You can then compare the telephone numbers of the caller with the telephone number of the valid user stored in the system or found in the enterprise's telephone directory. Also have the user send an email with regard to the matter to identify the person based on the email address. You can keep this email for documentation purposes. You then send the new password via the reply function of your email program. In this way, you avoid someone overhearing the reset password. Generated random passwords can also be better conveyed in written form than by telephone.

Some enterprises use a secret keyword that is used to check the user's identity on the telephone. Banks use a similar method to identify the caller. However, this method also has security risks because the secret keyword can be overheard by third parties.

Implement the following steps to reset a user password:

1. Call Transaction SU01.
2. Enter the user ID (e.g., "BCUSER") whose password is to be reset, and click on CHANGE PASSWORD (refer to Figure 13.1).
3. Click on GENERATE PASSWORD in the CHANGE PASSWORD dialog box to generate a new password via a random number generator (see Figure 13.15). You can also enter a password manually in the NEW PASSWORD field (e.g., "Initial1"). In this case, you need to reenter it in the REPEAT PASSWORD field.
4. Click on TRANSFER .

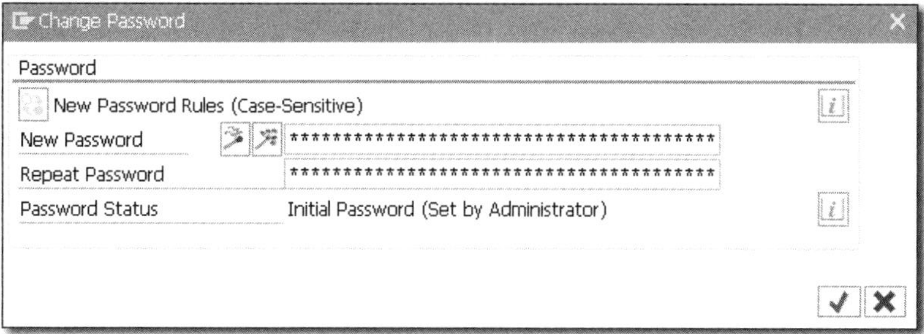

Figure 13.15 Entering a New Password

Passwords [⚙]

For security reasons, you can only specify an initial password for the user. The user must then change this initial password when he logs on to the system. You can neither display the current password nor define a permanent password for dialog users.

13.6 Locking or Unlocking a User

The locking/unlocking function is part of the logon check that enables or prevents the user from logging on to the SAP system.

Locking Users

Using the lock function, you can prevent the user from logging on to the SAP system; however, the user ID and the assigned authorizations persist. This function is suitable, for example, for temporary employees or consultants whose user ID is locked if they don't need to access the system. To lock a user, follow these steps:

1. Call Transaction SU01.
2. Enter the user ID (e.g., "BCUSER") to be locked, and click on LOCK/UNLOCK (refer to Figure 13.1).
3. A dialog window appears, which displays that the user isn't locked currently. To lock the user, click on LOCK (see Figure 13.16).

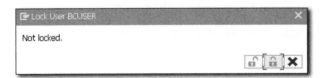

Figure 13.16 Locking a User

4. A message in the status bar confirms that the user has been successfully locked.

Unlocking Users

Users are automatically locked when they have exceeded the permissible number of unsuccessful logon attempts. In this case, the system administrator must unlock the user ID and might also have to reset the password.

[!] **Checking the Reason for Locking**

Make sure that you have a valid request before you reset a user. Don't unlock any manually locked user before you've determined the reason why the user has been locked. There may be an important reason as to why the user must not access the system.

1. Call Transaction SU01.
2. Enter the user ID (e.g., "BCUSER") to be unlocked, and click on LOCK/UNLOCK (refer to Figure 13.1).
3. A dialog window is displayed (see Figure 13.17). In this example, the system administrator has locked the user ID manually. The message could also read LOCKED DUE TO INCORRECT LOGONS.

Figure 13.17 Lock Status of a User

[!]

Locking by System Administrator

Also make inquiries if a user has been locked by a system administrator. The user may not be allowed to be unlocked. Via the INFORMATION • CHANGE DOCUMENTS FOR USERS menu path, you can determine who has locked the user and make specific inquires.

4. Unlock the user via the UNLOCK button. A message in the status bar confirms that the user has been successfully unlocked (see Figure 13.18). The addition, IF THIS IS PERMITTED IN THIS SYSTEM, is only relevant if the system is integrated with a Central User Administration. In this case, unlocking a user may only be possible in the central system.

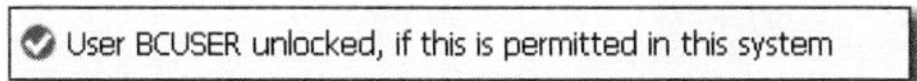

Figure 13.18 Confirmation for User Lock

13.7 Central User Administration

If you have to manage several SAP systems with a large number of users, setting up a *Central User Administration* (CUA) can significantly reduce your amount of work. Whether this is worth doing mainly depends on how many systems and clients you manage, whether many of the users have access to several clients or systems, and how frequently you process user requests.

Already in a three-system landscape consisting of a development, QA, and production system, it can be tedious when you have dozens of requests a week to create or change every user both in the production and QA system.

In a CUA, the user master data is maintained in the central system and distributed to the child systems via *Application Link Enabling* (ALE) technology. Maintenance directly in the child systems themselves is only possible with restrictions. However, it can be configured in relative detail.

[+]

Additional Information

The following section describes how you set up the CUA in a robust standard configuration. In SAP Service Marketplace (*www.service.sap.com*), you can find a variety of notes that you can use to reach further optimization.

13.7.1 Setting Up a Central User Administration

To operate a CUA, you must carry out a sequence of individual steps:

1. Create communication users for the CUA and provide them with authorizations.
2. Define and assign logical systems.
3. Set up RFC connections between the systems.
4. Generate a distribution model for the CUA.
5. Synchronize company addresses and users.
6. Customize authorizations for communication users for operation.
7. Configure the distribution of user fields (field selection).

The following sections describe these steps in more detail.

Creating and Allocating Communication Users and Authorization Roles

In each logical system, a user ID with special authorizations is required for the communication between the systems of the CUA. First, create these communication users:

1. Log on to the central system.
2. Create a user ID, for example, CUA, as described in Section 13.2 by using Transaction SU01.
3. Select the SYSTEM user type in the LOGON DATA tab.

4. Write down the password that you've assigned or generated.
5. Save the user master record.
6. Perform steps 1 to 5 in all your child systems.

You've now created a user ID by which the communication between the systems of the CUA takes place. Next, you must provide this user with the necessary authorizations for the communication. For these purposes, SAP provides template authorization roles:

- SAP_BC_USR_CUA_SETUP_CENTRAL
  Authorization in the central system to set up the CUA.
- SAP_BC_USR_CUA_CENTRAL
  Authorization in the central system to operate the CUA.
- SAP_BC_USR_CUA_CENTRAL_BDIST
  Authorization required if you use the redistribution function (see the "Configuring the Distribution of User Fields [Field Selection]" section).
- SAP_BC_USR_CUA_SETUP_CLIENT
  Authorization in the child system to set up the CUA.
- SAP_BC_USR_CUA_CLIENT
  Authorization in the child system to set up the CUA.

To use the templates, follow these steps:

1. Log on to the central system.
2. Copy the roles SAP_BC_USR_CUA_SETUP_CENTRAL, SAP_BC_USR_CUA_CENTRAL and SAP_BC_USR_CUA_CENTRAL_BDIST into your customer naming space (e.g., Z_BC_USR_CUA_SETUP_CENTRAL), as described in Chapter 14.

Using No Original Roles [!]

Don't use the original roles provided because these roles may be overwritten when a support package is imported.

3. Generate the authorization profile for each of the two roles in the AUTHORIZATIONS tab.
4. Assign each of the two roles to your communication user (e.g., "CUA") in the USER tab.
5. Execute the user comparison, and save.

6. Repeat steps 1 to 5 in each of your child systems using the two roles SAP_BC_USR_CUA_SETUP_CLIENT and SAP_BC_USR_CUA_CLIENT.

[+] **Transport Request**

You can also distribute the authorization roles for the child systems via a transport request to several child systems.

Creating and Allocating Logical Systems

In a CUA, the term *system* doesn't refer to an application server or an instance but instead to *logical systems*. These logical systems must be defined in the SAP system and are then assigned to a client of a system.

[+] **Logical Systems**

A logical system represents one client in a specific system. The ID of a logical system must not be used several times; otherwise, this could result in communication errors in the system network. It's therefore best to stick to the usual naming convention <SID>CLNT<client> (e.g., V14CLNT100).

In the central system of the CUA, all logical systems taking part in the CUA must be known. Only the logical system of the respective child system and the logical system of the central system need to be available in the child systems, respectively.

In this example, a CUA is to be created in one individual system using the system ID NSP. Client 000 assumes the function of the central system; client 001 is supposed to be integrated into the CUA as a child system and is provided with user master data. Modify the example accordingly to your framework conditions. First, create the logical systems:

1. Log on to the central system.
2. Call Transaction BD54 (Maintain Logical Systems), and click on the New Entries button (see Figure 13.19).
3. Create an entry for your central system and for each of your child systems (see Figure 13.20). Save your entries. You must add your changes to a workbench transport request, which the system prompts automatically.
4. Implement steps 1 to 3 in your child systems, or, even better, transport the logical systems created in the central system to the child systems using the transport request created in step 3.

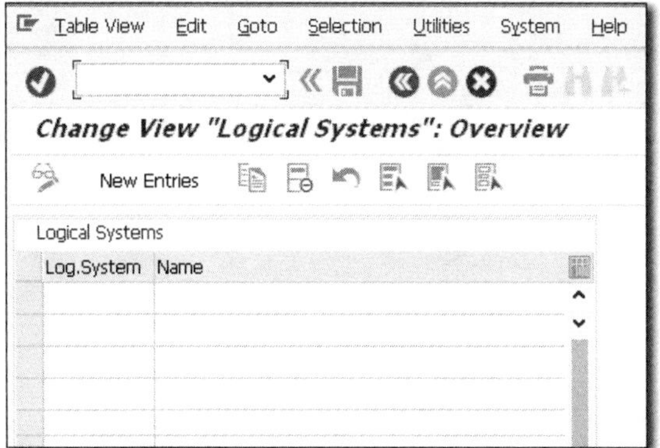

Figure 13.19 Initial Screen for Maintaining Logical Systems

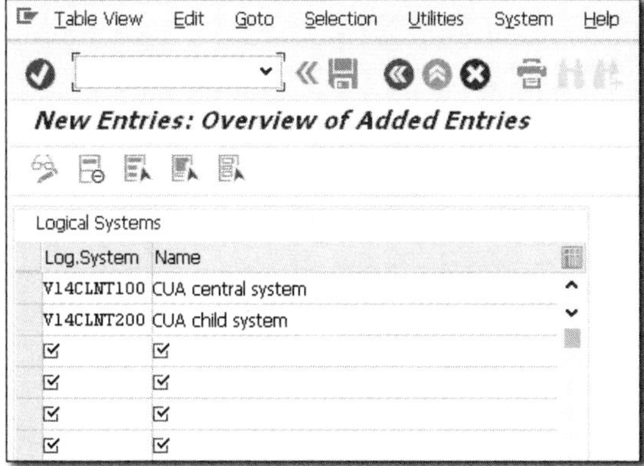

Figure 13.20 Creating New Logical Systems

If all required logical systems have been created, assign them to the respective systems' clients:

1. Log on to the central system once again.
2. Enter Transaction SCC4 in the command field and press the Enter key (or select the menu option Tools • Administration • Administration • Client Administration • SCC4—Client Maintenance; see Figure 13.21).
3. Switch to the change mode using the button, and double-click to select the client who is intended as the central system of your CUA (e.g., 100).
4. Enter the logical system in the field intended for this (e.g., "V14CLNT100"; see Figure 13.22), and Save.

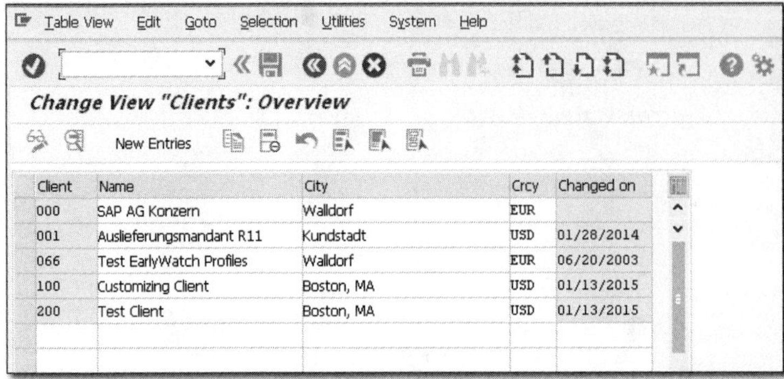

Figure 13.21 Initial Screen of Client Maintenance

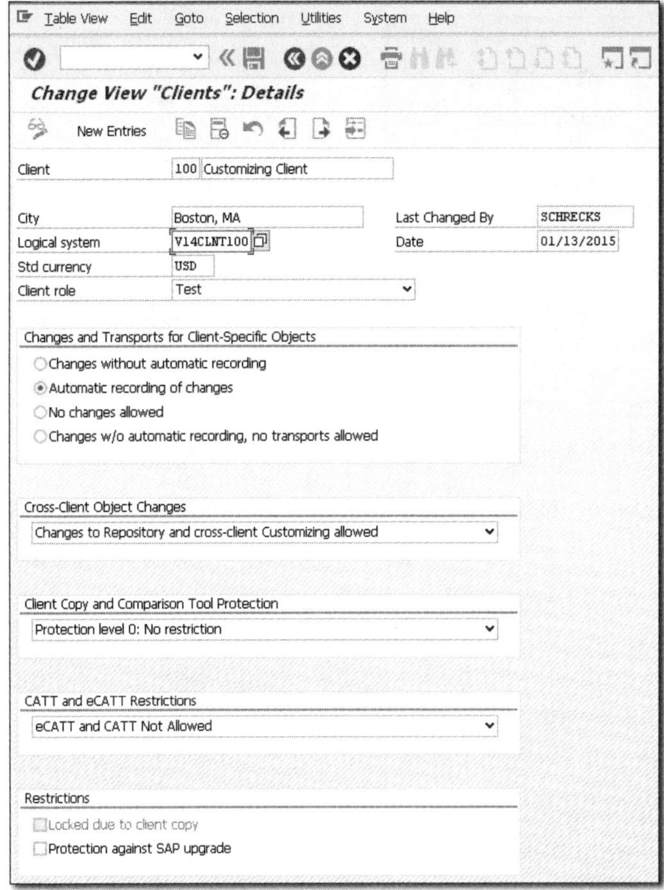

Figure 13.22 Assigning a Logical System to the Client

5. Exit the view by clicking on BACK, and save again.
6. Assign the remaining logical systems to the respective clients by repeating steps 1 to 4 in the respective systems (e.g., "V14CLNT200" for the logical system).

You've now defined and assigned logical systems for the systems or clients that are supposed to belong to your CUA.

Set Up RFC Connections Between the Systems

After the communication user and systems of your CUA have been set up, you can define the communication connections between the systems of the CUA, which are required to exchange data via ALE. A connection must be set up from the central system to each child system and from the respective child system to the central system. Furthermore, an RFC connection to the central system itself is required because the central system is handled as a child system when a user is assigned to the central system.

1. Log on to the central system.
2. Enter Transaction SM59 in the command field and press the Enter key (or select TOOLS • ADMINISTRATION • ADMINISTRATION • NETWORK • SM59—RFC DESTINATIONS in the standard SAP menu).
3. Click on CREATE (see Figure 13.23).

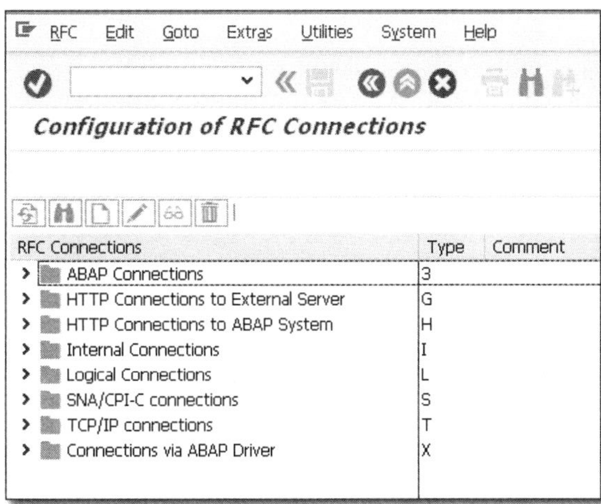

Figure 13.23 Initial Screen for Maintaining RFC Connections

4. First, create the RFC connection to the central system (e.g., V14CLNT100). Enter "3" as the connection type (ABAP CONNECTION), and provide a self-explanatory description.
5. Press the Enter key.

[!] **Description of the RFC Connections**

Note that the RFC connections that you create for a CUA must always have the same name as the logical system to which they point.

6. Enter the server name or the IP address of the application server (e.g., "v14") in the TARGET HOST field in the TECHNICAL SETTINGS tab , and define the respective system number (e.g., "00"; see Figure 13.24).

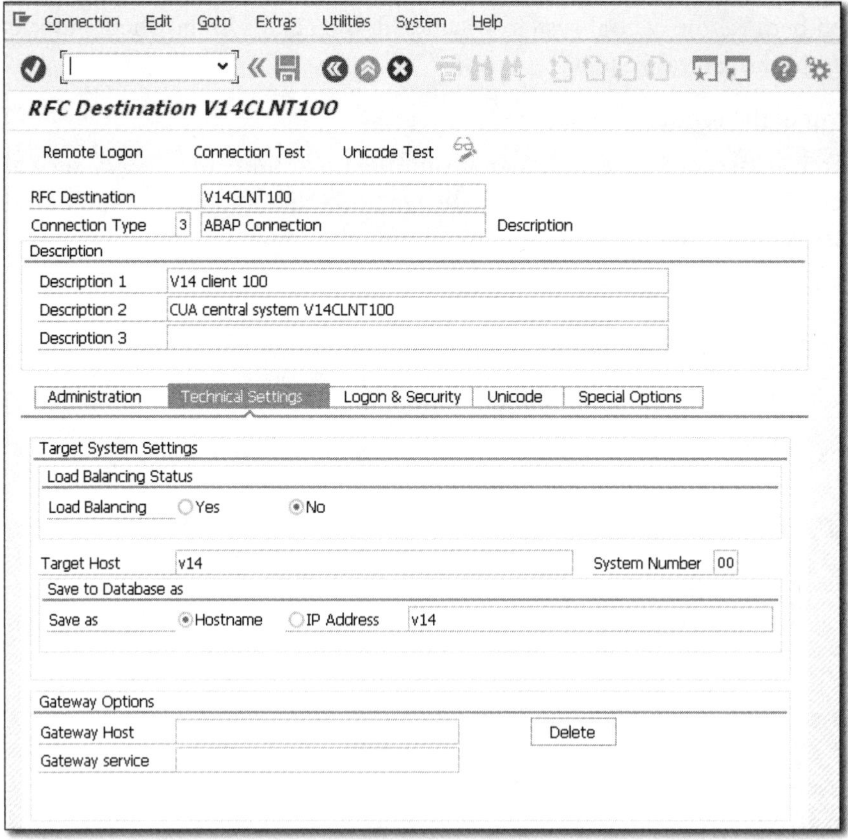

Figure 13.24 Creating an RFC Connection

7. Switch to the LOGON & SECURITY tab (see Figure 13.25):
   - Enter a LANGUAGE key (e.g., "EN") in the LOGON PROCEDURE area.
   - Enter the CLIENT that is supposed to function as the central system on the server (e.g., "100").
   - Enter the user ID of your communication user in the USER field (e.g., "CUA").
   - In the PASSWORD field, define the password of the communication user that has been generated or manually assigned by you.

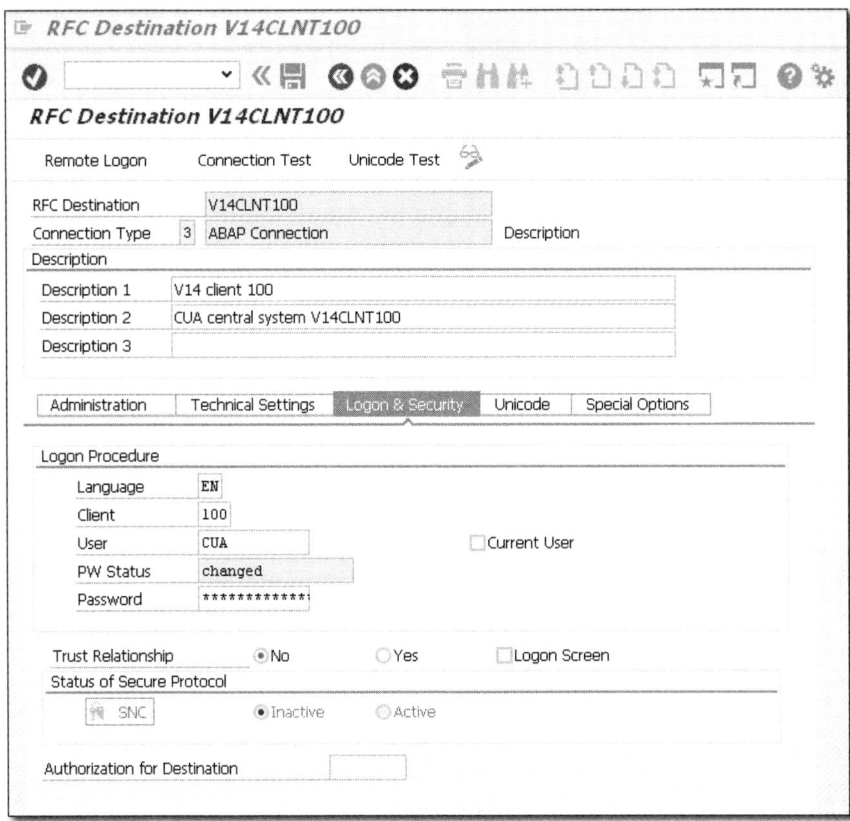

Figure 13.25 Defining Logon Data

8. Save the RFC connection.
9. Test the connection by clicking first on the CONNECTION TEST button.

[+] **Connection Test**

With the Connection Test, the information that you created in the Technical Settings tab is checked to determine whether the server is accessible and whether the system number exists (see Figure 13.26).

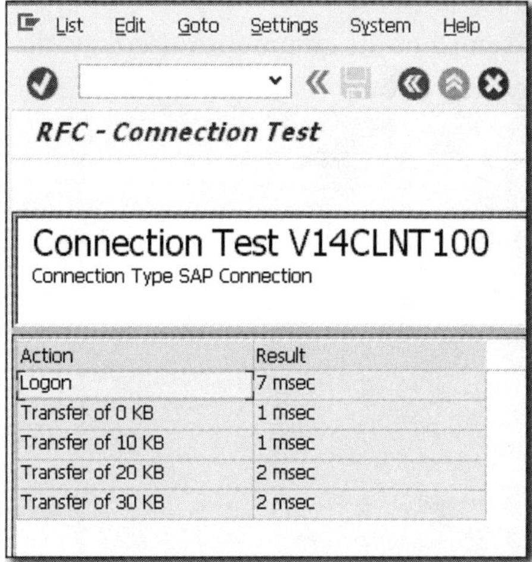

Figure 13.26 Testing an RFC Connection

10. Then click on the Remote Logon button (refer to Figure 13.25). The test is successful if *no* logon screen appears.

Connection Test Result

Don't worry if nothing happens in a successful remote login test—that's a good sign! The remote login checks the data in the Logon & Security tab. If a logon window appears, the remote login was unsuccessful. Then check whether you've entered the user ID and password correctly, and ensure that the user isn't locked.

To make sure that the connection is working, run an authorization test using Utilities • Test • Authorization Test. It includes both the connection test and the remote logon, and additionally checks the basic authorizations of the logon user.

11. Now create the RFC connections for the child systems (e.g., V14CLNT200) by repeating steps 3 to 9 in the central system.
12. Then log on to the child systems, and define the RFC connections to the central system. Repeat the same procedure for steps 2 to 9.

Generate a Distribution Model for the CUA

The communication between your systems is now prepared in such a way that the rest of the work can be done by the SAP system. The ALE settings still to be set up (distribution model) can be automatically generated via a custom transaction. To do this, follow these steps:

1. Log on to the central system.
2. Enter Transaction SCUA in the command field and press the Enter key (or select Tools • Administration • User Maintenance • Central User Administration • SCUA—Distribution Model).
3. Assign a name for your CUA distribution model in the Model view field (e.g., "CUA_V14"; see Figure 13.27). Click on Create.

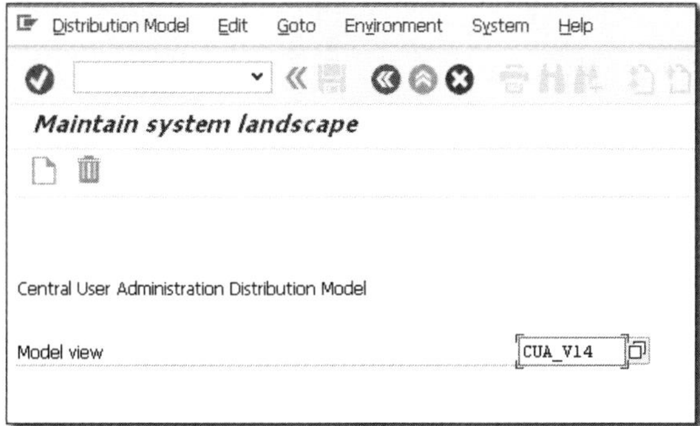

Figure 13.27 Creating a CUA Distribution Model

4. The logical system of the central system appears in the Sending system field (see Figure 13.28). Under Recipient, enter the logical systems of your child systems (e.g., "V14CLNT200"), and press Enter.

Checking the RFC Connections [⚙]

The connection to the selected receiving systems is checked in the background. If all of the columns for one of the receiving systems aren't filled by the system or if a red traffic light icon appears in the RFC Status field, you must check your RFC connections. The authorizations, which you assigned to the communication user in the child system, may sometimes not suffice. Then, extend the authorizations accordingly, for example, by using authorization traces in Transaction ST01 (System Trace; see Chapter 14, Section 14.4.2).

5. Click on Complete Save.

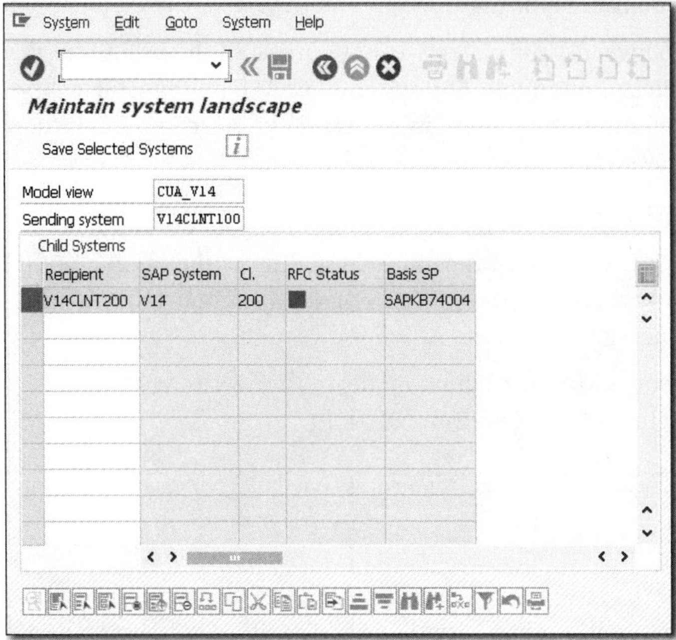

Figure 13.28 Entering Child Systems

6. A log is displayed (see Figure 13.29). Check the log, and eliminate errors that may have arisen (e.g., incorrect RFC connections or insufficient user authorizations).

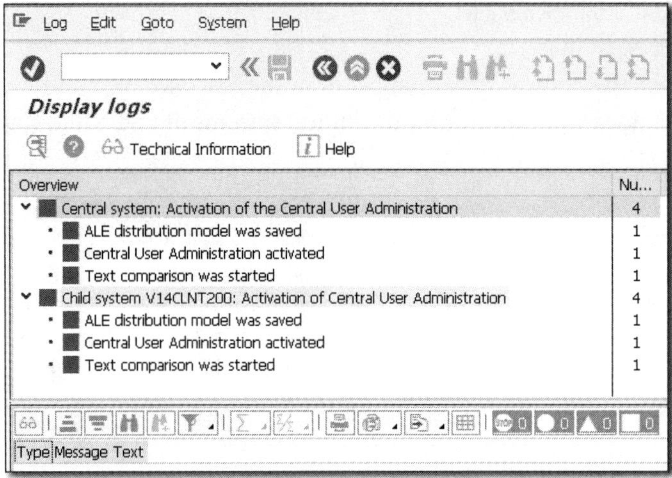

Figure 13.29 Log for Creating the Distribution Model

7. Click BACK twice. The distribution model is displayed in gray in the initial screen (see Figure 13.30).

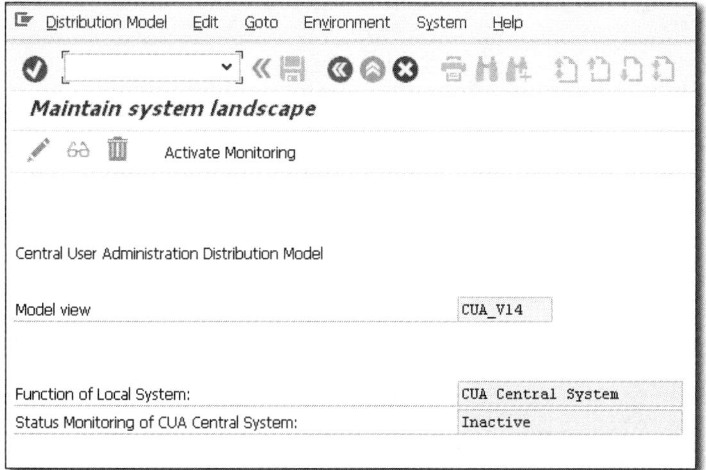

Figure 13.30 Created CUA Distribution Model

The distribution model is now configured, which means that the communication paths for the CUA are fundamentally set up.

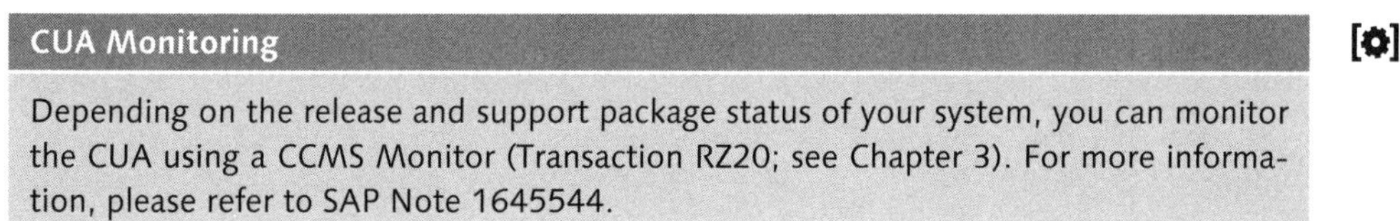

CUA Monitoring

Depending on the release and support package status of your system, you can monitor the CUA using a CCMS Monitor (Transaction RZ20; see Chapter 3). For more information, please refer to SAP Note 1645544.

Synchronize Company Addresses and Users

The technical settings for the communication of the CUA are completed when the distribution model is created. To use the CUA in operation, you must now fill it with the company addresses and the user data from the connected systems. To avert errors when you copy data, however, you should prepare it.

1. Log on to the central system.
2. Activate Transaction SA38 (ABAP Program Execution), and first execute Program `RSADRCK2` in the test run and then in the live run. Check the log output of the consistency check (see Figure 13.31).

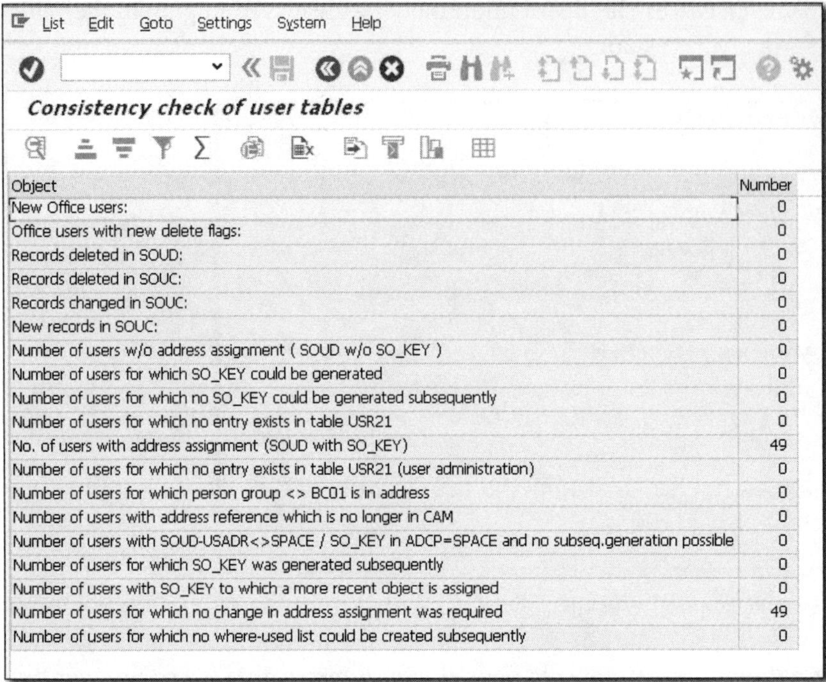

Object	Number
New Office users:	0
Office users with new delete flags:	0
Records deleted in SOUD:	0
Records deleted in SOUC:	0
Records changed in SOUC:	0
New records in SOUC:	0
Number of users w/o address assignment (SOUD w/o SO_KEY)	0
Number of users for which SO_KEY could be generated	0
Number of users for which no SO_KEY could be generated subsequently	0
Number of users for which no entry exists in table USR21	0
No. of users with address assignment (SOUD with SO_KEY)	49
Number of users for which no entry exists in table USR21 (user administration)	0
Number of users for which person group <> BC01 is in address	0
Number of users with address reference which is no longer in CAM	0
Number of users with SOUD-USADR<>SPACE / SO_KEY in ADCP=SPACE and no subseq.generation possible	0
Number of users for which SO_KEY was generated subsequently	0
Number of users with SO_KEY to which a more recent object is assigned	0
Number of users for which no change in address assignment was required	49
Number of users for which no where-used list could be created subsequently	0

Figure 13.31 Log of the Consistency Check Using Program RSADRCK2

Program RSADRCK2

Program RSADRCK2 remedies inconsistencies within the assignment of company addresses to users (table USR21).

3. Repeat steps 1 and 2 in all child systems.
4. Log on to the central system.
5. Activate Transaction SM30 (Table View Maintenance).
6. Enter "CUA_USERGROUPS_CHECK" in the Name field of table PRGN_CUST using the Value "C" (see Figure 13.32).

CUA_USERGROUPS_CHECK Entry

With this entry, the user groups, which aren't available in the central system, are created automatically when users are copied from the child systems. Without the entry, errors would arise when the users are copied. You can also ensure manually that all user groups exist in the central system.

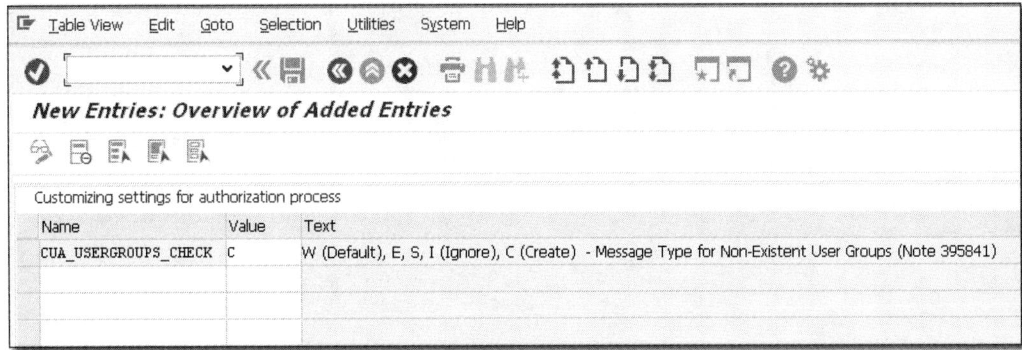
Table View Edit Goto Selection Utilities System Help

New Entries: Overview of Added Entries

Customizing settings for authorization process

Name	Value	Text
CUA_USERGROUPS_CHECK	C	W (Default), E, S, I (Ignore), C (Create) - Message Type for Non-Existent User Groups (Note 395841)

Figure 13.32 Creating a New Entry in Table PRGN_CUST

7. Implement steps 5 and 6 in the child systems as well, if user groups are to be created automatically when the users are distributed.
8. Enter Transaction SCUG in the command field and press the Enter key (or select TOOLS • ADMINISTRATION • USER MAINTENANCE • CENTRAL USER ADMINISTRATION • SCUG—TRANSFER USERS in the standard SAP menu).
9. Place the cursor on a child system (e.g., V14CLNT200), and click on SYNCHRONIZE COMPANY ADDRESSES IN THE CENTRAL SYSTEM (see Figure 13.33).

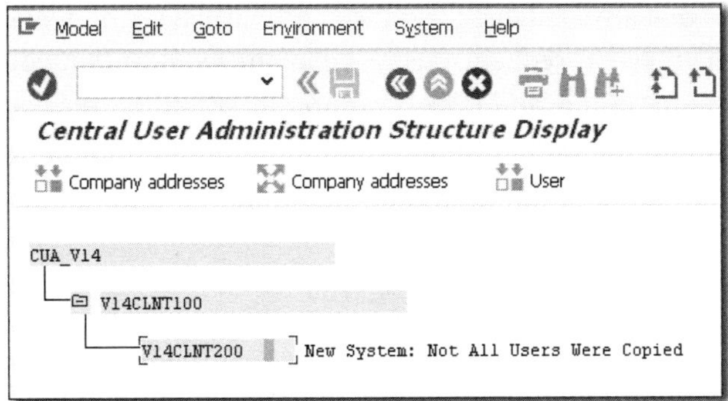

Figure 13.33 Synchronize Company Addresses in the Central System

10. Highlight the company addresses to be synchronized by expanding the areas and selecting either COPY FROM CHILD SYSTEM (e.g., for addresses that only exist in the child system) or the DISTRIBUTE TO CHILD SYSTEM button (e.g., for addresses that only exist in the central system) (see Figure 13.34).

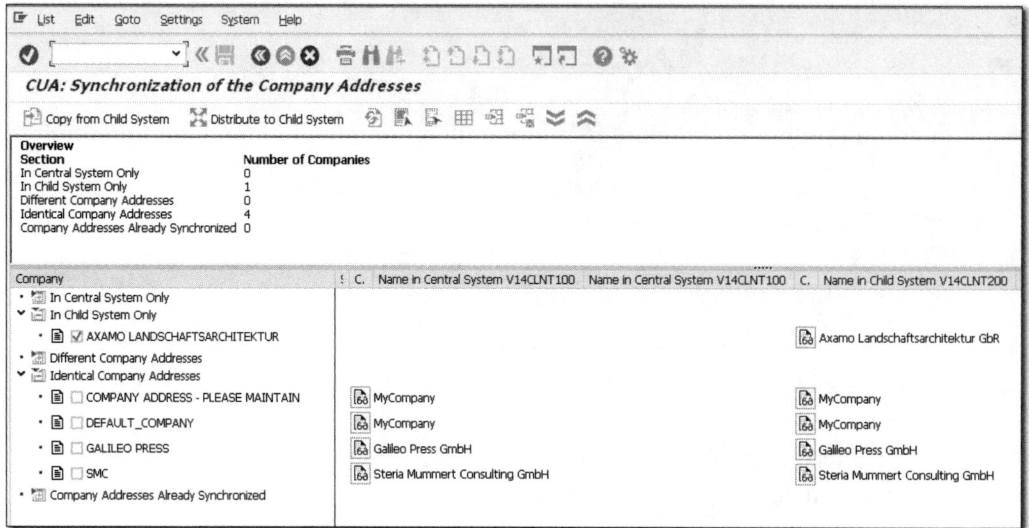

Figure 13.34 Selecting the Company Addresses to Be Synchronized

11. When you've completed the synchronization of the company addresses, click on BACK.
12. Click on the USER button to copy it to the central system.
13. The user master records that are available for transfer are displayed in several tabs, which you need to check in sequence. First highlight the data that you want to copy in the NEW USERS tab, and click on TRANSFER USERS (see Figure 13.35).

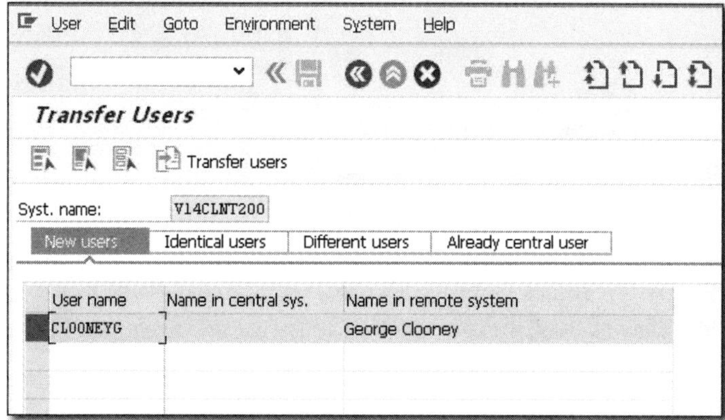

Figure 13.35 Highlighting Users for Transfer

14. Repeat the user transfer in the IDENTICAL USERS and DIFFERENT USERS tabs.
15. When you've completed the synchronization of the user data, click on BACK . In the structure display of the CUA, the status message NEW SYSTEM: NOT ALL USERS WERE COPIED no longer appears (see Figure 13.36).

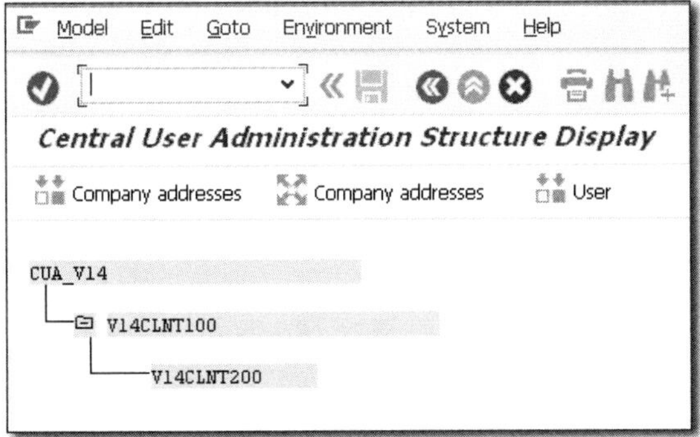

Figure 13.36 User Data Synchronization Completed

16. Repeat steps 10 to 15 for all remaining child systems.

You've now copied the company addresses and user master data from the connected child systems in your central system. All systems can now be found in a synchronized state. This is a fundamental prerequisite for consistent administration of user data.

Resynchronizing CUA [⚙]

To resynchronize user data, for example, according to a system or client copy, program RSCCUSND is provided. For further information, read SAP Notes 574094 and 503247.

Customize Authorizations for Communication Users for Operation

After you've synchronized the company addresses and user data, the CUA is ready. For security reasons, you should now withdraw the authorization roles again from the communication users for the setup of the CUA by following these steps:

1. Log on to the central system.
2. Call Transaction SU01.

3. Enter the user ID of the communication user (e.g., "CUA").
4. Click on CHANGE.
5. Go to the ROLES tab.
6. Highlight the authorization roles to set up the CUA (e.g., Z_BC_USR_CUA_SETUP_CENTRAL and Z_BC_USR_CUA_SETUP_CLIENT), and click on DELETE ROW (see Figure 13.37).

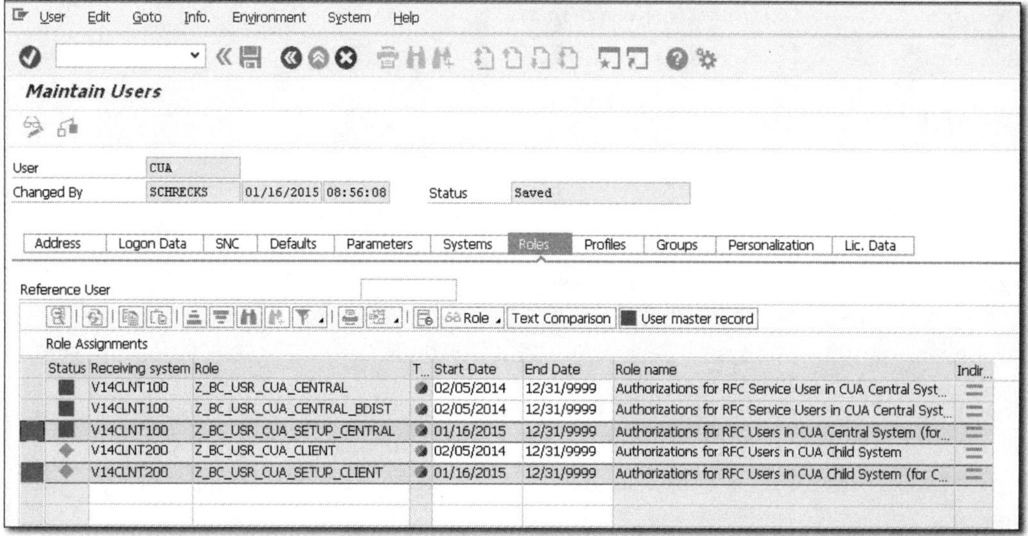

Figure 13.37 Deleting Roles for Setting Up the CUA

7. Click on SAVE.

You've now customized the communication user for operation.

Configure the Distribution of User Fields (Field Selection)

The main goal of the CUA is to bundle the maintenance of user master data in a system and at the same time minimize the administration effort. You can only create, copy, and delete users in the central system. Moreover, the default setting is provided so that all fields of the user master record can only be changed in the central system. You can customize these settings depending on the system landscape and the distribution of responsibilities within the enterprise. The CUA can be configured via *field selection* in such a way that many—but not all—fields can also be maintained in the child systems. You customize the default parameters as follows:

1. Log on to the central system.
2. Enter Transaction SCUM in the command field and press the [Enter] key (or select TOOLS • ADMINISTRATION • USER MAINTENANCE • CENTRAL USER ADMINISTRATION • SCUM—FIELD SELECTION).
3. Click on DISPLAY <-> CHANGE.
4. Select the distribution mode for the individual fields by navigating via the tabs and highlighting the respective radio buttons (see Figure 13.38).

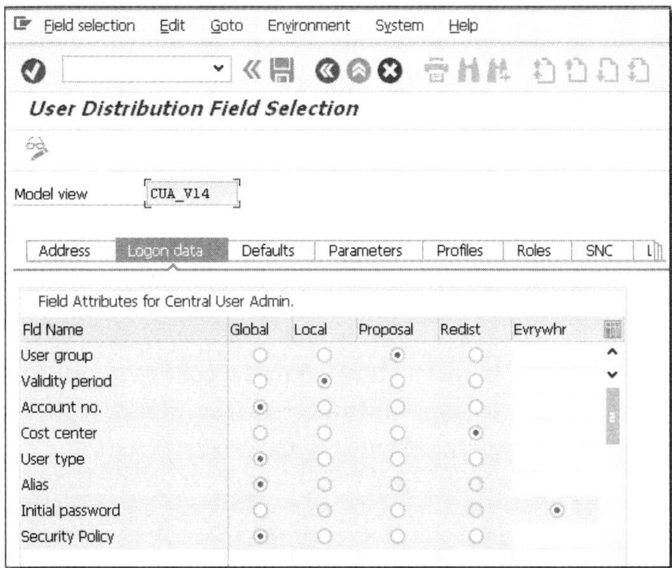

Figure 13.38 Adapting the Field Selection

5. When you've completed your settings, click on SAVE.

After saving, the configuration is copied to the child systems. The distribution options have the following meaning:

- GLOBAL
  The data can only be maintained in the central system. The settings made in the central system are distributed to the child systems. All fields are set to GLOBAL in the standard configuration.

- LOCAL
  The data can only be maintained in the child system. They are neither redistributed to the central system nor to other child systems. This setting makes sense for such fields, which can or need to be different in each system (e.g., the START menu).
- PROPOSAL
  The data can be changed in both the central and the child systems. However, the field value is distributed only when the user is created in the child system for the first time. No redistribution to the central system takes place if the field value is changed in a child system. Subsequent changes in the central system are also not transferred to the child systems.
- REDIST
  The data can be maintained both in the central and in the child systems. When you customize a setting in a child system, the user master record is notified of this change in the central system and edited there. Then it's distributed to all child systems. This mode is recommended for fields that are usually identical in all systems (e.g., name and address) because the settings of all systems are overwritten. For data that can exist in diverse ways in specific systems, redistribution isn't appropriate.
- EVRYWHR
  The data can be maintained both in the central and in the child systems. This option is only available for the initial password and certain user locks. If a child system is changed, this change isn't redistributed to the central system and the other child systems.

[+] **Distribution Modes**

Test the distribution modes until you find the setting suitable for your work environment. Various options aren't available for specific fields mainly due to the nature of the field and also often due to potential security threats. However, the setting options are usually adequate for common application scenarios.

13.7.2 Creating and Maintaining Users via a Central User Administration

After the CUA is used in live operation, you'll notice a few differences to the current system layout depending on the configuration of the field selection:

- In the child systems, the buttons to create, copy, and delete users are missing in the initial screen of Transaction SU01. The button to reset the password is also not available depending on the configuration of the field selection.
- If you select CHANGE in the child system, only the globally maintainable fields in the user master data are gray and can therefore not be changed.
- In the central system, the SYSTEMS tab is provided in the user master. The SYSTEM column is included both in the ROLES and PROFILES tabs.

The following sections now briefly describe the differences in the procedures already described in Section 13.2 through Section 13.6.

Creating New Users

Regardless of whether you create a user with or without a template, you must specify the systems in an active CUA in which the user is to be created. Enter the name of the desired logical system in Transaction SU01 (User Maintenance) in the SYSTEMS tab (see Figure 13.39). If you assign another logical system to a user in the SYSTEMS tab, the user is also created in this system. Authorizations are also assigned in a system-specific way. For this reason, the logical system is shown in the ROLES and PROFILES tabs as a new key column RECEIVING SYSTEM.

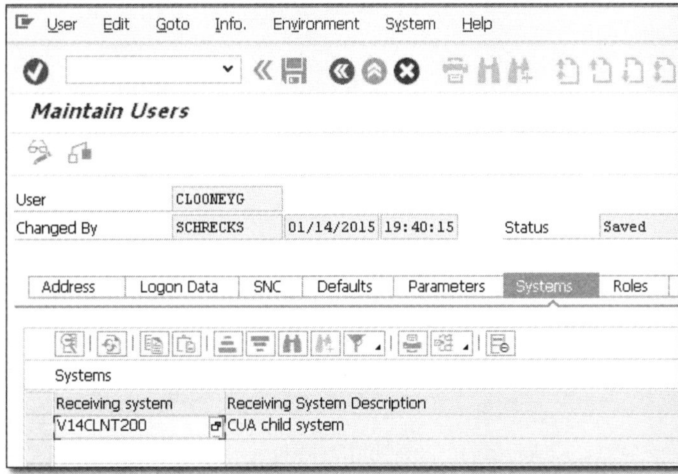

Figure 13.39 Defining Systems for Distributing the User Master Record

Assign authorization roles to the new user by filling an empty row with the logical system (RECEIVING SYSTEM column), the role name (ROLES column), and possibly varying validity dates in the ROLES tab in the ROLE ASSIGNMENTS area (see Figure 13.40).

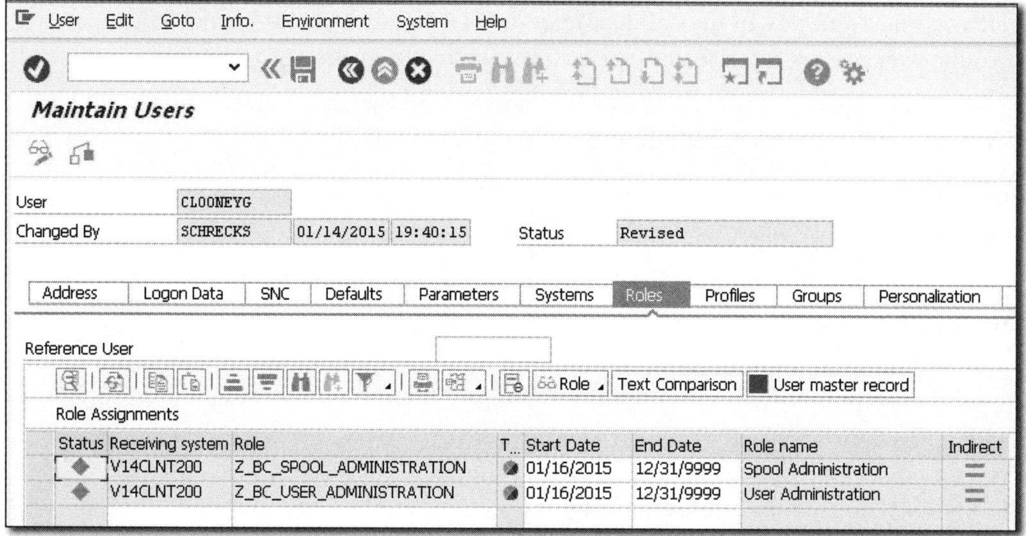

Figure 13.40 Assigning Roles in the Receiving System

Proceed in a similar way in the PROFILES tab in the ASSIGNED AUTHORIZATION PROFILES area (see Figure 13.41).

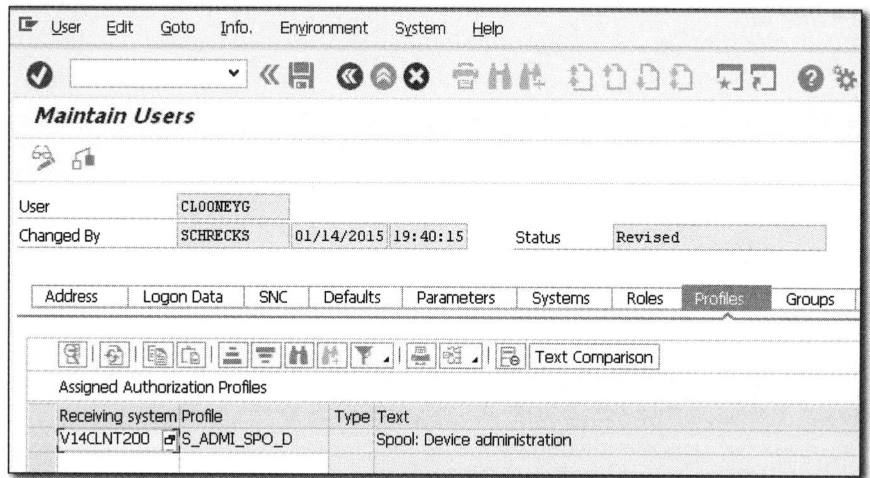

Figure 13.41 Assigning Profiles in the Receiving System

[+]

Text Comparison

If you receive messages such as ROLE/PROFILE ABC DOES NOT EXIST IN SYSTEM XYZ when assigning roles or profiles in a child system, first verify that you've spelled the names correctly, and then carry out a text comparison using the TEXT COMPARISON button. The text comparison reads all (text) data for roles and profiles from the selected child systems to the central system. You can then assign the role or profile.

User Maintenance and Mass Changes

When you change user master data and carry out mass maintenance via Transaction SU10, you must take into consideration that the same special features with regard to the assignment of logical systems are in an active CUA, as well as the system-specific assignment of authorization roles and profiles as when you create new users. If you want to delete a user, you can remove the respective logical system in the SYSTEMS tab. The user is then deleted in the target system. However, the user still remains in the central system as a master record. When you delete a user via the DELETE button, the user is removed globally in all systems, including the central system.

Resetting the Password

You can reset the user password from the central system for one or several systems (CHANGE PASSWORD button). The dialog window shows a list of systems in which the user exists. Select the systems to which you want the new initial password to be distributed by highlighting the rows (see Figure 13.42).

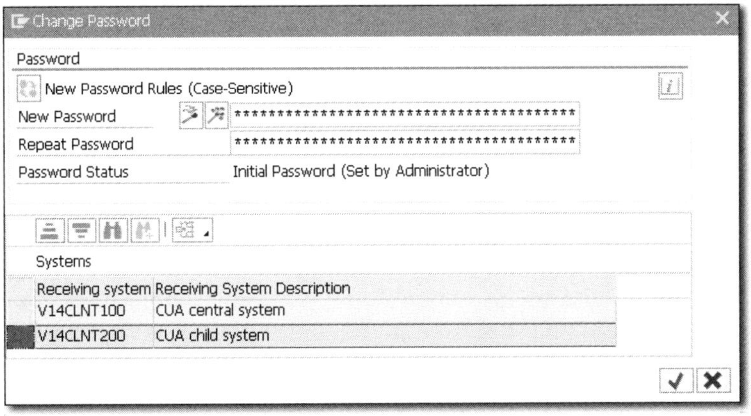

Change Password

Password

New Password Rules (Case-Sensitive)

New Password	**
Repeat Password	**
Password Status	Initial Password (Set by Administrator)

Systems

Receiving system	Receiving System Description
V14CLNT100	CUA central system
V14CLNT200	CUA child system

Figure 13.42 System Selection When Changing a Password

Locking or Unlocking a User

When you lock and unlock users, a differentiation is made between *local* and *global* locks in an active CUA.

- Local locks refer to exactly one system.
- Global locks are valid in all systems of the CUA.

The dialog window for setting and removing locks contains corresponding additional buttons (see Figure 13.43).

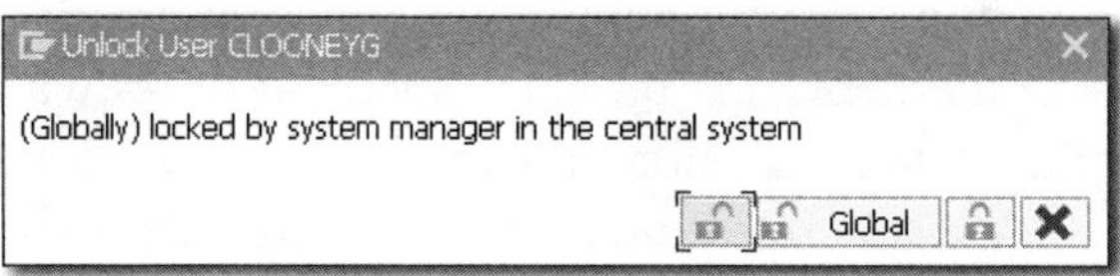

Figure 13.43 Lock Status in the Central User Administration

13.7.3 Troubleshooting

Problems in the CUA mainly arise from the communication between the systems involved and essentially manifest when maintained user data in the central system doesn't arrive in the child systems or when changes aren't passed to the CUA configuration. With regard to the error search, the first look applies to the CUA processing log in the central system. From the log, you can obtain initial notes with regard to the location and cause of the error.

1. Log on to the central system.
2. Enter Transaction SCUL in the command field and press the [Enter] key (or select TOOLS • ADMINISTRATION • USER MAINTENANCE • CENTRAL USER ADMINISTRATION • SCUL—LOG DISPLAY in the standard SAP menu) (see Figure 13.44).
3. In the selection screen, carry out any restrictions, and then click on EXECUTE .
4. Check the log for notes on the subsequent error search. With the DISTRIBUTE button , you can reactivate any incomplete processing operations (see Figure 13.45).

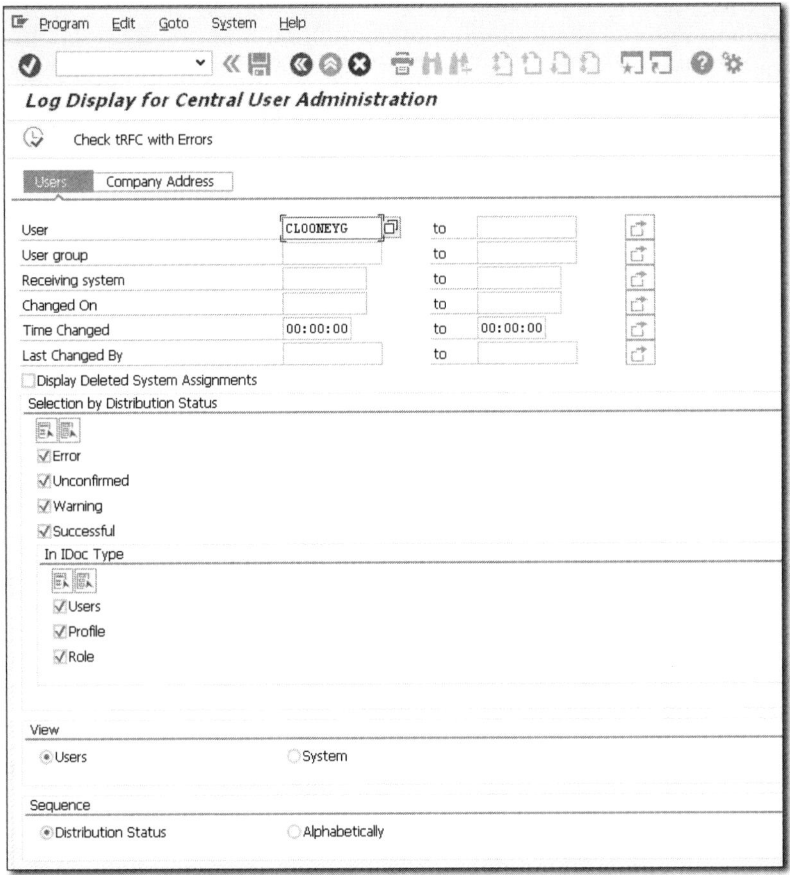

Figure 13.44 Selection Criteria for the Processing Log

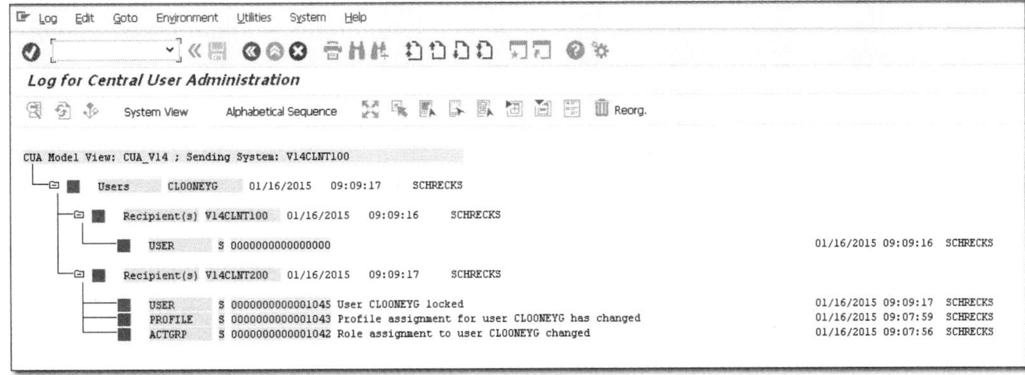

Figure 13.45 Processing Log

Using the IDoc Monitoring function, you can monitor data transfer.

1. Log on to the central system.
2. Enter Transaction BD87 in the command field and press the Enter key (or select TOOLS • ALE • ALE ADMINISTRATION • MONITORING • IDOC DISPLAY • BD87—STATUS MONITOR in the standard SAP menu).
3. Enter your selection options, and click on EXECUTE (see Figure 13.46).

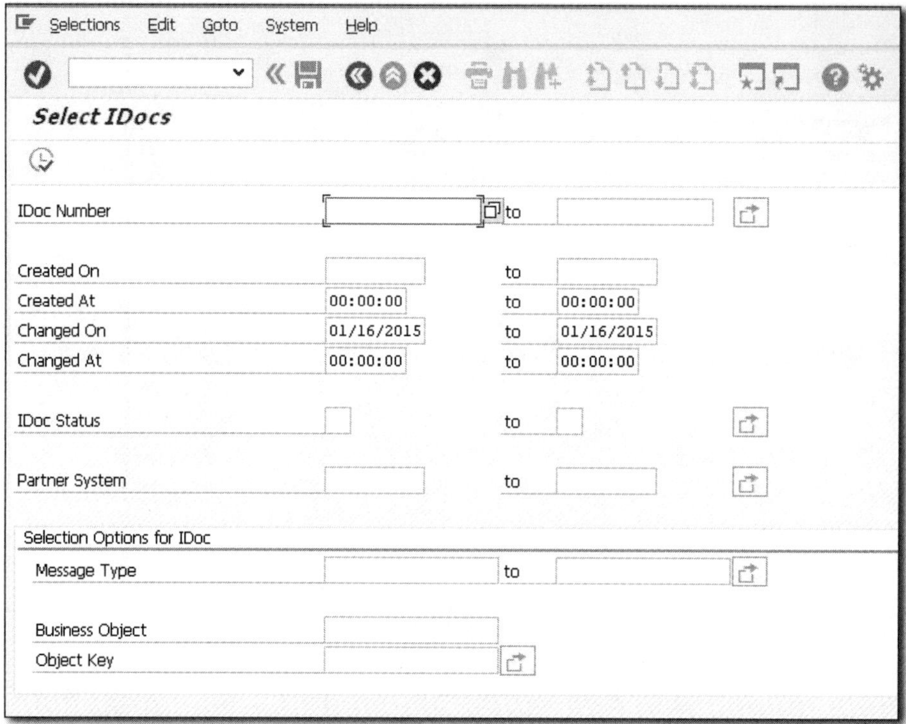

Figure 13.46 Selection Window for IDoc Monitoring

4. Search for errors in the tree structure in the processing of IDocs of type USER-CLONE or CCLONE (see Figure 13.47). Eliminate the cause of error indicated in the status message, and reactivate the distribution by clicking on the PROCESS button.
5. In the same way, check the IDoc processing in the child systems.

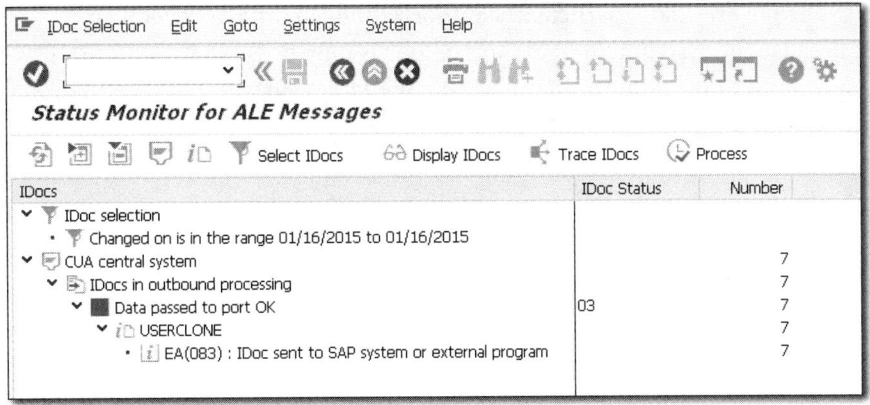

Figure 13.47 IDoc Monitor

By checking the CUA log or calling the IDoc monitoring, you'll have generally already obtained specific notes with regard to errors in your CUA. Here are some more error search tasks:

- Check your CUA system landscape for completeness and possible error messages (Transaction SCUA).
- Check the completeness of the distribution model (Transaction BD64).
- Examine the partner profiles (Transaction WE20).
- Make sure that the RFC connection is working (Transaction SM59).
- Check whether the communication users have been locked (Transaction SU01).
- Activate the authorization trace function, and evaluate missing authorizations of the communication users (Transaction ST01).

Helpful SAP Notes [+]

Read SAP Note 333441 (CUA: Tips for Problem Analysis) if errors occur in your CUA.

13.7.4 Deactivating or Deleting a Central User Administration

When you delete a CUA, you must first decide whether you want to remove individual target systems from the distribution or whether you want to deactivate the CUA. In an emergency scenario in which the central system has failed, you may have to change user data (particularly authorizations) in one or several target systems. Because the assignment of authorizations is only possible in the central system, such a situation requires that you take the target system from the CUA network.

Deleting Individual Target Systems or the Entire CUA

To specifically take individual systems from the CUA or to completely deactivate the CUA, you must maintain or remove the distribution model in the central system. For this purpose, the communication user requires authorizations to set up a CUA.

1. Log on to the central system.
2. Call Transaction SCUA (refer to Figure 13.30).
3. Click on DELETE. You're now in the DELETE CENTRAL USER ADMINISTRATION view (see Figure 13.48).

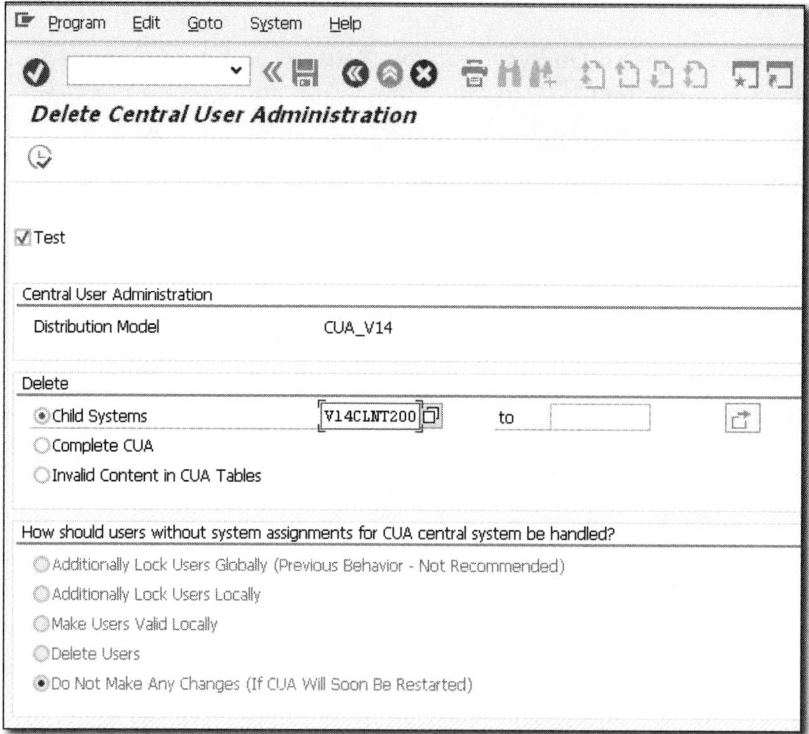

Figure 13.48 Deleting the Central User Administration

4. If you want to remove an individual target system from the CUA, select CHILD SYSTEMS in the DELETE area, and then enter the name of the logical system. If you want to completely deactivate the CUA, select COMPLETE CUA.
5. First leave the TEST checkbox marked, and then click on EXECUTE to activate the test run.
6. Check the log for error messages (see Figure 13.49). If no errors are displayed, click on the BACK button.

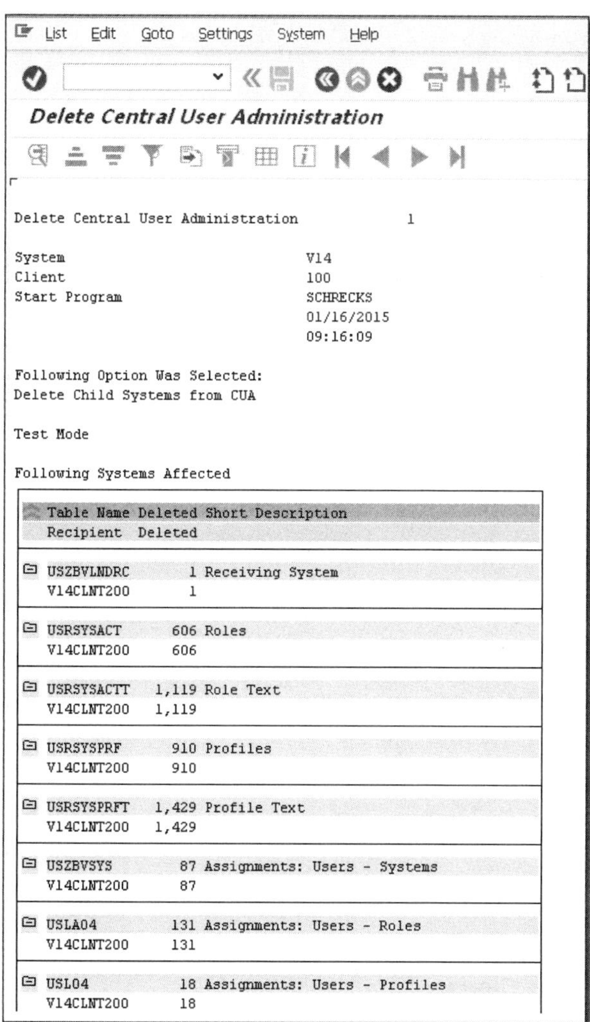

Figure 13.49 Checking the Test Run Log

7. Now deactivate the TEST checkbox, and then click again on EXECUTE. The completion of the live run is confirmed again via the log.

Deleting a Partner Profile in the Central System

You then delete the partner profiles among the logical systems, central system, and child system.

1. Log on to the central system.
2. Enter Transaction WE20 in the command field and press the Enter key (or select TOOLS • ALE • ALE ADMINISTRATION • RUNTIME SETTINGS • WE20—PARTNER PROFILES in the standard SAP menu).
3. In the folder structure, navigate to PARTNER PROFILES • PARTNER TYPE LS. Click on the child system that you've removed from the CUA (see Figure 13.50).

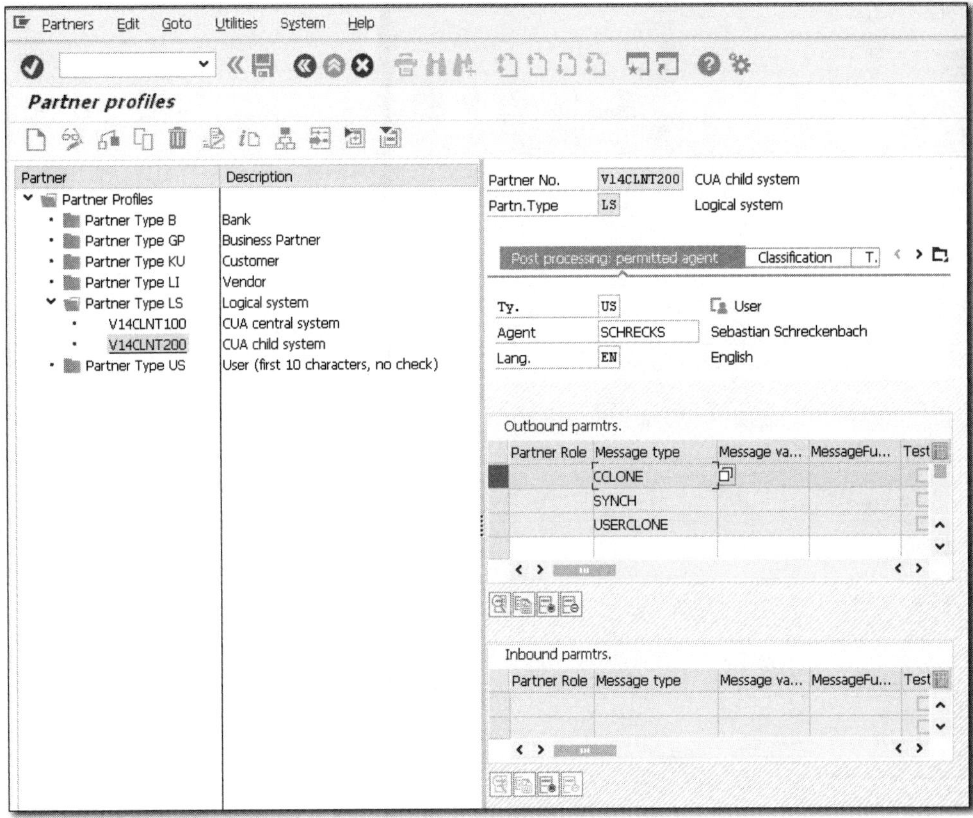

Figure 13.50 Deletion Partner Profiles for a Child System

4. Select the CCLONE and USERCLONE message type one by one in the OUTBOUND PARMTRS. area in the right half of the screen, and click on DELETE OUTBOUND PARAMETER.
5. Click YES each time when the confirmation prompt appears.

Message Type SYNCH [!]

You shouldn't delete the message type SYNCH because your changes are subsequently not transferred to the child system, and you need to repeat the steps there manually.

When you've deleted the entire CUA, highlight the PARTNER TYPE LS for the central system, and remove it by clicking on DELETE. In this case, you can also delete the message type SYNCH of the child system or the whole partner profile LS of the child system, as long as no other message type remains.

Deleting a Distribution Model in the Central System

After the partner profiles have been removed, you can clean up the distribution model.

1. Log on to the central system.
2. Activate Transaction BD64 (Maintenance of Distribution Model).
3. Go to the change mode by clicking SWITCH BETWEEN DISPLAY AND EDIT MODE.
4. Navigate in the tree structure to CENTRAL USER ADMINISTRATION. Expand the node of your central system and then your child system's node that you've deleted from the CUA (see Figure 13.51).
5. Highlight the BAPIs USER.CLONE and USERCOMPANY.CLONE one by one and delete them. If you completely deleted the CUA, highlight the model view CENTRAL USER ADMINISTRATION and delete it. The view is deleted with all its lower-level nodes (central and child systems).
6. Save your changes. Then highlight the CENTRAL USER ADMINISTRATION model view, and follow the path EDIT • MODEL VIEW • DISTRIBUTE to also remove the model in other systems.
7. In the dialog window, highlight the deleted child system, and confirm by clicking CONTINUE (see Figure 13.52). The distribution isn't needed as long as you've deleted the complete model view in the previous step.

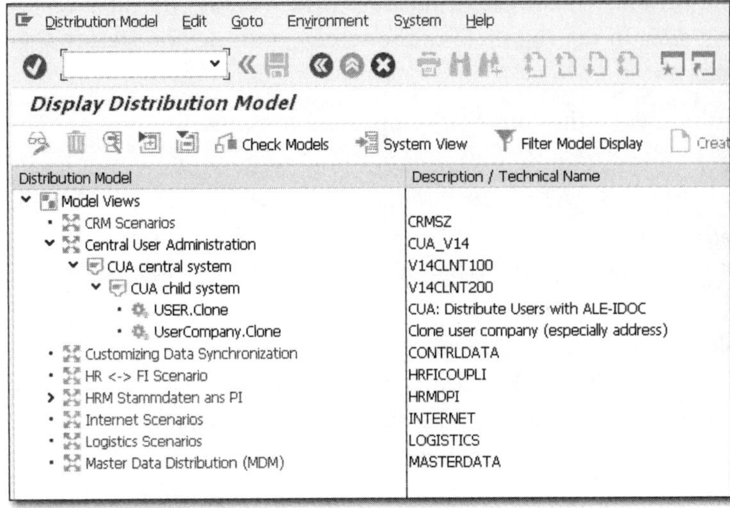

Figure 13.51 Displaying the Distribution Model

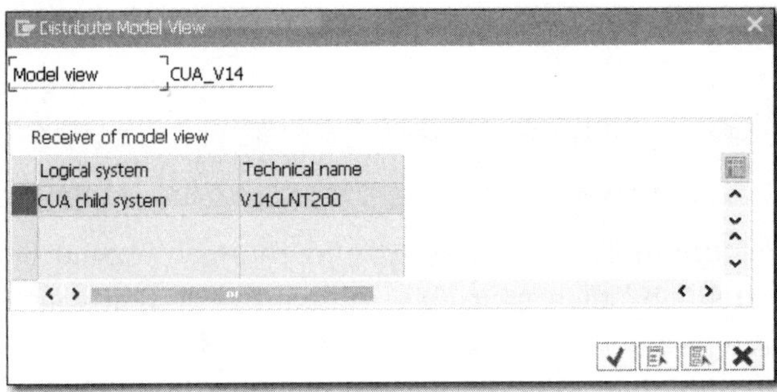

Figure 13.52 Distributing the Model View

8. Check the log, and click on CONTINUE ✓ (see Figure 13.53).

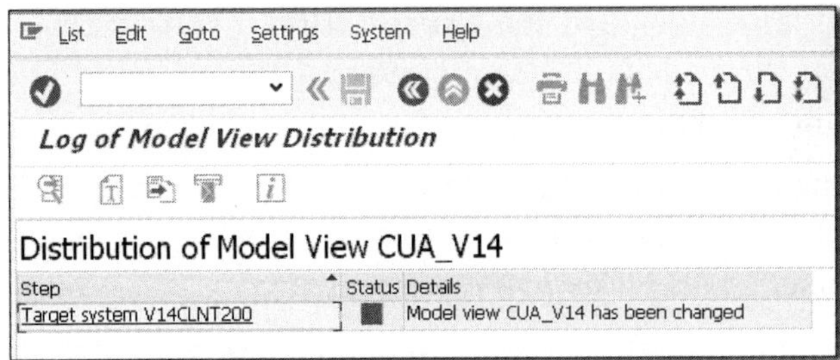

Figure 13.53 Log for Distributing the Model View

9. Via Transaction SCUA (Distribution Model), check whether the child system has been removed or whether the distribution model has been deleted from the model view.

Deleting a Partner Profile and Distribution Model in a Child System

After you've processed the steps in the central system, you still need to delete the partner profiles and the distribution model in the child system:

1. Delete the INBOUND PARMTRS. CCLONE and USERCLONE for the central system in Transaction WE20 (Partner Profiles) (see Figure 13.54).

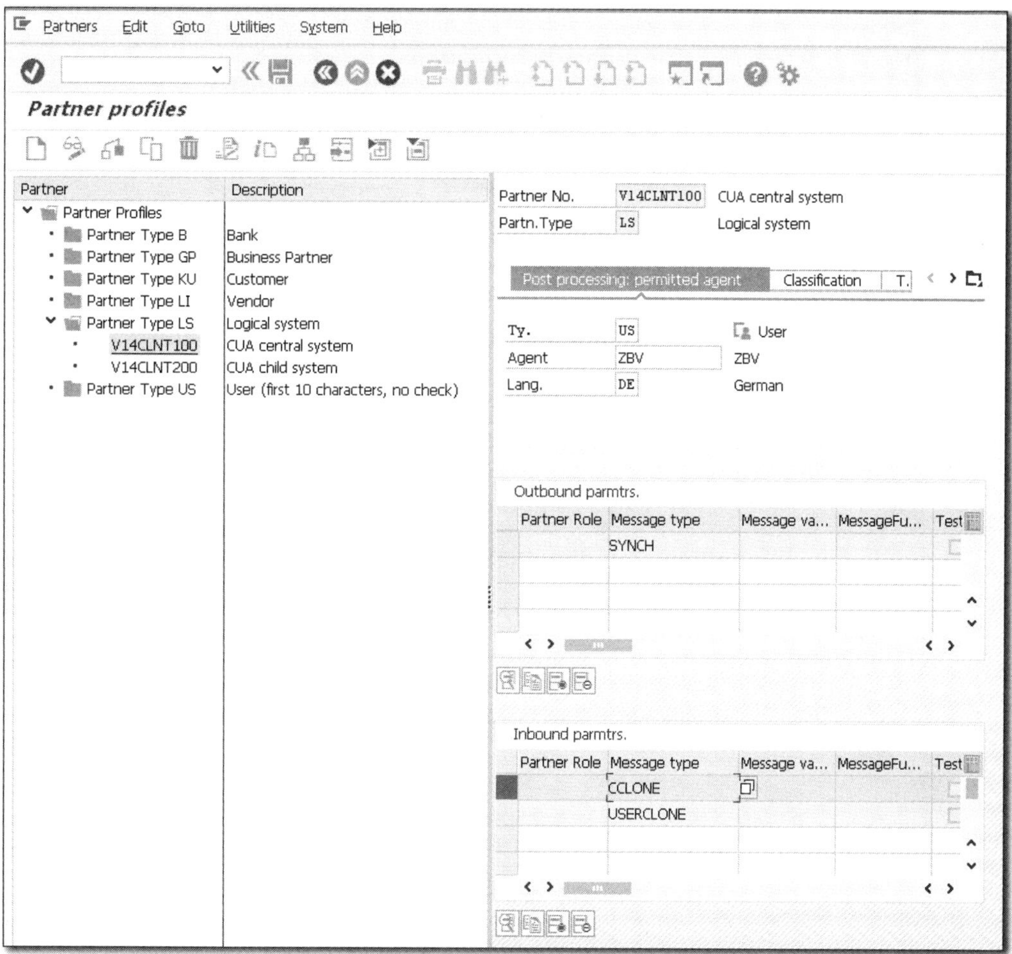

Figure 13.54 Deleting Input Parameters of the Central System in the Child System

2. Call Transaction BD64 (Maintenance of Distribution Model), and navigate to the change mode. Highlight the CENTRAL USER ADMINISTRATION model view, and click on DELETE.
3. In the dialog window, confirm with YES, and save the changes (see Figure 13.55).

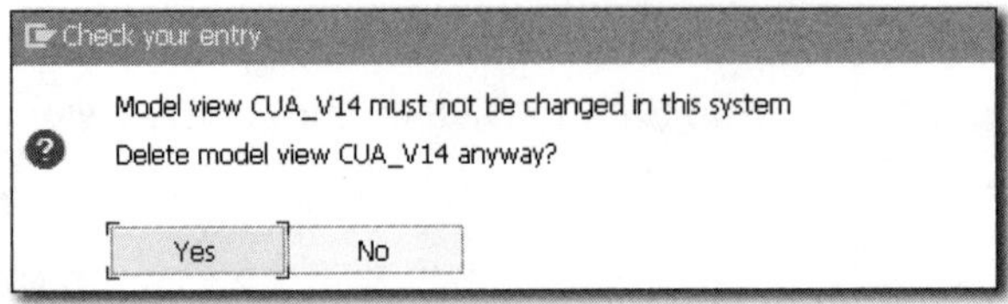

Figure 13.55 Confirming the Deletion of the Distribution Model

You've now completely removed the child system from the CUA.

Emergency Deactivation of the CUA in the Target System

In an emergency situation, the connection to the CUA can fail, for example, as a result of a breakdown in the central system. Depending on how you've configured the field distribution, changes to important user data may no longer be possible in the child system. You'll definitely neither be able to create any users nor assign authorization roles or profiles in the child system.

To quickly restore the capacity to act in the child system, you must take the child system from the CUA. To do this, follow these steps:

1. In the child system, start Transaction SCUA (Distribution Model). If there are any connection problems, the STATUS OF RFC CONNECTION TO CUA CENTRAL SYSTEM is indicated as INACTIVE (see Figure 13.56).
2. Click on DELETE.
3. Select CHILD SYSTEMS, and initially leave the TEST checkbox activated (see Figure 13.57).

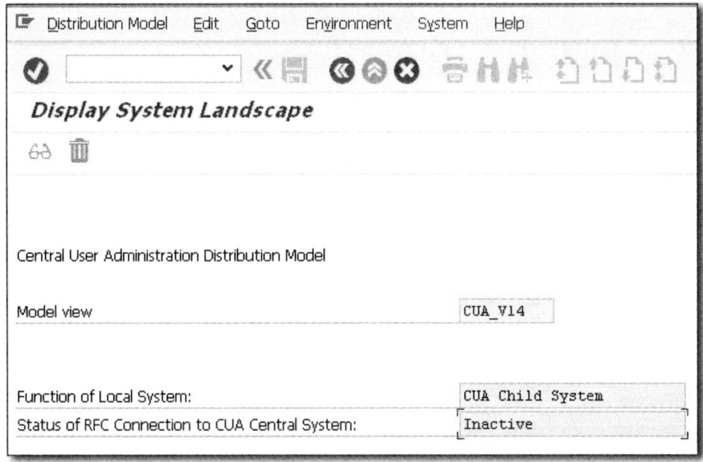

Figure 13.56 Deleting the Connection to the Central User Administration

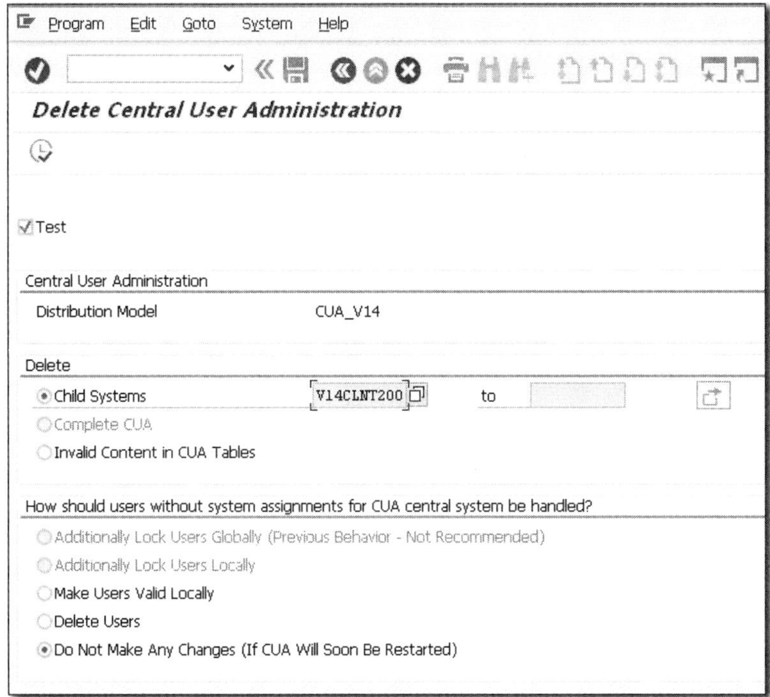

Figure 13.57 Testing the Deletion of the CUA

4. Click on EXECUTE .
5. Check the log, and click on BACK if no errors have occurred.
6. Deactivate the TEST checkbox in the previous screen, and execute the live run .

You can now create and maintain the user master data in the child system independently of the CUA. You can include the child system again into the CUA after you've dealt with the exceptional situation by calling the distribution model in the central system via Transaction SCUA in the change mode, highlighting the deleted target system, and distributing the CUA settings again to the child system via SAVE SELECTED SYSTEMS (see Figure 13.58).

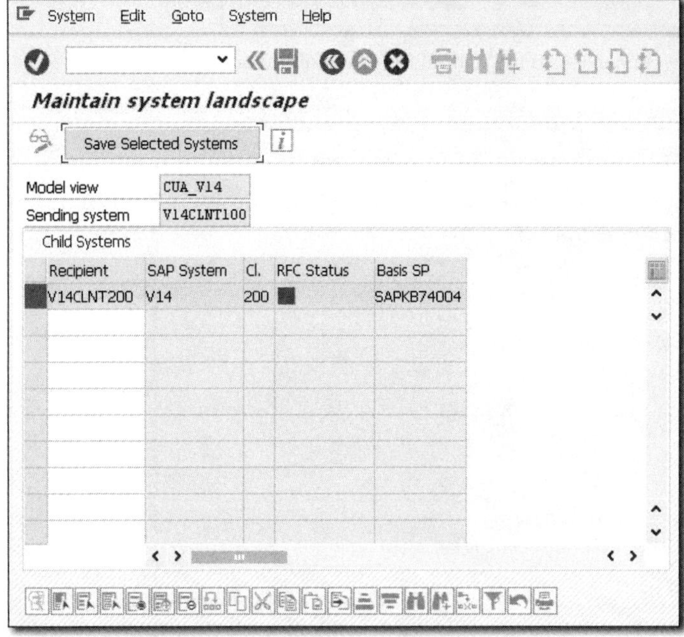

Figure 13.58 Adding a Child System to the Central User Administration Again

13.8 User Groups

A user group is a logical summary of users, for example, users in sales and distribution, incoming sales orders, or the financial accounting area. The following restrictions apply to user groups:

- A user can belong to several user groups. However, only the group that is entered in the LOGON DATA tab in the user maintenance (see Section 13.2) is included in the authorization checks (e.g., in the authorization object S_USER_GRP).
- A user group must be created before the user can be assigned to it.

The purpose of a user group is to restrict the access to specific user masters in the authorization check and also to facilitate the user administration (e.g., mass maintenance; see Section 13.4). It's recommended to use the special groups listed in Table 13.1.

Group	Definition
TERM	No longer current users. User data can then be retained in the system for identification purposes. ▸ All users of this group should be locked. ▸ When the users of the group aren't used as a template, the security profiles of the users are deleted.
SUPER	Users with full authorization (authorization profiles SAP_ALL or SAP_NEW).
TEMPLATE	Template users, which serve as a template to set up actual users.

Table 13.1 Recommended User Groups

When you define additional groups, you can orientate these to the requirements of your enterprise or the scope of the master data you manage.

Creating a User Group

Follow these steps to create a user group:

1. Enter Transaction SUGR in the command field and press the Enter key (or select the option TOOLS • ADMINISTRATION • USER MAINTENANCE • SUGR—USER GROUPS in the standard SAP menu).
2. Enter a name for the user group, which you want to set up (e.g., "SALES"), and click on the CREATE USER GROUP button (see Figure 13.59).
3. Enter a description of the user group in the TEXT field (see Figure 13.60).
4. Add users to the group under USER ASSIGNMENT.
5. Click on SAVE. A message confirms that the new user group has been set up.

Figure 13.59 Creating a User Group

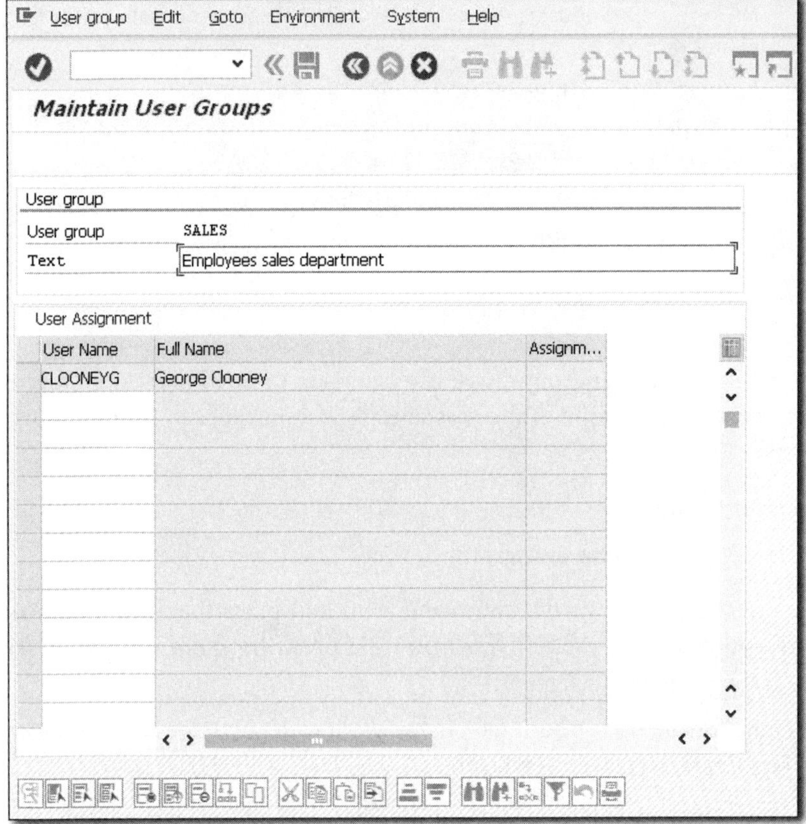

Figure 13.60 Adding Users to a User Group

Assignment via the User Group [+]

You can also assign users to user groups in the user maintenance (Transaction SU01) via the GROUPS tab.

13.9 Deleting User Sessions

System administration may need to delete a user session. For example, the user session may not have been closed by the user due to a program error, or the user may have forgotten to log off from the SAP system and locked data that needs to be urgently changed by another user.

Also in situations that threaten the system stability (e.g., if a user has activated comprehensive tools), the only secure path may be to end the session.

13.9.1 Displaying Active Users

First, check the user modes in the cases described. Using Transaction SM04 (User Overview), all users logged on to the system can be displayed. The user ID and the terminal name are displayed. If your system contains several instances, you can display the user sessions via Transaction AL08 (Global Users) extensively.

In a smaller enterprise, the system administrator can easily identify user IDs logged on to unusual terminals. An unusual terminal can mean that a person other than that belonging to the user ID has logged on under this name. If a user has logged on to more than one terminal, this could mean the following:

- The user ID is being used by another person.
- Several users are sharing this ID.

One User ID per User [+]

A user ID should not be used by several users for the following reasons:

- If a problem occurs, you can't find out who exactly was responsible for it. It therefore becomes difficult for you to eliminate the problem and ensure that it doesn't occur again.
- For security reasons, it isn't recommended to allow several users to share one ID. Use the profile parameter `login/disable_multi_gui_login` to prevent this from

occurring. Using the parameter `login/multi_login_users`, you can define exceptions in authorized cases.

- External auditors could run this test to check their security mechanisms.

System with Only One Instance

If your system only has one instance, use Transaction SM04 to display the active users.

1. Enter Transaction SM04 in the command field and press the Enter key (or select the menu option Tools • Administration • Monitor • System Monitoring • SM04—User Overview).
2. Select the desired user ID, and click on Session (see Figure 13.61).

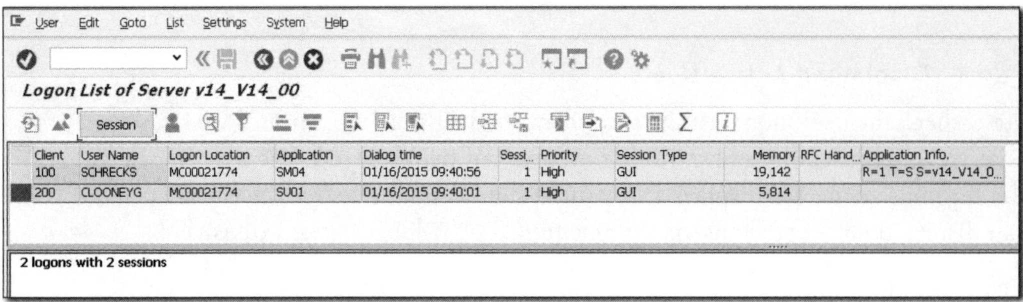

Figure 13.61 Displaying Logged On Users

3. The Overview of Sessions screen displays which sessions this user has generated (see Figure 13.62).

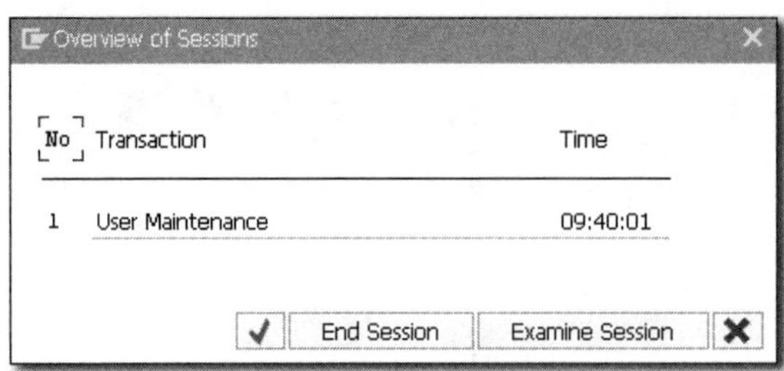

Figure 13.62 Session List

4. Click on Continue ✔.

System with Several Instances

If you have several instances in your system, it's easier to use Transaction AL08 because you can display all users in all instances of the system at the same time.

1. Enter Transaction AL08 in the command field and press [Enter] (or select menu option Tools • Administration • Monitor • Performance • Exceptions/Users • Active Users • AL08—Global Users).
2. All instances of your system and the number of active users are displayed (see Figure 13.63). You can view a list for each instance with the users who are currently logged on to an instance.

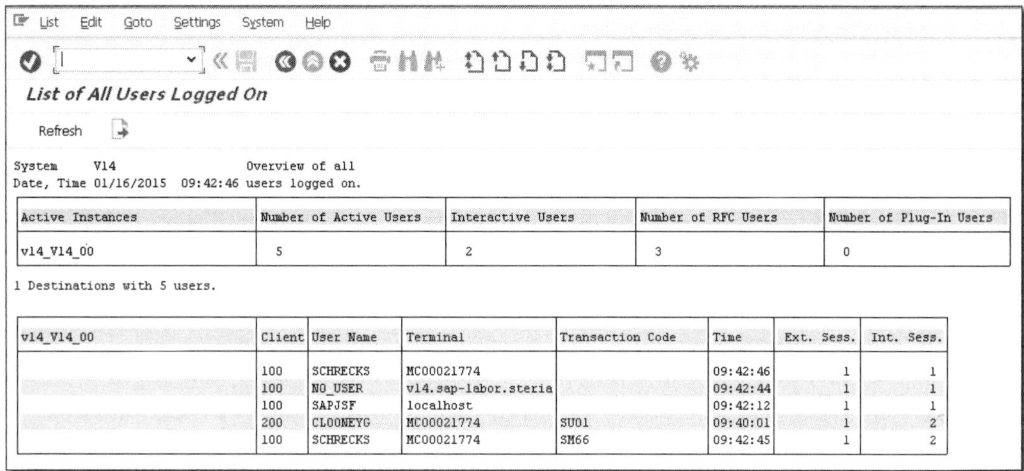

Figure 13.63 List of All Logged On Users

13.9.2 Deleting User Sessions

You must log on to the server to which the user concerned has logged on and process the following steps:

1. Check whether the user has actually logged off the SAP system and that no SAP GUI window is still open. Check the user's computer, if applicable.

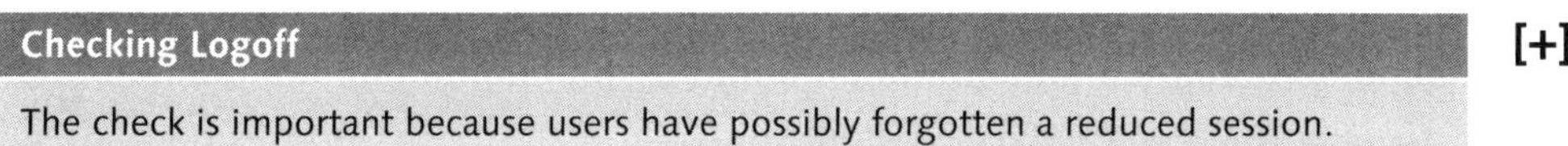

Checking Logoff [+]

The check is important because users have possibly forgotten a reduced session.

2. Call Transaction SM04.

3. Select the user ID concerned.
4. Click on the SESSION button (refer to Figure 13.61).
5. Select the session to be deleted, and click on END SESSION (see Figure 13.64). The end session process might take some time.
6. If required, repeat step 5 until all sessions for this user have been deleted.

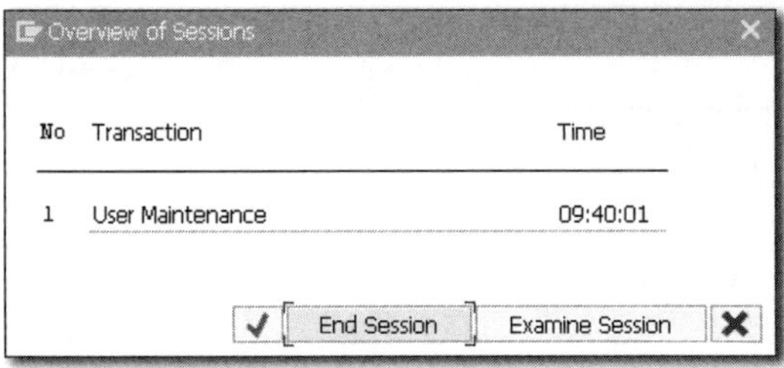

Figure 13.64 Deleting a User Session

Transaction SM04 can display a user that has already logged off the system as still active. This is the case, for example, when the user session hasn't been ended properly. This can be caused by the following:

- A network failure that results in the user no longer having access to the network or to the SAP system
- Users who switch off their computers without logging off the SAP system

You can, however, close these user sessions. If possible, consult the user in advance.

13.10 System Administration

As a system administrator, you need to take some special features into consideration. These include the usage of special standard users, how to deal with the assignment of full authorizations, and the options you have to improve password and logon security.

13.10.1 Special User IDs

Both user IDs SAP* and DDIC exist by default with full authorization in each client of the SAP system. Furthermore, the user EARLYWATCH is created in client 066 during the installation process. The default passwords of these users are generally known (see Table 13.2). You should therefore change them immediately to prevent the unauthorized use of these two special user IDs. In the case of user EARLYWATCH, it isn't quite so urgent because this user has very restricted authorizations.

Users	Standard Password
SAP*	06071992
DDIC	19920706
EARLYWATCH	support

Table 13.2 Standard Passwords

You should not use both SAP* and DDIC users for everyday administration tasks. You can use the DDIC user as an emergency user. Change the password and keep it in a safe place. You can also lock the user if you apply another emergency concept.

You must not delete user ID SAP*. Instead, you should change the password and lock the user ID. If the user ID SAP* is deleted, a logon with the user and the standard password "pass" is possible. The authorizations are replaced with rights, which are directly programmed in the SAP system. User ID SAP* therefore contains incalculable and unverifiable security rights.

13.10.2 Special Authorizations

Users SAP* und DDIC have the authorization profile SAP_ALL, which is equal to a full authorization in the system in conjunction with the supplementary authorization profile SAP_NEW. Assign these in a respectively restrictive way.

Particularly in medium and large enterprises, it's not usually appropriate to issue the profiles SAP_ALL und SAP_NEW to developers for development and test systems. For this, they should list special develop authorization roles. Avoid assigning SAP_ALL and SAP_NEW in production systems. Even system administrators should obtain customized authorization roles. For emergency cases, create special users with SAP_ALL and SAP_NEW, and keep the password safe.

Authorization Profiles SAP_ALL and SAP_NEW [!]

Authorization profiles SAP_ALL and SAP_NEW are extensive and pose a threat and a security risk to the system. Each person who requests similar security rights must be able to justify this *adequately*. Personal convenience is *not* considered a valid reason.

13.10.3 User Passwords

Using several profile parameters, you can specify conditions for user passwords (see Table 13.3). Acquaint yourself with the password rules in place for Microsoft Windows or for other applications. Also consider the explanations in Chapter 10:

- Passwords should be valid for a specific period.
- Passwords should have a certain minimum length.
- Passwords should consist of a combination of uppercase/lowercase letters, digits, and special characters.
- Certain letters and digit sequences should be prohibited (maintain table USR40 for this purpose).
- Users should be locked after a specific number of unsuccessful logon attempts.

Profile Parameter	Explanation
login/min_password_diff	Minimum number of different characters between old and new passwords
login/min_password_diff	Minimum number of digits in passwords
login/min_password_diff	Minimum number of letters in passwords
login/min_password_lng	Minimum length of passwords
login/min_password_diff	Minimum number of small digits in passwords
login/min_password_lng	Minimum number of special characters in passwords
login/min_password_diff	Minimum number of capital letters in passwords
login/password_max_new_valid	Minimum wait time between two changes of password via the user
login/password_compliance_to_-current_policy	Check the password for rule compliance upon each logon
login/password_expiration_time	Validity period of passwords
login/password_max_reset_valid	Scope of history for passwords already used
login/password_max_reset_valid	Validity period for unused initial passwords
login/failed_user_auto_unlock	Activate/deactivate automatic locking of users

Table 13.3 Important Profile Parameters for User Passwords

Profile Parameter	Explanation
login/fails_to_session_end	Number of failed logons until closing of logon screen
login/fails_to_user_lock	Number of failed logons until locking of user

Table 13.3 Important Profile Parameters for User Passwords (Cont.)

[+]

SAP Note 2467

You can find general information on passwords in the SAP system in SAP Note 2467.

13.11 Summary

In this chapter, the fundamental tasks of user administration have been described, for example, how to create, change, lock, or delete user master records. Mass maintenance facilitates the administration of many users, and a CUA is of great benefit in a large system landscape. You can bring structure into your user master records via user groups.

User administration is among the most security-relevant aspects of system administration. Use it with due care. The next chapter deals with the authorization administration in the SAP system, a topic closely linked to user administration.

With authorizations, you control which user obtains which permissions within the SAP system. This chapter describes how the SAP system checks the authorizations of a user. You also learn how to create and assign authorization roles and profiles.

14 Authorization Management

Besides user administration, the assignment of authorization is another security-relevant task area of SAP administration. In contrast to user administration, the authorization system is mainly characterized by business needs; in other words, the user's departments of your enterprise will determine to a large extent how authorizations are assigned. For example, the HR department must be consulted when the HR component is implemented or when personal data of employees are managed in the system. Furthermore, coordination with external auditors, legal, and other regulations (enterprise-internal) should be in place. Consult your external auditors with regard to requirements that are made on the audit-related internal control of user administration.

Usually, enterprises organize their user and authorization administration according to the segregation of duties (SOD) principle and implement it technically (via appropriate authorizations). The administrator who creates and maintains users usually can't edit authorizations and vice versa (at least in production systems). This can't always be implemented in small enterprises. In these cases, you must ensure that at least the user request procedure strictly implements the required approval steps.

This book limits the authorization management topic to a general, technically oriented introduction. For more in-depth information, please refer to *Authorizations in SAP Software: Design and Configuration* by Volker Lehnert, Katharina Stelzner, and Larry Justice (SAP PRESS, 2010).

14.1 Authorization Check Process

The authorization check entails multiple phases in the SAP system. When a transaction is started, the system first checks whether the user is authorized to execute the transaction based on the authorization object S_TCODE. If the user doesn't have this authorization, the transaction isn't called. Besides the check of the transaction authorization, the system runs additional authorization checks within the transaction if specific actions are carried out. Which authorization objects are addressed with which click and how many checks are made depends on the source code and therefore varies considerably for every transaction.

Authorization objects bundle one or more *fields* whose combination maps an action in the SAP system. This usually involves multiple possible activities (e.g., create, change, or display) in connection with an object in the system (e.g., a table or an authorization role). In this context, the activity and the object represent a field within the authorization object. The respective activity or the explicit object is entered as a *field value* in the authorization field. The combination of several field values represents an *authorization* (e.g., change the SAP_BC_SEC_AUTH_ADMIN role). For reasons of manageability, related authorization objects are grouped in *object classes*, which are organized by application areas or components.

Users may only execute actions in the SAP system if they have the relevant permission. If they don't have permission for specific actions, they may not execute them. Users obtain permission to execute an action by having the required authorization assigned either via *authorization roles* or *authorization profiles*.

14.2 Authorization Roles

Authorization roles—in contrast to authorization profiles—are the technically up-to-date form for assigning authorizations. They are based on the technology of authorization profiles but are considerably easier to maintain and manage and provide many more options. The role concept seizes the approach to bundle all authorizations required for a specific task. To what extent a technical role actually maps the respective workplace within your enterprise mainly depends on the enterprise's size, structure, and security or confidentiality requirement. The SAP components used also play a role here. An employee usually has several authorization roles whose combination describes the workplace. You define and describe the structure according to which you organize your authorization roles (e.g., according to components, tasks, business areas, etc.) in an *authorization concept*.

There are two types of authorization roles:

- Single roles
- Composite roles

In *single roles*, you can add authorization objects to assign them to users. *Composite roles*, by contrast, enable you to combine single roles for easier management. Authorizations can't be added to composite roles.

14.2.1 Creating and Maintaining Single Roles

The Profile Generator is the central access point for all tasks with regard to the maintenance of authorization roles. Here you create, change, and copy single and composite roles; assign them to users; and transfer them to other SAP systems.

Creating a Single Role

Carry out the following steps to create a single role:

1. Enter Transaction PFCG in the command field and press the Enter key (or select the menu option Tools • Administration • User Maintenance • Role Administration • PFCG—Roles).
2. Enter a suitable name for the new authorization role in the Role field, and click Single Role (see Figure 14.1).
3. In the next screen (see Figure 14.2), enter a meaningful Description. You can use the Long Text field for a more comprehensive description on the content and purpose or also for a change history.

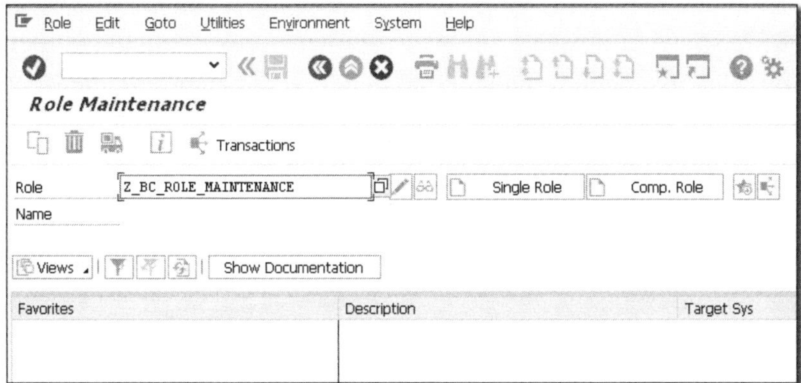

Figure 14.1 Creating a Single Role

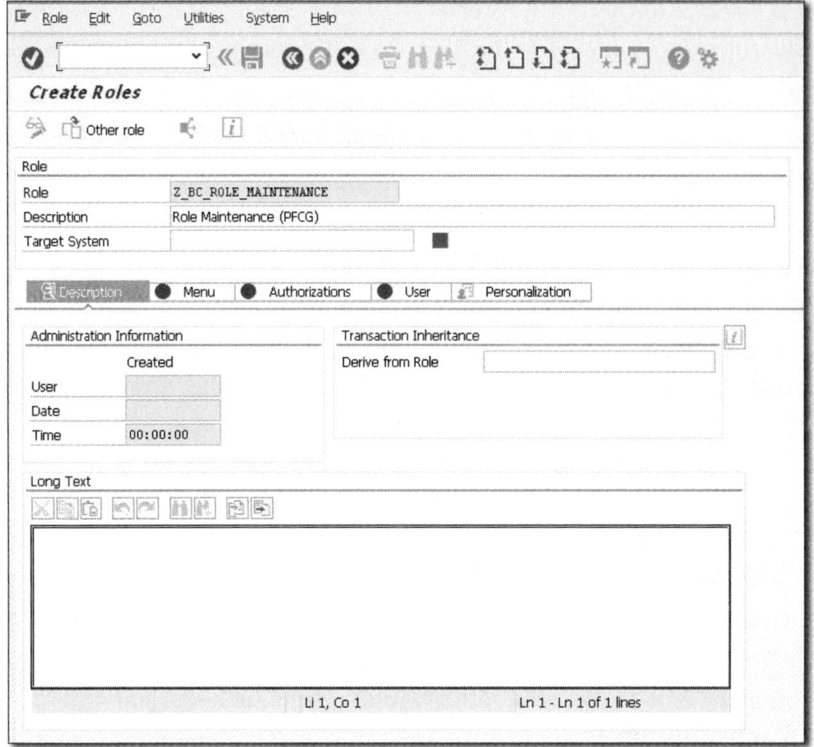

Figure 14.2 Defining a Description for the Single Role

4. Go to the Menu tab. The system prompts you to save the role. Choose Yes.

Maintaining the Single Role Menu

Authorization roles provide the option to structure the transaction authorizations contained therein in the form of a Role Menu to facilitate the users' access to transactions. Continue with the Role Menu maintenance:

1. Create a new folder in the Role Menu using the Create Folder button .
2. The system opens a dialog window, Create a folder, where you enter a name. Click on Continue .
3. The system creates the folder in the Role Menu (see Figure 14.3). Select this folder, and click the Transaction button.

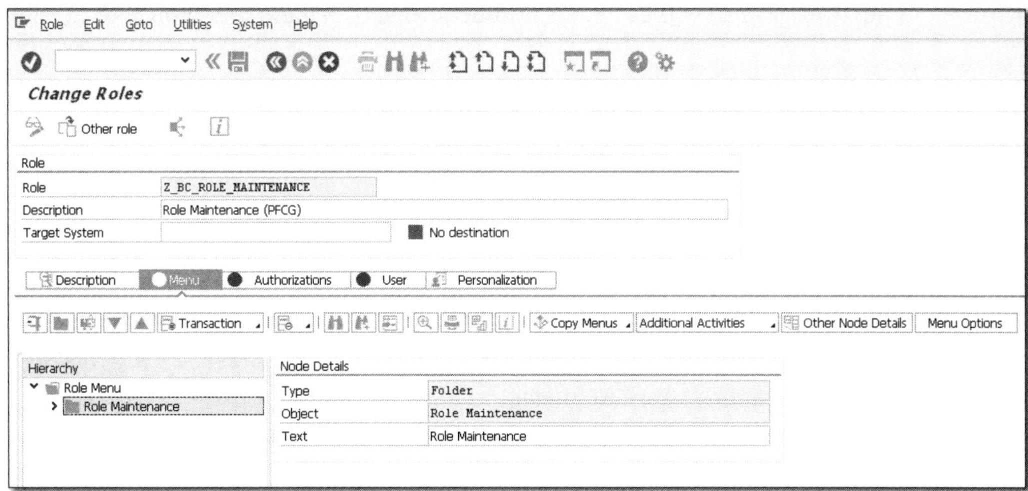

Figure 14.3 New Folder in the Role Menu

4. Enter the transaction that is supposed to be assigned to the role, and press the Enter key to confirm. The system determines the text for the transaction selected (see Figure 14.4). Click ASSIGN TRANSACTIONS.

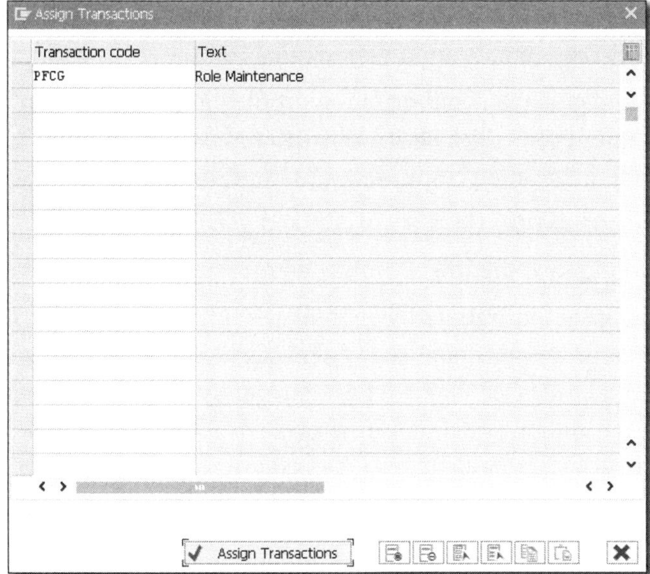

Figure 14.4 Assigning a Transaction to a Role

In the Role Menu, you can enter transactions and also the following:

- Programs (ABAP reports)
- Queries
- Transaction variants
- URLs
- Files
- SAP Business Warehouse (SAP BW) reports

Besides the manual menu maintenance, you can also import into your role specific menu parts from the SAP menu or the SAP area menu, from already existing menus of other authorization roles, and from external files. You can sort the Role Menu via drag-and-drop.

Maintaining the Authorization Profile

As soon as you've added transactions to the menu, the status of the Menu tab changes to green. For the role to function, you maintain the role's authorization profile in the next step:

1. Go to the Authorizations tab (see Figure 14.5). The Information About Authorization Profile area is empty for newly created roles.

   Without a maintained and generated authorization profile, however, you can't assign authorizations using a role. Click Propose Profile Names to have the system generate a profile name and profile text.
2. Then click Change Authorization Data to edit and generate the profile.
3. The system prompts you to save the role. Confirm with Yes.
4. In the next view, you assign authorizations by defining the authorization objects. Based on the check indicator (see note box), the system has already added several authorization objects to the role (see Figure 14.6). Expand the tree structure to obtain an overview of the authorization objects suggested. For example, under Cross-Application Authorization Objects • Transaction Code Check at Transaction Start, you can find the transaction added to the menu.

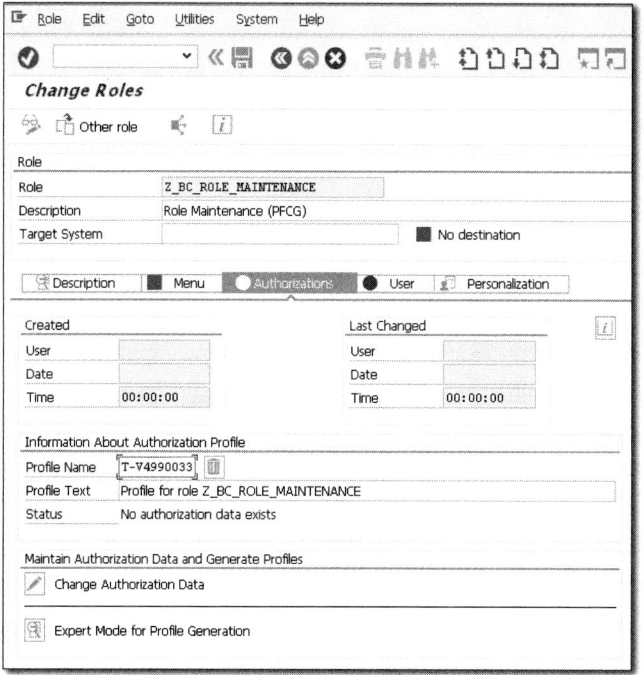

Figure 14.5 Generating an Authorization Profile for the Role

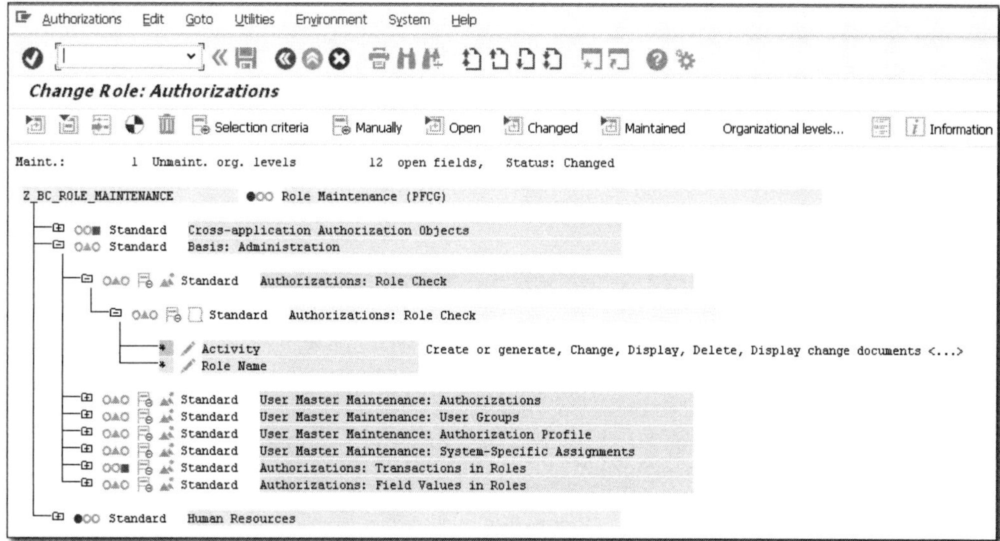

Figure 14.6 Displaying Authorization Objects of the Single Role

[⚙]

Check Indicator

After you've entered transactions in the menu, the system automatically suggests authorization objects that are relevant for the transaction selected. These default values are determined based on the check indicator defined in the system (see Section 14.4.1). You can add more authorization objects or delete suggested objects.

5. In the structure, navigate to an authorization object (and the corresponding authorization fields) that is indicated with MISSING VALUES (e.g., BASIS: ADMINISTRATION • AUTHORIZATIONS: ROLE CHECK). Click on the CHANGE icon in front of the ROLE NAME field to enter or change field values.
6. A FIELD VALUES dialog window opens (see Figure 14.7). Maintain the desired values in the table. Click on TRANSFER when you're done.

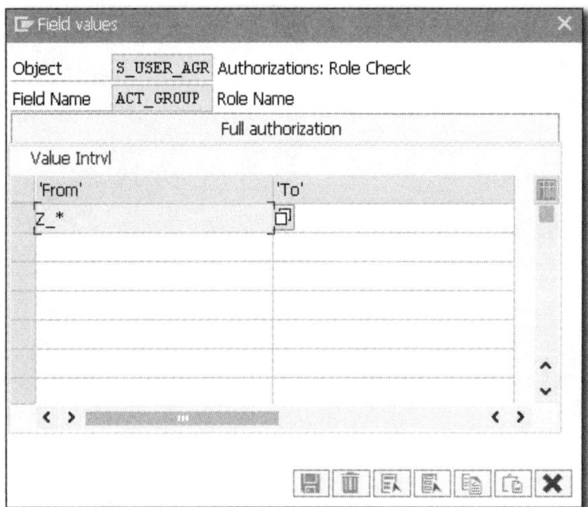

Figure 14.7 Maintaining Field Values

7. The field values are transferred. If values are defined for all fields of an object, the status display changes to ALL MAINTAINED. Repeat these steps for all of the other authorization objects with the MISSING VALUES status.

Activating the Technical Name [+]

If you frequently work with authorizations, you'll find it useful to switch the view to technical IDs via the UTILITIES • TECHNICAL NAMES ON menu path. This enables you to find specific authorization objects more easily. Via UTILITIES • SETTINGS, you can have the system display additional icons for processing authorizations.

8. The VARIABLES MISSING status means that not all organizational levels have been maintained yet (see Figure 14.8). Click the ORGANIZATIONAL LEVELS button to fill the variables.

Organizational Levels [!]

Organizational levels are field values used in many authorization objects with the same value and can therefore be maintained comprehensively as variables (e.g., company code, controlling area, etc.). Try to avoid maintaining accordingly highlighted fields directly in the authorization object because you then override the role-wide value of the variables.

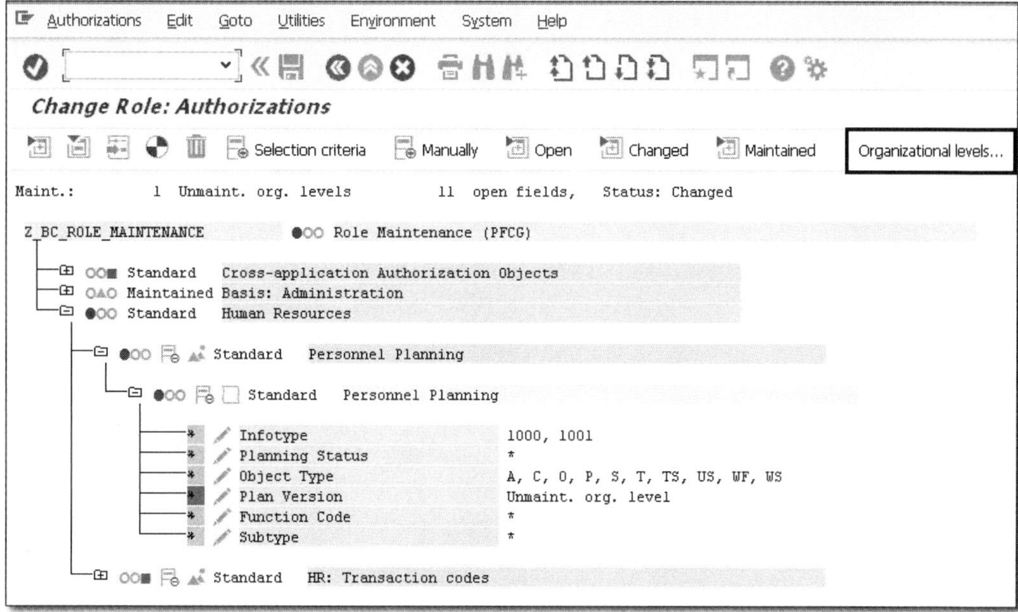

Figure 14.8 Organizational Levels Not Maintained

[⚙]

Defining Your Own Organizational Levels

Using program PFCG_ORGFIELD_CREATE, you can define additional fields as organizational levels to simplify the maintenance of frequently used authorizations. For more detailed information, please refer to SAP Note 727536.

9. Enter a value for the variable (see Figure 14.9), and click SAVE [save icon].

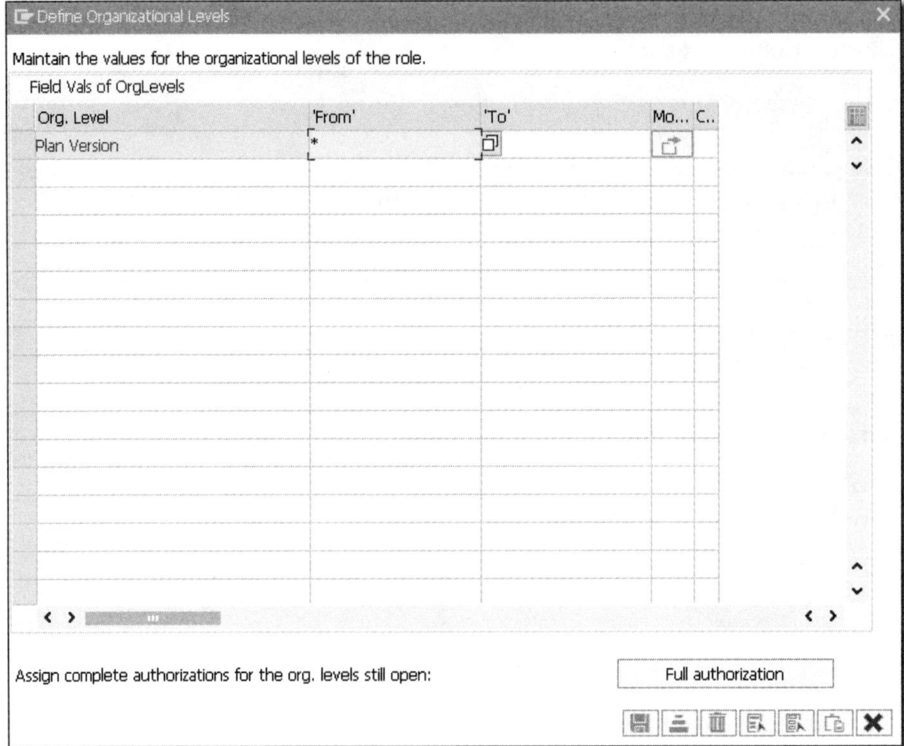

Figure 14.9 Maintaining a Value for Organizational Level

[⚙]

Value *

In the authorization system, the value * stands for the full authorization. It can be assigned for all types of authorization fields, that is, both for application objects (e.g., role names) and for activities. For activities, the value * authorizes the user to execute all actions for the respective application object.

10. After you've maintained all authorization objects, click SAVE.
11. Click GENERATE to create the authorization profile of the role (see Figure 14.10).
12. Click BACK to exit the view.

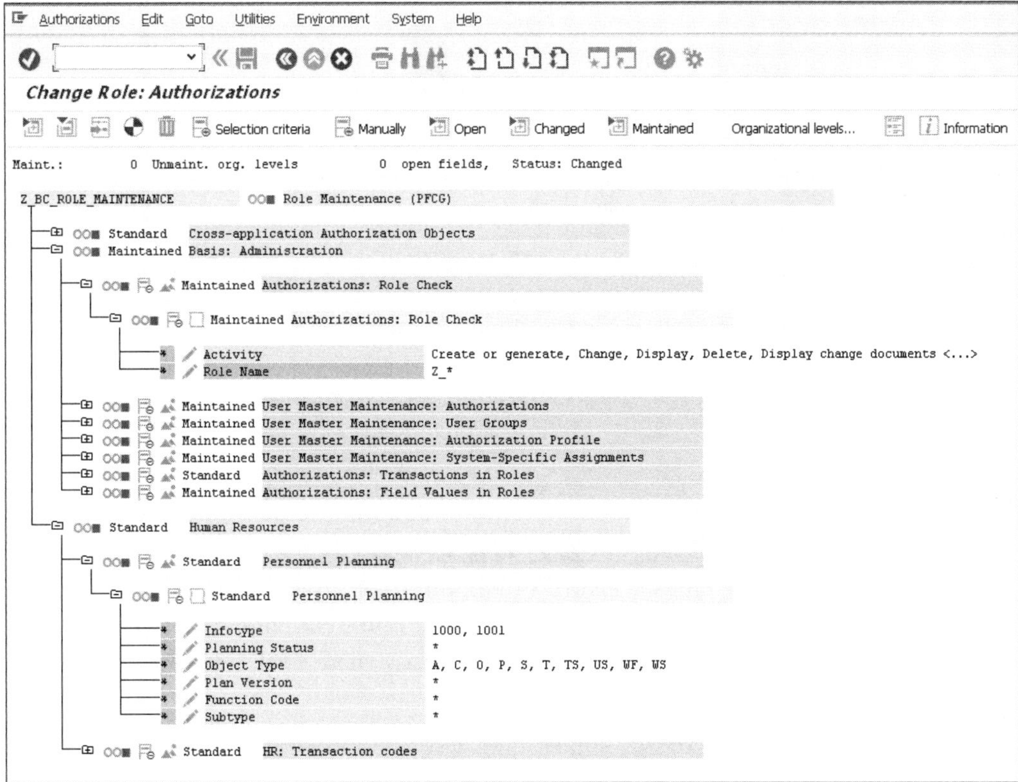

Figure 14.10 Completed Authorization Maintenance

The status of the AUTHORIZATIONS tab is green now; the STATUS of the authorization profile is GENERATED (see Figure 14.11).

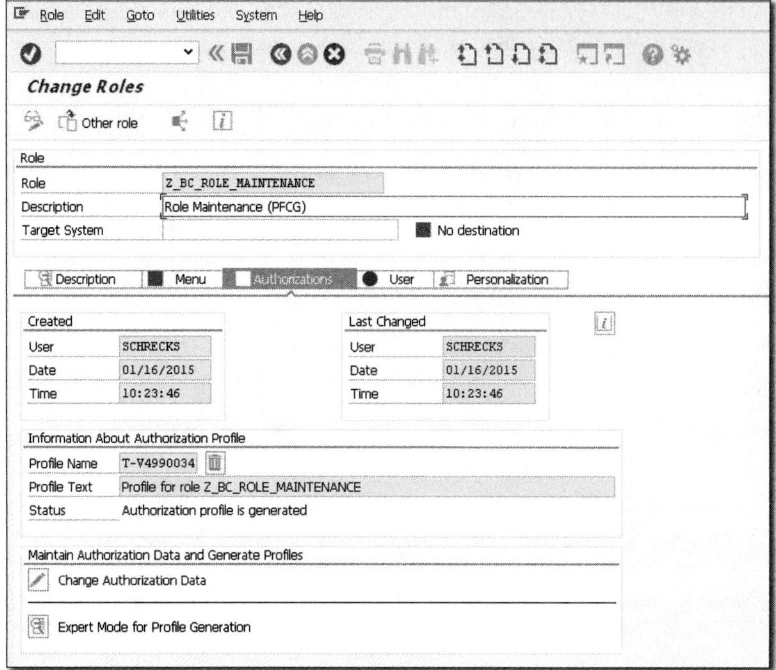

Figure 14.11 Generated Authorization Profile

User Assignment

In the next step, you must assign the users to the role created:

1. Go to the USER tab (see Figure 14.12). Enter the USER ID you want to assign to the role in the USER ASSIGNMENTS area. If required, enter a validity period in which the authorization is supposed to be assigned. Click SAVE to save your entries.
2. To provide the authorization immediately to the newly assigned user, select the USER COMPARISON button.
3. A new dialog window opens. Click on COMPLETE COMPARISON (see Figure 14.13).

The single role maintenance is now complete. Because you usually create roles in a development system, you must now transport them. The authorization profiles that belong to the single roles are transported as well.

Automating the User Comparison [+]

Via the UTILITIES • SETTINGS menu path, you can define that the user comparison is automatically run when the role is saved. You can also start the comparison using Transaction PFUD (User Master Data Reconciliation). Additionally, you should schedule report PFCG_TIME_DEPENDENCY at least once per day, which compares all roles and users. This especially applies to the systems to which you transport roles because the transport doesn't automatically trigger a user comparison.

Figure 14.12 Assigning Users

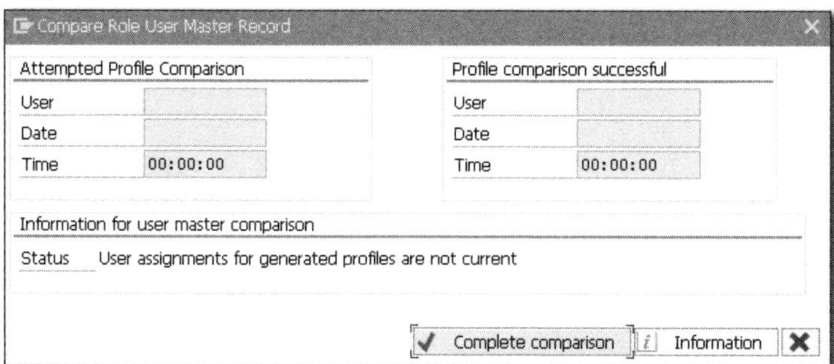

Figure 14.13 Running a User Comparison

14.2.2 Creating and Maintaining Composite Roles

You can simplify authorization management by grouping several single roles that are related or are usually assigned in combination into composite roles. Instead of several single roles, only the composite role is explicitly assigned to the users. As a result, the single roles contained in the composite role are automatically assigned.

Creating Composite Roles

Follow these steps to create a composite role in the Profile Generator:

1. Start Transaction PFCG.
2. Enter a suitable name for the new authorization role in the ROLE field (see Figure 14.14), and click the COMP. ROLE button.

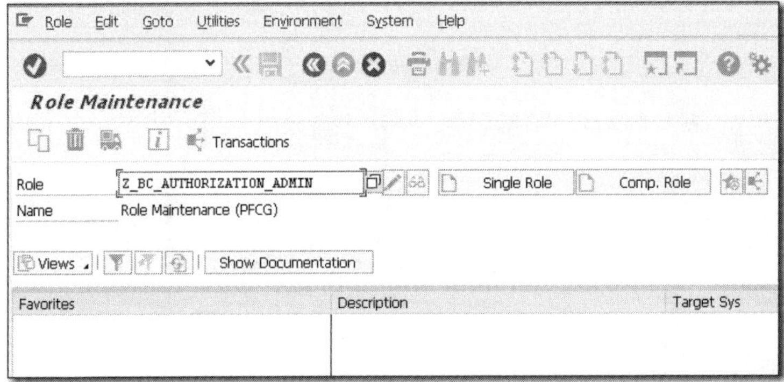

Figure 14.14 Creating Composite Roles

[+]

> **Naming Convention for Single and Composite Roles**
>
> In real life, it has proven beneficial to mark single and composite roles as such via the technical name, for example, by adding the _SR suffix to composite roles and _ER to single roles. It would also be possible to only add a special suffix to single roles, for instance, -E. For evaluations, for example, you can then determine the role type from the name of the role.

3. In the next screen, enter a meaningful DESCRIPTION (see Figure 14.15). You can use the LONG TEXT field for a more comprehensive description on the content and purpose or also for a change history.

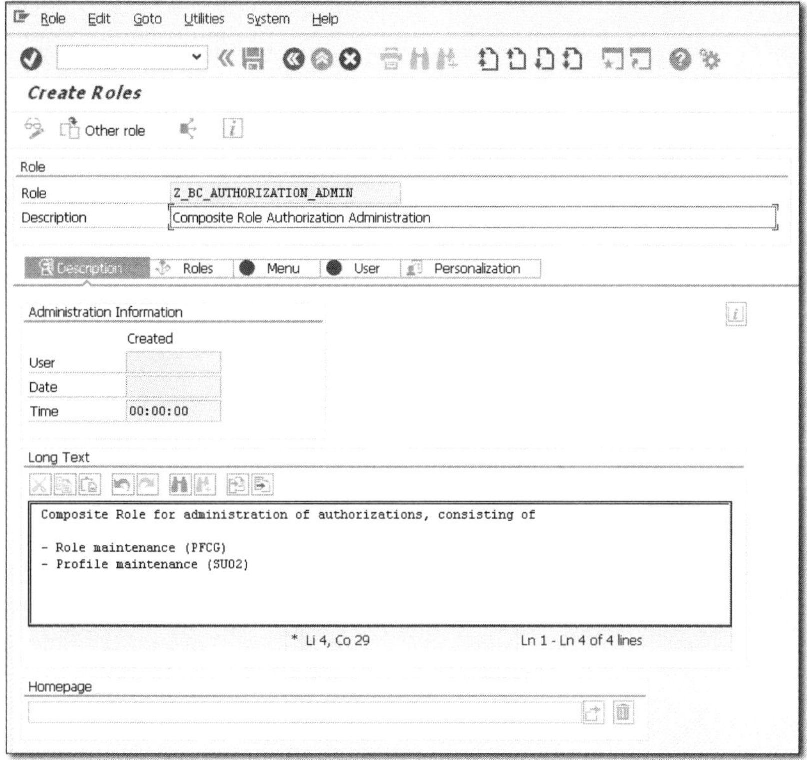

Figure 14.15 Maintaining the Description for the Composite Role

4. Go to the Roles tab (again, the system prompts you to save the role; confirm with Yes). In the Roles tab, enter the single roles you want to group in the composite role (see Figure 14.16).
5. Go to the Menu tab. Copy the menus of the single roles by clicking on Import Menu (see Figure 14.17).

Menu of Single and Composite Roles [!]

Provided that the composite role has a separate menu, the menus of the single roles belonging to the composite role are overridden in the user menu. If the composite role doesn't have a menu, the system shows the single roles' menu entries in the user menu as usual.

Note that changes to the menus of the single roles aren't automatically added to the menu of the composite role. You must compare the composite role menu anew for each change.

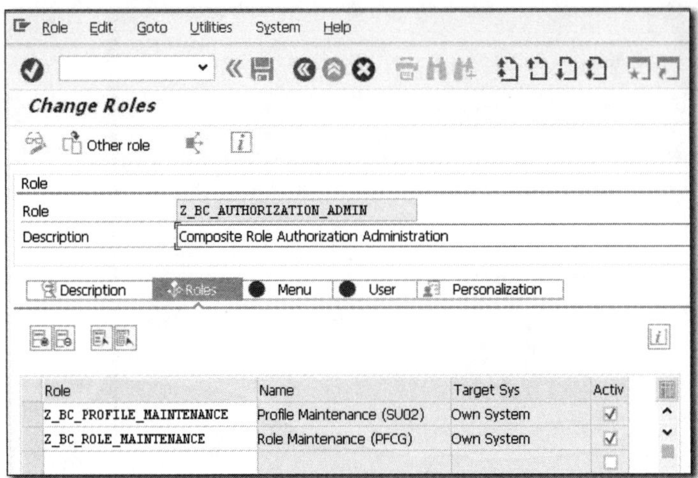

Figure 14.16 Assigning Single Roles to a Composite Role

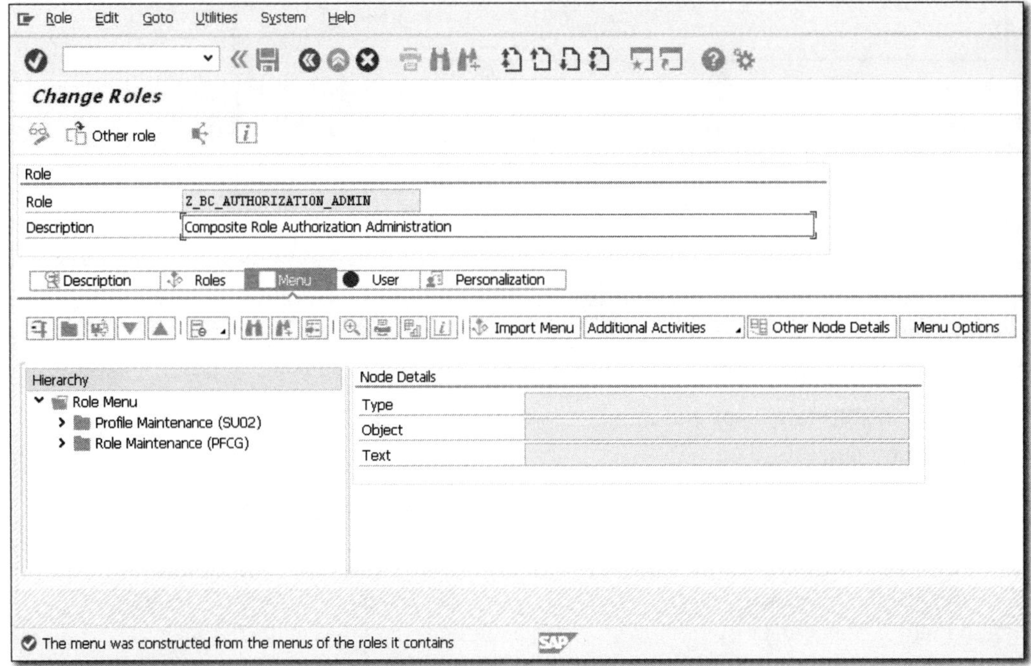

Figure 14.17 Transferring Menus of the Assigned Single Roles

6. Again, the system prompts you to save the role. Confirm with Yes.

Editing Composite Role Menus

The role descriptions of the single roles are displayed at the first level of the composite role menu. The menus of the single roles are available on the subordinate levels (see Figure 14.18). You can change the menu structure as required.

1. Create a new folder in the ROLE MENU using the CREATE FOLDER button, and enter a name.

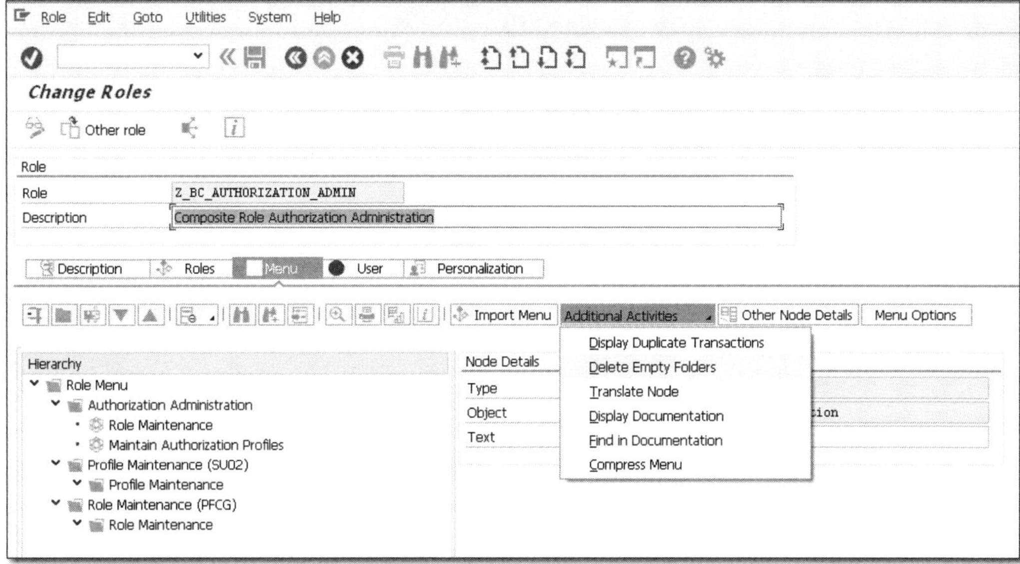

Figure 14.18 Structuring the Composite Role Menu

2. Drag and drop the transactions of the single roles to the newly created folder. Remove the subfolders no longer required by clicking ADDITIONAL ACTIONS • DELETE EMPTY FOLDERS. As soon as you've added transactions to the menu, the status of the MENU tab changes to green.

User Assignment

To assign users, follow these steps:

1. Go to the USER tab (see Figure 14.19). Enter the USER ID you want to assign to the role in the USER ASSIGNMENTS area.

2. If required, enter a validity period in which the authorization is supposed to be assigned. Click SAVE [save icon] to save your entries. Run the user comparison if required.

The composite role was assigned to the user. In the USER MENU, you can view the entries of the composite role menu (see Figure 14.20).

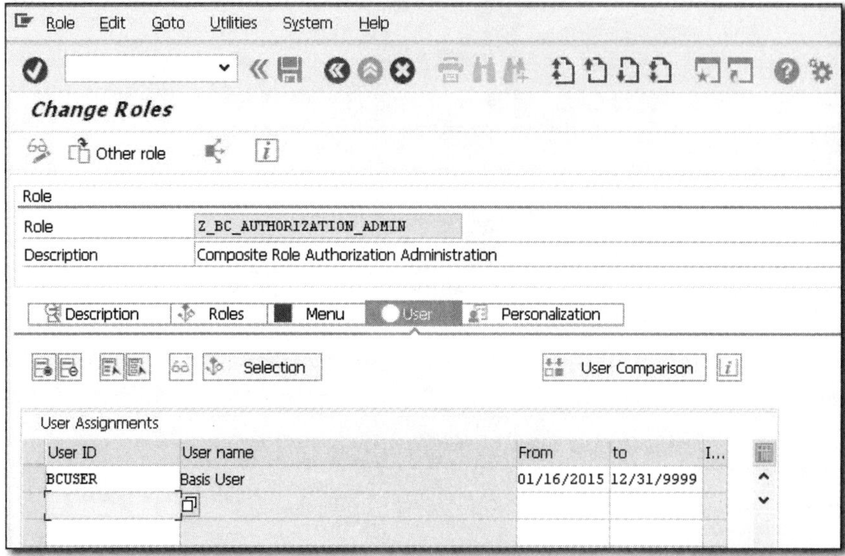

Figure 14.19 Assigning Users to a Composite Role

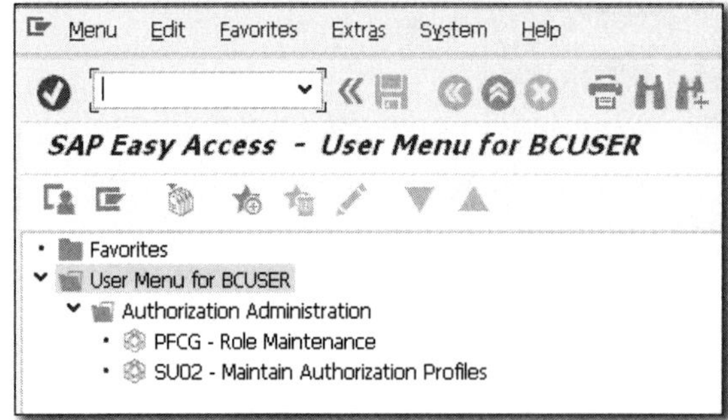

Figure 14.20 User Menu with Role Menu of the Composite Role

If you assign the single roles directly, the menus of the single roles are assigned separately in the USER MENU (see Figure 14.21).

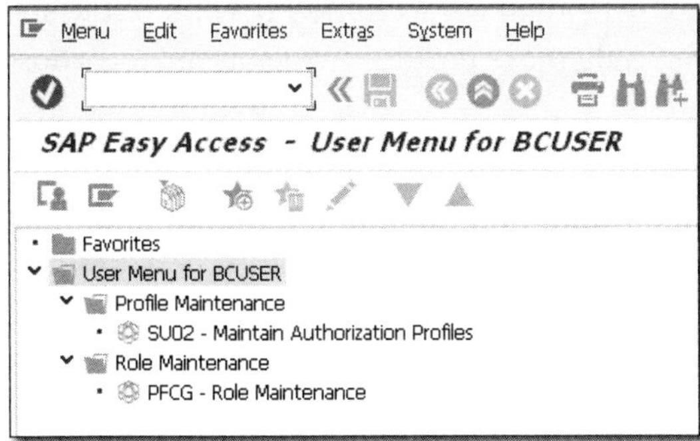

Figure 14.21 User Menu with Role Menus of the Single Roles

If you have the user master record displayed using Transaction SU01 (User Maintenance) and go to the Roles tab, you can see that both the composite and the single roles have been assigned (see Figure 14.22). Directly assigned roles are displayed in black. Single roles assigned via composite roles are indicated in blue. Single roles have the icon in the Type column; composite roles are represented via the icon. Roles for which the user comparison was not run completely are indicated in red in the Status column and presented with the note (tooltip) Profile Comparison required.

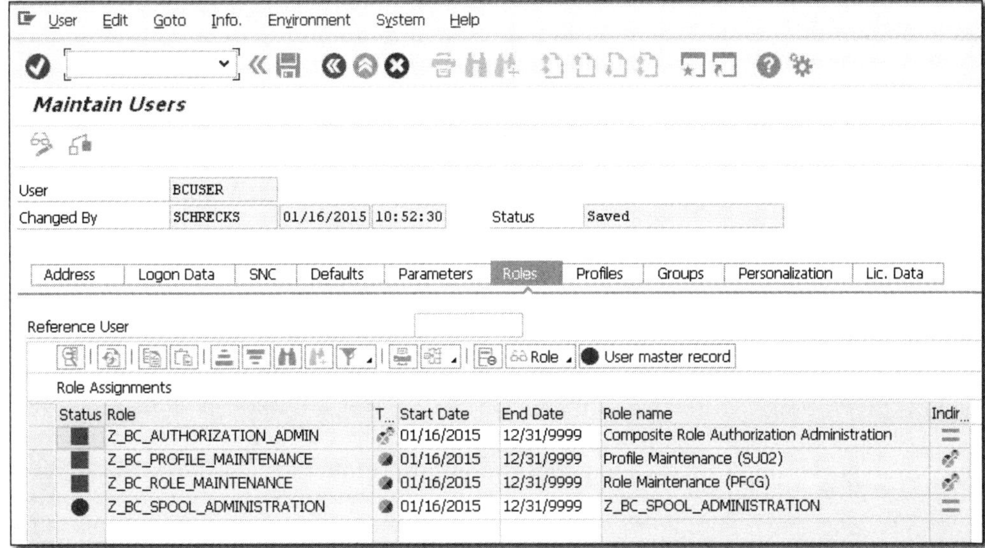

Figure 14.22 Role Display in the User Master Record

In the PROFILES tab, you can view the generated authorization profiles of the single roles (see Figure 14.23). However, only those profiles are displayed for whose roles the user comparison was run.

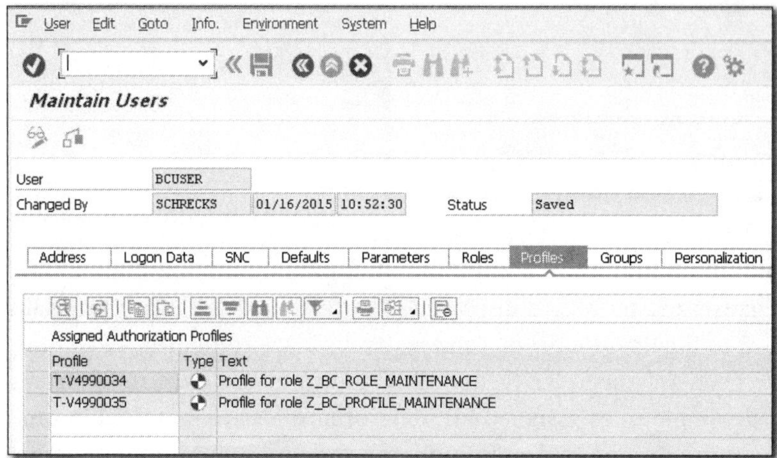

Figure 14.23 Displaying Authorization Profiles in the User Master Record

You can only withdraw the single roles assigned via a composite role by removing the composite role from the user master. You can't withdraw such a single role separately.

14.3 Authorization Profiles

In previous SAP releases, authorization profiles used to be the only option to assign authorizations. Today, you should work with authorization roles (refer to Section 14.2). Although not recommended, you still have the option to implement an authorization concept with authorization profiles or use standard SAP profiles.

Authorization profiles are also differentiated into *single profiles* and *composite profiles*. The purpose of a composite profile—as is the case for authorization roles—is to group single profiles to simplify administration.

Creating and maintaining authorization profiles isn't discussed in this book because we highly recommend using authorization roles. However, you should know how to obtain an overview of the content of a profile and how to assign authorization profiles to users.

Displaying Authorization Profiles

Because some administrators still work with authorization profiles or because standard SAP profiles (e.g., SAP_ALL) are used occasionally, you may want to take a closer look at an authorization profile.

1. Enter Transaction SU02 in the command field and press the Enter key (or select the menu option Tools • Administration • User Maintenance • Authorizations and Profiles (Manual Maintenance) • SU02—Edit Profiles Manually).

[+]

Using the Profile Generator Instead of the Manual Maintenance

Already in the initial screen of Transaction SU02 for profile maintenance, a note is displayed informing you to use the Profile Generator. Using the To Profile Generator button, you can directly navigate to Transaction PFCG.

2. Enter the name of the authorization profile in the Profile field if you want to view a specific profile. Leave the field blank to obtain a complete list of profiles. Click on Create work area for profiles (see Figure 14.24).

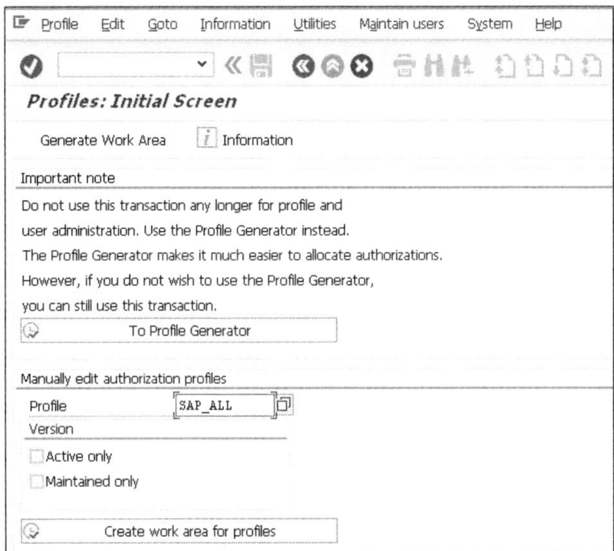

Figure 14.24 Displaying the Authorization Profile

3. In the next screen, the system displays the authorization profiles to which your selection criteria apply. Open the profile by double-clicking on the profile name or clicking on CHANGE PROFILE (see Figure 14.25).

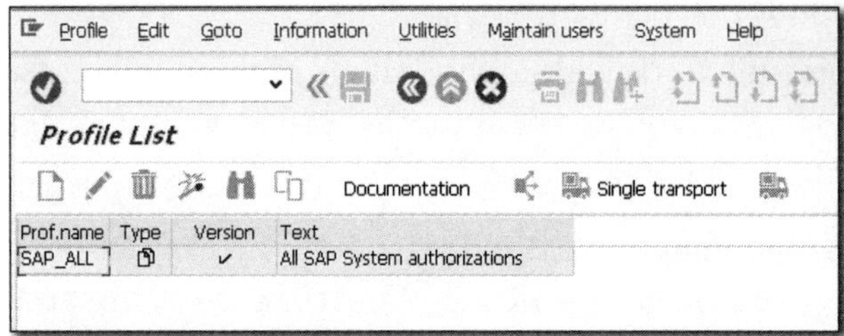

Figure 14.25 Editing the Authorization Profile

4. Via the TEXTS IN USER MASTER field, you can determine whether it's a single or composite profile (see Figure 14.26). For composite roles, the CONSISTING OF PROFILES area lists the single profiles that are included in the composite profile. Double-click on the profile name of a single profile to navigate to the next view.

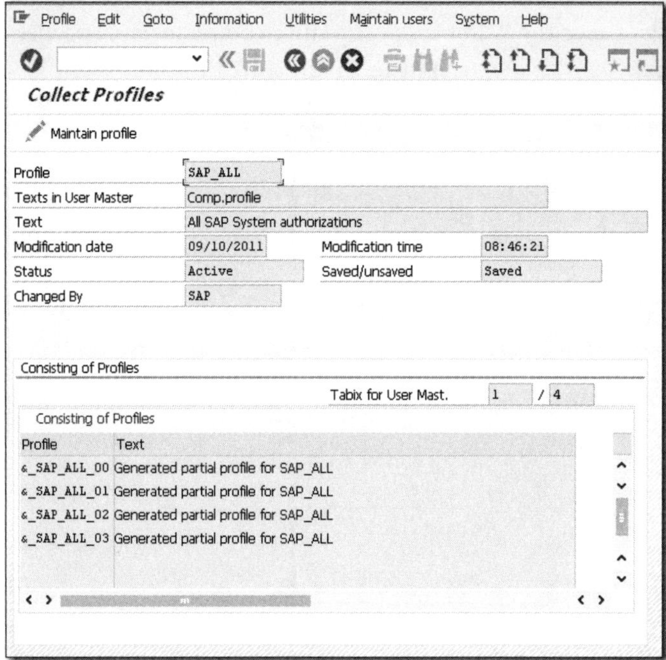

Figure 14.26 Composite Profile

5. At the level of single profiles, the CONSISTING OF AUTHORIZATIONS area lists the authorization objects contained in the profile (see Figure 14.27). Double-click on an object to open the field values.

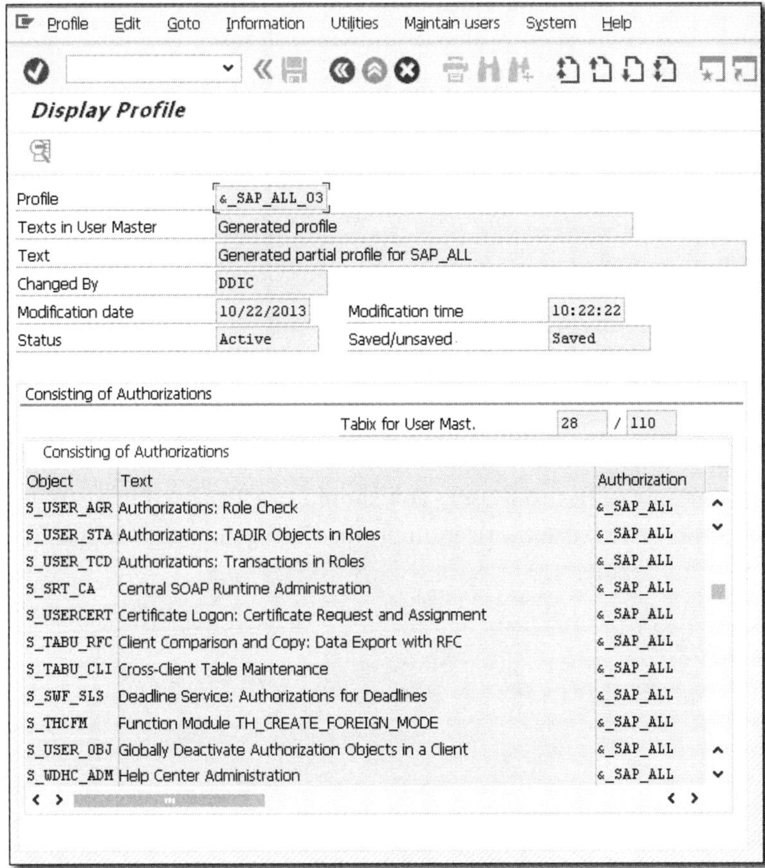

Figure 14.27 Display of the Authorization Objects Assigned

6. You're now in the display of the authorization fields of the authorization object (see Figure 14.28). Below each field, you can view the field values that were defined in the authorization profile.

With this approach, you can examine the content of specific authorization profiles.

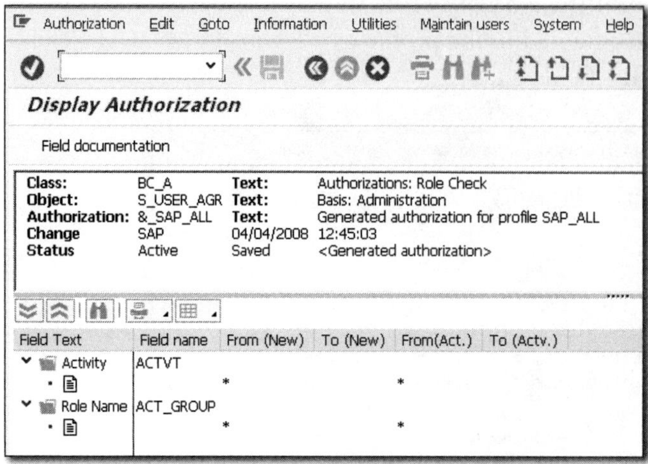

Figure 14.28 Authorization Fields of an Authorization Object

Assigning Authorization Profiles

To assign authorization profiles to a user, you should use Transaction SU01 for user maintenance and enter the authorization profiles in the PROFILES tab (see Figure 14.29 and refer to Chapter 13).

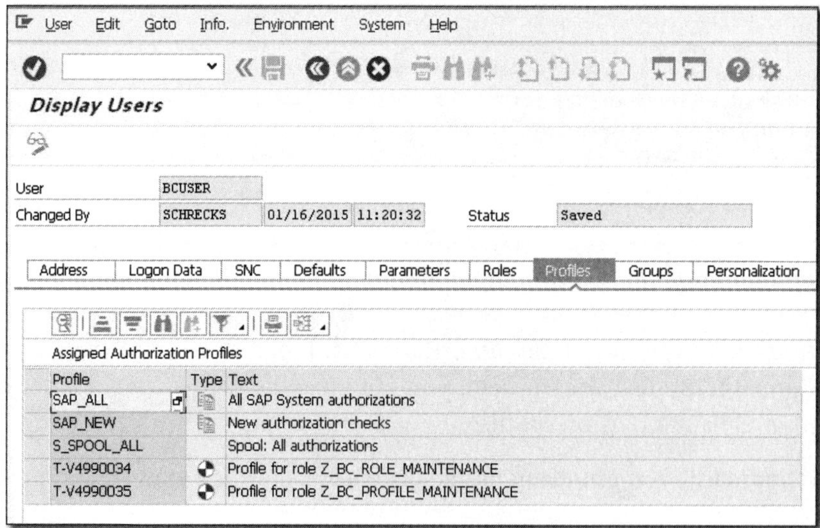

Figure 14.29 Authorization Profiles in the User Maintenance

The various profiles are displayed as follows:

- Profiles that have been created automatically for an authorization role are displayed as GENERATED PROFILE.
- A composite profile is presented using the COMPOSITE PROFILE icon.
- Single profiles don't have any entry in the TYPE column.

You can only withdraw generated authorization profiles by deleting the relevant authorization role.

14.4 Utilities for Authorization Management

As the administrator, you'll determine during the creation of authorization roles that the authorization objects the system added to the role sometimes don't correspond to the authorization objects that are actually checked in a transaction.

To understand and optimize the system behavior, you should well know the check indicators and authorization traces.

14.4.1 Default Values and Check Indicators

Section 14.2.1 describes that authorization objects are automatically added to the role profile after a transaction is added to the role menu. These default values depend on the check indicators defined in the system for each transaction. Implement the following steps to display the check indicators and default values.

1. Start Transaction SU24 (Maintain the Assignments of Authorization Objects).
2. In the TRANSACTION CODE field, enter the transaction for which you want to display the default values and check indicators, and select EXECUTE (see Figure 14.30).
3. The check indicators for the transaction are shown on the right side of the screen (see Figure 14.31). The value YES in the PROPOSAL field means that the object is automatically inserted in authorization roles. Click the FIELD VALUES button to show the default values of the authorization fields.

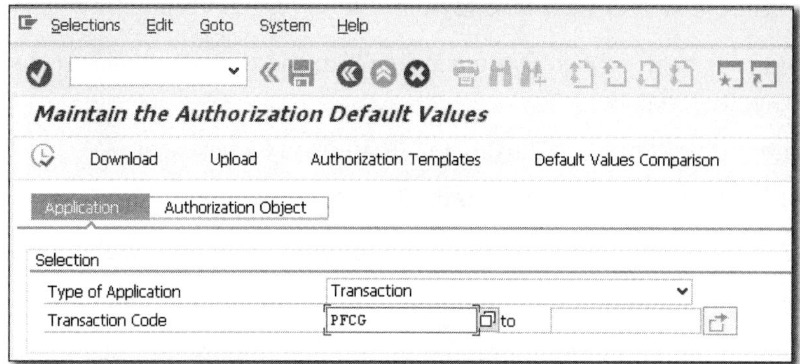

Figure 14.30 Displaying Check Indicators and Default Values

Application Edit Goto Utilities System Help

Display Transaction PFCG

SAP Data Authorization Trace: Off

Selection Result

Name	Short Description
PFCG	Role Maintenance

Transaction Code PFCG Saved

Object Field Values Trace

Authorization Objects

Status	Object	Object Description	TSTCA	Check Ind.	Proposal	Package	Component ID
■	P_ABAP			Check	No		
■	P_ORGIN			Check	No		
■	P_ORGXX			Check	No		
■	P_PCLX			Check	No		
■	P_PERNR			Check	No		
■	P_TCODE	HR: Transaction codes		Check	Yes	SP00	BC-BMT-OM
■	PLOG	Personnel Planning		Check	Yes	SP00	BC-BMT-OM
■	S_ALV_LAYO	ALV Standard Layout		Check	No	SLIS	BC-SRV-ALV
■	S_CTS_ADMI	Administration Functions in Change and Transport System		Check	No	SCTS_BAS	BC-CTS-ORG
■	S_DATASET	Authorization for file access		Check	No	SECC	BC-SEC
■	S_DEVELOP	ABAP Workbench		Check	No	SEU	BC-DWB-UTL-BRR
■	S_DOKU_AUT	SE61 Documentation Maintenance Authorization		Check	No	SDOC	BC-DOC-DTL
■	S_GUI	Authorization for GUI activities		Check	No	SABP_LIST	BC-ABA-LI
■	S_PROJECT	Project Management: Project authorization		Check	No	SPROJECT	BC-CUS-TOL-IMG
■	S_RFC	Authorization Check for RFC Access		Check	No	SRCX	BC-MID-RFC
■	S_TABU_DIS	Table Maintenance (via standard tools such as SM30)		Check	No	SVIM	BC-CUS-TOL-TME
■	S_TCODE	Transaction Code Check at Transaction Start		Check	No	SUSR	BC-SEC-USR-ADM
■	S_TRANSLAT	Translation environment authorization object		Check	No	STRO	BC-DOC-TTL
■	S_TRANSPRT	Transport Organizer		Check	No	SCTS_BAS	BC-CTS-ORG
■	S_USER_AGR	Authorizations: Role Check		Check	Yes	S_PROFGEN	BC-SEC-AUT-PFC
■	S_USER_AUT	User Master Maintenance: Authorizations		Check	Yes	SUSR	BC-SEC-USR-ADM
■	S_USER_GRP	User Master Maintenance: User Groups		Check	Yes	SUSR	BC-SEC-USR-ADM
■	S_USER_PRO	User Master Maintenance: Authorization Profile		Check	Yes	SUSR	BC-SEC-USR-ADM
■	S_USER_SAS	User Master Maintenance: System-Specific Assignments		Check	Yes	SUSR	BC-SEC-USR-ADM
■	S_USER_SYS	User Master Maintenance: System for Central User Maintenance		Check	No	SUSR	BC-SEC-USR-ADM
■	S_USER_TCD	Authorizations: Transactions in Roles		Check	Yes	S_PROFGEN	BC-SEC-AUT-PFC
■	S_USER_VAL	Authorizations: Field Values in Roles		Check	Yes	S_PROFGEN	BC-SEC-AUT-PFC
■	S_WFAR_OBJ	ArchiveLink: Authorizations for access to documents		Check	No	SWI	BC-BMT-WFM

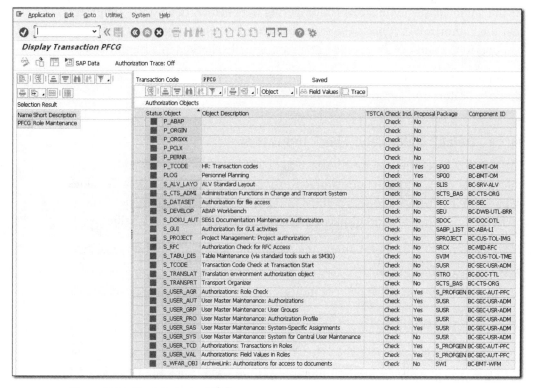

Figure 14.31 Check Indicator Display

4. Details on the field values, which the system uses as default values, are shown in the lower-right of the screen (see Figure 14.32).

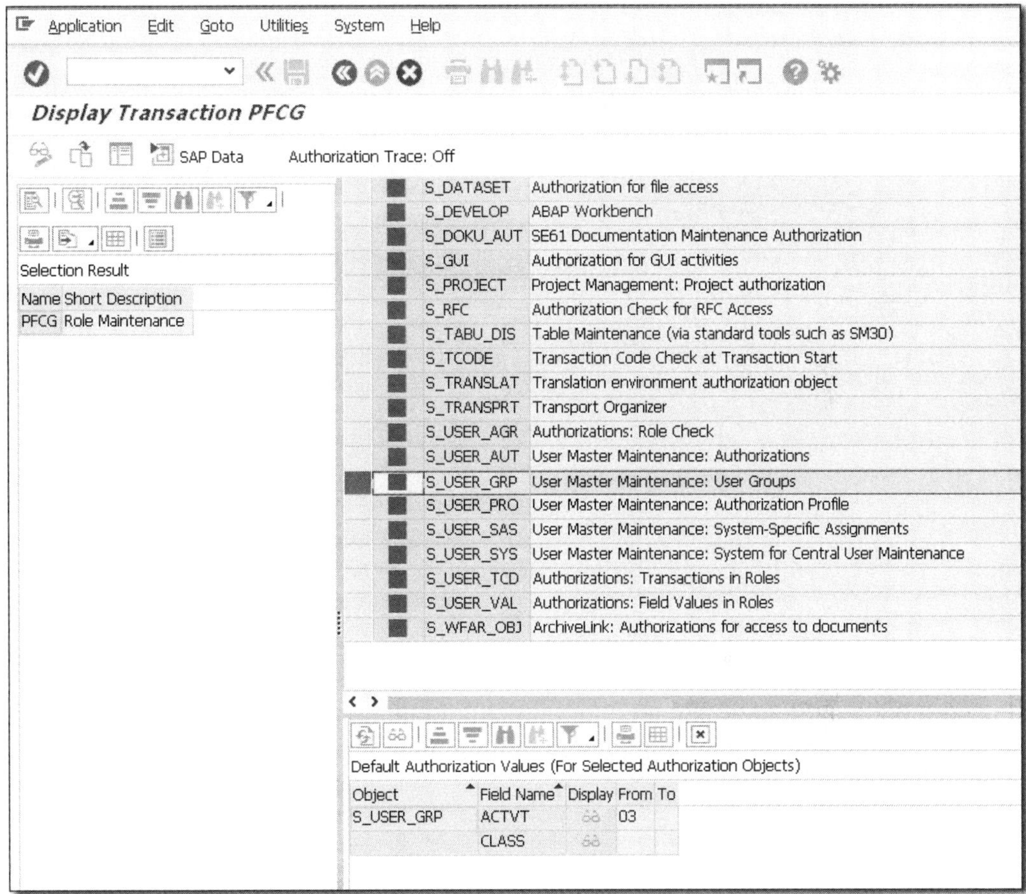

Figure 14.32 Default Value Display

5. To edit the objects proposed, switch to the change mode via DISPLAY <-> CHANGE. For example, in the AUTHORIZATION OBJECTS area, use the PROPOSAL button to choose SET STATUS "NO" if no default values are supposed to be added to the roles for the authorization object (see Figure 14.33).
6. If you want to change the default values, click CHANGE in the DEFAULT AUTHORIZATION VALUES area, and enter further activities as new default values, for example (see Figure 14.34).

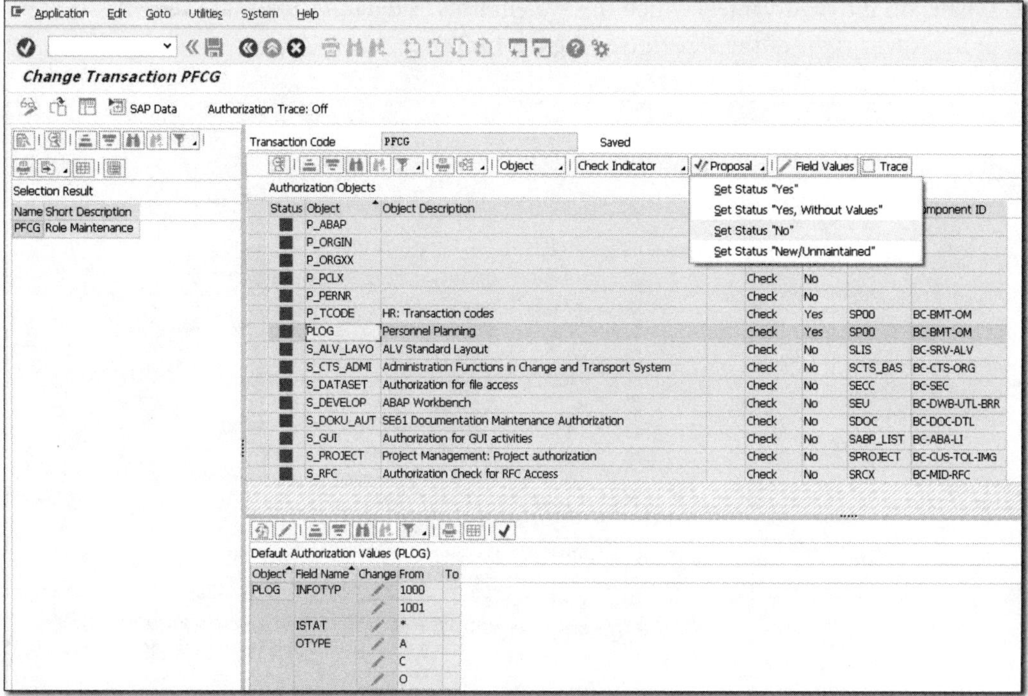

Figure 14.33 Editing the Default Values

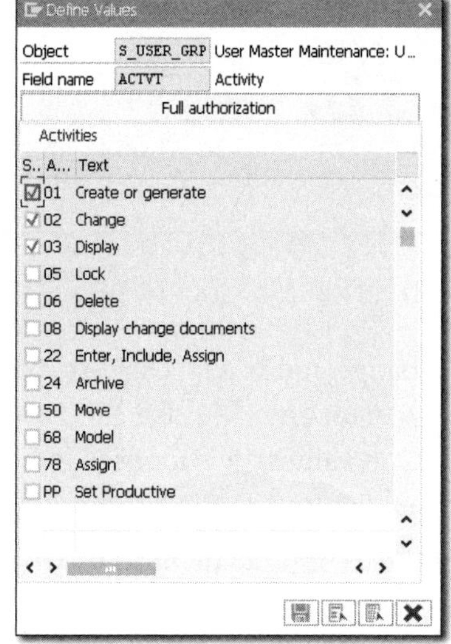

Figure 14.34 Adding Further Activities as Default Values

7. Click on SAVE.

[!]

Copying the Delivery Version

Before you change the default values or check indicators, you must copy the delivery version of this data to your customer namespace. To do so, start Transaction SU25 (Upgrade Tool for Profile Generator), and run the action INSTALLING THE PROFILE GENERATOR • INITIALLY FILL THE CUSTOMER TABLES.

8. Use Transaction SU24 to deactivate authorization checks in transactions in a targeted manner by changing the check indicators. For this purpose, select the relevant authorization object, and click on CHECK INDICATOR • DO NOT CHECK (see Figure 14.35).

[!]

Functions of the Check Indicator

Note that you can deactivate checks, but you can't use the check indicators to have the system check additional authorization objects in a transaction. If an object isn't checked in the source code of the transaction, this can only be changed by editing the program—not by setting a check indicator.

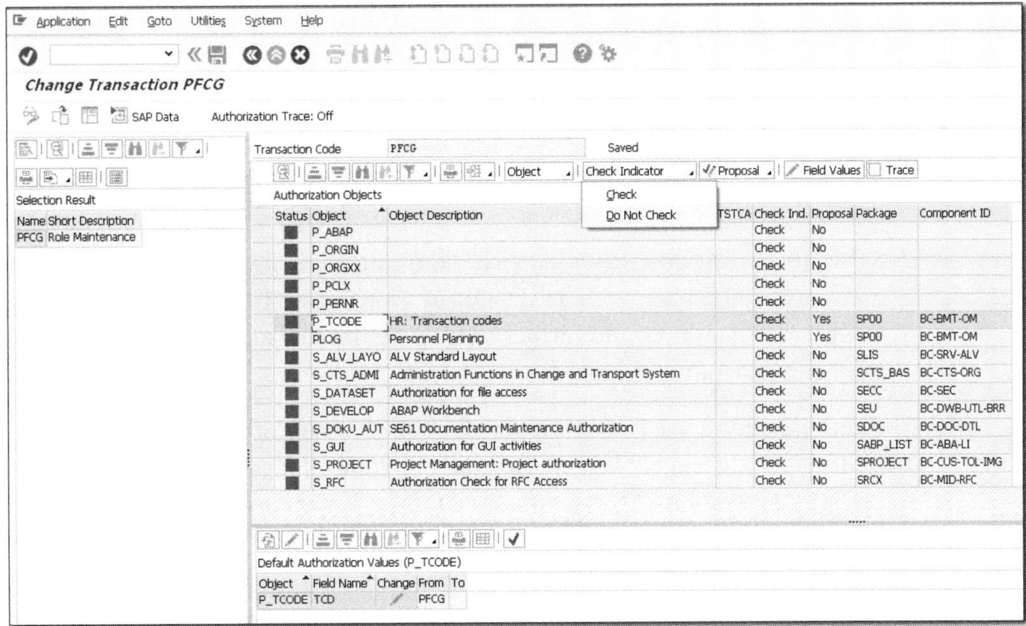

Figure 14.35 Changing the Check Indicator

9. You can also add further default values (choose OBJECT • ADD AUTHORIZATION OBJECT) or remove objects from the default values (choose OBJECT • REMOVE AUTHORIZATION OBJECT).
10. With the SAP DATA button, you can compare your modifications with the delivery data from SAP.

You can use the default values in Transaction SU24 to map or document your authorization concept directly in the SAP system. But you can also leave the default values unchanged and ignore them.

14.4.2 Authorization Trace

The authorization trace is probably the most essential utility of the (authorization) administrator. If you don't have any programming knowledge or don't want to go through source coding indefinitely when searching for authorization objects required for a transaction, the authorization trace is the right tool to find which authorization checks are run in a transaction.

Activating the Authorization Trace

The authorization trace is part of the system trace. Activate the trace in the first step to then evaluate it:

1. Enter Transaction ST01 in the command field and press the [Enter] key (or select the menu option TOOLS • ADMINISTRATION • MONITOR • TRACES • ST01—SYSTEM TRACE).
2. Select the AUTHORIZATION CHECK checkbox (in the TRACE COMPONENTS area), and activate the trace with TRACE ON (see Figure 14.36). You can use the GENERAL FILTERS button to further restrict the trace to a specific user, a transaction, or a program if required.

The authorization trace is now activated; in other words, all authorization checks that run in the system are logged according to your filter criteria. You can use the trace for the creation of new authorization roles by running the transactions whose authorization checks you want to analyze with the activated trace with a test user. The authorization trace can also be useful if you want to investigate a specific error message. Activate the trace, and ask the reporting person to repeat the action that failed.

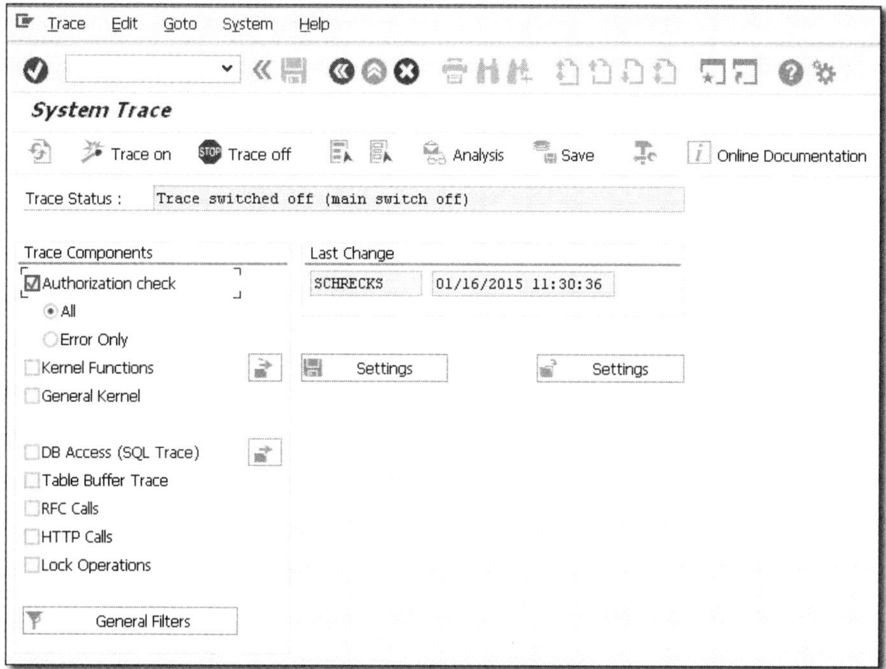

Figure 14.36 Activating the Authorization Trace

Evaluating the Authorization Trace

After you've run the test or reproduced the error, you start to evaluate the authorization trace by following these steps:

1. Start Transaction ST01.
2. In the options, you can restrict the system trace evaluations, for instance, to a specific user name or period of time. Deactivate all entries except for Authorization check under Trace Records (see Figure 14.37). Display the trace entries using Start Reporting.

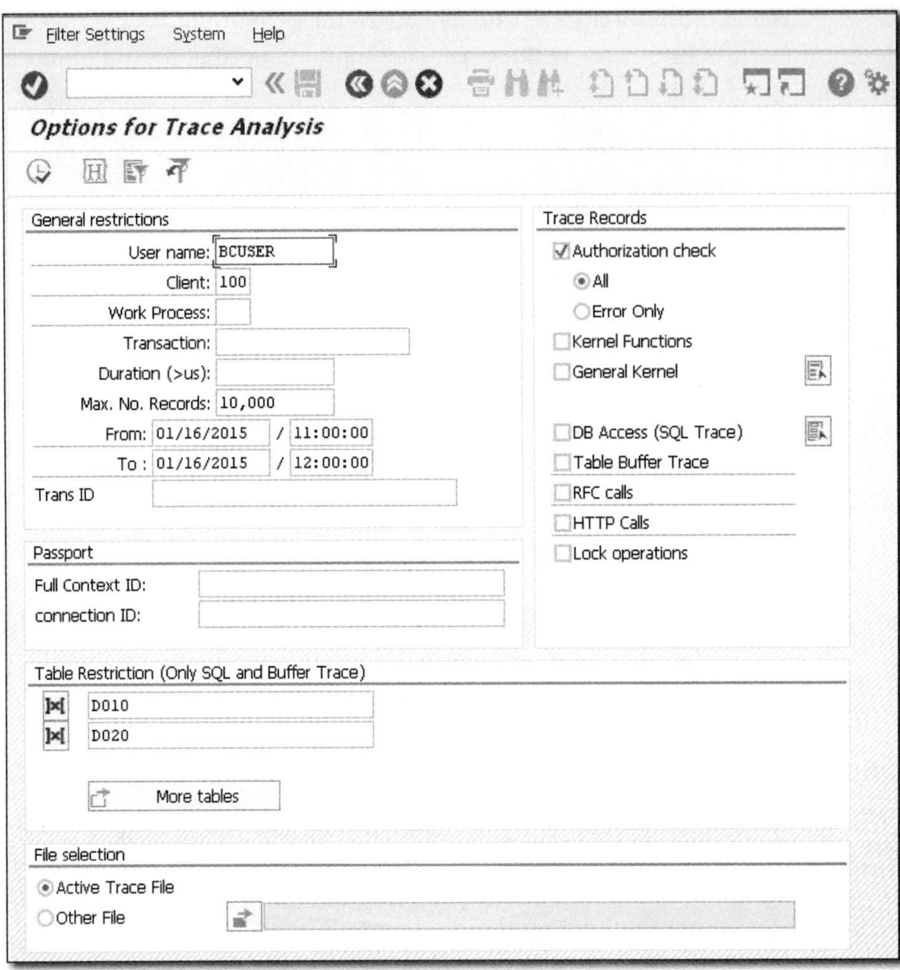

Figure 14.37 Restricting the Authorization Trace Evaluation

3. All authorization checks processed for the selected user are displayed in the next screen (see Figure 14.38). The first column indicates the exact time of the check. The OBJECT column shows the checked authorization object and the return code returned by the system. The TEXT column specifies which fields and field values were checked.

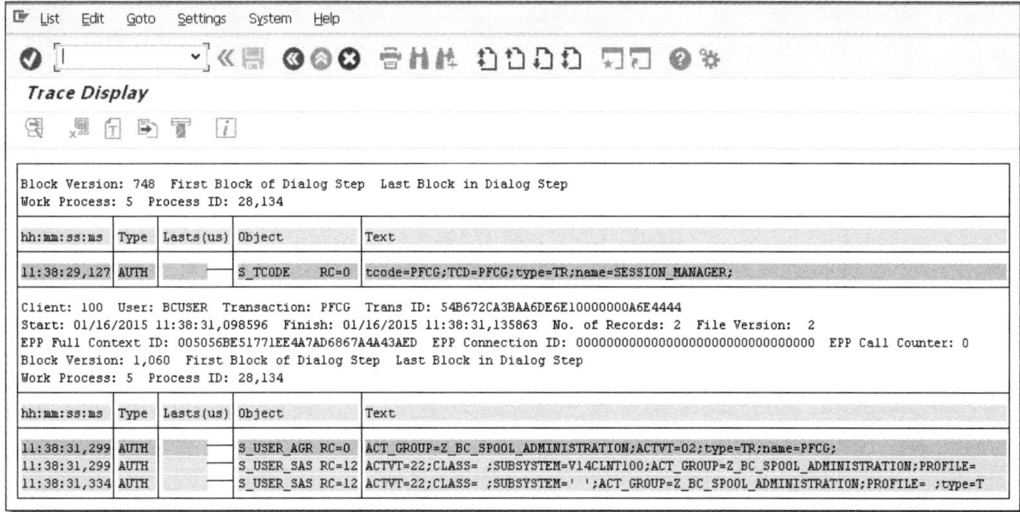

Figure 14.38 Evaluating the Authorization Trace

Return Code

Whether an action may be performed by a user depends on the *return code*, which the authorization check returns. Return code 0 means that the check was successful and the action was permitted. All other return codes (4, 8, or 16) indicate that the authorization check failed, and the user must not perform the action.

Interpreting the Trace Log

Interpreting the trace log is just a matter of practice. In the example of Figure 14.38, you can see that the user calls Transaction PFCG (object S_TCODE) and then creates a new authorization role (object S_USER_AGR with activity 02 (Change) and role Z_BC_BENUTZERADMINISTRATION). Both object checks finished with return code 0 and were thus permitted by the system. Assignment of the role to a user master record was denied with return code 4 because the BCUSER user doesn't have the authorization object S_USER_SAS with activity 22 (Assign). After you've evaluated the authorization trace, you can make the necessary corrections in the relevant authorization role (e.g., add activity 22 to object S_USER_GRP) and repeat the test.

Evaluating the Authorization Check

Besides the authorization trace described, there is another option to evaluate failed authorization checks: Transaction SU53 (Evaluate Authorization Check).

The authorization check is only available for selected users. Transaction SU53, however, should be available for all users in the system. With Transaction SU53, the system displays the log of the authorization check that failed last. In many cases, this can save you the work with the authorization trace; in case of an error, you can have the reporting person send the result of Transaction SU53 (e.g., as a screenshot). This information may already be sufficient to solve the problem.

1. Open a new session after the failed authorization check, and start Transaction SU53, or call the transaction in the same session using "/nSU53" or "/oSU53". Expand the tree structure to analyze the authorization check (see Figure 14.39).

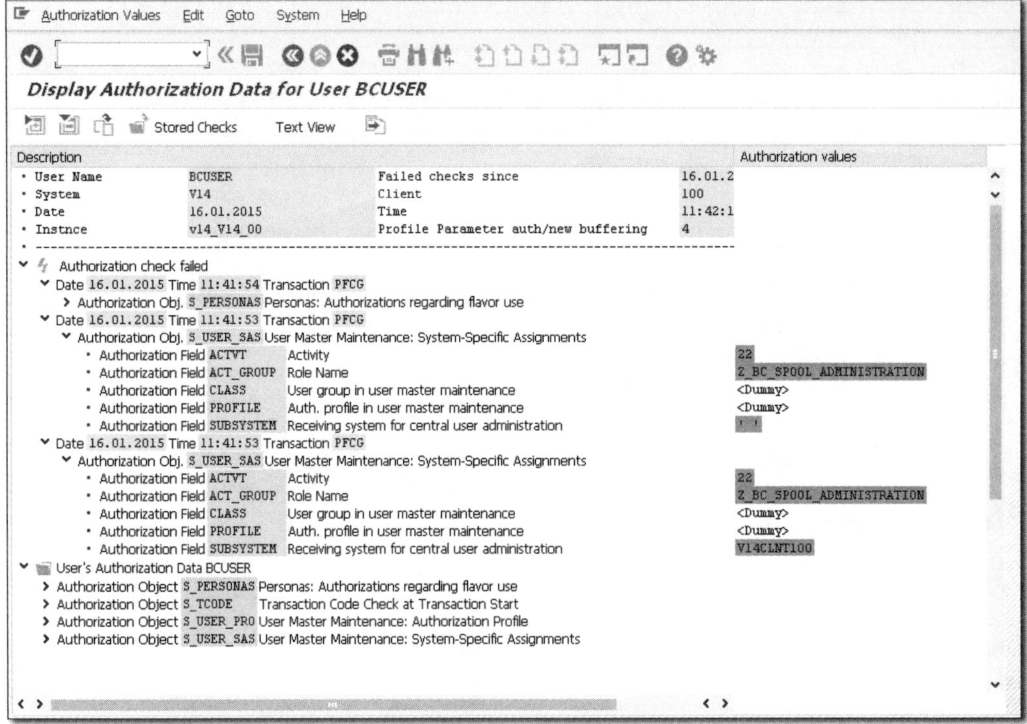

Figure 14.39 Evaluating the Authorization Check in Transaction SU53

2. Rejected authorization checks are highlighted in red. Below the checks, the system lists the authorizations that are currently assigned to the user for the relevant object.
3. Check the log entries, and correct the roles. Then try again.

[!]

Evaluation of Transaction SU53

The evaluation shown in Transaction SU53 had to be handled with due care for a long time because only the result of the *last* failed authorization check was output. The logged object (e.g., S_ALV_LAYO) wasn't necessarily responsible for the action in question not being executed. It could only be the last link in the chain of rejected checks. If in doubt, consult the authorization trace where the authorization checks are logged completely and in the sequence in which they were run.

With SAP Note 1671117, the display was improved considerably so that multiple erroneous checks can be displayed making evaluation more meaningful. This note can be implemented for all SAP releases as of 7.0 if they run on kernel release 7.21 or higher.

14.4.3 Infosystem Authorizations

Transaction SUIM or the area menu AUTH provides various options for evaluations on the authorizations topic in the form of predefined reports. To open the area menu or Transaction SUIM, enter "AUTH" or Transaction "SUIM" in the transaction field of the SAP Easy Access menu, and press the [Enter] key. The area menu will be presented, which contains evaluation programs sorted by topics (see Figure 14.40). The menu of Transaction SUIM is identical in terms of content.

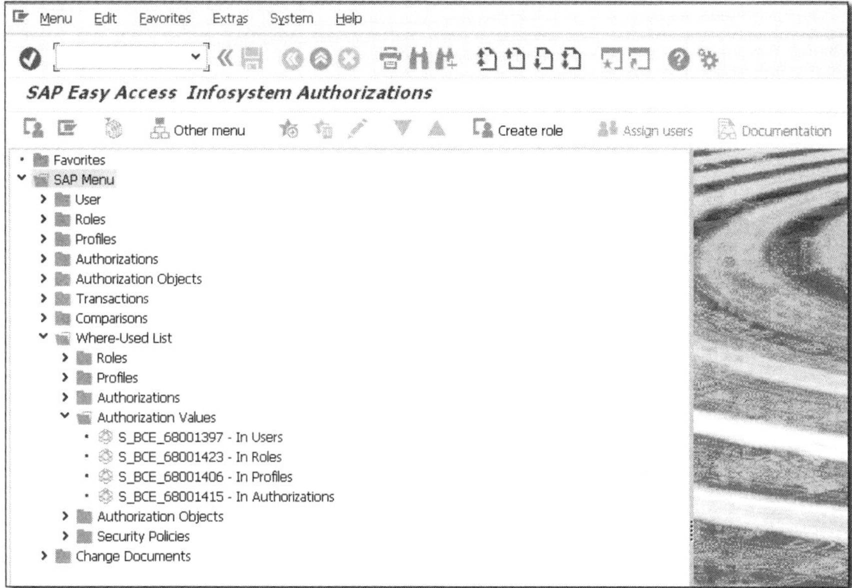

Figure 14.40 Area Menu AUTH

[+]

Returning to the SAP Menu

To return from the area menu AUTH to the standard SAP menu, either click on the SAP MENU button or enter "S000" in the transaction field, and press the Enter key.

The Infosystem Authorizations offers a variety of evaluation options for users, roles, and profiles. For example, you can evaluate the user master records that exist in the system using a wide range of selection criteria, for instance, based on assigned roles, available authorization objects and values, and user locks (see Figure 14.41).

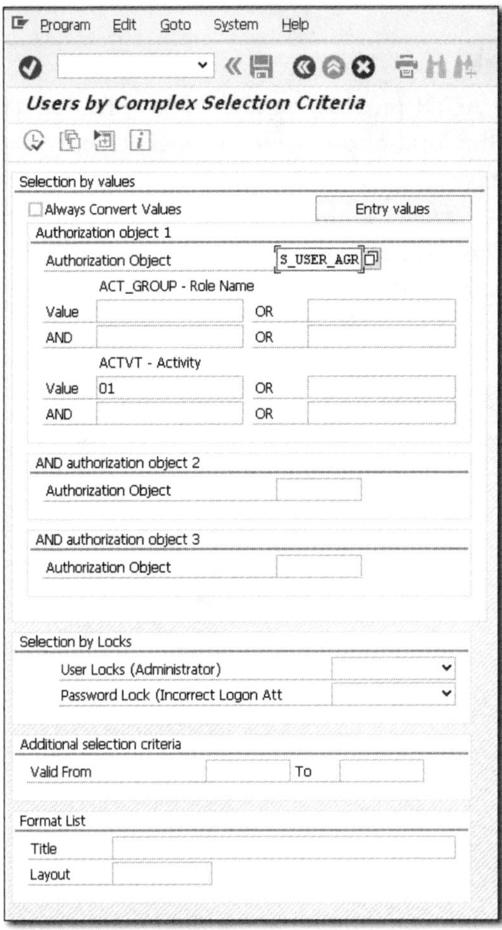

Figure 14.41 User Evaluation Using Complex Selection Criteria

Depending on the report, you can address questions with different levels of complexity. So, first take a look at the Infosystem Authorizations before you run elaborate evaluations for various system tables (see Appendix C).

14.5 Summary

SAP systems are provided with a sophisticated system for controlling authorizations. This is required because the access to business data must be customized with a very high level of detail due to legal, security-specific, or other reasons. In this chapter, you've learned how authorization checks work, how to create authorization roles or profiles, and how to assign authorizations to users. Create an authorization concept for your systems where you consider both of these closely linked topic areas of user and authorization administration.

In the SAP system, you can execute transactions and programs in dialog mode or in the background. You can flexibly control the start time and recurrence frequency of these background jobs. This chapter describes how to schedule programs with a long runtime for overnight processing and how to monitor background jobs.

15 Background Processing

In the SAP system, batch jobs are called *background jobs*. They are executed whether a user is logged on to the system or not. This is the main difference from the execution of a program in dialog mode. Background jobs provide the following advantages:

- Users can run jobs after work or on the weekend.
- The program can run without locking a user session.
- Jobs that take a lot of time might be canceled if they are executed online as soon as they exceed a certain time limit.

Numerous SAP transactions let you choose between an execution in dialog mode or in the background. For dialog and background processing, the SAP system provides different work process categories (see Chapter 2). If you choose background processing, a background job is created that uses a batch work process (BTC category). If you run the transaction in dialog mode, a dialog work process (DIA category) is blocked. As an alternative to creating a background job from a specific transaction, you can also create and schedule background jobs yourself.

15.1 Creating Background Jobs

In the SAP system, background processing is mainly used for the execution of regularly scheduled jobs. Regularly scheduled jobs are background jobs that are executed according to a schedule, for example, every day at 11am or every Sunday at 5am.

Unlike spontaneously performed background jobs, the start is specifically planned, and the execution is repeated at certain intervals. Regularly scheduled jobs are used for the following tasks, for example:

- Collecting performance data for statistics
- Importing data into an information system, for example, Special Ledger
- Generating reports
- Generating a data file for an outbound interface
- Processing an inbound interface
- Performing cleanup tasks, for example, deleting obsolete spool requests

[+]

Documenting Critical Jobs

You should list all critical scheduled jobs. This refers in particular to job runs that are important for the business processes of your enterprise, such as interfaces or overnight processing programs. You should record the following for every job of this category:

- Day/time of the planned start
- Expected duration
- Contact persons (name and telephone numbers) in case problems occur
- Restart or troubleshooting procedures

15.1.1 General

You must generally consider the following aspects when scheduling regular or spontaneous background jobs.

User ID

Like dialog mode, background processing requires an SAP user with ID and the corresponding authorizations. In dialog processing, programs are usually executed with the ID of the user who is currently logged on to the system. For background processing, a job is normally always started with the user ID of its creator. However, you can also define another user ID afterward (see Section 15.1.2).

You can create specific user IDs that are solely used for the scheduling of batch jobs, for example, `BATCH1`. You should work with several user IDs for the different task areas if batch jobs are scheduled by different organizations or groups or if they are scheduled for them. The disadvantage is that you have to administer multiple accounts.

Using Multiple User IDs [Ex]

You can assign the user IDs as follows, for example:

- BATCH_BC: System jobs
- BATCH_FI: Financial accounting
- BATCH_KR: Vendors
- BATCH_WH: Warehouse
- BATCH_MM: Material planning/stock

These special user IDs enable you to schedule jobs independently of the person. So you avoid jobs that can't be executed when an employee leaves the enterprise, for example, because the user ID of the employee has been locked or deleted. Another advantage of this procedure is that background users can also be of the system type (see Chapter 13); in other words, in a security-oriented environment, they can have more authorizations than would be acceptable for dialog users.

Variants

For the execution of a program with specific settings or selection parameters, a batch job may require the creation of a *variant*. Variants enable you to start jobs with default parameters, for example, predefined selection criteria. You have to create this variant in the dialog mode before you schedule the job. You can then specify this variant when scheduling the job.

Other

Various components and functions may require specific regularly scheduled jobs. The Special Ledger, for example, requires a regular job for copying data from the Financial Accounting/Controlling (FI/CO) components and for generating sets in the Special Ledger. Furthermore, several cleanup jobs may have to be executed at the database and operating system level.

15.1.2 Creating and Scheduling Background Jobs

Follow these steps to create and schedule new background jobs:

1. Enter Transaction SM63 in the command field and press the Enter key (or select the menu option Tools • CCMS • Background Processing • SM36—Define Job).
2. Make the following settings (see Figure 15.1):
   - Enter a name in Job Name.
   - Define the start priority of the job with Job Class.
   - Optionally, define a specific server as the Exec. Target provided that your SAP system comprises various application servers. The Status is preset.

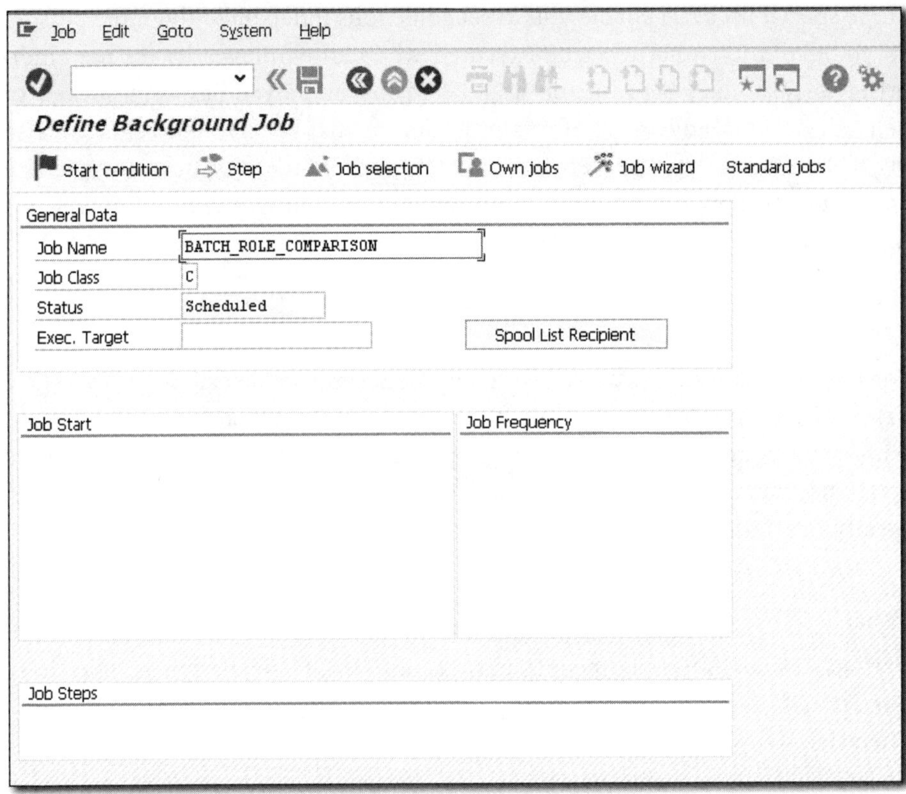

Figure 15.1 Creating a Background Job

Naming Convention for Background Jobs [+]

Using standard naming conventions facilitates the administration of jobs.

Job Classes [⚙]

The job class defines the start priority of a background job, that is, the sequence in which a free batch work process is assigned to the jobs. A job of class A is started before a job of class B, and a job of class B before a job of class C. Class C is the default job class.

After the start, all jobs have the same priority. That means a job of class A doesn't occupy processing resources of jobs of class B to accelerate the execution. Queued jobs don't have an effect on running jobs. A queued class A job doesn't replace a class C job that is currently running.

You can reserve batch work processes for jobs of class A in an SAP system (see Chapter 2). This enables you to control that the execution of very critical background jobs isn't blocked by unimportant jobs because no work processes are available.

3. Now, select STEP, and click on the ABAP PROGRAM button in the subsequent dialog box to schedule an ABAP program (see Figure 15.2).

Using Job Classes Efficiently [!]

Use job classes efficiently. For example, it doesn't make sense to assign every job to class A because all jobs are executed with the same priority then. Usually, jobs should be assigned to class C. Only jobs that must be started as preferred should be assigned to class A. There should be a reason for the assignment to a higher priority. You can use the SAP authorization concept as a reference.

Job Steps [+]

Each job consists of one or several *steps* that need to be defined individually. The steps are executed in succession.

4. Enter the following data here:
   - In USER, you can optionally define a user ID under which the job will be executed.
   - In the ABAP PROGRAM area, enter the name of the program in NAME.
   - If there are variants of the program, you can also enter a VARIANT.
   - Click on CHECK to check the consistency of your entries.

[!]

User IDs in Background Jobs

The USER of the job step provides the authorizations with which the job is executed; irrespective of this entry, the job overview (see Section 15.2) lists the job with the user ID of the creator. You can only use user IDs of the user type dialog, system, or service for background processing.

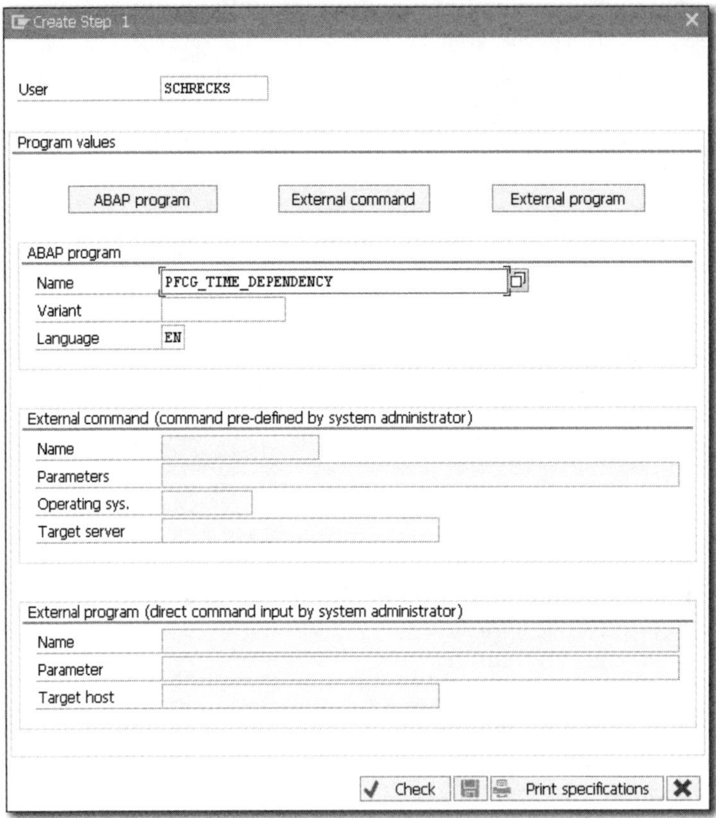

Figure 15.2 Creating a Background Job for Executing an ABAP Program

5. Click on PRINT SPECIFICATIONS. If the program generates a spool or output request, enter the name of the printer in OUTPUT DEVICE (see Figure 15.3).
6. Click on PROPERTIES to define the required spool control options in the SPOOL REQUEST PROPERTIES screen (see Figure 15.4). Your settings depend on whether you want to print the lists directly and for how long you want to retain them. When you're finished, choose CONTINUE ✓.

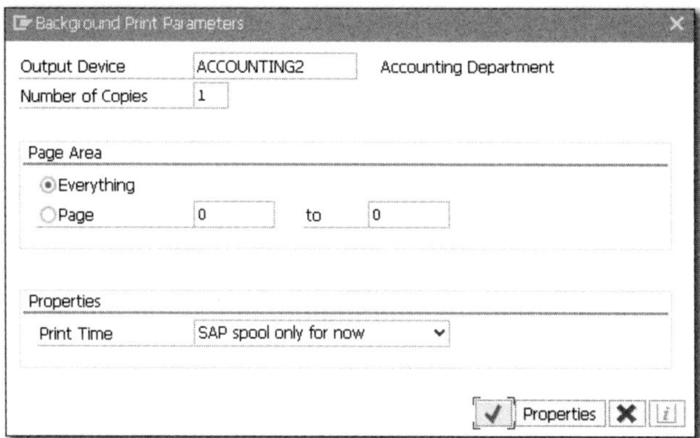

Figure 15.3 Defining the Output Device

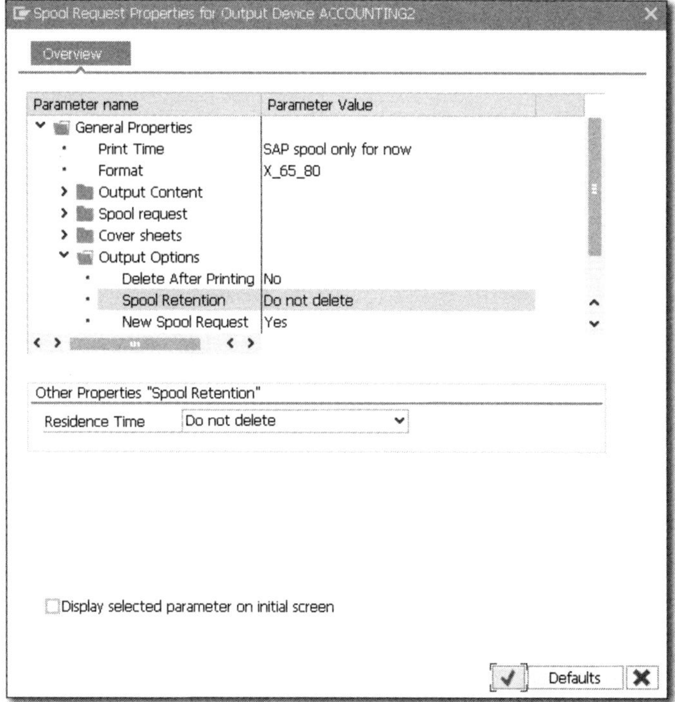

Figure 15.4 Setting the Spool Request Attributes

7. Also confirm the selection of the printer in the previous screen, BACKGROUND PRINT PARAMETERS, with CONTINUE.

8. Save your entries in the initial dialog box, CREATE STEP 1 (refer to Figure 15.2) using SAVE.
9. The overview of the already-defined steps is displayed (see Figure 15.5). Here you can add more steps and change or delete already-defined steps if necessary. Select BACK, to return to the initial screen of the job definition (refer to Figure 15.1).

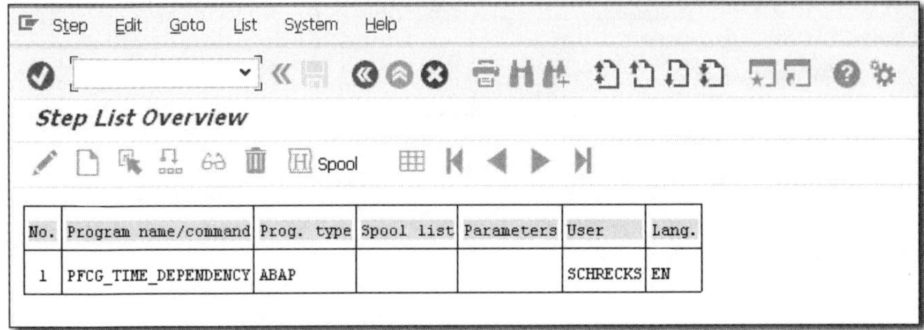

No.	Program name/command	Prog. type	Spool list	Parameters	User	Lang.
1	PFCG_TIME_DEPENDENCY	ABAP			SCHRECKS	EN

Figure 15.5 Overview of Defined Steps

10. Click on START CONDITION. If you schedule a regular job, select the DATE/TIME button (see Figure 15.6). Enter a date and time in SCHEDULED START. For NO START AFTER, enter the last possible date and time for the program start. If you want to start the execution of the program immediately, select the IMMEDIATE button.

[!] **Considering the Time Zones of the Database Server**

The date and time of the scheduled start refer to the database server and not to the local time.

[!] **Don't Schedule Jobs for 24:00**

Never set the start time for a job to 24:00 because this job will not start. In the SAP system, 23:59 is always followed by 00:00; that is, the time 24:00 doesn't exist from the technical point of view.

[+] **Option "No Start After"**

The entry in the NO START AFTER field is important if performance-intensive programs mustn't start at certain times to avoid jeopardizing running operations or to prevent one job from passing the other.

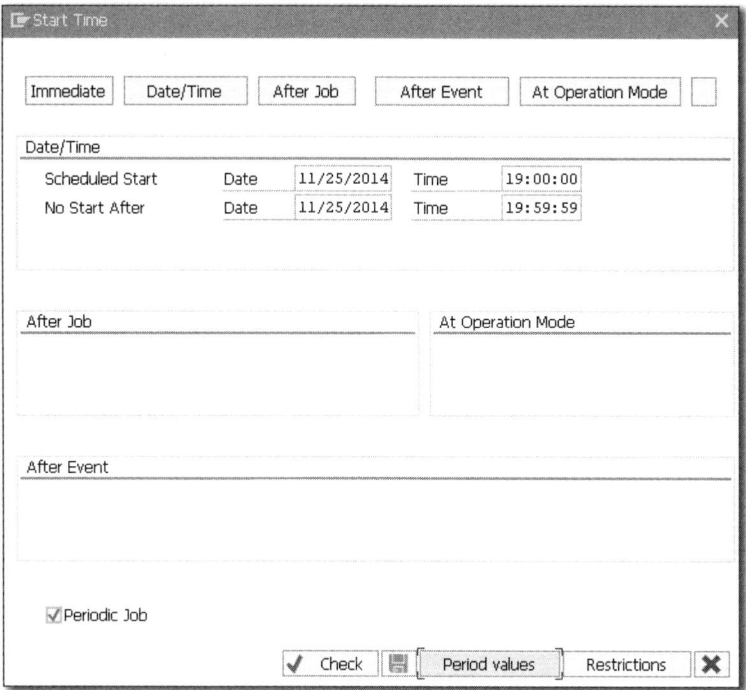

Figure 15.6 Defining the Start Time

11. Activate the Periodic Job checkbox, and click on the Period values button.
12. In the dialog box, select the required period (e.g., Daily), and click on Check. If the system doesn't output an error message, select Save (see Figure 15.7).

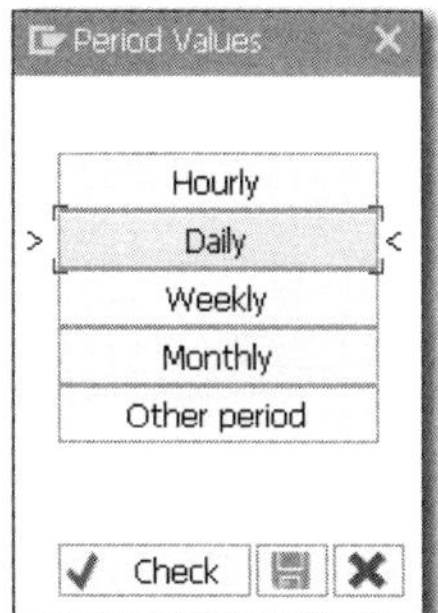

Figure 15.7 Defining the Period Values

13. Verify your entries in the START TIME screen (refer to Figure 15.6) using the CHECK button, and confirm them with SAVE [save icon]. This navigates you back to the DEFINE BACKGROUND JOB screen.
14. Again, click on SAVE. The status bar now displays a message that confirms the creation of the background job (see Figure 15.8).

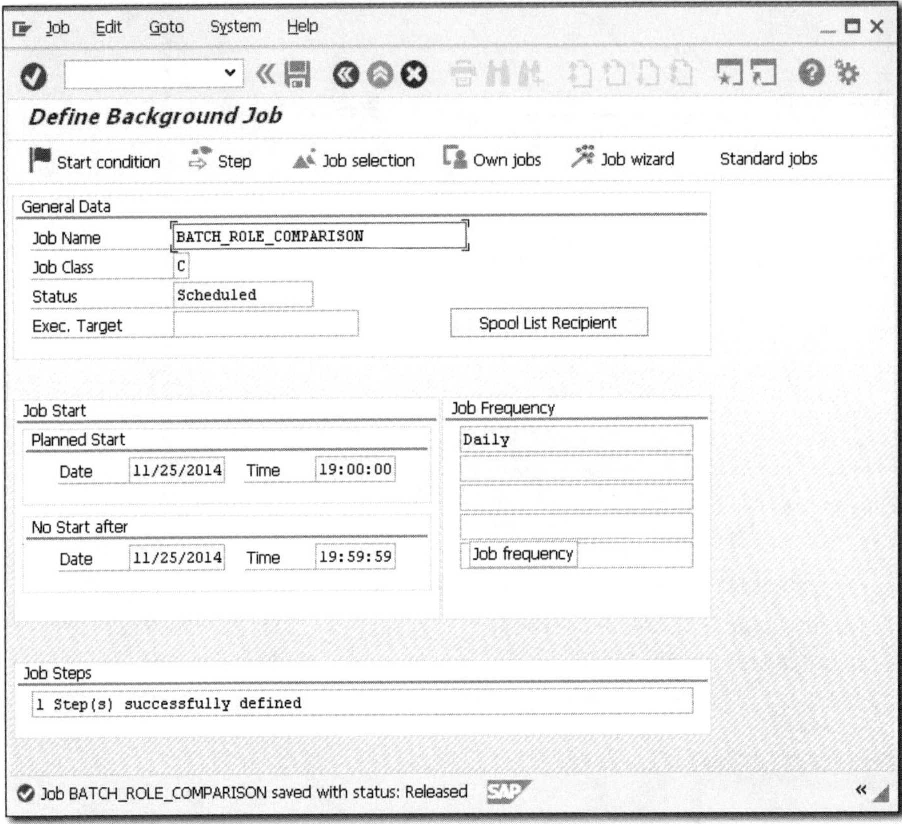

Figure 15.8 Status Message to Confirm Job Scheduling

[+]

Job Wizard

As an alternative to referring to these instructions, you can call the Job Wizard. It guides you through the individual steps of the process described.

[⚙]

SAP Central Process Scheduling

The standard means of SAP background processing provide a wide range of functions for job scheduling and monitoring. However, execution and linking of background jobs (e.g., across various systems) may reach a level of complexity that stretches the limits of these standard means. Here, a professional job scheduling tool such as *SAP Central Process Scheduling* (SAP CPS) can support you. You can deploy it to create complex job chains with advanced scheduling parameters and control and monitor them centrally. For more information, refer to the SAP help or SCN at *http://scn.sap.com/community/cps-by-redwood*.

15.2 Monitoring Background Jobs

If you execute critical jobs that are important for your business processes or for operating the system, you have to know if jobs are canceled because other processes, activities, or tasks may depend on these jobs. Follow these steps to monitor the background jobs:

1. Enter Transaction SM37 in the command field and press the [Enter] key (or select the menu option Tools • CCMS • Background Processing • Transaction SM37—Job Overview and Administration).
2. Make the following settings (see Figure 15.9):
   - In Job Name, enter the name of the background job, or use the * wildcard to view all jobs.
   - Enter the user ID of the creator of the job in User Name, or use the * wildcard to view the jobs of all users.
   - Under Job Status, activate the checkboxes for Active, Finished, and Canceled to view the jobs with these statuses.
   - Restrict the evaluation period by defining a start date in From and an end date in To in the Job Start Condition section.
   - Click on Execute.
3. In the Job Overview, check the job list for canceled or erroneous jobs (see Figure 15.10). Look for jobs that have the Canceled entry in the Status column. Monitor critical jobs in particular, for example, for material planning or payments by check (you have to know the name of the job in this case).

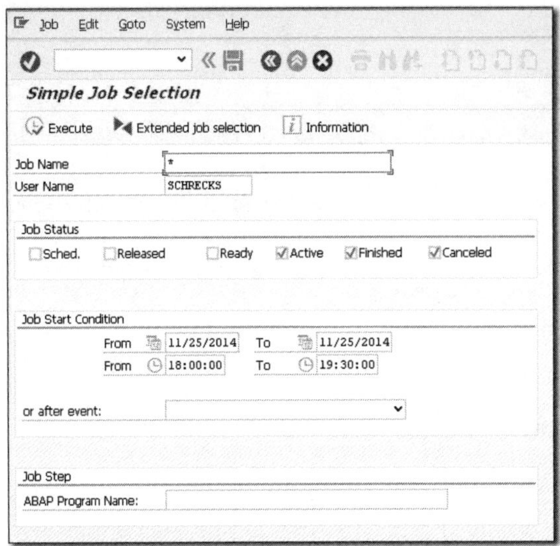

Figure 15.9 Selecting Jobs

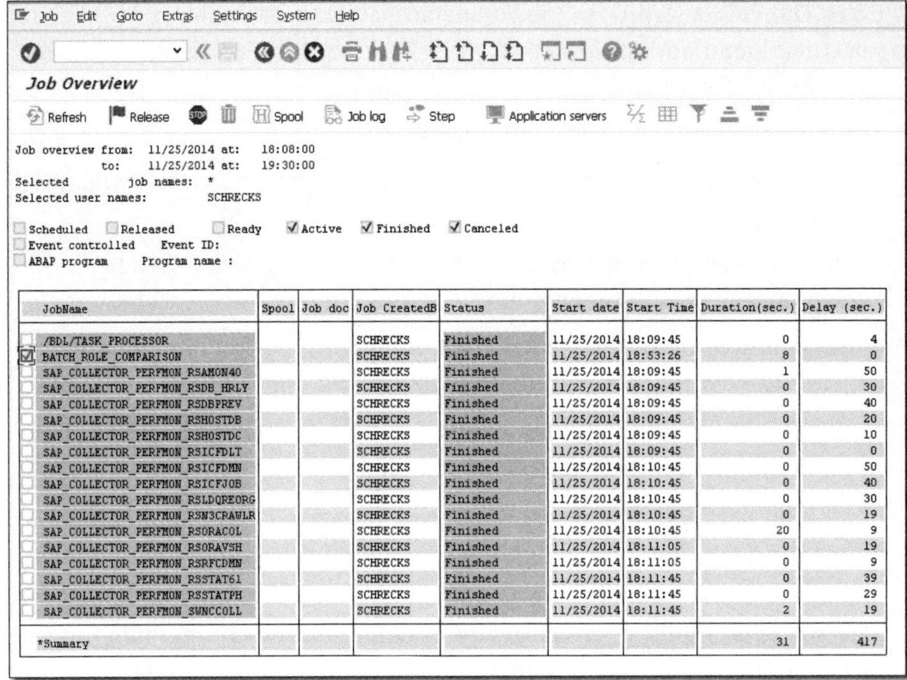

Figure 15.10 Job List

4. Double-click on a row to call the basic data of the background job (see Figure 15.11).

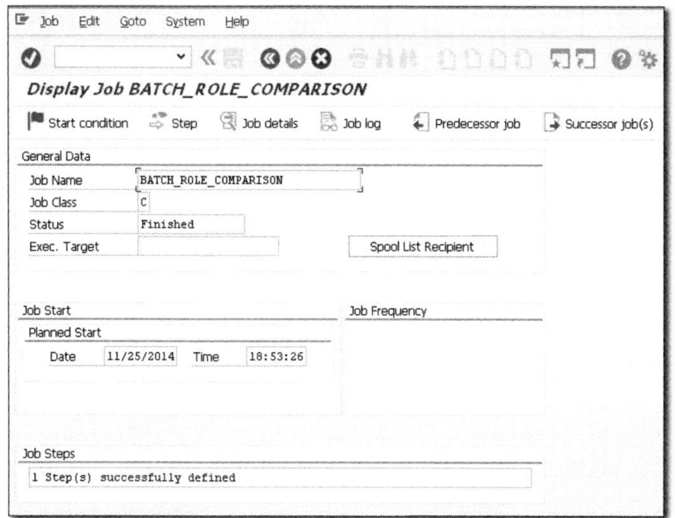

Figure 15.11 Displaying Basic Data of a Background Job

5. Click on the Job Log button to view the log (see Figure 15.12).

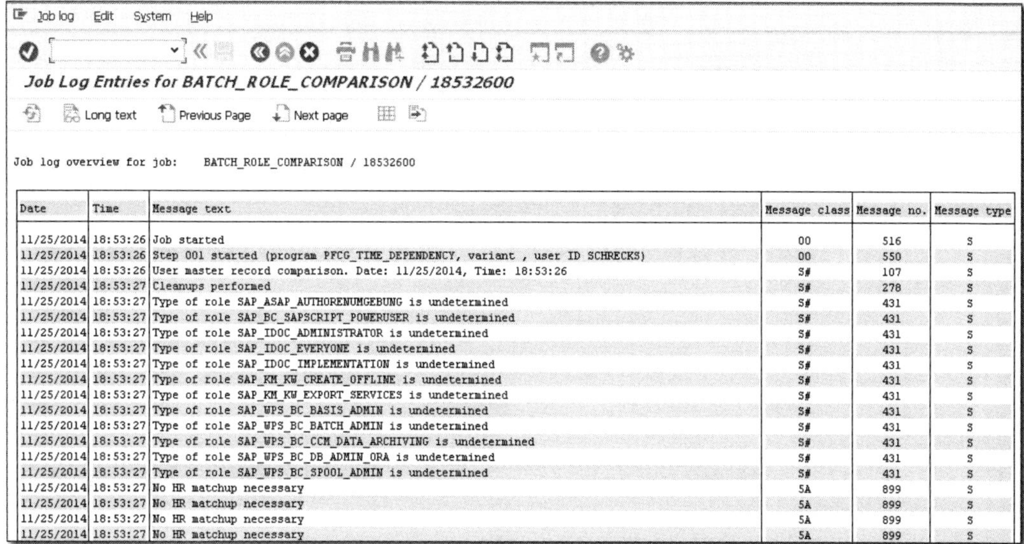

Job log overview for job: BATCH_ROLE_COMPARISON / 18532600

Date	Time	Message text	Message class	Message no.	Message type
11/25/2014	18:53:26	Job started	00	516	S
11/25/2014	18:53:26	Step 001 started (program PFCG_TIME_DEPENDENCY, variant , user ID SCHRECKS)	00	550	S
11/25/2014	18:53:26	User master record comparison. Date: 11/25/2014, Time: 18:53:26	S#	107	S
11/25/2014	18:53:27	Cleanups performed	S#	278	S
11/25/2014	18:53:27	Type of role SAP_ASAP_AUTHORENUMGEBUNG is undetermined	S#	431	S
11/25/2014	18:53:27	Type of role SAP_BC_SAPSCRIPT_POWERUSER is undetermined	S#	431	S
11/25/2014	18:53:27	Type of role SAP_IDOC_ADMINISTRATOR is undetermined	S#	431	S
11/25/2014	18:53:27	Type of role SAP_IDOC_EVERYONE is undetermined	S#	431	S
11/25/2014	18:53:27	Type of role SAP_IDOC_IMPLEMENTATION is undetermined	S#	431	S
11/25/2014	18:53:27	Type of role SAP_KM_KW_CREATE_OFFLINE is undetermined	S#	431	S
11/25/2014	18:53:27	Type of role SAP_KM_KW_EXPORT_SERVICES is undetermined	S#	431	S
11/25/2014	18:53:27	Type of role SAP_WPS_BC_BASIS_ADMIN is undetermined	S#	431	S
11/25/2014	18:53:27	Type of role SAP_WPS_BC_BATCH_ADMIN is undetermined	S#	431	S
11/25/2014	18:53:27	Type of role SAP_WPS_BC_CCM_DATA_ARCHIVING is undetermined	S#	431	S
11/25/2014	18:53:27	Type of role SAP_WPS_BC_DB_ADMIN_ORA is undetermined	S#	431	S
11/25/2014	18:53:27	Type of role SAP_WPS_BC_SPOOL_ADMIN is undetermined	S#	431	S
11/25/2014	18:53:27	No HR matchup necessary	5A	899	S
11/25/2014	18:53:27	No HR matchup necessary	5A	899	S
11/25/2014	18:53:27	No HR matchup necessary	5A	899	S
11/25/2014	18:53:27	No HR matchup necessary	5A	899	S

Figure 15.12 Displaying the Job Log

6. Use BACK to return to the JOB OVERVIEW, and check the runtimes of the jobs in the DURATION (SEC.) column. If the runtime deviates from the normal runtime, this can indicate a problem and should be analyzed. To evaluate the runtime, you have to monitor it over a long period of time and compare it to previous runs of this job.

[+]

Displaying Additional Columns

The CHANGE LAYOUT button enables you to display additional useful columns in the job overview, for example, the client in which the jobs are executed or the date and time for which the start of the job is scheduled.

15.3 Graphical Job Scheduling Monitor

The Job Scheduling Monitor is a graphical tool that supports job scheduling. It displays the individual background jobs in a diagram (see Figure 15.13). You start the Job Scheduling Monitor as follows:

1. Enter Transaction RZ01 in the command field and press the [Enter] key (or select the menu option TOOLS • CCMS • BACKGROUND PROCESSING • RZ01—JOB SCHEDULING MONITOR).

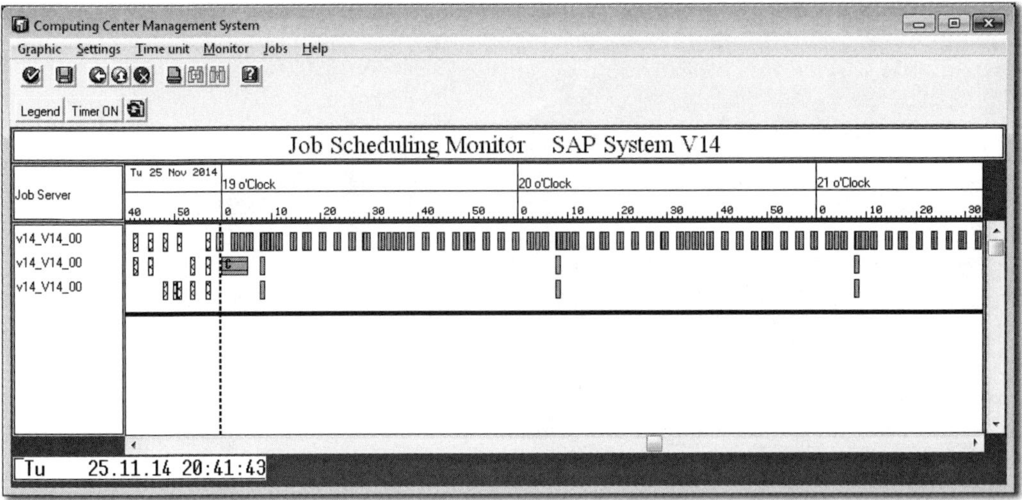

Figure 15.13 Using the Job Scheduling Monitor for Job Scheduling

2. In the menu, select TIME UNIT to change the scale.
3. To view a legend in a dialog box, click on the LEGEND button. The legend displays the colors and patterns used.
4. If you select TIMER ON, the system updates the display every three minutes.

Due to the graphical formatting of the scheduling data, the monitor is particularly well suited for the coordination of numerous background jobs.

15.4 Performance Factors for Background Jobs

Background jobs occupy a large part of the system resources. Therefore, they can have a negative effect on the online system performance. However, background jobs don't have a higher priority than dialog work processes; that is, they aren't assigned more system resources. There are various methods for optimizing system performance during the execution of background jobs. Online users benefit from these methods, and background jobs can be executed more efficiently.

To reduce the influence of background jobs on the system, you can run batch jobs on a standalone batch application instance or batch application server. For a small central instance with only 10 users, two batch jobs can already significantly impair the system performance. For small installations, it can therefore also be necessary to use additional application servers to isolate the batch processing from the central instance. The instance profile for this application server would then rather aim at background jobs than at the dialog (online) performance (e.g., five background work processes and only two dialog work processes).

Number of Available Background Processes [+]

As a rule of thumb, the number of background processes shouldn't be larger than twice the CPU number. You can determine whether your system has enough batch work processes if all processes of type BTC in the process overview (Transaction SM50; see Chapter 2, Section 2.4.3) have long CPU times. This means that the processes are used almost to their full extent, and only a little capacity is left in the system. At least one BTC process should have a very low CPU time (depending on the last system start; value <1 minute).

However, the definition of a target host can lead to problems. If you specify the target host, the system doesn't perform load balancing. So it's possible that the maximum number of batch work processes is occupied on the batch application server, but other applications aren't used at all. If you define that the job is supposed to be executed on the batch application server, you prevent it from being executed on another application server that is available. The job then waits until a batch work process on the specified batch application server is available.

When you schedule jobs, you should bear the following in mind:

- **Consider the time of the execution**
  Schedule background jobs so that they aren't executed during peak times, that is, preferably overnight or during lunch. If no users are logged on to the system, it's no problem if the system performance decreases.
- **Minimize job conflicts**
  Two background jobs that run at the same time might access the same files or even data records, which may lead to a cancellation of the jobs. You can avoid this conflict by coordinating these background jobs (e.g., two reports on due payments should not run simultaneously). For time reasons, the reports should run in succession in such cases.
- **Consider the local time for the respective users in case of global jobs**
  For example, if a resource-intensive background jobs is scheduled for 10am local time in Germany (9am GMT), this corresponds to a local time of 1am in California.
  The time is advantageous in California because it's in the middle of the night, but in Germany, the job would be executed during working time. For certain jobs, for example, backups of files at the operating system level, the execution time is very critical for the following reasons:
  - A backup of these files may require that the files aren't changed or used during the backup process because the backup fails otherwise.
  - Programs that try to change a specific file are canceled because the file is locked due to the backup process.

[+] **Background Jobs for Multiple Time Zones**

List the respective local times for all affected global locations. This way you can easily determine the local time in the affected locations when scheduling a job.

You should also define an enterprise timer (e.g., a specific server) or an enterprise time for organizations with locations in different time zones. You have several options here, for example:

- As the enterprise time, you use the time zone in which the enterprise is headquartered.
  - For SAP in Walldorf, Germany, this is CET (Central European Time)
  - For United Airlines in Chicago, Illinois, this is CST (Central Standard Time).
- UTC (Coordinated Universal Time) is used as the enterprise time, previously known as GMT (Greenwich Mean Time). This time is used by global organizations, such as airlines.

For daylight savings time, you have to consider the days at which the clocks change:

- **Beginning of daylight savings time**
  The clocks are adjusted forward one hour. Jobs that were scheduled for this hour aren't executed or are executed with a delay. Tasks that are carried out after the clock shift and that depend on a job that should have been executed in the missing hour need to be checked.
- **End of daylight saving time**
  At the end of daylight savings time, a problem occurs because an hour is "repeated." For example, if the clock is adjusted backward from 3am to 2am, the hour exists twice for the system.

You can avoid these clock shift difficulties by using UTC (GMT) as the enterprise timer.

Standard Time and Daylight Saving Time [!]

Clocks don't shift at the same time in all countries, which may result in time differences during this phase.

15.5 Summary

Background jobs are a useful alternative to dialog mode, in particular for program runs that must be executed periodically. You can run nearly all reports in the background. The SAP system offers various options for starting programs automatically in the required interval. Specifically, evaluations or reports that have a long runtime due to the amount of data that is processed should run in the background and not during peak load times of the SAP system to avoid negative effects on performance. Background processing enables you to schedule this kind of job for overnight processing, for example. You then simply have to check the results of the job runs the next morning.

In an SAP system, printing data, such as purchase orders, invoices, or similar documents, plays an important role. This chapter describes how to configure the output infrastructure of the SAP system and manage output requests.

16 Output Management

Within the SAP system, the spool system fulfills several functions that are essential for the output of data. It receives documents to be printed from the user (*spool request*), saves the data in a separate database (*TemSe*), and then generates an *output request*, which is sent platform-independently to the print system of the operating system (*host spool system*). The operating system's host spool system then transfers the print job to the printer or a similar output device. As the administrator, it's your task to manage the output devices within the SAP system and configure and monitor the SAP spool system.

16.1 Setting Up the Spool Servers

If users use the PRINT button to notify the system that they want to output a list or a screen view on a printer, the SAP system initially creates a spool request. To turn this spool request into an output request that can be forwarded to the printer, you require a *spool work process*. A spool work process, in turn, is provided by a *spool server*.

The SAP application server is usually the first spool server of your SAP system. Beyond that, you can define additional *real* or *logical* spool servers. An additional real spool server can be another physical SAP system (e.g., your QA system), which assumes the formatting of spool requests in case of bottlenecks as the *alternative server*. A logical spool server, however, isn't a separate physical device but only a mapping of a real server. You use logical servers, for example, to optimize the management of output devices by assigning a logical spool server to your printers (see Section 16.2). For example, if you transport your output devices and define logical spool servers that are identical in all systems, you don't need to switch the output servers after you've imported the printers.

[⚙]

Several Spool Work Processes

Depending on your enterprise's requirements, the spool server must manage a more or less large number of spool requests; in other words, several spool work processes are required to master the mass of accumulating spool requests. The number of spool work processes of the application server is controlled using profile parameter `rdisp/wp_no_spo`. SAP Note 108799 provides information on how many spool work processes you must provide.

The following sections describe a common scenario in which a real spool server was mapped by a logical spool server. Load balancing is set up between the various spool servers, which passes spool requests to the alternative server if the first server is overloaded. Follow these steps:

1. Enter Transaction SPAD in the command field and press the [Enter] key (or select the menu option TOOLS • CCMS • PRINT • SPAD—SPOOL ADMINISTRATION).
2. Select the DISPLAY option for the SPOOL SERVERS in the DEVICES/SERVERS tab (see Figure 16.1).

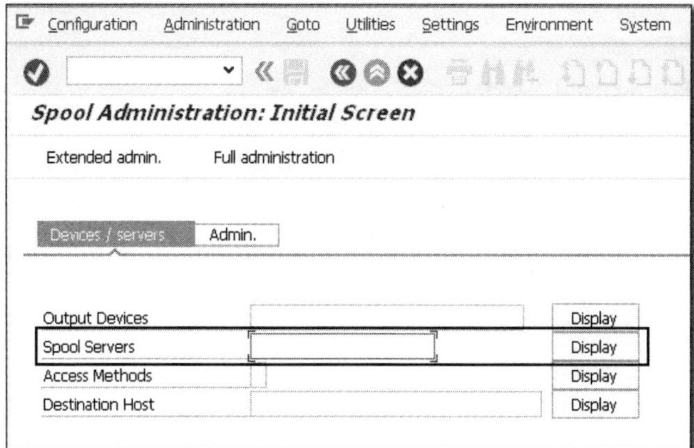

Figure 16.1 Displaying Spool Servers

3. The system displays the spool servers that are currently defined in the system (see Figure 16.2). To change the settings of an existing server or create a new spool server, you must first switch to change mode. To do so, click on CHANGE ✎.

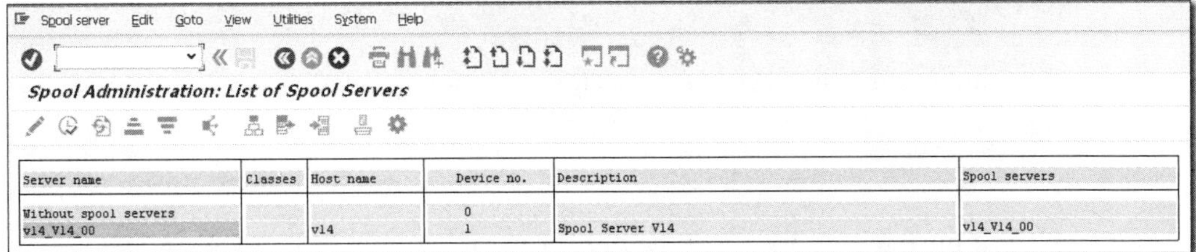

Figure 16.2 List of Spool Servers Defined in the System

4. Create a new *logical* spool server by clicking on the CREATE button (see Figure 16.3).

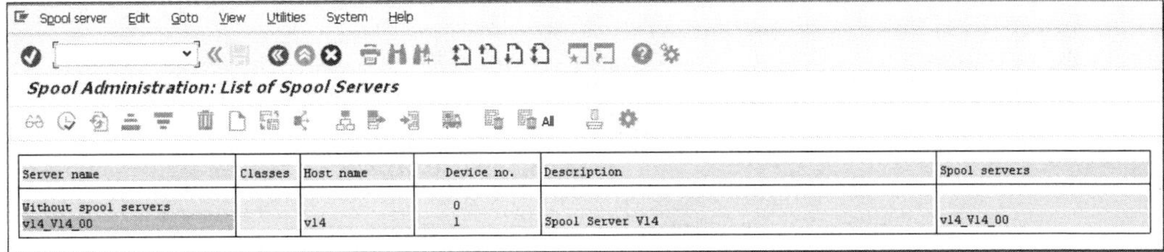

Figure 16.3 Creating a New Logical Spool Server

5. Enter a SERVER NAME and a DESCRIPTION, and activate the LOGICAL SERVER checkbox (see Figure 16.4). Enter a real spool server in the MAPPING field. Click on SAVE to save your entries.

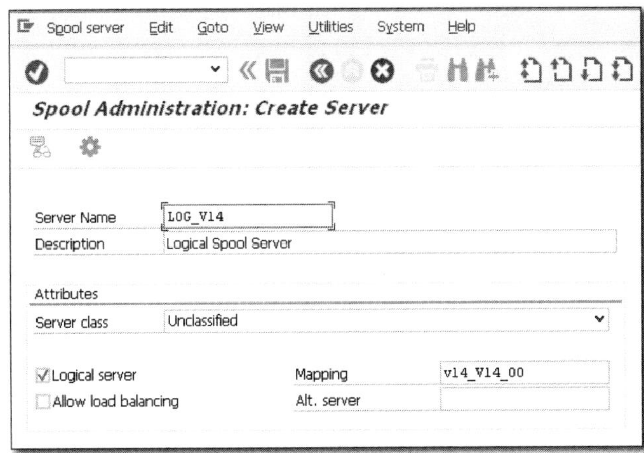

Figure 16.4 Configuring a Logical Server

[+]

Server Class

The entry in the SERVER CLASS field mainly serves informational purposes and should primarily ensure higher clarity. You can leave the entry as UNCLASSIFIED if you don't want to use the server classes.

6. Click on BACK to return to the list of spool servers (see Figure 16.5). As a result, you now have a real spool server and also another logical server that maps the real server.

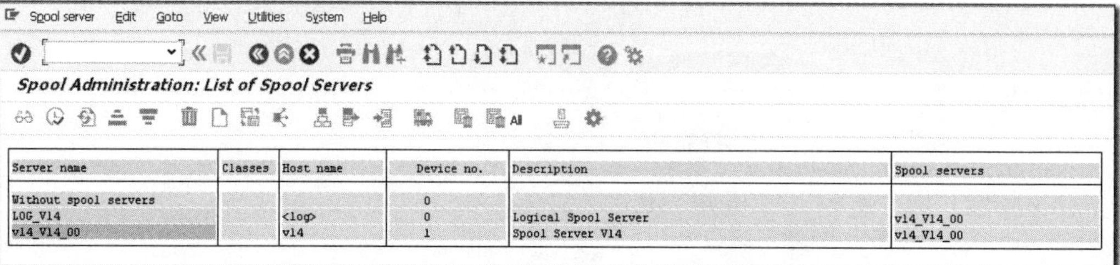

Figure 16.5 Display of Spool Servers

7. To define load balancing as an example, position the cursor on the first logical server, and then click on CHOOSE to reopen the detail view. Now activate the ALLOW LOAD BALANCING checkbox, and enter the name of the logical server in the ALT. SERVER field (see Figure 16.6). Save your entries.

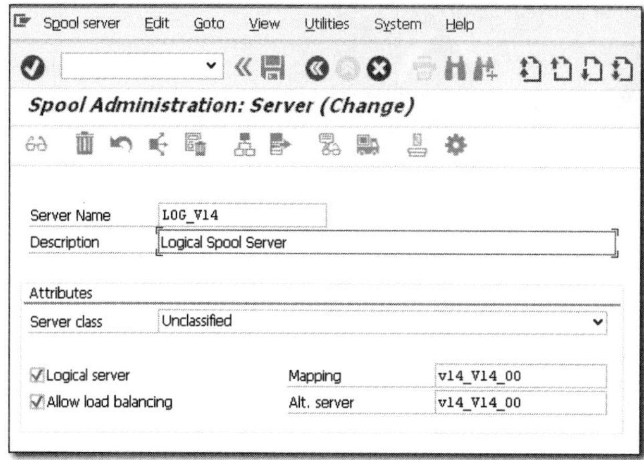

Figure 16.6 Defining Load Balancing

If all spool work process of the logical server `LOG_V14` should be fully utilized, the system will now pass the spool requests to the real spool server `v14_V14_00`. We should mention that we made up this scenario because the logical server `LOG_V14` only maps the real server `v14_V14_00`. Load balancing can only be set up meaningfully in a system landscape with various servers and instances.

16.2 Setting Up Printers

Before you can print from the SAP system, you must first define the output device, that is, the physical printer. This applies to network printers as well as to local devices connected to your PC.

16.2.1 Configuring Network Printers

To ensure that the print coupling between the SAP system and the operating system works, you must first set up the network printer at the operating system level. Perform the following steps before setting up a printer:

1. Set up the printer at the operating system level.
2. Write down the network name of the printer (e.g., `FIN3` or `\ACCOUNTING\ACCOUNT2`, *not* the printer type such as OKI C9500).
3. Write down the printer type. The printer type is a combination of the manufacturer name and the printer model (e.g., HP OKI C9500).

To set up the printer in the SAP system, follow these steps:

1. Call Transaction SPAD.
2. Select the DISPLAY option for the OUTPUT DEVICES in the DEVICES/SERVERS tab (see Figure 16.7).
3. The system displays the printers that are currently available in the system (see Figure 16.8). To change the settings of an existing server or create a new printer, click on CHANGE .

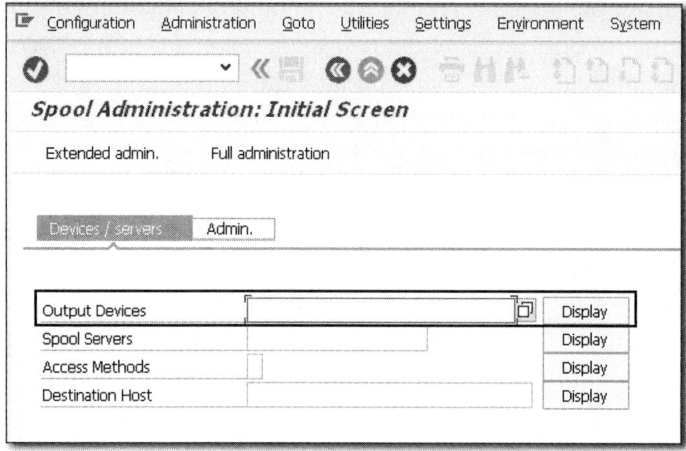

Figure 16.7 Displaying Output Devices

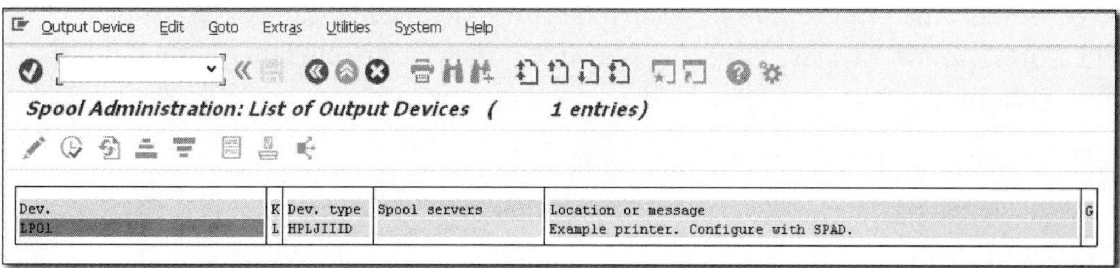

Figure 16.8 Changing the Output Device

4. Create a new printer by clicking on the CREATE button . The system displays the SPOOLER ADMINISTRATION: CREATE OUTPUT DEVICE view. Make the following settings (see Figure 16.9):
   - Enter the name of the printer, with which the printer is supposed to be managed in the SAP system, in the OUTPUT DEVICE field in the header data.
   - If required, enter a SHORT NAME. If you don't make any entries here, the system generates the short name.
   - Select the printer model from the DEVICE TYPE dropdown list in the DEVICE-ATTRIBUTES tab.
   - Define a SPOOL SERVER.

- Select an appropriate Device Class.
- Specify further information on the Model and Location of the printer as required.

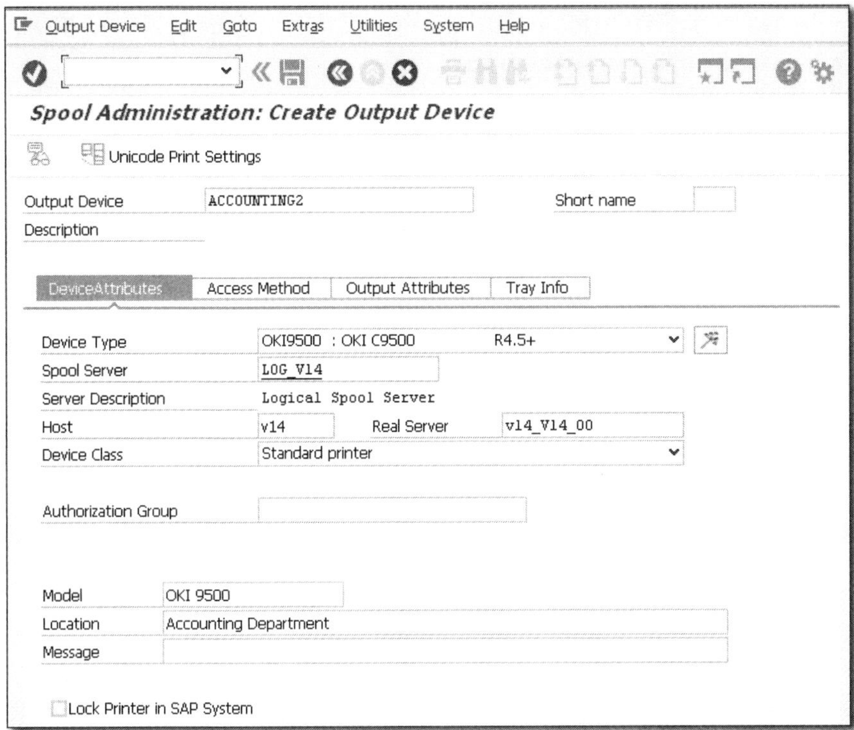

Figure 16.9 Creating a New Output Device

Model and Location [+]

The Model and Location fields are essential for the administration of output devices and facilitate the assignment of SAP printers to physical devices. Don't forget to update the Location field if you move the printer to another location.

5. Go to the Access Method tab (see Figure 16.10). Perform the following:
   - Select a Host Spool Access Method. The access method defines how the SAP spool system forwards the print data to the operating system's spool system. The access method depends on the operating system on which the

spool server runs (e.g., UNIX) and to which operating system the printer is connected (e.g., Microsoft Windows for desktop printers). Ask the administrator who is responsible for the network printers if you're unsure about the access method.

- In the HOST PRINTER field, enter the network name of the printer as it was defined at the operating system level.
- In the DESTINATION HOST field, enter the PC or operating system print server to which the printer is connected.

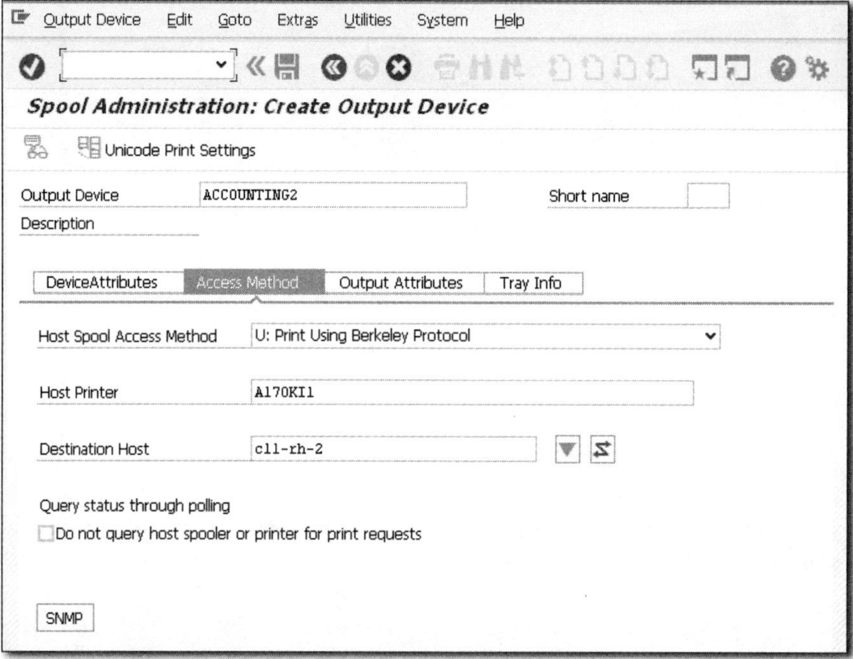

Figure 16.10 Configuring the Access Method

6. Depending on the access method selected, you can check your entries on the host spool access by clicking on CHECK CONNECTION. (In our example, this option is available after saving only.) If you check the connection, the system informs you whether the host spool system is available. Confirm the dialog window (see Figure 16.11).

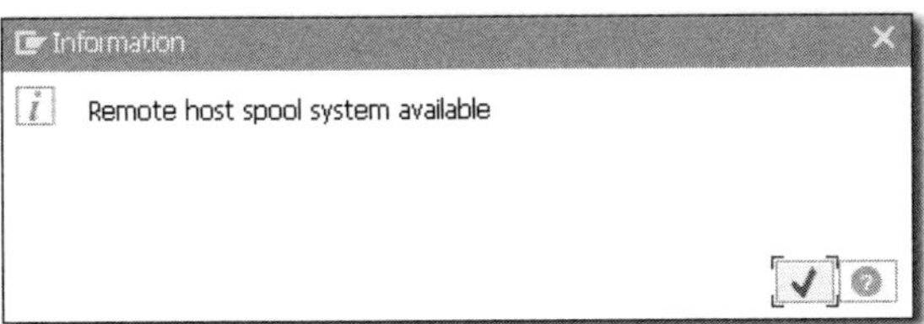

Figure 16.11 Testing the Host Spool Connection

7. Select the Output Attributes tab. Here, you can optionally maintain other settings for the printer, for instance, whether a cover page is to be printed (see Figure 16.12).

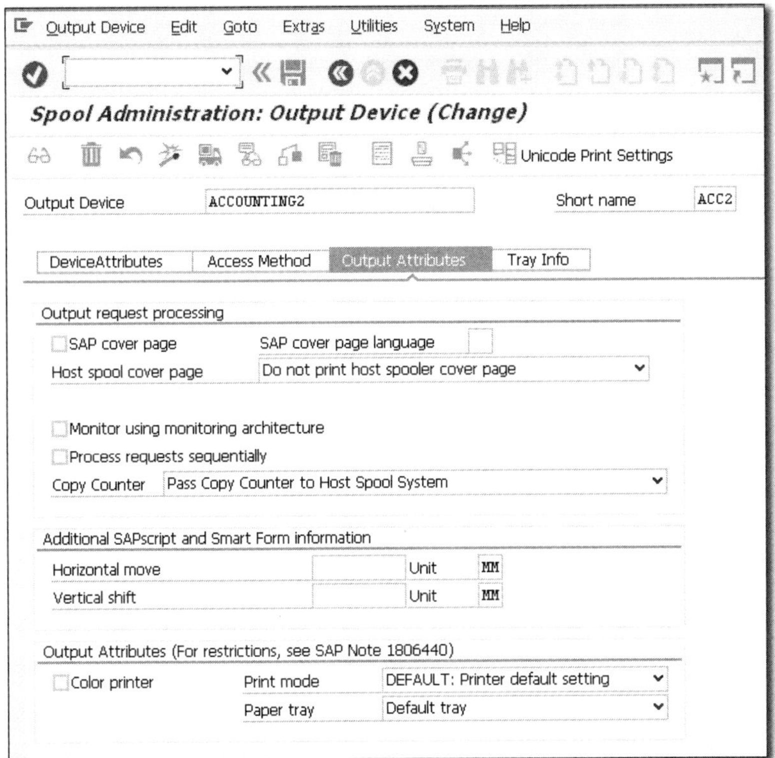

Figure 16.12 Maintaining Output Attributes

8. Open the Tray Info tab, and maintain the page formats of the paper trays if required (see Figure 16.13). After you've made all entries, click on Save.

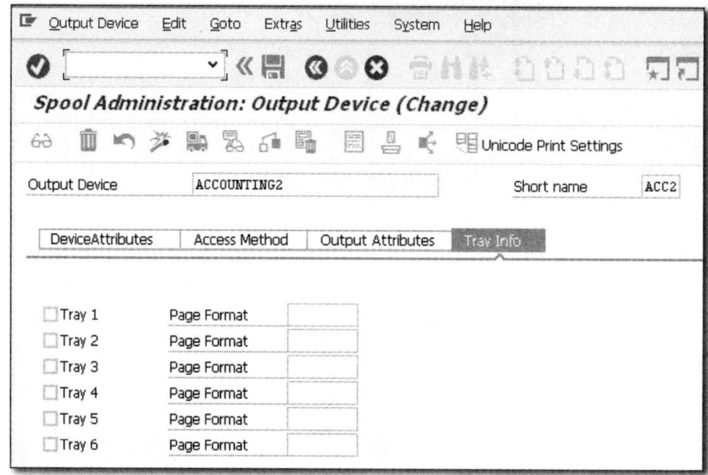

Figure 16.13 Setting the Trays

9. Provided that you haven't specified a short name yourself, a dialog window opens where you can generate a short name for the printer (see Figure 16.14). Click on YES. The dialog window closes automatically.

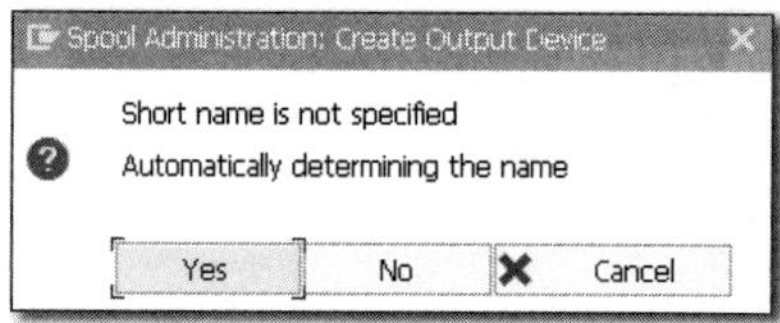

Figure 16.14 Confirming an Automatically Generated Short Name

10. Click on BACK to return to the list of output devices. The new printer is now displayed in the printer list (see Figure 16.15).

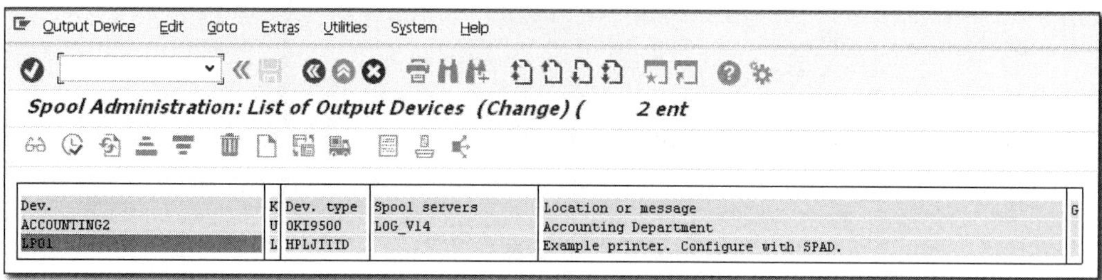

Figure 16.15 Updated List of Output Devices

11. To test the printer, select the OUTPUT DEVICE • PRINT THIS LIST option in the menu bar, and specify the newly created printer as the OUTPUT DEVICE in the PRINT SCREEN LIST dialog window (see Figure 16.16). Click on CONTINUE ✓. Proceed as described in Section 16.3 to check the result of the print process.

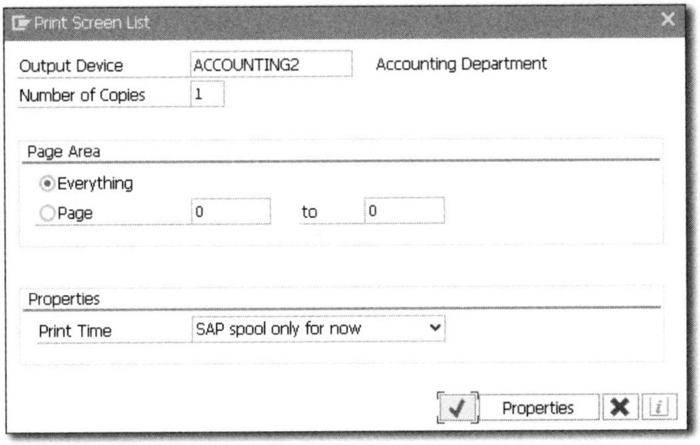

Figure 16.16 Testing Printers

The network printer has been set up and can now be used.

16.2.2 Setting Up Frontend Printers

It's possible that not all printers of your enterprise are network-compatible but are partly connected via USB to a PC, for example. You can also print with these devices from the SAP system.

Set up a frontend printer for this purpose. The following example assumes that the Windows operating system is used on the desktop PCs:

1. Implement steps 1 to 3 as described in Section 16.2.1.
2. Create a new printer by clicking on the CREATE button (see Figure 16.17).
   - Enter a name for the printer (e.g., "LOCL") for the local default printer in the header data in the OUTPUT DEVICE field.
   - In this example, enter "LOCL" in the SHORT NAME field.
   - Select the SAPWIN entry from the DEVICE TYPE dropdown list in the DEVICE-ATTRIBUTES tab.

- Select an appropriate DEVICE CLASS, for instance, STANDARD PRINTER.
- If required, define a general description of the device in the MESSAGE field.

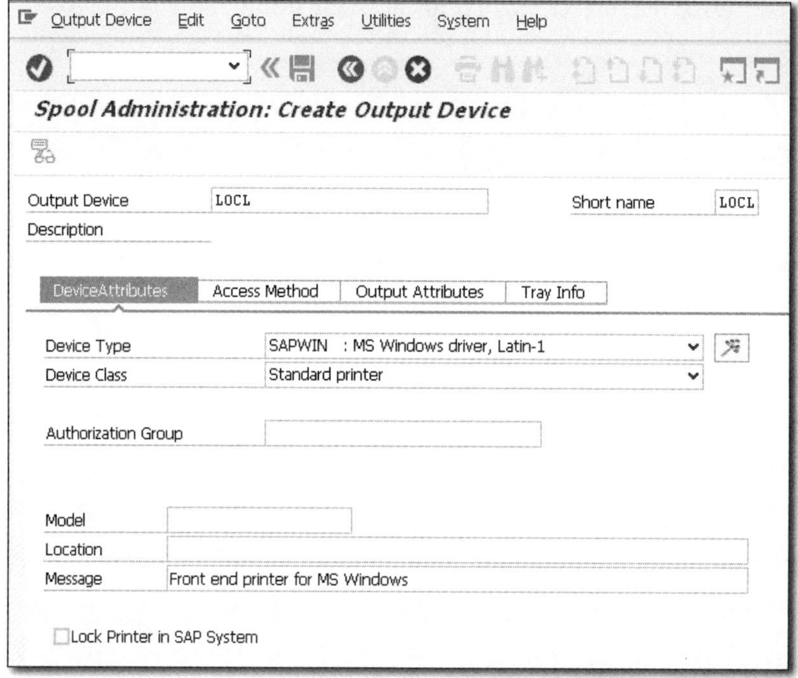

Figure 16.17 Creating a New Front end Printer

3. Go to the ACCESS METHOD tab (see Figure 16.18).
   - In the HOST SPOOL ACCESS METHOD field, select F: PRINTING ON FRONT END DEVICE.
   - Enter the "__DEFAULT" value in the HOST PRINTER field.

[⚙]

Access Methods F and G

The access method F works with the transfer program SAPlpd, which is installed with SAP GUI on PCs (see Chapter 5). You shouldn't use access method G because it's no longer supported by SAP. SAP Note 128105 provides further information on frontend printing.

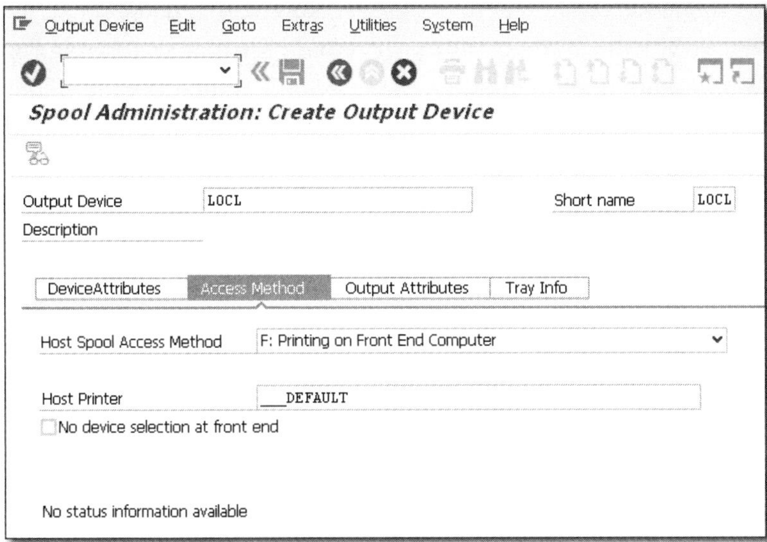

Figure 16.18 Configuring the Access Method

Host Printer "__DEFAULT"

[+]

By entering "__DEFAULT", the system addresses the output device which is defined as the default printer in the Windows operating system of the desktop computer.

4. Leave the default settings in the OUTPUT ATTRIBUTES and TRAY INFO tabs unchanged.
5. Choose SAVE, and click on BACK to return to the list of output devices. The new printer (e.g., LOCL) is included in the printer list (see Figure 16.19).

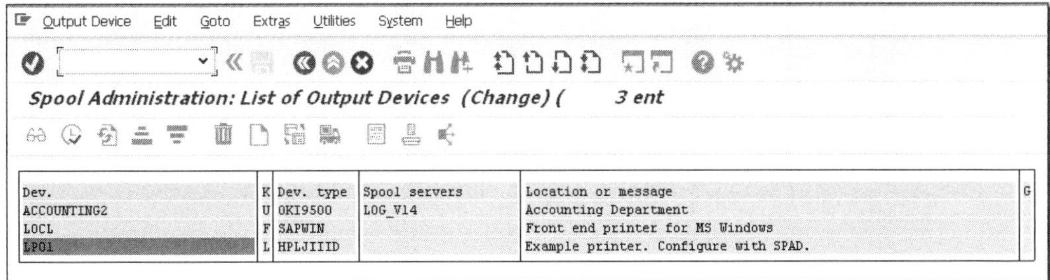

Figure 16.19 Updated List of Output Devices

6. To test the printer, select the OUTPUT DEVICE • PRINT THIS LIST option in the menu bar, and specify the newly created printer as the OUTPUT DEVICE (see Figure 16.20). If you set HOST SPOOL ACCESS METHOD F, the system determines the default printer of the PC when printing and enters it in the WINDOWS DEVICE field. Click on CONTINUE ✓.

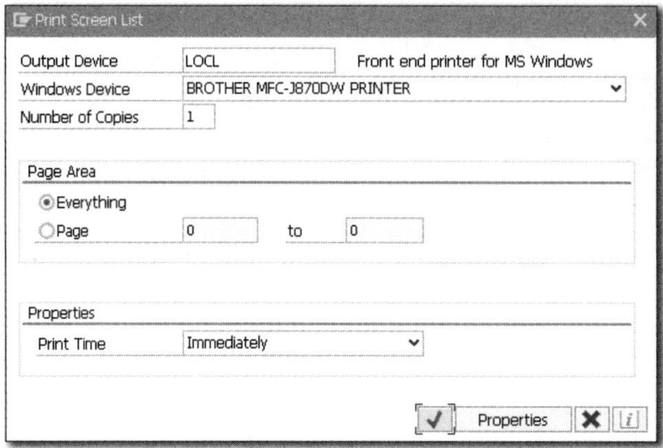

Figure 16.20 Testing a New Frontend Printer

You've now set up the Windows standard printer in the SAP system. You can use this procedure particularly if you don't use any network printer but a USB printer, for example. In print dialog windows, you can now select the printer as device LOCL.

16.2.3 Transporting Output Devices

If you operate more than one SAP system in your enterprise and if printing on physical printers is supposed to be possible from various systems, you don't have to redefine the output devices in each SAP system. For this purpose, you can use the option of transporting already configured printers.

1. Call Transaction SPAD.
2. Select the DISPLAY option for the OUTPUT DEVICES in the DEVICES/SERVERS tab.
3. Switch to change mode using the CHANGE button. Now position your cursor on a printer, and choose TRANSPORT to transport an individual device. If you want to transfer the entire list of output devices, select EDIT • TRANSPORT • TRANSPORT ALL (see Figure 16.21).

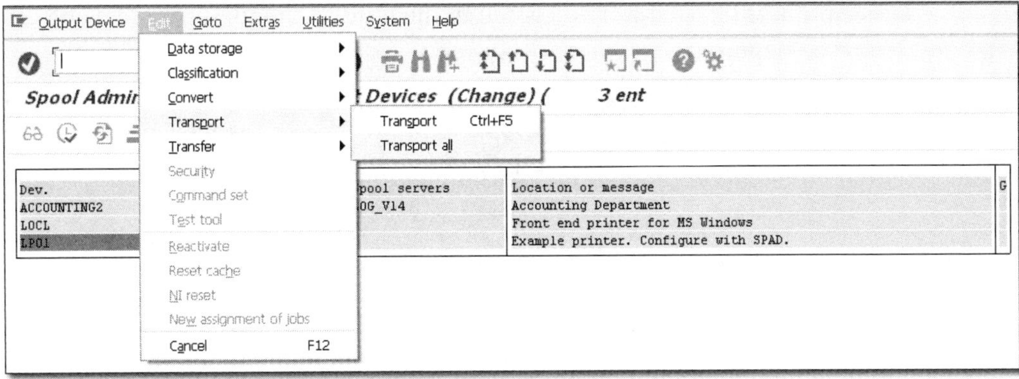

Figure 16.21 Transporting a New Output Device

4. A dialog window opens (see Figure 16.22) with the message that you need to process the printers later on in the target system. This message refers to the spool server defined in the output devices and can be ignored if you use logical spool servers that are defined identically in all systems (see also Section 16.1). Confirm with CONTINUE ✓.

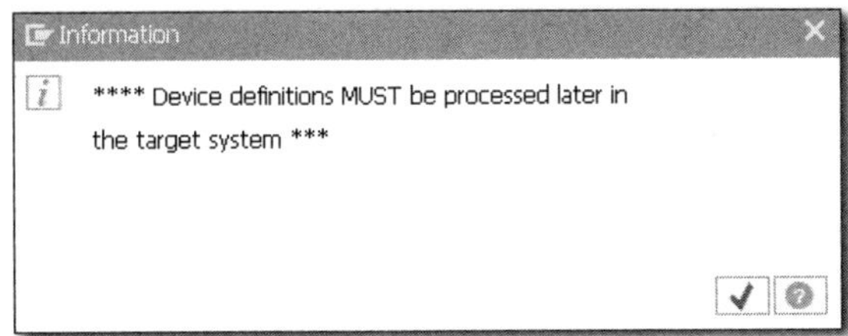

Figure 16.22 Confirming the Transport

5. In the next dialog window (see Figure 16.23), use the input help to select a workbench transport request, or create a new request. Click on CONTINUE ✓.

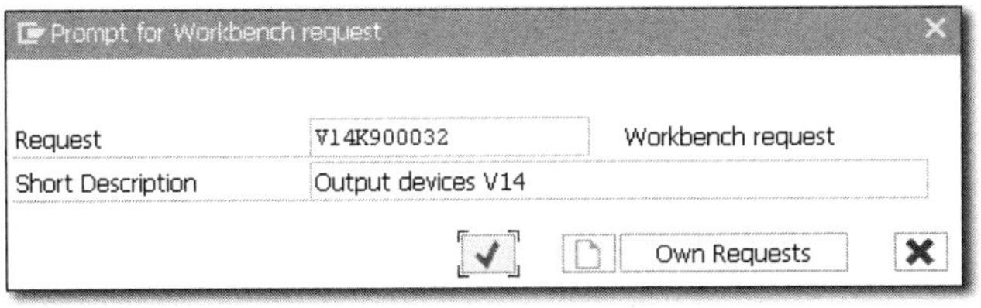

Prompt for Workbench request

Request V14K900032 Workbench request

Short Description Output devices V14

Own Requests

Figure 16.23 Selecting the Workbench Transport Request

6. The printers selected were recorded in the transport request specified and can now be imported into other SAP systems (see Chapter 17).

[+] **Transporting Spool Servers**

Spool servers can be transported similarly.

16.3 Outputting Data

The SAP system distinguishes two different types of requests: spool requests and output requests. Whenever you click on the PRINT icon, the system initially creates a spool request. The spool request includes the document to be printed; the data of this document is stored in the TemSe database. The spool request and the TemSe data are then used as the basis to create an output request, which now also includes attributes such as the target printer and the number of copies to be printed.

To print, follow these steps:

1. Click on the PRINT icon in any view or list. The PRINT SCREEN LIST dialog window appears (see Figure 16.24) where you're prompted to specify a printer. Depending on the spool control fixed values defined in your user master record, a printer is already displayed in the OUTPUT DEVICE field. Call the details for the spool request by selecting the PROPERTIES button.

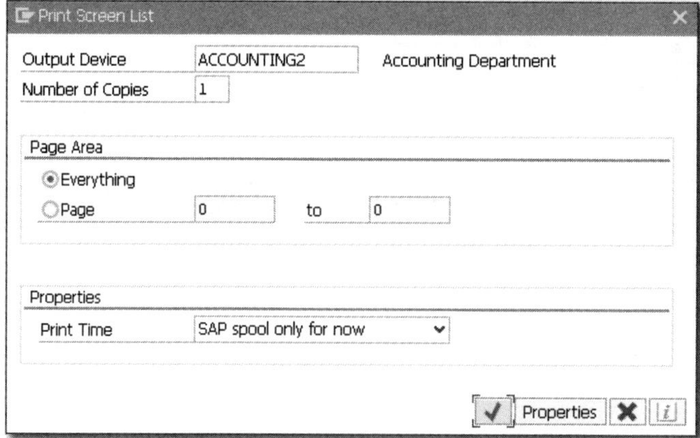

Figure 16.24 Print Menu

[+]

Different Print Menu Layouts

The layout of the dialog window may vary depending on what you want to print. For example, if you print authorization roles, you can set the print properties already in the dialog window; for screen lists, the detailed settings can be found via the PROPERTIES button.

2. You can edit the properties of the spool request (see Figure 16.25). For example, you can select the priority, print a cover sheet, or specify the deletion time for the request. The presettings are mainly determined from the print configuration.

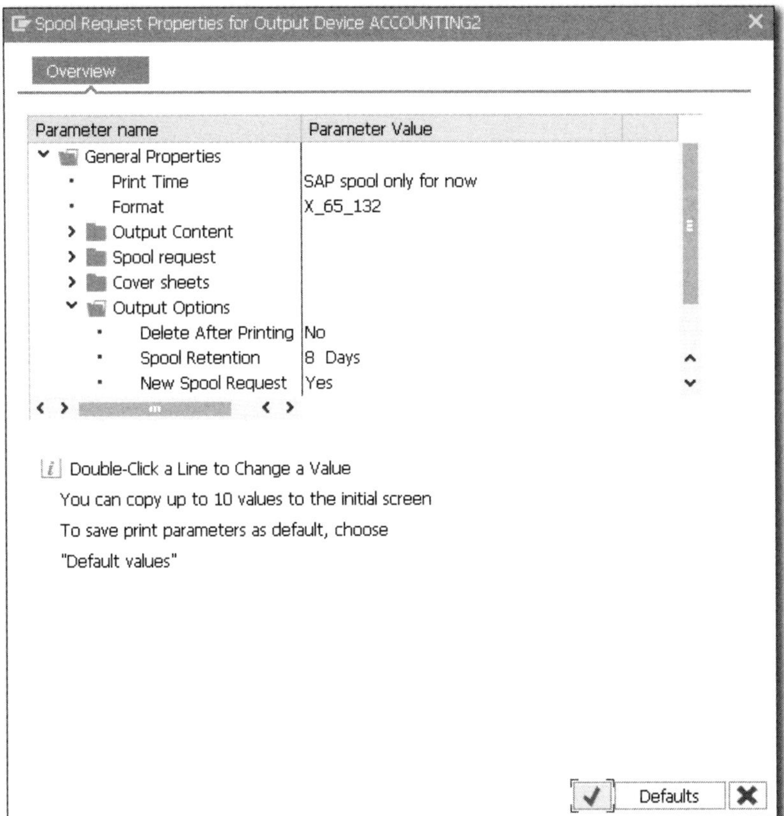

Figure 16.25 Editing the Properties of the Spool Request

[!]

Time of Printing

Particularly note the settings for the PRINT TIME option, which specifies when an output request is generated from the spool request. The following times of print are possible:

- SAP SPOOL ONLY FOR NOW
  Only a spool request is created. You must create the output request manually via Transaction SP01 (see Section 16.4). This setting is recommended for comprehensive print requests whose content you want to check prior to output.
- PRINT IMMEDIATELY
  After you've created a spool request, the system immediately creates an output request that is sent to the printer. This is the typical option for printing small lists and screen views.
- PRINT LATER
  With this setting, you specify the date and time when an output request is generated from a spool request and is sent to the printer. Use this time of print, for example, if you want to output a spool request at night, which you've created during the day.

3. When you're done, click on CONTINUE ✓ to return to the previous screen.
4. Start the print process via CONTINUE ✓ in the PRINT SCREEN LIST screen. A message in the lower part of the screen informs you about the number under which the spool request was saved (see Figure 16.26).

Spool request (number 0000005303) created without immediate output

Figure 16.26 Spool Request Number

A spool request has been generated that contains your print data. You can now check it and print it.

16.4 Output Control

Using the output control, you can check the content of spool requests, initiate the creation of output requests, and monitor the print process. Transaction SP01 provides you with a wide range of options for data output management and problem analysis.

1. Enter Transaction SP01 in the command field and press the Enter key (or select the menu option TOOLS • CCMS • SPOOL • SP01—OUTPUT CONTROLLER).
2. In the SPOOL REQUESTS tab (see Figure 16.27), modify the restrictions for your search, and then click on EXECUTE.

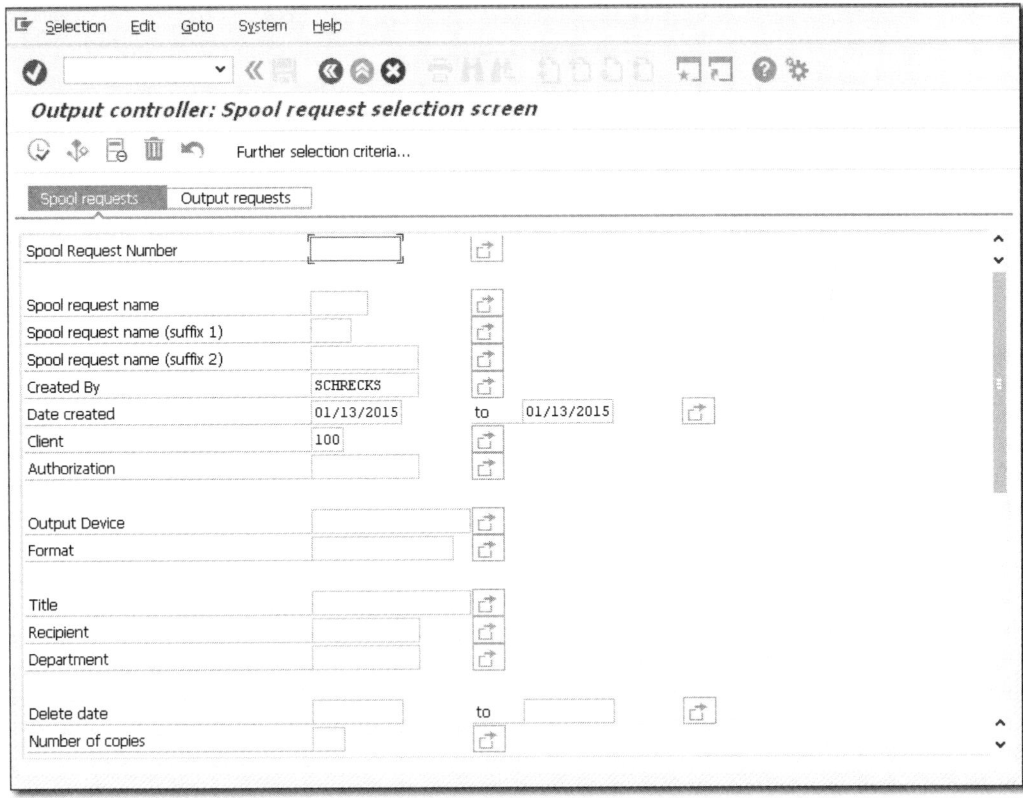

Figure 16.27 Defining the Search Criteria

3. The STATUS column indicates that the list of this example has a completed (COMPL.), failed (WAITING), and an unprocessed (-) spool request (see Figure 16.28). We'll examine the error later. Let's first take a close look at the open spool request (-), that is, the spool request for which no value is displayed in the STATUS column. No output request has yet been created for this spool request; in other words, it hasn't been printed yet.

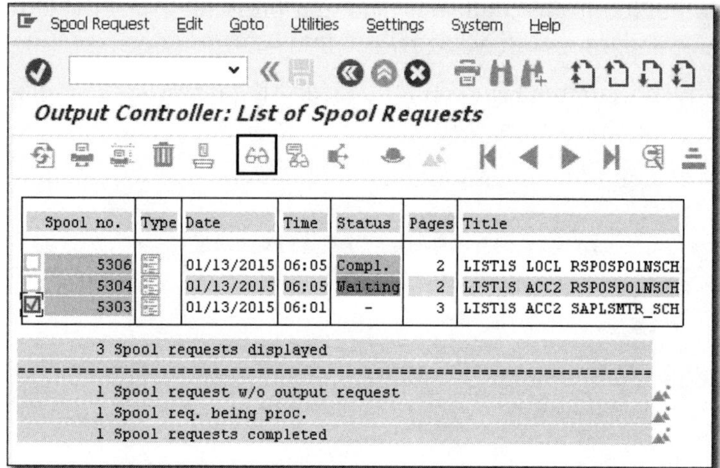

Figure 16.28 List of Spool Requests

To have the system display the content of a spool request, select a spool request, and click on Display Contents.

4. The content of the spool request is displayed (in Figure 16.29 it's an overview list of the printers that exist in the system). These data are now available for printing. Click on Back to return to the overview of spool requests.

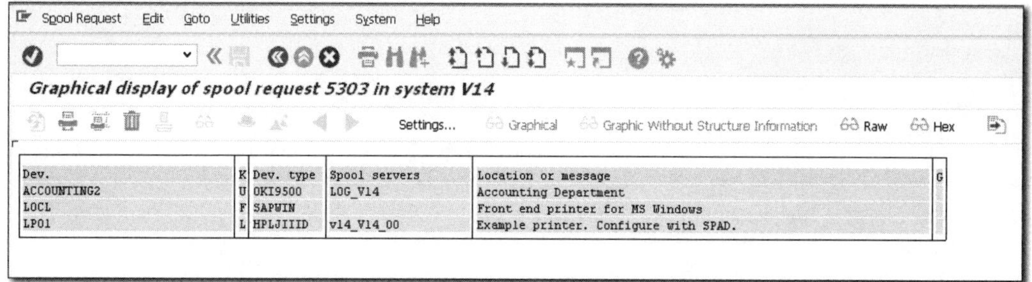

Figure 16.29 Content of the Spool Request

5. Via the Request Attributes button, you can call the request's print settings (refer to Figure 16.28).

6. Here you can view the technical data of the spool request, for instance, which user created it, the printer on which it's supposed to be printed, and when it's scheduled for deletion (see Figure 16.30). Choose BACK to exit the view.

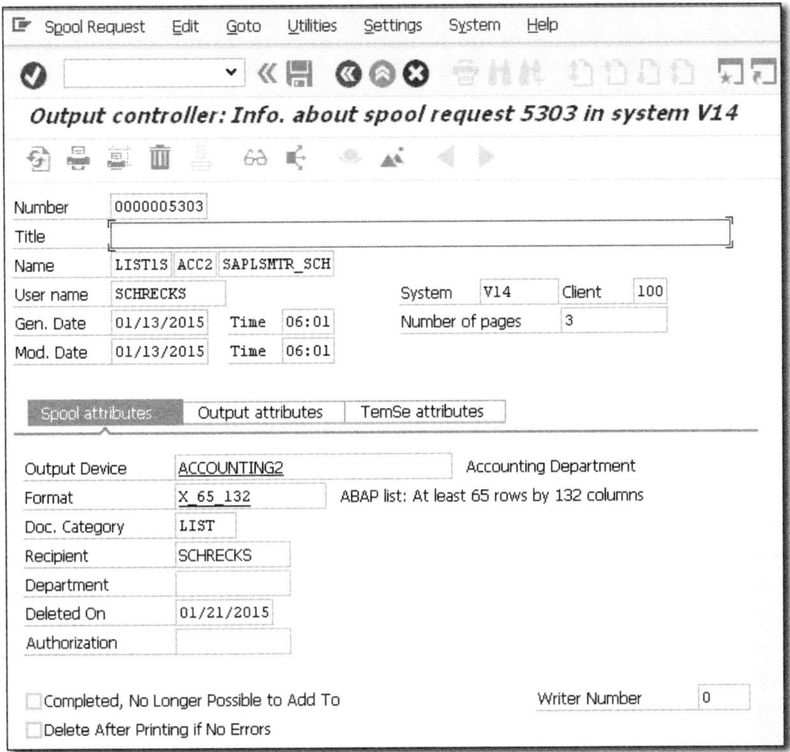

Figure 16.30 Technical Data for the Spool Request

7. After you've exited the request information view, you return to the initial list of spool requests (see Figure 16.28). Next, you print the open spool request. Select PRINT DIRECTLY to send the print request to the printer.

8. The system displays a message that an output request has been created (see Figure 16.31). Simultaneously, the entry in the STATUS column changes to WAITING. The spool request has been transferred to the spool system and now waits for the output request processing.

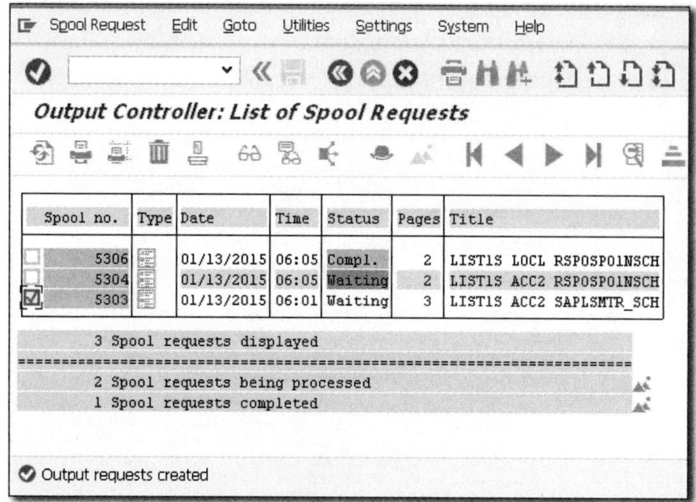

Figure 16.31 Confirmation of the Output Request in the Status Bar

9. Click on the REFRESH button to track the status change of the request.
10. When processing the spool request, the status will change to BEING PROCESSED (not shown here). Refresh the display several times. If the status changes to COMPLETED, the system has successfully generated your output request and transferred it to the host spool system (see Figure 16.32).

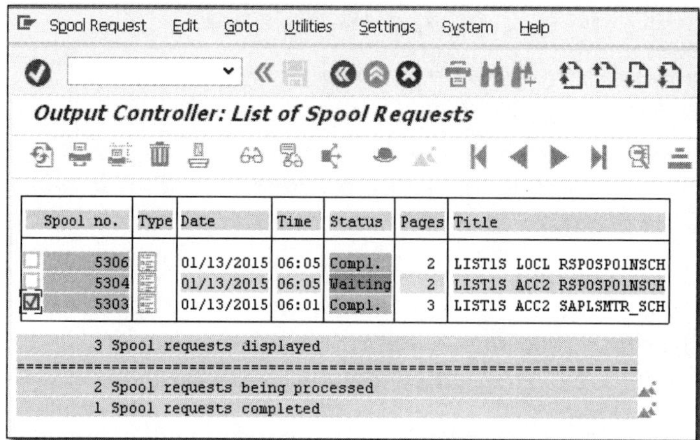

Figure 16.32 Tracking the Status of the Spool Request

11. Now, let's discuss troubleshooting. Search for a spool request for which an error is shown in the STATUS column (ERROR or—as shown in Figure 16.32—WAITING status, displayed in red), and select the checkmark in the SPOOL NO. column.
12. Double-click on the entry in the STATUS column to go to the overview of output requests. Check the error by selecting the OUTPUT REQUEST STATUS button (see Figure 16.33).

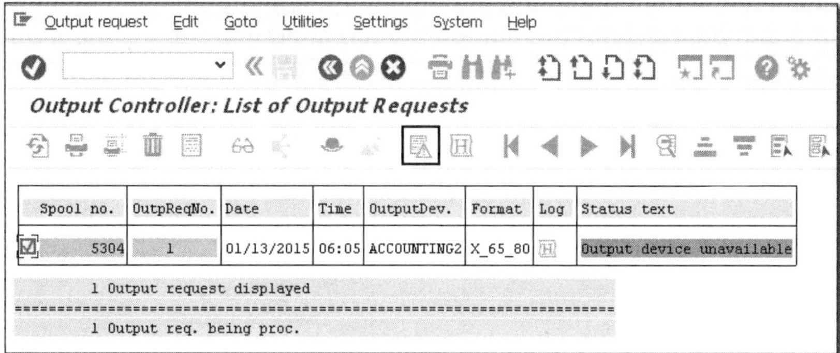

Figure 16.33 Querying the Status of the Output Request

13. A dialog window opens containing information on the print problem (see Figure 16.34). Use the OUTPUT REQUEST LOG button (refer to Figure 16.33) to display the SAP SPOOL ERROR LOG.

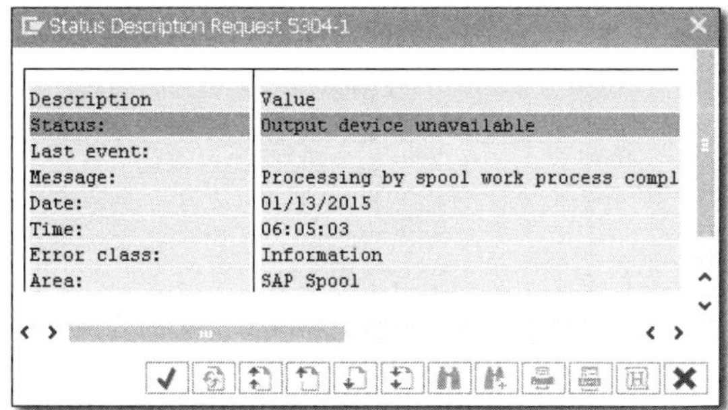

Figure 16.34 Status Details of an Output Request

14. Analyze the information in the log, and remedy the cause of error. In the example shown in Figure 16.35, there is a problem with the printer service on the destination host.

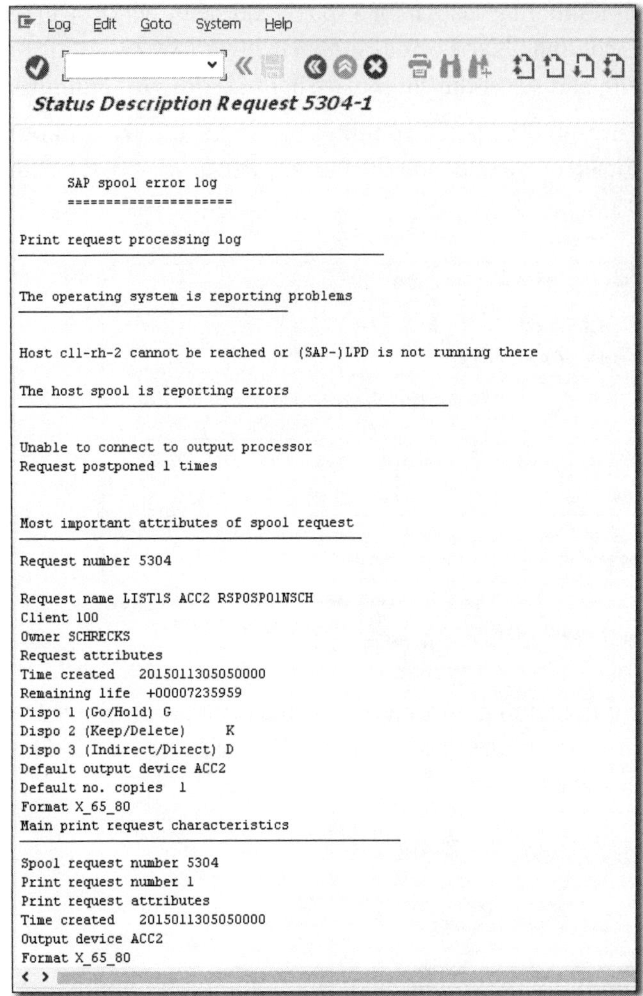
Log Edit Goto System Help

Status Description Request 5304-1

SAP spool error log
=====================

Print request processing log

The operating system is reporting problems

Host c11-rh-2 cannot be reached or (SAP-)LPD is not running there

The host spool is reporting errors

Unable to connect to output processor
Request postponed 1 times

Most important attributes of spool request

Request number 5304

Request name LIST1S ACC2 RSPOSP01NSCH
Client 100
Owner SCHRECKS
Request attributes
Time created 2015011305050000
Remaining life +00007235959
Dispo 1 (Go/Hold) G
Dispo 2 (Keep/Delete) K
Dispo 3 (Indirect/Direct) D
Default output device ACC2
Default no. copies 1
Format X_65_80
Main print request characteristics

Spool request number 5304
Print request number 1
Print request attributes
Time created 2015011305050000
Output device ACC2
Format X_65_80

Figure 16.35 Analyzing the SAP Spool Error Log

15. Click on BACK to return to the dialog window of Figure 16.34, and then close it with CONTINUE to return to the list view. Restart the output by clicking on PRINT DIRECTLY. Check the printout and the status change of the new output request using the REFRESH button (see Figure 16.36).

16. If the system was able to process the output request successfully (COMPLETED status), use BACK to return to the overview of spool requests. There, the status display for the spool request that has just been processed has changed yet

again: Spool requests with several output requests, for which errors occurred partly, are indicated with value <F5> in the STATUS column (see Figure 16.37, corresponds to the keyboard shortcut for the OUTPUT REQUESTS button).

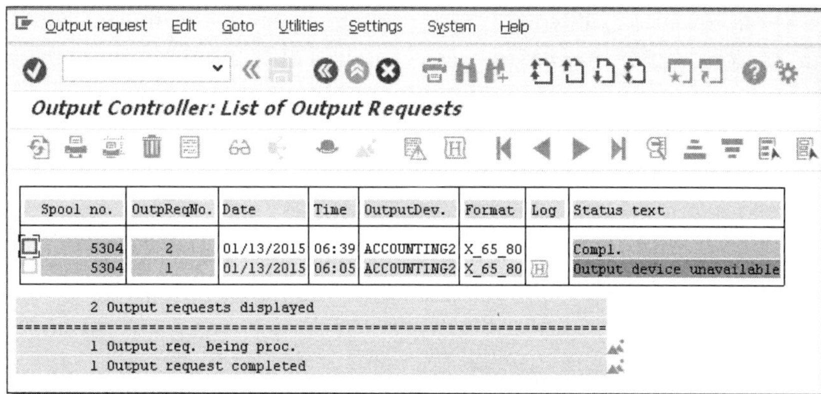

Figure 16.36 Checking the Status Change

Spool Request Edit Goto Utilities Settings System Help

Output Controller: List of Spool Requests

Spool no.	Type	Date	Time	Status	Pages	Title
5306		01/13/2015	06:05	Compl.	2	LIST1S LOCL RSPOSP01NSCH
5304		01/13/2015	06:05	<F5>	2	LIST1S ACC2 RSPOSP01NSCH
5303		01/13/2015	06:01	Compl.	3	LIST1S ACC2 SAPLSMTR_SCH

3 Spool requests displayed

2 Spool requests being processed

1 Spool requests completed

Figure 16.37 <F5> – Errors in Individual Output Requests

The COMPL. status only indicates that the transfer of the output request to the operating system's host spool system has run without any errors. Errors at the operating system level or in the device itself (e.g., a paper jam) can cause the printout to fail; however, Transaction SP01 doesn't display all of the possible problems. In case of a problem, revert to the monitoring tools of the operating system or the printer.

16.5 Deleting Old Spool Requests

Depending on how your spool system has been configured, old spool requests may consume memory in your database or your file system (parameter `rspo/store_location`; see also SAP Note 20176). In both cases, this memory could be used more reasonably for other purposes or can result in memory problems in extreme cases.

[⚙]

Spool Requests

Spool requests are stored at the operating system level of the spool server under */usr/sap/<SID>/SYS/global/<client>SPOOL*. The file name includes the number of the SAP spool request.

[⚙]

Parameter rspo/store_location

By means of the parameter `rspo/store_location`, you can define whether to store the files on the database or hard disk.

Report RSPO0041 exists for deleting old spool requests, which can also be scheduled as standard job report SAP_REORG_SPOOL and should be run on a daily basis. The job deletes all spool requests completed whose minimum retention period (usually, eight days) has been exceeded. If output requests still exist for an expired spool request that hasn't been completed (e.g., due to error messages), the spool request isn't removed. You must therefore regularly use the output controller (see Section 16.4) to check whether obsolete or undeleted spool requests exist, and remedy possible errors in the system.

16.6 Checking the Spool Consistency

In the spool consistency check, the system compares the spool data and the data in the tables of the output request (tables `TSP01` and `TSP02`) with the entries in the TemSe tables (tables `TST01` and `TST03`—see Section 16.7) as well as tables `TSP0E` (Archive) and `TSP02F` (Frontend Print Job). Moreover, it displays a list with obsolete write locks that can be deleted.

If you manually delete entries from the spool and from TemSe tables or spool and TemSe objects from the directories, this may lead to inconsistencies. Other causes for inconsistencies may be the cancellation of reports and transactions or incorrect execution of a client copy. Implement the following steps to check the spool consistency:

1. Call Transaction SPAD.
2. Select the ADMIN. tab, and click on CONSISTENCY CHECK OF SPOOL DATABASE (see Figure 16.38).

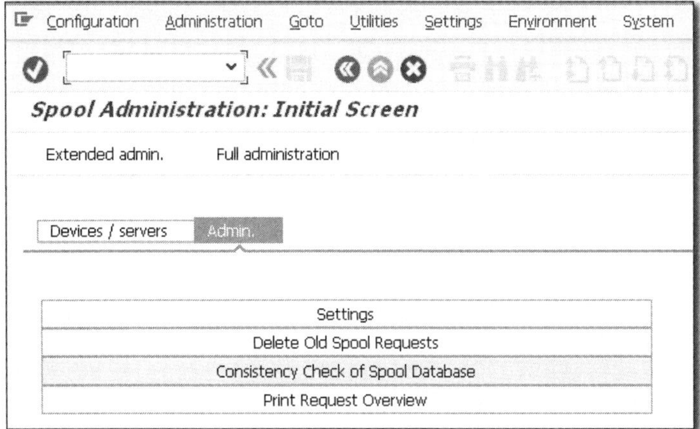

Figure 16.38 Starting the Consistency Check of the Spool Database

3. The system checks the spool and TemSe tables to ensure that the entries for each spool object match in the individual tables (see Figure 16.39). You can undo any possible locks or error messages by selecting them and clicking on DELETE SELECTED ENTRIES.

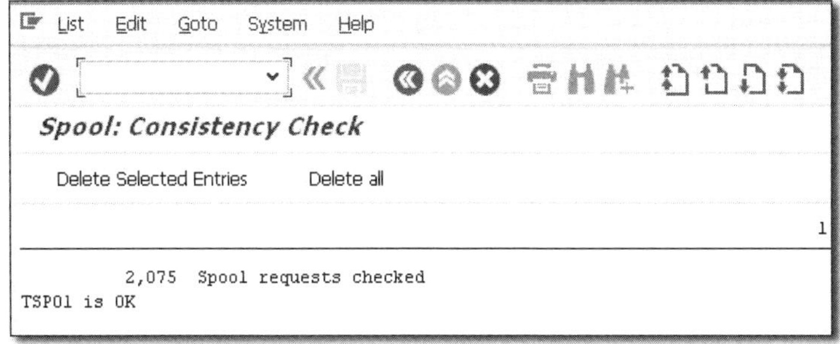

Figure 16.39 Reviewing the Results of the Consistency Check

[+]

Background Job for Checking the Spool Consistency

You can also use report RSPO1043 for checking the spool consistency. You should schedule this report as a periodic background job (see SAP Note 98065).

16.7 Checking the TemSe Consistency

The TemSe consistency check checks data in tables TST01 (Temporary Database Objects, TemSe Objects) and TST03 (TemSe Data). The TemSe database contains temporary objects such as job logs and temporary HR administration data. Report RSTS0020 executes the consistency check.

The relationship between the object and the data in the TemSe database may be corrupted with the following tasks:

- Recovery from backups
- Copying databases
- Copying clients using unsuitable tools
- Deleting clients without prior deletion of the associated objects

Implement the following steps to detect and remove inconsistencies in the TemSe database:

1. Enter Transaction SP12 in the command field and press the [Enter] key (or select the menu option Tools • CCMS • Print • SP12—TemSe Administration).
2. In the menu bar, select TemSe Data Storage • Consistency Check. The system checks the TemSe objects (table TST01). In the example in Figure 16.40, five files at the operating system level aren't accessible because they have already been deleted there. But there could also be serious problems in the file system. You can remove any inconsistencies by clicking on Delete Selected Objects.
3. Select table TST03 using the appropriate button in the toolbar to view the result of the TemSe data check (see Figure 16.41). Again, use the Delete Selected Objects button to delete defective data in TemSe.

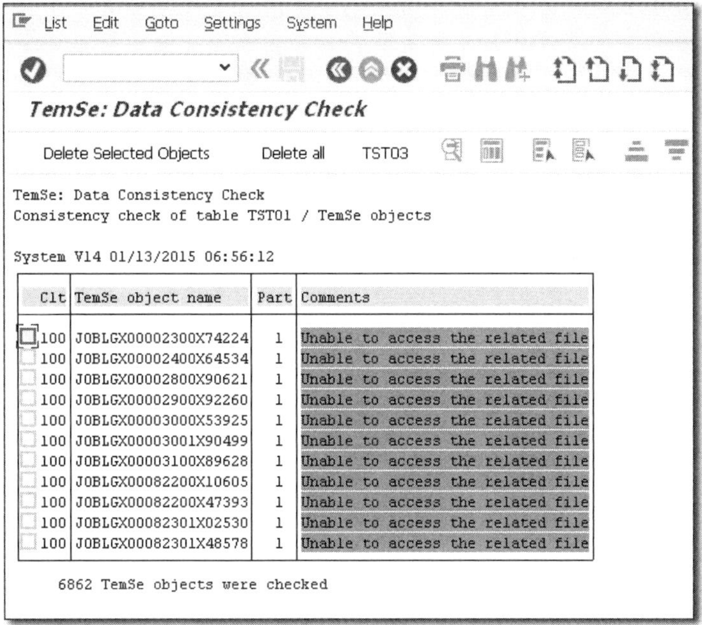

Figure 16.40 Result View of the TemSe Consistency Check

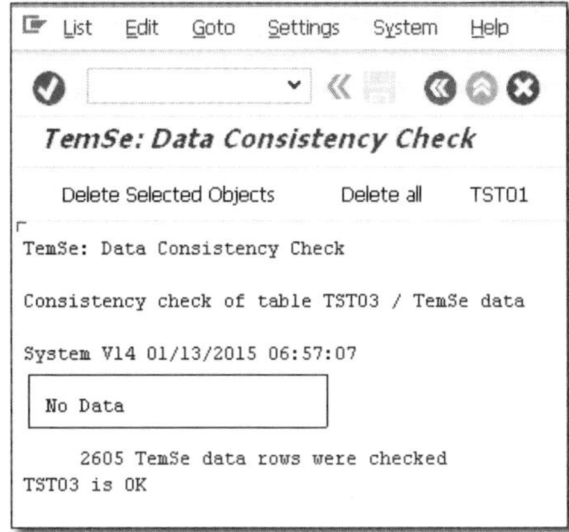

Figure 16.41 Checking the TemSe Data in Table TST03

Check TemSe for inconsistencies and delete them at regular intervals, for instance, every week (see Chapter 5).

16.8 Summary

This chapter presented the architecture of the SAP print and spool system. The print data are processed by spool servers and sent to printers, which you can configure locally or in a network. With the output control, you manage and delete the spool jobs and repeat the print job.

Usually, you only have to deal with the administration of TemSe in rare cases, but you should nevertheless know where you can start with problem analysis in case of an error. Answers to some questions are available in SAP Note 504952 discussing the spool and print system.

With the transport system, SAP provides a unique concept for recording, managing, and distributing changes, which contributes considerably to the stability of the entire system. This chapter describes how you create transport requests, use containers for changes, and finally carry out transports.

17 Change and Transport Management

The configuration of an SAP system is changed continuously due to new requirements of the users within the scope of an SAP project—for example, when a new SAP component is introduced—or simply because errors are corrected. Because the SAP system is integrated, minor changes to an object can affect numerous other components. In a worst-case scenario, this can lead to an interruption of entire business processes—and consequently to corresponding economic damage.

Changes in the SAP system must be controlled carefully to avoid these problems. *Change management* enables you to control changes in the SAP system in a defined process and minimize the related risks. This process begins with formulating a *change request* (or request for change). You can also define how the change is planned, checked, and approved. Finally, you coordinate the realization, testing processes, and implementation before the change is finally used in live operations. *IT Service Management in SAP Solution Manager* by Nathan Williams (SAP PRESS, 2013) describes in detail how you can implement a change management process using SAP Solution Manager.

Technically, the SAP system supports your organizational change process with the *transport system*. Changes that you make to the system are automatically recorded and bundled in *transport requests*. When a transport request has been released, you can transport the changes to downstream systems within multisystem landscapes—usually consisting of at least a development, testing, and production system—that is, you don't have to implement the change manually in each system. This chapter focuses on the basic principles of transport management. For more information on this complex topic, refer to *SAP Change and Transport Management* by Armin Kösegi and Rainer Nerding (3rd edition, SAP PRESS, 2009).

17.1 General Notes on Change Management

You need to define what the change process is supposed to look like in your enterprise so that you can track the implementation of the changes and avoid risks during live operation. In this coordination process, involve the persons responsible from the system administration, programming, and application support teams.

At a minimum, the following steps should be part of the change process:

1. **Specifying the change**
   Specify the change to be implemented. Describe the reasons, scope, target, and effects of the modification in detail.
2. **Obtaining approvals**
   Obtain the necessary approvals (see Appendix D). The necessary approval process can vary depending on the enterprise. In some enterprises, the approval needs to be granted by one person only; in other enterprises, approval is required from several persons.
   - *Approval by functional areas (end users)*
     - Checking the effects of changes to the respective functional area
     - Performing additional tests in coordination with other functional areas that might also be affected
   - *Approval by system administrator*
     - Checking the changes that might affect the system administrator
     - Scheduling new jobs
     - Performing program error procedures or troubleshooting procedures

[+]

Approval by End Users

The main objective of the approval process is to inform other functional areas of the objects to be transported. If the transport affects a functional area, the respective employees can perform checks or tests, for example. However, this may delay your transport until the end users are satisfied.

3. **Creating a transport request**
   Create a transport request, implement the changes, and record the changes in your transport request.

4. **Documenting changes**
   Document all changes to the programming code, configuration, and so on.
5. **Defining other critical data**
   Define other critical data for transport management, for example:
   - Contact person in case of problems. (The employee who implements the transport is usually not a developer. If a problem occurs during the transport, the employee needs help for the troubleshooting process.)
   - Recovery process in case of transport errors.
   - Employee who checks whether the transport has been implemented properly in the target system.
   - Transport number.
   - Source system.
   - Target system(s).
   - Relation to other transports, for example, previous and subsequent transports.
6. **Creating a recovery plan**
   The change control should also include a recovery plan that answers the following questions:
   - Which measures must be taken if problems occur during the import into the production system?
   - How is the rollback supposed to be implemented? Is a rollback possible?
   - Does the problem require a database recovery?
7. **Releasing a transport request**
   Release the transport request in the development system for the import to the test or QA system. Have developers and functionality analysts test the changes there.
8. **Importing the transport request to the production system**
   After the tests have been completed successfully, import the transport to the production system. Check the transport log, and check whether the changes have reached the target system as expected.
9. **Making the change known**
   Inform the persons affected that the change is used in live operations.

Objects may be overwritten during the transport. If an object is used in the target system during the transport, the transport can have inconsistent results or lead to a termination of the transaction. In a worst case scenario, a transport can result in a shutdown of the production system and require a system recovery. Consequently, implement the transport to the production system outside of peak user activity times (e.g., Sunday afternoon or evening) when no users are logged on to the system. Define at which times transports are usually carried out. However, in urgent cases, a transport may be necessary outside of the agreed weekly transport times. Specify in advance how this kind of emergency transport is handled.

17.2 Transporting Objects

The target and purpose of transports is to transfer objects and configurations from one system to another. In the common three-system landscape, a transport is generated in the development system, transported to the QA system where it's tested, and finally imported to the production system.

[+]

Names for the Transport System

The transport system was changed significantly in release 4.x. Previously, it was referred to as *Correction and Transport System*. The acronym *CTS* is still used but now stands for Change and Transport System. The CTS includes the *Transport Management System* (TMS, Transaction STMS) and the *Change and Transport Organizer* (CTO, Transaction SE10).

The following transfers of changes are referred to as *transports* in the SAP system:

- From one client to another within the same system
- From one system to another for the same client
- From one system to another and from one client to another

Use the Transport Management System (TMS) to transport objects. This enables you to control the transports in the SAP system without working at the operating system level. Additionally, you can do the following in the TMS:

- Define transport routes.
- Bundle transport requests in projects.
- Schedule imports of requests for later.
- Use the functions of the Advanced Quality Assurance function.

Advanced Quality Assurance [+]

As of release 4.6, the TMS provides the *Advanced Quality Assurance* function, which requires that requests imported to the QA system are approved there to be transported to the production system.

This prevents requests that haven't been fully tested in the QA system from being transported accidentally. This change is a significant enhancement in the change management process and should be generally used in three-system landscapes.

Basically, you can also implement transports at the operating system level using the `tp` transport program; this procedure, however, is less comfortable and prone to operating errors.

Prerequisite for Subsequent Sections [!]

The transport scenario described in the following sections requires that the TMS is set up completely and properly.

17.2.1 Creating a Transport Request

To transport an object, you first have to create a transport request in which you enter your change. You can create the transport request before implementing the change or during the recording in a respective dialog. In the following example, the transport request is created *before* the implementation of the change. You can find a reference to the alternative dialog in the appropriate step.

Authorization for the Creation of Transports [!]

If you aren't authorized to create transport requests, you should ask your transport administrator for a transport request before implementing the change. Otherwise, if a transport request is missing, you have to terminate your work for specific objects (e.g., Customizing tables) and repeat the steps later.

1. Enter Transaction SE10 in the command field and press the Enter key, or select the menu option Tools • Customizing • IMG • SE10—Transport Organizer (Extended View).

Alternative Transactions [!]

Alternatively, you can also use Transaction SE09 (Transport Organizer)—it provides the same functions. Use Transaction SE01 to call the extended Transport Organizer view. Here you can specifically look for individual transport requests.

2. Transaction SE03 (Transport Organizer Tools) is an additional useful transaction in the transport system: It enables you to perform researches and implement settings. In the TRANSPORT ORGANIZER window, click on CREATE (see Figure 17.1).

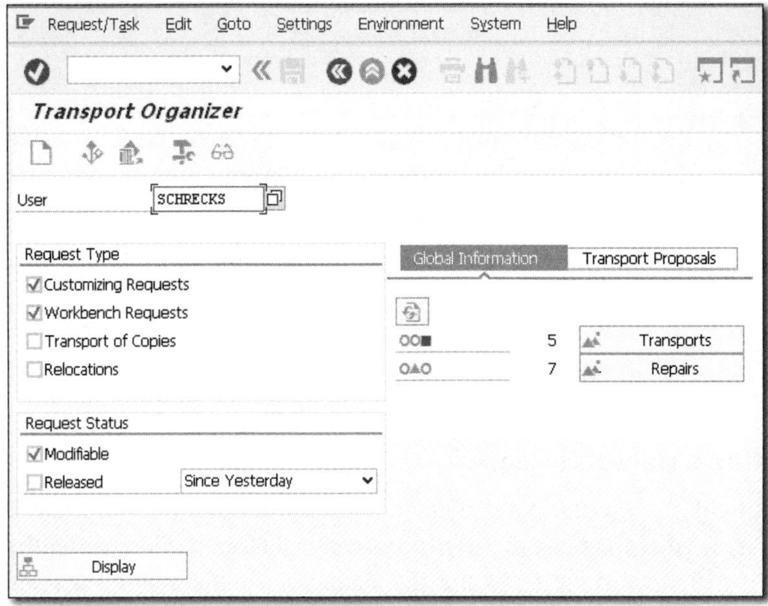

Figure 17.1 Creating a Transport Request in Transport Organizer

3. A dialog box opens in which you can define the type of the transport request to be created (see Figure 17.2). For example, activate the WORKBENCH REQUEST radio button, and click on COPY.

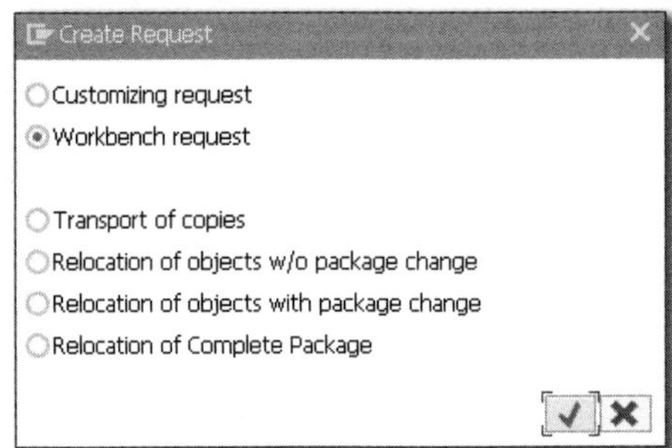

Figure 17.2 Defining the Transport Request Type

[!]

Transport Request Type

The request type depends on the object that will be transported.

- *Customizing requests* are used for Customizing changes, such as the maintenance of tables.
- *Workbench requests* are used for repository changes (e.g., programs).

Note that changes to Customizing can't be transported with a workbench request and vice versa. When creating the transport request, you need to know if you want to change a Customizing or repository object.

For this reason, it's advisable to first create the transport request during a change recording (see Section 17.2.2) because the correct type is selected there automatically. You can't change the transport request type retroactively.

4. In the next screen, enter the administration data for the transport request (see Figure 17.3):
   - Enter a meaningful SHORT DESCRIPTION.
   - If necessary, assign the request to a PROJECT. Depending on the configuration of your transport system, this may be a required entry field.
   - In the TARGET field, select the system to which the request will be transported. Usually, this is your production system.
   - In TASKS, enter the user IDs of all employees that are supposed to enter changes in this transport request.
   - When you've finished, click on SAVE.

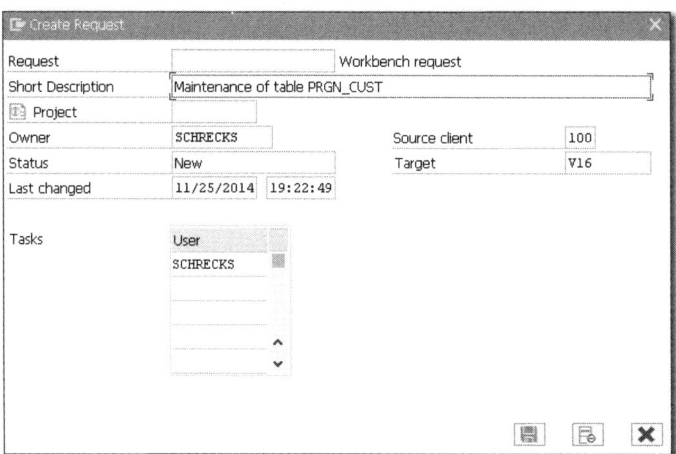

Figure 17.3 Maintaining Administrative Data for a Transport Request

5. The system creates the transport request and the related tasks. The system automatically assigns a request number according to the following pattern: *<system ID>K9<consecutive number>* (see Figure 17.4).

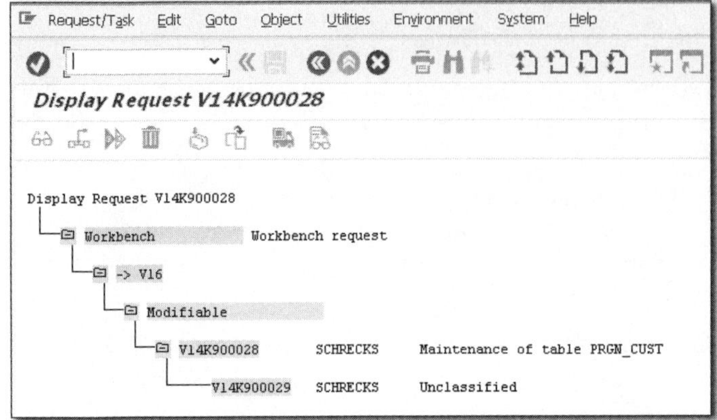

Figure 17.4 Transport Request with Request Number

The transport request is created and can be used to enter changes. The system creates a specific task for every user that you specified.

17.2.2 Recording Changes in a Transport Request

Now, you can make your changes. Start the corresponding transaction, Customizing activity, or maintenance dialog.

1. For example, start Transaction SM30 for table maintenance (see Section 17.3), and add a new entry to table `PRGN_CUST` (see Figure 17.5).

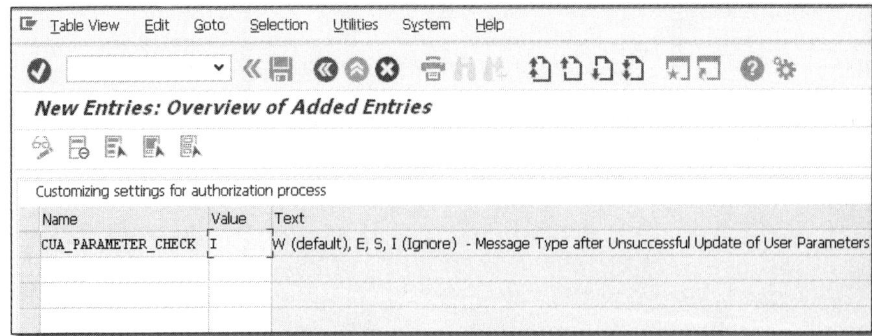

Figure 17.5 Adding a New Table Entry

2. If you save your entry, a dialog box opens that prompts you to specify the transport request in which the change will be entered. Open the input help to select a transport request (see Figure 17.6).

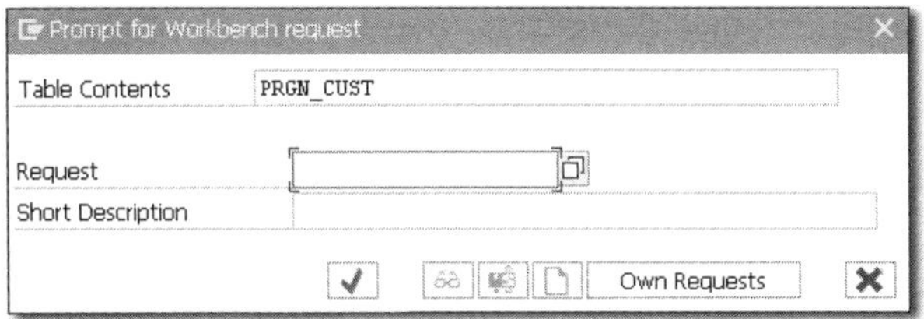

Figure 17.6 Dialog Box for Querying a Transport Request

[+]

Creating a Transport Request

Here, the CREATE REQUEST button also enables you to create a new transport request if you haven't done this yet. The advantage of this variant is that the request type is determined from the object to be changed, and you can't create a request of the wrong type by mistake.

3. Another dialog box opens that displays the available transport requests; that is, it only offers the transports of the required type (e.g., workbench requests) that contain a tasks for your user ID (see Figure 17.7). Position your cursor on the transport request or task, and click on CONTINUE.

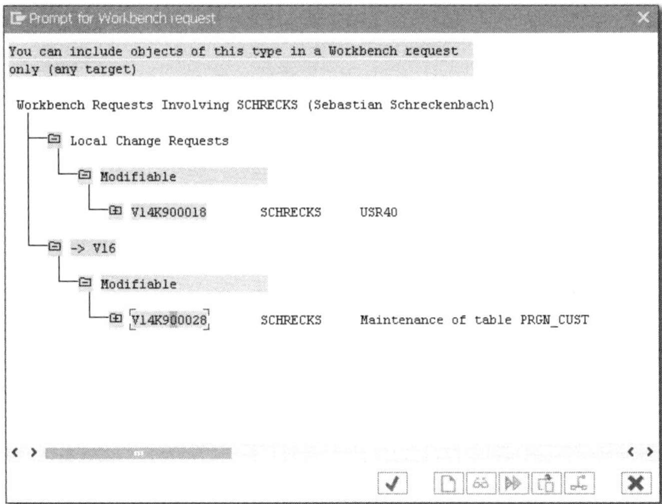

Figure 17.7 Selecting a Request from the Available Transport Requests

4. This takes you back to the prompt dialog box; the selected transport request is now specified in the REQUEST field. Click on CONTINUE ✓ (see Figure 17.8).

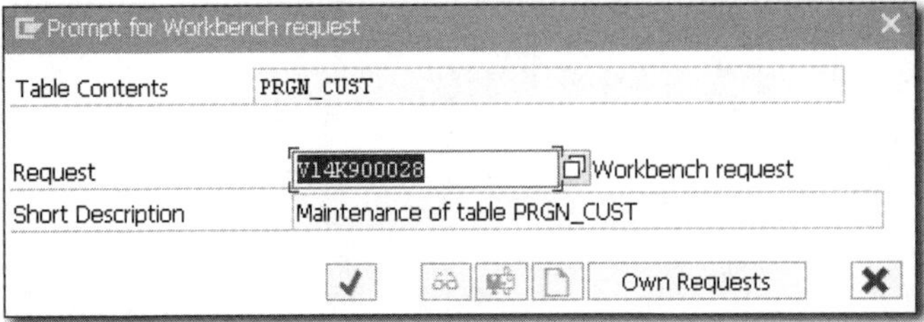

Figure 17.8 Confirming the Selected Request

You've now recorded the change in the transport request. You can exit the transaction and release the transport request for transport.

17.2.3 Releasing a Transport Request

Prior to the transport, you must release all tasks related to the request and then the request itself.

1. Call Transaction SE10.
2. In the TRANSPORT ORGANIZER window, ensure that the user ID of the owner of the transport request to be released is specified in the USER field. Select the REQUEST TYPES to be displayed and the MODIFIABLE request status. Click on DISPLAY (see Figure 17.9).
3. Position your cursor on the request to be released, and click on RELEASE DIRECTLY (see Figure 17.10).

[+] **Releasing Tasks**

All tasks that are related to the request have to be released before the request itself can be released.

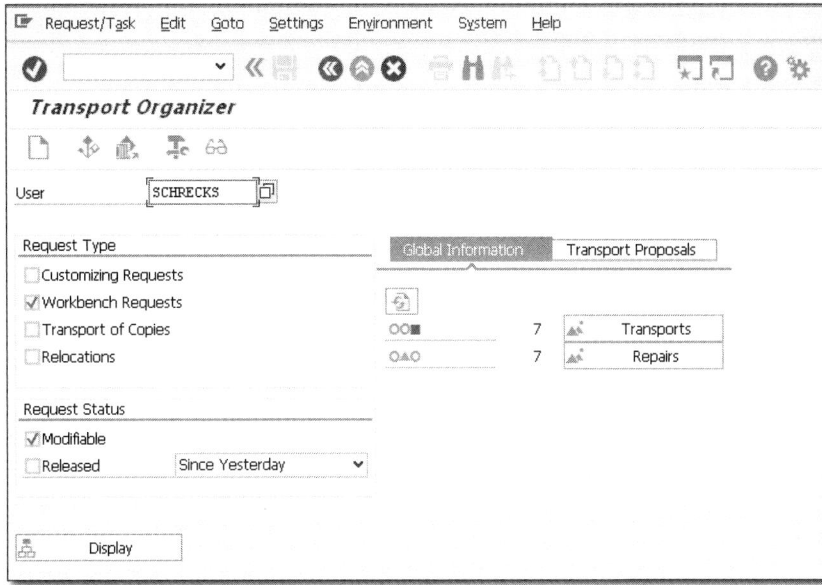

Figure 17.9 Specifying the Request Type and Status in Transport Organizer

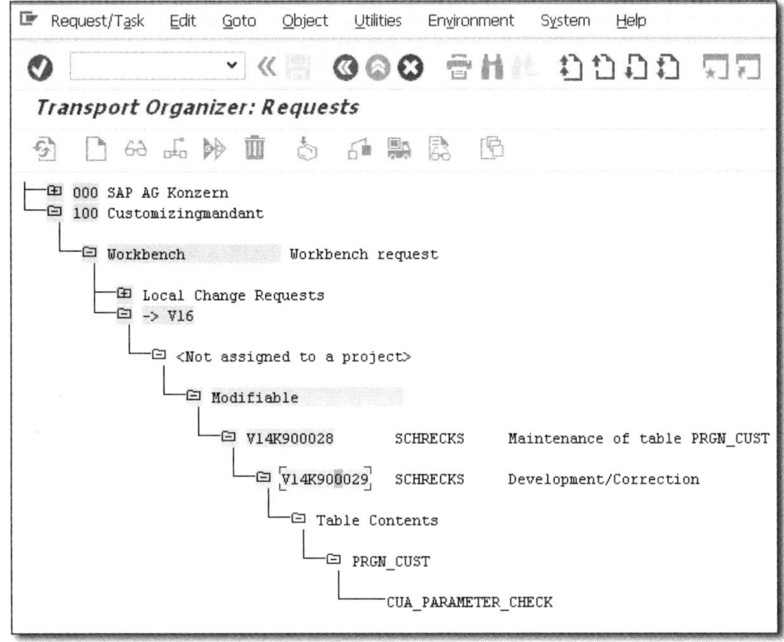

Figure 17.10 Selecting a Task for Release

4. In the next step, release the transport request by positioning the cursor on the request and clicking on RELEASE DIRECTLY (see Figure 17.11).

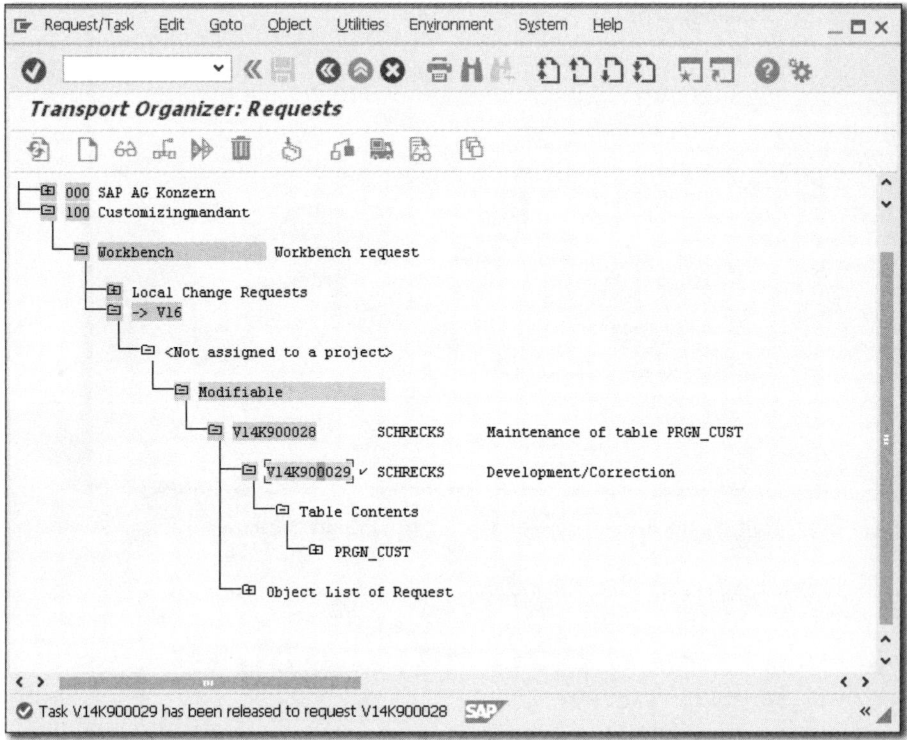

Figure 17.11 Releasing the Transport Request

5. The system switches to the transport log view. For the EXPORT step, the system displays the message IN PROCESS: REQUIRES UPDATE (see Figure 17.12). Click on REFRESH to update the status.

[⚙]

Transport Files

In this step, the values of the implemented changes are defined and the transport files are created at the operating system level. Up to this point, your transport request has simply "pointed" to the changed object (e.g., to the field in a table). During the export, the value that the object has when it's released is determined and stored in the transport files.

A transport request consists of a control file and a data file:

- The *control files* start with K and are stored in the */usr/sap/trans/ cofiles* (Linux/UNIX) or *<drive>:\usr\sap\trans\cofiles* (Windows) directory.
- The *data files* start with R and are stored in the */usr/sap/trans/data* (Linux/UNIX) or *<drive>:\usr\sap\trans\data* (Windows) directory.

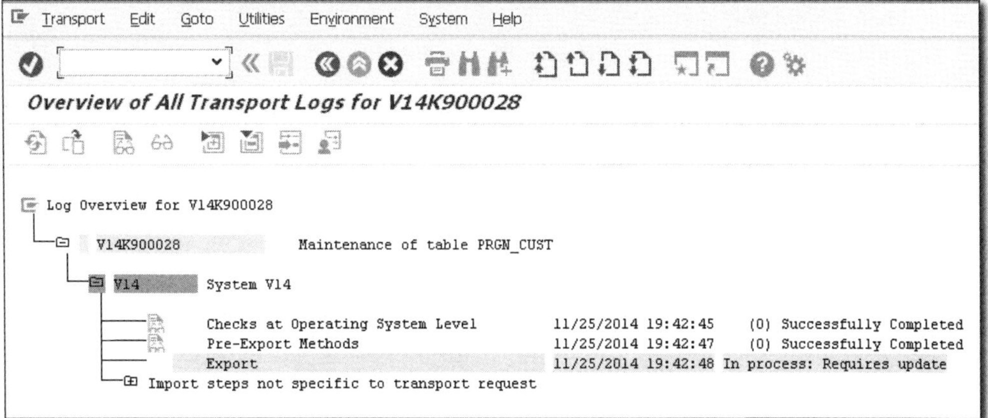

Figure 17.12 Updating the Transport Log

6. After the export has been completed successfully, the status message is set to Successfully Completed. Check the *return code* in parentheses before the status message (e.g., 0 in Figure 17.13). Then click on Back.

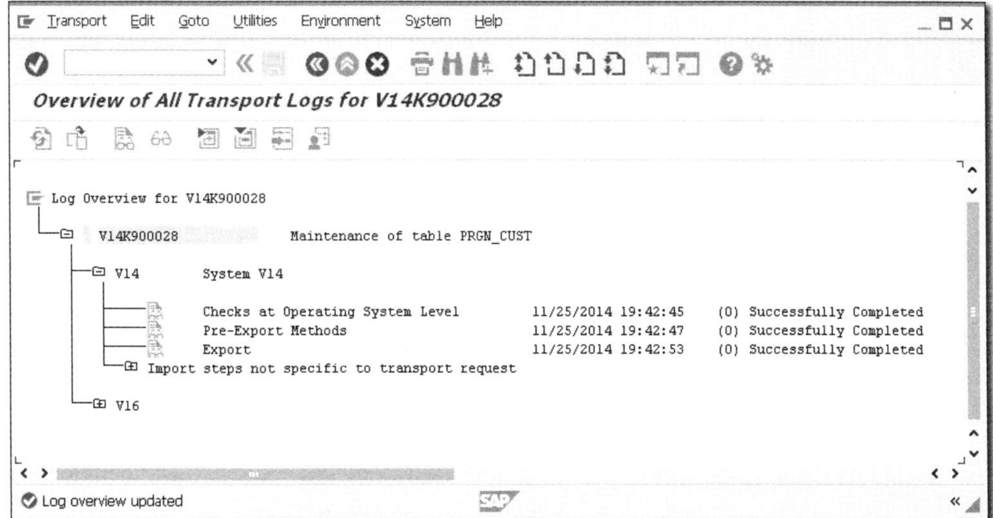

Figure 17.13 Checking the Return Code

[+]

Possible Return Codes

The following return codes are possible:

- 0: Successfully Completed
- 4: Ended with Warning
- 8: Ended with errors
- 12 or higher: Export was terminated unexpectedly

A return code of 8 or higher indicates that an error occurred during the export. Check the transport log using Display Log, eliminate the error, and repeat the export.

7. The transport request overview displays the status of the transport as Released (see Figure 17.14). Exit the Transport Organizer screen via Back.

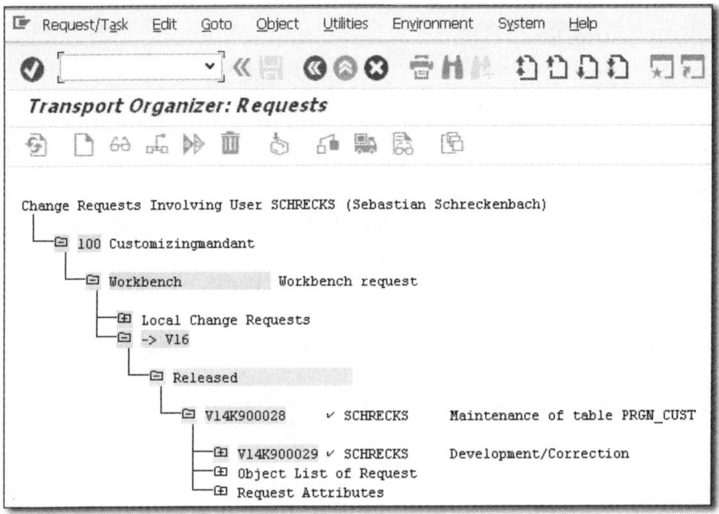

Figure 17.14 Released Transport

After the release and successful export, the transport request is now ready for import to downstream systems.

17.2.4 Importing Transport Requests

After the release, the system automatically queues the transport request in the *import queue* (the list of requests to be imported) of the downstream system. The import queue enables you to control the requests' import.

1. Enter Transaction STMS in the command field and press the [Enter] key (or select the menu option TOOLS • ADMINISTRATION • TRANSPORTS • STMS—TRANSPORT MANAGEMENT SYSTEM).

Domain Controller

Transaction STMS (Transport Management System) is a very complex tool for the configuration, control, and monitoring of the transport system. Certain settings can only be made centrally in client 000 of the system. It's used as the *domain controller*. The TMS configuration is distributed from the domain controller to the connected child systems.

2. The TRANSPORT MANAGEMENT SYSTEM window is displayed (see Figure 17.15). Click on the IMPORT OVERVIEW button.

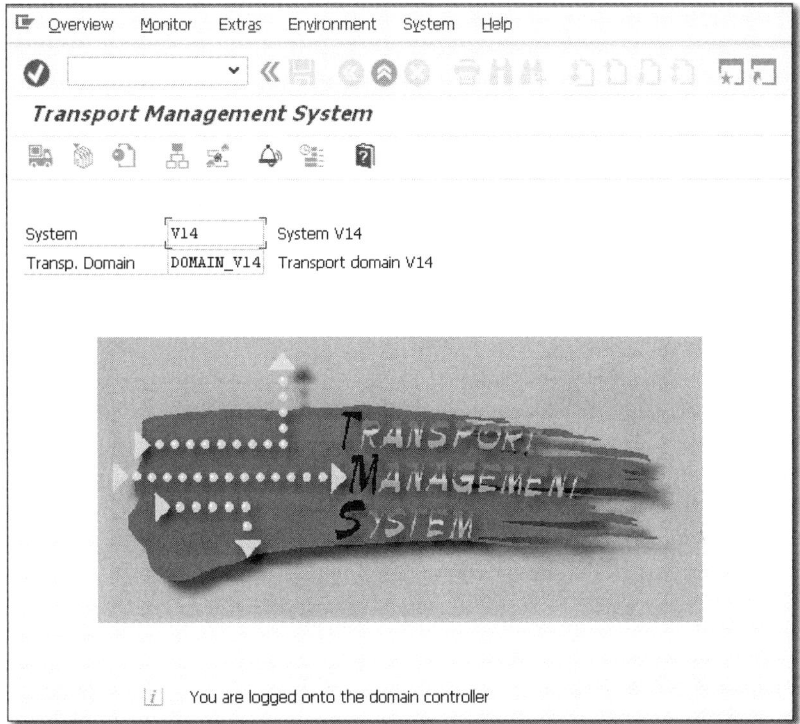

Figure 17.15 Initial Screen of the Transport Management System

3. Position your cursor on the system to which you want to import the transport request, and click on DISPLAY IMPORT QUEUE (see Figure 17.16).

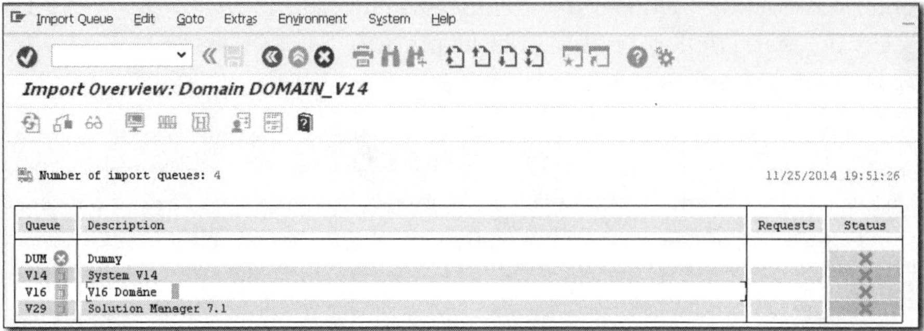

Figure 17.16 Selecting a System for Import

4. The system displays the list of the transport requests to be imported (*import queue*, see Figure 17.17). Position your cursor on the request to be imported, and click on IMPORT REQUEST.

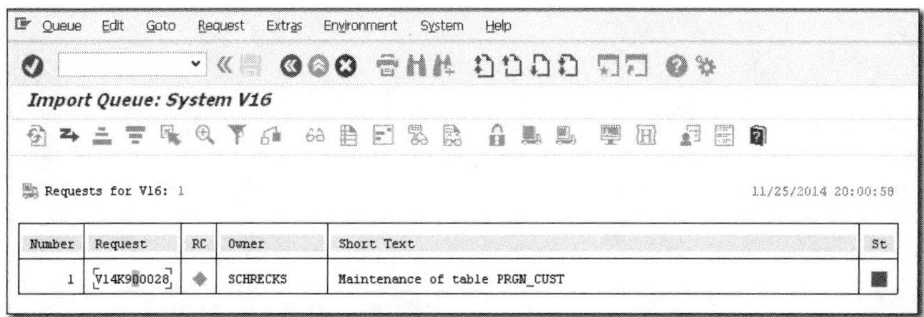

Figure 17.17 Selecting a Request for Import

[!]

Transport Buttons

Two of the icons are quite similar, so ensure that you select the appropriate icon. With the IMPORT ALL REQUESTS button, you import the entire import queue, that is, all transport requests to be imported.

5. If required, in the DATE tab of the IMPORT TRANSPORT REQUEST dialog box, enter the number of the client to which the request is to be imported in the TARGET CLIENT field. Here, you can also define a later execution date if you don't want the import to start immediately (see Figure 17.18).
6. Navigate to the EXECUTION tab. Select the SYNCHRONOUS option (see Figure 17.19).

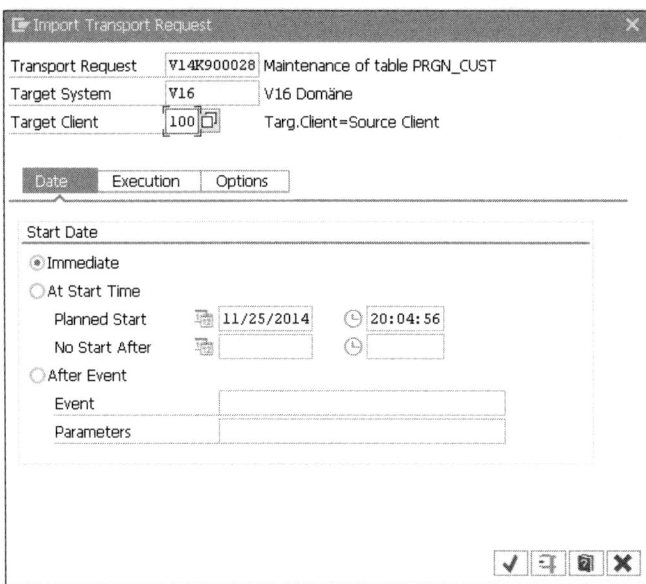

Figure 17.18 Defining the Target and Date for the Import

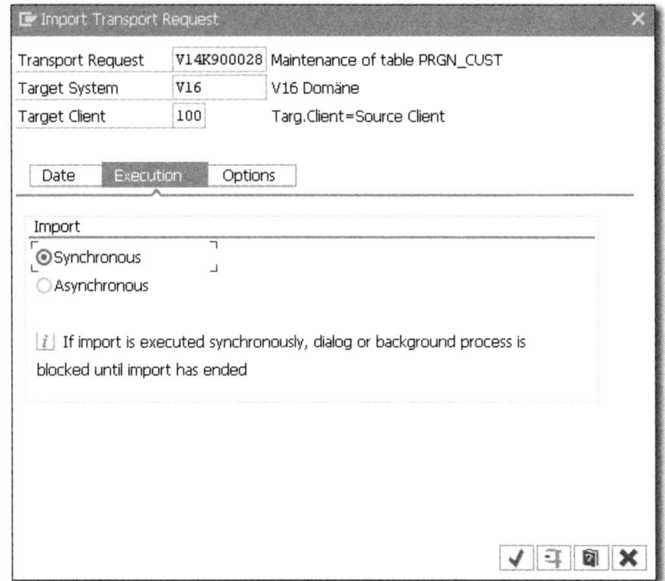

Figure 17.19 Defining the Execution Type of the Import

[⚙]

Import Options

The TMS calls the transport control program, `tp`, at the operating system level during the import. This program then executes the transport. To start the `tp` program, an SAP work process is used. You can choose between the following options:

- Synchronous
  The work process remains blocked until the `tp` program has been terminated. Select this option if you want to monitor the import process in detail or if you want to carry out subsequent actions. Bear in mind that the work process is locked as long as the import runs. In extreme cases (multiple parallel imports), this may block the system.
- Asynchronous
  The work process is released when `tp` is started. Use this option if many or very large transport requests queue for an import to avoid unnecessarily binding system resources.

7. Now select the Options tab. Here, you can set specific import options, if required, called *unconditional modes*. Click on Continue ✔ (see Figure 17.20).

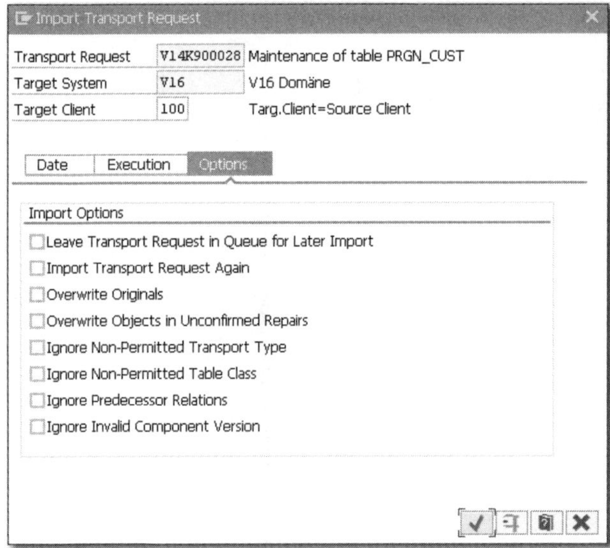

Figure 17.20 Unconditional Modes

[!]

Unconditional Modes

You should use unconditional modes carefully. They enable you to purposefully override security precautions if this is absolutely necessary. Because they bypass the protection of the transport landscape, wrongly setting unconditional modes can cause a lot of damage. Normally, no option should be selected, and you should select the appropriate checkbox for the error after a problem occurs during the import and after you've consulted the developer.

8. Click YES to confirm the security prompt (see Figure 17.21).

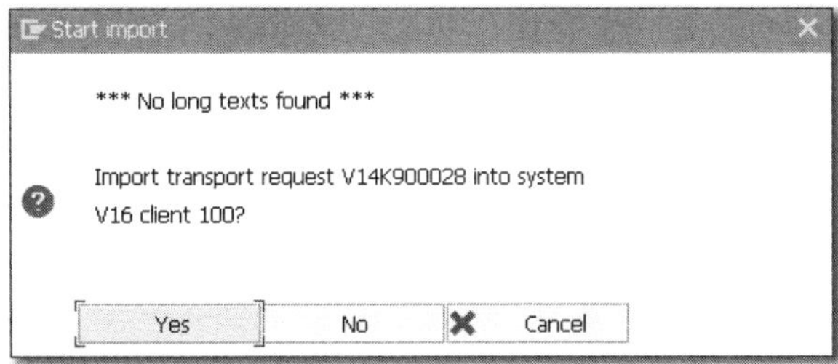

Figure 17.21 Confirming an Import

9. Depending on the configuration of the transport system and which system you're logged on to, you must authenticate your user ID and password for the target client.
10. The import process starts and may take some time. The system displays the request number with a green checkmark in the ST column (for import status). This status indicates that the request has already been imported. In the RC column (for Max. Return Code), the return code of the import is symbolically displayed in traffic light colors (see Figure 17.22).

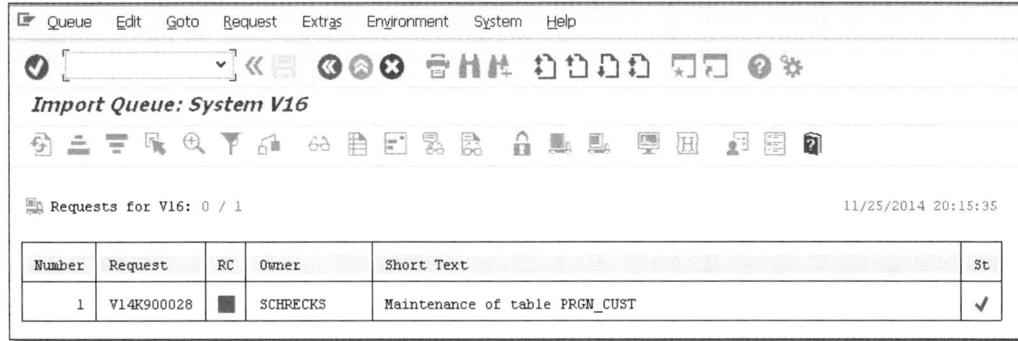

Figure 17.22 Checking the Import Status

[+]

Return Codes

The following return codes are common:

- 0 ■: The import was completed successfully.
- 1 or 4 ▲: Warnings occurred.
- 8 ●: An error occurred during the execution; all or individual objects couldn't be imported properly.
- 12 or higher ▮: The transport wasn't executed.

If the system displays a return code of 4 or higher, you should check the transport log.

[+]

Return Code 1

Note that return codes 1 (NOTHING DONE) and 4 (WARNING) use the same status icon ▲. Return code 1 occurs if you repeat an import without activating the unconditional mode IMPORT TRANSPORT REQUEST AGAIN. In this case, the import is *not* executed again. However, you can only see this if you move the mouse pointer over the icon, and the system displays an appropriate tooltip (NOTHING DONE). You can also check the import history.

After a successful import, you can exit the import queue view; the transport of the request is then completed. If warnings or error messages have occurred, check the transport log.

17.2.5 Checking the Transport Log

You can use the TMS to check transport logs.

1. In the import queue view, position the cursor on the transport request whose log you want to view, and click on LOGS (see Figure 17.23).

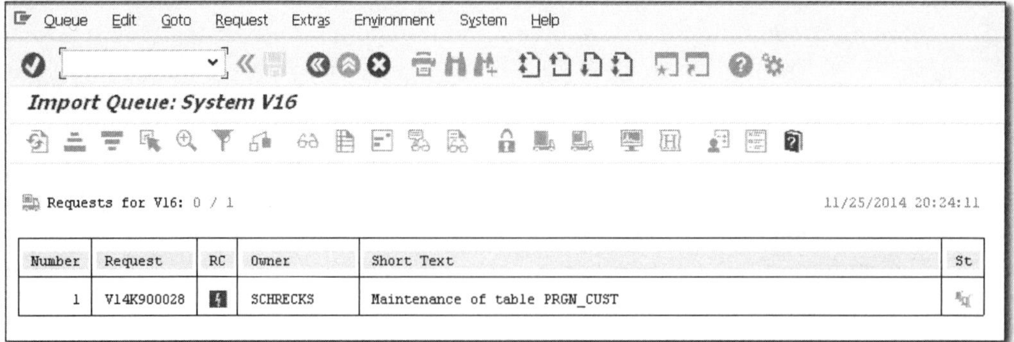

Figure 17.23 Selecting the Transport Request

2. In the Overview of Transport Logs screen, position the cursor on the log entry that you want to check, and click on Display Log (see Figure 17.24).

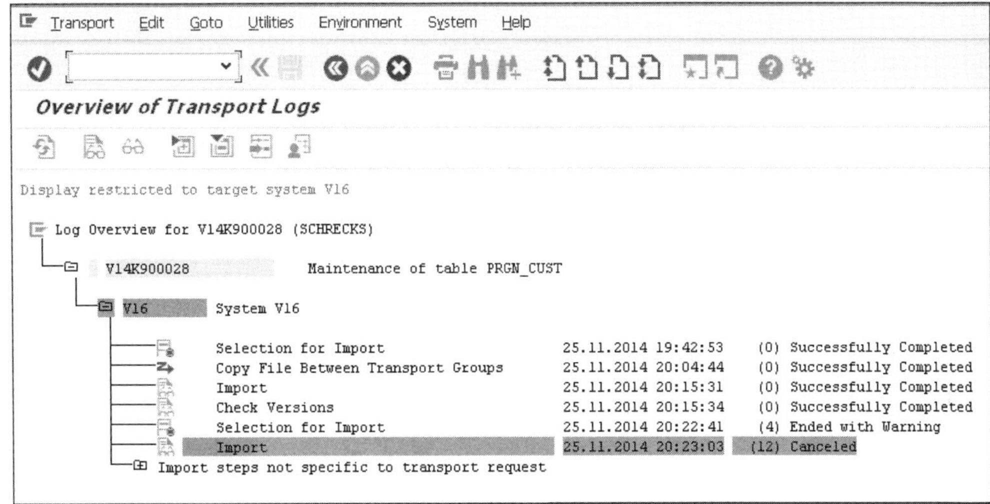

Figure 17.24 Selecting a Log Entry for Check

3. View the detailed messages in the log display by clicking on Expand (see Figure 17.25).

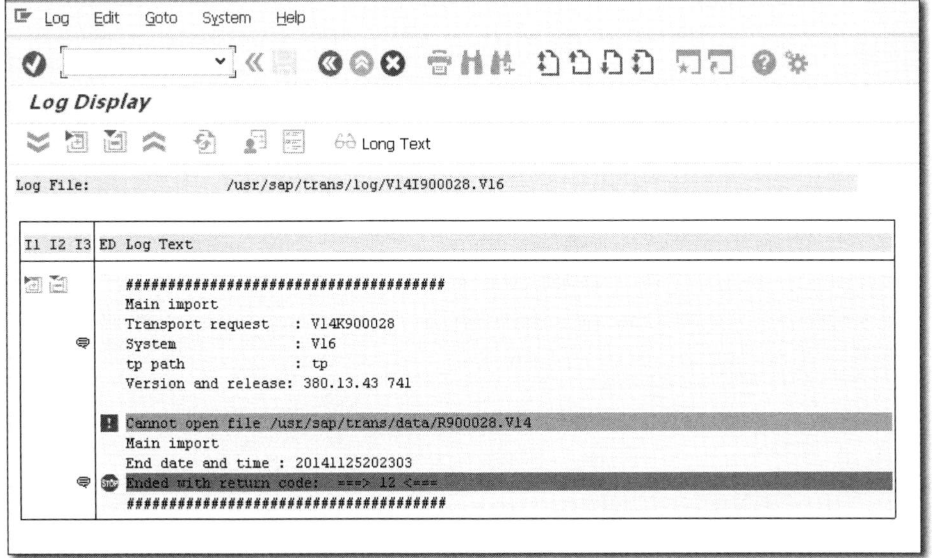

Figure 17.25 Displaying the Transport Log

4. Check the warning or error message, and have the system display the LONG TEXT if required. Eliminate the cause of the error, and then restart the import as described in Section 17.2.4.

[!]

Checking the Result of the Transport

It's possible that the transport wasn't successful even if you haven't received the corresponding return code. You therefore have to use a final test to determine whether the transport has been implemented properly. Ensure that the changes made in the original system have been correctly and fully transferred to the target system.

17.2.6 Checking the History

An essential transport system function is that all transports made can be traced in the history. This applies to both imports and exports. Proceed as follows to check the history:

1. In the import queue view, select the menu option GOTO • IMPORT HISTORY (see Figure 17.26).
2. If required, adapt the time interval displayed to your desired evaluation period (see Figure 17.27). At this point, you can go to the logs by selecting the button.

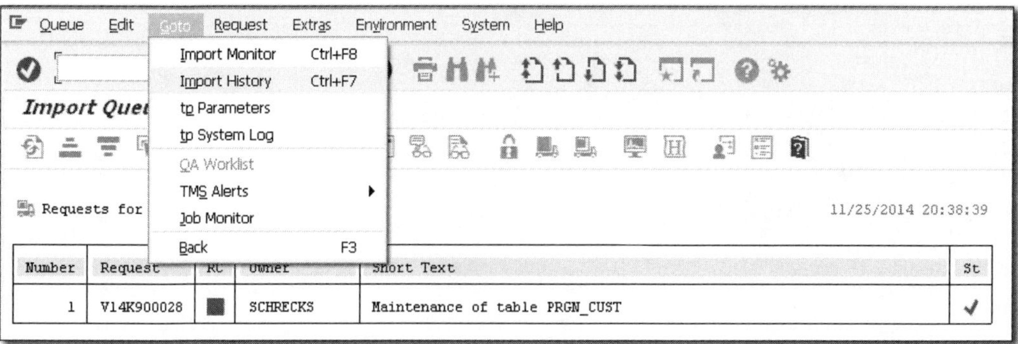

Figure 17.26 Calling the Import History

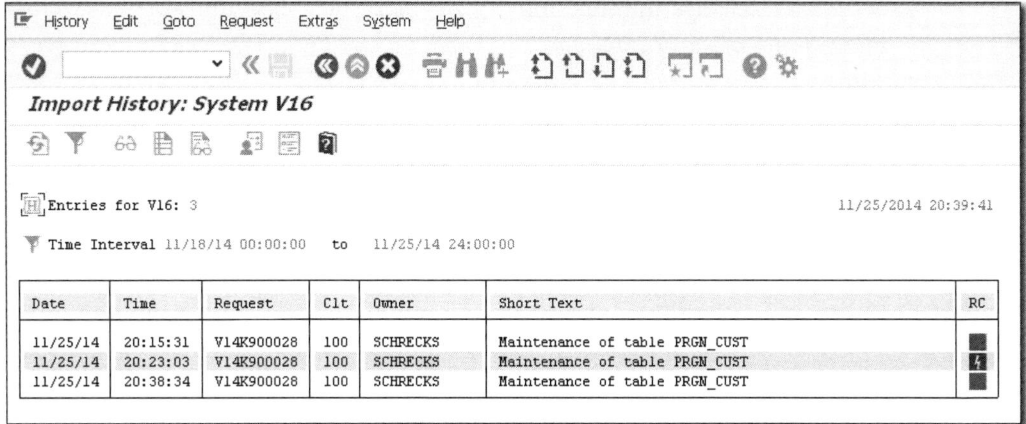

Figure 17.27 Checking the Import History

Additionally, the Export History function is interesting for your development systems. It provides an overview of the transport requests released in a system. To call this history, proceed as follows:

1. In the Import Overview, position the cursor on the required system, and select the menu option Goto • History • Export History (see Figure 17.28).

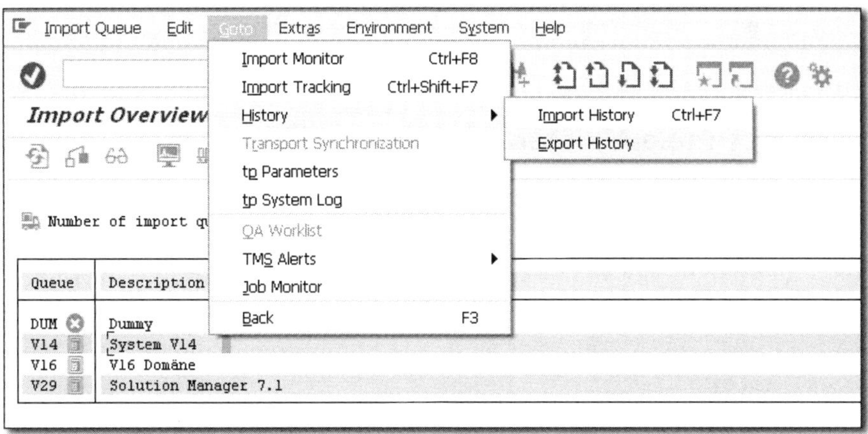

Figure 17.28 Calling the Export History

2. If required, change the time interval of the display list to meet your requirements (see Figure 17.29).

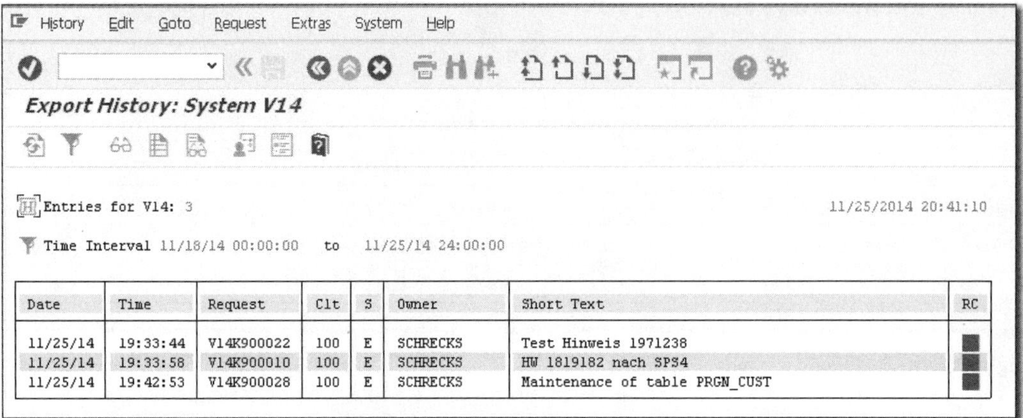

Figure 17.29 Displaying the Export History

EXPORT HISTORY is particularly interesting for evaluating the export sequence of transports or for use as a mass comparison of released and imported transport requests (e.g., if transports, which were imported to the test system but not the production system before the copy process started, need to be traced after a system copy from the production system to the QA system).

17.3 Direct Table Maintenance

Most of the changes are made via specific transactions or Customizing paths with the respective technical reference. In some cases, however, you have to maintain tables for which no transaction is available. If a maintenance view for the respective table is available (usually for Customizing tables; maintenance views aren't available for user tables), you can directly modify it using Transaction SM30 or Transaction SM31.

[!]

Direct Table Maintenance

Only use direct table maintenance if no other transaction is available for table maintenance. For the direct maintenance of a table, all processes and validations in the system are ignored. If you directly change a table and save it, the change is immediately applied. You can't undo the change.

To process the entries in a table via a maintenance view, follow these steps:

1. Enter Transaction SM30 in the command field and press the Enter key (or select the menu option SYSTEM • SERVICES • TABLE MAINTENANCE • EXTENDED TABLE MAINTENANCE).
2. In the TABLE/VIEW field, enter the table name (e.g., "USR40"). Ensure that no Customizing activity exists for the maintenance of the table by clicking on CUSTOMIZING.

[+]

Navigating to the Customizing

If you can maintain the table in Customizing, the system automatically navigates to the corresponding step in the Implementation Guide (IMG). If no Customizing activity is available for the maintenance of the table, the system displays the error message NO OBJECT MAINTENANCE IMG ACTIVITY EXISTS.

3. Now ensure that a maintenance view dialog exists for the table by selecting FIND MAINTENANCE DIALOG (see Figure 17.30).

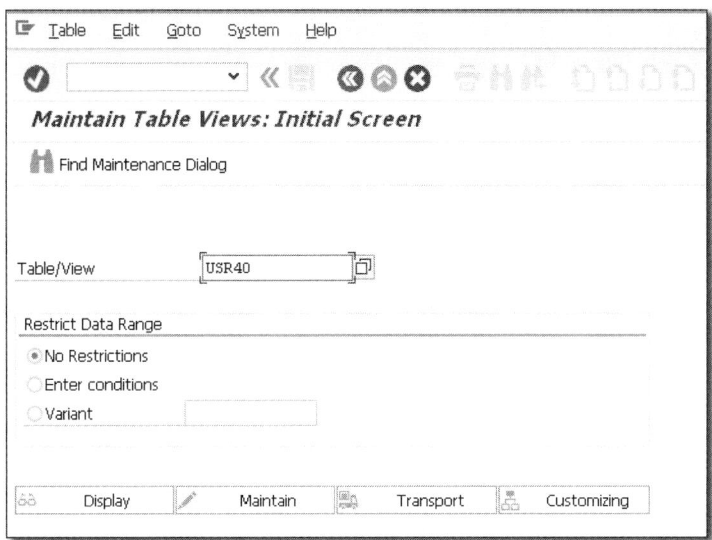

Figure 17.30 Searching the Maintenance Dialog

4. A dialog box with the selected table name opens. Click on CONTINUE (see Figure 17.31).

Figure 17.31 Confirming Table Names

[+]

Maintenance Views for Tables

If a maintenance view exists, the system returns to the initial screen without displaying a message, and you can proceed with the next step. If no maintenance view is available for the respective table, a dialog box opens that shows the message NO MAINTENANCE OBJECTS FOUND FOR TABLE/VIEW. Then you can't maintain the table using Transaction SM30.

5. Click on MAINTAIN (see Figure 17.32).

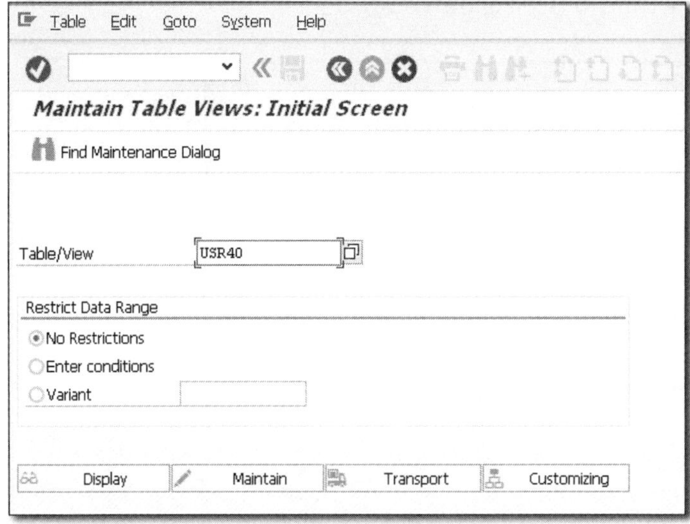

Figure 17.32 Starting the Table Maintenance

6. If the table that you modify is *cross-client*, the system displays an information dialog box. Click on CONTINUE ✓ (see Figure 17.33).

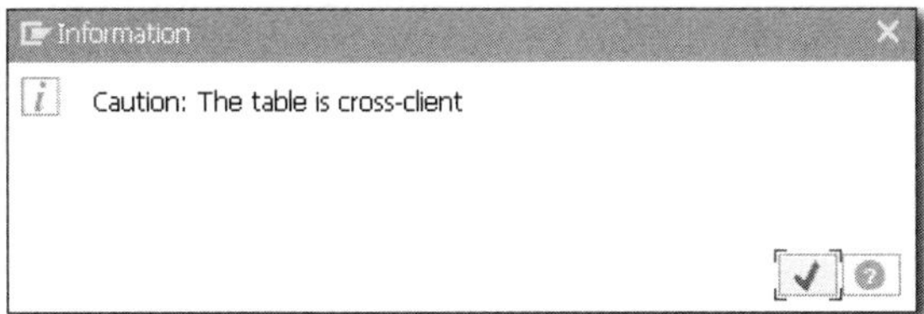

Figure 17.33 Cross-Client Message for a Table

Cross-Client Data [!]

Cross-client changes apply to *all* clients in a system and not only to the client that you're currently processing.

7. In the next window, select the New Entries option. You can also use the respective buttons to change, copy, or delete existing entries (see Figure 17.34).

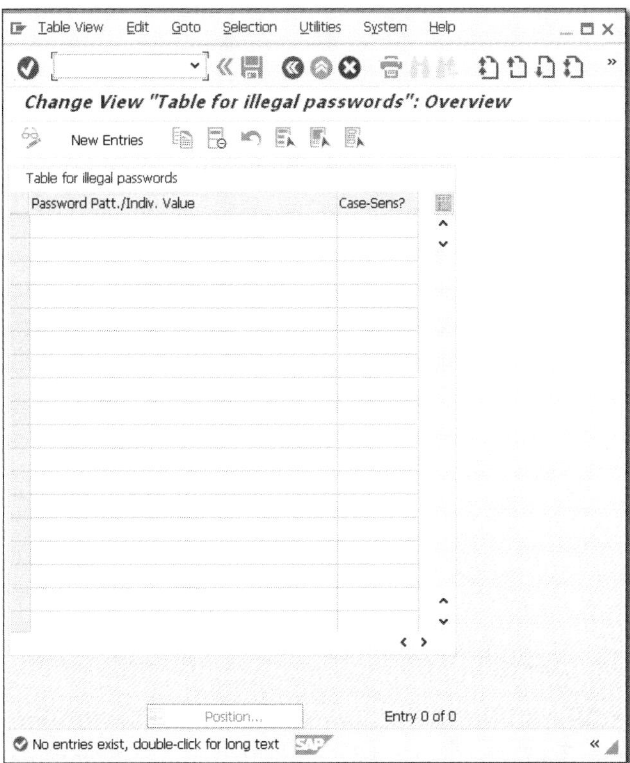

Figure 17.34 Editing Table Entries

8. Maintain the new entries. The number and names of the columns depend on the selected table. Then click on SAVE (see Figure 17.35).

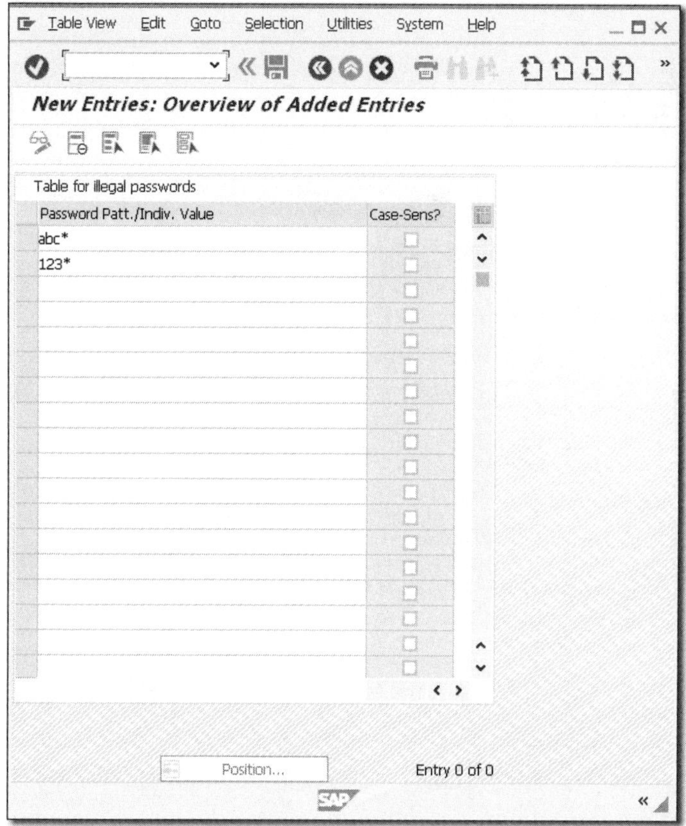

Figure 17.35 Adding Table Entries

9. If the table can be transported and if automatic recording is activated in the corresponding client, a dialog box opens that prompts you to enter a transport request. Proceed as described in Section 17.2.1 or Section 17.2.2. After you specify a transport request, click on CONTINUE (see Figure 17.36).

[+] **Recording Changes**

If the client has been configured in such a way that changes to client-specific tables are not to be recorded in transport requests, this dialog box isn't displayed (see Chapter 2, Section 2.7)—provided that you currently maintain a client-specific table. If you change cross-client tables (refer to Figure 17.33), the system always queries a transport request.

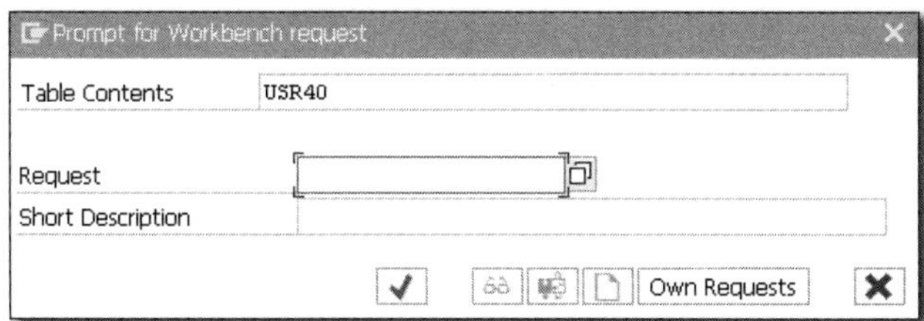

Figure 17.36 Entering a Transport Request

10. The status bar shows the message DATA WAS SAVED confirming that the entries have been saved. Click on BACK.
11. The table contains the new entries (see Figure 17.37). Click on the BACK button.

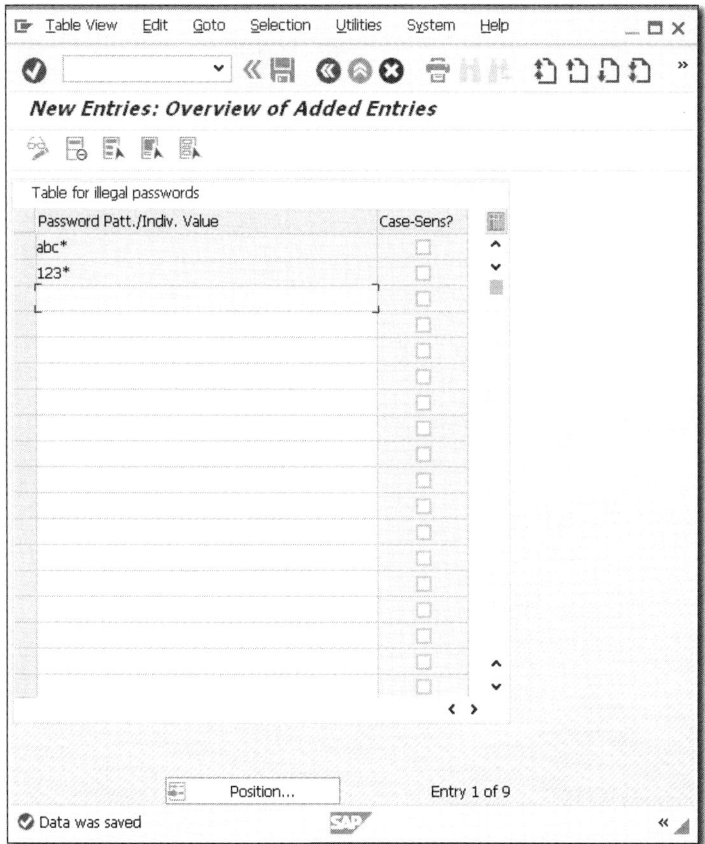

Figure 17.37 Display of New Table Entries

After making your changes, you can exit Transaction SM30 and transport the modification to other systems according to the procedure described in Section 17.2.

17.4 Summary

The Transport Management System enables you to apply changes to a multisystem landscape in a comfortable and secure way. The transport process ensures that most of the changes can only be implemented in the development system and transferred to the production system after having been tested in the QA system. This reduces the risks of errors and system failures considerably. This chapter described how you can create transport requests, include objects to be transported in a transport request, and finally implement the transport.

This chapter describes how to maintain SAP systems with support packages and patches. You'll learn how to download software updates from the SAP Support Portal, how to perform a kernel update, and how to maintain the ABAP components in your SAP system.

18 System Maintenance

SAP software is largely maintained using *support packages*. A support package is a set of corrections for errors in ABAP programs. These corrections are usually already available as SAP Notes. A support package bundles the corrections that have been provided over a certain period in a consolidated package. In most cases, support packages contain error corrections only, while functional enhancements are less common. The latter are usually provided as *enhancement packages*.

Support packages are provided for specific products, releases, and components. They provide corrections both for the system basis and for the functional components. Because the individual components of an SAP system interact with one another, the support package versions of the various components must be compatible. For example, if you import a support package for an application component that requires a specific SAP Basis support package, serious errors may occur if both packages aren't implemented.

To resolve such conflicts, SAP delivers *support package stacks* that contain compatible kernel and support package versions for all components in a system. You should use the support package stacks available, rather than importing support packages in isolation.

Support packages enable the early detection and resolution of problems in your system. There is some controversy regarding the best time to import support packages. SAP recommends customers import all support packages as soon as they are released to avoid the occurrence of serious problems. However, many customers believe that regression tests should be performed for all system changes; in other words, all business processes should be tested after maintenance.

Because support packages are released on a frequent basis, they're often not imported upon release because the required tests are too extensive to be completed in sufficient time.

Against this backdrop, you should create a maintenance concept for your SAP systems. Give some thought to the frequency with which you want to implement SAP Notes and import support packages and support package stacks. Have the concept agreed on by all business departments because most of the regression testing will have to be done by users from these departments.

[✪] **Maintenance Strategy Recommendation**

You should base your maintenance strategy on the intervals at which the support package stacks are published, and you should import these on a quarterly or annual basis. For short-term troubleshooting, it's best to refer to the corrections provided in SAP Notes (see Chapter 19). Support packages shouldn't be imported in isolation.

If necessary, you can perform a kernel update independently of the ABAP support package version. The ABAP components only ever require a minimum kernel version, which means that the kernel may always have a higher version than that contained in the most recent support package stack.

18.1 Downloading SAP Support Packages

Support packages and support package stacks can be downloaded from the SAP Support Portal. ABAP support packages for all SAP systems as of SAP NetWeaver 7.0 can only be downloaded with the Maintenance Optimizer in SAP Solution Manager (see Chapter 4, Section 4.4). While the support packages you require can also be selected in the SAP Support Portal directly, you need SAP Solution Manager to confirm (or approve) the downloads. Because the Maintenance Optimizer greatly simplifies the selection of support packages and helps avoid errors, we strongly recommend that you use SAP Solution Manager.

Kernel updates and updates for the SPAM/SAINT version can be downloaded without SAP Solution Manager. The steps involved in downloading the software from the SAP Support Portal are described next.

[✪] **SPAM/SAINT Version**

Transactions SPAM (Support Package Manager) and SAINT (Add-On Installation Tool) are used to import updates and add-ons. Both transactions are updated using a separate SPAM/SAINT update.

The SPAM/SAINT version is important because certain ABAP support packages require a minimum version. If the minimum SPAM/SAINT version required isn't in your system, serious errors may occur when you import support packages.

[+]

Logon to the SAP Support Portal

The following instructions assume that you can access the SAP Support Portal and that you're familiar with the logon and navigation procedure.

You also require authorization to download software from the SAP Support Portal. For more information, see Chapter 19.

18.1.1 Determining the System's Current Support Package Level

Before you download support packages, you need to determine which components are contained in your system and which updates have already been imported. There are two ways to do this as described next.

Method 1—System Status

Check the system status. Information about support package levels is included in the status display. Follow these steps:

1. Choose the menu option SYSTEM • STATUS. This function is accessible from all transactions and menus (see Figure 18.1).

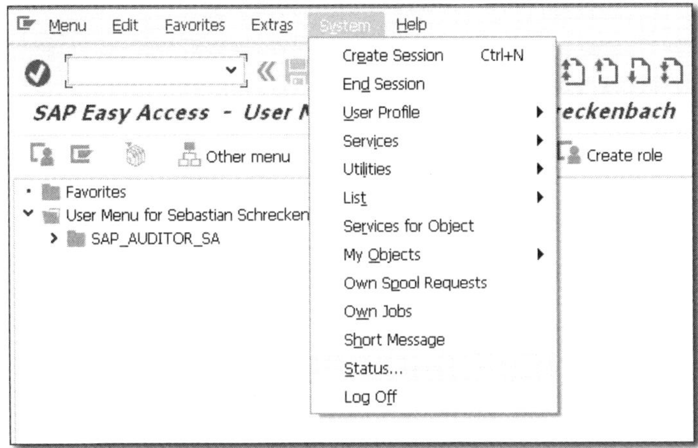

Figure 18.1 Calling the System Status

2. Write down the following information under SAP SYSTEM DATA in the SYSTEM: STATUS window (see Figure 18.2):
   - COMPONENT VERSION (e.g., SAP NETWEAVER 7.40)
   - UNICODE SYSTEM (e.g., YES)

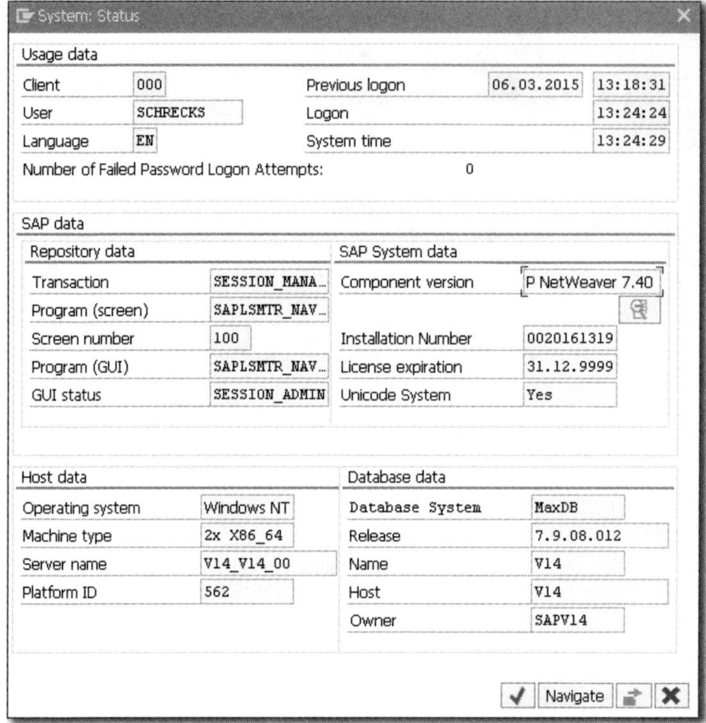

Figure 18.2 System Information Relevant for Maintenance

You also need the following details for the kernel update shown under HOST DATA and DATABASE DATA:

- OPERATING SYSTEM (e.g., LINUX)
- MACHINE TYPE (e.g., x86_64)
- DATABASE SYSTEM (e.g., ORACLE)

Then click on the COMPONENT INFORMATION icon.

3. The table displayed indicates which components are contained in your system, their version (release), and their support package level (see Figure 18.3):

- COMPONENT (e.g., SAP_BASIS)
- RELEASE (e.g., 740)
- SP-LEVEL (e.g., 0005)

Choose the PRINT icon, to print the list, or take note of the component information. Choose CONTINUE to return to the previous screen.

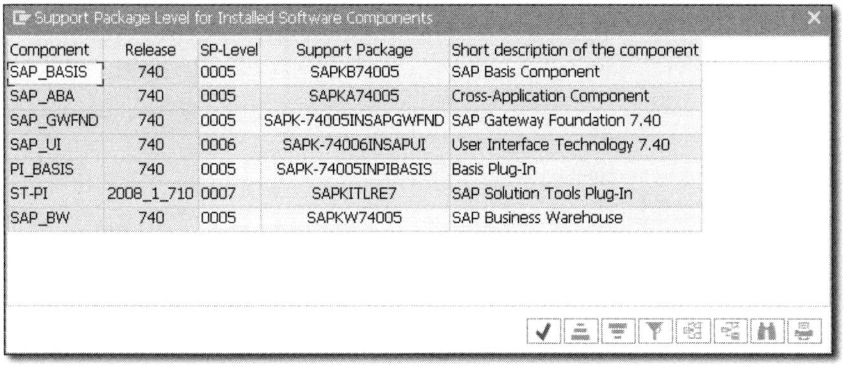

Support Package Level for Installed Software Components

Component	Release	SP-Level	Support Package	Short description of the component
SAP_BASIS	740	0005	SAPKB74005	SAP Basis Component
SAP_ABA	740	0005	SAPKA74005	Cross-Application Component
SAP_GWFND	740	0005	SAPK-74005INSAPGWFND	SAP Gateway Foundation 7.40
SAP_UI	740	0006	SAPK-74006INSAPUI	User Interface Technology 7.40
PI_BASIS	740	0005	SAPK-74005INPIBASIS	Basis Plug-In
ST-PI	2008_1_710	0007	SAPKITLRE7	SAP Solution Tools Plug-In
SAP_BW	740	0005	SAPKW74005	SAP Business Warehouse

Figure 18.3 Detailed Information about the Software Components

Technical Support Package Name [+]

The names of support packages (see the SUPPORT PACKAGE column) comprise the following elements:

SAPK<Component><Release><Level>

SAPKB74005 is the fifth support package of the SAP Basis component for release 7.40. You'll need to understand this naming convention when you receive the support packages as files.

4. On the SYSTEM: STATUS screen, click on the OTHER KERNEL INFO icon.
5. You need the following details from the kernel information to download the kernel (see Figure 18.4):
   - KERNEL RELEASE (e.g., 741)
   - SUP. PKG. LVL (e.g., 11)

   Take note of this information, and click on CONTINUE.

You now have all of the information you need to download ABAP and kernel patches.

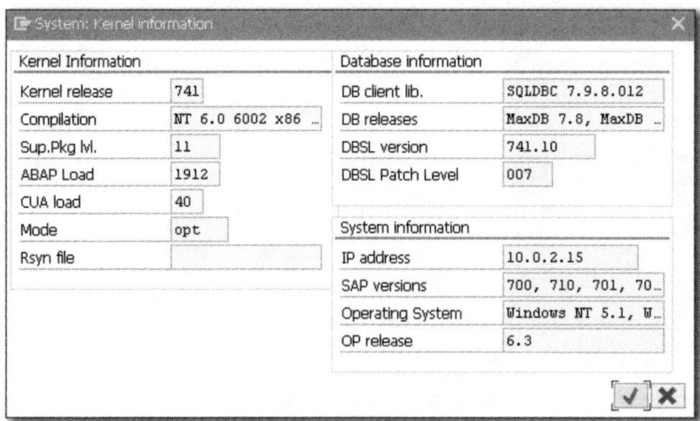

Figure 18.4 Kernel Version Information

Method 2—Support Package Manager

With the second method, you access more detailed information about which support packages have been imported. You also determine your system's current SPAM/SAINT version.

1. Enter Transaction SPAM in the command field and press the Enter key (or select the menu option Tools • ABAP Workbench • Utilities • Maintenance • SPAM—Support Package Manager).
2. Under Directory, select the Imported Support Packages option, and click on Display (see Figure 18.5).

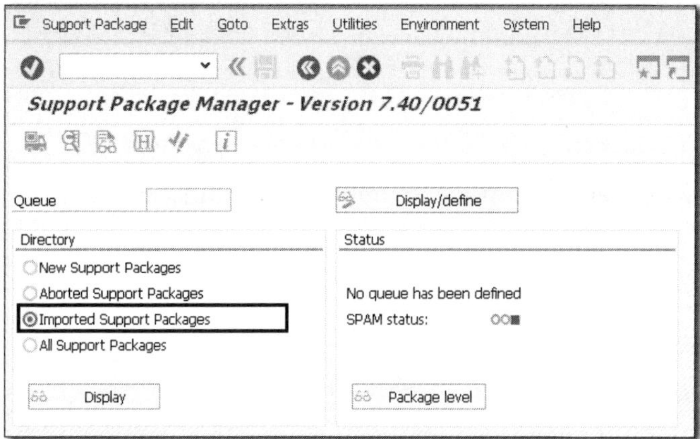

Figure 18.5 Initial Screen of the Support Package Manager

3. A list of the updates that have been imported is displayed (see Figure 18.6). Take note of the components and the highest support package levels. Pay particular attention to the information about the SPAM/SAINT UPDATE.

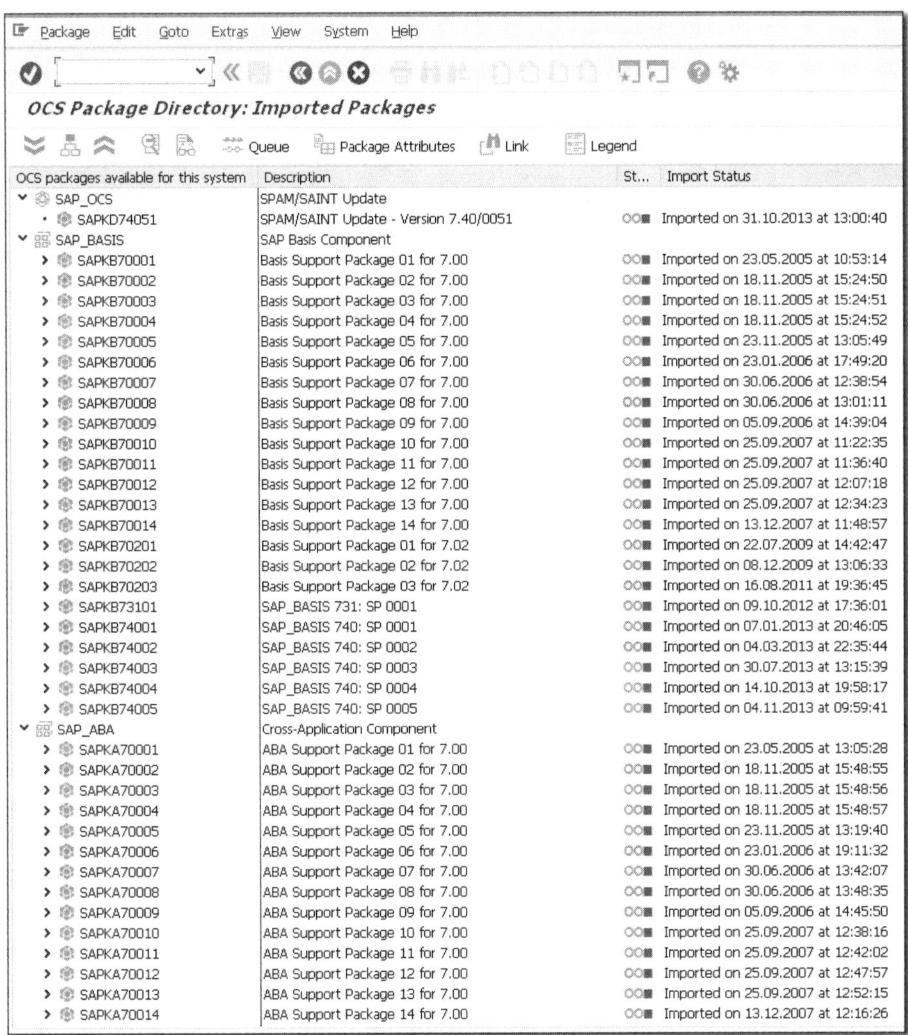

OCS packages available for this system	Description	St...	Import Status
SAP_OCS	SPAM/SAINT Update		
SAPKD74051	SPAM/SAINT Update - Version 7.40/0051		Imported on 31.10.2013 at 13:00:40
SAP_BASIS	SAP Basis Component		
SAPKB70001	Basis Support Package 01 for 7.00		Imported on 23.05.2005 at 10:53:14
SAPKB70002	Basis Support Package 02 for 7.00		Imported on 18.11.2005 at 15:24:50
SAPKB70003	Basis Support Package 03 for 7.00		Imported on 18.11.2005 at 15:24:51
SAPKB70004	Basis Support Package 04 for 7.00		Imported on 18.11.2005 at 15:24:52
SAPKB70005	Basis Support Package 05 for 7.00		Imported on 23.11.2005 at 13:05:49
SAPKB70006	Basis Support Package 06 for 7.00		Imported on 23.01.2006 at 17:49:20
SAPKB70007	Basis Support Package 07 for 7.00		Imported on 30.06.2006 at 12:38:54
SAPKB70008	Basis Support Package 08 for 7.00		Imported on 30.06.2006 at 13:01:11
SAPKB70009	Basis Support Package 09 for 7.00		Imported on 05.09.2006 at 14:39:04
SAPKB70010	Basis Support Package 10 for 7.00		Imported on 25.09.2007 at 11:22:35
SAPKB70011	Basis Support Package 11 for 7.00		Imported on 25.09.2007 at 11:36:40
SAPKB70012	Basis Support Package 12 for 7.00		Imported on 25.09.2007 at 12:07:18
SAPKB70013	Basis Support Package 13 for 7.00		Imported on 25.09.2007 at 12:34:23
SAPKB70014	Basis Support Package 14 for 7.00		Imported on 13.12.2007 at 11:48:57
SAPKB70201	Basis Support Package 01 for 7.02		Imported on 22.07.2009 at 14:42:47
SAPKB70202	Basis Support Package 02 for 7.02		Imported on 08.12.2009 at 13:06:33
SAPKB70203	Basis Support Package 03 for 7.02		Imported on 16.08.2011 at 19:36:45
SAPKB73101	SAP_BASIS 731: SP 0001		Imported on 09.10.2012 at 17:36:01
SAPKB74001	SAP_BASIS 740: SP 0001		Imported on 07.01.2013 at 20:46:05
SAPKB74002	SAP_BASIS 740: SP 0002		Imported on 04.03.2013 at 22:35:44
SAPKB74003	SAP_BASIS 740: SP 0003		Imported on 30.07.2013 at 13:15:39
SAPKB74004	SAP_BASIS 740: SP 0004		Imported on 14.10.2013 at 19:58:17
SAPKB74005	SAP_BASIS 740: SP 0005		Imported on 04.11.2013 at 09:59:41
SAP_ABA	Cross-Application Component		
SAPKA70001	ABA Support Package 01 for 7.00		Imported on 23.05.2005 at 13:05:28
SAPKA70002	ABA Support Package 02 for 7.00		Imported on 18.11.2005 at 15:48:55
SAPKA70003	ABA Support Package 03 for 7.00		Imported on 18.11.2005 at 15:48:56
SAPKA70004	ABA Support Package 04 for 7.00		Imported on 18.11.2005 at 15:48:57
SAPKA70005	ABA Support Package 05 for 7.00		Imported on 23.11.2005 at 13:19:40
SAPKA70006	ABA Support Package 06 for 7.00		Imported on 23.01.2006 at 19:11:32
SAPKA70007	ABA Support Package 07 for 7.00		Imported on 30.06.2006 at 13:42:07
SAPKA70008	ABA Support Package 08 for 7.00		Imported on 30.06.2006 at 13:48:35
SAPKA70009	ABA Support Package 09 for 7.00		Imported on 05.09.2006 at 14:45:50
SAPKA70010	ABA Support Package 10 for 7.00		Imported on 25.09.2007 at 12:38:16
SAPKA70011	ABA Support Package 11 for 7.00		Imported on 25.09.2007 at 12:42:02
SAPKA70012	ABA Support Package 12 for 7.00		Imported on 25.09.2007 at 12:47:57
SAPKA70013	ABA Support Package 13 for 7.00		Imported on 25.09.2007 at 12:52:15
SAPKA70014	ABA Support Package 14 for 7.00		Imported on 13.12.2007 at 12:16:26

Figure 18.6 List of Imported Support Packages

The SPAM/SAINT version is the last piece of information you need. You can now start downloading support packages from the SAP Support Portal.

18.1.2 Finding Support Packages

After you've gathered all of the details you need about the components in your system, you can search for available support packages in the SAP Support Portal. Use the details you noted to make your selection.

1. Access the SAP Support Portal, and go to the DOWNLOAD SOFTWARE tab (see Figure 18.7).

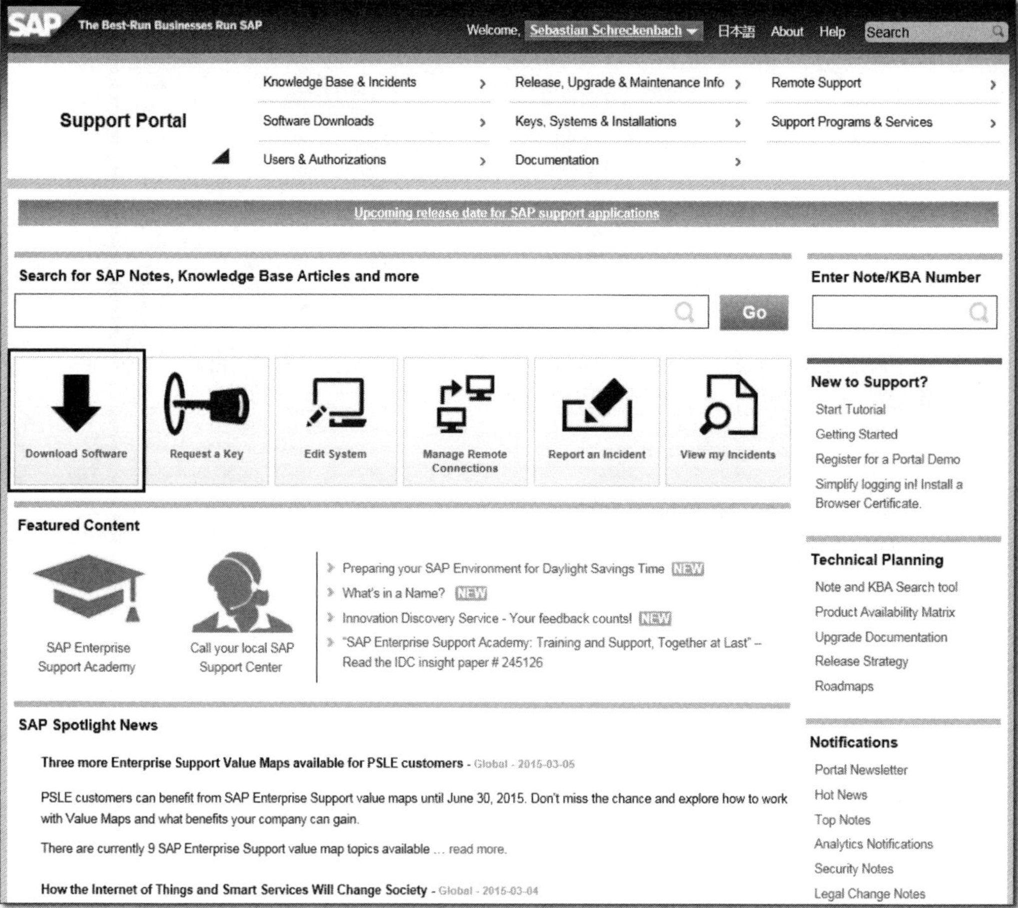

Figure 18.7 Initial Screen of the SAP Support Portal

2. Click on the SUPPORT PACKAGES AND PATCHES link (see Figure 18.8).

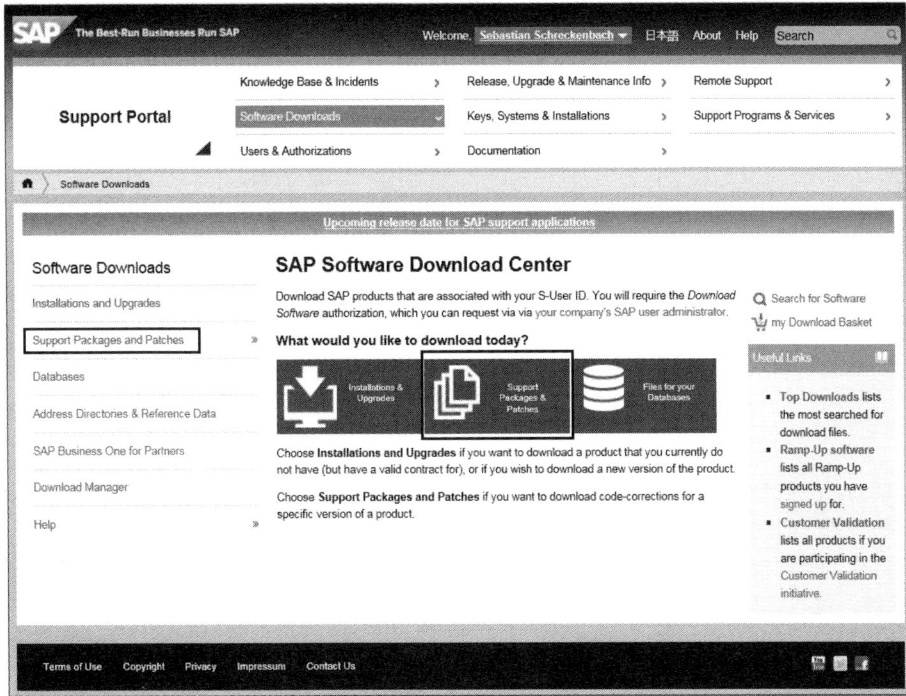

Figure 18.8 SAP Software Download Center

3. You now have various options for selecting support packages to be imported (see Figure 18.9):

   - A – Z Alphabetical List of Products: Here you can browse the support packages in an alphabetically sorted product hierarchy.
   - My Company's Application Components: Here you can find the products and components your company has registered with SAP.
   - Browse Download Catalog: Here you can browse the support packages for your product version.
   - Search for Software: Here you can enter any search text to find the appropriate support packages.

   Simply choose the search method that suits you best. In this example, click on the Browse Download Catalog link.

4. Select a product group, for example, SAP NetWeaver and complementary products (see Figure 18.10).

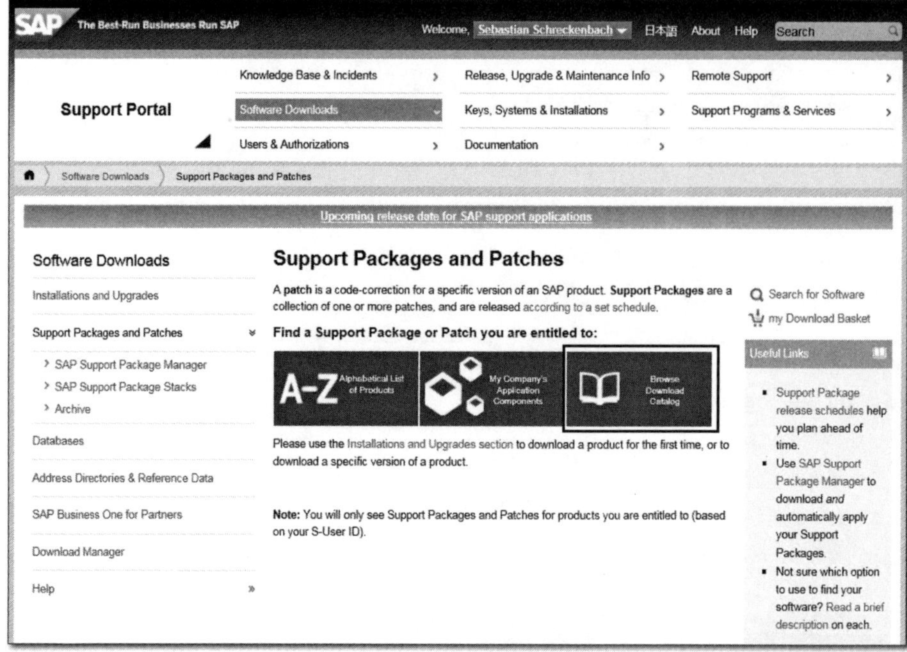

Figure 18.9 Search Options for Selecting Support Packages

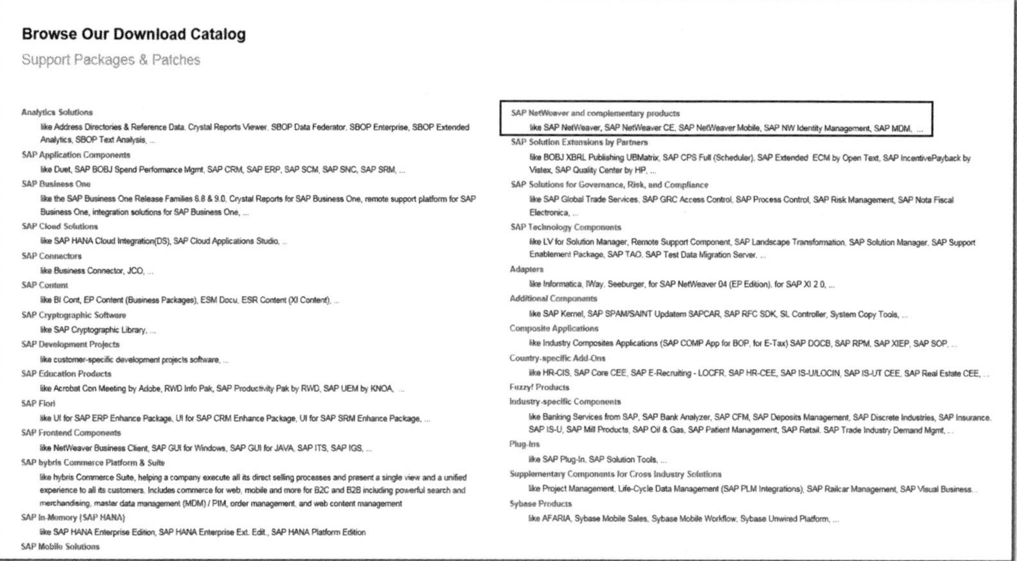

Figure 18.10 Selecting a Product Group

5. Select the subgroup, for example, SAP NetWeaver (see Figure 18.11).

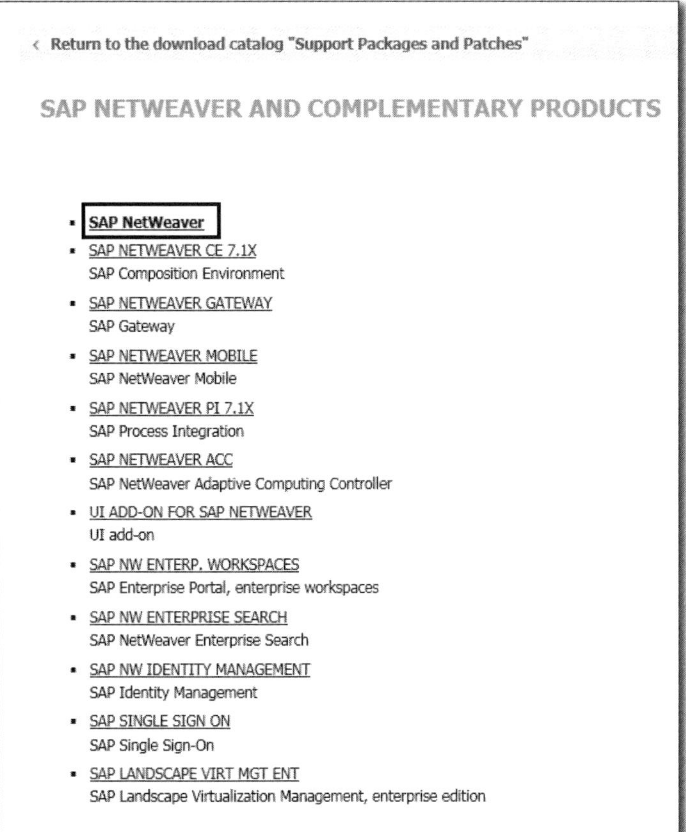

Figure 18.11 Selecting a Product Subgroup

6. Select your product version (see Figure 18.12), which you checked as described in Section 18.1.1, for example, SAP NetWeaver 7.4. The product version corresponds to the Component Version shown earlier in Figure 18.2.
7. Click on Entry by Component (see Figure 18.13).

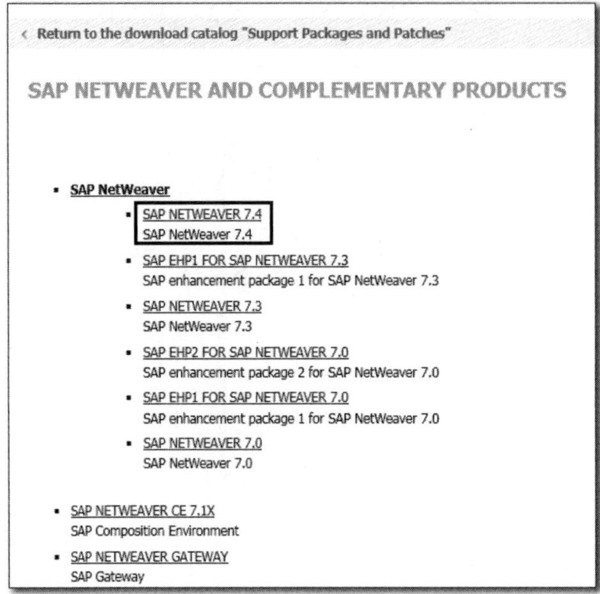

Figure 18.12 Selecting the Product Version

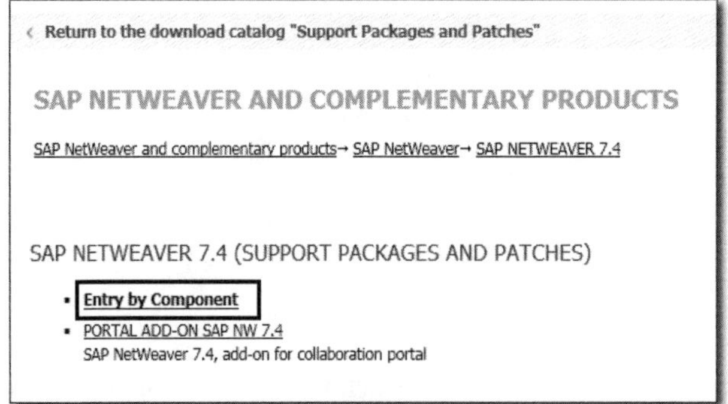

Figure 18.13 Entry by Component

8. The system opens a tree structure. Choose the product instance APPLICATION SERVER ABAP (see Figure 18.14).
9. Now go through the list of your product's components in detail, and select the support packages to download. Start by clicking on the PI_BASIS 7.40 component, for example (see Figure 18.15).

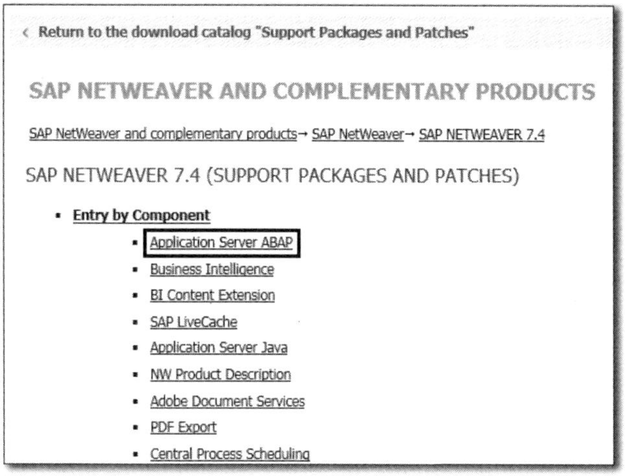

‹ Return to the download catalog "Support Packages and Patches"

SAP NETWEAVER AND COMPLEMENTARY PRODUCTS

SAP NetWeaver and complementary products → SAP NetWeaver → SAP NETWEAVER 7.4

SAP NETWEAVER 7.4 (SUPPORT PACKAGES AND PATCHES)

- Entry by Component
  - Application Server ABAP
  - Business Intelligence
  - BI Content Extension
  - SAP LiveCache
  - Application Server Java
  - NW Product Description
  - Adobe Document Services
  - PDF Export
  - Central Process Scheduling

Figure 18.14 Selecting the Product Instance

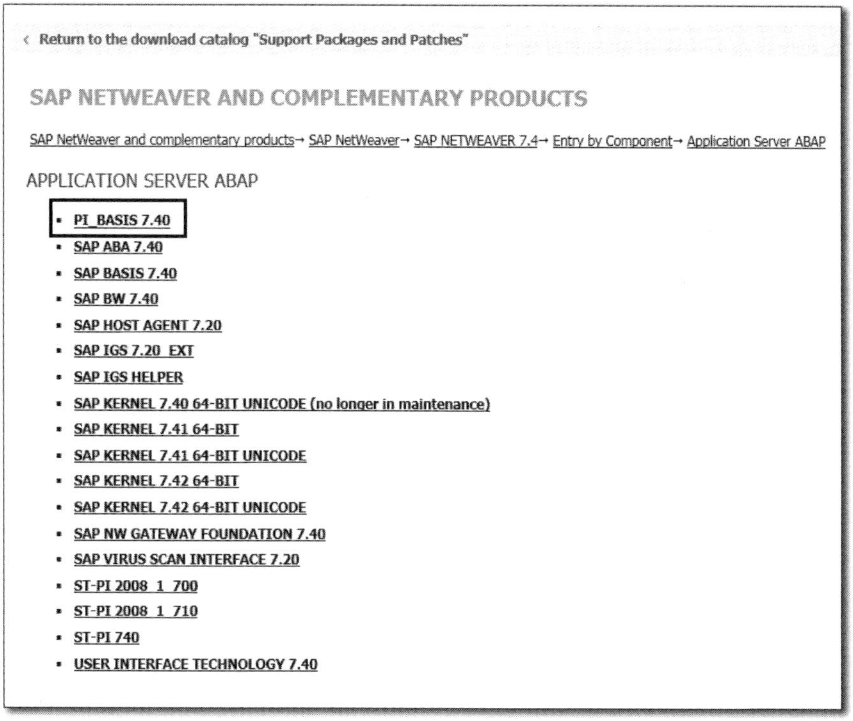

‹ Return to the download catalog "Support Packages and Patches"

SAP NETWEAVER AND COMPLEMENTARY PRODUCTS

SAP NetWeaver and complementary products → SAP NetWeaver → SAP NETWEAVER 7.4 → Entry by Component → Application Server ABAP

APPLICATION SERVER ABAP

- PI_BASIS 7.40
- SAP ABA 7.40
- SAP BASIS 7.40
- SAP BW 7.40
- SAP HOST AGENT 7.20
- SAP IGS 7.20_EXT
- SAP IGS HELPER
- SAP KERNEL 7.40 64-BIT UNICODE (no longer in maintenance)
- SAP KERNEL 7.41 64-BIT
- SAP KERNEL 7.41 64-BIT UNICODE
- SAP KERNEL 7.42 64-BIT
- SAP KERNEL 7.42 64-BIT UNICODE
- SAP NW GATEWAY FOUNDATION 7.40
- SAP VIRUS SCAN INTERFACE 7.20
- ST-PI 2008_1_700
- ST-PI 2008_1_710
- ST-PI 740
- USER INTERFACE TECHNOLOGY 7.40

Figure 18.15 Selecting the Component

10. Click on SUPPORT PACKAGES (see Figure 18.16).

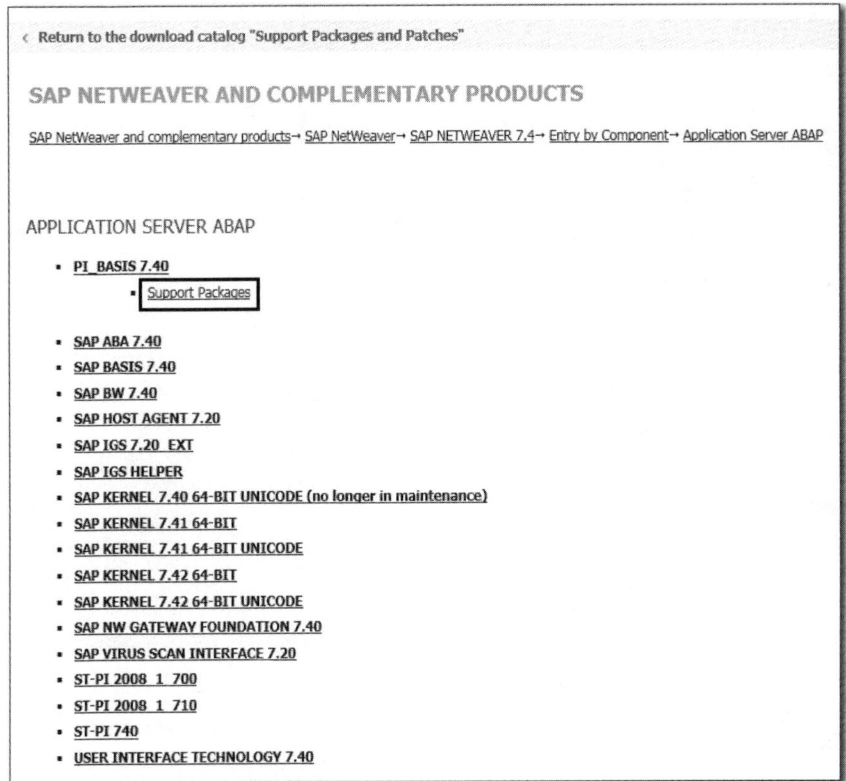

Figure 18.16 Displaying Support Packages

11. A list of download objects is displayed at the bottom of the screen. Scroll down through this list, and select one or more support packages with a higher support package level than the current level in your system (e.g., PI_BASIS 7.40: SP 0006 and PI_BASIS 7.40: SP 0007; see Figure 18.17). Click on ADD TO DOWNLOAD BASKET.

[!]

Skipping Support Package Levels

If you haven't imported any support packages for a long time, several new levels may have been made available since your last import (e.g., your system may currently have patch level 5, and patch level 7 is now available). If you want to update your system to the latest level (in this case, level 7) and skip one or several patch levels (here, level 6), you must download *all* files available (levels 6 and 7).

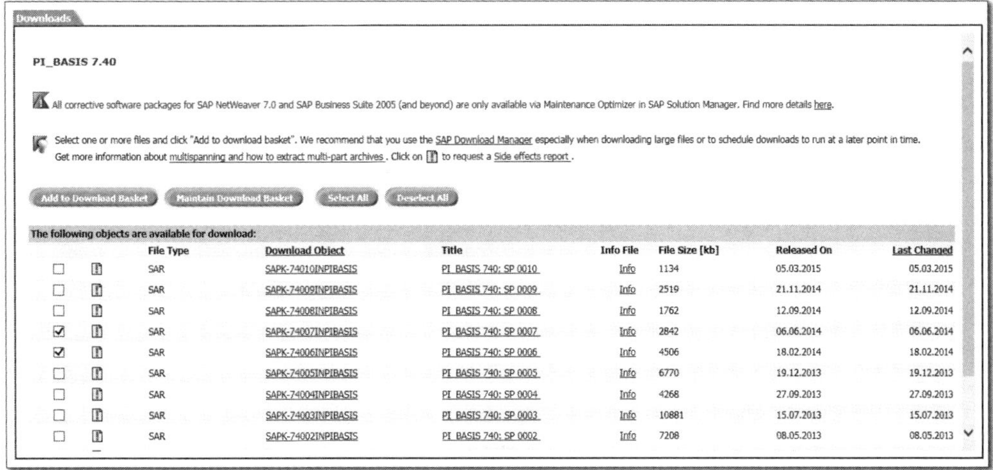

Figure 18.17 Selecting Support Packages for Download

12. Another browser window opens, confirming that the file has been added to your Download Basket (see Figure 18.18). Click on Close.

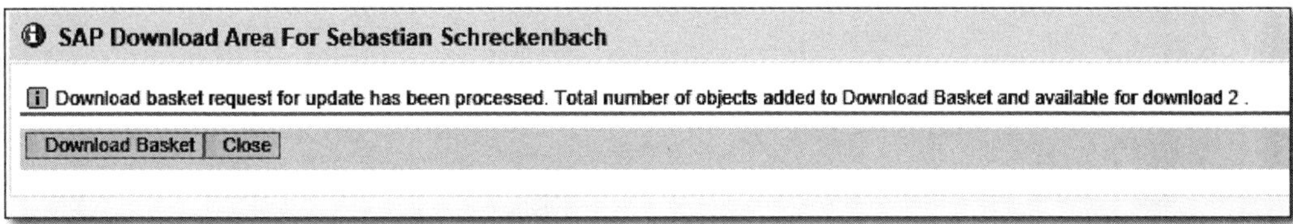

Figure 18.18 Confirmation for Download Basket

13. Continue with the other ABAP components, in this example (see Figure 18.19):
    - SAP_ABA 7.40
    - SAP_BASIS 7.40
    - SAP_BW 7.40
    - SAP NW Gateway Foundation 7.40
    - ST-PI 2008_1_710
    - User Interface Technology 7.40

    Go through the individual components, adding the support packages to your Download Basket one after another, as described in steps 9 to 12.

‹ Return to the download catalog "Support Packages and Patches"

SAP NETWEAVER AND COMPLEMENTARY PRODUCTS

SAP NetWeaver and complementary products→ SAP NetWeaver→ SAP NETWEAVER 7.4→ Entry by Component→ Application Server ABAP

APPLICATION SERVER ABAP

- PI_BASIS 7.40
  - Support Packages
- SAP ABA 7.40
  - Support Packages
- SAP BASIS 7.40
  - Support Packages
- SAP BW 7.40
  - Support Packages
- SAP HOST AGENT 7.20
- SAP IGS 7.20 EXT
- SAP IGS HELPER
- SAP KERNEL 7.40 64-BIT UNICODE (no longer in maintenance)
- SAP KERNEL 7.41 64-BIT
- SAP KERNEL 7.41 64-BIT UNICODE
- SAP KERNEL 7.42 64-BIT
- SAP KERNEL 7.42 64-BIT UNICODE
- SAP NW GATEWAY FOUNDATION 7.40
  - Support Packages
- SAP VIRUS SCAN INTERFACE 7.20
- ST-PI 2008 1 700
- ST-PI 2008 1 710
  - Support Packages
- ST-PI 740
- USER INTERFACE TECHNOLOGY 7.40

Figure 18.19 Expanded Download Links for ABAP Components

Next, you select the support packages for the operating system-dependent components of your system, that is, kernel und SAP Internet Graphic Service (SAP IGS):

1. Select the entry SAP IGS 7.20 EXT (see Figure 18.20). A tree structure is expanded, in which you can select your server's operating system (e.g., LINUX ON X86_64 64BIT).

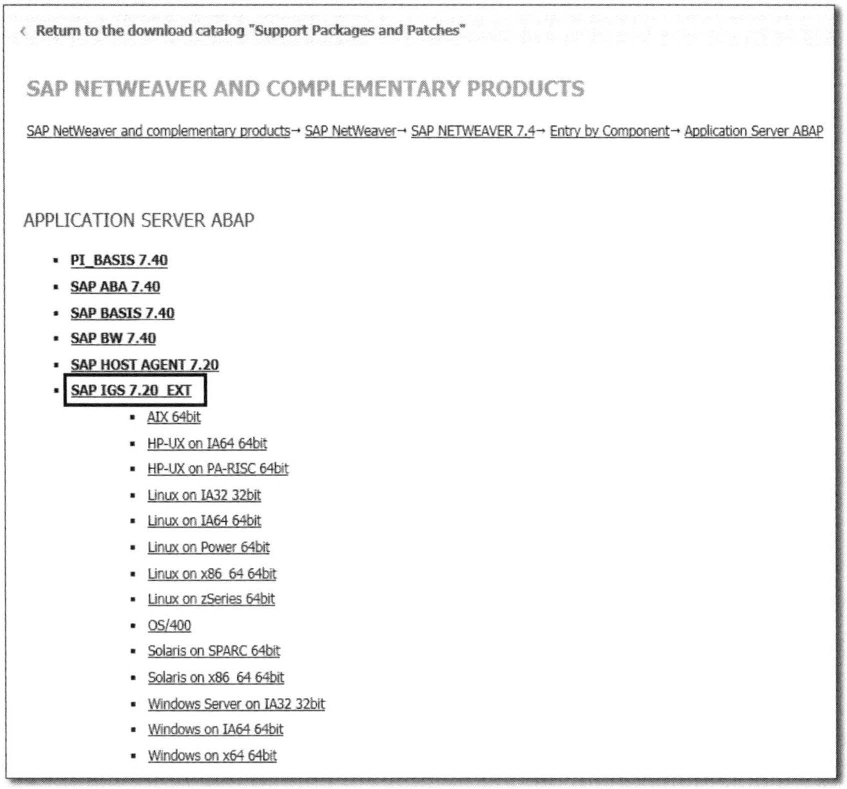

< Return to the download catalog "Support Packages and Patches"

SAP NETWEAVER AND COMPLEMENTARY PRODUCTS

SAP NetWeaver and complementary products→ SAP NetWeaver→ SAP NETWEAVER 7.4→ Entry by Component→ Application Server ABAP

APPLICATION SERVER ABAP

- PI_BASIS 7.40
- SAP ABA 7.40
- SAP BASIS 7.40
- SAP BW 7.40
- SAP HOST AGENT 7.20
- SAP IGS 7.20_EXT
  - AIX 64bit
  - HP-UX on IA64 64bit
  - HP-UX on PA-RISC 64bit
  - Linux on IA32 32bit
  - Linux on IA64 64bit
  - Linux on Power 64bit
  - Linux on x86_64 64bit
  - Linux on zSeries 64bit
  - OS/400
  - Solaris on SPARC 64bit
  - Solaris on x86_64 64bit
  - Windows Server on IA32 32bit
  - Windows on IA64 64bit
  - Windows on x64 64bit

Figure 18.20 Selecting the SAP IGS Component

SAP IGS [⚙]

The SAP IGS ensures that graphical content can be displayed in the SAP system. This technology is used for Web Dynpros, for example. As of release 6.40 of the Web Application Server (now SAP NetWeaver Application Server, AS), the SAP IGS is part of the kernel and is installed as standard. If you don't perform a kernel update, you should also update SAP IGS to the latest level immediately. Always use the most recent update available.

You can use Transaction SIGS (Internet Graphics Service Administration) to check which version of SAP IGS is running in your SAP system.

2. Select the latest version (e.g., Patch Level 8), and add it to your Download Basket (see Figure 18.21).

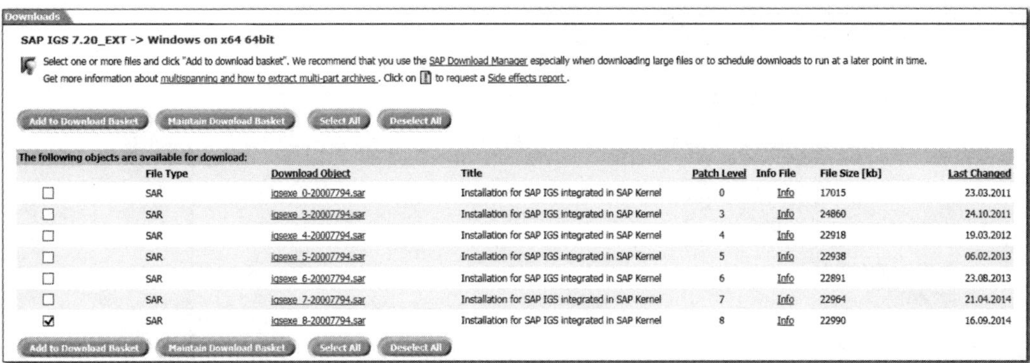

Figure 18.21 Selecting the Latest Support Packages of the SAP IGS

3. Continue with the download of the SAP kernel. Make sure to select the appropriate version for your operating system (e.g., 7.40/7.41 64 bit), and base your selection on whether your SAP system is a Unicode or non-Unicode system. In our example, we'll select SAP KERNEL 7.41 64-BIT UNICODE (see Figure 18.22) and the operating system LINUX ON X86_64 64BIT.

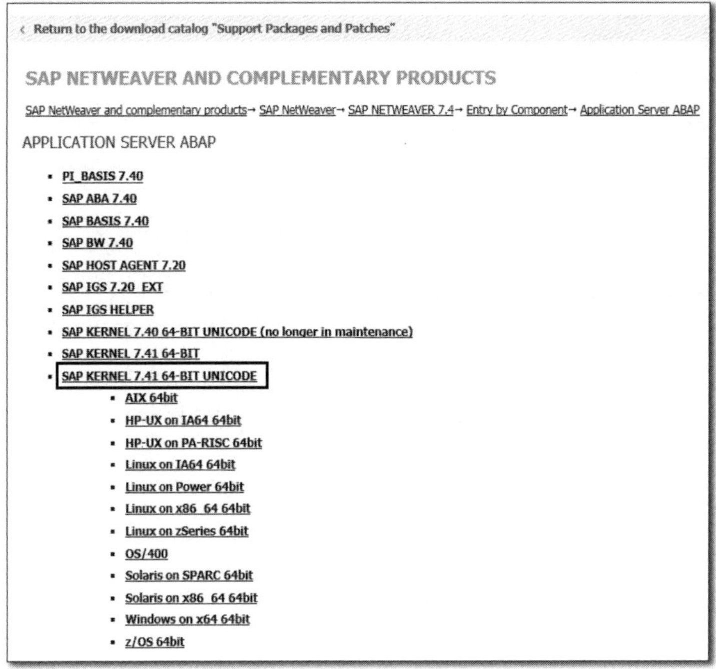

Figure 18.22 Selecting the SAP Kernel Version

4. Click on the #DATABASE INDEPENDENT link (see Figure 18.23).

Contents of a Kernel Patch [⚙]

The SAP kernel consists of a large, *database-independent* part (kernel part I) and a smaller, *database-dependent* part (kernel part II). You must always download both parts and install them together.

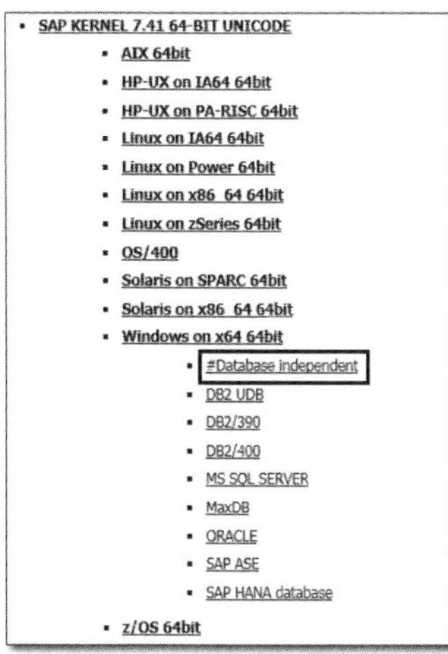

Figure 18.23 Selecting the Database-Independent Kernel Parts

5. Scroll down through the list, and add KERNEL PART I with the latest version (e.g., PATCH LEVEL 200) to your download basket on the DOWNLOADS tab (which is now displayed, see Figure 18.24).

Downloads

SAP KERNEL 7.41 64-BIT UNICODE -> Windows on x64 64bit -> #Database independent

Select one or more files and click "Add to download basket". We recommend that you use the SAP Download Manager especially when downloading large files or to schedule downloads to run at a later point in time. Get more information about multispanning and how to extract multi-part archives . Click on [ ] to request a Side effects report .

Add to Download Basket | Maintain Download Basket | Select All | Deselect All

The following objects are available for download:

	File Type	Download Object	Title	Patch Level	Info File	File Size [kb]	Last Changed
☐	SAR	R3ta_33-10012501.SAR	R3ta	33	Info	1435	08.05.2014
☐	SAR	R3trans_213-10012501.SAR	R3TRANS	213	Info	6891	06.03.2015
☐	SAR	SAPEXE_100-10012501.SAR	Kernel Part I	100	Info	494049	14.10.2014
☑	SAR	SAPEXE_200-10012501.SAR	Kernel Part I	200	Info	497374	06.02.2015
☐	SAR	SAPEXE_26-10012501.SAR	Kernel Part I	26	Info	488520	27.03.2014
☐	SAR	SAPEXE_31-10012501.SAR	Kernel Part I	31	Info	489220	11.06.2014
☐	SAR	SAPEXE_50-10012501.SAR	Kernel Part I	50	Info	493995	15.09.2014
☐	SAR	SSO22KerbMap_14-10012501.SAR	SSO2 To Kerberos Mapping Filter	14	Info	572	05.06.2014
☐	SAR	ccmagent_111-10012501.sar	CCMAGENT	111	Info	19481	31.10.2014
☐	SAR	dw_213-10012501.sar	disp+work package	213	Info	283394	06.03.2015
☐	SAR	dw_utils_210-10012501.sar	Kernel utilities	210	Info	15874	13.02.2015

Figure 18.24 Adding Kernel Part I to the Download Basket

Contents of a Kernel

The SAP kernel comprises a range of components, including the *startsap* and *stopsap* files for starting and stopping the SAP server, and the `tp` program for the transport system (see Chapter 17). We recommend that you use the kernel packages I and II compiled by SAP. These contain a stable, functioning, and complete version of the kernel. You should only download the individual components in the event of an emergency, or if requested to do so by SAP Support.

6. Scroll back up through the list, and select the database-dependent part of the kernel by clicking on the link for your database system (e.g., MaxDB; see Figure 18.25).
7. Next, scroll down through the list again, and add Kernel Part II with the latest version (e.g., Patch Level 200) to your download basket on the Downloads tab (see Figure 18.26). You must select the same patch level you selected for Kernel Part I.

   If you use an Oracle database, you should also download the patch for the BR*tools (see Section 18.6). You can find it via the same download path as Kernel Part II: DBATOOLS Package for Oracle <version>.

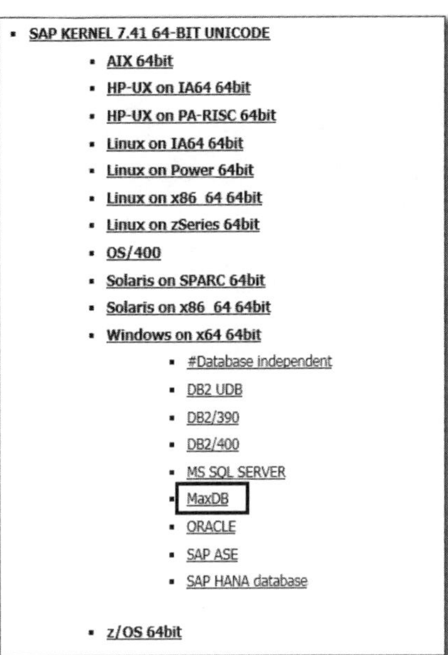

Figure 18.25 Selecting the Database-Independent Part of the Kernel

Downloads

SAP KERNEL 7.41 64-BIT UNICODE -> Windows on x64 64bit -> MaxDB

Select one or more files and click "Add to download basket". We recommend that you use the SAP Download Manager especially when downloading large files or to schedule downloads to run at a later point in time.
Get more information about multispanning and how to extract multi-part archives. Click on [i] to request a Side effects report.

Add to Download Basket | Maintain Download Basket | Select All | Deselect All

The following objects are available for download:

	File Type	Download Object	Title	Patch Level	Info File	File Size [kb]	Last Changed
☐	SAR	R3ldctl_48-10012498.SAR	R3load Control	48	Info	984	20.08.2014
☐	SAR	R3load_210-10012498.SAR	R3LOAD	210	Info	2609	13.02.2015
☐	SAR	SAPEXEDB_100-10012498.SAR	Kernel Part II	100	Info	28210	14.10.2014
☑	SAR	SAPEXEDB_200-10012498.SAR	Kernel Part II	200	Info	28908	06.02.2015
☐	SAR	SAPEXEDB_26-10012498.SAR	Kernel Part II	26	Info	26729	27.03.2014
☐	SAR	SAPEXEDB_31-10012498.SAR	Kernel Part II	31	Info	26994	11.06.2014
☐	SAR	SAPEXEDB_50-10012498.SAR	Kernel Part II	50	Info	28148	15.09.2014
☐	SAR	lib_dbsl_210-10012498.sar	Database Library	210	Info	2064	13.02.2015

Add to Download Basket | Maintain Download Basket | Select All | Deselect All

Figure 18.26 Adding Kernel Part II to the Download Basket

You've now selected all of the ABAP support packages and kernel patches you need. You can now search for the latest SPAM/SAINT version:

1. To do this, select the download menu option SUPPORT PACKAGES AND PATCHES • BROWSE DOWNLOAD CATALOG • ADDITIONAL COMPONENTS • SAP SPAM/SAINT UPDATE (see Figure 18.27), or search for the keyword SPAM under SEARCH FOR SOFTWARE.
2. Select your SPAM/SAINT version, for example, SPAM/SAINT UPDATE 740 (see Figure 18.28).
3. Click on SUPPORT PACKAGES, and add the latest version (e.g., SPAM/SAINT UPDATE – VERSION 7.40/0056) to your download basket (see Figure 18.29).

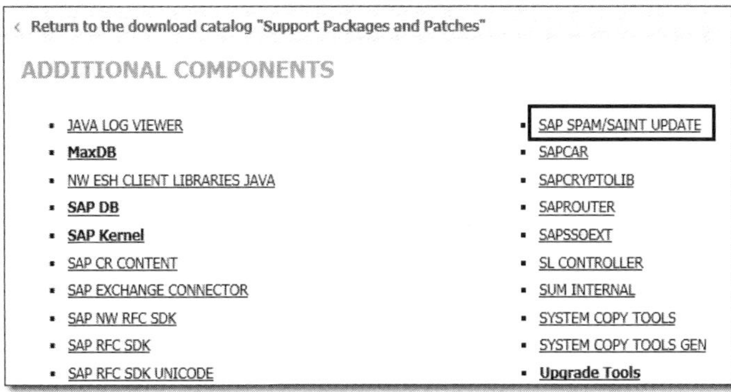

Figure 18.27 Opening the Update Section for the SPAM/SAINT Version

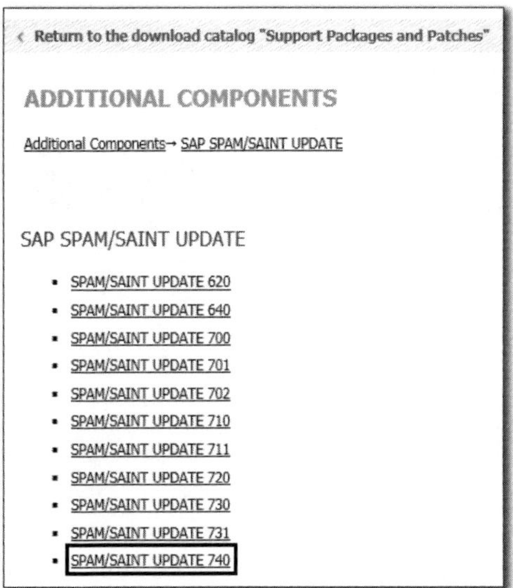

Figure 18.28 Selecting the Spam/Saint Version

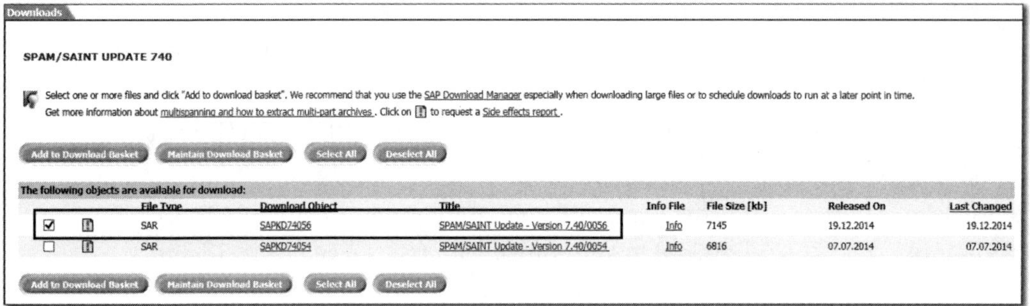

Figure 18.29 Adding the Latest SPAM/SAINT Support Package to the Download Basket

Your download list is now complete, and all files have been added to your download basket. You can now start downloading the software packages.

[+]

Maintenance Optimizer

As a guiding principle, you should use SAP Solution Manager to download support packages as a support package stack rather than in isolation (see Chapter 4, Section 4.4).

18.1.3 Downloading Support Packages

After adding all support packages to your download basket, you can begin the download by following these steps:

1. Access the SAP Support Portal, click on SOFTWARE DOWNLOADS and then on DOWNLOAD BASKET to open your download basket (see Figure 18.30).

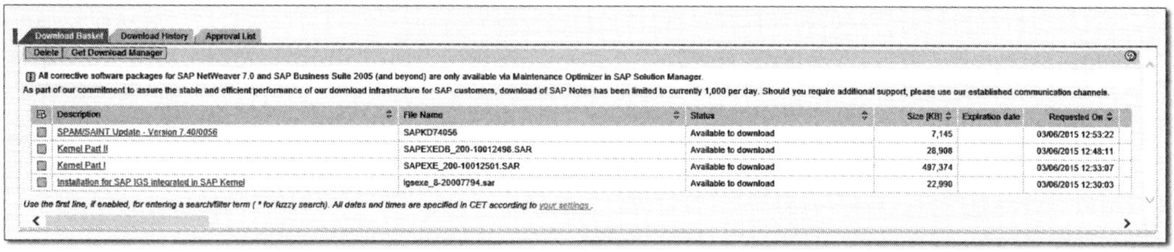

Figure 18.30 Displaying the Content of the Download Basket

2. The DOWNLOAD BASKET tab lists all of the files you can download. In our example, the list only shows the freely available kernel components.
3. Switch to the APPROVAL LIST tab. It shows the files for which a download needs to be approved with SAP Solution Manager (see Figure 18.31). This is indicated by the REQUEST APPROVAL entry in the STATUS column. The approval process is described in Chapter 4, Section 4.4.

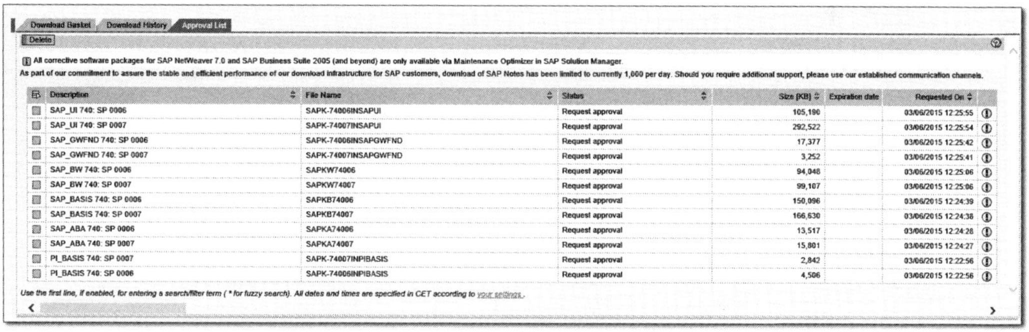

Figure 18.31 Calling the Approval List

4. As soon as the download has been approved, the ABAP support packages that require approval are also displayed on the DOWNLOAD BASKET tab (see Figure 18.32).

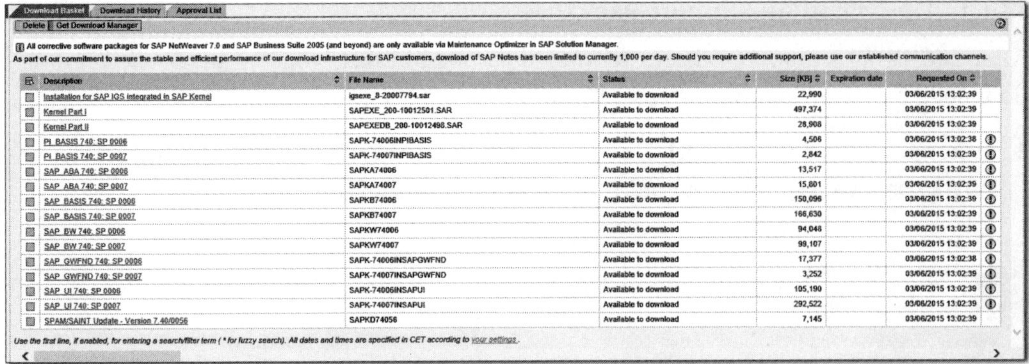

Download Basket | Download History | Approval List

Delete | Get Download Manager

All corrective software packages for SAP NetWeaver 7.0 and SAP Business Suite 2005 (and beyond) are only available via Maintenance Optimizer in SAP Solution Manager.
As part of our commitment to assure the stable and efficient performance of our download infrastructure for SAP customers, download of SAP Notes has been limited to currently 1,000 per day. Should you require additional support, please use our established communication channels.

Description	File Name	Status	Size [KB]	Expiration date	Requested On
Installation for SAP IGS integrated in SAP Kernel	igsexe_8-20007794.sar	Available to download	22,990		03/06/2015 13:02:39
Kernel Part I	SAPEXE_200-10012501.SAR	Available to download	497,374		03/06/2015 13:02:39
Kernel Part II	SAPEXEDB_200-10012498.SAR	Available to download	28,908		03/06/2015 13:02:39
PI_BASIS 740: SP 0006	SAPK-74006INPIBASIS	Available to download	4,506		03/06/2015 13:02:38
PI_BASIS 740: SP 0007	SAPK-74007INPIBASIS	Available to download	2,842		03/06/2015 13:02:39
SAP_ABA 740: SP 0006	SAPKA74006	Available to download	13,517		03/06/2015 13:02:39
SAP_ABA 740: SP 0007	SAPKA74007	Available to download	15,801		03/06/2015 13:02:39
SAP_BASIS 740: SP 0006	SAPKB74006	Available to download	150,096		03/06/2015 13:02:39
SAP_BASIS 740: SP 0007	SAPKB74007	Available to download	166,630		03/06/2015 13:02:39
SAP_BW 740: SP 0006	SAPKW74006	Available to download	94,048		03/06/2015 13:02:39
SAP_BW 740: SP 0007	SAPKW74007	Available to download	99,107		03/06/2015 13:02:39
SAP_GWFND 740: SP 0006	SAPK-74006INSAPGWFND	Available to download	17,377		03/06/2015 13:02:38
SAP_GWFND 740: SP 0007	SAPK-74007INSAPGWFND	Available to download	3,252		03/06/2015 13:02:39
SAP_UI 740: SP 0006	SAPK-74006INSAPUI	Available to download	105,190		03/06/2015 13:02:39
SAP_UI 740: SP 0007	SAPK-74007INSAPUI	Available to download	292,522		03/06/2015 13:02:39
SPAM/SAINT Update - Version 7.40/0056	SAPKD74056	Available to download	7,145		03/06/2015 13:02:39

Use the first line, if enabled, for entering a search/filter term (* for fuzzy search). All dates and times are specified in CET according to your settings.

Figure 18.32 Download Basket after Approval

5. Now click the Get Download Manager button to open the SAP Download Manager, and click on Download All Objects (see Figure 18.33).

Object Edit View Help

Object	Size	Date and time	Download status
Installation for SAP IGS integrated in SAP Kernel	22.990 KB	06.03.2015 13:02:39	Download not started.
Kernel Part I	497.374 KB	06.03.2015 13:02:39	Download not started.
Kernel Part II	28.908 KB	06.03.2015 13:02:39	Download not started.
PI_BASIS 740: SP 0006	4.506 KB	06.03.2015 13:02:38	Download not started.
PI_BASIS 740: SP 0007	2.842 KB	06.03.2015 13:02:39	Download not started.
SAP Download Manager for Windows	13.085 KB	06.03.2015 13:07:25	Download not started.
SAP_ABA 740: SP 0006	13.517 KB	06.03.2015 13:02:39	Download not started.
SAP_ABA 740: SP 0007	15.801 KB	06.03.2015 13:02:39	Download not started.
SAP_BASIS 740: SP 0006	150.096 KB	06.03.2015 13:02:39	Download not started.
SAP_BASIS 740: SP 0007	166.630 KB	06.03.2015 13:02:39	Download not started.
SAP_BW 740: SP 0006	94.048 KB	06.03.2015 13:02:39	Download not started.
SAP_BW 740: SP 0007	99.107 KB	06.03.2015 13:02:39	Download not started.
SAP_GWFND 740: SP 0006	17.377 KB	06.03.2015 13:02:38	Download not started.
SAP_GWFND 740: SP 0007	3.252 KB	06.03.2015 13:02:39	Download not started.
SAP_UI 740: SP 0006	105.190 KB	06.03.2015 13:02:39	Download not started.
SAP_UI 740: SP 0007	292.522 KB	06.03.2015 13:02:39	Download not started.
SPAM/SAINT Update - Version 7.40/0056	7.145 KB	06.03.2015 13:02:39	Download not started.

websmp110.sap-ag.de

Figure 18.33 SAP Download Manager

[+]

SAP Download Manager

Download the SAP Download Manager from the download basket by choosing Get Download Manager, and install it locally on your PC. Follow the instructions for installation and configuration.

Alternatively, you can download the files individually from the download basket by clicking on the corresponding links. In many cases, however, downloading files manually is very time-consuming.

SAP Download Manager downloads the files from the SAP Support Portal. When the download is finished, the files are available locally on your PC. You can then start to import the support packages.

18.2 Important Notes on Preparing and Executing System Maintenance

Note the following points before you begin to import the support packages:

1. Lock all users in your SAP system before the import.
2. Read all SAP Notes and instructions relating to the support packages. Refer to the information provided about the minimum requirements for the updates.
3. Import the support packages into a test system or sandbox system first, assuming that you have a four-system landscape. If you only have a three-system landscape, comprising a development, QA, and production system, start by importing the support packages into the development system.
4. If the development system remains stable, import the support packages into the QA system next. Perform a regression test, or have one performed by the end users in the business departments.
5. If testing is successful, import the support packages into your production system. Note that users can't work in the system during the import. You should therefore consult with the business departments to ensure that disruptions to normal operation are minimized.
6. Only download the patches once, and always use the same files for all systems.
7. Always make a full offline backup of the system before the import. You can use the backup to restore your system in case anything goes wrong.
8. Start with the kernel update. Save the old kernel at the operating system level before you import the new version.
9. Next, perform the SPAM/SAINT update.
10. Finally, import the ABAP support packages in test mode first and then in standard mode.

[!]

Caution When Importing Support Packages

Proceed with caution when importing support packages. If you make a mistake, you may no longer be able to start your SAP system, or serious errors may occur in the components. You should therefore approach this task with great care. Take your time, read all relevant SAP Notes, concentrate on the task, and be precise. If necessary, ask for help from an experienced colleague or an external consultant. If errors occur during a support package import, the situation may quickly become a system administrator's worst nightmare!

The following describes how to import support packages "traditionally," that is, using Transaction SPAM or at the operating system level (kernel). For maintenance and upgrades, SAP also provides the *Software Update Manager* (SUM), which is particularly recommended for systems that consist of both an ABAP and a Java stack. With SUM, you can also handle "smaller" updates, such as the one described in the following sections.

The benefit of SUM is the high degree of automation and standardization of the maintenance process. For example, the SUM updates the kernel automatically. The disadvantage is that you usually need to provide more disk space (for a shadow instance) and schedule more time.

18.3 Performing a Kernel Update

Now we come to the process of the update itself. As explained earlier, you should always start with the kernel update. The operating files of the SAP system are updated in a kernel update. Kernel updates are normally used to eliminate bugs and other errors in the kernel. In other words, they are used when problems occur in the communication between the SAP system and the operating system.

The kernel depends on the operations system and on the database of the SAP server. The same kernel version should be installed on all servers in a system (the central instance and other application servers).

A kernel update comprises the following steps:

1. Save the old kernel.
2. Copy the new kernel to the SAP server and unpack it.

3. Stop the SAP system and services.
4. Replace the kernel files.
5. Start the SAP system, and check the logs.

You update the kernel at the operating system level. You therefore require direct access to the server (user data, sufficient authorizations, and, in some cases, a shell program). You should also be able to use the operating system; that is, you should be familiar with the commonly used commands. If you usually only use Windows, and you now need to execute a kernel update, you may be unsuccessful if you're not familiar with the `ls` and `cp` commands. If necessary, ask for help from an operating system administrator.

Your backup of the old kernel files is your most effective safeguard against data loss and is therefore the most important part of the kernel update. This backup allows you to get the system up and running again very easily if it can no longer be started after the patch is installed (things aren't as simple in the case of ABAP support packages). You generally know that the update has been a success if you can start the system and log on with the SAP GUI.

SAP Note on Kernel Patches [+]

You can find more information on downloading and implementing (release-dependent) kernel patches in SAP Note 19466.

18.3.1 Kernel Backup

Begin by making a backup of the old kernel files by copying the entire kernel directory at the operating system level. This can be done while the SAP system is running.

1. Use the user `<SID>adm` to log on to your SAP server.
2. Create a backup directory, for example:
   - *<drive>:\<temporary directory>\kernel_701_69\bak* (Microsoft Windows)
   - *<temporary directory>/kernel_741_200/bak* (UNIX/Linux)

   If you want to save the update data permanently, give your directory a name that is as meaningful as possible. You also need to ensure that there is sufficient memory available on your drives.

3. Copy the entire kernel directory *<drive>:\usr\sap\<SID>\SYS\exe\run* (Windows) or */usr/sap/<SID>/SYS/exe/run* (UNIX/Linux), including all subdirectories, into your backup directory.

This completes the kernel backup. If necessary, save your backup directory on a separate server on your local PC or on tape. Ensure that you comply with all security measures so that your directory can't be deleted by another user while you're busy with the kernel update.

18.3.2 Unpacking a New Kernel

The kernel files you downloaded from the SAP Support Portal exist in a compressed format in your system. You need to transfer them to the server and unpack them with program `SAPCAR`.

1. Use the user `<SID>adm` to log on to your SAP server.
2. Create a directory for the new kernel files, for example:
   - *<Drive>:\temporary directory\kernel_701_69\new*
   - *<temporary directory>/kernel_741_200/new*

   The size of the SAP kernel is several hundred megabytes, even when compressed. Ensure that a sufficient amount of memory is available to store the packed files, and make a sufficient number of hard disk reserves available for decompression of the files.
3. Copy all new kernel files to your server into the newly created directory:
   - *SAPEXE_<patch level>-<identifier>.SAR*
   - *SAPEXEDB_<patch level>-<identifier>.SAR*
   - *igsexe_<patch level>-<identifier>.sar*
   - *DBATL<Release>_<patch level>-<identifier>.SAR* (for systems based on an Oracle database)
4. Create a directory in which to unpack the files, for example:
   - *<drive>:\<temporary directory>\kernel_701_69\new\unpacked*
   - *<temporary directory>/kernel_741_200/new/unpacked*
5. Open a shell session, and switch to the *<drive:\<temporary directory>\kernel_741_200\new* or *<temporary directory>/kernel_741_200/new* directory.

6. Unpack the kernel files with `SAPCAR`, for example:
   - `SAPCAR -xvf SAPEXE_<patch level>-<identifier>.SAR -R .\unpacked`
   - `SAPCAR -xvf SAPEXE_<patch level>-<identifier>.SAR -R ./unpacked`

The sequence in which you unpack the files is irrelevant. When you've finished, the decompressed kernel is saved in the directory you selected for unpacking.

Troubleshooting When Unpacking with SAPCAR [+]

`SAPCAR` lists the unpacked files in the shell. If the SAPCAR: NOT ALL FILES COULD BE EXTRACTED message is displayed, check first whether the syntax in your `SAPCAR` command was correct. Enter "SAPCAR" to display the HELP menu.

Errors may also occur if case sensitivity isn't taken into account, in particular in the UNIX/Linux environment. In rare cases, an archive may be damaged during the download, for example. If this occurs, download it a second time and try again.

18.3.3 Stopping the SAP System

During the kernel update, you replace the files at the operating system level. To do this, you must stop the SAP system and the database. You also need to ensure that files in use by running programs aren't deleted or overwritten. You therefore need to end all running SAP services. To do this, follow these steps:

1. Open a shell session, and log on to the SAP server with user `<SID>adm`.
2. Switch to the */usr/sap/<SID>/<instance>/exe* or *<drive>:\usr\sap\<SID>\<instance>\exe* directory.
3. Stop the SAP system and database first with the `stopsap -all` command or by using the SAP Microsoft Management Console (SAP MMC; see Chapter 2, Section 2.1.1).
4. Stop all SAP services that are currently running. Your operating system, the system's release, and the scope of its installation will determine how many services are still running and which services these are. Therefore, the following list of services and related stop commands may not be complete in all cases:
   - saposcol: `saposcol -k`
   - CCMS agents: `sapccm4x -stop/sapccmsr -stop`

- SAProuter: `saprouter -s`
- Service `SAPService<SID>` (Windows): via Windows Services Administration

5. Depending on your operating system, you may also need to clean the kernel libraries in the buffer with the following command under UNIX, for example: `/usr/sbin/slibclean`.

You can also stop all services that are currently running with the task manager or a similar operating system tool. When you've finished, you should be able to overwrite all old files when you copy the new kernel version.

It you're unable to replace all files due to programs that are currently running, errors are very likely to occur during SAP system operation.

18.3.4 Replacing Kernel Files

After you've made a backup copy of the old kernel, unpacked the new files on the server, and completely stopped the SAP system, you can begin to replace the old kernel files with the new version. Follow these steps:

1. Log on to your SAP server at the operating system level. Under Windows, you can use the user `<SID>adm`; under UNIX/Linux, you must use the user `root` due to different authorization administration because the user `<SID>adm` must not overwrite all old kernel files.
2. Copy all files and subdirectories from your *unpacked* directory into the kernel directory *<drive>:\usr\sap\<SID>\SYS\exe\run* or */usr/sap/<SID>/SYS/exe/run*.
3. Overwrite the existing files if the operating system prompts you to do so.
4. Switch to the kernel directory *<drive>:\usr\sap\<SID>\SYS\exe\run* or */usr/sap/<SID>/SYS/exe/run*, and use the user `root` under UNIX/Linux to run the script *saproot.sh* (additionally *oraroot.sh* under Oracle). The script sets all owner, group, and authorization settings correctly for the kernel files at the operating system level.

Pay particular attention to messages indicating that certain files could not be overwritten because they are in use by a program. This means that you haven't stopped all SAP services. If this occurs, find the applications that are still running and stop them. Then copy the files again.

Errors Caused by Authorizations [⚙]

The authorizations on your server for the old kernel files may be configured differently before and after the update in certain cases. This may result in errors when functions are executed in the SAP system. Compare the authorizations in your kernel backup with the new version, and make adjustments so that they are identical. If necessary, ask an operating system administrator for help.

18.3.5 Starting the SAP System and Checking the Logs

When the kernel files have been copied successfully, start the SAP system again:

1. Open a shell session, and log on to the SAP server with user `<SID>adm`.
2. Start the database and SAP system with the command `startsap` or by using the SAP MMC (see Chapter 2, Section 2.1.1).

Longer Startup Times after Kernel Updates [+]

After a kernel update, it takes longer to restart your SAP system than normal the first time you do so because program `sapcpe` first distributes the new kernel files to all instance directories at the operating system level. Prepare yourself for the longer startup time, and don't be unsettled by it. Check the log files for errors.

3. Check the operating system log, database log, and SAP system log for error messages (refer to Chapter 2, Section 2.1). If problems occur, pay particular attention to the trace files of the work processes and especially the *dev_w0* file in *<drive>:\usr\sap\<SID>\<instance>\work* or */usr/sap/<SID>/<instance>/work*.
4. Try to log on to the system with the SAP GUI. If a logon screen is displayed, this indicates that the SAP system is running.
5. Log on, and check the kernel version under SYSTEM • STATUS. If the new kernel version is displayed in the status view, you know that you've performed the kernel update successfully (see Figure 18.34).

As a precautionary measure, keep your kernel backup for a number of weeks. If the system starts with the new kernel version, it's unlikely that any errors are to be expected. However, you can never rule out the possibility of a problem occurring, and a backup of the operating system files that you know can be run may be useful in the event of an error.

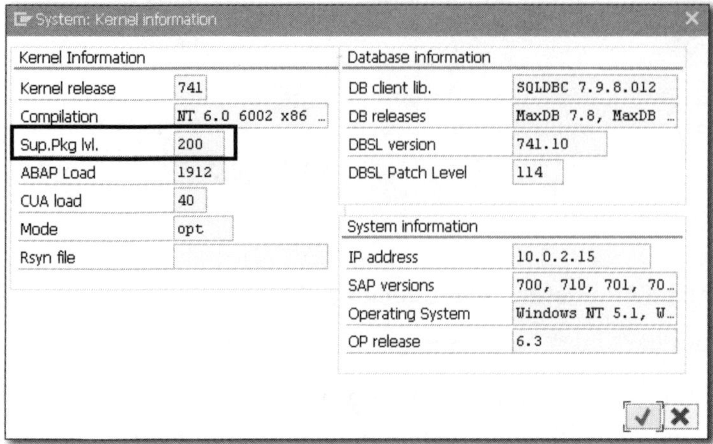

Figure 18.34 Checking the Kernel Version

18.4 Applying the SPAM/SAINT Update

ABAP components are maintained using the following two SAP tools:

- Support Package Manager (Transaction SPAM)
- Add-On Installation Tool (Transaction SAINT)

These tools are enhanced on an ongoing basis, and updates are delivered with the *SPAM/SAINT update*. Before you import an ABAP support package or an add-on into your system, you should always import the latest SPAM/SAINT update *first* to avoid errors and problems. Some support packages even require a certain minimum SPAM/SAINT version before they can be imported. You should therefore always download the *latest* SPAM/SAINT update from the SAP Support Portal together with the support packages.

To install the update, follow these steps:

1. Log on to the SAP system in client `000`.
2. Call Transaction SPAM.

[+]

Current SPAM/SAINT Version

The current SPAM/SAINT version in your system is displayed in the title bar of Transactions SPAM and SAINT.

3. Select the menu option SUPPORT PACKAGE • LOAD PACKAGES • FROM FRONT END (see Figure 18.35).

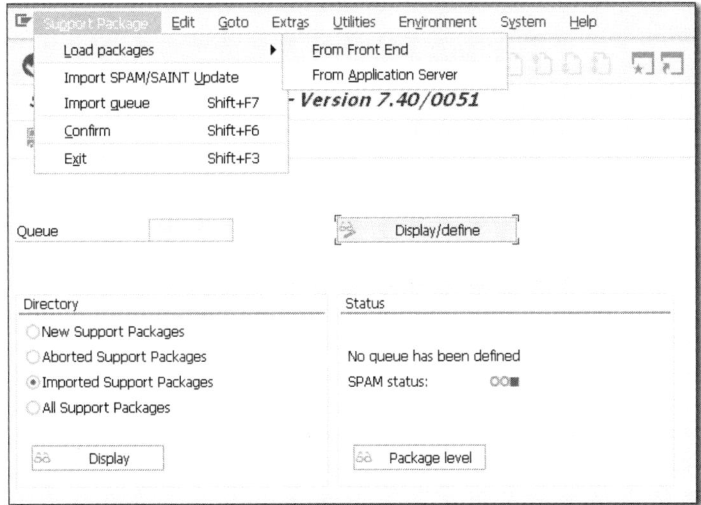

Figure 18.35 Initial Screen of Transaction SPAM

4. Navigate to where the file is stored on your local PC, and choose OPEN (see Figure 18.36).

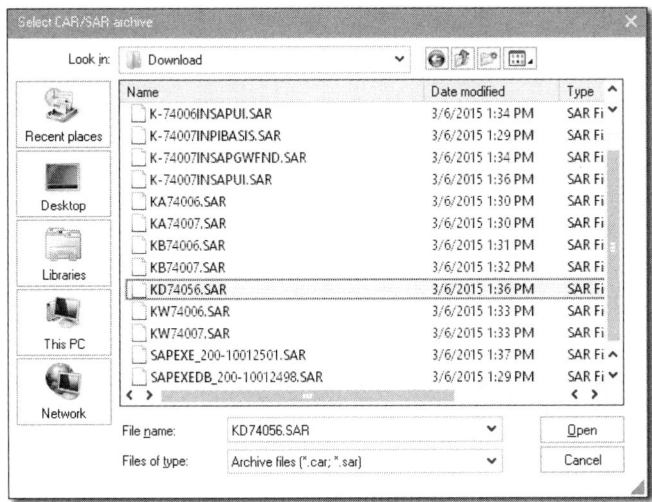

Figure 18.36 Selecting the Spam Support Package

5. The system copies the archive to the application server and displays the files that are to be unpacked. Click on DECOMPRESS (see Figure 18.37).

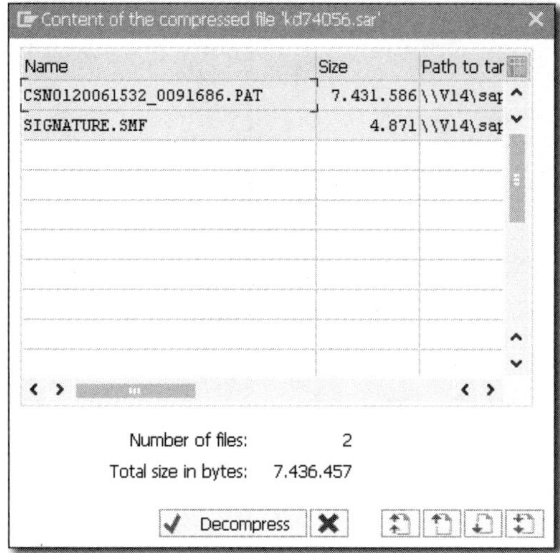

Figure 18.37 Decompressing the Support Package File

6. To import the SPAM update, select the menu option SUPPORT PACKAGE • IMPORT SPAM/SAINT UPDATE (refer to Figure 18.35).
7. Read the SAP Note displayed to determine possible prerequisites or known problems associated with importing the update (see Figure 18.38). Then click on IMPORT .

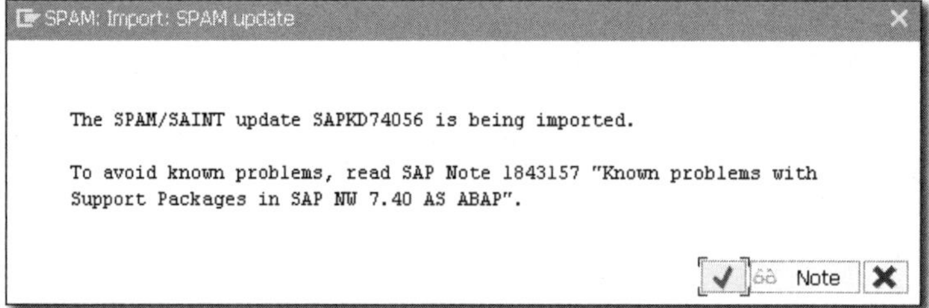

Figure 18.38 Reading the SAP Note on the SPAM Update

8. The update is imported. When the update is completed, you're prompted to restart Transaction SPAM (see Figure 18.39). Choose CONTINUE to close the dialog box, and then restart Transaction SPAM.

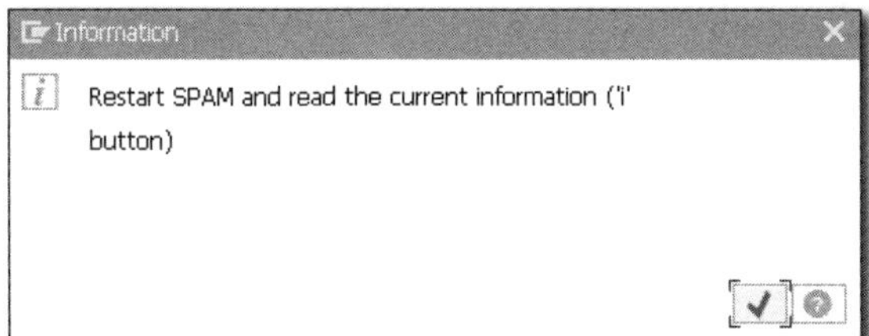

Figure 18.39 Confirming the Dialog Box with Prompt for Restart

The update is now complete. The new SPAM/SAINT version is now displayed in the title bar of the transaction (see Figure 18.40). Unlike ABAP packages and add-ons, you don't need to confirm the update.

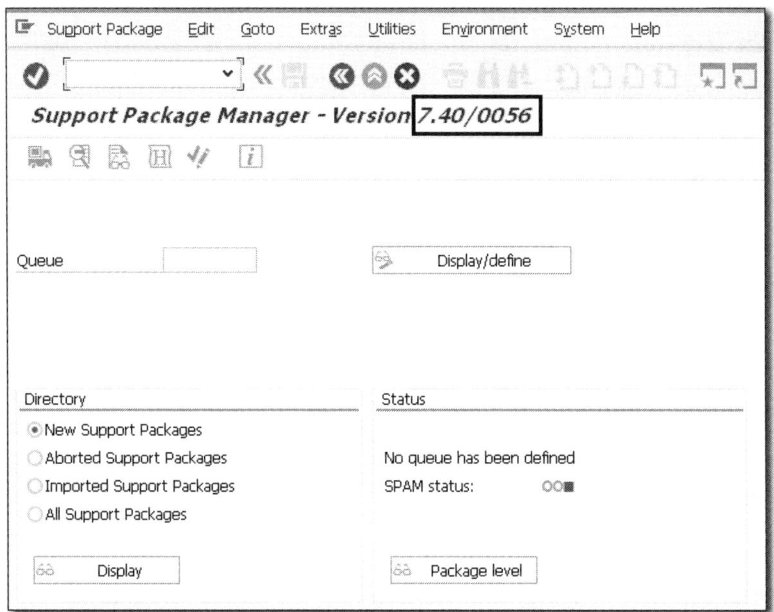

Figure 18.40 Display of the New SPAM/SAINT Version in Transaction SPAM

Short Dump During the SPAM/SAINT update [+]

Because Transaction SPAM virtually updates itself while it's running, it's not unusual for a short dump to occur during the update. If this occurs, close the short dump, and restart Transaction SPAM. To continue the update, select the menu option Support Package • Import SPAM/SAINT Update.

After you import the SPAM/SAINT update, you can proceed to import ABAP support packages or install add-ons.

18.5 Importing ABAP Support Packages

You've updated your SAP system kernel and imported the SPAM/SAINT update. You can now proceed to import the ABAP support packages. You use the Support Package Manager (Transaction SPAM) for this purpose, which you updated to the latest version in the previous step. To import the ABAP support packages, follow these steps:

1. Make the support packages available:
   - Transfer files to the server.
   - Unpack the archives.
2. Import the support packages:
   - Lock users and deallocate jobs.
   - Import the support packages in test mode.
   - Import the support packages in production mode.
3. Perform modification adjustment.
4. Regenerate objects.
5. Execute a regression test.

As in the procedure for SPAM/SAINT updates, you log on to the SAP system in client `000` to import ABAP support packages. Ensure that your user has sufficient authorization (the minimum authorization required is contained in the `S_A.SYSTEM` authorization profile).

[!]

Offline Backup

Create a complete offline backup of your SAP system before you start to import the ABAP support packages. This backup will allow you to easily restore the system in the event of a serious error.

18.5.1 Making the Support Packages Available

You've already downloaded the support package files from the SAP Support Portal and stored them locally on your PC. You now need to make these files available to the SAP server. In other words, you must load the support packages. There are two ways to do this:

- Load the support packages from the frontend.
- Load the support packages from the application server.

Loading the support packages from the frontend (i.e., from your local PC) is very simple if you use the Support Package Manager because you aren't required to manually copy the files to the server and unpack them there. However, you should only use this option if the archive is *smaller than 10MB*. The procedure for loading support packages from the frontend is explained in Section 18.4 and Section 18.6.

Loading from the application server is explained here. To do this, you transfer the compressed support package files to the SAP server, unpack them with program `SAPCAR`, and then load them into the Support Package Manager. Follow these steps:

1. Use the user `<SID>adm` to log on to your SAP server.
2. Create a temporary directory for the support package files, for example:
   - *<drive>:\<temporary directory>\sps7* (Windows)
   - */<temporary directory>/sps7* (UNIX/Linux)
3. Copy all support package archives into the temporary directory on your server.
4. Open a shell session on the SAP server, and switch to the transport directory, for example, *<drive>:\usr\sap\trans* or */usr/sap/trans*.
5. Unpack the support packages with `SAPCAR`:
   ```
   SAPCAR -xvf <drive>:\<temporary directory>\sps7\<file name>
   ```
   or
   ```
   SAPCAR -xvf /<temporary directory>/sps7/<file name>
   ```
6. Execute the command for all files in sequence, or use `SAPCAR` with a wildcard to unpack all files at once, for example:
   `SAPCAR -xvf <drive>:\<temporary directory>\sps7\*.SAR` or
   ```
   SAPCAR -xvf /<temporary directory>/sps7/*.SAR
   ```

Unpacking Support Packages [⚙]

`SAPCAR` unpacks the archives into two files:

- *CSR<name>.ATT*
- *CSR<name>.PAT*

These files belong to the EPS inbox, that is, in the *<drive>:\usr\sap\trans\EPS\in* or */usr/sap/trans/EPS/in* directory. If you execute the SAPCAR command while you're in the transport directory, the files are automatically saved to the EPS inbox. If you execute the command in another directory, a new *EPS\in* (or *EPS/in*) structure is created within this directory. You then need to move the **.ATT* and **.PAT* files manually into the correct EPS inbox.

7. Check the EPS inbox. Assuming that your EPS inbox was previously empty, the *<drive>:\usr\sap\trans\EPS\in* or */usr/sap/trans/EPS/in* directory should now contain support packages numbering twice the number of support packages you unpacked.

After you unpack the support package files and place them in the EPS inbox as just described, you can load the support packages into the Support Package Manager by following these steps:

1. Log on to the SAP system in client 000.
2. Call Transaction SPAM.
3. Select the menu option SUPPORT PACKAGE • LOAD PACKAGES • FROM APPLICATION SERVER (see Figure 18.41).

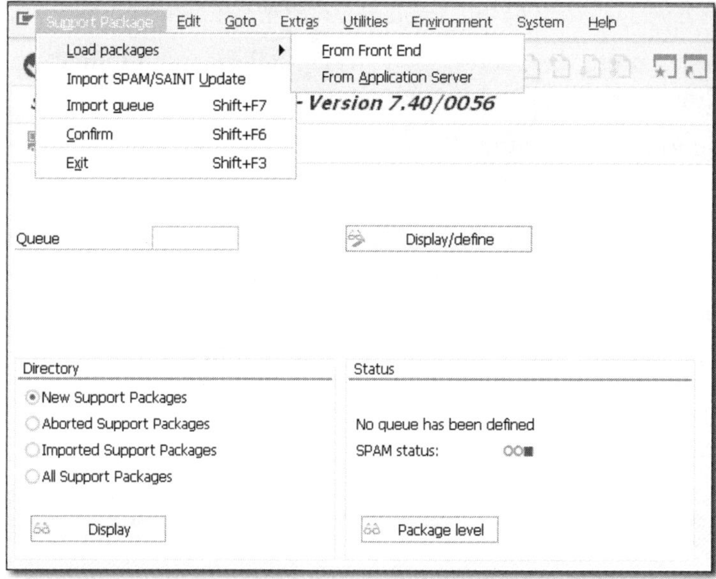

Figure 18.41 Uploading Support Packages from the Application Server

4. Choose Yes to confirm the dialog box that opens (see Figure 18.42).

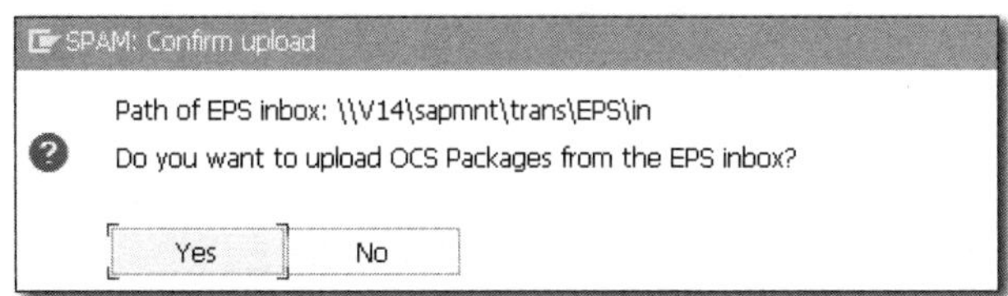

Figure 18.42 Confirming the Security Prompt

5. The support packages you loaded are displayed (see Figure 18.43). Make sure that no warning or error messages were issued. Choose Back to exit the view.

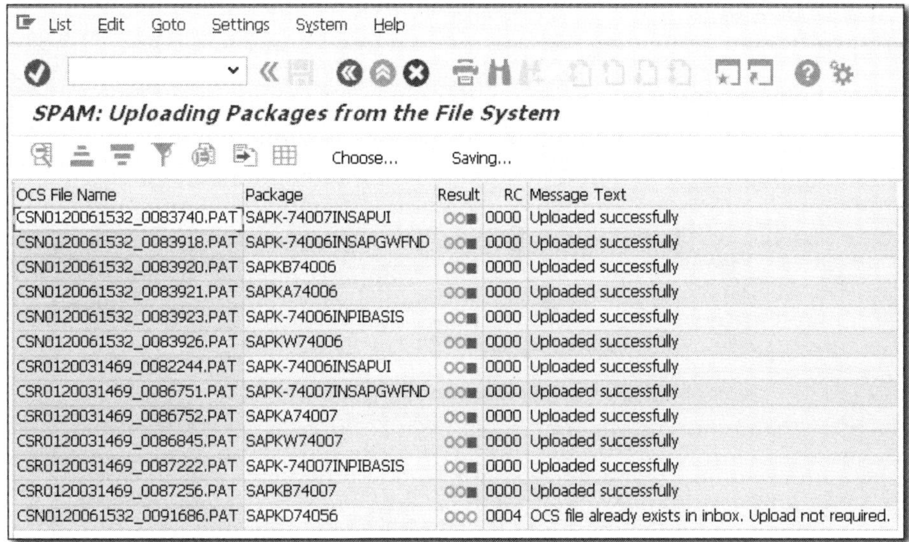

Figure 18.43 List of Loaded Support Packages

6. Check the packages by selecting the New Support Packages option under Directory and clicking on the Display button (see Figure 18.44).
7. The new updates are listed with the status Not imported (see Figure 18.45). Choose Back to exit the display.

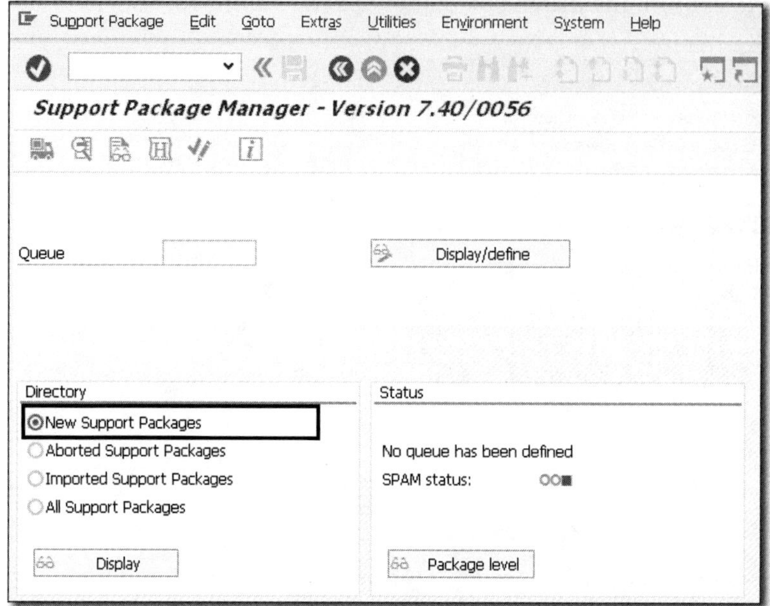

Figure 18.44 Displaying New Support Packages

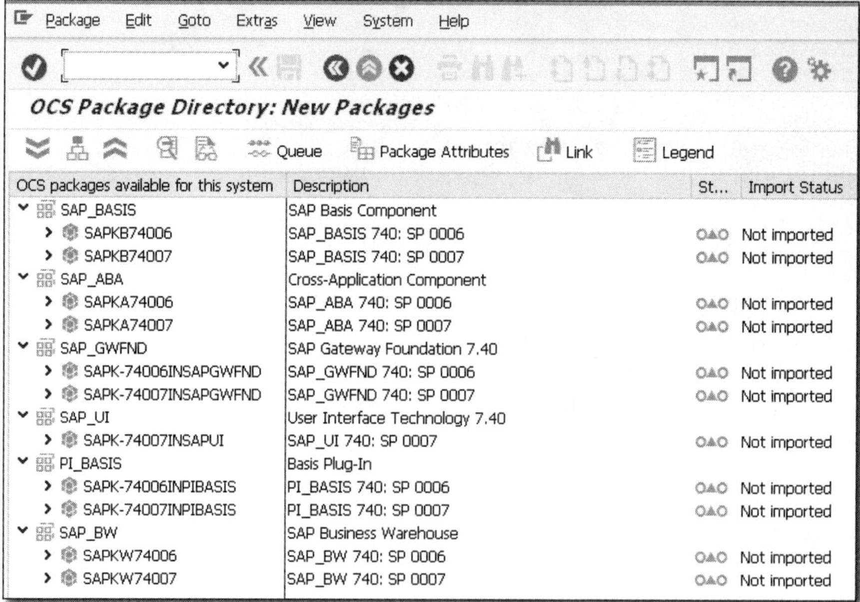

Figure 18.45 List of Packages Not Imported

Your preparations for importing the support packages are now complete. The Support Package Manager now has access to the files. In the next step, you can start the import.

18.5.2 Importing the Support Packages

Users must not work in the SAP system while the ABAP support packages are being imported. You must ensure that the following prerequisites are in place:

- All users are locked and logged off (Transaction SM04).
- No jobs are running or scheduled (Transaction SM37).

Importing the updates will cause changes to ABAP programs and objects. Any users working with these programs or objects during the import will receive error messages, and, in the worst case scenario, their data may be lost.

The import of ABAP support packages can be subdivided into three phases: definition of the queue, import in test mode, and import in standard (real) mode.

Import Queue [+]

Support packages for various system components must be imported in a specific sequence, known as a *queue*. The system calculates the queue itself, which is particularly important if you skip one or more support package levels.

Defining the Queue

To define the support package queue, follow these steps:

1. Log on to the SAP system in client `000`.
2. Call Transaction SPAM.
3. Click on the DISPLAY/DEFINE button (refer to Figure 18.44).
4. You can now select the components you want to update. Click on ALL COMPONENTS (see Figure 18.46).
5. The components are listed, together with the corresponding target support packages. Click on CALCULATE QUEUE (see Figure 18.47).

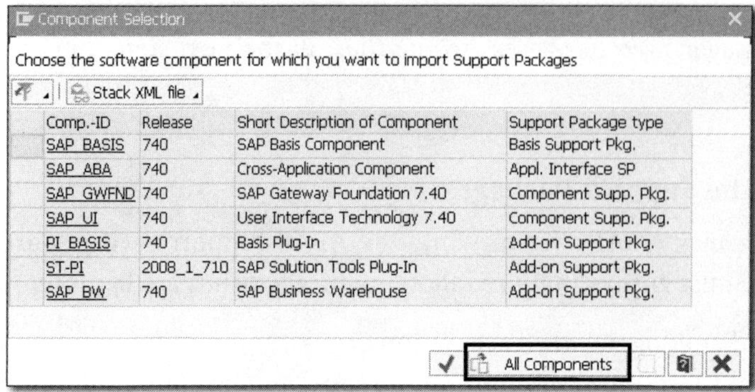

Figure 18.46 Selecting the Components to Be Updated

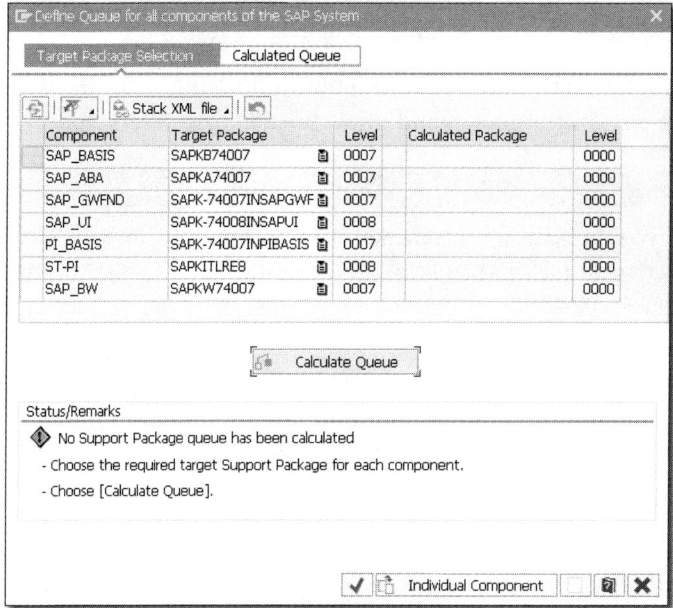

Figure 18.47 Calculating the Import Queue

6. The system calculates the sequence in which the support packages are to be imported. Check under Status/Remarks that no warning or error messages were issued (see Figure 18.48). Switch to the Calculated Queue tab.
7. The calculated sequence is displayed here again (see Figure 18.49). Click on Confirm Queue.

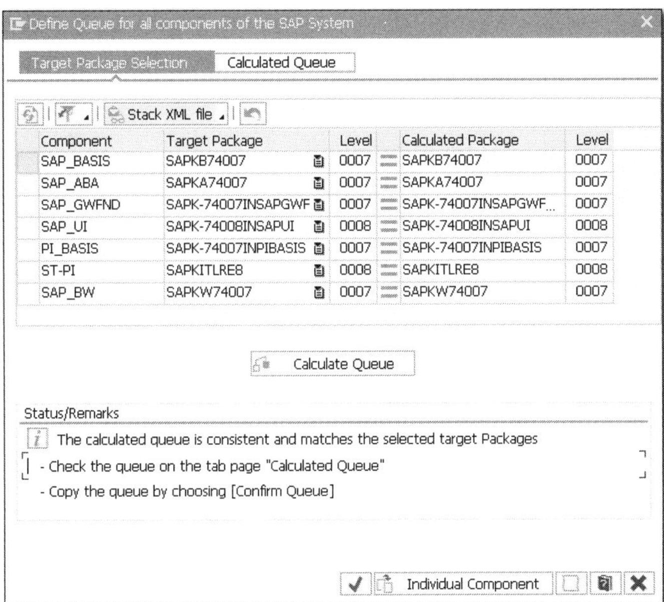

Figure 18.48 Checking the Calculation Status

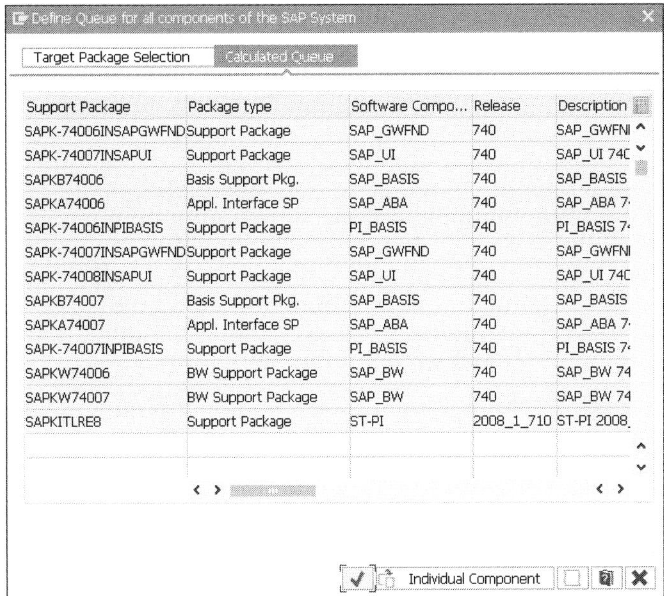

Figure 18.49 Confirming the Import Queue

8. The system asks you whether you want to create a modification adjustment transport (see Figure 18.50). In our example, modification adjustment transports aren't used, so click on No.

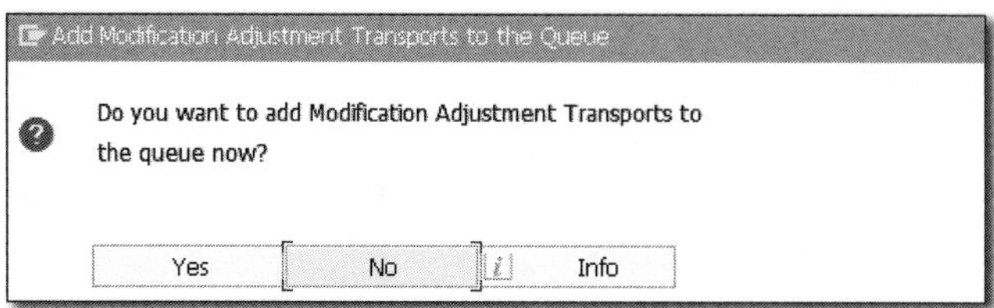

Figure 18.50 Rejecting the Modification Adjustment Transport

9. When the queue has been calculated, check the messages in the STATUS area (see Figure 18.51).

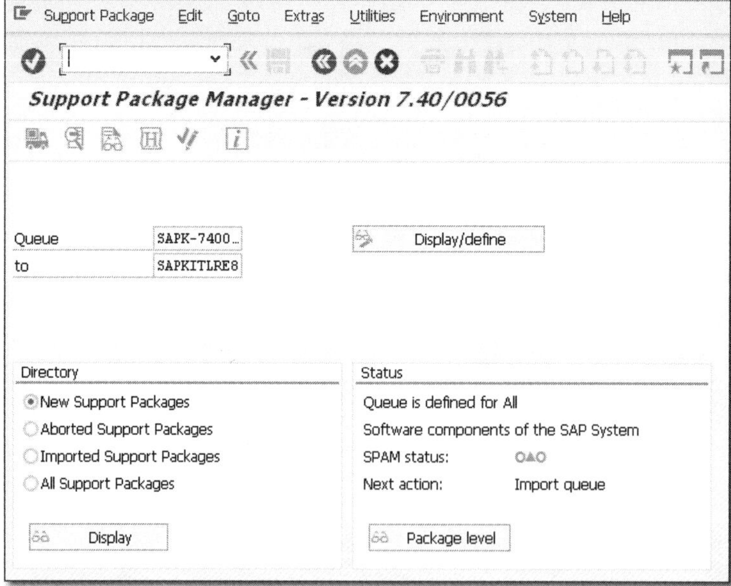

Figure 18.51 Checking the Status Messages

[+]

Modification Adjustment Transports

Modification adjustment transports are created when you perform a modification adjustment (see Section 18.5.3). In a multisystem landscape, it's highly recommended to transport the result of your modification adjustment instead of performing a new adjustment in each system. To avoid unnecessary delays during system maintenance, you can integrate the modification adjustment transport with the update process.

You can include the transport request created in the development system as part of the modification adjustment in the support package queue if you import the support packages into the QA and production system, for example. The request is then imported with the queue. After the SPDD or SPAU adjustment, you must first mark the transport request as a modification adjustment transport in the respective transaction using the menu option UTILITIES • ASSIGN TRANSPORT. You can then release it. Otherwise, it can't be used as a modification adjustment transport.

Import in Test Mode

After you've defined a valid support package queue as described, you can now continue with the import in test mode:

1. Before you start the import, test the functionality of the transport programs. To do this, choose the menu option UTILITIES • CHECK TRANSPORT TOOL (see Figure 18.52).

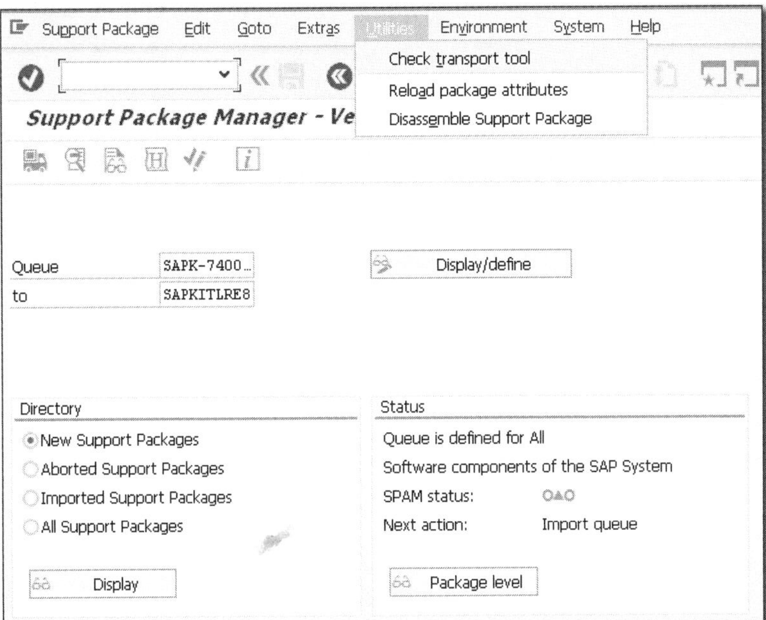

Figure 18.52 Checking the Functionality of the Transport Programs

2. Make sure that no error messages were issued (see Figure 18.53). Choose BACK to exit the view.
3. Begin by importing the support packages in test mode. Choose the menu option EXTRAS • SETTINGS.
4. Select the TEST option under SCENARIO on the IMPORT QUEUE tab to simulate the import into the system. Click on CONFIRM (see Figure 18.54).

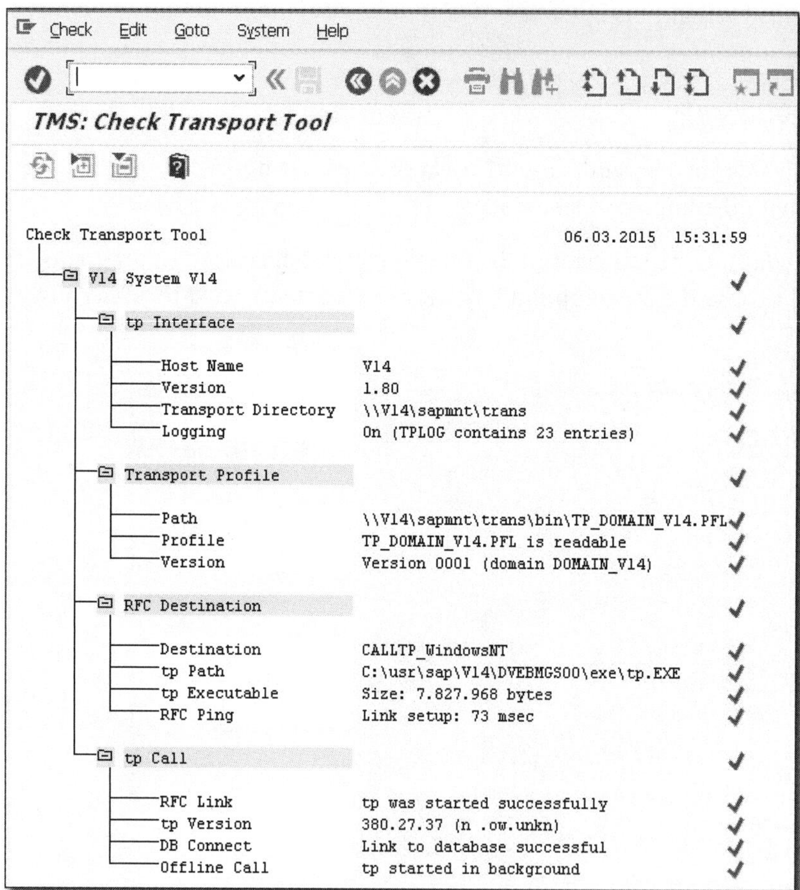

Figure 18.53 Results for Transport Programs

Figure 18.54 Switching the Import Scenario to Test

5. Choose CONTINUE ✔ to close the dialog box (see Figure 18.55).

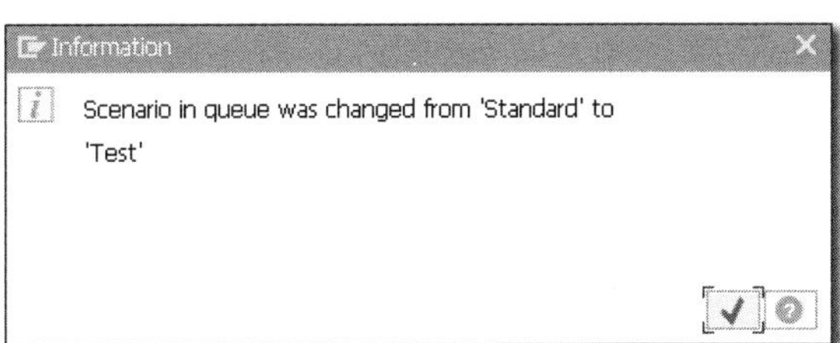

Figure 18.55 Confirmation for the Test Scenario Selection

6. On the SPAM main view (refer to Figure 18.52), click on the IMPORT QUEUE icon in the toolbar.
7. A dialog box is displayed to confirm that the queue has now been imported. Read the specified SAP Note (e.g., SAP Note 822379; see Figure 18.56) to determine whether any prerequisites apply to the import. Then click on IMPORT.

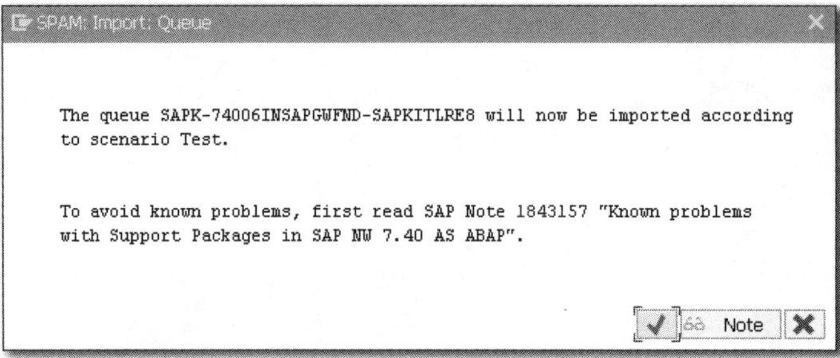

Figure 18.56 Reading the SAP Note on Importing Support Packages

[!]

Referring to SAP Notes

Carefully read any SAP Notes mentioned during the import. Certain prerequisites must be fulfilled before you can import some support packages. Some support packages need to be imported together, while others must be imported individually. SAP Notes also tell you how to handle known error messages.

8. The updates are then imported. You can track the progress of the update in the status bar in the bottom-left corner of the screen. An information message is displayed as soon as the process is complete (see Figure 18.57). Click on CONTINUE.

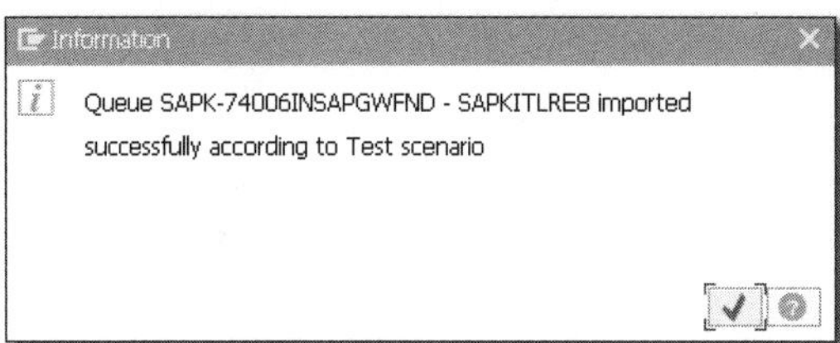

Figure 18.57 Confirmation for the Import in Test Mode

[+]

Duration of the Import

The process of importing the queue may take a long time to complete, depending on the number and size of the support packages involved. Depending on the performance of your system, it may take hours to import a large queue.

9. Now check the log. In the menu, choose GOTO • IMPORT HISTORY • QUEUE.
10. Expand the tree structure, and check the log for error messages (see Figure 18.58). If an error occurred, you can choose the IMPORT LOGS icon to go to the detail view to analyze the error. Then choose BACK to exit the view.

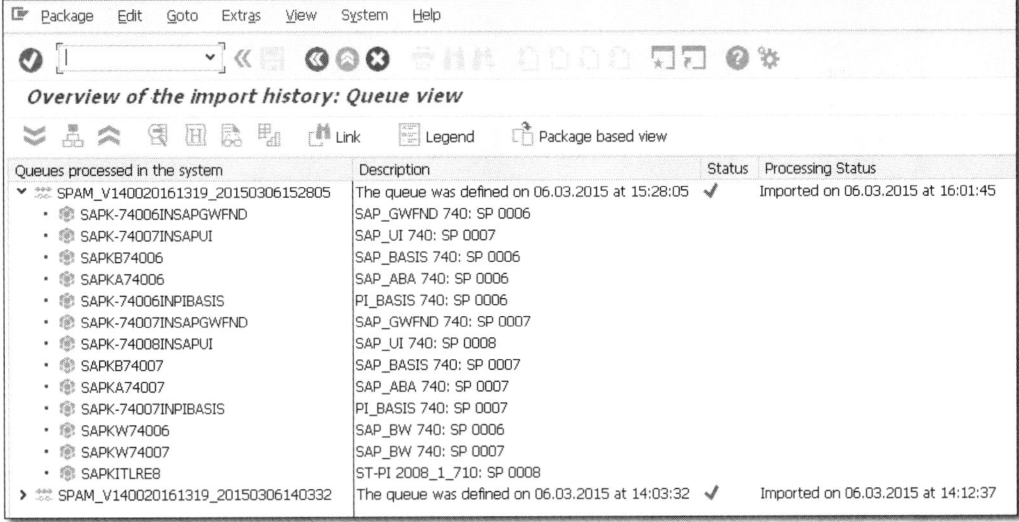

Figure 18.58 Checking the Import Logs

Import in Standard Mode

You need to define the queue again to import the support packages in production mode. Repeat steps 3 to 9 of the "defining the queue" phase. Then repeat steps 3 and 4, which you performed when importing in test mode, and activate the STANDARD scenario (see Figure 18.59). Click on CONFIRM.

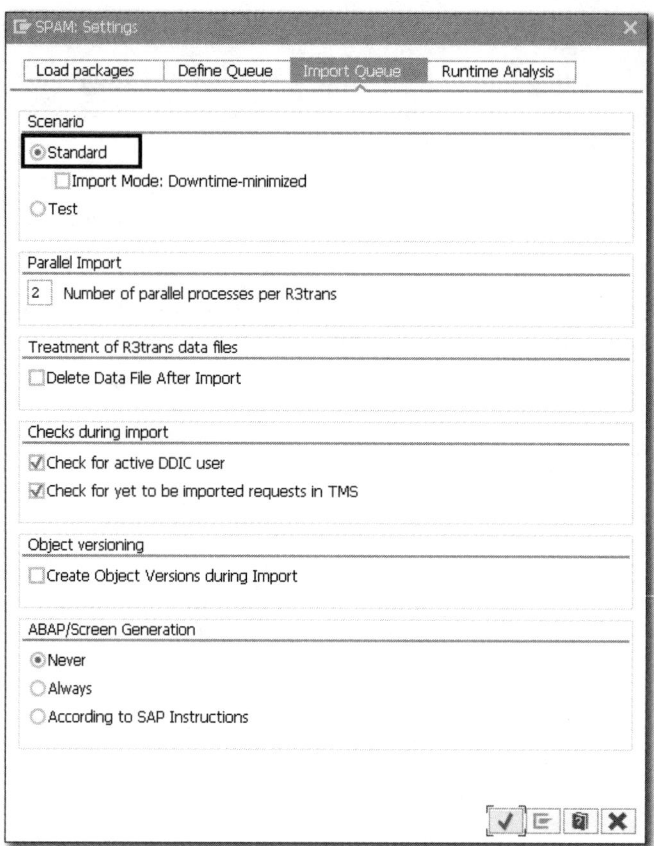

Figure 18.59 Selecting the Standard Scenario for Importing Support Packages

[⚙]

"Downtime-Minimized" Import Mode

In the STANDARD import scenario, you can choose the additional IMPORT MODE: DOWNTIME-MINIMIZED option. This is an import mode that minimizes the time period during which the SAP system is unavailable. This mode is generally only useful for production systems under specific circumstances. For more information about this function, refer to the online SAP Help Portal.

1. Click the IMPORT QUEUE icon in the toolbar of the SPAM main view (refer to Figure 18.52).
2. Here you can make a setting to determine whether updates are to be imported in dialog mode or as a background job. We recommend using background pro-

cessing for production mode. Click the START OPTIONS button to change configurations (see Figure 18.60). Then click on IMPORT.

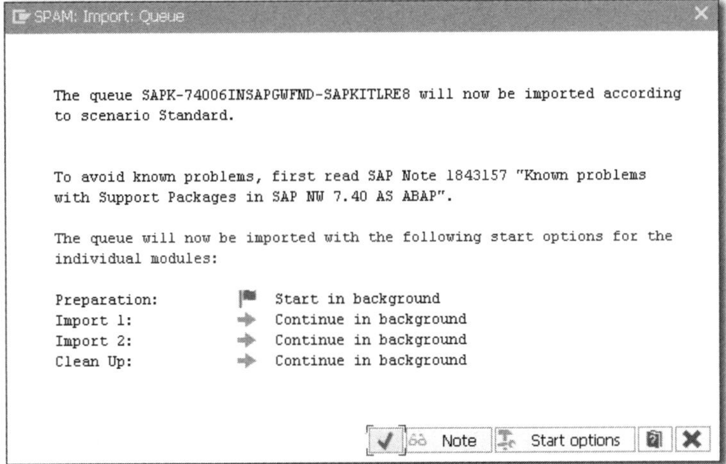

Figure 18.60 Checking the Start Options for the Update

3. You're informed as soon as the import is complete (see Figure 18.61). Choose CONTINUE to close the dialog box.

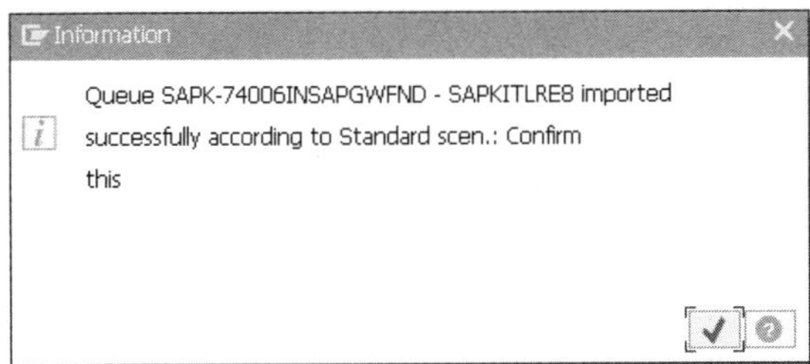

Figure 18.61 Confirmation for the Import of Support Packages

Duration of the Import in Production Mode [!]

In production mode, the import may take more time to complete than in test mode. Take account of this when scheduling and monitoring the import.

4. Choose the IMPORT LOGS OF THE QUEUE icon to check the import log again. If no errors occurred, choose the CONFIRM QUEUE icon to confirm a successful import (see Figure 18.62).

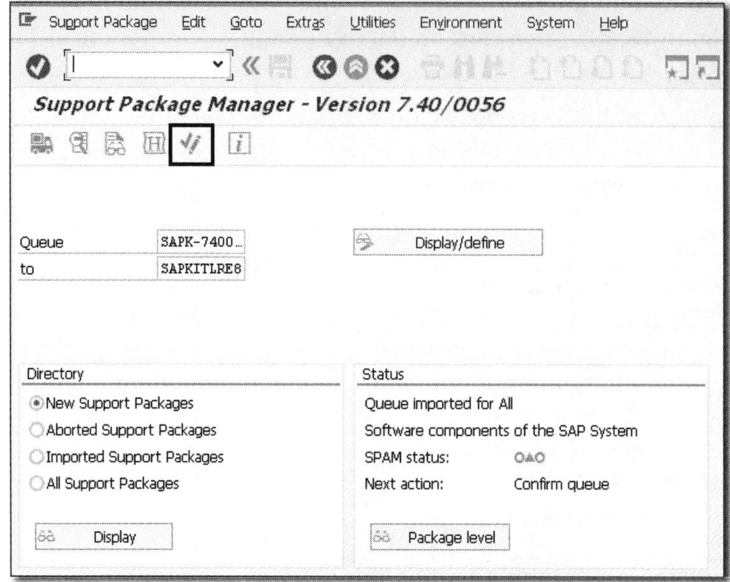

Figure 18.62 Checking the Import Logs and Confirming the Queues

5. A message appears in the status bar, indicating that the queue has been confirmed. You must confirm the queue before new support packages can be imported. You can view the support packages that have been imported by selecting the IMPORTED SUPPORT PACKAGES option.

Confirming the queue completes the import procedure, and the updates have now been imported into your SAP system. Next, perform the modification adjustment if the system prompts you to do so. You have the option of regenerating the updated ABAP objects to improve system performance after the update. Perform a regression test to verify functionality in the system.

18.5.3 Performing a Modification Adjustment

If a support package contains SAP objects (such as programs or tables) that you've changed (*modified*) in your system, conflicts occur when you import the update. The Support Package Manager provides you with information about these object conflicts and prompts you to perform a *modification adjustment*. As part of this adjustment, you must choose between retaining your modifications and accepting the newly delivered SAP version of the objects.

Depending on whether the objects in question are *ABAP Dictionary objects* (e.g., tables) or *repository objects* (e.g., programs), start the modification adjustment in Transaction SPDD (ABAP Dictionary) or Transaction SPAU (Repository). During the import of the support packages, you can skip the Transaction SPAU adjustment and return to it after the import has been completed. However, the ABAP Dictionary adjustment can't be skipped.

Use Transaction SPDD or Transaction SPAU to check whether your change is contained in the support package and whether it's identical to the version in the imported update. Revert, where possible, to the SAP standard to simplify future system maintenance. If your modification isn't contained in the support package, determine which steps are required to import the modification again. Import the modification again and test it.

Modification Adjustment [+]

As an SAP Basis administrator, you may not be able to perform the modification adjustment yourself, for example, if you didn't personally make the change or if you don't have sufficient programming experience. Ask for assistance from the user who modified the SAP object or your programming department if a modification adjustment is required when importing support packages.

18.5.4 Regenerating Objects

Importing support packages involves the large-scale replacement of SAP objects with new versions. These objects need to be compiled or regenerated the first time they are called. As a result, system performance is temporarily very slow immediately after updates are imported. In general, these restrictions don't pose a major problem because they no longer apply as of the second call, for example, the second call of a transaction. However, users may find them very disruptive, in particular if they affect time-critical production.

To counteract these effects, you can choose to only regenerate objects that were already in use before the support package import, using the SAP Load Generator (Transaction SGEN). The benefit of this approach is that it has hardly any effect on performance. The drawback, however, is that the generation of the objects requires storage space in the database, which you could possibly save temporarily. If you detect a shortage of database capacity, it's best to avoid regeneration. However, you should regenerate the objects if capacity problems don't apply.

Consider the needs of your end users when making this decision. Depending on the application area, the generation may not be strictly essential for performance reasons.

1. Enter Transaction SGEN in the command field and press the Enter key.
2. Under GENERATION TASK, select the REGENERATE ALREADY EXISTING LOADS and the REGENERATE ONLY INVALID LOADS (MODE INVALID) suboption (see Figure 18.63). Click on CONTINUE.

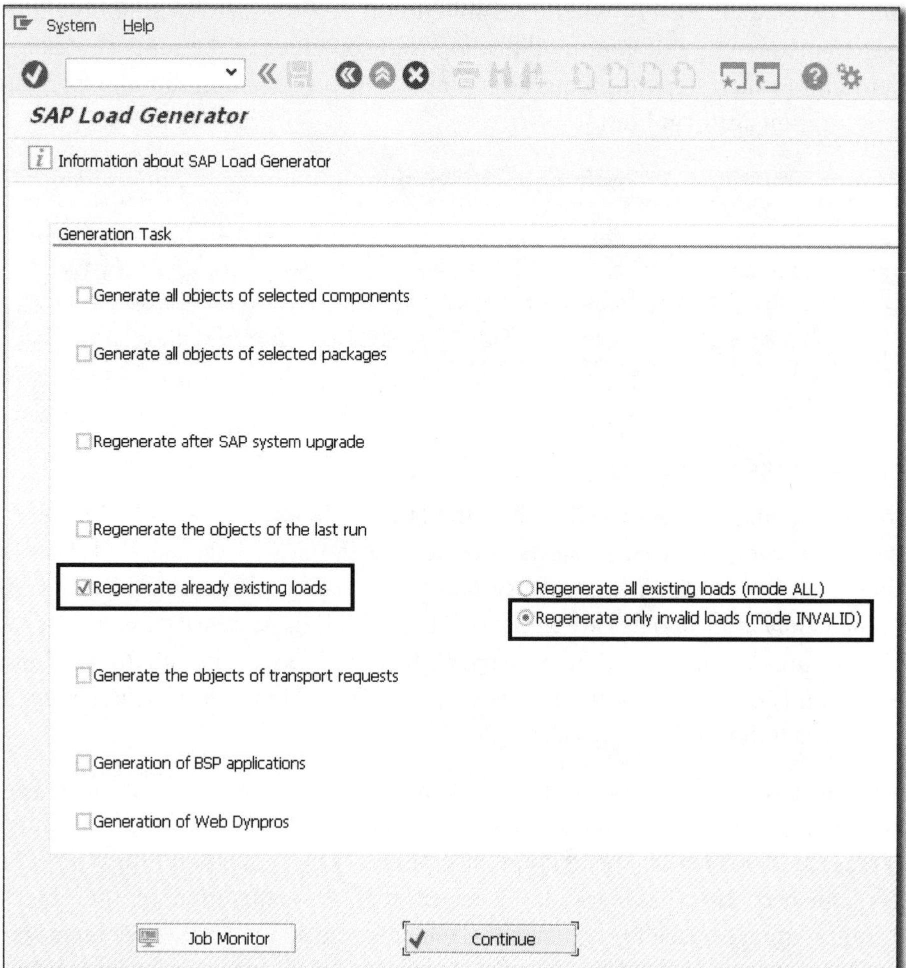

Figure 18.63 SAP Load Generator

3. The generation is executed in the background. You can choose to execute the job immediately or at a specific time. Select the job, and, for example, click on START JOB DIRECTLY (see Figure 18.64).

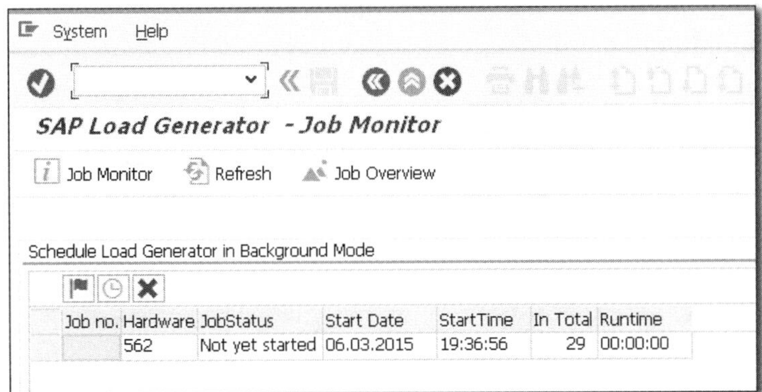

Figure 18.64 Starting the Background Job for Load Generation

4. You can monitor the progress of the generation directly in Transaction SGEN (REFRESH button). When the job is completed, it's no longer displayed in the table after you've refreshed the view. Alternatively, monitor the job in the Job Monitor (Transaction SM37; see Figure 18.65).

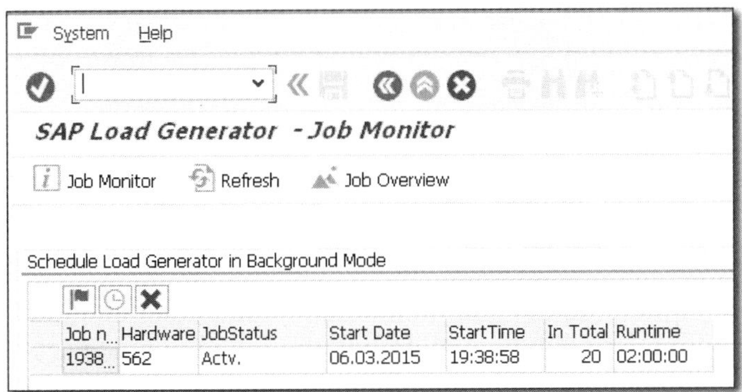

Figure 18.65 Monitoring the Generation Job in the Job Monitor

If you run the SAP Load Generator with the options specified earlier, only the following objects are regenerated:

- Objects that were already loaded once (existing load)
- Objects that were updated (invalidated) by the support package

You can also select other options in Transaction SGEN. However, in the case of support packages, the settings shown here are optimal.

18.5.5 Performing Regression Tests

Regression tests are required because support packages may cause changes to many objects across many different components. All business departments that use the SAP system must use regression tests to check whether all functions are still available without errors after the import or whether the support package has produced new problems. A support package or support package stack must be treated as a mini-upgrade, in particular if it contains extensive changes.

All existing processes must continue to function in exactly the same way they did before the support package was imported. The SAP Notes that are relevant for a support package specify the precise tests that are to be conducted by the technical team and end users. The testing procedure can be accelerated if the business departments have recorded test cases or a script for the tests to be processed.

To perform regression testing, you can, for example, use Test Management in SAP Solution Manager (see Chapter 4). Another option is to automate testing with the SAP eCATT tool (extended Computer-Aided Test Tool).

18.6 Installing Add-Ons

Add-ons enhance the functional scope of standard SAP systems. Examples of add-ons include industry solutions and plug-ins. You can download add-ons from the SAP Support Portal in just the same way as support packages.

Add-ons that have been downloaded can be installed with the *Add-On Installation Tool* (Transaction SAINT). This tool is similar to the Support Package Manager (Transaction SPAM), which is used to maintain the SPAM/SAINT update. In contrast to the import of support packages, you can't use the Add-on Installation Tool to install packages in the test scenario. The installation is always done in standard mode.

If you've downloaded an add-on from the SAP Support Portal, follow these steps to install it:

1. Log on to the SAP system in client `000`.
2. Enter Transaction SAINT in the command field and press the Enter key.
3. On the initial screen of the Add-On Installation Tool, click on the START button (see Figure 18.66).
4. You can upload the add-on from your PC or from the SAP server. Select the menu option SUPPORT PACKAGE • LOAD PACKAGES • FROM FRONT END.

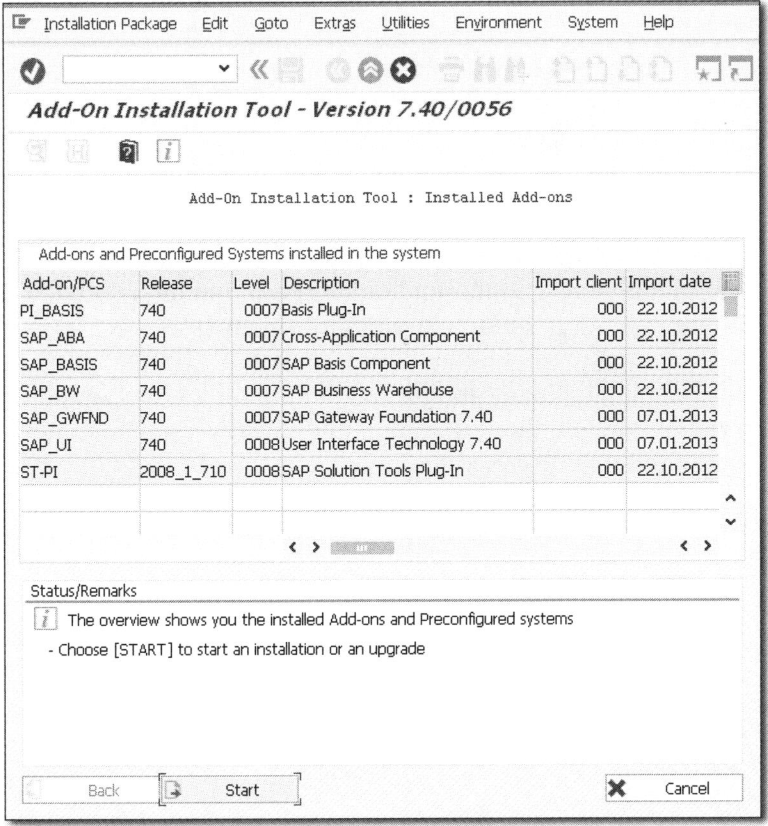

Figure 18.66 Initial Screen of the Add-on Installation Tool

5. Navigate to where the file is stored, and choose OPEN (see Figure 18.67).

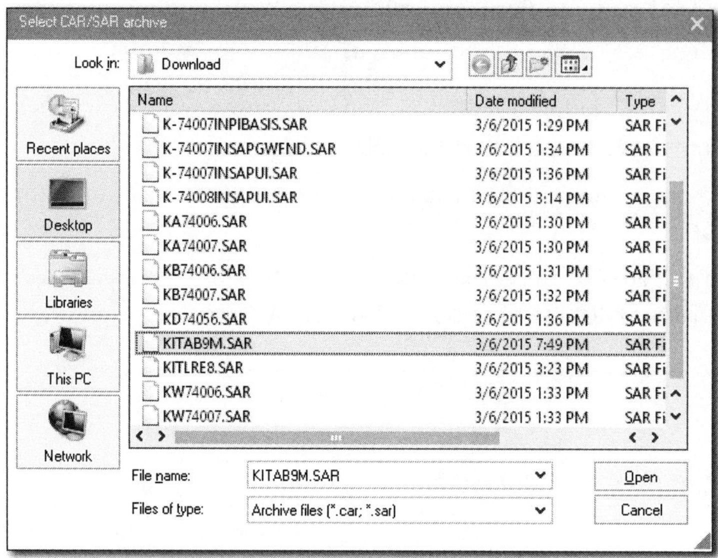

Figure 18.67 Selecting the File in Which the Add-on Is Stored

6. The system copies the archive to the application server and displays the files that are to be unpacked. Click on DECOMPRESS (see Figure 18.68).

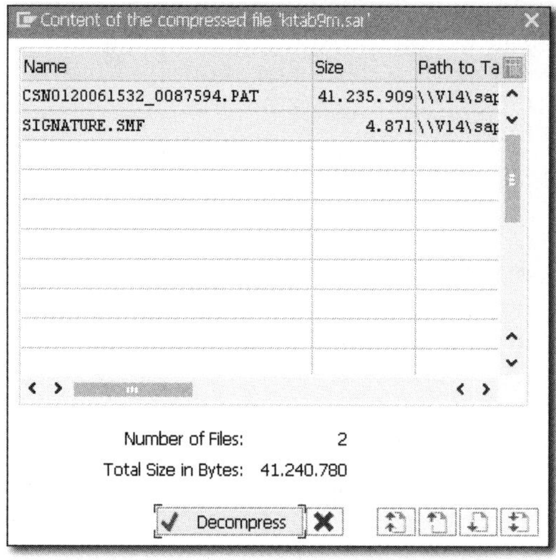

Figure 18.68 Decompressing the Add-on Files

7. The uploaded add-on is now displayed in the list of packages that can be installed (see Figure 18.69). Select the add-on, and click on CONTINUE.

Figure 18.69 List of Add-on Packages That Can Be Installed

Installation Requirements for Add-Ons Not Met [+]

If the requirements for installing an add-on (e.g., a specific release of the component SAP_BASIS) aren't met, the add-on isn't available in the list of installable packages.

The system doesn't list it "without comment." It doesn't provide any error message after uploading and decompressing an add-on. Installation is still not possible if you upload it again. In this case, you can only check the information file of the relevant package in the download area of the SAP Support Portal to see if your system meets all *import conditions*.

8. The add-on to be installed and the calculated support package are displayed on the SUPPORT PACKAGE SELECTION tab (see Figure 18.70). In this view, you can still make changes to the packages to be imported. Click on CONTINUE.

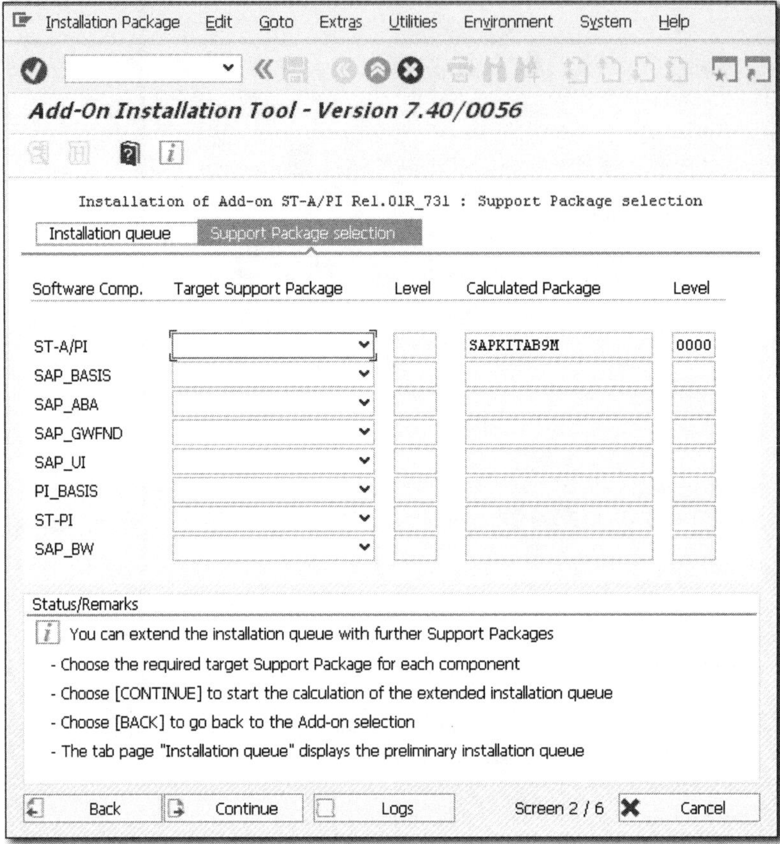

Figure 18.70 Checking the Add-On/Support Package

9. The calculated import queue is displayed. Check whether all required packages are available for import in the intended version (see Figure 18.71). Again, click on CONTINUE.

10. Add a modification adjustment transport to the installation queue if required, or, alternatively, click on NO (see Figure 18.72).

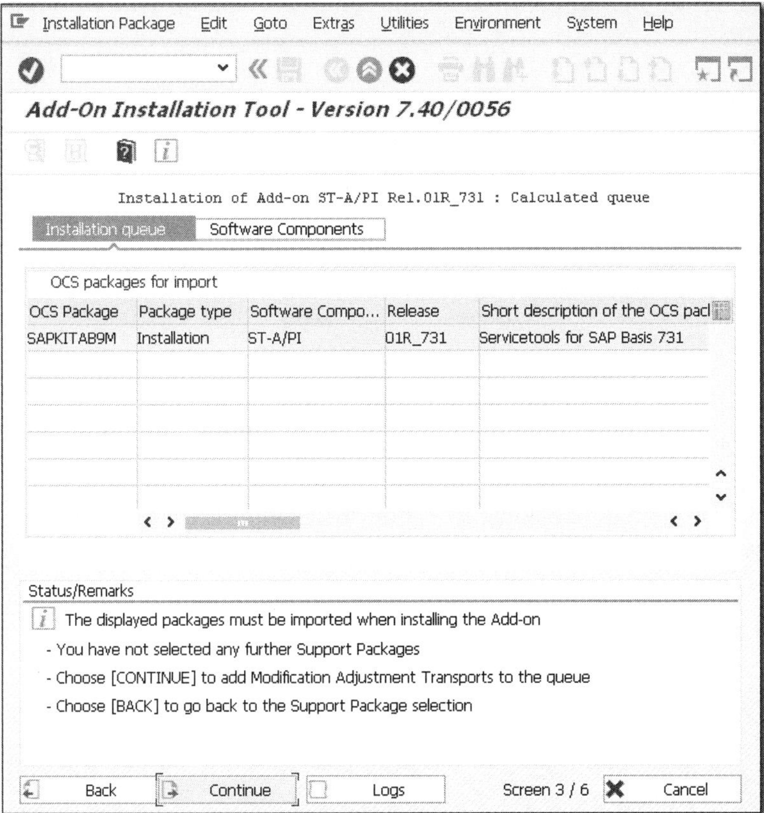

Figure 18.71 Checking the Installation Queue

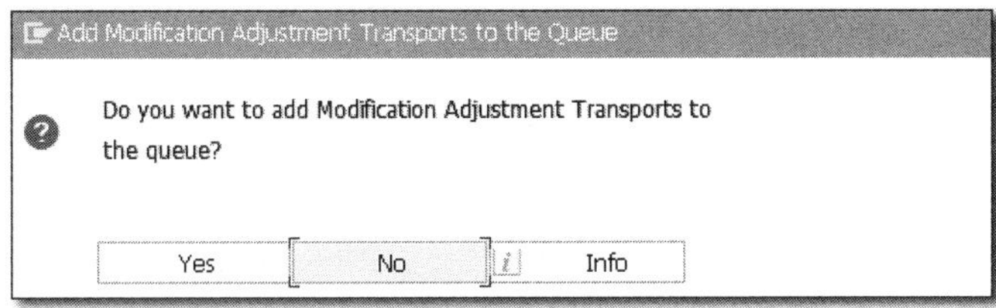

Figure 18.72 Querying Modification Adjustment Transports

11. The queue is imported in the dialog by default. If required, you can change the mode to BACKGROUND under START OPTIONS to run the import as a batch job. Choose IMPORT to start the import (see Figure 18.73).

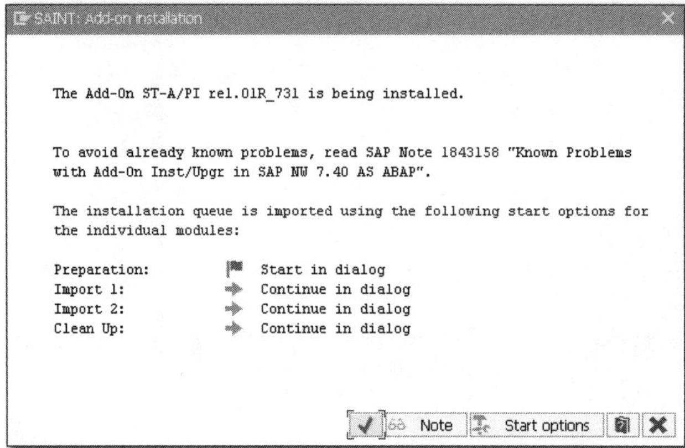

Figure 18.73 Starting the Installation

12. The add-on is installed. Check the logs after installation is complete (see Figure 18.74).

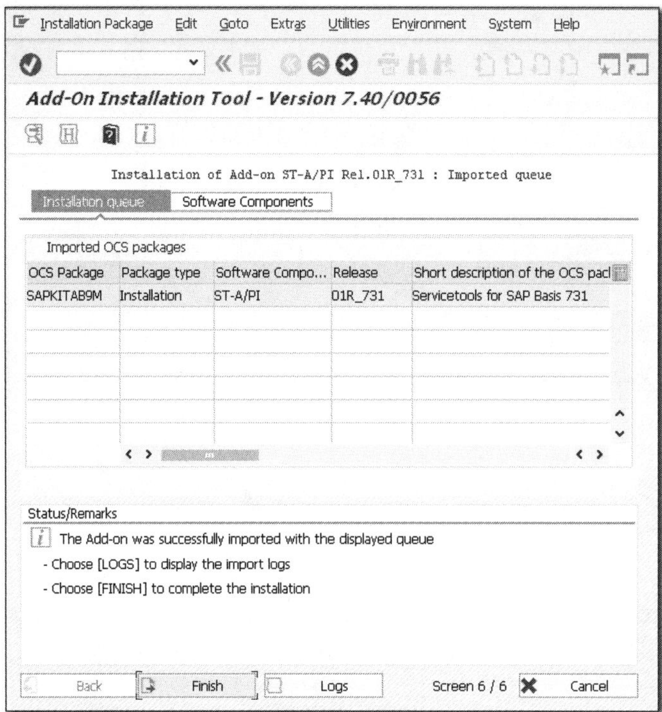

Figure 18.74 Checking the Logs and Completing the Installation

13. Then click on FINISH.

The add-on is now implemented. If you now select the menu option SYSTEM • STATUS to view the component information, the add-on is included in the list of installed components.

Uninstalling Add-ons [+]

In principle, add-ons can't be uninstalled; that is, you can only undo the installation with a system recovery. As of SPAM/SAINT version 53, however, it's possible to uninstall specific add-ons using Transaction SAINT if certain requirements are met. Read SAP Note 2011192 to learn more about the requirements and the add-ons that support this function.

A modification adjustment may also be necessary for add-ons. If you want to perform load generation, activate the GENERATE ALL OBJECTS OF SELECTED SOFTWARE COMPONENTS option in Transaction SGEN, and only select the add-on you've just installed for generation.

18.7 Summary

This chapter described how to maintain an SAP system. You now know how to download support packages and add-ons from the SAP Service Marketplace, and how to implement them in your system using the Support Package Manager or Add-On Installation Tool. You also know how to perform a kernel update.

You should use support package stacks instead of individual support packages because the support package stacks deliver stable combinations of support packages for all components in your system. Ideally, you should use the Maintenance Optimizer in SAP Solution Manager to download support package.

This chapter addresses some fundamental issues related to troubleshooting. You'll become familiar with a number of tools and methods that you can use to resolve problems yourself. You'll also learn how to make the most of the support channels offered by SAP.

19 Diagnostics and Troubleshooting

In every SAP system, errors will sometimes occur that you'll be required to resolve yourself, or you'll need to at least collaborate in their correction. Some errors are trivial and can be solved after you read the error message. Other issues are caused by an application error, incorrect system settings, or by an actual programming error.

SAP provides the *SAP Support Portal* to help you find solutions to system errors. The Portal has an extensive database of solutions and SAP Notes to help you resolve issues. This chapter outlines the basic principle of error handling, demonstrates how to use the SAP Support Portal for troubleshooting, and shows you how to implement SAP Notes in your SAP System.

19.1 Basic Procedure

The general procedure for troubleshooting described here isn't a new one—it has been used for many years in a range of industries:

1. Gather data.
2. Analyze the problem.
3. Determine solution options.
4. Eliminate the error.
5. Make the necessary adjustments.
6. Document the changes.
7. Test the results.

Some of these steps are described in more detail next.

Gather Data

When an error occurs, the first step is to gather data. Pay particular attention to the following questions:

- What is the precise nature of the problem?
- What causes the problem?
- Is it possible that the problem will occur frequently, or has it already occurred several times?
- Can the problem be systematically reproduced?
- Which error messages, dumps, or other diagnostic information was displayed in connection with this problem?

Use the available system tools to analyze the error messages, for example:

- System log (Transaction SM21)
- Dump analysis (Transaction ST22)
- Update system (Transactions SM13 and SM14)
- Output controller (Transaction SP01)

Then analyze the problem.

Analyze the Problem

After you've formed a detailed picture of the situation, proceed with the analysis of the problem. Use the resources available to you for solving the problem for this purpose:

- Online documentation in the SAP Help Portal (*http://help.sap.com*)
- Reference manuals
- SAP Notes and documentations in the SAP Support Portal (*https://support.sap.com* or *https://service.sap.com/support*)
- SAP Community Network (*http://scn.sap.com*)

If you're unable to turn up any useful information, seek the assistance of an expert:

- Internal specialists and administrators
- External consultants
- Other SAP customers (in your network)

[+]

Excluding User Error

Errors may have many different causes. For example, a problem may occur because of a user error, incomplete or missing system settings, or program errors. In every case, you should begin by excluding the possibility of incorrect use or configuration of the system before consulting external partners.

Eliminate the Error

After you've identified one or more approaches to eliminating the error, take care not to jump the gun. For one thing, not every solution will suit your situation every time. And, for another, you may cause further problems by making a snap decision. Take a levelheaded approach, and consider the following aspects:

- **Comparing the solution options**
  Compare the various solutions options you've identified. Check which changes would be necessary in each case and how these changes would impact on the behavior and stability of your SAP system. Compare the impact to be expected (*costs*) with the result foreseen (*benefits*) for each individual option.
- **Implement changes one at a time**
  Only implement one change at a time if possible. If a problem occurs and you implement several changes simultaneously, you may then be unable to identify which change solved the original problem or which change caused a new one. In some cases, however, you need to make several changes to solve a problem. Only implement more than one change at a time if this is *absolutely* essential, for example, in the case of related program changes.
- **Documenting changes**
  All changes are to be documented thoroughly. If a change produces an additional problem, you must undo that change. To do this, you need to know what the configuration was before the change was implemented and exactly what change was made. If changes are to be applied across various systems, you must know *exactly* what changes are to be made and how this is to be done. The same steps must be performed in *exactly the same way* in all systems.

When it comes to troubleshooting, the concept of "learning by doing" applies. The more experience you have, the less time it will take you to solve the problems that arise. The next section explains how to use the SAP Support Portal for diagnostics and troubleshooting.

19.2 Troubleshooting with the SAP Support Portal

The SAP Support Portal is an Internet platform on which SAP provides information, as well as support functions and resources. As part of the SAP Service Marketplace (*https://service.sap.com*), you can do the following with the resources and functions provided by the SAP Support Portal:

- Search for SAP Notes.
- Download support packages.
- Register developers and namespaces.
- Maintain connection data to allow SAP to access your systems.

[+]

New SAP Support Portal

When this book was written, SAP was about to build a new support portal. The new portal is available under *https://support.sap.com* and is supposed to provide a simplified navigation and clearly structured content. The functions of the old SAP Support Portal (*https://service.sap.com/support*) will be moved gradually to the new portal. As far as possible, this book describes all functions using the new SAP Support Portal.

The SAP Support Portal is your first external point of contact when you need to analyze an error or search for troubleshooting documentation and guides. Following are the prerequisites for using the SAP Service Marketplace:

- An Internet connection
- A browser (the SAP Service Marketplace is optimized for Microsoft Internet Explorer)
- A valid user ID and a valid password for the SAP Support Portal

Within the SAP Support Portal, access is controlled by authorizations. If you're denied access to certain functions, notify the relevant super administrator. The SAP Support Portal indicates your super administrator as soon as you call a function for which you don't have any authorization.

[!]

Older Names for the SAP Service Marketplace

The SAP Service Marketplace has been rechristened a number of times in the past and was formerly known, for example, as *SAPNet*, *OSS*, *www.sap.com*, and *service.sap.com*. All of these names refer to the central service platform of SAP AG.

19.2.1 Searching for SAP Notes with the SAP Support Portal

SAP Notes (formerly known as *OSS Notes*) help you eliminate specific problems in SAP systems and enhance the general documentation and help topics available. Follow these steps to search for an SAP Note dealing with a specific problem:

1. Access the URL *https://support.sap.com* in your web browser. (Alternatively, access the SAP Service Marketplace at *https://service.sap.com*, and click on the SAP SUPPORT PORTAL link.) The welcome page of the SAP Support Portal is displayed (see Figure 19.1).

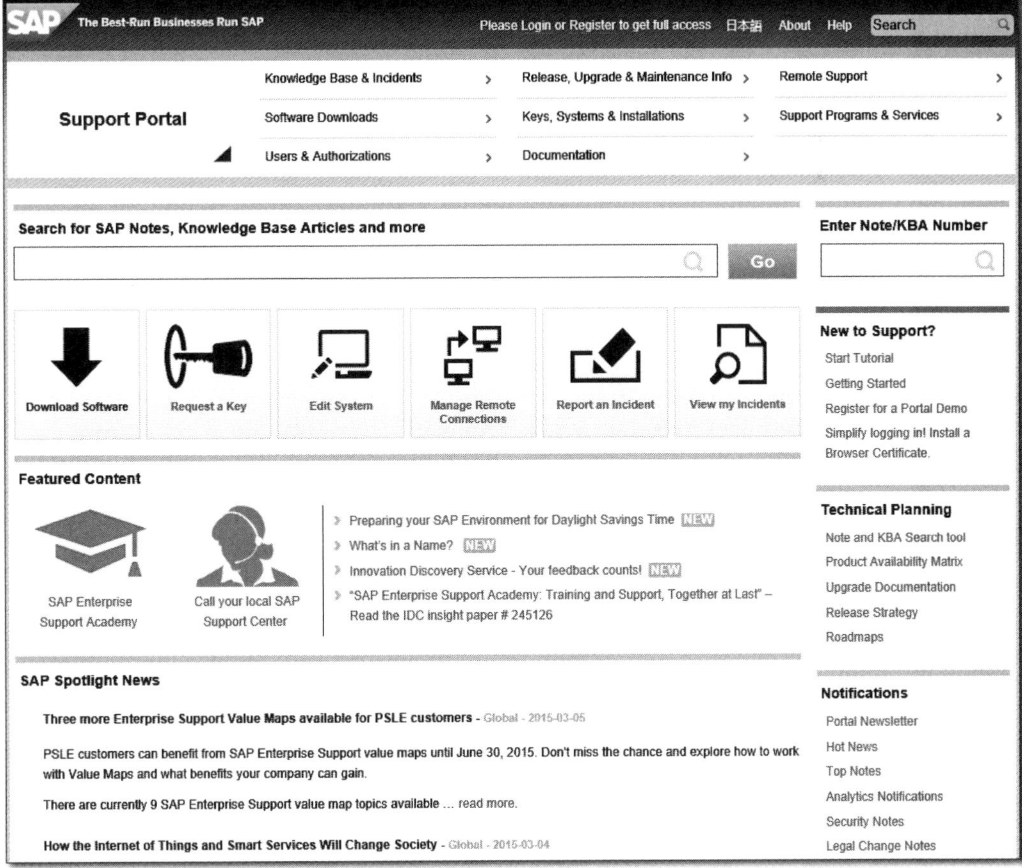

Figure 19.1 Initial Screen of the SAP Support Portal

2. On the initial screen, you can perform a text search (see Figure 19.2). Here, the system searches all sources connected, that is, the SAP Note database, documentations, the SAP Community Network (*http://scn.sap.com*), and so on. This function corresponds to the *xSearch* function of the old SAP Support Portal. Enter your search term in the search field under SEARCH FOR SAP NOTES, KNOWLEDGE BASE ARTICLES AND MORE, and start the search by clicking the GO button.

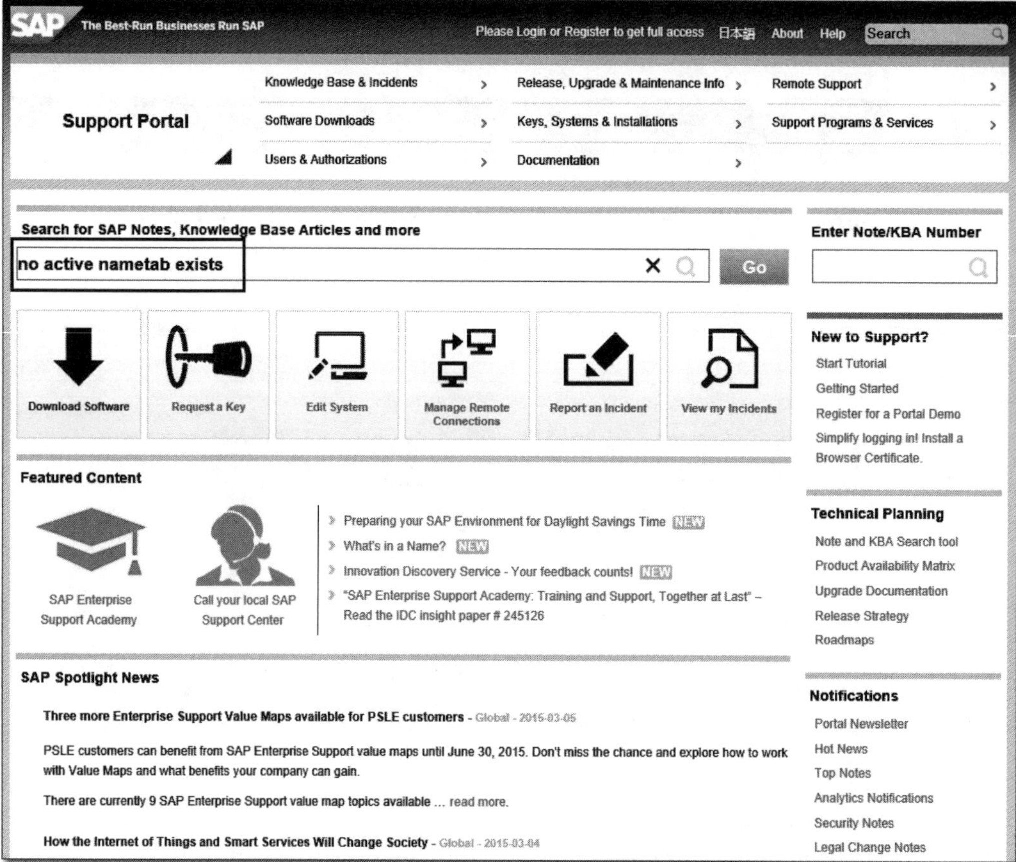

Figure 19.2 Text Search by Keywords

[+]

Displaying Notes Directly

You can also access an SAP Note directly by entering the number in the ENTER NOTE/KBA NUMBER field and clicking the GO icon.

3. Use your user ID (S000...) and password to log on (see Figure 19.3).

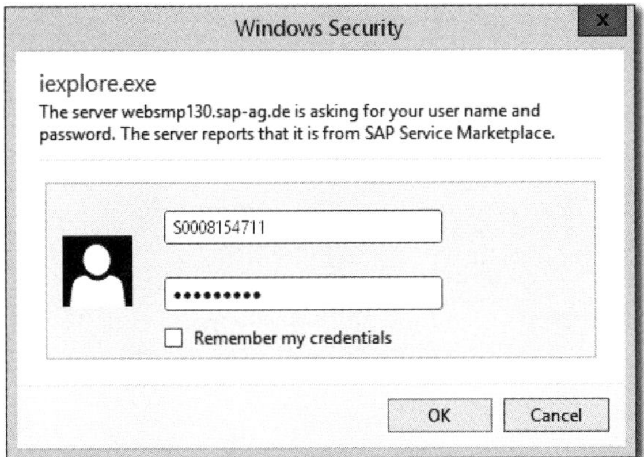

Figure 19.3 Entering Logon Data (S-User)

[+]

Single Sign-on

In certain cases, you may need to enter your use ID and password several times over the course of your SAP Support Portal session. If you want to use the portal's *single-sign-on function*, you must request an *SAP Passport*. To do this, follow the instructions provided in the SAP Service Marketplace under *https://support.sap.com* • Install a Browser Certificate or via the quick link of the old SAP Support Portal *https://service.sap.com/sso-smp*. Thanks to a certificate installed in your browser, you can save yourself the task of entering your user name and password in the future.

[+]

Quick Links

Quick links exist for many functions within the old SAP Support Portal. You can use these links to directly call the desired function, for example, the maintenance of service connections or the training catalog. The direct call is usually far more convenient than browsing through the website. You can find an overview of available quick links in the old SAP Support Portal under Quick Links (top right, directly under the search field) or via the quick link *https://service.sap.com/quicklinks*. In the new SAP Support Portal *https://support.sap.com*, the idea of quick links had not been fully implemented when this book went to press—but it will definitely be implemented in the near future.

4. The search results are then displayed (see Figure 19.4). To open an SAP Note, click on the corresponding link.

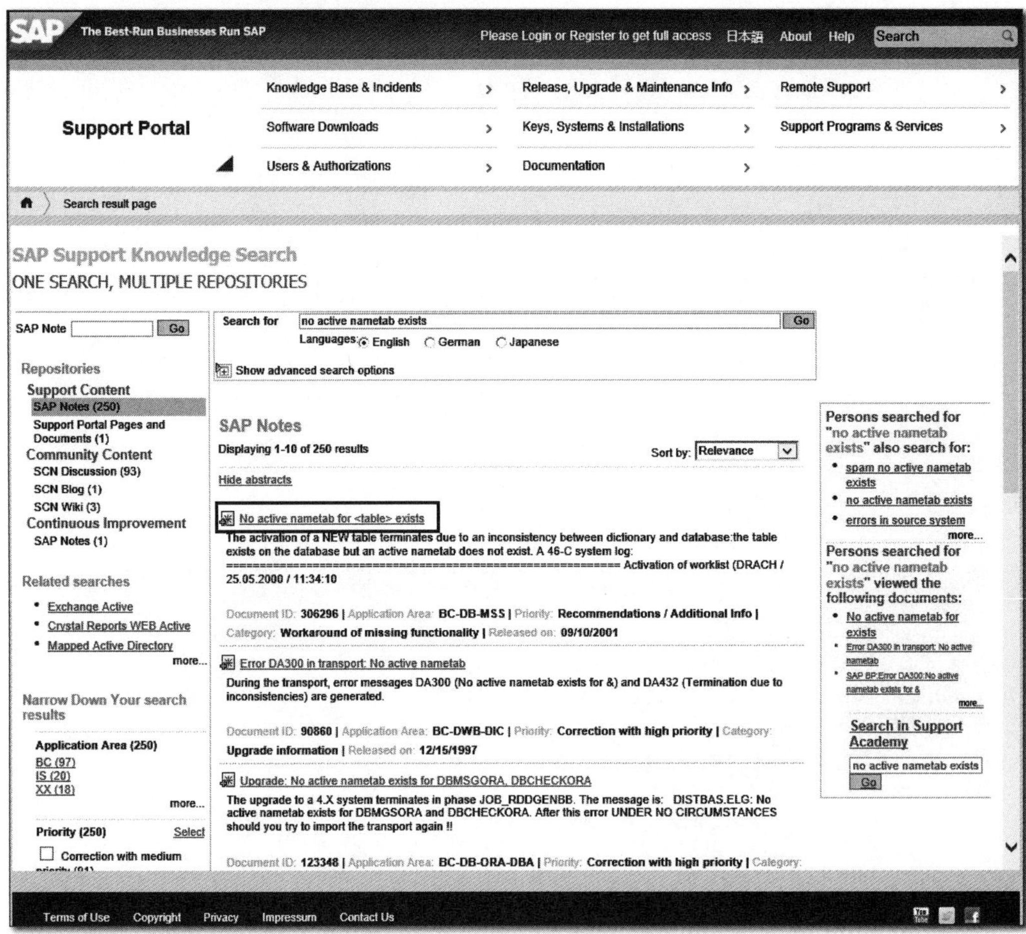

Figure 19.4 Display of Search Results

5. The SAP Note then opens in a new window or on a new browser tab (see Figure 19.5).

Check whether the SAP Notes found describe the problem that has occurred in your system. Check whether your release or support package level is affected by the problem described (see Chapter 18, Section 18.1.1). If the SAP Note describes your problem, follow the instructions provided in the solution description (e.g., implement the corrections provided in your SAP system—see Section 19.4). If your search in the SAP Support Portal is unsuccessful, create a *customer incident (message)*.

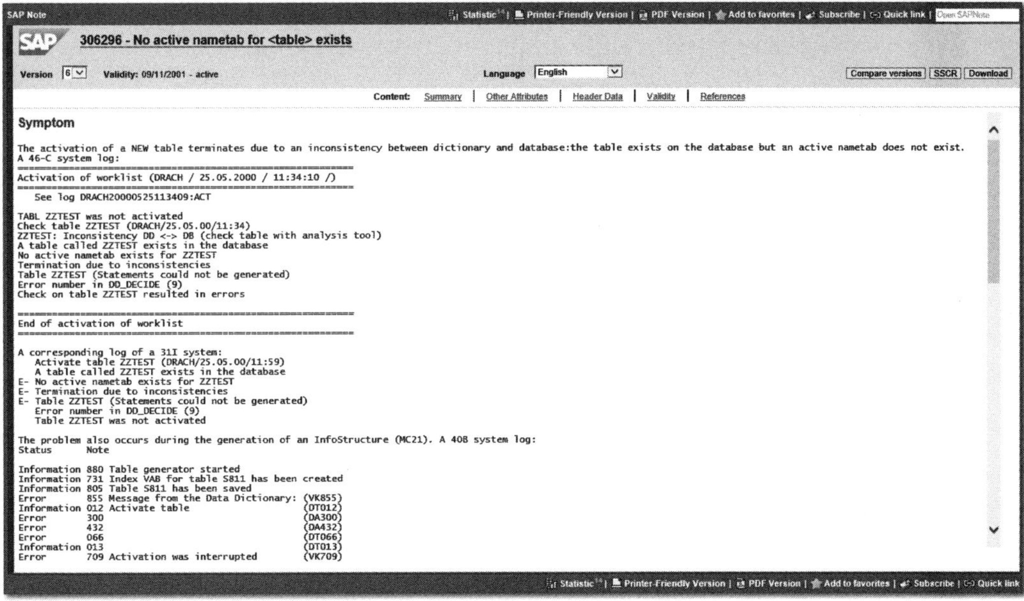

Figure 19.5 Displaying the SAP Note

19.2.2 Customer Incident Messages

If you can't find an answer to your question or a solution to your problem in the online documentation or SAP Notes, you should send a customer incident to SAP Global Support.

Error Message and Consulting Services [+]

Customer incidents aren't intended to replace consulting services. Customer incidents are used primarily for reporting purposes and for the elimination of SAP errors and bugs. If an incident message is merely a veiled request for consulting services, it will be returned to the sender, who will be advised to contact consulting services. For this reason, phrase your message in such a way that the product error is described clearly.

The following list contains some useful tips for reducing the time required to troubleshoot your customer incident:

- Describe your problem clearly and precisely. The better the quality of the information you provide, the better the results will be. Information that appears self-evident to you may be anything but obvious for the hotline consultant.

- Provide a sufficient amount of detail so that the SAP hotline team members don't need to ask additional questions before starting the troubleshooting process.
- Pay particular attention to the following aspects when describing the error:
  - If an error message was displayed, specify the error message exactly as it appeared on the screen. Where relevant, create a screenshot to attach to your incident.
  - Specify the relevant transaction or menu path.
  - Indicate whether the problem can be reproduced in your test system.
  - Describe the circumstances in which the problem occurred.
  - Describe any special features of the data entered.
  - Include a list of the SAP Notes you consulted in connection with the problem and of those that you implemented.
  - List the measures you've already introduced and the investigations you've already undertaken.

If the SAP hotline team receives incident messages such as FB01 IS NOT WORKING or THE SYSTEM IS SLOW, it requires additional information before it can begin to resolve the issue.

[!]

Information about the System Landscape

Keep the technical information about your system landscape up to date on the SAP Support Portal, and make sure that it's accurate. This information is used by the hotline team when working on your problem.

Creating a Customer Incident Message

Creating a customer incident message takes four steps:

1. Select the relevant system.
2. Search for a solution to the problem.
3. Check SAP Notes for a description of your problem.
4. Create a customer incident message.

You must search for SAP Notes before you create a customer incident message. This process avoids the creation of unnecessary support incident messages for problems already described by SAP Notes in the SAP Notes database.

[+]

Second Notes Search

In most cases, you've already searched once for SAP Notes when you create a customer incident message. Try searching a second time using different search terms—you may find an SAP Note describing your problem and avoid having to create a customer incident message.

To create a customer incident message, you follow these steps:

1. Access the SAP Support Portal, and click on REPORT AN INCIDENT (see Figure 19.6).

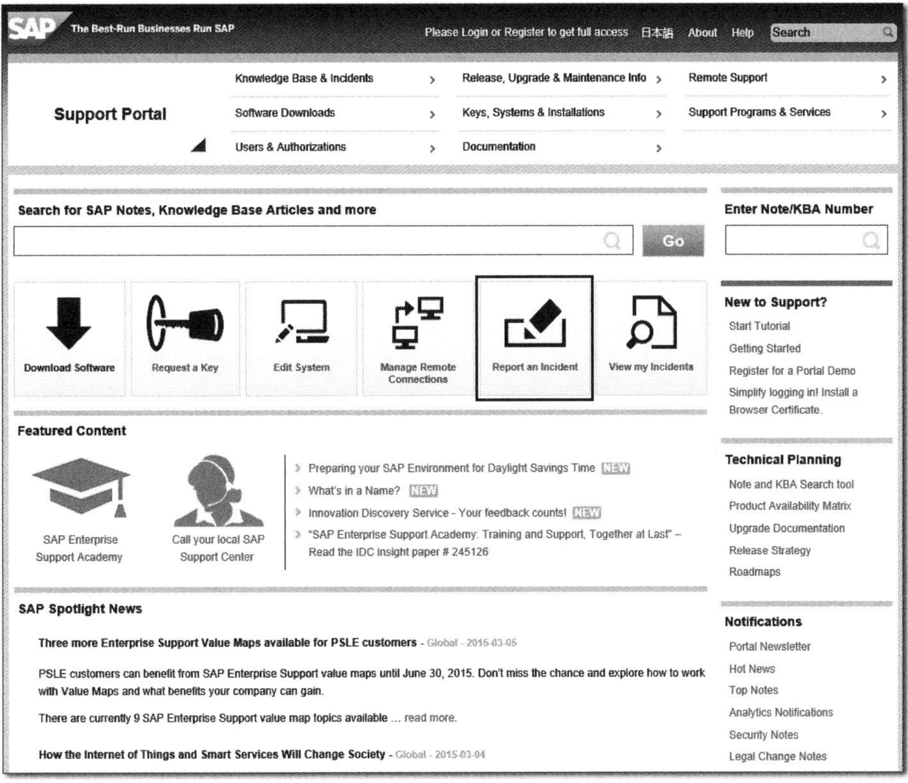

Figure 19.6 Reporting an Error to the SAP Global Support

2. In the SYSTEM SEARCH area, select the SAP system in which the problem occurred. Enter the SYSTEM ID in the field provided, and choose SEARCH (see Figure 19.7). Alternatively, use the CUSTOMER and INSTALLATION dropdown list boxes to restrict the search step by step. Or you can choose the system directly from the YOUR RECENTLY USED SYSTEMS list.

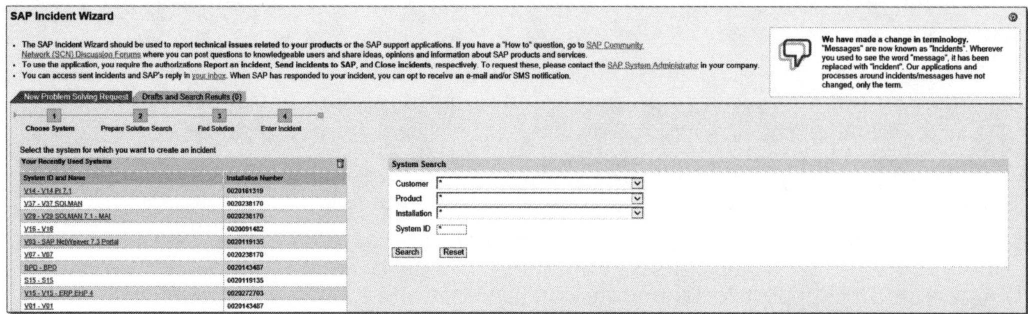

Figure 19.7 Selecting the System

3. Use the SEARCH TERM field to search for SAP Notes relating to your error. Click on CONTINUE to start the search (see Figure 19.8).

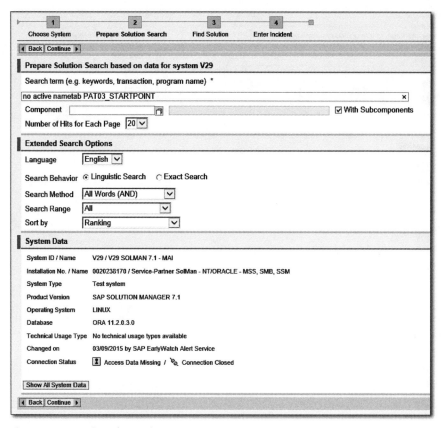

1 Choose System | 2 Prepare Solution Search | 3 Find Solution | 4 Enter Incident

Back | Continue

Prepare Solution Search based on data for system V29

Search term (e.g. keywords, transaction, program name) *

no active nametab PAT03_STARTPOINT

Component ☑ With Subcomponents

Number of Hits for Each Page 20

Extended Search Options

Language English

Search Behavior ◉ Linguistic Search ○ Exact Search

Search Method All Words (AND)

Search Range All

Sort by Ranking

System Data

System ID / Name	V29 / V29 SOLMAN 7.1 - MAI
Installation No. / Name	0020238170 / Service-Partner SolMan - NT/ORACLE - MSS, SMB, SSM
System Type	Test system
Product Version	SAP SOLUTION MANAGER 7.1
Operating System	LINUX
Database	ORA 11.2.0.3.0
Technical Usage Type	No technical usage types available
Changed on	03/09/2015 by SAP EarlyWatch Alert Service
Connection Status	Access Data Missing / Connection Closed

Show All System Data

Back | Continue

Figure 19.8 Searching for a Solution

4. The result of the SAP Notes search is then displayed. Consult the SAP Notes that may describe your problem. Click on the link in the TITLE column to open the corresponding SAP Note. You can repeat the search with modified search terms by clicking on SEARCH or NEW SEARCH. If your search for a relevant SAP Note is unsuccessful, click on CREATE INCIDENT (see Figure 19.9).

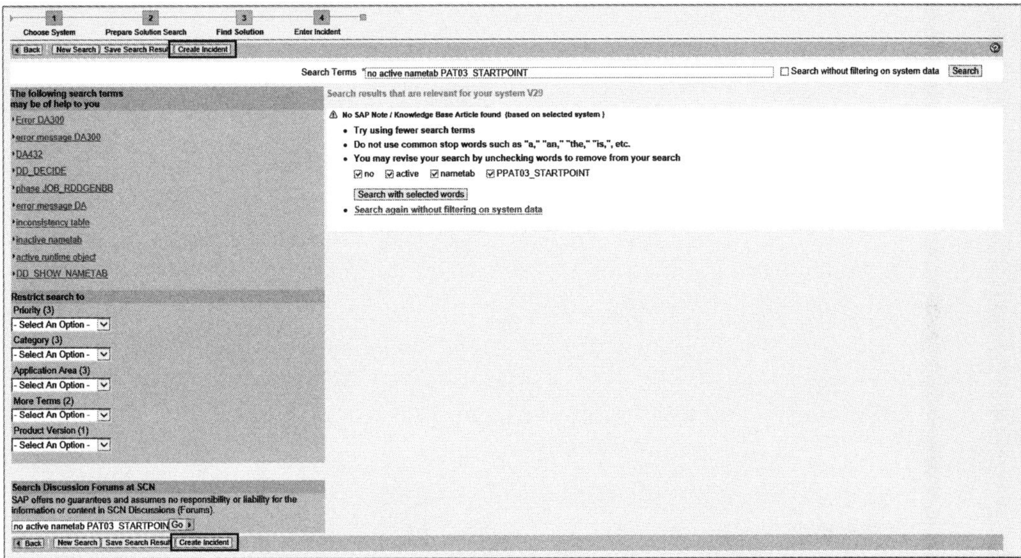

Figure 19.9 Creating a Customer Incident for a Problem

5. The following steps comprise the process of creating the customer incident (see Figure 19.10). Start by selecting the relevant language if the default setting isn't correct.

6. If you haven't already entered an application component in the search, you're required to do so now (see Figure 19.11). Enter the component in the COMPONENT field, or use the input help ❐. If you use the input help, a dialog box opens, displaying the component hierarchy. Expand the tree view, or search by keyword.

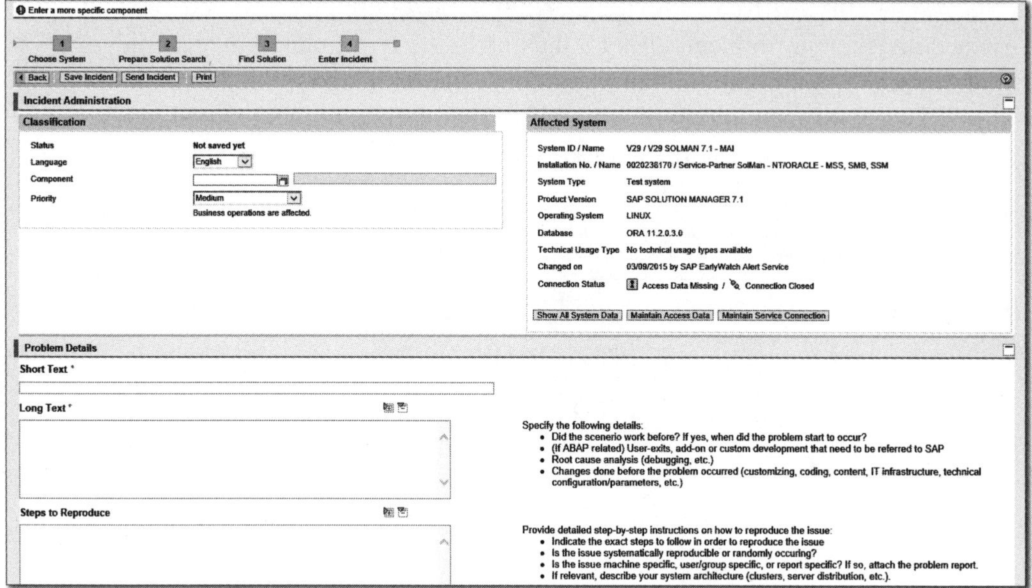

Figure 19.10 Selecting the Language for the Customer Incident Message

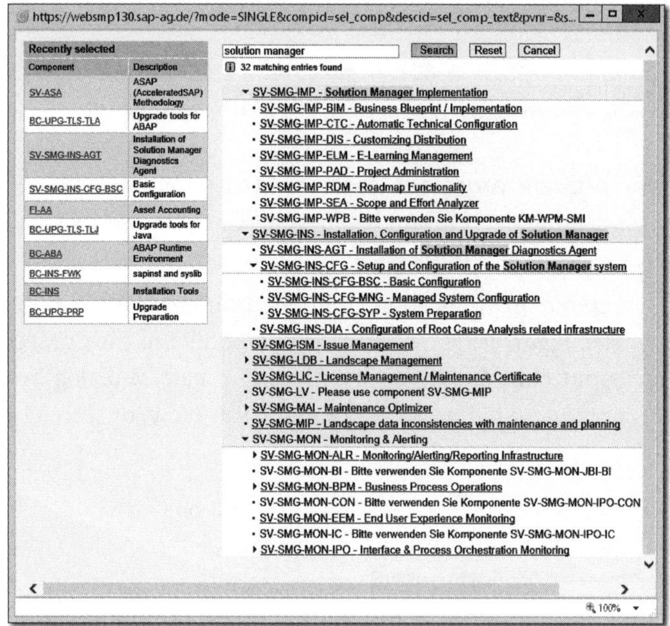

Figure 19.11 Selecting an Application Component

[!]

Selecting the Application Component

Assign the relevant component if you know it. If you don't know the component, assign the incident to a less detailed component level (e.g., assign level 3 BC-CCM-PRN, rather than level 4 BC-CCM-PRN-DVM). The SAP hotline consultant can assign a specific component. Valuable time may be lost if you assign the wrong component to the incident and it's forwarded to the wrong person as a result.

Note, however, that the cause of the error may originate in a component other than the component in which you currently work.

7. Define a priority. You can choose between the following priorities:

   - VERY HIGH

     In production systems:

     - Only to be used for serious, business-critical problems, which must be resolved immediately

     In nonproduction systems:

     - Only to be used for critical project phases.
     - An SAP Support Portal consultant will process these incident messages within 30 minutes of receiving them. If the problem isn't in the VERY HIGH category, it's automatically treated with a lower priority.

[+]

Ensuring Availability

Don't assign the VERY HIGH priority if you're unable to take a return call from SAP. If SAP tries to call you back and can't reach you, the priority of your incident message may be reduced.

   - HIGH
     Indicates functional failure of important applications in a production system that is critical to the business process, or an issue that threatens the go-live or upgrade date.
   - MEDIUM
     Indicates errors with less serious consequences than those specified in the two categories just described. Errors in this category affect business processes but don't represent a serious threat to the operation of the production system.
   - LOW
     Indicates minor errors that don't disrupt or threaten daily work (e.g., documentation errors or spelling errors).

[!]

Selecting a Priority

Take great care when assigning priorities. If your problem doesn't really belong in the VERY HIGH category, assigning this priority won't guarantee a quick response time.

8. Describe your problem. Use the following fields (see Figure 19.12):
   - SHORT TEXT: A description of the problem using key words (60 characters).
   - LONG TEXT: A detailed description of the problem.
   - STEPS TO REPRODUCE: Instructions for reproducing the error that occurred.

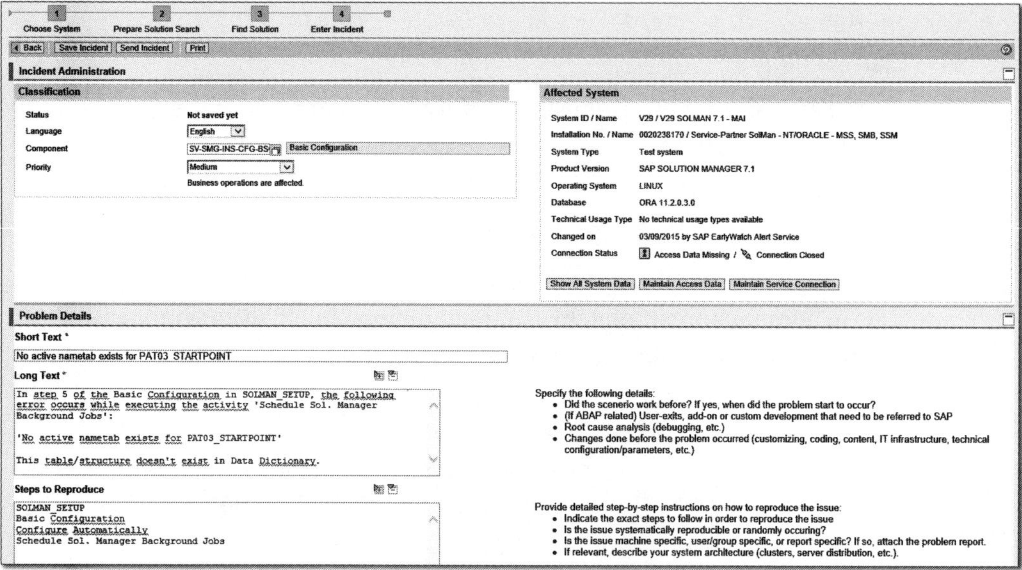

Figure 19.12 Phrasing the Problem Description

[+]

Information Content of the Incident Message

Include as much information as possible in your incident message, so that the SAP support team member can minimize the amount of information they need to request.

9. Upload an attachment if required (e.g., screenshots, a short dump, or a trace file; see Figure 19.13). Enter a meaningful short description under ATTACHMENTS, and click on BROWSE to select the relevant file on your PC.
10. Select the file for upload, and click on OPEN (see Figure 19.14).

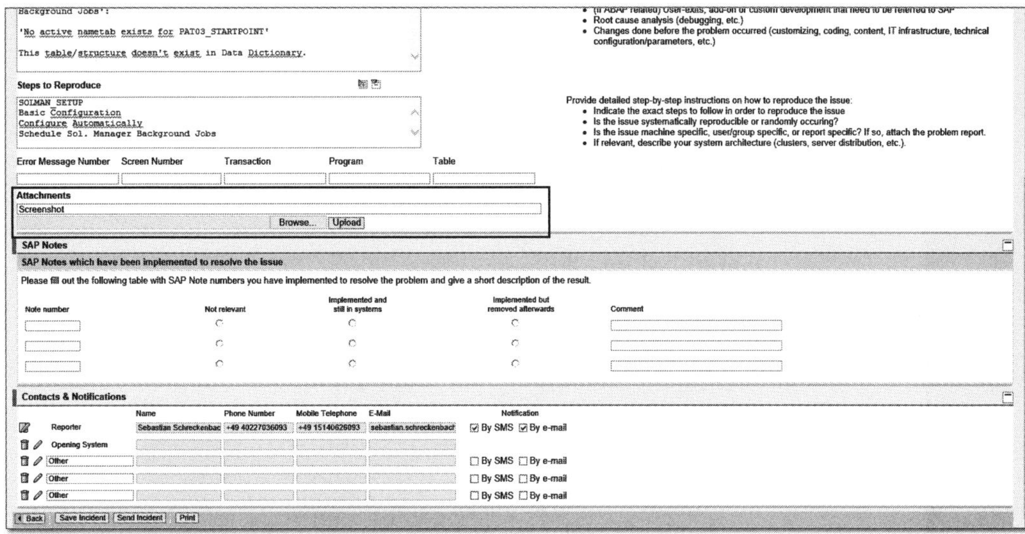

Figure 19.13 Entering a Short Descripting for Attachments

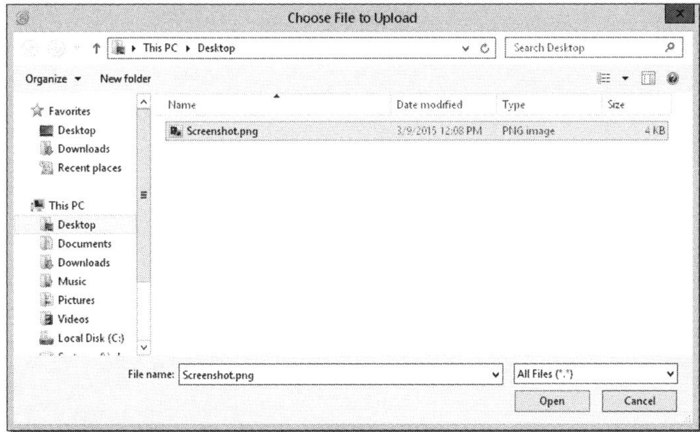

Figure 19.14 Selecting an Attachment for Upload

11. Click on UPLOAD in the message view to add the file to the incident.
12. In the SAP NOTES screen area, specify which SAP Notes, if any, you've already consulted without success.
13. Check that your telephone number and email address are entered correctly under CONTACTS & NOTIFICATIONS. If necessary, enter other contact persons who can be contacted by the SAP hotline team members should they have any

queries. This may be, for example, the person acting as your vacation substitute or a contact from the data center for issues relating to database administration.

[+]

Maintaining Contact Details

If your contact details are incorrect, you can change them in the SAP Support Portal under WELCOME, <YOUR NAME> • EDIT MY PERSONAL DATA after you've logged on.

14. When you've finished entering the details, click on SEND INCIDENT. The system confirms that the incident was created (see Figure 19.15).

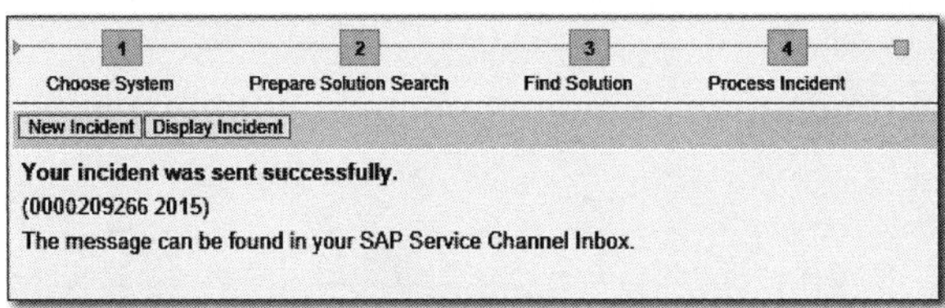

Figure 19.15 Transmission Confirmation for the Incident

15. Click on DISPLAY INCIDENT to display the incident again (see Figure 19.16).

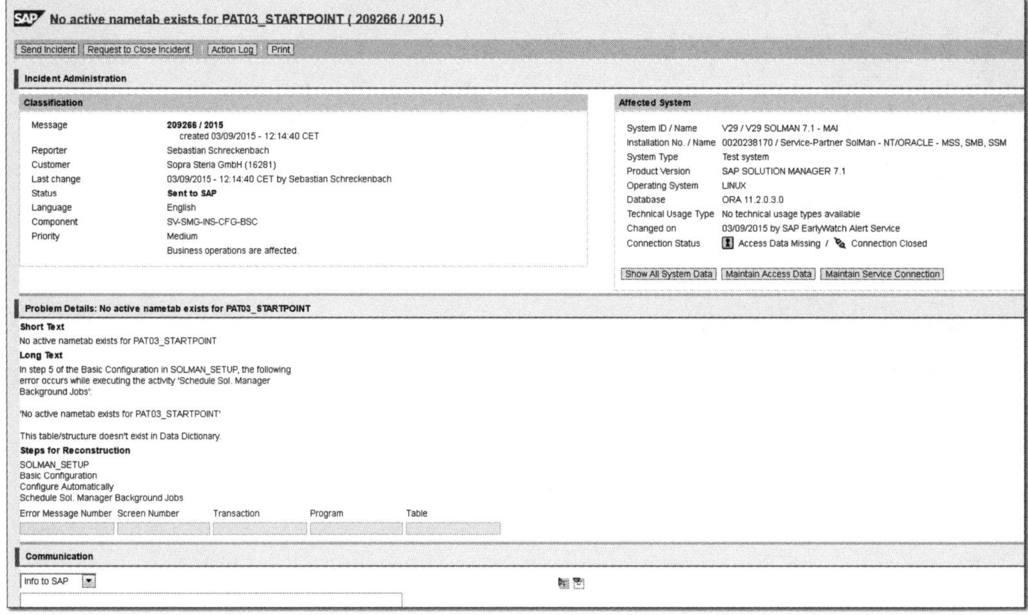

Figure 19.16 Display of the Customer Incident

Your customer incident has been created, and a member of the SAP hotline team is handling your problem. You'll be informed by email or SMS when the processing status of your incident changes. The hotline employee may contact you by telephone to clarify any open questions.

Monitoring the Status of Customer Incidents

While your incident is being processed, you can display it and check its status at any time:

1. Access the SAP Support Portal, and go to ACCESS MY INBOX. While SAP is still working on your problem, the incident is displayed on the SENT ITEMS tab (with the status SENT TO SAP or IN PROCESSING BY SAP, see Figure 19.17). Incidents that have been saved but not yet sent are located on the DRAFTS tab.

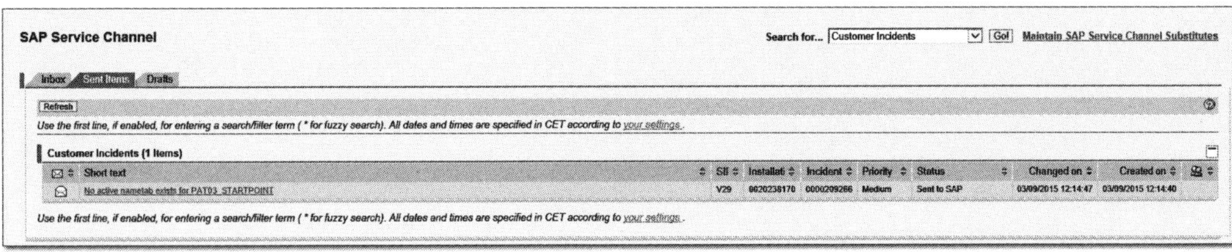

Figure 19.17 Sent Items in the SAP Service Channel

2. Click on the link in the SHORT TEXT column to open the incident. You can add supplementary information, such as an additional explanation (INFO TO SAP field) or other attachments (in the ATTACHMENTS area). Click on SEND INCIDENT (see Figure 19.18).
3. As soon as your help is required to process the incident, you'll receive an email notification. Open the incident in the SAP Support Portal. You can find it on the INBOX tab, with the status CUSTOMER ACTION, for example (see Figure 19.19).
4. Open the incident, and check which action you need to take (see Figure 19.20). For example, you may be asked to open a service connection. Proceed as described in Section 19.3. You can define the access data for external analysis of the problem in the incident itself. To do this, click the MAINTAIN ACCESS DATA button.

No active nametab exists for PAT03_STARTPOINT (209266 / 2015)

Send Incident | Request to Close Incident | Action Log | Print

Incident Administration

Classification

Message	**209266 / 2015** created 03/09/2015 - 12:14:40 CET
Reporter	Sebastian Schreckenbach
Customer	Sopra Steria GmbH (16281)
Last change	03/09/2015 - 12:14:40 CET by Sebastian Schreckenbach
Status	**Sent to SAP**
Language	English
Component	SV-SMG-INS-CFG-BSC
Priority	Medium Business operations are affected.

Affected System

System ID / Name	V29 / V29 SOLMAN 7.1 - MAI
Installation No. / Name	0020238170 / Service-Partner SolMan - NT/ORACLE - MSS, SMB, SSM
System Type	Test system
Product Version	SAP SOLUTION MANAGER 7.1
Operating System	LINUX
Database	ORA 11.2.0.3.0
Technical Usage Type	No technical usage types available
Changed on	03/09/2015 by SAP EarlyWatch Alert Service
Connection Status	Access Data Missing / Connection Closed

Show All System Data | Maintain Access Data | Maintain Service Connection

Problem Details: No active nametab exists for PAT03_STARTPOINT

Communication

Info to SAP

See attachment for further screenshots.

Contacts & Notifications

Attachments

Screenshots2 | Browse... | No file selected. | Upload

Description	File Name	Created from	Date	Time
Screenshot	Screenshot.png	Sebastian Schreckenbach	03/09/2015	12:13

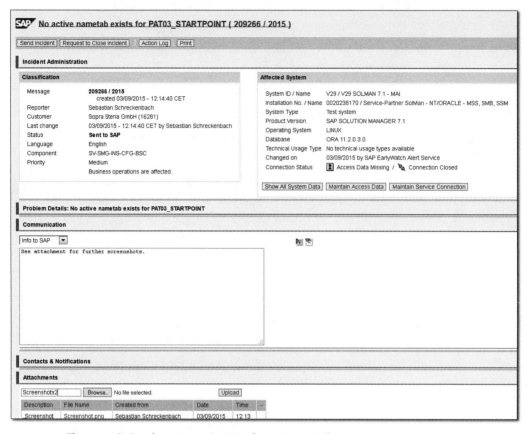

Figure 19.18 Supplementing a Sent Incident Retroactively

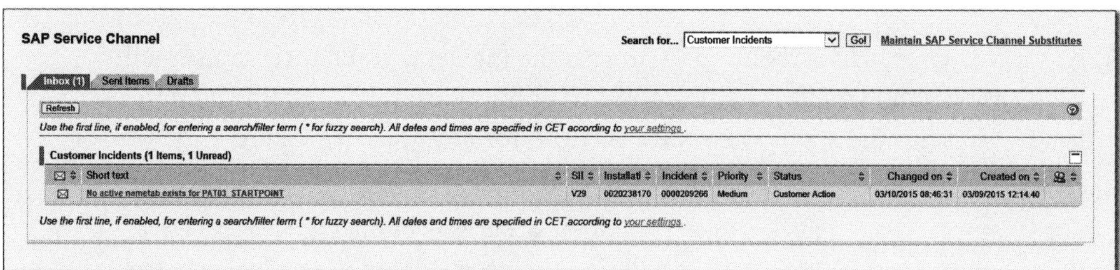

Figure 19.19 Notification on Customer Action in the Incidents Inbox

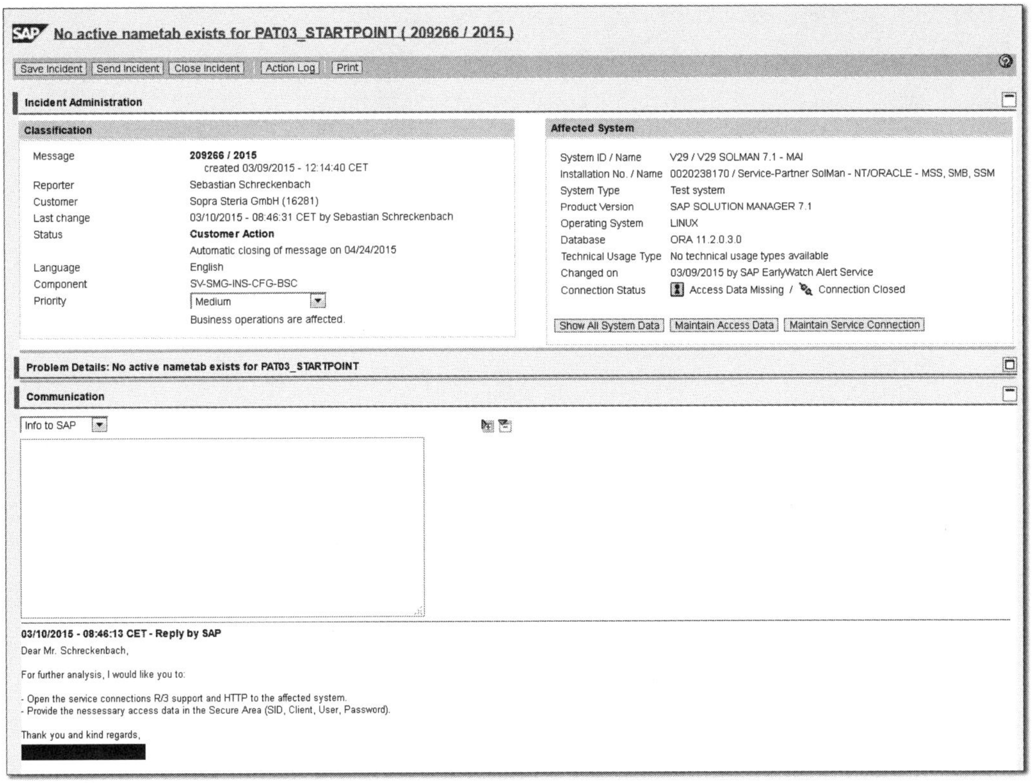

Figure 19.20 Displaying the SAP Support Team's Response

5. In the new window that opens, click on MODIFY (see Figure 19.21).

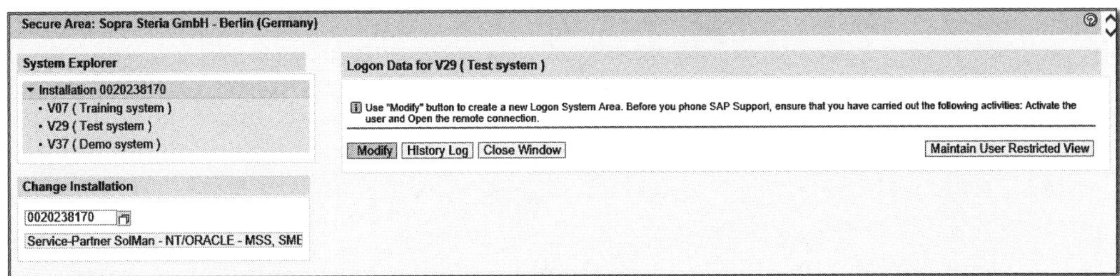

Figure 19.21 Providing Logon Data for the SAP Support Team

6. Enter the user data in the fields provided. Remember to create the user in the SAP system also (see Chapter 13). Click on SAVE (see Figure 19.22).

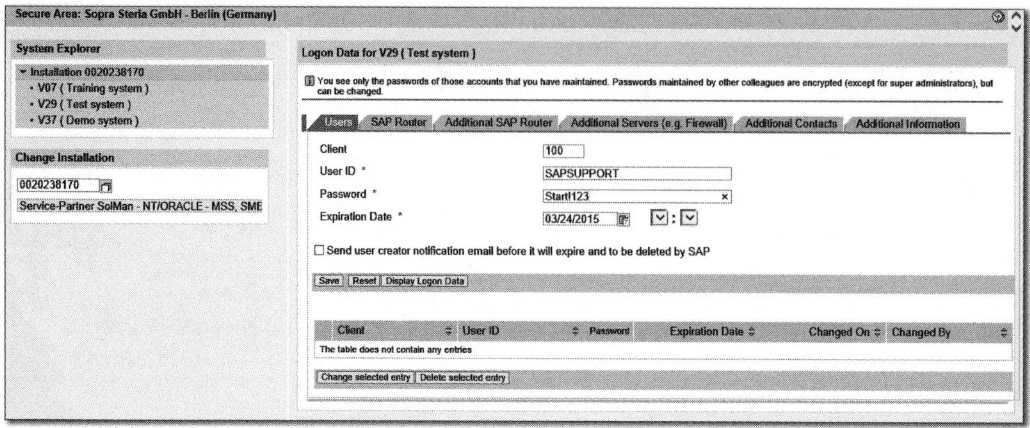

Figure 19.22 Saving the Access Data

7. The data are transferred (see Figure 19.23). Close the browser window.

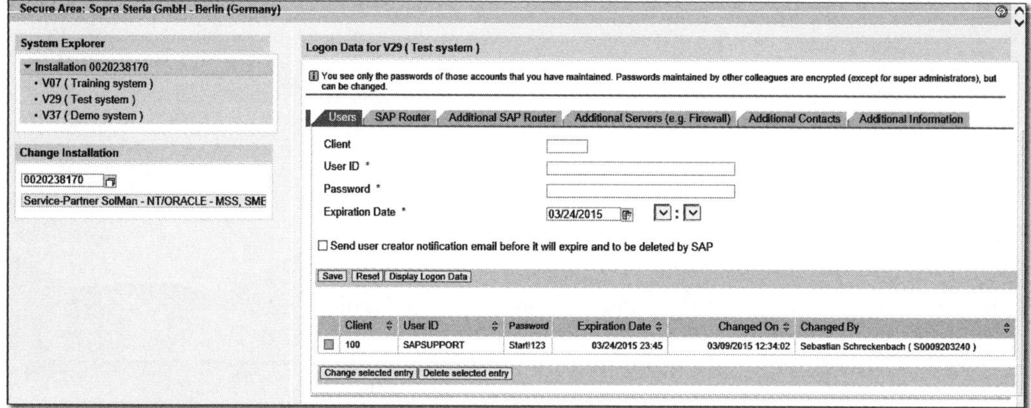

Figure 19.23 Saved Logon Data in the Secure Area

[+] **Secure Area for Access Data**

The access data are stored in encrypted form in a "secure area" within the incident. Only you and the SAP hotline incident processor can see the passwords defined there.

8. The ACCESS DATA MAINTAINED status is displayed in the incident. Enter explanatory text, and click on SEND INCIDENT to return the incident to SAP (see Figure 19.24).

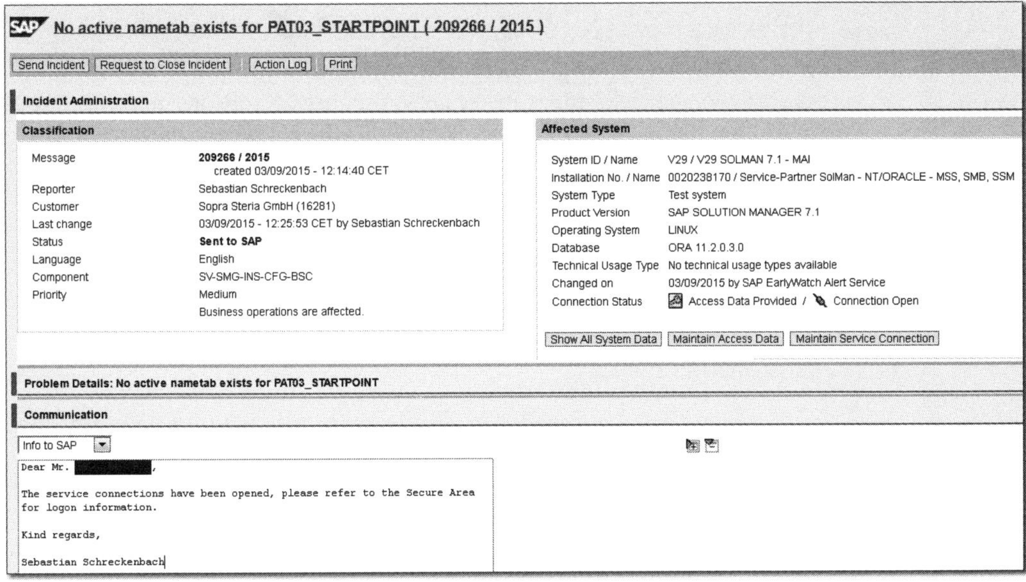

Figure 19.24 Sending a Response to the SAP Support Team

9. The system confirms that the incident was sent. To display the incident again, click on the DISPLAY INCIDENT button.
10. The information you added is displayed in the communication history. The AFFECTED SYSTEM area shows whether access data has been maintained and whether a service connection has been created (see Figure 19.25).

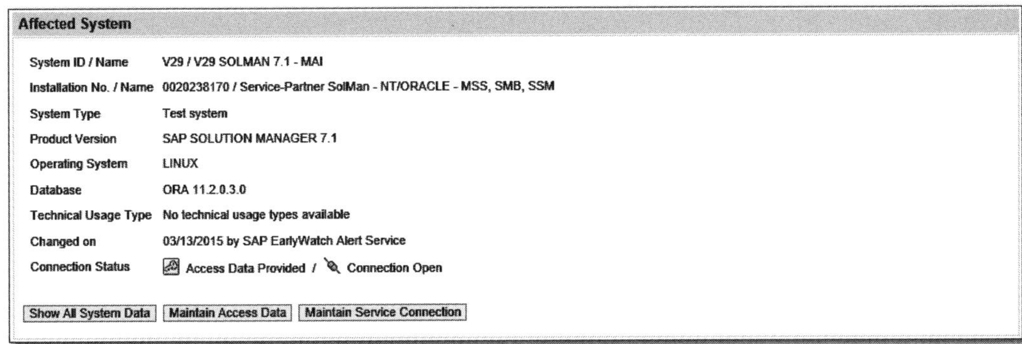

Figure 19.25 Affected System – Status Information

[!]

Accelerating Incident Processing

You can't change the priority of your incident while SAP is processing it. If you wait for an exceptionally long time without receiving a response to your incident, or if you require a faster solution due to unforeseen follow-on errors, you can contact your local *Global Support Customer Interaction Center* by phone. You can find more information in the SAP Support Portal under REPORT AN INCIDENT • REPORT AN INCIDENT – HELP • HOW TO SPEED UP A MESSAGE: Here, you're referred to SAP Note 560499, which includes the relevant telephone numbers. SAP Note 1281633 describes the requirements for accelerating the processing of incidents.

Closing an Incident

When your problem has been solved, you can close the incident by confirming the solution:

1. Access the SAP Support Portal, and click on VIEW MY INCIDENTS. Your incident will be on the INBOX tab, with the status SAP PROPOSED SOLUT., for example (see Figure 19.26).

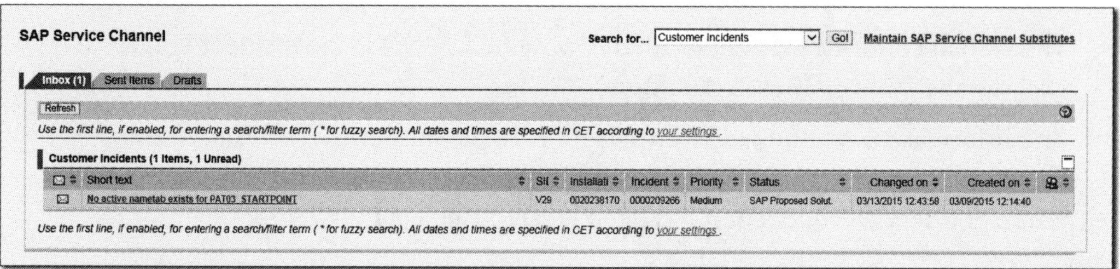

Figure 19.26 Incident with the SAP Proposed Solution Status

2. Open the incident, and check the proposed solution. If the solution eliminates your problem, click on CLOSE INCIDENT (see Figure 19.27).
3. A dialog box opens in which you're asked to confirm closing of the incident. Click on YES (see Figure 19.28).
4. After you confirm the incident, you're asked to participate in the support desk evaluation or POSITIVE CALL CLOSURE SURVEY (see Figure 19.29). Here you can rate the various aspects of the service provided by SAP Support. Click on CONTINUE.

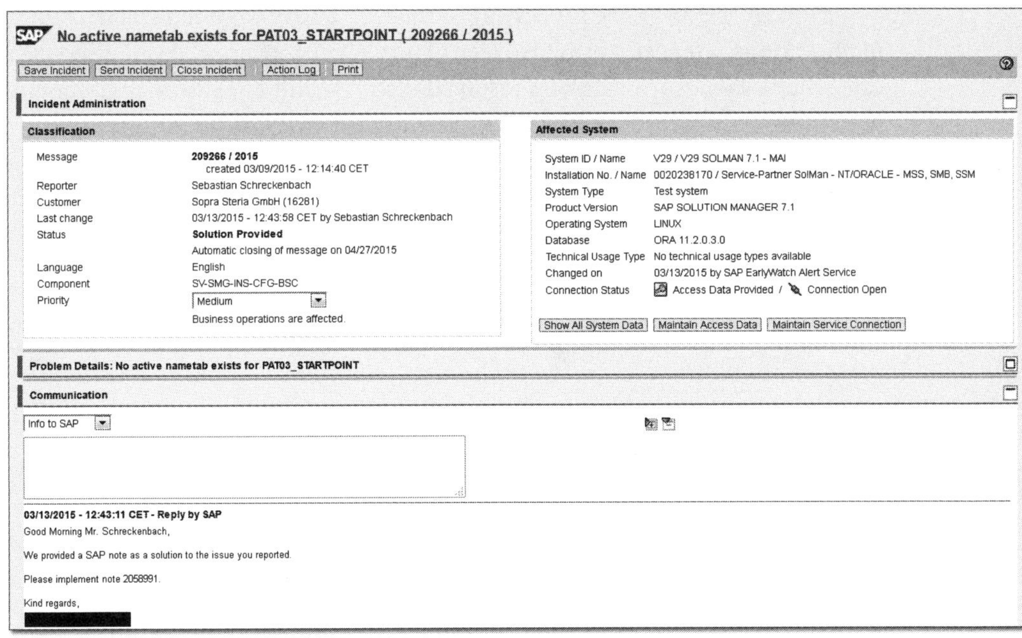

Figure 19.27 Checking the Proposed Solution

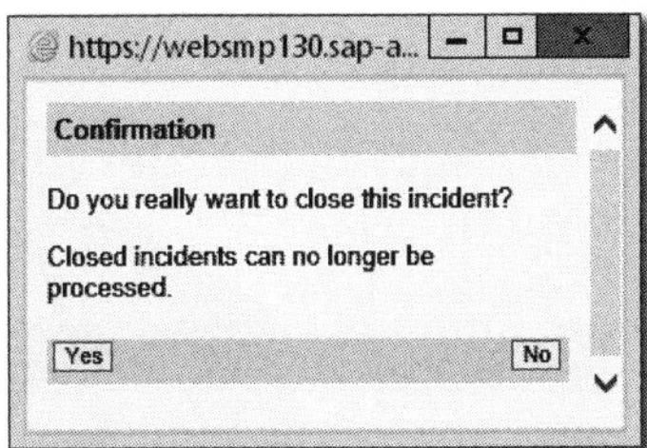

Figure 19.28 Confirming the Closure of the Incident

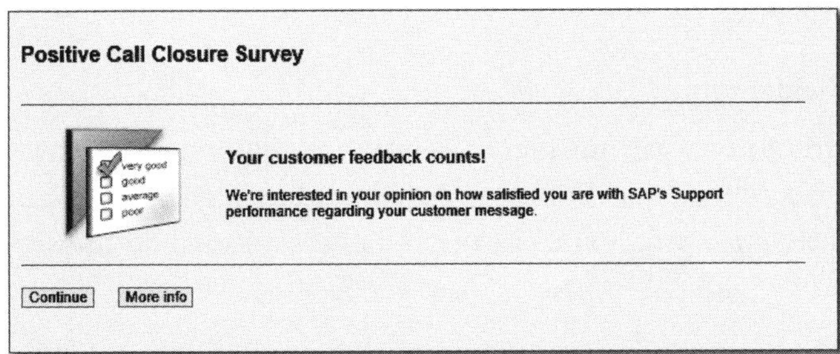

Figure 19.29 Invitation to the Evaluation Survey

5. You evaluate the incident processing service by awarding points from 1 to 10 in the various categories provided (see Figure 19.30). You're also asked to indicate whether your problem was resolved. You can enter any further comments in the user-defined text field. When you've finished, click on SUBMIT.

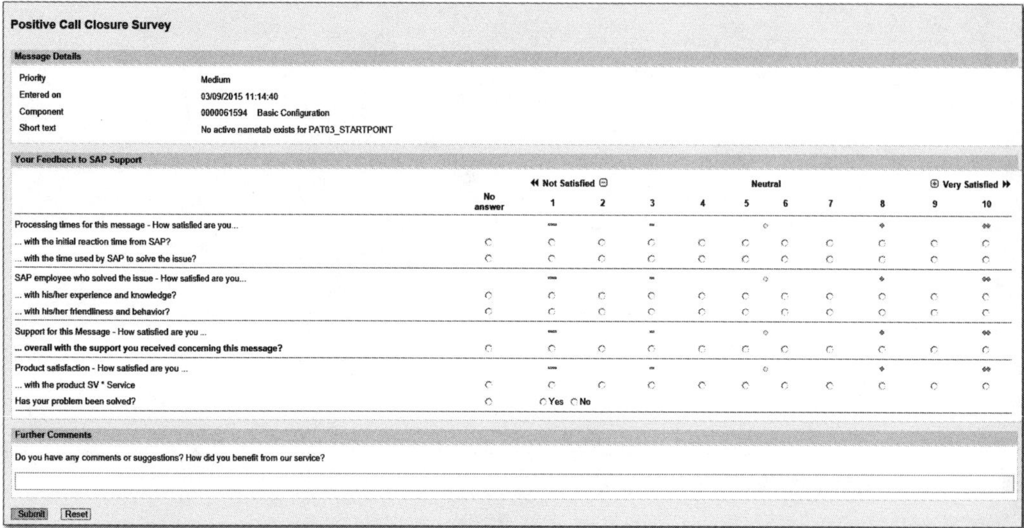

Figure 19.30 Evaluating Incident Processing

6. Your participation is confirmed on the next screen, and you can then close the browser window.

[+]

Authorization for Support Desk Evaluation

The request to participate in a support desk evaluation depends on the authorizations assigned to your SAP Support Portal user. You won't have an opportunity to express your opinion if your administrator hasn't assigned you the relevant authorizations.

Displaying Archived Incidents

After an incident is closed, you can no longer display it under VIEW MY INCIDENTS. However, you may occasionally want to reopen old incidents, for example, to look up the solution to a problem that occurred in the past. To do this, follow these steps:

1. Access the SAP Support Portal, and navigate to Knowledge Base & Incidents • Search Incidents. A search form is displayed where you can enter various search criteria (see Figure 19.31). Click on Search to begin the search. If you're certain that you created the incident yourself, click on the Reported by me button.

Basic Search | Advanced Search

Customer number: *
Installation: *
Reporter name:
Status: *
Create date from: to 03/09/2015 ☐ Archived Incidents
Changed within the last: days
Priority: *
Component:
Incident Number / Year: /
Number of results per page: 10

Search | Reported by me | Reset

Figure 19.31 Searching for Closed Incidents

2. A list of the incidents found is displayed (see Figure 19.32). Click on the link in the Short text column to display your incident.

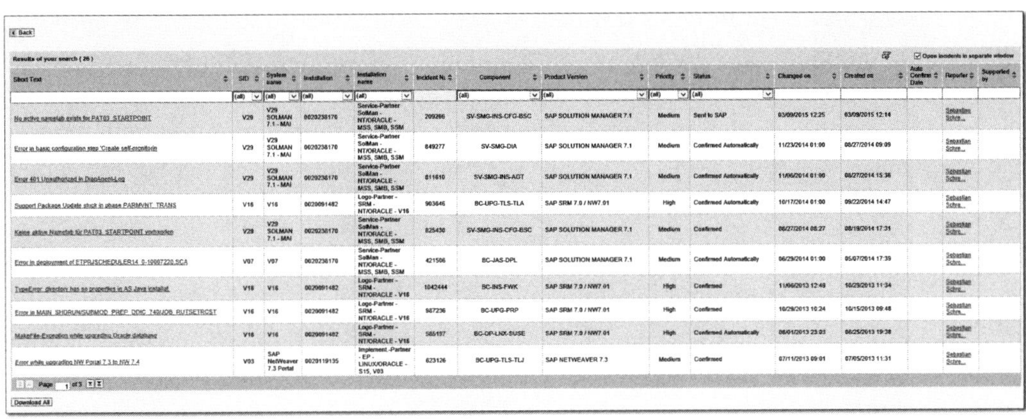

Figure 19.32 List of Incidents Found

[+]

Archived Incidents

All information is retained in the archived incident, for example, problem description, file attachments, proposed solution, and similar correspondence.

19.3 Creating a Remote Service Connection

If you've created an incident, you may be asked to open a *remote service connection* and provide SAP Support with direct access to your system. If the service connection is open, and a user ID has been provided, a member of the SAP hotline team can log on to your system to investigate the problem.

For security reasons, a service connection can only be set up by you, the customer. SAP can't initiate a service connection from its end. Note also that a service connection may incur high telephone charges that must be paid by your enterprise. You should therefore only open a connection if you're asked to do so, and you should only make the service connection available for the expected time required to investigate the problem.

[+]

SAP Notes Relating to Service Connections

For more information about service connections, refer to SAP Notes 35010 and 31515, and consult the SAP Support Portal under MANAGE REMOTE CONNECTIONS.

You may need to enter test data in your system for troubleshooting purposes. This testing should not be conducted in the production system. Try first to reproduce the problem in your development or test system, and provide SAP with access to the relevant server. You should only grant SAP access to your production server if the problem can't be reproduced on the development or test server. The prerequisites for opening a remote service connection are as follows:

- The remote network connection to SAP must be set up. (This includes, for example, configuration of the *SAProuter*.)
- The *SAP Service Connector* must be installed on the PC on which the connection is to be created.
- SAP GUI must also be installed on the PC to enable use of the SAP Service Connector.

[+]

Setting Up Remote Network Connections

A discussion of how to set up remote network connections falls outside the scope of this chapter. For more information about this topic, refer to the documentation provided in the SAP Support Portal (Link in the HAVING TROUBLE box on the MANAGE REMOTE CONNECTIONS page). You can download the SAP Service Connector from the SAP Support Portal under MANAGE REMOTE CONNECTIONS • SAPROUTER • SERVICE CONNECTOR.

Chapter 4 explains how to open and manage service connections conveniently using SAP Solution Manager. The following section describes the manual method via the SAP Support Portal. The following discussion assumes that the technical prerequisites set out previously are already in place. To create a service connection, follow these steps:

1. Log on to the SAP Support Portal (*https://support.sap.com*), and choose MANAGE REMOTE CONNECTIONS and CONNECT TO SAP (see Figure 19.33).

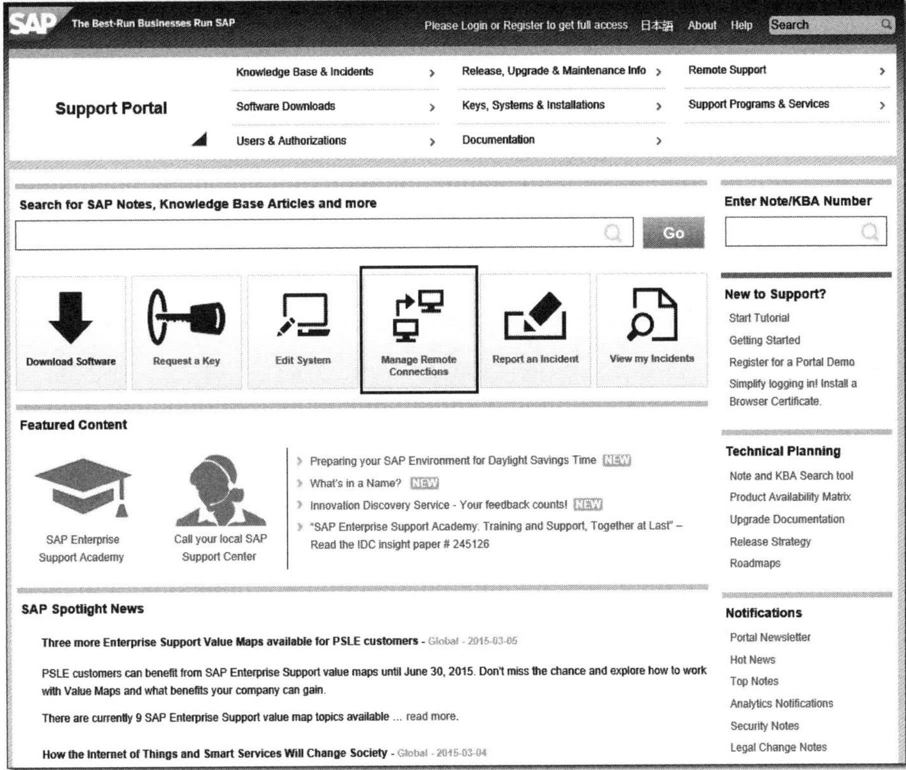

Figure 19.33 Opening a Service Connection via the SAP Support Portal

[+]

Remote Support Page in the Old SAP Support Portal

In the old SAP Support Portal (*https://service.sap.com*), you can reach the remote support page under HELP & SUPPORT • CONNECT TO SAP.

2. Click on MAINTAIN CONNECTIONS (see Figure 19.34).

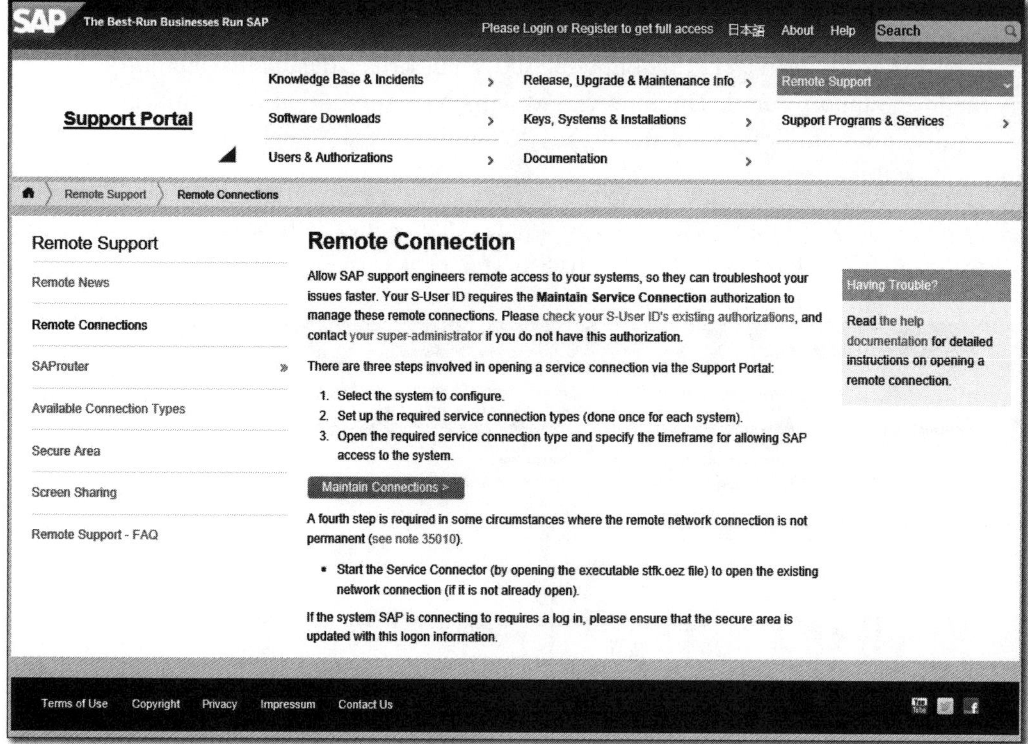

Figure 19.34 Administration of the Remote Service Connections

3. Use the fields in the SYSTEM SEARCH area to define the SAP system for which you want to create the service connection (see Figure 19.35). If you already created a connection for this system in the past, you can select this connection from the YOUR RECENTLY USED SYSTEMS list.

4. For external access to an ABAP system, you usually require a connection of the R/3 SUPPORT type. However, if you've never used this before, you must set it up first. To do this, click on the R/3 SUPPORT link in the CONNECTION TYPE column under SET UP CONNECTION TYPES (see Figure 19.36).

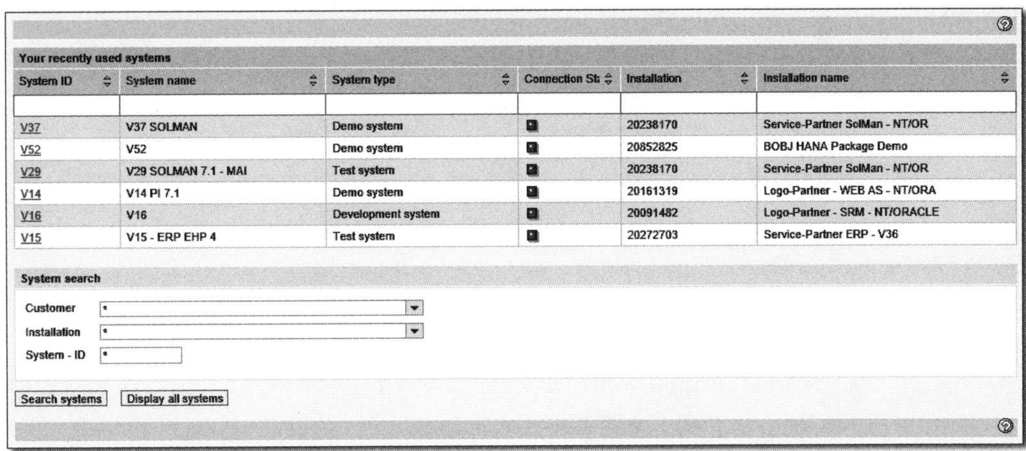

Figure 19.35 System Search or Selection

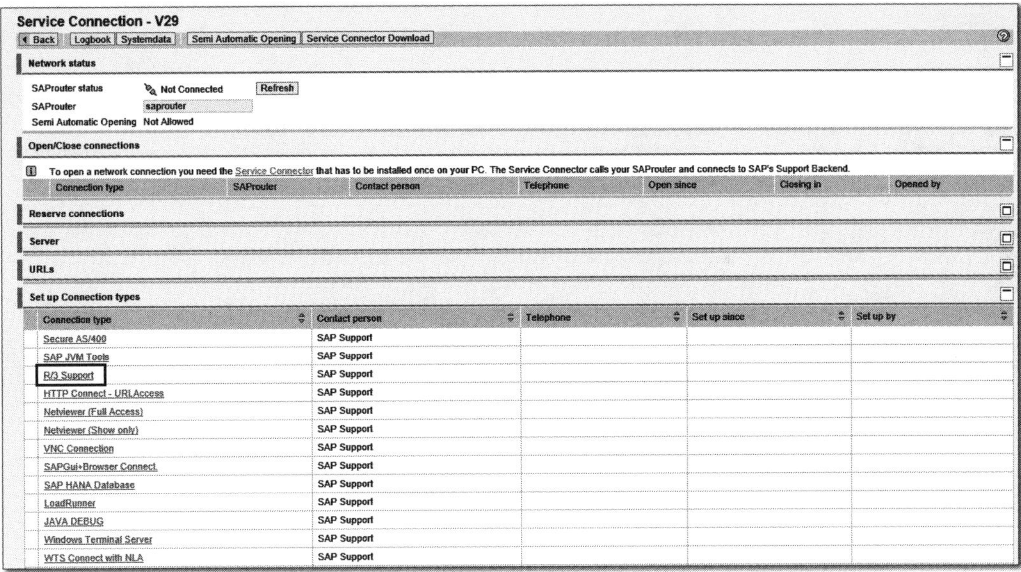

Figure 19.36 Setting Up a Connection Once

5. On the next screen, your contact details are displayed under Contact person. You can use the input help to select a different or an additional contact person if necessary. Otherwise, all you need to do to set up the connection is to save your contact details (see Figure 19.37).

Figure 19.37 Selecting the Contact Person for the SAP Support Team

6. When you've finished, click on SAVE.
7. The connection type you've set up is then displayed under OPEN/CLOSE CONNECTIONS. Click on the connection (e.g., R/3 SUPPORT) in the CONNECTION TYPE column to open it (see Figure 19.38).

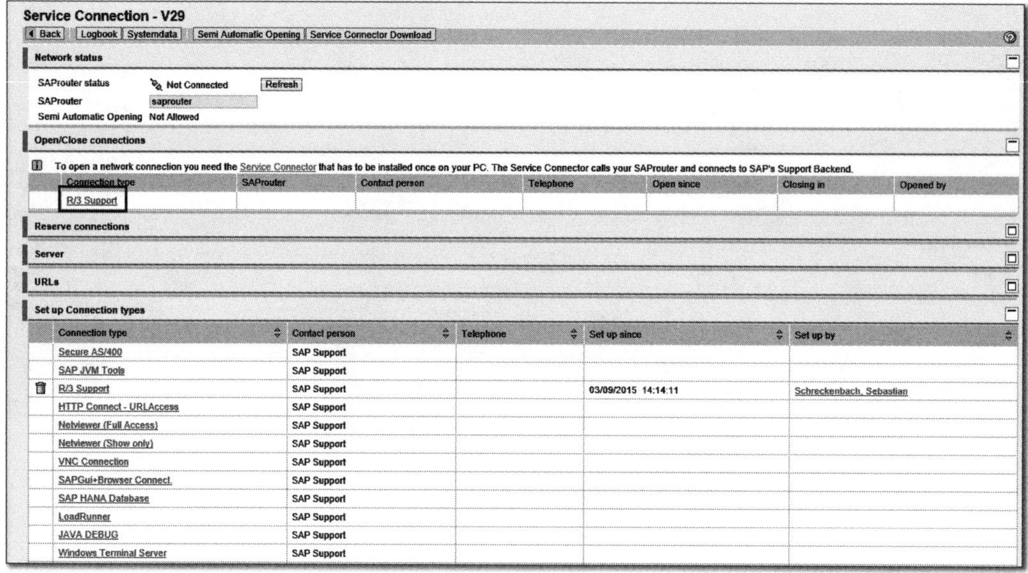

Figure 19.38 Opening the Service Connection

8. Under DEFINE TIME, you can define the period for which the service connection is to remain open. If necessary, enter another contact person or telephone number under CONTACT DATA. You may need to enter the IP address and outbound port of your SAProuter server in the ROUTESTRING field. Then click on START SERVICE CONNECTOR (see Figure 19.39).

Using the SAP Service Connector [+]

If the SAProuter status is already displayed as CONNECTED when you select the service connection, your enterprise may use an Internet connection (VPN or SNC) as a remote network connection, or—if ISDN is used—a connection is already set up. In both cases, the usage of the SAP Service Connector is obsolete, and the connection is opened immediately. Continue with step 14 of these instructions in this case.

SAProuter [⚙]

SAProuter is a program that runs on a server in your network and can act as a proxy to create a connection to another network. This allows you to bundle, control, and log SAP-specific accesses to your corporate network as an enhancement of your firewall.

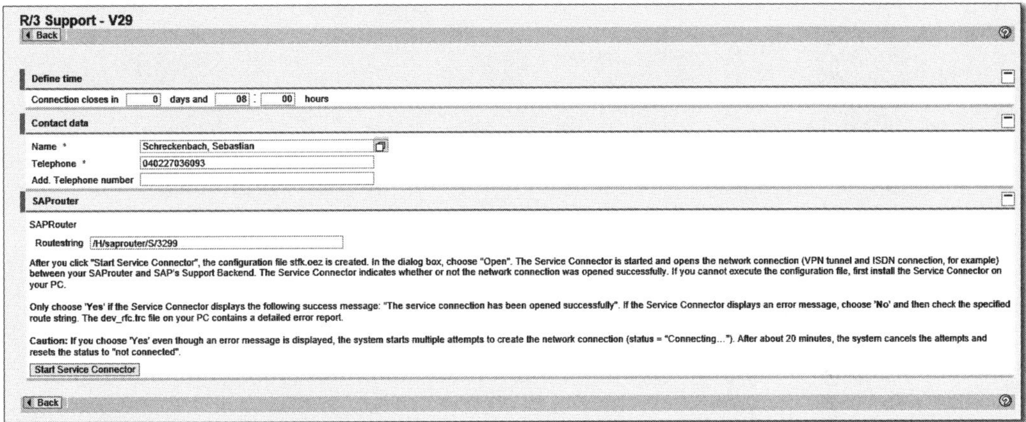

Figure 19.39 Entering Connection Data

9. A file named *stfk.oez* is generated that contains all parameters for the SAP Service Connector for your service connection. A dialog box opens in your browser (see Figure 19.40). The file must be opened with the SAP Server Connector.
   - Some browsers or browser versions don't allow files to be opened directly for security reasons. If you use such a browser, you must store the file temporarily on your PC and start it manually using the SAP Service Connector.

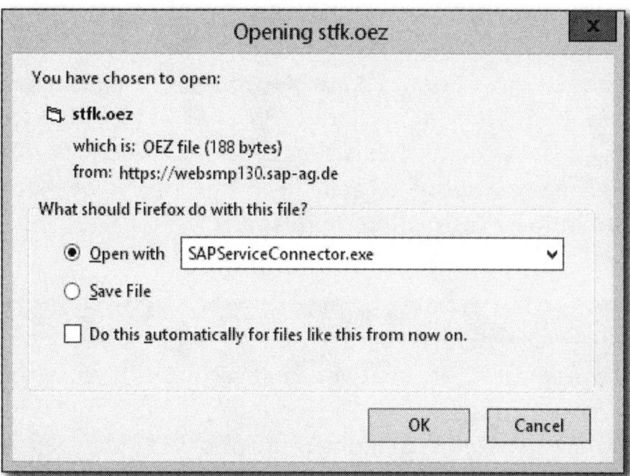

Figure 19.40 Opening a File Dialog Box

[⚙]

Opening a Connection without the SAP Service Connector

If you're unable to install the SAP Service Connector and/or SAP GUI on your PC, the following actions may be useful:

- Cancel opening the *stfk.oez* file.
- Log on to the SAP system for which you want to create the service connection.
- Start Transaction SM59 (RFC Connections), and access the RFC connection SAPOSS. Perform a connection test.

Then go back to the SAP Support Portal, and confirm that the service connection has been successfully opened (see step 14).

10. Another dialog box opens to inform you that the Service Connector has started (see Figure 19.41). Click on OK.

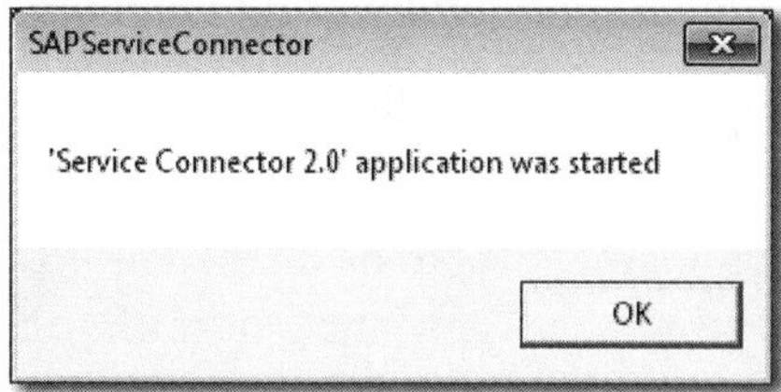

Figure 19.41 Starting Message of the SAP Service Connector

11. It may take a while for the next dialog box to open, signaling that the service connection has been successfully created (see Figure 19.42). Therefore, wait a while until it appears, and then choose OK to close it.

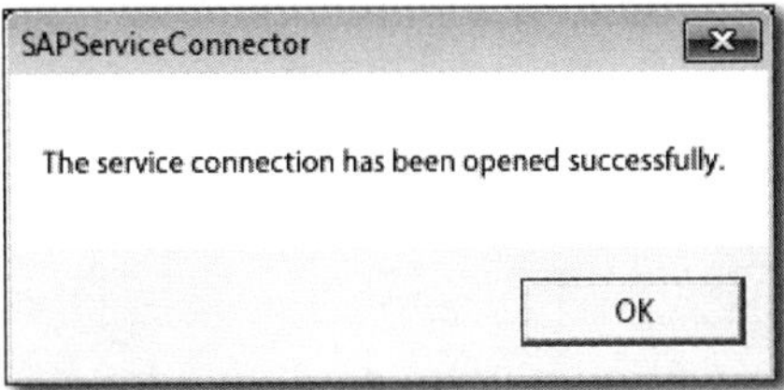

Figure 19.42 Connection Confirmation

12. In the browser window containing the connection view, you'll now see a question asking whether the network connection was opened successfully. Answer YES to this question (see Figure 19.43).

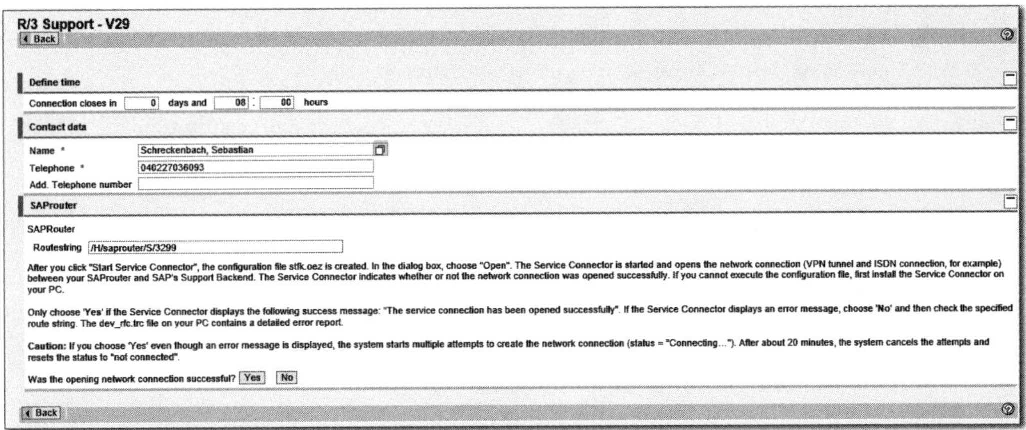

Figure 19.43 Confirmation to Open the Service Connection in the Connection View

13. This automatically brings you back to the initial connection setup screen (see Figure 19.44). The NETWORK STATUS area indicates that the connection has been set up. It may actually take a few minutes for the connection to be set up. Click on the REFRESH button to update the status.

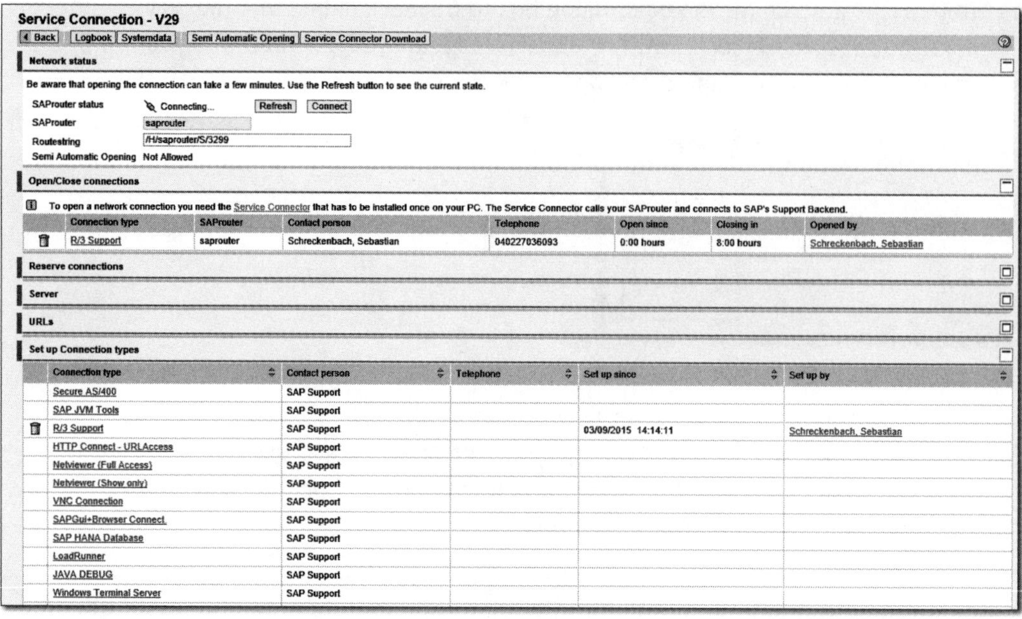

Figure 19.44 Status Display for the Connection Setup

14. The status changes to CONNECTED when the service connection has been created. You can now click the BACK button to exit the view for opening a connection (see Figure 19.45).

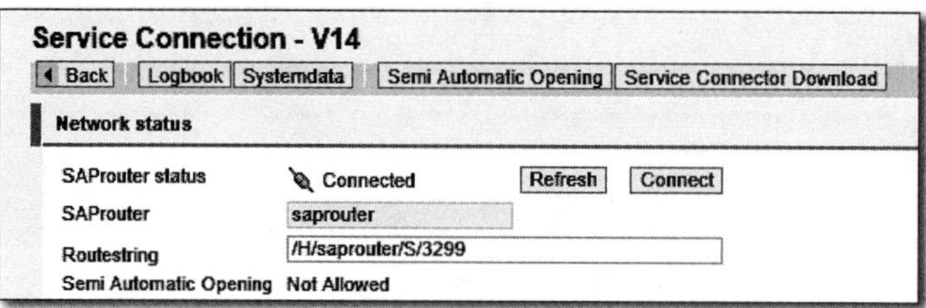

Figure 19.45 Successfully Created Service Connection

[+] **Closing Connections**

To close the connection manually, click on CLOSE in the row that corresponds to the service connection under OPEN/CLOSE CONNECTIONS.

15. The open connection is displayed with a green traffic light icon in the system list (see Figure 19.46). You can now close the browser.

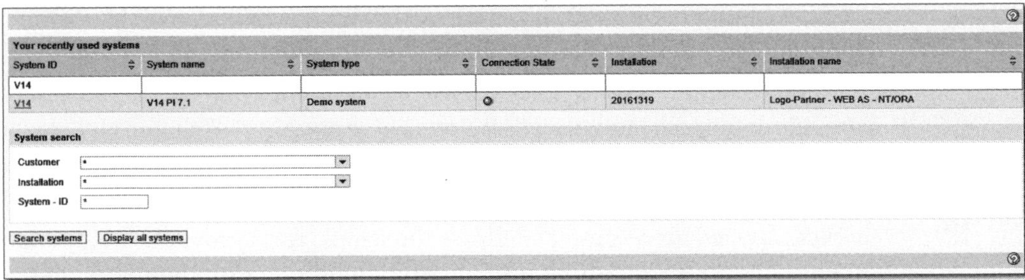

Figure 19.46 System List with Opened Connection

After you've opened the service connection, the SAP hotline team can analyze the problem in your SAP system. Remember to provide them with a user ID with sufficient authorization to log on to your system (see Section 19.2.2).

Opening Service Connections Using SAP Solution Manager [+]

As an alternative to managing service connection in the SAP Support Portal, you can also open them via SAP Solution Manager. Chapter 4, Section 4.3.6, provides more information on this subject.

19.4 Implementing SAP Notes

SAP provides program corrections to eliminate program errors that cause specific problems. These corrections are provided in the form of SAP Notes, which describe the error and the solution, which consists of program corrections attached to the SAP Note. To copy the corrections into your system, you *need to implement the SAP Note* by implementing the program corrections.

SAP Note Implementation [+]

Not all SAP Notes can be implemented automatically using Transaction SNOTE. Many SAP Notes describe Customizing settings or system configurations that have to be performed manually to eliminate the error. An "implementable" SAP Note is one that has *correction instructions* attached.

Document the implementation of SAP Notes as thoroughly as possible. Pay particular attention to the following aspects:

- Document all SAP Notes applied to your system, and specify both the systems and instances in which they were applied.
- You should create a table to track all SAP Notes applied and also keep detailed data records for each individual SAP Note. These data records should include the following information: the object changed, the release in which the SAP Note was implemented (important for updates), and other SAP Notes that have been checked, applied, or recommended (see the sample form provided in Appendix D). You should also keep a record of the problem for which the SAP Note was used. Provide an example so that the error can be retested if necessary.
- Document any required manual changes associated with the implementation of an SAP Note.
- In the case of system upgrades, it's essential to know which SAP Notes have been implemented to resolve problems. The following SAP Notes are relevant:
  - SAP Notes that are part of the upgrade, to allow you to return to the SAP standard code
  - SAP Notes that are applied again because they aren't part of the upgrade
- Document all relevant SAP Notes that don't require changes in the system (e.g., informative notes or instructions).
- Document the SAP Notes that were *not* applied in your system. There may well be cases where you check an SAP Note and decide that it's not relevant for your problem. You should document the reasons for this. If your SAP contact person then asks why a certain SAP Note hasn't been applied, you can quickly check the reasons in your records.

SAP Notes often provide important advance corrections, before these are delivered with other SAP Notes and further developments in a support package. For this reason, SAP Notes are usually relevant for specific SAP versions (*releases*), support package versions, or kernel patch levels. Details of an SAP Note's validity are provided in the SAP Note itself under VALID RELEASES and LINKS TO SUPPORT PACKAGES.

If you recognize the problem described in an SAP Note as your own problem, and you want to apply this SAP Note, check first whether the SAP Note is relevant for your SAP system by opening the system information. To do this, proceed as described in Chapter 18, Section 18.1.1. Compare your system's version and support package level with the relevant components specified in the SAP Note (the VALIDITY and SUPPORT PACKAGES & PATCHES sections at the bottom of the note display).

Let's assume you've determined that an SAP Note must be implemented in your system to eliminate an error and that the patch level version specified is relevant for your system. To implement the SAP Note, you can then use the *Note Assistant* in your SAP system.

The Note Assistant (Transaction SNOTE) is a tool that enables a quick implementation of SAP Notes. It downloads SAP Notes from the SAP Support Portal automatically and checks during the import whether dependencies exist among support packages, SAP Notes, and changes you may have implemented previously. The tool optimizes the implementation of SAP Notes-based corrections in a consistent and user-friendly way. The Note Assistant may also help you avoid errors because it applies automatic code changes to SAP Notes.

The Note Assistant logs all processing steps automatically. It provides an overview of all SAP Notes that were previously implemented in your system. In addition, it shows the processing statuses of the SAP Notes and all corrections already made to the source code. As a result, you can keep track of which SAP Notes have been implemented successfully and which still need to be processed.

The steps involved in downloading SAP Notes with the Note Assistant and implementing them in your system are described here:

1. Enter Transaction SNOTE in the command field, and press the Enter key.
2. Click on DOWNLOAD SAP NOTE (see Figure 19.47).

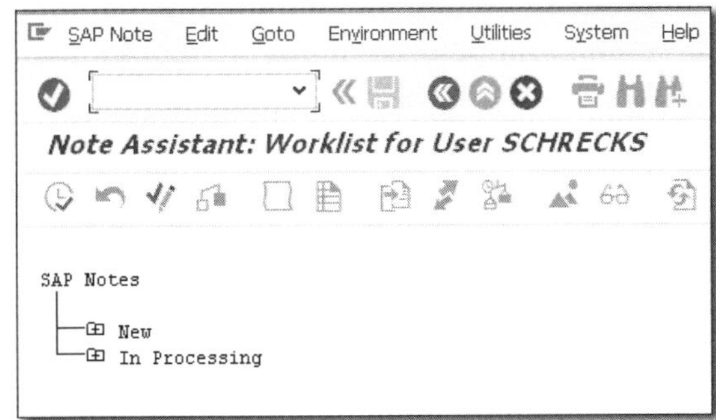

Figure 19.47 Initial Screen of the Note Assistant

3. In the dialog box that opens, enter the NOTE NUMBER of the SAP Note you want to download (see Figure 19.48). Then click on EXECUTE.

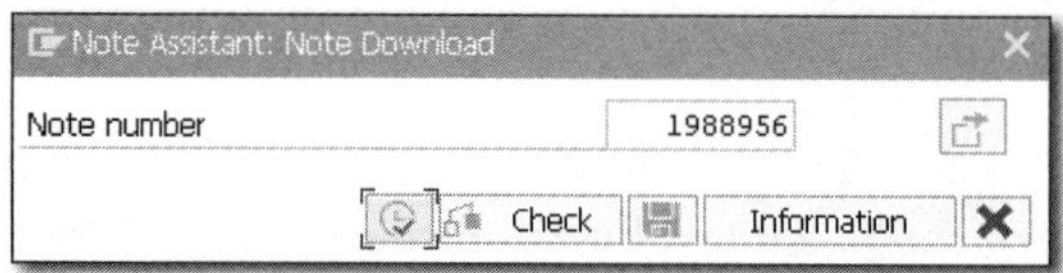

Figure 19.48 Specifying the SAP Notes to Be Downloaded

4. The SAP Note is then downloaded from the SAP Support Portal. This process may take some minutes to complete, after which the SAP Note appears with the status NEW in the worklist. The CAN BE IMPLEMENTED icon indicates that this SAP Note can be implemented (see Figure 19.49). Position the cursor on the SAP Note, and choose IMPLEMENT SAP NOTE.

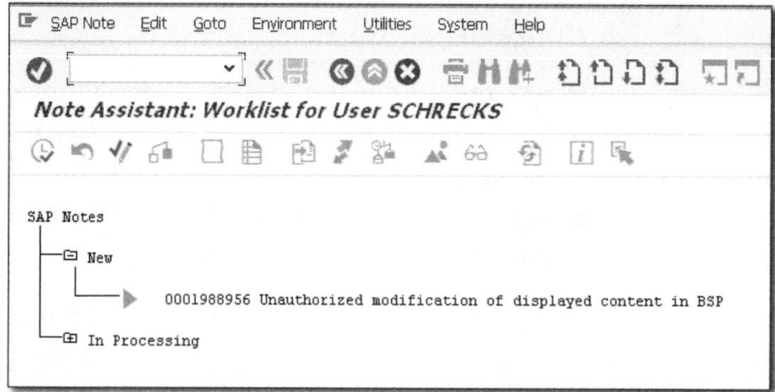

Figure 19.49 SAP Note That Can Be Implemented

[+]

SAP Notes That Can/Cannot Be Implemented

Only SAP Notes that contain correction instructions valid for your system's support package level are marked as CAN BE IMPLEMENTED in the Note Assistant. *Correction instructions* involve a technical description of the source code changes that are included in an SAP Note (CORRECTION INSTRUCTIONS section at the bottom of the note display). The note text itself is *not* part of the correction instructions.

When you download an SAP Note and then determine that it has the CANNOT BE IMPLEMENTED status, this can be due to various reasons:

- The SAP Note doesn't contain any correction instructions. This can be the case if it doesn't involve a program error that can't be corrected by changing the repository objects but a general recommended action, for example.

- Although the SAP Note contains correction instructions, they don't match the version or support package level of your system. In most cases, the corrections have already been implemented in your system during maintenance and the SAP Note no longer applies to your error.

If, during your error search, you come across an SAP Note that can't be implemented, you must check whether it's already obsolete or whether it only provides a "manual" solution to your problem.

5. For security reasons, a dialog box is displayed asking whether the SAP Note to be implemented has been read (see Figure 19.50). Click the SAP NOTE button to open and read the SAP Note. Click on YES to continue with the implementation.

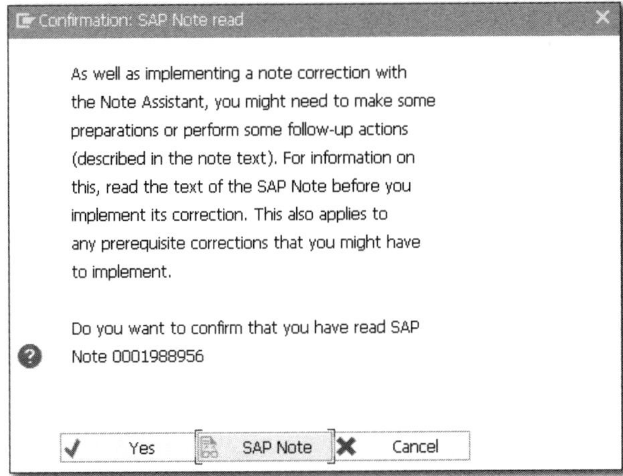

Figure 19.50 Security Prompt for Confirming the Conent of the SAP Note

6. Next, a warning message is displayed, which you can confirm by clicking CONTINUE (see Figure 19.51).

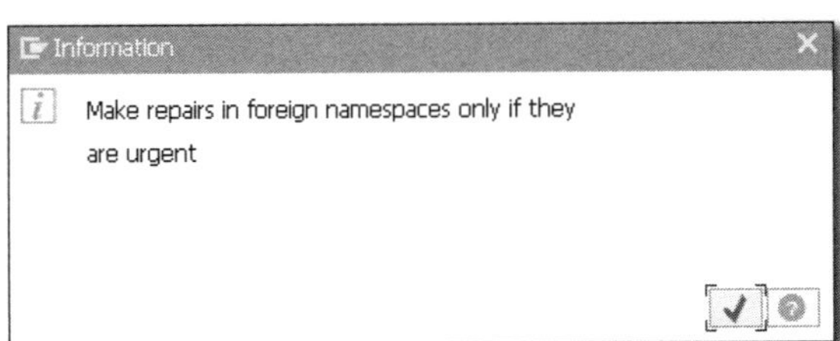

Figure 19.51 Confirming an Information Message

7. Another dialog box opens, where you're required to enter a transport request, specifying the change to the system (see Figure 19.52). Enter a request number here, or create a new workbench request as described in Chapter 17. Choose CONTINUE ✔ to proceed.

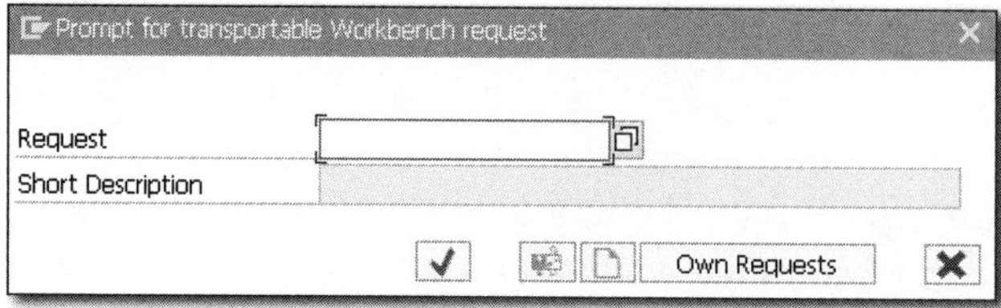

Figure 19.52 Entering a Transport Request

8. In certain cases, another dialog box opens, where you're prompted to confirm the changes, as shown in Figure 19.53. Click on CONTINUE ✔.

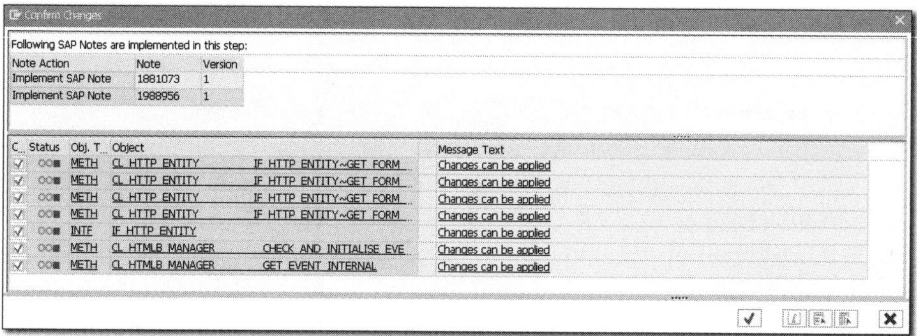

Figure 19.53 Checking and Confirming the Copy of Changes

[⚙]

Incomplete Copying of Changes

When you confirm the copying of changes, you must consider the traffic light icon in the STATUS column. A green traffic light means that the changes from the correction instructions have been implemented automatically and completely. No further action is required.

A yellow or red traffic light means, however, that the corrections were *not* implemented or only *incompletely*. In this case, you need to carefully check the copy of changes because otherwise the SAP Note isn't implemented correctly. If in doubt, consult an experienced programmer.

9. You may need to activate objects, depending on the type of correction involved (see Figure 19.54). Confirm with CONTINUE ✔.

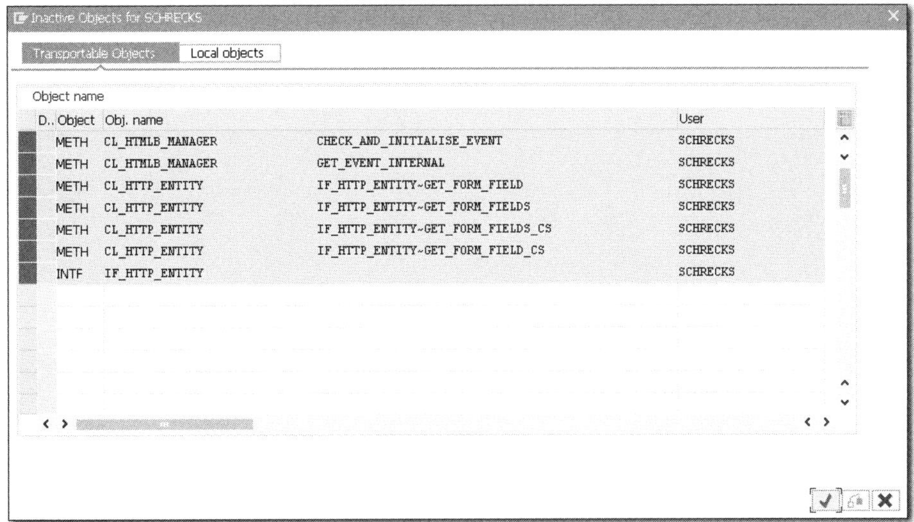

Figure 19.54 Activating Objects

10. The view switches back to your task worklist (see Figure 19.55). The SAP Note you've just implemented is displayed with the status IN PROCESSING. An icon indicating COMPLETELY IMPLEMENTED ✔ precedes this line. You can now test whether the SAP Note succeeded in eliminating your system errors. When you've completed the test, click on SET PROCESSING STATUS.

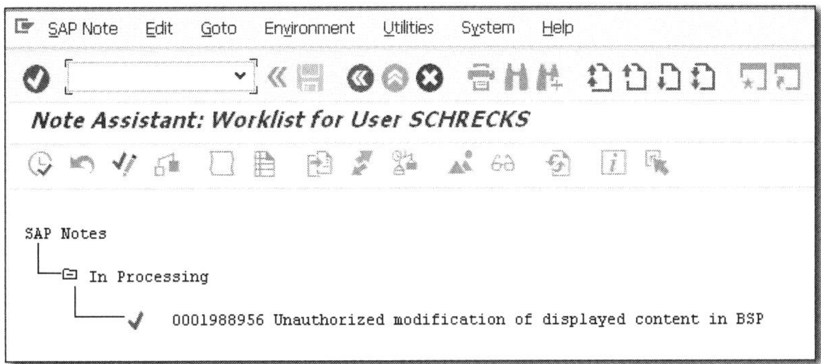

Figure 19.55 SAP Note Implemented Completely

11. Set the status as COMPLTD, and click on CONTINUE (see Figure 19.56). The SAP Note is then no longer displayed in your worklist.

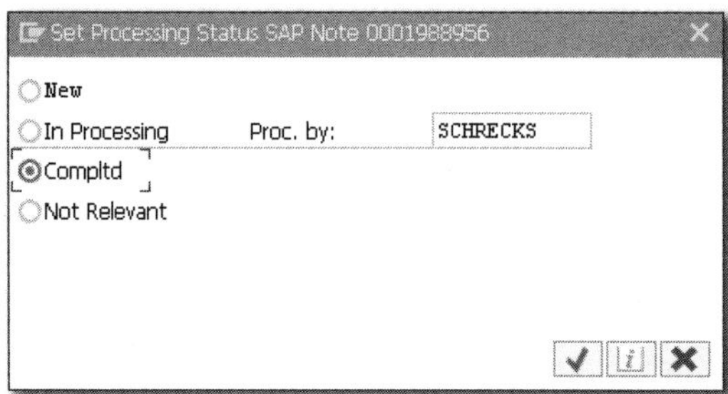

Figure 19.56 Classifying an SAP Note as Completed

[+] **Undoing SAP Note Implementation**

If, after performing testing and contacting the SAP hotline again (if necessary), it turns out that the implementation of a specific SAP Note doesn't solve the issue, remove the software from your system again as a precautionary measure. To do this, click on RESET SAP NOTE IMPLEMENTATION in the Note Assistant. Then set the processing status as NOT RELEVANT, and document your findings.

19.5 Summary

This chapter focused on the basic procedures used to analyze and eliminate errors in SAP systems. It explained how you can use the SAP Support Portal to find solutions quickly or to create incidents. You now know how to open service connections to SAP to troubleshoot problems in your system. You also know how to download SAP Notes and implement these in your system.

Appendices

A Useful Transactions

This appendix contains a reference list of useful transactions for nearly every topic covered in this book.

- **System administration**
  - AL11—Display System Paths
  - BD54—Logical Systems
  - RZ03—Display Instances and Operation Modes
  - RZ04—Maintain Instances and Operation Modes
  - RZ10—Maintain Profiles
  - RZ11—Display Profile Parameters
  - SE16—Display Tables
  - SA37/SE37—Execute Function Modules
  - SA38/SE38—Run Programs and Reports
  - SBWP—SAP Business Workplace
  - SCC1—Client Copy Using Transport Requests
  - SCC3—Client Copy Log
  - SCC4—Client Administration
  - SCC5—Delete Client
  - SCC7—Post-Processing for Client Import
  - SCC8—Export Client
  - SCC9—Remote Client Copy
  - SCCL—Local Client Copy
  - SCON/SCOT—SAPconnect Administration
  - SICF—HTTP Services
  - SM02—System Messages
  - SM04—List of Active Users
  - SM12—Lock Entries
  - SM13—Update Requests
  - SM14—Update System Administration

- SM21—System Log
- SM50—Process Overview
- SM51—Server List
- SM59—RFC Connections
- SM63—Operation Mode Sets
- SMGW—Gateway Monitor
- SMICM—Internet Communication Manager Monitor
- SMLG—Logon Groups
- SMMS—Message Server Monitor
- SMT1—Trusted Systems
- SMT2—Trusting Systems
- SR13—Configure Online Help
- SSAA—System Administrations Assistant
- ST22—ABAP Dump Analysis (Runtime Error)

- **System monitoring**
  - RZ20—CCMS Alert Monitor
  - RZ21—Configuration of CCMS Alert Monitor
  - RZ23N—Central Performance History
  - SM04—List of Active Users
  - SM50—Process Overview
  - SM51—Server List
  - SMGW—Gateway Monitor
  - SMICM—Internet Communication Manager Monitor
  - SMMS—Message Server Monitor
- **SAP Solution Manager**
  - AISUSER—Maintain User for Connection to SAP Support Portal
  - LMDB—Landscape Management Database
  - RZ70—System Landscape Directory Administration (local)
  - SCOUT—Customizing Comparison
  - SDCCN—Service Data Control Center
  - SM_WORKCENTER—Work Center (start in browser window)

- SMSY—System Landscape Maintenance
- SOLAR_PROJECT_ADMIN—Project Management
- SOLMAN_CONNECT—Service Connections
- SOLMAN_SETUP—SAP Solution Manager Configurations
- SOLMAN_WORKCENTER—Work Center (start in SAP GUI)
- STWB_1—Test Management—Test Catalogs
- STWB_2—Test Management—Test Plans
- STWB_TC—Test Management—Test Cases
- STWB_TC—Test Management—Worklist

- **Backup and restore**
  - DB12—DBA Backup Logs
  - DB13—DBA Planning Calendar
- **Database administration**
  - DB01—Display SQL Locks
  - DB02—Database Analysis
  - DB03—Maintain Database Parameters
  - DB05—Table Analysis
  - DB11—Maintain Connection between SAP System and Database
  - DB12—DBA Backup Logs
  - DB13—DBA Planning Calendar
  - SE14—ABAP Tools for Database Objects
  - ST04—Database Performance Monitor
  - ST10—Statistics for Table Calls
- **Operating system administration**
  - OS01—Network Check (ping)
  - OS02—Display Operating System Configuration
  - OS03—Maintain Operating System Parameters
  - OS04—Display Operating System Parameters (local)
  - OS05—Display Operating System Parameters (remote)
  - OS06—Operating System Monitor (local)
  - OS07—Operating System Monitor (remote)

- **Security administration**
  - SCC4—Set Changeability of Clients
  - SE03—Set System Changeability
  - SM01—Lock Transactions
  - SM18—Delete Security Audit Log Files
  - SM19—Configure Security Audit Log
  - SM20—Analyze Security Audit Log (global)
- **Performance**
  - DB02—Database Analysis
  - ST02—Performance Tuning Analysis
  - ST03N—Workload Monitor
  - ST04—Database Performance Monitor
  - ST05—Performance Analysis (traces)
  - ST06—OS Performance Monitor
  - ST07—Application Monitor
  - ST10—Statistics for Table Calls
  - STAD—Transaction Analysis
- **User administration**
  - AL08—Overview of Active Users (multiple instances)
  - BD87—Status Monitor for IDocs (CUA)
  - SA03—Maintain Titles
  - SCUA—Create Distribution Model (CUA)
  - SCUG—Synchronization of Users and Company Addresses (CUA)
  - SCUM—Field Selection for User Distribution (CUA)
  - SM04—Overview of Active Users, Exit User Modes
  - SU01—Maintain User
  - SU10—User Mass Maintenance
  - SUCOMP—Maintain Company Address
  - SUGR—Maintain User Groups
  - SUIM—User Information System

  - USMM—System Measurement (license data)
  - WE20—Partner Agreements
- **Authorization management**
  - PFCG—Profile Generator for Maintaining Authorization Roles
  - PFUD—User Comparison for Roles and Profiles
  - ROLE_CMP—Compare Role Menus
  - SE43N—Create and Maintain Area Menus
  - SE54—Assign Authorization Groups to Tables
  - SE97—Check Indicators for Transaction Calls (see SAP Note 358122)
  - SU02—Maintain Authorization Profiles
  - SU03—Authorization Classes and Objects
  - SU20—Authorization Fields (see Table `AUTHX`)
  - SU21—Authorization Objects
  - SU22/SU24—Maintain Check Indicators for Transactions
  - SU25—Initially Fill Customer Tables for Check Indicators
  - SU53—Display Data of Last Authorization Check
  - SU56—User Buffer
  - SUPC—Mass Generation of Authorization Profiles for Roles
  - SSM2—Set Initial Menu Across the System
  - ST01—System Trace
- **Background processing**
  - RZ01—Job Scheduling Monitor
  - SM35—Run Batch Input Sessions
  - SM35P—Batch Input Log
  - SM36—Define Batch Jobs
  - SM36WIZ—Batch Job Wizard
  - SM37—Batch Job Monitor
  - SM61—Background Processing Control
  - SM62—Event Management for Background Processing
  - SM65—Analysis Tool for Background Processing
  - SM69—External Operating System Commands

- **Output management**
  - SP01—Output Control (spool and output requests)
  - SP02—Output Request Display
  - SPAD—Spool Administration
  - SP11—Display TemSe Objects
  - SP12—TemSe Administration
- **Change and Transport Management**
  - SE01—Transport Organizer (extended view)
  - SE03—Transport Organizer Tools
  - SE06—Installation Wizard for Transport Organizer
  - SE07—Import Monitor (transport system status display)
  - SE09/SE10—Transport Organizer
  - SM30/SM31—Table Maintenance
  - SNOTE—Note Assistant (import SAP Notes)
  - STMS—Transport Management System
- **System maintenance**
  - SAINT—Add-On Installation Tool
  - SGEN—SAP Load Generator
  - SPAM—Support Package Manager
  - SPDD—Modification Reconciliation for Data Dictionary Objects
  - SPAU—Modification Reconciliation for Repository Objects
- **Diagnostics and troubleshooting**
  - SM21—System Log
  - SNOTE—Note Assistant (import SAP Notes)
  - SR13—Configure Online Help
  - ST22—ABAP Dump Analysis (runtime error)

B Security-Relevant Transactions

Table B.1 contains security-relevant transactions that you should lock in SAP systems. Chapter 10 explains why and how you should lock these transactions. Table B.1 was created in collaboration with SAP Basis consultants and end users. The transactions are categorized as follows:

- Critical
- Impairing security
- Impairing performance

Contact your technical consultants and the persons responsible for the specific components. They can provide you with more information on further critical transactions in your components.

Transaction	Description	Critical	Impairing Security	Impairing Performance
F040	Reorganization	✓		
F041	Archiving Bank Master Data	✓		
F042	Archiving GL Accounts	✓		
F043	Archiving Customers	✓		
F044	Archiving Vendors	✓		
F045	Archiving Documents	✓		
F046	Archiving Transaction Figures	✓		
GCE2	Profiles		✓	
GCE3	Object Classes		✓	
KA10	Archive Cost Centers (Total)	✓		
KA12	Archive Cost Centers (Plan)	✓		
KA16	Archive Cost Centers (Line Items)	✓		
KA18	Archive Administration: Assessment, Distribution, and so on	✓		
KA20	Archiving Cost Centers (Total)	✓		

Table B.1 Security-Relevant Transactions

Transaction	Description	Critical	Impairing Security	Impairing Performance
O001	C CL User Maintenance		✓	
O002	C CL User Profiles		✓	
O016	C CL Authorizations		✓	
OBR1	Delete Documents	✓		
OBZ7	C FI Users		✓	
OBZ8	C FI Profiles		✓	
OBZ9	C FI Authorizations		✓	
OD02	Define Role for DMS		✓	
OD03	CV User Profiles		✓	
OD04	CV User Maintenance		✓	
OIBA	Authorizations		✓	
OIBB	User Maintenance		✓	
OIBP	User Profiles		✓	
OMDL	C MM-MRP User Maintenance		✓	
OMDM	C MM-MRP User Profiles		✓	
OMEH	C MM-PUR User Maintenance		✓	
OMEI	C MM-PUR User Profiles		✓	
OMG7	C MM-PUR Authorizations		✓	
OMI6	C MM-MRP Authorizations		✓	
OML0	MM: Warehouse Management User Maintenance		✓	
OMM0	MM: Warehouse Management User Profiles		✓	
OMNP	Authorizations in MM-WM		✓	
OMSN	C MM-BD User Maintenance		✓	
OMSO	C MM-BD User Profiles		✓	
OMSZ	C MM-BD Authorizations		✓	
OMWF	C MM-IV User Maintenance		✓	
OMWG	C MM-IV User Profiles		✓	

Table B.1 Security-Relevant Transactions (Cont.)

Transaction	Description	Critical	Impairing Security	Impairing Performance
OMWK	C MM-IV Authorizations		✓	
OOPR	Authorization Profile Maintenance		✓	
OOSB	Users (Structural Authorization)		✓	
OOSP	Authorization Profiles		✓	
OOUS	Maintain User		✓	
OP15	Production User Profiles		✓	
OP29	Production User Maintenance		✓	
OPCA	User Maintenance		✓	
OPCB	User Profiles		✓	
OPCC	Authorizations		✓	
OPE9	User Profile Maintenance		✓	
OPF0	User Maintenance		✓	
OPF1	C CAP Authorizations		✓	
OPJ0	Maintain User		✓	
OPJ1	User Profile Maintenance		✓	
OPJ3	Maintain Authorizations		✓	
OSSZ	C PP Authorizations		✓	
OTZ1	C FI Users		✓	
OTZ2	C FI Profiles		✓	
OTZ3	C FI Authorizations		✓	
OVZ5	C RV User Maintenance		✓	
OVZ6	C RV Maintain User Profile V_SD_ALL		✓	
OY20	Customizing Authorizations		✓	
OY21	Customizing User Profiles		✓	
OY22	Create Subadministrator Customizing		✓	
OY27	Create Superuser Customizing		✓	
OY28	Deactivate SAP*		✓	

Table B.1 Security-Relevant Transactions (Cont.)

Transaction	Description	Critical	Impairing Security	Impairing Performance
OY29	Documentation Developer		✓	
OY30	Documentation Developer		✓	
SARA	Archive Administration	✓		
SCC5	Delete Client	✓		
SE01	Transport Organizer (Extended View)			
SE06	Set Up Transport Organizer	✓	✓	
SE09	Transport Organizer			
SE10	Transport Organizer			
SE11	R/3 Data Dictionary	✓		
SE13	Maintain Storage Parameters for Tables	✓		
SE14	Utilities for Dictionary Tables	✓		
SE15	Dictionary Info System			
SE16	Data Browser			✓
SE17	General Table Display			✓
SE38	ABAP Editor	✓		
SM49	Execute External OS Commands	✓	✓	
SM59	RFC Destinations (Display and Maintenance)			
SM69	Execute External OS Commands	✓	✓	
ST05	Performance Trace			✓
SU12	Mass Changes to User Master	✓	✓	

Table B.1 Security-Relevant Transactions (Cont.)

Table B.2 contains transactions that can possibly not be locked because they are used regularly. These transactions are used in production systems for specific reasons. Because they are critical, access to these transactions should be granted via authorization roles to a limited extent only.

Transaction	Description	Critical	Impairing Security	Impairing Performance
RZ10	Maintain Profile Parameters	✓		
SA38	ABAP/4 Reporting	✓		
SM04	User List		✓	
SM12	Display and Delete Locks	✓		
SM13	Display Update Records	✓		
SM30	Call View Maintenance	✓		
SM31	Call View Maintenance, Analogous to SM30	✓		
STMS	Transport Management System	✓		
SU01	User Maintenance		✓	
SU02	Maintain Authorization Profiles		✓	
SU03	Maintain Authorizations		✓	

Table B.2 Transactions (Can Possibly Not Be Locked)

C Useful Tables

This appendix contains a list of database tables for nearly every topic covered in this book. These tables store the most important data. Sometimes, it can be helpful to download specific data from the system using Transaction SE16 to be able to analyze it.

Occasionally, you can determine the table that stores the data by positioning the cursor in the corresponding field and using the F1 key to call the help. Then, select the Technical Information button, and read the name of the corresponding table from the Table Name field. (This is only possible if it is a *transparent table*.)

- **System administration**
  - BTCOMSET—operation mode sets
  - LTDX—user-specific layout variants
  - PATH—system paths
  - RFCDES—RFC connections
  - RFCSYSACL—trusted systems
  - RFCTRUST—trusting systems
  - SNAP—ABAP short dumps
  - T000—clients
  - TPFBA—operation modes
  - TPFYPRBTY—profile parameters
  - TSTC—transactions
  - V_TBDLS—logical systems
- **System monitoring**
  - ALMONISETS—CCMS Alert Monitor sets
  - ALMSETS—CCMS Alert Monitors
- **SAP Solution Manager**
  - SMSY_DB_SYS—system landscape – databases
  - SMSY_SYS_CLIENTS—system landscape – clients
  - SMSY_SYST_CLIENT—system landscape – product systems

  - SMSY_SYST_COMP—system landscape – installed components
  - SMSY_SYSTEM—system landscape – systems
  - TPROJECT/TPROJECTT—projects
- **Database administration**
  - SDBAC—available database activities
  - SDBAP—planning data for database activities
  - TCPDB—database code page
- **Operating system administration**
  - OPSYSTEM—directory of operating system identifiers
  - OSMON—operating system monitor data
  - TSLE4—operating systems of instances
- **Security administration**
  - RSAUPROF—security audit profiles
- **Performance**
  - TCOLL—time when Performance Collector runs
- **User administration**
  - SMEN_BUFFC—favorites in SAP Easy Access menu of each user
  - USER_ADDR—user name/address
  - USR02—user logon data
  - USR05—user parameters
  - USR06—user license category (texts—TUTYPNOW)
  - USR21—user company address (via table ADRC)
  - USR40—excluded passwords
  - USLA04—user assignments to roles for each system (CUA)
  - USZBVSYS—users for each system (CUA)
- **Authorization management**
  - AGR_1251—authorization values in roles
  - AGR_1252—organizational level characteristic in roles

- AGR_AGRS—single roles in composite roles
- AGR_DEFINE—texts and change dates for roles
- AGR_HIER—menu structure for roles
- AGR_HIERT—menu structure texts for roles
- AGR_PROF—generated profiles for authorization roles
- AGR_TCODES—transactions in role menus
- AGR_TEXTS—long texts for roles
- AGR_USERS—user assignments to roles
- AUTHX—authorization fields (see Transaction SU20)
- PRGN_CUST—Customizing table for authorization check
- SSM_CUST—Customizing table for profile generator
- TACT—activities with texts
- TACTZ—activities for authorization objects
- TBRG—authorization groups for authorization objects
- TCDCOUPLES—check identifier for transactions called
- TDDAT—authorization groups for tables
- TOBJ—fields for authorization objects
- TOBJT—texts for authorization objects
- USLA04—user assignments to roles for each system (CUA)
- USOBT_C—check indicator for transactions (customer-specific)
- USR11—texts for profiles
- USRBF2—user buffer
- UST04—profile assignments to users
- UST12—authorization values in profiles
- USZBVSYS—users for each system (CUA)

- **Background processing**
  - TBTCO—planning data for batch jobs
  - TBTCP—steps in batch jobs (including program names)

- **Output management**
  - `TSP01`—spool requests
  - `TSP02`—output requests
  - `TSP03`—output devices
  - `TSP6D`—access method
  - `TSPSV`—spool server
  - `TST01`—TemSe objects
  - `TST03`—TemSe data
- **Change and transport management**
  - `TMSCSYS`—systems in transport management
  - `TMSBUFFER`—transports in transport queue
- **System maintenance**
  - `CVERS`—system software components (including releases)
  - `PATCHHIST`—history of the kernel version
  - `PATHISTQ`—history of the SPAM/SAINT queue
- **Diagnostics and troubleshooting**
  - `DEVACCESS`—developer key

D Forms

This appendix contains some sample form templates that you can use for the respective work area in live operations.

User Request

Use a form as shown in Table D.1 to document requests for SAP access and to track approval procedures (see Chapter 13).

SAP User Request	Company Identification or Personnel Number:	
	System/clients	▸ PRD 300 ▸ QAS 200 210 220 ▸ DEV 100 110 120
Employee:	Change type	▸ Create user ▸ Change user ▸ Delete user
Department/cost center number:		
User ID:		
Position:	Valid until (mandatory for short-term employees)	
Password:	Degree of urgency	▸ High ▸ Medium ▸ Low
Requester:		
Requester's position:		
Requester's telephone number:		
Position of the employee (if similar to already-existing employees in the same department, name, and user ID of a person with similar position):		

Table D.1 Documenting User Requests and Approval Procedures

SAP User Request	Company Identification or Personnel Number:		
Authorizations:			
Requester's signature			
	(Name)	(Signature)	(Date)
Manager's signature			
	(Name)	(Signature)	(Date)
Signature of the person responsible			
	(Name)	(Signature)	(Date)
	(Name)	(Signature)	(Date)
	(Name)	(Signature)	(Date)
Security			
	(Name)	(Signature)	(Date)
Is a signed copy of the document on the computer security and policy additionally attached to the security approval? ▸ Yes ▸ No			

Table D.1 Documenting User Requests and Approval Procedures (Cont.)

Changing Authorization Roles

Document changes to authorization roles or profiles to track the reason for a change later on (see Table D.2 and Chapter 14). You might discover a security gap during a check and want to delete specific authorizations from a role. In this case, it's helpful to know why an authorization was given to avoid unwanted side effects.

Change to Authorization	
Authorization role(s) or profile(s):	
Change type:	
▸ Transaction(s)	▸ Added ▸ Removed

Table D.2 Documenting Changes to Authorization Roles

Change to Authorization				
▸ Authorization object(s)			▸ Added ▸ Removed	
▸ Field value(s)			▸ Added ▸ Removed	
Reason for change:				
Contact person in user department:				
Consequences/side effects/risks:				
Approval of security officer:				
Implementation:				
System	**Client**	**Date**	**Transport Request**	**Done/ Initials**

Table D.2 Documenting Changes to Authorization Roles (Cont.)

Approving Transports

You can use the form in Table D.3 to document which transport requests have been imported to your production system for which reasons. It's particularly important that you can track the approval by the user's department (see Chapter 17).

Transport Request			
Transport number:			
Title/description:			
Objects:			
SAP Notes used: (SAP Note form required for each note)			
Consequences for other functional areas:			
Special instructions for transport:			
Special request	Idle time required: Yes/No		

Table D.3 Documenting Approved Transport Requests

Transport Request						
Transport request created by:						
Tested by:						
Checked and approved by functional area:						
FI		MM		IT area		
SD		and so on				
Transport approved by:						
Transport details:						
System	**Client**	**Date**	**Start Time**	**End Time**	**Return Code**	**Done/ Initials**
QAS	200					
	210					
PRD	300					

Table D.3 Documenting Approved Transport Requests (Cont.)

Documenting Imported SAP Notes

This form (see Table D.4) enables you to document the import of SAP Notes from the SAP Support Portal (see Chapter 19).

SAP Note			
SAP Note number:			
Short description:			
Component:			
Problem to be solved:			
Changed objects:			
Installed in release:			
Remarks:			
Other SAP Notes used:			

Table D.4 Documenting Imported SAP Notes

SAP Note					
Used for:					
System	**Client**	**Transport Request Number**	**Import Date**	**Return Code**	**Done/ Initials**
DEV	100				
	110				
QAS	200				
	210				
PRD	300				

Table D.4 Documenting Imported SAP Notes (Cont.)

E Bibliography

Bremer, Richard; Breddemann, Lars. *SAP HANA Administration*. Boston: SAP PRESS, 2014.

Caesar, Daniel; Friebel, Michael R. *Schnelleinstieg SQL Server 2012*. Bonn: Galileo Computing, 2013.

Cavalleri, Andrea; Manara, Massimo. *100 Things You Should Know About Authorizations in SAP*. Boston: SAP PRESS, 2012.

Chuprunov, Maxim. *Handbuch SAP-Revision—Internes Kontrollsystem und GRC*. Bonn: SAP PRESS, 2012.

de Boer, Martijn; Essenpreis, Mathias; Garcia Laule, Stefanie; Raepple, Martin. *Single Sign-on mit SAP*. Bonn: SAP PRESS, 2010.

Dröge, Ruprecht; Knuth, Jörg; Raatz, Markus. *Microsoft SQL Server 2012. Überblick über Konfiguration, Administration, Programmierung*. Munich: Microsoft Press Deutschland, 2012.

Faustmann, André; Greulich, Michael; Siegling, André; Wegener, Benjamin; Zimmermann, Ronny. *SAP Database Administration with IBM DB2*. Boston: SAP PRESS, 2013.

Föse, Frank; Hagemann, Sigrid; Will, Liane. *SAP NetWeaver AS ABAP—System Administration* (4th ed.). Boston: SAP PRESS, 2012.

Hartke, Lars; Hohnhorst, Georg; Sattler, Gernot. *SAP Handbuch Sicherheit und Prüfung—Praxisorientierter Revisionsleitfaden für SAP-Systeme*. IDW Verlag, 2010.

Heilig, Loren; Gergen, Peter. *Understanding SAP NetWeaver Identity Management*. Boston: SAP PRESS, 2010.

Held, Andrea; Hotzy, Mirko; Fröhlich, Lutz; Adar, Marek. *Der Oracle DBA—Handbuch für die Administration der Oracle Database 11g R2*. Carl Hanser Verlag, 2011.

Hennermann, Frank. *Implementierungs und Upgrade Projekte mit dem SAP Solution Manager*. Bonn: SAP PRESS, 2009.

Kösegi, Armin; Nerding, Rainer. *SAP Change and Transport Management* (3rd ed.). Boston: SAP PRESS, 2009.

Lehnert, Volker; Otto, Anna; Stelzner, Katharina. *Datenschutz in SAP-Systemen—Konzeption und Implementierung*. Bonn: SAP PRESS, 2011.

Lehnert, Volker; Stelzner, Katharina; Justice, Larry. *Authorizations in SAP Software: Design and Configuration*. Boston: SAP PRESS, 2010.

Linkies, Mario; Karin, Horst. *SAP Security and Risk Management* (2nd ed.). Boston: SAP PRESS, 2010.

Naumann, Jacqueline. *Praxisbuch eCATT*. Bonn: SAP PRESS, 2009.

Schäfer, Marc O.; Melich, Matthias. *SAP Solution Manager* (3rd ed.). Boston: SAP PRESS, 2012.

Schneider, Thomas. *SAP Performance Optimization Guide: Analyzing and Tuning SAP Systems* (7th ed.). Boston: SAP PRESS, 2013.

Teuber, Lars; Weidmann, Corina; Will, Liane. *Monitoring and Operations with SAP Solution Manager*. Boston: SAP PRESS, 2014.

Williams, Nathan. *IT Service Management in SAP Solution Manager*. Boston: SAP PRESS, 2013.

F The Author

Sebastian Schreckenbach has worked as an SAP Basis consultant at Steria Mummert Consulting GmbH since 2012, assuming responsibility for various customers in different projects. Prior to that, he worked as an SAP system administrator for the city administration of Dresden, the capital of Saxony, Germany.

During and after his studies of information management at the University of Cooperative Education in Dresden, Germany, from 2002 to 2005, he worked at SSC Procurement Germany of Deutsche Post AG in Koblenz, Germany. There he took care of the implementation of SAP Enterprise Buyer Professional and was responsible for the technical support of SAP SRM and EBP.

Contributors to this Book

Benjamin Wegener studied information management at the Otto von Guericke University in Magdeburg, Germany, and has been a member of the SAP Basis administration team at the SAP University Competence Center (SAP UCC) Magdeburg since 2010. He's responsible for the implementation, operation, and content management of SAP HANA as well as SAP HANA-based technologies. For more than two years, he's contributed to various projects that use the in-memory database. Additionally, he has vast experience in SAP ERP, SAP CRM, and SAP Solution Manager. Wegener is responsible for Section 8.9, "Database Administration—SAP HANA" in Chapter 8.

André Faustmann studied information management at the Otto von Guericke University in Magdeburg, Germany. Since 2000, he has worked for the SAP University Competence Center (SAP UCC) in Magdeburg, where he assumes responsibility for hosting various SAP solutions that are operated for universities, universities of applied sciences, universities of cooperative education, and professional schools in Germany, Europe, the Middle East, and Africa. His many years of experience in handling SAP systems range from Release 4.6 to the latest version of SAP NetWeaver 7.4. For more than 10 years, he has been a certified technology consultant for SAP NetWeaver AS as well as SAP Enterprise Portal and Knowledge Management. André Faustmann is responsible for Section 8.5, "Database Administration—DB2" in Chapter 8.

Index

A

B

C

E

F

G

H

I

P

Q

R

S

T

U

V

W

X